Queen Alexandra

Loyalty and Love

1 Alexandra, Princess of Wales, c 1887. *Lafayette*
RCIN 2941847

Queen Alexandra

Loyalty and Love

FRANCES DIMOND

History & Heritage
Publishing

First published in the United Kingdom in 2022 by
History and Heritage Publishing

ISBN 978–1-914280–05-4

Contents

Preface

W

As a small child I was captivated by royal history. Articles about Queen Victoria and her family assisted my recovery from something which I claimed must have been German measles, because of Prince Albert. The death of King George VI, followed a year later by the coronation of HM the Queen, brought awareness of the Royal Family closer and, living in St Marylebone, not far from areas associated with them, I was able, early one morning, to go through to Oxford Street with my mother and wait in the rain for the coronation procession later that afternoon. In between these two events, Queen Mary died and we walked to the Mall to see her funeral procession. I was sorry not to see her in person, but studied magazine photographs of her throughout her life. They included other people and I noticed one lady, similarly dressed but prettier. This was Queen Alexandra.

The immediate attraction was that her name began with A, then my favourite letter of the alphabet; sadly my own name only contained one A, whereas here was someone with three of them and, crucially, one at the end. I began to take note of Queen Alexandra; my mother told me that she herself, as a child, had seen her riding in her carriage down Sloane Street, and had always rather liked her. There were many local echoes of her; close by, in Wigmore Street, was a Danish restaurant, and if the door was open you could see a photograph of the Queen at the back. There was a Danish laundry in Marylebone Lane, and we used to go to Hertford House where, I discovered later, Alexandra and her husband had visited Sir Richard Wallace before his art collection was open to the public. Her singing teacher, Tosti, had lived in a house in Mandeville Place. Further off, a stationer's shop in Albemarle Street had a mosaic doorstep proclaiming her patronage, but disappointingly, the memorial to her outside Marlborough House showed an allegorical figure rather than the Queen herself.

By the time I was eleven the Russian Imperial Family was my lode star and Queen Alexandra stood modestly aside, but she never went away; she was, after all, their aunt. In seeking information about them I read about other royalties, including her. My mother and I used to talk about her and "the Wales family", imagining what their life had been like, and drawing pictures of them – and my mother nobly allowed me to write out Royal Family trees all over the kitchen walls. I also made a large number of dolls representing royalties in 1909 and of course took particular care with the one of Queen Alexandra. Every year I would look forward to Alexandra Rose Day and those delightful little pink fabric roses, and for two years in my late teens I sold them in Euston Road. Deciding to apply to study for my degree at Bedford College might have been at least partly because she was its former patron.

Surely there is nothing like perseverance, and I was fortunate enough to secure a job which was as nearly perfect as a job could be. In the course of it I looked after and researched Queen Alexandra's photograph albums and began to feel that I was encountering the real person at last. What I found was so positively at odds with the gushing or dismissive biographies I had read, that I made a decision. My suggestion was kindly received and permission was given; hence this book.

In memory of my mother,
Phyllis Dimond, 1911–2008

Acknowledgments

꧁

The Royal Archives is an essential resource for a royal biography, and my greatest thanks are to Her Majesty The Queen, for so kindly consenting to my writing this book, with full use of such a valuable tool; and to my commenting on a selection of books which belonged to Queen Alexandra; and for permission to reproduce photographs and the painting by Josefine Swoboda from the Royal Collection. It is a privilege to have been allowed to develop my interest in the life of Queen Alexandra in this way. My colleagues, past and present, in the Royal Household have always encouraged my aspirations; in thanking just a few of them by name, I am not forgetting all the others; specific thanks to Sheila de Bellaigue, Pam Clark, Bill Stockting, Allison Derrett, Julie Crocker, Laura Hobbs, Angeline Barker, Lynnette Beeche, Lisa Heighway, Stella Panayotova, Bridget Wright, Emma Stuart, Megan Gent, Karen Lawson, Daniel Partridge, Alessandro Nasini and Siân Cooksey extend to many more.

I have also been assisted and encouraged by many other people and organisations, including Kristen Mercier at St George's Chapel Archives; Nicholas Robinson at the Fitzwilliam Museum; the Bodleian Library; Sally Dobinson at Leighton House; the Hampshire Record Office; the Norfolk Record Office; The Harrison Sisters' Trust; Eric Birbeck; Mary Etherington and Helen Mckillop at QARNNS; Richard Davies at Leeds Russian Archive; Simon Evans at the National Library of Wales; James Page-Roberts; Stephen Patterson; Roger Taylor; Robin Piguet; Dr Hendrik Weingarten at the Niedersächsisches Landesarchiv; Camille Koutoulakis at Lambeth Palace Library; Preben Ulstrup; Steffen Løvkjær, Susan Bennett; Anna Halager; Marianne Kouwenhoven; Tom Cridford at the Royal College of Art; Juan Martin, Director of the Archivo General de Palacio in Madrid; the Anglo-Danish Society; the Society of Authors; the late Duke of Fife; and the Countess of Rosebery. Michael Turner, Ricardo Mateos y Sainz de Medrano, Hugo Vickers, Peter Galloway, Ian Shapiro, Charlotte Zeepvat, Sue Woolmans, Michael Boag and Richard Keeler have been particularly helpful. Paul Rothe & Son in Marylebone Lane sustained me with coffee and sandwiches at crucial moments. Most importantly, I am very grateful to Miles Bailey, Rachel Woodman and Adrian Sysum at The Choir Press and History & Heritage Publishing, and my editor, Joshua Lambert, for turning the project into a book.

I have done my best to find and acknowledge copyright ownership in all the documents and photographs used in producing this book, but in a few cases it has eluded me, especially as some ownership has changed and knowledge of the new ownership is lacking. If anyone feels that I have overstepped the mark and used their material without their permission, the publisher and I will be delighted to acknowledge this and put it right in any future edition. In a work of this size and density it is also inevitable that inadvertent errors have crept in, for which I also apologise.

It would be fair to say that, during the fifteen years it has taken me to write the book, just about everyone I know has been made aware of its subject, although not its details, and I thank them for their forbearance in the face of what must often have seemed like "crying wolf" about an invisible project. Sadly, some of my most loyal allies did not survive long enough to see it, but other people, whom I never met, appeared to come closer. It was gratifying to find that Queen Alexandra's faithful old servants, Sir Dighton Probyn and Miss Charlotte Knollys, were both born in St Marylebone, the part of London where I too grew up. I sympathised deeply with Sir Arthur Davidson (a fellow Scorpio) in his strenuous efforts to do justice to King Edward's memory, and took heed of his resulting ill health. From what I discovered, King Edward himself (another Scorpio), despite all, justified his wife's devotion.

Writing a biography is a huge responsibility, taking someone's life in your hands and trying to make sense of it, while wondering what they would have thought and whether they would have approved. I will never know whether Queen Alexandra would have applauded my efforts, but I was encouraged by the ease with which her character emerged from documents; by her interests, some of which are mine too; and a certain sense of friendliness, which encouraged me to persevere with the task despite all sorts of hindrances. The happy atmosphere of my youthful talks with my mother about Queen Alexandra was somehow reproduced. It went further; when I was researching Alexandra's photographic concerns some years ago at Sandringham, I had reached the last day of my work there having failed to find a specific book, *The Flag*, produced by the Union Jack Club in 1908 and using some of her photographs with her permission. I was in her small library, almost at the end of the afternoon, my notebook full except for two lines at the bottom of the page. Tired and frustrated at not finding the book, I shut my eyes and just pointed at the shelves at random. When I opened them – there it was. I could almost hear her laughing.

Illustrations

Genealogical tables showing:

Acknowledgements:
Nos 1, 2, 3, 4, 5, 9, 10, 14, 15 are Royal Collection Trust/©Her Majesty Queen Elizabeth II 2021
No 6 is reproduced by kind permission of the National Library of Wales
Nos 7, 8, 12 are from a private collection
Nos 11, 13 are from another private collection

Introduction

"The position is, for me, actually the only 'down'". Princess Alexandra of Denmark, just engaged to the Prince of Wales, was sure that she loved him, while viewing her new place in society with considerable trepidation. Her love for her husband never seriously faltered and she came to terms, in her own way, with her new rank, and made a success of her job. She used her time to the full and, despite being hindered by progressively severe hearing loss, played an increasing part in royal duties while still pursuing her interest in the arts and humanitarian projects. Above all, she was devoted to her children; remained loyally in touch with her friends; and cherished her Danish family, who relied on her help and sympathy. Alexandra was far more interesting than the one-dimensional figure in popular memory and, as someone who believed in fair play and always supported people she felt had been misjudged, she should now, as far as possible, be assessed on her own terms.

As public figures, King Edward VII and Queen Alexandra particularly guarded their private life. The King directed that much of his archive should be destroyed after his death, and many of Queen Alexandra's private papers no longer exist; she tore up some of them herself and left instructions to burn others, which she had every right to do. This could be daunting to a biographer, but plenty of material remains, perhaps by courtesy of King George V and Queen Mary, who seem not to have shared their predecessors' incendiary predilections. Surviving letters and other documents, the engagement diaries of both King Edward and Queen Alexandra, and court circulars over six decades, mean that actually there is far too much. A lot of it, as well as some often-repeated stories, had to be set aside. Nevertheless, it seemed important to attempt as full a picture as possible of what royalty have to accomplish, all the time, in the public eye, happily or unhappily, and often despite their state of health. Alexandra balanced duty with social events, a private family life, interests and hobbies, while coping at the same time with tragic personal loss, such as the deaths of her eldest and youngest sons and husband, and the assassination of her brother, her nephew and his family.

By following this book chronologically, readers may feel that they are gradually getting to know "the Wales family", and understanding how and why events happened as they did, but as the book contains so much detail, it may be more comfortable to dip in and out, taking particular years or topics as preferred. Lesser-known aspects, what is known of their family life and interests, and the remarkable number and variety of the people they met, have been preferred, although each one could open the way to more stories for which there is no room. Politics and King Edward's friendships with other women cannot be ignored, but thankfully they have been amply and ably covered by other authors. It proved impractical to make a thorough incursion into Alexandra's letters to her sister, Empress Marie Feodorovna, in Russia; two devoted sisters gossiping and saying exactly what they thought about other people and events in a way that no-one else was supposed to see. However, surely Alexandra deserves that amount of privacy, and, if she had had the disposal of the letters, would probably have burned them.

One topic which continues to intrigue is Alexandra's alliance with face make-up, which some people suspected was too close. However, not only did she inherit a naturally good complexion, but she kept it in good order with a healthy diet (including poultry, fish, seafood and fruit), fresh air and exercise, and a simple regime of soap and water, with cold cream as a protective base. She sometimes used powder as well, and perhaps occasionally needed slightly more of it, but the astonishing plaster-saint-perfection in some formal portraits came from the photographers' workroom rather than the stage make-up box. The common practice of re-touching and over-painting photographs made people think she had "enamelled" her face, which she never did.

Queen Alexandra was personally virtuous and followed the rules of good behaviour and propriety, but had a mischievous sense of humour, some sympathy with transgressors, and could be broad-minded and understanding. She would often support people being criticised, sometimes unfairly, such as the Duchess of Manchester, Lady Lonsdale, Princess Louise, Marchioness of Lorne, the Munshi or Infanta Eulalie. She stood up for people in trouble, such as Jacques Fehr, the courier, and she apologised to Henry Bell of Garrard's when he had been wrongly accused. She felt compassion for people in self-inflicted adversity, such as Mr Farrar at Sandringham and she even felt sorry for the widowed and exiled Emperor William II of Germany. She owned a copy of *The Ballad of Reading Gaol* and so evidently knew something about Oscar Wilde (1854–1900). She supported the education of women and was interested in women's issues: she read *The Woman who Did*, by Grant Allen – the story of a young, intelligent and virtuous woman who decides that she wants to have a baby without a husband, despite social stigma; she was sorry for the young Duchess Marie of Mecklenburg-Strelitz, who was raped by a footman and gave birth; and she was extremely anxious to help any women who had had babies after being raped by German soldiers in the First World War. At this time she also supported the work of the suffragettes running the military hospital in Endell Street.

This tolerance and imagination helped Alexandra cope with a husband who often fell morally by the wayside, but knew when he had done wrong and regretted it. In fact he could be quite prudish: he thought Rodin's sculptures immoral and some French plays indecent. King Edward was sometimes naïve and thoughtless, and occasionally "blew up" or put his foot down, but would never have been intentionally and deliberately cruel to his wife. Nevertheless, although she seemed to accommodate and accept his "other women", did he ever appreciate not only the hurt she felt, but also the love which helped her overcome it? Perhaps he did; he told his mother that "Alix was much too good for him." Alexandra herself had been a tempestuous child and could still be furiously upset; as an adult she usually kept her strong emotions under control, but they had not disappeared. However, she and her husband both recovered quite quickly from bursts of anger, resumed their affectionate relationship, and spent more time together than is often reported. Alexandra could equally be critical of other people's behaviour before, on reflection, coming to a more sympathetic conclusion.

Alexandra's own relationship to "other men" was clear-cut; she liked men, found them amusing and enjoyed talking to them (as her mother, Queen Louise, and her daughter, Princess Victoria also did) and had several male friends, such as Oliver Montagu, the Marquis de Soveral, Lord Knutsford and others. But she was not in love with any of them. She was devoted to Montagu, but it is plain from her letters to her son Prince George and others that she regarded him as mainly a family friend, as she did Soveral. She and the Marquis exchanged gossipy letters; hers were written in French, but she addressed him as "M de Soveral" and "Vous", rather than the more familiar "Tu". Lord Knutsford, with his connection to the London Hospital, was more of a business associate; they become quite close friends, but always within the rules of propriety.

Alexandra's relationship with her children was one of great love; she adored them and allowed them a certain amount of freedom, but, as a conscientious mother, was also quite strict, especially about good behaviour regarding other people. She had a particular rapport with Prince George, who was, by mid-January 1892, the only one of her three sons to have survived, and, in a different context, important as the heir. He was indeed on good terms with both his parents, while his elder brother, Prince Albert Victor, devoted to his mother, was rather afraid of his father. Alexandra has been criticised for her sentimental style of letter-writing to George, but this was private, affectionate family banter, not meant for anyone outside the family to read. She could be sensible and matter-of-fact when required. Her relationship with her three daughters has also been criticised as being too sheltering. In fact she was behaving much as her own mother had – bringing them up strictly but with great love. They all had poor health and were frequently unwell but when Princess Louise chose the middle-aged Lord Fife as a husband, her mother was glad that she had found a considerate partner and would be comfortable in a successful marriage. Alexandra did not bully her younger daughters into marrying against their will;

they were both happy at home, but when Princess Maud decided to marry her cousin, Prince Charles of Denmark, her mother rejoiced with her.

Princess Victoria, the unmarried daughter, has often been regarded as hard-done-by and in thrall to her mother. This is not strictly true. Victoria was vulnerable; her health was precarious and, although she was much loved by friends and close relatives, her personality could sometimes be challenging. Her mother was, to a certain extent, trying to protect her. When in good health Victoria was lively, kind, friendly and a great asset to her parents as a sort of "personal assistant" in their dealings with guests and officials; she could put people at their ease and advise them what was required, or what the King and Queen would want. Alexandra's view of children's responsibilities towards their parents was based on her own family traditions; when needed, she would always go back to Denmark, for example, to care for her mother in her last illness, or take it turns with her sisters to stay with their elderly widowed father in case he should be lonely. Naturally she hoped her own children would do likewise, and she did depend a great deal on Victoria, but without stopping her from taking holidays away from time to time. Whether marriage would have given Victoria better health and more consequence cannot be guessed; she was not ambitious for a throne or high position and after several unfulfilled dreams, fell in love with a member of the household who was simultaneously perfect for her, but, in those days, out of bounds. Paradoxically, as her mother's companion, she still spent much of her life in his company when he was on duty.

During Alexandra's lifetime, illness was a serious matter. Even royalty were adversely affected by bad drainage (such as at Marlborough House); antibiotics and most vaccines were not yet in use; colds and influenza (to which royalties, meeting so many people, were particularly vulnerable) lasted longer and could be severe. Medical knowledge was less developed, although rapidly advancing. Dentistry relied largely on extracting teeth, rather than preserving them in situ for as long as possible, as poor Princess Victoria discovered. There was no National Health Service and medical attendance and medicine could be expensive; public welfare services outside the range of hospitals and formal medical attendance might be provided by charity groups, often run voluntarily by the upper or upper-middle classes; charity matinees would raise funds for deserving causes. In this milieu, Alexandra's compassionate instincts and support of hospitals and nursing were invaluable.

Patronage of the arts is a royal tradition, which Alexandra followed completely. She enjoyed music personally as a good amateur performer, and was a devotee of opera and concerts. She loved the theatre, and had been brought up to appreciate art in many forms, from sculpture, painting and drawing to photography, the new tool with elements of both science and art. She herself was an amateur artist and photographer, and visiting galleries, studios and exhibitions was one of her principal activities. She took an interest in the Arts and Crafts movement, appreciating its fostering of creative talent, which could then help people earn a living. By founding the technical school at Sandringham as part of this, and enabling its products to be sold, Alexandra invented a modest forerunner of later ventures such as Royal Collection Enterprises and Duchy Organics, albeit without the biscuits.

Past lives have their own context and cannot always be slotted neatly into modern conceptions, but human endeavour arouses interest at all times. Constantly doing her best to fulfil her duties and follow her ideals, Queen Alexandra evokes sympathy and admiration even many years after her death.

Frances Dimond, Windsor, January 2021

Queen Alexandra's descent from King Henry VII of England

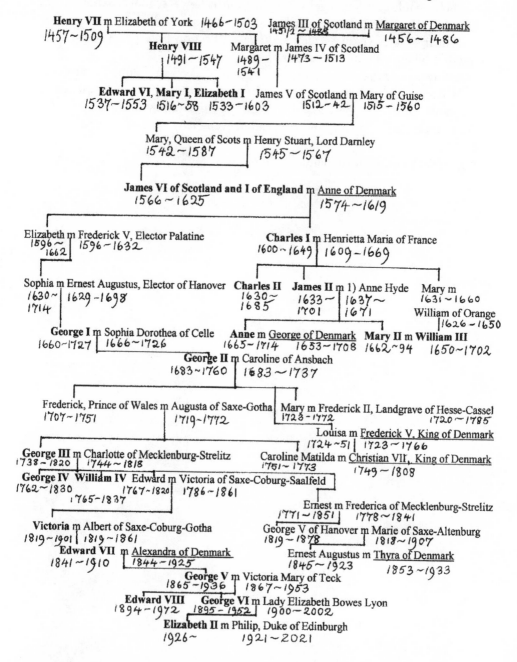

This table is incomplete; it has been simplified to show the main lines of descent. Reigning British monarchs are in bold type and Danish connections are underlined.

Chapter 1

1844–1860

A Danish Childhood

ꕥ

The little princess who became Queen Alexandra[1] was born in Denmark when it was changing politically and redefining its relationship to its close neighbour, the German Confederation, headed by Prussia.[2] This shaped her lifelong Danish patriotism and hatred of Prussian domination, but an equally strong influence was her connection with the Hesse-Cassel family, from which, in addition to their Danish roots, both her parents came. The Danish and Hesse-Cassel families also had marriage alliances with British royalty, which linked Alexandra to Britain even before she became its queen.

Rumpenheim Castle[3] on the banks of the River Main, opposite Frankfort, belonged to the Hesse-Cassel line of the house of Hesse and was renovated for Princess Mary,[4] fourth daughter of the British King George II,[5] who married Frederick II, Landgrave of Hesse-Cassel[6] in 1740. The couple separated in 1755; Mary died in 1772 and their fourth son, Frederick,[7] inherited Rumpenheim; he, his wife, Caroline,[8] and their children often held family reunions there. Caroline died in 1823 and, wishing the gatherings to continue after his own death, Frederick bequeathed Rumpenheim to his three sons and three daughters, requesting that they and their descendants meet there every second year. His eldest son, Landgrave[9] William, had married Princess (Louise) Charlotte of Denmark,[10] a granddaughter of Frederick V,[11] and their third daughter, Louise,[12] was born in 1817. William's sister, Augusta,[13] married Adolphus, Duke of Cambridge.[14]

Karl,[15] Landgrave Frederick II and Princess Mary's third son, had married, in 1766, Princess Louise of Denmark,[16] third daughter of Frederick V. He became a field marshal in the Danish army and Governor of Slesvig-Holstein. Their youngest daughter, Louise,[17] married Frederick William, Duke of Glücksburg[18] in 1810, but his death in 1831 left her and their ten children somewhat impoverished. Her Danish relatives were sympathetic and Frederick VI,[19] whose own sons had died, offered to adopt one of the boys. The fourth, Christian,[20] aged thirteen, was chosen and went to live in Denmark, where he was educated at the military college, rising to Captain of the Life Guards. Like other relatives of Landgrave Frederick, he went to the Rumpenheim reunions and in 1841 became engaged there to his third cousin, Louise (daughter of Landgrave William), whom he had probably already met in Copenhagen, where her parents had a residence. They were in love, and the match pleased their relatives as well as Emperor Nicholas I of Russia.[21]

Christian and Louise were married at Copenhagen on 26 May 1842. Frederick VI had died in 1839 and his cousin, Christian VIII,[22] in 1848. Christian VIII's only surviving son, Frederick VII,[23] despite three marriages (the last to Louise Rasmussen,[24] a former dancer and milliner, whom he created Countess Danner), was childless, as was the heir apparent, his cousin Ferdinand, Hereditary Prince of Denmark.[25] Meanwhile, in 1849, the autocratic Danish monarchy was made constitutional and almost simultaneously an uprising in Holstein sought independence. Denmark accepted Holstein's German sympathies but, as Slesvig and Holstein were "forever undivided", saw Holstein as being permanently bound to Danish Slesvig and therefore to Denmark, although this was not absolutely clear in the original mediaeval document. Now the Holsteiners asserted that they were aligning with Germany and would take Slesvig with them, because the two provinces were bound to stay together. In fact southern Slesvig had also become pro-German and in order to keep Slesvig, Denmark went to war against the revolutionary Holstein army.

Holstein's force was immediately boosted by volunteers from the other German states, including Prussia. The war ended with a Danish victory in 1850, and the pro-German Duke of Augustenburg[26] and 30 revolutionary leaders were exiled. The peace treaty made Slesvig and Holstein Danish again and the London Protocol of 2 August 1850 confirmed the integrity of the Danish monarchy. In North Slesvig the official language would be Danish and in South Slesvig, German. Denmark's new democratic constitution would also apply to Slesvig, but the king was obliged to continue autocratic rule there because Prussia and Austria protested that being democratic would bind Slesvig closer to Denmark than Holstein. It was thus only attached to Denmark through the person of the king.

As Frederick VII had no sons, the Danish succession needed international endorsement. The heir presumptive was Landgravine Charlotte, granddaughter of Frederick V, wife of Landgrave William of Hesse-Cassel and mother of Louise, who was married to Christian of Glücksburg.[27] Although there was no Salic law in Denmark and the succession could descend in the female line, women could not rule in their own right.[28] Charlotte therefore renounced her claim in favour of her daughter, Louise, Princess Christian, who then waived it in favour of her husband, considered more suitable than Charlotte's son, Frederick,[29] besides being, like his wife, a great-grandchild of Frederick V. In the Treaty of London of 8 May 1852, signed by Denmark, the Swedish–Norwegian Union, England, France, Russia, Austria and Prussia, Prince Christian of Glücksburg, good looking, pleasant, modest and of exemplary character, was acknowledged as heir. The Danish parliament approved the treaty and the Duke of Augustenburg (a grandson of King Christian VII through his mother) promised to abandon further claims to the throne on behalf of his family, in return for compensation for his estates on the island of Als. He also renounced his ducal rights in favour of his son, Frederick.[30] Slesvig and Holstein would remain under Danish influence, despite Holstein being a member of the German Confederation and there being some German sympathisers in South Slesvig. Some minor German states refused to sign the Treaty of London, but the unity and future of the realm generally seemed secure.

Prince and Princess Christian were given the Yellow Palace as a residence in Copenhagen and their first child, Frederick,[31] had been born on 3 June 1843. Seven months later, Princess Christian's brother Frederick married Grand Duchess Alexandra,[32] youngest surviving daughter of Emperor Nicholas I. She became pregnant and her sister-in-law Louise was expecting her second child; both babies were due towards the end of 1844, but Alexandra and her premature son both died on 10 August during a visit to St Petersburg. On 1 December Princess Christian gave birth to a daughter, who was named in memory of the young Grand Duchess.

Princess Alexandra Caroline Marie Charlotte Louise Julie was born in a room with a window overlooking the courtyard[33] in the Yellow Palace. She was christened at the palace, in the silver-gilt font traditionally used in the Danish Royal Family.[34] Alexandra had an English nurse, so became familiar with the language from an early age. Soon, she had more brothers and sisters: William,[35] born on Christmas Eve 1845, Dagmar[36] on 26 November 1847, Thyra[37] on 29 September 1853 and Waldemar[38] on 27 October 1858. The elder children tended to group together, while the two youngest were company for one another, but the family was always united and devoted. Other relatives were also valued; in August 1847 Princess Christian and her children were at Rumpenheim, as were the Duchess of Cambridge and her thirteen-year-old daughter, Mary,[39] who, writing in French to a friend, mentioned the swing and carousel in the garden and the little cart, in which they sometimes pulled "la petite Alexandrine". Princess Christian was her favourite cousin and she thought her three little children quite charming.[40] The household in the Yellow Palace was happy, well-disciplined and economical, relying at first solely on Prince Christian's army salary. His wife was sensible, tactful, shrewd and clear-sighted, supporting and perhaps guiding her husband, thus demonstrating a good wife's role to her daughters. She supervised everything, designed her daughters' dresses and gave them the left-over scraps of material for dolls' clothes; they would all sew together while someone read aloud. Prince and Princess Christian were quite strict parents, but loved their children dearly. Alexandra was apparently the favourite and the others would get her to ask their parents for special concessions. The whole family always relied on her as "big sister" and eldest daughter.

In 1848, the year of European revolutions, Frederick VII became King and the Danes, ruled by autocratic, albeit non-tyrannical, monarchs, demanded a constitution, which he granted. It was ratified on 5 June 1849; Denmark would be governed by a two-tiered assembly, the Folketing, (Lower House) and the Landsting (Upper House). There was a great national celebration, which four-year-old Alexandra witnessed.[41] The King became a constitutional monarch and all Danish men over 30 were given the vote. Prince Christian supported democracy and Alexandra thus grew up with some understanding of constitutional monarchy, like that in England.

Meanwhile, she continued travelling abroad with her family and in the autumn of 1851, the Christians, now with four children, stayed with their Cambridge cousins at Dresden. Alexandra was now nearly seven and from an early age she and Dagmar (known in the family as Minny) received their first lessons in general knowledge, music and drawing from their mother, an accomplished artist who also passed on her love of music to them. Leading singers (including Jenny Lind)[42] and musicians were invited to the palace to perform; Alexandra later continued this custom in England. She and her sisters became good pianists and their artistic education continued. Danish kings were noted antiquarian and art collectors and during Alexandra's childhood, Christian VIII held court in the Palace of Christiansborg[43] where there were fine picture galleries, a natural history museum occupying twelve salons and a library with some 400,000 books. Under the King's supervision, Thorwaldsen's[44] marble sculptures and casts were being collected in a museum next to the palace; Thorwaldsen had been honoured at the Danish Court and Alexandra was often taken to see his work. Rosenborg Castle also contained treasures collected by former kings. Regarding literature, Hans Christian Andersen[45] enjoyed royal patronage and was often invited to the Yellow Palace. Alexandra was allowed to read his stories as a reward for good behaviour. When Andersen died in 1875 Queen Louise placed a wreath of laurels and lilies on his coffin. Princess Alexandra loved the arts; regarding studies in general, she is quoted as saying, "We had to learn, for we were made to understand that it was necessary."

The girls were taught needlework, sewing Christmas presents for relatives and friends. Alexandra was a good needlewoman and loved pretty clothes; apparently disliking her gymnastics dress, she was told she could wear a different one if she made it herself, which she promptly did. Her sense of style later made her a leader of fashion; while her youthful clothes were always plain and simple, she was able to follow her own ideas in adulthood. The children's physical education included drill for deportment, gymnastics, and riding lessons from their father. Alexandra was always a fearless rider and also loved dancing; she is said to have invented some dances. She used to go to her grandparents' little evening parties in their palace in Copenhagen and occasionally was allowed to attend dances given by her mother's friends, although her mother did not believe in late hours or too much excitement for young people.[46] The Yellow Palace was not far from the sea and Alexandra liked watching the ships in the sound from the harbour. Winters were spent in the old-fashioned palace, with its small rooms, winding stairs and passages, and Christmas was celebrated there. Each child had a small tree and they all danced round a large central tree, laden with presents and shimmering lights. Alexandra's birthday was also spent in Copenhagen and for this her young friends would be invited.[47] There were not many servants and the girls had to dust their own rooms and help at mealtimes; on one occasion the butter was running low and Princess Christian asked Alexandra to fetch some more, which she willingly did. She and her sisters were always taught to behave naturally and graciously, with simple good manners. Punctuality was important and while their mother was very lenient in some ways, they would be punished for lateness at lessons or meals. Alexandra sometimes arrived late in the dining room and for this she had to drink her coffee standing up.[48] She never entirely mastered the art of punctuality.

The Law of Succession, passed in 1853, made Prince Christian's family slightly better off, although by royal standards they were still quite poor. He became a member of the King's Council, with an allowance of 80,000 rigsdaler. Bernstorff Palace, a pleasant, white-painted country house in extensive grounds on the outskirts of Copenhagen, was made available for his use. Alexandra's life was now divided in two; winters in Copenhagen and summers at Bernstorff. As soon as the weather improved, the family would sail from Copenhagen Harbour to the little landing stage at Klampenborg, and drive along the sea road to Bernstorff, with miles of deer forest beyond. There was also an approach through an avenue of elms, a mile and a half long. Bernstorff was beautiful and serene and studies were relaxed, although the girls went into Copenhagen for lessons on Tuesdays and Fridays. The children lived mostly in the open air, walking, riding with their father and playing in the park, or helping their mother with gardening and cutting and arranging flowers for the house. Early hours and plain living were the rule; after a light breakfast, they played in the woods until their mother's gong[49] or their father's whistle summoned them home for *déjeuner*. After this, there were lessons and then walking or driving in the afternoon until dinner at 4 o'clock. Then coffee, often served in the garden, was followed by reading and needlework, or walking to the village of Gjentofte, about a mile away, as Princess Christian encouraged her daughters to take a friendly interest in the inhabitants. On Sundays the family attended the red-tiled church there informally and the pastor was always welcome at Bernstorff. Friends from Copenhagen would also visit, for boating excursions and picnics in the woods.[50]

The Christians and their five children were at Rumpenheim again in August

1857, where the young Lady Geraldine Somerset,[51] lady-in-waiting to the Duchess of Cambridge, met them for the first time. They went on trips to Frankfort, shopping and visiting confectioners, and spent a day at Biberich. At Rumpenheim again in August and September 1859, they had a *"parti champêtre"* at Dorfeld on 11 September, with a picnic lunch in the picturesque old farmhouse.[52] Alexandra had her English exercise book[53] with her, dated 16 September 1859; it was later used for French, Danish and German exercises as well. One of her early English exercises contained the sentence, "at last perseverance was crowned with success"; "Nothing like perseverance" she would say in later life. At thirteen, she had begun formal English lessons on 5 January 1858 with Miss Mathilde Knudsen, a bright and cheerful person with whom Alexandra remained friendly for the rest of her life; calling on her in Denmark and in England, which the teacher sometimes visited. Miss Knudsen would be invited to tea, lunch and, once, dinner.[54] [55] She was at the garden party held on the day before the Duke of York's[56] marriage in 1893 and eventually received an invitation to the coronation in 1902. Other teachers were the Swiss Mademoiselle Schwiedland, Alexandra's resident French governess; Monsieur Siboni (music); Pastor Theobald, the clergyman from the German Reformed Church, (German); Professor Buntzen[57] (drawing) and Professor Petersen (history and geography). Alexandra's surviving lesson books,[58] dating from 1854–1862, included English, French, Danish and German; *Cours d'Analyse Logique,* 1859, *and Histoire Naturelle,* with essays about animals, vegetables and minerals. She also studied Swiss and Danish history, a list of the kings of Norway from 930–1412, and ancient history, including Rome and Greece. She wrote a long essay in French on this topic in 1855. Lessons also referred to Shakespeare's plays, providing an English cultural influence, and she seems to have been fond of amateur dramatics, spending so much time studying plays that in the end her mother intervened to stop her.[59] Alexandra always loved the theatre and later would often show a feeling for drama in the clothes and colours she chose to wear, her fondness for reading aloud and in her dignified bearing and "sense of occasion" at important ceremonies. She had the gift of easy conversation and spoke well.

Pastor Paulli,[60] who prepared Alexandra for confirmation, was impressed by her strong religious faith. She and her brother Frederick were confirmed on 18 October 1860 in the presence of the King at the Chapel Royal (Slots Kirken) in Copenhagen when she was nearly sixteen. Previously sharing a bedroom and sitting room with Minny, Alexandra was now given her own room in the Yellow Palace, which she loved. It was simply upholstered in blue and contained her piano, her worktable and a little cabinet for her treasures, which she later took to Sandringham.[61]

In England, Albert Edward, Prince of Wales[62] was also growing up. Very slight, with blue eyes and a sweet smile, he looked young for his age. He was shy and diffident but very charming; Miss Ella Taylor,[63] lectrice to the Duchess of

Cambridge, wrote half-jokingly to her mother, "I can't tell you what a duck he is. I am quite in love with him".[64] On 9 November, his seventeenth birthday, the Prince received the uniform of an "unattached Colonel" and, without any examination, was gazetted a lieutenant-colonel. He had begged his parents[65] for military training, but starting at the bottom of the ladder, and he found the unearned high rank embarrassing, for example, when reporting to the Duke of Cambridge,[66] Commander-in-Chief. At the same time, he was given a memorandum about his future, drafted by Prince Albert and signed by both parents. His tutor, Mr Gibbs,[67] would be replaced by a governor, General Bruce,[68] to guide, supervise and convey his parents' wishes to him. He would become a Knight of the Garter, denoting "the Christian fight ... with the temptations and difficulties of this transient life" and should understand that "Life is composed of duties and in the due, punctual and cheerful performance of them the true Christian, true soldier and true Gentleman is recognised." He would have his own rooms and, when not having lessons, exercise or recreation would learn how to occupy himself constructively on his own responsibility. Above all he would be taught how to become a good man and a thorough gentleman. His allowance would be increased to £500 a year, within which limit he was expected to keep. He should always be kind and courteous to his staff and servants, who, although salaried, had not "surrendered that dignity which belongs to them as brother men and brother Christians" but should not depend abjectly on servants for his daily needs; "the more you can do for yourself and the less you need their help, the greater will be your independence and real comfort." Most importantly, his conduct should be ruled by the precepts of the Church catechism, the most important being to "love your neighbour as yourself and do unto all men as you would they should do unto you."[69]

Albert Edward did indeed absorb many of the plan's good intentions, but placing a barrier between him and his parents was problematic. He loved and respected General Bruce but should also have been encouraged to confide in his father.[70] The plan was silent about women; being a thorough gentleman was a good start, but an attractive, susceptible seventeen-year-old needed more; shy of discussing such personal matters with his father, he would fall into a predictable trap. Advice on sexual awareness and appropriate pro-creation, both crucial to the survival of the monarchy, seems to have been carefully avoided. Prince Albert, intelligent and far-sighted, would not have hesitated in giving this if he had felt it to be his duty, but he and the Queen deplored the immorality of some of their own relatives and perhaps felt that explaining things to Bertie was likely to encourage him. The Duchess of Cambridge had indeed told Ella Taylor how "pure minded" the royal couple were and that if anyone told a "naughty" story or repeated a *"double entendre"* in Albert's presence, he "either did not understand the drift of what was said – or if he did – he blushed with shame & indignation."[71]

Nevertheless, the couple had begun to look for a wife for their son. They worried incessantly about him, as the Queen told her daughter,[72] "Bertie continues such an anxiety!... His only safety & the Country's is his implicit reliance in everything on dearest Papa, that perfection of human beings!"[73] Unfortunately this made dearest Papa virtually unapproachable, however much he may have wished otherwise. Bertie was improving slowly but "certainly the wife will be of immense importance! I trust we may find somebody at last but it is very difficult."[74] It was essential to get a Protestant princess, who was most likely to be found in Germany. Vicky sent a disappointing report about Princess Elizabeth of Wied;[75] others failed to qualify, although another two years could make a great difference. "Looks, health, education, character, intellect & a good disposition we want; great rank & riches we do not."[76] Bertie continued with his studies, passing a good examination by 31 March 1860, when the Dean of Christ Church College,[77] Oxford, reported him decidedly improved. The Queen found him "not in good looks" and was irritated by his "frightful inactivity".[78] This was probably due to boredom and a lack of stimulating projects; when he travelled to Coburg and Gotha, and later Canada and America, he made a favourable impression, began developing his social skills and returned home "quite bright & lively".[79]

Princess Alice[80] (seventeen) became engaged to Prince Louis of Hesse[81] on 30 November. Vicky was delighted at her sister's happiness, and, interestingly, had heard recently from several people about the daughter of Prince Christian, heir to the Danish throne, giving rapturous accounts of her beauty, charm, amiability, frank, natural manner and other excellent qualities. As Vicky told her mother on 7 December, "I thought it right to tell you all this in Bertie's interest, though I as Prussian cannot wish that Bertie should ever marry her. I know her nurse who tells me that she is strong in health and has never ailed anything. I must say in the Photograph I think her lovely, & just the style Bertie admires, but I repeat again that an Alliance with Denmark wd be a misfortune for us here."[82] Ten days later she sent another photograph which was "unashamedly pretty".[83] She had never seen anything so sweet, "do not let Bertie see it or he must fall in love with it."[84] Vicky had already heard from her father, who, as she had expected, had admired the first photograph, commenting, "Gott sei uns gnädig".[85] Nevertheless, as Queen Victoria made very clear on the 18th; "We are anxious to know as much about Pcess Eliz[abeth] of Wied and Anna of Hesse[86] as possible, as I think the future choice of Bertie must lie between them ... You know, dearest, we must feel vy anxious about this choice, & the beauty at Denmark is much agst our wishes. I do wish somebody wld go & marry her off – at once. If Bertie cld see & like one of the others 1st, then I am sure we shld be safe."[87]

The House of Glücksburg's descent from the Danish Royal Family

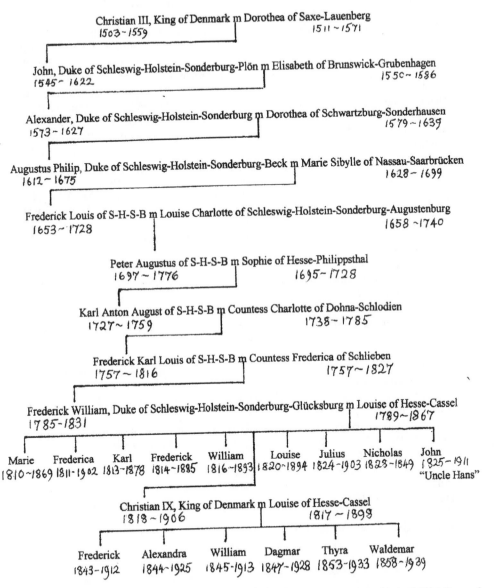

Christian III, King of Denmark m Dorothea of Saxe-Lauenberg
1503-1559 · 1511~1571

John, Duke of Schleswig-Holstein-Sonderburg-Plön m Elisabeth of Brunswick-Grubenhagen
1545~1622 · 1550~1586

Alexander, Duke of Schleswig-Holstein-Sonderburg m Dorothea of Schwartzburg-Sonderhausen
1573-1627 · 1579~1639

Augustus Philip, Duke of Schleswig-Holstein-Sonderburg-Beck m Marie Sibylle of Nassau-Saarbrücken
1612~1675 · 1628~1699

Frederick Louis of S-H-S-B m Louise Charlotte of Schleswig-Holstein-Sonderburg-Augustenburg
1653~1728 · 1658~1740

Peter Augustus of S-H-S-B m Sophie of Hesse-Philippsthal
1697~1776 · 1695~1728

Karl Anton August of S-H-S-B m Countess Charlotte of Dohna-Schlodien
1727~1759 · 1738~1785

Frederick Karl Louis of S-H-S-B m Countess Frederica of Schlieben
1757~1816 · 1757~1827

Frederick William, Duke of Schleswig-Holstein-Sonderburg-Glücksburg m Louise of Hesse-Cassel
1785-1831 · 1789~1867

| Marie | Frederica | Karl | Frederick | William | Louise | Julius | Nicholas | John |
| 1810~1869 | 1811~1902 | 1813~1878 | 1814~1885 | 1816~1893 | 1820~1894 | 1824~1903 | 1823~1849 | 1825~1911 "Uncle Hans" |

Christian IX, King of Denmark m Louise of Hesse-Cassel
1818~1906 · 1817~1898

| Frederick | Alexandra | William | Dagmar | Thyra | Waldemar |
| 1843-1912 | 1844~1925 | 1845-1913 | 1847~1928 | 1853-1933 | 1858-1939 |

who became King Frederick VIII of Denmark, Queen Alexandra of Great Britain and Ireland, King George I of the Hellenes, Empress Marie Feodorovna of Russia, Thyra, Duchess of Cumberland, and Prince Waldemar of Denmark

This table is incomplete and some abbreviations have been used

Notes

1 Princess Alexandra of Slesvig-Holstein-Sonderburg-Glücksburg (1844–1925), later of Denmark; m future King Edward VII and became Queen Alexandra

2 The author acknowledges *A History of Denmark* by Palle Lauring, translated from Danish by David Hohnen, for valuable help. Traditionally, problems arose from the complicated politics of the provinces of Slesvig and Holstein, which linked Denmark geographically with Germany. Slesvig was originally Danish land, administered as an independent duchy, while Holstein, although German, was more or less united to it. In 1460 King Christian I of Denmark was elected sovereign duke of Slesvig and feudal lord in Holstein, bringing them together under the Danish crown and putting a clause into the agreement that they were never to be separated: "Up ewig ungedeelt". He could have had no idea of the trouble this would cause in the future.

When Denmark (supported by Napoleon) lost the Seven Years' War of 1807–1814 to England, its long-standing union with Norway was dissolved at the Congress of Vienna in 1814 and the strong Norwegian influence in Danish intellectual life and the civil service began to be replaced by a German element. Holstein, where German nationalism was growing, started looking to Germany rather than Denmark

3 Damaged in the Second World War but restored in the 21st century as flats

4 Princess Mary of Great Britain (1723–1772)

5 King George II (1683–1760)

6 Frederick II, Landgrave of Hesse-Cassel (1720–1785)

7 Landgrave Frederick of Hesse-Cassel (1747–1837)

8 Princess Caroline of Nassau-Usingen (1762–1823)

9 Landgrave William of Hesse-Cassel (1787–1867); the title "Landgrave" was not only borne by the head of the house; it seems to be have been used by the other male descendants as well.

10 Princess Charlotte of Denmark (1789–1864), m Landgrave William of Hesse-Cassel

11 King Frederick V of Denmark (1723–1766)

12 Princess Louise of Hesse-Cassel (1817–1898), m future King Christian IX of Denmark (Queen Alexandra's parents)

13 Princess Augusta of Hesse-Cassel (1797–1889), m Adolphus, Duke of Cambridge

14 Adolphus, Duke of Cambridge (1774–1850), seventh son of King George III

15 Landgrave Karl of Hesse-Cassel (1744–1836)

16 Princess Louise of Denmark (1750–1831) m Landgrave Karl of Hesse-Cassel

17 Princess Louise of Hesse-Cassel (1789–1867) m Frederick William, Duke of Glücksburg

18 Frederick William Duke of Glücksburg (1785–1831); Glücksburg was in Slesvig, close to Denmark

19 King Frederick VI of Denmark (1768–1839)

20 Prince Christian of Slesvig-Holstein-Sonderburg-Glücksburg (1818–1906), King Christian IX of Denmark

21 Emperor Nicholas I of Russia (1796–1855)

22 King Christian VIII of Denmark (1786–1848)

23 King Frederick VII of Denmark (1808–1863)

24 Louise Rasmussen (1815–1874) Countess Danner, m King Frederick VII of Denmark

25 Ferdinand, Hereditary Prince of Denmark (1792–1863)

26 Christian, Duke of Slesvig-Holstein-Sonderburg-Augustenburg (1798–1869)

27 Full title, Prince Christian of Slesvig-Holstein-Sonderburg-Glücksburg

28 The Salic law applied in Slesvig and Holstein, (united under the Danish Crown since 1460)

29 Landgrave Frederick of Hesse-Cassel (1820–1884)

30   Frederick, Duke of Slesvig-Holstein-Sonderburg-Augustenburg (1829–1880)

31   1843–1912; later King Frederick VIII of Denmark

32   Grand Duchess Alexandra Nicholaievna of Russia (1825–1844), m Landgrave Frederick of Hesse-Cassel

33   Sarah A Tooley, *The Life of Queen Alexandra*, p 8

34   Tooley, p 5

35   Prince William of Denmark (1845–1913), later elected King George I of the Hellenes

36   Princess Dagmar of Denmark (1847–1928), m the future Emperor Alexander II of Russia

37   Princess Thyra of Denmark (1853–1933), m Ernest Augustus, Duke of Cumberland

38   Prince Waldemar of Denmark (1858–1939)

39   Princess Mary Adelaide of Cambridge (1833–1897), later Duchess of Teck

40   Clement Kinloch Cooke, *A Memoir of Princess Mary Adelaide, Duchess of Teck*, Vol.I, pp 77,79,121

41   Tooley, p 9

42   Jenny Lind (1820–1887), Swedish opera singer

43   Gutted by fire in 1884

44   (Albert) Bertel Thorwaldsen (1770–1844), leading sculptor

45   Hans Christian Andersen (1805–1875), well-known Danish author

46   Details about Alexandra's youth are from Tooley, p 8 and elsewhere

47   Tooley, pp 10–11

48   Tooley, p 40

49   Later taken to Fredensborg and used to summon grandchildren

50   Tooley, pp 13–14

51   Lady Geraldine Somerset (1832–1915)

52   RA VIC/ADDC6/1/1857:7 August; 1859:1 September, diary kept by Lady Geraldine Somerset for the Duchess of Cambridge

53   Private collection

54   Tooley, pp 10–11

55   RA VIC/MAIN/QAD/1880: 27 October

56   Prince George (1865–1936), later Duke of York, Prince of Wales and then King George V

57   Heinrich Buntzen (1803–1892), Professor of the Royal Academy in Copenhagen, and also Princess Christian's art teacher

58   Private collection

59   David Williamson, *Queen Alexandra*, p 21

60   Just Henrik Voltelen Paulli, (1809–1865), Danish priest

61   Tooley, p 16

62   Albert Edward, Prince of Wales (1841–1910), later King Edward VII

63   Miss Ella Taylor (1827–1914)

64   RA VIC/ADDA8/390, Ella Taylor's Reminscences. 1827–1889, p 32, letter to her mother, 1858:31 October

65   Queen Victoria (1819–1901), and Albert, Prince Consort (1819–1861)

66   George, Duke of Cambridge (1819–1904), Queen Victoria's first cousin

67   Frederick Waymouth Gibbs (1821–1898), barrister and tutor to Albert Edward, Prince of Wales

68   Major General Robert Bruce (1813–1862), army officer who served as governor to the Prince of Wales

69   RA VIC/MAIN/Z/141/36, Queen Victoria and the Prince Consort to the Prince of Wales, 1858: 9 November

70   As indeed Albert Edward encouraged his own sons, when the time came

71   RA VIC/ADDA8/390, Taylor, p 49

72   Victoria, Princess Royal, (Vicky) (1840–1901), m Prince Frederick William of Prussia, later Emperor Frederick III

73   RA VIC/ADDU/32/1859:9 April, Queen Victoria to Princess Frederick William of Prussia

74   RA VIC/ADDU/32/1859:16 April, Queen Victoria to Princess Frederick William of Prussia

75   Princess Elizabeth of Wied (1843–1916), m King Carol I of Roumania; she wrote under the pen-name of "Carmen Sylva"

76   RA VIC/ADDU/32/1859:10 December, Queen Victoria to Princess Frederick William of Prussia

77   Henry George Liddell (1811–1898), dean from 1855–1891

78   In German, "grässliche Unthäthigkeit"; RA VIC/ADDU/32/1860:9 April, Queen Victoria to Princess Frederick William of Prussia

79   RA VIC/ADDU/32/1860:25 April, Queen Victoria to Princess Frederick William of Prussia

80   Princess Alice (1843–1878), m Prince Louis, later Grand Duke Louis IV of Hesse and By Rhine

81   Prince Louis of Hesse (1837–1892), later Louis IV, Grand Duke of Hesse and by Rhine

82   RA VIC/MAIN/Z//10/22/1860:7 December, Princess Frederick William of Prussia to Queen Victoria

83   In German, "unverschämt hubsch"

84   RA VIC/MAIN/Z/10/25, Princess Frederick William of Prussia to Queen Victoria, 1860: 17 December

85   "May God be gracious to us"; RA VIC/MAIN/Z/3/50, Princess Frederick William of Prussia to Prince Consort, 1860; 15 December

86   Princess Anna of Hesse (1843–1865), Louis' sister, m Frederick Franz II, Grand Duke of Mecklenburg-Schwerin

87   RA VIC/ADDU/32/1860:18 December, Queen Victoria to Princess Frederick William of Prussia

Chapter 2

1861–1862

"She ... longs to go to England"

꧁

In February 1861 the Queen reluctantly began reconsidering, although a "connection with a certain beauty" would never be desirable; her gentleness could provoke rudeness and bullying, unless she was also intelligent, determined, good-tempered and cheerful. "Those who never knock under, but hold their own, are always those most liked & who get on best with the nameless individual."[1] When by the 25th Vicky reported that Elizabeth of Wied was highly intelligent but utterly tactless, and Anna of Hesse and even Alexandra of Denmark should be considered, Victoria replied; "get Wally[2] to find out everything about [Alexandra's] education & general character; whether she is clever, quiet, not frivolous or vain, fond of preoccupation etc ... & whether she seems very *outré* Danish. The Mother's family are bad, the Father's foolish. Valérie[3] cld write to Wally to find it all out." This vital matter needed prompt action. "It is so very important, with the peculiar character we have to deal with. The Pcess of Meiningen[4] he did not like, & she is not strong, Marie of the Netherlands[5] is clever & ladylike, but too plain & not strong, & poor Addy[6] not clever or pretty."[7] Anna of Hesse was a nice girl, but had bad teeth and a nervous twitch.[8] Marie of Altenburg[9] was good looking, but badly dressed and "always with her <u>most</u> disagreeable Mother".[10] Only Princess Marie of Hohenzollern[11] had everything – but she was Roman Catholic.[12] However, Walburga Paget was making further enquiries about Princess Alexandra; as Vicky, now Crown Princess of Prussia, wrote on 11 March, "At present, although I do not like to own it, even to my own self, the balance is inclining on the side of the Danish beauty, but ... how can one judge without having seen a person!"[13]

The Queen was heartbroken at her mother the Duchess of Kent's[14] death on 16 March, but within a month Vicky was sending more information from Alexandra's former nurse (a friend of Mrs Hobbs,[15] who was Vicky's children's nurse). She had been with Alexandra for ten years[16] and remembered her as "the sweetest girl [who] ever lived, & full of life and spirits. She says she has <u>always</u> been as strong and healthy as possible & has a very good constitution; that she has never ailed anything in her life except having the measles." Vicky's mother-in-law, Queen Augusta,[17] had concluded that, although this sounded better than what she knew about any German princesses, the match was politically undesirable, especially because of the Hesse-Cassel connection and the Duchess of Cambridge's influence. Queen Augusta was willing to help initiate the chosen princess into her future life and duties, but could not do so with the beautiful Dane, because all the unmarried Prussian princes in Berlin would fall in love with her.[18] Later, Vicky told her mother she had seen a letter, in German, from Alexandra to her nurse, saying how seriously she regarded her confirmation and how she would miss her lessons[19] when it was over.[20]

Evidently a meeting should be arranged. Berlin was impossible but Vicky had heard that Princess Christian and her daughters were expected at Strelitz on 29 May. Without saying why, she asked Augusta, Grand Duchess of Mecklenburg-Strelitz[21] whether she (Vicky) and her husband[22] could visit; this was agreed[23] and they arrived on 3 June. Vicky was nervous enough about her under-cover mission but also acutely self-conscious; travelling there in an open carriage, she had caught the sun on her forehead and right cheek and had a swollen, red and painful face;[24] "it is so odious arriving at a strange place looking such a figure, and everybody asking what had happened." Augusta and her husband Frederick[25] were most kind but his mother, the Dowager[26] (the Duchess of Cambridge's sister), was "the most vulgar, common, disagreeable woman I ever saw, and leads poor Augusta a dreadful life, as I have had plenty of opportunity of seeing." The house was badly run; unpunctual, haphazard and rudderless, while the fine park and garden were ill-kept. It seemed "uncommonly dull", but fortunately some of the people were agreeable. Frederick and Augusta's son, Adolphus,[27] was a "dear boy"; Princess Dagmar of Denmark a "dear little thing" and her mother, Princess Christian, although very deaf, "very amiable". Vicky was "all in a tremble and almost ready to cry" when she first saw Princess Alexandra. A slender young girl, taller than her,[28] and with a lovely figure, faced her. She had a beautiful complexion, fine, regular white teeth and lovely large eyes, with very prettily-marked eyebrows. Her nose was narrow and well-shaped, although a little long; "her whole face is very narrow, her forehead too, but well-shaped and not at all flat." She looked rather severe, but when she began to talk and smile her face lit up and her expression became infinitely sweet. She was unpretentious, childlike but not childish, and apparently not at all shy. After more meetings, Vicky was utterly entranced; "She is lovely! not a dazzling, striking beauty but an indescribable [sic] charming one." Alix, as she was called, was evidently exceedingly well brought up and could speak English, German, some Swedish and French, although usually she spoke Danish. She was soon comfortable with Vicky, talking away about her life. She was still having lessons, which she enjoyed, although she found writing essays difficult. History she liked immensely.[29] "She says she likes being in Germany very much indeed, and longs to go to England. She seems very lively and merry, but as she is so very graceful, it suits her very well." Alix was only sixteen, but "her voice, her walk, carriage and manner are perfect, she is one of the most ladylike and aristocratic people I ever saw." She seemed completely unaware of her own beauty and was very modest.[30]

As the meeting seemed to have happened quite naturally, Vicky optimistically hoped no-one there would suspect otherwise. She would try to talk to Alix a little more, to find out what she was like. "She tells me she is very fond of music and plays, and very fond of pictures." However, Vicky dared not talk to her too much, "for fear of attracting attention, & with Hessian eyes in every direction one must mind what one is about." If Alix was to be "the one", once engaged, she could perhaps stay briefly in Germany with Vicky or Queen Augusta, to be initiated into her future life. Vicky had no doubt Bertie would admire her "as she is just what he likes"[31] and told her father on 6 June that it was not just Alix's beauty but "the sweetness of her expression, her voice and manner, the grace in every movement, the perfect, easy charm[32] which draws one to this sweet young girl! Her education seems to have been a very good one, ie a natural one, and one of the heart; it is so nice to see her with her Mother and with her little Sister." There had been "but one voice about her" at Strelitz "and our people" were quite carried away.[33] [34] Alix was refined and tactful; although probably not as clever as Elizabeth of Wied, she was gentle and modest and knew instinctively how to behave. She had been strictly brought up, had never read a novel except an English book called *Home Influence* and, although not yet "out in the world" had perfect manners in company and something spontaneous to say to everyone. Having won Vicky's heart, she reciprocated by begging Vicky to call her "Du"[35] and "Alix". When Vicky and Fritz joked that she would not like them because they were Prussians, she replied, "When I hear grumbling in Denmark about the Germans, then I grumble about the Danes, because it annoys me so."[36] This was pleasing, and diplomatic. Alix sang some Swedish songs with a very pretty voice and could play charmingly. She liked drawing, preferring figures to landscapes, and also riding, dancing and pony carriage driving. "You could not see a nicer girl anywhere. She looks a born Queen or Empress!" Something, but not too much, had to be said to her mother; Vicky hazarded saying she would tell the Queen how charming Alix was. "Please don't say too much or she might be disappointed!"[37] was the reply. Vicky joked that she looked at every pretty face for her brother. "Even the Prince of Wales is obliged to have the best available",[38] said Princess Christian.

The Queen and Prince Albert knew that Vicky and Fritz, as Germans, would be against Bertie marrying a Dane, but as family members they could only rejoice at his union with such a charming girl. Politics and personal feelings conflicted. Also, while Alix's parents could not be faulted, other relatives appeared highly objectionable. If Countess Danner heard that Alix might be going to England, she would do everything she could to make her as Danish as possible, confounding the Queen and Prince Albert's wish to encourage her

German sympathies. Crucially, another Prince might carry her off before Bertie was 22, in 1863.[39] Prince Albert sent Vicky's letter and others, with some photographs of Alexandra, to Bertie, then at Madingley Hall at Cambridge. After carefully studying them, Bertie thanked his relatives on 11 June for all their efforts on his behalf. "The accounts of the Pss are so very good, that it leaves me really nothing to say; but of course how to find a way of securing her, is a very difficult matter." Returning the letters, which he had shown General Bruce, and the photographs, "which I am quite loath to part with",[40] he asked for time to consider. General Bruce told Prince Albert his son was "evidently most interested in the project, more so than I have ever seen him in any point seriously affecting his future, and most captivated by the description contained in these letters."[41] On the 12th the Queen thanked the Prussians for their letters. Vicky seemed rather "carried away" about Alix, but as the much more level-headed Fritz agreed, then "she really must be charming in every sense of the word, & really a pearl not to be lost. The thought of having in Bertie's wife so charming a daughter, wld be a great comfort for me & there is nothing I wld not do to be quite a real Mother to her." But would this pearl accept him? Alice had said she personally would strongly object to being selected without knowing for whom. Meanwhile, "I am so glad that Augusta suspects nothing. I only hope you cautioned the mother to be discreet, so that the Cambridges don't get wind of it? They always made more of the 2nd, Dagmar, who you say is plain, but who they thought so very pretty. Is the Mother still good looking? I suppose the Father did not come."[42]

Vicky had heard that the Dutch queen[43] was interested in Alexandra for her son, the Prince of Orange[44] and had approached Princess Christian. "You know what an intriguing, sly woman the Queen of the Netherlands is – it wld be dreadful if she caught the Princess, wh if she has an idea that she is wanted for Bertie, she will do forthwith," she told her father on the 14th. Augusta had reported this, probably "to hear what my answer wld be, so I was careful & only said, the Prince of Orange was a bad lot,[45] and I did not know whether a mother wld like to sacrifice her child. Augusta said he had much improved and it wld be a nice position, in short seemed to wish it, so I dropped the subject." Obviously Alix would have plenty of suitors; something must be done – "what I do not know." People in Berlin were suspecting Vicky of going to Strelitz to look at her, although some thought it was for Prince Albert of Prussia.[46] Now Vicky had some suggestions; there would be military manoeuvres on the Rhine in September and she would be at Brühl or Coblentz and could perhaps invite Princess Christian and her daughter over from Rumpenheim; Prince Albert or even Bertie could come for the day and see Alix. Or, if her father agreed, she could ask Princess Christian not to settle anything with the Prince of Orange until she had heard further from her; perhaps they could invite Princess Christian and Alix to England in 1862, having sent Bertie away, and ask her not to give the Dutch queen a decisive answer before then. As to whether Alix would accept him, "I have not much doubt on that score; he turns most Ladies' heads as you know!"[47]

Vicky had something else to tell her father on 14 June, having briefly mentioned it to her mother on the 4th. When she saw Alexandra at Strelitz, she heard about a mark on her neck, which she would never have noticed if Alix had not revealed it herself; it was normally hidden during the day by her high-cut dress or, in the evening, by a necklace or her long curls over her shoulders. It seems odd to show this to a comparative stranger but Alix was very conscious of the mark and often talked about it. Perhaps it was kindly fellow-feeling because of Vicky's embarrassing sunburn. Of course they all knew about it and Augusta later began, unasked, to explain that it was not scrofula, but a careless doctor's mistake; Alix's delicate skin had reacted badly to his treatment. Vicky had to respond cautiously but determined to find out more, as Dr Wegner had said it could be scrofula or an abscess after swollen glands.[48] Wally Paget spoke to Alexandra's Aunt Anna, Landgrave Frederick's second wife,[49] who said Alix was upset about the scar, "because she says people would think she had been cut there, and that was not the case at all."[50] She had had a bad cold with swollen glands the year before; a clumsy doctor had experimented, causing an ulcer, which failed to heal properly. There was no scrofula in the family and everyone seemed healthy, even Alix's grandparents, in their early 70s; Landgravine Charlotte had a complexion like a young girl.

Prince Albert had finally allowed Bertie a strictly-disciplined ten-week course of military training with the 1st Battalion, Grenadier Guards at the Curragh Camp near Dublin, during the summer vacation from Cambridge. He would learn the duties of every grade from ensign upwards, thoroughly and promptly, and should try to earn promotion every fortnight. With "some exertion" he should, within ten weeks, be able to command a battalion and manoeuvre a brigade in the field.[51] Bertie was delighted, although the plan was unrealistically ambitious. He left for the Curragh on 2 June and heard there about negotiations for a meeting with Princess Alexandra. On 13 July his father told him Princess Christian had agreed, but the location was not yet decided. Ostend was a possibility but meeting there without King Leopold[52] might look odd and suspicious. It was essential to avoid Rumpenheim and the "43 disagreeable or objectionable relatives" there. Even with the Rhineland manoeuvres as an excuse, it was not known whether Princess Christian and her daughter could stay in Germany until the end of September.[53] Princess Christian had suggested Wiesbaden or Biberich but Bertie thought they would not do at all and neither would Ostend, just a popular seaside resort; he preferred Coblentz or Düsseldorf[54] and also wanted Vicky to be present.[55]

One objection to meeting at the manoeuvres was that the French emperor[56] was expected and encountering him there might seem politically significant.

Meanwhile Ernest II of Saxe-Coburg-Gotha[57] had got wind of the proposed match and was vociferous in his disapproval. Bertie had had enough, writing, rather bitterly, to his father, "Though it seems settled that the Emperor Napoleon is going to be at the Manoeuvres on the Rhine, I should hardly think that meeting him there with so many other Princes of Foreign Nations would do any harm, & could hardly be looked upon as a political object; of course I merely give this as my idea, & know full well that any reasons you may have agst it are of course very good, & mine next to yours are worth nothing; but it seems such a pity to give up the idea of going to the Rhine, as the people in England would consider it quite natural my going there, after my military duties here, especially if I could meet the Princess there."[58] This made sense, but finally his father told him that, as Napoleon III would not be at the manoeuvres after all, Bertie could attend from 16–20 September. He would have to be at Cologne on the evening of the 15th and then accompany Vicky in her choice of opportunity and *rendezvous* for the other meeting.[59] Bertie thanked him delightedly "for all the trouble you have taken in my affairs." He was glad his father was "satisfied with my progress here, & every day my work becomes more interesting as I go on, & understand more about it; but I quite agree that one must study books at the same time."[60] He was enjoying army life but finding it hard to keep up. Performing a subaltern's duties in his colonel's uniform was not edifying; he made slow progress with drill, was not ready to command a company, let alone a battalion, and felt humiliated by his inadequacy.

At Osborne on 9 August the Queen and Vicky, who was staying there, discussed the meeting and what was to be said to Princess Christian. At the Curragh, Bertie was thinking about his marriage and the girl he would soon meet. It was almost the end of his time there, and being with officers who were so much more worldly-wise than he was, had opened his eyes. He was an amiable young man, who wanted to fit in and make friends, but his royal rank and military inexperience were stumbling blocks. He could not compete with the others, except perhaps in one way. There were certain things he should know about marriage. Perhaps he had already confided in his companions; they obliged by introducing him to a young actress, Nellie Clifden, and on three occasions she gave him the instruction he wanted.[61] He had managed to evade General Bruce and felt it was not necessary to tell his father; this was between men of the world and a gentleman did not bring a lady's name into disrepute. It was all part of his education. On the 11th he left for Dublin, arriving in London early on the 13th.

His father had told him that Uncle Ernest, who was also going to the manoeuvres, was dead set against the marriage and had threatened to try to dissuade Bertie from it. "Your safest defence will be, to be on your guard & not to enter upon the subject when he should broach it; saying nothing is not difficult & 'least said is easiest mended'. He also said: the great point was to prevent your meeting the Pss. You will see from this that he does not dream of such a meeting being contemplated ... Should you be told, that it is well known that you will meet Pss A, your answer should simply be, that you will be very glad to have an opportunity of seeing a young lady of whom you have heard much good ... In all things, while at the Rhine, you will act in nothing without Genl Bruce's knowledge & concurrence, & will take the advice of Fritz alone, refusing all suggestions for whatever purpose they may be, & from whatever other source they may proceed." The only way to avoid mistakes and succeed in a difficult situation was to follow a well-considered plan.[62] Bertie promised to follow this good advice but would not show his uncle, who had always been kind to him, any ill will.[63] His father agreed; "One may differ from others on important points without allowing such differences to interfere with the general feelings of love or gratitude which one bears or owes to them."[64]

It was time for the Rumpenheim reunion and among those greeting the Duchess of Cambridge, Princess Mary and Lady Geraldine Somerset on 10 August were Princess Christian and her daughters; "Pss Alix (who is very, very pretty! oh, so pretty!!)" On the 17th they all drove to Frankfort for the zoo, eating at Roeder's and going to the horse market to see the torch procession celebrating the Austrian emperor's[65] birthday, which, however, turned away unexpectedly before passing the hotel balcony on which they were standing.[66] The newspapers had of course scented intrigue and the *Morning Post, Globe* and *Spectator* of 13 and 14 September hinted about the Prince's possible marriage and future. *The Spectator* was perceptive; "The education of a Constitutional King should not be intended to make him either a general or a savant, or even a very keen politician, but simply an accomplished, and therefore tolerant, man of the world."[67] Now the Prussians would go to Coblentz on the 20th and then, on the 23rd, with Bertie, to Speyer Cathedral, meet the Christians and Alix there and accompany them to Heidelberg, staying till the 25th. "Uncle George"[68] had asked Vicky whether the charming Princess A "wld not be the right wife for somebody"; she replied that she did not know somebody's taste.[69] Rumpenheim was quivering with anticipation; on the 22nd everyone gathered to wish the Christians[70] and Alix God speed on their interesting journey. It had poured with rain all morning but cleared as they drove off to the station at 3pm, in bright sunshine. "Tonight, they are to go to Speyer, & there, I believe, meet him! & tomorrow go together to Heidelberg", wrote Lady Geraldine.[71]

Bertie left for Dover on 13 September, crossing the next day and later reaching Brühl. He attended the manoeuvres as planned and stayed at Coblentz until the 23rd, having met Vicky and Fritz.[72] But Alexandra had no idea what was to happen or whom she would see and had been rather perturbed when, on the 22nd, her mother told her to wear her best gown. Would it not get dusty on the train?[73] Their journey was delayed and very trying; they did not reach Speyer till 1am and the hotel was not good. In the morning they went over the cathedral, returning to the hotel at midday, when a message came from the railway that Vicky's party had arrived. So they went back to the cathedral, where, of course, they encountered the Prussian couple and Bertie, who thus "Saw Pss A for the 1st time."[74] Initially he seemed "disappointed about her beauty, and did not think her as pretty as he expected" but as there was nothing striking about her looks and her beauty consisted in a sweet expression, graceful manner and extremely refined appearance, she "grows upon one the more one sees her, and in a quarter of an hour he thought her lovely but said her nose was too long and her forehead too low." Even so, she had made an impression on him. In a slightly awkward situation, her parents quietly and tactfully put everyone at their ease and soon Alexandra was talking away to Bertie, unaffectedly and confidently. Vicky marvelled at the sixteen-year-old's poise; "Her manners are more like 24". Alexandra always travelled without her governess when she was with her mother, and Vicky never saw her mother "say a word or give a sign to her about anything". She behaved perfectly.

They toured the cathedral together and Vicky began conversing with Princess Christian as planned; Bertie was very glad to make their acquaintance. Princess Christian was happy the meeting was making everything so much easier; she had perceived "that Bertie was not indifferent to her daughter, but he had seen few young Princesses, she supposed, & he might see many others who pleased him better." On Vicky's asking her whether, if the idea became more serious, she would let Alexandra stay with Queen Victoria for a while, she replied "Oh yes, to be sure." However, if it did become serious and if Alix ever did go to England, she would not wish her to have anything to do with the Duchess of Cambridge, Augusta or Mary, "as they cultivated acquaintances and frequented society wh she wd never allow her daughter to go near; that at Rumpenheim she had had hard work to keep her children away from them as Mary's conversation was not fit for young girls." She had seen Mary flirt so outrageously that she had warned Alix she would get her ears boxed if she ever behaved like that. Alix had agreed this would be deserved. The Duchess of Cambridge and Augusta had almost teased her life out about Bertie and Alix and Augusta had made a great scene, saying she knew all. "I am very glad you do, as for myself, I know nothing!" replied Princess Christian. Augusta was jealous, untrustworthy and often invented things; she was much against the suggested marriage, but if it took place she wanted it to look as though she had arranged it all, and was telling everyone so. Princess Christian was thankful that, if it happened, it would be for purely personal, not political, reasons. She had thus anticipated the points raised by Queen Victoria at Osborne,[75] without being prompted.[76]

Vicky was struck by Princess Christian's intelligence. She was quick and sharp; nothing escaped her and everything she said was so sensible that Vicky only wished Prince Albert had been there and seen there would be no difficulty with her. "I think she 'hears the grass grow'[77] and withal is so gentle and amiable and ladylike." Prince Christian was "handsome in appearance and a perfect gentleman in all he says and does; it is impossible not to like him, and he seems such a good Husband and Father." Tactfully, he did not "make up" to the Prince of Wales, but treated him just as he did the Crown Prince.[78] After leaving the cathedral, they all went to the Christians' hotel, which was so full and ill-prepared that they "knew not what to do with the P of W etc.!!"[79] Finally they went to Heidelberg, arriving at about 6pm, dining and staying together till 9pm. The next day they breakfasted together and, having explored the local Schloss, went on a trip to Neckarthal. After dinner, Bertie and Alix, sitting together, started looking at photographs, the latest craze. He gave her one of his and then, very politely, asked her mother if she would allow Alexandra to give him one of hers. At 10am the next day the two groups parted.

Bertie told his mother on 24 September that he had met "the young lady of whom I had heard so much, & I can now candidly say that I think her charming & very pretty; I must ask you to wait till I see you & then I will give you my impressions about her." Princess Christian was very nice, but unfortunately very deaf; Prince Christian was "a most gentlemanlike & agreeable person". The Danes were going back to Rumpenheim on the 25th.[80] On that day the Queen wrote to Vicky, still anxious, "but we both feel that we can't help ourselves & that there is no-one else." Her half-sister, the Dowager Princess of Hohenlohe-Langenburg[81] had been kind and sensible and had written to Fritz H[82] "to urge perfect passivity upon the subject." But the Queen longed for Bertie to confide in his parents.[83] Lady Geraldine and all at Rumpenheim witnessed the return of the Christians and their daughter, happy and smiling, "all seeming to promise favourably for the one topic that filled <u>all</u> our minds & might pass none of our lips." She heard about it later from Countess Reventlow,[84] Princess Christian's lady-in-waiting.[85] Alexandra's cousins were longing to hear about the meeting at Speyer and were thrilled when she took the photograph out of her pocket and said "I have got him here!"[86] The Danes left on the 27th for Copenhagen via an art exhibition at Cologne. "They are an inexpressible loss! all the life & animation of the place!" Lady Geraldine was in despair at their departure.[87]

Vicky told her father that she was not sure whether Alix was clever or not but she was obviously not stupid and her great tactfulness was probably worth just as much as great cleverness. "But I am afraid of being too hasty, as she may be cleverer than I think."[88] She told her mother about more lamentations, this time from Duncker,[89] who deplored the proposed marriage politically but also because he said the family was notoriously bad, the father was a very wretched creature and the mother was disreputable. Vicky's sister-in-law, Louise, Grand Duchess of Baden,[90] said, surprisingly, that there were no political disadvantages to Germany in the Prince of Wales marrying a Danish princess (the current view of the King[91] and Queen of Prussia) but she too accused Prince Christian of being a drunkard and his wife ill-famed and nothing would shake her. Vicky was shocked at how many people held this completely unjust view,[92] and later, that diplomats on all sides knew about the meetings at Strelitz and Heidelberg and there was universal wailing, blaming her for her part in it.[93] On 1 October the Queen had thanked the Prussians for all their kind help; "Bertie is certainly much pleased with her, but as for being in love, I don't think he can be, or that he is capable of enthusiasm about anything in the world. But he is shy & I dare say we shall hear more from Alice, to whom he is sure to open his heart." She was reassured by Princess Christian's opinion of the Cambridges and trusted Bertie's eyes had thereby been opened about them.[94] Victoria wrote again, deploring the slurs on Princess Christian; she had heard that in about 1856 there had been money transactions which reflected on Prince Christian but the family life was always perfect and nothing could be said against his wife; it was her mother and sisters who were ill-reputed. Strangely, Bertie seemed far more interested in his coming tour than his marriage; he was clearly incapable of deep feelings.[95]

Bertie was neither shallow nor unfeeling; he was immature and lacked confidence but was learning how to keep his own counsel. His parents, although uneasy about him, did not know that he was indeed thinking deeply about the future. The affair in Ireland was always in his mind, unconfessable and overwhelming. "A sudden fear of marrying, & above all of having children (wh for a young man is so strange a fear) seems to have got hold of him, but I hope he will see this in its right light ere long; he does now, when talked to", his mother wrote.[96] Five days later she was determined not to give up hope; "In his way he is occupied with [Alexandra]; for on Sunday evng he complained to me for not having recd the promised photographs, wh I think a good sign."[97] But how could Bertie think clearly about Alix when he was so beset with worries? He was ashamed of his behaviour at the Curragh; how could he approach an innocent young girl after that?

On 7 October Prince Albert sent him a memorandum, plainly stating the position. Bertie had desired an early marriage; endless trouble had been taken and a charming princess had been found, whom he had been given a chance to meet. He had been favourably impressed but now some decisions must be made. Of course it would be right to see her again before finally making up his mind, but he must understand that a second meeting would compromise them further and increase the pressure for him to propose. It would be foolish to decline on the vague possibility that he might one day see someone he liked better, which might never happen, and to refuse her in these circumstances would be insulting and ungentlemanly. Alexandra might any day see another prince she liked, who might carry her off, to be forever lost to them. An early engagement need not lead to immediate marriage; possibly not for two years.[98] However, Prince Albert made it clear that if Bertie decided, on further acquaintance, that she was not for him, negotiations would be quietly stopped. But what did Alexandra think? On the 18th, Princess Christian, replying to Vicky, said that the impression which, she understood, her daughter had made on Bertie, was returned. They were all very taken with his kindness and amiability and Alix had lamented that "the beautiful days" had passed so quickly. Obviously she was impressed, as she had kept very quiet about it. Her parents completely agreed with the Queen that the young people should get to know each other better; Princess Christian was also anxious to meet Bertie's parents.[99] Vicky had not been sure how to respond. She was also feeling very sorry for the Augustenburgs "when I think of them defrauded of their rights and what their feelings must be when they think of the Glücksburgs and of a possible marriage with Bertie."[100]

Soon after Bertie's twentieth birthday on 9 November, the Curragh episode became public knowledge; Nellie Clifden was vulgarly called "the Princess of Wales" and of course Prince Albert learned what had happened. He was utterly devastated and poured out his grief and disappointment; "I knew that you were thoughtless & weak, & often trembled at the thought that you might get into some scrape through ignorance & a silly love of doing what you may have heard of others doing without further reflection or enquiry whether it was in itself right or wrong, but I could not think you depraved." Where was Bertie's sense of religion, morality, decency and honour, entrusting himself to "one of the most abject of the human species, to be by her initiated in the sacred mysteries of creation, which ought to remain shrouded in holy awe until touched by pure & undefiled hands?" Young men needed explanation about sexual passions, but "Why did you not open yourself to your father, who would with tender care, have instructed you and pointed out at the same time the dangers which surround you?" Instead, he had confided in new friends, who then urged him towards his final destruction. The desires themselves were not evil, but their gratification must be controlled by reason. The unhappy father pointed out, sparing no detail, that Nellie Clifden would probably have a child, or get one, and claim the Prince of Wales as its father; his name would be dragged through the gutter and catastrophe would follow.[101]

While no one would have expected Prince Albert to rejoice at Bertie's behaviour, his reaction was excessive, partly because he was exhausted and unwell through over-work and partly because he and the Queen had striven for years, successfully, to create a wholesome, domestic view of the Royal Family, through their own blameless home life. Bertie, only by exploring fundamental human behaviour, now seemed blighted by his forebears, the sons of George III,[102] or his uncle, Ernest II of Saxe-Coburg-Gotha. He had had an affair with an actress; it was hardly that, but the shade of his great-uncle, the Duke of Clarence (later William IV)[103] and the actress, Mrs Dora Jordan,[104] with their ten illegitimate children, loomed before him. Closer at hand was George, Duke of Cambridge, who had married his actress, Louisa Fairbrother[105] (without the Queen's requisite consent), but not before they had already had two sons and another was expected. Mrs FitzGeorge, as she was known, although respected by everyone who knew her, was not acknowledged publicly and lived separately from her husband. Perhaps the worst part of Prince Albert's grief was that Bertie had not confided in him at a crucial time. Did he ever reflect that he himself had not made this easy, or even that he should have taken the initiative earlier with some kind of sex education? If he did, his thoughts must indeed have been bitter. He sent another long letter; poor Bertie had been very contrite and deserved to be forgiven by "ever your still affectionate father".[106] At least he had honourably refused to name those who had led him astray. Nellie Clifden too, seems to have been good-natured enough not to cause him trouble.

On 20 November, Baron Stockmar[107] wrote objecting to the proposed match. Vicky regretted this and had her own misgivings; her brother must marry early, she insisted, but whether Princess Alix possessed all the qualities he lacked was another matter. Even if not, there was no-one else remotely in the running. "I think he is too indolent to choose himself a wife and if he did … it would most likely not be for her great mind and cleverness, as I think he would shun more than anything the idea of being ruled by his wife."[108] Matters were in this unhappy limbo, when everything changed. Prince Albert had been sleeping badly since the 10th but went to see Bertie at Cambridge on the 25th, returning the next day feeling wretchedly ill. Beset with political and family worries, he could not rest; working relentlessly, despite rheumatic pain and exhaustion, he became feverish and the doctors diagnosed typhoid.[109] He was listless and irritable but by 10 December seemed to be rallying and on the 14th was at first thought to be much better. Bertie had arrived and was with him. The Queen went in and out of the bedroom all day; she had to keep leaving to give way to her grief. Other members of the family were also present. Finally, during the evening, a rapid change set in; when the Queen took her husband's hand, it was already cold, although he was still breathing. He died just after 10pm on 14 December.[110]

In the immediate shock Victoria felt abandoned and distraught. She and her daughters did not attend the funeral on 23 December at St George's Chapel; the chief mourner was Bertie, supported by his little brother Arthur[111] and his Uncle Ernest. The Queen wrote from Osborne on the 27th to Vicky, thanking Fritz for having talked to "poor unhappy Bertie". In her opinion, grief at his behaviour had directly caused his father's death. "Tell [Fritz] that Bertie (Oh! that boy – much as I pity I never can or shall look at him without a shudder as you may imagine) does not know, that I know all. Beloved Papa, told him that I cld not be told 'the disgusting details'. That I try to employ & use him, but I am not hopeful. I believe firmly in all Papa foresaw."[112] Vicky replied two days later, "Poor Bertie how I pity him, but what sorrow he does cause, perhaps you do not even know <u>how</u> much I grieved over his 'fall'. It was the 1st step to sin; whether it will be the last no one knows, I fear <u>not</u>! … I have written <u>3</u> long letters to poor Bertie, saying all I could possibly think of calculated to make an impression on him in

this dread and solemn time, but I fear what I can say, can only be of little use."[113]
In their despair they were laying the cruellest burden on Bertie, who was also
grieving deeply for his father and undermining his fragile self-confidence with
guilt. It was time for a new chapter and just at this time he acquired Victor
Hugo's[114] *Les Misérables,* in the original French. It was so gripping that he could
not put it down until he had finished it.[115] The story of a man, severely punished
for a small mistake, making his difficult way through life towards respect,
honour and almost sainthood, was irresistible.

Despite the Queen's anxiety, "let us hope that all may yet turn out better than we
are sometimes led to expect, and [Bertie] himself is much to be pitied" wrote
Vicky on 4 January 1862.[116] She was still investigating claims of immorality;
Princess Christian had had illegitimate children and Alix had flirted with young
officers, one consequently being sent away. Baron Stockmar, his son Ernest,[117]
Dr Meyer, Frederick of Augustenburg and Uncle Ernest all believed this, having
been told by a Monsieur de Roggenbach,[118] who had it, in confidence, from the
Duchess of Nassau,[119] Princess Christian's niece. "Of course this staggered me
still more", wrote Vicky, "I thought the Duchess must be either very wicked to
blacken her aunt and cousin, or that there must be some extraordinary
'mésentendre' wh wanted clearing up".[120] In fact it was the Duchess' mother[121]
who had had an illegitimate child. Either she had told her daughter the child was
Princess Christian's, or, to shield her mother, the Duchess was blaming her aunt
instead. This was inexcusable, although all too likely, and enough to start all
kinds of stories. "God knows the wickedness of this world passes all belief and
who can screen poor unsuspecting Pcesses from the breath of scandal", wrote
Vicky, indignantly. Meanwhile Bertie sorely needed his mother's forgiveness; he
was well-intentioned and should not be given up for lost at twenty. His Near
Eastern tour would be very beneficial to him. That was all settled, replied the
Queen, but "The marriage is the thing & beloved Papa was most anxious for it."
He had been shocked by Stockmar's disapproval and had said, latterly, "We will
have trouble on all sides about the marriage"[122] while being determined it
should go ahead.[123] The Queen wanted Stockmar to hear the truth about Bertie
and that it had "made beloved Papa so ill, for there must be no illusion about
that – it was so; He was struck down, & I never can see B without a shudder."[124]
She also wanted Princess Christian to be told, "for were the poor girl to be very
unhappy, I cld not answer it before God if she had been entrapped into it."[125]
    Vindications had arrived, which Vicky sent to the Queen. Mrs Paget's letter to
Countess Blücher[126] mentioned that Princess Christian had sometimes caused
comment because she was very lively and "let her hair down"[127] with people she
liked, but appeared to be a model wife and mother to a happy and united family.

The story about Alexandra was absurd; she was barely seventeen and still in the nursery until early 1862. She had been to two large parties, one concert and a ball for her seventeenth birthday, and her behaviour was utterly innocent and dignified. Even those who disliked her father politically (it was impossible to dislike him personally) praised her unreservedly. Landgravine Anna had assured Mrs Paget that the story against Alexandra, whom she knew very well, was completely untrue.[128] Augustus Paget[129] championed the young princess, having known her since July 1859, never seen anything amiss in her behaviour and often thought she would be a suitable wife for the Prince of Wales. "I can and do most solemnly affirm that I have never until now heard the faintest whisper of any such rumour as the one alluded to and you may depend upon it I should have done so, for the Family has enemies here as well as elsewhere who would be only too glad to set about any story calculated to frustrate their hopes if they could do so with any show of plausibility." Neither had he heard anything against Princess Christian, except that perhaps she was "rather too affable and what some people might think perhaps not sufficiently dignified for a Princess." If this was all, there was surely nothing worse to accuse her of.[130]

Writing to Stockmar, Paget went further. His friend, Monsieur Dotezac, French Minister at Copenhagen for twenty years, knew all about Prince Christian's family and gave his word of honour that the report was false; in fact Alexandra had been protected from encountering anyone with whom she could have had an affair. She usually only went to family parties and only danced with pre-approved partners. Her parents' whole object appeared to be to prevent her name being linked with anyone else's. Princess Christian, who had had disagreements with some high-ranking Danes, unfortunately became embroiled in 'a paper warfare' and involved a newspaper. The other side vengefully invented a story about her, drawing on her mother's and sister's bad reputations.[131] Dotezac insisted that her only problem was a tendency to meddle in politics, but "She has always been the best of wives just as she is the best of mothers. Look how she brings up her children."[132] The Queen was determined to see Alexandra before Bertie did, "so that I cld judge before it is too late – whether she will suit me. The whole affair is our 'forlorn hope' & if it were not to be successful, or she not to take to me, all wld be lost!"[133] Vicky had been pleasantly surprised when Bertie wished her joy on her wedding anniversary, 28 January, writing compassionately about their mother's terrible grief; "Oh! How glad we shld also be if we could possibly bear some part of that heavy burden laid upon her." Clearly he had good intentions.[134] Vicky had assured Princess Christian that nothing relevant had changed since Prince Albert's death and the Queen still hoped to meet her and Alexandra in 1862.[135] Victoria told Bertie on 20 February that Brussels or Laeken seemed the only quiet places for the meeting, in the autumn, when he too could see the princesses. She had heard nothing but praise for Alexandra, who had been very carefully brought up and had also expressed sympathy, especially with Bertie, in their sad loss.[136]

The Queen asked Lord Palmerston[137] to discourage all discussion about the proposed marriage[138] but was told it was already being talked about in society, mostly favourably.[139] On 2 March, on her mother's instructions, Vicky mentioned to Bertie that Palmerston had told her some salon gossip; the Russian emperor[140] very much wanted Alexandra for his son, Tsesarevitch Nicholas,[141] and there were hopes for a match.[142] Vicky thought it might well worry him. Bertie wrote from Cairo on 24 March; "I only trust that I may be able soon to have another interview with the young Princess & that matters will be arranged satisfactorily, as it would certainly not be pleasant to see her carried off as a Russian prize."[143] King Leopold had been asked if the meeting could take place in Belgium and he was happy to help.[144] Stockmar still adamantly opposed the match[145] although his son had now accepted it. Vicky sent her mother more details from Valérie Hohenthal, who had often seen Alexandra in company and could hardly believe her youth, being so composed, quiet, self-possessed, tactful and modest, just as Vicky had seen for herself. She had asked for more information on Alix's temper and disposition, which all seemed to be favourable. Alix had been "very violent and passionate as a child, wh she is not at all now, though she is naturally lively and can be quick." This was good news; she had spirit to defend herself if necessary. Valérie had not thought Alix "<u>very</u> clever" but she was renowned for tact, appropriate behaviour and common sense and Valérie had never heard her say the wrong thing. Vicky thought these far more valuable than any amount of "cleverness".[146] Alix had now stopped all but her music lessons but was well-informed and no pains had been spared with her education.[147] The Queen was very happy to hear this. Prince Alfred[148] (who would really have liked to marry Alexandra himself) had nobly offered to "talk sense to B on the subject ... & promises if Uncle Ernest shld come here never to leave him & B alone but to stick to them!"[149]

Vicky had heard more stories; a pantomimic catalogue of frightfulness. Alexandra's grandmother, Landgravine Charlotte, was "said to be wicked and very intriguing, besides not being at all respectable," having contributed to Frederick VII's divorce from Princess Caroline of Strelitz,[150] because she wanted him to marry her own daughter, Princess Augusta.[151] Another daughter, Princess Marie, who had had the illegitimate child, had, supposedly with her mother's encouragement, had an illicit affair with a groom in the stables of her mother's house in Copenhagen. Landgrave William was not ill-natured but was weak and "dreadfully mean and avaricious". Prince and Princess Christian were very poor indeed. Landgrave Frederick had inherited his parents' faults and his sister, Princess Augusta was not at all respectable; she had been married to Carl, Baron von Blixen-Finecke,[152] an adventurer, "and the worst enemy Pce & Pcess Christian have." Thankfully, "the old Queen of Denmark[153] is said to be a most excellent person." Even allowing that one person's nest of vipers could simultaneously be another's beloved family, Bertie should certainly be warned, in case he met them. But he had met Uncle Ernest, notoriously against the match, at Thebes.[154] Ernest Stockmar reported that Princess Christian was slightly uneasy about the lull in negotiations, but had still, without consulting Alexandra, given an initially negative answer to the Tsesarevitch's proposals. She was now doubly anxious not to lose the Prince of Wales but was very nervous lest he should not be in earnest after all; if so, she would still like to have the Tsesarevitch in reserve.[155] Vicky thought it would be a pity if anything were decided for Dagmar, who could otherwise be considered for Alfred.[156]

Queen Victoria was interested in all this, but wondered whether Princess Christian might have heard (perhaps from the Duchess of Cambridge) about the Curragh episode and thought Bertie a regular bad lot. "I fear we can say no more. The Meeting must be at Laeken & can't be before the 2nd or 3rd Sept. I will however let Bertie know that [Alix] is much sought after; but more we cannot do. Your acct of the family is certainly as bad as possible, and that is the weak point in the whole affair, but dearest Papa said we cld not help it. Oh! the whole thing is so disheartening to me!" She was very anxious that Alexandra should be modestly dressed at the "Meeting"; "don't encourage too much dressing or smartness; gt quietness & simplicity – going to the opposite of loud or fast dress, like our foolish English girls; for God's sake don't let Wally try to encourage them to catch the poor Boy by that fashionable dressing – anything but that."[157] Vicky reassured her; Princess Christian's taste was very simple and quiet and she had a horror of "fast" or showy clothes. Alexandra's were as simple as could be; in any case, her parents could not afford to spend much on dress.[158]

Queen Victoria sympathised with Princess Christian's anxiety, but could only tell Bertie he was in danger of losing the only wife who was suitable and they must encourage her mother to hope he would choose Alexandra. As for Dagmar: "let the Empr have her." Two marriages from that family were undesirable; there had been enough outcry about one and Alfred, as future Duke of Saxe-Coburg-Gotha, should not antagonise the Germans further.[159] Bertie had written, thanking her and Vicky for their trouble "& I only trust that everything will succeed according to your wishes, & that you will be pleased with the young Pcess when you see her." Vicky could safely tell Princess Christian "that you know your brother's feelings have not changed & that you hope all will end as we cld wish."[160] The Queen had shown much of the recent correspondence to Sir Charles Phipps [161] who, with General Grey,[162] had read it carefully. He too regretted the relatives' disreputability but because of Alexandra's excellent personal qualities, because she seemed the only possible available bride and because it was imperative for the Prince to marry early, to guard against temptation, it should be settled as soon as possible. He need not see much of the relatives and as for Alexandra, "with a virtuous and well educated girl, the ill repute of some members of her family usually adds to her hatred & horror of vice."[163]

Now Baron von Blixen-Finecke announced his intention of visiting England. According to Mrs Paget, he was "a worthless & dangerous man" who had divorced "a vy good wife" in order to marry Princess Augusta and the connection with him was one of the many disadvantages of the match. He would present himself as Alexandra's uncle and behave as though he knew all the family secrets. Princess Christian anxiously sent word to the Queen that Blixen had never been in her confidence; whatever he might say was untrue. He was determined to break off the match and they were afraid of him doing them harm in England. Lord Russell[164] assured the Queen that Paget had warned him about Blixen's dangerous and mischievous character; he would merely receive him formally at the Foreign Office.[165]

More photographs of Alix had arrived and her mother had requested a large one of Bertie. He was enjoying his tour and seemed much improved, getting on well with his governor and Dr Stanley,[166] who had a very good influence on him. He hoped to meet Alexandra in the autumn, informing his mother, from Constantinople, how glad he was that Princess Christian was to be told his feelings for her daughter were unchanged.[167] Mrs Paget had told Vicky that Alix was not brilliantly witty or talented, although her abilities were usually underrated as she was very diffident and humble about herself. Very shy but never at a loss about what to do or say, her judgement was good and she was the soul of truth. Everyone, even the older people, relied on her; she was the one who made peace, put things right and performed kindly acts unostentatiously. She could always be trusted to do her duty conscientiously, pleasant or not, but was chary about revealing her feelings or opinions; before knowing her well it was difficult to appraise her correctly. Mrs Paget hoped "you will not judge of her by the first few moments, as she is doubly shy before her own Mama." But Alix had a tender, loving heart and would give true affection and devotion to the Queen.[168] Vicky admitted, "It is not everyone one would wish as a Sister in Law, in one's own dear home at your side as your Daughter, when we are away from you, but of this one no one could be jealous, she is so worthy to fill a daughter's place. I am sure dear Papa would have loved her very much, in fact he did like her even though he had only seen her photograph, & that makes me feel doubly for her." She hoped that, if by then engaged to Bertie, Alexandra could stay briefly in Germany with them, perhaps in January 1863.[169] Vicky was glad that Bertie was doing his best to please his mother; "his heart is not at fault I am sure!"[170] On 3 June she sent a little oil sketch of Alexandra by a Danish artist, Madame Jerichau.[171]

On 7 June the Queen's half-nephew, Ernest Leiningen,[172] on board *Magicienne*, wrote to her as they steamed along the Sicilian shore. Bertie, after his tour and visits to Turkey, Greece and Malta, was there. He had been well received everywhere; "Nobody knows better than himself how to please people, when he likes!" He seemed improved, was more inclined towards marriage than before and full of good impulses, although, unfortunately, he still liked and was easily led by people who amused him. He was too old for a tutor and too sharp not to realise if a mentor were placed with him, but it was vital that his entourage included someone who could guide him imperceptibly. Ernest thought this, ideally, would be "a young and handsome wife" to "keep him straight in every way ... The country would never stand a '<u>fast</u>' Prince of Wales."[173]

Vicky wrote on 10 June, sorry the Queen had vetoed her suggestion that Bertie should visit them on his way home.[174] Writing again, she was concerned lest Uncle Leopold could not see them during the meeting in Belgium; should they not make an alternative plan? She had discovered that the garrulous, ill-natured Olympia Usedom,[175] wife of an anti-Danish German liberal, had been one of those spreading lies about Princess Christian and Alix.[176] Vicky hoped the Queen could see the Pagets in August; they would be staying at Gordon Castle and could come to Balmoral.[177] On the 17th she had heard, annoyingly, that Uncle George had told Princess Christian "Bertie's unfortunate story", adding that the Queen was very angry with him and there was complete discord between them. Mrs Paget had found poor Princess Christian holding the letter, in floods of tears at the thought of Alexandra being unhappy and the Queen disliking her too, if she married Bertie. It was the first time she had heard the story, which of course the Duke had not imparted mischievously, but it was foolish, indiscreet and typical of the insatiable love of gossip which made that family so dangerous.[178] The Queen replied on the 26th; Bertie had returned and was amiable, good and sensible; General Bruce's efforts had not been in vain. He was most anxious about his marriage, hoped it could be in March or April and had brought "numbers of pretty things for the young lady." He was furious at Uncle George's intervention. The Queen thought Mrs Paget should tell Princess Christian the truth; "that wicked wretches had led our poor innocent boy into a scrape which had caused his beloved father & myself the deepest pain ... but that both of us had forgiven him this (one) sad mistake, & that I was very confident that he wld make a steady Husband." She looked to his wife to be his salvation, as he was very domestically-minded and longed to be at home; he was now immensely improved and she was very pleased with him.[179] This, Vicky passed to Mrs Paget.

Now General Bruce, who had, despite ill health, accompanied the Prince on his tour, died. "We have lost the most dear & valued friend we had – our poor Bertie, his 2nd father! Dear General Bruce! he has sacrificed his valued life for our poor dear child! And Bertie is quite overwhelmed by it ... he is indeed very forlorn!"[180] Vicky suggested Bertie should join them on an autumn tour to Switzerland and along the Mediterranean coast after the meeting in September. Greatly daring, she asked to borrow *Osborne*.[181] She kept thinking about the other Slesvig-Holstein family, the pro-German Fritz and Ada[182] of Augustenburg, fearing they might be hurt by Bertie's marriage to a pro-Danish

Glücksburg and feeling guilty, but there was no other option left. She suspected Bertie "wd be just as likely to marry [Alix] if Fritz and I did not wish it at all, as I really do not see who else he is to take." It was, after all, not a political marriage and really not a misfortune for Germany. Stockmar had accepted that Alexandra's and her mother's reputations were spotless, but had heard about the mark on Alix's neck and people were trying to frighten him about scrofula.[183]

The Queen had decided General William Knollys[184] should succeed General Bruce, although he would not be called governor. Prince Albert had regarded him highly and considered employing him for Bertie, thus now provided with an excellent ally, whose family would continue to serve the Royal Family into the 20th century. Just at present, however, Bertie was still grieving for General Bruce.[185] After a satisfactory meeting with the Pagets, the Queen, travelling as Duchess of Lancaster, would leave for Laeken on 1 September and stay there until the 4th, meanwhile meeting the Danes. She would then go straight to Reinhardtsbrunn and remain in Germany till mid-October. Bertie would join her there after having proposed to Alexandra.[186] Vicky had heard from Stockmar that "the Schleswig-Holsteiners" were excitedly insisting the marriage was impossible because Alix was "eaten up by scrofula". This was annoying enough, but apparently Blixen had said all he could in London to harm Alexandra and her mother, naturally emphasising his near relationship.[187] Bertie had gone to Birkhall; the Queen was finding him affectionate and dutiful but also very trying. He was still idle and off-hand with his siblings but was anxious to do what was right.[188] It must have been a frustrating time for him. King Leopold had agreed to the Danes staying at the palace at Brussels.[189] Mrs Paget had assured the anxious Stockmar that, apparently, the doctor, instead of just keeping Alexandra's swollen glands warm, had put a plaster on her neck, which had left an intractable red mark. Other accusations would melt away like snow in the sun.[190] Mrs Paget told the Queen that Princess Christian had now found out exactly how her daughter felt about Bertie. Alix had said "No, but how can you assume that he is thinking about me?" Her mother answered "Yes, but if the Prince were to see you, and asked you, what would you reply?" "Yes, but I am much too insignificant", Alix responded, but finally admitted "Yes Mama, if he had displeased me, I should have said No, shouldn't I? but he did not, but if I had seen him for longer, I would have got to know him more and then I could have made a better judgement of how much I liked him." Princess Christian explained that she had set all this down, verbatim, to show Bertie that, clearly, Alix wanted a love match. If she judged her correctly, Alix would be happy to see him again, but if she had to give an answer now, she might not be quite sure. The Queen would see, however, that only great modesty was holding Alix back; Bertie had impressed her, even if she perhaps had hardly admitted it to herself.[191]

On 23 August, Queen Victoria sent her son a memorandum regarding the forthcoming Belgian visit. She would see the Danes first; he would come to Brussels on the 7th, see Princess Alix again and then, a day or two later, ask for her hand. He would then telegraph the result to his mother, in Germany. He would probably stay two days longer and be allowed to see Alix alone in a room next to her mother's, with the door open.[192] Bertie thanked his mother for her trouble and thought the plan excellent.[193] In her next letter, the Queen wrote "earnestly & lovingly" about the important step he was about to take. In stressing Alexandra's goodness, she mentioned his selfish attitude and the Curragh affair. He had improved, but "Do you think you have ever <u>done</u> anything yet to deserve being <u>very</u> <u>happy</u>?"[194] Bertie took this well, but was hurt at being accused of marrying just for selfish reasons; he would "do all in my power to show [Alexandra] that her love is returned, & make her life as happy as I possibly can in her future home." He had no wish to fritter away his time but wanted to be useful; "I shall always consider my first duty, as towards my wife, & then to you, dearest Mama, & to my country." If she knew how much he felt for her and how often he wished to allay her suffering and sorrow, she would not consider him so very selfish. As to "that unhappy subject", he hoped his present and future conduct would make amends, as he had been trying very hard to improve himself.[195] Vicky wrote sympathetically; she was thinking continually of her mother and brother "and of the poor young Princess who I am sure <u>must</u> feel so shy and frightened and her parents so anxious and nervous."[196] Vicky would soon be completely reassured.[197] As Victoria told her son on 3 September, "I have seen the Pce & Pss of Denmark & their sweet Daughter, please God, <u>our</u> sweet Daughter ... <u>she seems a pearl</u>. She is lovely & above all so sweet, gentle & good, so quiet & dignified." The Christians had assured her that, if Alix accepted Bertie, it would be with her whole heart and will; she would not do it if she was not sure of her feelings but hoped he felt a real inclination towards her and it was not just "<u>an arranged thing</u>." They were sure she would be in good hands with Queen Victoria. "The Princess' Mother seems a kind, good person. The Prince a good, <u>not</u> bright man. Dagmar, the other sister, we find plain & not distinguée looking. Alexandra looks as if she were quite different and above them all." The Queen confided to her journal that Prince Christian had told her Alix was "a good child, not brilliant, but had a will of her own" while being sensible and reasonable.[198]

At dinner; Alix had sat next to Aunt Feodore,[199] who was charmed with her. The Queen handed her a little bunch of "our dear white Highland Heather" which Bertie had given her, saying that although she herself could expect no luck from it, she hoped it would bring Alexandra luck; "the dear Child looked so aff[ectionately] & kindly at me." Victoria had not found the parents "sympatique, but that don't signify."[200] Bertie replied on the 4th from Windsor, thanking her for preparing the way for him. He was feeling rather nervous but had been to his father's rooms, which "looked so quiet & peaceful, with the morning sun shining through the windows" and also to the Wolsey Chapel, next to St George's Chapel, where decorative works were being carried out; "it will be quite beautiful when completed."[201] He wrote again on the 5th, delighted his mother was so pleased with Alix; "If, when I propose, she will accept to share my life with her 'for better or for worse', I hope that we shall both prove to you by our after conduct that we are grateful to you for bringing about the marriage." Unfortunately the papers were full of it; "But I suppose it is our lot that all one's actions, or rather one's intended actions should come before the public." He had visited Prince Albert's rapidly-progressing mausoleum at Frogmore, discussed it all with Mr Humbert[202] and also been several times to Marlborough House, which was nearly finished.[203]

Sir Charles Phipps told the Queen on the 5th of her son's gratitude for her letter. He had never seen him "so very happy as he seemed, his countenance quite beamed, and he said it was the kindest letter that he had ever received in his life." He would be at Ostend on the 7th and, when he had called on the Danes, the party would proceed to Brussels.[204] The Queen was now at Reinhardtsbrunn and Bertie wrote to her there. The Danes had told him how kind she had been to them and how they felt for her in her sorrow. He had "quite made up my mind about the young Princess & that I should be very happy with her, & make her so also."[205] Sir Charles Phipps thought he seemed "very much struck with his new visit to the young Princess ... Sir Charles never heard the Prince of Wales speak in such strong terms as today, and His Royal Highness seemed very happy."[206] Praising Alexandra, General Knollys agreed.[207] On 9 September, Bertie telegraphed to his mother, using a numerical cypher; "I have proposed & have been accepted. You will I am sure, congratulate me, we only now beg for your consent & blessing."[208]

Later he sent her a full description; "I cannot tell you how grateful I am for it. Though I still feel as if I was in a dream, I will give you an account of everything from the beginning." He had asked Prince Christian to come to his room after lunch on the 8th; "& then I told him how I loved his daughter, & how anxious I was that she should one day be my wife. He thanked me, & spoke most kindly, hoping that I would not be too rash in my choice. I told him that I had quite made up my mind, & I knew that you had told him the same; I don't think I ever saw anybody so much pleased as he was." Later they all drove round the town and to the zoo, Bertie sitting in the first carriage with the Duchess of Brabant,[209] Princess Christian and Alexandra. On their return, he told Princess Christian what he had said to her husband. She was sure he would be kind to Alix and that Queen Victoria would take care of her, although she dreaded parting with her beyond everything. It was arranged that he would propose next day out walking; meanwhile they sat together at dinner that evening (her mother on his other side) and talked to each other, rather shyly, "& I felt an increasing love towards her every moment." The next day, at 12.00, they all arrived at Laeken and the

King suggested going into the garden. "Princess Christian & Marie[210] walked in front & I walked with Alexandra some distance behind; Philip[211] took charge of the rest of the party. After a few commonplace remarks, Alexandra said that you had given her the white heather, I said I hoped it would bring her good luck. I asked her how she liked her own country & if she would some day visit England, & how long she would remain, she said she hoped some time; I then said that I hoped she would always remain there, & then offered her my hand & my heart; she immediately said Yes; but I told her not to answer too quickly but to consider over it. She said she had, long ago. I then asked her if she liked me – she said <u>Yes</u> – I then kissed her hand & she kissed me. We then talked for some time, & I told her, that I was sure you would love her as your own daughter, & make her happy in her new home, though she would find it very sad after the terrible loss we had sustained. I also said <u>how</u> sorry I was that she could never know beloved Papa. She said she regretted it deeply, & hoped that he would have approved of my choice. I told her that it had always been his greatest wish; I only feared that I was not worthy of her."

Bertie then spoke to Princess Christian and, back at Laeken, saw the parents and Alexandra alone, when he asked for their permission to marry her. They consented at once, and the young couple kissed one another. After lunch, he told King Leopold, "who was most kind" and later they returned to Brussels. "I cannot tell you with what feelings my heart is filled, & how happy I feel, I only hope that it may be for her happiness, & that I may do my duty towards her. Love her & cherish her, you may be sure I will to the end of my life. May God grant that <u>our</u> happiness may throw a ray of light on your once so happy & now so desolate home. You may be sure that we shall both strive to be a comfort to you." He still didn't know whether he was on his head or his feet.[212] On the same day Alexandra wrote in German; "Dear Mama, May I just begin like this, as I am now the <u>happy</u> <u>Bride</u> of your dear son. May God give me His blessing and the strength ever to fulfil all the duties towards him, so that, as his future wife, I may stand by his side as a true support in joyful and in difficult times. His and my wish is that he should be as happy in his marriage as <u>his</u> and <u>my</u> parents. Bertie wants to have the letter; I close this as your happy and grateful daughter, Alix."[213] King Leopold also wrote, delighted at his great-nephew's happiness; it was really a match of affection. Alexandra was also "much pleased, as well she may, and I was flattered by her seeming to place great confidence in her future Grand Uncle." Her parents were anxious for Bertie to visit Copenhagen; they did not wish Alexandra to stay too long in England at the moment and Prince Christian "of course thinks also a little of his <u>own</u> position, which poor man is natural enough."[214] Sir Charles Phipps had met Alexandra on the 8th and been struck by her "great sweetness of manner and intelligence." "There is in her mode of conversation a happy mixture of simplicity and dignity." It had been difficult for the young couple at dinner, with everyone watching to see "<u>how they got on</u>

together". Sir Charles had been able to spy unnoticed, as there was a convenient mirror reflecting them; they were both looking very happy. He thought the Prince's chief feeling was great pride in his fiancée; she was universally admired but was going to be his. She herself was "very much taken with him" and indeed Sir Charles had never seen him appear so advantageously; he was bright, happy, polite and considerate to everybody, which had produced an excellent impression.[215] On hearing later of the engagement Sir Charles sent congratulations to the Queen, believing most sincerely "that no person, of any rank, had ever a better prospect of happiness open to them than the Prince of Wales."[216]

Queen Victoria wrote affectionately to Alexandra on the 11th from Reinhardtsbrunn, assuring her that if she and Bertie enjoyed only a third part of her own married happiness, they would still be extremely happy.[217] Vicky heard from them as well as from Princess Christian, who feared seeming stupid to the Queen earlier, having been so overcome by the situation and thoughts of her daughter's future that "it made me deaf and dumb!"[218] Alexandra's parents did not want her to go to Berlin, or to stay as long as six weeks in England. Vicky was adamant that Bertie should not go to Copenhagen; Papa had not meant him to go there, Fritz was strongly against it and there were so many other reasons. Uncle Ernest still opposed the marriage, although of course he had not yet met Alexandra. The engagement had happened but the problems were still there.[219] Bertie, however was basking in happiness; "[Alexandra] is such a dear being & I am sure will do everything that is right; I frankly avow to you, that I did not think it possible to love a person so, as I do her, & she is so kind & good, & I feel sure will render my life a happy one, I only trust that God will give me strength to do the same for her." They had been riding; she rode fearlessly and well. After dinner she and Marie Brabant played and sang; Alexandra had a particularly sweet voice and was a good pianist. Her parents were kindness itself; Dagmar was not pretty but she was a nice, clever girl; Frederick, though not very clever, was very gentlemanlike; Thyra and Waldemar were nice children but the little boy was rather spoiled. They had visited a ruined abbey at Villers and lunched there. He rather wanted to accept the invitation to Copenhagen, provided, as they had promised, he did not have to meet Countess Danner or any disagreeable relatives; although a private visit, the Danes would still be keen to see him. It could be discussed later; meanwhile, he and Alexandra were going to be photographed together the next day.[220]

Uncle George sent congratulations, delighted that Bertie had chosen such an "amiable, affectionate [and] distinguished girl" who, he had been convinced during family meetings at Rumpenheim, deserved a high social position.[221] The Queen, as she told King Leopold, was determined to have Alexandra to stay with her, so as to get to know her properly, which otherwise might never happen.[222] The visit was nearly over; the young couple would be parted for a time but they had been successfully photographed at two different studios.[223] Alexandra had told the Queen the ten days had been the happiest of her life. Her future sisters-in-law had sent kind letters and she thanked the Queen for hers; her life would now be devoted to "dear beloved Bertie".[224] Although King Leopold saw the young couple's sadness at parting, he thought it best that Bertie did not go to Copenhagen and was also slightly doubtful about Alexandra's visiting England, thinking it better if she first arrived there to be married; if she were seen in public in advance, "the shine would be taken out of it." If she did go sooner, she could not possibly travel without her mother; "it would be considered odd if she came so, and give it a look as if she was a poor girl taken over to give her some manners, to style her." Neither could she leave England without her mother, as to "ship her off with some dame or other" would be undignified. However, there was enough time to consider all this. He had been so pleased to have assisted; when Prince Albert had told him "You must help us in the business" it had given him so much pleasure.[225] On being told that Prince Albert had specifically advised Alexandra's staying with the Queen before the marriage, he acquiesced at once, adding; "As far as one can judge, there is something frank and cheerful in Alix's character, which will greatly assist her to take things without being too much overpowered or alarmed by them."[226] Perhaps he spoke too soon; by 3 October he had heard from Prince Christian, who seemed worried about Alexandra's journey to England; she herself, not surprisingly, was rather overcome by the idea;[227] she had never stayed away from home alone before and now she was being summoned "on approval".[228] It was decided that her father would accompany her.[229]

The Queen wrote to Princess Christian, hoping Alexandra would arrive by 6 or 7 November at Osborne, and then go with her to Windsor on the 11th or the 13th, when Prince and Princess Louis of Hesse[230] would be there. She asked whether the girl had any health concerns she should be aware of; as they lived privately *en famille*, she could go to bed early if necessary. She noted Princess Christian's wish that civility towards the Cambridges should not be neglected.[231] Stockmar was reconciled, although perhaps the marriage should have been postponed for a few years. He was "most kind about it, & simply said it was an experiment which he most devoutly hoped, would turn out as Your Majesty wished."[232] A new player now appeared on the stage; King Frederick VII of Denmark sent official congratulations, expressing his wish for the wedding to be in London, "as it can then be celebrated with more fitting ceremony than at Copenhagen." This was considered rather impertinent, but it led to what was probably the real point; Frederick thought they should have sought his permission for the match. This was unwelcome, but nothing was to be done at present.[233]

Mrs Paget and Lady Augusta Bruce[234] were now discussing Alexandra's trousseau. Princess Christian was in touch with the Duchess of Brabant about three dresses, to be made at Brussels, but thought it would gratify English feelings if her daughter were married in Honiton lace, so Mrs Paget had ordered patterns, commenting that "as much as I know of Pss Xtian's intentions, the trousseau will be very handsome." The mother wished to know if Alix would need a great many *grandes toilettes* and trains for drawing rooms or similar occasions. "You cld perhaps let me know if the wedding is to be quiet or not, for they are rather anxious to know here, also Pss Xtian wd like to know if she herself and her entourage wd be expected to appear at the wedding in mourning or in colours. The sooner you let me know the better, for in this out of the way place things are so difficult to get. It is excessively cold here already & Pss Xtian is in a gt state of mind lest Pss Alix shd catch cold on the journey."[235] Lady Augusta replied that King Leopold wished to give the wedding dress and would be hurt if it were not worn; it not being of Honiton lace would not signify. Three or four trains and *grandes toilettes* would be sufficient. The princesses and their attendants would be in lilac or grey and white at the wedding but non-family members could wear what they liked.[236]

Alexandra was to stay in England for three weeks, returning home for her 18th birthday. She and her father arrived on board *HMS Black Eagle*, at 9pm on 5 November and were met at Calais by Colonel the Hon. Augustus[237] Liddell and then at Osborne Pier by Princess Helena,[238] Prince Leopold,[239] Lady Caroline Barrington[240] and Lady Augusta Bruce. It was pouring with rain but Alexandra looked as pretty as ever, according to Princess Louise,[241] who went with the Queen, Alexandra and her father, to see Barton Farm on the 7th; "then we drove about a little in the open carriage and it was raining the whole time and so very foggy that one could hardly see anything."[242] Prince Christian then left for London before going home. He visited the Cambridges at Kew, arriving on a stormy afternoon and leaving next morning in bright sunshine. There was much to discuss; everyone was happy about the marriage but the Cambridges sympathised with his anxiety at leaving Alexandra alone and forlorn, for the first time, with people she did not really know very well.[243] Bertie, in Naples, wondered how she was getting on. Writing to his sister Louise, he hoped that "now Alexandra feels herself quite at home with you all, & that she likes what will be her new home. It was a great trial to her quitting her home, her Mama & brothers & sisters, but as I am sure you will do all you can to make her happy, she will soon get accustomed to the separation."[244]

The Queen wrote ecstatically to King Leopold on 11 November; "Dearest Uncle, she is a pearl! I almost tremble for the soul seems fully as lovely as that bright robe which clothes it! She is most dear, quite at home with us, just like a daughter, full of affection & tenderness, most anxious to do all that is right. So simple & unspoilt, extremely well brought up, so pure minded, religious, so very frank & natural, something so fearless about her, so refined! and so wonderfully unconscious of her great loveliness." When the Queen spoke about her duties and her engagement, Alexandra admitted she had never thought the meeting at Heidelberg had meant anything. By early 1862 rumours had started, which made her very angry, as she objected to being talked about like that and it was only in the spring that her mother had mentioned "the possibility & spoken of the meeting". When Victoria asked her if she had really felt at once that she liked Bertie well enough to marry him, she answered yes, otherwise she would never have taken him, as she had told him herself. The Queen suggested that many people thought the position would attract her, but "Oh! no, she said, not her, 'as the position is, for me, actually the only "down"'". This was highly satisfactory.[245] Victoria described her hopes for Bertie in a letter for Alexandra; it was mainly in German except for one paragraph: "To be like his beloved father is impossible, for no-one possessed such rare & extraordinary talents & qualities as he did, but to try, to do his best, to try & live for you, for me, for his Country, & to lead a happy & exemplary life – that is in his power & you, beloved Child, can be of the most unbounded use to him, if you will ever remind him of this, encourage him, if he thinks he cannot do a thing, & with your tender love & affection cheer him & urge him always to do what is for his real good, even if it be not always what he should most like, & you will be a blessing to this sad house & to this Country!"[246]

Bertie had been sent abroad; after Reinhardtsbrunn he joined the Prussians on *Osborne* for their Mediterranean trip. Vicky found him, at 21, "extremely amiable, accommodating and good natured and we are as happy as possible together. I think he enjoys himself very much and really I must say he has made a gt deal of progress, he takes so much more notice of what he sees and hears, & I am sure travelling in that respect is very good for him."[247] The Queen was also writing to Vicky; Alix had won all their hearts. She was cheerful and bright but could also be so quiet and gentle and her presence was very soothing to the Queen. "Then how lovely! She is quite at home, comes in & out of the room to me as the Sisters, is most attentive & dear in her manner to me, & quite at ease with us all." She got on well with all the children, especially sixteen-year-old Helena. She seemed very religious, had brought some serious, well-worn books with her, was thoughtful,[248] truly anxious to improve herself and be of real use to her future husband; she already spoke English well but wanted more practice in reading and writing; "she will read English with Mrs Bruce[249] [and write] with Mr Ogg." She was also going to take French lessons with Madame Hocédé[250] and drawing lessons with Mr Leitch.[251] She went to bed regularly at 10pm, as her parents wished, and was reasonable and sensible about her health. The question of her maids had arisen but the Queen was going to settle that later.[252]

Four days later Victoria was still ecstatic; "She is one of those sweet creatures who seem to come from the skies to help & bless poor mortals & lighten for a time their path!" Alexandra had been sitting for an hour with her that evening, hearing all about former happy times and a good deal about Prince Albert and his last illness. The sensitive girl "showed such feeling – laid her dear head on my shoulder & cried – said how she prayed God to help her to do all she cld to help me, & comfort me, & I told her – I felt sure when I was gone, she wld watch over all darling Papa loved, & I can't describe the look of tender pity & affection she gave me." She would indeed be a blessing to the family "& certainly who wld have expected it from that quarter." Alexandra had plenty of sense and intelligence and, although she enjoyed amusements and was very cheerful and merry, had also a serious, solid side to her character and loved "her Home & quiet – as much or more." Spending this time together had been so valuable; they could not have got to know each other so well otherwise. The only slight cloud was that the Christians, or their associates, wanted to stress the Danish element, including suggesting a Danish maid. The Queen strongly disapproved; it might be divisive if Alexandra had someone with whom she could chatter in a language her husband did not understand. Perhaps a Danish man-servant might be employed; someone to deal with her letters home, for example. Otherwise she would have a dresser, possibly the Queen's own *couturière*, Miss Skerrett,[253] and two wardrobe maids, Ellen Roberts and a German girl.[254]

Vicky, writing from Rome, was delighted and relieved that her mother had taken so wholeheartedly to Alix, and that a happy marriage seemed more likely than she had feared. Bertie had been so kind and amiable, helpful, accommodating and very good-humoured. "I find him far from a dull companion, he is very amusing when he likes and has a very quick *répartee*. I am quite struck at his knowing so much about Pictures, his taste is really very good and I find he understands much more about art than I thought." She had realised that "His is a nature wh develops itself slowly, & I think you will find that his marriage will do a great deal for him in that way."[255] Later, her enthusiasm for Alix rose impossibly high; "Ah, may [beloved Papa's] spirit rest on her – it seems as if he had left his mission of being a blessing to all around to her and that when she has fulfilled hers, as he has done, they will meet in that happier world and love each other as they would have done here, only tenfold more."[256] This romantic vision put a heavy burden on Alexandra, who deserved reassurance and understanding in her new role. She was being expected to support the Prince of Wales, comfort his mother, carry out official obligations on the Queen's behalf, produce a healthy family, give up her Danish allegiance and above all, assume the angelic mantle of the Prince Consort. It was almost unkind, but the Queen and her daughter, still shocked after bereavement, were not yet thinking very straight.

King Leopold found Alexandra "a dear creature ... right minded and unsophisticated", the latter being of great importance, as a worldly attitude could spoil everything else. He was sure her sweet face would be like a sunbeam[257] to the sorrowful queen.[258] Alexandra accompanied the Queen, Helena, Louise and Leopold to Windsor on 14 November and went for drives with them and the Hessians. On the 21st, however, the Duchess of Cambridge and Mary came for the day. When Alexandra saw them she was speechless; relief at seeing their familiar faces was so great that all she could do was throw herself into their arms. The subdued atmosphere, tears, expectations, exalted feelings and best behaviour must have been a considerable strain. On the 24th, with the Hessians and Helena, she went to see "Aunt Cambridge" at Kew and, wonderfully, her father suddenly appeared; he had arrived on the 23rd. Mary told a friend that Alexandra was prettier than ever and her bright, joyous presence had greatly roused the Queen, "who is able to smile and even laugh cheerfully at times and talks readily and with interest on every subject, tho' of course often recurring to the sad, sad past with an expression of sorrow in her face, that pained one to the heart." Prince Christian would go to Windsor on the 25th, to collect his daughter, Bertie would meet them somewhere en route and escort them perhaps to Hamburg; Alexandra was "as much in love with [him] as even you could possibly desire." Both were looking forward to the meeting, although it would only be short. Alexandra seemed on affectionate terms with her new relatives and had much enjoyed her brief glimpse of England.[259]

On the morning of 25 November the Queen drove to the Flemish Farm in the Home Park at Windsor to plant an oak tree on the spot where her husband's last shooting expedition had finished. With her were the Hessians, Alexandra, Louise, Leopold, Count Gleichen,[260] attendants and park employees. The Prince Consort's Oak was successfully planted, "the Queen taking it not at all *au tragique* but doing it in her own pleasant cheerful manner that was quite delightful to see again ... I had a photographic man all ready in case of her liking a record of the proceeding, which she approved of highly, & a very successful one was obtained", as Francis Seymour[261] wrote to his father on the 26th. Seymour and Victor were charmed by Alexandra; she was prettier than her photograph and had such a nice manner.[262] Prince Christian arrived later; they planned to leave on the 26th, but Bertie telegraphed that a heavy gale had delayed him; could his bride wait another day? So Alexandra and her father left for Dover on the 27th. She had passed with flying colours; the appointment was confirmed. Bertie arrived in Paris on the same evening and met her at Lille next day. General Knollys was touched at their happiness together, sincerely believing "the Prince of Wales is as much attracted to the Princess Alexandra as Her Royal Highness is to him."[263] They continued to Cologne and to Hanover; on the 30th the Prince escorted his fiancée and her father to Harburg, where they parted. The Danes managed to reach Copenhagen at 11am on 1 December and were greeted enthusiastically through streets decorated with English and Danish flags. All the houses near the Yellow Palace were splendidly illuminated later. King Leopold considered Alexandra's arrival, on her birthday, "*a great tour de force*". Bertie had been tempted to accompany her but had had second thoughts as to the propriety of another journey so soon; however, he looked well in spite of all his recent travelling.[264]

The little difficulty with the King of Denmark was resolved; Mr Paget had an audience with him on 14 November and, on the Queen's behalf, announced Princess Alexandra's marriage with the Prince of Wales.[265] There was another problem; the wedding was tentatively arranged for early March, in Lent and "while there is no prohibition against the solemnization of Marriages at that time, yet the light in which Lent is viewed by our Church has led her intelligent members generally to refrain from fixing that period for their Marriages", wrote the Archbishop of Canterbury,[266] somewhat reproachfully, on the 19th. However, there was no divine rule against it, and the present instance was exceptional; he would conduct the service, in St George's Chapel at Windsor.[267] Support from the Queen's relatives was growing. Her sister-in-law, Duchess Alexandrine of Saxe-Coburg-Gotha,[268] wrote kindly of her pleasure that the Queen was so happy with Alexandra.[269] Her half-sister, Feodore, was "<u>delighted</u> to hear you like Alix so much, she is very charming and your finding her so the more you see her, is really a great blessing, for which we can not be thankful enough. It is not otherwise possible than that she <u>must</u> have a good influence on him gradually, as he is so fond of her and she devoted to him." She wrote again: "Knowing you all now as she does, makes her marriage so much easier for her, poor child. The parents must feel the separation dreadfully, they cannot see her often, and what a loss in the family. At the same time, it is what they brought her up for, and to see their daughter Princess of W will reconcile them, I dare say!"[270]

Vicky had been sorry to part with Bertie, who had really been very agreeable; everyone had liked him. They should all take every opportunity of meeting, especially as their father was dead. She was delighted the Queen was pleased with Bertie, "he has indeed a heart full of good and kind feeling, it only requires to be called forth and no one will be able to do that better than dear Alix!"[271] Alexandra had telegraphed her thanks[272] and the next day wrote Victoria a long letter in German, saying she often thought of the evening at Osborne when she had sat with the Queen in her room and been told everything, just like one of the Queen's own daughters; it had felt like talking to her own mother.[273] Frederick VII had appointed an official to conclude the marriage treaty and had also promised Alexandra a dowry of 100,000 rigsdaler as soon as the government agreed.[274] At Windsor, Francis Seymour found the Queen much happier, "and can now see my way to her settling down to a cheerful old age tho' of course frequently subject to great fits of depression & very different to what it would have been had the Almighty seen fit to spare the loved companion & guide of her life." He drove her through the park and Belvedere for two hours, "during which she talked & chatted quite as of old on all sorts of subjects." The mausoleum, although unfinished, would be consecrated on the 17th and Prince Albert's remains taken there on the 18th, so that the workmen could begin work at St George's Chapel for the wedding. "The space is sadly small, but it is the only

Chapel where the Q could attend it in private, the Royal Closet being well adapted for it." Victoria had been full of admiration for Alexandra, "winding it all up by saying that her beauty was the least of her merits. She is afraid, however, that she is still growing & will be taller than her husband who is growing, she says, as fat as Victor & to look like a farmer!"[275] Richard Lauchert[276] was to paint an official portrait of Alexandra in a simple white gown and on the 29th Vicky asked him to paint it very light, with all the colours as brilliant and fresh as he could, as he rather tended to paint "leaden skies". Lauchert's depiction of folded material was incomparable, "& I never saw an ugly picture of his, they are all fine, and he paints extremely quick."[277]

Notes

[1] RA VIC/ADDU/32/1861:23 February, Queen Victoria to Princess Frederick William of Prussia

[2] Walburga von Hohenthal (1839–1929) wife of Sir Augustus Paget, then British ambassador at Copenhagen

[3] Valerie von Hohenthal (1841–1878), Walburga's sister; lady-in-waiting to Princess Frederick William

[4] Princess Augusta of Saxe-Meiningen (1843–1919)

[5] Princess Marie of the Netherlands (1841–1910)

[6] Princess Alexandrine of Prussia (1842–1906), m Duke William of Mecklenburg-Schwerin

[7] RA VIC/ADDU/32/1861:25 February, Princess Frederick William of Prussia to Queen Victoria

[8] RA VIC/MAIN/Z/10/63, Princess Frederick William of Prussia to Queen Victoria,1861:4 March

[9] Princess Marie of Saxe-Altenburg (1845–1930)

[10] RA VIC/MAIN/Z/10/67, Princess Frederick William of Prussia to Queen Victoria,1861: 11 March

[11] Princess Marie of Hohenzollern-Sigmaringen (1845–1912)

[12] RA VIC/MAIN/Z/10/63, Princess Frederick William of Prussia to Queen Victoria,1861: 4 March

[13] RA VIC/MAIN/Z/10/67, Princess Frederick William of Prussia to Queen Victoria,1861: 11 March

[14] Princess Victoria of Saxe-Coburg-Saalfeld (1786–1861), m (1) Carl, Prince of Leiningen and (2) Edward, Duke of Kent

[15] Emma Hobbs (b 1826/7)

[16] She now looked after Prince and Princess Frederick Charles of Prussia's children

[17] Princess Augusta of Saxe-Weimar-Eisenach (1811–1890), m William I, King of Prussia, later German Emperor

[18] RA VIC/MAIN/Z/11/3, Princess Frederick William of Prussia to Queen Victoria,1861:17 April

[19] In preparation for Confirmation; she continued other lessons afterwards

[20] RA VIC/MAIN/Z/11/6, Princess Frederick William of Prussia to Queen Victoria,1861: 26 April

[21] Princess Augusta of Cambridge (1822–1916), m Frederick William, Grand Duke of Mecklenburg-Strelitz

22   Prince Frederick William of Prussia (1831–1888), later Emperor Frederick III of Germany
23   RA VIC/MAIN/Z/4/19, Princess Frederick William of Prussia to Prince Consort,1861: 25 May
24   RA VIC/MAIN/Z/11/18, Princess Frederick William of Prussia to Queen Victoria,1861: 4 June
25   Frederick, Grand Duke of Mecklenburg-Strelitz (1819–1904)
26   Princess Marie of Hesse-Cassel (1796–1880), m George, Grand Duke of Mecklenburg-Strelitz
27   Adolphus (1848–1914), later Grand Duke of Mecklenburg-Strelitz
28   Vicky was 5'2"
29   Alexandra's studies in ancient history piqued her later interest in Egyptian tombs, Roman, Pompeiian and Greek architecture and ruins, when she had the opportunity of visiting them
30   *bescheiden*
31   RA VIC/MAIN/Z/11/18, Princess Frederick William of Prussia to Queen Victoria, 1861: 4 June
32   *unbefangenheit Anmuth*
33   *weg*
34   RA VIC/MAIN/Z/462/43, Princess Frederick William of Prussia to Prince Consort, 1861: 6 June
35   German for "You", used for children, relatives and close friends, as opposed to "Sie", which was more formal
36   *Wenn ich in Dänemark über die Deutschen raisonnieren höre, dann raisonniere ich über die Dänen, weil es mir so ärgert.* In Denmark, Prince Christian and his family were sometimes criticised for being too German
37   *Bitte sagen Sie nicht zu viel sonst könnte man sich enttäuscht fühlen!*
38   *Auch der Prinz von Wales müss das beste haben was es giebt*
39   RA VIC/MAIN/Z/462/43, Princess Frederick William of Prussia to Prince Consort, 1861: 6 June
40   RA VIC/MAIN/Z/462/46, Prince of Wales to Prince Consort, 1861: 11 June
41   RA VIC/MAIN/Z/462/47, General Bruce to Prince Consort, 1861: 11 June
42   RA VIC/ADDU/32/1861:12 June, Queen Victoria to Princess Frederick William of Prussia
43   Princess Sophie of Württemberg (1818–1877), m King William III of the Netherlands
44   William, Prince of Orange (1840–1879)
45   *mauvais sujêt*
46   Prince Albert of Prussia (1837–1906)
47   RA VIC/MAIN/Z/4/22, Princess Frederick William of Prussia to Prince Albert, 1861:14 June
48   RA VIC/MAIN/Z/462/50, Princess Frederick William of Prussia to Prince Consort, 1861: 14 June
49   Princess Anna of Prussia (1836–1918), m Landgrave Frederick of Hesse-Cassel (1820–1884)
50   RA VIC/MAIN/Z/462/51, Walburga Paget to Princess Frederick William of Prussia, 1861: 9 June; as Princess Alix feared, the story of the scar became exaggerated and, even as late as the early 21st century, people were still saying that she had tried to cut her throat.
51   RA VIC/MAIN/Z/446 /14,15, Prince Consort to Prince of Wales, 1861
52   Leopold I, King of the Belgians (1790–1865)
53   RA VIC/MAIN/Z/462/57, Prince Consort to Prince of Wales, 1861: 13 July
54   RA VIC/MAIN/Z/462/60, Prince of Wales to Prince Consort, 1861: 16 July
55   RA VIC/MAIN/Z/462/66, Colonel Bruce to Prince Consort, 1861: 18 July
56   Louis Napoleon Bonaparte (1808–1873), Emperor Napoleon III of the French

57   Duke Ernest II of Saxe-Coburg-Gotha (1818–1893), Prince Albert's elder brother
58   RA VIC/MAIN/Z/462/69, Prince of Wales to Prince Consort, 1861: 24 July
59   RA VIC/MAIN/Z/141/88, Prince Consort to Prince of Wales, 1861: 7 August
60   RA VIC/MAIN/Z/462/72, Prince of Wales to Prince Consort, 1861: 9 August
61   RA VIC/MAIN/EVIID/1861:September 6, 9, 10
62   RA VIC/MAIN/Z/141/89, Prince Consort to Prince of Wales, 1861: 4 September
63   RA VIC/MAIN/Z/462/81, Prince of Wales to Prince Consort, 1861: 8 September
64   RA VIC/MAIN/Z/141/90, Prince Consort to Prince of Wales, 1861: 12 September
65   Francis Joseph (1830–1916), Emperor of Austria and King of Hungary
66   RA VIC/ADDC6/1/1861:17 August, Lady Geraldine Somerset's diary
67   *The Spectator*, 1861:14 September
68   George, Duke of Cambridge (1819–1904)
69   RA VIC/MAIN/Z/462/83, Princess Frederick William of Prussia to Prince Consort, 1861: 17 September
70   Travelling as Count and Countess Holk
71   RA VIC/ADDC6/1/1861:22 September, Lady Geraldine Somerset's diary
72   Travelling incognito under the name Berg
73   RA VIC/ADDA8/390, Taylor, p 53
74   RA VIC/MAIN/EVII/1861:23 September
75   These have been reproduced in Battiscombe, pp 25–26
76   RA VIC/MAIN/Z/462/87, Crown Princess of Prussia to her parents, 1861: 26 September
77   Ironically, Princess Christian was very deaf, but could sense the nuances of a situation instinctively
78   RA VIC/MAIN/Z/462/87, Crown Princess of Prussia to her parents, 1861: 26 September
79   RA VIC/ADDC6/1/1861: September, Lady Geraldine Somerset's diary
80   RA VIC/MAIN/Z/462/85, Prince of Wales to Queen Victoria, 1861: 24 September
81   Princess Feodore of Leiningen (1807–1872) m Ernst, 4th Prince of Hohenlohe-Langenburg
82   Feodore's son-in-law, later Duke Frederick VIII of Augustenburg (Fritz Holstein)
83   RA VIC/ADDU/32/11/1861:24 September, Queen Victoria to Crown Princess of Prussia
84   Countess Hilda Reventlow (1828–1900)
85   RA VIC/ADDC6/1/1861:23,25 September, Lady Geraldine Somerset's diary
86   Kinloch Cooke, Vol I, pp 369, 396
87   RA VIC/ADDC6/1/1861:27 September, Lady Geraldine Somerset's diary
88   RA VIC/MAIN/Z/4/29, Crown Princess of Prussia to Prince Albert,1861:28 September
89   Professor Maximilian Duncker (1811–1886), a Prussian deputy and the Crown Prince's political adviser
90   Princess Louise of Prussia (1838–1923), m Frederick I, Grand Duke of Baden
91   Later William I, Emperor of Germany (1797–1888)
92   RA VIC/MAIN/Z/12/14, Crown Princess of Prussia to Queen Victoria, 1861: 28 September
93   RA VIC/MAIN/Z/12/19, Crown Princess of Prussia to Queen Victoria, 1861: 7 October
94   RA VIC/ADDU/32/13/1861:1 October, Queen Victoria to Crown Princess of Prussia; in fact, the Prince and his future wife always remained on good terms with the Cambridges
95   RA VIC/ADDU/32/15/1861:5 October, Crown Princess of Prussia to Queen Victoria
96   RA VIC/ADDU/32/16/1861: 10 October, Queen Victoria to Crown Princess of Prussia
97   RA VIC/ADDU/32/17/1861: 15 October, Queen Victoria to Crown Princess of Prussia
98   RA VIC/MAIN/Z/141/91, Prince Consort to Prince of Wales, 1861: 7 October
99   RA VIC/MAIN/Z/141/93, Princess Christian to Crown Princess of Prussia, 1861: 18 October
100 RA VIC/MAIN/Z/12/24, Crown Princess of Prussia to Queen Victoria, 1861: 24 October
101 RA VIC/MAIN/Z/141/94, Prince Consort to Prince of Wales, 1861: 16 November

102 King George III (1738–1820)
103 King William IV (1765–1837)
104 Dorothea Jordan (1761–1816), actress, companion of the Duke of Clarence
105 Sarah (known as Louisa) Fairbrother (1814–1890), actress, m George, Duke of Cambridge
106 RA VIC/MAIN/Z/141/95, Prince Consort to Prince of Wales, 1861: 20 November
107 Christian Frederick, Baron Stockmar (1787–1863), German physician and statesman and the revered mentor of the Queen and Prince Albert
108 RA VIC/MAIN/Z/462/99,101, Crown Princess of Prussia to Queen Victoria, writing (101) about Baron Stockmar's letter of 1861: 20 November (99)
109 Later medical research cast doubt on this diagnosis, but the Royal Family accepted it at the time and their reactions to typhoid cases such as the Prince of Wales's in 1871 were governed by their experience of the Prince Consort's fate.
110 Theodore Martin, *The Life of His Royal Highness The Prince Consort*, Vol V, Chapter CXVI
111 Prince Arthur (1850–1942), later Duke of Connaught
112 RA VIC/ADDU/32/1861:27 December, Queen Victoria to Crown Princess of Prussia
113 RA VIC/MAIN/Z/12/57, Crown Princess of Prussia to Queen Victoria, 1861: 29 December
114 Victor Hugo (1802–1885), French poet, novelist and dramatist
115 RA GV/PRIV/AA16/11, Prince of Wales to Prince George, 1886: 16 October
116 RA VIC/MAIN/Z/12/60, Crown Princess of Prussia to Queen Victoria, 1862: 4 January
117 Ernest, son of Baron Stockmar (1823–1886)
118 Probably Franz von Roggenbach (1825–1907), a leading Baden politician
119 Princess Adelaide of Anhalt-Dessau (1833–1916), m Adolf, Duke of Nassau, later Grand Duke of Luxemburg
120 RA VIC/MAIN/Z/12/64, Crown Princess of Prussia to Queen Victoria, 1862: 14 January
121 Princess Marie of Hesse-Cassel (1814–1895), m Prince Frederick of Anhalt-Dessau (1799–1864)
122 *Wir werden aller Hand Mühe haben mit der Heirath*
123 RA VIC/ADDU/32/1862:11 January, Queen Victoria to Crown Princess of Prussia
124 RA VIC/ADDU/32/1862:15 January, Queen Victoria to Crown Princess of Prussia
125 RA VIC/ADDU/32/1862:22 January, Queen Victoria to Crown Princess of Prussia
126 Madeline, Countess Blücher von Wahlstatt (1810–1870)
127 *se laisse aller*
128 RA VIC/MAIN/Z/462/102, Walburga Paget to Countess Blucher, 1862: 5 January
129 Augustus Berkeley Paget (1823–1896), later Sir, diplomat
130 RA VIC/MAIN/Z/462/103, Augustus Paget to Countess Blücher, 1862: 8 January
131 RA VIC/MAIN/Z/462/108 Augustus Paget to Baron Stockmar, 1862: 17 January
132 RA VIC/MAIN/Z/462/110 (from French), Augustus Paget to Countess Blücher, 1862: 9 February
133 RA VIC/ADDU/32/1862:24 January, Queen Victoria to Crown Princess of Prussia
134 RA VIC/MAIN/Z/12/71, Crown Princess of Prussia to Queen Victoria, 1862: 31 January
135 RA VIC/MAIN/Z/462/111, Crown Princess of Prussia to Princess Christian, 1862: 20 February
136 RA VIC/MAIN/Z/462/112, Queen Victoria to Prince of Wales, 1862: 20 February
137 Henry John Temple, 3rd Viscount Palmerston (1784–1865), statesman, then Prime Minister
138 RA VIC/MAIN/Z/463/2, Queen Victoria to Lord Palmerston, 1862: 27 February
139 RA VIC/MAIN/Z/463/3, Lord Palmerston to Queen Victoria, 1862: 27 February
140 Emperor Alexander II of Russia (1818–1881)
141 Tsesarevitch Nicholas Alexandrovitch (1843–1865), heir of Emperor Alexander II of Russia
142 RA VIC/MAIN/Z/463/4, Crown Princess of Prussia to Prince of Wales, 1862: 2 March

143 RA VIC/MAIN/Z/463/20, Prince of Wales to Crown Princess of Prussia, 1862: 24 March

144 RA VIC/MAIN/Z/13/1, Crown Princess of Prussia to Queen Victoria, 1862: 1 April

145 RA VIC/MAIN/Z/13/2, Crown Princess of Prussia to Queen Victoria, 1862:5 April

146 She might well have reflected that her own high intelligence had not done her any favours in Berlin

147 RA VIC/MAIN/Z/13/3, Crown Princess of Prussia to Queen Victoria, 1862: 8 April

148 Prince Alfred (1844–1900), later Duke of Edinburgh, and of Saxe-Coburg-Gotha

149 RA VIC/ADDU/32/1862:12 April, Queen Victoria to Crown Princess of Prussia

150 Princess Caroline of Mecklenburg-Strelitz (1821–1876) had been the second wife of Crown Prince, later King Frederick VII of Denmark

151 Princess Augusta of Hesse-Cassel (1823–1889), m Carl, Baron von Blixen-Fineke

152 Carl, Baron von Blixen-Fineke (1822–1873)

153 Caroline (of Slesvig-Holstein-Sonderburg-Augustenburg, 1796–1881), widow of Christian VIII

154 RA VIC/MAIN/Z/13/4, Crown Princess of Prussia to Queen Victoria, 1862: 11 April

155 RA VIC/MAIN/Z/463/11, Baron Ernest Stockmar to Queen Victoria, 1862: 12 April

156 RA VIC/MAIN/Z/13/5, Crown Princess of Prussia to Queen Victoria, 1862: 15 April

157 RA VIC/ADDU/32/1862:16April, Queen Victoria to Crown Princess of Prussia

158 RA VIC/MAIN/Z/13/6, Crown Princess of Prussia to Queen Victoria, 1862: 19 April

159 RA VIC/ADDU/32/1862:19 April, Queen Victoria to Crown Princess of Prussia

160 RA VIC/ADDU/32/1862:21 April, Queen Victoria to Crown Princess of Prussia

161 Sir Charles Phipps (1801–1866), soldier and courtier

162 General Charles Grey (1804–1870), soldier, politician, private secretary to Prince Albert and Queen Victoria

163 RA VIC/MAIN/Z/463/18, Sir Charles Phipps to Queen Victoria, 1862: 22 April

164 John Russell, 1st Earl Russell (1792–1878), politician (at this time Foreign Secretary)

165 RA VIC/MAIN/Z/463/24, Lord Russell to Queen Victoria, 1862: 15 May

166 Arthur Penrhyn Stanley (1815–1881), priest and historian, Dean of Westminster

167 RA VIC/MAIN/Z/463/26, Prince of Wales to Queen Victoria, 1862: 21 May

168 RA VIC/MAIN/Z/463/27, copy extract from undated letter from Walburga Paget, 1862

169 RA VIC/MAIN/Z/463/28, Crown Princess of Prussia to Queen Victoria, 1862, sending the above

170 RA VIC/MAIN/Z/13/20, Crown Princess of Prussia to Queen Victoria, 1862: 27 May

171 RA VIC/MAIN/Z/13/23, Crown Princess of Prussia to Queen Victoria, 1862: 3 June; Madame Jerichau was Elisabeth Jerichau-Baumann (1819–1881), Polish-Danish painter

172 Ernest, 4th Prince of Leiningen (1830–1904), Admiral in the British Navy; son of the Queen's half-brother, Charles, Prince of Leiningen

173 RA VIC/MAIN/Z/463/30, Prince Ernest of Leiningen to Queen Victoria, 1862: 7 June

174 RA VIC/MAIN/Z/13/25, Crown Princess of Prussia to Queen Victoria, 1862: 10 June

175 Olympia Malcolm (1811–1886), m Karl, Graf von Usedom (1805–1884)

176 RA VIC/MAIN/Z/13/26, Crown Princess of Prussia to Queen Victoria, 1862: 14 June

177 RA VIC/MAIN/Z/13/27, Crown Princess of Prussia to Queen Victoria, 1862: 17 June

178 RA VIC/MAIN/Z/13/28, Crown Princess of Prussia to Queen Victoria, 1862: 21 June

179 RA VIC/ADDU/32/1862:26 June, Queen Victoria to Crown Princess of Prussia

180 RA VIC/ADDU/32/1862:28 June, Queen Victoria to Crown Princess of Prussia

181 RA VIC/MAIN/Z/13/33, Crown Princess of Prussia to Queen Victoria, 1862: 5 July; Osborne was one of the Royal Yachts

182 Duke Frederick and his wife Duchess Adelaide (1835–1900), daughter of the Princess of Hohenlohe-Langenburg and thus a half-niece to Queen Victoria

183 RA VIC/MAIN/Z/463/36, Crown Princess of Prussia to Queen Victoria, 1862: 12 July

184 General Sir William Knollys (1797–1883), soldier, and treasurer and comptroller to the Prince of Wales

185 RA VIC/ADDU/32/1862:10 July, Queen Victoria to Crown Princess of Prussia

186 RA VIC/MAIN/Z/463/37, Sir Charles Phipps to Earl Russell, 1862: 17 July

187 RA VIC/MAIN/Z/463/41, Crown Princess of Prussia to Queen Victoria, 1862: 26 July

188 RA VIC/ADDU/32/1862:29 July, Queen Victoria to Crown Princess of Prussia

189 RA VIC/MAIN/Y/84/44, King Leopold of the Belgians to Queen Victoria, 1862: 15 July

190 RA VIC/MAIN/Y/154/70, Walburga Paget to Baron Stockmar, 1862: 30 July

191 RA VIC/MAIN/Z/463/43, Walburga Paget to Queen Victoria, 1862: 2 August

192 RA VIC/MAIN/Z/463/46, Queen Victoria to Prince of Wales, 1862: 23 August

193 RA VIC/MAIN/Z/463/47, Prince of Wales to Queen Victoria, 1862: 24 August

194 RA VIC/MAIN/Z/463/50, Queen Victoria to Prince of Wales, 1862: 28 August

195 RA VIC/MAIN/Z/463/52, Prince of Wales to Queen Victoria, 1862: 31 August

196 RA VIC/MAIN/Z/13/46, Crown Princess of Prussia to Queen Victoria, 1862: 26 August

197 RA VIC/MAIN/Z/13/49, Crown Princess of Prussia to Queen Victoria, 6 September

198 RA VIC/MAIN/QVJ/1862:3 September

199 The Queen's half-sister, Dowager Princess of Hohenlohe-Langenburg

200 RA VIC/MAIN/Z/463/55, Queen Victoria to Crown Princess of Prussia, 1862: 3–4 September

201 RA VIC/MAIN/Z/463/56, Prince of Wales to Queen Victoria, 1862: 4 September; the chapel was later re-named the Albert Memorial Chapel

202 Albert Jenkins Humbert (1822–1877), architect who worked extensively for the royal family

203 RA VIC/MAIN/Z/463/57, Prince of Wales to Queen Victoria, 1862: 5 September. Marlborough House was his future London residence

204 RA VIC/MAIN/Z/463/58, Sir Charles Phipps to Queen Victoria, 1862: 5 September

205 RA VIC/MAIN/Z/463/60, Prince of Wales to Queen Victoria, 2862: 7 September

206 RA VIC/MAIN/Z/463/61, Sir Charles Phipps to Queen Victoria, 1862: 7 September

207 RA VIC/MAIN/Z/463/62, General Knollys to Queen Victoria, 1862: 8 September

208 RA VIC/MAIN/Z/463/64, Prince of Wales to Queen Victoria, 1862: 9 September

209 Marie Henriette of Austria (1836–1902), m the Duke of Brabant, later King Leopold II (1835–1909)

210 Duchess of Brabant

211 Philip, Count of Flanders (1837–1905), brother of the Duke of Brabant

212 RA VIC/MAIN/Z/463/67, Prince of Wales to Queen Victoria, 1862: 9 September

213 RA VIC/MAIN/Y/154/73, Princess Alexandra of Denmark to Queen Victoria, 1862: 9 September (translation)

214 RA VIC/MAIN/Z/463/71, King Leopold of the Belgians to Queen Victoria, 1862: 9 September

215 RA VIC/MAIN/Z/463/72, Sir Charles Phipps to Queen Victoria, 1862: 9 September

216 RA VIC/MAIN/Z/463/73, Sir Charles Phipps to Queen Victoria, 1862: 9 September

217 RA VIC/MAIN/Z/463/81, Queen Victoria to Princess Alexandra of Denmark, 1862: 11 September

218 *me rendre sourde et muette!*

219 RA VIC/MAIN/Z/463/82, Crown Princess of Prussia to Queen Victoria, 1862: 11 September

220 RA VIC/MAIN/Z/463/83, Prince of Wales to Queen Victoria, 1862: 11 September

221 RA VIC/MAIN/Z/463/94, Duke of Cambridge to Queen Victoria, 1862: 14 September

222 RA VIC/MAIN/Z/463/100, Queen Victoria to King Leopold of the Belgians, 1862: 17 September

[223] RA VIC/MAIN/Z/463/96, Prince of Wales to Queen Victoria, 1862: 14 September

[224] RA VIC/MAIN/Z/463/102, Princess Alexandra of Denmark to Queen Victoria, 1862: 16 September

[225] RA VIC/MAIN/Y/84/52, King Leopold of the Belgians to Queen Victoria, 1862: 15 September; *Du müsst uns helfen in der Sache*

[226] RA VIC/MAIN/Y/84/53, King Leopold of the Belgians to Queen Victoria, 1862: 22 September

[227] *ein wenig angegriffen*

[228] RA VIC/MAIN/Y/84/55, King Leopold of the Belgians to Queen Victoria, 1862: 3 October

[229] RA VIC/MAIN/Y/84/56, King Leopold of the Belgians to Queen Victoria, 1862: 10 October

[230] Princess Alice had married Prince Louis of Hesse earlier in 1862

[231] RA VIC/MAIN/Z/463/108, Queen Victoria to Princess Christian, 1862: 7 October

[232] RA VIC/MAIN/Z/463/110, General Grey to Queen Victoria, 1862: undated, c October; in fact, there had been a number of Anglo–Danish royal marriages in the past

[233] RA VIC/MAIN/Z/463/112, Earl Russell to Queen Victoria, 1862: 13 October, also see 113, 117 and 118

[234] Lady Augusta Bruce (1822–1876), lady-in-waiting to Queen Victoria. She later married Dean Stanley

[235] RA VIC/MAIN/Z/463/120, Walburga Paget to Lady Augusta Bruce, 1862: 28 October

[236] RA VIC/MAIN/Z/463/123, Lady Augusta Bruce to Walburga Paget, 1862: 1 November (123)

[237] Colonel Hon Augustus Liddell (1812–1888), soldier, groom-in-waiting to Queen Victoria, Deputy Ranger of Windsor Great Park

[238] Princess Helena (1846–1923), 3rd daughter of Queen Victoria, m Prince Christian of Schleswig-Holstein-Sonderburg-Augustenburg

[239] Prince Leopold (1853–1884), 4th son of Queen Victoria, later Duke of Albany

[240] Lady Caroline, née Grey (1799–1875), m Hon George Barrington. She was governess to Queen Victoria's children.

[241] Princess Louise (1848–1939), 4th daughter of Queen Victoria, later married the Marquess of Lorne

[242] RA VIC/ADDA15/201, Princess Louise to Prince Arthur, 1862: 7 November

[243] RA VIC/ADDA8/384, Princess Mary of Cambridge to Ella [Taylor], 1862:25 November

[244] RA VIC/ADDA/17/59, Prince of Wales to Princess Louise, 1862: 10 November

[245] RA VIC/MAIN/Z/463/132, Qjueen Victoria to King Leopold of the Belgians, 1862: 11 November. Alexandra had spoken in German, *'den die Stellung ist, für mich, eigentlich der einzige 'down'*

[246] RA VIC/MAIN/Z/463/130, Queen Victoria to Princess Alexandra of Denmark, 1862: 9 November

[247] RA VIC/MAIN/Z/14/11, Crown Princess of Prussia to Queen Victoria, 1862: 8 November

[248] *ein tiefes, ernstes Gemüth*

[249] Katherine Stewart (1824–1889), m General Robert Bruce. Woman of the Bedchamber to Queen Victoria

[250] Madame Hocédé (died 1901), French teacher to Queen Victoria's daughters

[251] William Leighton Leitch (1804–1883), painter and illustrator, drawing master to Queen Victoria

[252] RA VIC/ADDU/32/1862:8 November, Queen Victoria to Crown Princess of Prussia

[253] Marianne Skerrett (1793–1887), dresser to Queen Victoria from 1837–1862

[254] RA VIC/ADDU/32/1862:12 November, Queen Victoria to Crown Princess of Prussia

[255] RA VIC/MAIN/Z/14/13, Crown Princess of Prussia to Queen Victoria, 1862: 15 November

[256] RA VIC/MAIN/Z/14/14, Crown Princess of Prussia to Queen Victoria, 1862: 19 November

257 French, "un rayon de soleil"

258 RA VIC/MAIN/Y/84/61,63, King Leopold of the Belgians to Queen Victoria, 1862: 14 and 20 November

259 RA VIC/ADDA8/384, Princess Mary of Cambridge to Ella [Taylor], 1862: 25 November

260 Prince Victor of Hohenlohe-Langenburg (1833–1891), Queen Victoria's half-nephew, m, morganatically, Miss Laura Seymour (1832–1912); the couple took the titles of Count and Countess Gleichen

261 Francis Seymour (1812–1884), later 5th Marquess of Hertford, soldier, politician and courtier

262 RA VIC/ADDC10/72, Francis Seymour to Admiral Sir George Seymour, 1862: 26 November

263 RA VIC/MAIN/Z/447/47, General Knollys to Queen Victoria, 1862: 1 December

264 RA VIC/MAIN/Y/84/65, King Leopold of the Belgians to Queen Victoria, 1862: 4 December

265 RA VIC/MAIN/Z/463/141, *Berlingske Tidende*, 1862:14 November

266 Charles Longley (1794–1868) was Archbishop of Canterbury from 1862–1868

267 RA VIC/MAIN/Z/463/145, Archbishop of Canterbury to Dean of Windsor, 1862: 19 November

268 Princess Alexandrine of Baden (1820–1904), m Duke Ernest II of Saxe-Coburg-Gotha

269 RA VIC/MAIN/Y/29/59, Duchess of Saxe-Coburg-Gotha to Queen Victoria, 1862: 14 November

270 RA VIC/MAIN/Y/43/44,46, Dowager Princess of Hohenlohe-Langenburg to Queen Victoria, 1862: 12 and 26 November

271 RA VIC/MAIN/Z/14/15,19, Crown Princess of Prussia to Queen Victoria, 1862 : 19 November, 11 December

272 RA VIC/MAIN/Z/463/155, Princess Alexandra of Denmark to Queen Victoria, 1862: 2 December

273 RA VIC/MAIN/Z/464/1, Princess Alexandra of Denmark to Queen Victoria, 1862: 3 December

274 RA VIC/MAIN/Z/464/7, Augustus Paget to Foreign Office, 1862: 23 December

275 RA VIC/ADDC10/73, Francis Seymour to his father, 1862: 3 December

276 Richard Lauchert (1823–1868), portrait painter, m Princess Amalie of Hohenlohe-Waldenburg-Schillingsfürst

277 RA VIC/MAIN/Z/14/26, Crown Princess of Prussia to Queen Victoria, 1862: 29 December

Chapter 3

1863–1864

"We love each other greatly"

꙳

On 4 January 1863 Alexandra told Queen Victoria that her greatest wish was to make her future husband happy and contented and to "prove worthy of him."[1] Like other letters to the Queen, it was mostly in German.[2] On the 6th, Bertie, with horses and carriages, left by train for his estate at Sandringham, where the house was being renovated. Three weeks later he returned to inspect Marlborough House twice. Meanwhile the marriage contract was signed on the 15th at Copenhagen.

One problem was solved, although a king for Greece and a husband for Princess Mary of Cambridge (30) were still required. Vicky wrote on the 12th, anticipating the wedding and delighted that her four-year-old son, William,[3] was coming too. "He thinks and talks of nothing else and is so excited about it, that we have to say, if he is not quiet we shall leave him at home. He is much occupied with his Scotch dress; whether Uncle Arthur and Uncle Leopold will put on theirs."[4] She thought the trip would do him good; "he fancies he is going to take care of me." Frederick of Augustenburg was with them; happily the ice had been broken and he was ready to forget any ill feelings towards Alexandra.[5] Queen Victoria gloomily told King Leopold that Bertie was indiscreet, contradictory, noisy and showing off; "The sooner the marriage takes place the better, but I am very anxious for the result; I fear dear Alix is under a complete delusion."[6]

Princess Mary was helping with her cousin's trousseau, consulting a Mrs James[7] about lace patterns and gowns in November 1862. Mrs James brought the lace on 7 February and was asked about the orange blossom on the 25th.[8] On 3 March, Mary saw "the wedding lace and veil for Alix, which is of Honiton manufacture and quite beautiful!"[9] According to the Danish paper, *Danemark*, Alexandra was living quietly, observing mourning for Prince Albert. The Revd MS Ellis, Chaplain to the British Embassy at Copenhagen, was instructing her in the Anglican rites. She often walked arm-in-arm with her father along the Lange Linie, a fashionable promenade by the sea where people skated in January, although this year the water had not frozen. The *Court Circular* had announced that she would receive an annual personal allowance of £10,000, from revenues belonging to the Prince and a parliamentary grant, to be paid half yearly during the marriage. On the 22nd Alexandra went for the last time to St Mary's Church, (where Thorwaldsen's religious sculptures were) and her old friend, Pastor Paulli, gave the address.

Several big parties in Copenhagen marked her departure. The whole Danish Royal Family attended Mr Paget's British Embassy ball for the English community, Landgrave William gave a ball at his palace, and Prince Christian held a reception, after which Alexandra took leave of her friends. She bade her teachers farewell at a private audience at the Yellow Palace but only temporarily; one later referred to her as 'Alexandra the Faithful'; "she will never give up an old friend."[10] On the 24th Frederick VII came from Fredericksborg with his present, a diamond necklace bearing a facsimile of the celebrated Dagmar Cross.[11] Alexandra had a cold but all morning received deputations with more gifts; Flora Danica porcelain from the ladies of Denmark; paintings, sculptures, jewels, a 100-year-old English Bible; and a prayer book with the twelve chief Anglican prayers painted in mediaeval style on vellum by her aunt, Princess Augusta. Alexandra herself had allotted 3,000 rigsdaler as a dowry for six brides from the poorer classes.

Miss Knudsen had lent her Charlotte M. Yonge's[12] *The Heir of Redclyffe*, the first and only novel she read before her marriage, finishing it the evening before leaving. When Miss Knudsen went to Alexandra's forsaken room the next day she found it on the dressing table.[13] Just as Alexandra was about to drive off on 26 February, she ran back upstairs to say goodbye to her room again.[14] Houses from the palace to the station were hung with garlands and English and Danish flags, and medals of Alexandra were in all the shop windows. There was great interest in her trousseau, made by Mr Levysohn's company and exhibited earlier at his establishment in Kjöbmagergade. It was all beautifully hand-made, with Alexandra's initials and the English crown embroidered on each piece; 600 embroideries altogether, done by several hundred workers. The handkerchiefs had been ordered from Paris.[15] Immense crowds had gathered to see Alexandra off; she, her parents and eldest brother drove in an open carriage, escorted by hussars, while quantities of flowers were thrown from windows. Prince Christian had invited Augustus Paget to join the procession, and there was immense patriotic enthusiasm along the route. Streets were packed and bouquets were showered on Alexandra; everyone seemed pleased she was joining the British Royal Family and "God Save the Queen" was heard as well as the Danish national anthem.[16] A guard of honour and all the ministers, high officials, municipal authorities and elite of Copenhagen were waiting at the splendidly decorated railway station. Copenhagen's council president[17] gave a farewell address and Prince Christian thanked him.

Accompanied by cheering crowds, militia and a dragoon regiment, they left at 4.30pm for Korsör, which was illuminated, and there was a firework display; the mayor presented an address and the Burgomaster made a speech. Early on the

2 Group, 9 March 1863, showing, left to right: *seated in foreground*, Prince and Princess Christian of Denmark; Alice, Princess Louis of Hesse; Princess Helena; Victoria, Crown Princess of Prussia. Princess Louise is standing. *In the background are*, left to right: Prince Frederick of Denmark; Crown Prince Frederick William of Prussia; Prince Louis of Hesse; Princess Alexandra of Denmark; Albert Edward, Prince of Wales; Princess Dagmar of Denmark; Prince William of Denmark.

RCIN 2927053

27th the royal party left on the royal steam ship, *Slesvig*, for Kiel, where young ladies, with bouquets, gave Alexandra a welcoming poem by JF Horn, printed on silk. At Hamburg, hundreds of spectators applauded as the cavalry escorted the party through the streets. A deputation from the Hamburg Senate greeted them at the Hotel de l'Europe and later, a huge crowd stood outside, cheering and calling for Alexandra until she eventually appeared at the window. On the 28th they left for Hanover, stayed overnight with the King, left next day and, via Cologne, reached Brussels, where they were received on 2 March with great ceremony and driven to the palace in open state carriages. In beautiful weather, a vast crowd gathered along the route; later there was a state dinner. However, Alexandra's cold seemed worse and she was advised to go to bed at once. It was hoped that two days' rest would cure it.[18]

King Leopold was delighted to see them and very sad that his poor health would prevent him attending the wedding itself.[19] Queen Victoria confided on 3 March; "I do not deny that my poor broken heart rejoices to possess so sweet, dear & good a daughter-in-law. Poor Bertie, he means to do his very best, & I do feel so much for him, he is so forlorn, so helpless, that what I can do for him, I will, for my own precious darling's sake!" The magnificent memorial window in St George's Chapel would be finished and the couple would be married beneath it. "His blessed Spirit will be near us & bless us, tho' we cannot see Him!"[20] The Danish party left Brussels and, on board HM Yacht *Victoria and Albert*, with a naval escort, arrived in Margate Roads late on the 5th, anchored near the head of the jetty and, in the clear moonlight, were easily visible on shore. On the gloriously fine morning of the 6th a deputation came to enquire whether a welcome address could be presented, and consequently, at half past two, the Mayor of Margate and about twenty officials, with the address, were received by Alexandra in the state cabin. She went on deck with her family and thanked the deputation, captivating them with her friendliness and charm.

In squally, rainy weather, the yacht continued, anchoring at the Girdler Deeps at the Great Nore shortly after 5pm on the 6th. A 21-gun salute was fired at Shoeburyness and from HMS *Formidable, Cumberland* and *Leander*. The Royal Artillery fired a royal salute at the Nore, the Danish colours were hoisted and the commander-in-chief there[21] boarded the yacht to meet Alexandra. Brilliant illuminations shone on the beach at Sheerness, with "Welcome" in gigantic letters with blue lights, a torchlight procession and several large bonfires along the shore. On the 7th the yacht arrived at Gravesend, where the bridal couple were joyfully reunited. Londoners were disappointed the wedding was to be at Windsor but gave Alexandra a magnificent reception as she drove with her fiancé through the City. Huge crowds had gathered, despite changeable weather, and all the troops currently in London were drawn up at open spaces; lining the streets was only done for crowned heads.

Guests at Windsor Castle greeted them at 5.45pm. Alexandra and her parents were housed in the state apartments. Her three brothers and Thyra had rooms on the North Front, Minny[22] was in the Star Building on the West Front and the Duke of Glücksburg[23] and Landgrave Frederick were in Lancaster Tower.[24] A private family dinner in the Oak Room was followed the next day by a service in the private chapel. On the 9th the Lord Mayor[25] and Corporation of the City of London brought their gift for Alexandra and were given a meal and shown round the chapel to see the preparations. The gift was a magnificent diamond necklace and earrings, costing £10,000. The necklace had 32 Golconda diamonds, the central one weighing over 13 carats, all cut in the Old English style. The earrings were equally splendid and Alexandra often wore "the City diamonds" on future formal occasions. During the morning of the 9th, the Queen, the Prussians and the bridal pair visited Prince Albert's unfinished mausoleum at Frogmore; later, the couple and Princess Christian went for a carriage drive. A grand dinner in St George's Hall was followed by an evening party.

On the 10th, the wedding day, the guests processed to St George's Chapel at 11.30 and the Queen left privately for the Royal Closet, above and to the left of the altar. Albert Edward left for the chapel at 12.00. At 12.15, Alexandra, supported by her father and the Duke of Cambridge, drove to the West Door, close to where her eight bridesmaids, all young British noblewomen, were waiting. As Alexandra entered the chapel, wearing Honiton lace over a florally-garlanded dress made of British ivory silk, woven with a silver weft,[26] the organ and the Queen's Band struck up Handel's[27] March from *Joseph*. As the couple stood before the altar Prince Albert's *Chorale*, with words by Thomas Oliphant,[28] was sung; a very emotional moment for the Royal Family. The Archbishop of Canterbury conducted the service and the choir sang the 67th Psalm. The couple exchanged rings; Albert Edward gave his bride a ring in which the six stones, Beryl, Emerald, Ruby, Turquoise, Jacynth and Emerald, spelled BERTIE, while she gave him a plain gold ring, inscribed "Alexandra". As the wedding procession left the chapel, Beethoven's[29] *Hallelujah Chorus* from *The Mount of Olives* was sung and guns fired in the Long Walk. The Queen welcomed the Prince and Princess of Wales at the Grand Entrance, embracing them and leading them to Alexandra's rooms. They signed the register in the White Drawing Room and various documents were signed by the Queen and other royalty, officials and members of the household.[30] A *déjeuner* was then served to the royal guests in the dining room and to 400 others in St George's Hall; there was a wedding cake in each room. At 4pm, Alexandra parted from her family at the Grand Entrance; the young couple, in an open carriage preceded by outriders in scarlet liveries, drove slowly round the quadrangle, through the George IV Gateway and down to the Great Western Railway Station, en route for their honeymoon at Osborne House.

People who had seen Alexandra were impressed, among them the staff of the

3 The Prince and Princess of Wales, married on 10th and photographed on 18 March 1863.
JJE Mayall
RCIN 2926335

humorous magazine, *Punch.* Comments at their dinner on 11 March were noted by Henry Silver; "The Beauty of Alexandra is not merely in her features – looks good and amiable and wishing to please, and as if she had brains and used them."[31] Details of her household were now published. Her chamberlain was Lord Harris,[32] while her ladies of the bedchamber were the Marchioness of Carmarthen[33] and three countesses, of Macclesfield,[34] Morton,[35] and de Grey and Ripon.[36] The bedchamber women were the Hon Mrs Robert Bruce[37] (General Bruce's widow), the Hon Mrs Edward Coke,[38] the Hon Mrs William George Grey [39] and the Hon Mrs Francis Stonor:[40] all British, except the Swedish Mrs Grey, who spoke some Danish. The only Dane was Soren Neilsen, who would be Alexandra's page-in-waiting for 38 years. He had worked in her father's household since she was eight and, being a good linguist, acted as courier to the family abroad; he was present when the young couple first met in Speyer Cathedral. Neilsen was very popular with the family and Prince William wanted to take him to Greece[41] but at Princess Christian's and Queen Victoria's special request, he came to England, two months before Alexandra, to superintend the arrangement of her rooms at Marlborough House and receive her there. Queen Victoria later employed his son in her household, on Alexandra's recommendation.[42]

Meanwhile, the young couple crossed to the Isle of Wight in HMS *Fairy.* Just as they disembarked at Trinity Pier, a heavy shower started and a deputation, with an address, met them in the pouring rain. The road to Osborne House's park gates was lit by torches and lights and lined by troops.[43] Stockmar had prayed "that this union may be attended with all the blessings of which human life admits and may prove a source of comfort and contentment to Your Majesty personally."[44]

The next day, Princess Christian received two letters. One, in Danish, was from Alexandra, blissfully happy: "As a wife I write today to you, and as the happiest one on earth. Yes, my own beloved Mama, now I am his – completely his wife. We love each other greatly and I feel so good and am so happy about him, my beloved Bertie! I have only about five minutes left to write in and my beloved Bertie, my husband, is sitting at his desk opposite me also writing to you, we just came back from a drive and this morning we went walking together! I made the tea and had my little cap on just like a little housewife, I had to laugh at myself! Just this moment I got your loving letter, thousand thanks for everything. Please give my love to dear Papa and all my brothers and sisters." She signed it "Your loving daughter Alix. Alexandra of Wales."[45] The other letter, in English, was from "Ever your most devoted & grateful son-in-law, Bertie"; "As I thought that you might like to have a few lines from me the day after I robbed you of your angelic Alix, I hasten to do so, although in five minutes my letter must go. I am happy to be able to give you the best possible accounts of my darling. She bore all the fatigue and excitement of yesterday wonderfully well, but I have taken care that she should have plenty of rest today. I only took a short walk with her in the morning, & this afternoon drove her out. Her cold is much better, & she is in excellent spirits. All seems to me still as a dream, but I am afraid not so to you as it was a most trying day for you to part with her. You may be assured that <u>everything</u> <u>I</u> can do to make her happy I shall do, & I can never sufficiently thank you & dear Papa for giving her to me."[46]

For the rest of that week and part of the next, St George's Chapel and the temporary state rooms nearby were open to the public. On 11 March the Danes left for two weeks at the Palace Hotel in Buckingham Gate. Of course they socialised with the Duchess of Cambridge and her family. On the 15th they attended the Danish church in the City and on the 16th the British Museum. Princess Christian and Thyra went to the flower show at the Horticultural Gardens, the 1862 International Exhibition building and the South Kensington Museum and afterwards visited the Duchess of Inverness at Kensington Palace. From Osborne on the 15th, General Knollys told the Queen that the young couple were in "apparent perfect enjoyment in each others' society." They were well, relaxing after the celebrations in reasonably fine weather. The Prussians had called on their way home and the Waleses had accompanied *Osborne* in *Fairy* as far as the Nab Light, beyond Spithead, which "the Princess of Wales seemed to enjoy much." She had been out every day in the phaeton and attended a service at Whippingham Church.[47] On 17 March the couple left for Windsor; while waiting for them, the Queen told King Leopold that apparently "the effect of this sweet young Wife has already been most favourable to Bertie." They had all greatly admired the beautiful dress the King had given her.[48] On the 18th the young couple were photographed in wedding clothes by JJE Mayall.[49] Alexandra's family visited the castle on the 19th, attending a play at the Lyceum in London afterwards. Replying to the Queen that day, King Leopold mentioned the Duchess of Kent, his sister, who would have been so happy at her grandson's marriage; "I am glad Bertie felt that a little, as she was always so kind to him. I want constantly to write to her and to let her know what might interest her."[50] The wedding presents were, by the Prince's wish, exhibited at the South Kensington Museum, including the Queen's gift of Indian emerald, pearl and diamond ornaments, which Alexandra often wore later at special events.

An evening party in the couple's honour was held at St James's Palace on the 20th, the first time Alexandra (in a white satin moiré dress beneath an over-dress of Brussels lace)[51] attended an event including a wider circle of London society. The Waleses were living at Buckingham Palace, although they inspected Marlborough House on the 21st. Alexandra still saw her own family, driving with her husband, mother and Minny; receiving them as visitors or calling on them at the Palace Hotel. On the 22nd the Christians took their family to the zoo; the next day they and Minny visited the Tower of London. But early on the 24th the Waleses called at the hotel, Alexandra took leave of her family and her husband

and Uncle George saw them off at London Bridge Station. Later, the Waleses left for Windsor, where Alexandra rode and drove with her husband and with the Queen. She was getting used to her new life.

On 28 March Alexandra saw for the first time the Norfolk mansion which would become so dear to her: Sandringham Hall, later known as Sandringham House. Mrs Bruce told the Queen on the 29th that, after much enthusiasm from crowds en route, the Waleses, via Lynn, had reached Wolferton by train, "& there got into carriages followed by vehicles of every description. It was a strange scene & the dust of this sandy country was blinding." Bleak and wild, it reminded Colonel Keppel[52] of Aldershot. Along the roads people waited in donkey carts, all decorated with laurels. At the gates, Alexandra was met by a bevy of young ladies in white muslin dresses and blue and red "opera cloaks", with baskets of violets and primroses, which they scattered before her. The house, with its brown stone porch and white-painted walls, looked rather odd, but inside it was comfortable, clean and fresh. The royal apartments; a very nice sitting room, bedroom and drawing room, were on the first floor, shut off by *portières* from the rest of the passage. Downstairs, a pleasant drawing room, library and a cheerful, well-furnished, but not very large dining room stood ready. "The Princess I think likes the house. We dined with them last evening & nothing could have been better than her manner, so graceful & pleasing & dignified." After dinner she had played duets with Lady Morton, and then "worked[53] & talked to us while the Prince played a rubber."[54] The next day, Sunday, they attended Sandringham Church for the first time. Inquisitive people had come from Lynn and 200 who had been unable to get inside were in the churchyard. It was "a curious & disgraceful scene, crammed with people standing & staring through the 2 hours service at the poor Princess. I felt quite ashamed of my countrymen & women." However, despite the deaf and slow rector[55] and the badly-performed service, the church was beautiful. The Prince had sensibly invited Dr Stanley to administer the Sacrament early and privately on Easter Sunday, and precautions were being taken against such a large congregation then. The young couple seemed very happy together and quite at home, going for walks and sometimes dining alone.[56] The Prince, whose smoking had annoyed his mother, appeared not to smoke here; he was now completely relaxed and happy with his wife all day, walking, driving and riding. As Mrs Bruce noted; "The country seems well adapted for riding & the walks in the woods are pleasant – so dry – sand covered with moss or heather – the sea seen at a distance. I think they will like this place. A great deal must be done to it by degrees, & this will give them both an interest in it." Alexandra continued playing duets with Lady Morton and Albert Edward played whist occasionally, but they always went to bed before 11pm. She seemed very well and very happy and her husband was kind to her and so proud of her appearance.[57]

On 5 April, Princess Alice who, with her husband, had stayed on after the wedding gave birth to her first child at Windsor Castle. At Sandringham on the 7th, the Waleses received, from the Earl of Leicester[58] and other officials, Norfolk's splendid wedding gift: the "Norwich Gates", impressive, iron-worked portals at the main entrance to the grounds.[59] On the 18th the Waleses returned to Windsor, where Alexandra drove with the Queen several times before the couple returned to London on the 22nd. At Marlborough House, they received congratulations from the Lord Mayor and Corporation and deputations from Oxford, Cambridge, Edinburgh, and Dublin, as well as Presbyterian ministers from London. Afterwards, they went to the South Kensington Museum, where their wedding presents were, before returning to Windsor.

Princess Victoria of Hesse[60] was christened in the Green Drawing Room on 27 April in a German Lutheran service led by the Hessian Grand Ducal family's court chamberlain, summoned specially. Albert Edward was a sponsor and his wife now took her place at a family ceremony in England but it was not so very strange; she was used to Lutheran rites. The next day the young couple paid their first formal visit to a theatre, for *Masaniello*, given by the Royal Italian Opera Company at Covent Garden to a completely full house, even with raised prices. Alexandra, like her husband, loved the theatre, especially opera; this time, however, the audience's appreciation was concentrated firmly on the royal box. Alexandra seemed intent on the stage and unconscious of being their focus, although she may well have felt overwhelmed or even frightened. In dazzling finale, the entire company, aided by a double chorus and two military bands, performed the national anthem, bringing the sparkling, evening-dressed audience to its feet.

The London season had started and it was Alexandra's first foray into it, like a debutante, although she was already a married woman. The couple continued receiving congratulatory addresses and wedding presents, went driving, sometimes in an open carriage, visited the Royal Academy exhibition, entertained guests at small dinner parties, paid visits and dined at noble houses and attended more operas and plays. Few had seen the Queen since 1861 but the Waleses were delightfully visible: two happy young people enjoying their new role. The public gazed admiringly, just as Alexandra loved watching the beautiful gold fish swimming in their ornamental aquarium at Marlborough House.[61] Albert Edward was finding his feet as a speaker and consequential person; at the Royal Academy banquet on 2 May he spoke emotionally but impressively. Like him, Alexandra had begun sitting to artists: Theodore Jensen,[62] Marshall Wood,[63] Mr Thomas,[64] WP Frith,[65] Madame Jerichau, Mr Gibson,[66] Henry Weigall,[67] Joseph Wyon,[68] Miss Dixon,[69] R Dowling[70] and photographers, Vernon Heath[71] and Southwell.[72] The couple also visited galleries and studios and attended concerts, such as those at the Hanover Square Rooms. Popular resorts were the Horticultural Gardens at South Kensington, the Royal Botanic Gardens and zoo in Regent's Park. In contrast, Alexandra sat in the Ladies' Gallery for a debate in the House of Lords on 8 May. On the 15th the couple visited the Queen at Windsor. The next day there was an afternoon "drawing room" reception of about 3,000 ladies, lasting till 6pm. Alexandra, with her husband, stood in front of the throne to "receive" them as they passed by. These and other receptions, such as courts, meant standing still for about two hours, in evening dress, being amiable to a lot of, mostly, complete strangers. The receptions took place several times during the season. They were probably more enjoyable for the guests than the hosts but despite her weariness, Alexandra always appeared happy and gracious. On this first occasion she wore a white silk train with a deep trimming of white crêpe, a wreath of white lilac and Honiton lace. Her dress was trimmed to match the train and on her head she wore a diamond tiara, feathers and a tulle veil; she also wore diamond and opal ornaments. But the Queen thought she looked tired and sallow and "Alas! she is deaf and everyone observes it, which is a sad misfortune."[73]

Not long afterwards the couple visited the Royal Polytechnic Institution for Professor Pepper's[74] "Ghost lecture", were shown round the rooms and behind the scenes to see how the "ghost" was produced. They saw submarine experiments with a diver and apparatus and ended their two-hour visit viewing the "Incantation" and other scenes from Weber's[75] opera, *Der Freischutz*. In the same week a reception was given for them in the state rooms at St James's Palace, with masses of flowers, chandeliers and candelabra, and supper in the Grand Banquet Room. Guests included the Royal Family, household, ambassadors, politicians, nobility and the armed forces. On 20 May the couple visited the Royal Institution in Albemarle Street and later attended the opera with the Hessians, who were in London with their daughter until the 23rd. Then it was the International Dog Show at the Agricultural Hall, Islington, driving, and visiting galleries, studios, the Horticultural Gardens and South Kensington Museum. Alexandra had started to receive musicians at Marlborough House: on the 27th the pianist, Mademoiselle Emilie Kupsch.

The young couple, kindly and thoughtful, often called on their relatives. Princess Christian's previous unwillingness to let Alexandra associate with the Cambridges was only to protect her from unsuitable conversation and interference in the marriage plans. Once safely married, it would have been impractical and unkind to ignore them; Alexandra and her husband were very fond of them and they were a cherished link in England with her earlier life. The Waleses therefore regularly visited the Duchess of Cambridge (their mutual great-aunt) and her son and daughter, as well as the Duchess of Inverness,[76] widow of the Prince's great-uncle, Augustus, Duke of Sussex.[77] She was a tiny, old-fashioned elderly lady, kind, generous, hospitable and very popular, who lived modestly, never claiming royal rank or precedence.[78]

In early June, with Prince Leiningen, the couple went to Ascot, then Frogmore, until the 8th. They attended celebrations for the 4th at Eton College[79] in steady rain, causing comments that the Prince had not inherited the Queen's good fortune with the weather. The couple visited her at Windsor but returned to London as Albert Edward had to hold a levee on her behalf on the 9th at St James's Palace. On the same evening there was a grand assembly with dancing at the Guildhall; the Prince appeared in field marshal's uniform, with the Order of the Garter, while Alexandra wore a "rich but simple" white dress, with, tactfully, the coronet and diamond brooch from her husband, and the diamond necklace from the City. She looked radiant and, as the *Spectator* commented, "her manner, so English in other respects, was un-Englishly cordial, and is rapidly making her the pet of the country." Her kind, innocent but slightly arch expression seemed to "deprecate the formality of the occasion."[80] Albert Edward was given the Freedom of the City and there was a surprise for Alexandra. In a deep recess along one side of the Court of Aldermen a moonlit scene showed Bernstorff, with the lawn reaching down to the foreground, where real plants had been arranged. In the middle of the lawn was a picture of Alexandra. She was quite delighted; it probably gave her more pleasure than anything else that evening. The next day, with five of the Prince's siblings, they went to South Kensington, where Albert Edward unveiled the memorial to the 1851 Exhibition and a statue of Prince Albert, in the Horticultural Society's gardens.

The Royal Family were friendly with the exiled members of the French Royal Family[81] living in England. The Waleses visited the Duke and Duchess d'Aumale[82] on 12 June and would later attend the wedding of the Duke de Chartres[83] and Princess Françoise d'Orléans[84] in the Chapel of St Raphael at Kingston-upon-Thames. They themselves received more wedding presents, attended a charity military concert at the 1862 International Exhibition building, and the theatre. On the 13th the Prince received some Maori chiefs from New Zealand. The couple visited Oxford on the 16th. On the 20th Alexandra held another drawing room at St James's Palace. They attended the opening of the British Orphan Asylum at Slough on the 24th and on the 25th gave a dinner party at Marlborough House; the Queen lent her private band to play during the evening. On the 29th they gave an evening party and dance. On 3 July the Prince saw a trial of steam fire engines at the Crystal Palace; fire was a common hazard and he was interested in fire-fighting. On the 8th he received the Freedom of the Mercers' Company and on the 11th laid the foundation stone of buildings for schools for the orphan children of members of the Warehousemen and Clerks' Charity, at Caterham.

After a few days at Frogmore, the couple went on 13 July to the National Rifle Association's shooting competitions at Wimbledon. On the 24th, with Princess Mary and their suite, they left for Aldershot, where the Duke of Cambridge was holding a state review. Albert Edward, in full uniform, and Alexandra in black, deeply interested in everything, drove slowly down the line. After some manoeuvres, a sham fight began, which the royal party watched from a hill before driving down to the reservoir supplying the camp with water. It was fearfully hot, but Alexandra was thoroughly enjoying herself and, with Uncle George, climbed some steps to the top of a bank, to get a good view. The others followed, but the fighting had raised a lot of dust and it was difficult to see what was happening. Alexandra, beside herself with excitement, could see a vantage point on the next hill and, ignoring the steps, went skimming like an arrow down the steep and slippery bank. Uncle George gallantly followed, hampered by greater age and weight and the panoply of Commander-in-Chief. Lady Macclesfield and Mary, laughing, flatly refused to go down the same way; Albert Edward had prudently remained behind and could therefore escort them down the steps. Meanwhile Alexandra, picking up her skirts, ran across a wide area of thick, stunted gorse to the foot of her chosen hill, where she had to stop; it was too steep and she was too hot. There was nothing for it but to wait for the others and the carriages, which took them up for a splendid view of the Long Valley, along which the battle was raging fiercely. Victory was declared at 3pm,[85] and the Waleses went back to Frogmore, where Vernon Heath took photographs for them. Returning to London on 20 July, they left for ten peaceful days with the Queen at Osborne. The main excitement was Princess Leiningen[86] giving birth to a daughter on the 24th.

After her initial enthusiasm, and as she saw how the late hours and festivities were tiring Alexandra out, the Queen rediscovered her anti-Danish feelings. She insisted to King Leopold that Helena's future certainly did not include marriage to Alexandra's elder brother; "My Angel, as well as I, long ago decided never to hear of any of our daughters going to Denmark under any circumstances, & much as I love dear Alix, as much do I dislike her family." She was trying hard to preserve a precious aspect of her own family life; "One of the things wh I feel so dreadfully now is the want of that beloved German element, that Gemüth, that German herzlichkeit wh I have lived with from my birth & without wh I never cld exist. Our 2 [elder] sons have alas! (particularly Bertie) but little of it, & that is what I require like food & air ... & I won't have either Dane, or Dutchman or Swede, for sons or daughters."[87] Victoria despaired about her family and had confided in her half-sister, who had sent a wise and comforting reply on 8 July; "It won't do to trace, prevent or guide as we think fit. Even the faults and falls of the young must be, it is a part of that education everyone has to go through in life. The struggles are necessary for the development of the character, the good and the bad parts must come into play; if you prevent every temptation, how is a young man or girl to get a certain degree of self awareness.[88] And so it is with the marriages too. Where can you find perfections, for so many young people? Let us try to find what we wish, but leave it to Him who knows best, to work out the way they are destined to go in life." The Queen had mentioned that Alexandra was not looking well; Feodore wondered whether the young woman was "in a way to account for her looking so ill? I was in hopes it was so!" Later, she confessed her curiosity about her and how she would like to get to know her properly.[89] Feodore was right; Alexandra was pregnant. The Waleses left for London on 1 August and the next day, as usual, attended a service at the Chapel Royal, St James's. On the 3rd the Prince went to stay overnight at Halifax, where he opened the town hall; he and Alexandra then left on the 5th for Studley Park, to stay with Lord and Lady de Grey and Ripon[90] en route to Scotland. They arrived at Edinburgh on the 6th and, visiting the castle and palace of Holyroodhouse next day, were welcomed enthusiastically in their open carriage, but at 2.00 heavy rain started and by 3.30 it was pouring down in torrents. They finally reached Abergeldie on 8 August.

It was time to relax. Alexandra had been cherishing a plan to visit Rumpenheim but, greatly to her disappointment, although Doctors Farre,[91] Jenner[92] and Sieveking[93] thought the journey, with care, would not hurt her, the Queen was much against it. She had agreed earlier and Alexandra's delighted grandfather had made all the arrangements. Princess Christian also had been pleased, as she had been unwell and was very depressed about her second son, William, the elected Greek king. It was hard to deprive her of her eldest daughter's company but, sadly, Alexandra had to give up the Rumpenheim plan. But she wrote a long letter in German to the Queen on Prince Albert's birthday[94] and Uncle George promised to explain things at Rumpenheim; "I think it would be most improper & unwise to run the slightest risk, & I am confident, that that is the feeling of the whole family here, amongst whom I have heard the subject discussed. Doubtless the disappointment at Alix & Bertie not coming will be great but the necessity for prudence under present circumstances is fully appreciated & by nobody more so, that by the old Landgrave & Landgravine." [95] In fact, Alexandra enjoyed the long drives round the Balmoral estate with her husband; they admired the romantic scenery and he went deer-stalking and grouse-shooting. The Hessians arrived on 17 September and on 1 October the Waleses returned to Edinburgh, where Alexandra received a present at Holyroodhouse from Edinburgh ladies and also crossed paths with the Prussians and their children, on the way to Balmoral.

They arrived at Marlborough House late on 3 October, anticipating an important visitor the next day; King George of the Hellenes, "Willy", whose fortunes had so greatly changed and who was still under eighteen. They all enjoyed the next ten days of riding, driving, dinner parties in the King's honour and theatres. Albert Edward took him and Uncle George Cambridge shooting in Richmond Park and the King received deputations and gave audiences at Marlborough House. Even better, the Christians, Frederick and Minny arrived at Victoria Station on the 10th, to stay at Marlborough House. Alexandra drove with her mother and sister in the afternoon, while Albert Edward rode out with Prince Christian and his two sons. When the gentlemen went to Newmarket, the ladies were photographed by Mr Southwell in Baker Street. The Waleses took their guests to Theodore Jensen's studio, to the theatre and for drives and on the 14th they all, except King George, who left for Paris, went to Sandringham. Frederick left on the 19th to resume his studies at Oxford; the others stayed a little longer but there was solemn news from Denmark and by 4 November they had gone.

There had for some time been trouble with Slesvig and Holstein; the German Confederation kept interfering in Denmark's relationship with them, even though Slesvig, unlike Holstein, was not a member. Obviously the aim was to drag Slesvig in, and the Danish government had had enough. It decided to incorporate Slesvig into Denmark, with its constitutional monarchy. This was dangerous; Denmark would be breaking the peace treaty, separating the two provinces and extending its authority down to the River Eider. Fully aware of this, the Danish parliament passed an Act on 13 November, but Frederick VII died on the 15th before he could sign it. Alexandra's parents were now King and Queen of Denmark. On that day, the Waleses went to St Lawrence's Church at Castle Rising; the next day the Prince and his suite went for shooting to Rising and on the 17th to Marham House. Flags were flying at half-mast for the King of Denmark; on the 24th the Waleses passed through London to Windsor Castle for a few days with the Queen, before moving on the 29th to Frogmore. The Prince went shooting and hunting, while Alexandra sat to Frith for his painting of the wedding. On her nineteenth birthday, the Queen, her children including the Prussians, and Feodore, visited Alexandra at Frogmore, for dinner and an evening party. The Waleses dined at the castle twice and on the 8th the Queen held a Privy Council meeting, formally introducing Albert Edward as a member.

There were more artists' sittings; the Prince presided at a Duchy of Cornwall meeting in London on the 11th and the Prussians dined twice at Frogmore. Then on the 14th, the Queen and all the Royal Family went early in the morning to the Prince Consort's almost-completed mausoleum at Frogmore for a memorial service. Dramatically, a fire started in the Brunswick Tower of the Castle on the 17th, but it was brought under control. On Sunday the 20th the couple attended afternoon service in St George's Chapel; the Prince in his own stall as a Knight of the Garter, and the Princess in the royal stall adjoining. The next day they left for Christmas at Osborne. On Christmas Eve, Alexandra went out driving with Helena; later, Osborne estate workers' children assembled in the Servants' Hall, for their Christmas tree and presents. At half past four the Queen and her family handed out toys, books and clothes to the children and later, greatcoats and blankets to the men and women. On Christmas Day the Royal Family attended Whippingham Church and for the rest of 1863, Albert Edward and Alfred went shooting, while the Queen, her daughters and Alexandra went for drives.

Everyone in Denmark realised how grave things were. There was some resentment that, after becoming King on 15 November, Christian IX had, not surprisingly, hesitated three days before endorsing the "November Constitution" incorporating Slesvig into Denmark. When he did so, Germany immediately reacted; the new Act violated the treaty and the Duke of Augustenburg had himself proclaimed Duke of Slesvig-Holstein. Otto von Bismarck,[96] Prussia's Minister of State, seized his chance, supported Augustenburg and accepted Austria as an ally. Denmark was given an ultimatum to repeal the November Constitution, with an expiry time so short as to make this impossible, giving Bismarck an opportunity of winning prestige for himself and Prussia, proving to King William what the new German Army he had built up was worth, and trying it out.

Although Alexandra had a bad cold and sore throat, they returned to Frogmore on 2 January 1864 and celebrated on the 6th with a Christmas tree for about twenty children. By Friday the 8th it was cold enough for the ice to freeze hard on Virginia Water, so Albert Edward set out at 11.15am to test it for skating. Alexandra had back pain but, despite Lady Macclesfield's advice, decided to join him, following in a close carriage. Other skaters were already there; two sides were chosen to play hockey, the Prince's team wearing a white ribbon on the left arm. They played enthusiastically till 2pm, lunched at the Fishing Temple and continued the game until 5pm, when Albert Edward returned to Frogmore. About 500 had gathered; news of the excellent skating conditions and the royal presence had spread. The Royal Horse Guards band, seated round a large charcoal fire near the Fishing Temple, played while people skated.

Alexandra had enjoyed being driven about in a sledge but by 4pm felt uncomfortable and returned to Frogmore; her labour had begun. Her husband summoned Dr Sieveking, Dr Farre and the midwife, Mrs Innocent,[97] but they could not get there before she gave birth to "a fine boy"[98] at 9pm. Albert Edward was present when Henry Brown, the Windsor doctor, delivered him, with Lady Macclesfield as midwife. Alexandra's suffering seemed intense but Lady Macclesfield, mother of fifteen, assured them it was much less than usual and the emotional young mother was calm and composed again by 10.30. However, the baby, healthy and pretty, with a fine forehead and well-shaped head, beautiful eyes and a distinctive nose,[99] had not been expected for some weeks, and nothing was ready. Everything was in confusion, space was limited "& poor baby even has no clothes. Lady Macclesfield has been most kind & energetic, & won't give the baby up to anyone but Mrs Innocent, but she has not yet arrived", the young father told the Queen. He apologised for his writing; he was in a great hurry and had "an empty stomach & … a dizzy head" but "I cannot tell you dear Mama how grateful I feel to Providence for having granted us all this happiness & especially that everything went off so well. We were evidently mistaken in one month, possibly nearly two, & Dr Sieveking who arrived just after the event took place, is quite of that opinion, as the child is so full grown."[100]

Lord Granville[101] had visited Albert Edward on business that evening; he saw the baby and was touched by the Prince's emotion. The Princess was very well, "but almost too happy."[102] An outfit was hastily provided; the Windsor draper, Messrs Caley supplied 2 yards of coarse flannel and 6 yards of superfine flannel; Mrs Knollys[103] lent a sheet of wadding and there was a superb lace robe.[104] The Queen left for Windsor on the 9th with Helena and Beatrice;[105] her son met her at Windsor Station and took her to Frogmore, where she spent most of the afternoon and evening. Press reports noted; "The Prince of Wales seems much pleased with the addition to his family, while the town and neighbourhood all day yesterday were in a state of joyous excitement." There were now two generations of heirs to follow the Queen. Feodore had been at Osborne with her and wrote on the 10th; "What a blessing that Lady Macclesfield was there! Poor Alix, I hope the child will go on well, anxious it always is, but it may grow up quite strong. I hope Alix is not uneasy, and is as well as she can be. Will you give her my love when you see her."[106]

The Queen told King Leopold more on the 12th. Alexandra had been "wonderfully well" all through her pregnancy "& showed it less than anyone ever did. She was not imprudent in any way, beyond perhaps not lying down quite enough, but she felt no inconvenience." Bertie had "behaved extremely well & was much affected." Victoria was pleased the baby had been born at Frogmore, her mother's house, so near the mausoleum; he was "under their special protection."[107] She and her daughters visited Frogmore several more times before going back to Osborne on the 13th but returned after ten days. Alexandra and the baby received more visitors but those whom she most wanted, especially her mother,[108] could not come because of Danish troubles. The government had resigned and a new one formed; the Danish army immediately withdrew from Holstein and positioned itself along the Danevirke, the over 1,000-year-old border embankment defence, which followed the southern border of Slesvig. Some 40,000 men were deployed along a front about 60 miles long. On 1 February the Prusso–Austrian army crossed the border at the River Eider and marched northwards. The Danevirke was incomplete and too short to withstand 60,000 enemy troops and the Danish army's old-fashioned weapons were no match for the enemy's modern ones. The Danes were forced to retreat, hoping, vainly, that England would send help or offer to arbitrate.

The Prince hunted with the harriers, attended a military dinner, a debate in the House of Lords and a Duchy of Cornwall meeting in London. On 2 February in the castle's private chapel, Alexandra gave thanks for her recovery. Her Danish family were thinking of her and on the 12th Minny told Louise; "We are all so happy to get so good news from darling Alix and her baby, I quite envy you to be so near her and to see her every day. I am sure she must be very affected by what is passing here as she always loved her country so much and felt so deeply for dear Papa and Mama, for they really have a great many troubles to go through, but we must hope for the best and put faith in God."[109] The Wales family spent ten days at St Leonard's, the Prince going hunting while his wife went out for drives. They visited Battle Abbey and attended St Leonard's Parish Church. On the 22nd Alexandra thanked a friend, Mrs Emily Alston for her congratulations; she was looking forward to seeing Mrs Alston's son (to whom she was Godmother) so that "our two boys" could meet. She was fearful about Danish affairs; "Very sad and anxious I feel about the present dark state of affairs in Denmark, and the terrible war. My poor Parents have certainly felt since the first day of their accession to the throne, the <u>weight</u> of the crown, but none of the <u>pleasures</u> yet."[110] Back in London, the Prince rode, attended the House of Lords and other events, as usual. Alexandra went for drives, received many visitors and dined with "Aunt Cambridge" at St James's Palace on the 26th. The next day the Waleses drove together and later went to the Princess's Theatre.

On the 29th, state-robed deputations from the City of London, Dublin, Edinburgh and York came to Marlborough House with congratulations on the baby's birth. Messrs Southwell took photographs on 1 March and the couple gave a dinner party later. Alexandra also received four deputations with gifts; from South Wales, North Jutland, Danes in London, and South Australia. There were drives to Kew Gardens and elsewhere; an overnight stay with the Queen at Windsor and a visit to the Lyceum on the 8th, with Alexandra's uncle, Prince John of Glücksburg.[111] The baby's names and sponsors had been much discussed between the Queen and his parents. He was christened in Buckingham Palace's private chapel on his parents' first wedding anniversary, watched by many royalties. Prince John represented Alexandra's father and the Queen, also a sponsor, told the Archbishop of Canterbury the baby's names; Albert Victor Christian Edward. He wore the Honiton lace robe worn by all Queen Victoria's children, with a crimson velvet cloak lined with ermine and a white satin mantle, edged with Honiton lace. There was a reception in the state apartments and, during the day, Vernon Heath came to take photographs. Later, the Waleses gave a banquet.

Sir James Clark[112] had agreed with the Queen, on 9 March, that Alexandra needed rest; Dr Sieveking had spoken strongly about it to Albert Edward. Lady de Grey thought she was being overworked; Dr Sieveking considered she was still recovering from her confinement.[113] The real trouble was her despair about the war between Denmark and Prussia. The Queen urged General Knollys to insist "in the strongest terms upon all the Prince & Princess of Wales's establishment the imperative necessity of not talking at the Prince's table or in Society about this wretched 'Dano-German question'. The Queen has almost been worn out with anxiety upon this subject, and with the wish to keep things quiet, and to take an impartial line … smoothing down difficulties and calming instead of exciting the Prince & Princess. The contrary may have <u>very</u> serious consequences."[114] Knollys agreed; however, he was not aware her ban was needed "as far as the Ladies and Gentlemen of His Royal Highness's Establishment are in question." Tactfully he said nothing about the couple themselves; Albert Edward saw Alexandra's distress and was inclined to support her views. Knollys prayed the "unhappy question" would soon be settled.[115]

On 11 March, two more deputations brought gifts. Alexandra went driving; her husband and uncle went to the zoo, and there were more visitors and call-paying. King Leopold had come for the christening; the Waleses gave him lunch and dinner and visited him at Buckingham Palace. He told the Queen he had seen "the little gentleman, he is very small but lively", but "Alix looked very transparent". King Leopold had gathered from Albert Edward that she was "more taken up with those unfortunate Danish affairs than one generally thinks." He felt the problem was insoluble without war, unless a Great Power conference was called, and he intended to use his powers of dissuasion on the Austrians and Prussians. He had also discussed the matter with Prince John.[116] He wrote again to Victoria on the 12th; she continued complaining about her eldest son and exhorting her uncle to further remonstrances. "<u>The</u> things I wld beg you to impress upon him are that in <u>his</u> position (as <u>in mine</u>) he <u>must</u> <u>never</u> <u>become</u> a <u>partisan</u> (wh he has <u>always</u> been in <u>everything</u>) – that he must never let his <u>personal</u> feeling for Alix's parents <u>affect</u> his political views, or make him <u>one-sided</u>, for that wld be fatal, & besides that, he must <u>not</u> forget, that his connection with <u>Denmark</u> is only of <u>1 year's standing</u>, & <u>only</u> by his wife, whereas that with Germany <u>is from his birth</u>, & on <u>all sides</u>, as much as with <u>this</u> <u>country</u> – he being a <u>German</u> <u>Prince</u> as well as an <u>English</u> <u>one</u>. If <u>beloved</u> Albert had been here, <u>He</u> wld have kept this all straight. Above all, let our <u>family</u> relations remain unimpaired, & let us be <u>loving</u> & <u>peaceful</u> & let there be a true <u>Christian</u> <u>Spirit</u> in our family at least. Bertie is weak minded, <u>narrow</u> minded & <u>intolerant</u>, <u>& I</u> will <u>not</u> <u>stand</u> partisanship or <u>quarrels</u>. I have all along had this difficulty to contend with & yet I have <u>perfectly</u> steered <u>clear</u> of anything & kept my <u>own sympathies</u> <u>to myself</u>. If poor Bertie were <u>clever</u>, all wld do well, but he is not, & dear Alix is unfortunately <u>very</u> <u>ignorant</u> & does not understand the question."[117] There was something else: Alfred seemed to be spending too much time at Marlborough House with "Bertie & his wife (whom [Affie] only likes & admires <u>too</u> <u>much</u>.)" He was causing her as much anxiety as Bertie.

The Waleses and Prince John went to the Princess's Theatre on 14 March and lunched at Woolwich next day on the Sultan's new yacht, with the Turkish ambassador[118] and his wife. On the 17th Alexandra sat to Henry Weigall for her portrait and to Joseph Wyon for the medal he was making for the City of London. The next day she visited Westminster Abbey and, with her husband, saw the Mulready Collection at the South Kensington Museum. On the 19th Albert Edward and Uncle Hans watched the Oxford and Cambridge University Boat Race[119] but Alexandra, in blue and white, had to hold a drawing room on behalf of the Queen that afternoon at St James's Palace. After church the next day, she drove with her husband and uncle to Richmond Park. The baby, officially Prince Albert Victor of Wales but always Eddy to his family, had been vaccinated satisfactorily on 16 March. Alexandra was hugely proud of him and loved showing him off to visitors, so Albert Edward had a lift installed at Marlborough House on which Eddy could be lowered undisturbed in his cradle from the nursery to his mother's boudoir below.[120]

Uncle Hans left on the 22nd. Alexandra sat again to Weigall; the next day the Wales family went to Windsor for Easter and for sittings to George Thomas, Weigall and Henry O'Neill.[121] However, Alexandra received the sad news of her grandmother, Landgravine Charlotte's death on 28 March, and felt too miserable to join the dinner party at Windsor that evening. It had, after all, been a momentous year and she had been faced with marriage, a foreign country, public life and motherhood before she was twenty. In many ways she loved her new life, but never forgot her former loyalties; the terrible war had prevented her parents and siblings from attending Eddy's christening or even meeting him. Uncle Hans, of whom the Waleses were very fond, had managed to visit, but Alexandra's beloved grandmother would never see her happily established in her own home; worst of all, she had been deprived of seeing Landgravine Charlotte for the last time at Rumpenheim in 1863. A comforting plan, to visit Denmark this year, was forming in Alexandra's mind.

They left on 30 March for London and the congenial Cambridges and saw Henry Tidey's[122] three-part picture, *The Night of the Betrayal* on the 31st. On 1 April the family left for Sandringham in the Great Eastern Railway's new royal carriage from Bishopsgate to Wolferton and thence by horse and carriage. This was Alexandra's second visit and after nearly a month there it must have started to feel like home. Vernon Heath was commissioned to photograph the house and grounds, for a birthday present album for the Queen on 24 May. Back in London, they visited the Royal Academy and called on the great-aunts. On 3 May Alexandra, in mourning for her grandmother, had to hold a drawing room at St James's Palace. Lacking a head-dress, she had asked Mary for the address of the jet diadem maker, "as I must get a diadem made as soon as possible for the Drawing room on Tuesday next."[123] She wore similar deep mourning at receptions and state concerts, but continued driving, theatre-going and dinner parties as usual. On 12 May it was an evening party at the South Kensington Museum. The next day, Alexandra lunched at Windsor with the Queen, who was going to Balmoral. On the 17th the Waleses attended a bazaar for the French Protestant Free School, at St James's Hall. The next day Alexandra received more deputations and presents; Irish ladies with lace and the Marquis of Kildare[124] with an oak casket; ladies with three Limoges enamel vases and gentlemen with a breakfast service, all from Worcester.

Despite the war, the young couple were considering a Danish visit. Both the Queen and Lord Palmerston were against it, unless a satisfactory peace was declared first.[125] Danish sea power had successfully blockaded the German coastline but Denmark was vanquished at Dybboel Hill, with 4,904 casualties, killed, wounded, missing or captured. After further action elsewhere a truce was signed on 9 May and England called a conference in London. However, Prussia and Austria wanted Slesvig divided so as to leave only negligible Danish territories in the north, while Denmark demanded land down as far as the Danevirke. Inevitably, war began again. This time Denmark was defeated and forced to cede Slesvig (now Schleswig) and Holstein to Prussia and Austria in the peace treaty of Vienna. The Duke of Augustenburg advanced his own claims again but Bismarck's legal advisers submitted that his family had relinquished them long ago. The lawful lord and master of the duchies was Christian IX of Denmark and he had surrendered his rights at Vienna.

The Waleses went for drives, including to Hampton Court, and also attended the Queen's birthday parade at Horse Guards. They went to a service in Westminster Abbey on 25 May; the Hessians arrived and all called on the Mecklenburg-Strelitz couple,[126] and later attended the Italian Opera. The next day Alexandra, with Mary, heard a concert at St James's Hall and later went driving with Alice. Madame Jerichau had sittings for a portrait of Eddy. After church on the 29th they all went to White Lodge, Richmond Park, for a dinner party and overnight stay. Alexandra and Alice visited a flower show at the Horticultural Gardens on the 31st and later, with their husbands, a French art exhibition in Pall Mall; in the evening it was the Haymarket Theatre. The Waleses left on 3 June for a function at Cambridge and further London activities included giving a dinner and an evening party, with music, on the 7th.

The next day the couple left for Frogmore, while the Hessians stayed with the Queen at the castle. On 9 June they went to Ascot Races, lunched with the Queen on the 10th and later returned to London for the state ball. This time Alexandra wore white, another royal mourning colour, as she did when holding a drawing room on 14 June; she then went out driving and to the opera and in the evening, with Albert Edward, Alfred and Louis of Hesse, the Caledonian Ball. On the 16th the Waleses inspected the Civil Service Volunteers at Somerset House. An artist, Miss Westphal took a portrait of Alexandra on the 17th. On the 18th Lady Young[127] and the ladies of New South Wales gave her the wedding gift of a gold casket. Later, Albert Edward, Alexandra, the Hessians and Alfred went to the Marchioness of Westminster's Ball, where Alexandra happened to mention to the Marquess[128] that figs were a favourite fruit of hers. He therefore arranged for a small basket of fresh figs, from his country estate, to be sent to her.[129] The season was well under way and evenings were mostly occupied by dinner parties, balls, plays and operas. The couple went to a charity bazaar for the Female School of Art at the Horticultural Gardens on the 23rd. Alexandra and Mary heard H Matthison Hansen,[130] organist of Roskilde Cathedral in Denmark, play in Westminster Abbey on the 24th; later, the Waleses attended a dinner and ball at Devonshire House. They and Eddy visited the Queen at Windsor at the weekend and on the 27th it was the philharmonic concert at Hanover Square Rooms. The Leiningens arrived on a visit the same day; the two couples went driving and visited the Museum of the Geological Survey and the Royal School of Mines in Jermyn Street. Later they went to the Adelphi and on the 29th to the Royal and Honourable Artillery Company's training ground, where the Prince inspected the Corps and Alexandra presented new colours. On the 30 June the couple drove to Harrow School and on July 1 to Wellington College, for their "speech days". On the 2nd they attended a charity bazaar at the Hanover Square Rooms for Earlswood Idiot Asylum and on the 4th went to the London Hospital, where the Prince laid the foundation stone of the new "Alexandra Wing". They inspected the wards, lunched with the President and governors, and later gave a dance at Marlborough House.

Between 5 and 7 July the couple attended the horse show at the Agricultural Hall, the flower show at the Horticultural Gardens, the French Gallery in Pall Mall, (to see M Gudin's[131] picture of *The Arrival of Napoleon III at Genoa during the Italian War*) and the Italian Opera at Covent Garden. From the 8th to the 12th they watched the Eton and Harrow match at Lord's Cricket Ground, and drove to the House of Lords; went to the Adelphi and for an overnight stay at Windsor Castle; visited the Clothworkers' Hall in the City, where Albert Edward was enrolled as a Freeman of the Company, and received a deputation with a Bible for Alexandra from the women of the United Kingdom. On the 13th it was the Duke of Buccleuch's[132] evening *conversazione* at the Horticultural Gardens. After another theatre visit, various engagements and sittings to M Desanges[133] and Henry Barraud,[134] they left to stay at White Lodge from 16–21 July, followed by Frogmore, then Goodwood, and from there on the 29th to Osborne, lodging at Osborne Cottage.

The couple had adopted a demanding social and official schedule, which became a permanent way of life as their presence and patronage were universally sought. Even while they were still young and energetic, it was exhausting, and although the Queen was glad "the Baby is much grown & improved & a very great darling," she thought his parents looked ill "& quite worn out by the most unhealthy life they have led. How thankful I shall be when this S Holstein question is finally shelved!"[135] She had already insisted on her right and duty as Queen to "interfere in the management & education of the Child"; Albert Edward should always consult her first. It was also her duty to see that Alexandra's health, about which she was seriously concerned, was properly safeguarded. She had asked King Leopold, to "break the ice" and speak strongly to the Prince about this.[136] Albert Edward had mentioned a Danish visit, possibly in time for Queen Louise's birthday on 7 September; they were keen to visit Stockholm, St Petersburg and Moscow as well, returning through Germany to see his sisters. The Queen thought it would be better to do this another year, but was "so anxious to do what cld give the Pss (who seems to have set her heart on seeing her Parents again) pleasure, that <u>she</u> wd not oppose this journey if Ld Russell & Ld Palmerston saw <u>no</u> political objection to it," but it must be private and the Prince must be scrupulously careful not to express any political opinion whatsoever. It looked as though peace between Denmark and Germany was about to be settled.[137] Alexandra was longing to show Eddy to his grandparents; Sir James Clark told the Queen that he and Dr Sieveking both saw a risk in this and thought Dr Farre would probably agree. However, Sir James advised that the Princess should deal directly with Dr Farre; it would all be better settled between Eddy's parents and the doctors. So Eddy was allowed to go to Denmark, but not as far as Russia.[138]

The holiday continued pleasantly; the Hessians and their daughter, Victoria, were also at Osborne, as was five-year-old William of Prussia. With Eddy, Alberta of Leiningen and Beatrice, who, although aunt to three of the others was only seven, this made a nice group of children. Their parents went on drives, excursions and short cruises. By 7 August, Edward Tayler[139] had had sittings for miniatures and Jabez Hughes[140] photographed them all. On the 8th, the Waleses left for London and, having called on Aunt Cambridge at Kew on the 10th, left for Scotland, halting at Stirling for breakfast and visiting the ancient castle. Later they saw Loch Lomond and Loch Katrine and drove to a suite of 22 rooms at the New Trossachs Hotel, Bridge of Turk. They continued to Abergeldie on the 12th. The weather was not good for outdoor activities but began to improve towards the end of August and they all rode to the top of Loch Nagar. While Albert Edward went shooting, Alexandra and Mary drove round by Ballater, had tea among the hills and then rode home to Abergeldie. The next day a picnic was held in the Balmoral woods and the Prince gave a ball at the castle for the tenantry and servants. The Queen arrived on the 31st and the Waleses received her and dined with her three times.

At last, on 3 September, the family embarked on *Osborne* for Denmark. The Prince had promised his mother not to say "anything imprudent" during their visit; all he wanted was to see "this unfortunate affair" settled.[141] The sea was rough; nearly everyone, especially Alexandra, was ill, although "baby preserved his excellent reputation as a traveller." Only Dr Minter[142] and Dr Sieveking were able to enjoy dinner on the Sunday. On the 6th Elsinore's landing place was crowded and the town was decorated; rain did not dampen the cordial reception and the Royal Family and Alexandra were overjoyed to be together again. The Danish people too were pleased to see their princess but the general mood was sombre, because of the war. Queen Louise held a small reception on her birthday, which her grandson attended. His parents were not going to Russia after all, but one of the guests, Tsesarevitch Nicholas, was to be betrothed to Minny.

Lord Spencer[143] thought the war had left King Christian much altered, sad and low spirited, but it was "delightful to see him & indeed all the family with the Princess, they are so exceedingly happy to have her with them; the poor King said the day of their arrival was the first happy moment he had had for a very long while." The King and Queen were very kind and Albert Edward seemed to be enjoying himself. It was "not easy to pick up much about politics; great hopes are held of the good the present Ministry will do, but it is questionable how far they are supported throughout the country, as the aristocracy they are supposed to represent seem very inert & without public spirit."[144] Prince Eddy had three teeth by 22 September and was thriving on chicken broth. By the 26th he had four teeth and such a good appetite that he was being given an egg every day, which he much enjoyed, learning also to appreciate the use of salt. As the wet-nurse's "supplies have diminished so much", it was decided that, at not quite nine months, he should be completely weaned. Dr Sieveking had just seen him in the park "and he was as cheery and merry as possible. He looks better than I have ever seen him and I trust that the return journey may not try him so as to impair his healthy looks." Everyone at the Danish court was kind and welcoming, while the Royal Family "were adorned with every social and domestic virtue."[145]

After two weeks of family activities, the Waleses left on 24 September for sightseeing and elk shooting in Sweden, while their son remained in Denmark. By now, Queen Victoria had decided he had been away long enough and should be sent back to stay with her until his parents returned. Reluctantly, they had agreed. She wanted him while she was still at Balmoral but her son wrote; "I must candidly tell you that both Dr Sieveking & Dr Minter do not much approve of his going to Scotland, as it is a long journey there, & a long journey south again, & tho' the weather may be fine now, it may become much colder, & after Lady Ely[146] having had the scarlet fever it is always a risk for so young a child." Not only this; "Alix will also feel very much parting with her little treasure." The Queen was annoyed at them staying at the palace at Stockholm, when she had insisted the visit was private. However, as her son explained, the King of Sweden[147] had been immensely gratified by their going to the palace; he himself would always try to meet the Queen's wishes, "but when circumstances change, if I am not allowed to use my own discretion, we had better give up travelling altogether." He knew she did not always receive foreign princes at her palace, "but Alix & I will always be most happy to put anyone up at Marlboro' House at any time, & so return any civility we may have received." They were planning to stay a little longer in Denmark, as Alexandra wanted to be with her family until later in October. This was not long compared with the usual two or three months that Vicky and Alice spent on holiday in England. He was aware the visit was no longer private but that was not his fault; they had been followed by three newspaper reporters who tried to make out that it was "a sort of Royal progress, & very often exaggerate very much the events that have taken place." They would go home via Hanover, as Alexandra wanted to see her old aunt there, also her grandmother, the Dowager Duchess of Glücksburg, whom she had not seen for a long time and who was hoping to meet them somewhere. They might also see the King of Hanover,[148] and then Vicky, but eventually gave up the idea of visiting Paris too.

The young parents had found Eddy thriving and completely weaned, with two front teeth and fast-growing hair. Minny and the Tsesarevitch were very happy and she had received some splendid presents from him and his parents. After deep thought, she had accepted the necessary religious change from Lutheran to Orthodox. Albert Edward considered the match a very good one in every way; it had been entirely arranged by the Emperor and Empress (the King and Queen of Denmark had had nothing to do with it) and it was also a marriage of affection. Minny was not going to Russia before the wedding "wh is an excellent arrangement, as the old plan was quite ridiculous."[149] This was rather a dubious remark; had he disagreed about Alexandra's prenuptial visit to England in 1862? Now Eddy's journey must be organised. General Knollys diplomatically told the Queen that he would leave Denmark for Scotland on 10 October, "although the medical gentlemen express some doubt whether the season is not too late for the journey to Scotland." The couple wanted to please the Queen, although "Her Royal Highness cannot help feeling it a little sacrifice – parting with her Baby."[150] It seems there was a delay; "Your Majesty's kind consideration will perhaps make a little allowance for a young Mother wishing to delay the first separation from her child, as long as she could." Eddy left on the 11th, with Lady de Grey and Dr Sieveking and placidly allowed his nurse to carry him on board *Osborne*. He arrived at Balmoral on the 18th.

Alexandra's parting from her family "was painful to witness – the King in particular showed much distress."[151] Although the Danes had been pleased to see her again, there was general depression at the outcome of the war, which the King shared, and no-one could see any way forward. Denmark had been reduced to one of Europe's smallest nations, in danger of obliteration or division between Germany and Sweden. There was deep bitterness, but the new Royal Family, considered too German by some Danes, was wholeheartedly Danish in allegiance. Denmark would improve significantly during Christian IX's reign and the family would become extremely popular. The Waleses arrived at Hanover on the 25th and went to see King Christian's mother at Ballenstädt. Staying with the King and Queen[152] of Hanover, they met a handsome young officer, Franz, Prince Teck,[153] son of Duke Alexander of Württemberg[154] and his morganatic wife, Countess Claudine Rhédey,[155] and invited him to stay at Sandringham in December. They returned to Marlborough House on 7 November; by now the Queen, Helena, Beatrice, Arthur, Leopold and Eddy were at Windsor and the *Court Circular* for 3 November had announced; "Prince Albert Victor took a carriage airing." His parents were delighted to reclaim him on the 8th. The next day was Albert Edward's birthday and the Band of the 2nd Regiment of Life Guards played music by the Prince Consort and the Duchess of Kent, as well as Mozart[156] and Mendelssohn,[157] in the quadrangle.

The Queen told King Leopold on 10 November; "I am thankful to say the dear little Baby is now quite well & has prospered under … good old Thurston's[158] care; but it was very unwell in Denmark, where they weaned it suddenly, & when it came back to me. Alix is rather childish & foolish about it. She refused to go & see our dear Queen of Prussia, wh I think injudicious. Bertie went. Alix does not sufficiently feel that she is now a Pcess of England & no longer of Denmark & that is her Mother's doing, I am sure." Later, she mentioned relying on her own daughters; "Alix I can't depend on as they are never with me for long, & besides she knows none of my most intimate *Angelegenheiten*[159] All this is independently of the necessity of my having someone to comfort & sustain me, for I feel wretchedly *verlassen*."[160] [161] Queen Victoria was trying to justify her unreasonable request. According to Dr Sieveking, Prince Eddy had looked better than ever before while in Denmark, although he had been unwell before leaving for Scotland and had then had to undergo the long sea voyage. It was unfair to blame Alexandra for being fond of her own child, or for feeling, at this early stage, more Danish than English; indeed sometimes it looked as though she was supposed to be more German than English, for which she would not have cared at all. It was all part of claiming responsibility for Eddy's care; Victoria had persuaded herself his parents were not sufficiently capable and had worked herself up, blaming and distrusting them, when she needed all their support. As to her son being partisan about Denmark, he had after all said at the time of his engagement that his first duty would be to Alexandra. The Queen herself was rather too partisan about Germany, but it was a comforting, Coburg-centred version for which she yearned, not the Prussian one, which was beginning to worry her. There was ground here for closer agreement with Alexandra, if she could have seen it.

Lady Macclesfield noticed that the household at Windsor spent a lot of time together, only seeing the Queen if she invited them to dine at her table. Then she would withdraw to her private drawing room, while the household and the guests mingled in the large one. "It is terribly dismal & sleepy work for our Prince and Princess, who are accustomed to much more sociability & the absence of formality in their own homes." The Queen walked and drove twice a day with members of her own family. One evening Lady Macclesfield went up to the nursery, while Alexandra prepared her son for bed. "She is a capital nurse, & really in a flannel apron, & with her sleeves tucked up to her shoulders, she looked almost prettier than ever!" She thought the Princess "quite lovely"; her beautiful expression was fascinating and even greater charm was given by the simplicity of her character and "utter unconsciousness of her own beauty, or perhaps her indifference to it, as she must have heard enough of it by this time to turn her head, if she had a particle of vanity or self esteem in her composition." Alexandra always tended to rate other people's merits far more highly than her own but she did not lack judgement, nor was she slow in observation. She was refined and tactful and quickly saw when others were not, "but the kindest feeling pervades all her actions and opinions." The Prince could not have found a more charming and beautiful wife but although the Queen seemed very fond of her, she treated her more as a petted child than as a companion. Victoria also refused to confide in her son, complaining he was childish and injudicious but never encouraging him to improve by letting him take any part in her affairs. She often conveyed her reproofs to him through members of the household, making them all the more galling, but "His spirit of obedience and dutifulness is admirable, & his forbearance frequently astonishing".[162]

The couple visited Queen Marie Amélie[163] at Claremont on the 14th and returned to Windsor the next day after the Prince's Duchy of Cornwall meeting. On the 16th, the Queen, Helena and Alexandra visited the British Orphan Asylum at Slough and on the 21st Alexandra and Helena attended the consecration of a new church in Windsor, of which Vicky had laid the first stone in 1863. Back in London on the 23rd the Waleses later went to the Princess's Theatre, and left for Sandringham the next day. On 3 December Alexandra thanked Louise for her birthday present of a hand-made cushion. They had had a delightful fine day on the 1st "and we were able to enjoy it <u>thoroughly</u>, in driving to a little cottage in the woods where we made a beautiful luncheon for the shooting party who came home with an immense appetite."[164] Winter covert shooting was taking place for the first time. Lady Macclesfield described how Alexandra had done some of the cooking "upon which fortunately we did not depend exclusively. The cutlets were not to be despised, but the pancakes <u>would</u> come out an inch thick, in spite of all efforts to moderate their proportions!" A dance that evening lasted till 1am.[165] The young couple spent their first Sandringham Christmas looking forward to 1865 and a new baby in the summer. On the 30th there was a meet of the West Norfolk Hunt.[166]

Notes

[1] RA VIC/MAIN/Z/464/12, Princess Alexandra of Denmark to Queen Victoria, 1863: 4 January

[2] Alexandra continued this for some years; the reason is not known. She wrote in English to other people at the same time; perhaps she felt her command of the language was not yet good enough for the Queen, or perhaps the Queen had asked her to do so, in an attempt to encourage her German sensibilities (which signally failed).

[3] Later William II, Emperor of Germany (1859–1941)

[4] RA VIC/MAIN/Z/14/35, Crown Princess of Prussia to Queen Victoria, 1863: 12 January

[5] RA VIC/MAIN/Z/14/40, Crown Princess of Prussia to Queen Victoria, 1863: 17 February

[6] RA VIC/MAIN/Y/109/10, Queen Victoria to King Leopold of the Belgians, 1863: 20 January

7   Dressmaker, with premises in Hanover Square, London; Queen Victoria had decided that Alexandra should wear a dress of British manufacture, rather than King Leopold's gift. *See Inside the Royal Wardrobe: a Dress History of Queen Alexandra*, by Kate Strasdin, pp 26–34

8   Kinloch Cooke, Vol I, pp 398, 405, 406

9   Kinloch Cooke, Vol I, p 407

10 Tooley, p 27

11 The original was a pectoral cross, found lying on the breast of Queen Dagmar of Denmark (c 1186–1212) when her tomb was opened in 1683, and subsequently donated to the National Gallery of Denmark. Queen Dagmar, who m King Valdemar II of Denmark, was popularly regarded as an ideal Christian queen

12 Charlotte Mary Yonge (1823–1901), leading novelist

13 Tooley, p 26

14 Tooley, p 16

15 Information from the Danemark, 26 February 1863

16 RA VIC/MAIN/Z/464/43, Augustus Paget to Earl Russell, 1863: 28 February

17 At this time the office was held by Carl Christian Hall (1812–88)

18 RA VIC/MAIN/Z/464/44, General Grey to Queen Victoria, 1863: 2 March

19 RA VIC/MAIN/Y/85/5,7, King Leopold of the Belgians to Queen Victoria, 1863; 20 February and 9 March

20 RA VIC/MAIN/Y/109/20, Queen Victoria to King Leopold of the Belgians, 1863: 3 March

21 Admiral Sir William James Hope-Johnstone (1798–1878)

22 Minny, the name by which Princess Dagmar was known to her family, will now be used, except when she is referred to as Dagmar in quotations from original documents.

23 Karl, Duke of Glücksburg (1813–78), elder brother of Alexandra's father

24 RA VIC/MAIN/Z/464/48, List of Her Majesty's Visitors at Windsor Castle on 7,8,9 March 1863

25 Sir William Lawrence (1818–1897)

26 Shimmering outfits became Alexandra's choice in years to come.

27 George Frederick Handel (1685–1759), leading German/British composer

28 Thomas Oliphant (1799–1873), Scottish musician, artist and author

29 Ludwig van Beethoven (1770–1827), leading German composer

30 RA VIC/MAIN/Z/464/49, Wedding ceremonial, 10 March 1863

31 *A History of Punch*, by RGG Price, p 105

32 George Harris, 3rd Baron Harris (1810–72), colonial administrator, politician and courtier

33 Frances Georgiana, née Pitt-Rivers (1836–96), wife of the Marquess of Carmarthen, later 9th Duke of Leeds

34 Mary Frances, née Grosvenor (1821–1912) wife of 6th Earl of Macclesfield

35 Alice Anne Caroline, née Lambton (1831–1907), wife of the 18th Earl of Morton

36 Henrietta, née Vyner, died 1907, wife of 1st Marquis of Ripon

37 Katherine Mary, née Stewart (d 1889)

38 Diana, née Agar-Ellis (1832–90), wife of Hon Edward Coke

39 Theresa, née Stedingk (1837–1901), wife of 1) William George Grey (d 1865), 2) in 1873, 5th Duke d'Otrante

40 Elise, née Peel (c 1832–83) wife of Hon Francis Stonor

41 Prince William of Denmark was elected King of the Hellenes in 1863, taking the name of George

42 Tooley, pp 117–8

43 RA VIC/MAIN/Z/464/52, General Knollys to Queen Victoria, 1863: 11 March

44 RA VIC/MAIN/Z/464/55, Baron Stockmar to Queen Victoria, 1863: 11 March

45 RA VIC/ADDA5/484, Princess of Wales to Princess Christian of Denmark, 1863: 11 March; translated from Danish

46 RA VIC/ADDA5/483, Prince of Wales to Princess Christian of Denmark, 1863: 11 March

47 RA VIC/MAIN/Z/464/63, General Knollys to Queen Victoria, 1863: 15 March

48 RA VIC/MAIN/Y/109/22, Queen Victoria to King Leopold of the Belgians, 1863: 17 March; she did not mention that the dress had not been worn at the wedding

49 John Jabez Edwin Mayall (1813–1901), photographer

50 RA VIC/MAIN/Y/85/10, King Leopold of the Belgians to Queen Victoria, 1863: 19 March

51 It is tempting to speculate that this may have been the dress given by King Leopold

52 Lt-Colonel Frederick Charles Keppel (1831–76), equerry to the Prince of Wales

53 Ladies often had some kind of handicraft, known as "work", to occupy their leisure moments, such as sewing, embroidery or knitting

54 Of whist

55 The Reverend George Browne Moxon (1794–1866), cleric and botanist

56 RA VIC/MAIN/Z/464/72, Mrs Bruce to Queen Victoria, 1863: 29 March

57 RA VIC/MAIN/Z/464/73, Mrs Bruce to Queen Victoria, 1863: 1 April

58 Thomas Coke (1822–1909), 2nd Earl of Leicester, Lord Lieutenant of Norfolk

59 They had been designed for showing at the Great Exhibition of 1862

60 Princess Victoria of Hesse (1863–1950), m Prince Louis Battenberg, later 1st Marquess of Milford Haven

61 Beavan, p 80; Alexandra seems to have had a liking for fish, aesthetically and gastronomically; after all, a silver stockfish with a golden crown was a feature of her Coat of Arms and fish is significant in Danish cuisine. Shining fish scales may also have influenced her taste for shimmering, sequinned gowns.

62 Theodore Jensen (1816–94), painter

63 Marshall Wood (c 1834–82), sculptor, medallist and artist

64 George Housman Thomas (1824–68), engraver, illustrator and painter (including of the Prince and Princess of Wales's wedding)

65 William Powell Frith (1819–1901), portrait and narrative painter

66 John Gibson (1790–1866), sculptor

67 Henry Weigall (1829–1925), portrait and genre painter

68 Joseph Wyon (1836–73), medallist and engraver

69 Annie Dixon (1817–1901), portrait miniaturist

70 Perhaps Robert Hawker Dowling (1827–86), Australian artist

71 Robert Vernon Heath (1819–95), photographer

72 The Southwell Brothers, William (1823–70), Frederick (1833–83) and Edwin (1840–82), photographers specialising in *cartes-de-visite*, who had three studios in the West End of London in the 1860s and 1870s

73 *Dearest Mama, Private Correspondence of Queen Victoria and the Crown Princess of Prussia, 1861–1864*, edited by Roger Fulford, 1968, p 212. Like her mother, Alexandra is believed to have suffered from otosclerosis, which worsened as she aged

74 "Professor" John Henry Pepper (1821–1900), scientist and inventor

75 Carl Maria von Weber (1786–1826), German composer, conductor, musician and critic

76 Lady Cecilia Underwood (c 1785–1873), daughter of the second Earl of Arran, m Duke of Sussex and was created Duchess of Inverness, after the death of her first husband, Sir George Buggin

77 Augustus, Duke of Sussex (1773–1843), sixth son of King George III

78 RA VIC/ADDA8/390, Taylor, p 19

79 King George III, who spent much time at Windsor, became an active friend of Eton College

and was greatly loved and respected there. His birthday, 4 June, was consequently made a school holiday.

80 Tooley, p 45–6
81 The family and descendants of King Louis Philippe (1773–1850)
82 Henri d'Orléans, Duc d'Aumale (1822–1897) and Maria Carolina (of the Two Sicilies) (1822–69)
83 Robert d'Orléans, Duc de Chartres (1840–1910)
84 Princess Françoise d'Orléans (1844–1925), d of Prince de Joinville; m Robert, Duc de Chartres
85 Information taken from a press report
86 Princess Marie of Baden (1834–99) wife of Prince Ernest of Leiningen (Queen Victoria's half-nephew); the baby was Princess Alberta of Leiningen (1863–1901)
87 RA VIC/MAIN/Y/109/32, Queen Victoria to King Leopold of the Belgians, 1863: 24 May
88 *selbstständigkeit*
89 RA VIC/MAIN/Y/43/78,81,88, Dowager Princess of Hohenlohe-Langenburg to Queen Victoria, 1863: 8 July, 27 July, 26 September
90 A double title; the holders were sometimes called by one title and sometimes the other one
91 Arthur Farre (1811–87), obstetric physician
92 Sir William Jenner, 1st Baronet (1815–98), royal physician
93 Edward Henry Sieveking (1816–1904), royal physician
94 RA VIC/MAIN/Z/447/73, Princess of Wales to Queen Victoria, 1863: 26 August
95 RA VIC/MAIN/Z/447/74, Duke of Cambridge to Queen Victoria, 1863: 31 August
96 Otto, Prince of Bismarck (1815–98), statesman and first chancellor of united Germany
97 Ellen Innocent, royal monthly nurse in the 1860s
98 Prince Albert Victor of Wales (1864–92), later Duke of Clarence and Avondale
99 RA VIC/MAIN/Z/447/84,85, Prince of Wales to Queen Victoria, 1864: both on 8 January
100 RA VIC/MAIN/Z/447/86, Prince of Wales to Queen Victoria, 1864: 8 January
101 Granville George Leveson-Gower, 2nd Earl Granville (1815–1891), statesman
102 RA VIC/MAIN/Z/447/89, Lord Granville to Sir Charles Phipps, 1864: 8 January
103 Elizabeth St Aubyn (1815–78), wife of General Knollys
104 RA VIC/MAIN/Z/447/90, Outfit provided for his Royal Highness the eldest son of the Prince of Wales
105 Princess Beatrice (1857–1944), fifth daughter of Queen Victoria, m Prince Henry of Battenberg
106 RA VIC/MAIN/Z/447/108, Dowager Princess of Hohenlohe-Langenburg to Queen Victoria, 1864: 10 January
107 RA VIC/MAIN/Z/447/117, Queen Victoria to King Leopold of the Belgians, 1864: 12 January
108 Who wrote on 28 January to thank Dr Sieveking for good news of Alexandra; "I trust the health of the hasty young gentleman will not be harmed by the premature entry on the stage of life." Queen Louise of Denmark to Dr EH Sieveking, 1863: 28 January, private collection
109 RA VIC/ADDA17/96, Princess Dagmar of Denmark to Princess Louise, 1864: 12 February
110 RA VIC/ADDA8/1461, Princess of Wales to Mrs Emily Alston, 1864: 22 February
111 Prince John of Glücksburg (1825–1911), often referred to as Uncle Hans
112 Sir James Clark, 1st Baronet (1788–1870), Queen Victoria's physician from 1837–1860
113 RA VIC/MAIN/Z/447/144, Sir James Clark to Queen Victoria, 1864: 9 March
114 RA VIC/MAIN/Z/447/149, Queen Victoria to General Knollys, 1864: 14 March
115 RA VIC/MAIN/Z/447/151, General Knollys to Queen Victoria, 1864: 15 March
116 RA VIC/MAIN/Y/86/15, King Leopold of the Belgians to Queen Victoria, 1864: 12 March

[117] RA VIC/MAIN/Y/111/25, Queen Victoria to King Leopold of the Belgians, 1864: 12 March

[118] Konstantinos Mousouros (1807–91) also known as Kostaki Musurus Pasha, Ottoman Greek diplomat

[119] The Prince backed Cambridge; Alexandra may also have done so, to support him or because her cousin Mary of Cambridge did, although, of course, her brother Frederick went to Oxford.

[120] Tooley, p 156

[121] Henry Nelson O'Neill (1817–80), historical genre painter

[122] Henry Tidey (1814–72), painter

[123] RA VIC/ADDA8/1465, Princess of Wales to Princess Mary of Cambridge, 1864: 29 April

[124] Charles FitzGerald (1819–87), Marquis of Kildare; succeeded his father as 4th Duke of Leinster in 1874

[125] RA VIC/MAIN/Z/448/9, Lord Palmerston to Earl Russell, 1864: 20 May

[126] Who were staying at St James's Palace

[127] Adelaide Dalton (1821–95) wife of Sir John Young (1807–76), later Baron Lisgar, who was Governor of New South Wales from 1861–7

[128] Hugh Grosvenor (1825–99), Marquess and then Duke of Westminster; his wife was Lady Constance Sutherland-Leveson-Gower (c1835–80)

[129] RA VIC/ADDC/07/1/0259, Marchioness of Westminster to General Knollys, 1864: 22 June

[130] Hans Matthison Hansen (1807–90), organist and composer

[131] Théodore Gudin (1802–80), French marine painter

[132] Walter Montagu-Douglas-Scott (1806–84), 5th Duke of Buccleuch and 7th Duke of Queensberry

[133] Louis William Desanges (1822–1905), painter mostly of military subjects

[134] Henry Barraud (1811–1874), painter

[135] RA VIC/MAIN/Y/112/17, Queen Victoria to King Leopold of the Belgians, 1864: 30 July

[136] RA VIC/MAIN/Y/113/18; RA VIC/MAIN/Y/111/24, memorandum by Queen Victoria for King Leopold, 1864; Queen Victoria to King Leopold, 1864: both 11 March

[137] RA VIC/MAIN/Z/448/23, Queen Victoria, memorandum, 1864: 1 August

[138] RA VIC/MAIN/Z/448/ 24, 29, Sir James Clark to Queen Victoria, 1864: August (undated); Earl Russell to Queen Victoria, 1864: 7 August

[139] Edward Tayler (1828–1906), painter of portraits, figures and miniatures

[140] Cornelius Jabez Hughes (1819–84), photographer, writer and lecturer

[141] RA VIC/MAIN/Z/448/35, Prince of Wales to Queen Victoria, 1864: c early September; he was referring to the war

[142] John Moolenburgh Minter (1815–91), royal physician

[143] John Poyntz Spencer (1835–1910), 5th Earl Spencer, courtier, politician, twice Lord Lieutenant of Ireland

[144] RA VIC/MAIN/Z/448/42, Earl Spencer to Sir Thomas Biddulph, 1864: 22 September

[145] RA VIC/MAIN/Z/448/43,44, Dr EH Sieveking to Queen Victoria,1864: 26 and 22 September

[146] Jane, née Hope-Vere (1821–90), m 3rd Marquess of Ely; Lady of the Bedchamber to Queen Victoria

[147] Carl XV (1826–72)

[148] King George V of Hanover (1819–78)

[149] RA VIC/MAIN/Z/448/54, Prince of Wales to Queen Victoria, 1864: 7 October

[150] RA VIC/MAIN/Z/448/55, General Knollys to Queen Victoria, 1864: 8 October

[151] RA VIC/MAIN/Z/448/75, General Knollys to Queen Victoria, 1864: 24 October

[152] Princess Marie of Saxe-Altenburg (1818–1907), m King George V of Hanover

153 Franz, Prince Teck (1837–1900), later Duke of Teck, m Princess Mary Adelaide of Cambridge

154 Duke Alexander of Württemberg (1804–85)

155 Countess Claudine Rhédey de Kis-Rhéde (1812–41), created Countess von Hohenstein

156 Wolfgang Amadeus Mozart (1756–91), prolific and significant German composer

157 Felix Mendelssohn Bartholdy (1809–47), noted German composer

158 Mrs Mary Anne Thurston (c 1810–96), nurse to Queen Victoria's children

159 Concerns

160 Forsaken

161 RA VIC/MAIN/Y/113/2,3, Queen Victoria to King Leopold of the Belgians, 1864: 10 and 15 November

162 RA VIC/ADDC18/93, Mary, Countess of Macclesfield (1821–1912) to her husband, Thomas Parker, 6th Earl of Macclesfield (1811–96), 1864: 11 November – 2 December

163 Princess Marie Amélie of the Two Sicilies (1782–1866) m Louis Philippe I, King of the French (1773–1850)

164 RA VIC/ADDA17/108, Princess of Wales to Princess Louise, 1864: 3 December

165 RA VIC/ADDC18/93, Countess of Macclesfield to her husband, 1864: 11 November – 2 December

166 The master of the hunt, Henry Villebois (1807–83), known as "The Squire", was a friend of the couple

Chapter 4

1865–1869

"An entirely new world"

～❦～

After dinner and a "snap dragon"[1] on 1 January 1865, the Waleses stayed until the 6th at Holkham Hall.[2] Back at Sandringham, the Knollys family dined with them, enjoying a Twelfth cake and another snapdragon. Eddy had a little first birthday present table on the 8th. The house party arrived and field sports began. Alexandra drove with Aunt Cambridge and Albert Edward showed the guests his new kitchen garden, pheasants and stables. The family left for London on the 19th but stayed with the Queen at Osborne for Princess Louise's confirmation at Whippingham Church on the 21st and some very successful theatricals by the servants later. It was still very cold but they went out every day; heavy snow and a gale on the 27th thwarted the Prince's hunting and shooting but the weather was improving when, on 3 February, they returned to London.

Albert Edward attended the House of Lords, rode, hunted and entertained friends with smoking and "b & s"[3] in the Turkish Room at Marlborough House. The couple went driving, dined either alone or with friends and relatives and often went to the theatre; on the 6th it was *Cinderella* at Covent Garden, where Donato,[4] a one-legged Spaniard, "danced wonderfully well."[5] On the 9th they heard that fire overnight at Sandringham had completely destroyed the bedroom used by Aunt Cambridge; dying embers in the next room's grate had smouldered and ignited, spreading along a beam at the back of the fireplace to the bedroom and then the billiard room below. It was contained and doused in a few hours but it fuelled Albert Edward's interest in patent fire extinguishers. Heavy snow fell in London on 11 February and Ernest Leiningen later accompanied the Waleses to a play and an amusing burlesque at St James's Theatre. The next day the two princes drove to the zoo; it was fashionable and Albert Edward liked to see new acquisitions. The popular porpoise had died but the new favourite was the orangutang. Alexandra also enjoyed zoos but in cold weather theatres or parties were more inviting, despite sometimes crowded and stuffy dancing rooms. The Prince constantly rode, hunted, socialised, chaired meetings, saw exhibitions, attended Parliament, visited galleries and studios, received visitors and discussed such projects as the Albert Hall. Alexandra would join him, for example, at a watercolour exhibition in the Egyptian Hall in Piccadilly on the 17th. M Desanges showed them his portrait of her on the 21st and on the 24th they visited Weigall's and Leighton's[6] studios.

On 19 February the Waleses met the Stonor family at the South Kensington Horticultural Gardens and strolled round the gardens, conservatory and colonnades. They watched Guards officers perform charity shows for the Guards' Industrial Home, at the Bijou Theatre, Haymarket, on the 25th and the 27th, taking Princes Arthur and Leopold (fourteen and eleven), who both enjoyed acting, on the 25th. Weigall was painting a portrait of Albert Edward as an anniversary surprise for Alexandra, but during a sitting on 2 March Francis Knollys[7] came to remind the Prince he was supposed to be at the South London Working Classes' Industrial Exhibition at Lambeth Baths. Hurrying there, he found it, after all, very interesting. That evening it was the Fifes'[8] ball at Grosvenor Place, in two rooms covered entirely in pink, with pink artificial roses. The next day, the Russian field marshal, Prince Bariatinsky[9] called. There were more artists' sittings,[10] social events and the zoo again. The dinner party at Marlborough House on the 6th was a typical gathering: nobility, politicians, friends, household and foreigners (Count Lavradio)[11]. Guests might also include royalty, diplomats, the Church, arts, sciences, forces, and interesting or amusing people. The important thing was that they should all get on well together and to assist this there would often be a military band, other music, or entertainers. The Waleses took Eddy to stay overnight with the Queen at Windsor on 7/8 March. The wedding anniversary ball on the 10th included a "sit-down" supper at 1.00 and dancing until 4.30am; the Prince and his friends smoked in the Turkish Room till 5.45. The next day the couple walked across to St James's Palace to see Aunt Cambridge; later the Prince, keenly interested in electricity, saw electric light experiments at a *conversazione* at the Royal Society.

Alexandra went driving nearly every day, while her husband rode or hunted; they gave dinner parties and attended more balls and theatres. On the 18th Alexandra and Mrs Stonor visited the botanical gardens in Regent's Park and the next day, Princess Bariatinsky,[12] "very dark and rather pretty", called on Alexandra. On the 20th Albert Edward, riding in Rotten Row with Alfred, was nearly blown away by piercingly cold wind; later the Waleses dined with the Duchess of Inverness at Kensington Palace. They stayed till 2am at the French Ambassador's[13] ball at Albert Gate on the 23rd; the two dancing rooms were rather small and supper, although very good, lasted too long.[14] Albert Edward met King Leopold at Waterloo Station on the 24th and took him to Windsor; the next day Alexandra held a drawing room at St James's Palace and on the 26th the couple gave a dinner for Uncle George's 46th birthday. They saw Edward Sothern[15] in *The Woman in Mauve* at the Haymarket on the 27th; "a ridiculous piece", evidently inspired by Wilkie Collins's[16] *The Woman in White*[17] and the new fashionable colour, invented by William Perkin[18] in 1856. On the 28th the couple received jewels, a shield, sword and shawls as wedding gifts from the Punjab. After the dinner they gave on the 29th, Lord Llanover's[19] Welsh harpist, Thomas Gruffydd,[20] played on the triple-stringed Welsh harp, accompanied on the piano by John Parry,[21] who also sang some comic songs. On the 30th the Waleses gave a dinner party for King Leopold and the next day saw *Faces in the Fire* at St James's Theatre.

Mr Window[22] photographed the family in the conservatory the next day. They spent two nights at Windsor before Alfred came to stay, and all attended the Philharmonic Society's concert at the Hanover Square Rooms. There were more plays and dinner parties; the two brothers attended several functions together, while Alexandra drove with her lady-in-waiting. Her new baby was expected in the summer. On 8 April they left for Sandringham; Albert Edward was keen to show the guests his estate, while Alexandra drove in the "Basket Carriage" with Lady de Grey. It was fine and warm and sightseeing included Castle Rising and the almshouse for old ladies, wearing their own special costume. On the 12th there was an excursion to Hunstanton for a picnic lunch on the grass in Mr Le Strange's[23] park; Mrs Knollys and her three daughters joined them. In view of his growing family, the Prince, with General Knollys, Mr Humbert (the London architect), and others, discussed alterations at Sandringham, and decided, for the present, to extend the existing house. After lunch, WR Pridgeon, from King's Lynn, photographed the whole party.

On Good Friday, the 14th, Albert Edward showed Mr Toward[24] round the grounds and the next day discussed estate improvements with his gardener, Carmichael[25] and local architect, Mr Goggs.[26] After church on Easter Sunday, they had tea "al fresco" in fine weather at Jocelyn Cottage in Jocelyn Wood. Alfred arrived on the 17th for three days of shooting, fishing and hawking with hawks lent by the Duke of St Albans.[27] There was a trip to the ruined abbey and castle at Castle Acre on the 19th and on the 21st Albert Edward and others rode his Icelandic ponies, bought in Copenhagen in 1864. But on the 24th came devastating news from Nice; Tsesarevitch Nicholas had died there from cerebrospinal meningitis. Minny, with her mother and eldest brother, had arrived only two days before his death. Alexandra, who had a cold, stayed in her room all day and wrote to Princess Mary: "No words can say how sad I am for her and for the dear kind brother we have lost! Still it is one great consolation that she found him alive, and that he knew her, they say he was so thankful for her coming to see him, poor darling remained with him to the last!!"[28] On the 26th a telegram announced that the American President Lincoln[29] had been shot at the theatre, dying next morning. Despite all this bad news, it was pleasant in the hot weather, with plenty to do; croquet, driving and a trip to Houghton,[30] to see all the pictures and rooms, followed by lunch outside on the grass. On the 29th Mr Merryweather,[31] inventor of the "Sandringham" fire engine, which the Prince had recently got from London, came to demonstrate it; "we pumped over the house, & I held the hose the whole time."[32] The next day the Prince chose the site of a new keeper's cottage, overlooking the partridge ground and some new ground rented from Lord Leicester; he also decided to lengthen the wall up to the church and put a new door near the royal pew.

Back in London, the Prince left to open the Exhibition in Dublin, without Alexandra, who was in advanced pregnancy. Much to her delight, her brother Frederick arrived on 6 May; they drove together and on the 9th had lunch at Kew with Aunt Cambridge. On the 11th Edward Cardwell,[33] colonial secretary, with a deputation of British residents from the Colony of Victoria, brought Alexandra an address and a gift. Her husband came back on the 13th and there were drives, theatre visits and the zoo. Sadly, the Waleses favourite dog, Muff, only two, died on the 14th "fr over excitement".[34] After Frederick went home on the 16th Alexandra attended the state ball, wearing mourning for the Tsesarevitch. There were more drives, theatres, a dinner party at Marlborough House on the 19th and on the 22nd the state concert at Buckingham Palace; earlier the couple had stood sponsors to Lord and Lady Alfred Paget's[35] daughter, to whom they gave a necklet. On the 23rd, with Princess Mary, they watched Uncle George's review of militia in Hyde Park. The Prince laid the foundation stone of St Mary's Hospital, Paddington's new wing; later the couple went to the opera. They both attended the Queen's birthday parade at Horse Guards the next day.

Stopping overnight at White Lodge, they attended a ball on the 25th at Orléans House, with French Royalty and the Duke of Brabant, who later stayed with them till the 31st. A ball at Stafford House on the 29th lasted till almost four in the morning, although Alexandra and the Duke left after 2am. On 1 June the Waleses went to see *Eleanor's Victory*, "a very good sensation play".[36] Perhaps it was too sensational; the next day, Alexandra was too unwell to attend dinner and felt worse later. Dr Farre, Mrs Clarke[37] and Lady Macclesfield were called and at 1.18am on 3 June her second son[38] was born, in the presence of his father, Mrs Clarke and the doctor; although reputedly an eight months child, he was much larger than Eddy had been.[39] He flourished, Alexandra slept, and they woke later to a fine, hot day. She moved from bed to sofa on the 10th and the next day her husband told his mother the baby's names and sponsors; they had decided to call him George, an English name they both liked, then Frederick, as he was born on the Danish crown prince's birthday and thirdly Ernest, after Ernest Leiningen,[40] a longstanding good friend. If the baby had been a girl, they would have called her Louise. The sponsors would be the Queen of Denmark, Princess Alice, the Duchess of Cambridge and the Duke, Crown Prince Frederick and Ernest Leiningen.[41] The Queen was not impressed by George as a first name, predictably asking them to add Albert and pressing them to invite Duke Ernest II to be a sponsor too. This was agreed and King George V of Hanover was also invited.[42] Albert Edward, delighted with his new son, continued with his usual engagements, while Alexandra, feeling very well, stayed quietly at home with the children, receiving family visitors on the 10th and the 17th. She went driving for the first time on the 24th, with her husband and the Brabants. More visitors called, she began driving more often, sometimes with Helena and Louise, or Lady Macclesfield, and on 30 June was churched at the Chapel Royal, St James's. Next evening the Waleses saw *Les Huguenots* at Covent Garden; on 2 July they attended a service at the chapel and on the 3rd gave a dinner for the Queen of the Netherlands.

After lunch on 4 July, Lt-Colonel Armytage,[43] Captain of the Coldstream Guards, on duty at St James's Palace, saw smoke coming from Marlborough House's roof, above the east wing, near the nurseries. He called the Guard out and they rushed a fire engine and hose across the road, where Albert Edward, in his shirt-sleeves, was already collecting pails and jugs of water to be taken onto the roof. Tearing up the floor (the Prince nearly falling through the rafters) they found the fire in the ventilating shaft and, with the help of some friends, "we all worked hard & got it down in an hour."[44] They had flooded the staircase and when Captain Shaw,[45] of the Metropolitan Fire Brigade, arrived with three engines, he was amazed at the unnecessary deluge. Alexandra, alarmed at the thought of danger, was reassured by Colonel Armytage, and she and the children moved to another part of the house but she could not resist coming back from time to time to see what was happening. With order restored[46] the family left for Windsor, as planned, at 5.45, driving in the grounds next morning and seeing the Queen, Helena and Louise. Albert Edward returned to London briefly, chairing and speaking at a meeting about the proposed Albert Central Hall of Arts and Sciences, for South Kensington, before, on 7 July, the Archbishop of Canterbury christened baby George Frederick Ernest Albert in Windsor Castle's private chapel. The whole of next morning was spent in the conservatory, being photographed by Mr Saunders[47] from Eton. On the 9th Alexandra drove with the Queen and the next day the Waleses attended the horse show at the Agricultural Hall, and *Faust* at Covent Garden.

On the 13th the family left for Osborne Cottage. They dined with the Queen and toured the estate, including Osborne Pier and the floating bath,[48] where Albert Edward enjoyed a pleasant dip. He drove Alexandra in her phaeton to Apley House, near Ryde, where the Prince and Princess of Thurn und Taxis[49] were staying. On the 16th he drove her, Louise and Leopold in his Irish car, to the Swiss Cottage for tea. Despite heavy thunderstorms and constant rain on the 17th, he went on a steam yacht to Spithead and back and at 10.30pm the Waleses boarded *Osborne*, for a short cruise, leaving at 3am next morning in deteriorating weather. They were both very seasick, but landed near Mount Edgcumbe at about 4pm, to stay with the Earl.[50] The next day they drove to the Royal Agricultural Society's show, which was so crowded that the prize animals were trotted round for them to see from their carriage. After lunch in a tent they drove to the Albert Bridge at Saltash, and, in *Osborne*, steamed along to the

Ironclad Squadron. After visiting the French ship, *Magenta* and others, the Prince rejoined the ladies on *Osborne*; later there was an impromptu dance at Mount Edgcumbe.

On the 20th their host gave a grand lunch in the Orangery, with music by the Band of the Royal Marines, Plymouth Division. In the bright, warm afternoon they walked about the park and the Prince sailed in the yacht, *Waterbaby*. That evening the Army and Navy gave a celebratory ball in the large rooms of the Melville Stores in the Royal William Victualling Yard. About 900 people attended and it became very hot. Alexandra had not really been expected to come, but was welcomed with delight. The couple left after supper at 1am and the next day gave a dinner on *Osborne*, to the Mount Edgcumbe party; the Duke of St Albans and Lord Mount Edgcumbe stayed with them and on 22 July the yacht left for Fowey, where they visited Mr and Mrs Trefry and the Fowey Consuls Mine, where some silver was being smithed from the copper ore.[51] They saw Restormel Castle, a picturesque ruin belonging to the Duchy of Cornwall and lunched with Mr and Mrs Robarts. Colonel Peard[52] ("Garibaldi's Englishman") accompanied them. They invited some of these people to a dinner that evening, and afterwards the sailors gave a singing concert on deck. Reaching Mount's Bay the next day, they lunched with the St Aubyns[53] at St Michael's Mount and Alexandra returned to *Osborne* while her husband and others sailed in one of the Revenue Cutters in the Bay. On the 24th the Waleses landed at Penzance and drove to Botallack Mine, where they donned mining dress and, in a truck worked by a steam engine, went down a quarter of a mile below sea level into a tin and copper mine, where they saw miners at work and "knocked off a little of the ore ourselves."[54] Alexandra and some of the party then went straight back to *Osborne,* while the Prince and others drove to Land's End. They met at dinner at St Michael's Mount, where the Prince left Alexandra overnight while he started at 4am for the Scilly Isles. She was rowed out to *Osborne* in Mr St Aubyn's barge and then went to Marazion, received an address and drove about near Penzance. Albert Edward returned on the 26th; they left for Falmouth, landed at the docks and drove round Pendennis Castle. After an excursion up the River Fal, they steamed away on *Osborne*, arriving at Cowes at 10pm on the 27th, and finding the children quite well at Osborne Cottage.

On the 31st, Alexandra, with Lady de Grey, took her first bathe. The Waleses, Louise, Beatrice and Leopold, on *Alberta*, watched the Town Regatta open on 2 August with tub and boat races and duck hunts in Cowes Roads; later, the Prince went sailing on his new cutter, *Dagmar* and Alexandra joined him on the 3rd. There were more trips on *Dagmar,* the annual Royal Yacht Squadron ball on the 4th, lunch with their relatives and a service at Whippingham Church on the 6th. Leaving their children at Osborne Cottage with Lady Caroline Barrington, the couple went to London on the 8th, for Albert Edward to register George's birth and various other matters; later on the 9th they saw *The Lady of Lyons* at the

Haymarket. The next day they were busy packing and at 12.30 set off, reaching Antwerp on 11 August, then Cologne, where they saw the cathedral and bought some local scent. Staying at the Hotel Giant at Coblenz, they visited the Queen of Prussia at the palace; "now <u>everybody</u> can be satisfied that we paid the necessary civility", Albert Edward told Louise.[55] They left next day for Rumpenheim, staying with Landgrave William and other relatives, for games of skittles, trips to Wiesbaden and Frankfort and shooting. On the 19th Uncle Hans arrived; he and Albert Edward went for drives. A group photograph was taken on the 22nd and on the 24th, after giving a dinner at the Hotel d'Angleterre at Frankfort, the Waleses left by late train for Coburg, for another family gathering. On 26 August, Prince Albert's birthday, Queen Victoria unveiled his statue in the market place; the next day Albert Edward, Alfred and Fritz called on his old tutor, the ailing Hofrath Florschütz.[56] Later, Alexandra and others drove with them to explore the house and grounds at Kallenberg, especially the model farm and horses. There was a large dinner in the Riesensaal, then Faust at the theatre and Lord Granville's little supper party, with guests including Madame Reuter, an illegitimate daughter of Duke Ernest II.[57]

It was rare for all nine of Queen Victoria's children to be together and Mr Bingham, from Paris, photographed them in groups at the Rosenau. Over the next two days Albert Edward, Duke Ernest, Alfred and others went to the Duke's shooting box at Oberhof, bagging some stags, while Alexandra stayed at Kallenberg with Duchess Alexandrine. On the 31st the Waleses returned by train to Rumpenheim for more shooting, skittles, whist, a visit to Kentz's famous circus and to Königstein, a charming villa near a ruined castle. There were more trips to Frankfort and on 7 September the Duke of Nassau's band played during the dinner and dance. The couple left on the 8th for Kranichstein,[58] staying overnight at Darmstadt. The next day the Prince went shooting, but at 4.15pm he and Alexandra, the Hessians and Princess Hilda of Anhalt-Dessau[59] left, reaching London on the 11th. The children had arrived on the 9th.

The Waleses took their guests all over the Crystal Palace on 12 September, lunched in one of the refreshment rooms, saw the fountains play and got back home soon after 5pm. Later that evening a Chinese giant was brought to Marlborough House. He was about twenty, a good-looking man of 7' 8", accompanied by his wife, a small Chinese lady, and a dwarf, 3' tall. Afterwards, it was the Adelphi for *Rip Van Winkle* a new play by Dion Boucicault.[60] Albert Edward and Uncle George went shooting in Richmond Park, while Alexandra, Alice and Hilda went to the Tower of London. On the 14th they spent an hour at the zoo and later saw *Arrah na Pogue* at the Princess's Theatre. The next day the princesses watched the Prince and Prince Louis play tennis at Prince's Club[61] and afterwards saw some exotic plants at the Subtropical Garden in Battersea Park. At 8pm they left by the limited mail train from Euston Square for Perth, arriving next morning starving and glad of breakfast at the station. Leaving for

Aboyne and then Ballater, they reached Abergeldie at 4.30pm; the Hessians went to Balmoral. The Scottish holiday lasted just over a month; as usual, there was shooting and fishing and frequent meetings with the Queen. The Waleses gave a dance on the 19th and a ball on the 22nd, the day Uncle Hans arrived; they danced reels, jigs and country dances till the early morning. On the 28th the Prince and Uncle Hans rode to the "Merchants" at Crathie, where Alexandra and Hilda joined them; later they gave a gillies' ball in the new ballroom at Abergeldie. More deer drives, shoots and excursions followed until 17 October, when the couple, Hilda and Uncle Hans left to stay at Floors Castle,[62] while General Knollys and Mr Holzmann[63] took the children back to London. Floors was large, comfortable and full of guests; on the 18th they went to Kelso Races and later there was a large ball. After shooting, another ball and a small dance, they left (after a group photograph and a last attempt at fishing) at 11.00 on the 21st by special train to London, reaching Marlborough House next morning; it poured with rain all day.

While Albert Edward went to the races and out shooting with Uncle Hans and others, Alexandra drove with Hilda; on the 26th she took her to Windsor Castle and there were several theatre visits for them all. On 27 October the Prince attended Lord Palmerston's funeral in Westminster Abbey, and burial. The couple dined with the Duchess of Inverness at Kensington Palace on the 28th. The following evening Uncle Hans started for Copenhagen; next morning Hilda left for Germany. Staying at Knowsley,[64] the Waleses went on the 31st to Liverpool and were met by enormous, enthusiastic crowds. They steamed up and down the Mersey, glimpsing the town, docks and shipping before lunch with the Mayor at the Town Hall and a visit to the Free Library and the Derby Collection. Afterwards they heard the fine organ being played in St George's Hall. At Knowsley, there was evening dancing and daytime shooting, despite rain, until 3 November, when they returned to Sandringham. The Prince inspected the new kennels and pheasantry next morning and later rode to Wolferton Station to meet the Prussians, who had come from Windsor for a few days. After church next day, the whole party walked to the new kitchen garden and home by the kennels and stables. This walk, extended as time went on, became a tradition and was known as the "Sunday Round"; a regular exercise for guests. On the 6th the Waleses and their party went to see Ely Cathedral. On the Prince's birthday a feast for the schoolchildren was held in one of the coach houses; later a large bonfire was lit "near Brereton's house". At 10.00 they gave a "first rate" dance for nearly 80, including as many neighbours as they could get, which went on till 4am. The Prussians returned to Windsor the next day; shooting continued and others, including the Hessians, arrived; Alexandra and Alice joined the shooters on the 14th for lunch. The West Norfolk Hounds met at Anmer on the 15th, when Alice rode "Norma" and Alexandra a new black horse. On the 20th the Prince inspected cottages with Mr White,[65] General Knollys and

Mr Beck,[66] the new agent; later he saw other new cottages at West Newton, Carmichael's new house and the wood yard. The party left and the couple stayed a few days at Melford;[67] while the Prince went shooting, Alexandra visited the parish church at Acton, the national schools and the hospital for aged inhabitants. Heavy rain and strong winds prevailed for most of the time, but there was a dance on the 21st and a little "hop" on the 23rd.

Despite the weather, field sports continued at Sandringham. For Alexandra's 21st birthday, her husband gave her, among other things, a hunter, a pair of bay ponies with harness and a chocolate-coloured carriage. She and the ladies joined the shooting party at lunch. The Danish minister, Baron Bülow[68] arrived and there was a feast in the coach house for the estate workers; later, there was a bonfire and a dance, lasting till nearly 5am. The next day, not surprisingly, they got up very late, but were determined to hunt, so drove to Houghton and met the hounds close by. Alexandra "rode like a bird"[69] to her husband's admiration. 3 December was very wet, so, apart from the "Sunday Round" there were no outings and they played games in the evening. On the 4th they went to stay with the Suffields[70] at Gunton, for shooting and a grand ball. On the 5th Princess Helena's engagement to Prince Christian of Augustenburg,[71] the Duke's brother, was announced. As well as being "an Augustenburg", he was fifteen years older than Helena, which the Waleses thought rather hard on her. However, she was happy, so they took the news "much better than we cld have expected & I have no doubt all will go smoothly", as the Queen told her uncle.[72] Alexandra's family was suspected of influencing her against Prince Christian and, as Sir Charles Phipps told General Knollys; "The Princess of Wales in this country should be an English Princess, and not a Dane, still less a Holsteiner, and if left alone, I feel sure that she would be." Differences between Glücksburgs and Augustenburgs should not be allowed to create coolness between the Queen's sons and daughters, and Prince Christian himself was determined to do his best to become an Englishman.[73] The Waleses had planned to visit Merton but on the 9th news came of King Leopold's death and, after the mausoleum service on the 14th, Albert Edward and Arthur left for the funeral at Laeken on the 16th. Albert Edward visited his mother at Osborne on the 21st, to report on the sad obsequies and try to comfort her. Back in London, he left on the 23rd for Sandringham and Christmas with his wife and children.

On 30 December the Queen castigated him about the amount of time they spent with the Sutherlands,[74] "he does not live as a Duke <u>ought</u> & she is a foolish injudicious little woman." They would soon have paid three visits to Lord Leicester's, "& it is so much remarked that you are so little quietly at home & go so much about, & I can't deny that I think 2 or 3 visits in <u>the year</u> are quite enough & especially I would not visit the same people every year, nor would I go to the same people <u>in London</u> & <u>in the country</u>, for that at once puts you on a footing of friendship & makes your visits no longer an honour & a distinction."[75]

This was not the only comment the Queen made about her son's friends. She felt that the monarchy should remain dignified and slightly distanced from others but also, being a grieving widow and very shy, often found meeting people difficult and tiring. Albert Edward, however, revelled in company, he was a good host and a good friend and Alexandra was ready to help him. Searching for a public role, he was striking out on a line of his own, which people welcomed. He saw the need for greater, not less, royal involvement in public life and with British institutions and people. Prince Albert, who had been committed to all kinds of British causes, might well have agreed.

When Albert Edward replied on 2 January 1866, he defended the Duke of Sutherland; "a clever & a most straightforward man, in spite of certain eccentricities & formerly faults." He was an intelligent individualist, the kind of person the Prince liked. Albert Edward also disputed that he and Alexandra "run about too much – as it is really not the case." Lord Leicester was a neighbour and visits to Holkham were really for the shooting. Of course "going about too much & making oneself common" was not desirable and was not his intention.[76] Accordingly, from 8–13 January the couple visited Holkham privately, leaving again on the 24th to stay at Lilleshall House with the Sutherlands, for shooting, and walking in the beautiful grounds. After a ball on the 25th, they went to Trentham. Back in London, the Waleses attended the Queen's State Opening of Parliament on 6 February, followed their usual occupations and on the 12th went fox-hunting at Thame, travelling from Paddington Station in hunting dress. The next day they visited Theed's[77] studio. They went to Cumberland Lodge, for hunting with harriers, but rain intervened. In London again, they received visitors and on the 20th dined with Uncle George at Gloucester House. They stayed briefly at Belvoir Castle[78] and then the Prince attended a meeting of the Commissioners for the 1867 International Exhibition in Paris, a Duchy of Cornwall meeting, and the House of Lords.

Prince Alfred sometimes joined the Waleses at social events, such as dinner with the Duchess of Inverness on 1 March, or riding with them on the 7th. There were dinner parties, theatres and Alexandra drove nearly every day, usually with her lady-in-waiting. She got on well with the now widowed and homeless Mrs William Grey, who was brought more permanently into Alexandra's household, to help with the children and as a companion.[79] The Queen, Helena and Louise visited the Waleses on their third wedding anniversary; later, the couple gave a dinner and evening party, entertained by the conjurer, Colonel Stodare[80] and the Coldstream Guards Band. On the 12th it was St James's Theatre and the next day they gave a dance.

Alexandra was very fond of Louise, and on her birthday, 18 March, sent her "a sealskin bag and a crystal locket with my hair in."[81] Sometimes they drove or rode together and, when her mother let her, Louise would come to Marlborough House. Meanwhile Alexandra visited the London Surgical Home at Notting Hill on the 21st and later the Waleses dined with the Marlboroughs[82] at St James's Square. They visited Uncle George on the 26th, later leaving condolences at Claremont.[83] Spending Easter at Windsor, the family went home after church. The Queen told Vicky that, while "Bertie" was most amiable and "all is right about Lenchen", she found "dear Alix" a little grand; "we never get more intimate or nearer to each other." Hers "was not a sympathetic nature, good & kind as she is" but perhaps the Queen's having stopped her hunting[84] ("which shocked everyone"), and the discord over Helena's marriage, had embarrassed her. The Queen insisted that Alexandra was getting haughty and frivolous; "what you say of her not being demonstrative is not the objection ... it is the want of softness & warmth ... Alix & I, never will or can be more intimate. She shows me no confidence whatever especially about the Children, who are not sufficiently cared for."[85] Victoria felt she was right, while Alexandra, with her own opinions, had become nervous and aloof. Lady Macclesfield's observation that the Queen treated her as a petted child was perceptive; Victoria (like many other people) failed to appreciate that, however fairy-like she appeared, Alexandra was a sensible adult who simply needed to be treated as such.

On 2 April, the couple, Princess Mary, the Prince of Hohenlohe-Langenburg[86] and Prince Teck went to a volunteer review at Brighton. They returned to London to greet the new Belgian king, Leopold II,[87] who had come for Queen Marie Amélie's[88] funeral on 3 April, which Albert Edward also attended. On the 9th Mary's engagement to Teck was announced. He had first come over in 1865 and made many friends in London society, attending the Marlborough House garden party and visiting Sandringham later. He was handsome, with perfect manners, high-principled, domestically-inclined, soldierly, artistic, musical – and strongly Protestant; could the Waleses have invited him for a purpose? Early in March 1866 he was asked to a dinner given by the Duchess of Cambridge, and he and Mary were mutually attracted. As she put it; "The wooing was but a short affair. Francis only arrived in England on the 6th of March, and we met for the first time on the 7th at St James's. One month's acquaintance settled the question and on the 6th of April he proposed in Kew Gardens and was accepted."[89]

The family spent most of April at Sandringham, returning on the 27th for Albert Edward's various commitments, as well as operas, plays and art exhibitions. With Alfred, they called on Augusta, Grand Duchess of Mecklenburg-Strelitz, visiting her brother at Gloucester House, on 7 May. The next day, Albert Edward rode with Prince Teck and also drove with Alexandra; later they attended the Royal Italian Opera. On the 9th they visited the botanical gardens at Regent's Park and following days included plays, a dinner party, opera and a court. On the 16th the couple went riding together. However, they really needed somewhere quiet but near London, to relax with their children. In early May they viewed the dilapidated Stud House and grounds near Hampton Court. Improvements might cost up to £2,000, which presumably the Board of Works would pay, as Albert Edward certainly could not afford to. He hoped the Queen might offer them White Lodge, the Phipps's residence, as Sir Charles had recently died. Perhaps Lady Phipps[90] could have an apartment at Kensington Palace instead. In any case, the Stud House would only do in the summer, as it must be very damp in the winter. The Queen was quite willing for them to have White Lodge after Lady Phipps had left, although Princess Mary had asked for it. It needed improvement and the Queen offered them part of Windsor Castle for Ascot week. She disapproved of them using private houses like Titness Park, although this year's arrangements there could not be cancelled.[91]

On 22 May, with Alfred and Helena, the Waleses visited the International Horticultural Exhibition at South Kensington; on the 23rd Alexandra, wearing pink, held a drawing room at St James's Palace. The next day, the Queen's birthday, the couple and Alfred visited her at Windsor, dining later with the Sutherlands at Stafford House. Then it was the state concert on the 25th, Horse Guards Parade on the 26th and later, the Sutherlands' daughter's christening. On the same day, Alexandra's brother Frederick arrived and they all went to the opera that evening. On the 29th the Wales family, Alfred (now Duke of Edinburgh) and Frederick all left for Ascot week at Titness Park, where, on 3 June, little George and his uncle celebrated their birthdays. Back in London, the Waleses and Frederick went driving on the 6th; and Alexandra sent some small presents to Mary and Teck, including a little horseshoe, which she hoped would bring them as much happiness "as yours brought us". Her best wish for them was "that you may be as happy as I am!"[92] The next day she, her husband, brother and Teck went to a divisional field day at Aldershot, lunching with the commander, General Sir James Scarlett.[93] In the evening the couple dined with Earl and Countess Vane.[94] On the 8th, the Waleses, Frederick and Alfred drove to Aunt Cambridge's party at Kew. Alexandra drove with her brother on the 9th and later held a drawing room at St James's Palace; she and Frederick visited the Duchess of Inverness on the 11th and, with Albert Edward, attended the philharmonic concert in the Hanover Square Rooms, and the Wiltons'[95] ball at Grosvenor Square.

Princess Mary was married at Kew Church on 12 June, in white satin and lace, with Prince Teck in uniform and the bridesmaids in blue and white. Pale blue ("Cambridge blue") was Mary's favourite colour[96] and many ladies there, including Alexandra, were in blue and white. It was a very happy occasion; Mary, who at nearly 33 had waited quite a long time for her wedding, wanted it celebrated at her local church, amid the friendly faces of her relatives, friends and neighbours, with the wedding breakfast at Cambridge Cottage. On the 13th,

Frederick left, and the Waleses, with Alfred, visited the Aumales at Orléans House, Twickenham, on the 15th. The next day the couple lunched with the Archbishop of Canterbury at Lambeth Palace. In the evening of the 18th they went to the Dudleys'[97] ball at Park Lane. A pianist, Mr Sanderson, played for them at Marlborough House. Alexandra drove with Duchess Caroline of Mecklenburg[98] on the 19th but they also learned, sadly, that Sigismund,[99] the Prussians' youngest son, had died, at not yet two.

Albert Edward had chaired another 1867 Paris Exhibition meeting on the 21st; on the 23rd he, Alexandra and Eddy went to stay for a few days with the Sutherlands at Trentham, returning for the state ball. Next morning, after inspecting the merchant officers' training ship, *Worcester* at Erith and giving prizes to the cadets, Albert Edward met Alexandra at the Merchant Orphan Asylum at Snaresbrook, to lay the foundation stone of the new dining room. With Alfred, they called on the Belgian sovereigns[100] at Claridges Hotel and afterwards saw the Tecks off to the continent. On the 29th the Waleses attended the De la Warrs'[101] fête at Knole. After driving with the Belgian queen the next day, Alexandra received Professor Fittig and Mr Schulz to play the zither, an instrument which interested her, at Marlborough House. She rode with her husband and drove again with Queen Marie Henriette on 2 July; later it was the Turkish ambassador's ball at the embassy at Bryanston Square and the Halifax's[102] ball at Belgrave Square next day. On the 4th, Messrs CF Hancock, of Bruton Street, showed them the Irish Volunteer Challenge Cup, for competition at Wimbledon.

The second royal wedding was on 5 July; Princess Helena married Prince Christian of Augustenburg in Windsor Castle's private chapel, followed by a buffet in the Waterloo Chamber. The Waleses gave Helena a diamond bandeau head-dress and a ruby and diamond ring. The next day it was the Mansion House banquet for the Belgians. On the 7th they visited Farningham, where Alexandra laid the foundation stone of new buildings for the Home for Little Boys; the Carringtons'[103] ball at Whitehall on the 10th and dinner with the Manchesters[104] on the 13th followed. Travelling to Sandringham on the 15th, they gave a dinner there for I Zingari[105] on the 18th, while the A Division Police band played. At Wimbledon on the 21st Alexandra gave prizes for shooting, including the cup they had seen at Hancock's, followed by the volunteer review. Shortly afterwards, the family went to Osborne until 7 August. Albert Edward had meetings on the 8th, and Aunt Cambridge and Uncle George called at Marlborough House.

On 9 August the family left for York, staying at Bishopsthorpe with the Archbishop and Mrs Thomson.[106] With a very full programme, they could only pay hurried visits to the Agricultural Show, Foxhounds Show, Fine Arts Exhibition, Philosophical Society Gardens and Guildhall, where the Prince unveiled a window celebrating his father's visit some twenty years earlier. Later, there was a banquet at the Archbishop's Palace and a ball at the Assembly Rooms. On the following day, a volunteer review was held on Knaresmire race course; the couple drove up to the royal stand, amid a wildly enthusiastic crowd. The Prince and the Duke of Cambridge stayed on the course while Alexandra went up to the royal box, and "all within the enclosure collected in front of it to cheer, wave handkerchiefs, and even throw up hats, and so prolonged was the greeting that some time elapsed before HRH could cease bowing her acknowledgments and take her seat."[107] The newly-built Lendal Bridge had the Royal Arms in the centre, supported by an angel modelled on Alexandra, but it did not do her justice and the Prince regretted not being told, as he would have given the bust made by Marshall Wood instead.[108]

The family, with Alfred, reached Abergeldie on the 18th. The Queen arrived at Balmoral the next day and they saw her frequently during the visit. On 14 September they gave a tenants' and servants' ball at Abergeldie; the ballroom was decorated inside and out with Chinese lanterns, the Queen attended, and during the evening Eddy and George were brought in to see her. There was dinner, and dancing until the early hours. After more excursions, shooting for the Prince and driving for the Princess, they and their sons left on the 24th to stay till 10 October at Dunrobin.[109] The drive on the 27th to Brora Water, where the gentlemen went fishing, was followed by the Sutherland Rifle Association's competition, and, later, a grand ball, followed the next day by a review of the Sutherland Volunteers in Bowman's Park, and Highland Games.

Affairs abroad had deteriorated since February. The Gastein Convention of August 1865 had ratified Prussia's and Austria's joint control of Schleswig and Holstein, but while Austria made it clear she would ultimately offer Holstein independence and had allowed campaigning there on behalf of the Augustenburgs, Prussia made it equally clear she would annex Schleswig, and consequently went to war with Austria and the other states in the German Confederation. It ended in September 1866, with the victorious Prussian army's triumphal entry into Berlin and Prussia's appropriation of the two duchies. Emperor Napoleon III[110] had a clause, Paragraph 5, inserted into the Prusso-Austrian peace treaty stating that northern Schleswig was to be returned to Denmark later, after a plebiscite.[111]

Queen Louise, Thyra and Waldemar arrived on the 13th; King Christian was disappointed not to come but his wife looked remarkably well and Alexandra was overjoyed to see her again. The children had grown and were charming, although Thyra was not pretty. That evening all except Waldemar went to the Lyceum. Albert Edward had made a decision; Minny was to be married at St Petersburg in early November; after her fiancé's death she had later become engaged to his brother, now Tsesarevitch Alexander.[112] Not only would Alexandra, who was pregnant, be unable to go, but such a grand occasion was too expensive for her parents. Lord Derby[113] thought Albert Edward's presence would be politically beneficial, so "I now write to say, that if you approve of it, dear Mama, I am quite ready to go, as besides the pleasure of being at Dagmar's marriage, it would interest me beyond everything to see Russia, altho' my visit would naturally be a short one." Queen Louise had told him "Dagmar is so anxious that I should come, as it would be a great support to her to see a familiar face at that time; the Queen also says that the Emperor & Empress[114] would be immensely gratified if I came."[115] Queen Victoria was less enthusiastic but agreed it was perfectly natural that Dagmar wished to see her kind brother-in-law's face at so trying a time, and consented. She did, however, regret "your remaining <u>so little</u> quiet at home, & always running about. The Country, & all of <u>us</u>, wd like to see you a little more stationary, & therefore I was in hopes that this autumn & winter this wd have been the case."[116]

On 15 October Alexandra took her mother and sister to see Aunt Cambridge at Kew and, later, the Olympic Theatre. Queen Louise and the Waleses dined with the Duchess of Inverness on the 16th and on the 18th, Alexandra took them for a drive; the next day they and Aunt Cambridge drove to Crystal Palace. On the 21st, after church, they went to stay at Sandringham until the 30th, when the Waleses and Queen Louise spent two days with the Staffords[117] at Costessey Hall. The couple paid their first visit to Norwich on the 31st and, with Queen Louise, went to the Guildhall and St Andrew's Hall for part of the Norwich Musical Festival; later, Albert Edward opened the Norwich Volunteers' recently-built drill-shed at Chapel Field and the couple planted two trees nearby. Back in London on 1 November, the Prince departed for Russia the next day. Queen Louise and her children left on the 3rd; Alexandra returned to Sandringham on the 5th.

Queen Victoria had criticised Alexandra sporadically throughout the year, sometimes while supporting her son; "poor Bertie breakfasts alone" and "dear Bertie … is so kind to the people here."[118] One source of complaint was the Danish family; "No more Northern Pcesses. We have quite enough with one; that has not been a gt blessing, forgive my saying, from her family & her want of knowledge & education & gt idleness." She had also heard that Queen Louise was "false, intriguing & not wise".[119] Victoria's dissatisfaction was out of control; her unreasonable dislike of Queen Louise may partly have been stoked unconsciously by envy of her harmonious family, and her still having a husband. Vicky, who spoke up for the Waleses whenever she could, thought she should let her mother into a secret, writing on the Queen's birthday that "I know Alix has the greatest <u>wish</u> to be now and then alone with you; she says she is not amusing, she knows, and she fears she bores you. But she loves you so much, and it seems to be a little ambition of hers to be allowed to be <u>alone</u> with you sometimes. It was <u>Bertie</u> that told me this, and it quite touched me, as I saw it sprang from their love to you. He has <u>not an idea</u> that I attached any importance to this remark, or that I wld ever say it to you. But I thought I should tell you, thinking that while he was away it wld please them both so much if you took her once for a drive or a walk <u>alone</u> with you. Please do not think I wish to meddle or interfere; I merely thought I could not be wrong in mentioning this little thing. You cannot be astonished that it should be a pleasure coveted by them. Bertie spoke kindly of Christian, & I was much relieved at that too."[120] Ironically, Victoria and Alexandra had really wanted the same thing but had alienated each other instead. When Alexandra and her little boys arrived at Windsor on 14 November, the Queen melted at once; "She is dear, & good & gentle but looking very thin & pale … I was some time alone with her yesterday evng & I shall take her out alone this afternoon. I had always hoped to be able to do this, but I never cld. I hope however to see more of her this year … I have taken a nice walk & drive with dear Alix, & nothing cld be dearer & nicer than she is. I never saw a purer mind, it is quite charming to see her & hear her. She looks delicate – I do love her dearly. She is a little embarrassed with Christian but still it does quite well."[121] There were still occasional grumbles but the Queen's relationship with Alexandra began improving as she got to know her better, and finally trusted her with personal confidences.

Over the next week Alexandra walked or drove with the Queen, Helena or Louise and on the 21st the Queen gave a dance in the Red Drawing Room to some local and castle-resident children, to celebrate Vicky's birthday. Alexandra and her siblings-in-law also attended and then she and her sons left on the 22nd for London and Sandringham. She thanked Louise for a locket containing Louise's hair, and would have liked her to stay for a while during Albert Edward's absence, but this had not been allowed; meanwhile, Alexandra was "looking forward to the return of my <u>beloved one</u> who I have missed most painfully ever since he left me, <u>6 weeks</u> ago, which seems an endless time and I hope <u>never</u> will happen again."[122] He returned on the 7th after a splendid trip; the Imperial Family had been delighted to see him. Minny, now Tsesarevna Marie Feodorovna, had been very touched to receive Queen Victoria's wedding present.[123] The Prince left next day for Sandringham but felt unwell and the couple did not attend the mausoleum service on the 14th. He was better by the 15th; drove with Alexandra, joined the Christmas guests for shooting, and on the 31st left with his wife and brother for Holkham.

January 1867 was the coldest in Norfolk since 1860. Snow disrupted sport at Holkham, but nevertheless on one day 2 tons 19cwt of game was sent to Leadenhall Market in London. There were evening entertainments too and the Waleses returned to Sandringham on 5 January after an enjoyable visit. After chairing Paris Exhibition meetings at the South Kensington Museum, the Prince returned to Sandringham on the 12th. The Duke of Edinburgh left and the Tecks arrived; in the intense cold, the chief amusement was skating. Like Alexandra and Helena, Mary was expecting a baby later in the year.

On the 27th the family returned to Marlborough House. While Albert Edward stayed briefly at Trentham, Alexandra went driving every day and called on Aunt Cambridge and Mary. On 5 February the Prince attended the Queen's Opening of Parliament and later the Waleses heard the debate in the House of Lords. There were more drives and theatre visits, hunting and shooting for the Prince and on the 13th the couple gave a dinner party. Alexandra was delighted with some violets from the Queen and Louise that day.[124] Albert Edward had a Duchy of Cornwall meeting and went riding as usual but Alexandra was feeling rheumatic and feverish. At 6.30 on the 20th "dearest Alix was safely delivered of a fine little girl.[125] I don't think she suffered more than last time, & the rheumatism did not produce such an obstruction as we expected. She had no chloroform tho' she wished for it very much, but Dr Farre thought it better not," the Prince told his mother. He, Dr Farre, (only just in time), and Mrs Clarke had witnessed the birth; "We are both immensely pleased that it is a little girl, as we were so anxious about it." He had hurried away to tell his mother as soon as possible and hoped Alexandra was now sleeping. As for himself; "with the exception of a baddish cold & being nervous and worried by dear Alix's illness, I feel pretty well."[126]

The baby flourished but Alexandra was still feverish, with persistent, excruciating pain in her right knee. It was announced on the 28th that she had recovered from her confinement and "the general disturbance from the acute rheumatism has ceased and the local affection limited to the right knee is less severe."[127] Her husband was still chairing meetings, hunting, attending the House of Lords and, on 1 March sitting to the photographer, Disderi[128] in Bond Street. He was anxious about Alexandra, but there was little he could do practically, except to have his writing desk moved into her room, so that he could be with her while attending to his correspondence.[129] On 3 March she was reported to be making good progress, although her knee's recovery would be slow. A nurse from St Bartholomew's Hospital, Mrs Elizabeth Jones, had been brought in to help her.[130] While Alexandra lay at Marlborough House, her husband's life continued relentlessly: receptions, meetings and hunting with staghounds. He wrote sometimes to his sister Louise about the patient's progress. On 8 March she was restless and feverish; three days later she was slightly better.[131] The Queen, with Helena or Louise, called four times. On the 14th Alexandra learned that her remaining grandmother, the Dowager Duchess of Glücksburg, had died and, overwhelmed with grief as well as physical pain, she cried piteously for her mother. Albert Edward was at an official function and the doctor, James Paget,[132] on his own initiative, telegraphed to Queen Louise; King Christian had gone to Ballenstadt, where his mother had died, but his wife came straight to London. As Paget later said, "If it had not been for the Queen of

Denmark, I fear we should have lost our Princess."[133] In fact there was better news on the 17th; the Prince really thought a corner had been turned "& the Doctors are immensely pleased, even Jenner did not look as mournful and *lugubre* as he generally does. Alix's Mama arrives here tomorrow & it will be an immense pleasure to her to see her again."[134] On the 18th Alexandra had the boundless relief of her mother's presence and, two days later, her father's too.

Queen Victoria visited them all on the 22nd and the 23rd. When they were not with Alexandra, Albert Edward took her parents out; the King accompanied him when inspecting the Honourable Artillery Company at Finsbury, visiting St Bartholomew's Hospital or riding. On 2 April the King received an address from the London Danes and thanked them for their loyalty while regretting he had no better news for them about the Schleswig Danes. One, Mr A Delcomyn, sent greetings to Queen Louise and Alexandra, assuring the latter of "the profound sympathy which all Danes here have constantly felt for Her Royal Highness during her illness." He sent best hopes for her speedy recovery, thanked the King for a large donation to the fund for indigent Danes in London, and Alexandra for "the many proofs she has given of her interest for that and other Danish institutions." The King assured them she would be very glad they thought of her so kindly.[135] Alexandra needed comfort as her knee had swelled up again[136] but it began to recover and her general health was improving. Her father went home on the 11th but Queen Louise stayed; now her daughter was a little better, she could go sightseeing. Albert Edward took her out several times to art galleries and exhibitions. On 1 May King George of the Hellenes came to stay overnight.

The new baby, born on 20 February, would normally have been christened in March but, because of her mother's illness, it was not until 10 May. Louise had sometimes been allowed to sit with Alexandra and the couple asked her to be a sponsor.[137] The christening started at 1.30pm in Alexandra's sitting room at Marlborough House; her bed, with a blue silk coverlet, had been wheeled in and stood near the centre window. She looked lovely in a white lace jacket trimmed with pink, with a pink bow in her hair. The font was in the middle of the room and the altar was where the piano usually stood, under her parents' portraits. About 26 people attended, including Eddy and George. Queen Louise told the Archbishop of Canterbury the names: Louise Victoria Alexandra Dagmar. Little Louise did not cry at all and her mother was not tired by the ceremony.[138] There had been some contention about the names; Queen Victoria thought the first one should be hers[139] but there had been warning signs after George's birth. The young parents wanted it to be Louise, after Queen Louise and the late Dowager Duchess of Glücksburg. Among many other Louises were the late Landgravine Charlotte (whose first name it was), Prince Albert's mother[140] and the baby's nineteen-year-old aunt.

It was still cold, with easterly winds; Alexandra's swollen knee would need careful treatment. Albert Edward had recently visited Paris about the Exhibition and on 20 May Queen Victoria laid the first stone of the Royal Albert Hall of Arts and Sciences; her eldest son, as Chairman of the Provisional Committee, was in attendance. Later she, Louise and Beatrice went to see Alexandra. Queen Louise, after three months in England, now had to go home to celebrate her silver wedding with King Christian on 26 May; Alexandra was naturally disappointed at being unable to go too.[141] On the 21st Helena's son, Christian Victor,[142] born on 14 April, was christened in Windsor Castle's private chapel. Albert Edward, with Colonel Kingscote,[143] Major Teesdale[144] and Oliver Montagu[145] attended the parade at Horse Guards on the 25th and later presided at the 10th Hussars' annual dinner. Mary's confinement was imminent, and on the 26th, at one minute to midnight, her daughter was born. Alexandra was much better but still almost immobile; her knee was less painful and a better shape but a shock or abrupt movement could set it back; her leg would probably have to be kept in a splint and swing for some time. It was desperately frustrating for someone normally so active but by 7 June she had been allowed to sit in a chair and the splints were to be adjusted to allow more freedom.

A few days later, the Hessians, with their children, Victoria, Elizabeth[146] and Irène[147] arrived at Marlborough House, staying until the 19th before going to Windsor and accompanying Albert Edward on various occasions, as Alexandra was still confined indoors. Alice held a drawing room and was present at other official events which Alexandra would normally have attended; the season had begun. The Queen of Prussia arrived and Albert Edward took her to Windsor to see Queen Victoria. He was still chairing meetings, visiting Paris on Exhibition business and, on 26 June, attending a concert in aid of repairs to Crystal Palace. The Queen called on Alexandra on 2 July, then, at last, on the 6th, the Princess was well enough to go out with her husband. After that she went driving nearly every day, although not taking her usual part in engagements. It was an eventful time; first the Viceroy of Egypt[148] arrived and the Prince had to play host in entertaining him and taking him to functions. Then he went to Dover to meet the Sultan of Turkey, Abdul Aziz Khan,[149] who arrived on the 12th and also needed entertaining and accompanying. The Viceroy left on the 18th, then, after more festivities and a visit to Marlborough House, the Sultan left on the 23rd; he had been so touched by his reception that he gave £2,500 to be distributed among the London poor.

Alexandra had received other visitors and continued her daily carriage drives, although she was not well enough to attend, as her husband did, the christening on 27 July of the Tecks' daughter at Kensington Palace. Victoria Mary Augusta Louise Olga Pauline Claudine Agnes, always known as May to her family, would assume great importance in the Wales family and the nation when she grew up.[150] King George of the Hellenes arrived and on 17 August, the Wales family left for Wiesbaden. Alexandra, seated on a small invalid carriage, was carried on to the yacht, leaving her 21-year-old brother at Marlborough House; he rode, attended theatres, received members of the Greek community in London, was photographed by Disderi and visited Mr Denman's establishment selling Greek wines in Piccadilly. By 4 September reports from Wiesbaden were reassuring; Alexandra was under James Paget's care and, despite her stiff knee, was recovering in spirits, strength, complexion and appetite, as General Knollys told the Queen.[151] However, in deep mourning for her grandfather, Landgrave William of Hesse-Cassel, who died on 5 September, Alexandra refused to receive the King of Prussia[152] who had proposed visiting her. His country had defeated Denmark in 1864 and seized some smaller German states[153] in 1866. By the 24th, Paget pronounced that when, within a week, Alexandra had finished her course of 30 baths, there would be no point in her remaining there; he was going back to London and had a poor opinion of Wiesbaden's healthiness in October.[154] The *Medical Times* reported that Alexandra was starting to walk and regain weight, having become very thin.

Albert Edward told his mother on 4 October that Alexandra had walked upstairs the day before, which was a decided improvement, but the Queen was very angry that she had rebuffed the King of Prussia. Albert Edward sprang to her defence: "I myself should have been glad if she had seen the King, but a lady may have feelings wh she cannot repress, while a man must overcome them. If Coburg had been taken away, as Hanover, Hesse (Cassel) and Nassau have been, I don't think you would much care to see the King either. You will not I hope be angry, dear Mama, at my last sentence, but it is the only way that I can express what dear Alix really feels."[155] Back home on the 17th, Alexandra wrote to Louise on 1 November; "I hope your Mama will excuse my being very slow and inactive at this moment, and I fear very stupid and botheross,[156] as I can only hump about on two sticks, which makes me rather shy before people, and I don't know quite at this moment how I am to manage about driving in an ordinary carriage like other people ... Now about your Mama's present for my Bertie; I am sorry to say I cannot think of a thing, as he has so many things and I am always in despair myself not knowing what to give him, but I know too that everything pleases him. Your suggestion 'the egg boiler' is, I am sure, very pretty and that is a thing we don't possess in 'our household' at present."[157] On the 6th they went to Windsor, where Alexandra drove with the Queen and Louise while the Prince hunted and shot. On Sunday the 10th, for the first time since her illness, Alexandra attended morning service in the castle's private chapel.

The Waleses both sat to Miss Durant[158] for their portraits and left for Sandringham on the 14th; the Christians went to stay with them soon afterwards. Alexandra wrote to Mary on her 34th birthday, 27 November, much looking forward to seeing May again "who must be a duck"; her own Louise "is grown very fat and tall and has got three teeth but no hair yet, but she is such a darling, and almost always good, smiling and bright looking."[159] On her own 23rd birthday Alexandra gave a dinner to 185 children from the four local schools and thanked Mary for presents including some "little puggies", probably ornaments.[160] Louise also gave her "the happy pug family which is quite delightful and nothing could have given me greater pleasure (as you know my weakness for pugs)." Her husband had given her "three lovely walking gowns, pearls! a lovely onyx cross and chain, a clock, a crystal brooch with his dear self on gold ground, a pair of little fish earrings and some very pretty cups and saucers – altogether most beautiful things much too good for stupid me." Alexandra also mentioned "dancing the perpetual jig", apparently meaning the endless round of official functions and entertaining that had to be done by the Christians and Louise because she could not yet fully participate.[161] She had been delighted that her husband was with her on her birthday, as last year he had been in Russia. She had had to entertain Prince Christian, but some of the others were more fun; "dear Uncle George who brought life into everybody and everything, General Hall,[162] who is getting more and more like a monkey than ever, Mr Montagu, Lord Blandford[163] and Mr Wellesley[164] and Colonel Hardinge,[165] who were altogether very cheery I must say." Alexandra longed to see Mary and May again; "after your description she must be getting lovely, our rival babies, I am afraid yours will win the prize!!"[166]

Alexandra also wrote to the Duchess of Manchester, who had asked Charlotte[167] and Francis Knollys to Kimbolton. Charlotte was "a very nice girl and I like her very much; she will be able to show you some patterns for the photo-book I have just been doing; a clock like yours and really it looks very nice."[168] This album contained 29 different designs, painted by Alexandra and embellished with cut-out photographs of her relatives and friends.[169] While the Prince visited Buckenham Tofts, Alexandra and the children remained at Sandringham; she took her usual daily drives, and by 24 December was well enough to ride with her husband and watch the West Norfolk hunt. He was busy discussing estate improvements with Mr Beck, and she gave gifts of beef to estate workers in the afternoon. On Christmas Day she received Holy Communion, at Sandringham Church, for the first time since her illness. Albert Edward and guests drove twice to Houghton, where he had shooting rights and on the 30th the Waleses went to Holkham for their annual visit.

When they returned on 4 January 1868, a telegraph system had been installed; a clerk dealt with telegrams by wire between Sandringham and London, other parts of England and the continent. Just now, however, the Prince wanted to be in London in person, to visit casualties at St Bartholomew's Hospital and other damage caused by a Fenian[170] explosion in Clerkenwell. On the 7th he visited the burned-out shell of Her Majesty's Theatre in Haymarket and offered help to James Mapleson[171] the manager. That day the Queen wrote to him about the immorality of the upper classes; in his position, he could take the lead against this, as could Alexandra, to whom she had often mentioned it.[172] Many of her subjects thought likewise and the behaviour of those who should know better reminded her of the period before the French Revolution. Albert Edward mostly agreed but would have felt uncomfortable in the role of public moralist. His main difficulty was lack of enough significant work; he fervently desired more responsibility and hated being idle, as boredom sometimes led him in later-regretted directions.

He joined Alexandra at Sandringham on the 8th. Meanwhile a farmer's son, Howell Haward, injured and unable to work as before, carved a wooden "true lover's knot" and offered it to her as a mark of "respectful attachment". Royalty did not usually accept personal gifts from strangers and it was therefore sent back, with Alexandra's thanks, regrets for Haward's injury and a cheque for ten guineas, as "a little pecuniary acknowledgement, to which she hopes there may be no objection."[173] The family arrived in London on 11 February and Alexandra resumed her daily carriage drives, while for the Prince there was the House of Lords and hunting. They attended the Haymarket Theatre on the 13th and on the 17th went to St Bartholomew's Hospital. Next evening they dined with Uncle George. On the 20th Albert Edward saw James Farie's experiments, showing Dick's patent, portable, self-acting fire engine, "L'Extincteur". He briefly visited the Queen at Osborne and on the 25th left for two days with the Beauforts[174] at Badminton. Alexandra stayed behind as she had not completely recovered and was also about four months pregnant; she enjoyed theatres, driving and some socialising but could not attend the Queen's Court on 6 March. However, on the 10th the couple gave a fifth wedding anniversary dinner and party, with music conducted by Charles Hallé.[175] On the 12th they went to observe Christ's Hospital's "public supper" in their great hall. About 750 boys each carried a bowl of milk and some bread and cheese into the hall in baskets, for a half-hour supper following a short service, with a hymn, an anthem and "The Old Hundredth". Afterwards, the older boys, in pairs, carried away the remains in the baskets and bowed to the Waleses as they passed them. After the national anthem, there were three cheers: for the president of the hospital,[176] the Prince of Wales and, "with extraordinary vigour", the Princess. They left, to more cheers from the boys and the crowd outside.

Alexandra had been driving with Mary Teck and the two families dined together on 29 February. Mary Teck thought her cousin much better; "though the knee is still stiff, it is scarcely perceptible when she walks, and the surgeons assure us that in time the joint will come right. She is delighted with our apartment."[177] On 12 March Alexandra attended the Queen's drawing room at Buckingham Palace; on the 16th she and her husband went to the Royal Amphitheatre and on the 18th to the New Royalty and to four more theatres by the end of March. Alexandra was resuming her full social life; on the 24th the couple went to the Van de Weyer's[178] dance at Arlington Street and on the 25th to Disraeli's[179] reception at the new Foreign Office. She was feeling so well that she asked the Queen if she could accompany her husband on his Irish visit in April; "I really think, and have a sort of conviction that it will do me no harm, and therefore have almost made up my mind to go with my Bertie." She was always nervous when they had to be separated and especially, given the uncertain state of Irish politics, shuddered to think of him going there alone. But "as it is some little time off yet, I can always see how I feel when the moment comes, and if then I should not feel as well, or as much inclined to go, as now, I could then even give it up, but now I feel like a sort of call and wish to go."[180]

There was another drawing room on 1 April and later, with Louise and Arthur, a visit to the Adelphi. The Queen, with Louise, Beatrice and Leopold, lunched at Marlborough House on the 3rd and went driving with Alexandra; the couple dined with her later. The next day, the Prince watched the boat race, and the pianists, Miss Lie, from Norway and Miss Jäle, from St Petersburg, played before Alexandra. Later it was Landseer's[181] studio and the opera at Drury Lane. On the 6th, the family went to Sandringham for Easter. Albert Edward inspected the improvements, Alexandra, apparently quite well, walked and drove, and they both toured the estate and neighbourhood. They returned on the 13th to prepare for the Irish visit, and left next day; Alexandra had achieved her wish. Eddy went to stay with the Queen at Windsor, his brother and sister joined him on the 16th and, with their grandmother and cousin, Christian Victor, they left for Osborne on the 17th. Princess Louise was twenty on the 18th; unlike her sisters at this age, there was still no husband in prospect. There are hints that she may have been interested in Alexandra's brother Frederick, or perhaps he in her,[182] but if so, there was no chance Queen Victoria would agree. This was possibly one reason why she did not often allow Louise to visit or stay with the Waleses, who might encourage a match. Instead, Frederick married another Louise, Princess of Sweden and Norway,[183] on 28 July 1869.

The Waleses arrived at Chester on 15 April and soon afterwards reached Dublin safely on a beautiful sunny day. Alexandra had had a cold but it soon disappeared. It was the first time a Princess of Wales had visited Ireland and she was welcomed with open arms as an exhausting but triumphant ten-day visit began. Everything interested her, but she carefully conserved her strength by resting before dinner.[184] There were Punchestown Races, the installation of the Prince as a Knight of St Patrick and the consequent banquet of the Knights in St Patrick's Hall on the 18th. Here the Lord Lieutenant[185] praised Alexandra: "There is no man worthy of the name of Irishman, whether he be the coroneted peer, the installed Knight or the hardy and stalwart son of the soil, who has not felt the fair presence of that illustrious lady as a ray of sunshine gilding the Irish horizon."[186] Alexandra wrote to the Queen, "delighted and thankful … to be with [Bertie] here, and how beautiful our reception has been, and how kind everybody, low and high, have been to us." The Abercorns[187] had made sure she was not too tired, "and I am happy to say that I feel very well and not at all the worse for my journey, or anything I have been doing here." She was glad the children were at Osborne and hoped the sea air would do them good.[188]

In the next few days, the Waleses attended a military review in Phoenix Park, a grand Ball at Dublin Castle, a grand dinner at Dublin Castle and a *conversazione* at the Royal Dublin Society, which they finally left at about 1am. They arrived at midnight on the 22nd at a Ball in the Exhibition Palace, with beautiful gas-lit decorations and supper at 2am. The Prince had been made a Lord of the Irish Privy Council, received the degree of LLD at Trinity College, unveiled Burke's statue,[189] and visited the Roman Catholic Maynooth University and the Dublin Cattle Show. The couple lunched at Powerscourt, where it rained heavily, making the waterfall in the deer park, which they saw while driving round the estate in an open carriage, even more impressive. After visiting the National Gallery and the College of Physicians on the 24th, Albert Edward met Alexandra at a flower show at the Rotunda. They saw the Mater Misericordiae College and the Constabulary depôt in Phoenix Park, drove to Viceregal Lodge and later, the Adelaide Hospital; enthusiastic crowds were everywhere. At 8pm they left for the yacht at Kingstown; later the fleet was illuminated with coloured lamps. Summing up the visit, one reporter described how Alexandra's presence had produced "a sentiment of the profoundest sympathy and respectful attachment." A committed Irish nationalist had exclaimed, "If she could only be seen by every man, woman and child in Ireland, moving about as she has done here in our crowded streets, the Government might withdraw every soldier tomorrow."[190] Ireland's troubles were too deep-rooted to be so easily solved, but, curiously, Dublin's crime and drunkenness decreased during the visit, as though "the whole people had entered into a compact with their consciences."[191]

The yacht left Dublin on the 25th but at Holyhead there was shocking news. In Australia, at a public picnic in aid of the Sailors' Home at Port Jackson, Sydney, the Duke of Edinburgh had been shot in the back by Henry James O'Farrell.[192] The two brothers had simultaneously experienced both sides of Irish opinion. Alfred recovered, but Albert Edward was very upset. As a lucky distraction, when they opened the new waterworks in Castle Square at Caernarvon, the water jet was accidentally turned on full, drenching part of the crowd, and the Waleses joined in the general hilarity. Before lunch they received a National Address and a gold medal from the National Eisteddfodd at Caernarvon Castle and were shown the Eagle Tower, where, by unreliable tradition, the first Prince of Wales[193] had been born. After a weekend at Trentham, they went home on the 27th. The season was beginning; they visited the Queen's Theatre, the Royal Italian Opera at Covent Garden and Her Majesty's Opera at Drury Lane, all in the first week after their return. They also saw the Royal Academy Exhibition. Albert Edward held a levee on 4 May and continued attending debates in both

Houses of Parliament. He presided on the 5th at the anniversary festival for the Society of Friends and Foreigners in Distress, at Willis's Rooms. On the 6th he watched the Royal Military Academy's cadets' athletic sports at Woolwich, and dined afterwards with one of them, his brother Arthur, at Ranger's Lodge, Blackheath. Alexandra attended the Italian Opera that evening, as they both did four more times. On the 12th they sat to Matthew Noble[194] for their busts, destined for the Leeds exhibition. Alexandra missed the drawing room on the 12th but the couple attended when the Queen laid the foundation stone of the new St Thomas's Hospital the next day, and also the state ball on the 15th. They and Arthur went to St James's Theatre on the 16th; two days later, Albert Edward left to open the Leeds Art Treasures Exhibition. Adolphe Beau[195] photographed Eddy and George, and Frits Hartvigson[196] played for Alexandra.

The Waleses attended the state concert on the 20th but for the next few days Albert Edward and Arthur went fishing at Balmoral. Alexandra's brother Frederick came to stay on the 23rd. She took her sons to Horse Guards Parade and later she and Frederick went to Her Majesty's Opera. When the Prince returned on the 25th, all three went to the Lyceum, dined the next day with the Ailesburys[197] at Pall Mall and on the 27th and 30th attended the Italian Opera. During the first week of June they went to St James's Theatre, the horse show at the Agricultural Hall, the matinee performance at the Haymarket (in aid of the Royal Dramatic College), and both opera houses. They stayed at Titness Park for Ascot week, 9–15 June, while the three children went to Windsor. The couple and Frederick attended the Italian Opera again on the 16th and the next day the two princes visited Oxford, where both had been students; Frederick received a diploma conferring the degree of DCL. The three later dined with the Danish Minister and Madame de Bülow in Wimpole Street. They attended the state concert on the 19th and the Queen's volunteer review in Windsor Great Park on the 20th. On 22 June the Queen invited them to a breakfast at Buckingham Palace; the next day they dined with the Sutherlands at Stafford House. On the 26th Alexandra and Louise went to Her Majesty's Opera. Mr Bierstadt[198] showed some pictures to the couple on the 27th, and Albert Edward met Alfred at Victoria Station; he dined at Marlborough House, with, undoubtedly, plenty to tell them, before leaving for Windsor. Alexandra drove with Frederick on the 29th and later they attended the Italian Opera together. The next day, with the Prince, they dined at Holderness House[199] and on 1 July all attended the state ball. On the 2nd it was the Italian Opera again, and Alexandra and Frederick had their last drive on the 3rd before he left.

A fête was held at the Crystal Palace on the 4th in honour of the Duke of Edinburgh, which the Waleses attended. Sunday 5th passed, then, early on 6 July, Alexandra realised her pregnancy was nearing its conclusion. She gave birth to a daughter[200] at 4.20am; both were well. Later, the Park and Tower guns were fired as usual in celebration but the pre-natal auditory influences on the baby probably had greater effect. In the previous two months her mother had been some fourteen times to the opera, twice to concerts and to other events including music; it was the height of the season. Naturally, in such a music-loving family, the child grew up enjoying opera and concerts, but music was particularly important to her.[201] Eddy, George and little Louise went to stay at Kent House, near Osborne on the 11th and on the 22nd their father told the Queen the baby's name; they had settled on Victoria "& we are anxious to ask you to be Godmother." [202] Two days later he wrote again; Alexandra was to have a course of bending exercises for her knee, supervised by Mr Paget "as he alone is capable of knowing what ought or ought not to be done, & as I think Alix owes almost her life to his care & attention last year."[203] The Prince was still attending or giving formal dinners, chairing meetings, distributing prizes, receiving visitors and attending the volunteer review at Wimbledon on the 25th. On the 27th the children returned and the next day their mother took her first carriage drive since Victoria's birth. Princess Alice had been staying with her, but had gone to Osborne with her husband on the 23rd. Alexandra drove with her sons then, on 1 August, Albert Edward returned from Goodwood and they went to Her Majesty's Opera. Briefly visiting the Queen at Osborne, before she went to Switzerland, the Prince came back for a Duchy of Cornwall meeting on the 5th. The next day, the Bishop of London[204] christened the baby at Marlborough House: Victoria Alexandra Olga Mary, the third name being after her new aunt, the Queen of the Hellenes.[205] The Grenadier Guards' band played during lunch afterwards. Later the Waleses went to the Royal Amphitheatre at Holborn.

The whole family arrived on 11 August at Abergeldie, where rain had been falling heavily for sixteen hours, after three dry months. This continued. On the 13th they heard that Mary Teck had given birth to a son, Adolphus.[206] Meanwhile Alexandra, still not fully recovered, told Louise on the 22nd that she did not "*entre nous soit dit*[207] exactly think the Highlands the most suitable place for a stiff leg!! I have now begun the dusch bathes for my knee, which I hope may do some good although I don't expect much, I must confess. Both Mr Paget and Hewitt are staying at Ballater and come over every day to bend my leg and pinch and hurt it!!" She was glad about the Tecks' son and also that in Greece Queen Olga had had a son; "I can hardly realize her being Mother already and Willy Father! They are both very, very happy and delighted with their little boy; he is called Constantine[208] after his maternal Grandfather, I am very pleased to have been asked to be Godmother to my little Nephew!!" Her parents and younger siblings were "with Minny and Sacha at Peterhof and I hear seem quite delighted with Minny's home, and her little boy,[209] how much I should like to see her again, as I can hardly say I saw much of her last year at Wiesbaden."[210] The Braemar Gathering was held in heavy rain on 3 September in the grounds of Old Mar Castle; the Fifes and their eighteen-year-old-son Lord Macduff[211] attended. Alexandra's Uncle Hans, staying at Abergeldie, accompanied the couple there, as did Charlotte Knollys, the General's eldest daughter. The Queen arrived at Balmoral on the 16th and visited Alexandra the next day; on the following two days the couple and their guests dined with her. Later in September the Waleses and their party left for Dunrobin, where on 30th Albert Edward sat to GE Ewing[212] of Glasgow, for a bust. They reached Edinburgh on 7 October, staying overnight at the Douglas Hotel before going to Glasgow, where the Prince laid the foundation stone of the new Glasgow University buildings at Gilmour's Hill. Returning by express train from Edinburgh, they found the children, who had come straight from Dunrobin on the 8th, at home.

A holiday, to aid Alexandra's recovery, was planned for early 1869, but a Danish visit beforehand was causing difficulties. Alexandra wanted to take the children; Queen Victoria was adamantly opposed, unless the doctors sanctioned it. She was prepared to let the boys go, but "the 2 Babies are totally out of the question"; Alexandra was behaving selfishly in wishing to take them. However, by the 6th the Prince was thanking his mother for "the very kind letter I received fr you this afternoon. I can hardly tell you how pleased [Alix] is, now that she can take little Louise with us, as she feared she was quite in disgrace, altho' I know you did not mean to impute selfishness as her character. We fully understand & appreciate your feelings regarding the child, & cannot expect you to change your opinion wh you have once formed, but we will readily undertake the responsibility ourselves, & with God's blessing our little darling will return back as well as she went out." Alexandra had had a chilblain so severe that she could hardly put her slipper on.[213] Uncle Hans accompanied them to three theatres, visiting the Duchess of Cambridge and shooting in Windsor Park before going home on the 13th. By the end of October the Waleses had attended five theatres and heard Mark Lemon[214] read *Falstaff* at the Gallery of Illustration in Regent Street. Alexandra visited the children's hospital in Great Ormond Street on the 19th; later, the couple dined with the Duchess of Inverness. The Queen of the Netherlands and members of the French Royal Family all called. While the Prince was away shooting, Alexandra went to the Queen's and Olympic Theatres with the Duke of Edinburgh and the Tecks. Albert Edward returned on the 29th; Vicky visited Marlborough House briefly before going to St Leonard's and Alfred left England in command of *HMS Galatea*. The Prince attended a funeral at Trentham on the 2nd; chaired a meeting of the Royal Agricultural Society in Hanover Square on the 3rd and on the 5th went with Alexandra and the Tecks to the Adelphi.

Negotiations had continued; the Queen wished to know all about the proposed January trip, especially the cost and Dr Minter's suitability as a medical attendant. Her son assured her on 25 October that it would be done as economically as possible (they would, after all, save on expenses in England); Dr Minter was an excellent attendant as he was used to warm climates. They would leave on 17 or 18 November, stay incognito at the Hotel Bristol in Paris for a few days, so that Alexandra could have a glimpse of it, "& buy some things we want to get", and continue to Copenhagen, arriving just before Alexandra's birthday. In January they would travel via Trieste or Venice to Alexandria, for a Nile trip. He would show his mother a sketch of the proposed journey when they came to Windsor for his birthday on the 9th.[215] Alexandra also told her the doctors' opinion of the children travelling to Denmark.[216] There was now some doubt about Louise, but this was because Sir William Jenner had not seen her since an indisposition in 1867. She had in fact "become so much stronger this last year, has most of her teeth & is nearly a year older." The Danish climate, although cold, was dry, not damp, as Jenner thought. Albert Edward added; "I think a child is always best looked after under the Mother's eye, & the children are so much with us, that I think [Alix's] whole visit to her old home would be spoiled, were she not to take her Mama's little God Child with her."[217] He did not mention that they would be separated from the children for several months during the longer trip; that was certainly long enough.

By the time he wrote again, the Queen had reverted to her former opinion about Louise, but the Waleses had consulted Sir Henry Holland[218] and Sir Charles Locock,[219] who both thought there would be no risk; in fact, Louise, at her age, would probably travel best. Albert Edward leapt to his wife's defence; "I regret very much that you should still oppose our wishes, but as you throw the responsibility entirely upon Alix, if we take Louise, I naturally shall share it, & have not the slightest hesitation or fear in doing so. Alix has made herself nearly quite ill with the worry of all this but what she has felt most, are the words you have used regarding her. Ever since she has been your daughter-in-law, I think she has tried to meet your wishes in every way & you have never said an unkind word to her or of her. You can therefore imagine how hurt & pained she has been by your accusing her of being 'very selfish' & 'unreasonable' & in fact risking her own child's life. None of us are perfect, & she may have her faults but she certainly is not selfish & her whole life is wrapt up in her children & it seems hard that because she wishes (with a natural mother's pride) to take her 3 eldest children with her to her Parents & Home every difficulty should be thrown in her way – enough to mar the prospect of her journey & when Vicky & Alice come here nearly every year with their children, whether it be winter or summer (& I maintain that ours are quite as strong as theirs) it seems rather inconsistent not to accord to the one what is accorded to the others."[220]

On the 6th, Alexandra had some cold cream made up, filling three large and six small pots, perhaps to protect her complexion against different climates. It may have been similar to the cream she later used habitually.[221] The family left on the 7th for Windsor and on the Prince's 27th birthday St George's Chapel choir, conducted by the Queen's organist, Dr Elvey, sang for him in the corridor. He went shooting with relatives; there was a dinner, the Queen's private band

and an evening party. The next day he left for Sandringham, while Alexandra drove with the Queen and Vicky and heard Agnes Zimmermann[222] play the piano. She and the children returned to London on the 13th. On the 16th the Dutch queen called and the Prince came back from Sandringham. A number of relatives lunched on the 17th and another visitor was Prince Hassan, the Viceroy of Egypt's second son. Later, the couple and their elder children left for the continent. Princess Victoria returned to Windsor to stay with her grandmother.

The Paris visit was getting out of hand, as it was not allowed to be private; "There was a marked desire on the part of the Emperor and Empress[223] to pay the greatest attention to the Prince and Princess", as General Knollys put it on 3 December. There had been a dinner, evening party and dancing at Compiègne, where "no lady in the room … in appearance came half way up to the Princess of Wales."[224] In Denmark George went down with measles. He was supposed to be isolated but "as Her Royal Highness the Princess Louise would not put up with any other nurse than her own, who was equally necessary for Prince George, the isolation amounted to nothing." Eddy and Louise were both well and it was hoped they would escape infection.[225] On the 14th Alexandra spared a thought for sister-in-law Louise and the others at the mausoleum, which was now quite finished. She had had a very happy birthday, including "a little <u>impromptu</u> dance, in which I joined to my <u>own</u> great surprise and delight" although she was not yet up to skating. The three children were flourishing, "But my poor <u>little baby</u> I miss all the time <u>very</u> much altho' I know you all take great care of her, the little pet. Tell May[226] that I thank her very much for the good news she gives me of my sweet little darling as well as for the flowers she sent me! I hope she will <u>be very</u> careful with her and wrap her well up for the long journey to Osborne." Alexandra had loved Paris "and went about all day long and to a great many shops which was most amusing." She had heard Louise was being bothered by Vicky and Fritz to consider marrying Prince Albert of Prussia and advised her to tell her mother she had no wish to do so.[227]

Dr Minter told the Queen in early 1869 that Alexandra had had a bad sore throat and her knee was no better. Constant attempts to bend it were essential and Minter and Mrs Jones had been investigating the Swedish system of calisthenics at the Gymnastic Institution in Copenhagen. The professor there had seen Alexandra and endorsed Paget's views.[228] By 16 January the family was at Hamburg and General Knollys took the children home[229] to stay at Osborne with the Queen and their baby sister while their parents were away.

Alexandra's hopes of meeting her brother Willy at Corfu had been dashed, as being politically inadvisable. By the 25th the Waleses had reached Berlin and then Vienna, after a tiring and intensely cold 22-hour journey between capitals.

They left for Trieste early on the 27th and travelled more comfortably for 15 hours,[230] with beautiful weather and magnificent snowy, alpine scenery. Alexandra was fascinated to see the barometer falling as the train travelled upwards, but did not look as well as when they left Copenhagen, after the festivities in the various capitals and seasickness. At Trieste, a large warehouse on fire lit up the surrounding area; a sublime sight but a local misfortune. Arriving at Alexandria on 2 February, their ship, *Ariadne* could not get in until the 3rd as the harbour was closed at night.[231]

The party travelled to Cairo with the Viceroy's son, Cerif Pasha and the next day went to stay in the newly-built Palace of the Nile, with enormous chandeliers, gigantic mirrors, richly ornate walls and furniture, including silver four-poster beds, heavily garnished with beaten silver and gold. At the opera, however, there was no ceremonial or fine evening dress. On the 5th they watched pilgrims starting for Mecca from the Grand Mosque; later, Alexandra, with Mrs Grey, drove informally through the bazaar and shopped. It was cool for Egypt and blankets were needed when they set off up the Nile on the 6th. The party reached Beni Hassan on the 10th and, while the Prince went shooting, Minter escorted Alexandra to the Viceroy's elegantly-decorated palace, "with good gardens, luxurious baths etc. We also went over the sugar factory, with which the Princess was much pleased, and walked about without fatigue the greater part of the day." On the 12th they reached Siout and rode on donkeys to the bazaars. Another steamer, with the Duke of Sutherland's party, dressed, as they thought, appropriately, joined them; "the cavalcade was as grotesque as it was amusing." They also inspected two schools. It was now much warmer; Alexandra had sprained her thumb but it was recovering. On Sunday the 14th the Prince read the service, which everyone attended. The most interesting part of the journey was about to begin.[232]

The couple were in good health and Alexandra was delighted with the Nile journey; "she said only last night that she never was happier in her life." By the 19th they had reached Edfoo, having seen the Temple at Dendera; Luxor, where excited shouting and gunpowder explosions greeted them; the Temple of Karnak; the tombs of the kings and queens; the Memnonium and the Colossi. Alexandra had climbed enthusiastically among the ruins and explored the ancient tombs. After dinner on the 18th, they returned to see Karnak by moonlight, with blue and white magnesium lights and a firework display; Alexandra and Mrs Grey wandered alone through the forest of gigantic columns.[233] Meanwhile, as doctors were scarce, the Prince had "lent" Minter to some sick English friends. Sadly, Alexandra's knee joint was scarcely better than three months earlier.[234] By the 21st the flotilla had arrived at Assouan, where they landed briefly. Houses were hung with bunting and a stage with coloured lanterns lit up at dusk. A great many camels were drawn up along the beach and some Arabs performed a display. On the 22nd, the party split up; the Prince, enjoying being back in Egypt, went on ahead, while Alexandra and Mrs Grey set forth together. They ended up riding donkeys with only unsecured pads on their backs. Alexandra was roaring with laughter as she tried to keep her balance, while the gentlemen, their feet sinking into the sand at every step, trudged three miles towards Philae under a burning sun. They met the Prince and Sir Samuel Baker[235] after about an hour and after watching some Arabs swimming down the boiling current of the First Cataract for money, they finally reached Philae at sunset, exhausted. In the morning, a leisurely breakfast, including fresh Nile fish, was served in a large marquee and observed with interest by vultures, which came slowly dropping in from Assouan.

There was good news of the children in England;[236] meanwhile, their parents continued up the Nile, returning to Cairo in mid-March and visiting the Pyramids of Ghizeh, where Alexandra again eagerly explored the underground passages and later rode round the Pyramid on her donkey to look at the Sphinx.[237] Albert Edward and Sir Samuel had unsuccessfully stalked two crocodiles and had no luck with the hyaenas either. The intense heat rose to 98° in the shade, but they were all perfectly well, except for Alexandra's knee. Looking pale and thin (perhaps an early sign of her fifth pregnancy), she was given an iron tonic. Thankfully, the temperature would soon cool down. The Prince asked Minter to attend a sick Englishwoman and a French lady's son with smallpox; he did so but was not sorry to get away the next day.[238] They arrived at Constantinople on *Ariadne* on 1 April and the next day, from the Sultan's kiosk, watched him depart in state for the Mosque of St Sophia. They received a deputation of British residents, shopped in the bazaars and went sightseeing.[239] The Sultan gave a state dinner in their honour on the 3rd; in return, there was a ball at the British Embassy on the 6th and the next day the Sultan and the Waleses visited the opera in state. On the 10th he gave them lunch at Dolmabakshi Palace and showed them the state apartments before they steamed up the Bosphorus in *Ariadne* to the Crimea, where reminders of the war were everywhere. For Albert Edward it was a dream fulfilled; since boyhood he had longed to go there and was now keen to establish better relations with the Russians. He inspected some Russian troops and saw Sevastopol, still devastated after the bombardment of 1854–5. Alexandra could hardly believe the heaps of rubble had been a city with 50,000 inhabitants, now reduced to about 5,000, most of whom were very poor. The Prince was touched by the kindness of the Russian officers who showed them round, and reflected grimly on the terrible wartime carnage, "for what? for a political object."[240] Continuing to Athens, they stayed in the palace with their relatives[241] and visited Paris on the way home.

The children returned on 11 May to Marlborough House, where their parents arrived the next day. The Queen had earlier told her son how sorry she would be to lose her grandchildren, who had been very well and were very fond of her. "You must let me see them often and sometimes let one or other of them come and stay with me for a little while, as I should not like them to become strangers to me." Regular hours were essential and it was best to see them one at a time: "Eddy is very good and very sensible when you have him with you alone." The tour must have been immensely expensive and they were unlikely to be given more money; "I hope dear Alix will not spend much on dress at Paris." There was a strong feeling against the "luxuriousness, extravagance & frivolity of society"; everyone praised the Queen's own unpretentious clothes. Alix should dress with "<u>great</u> <u>simplicity</u> which is more <u>elegant</u>." Chiswick House had been made available to them for spending peaceful Sundays "quietly for your repose with your dear children"[242] and, she hoped, not for parties.

Alexandra never forgot the Eastern tour, her first experience of intrepid travel in exotic surroundings; she did not accompany the Prince to India later and never visited America or the Dominions. She tried to recapture the same sense of adventure in Scandinavian and Mediterranean cruises, two of which included the Mediterranean coastal areas of North Africa. She loved talking about Egypt, telling stories, treasuring souvenirs[243] and, years later, writing a fictional account of just such another holiday.[244] But in 1869 she had brought back a live "souvenir". The royal party had attracted the attention of an engaging ten-year-old orphan, Ali Achmet, who had attached himself to them at Wadi Halfa. Enchanted by Egypt and its people, Alexandra wanted to help him; perhaps the picturesque child could serve coffee to the guests at Sandringham and perhaps her own sons would benefit from associating with a boy of such different background. Queen Victoria had sponsored Sally Bonetta Forbes,[245] Maharaja Duleep Singh[246] and Princess Victoria Gouramma of Coorg[247] in the 1850s. But they had been of high rank in their own countries, whereas Ali Achmet turned out to be an Artful Dodger.[248] He stole things, not just from the Sandringham House community, but from the guests too. The kind thought had failed, and he had to leave Sandringham House for the rector's household, where, eventually, he was baptised.

Normal life now resumed: the state concert on the 12th, driving, riding, paying calls, and the Flower Show at the Royal Botanic Gardens. Between 19 and 22 May Albert Edward inspected works at Sandringham and on the 20th Henry Holmes[249] played the violin to Alexandra; the pianist, Teresa Carreño[250] also played. Crown Prince Frederick arrived and on the 24th Albert Edward called on the Christians at Frogmore, while Alexandra drove with her brother; later, all three went to Epsom Races. Until 23 June Frederick accompanied them on family visits and at dinners, evening parties and balls given by the nobility and the Danish and Russian ambassadors. There were at least five theatre visits and they gave a dinner party on the 26th. On the 29th it was the "Annual View" of St Bartholomew's Hospital (of which Albert Edward was president), the horse show at the Agricultural Hall on the 31st, Horse Guards Parade and a dog show. On 2 June it was an inspection of the Honourable Artillery Company (of which

Albert Edward was Chairman) at the Finsbury Parade Ground; the next day Albert Edward took Frederick to a lecture at the Royal Institution. Alexandra had attended the Musical Union Concert on the 31st and Hallé's piano recital on 3 June, both at St James's Hall. On the 7th they all left for Ascot week at Coopers Hill.

On 12 June Alexandra went to a concert by Madame Norman Neruda[251] and Henri Vieuxtemps[252] at St James's Hall. Her husband attended debates in the House of Lords, and the state ball was on the 17th. Alexandra heard Henry Holmes's morning concert at the Queen's Concert Rooms in Hanover Square on the 21st. She was still driving with her brother and on the 22nd her husband was to meet and help entertain the Viceroy of Egypt, to repay his hospitality. On the 23rd there was a state concert. The Viceroy's son, Ibrahim Pasha lunched at Marlborough House on the 24th and events in the Viceroy's honour were arranged over the next few days by the Queen and the Waleses. The Prince laid the foundation stone of the Idiot Asylum's new wing at Earlswood and the couple attended the Philharmonic Concert at St James's Hall. On the 29th Albert Edward inspected the Royal Bodyguard of the Yeomen of the Guard in St James's Palace gardens and chaired a meeting of Wellington College's Governors at the Palace of Westminster the next day. The couple dined with the Aumales at Twickenham and later went to a ball at Strawberry Hill,[253] which the Viceroy also attended. He left on 1 July.

There was a state ball on the 2nd and, while the Prince presided at a banquet at Trinity House on the 3rd, Alexandra and Mrs Stonor went to the Italian Opera. On 5 July the Waleses gave a ball at Marlborough House; earlier, Eddy and Louise sat to Mr W Ewing[254] for their busts. On the 6th, Alexandra went to Lady Derby's[255] juvenile party in St James's Square; later, the couple attended St James's Theatre. The Prince opened the new dock at King's Lynn on the 7th and the couple stayed overnight at Sandringham, leaving the children at Windsor with the Queen until the 9th. The Waleses attended the opera on 10 July; a society wedding and the Rendleshams'[256] ball at Grosvenor Square, on the 12th. On the 13th they visited Watford, where the Prince laid the London Orphan Asylum's foundation stone; later, with Princess Teck and Prince Louis of Battenberg,[257] they went to the opera. After another wedding on the 14th, it was Lady Holland's[258] afternoon party at Holland House and the Wellingtons'[259] ball at Apsley House. The Christians visited Marlborough House on the 15th and Louis left for Portsmouth.

On 16 July the couple lunched with the Queen at Windsor, visiting Grand Duchess Marie of Russia[260] at Claridge's Hotel afterwards, and later taking her to the opera. Messrs Downey[261] came to photograph the three elder children and the next day the Prince attended a review at Wimbledon. On the 19th the Waleses went to stay with the Ellesmeres[262] at Worsley Hall while visiting Manchester. A dinner and evening party at Worsley Hall were followed the next day by a drive through Manchester to Salford and the Royal Agricultural Exhibition at Old Trafford. At Hull, they visited Christopher Sykes[263] MP at Brantingham Thorpe in the evening, and opened the Hull Western Dock (the "Albert Dock") on the 22nd, before returning to London. As the season concluded, they dined with the Marquess and Marchioness of Bath[264] on the 23rd, attended a fête at Crystal Palace in aid of the Dramatic College and on the 26th, with Arthur, went to the New Queen's Theatre. Messrs A Borgen,[265] of New Bond Street, had earlier shown them a vase made for the Danish Galleries by the Copenhagen Royal Porcelain Manufactory. On 27 July, the family left for the continent; Alexandra and children for Wildbad, a spa in the Black Forest. Her baby was due towards the end of the year and she needed rest. Also staying at Wildbad for her health was Sarah Angelina Acland,[266] daughter of the Prince's physician, Sir Henry Acland.[267] She became friendly with them and stayed in touch with Charlotte Knollys, recalling the "Wildbad days" with great pleasure. Miss Acland, like Alexandra, became a keen photographer; she was a fellow of the Royal Photographic Society and showed her work at its exhibitions between 1899 and 1909.[268]

From Wildbad's Hotel Klumpp on 7 August, James Paget reported to the Queen on Alexandra's health. She had arrived well but tired, and had seen Dr Burckhardt and Dr Hausmann, the principal physicians, who recommended a thorough local thermal water treatment of her right knee, beginning the next day. The spring produced naturally hot water, 93°, aerated similarly to Buxton water, which bubbled up constantly through the floor of the bath.[269] Alexandra placed her knee over it, and the water flowed up against the back, while the front and sides were douched with a heavy shower of similar water from another spring, for fifteen minutes. The joint was then massaged and manipulated to encourage bending, wrapped overnight in linen soaked with the hot water, and covered with oiled silk. As yet there was no discernible effect, but by the 16th it was a little more flexible and Alexandra felt it was less stiff when walking. She was in good health, took as much exercise as the weather allowed and on the Sunday had walked tirelessly for two hours. By the 28th she was still improving; the doctors agreed that, although the waters were useful, manual treatment was more important and with daily exercise, good mobility could be gained over months. The weather had been beautiful and Alexandra and her children spent hours outdoors every day. By 8 September her knee was even more flexible; it looked as though similar, continual treatment in England would work almost as well, but if it ceased, the knee would certainly stiffen again. Paget was back in England when he wrote again to the Queen but had left all well with Alexandra; he had told Mrs Jones what to do on the way home and had made arrangements for treatment to continue in Scotland; "I entreat Your Majesty to encourage the Princess to submit, with her usual patience, to the uninterrupted treatment which is essential to the good result which is certainly within reach."[270]

Between c1870 and 1872 Alexandra may have met a British-Jamaican woman, Mrs Mary Seacole,[271] who, although not officially qualified as a nurse, had greatly helped wounded officers and soldiers behind the lines during the Crimean War with refreshments and nursing assistance, using traditional Jamaican herbal remedies. Count Gleichen, the Duke of Cambridge and Prince Edward of Saxe-Weimar,[272] all having served in the war and met Mrs Seacole, contributed to a fund started to help her when she fell on hard times afterwards. The Prince of Wales also contributed. It seems that Mrs Seacole was a skilled masseuse, who treated Alexandra's knee problems. No documentary evidence of this has yet been found; the Princess's engagement diaries did not begin until 1873. However, there is certainly a possibility that the treatment took place, as the couple were interested in alternative medicines and Alexandra, with her recent happy memories of the people in Egypt, may well have been intrigued by Mrs Seacole's partly African heritage.

Having returned to London and spent a fortnight at Abergeldie, the Prince left on 11 September 1869 for Wildbad and brought them home on the 28th. Driving and visiting resumed but on 2 October he returned to Abergeldie while his family went to Chiswick. Alexandra was feeling "dreadfully low" at having to part from "my beloved husy" again, after such a long separation.[273] In Scotland, he went deer driving, attended two Privy Council meetings held by the Queen and gave a dance at Abergeldie. He left for Edinburgh on the 13th and opened the new Town Hall at Chester en route to London on the 16th, when Alexandra joined him from Chiswick. The next day, after church, she returned there and did not accompany her husband on several forthcoming visits because of her advancing pregnancy. He went for shooting to Gunton Hall, which Lord Suffield had offered them for the winter, as Sandringham was being enlarged and was uninhabitable. After other visits he returned to his family in London on 6 November and on the 8th the couple attended a double wedding in Westminster Abbey; the Marquis of Blandford married Lady Albertha Hamilton[274] and the Marquis of Lansdowne her sister, Lady Maude.[275] "Maud(e)" was fashionable; it was Princess Alice's second name, and Tennyson's[276] eponymous poem had been published in 1855. [277]

Louise was no nearer to finding a husband but at least she and her mother were united against a Prussian marriage. The Queen had seen Prussia's military and political ambitions grow since Vicky's marriage in 1858 and was determined not to send another daughter there. Neither was there any chance for Prince Albert of Solms.[278] In fact Victoria was quite in favour of Louise's marrying a British aristocrat, while Louise herself wanted to stay in Britain.[279] On Albert Edward's 28th birthday, Uncle George visited Marlborough House and afterwards the Waleses lunched with the Queen at Windsor. That evening they went to the Italian Opera. At about this time, Reginald Easton[280] had sittings for a miniature on ivory of Alexandra and little Louise. There were more visitors, an evening at the Gaiety on the 12th and several official functions for the Prince; on the 22nd Alexandra visited the South Kensington Museum. Albert Edward left to visit General Hall on the 23rd, but on the 25th Alexandra, who had felt uncomfortable all day, telegraphed to him at 5pm to come home, which he did immediately, arriving at 8.30pm. Later, he sent for Dr Farre; the baby was born at 12.20am on the 26th.[281] She was a fine, healthy child and both she and her mother continued to flourish.[282] Relatives, including the Belgian king, called to enquire and congratulate. The Prince chaired several meetings and dinners, went shooting at Windsor and Bagshot, stayed at Studley Royal for a few days but returned on 10 December for the Duchesse d'Aumale's funeral. He also attended the mausoleum service on the 14th.

The Queen now fully agreed that Marlborough House was too small; "the children have absolutely <u>no</u> room even <u>now</u>, and when Governesses and Tutors are required they <u>cannot</u> be lodged in the House." Disraeli had suggested demolishing the so-called German Chapel[283] nearby, which the Prince thought should be linked to the house's enlargement.[284] The chapel stayed, but the 1865 fire had revealed unsound timber in the house's old upper rooms; in 1870 that part was rebuilt and another storey added at the sides but not the centre of the house, and what became the comptroller's room and the schoolroom were built on the North Front at the same time. After further additions in 1874–5, a storey was added in 1885 to the east and west of the office buildings and by 1895 there were some 106 rooms altogether.[285]

By 8 December 1869 Alexandra was on the sofa in the drawing room, doing rather better than after previous confinements and enjoying her food. The baby also slept and ate well.[286] On the 20th Alexandra was churched at the Chapel Royal, St James's and on Christmas Eve the Bishop of London christened the baby Maud Charlotte Mary Victoria at Marlborough House. Christmas was spent there; Prince Leiningen came to lunch and Uncle George, the Tecks and Teck's sister Claudine[287] to dinner. On the 27th the Waleses and their sons left for Holkham.

Notes

1   A shallow dish of hot, burning raisins in spirits; these had to be snatched out of the flames
2   With the Earl and Countess of Leicester – this was the first royal visit since Princess Victoria's in 1831. "Holkham time" was 40 minutes ahead of "London time", to allow more daylight for shooting, so the Prince put "Sandringham time" 30 minutes ahead for the same reason.
3   Brandy and soda, a fashionable drink
4   Julio Donato (d 1865)
5   RA VIC/MAIN/EVIID/1865:6 February
6   Frederic Leighton, Baron Leighton (1830–96), painter, draughtsman and sculptor
7   Francis Knollys (1837–1924), later 1st Viscount Knollys, courtier; son of General Knollys, brother of Charlotte

8   James Duff (1814–79) 5th Earl Fife, m Lady Agnes, née Hay (1829–69)
9   RA VIC/MAIN/EVIID/1865:3 March Prince Alexander Ivanovitch Bariatinsky (1815–79), formerly commander of the Russian army in the Caucasus; he had retired to Devonshire, suffering from gout
10 Albert Edward to Weigall and Alexandra to Desanges
11 Francisco de Almeida Portugal, 2nd Count of Lavradio (1796–1870), Portuguese minister plenipotentiary
12 RA VIC/MAIN/EVIID/1865:19 March She was the Georgian wife of Prince Bariatinsky
13 Henri, prince de La Tour d'Auvergne (1823–71), French politician
14 RA VIC/MAIN/EVIID/1865:23 March
15 Edward Askew Sothern (1826–81), actor known for his comic roles
16 William Wilkie Collins (1824–89), novelist and playwright
17 RA VIC/MAIN/EVIID/1865:27 March; the book had been published in 1860
18 William Henry Perkin (1838–1907), later Sir, chemist and entrepreneur
19 Benjamin Hall, 1st Baron Llanover (1802–67), Welsh civil engineer and politician
20 Thomas Gruffydd (1815–87), famous Welsh harpist
21 John Orlando Parry (1810–79), actor, pianist, comedian and singer
22 Frederick Richard Window (1824–75), photographer, later in partnership with William Henry Grove (1847–1906) in Baker Street, W1
23 The Le Strange family had been established in Norfolk since 1066 and played a large part in local history. The head of the family in 1865 was Hamon Le Strange (1840–1918/19).
24 Andrew Toward (1796–1881), agent and farm bailiff at Osborne
25 William Carmichael (c 1816–1904), gardener at Sandringham in the 1860s
26 From the building firm of Goggs Brothers, of Swaffham
27 William Amelius Aubrey de Vere Beauclerk, 10th Duke of St Albans (1840–98)
28 RA VIC/ADDA8/1509, Princess of Wales to Princess Mary of Cambridge, 1865: 25 April
29 Abraham Lincoln (1809–65), the 16th president of the United States of America
30 Seat of the Marquess of Cholmondeley, then George Cholmondeley (1792–1870), 2nd Marquess
31 Moses Merryweather (1791–1872), founder of firm which built steam fire engines and tram engines, or his son Richard (1839–1877)
32 RA VIC/MAIN/EVIID/1865:29 April
33 Edward Cardwell, 1st Viscount Cardwell (1813–86), later Secretary of State for War
34 RA VIC/MAIN/EVIID/1865:14 May
35 Lord Alfred Paget (1816–88), soldier, courtier and politician, m Cecilia Wyndham; the baby may have been Alexandra (1863–1944), later m Baron Colebrooke
36 RA VIC/MAIN/EVIID/1865:1 June
37 Monthly nurse
38 Prince George (1865–1936), later King George V
39 RA VIC/MAIN/Z/448/106, Sir James Clark to Queen Victoria, 1865: 3 June
40 Who, curiously, shared the same birthday, 9 November, as the Prince
41 RA VIC/MAIN/Z/448/108, Prince of Wales to Queen Victoria, 1865: 11 June
42 RA VIC/MAIN/Z/448/109; Queen Victoria to Prince of Wales, 1865: 13 June; RA VIC/MAIN/EVIID/1865:7 July
43 Possibly Lt-Colonel A H Armytage
44 RA VIC/MAIN/EVIID/1865:4 July
45 Sir Eyre Massey Shaw (1830–1908), mentioned by the Fairy Queen in Gilbert and Sullivan's *Iolanthe*
46 *Marlborough House and Its Occupants, Present and Past*, by Arthur H. Beavan, pp 100–103

47   Hills & Saunders, well-known photographers; Robert Hills (1821–82) and his son-in-law, John Henry Saunders (1836–90)

48   A cordoned-off area, used by the Royal Family for bathing

49   Either Maximilian Karl, 6th Prince of Thurn und Taxis (1802–71) or his son, Maximilian Anton, Hereditary Prince (1831–67)

50   William Henry Edgcumbe, 4th Earl of Mount Edgcumbe (1833–1917), politician and courtier

51   RA VIC/MAIN/EVIID/1865:22 July

52   John Whitehead Peard, (1811–80) fought with Garibaldi's forces in Sicily and Naples and was raised to the rank of Colonel by him

53   Sir Edward St Aubyn, 1st Baronet (1799–1872) m Emma Knollys (c 1806–87), General Knollys' sister

54   RA VIC/MAIN/EVIID/1865:24 July

55   RA VIC/ADDA17/122, Prince of Wales to Princess Louise, 1865: 19 August

56   Johann Christoph Florschütz (1794–1882), tutor and mentor of Prince Albert and his brother

57   RA VIC/MAIN/EVIID/1865:27 August; Ida Magnus m Paul, Freiherr, later Baron von Reuter (1816–99) who founded Reuter's news agency

58   Residence of Prince and Princess Louis of Hesse

59   Princess Hilda of Anhalt-Dessau (1839–1926), Alexandra's cousin

60   Dionysius Lardner Boucicault (1820–90), Irish actor and playwright

61   Not a royal establishment; it was run by a Mr Prince

62   Seat of the Duke of Roxburghe, then James Innes-Ker (1816–79), 6th Duke

63   Maurice Holzmann (1835–1909), later Sir; courtier and mountaineer

64   Seat of the Earl of Derby, then Edward Stanley (1826–93), the 15th Earl

65   His solicitor, Arnold White (1830–93), later Sir

66   Edmund Beck

67   With Lord and Lady Alfred Paget

68   Bernhard Ernst von Bülow (1815–79), Danish and German statesman

69   RA VIC/MAIN/EVIID/1865:2 December

70   Charles Harbord, 5th Baron Suffield (1830–1914), courtier and politician; m Cecilia Baring (d 1911)

71   Prince Christian of Schleswig-Holstein-Sonderburg-Augustenburg (1831–1917)

72   RA VIC/MAIN/Y/114/32, Queen Victoria to King Leopold of the Belgians, 1865: 21 September

73   RA VIC/ADDCO7/1/0487, Sir Charles Phipps to General Knollys, 1865: 15 December. In fact, Prince Christian regarded himself as Danish rather than German (RA AEC/GG/9/1031)

74   George Granville Sutherland-Leveson-Gower, 3rd Duke of Sutherland (1828–92), m Anne, née Hay-Mackenzie (1829–1888)

75   RA VIC/MAIN/Z/448/118, Queen Victoria to Prince of Wales, 1865: 30 December

76   RA VIC/MAIN/Z/448/119, Prince of Wales to Queen Victoria, 1866: 2 January

77   William Theed (1804–91), sculptor

78   Seat of the Duke of Rutland

79   RA VIC/MAIN/Z/448/122, Prince of Wales to Queen Victoria, 1866: 5 March

80   Joseph Stoddart, magician and conjurer (1831–66), who died in October this year of tuberculosis

81   RA VIC/ADDA17/141, Princess of Wales to Princess Louise, 1866: 18 March

82   John Winston Spencer-Churchill, 7th Duke of Marlborough (1822–83) m Lady Frances, née Vane (1822–99)

83   Queen Marie Amélie had died on the 24th

84   In fact Alexandra continued to accompany hunts for many years

85   RA VIC/ADDU32/1866:31 March, 11 April, Queen Victoria to Crown Princess of Prussia

86   Hermann, 6th Prince of Hohenlohe-Langenburg (1832–1913)

87   Leopold II (1835–1909), King of the Belgians

88   The King's grandmother

89   Kinloch Cooke, Vol I, pp 412, 414

90   Margaret Anne, née Bathurst (d 1874)

91   RA VIC/MAIN/Z/448/123, 124, 125, Prince of Wales to Queen Victoria, 1866:10 May; Queen Victoria to Prince of Wales, 11 May; Prince of Wales to Queen Victoria, 12 May

92   RA VIC/ADDA8/1600, Princess of Wales to Princess Mary of Cambridge and Prince Teck, 1866: 6 June

93   General Sir James Yorke Scarlett (1799–1871), army officer who led the charge of the Light Brigade in the Crimean War

94   George Vane-Tempest, 5th Marquess of Londonderry (1821–84), known as Earl Vane from 1854–72, diplomat and Conservative politician, m Mary, née Edwards (d 1906)

95   Thomas Egerton, 2nd Earl of Wilton (1799–1882), courtier, politician and composer, m (2) Isabella, née Smith (d 1916)

96   Kinloch Cooke, Vol I, p 417

97   William Ward, 1st Earl of Dudley (1817–85), benefactor; m Georgina, née Moncreiffe (d 1929)

98   Duchess Caroline of Mecklenburg-Strelitz (1821–76), the divorced second wife of King Frederick VII of Denmark (who had died in 1863)

99   Prince Sigismund of Prussia (1864–66)

100   King Leopold II and Queen Marie Henriette

101   George John Sackville-West, 5th Earl De la Warr (1791–1869), courtier and politician, m Lady Elizabeth, née Sackville (1795–1870)

102   Charles Wood, 1st Viscount Halifax (1800–85), politician, m Lady Mary, née Grey (1807–1884)

103   Robert John Carrington, 2nd Baron Carrington (1796–1868), politician, m (2) Hon Charlotte, née Drummond-Willoughby (1815–1879)

104   William Montagu, 7th Duke of Manchester (1823–90), politician, m Countess Louise von Alten (1832–1911) who later married the Duke of Devonshire

105   An amateur and independent cricket club

106   William Thomson (1819–90) m Zoë, née Skene

107   *Evening Mail*, 13 August 1866

108   Tooley, page 54; Marshall Wood (c 1834–82) was a sculptor, medallist and artist

109   With the Duke and Duchess of Sutherland

110   France had been neutral during the war, but Napoleon III distrusted Prussia's possible goal of German unity, which he felt would threaten France. He wanted to limit Prussia's expansion.

111   However, the Prussian army defeated the French in 1871 and eight years later, with Austria's agreement, Bismarck deleted Paragraph 5; Slesvig was German

112   Tsesarevitch Alexander Alexandrovitch (1845–94), later Emperor Alexander III of Russia

113   Edward Smith-Stanley, the 14th Earl of Derby (1799–1869), statesman, three times Prime Minister

114   Marie Alexandrovna, née Princess Marie of Hesse (1824–80), m Emperor Alexander II of Russia

115   RA VIC/MAIN/Z/448/134, Prince of Wales to Queen Victoria, 1866: 14 October

116   RA VIC/MAIN/Z/448/135, Queen Victoria to Prince of Wales, 1866: 16 October

117 Henry Stafford-Jerningham, 9th Baron Stafford (1802–84), politician, m (2) Emma, née Gerard (d 1912)

118 RA VIC/ADDU32/1866:2 August, 23 September, Queen Victoria to Crown Princess of Prussia

119 RA VIC/ADDU32/1866:2 May, 2 August, Queen Victoria to Crown Princess of Prussia

120 RA VIC/MAIN/Z/19/29, Crown Princess of Prussia to Queen Victoria, 1866: 24 May

121 RA VIC/ADDU32/1866:14 November, Queen Victoria to Crown Princess of Prussia

122 RA VIC/ADDA17/165, Princess of Wales to Princess Louise, 1866: 5 December

123 RA VIC/MAIN/Z/448/141, Prince of Wales to Queen Victoria, 1866: 8 November

124 RA VIC/ADDA17/180, Princess of Wales to Princess Louise, 1867: 13 February

125 Princess Louise (1867–1931), Princess Royal from 1905; m 1st Duke of Fife

126 RA VIC/MAIN/Z/448/154, Prince of Wales to Queen Victoria, 1867: 20 February

127 *Court Circular,* 1867: 28 February

128 André Adolphe Eugène Disdéri (1819–89), French photographer

129 Tooley, p 60

130 Beavan, p 193

131 RA VIC/ADDA17/184, Prince of Wales to Princess Louise, 1867: 8 March

132 James Paget (1814–99), later Baronet; surgeon, pathologist and royal surgeon

133 Tooley, p 59

134 RA VIC/ADDA17/186, 187, Prince of Wales to Princess Louise, 1867: 11, 17 March

135 Information from press cuttings

136 Court Circular, 1867: 10 April

137 RA VIC/ADDA17/193, Prince of Wales to Princess Louise, 1867: 6 May

138 RA VIC/MAIN/Z/448/159, Mrs Stonor to Queen Victoria, 1867: 10 May

139 RA VIC/MAIN/Z/448/155, General Knollys to Queen Victoria, 1867: 20 February

140 Princess Louise of Saxe-Gotha-Altenburg (1800–31), w of Duke Ernest III of Saxe-Coburg-Saalfeld, later known as Duke Ernest I of Saxe-Coburg-Gotha

141 Tooley, p 60

142 Prince Chrstian Victor of Schleswig-Holstein-Sonderburg-Augustenburg (1867–1900), soldier and keen amateur cricketer

143 Colonel Nigel Kingscote (1830–1908), later Sir, army officer, politician, agriculturalist and courtier

144 Major-General Christopher Charles Teesdale, VC (1833–93), later Sir, army officer and courtier

145 Colonel the Hon Oliver George Paulet Montagu (1844–93), army officer and courtier

146 Princess Elizabeth of Hesse (1864–1918), m Grand Duke Serge Alexandrovitch of Russia (1857–1905)

147 Princess Irène of Hesse (1866–1953) m Prince Henry of Prussia (1862–1929)

148 Ismail Pasha (1830–1895), Viceroy, or Khedive, 1863–79

149 Abdulaziz (1830–1876), Sultan of Turkey, 1861–76

150 As Queen Mary (1867–1953)

151 RA VIC/MAIN/Z/448/180, General Knollys to Queen Victoria, 1867: 4 September

152 William I (1797–1888), later German Emperor from 1871

153 Including Hesse-Cassel

154 RA VIC/MAIN/Z/448/182, General Knollys to Queen Victoria, 1867: 24 September

155 RA VIC/ADDA3/96, Prince of Wales to Queen Victoria, 1867: 4 October

156 Seemingly her own word

157 RA VIC/ADDA17/219, Princess of Wales to Princess Louise, 1867: 1 November

158 Susan Durant (1827–73), artist and sculptress

159 RA VIC/ADDA8/1758, Princess of Wales to Princess Teck, 1867: 27 November

[160] RA VIC/ADDA8/1761, Princess of Wales to Princess Teck, 1867: 7 December

[161] RA VIC/ADDA17/230, Princess of Wales to Princess Louise, 1867: 1 December

[162] May be General John Hall (1799–1872), politician, lived on estate at Six Mile Bottom

[163] George Spencer-Churchill (1844–92), later 8th Duke of Marlborough

[164] May be Gerald Valerian Wellesley (1809–82), Dean of Windsor from 1854–1882

[165] May be Arthur Edward Hardinge (1828–92), later General Sir, courtier

[166] RA VIC/ADDA8/1761, Princess of Wales to Princess Teck, 1867: 7 December

[167] Elizabeth Charlotte Knollys (1835–1930), later woman of the bedchamber to Alexandra

[168] RA VIC/ADDC2/12, Princess of Wales to Duchess of Manchester, 1867: 7 December

[169] See *Developing the Picture: Queen Alexandra and the Art of Photography*, by Frances Dimond, pp 35–39 for more information about the album

[170] Perpetrated by the Irish republican group, Sinn Fein ("Ourselves alone")

[171] James Henry Mapleson (1830–1901), opera impresario

[172] RA VIC/MAIN/Z/448/186, Queen Victoria to Prince of Wales, 1868: 7 January

[173] Press cutting; this was an early example of Alexandra's compassion towards people in adversity.

[174] Henry Somerset (1824–99), 8th Duke of Beaufort, soldier, politician and courtier, m Lady Georgiana, née Curzon (1825–1906)

[175] (Karl Halle) Charles Hallé (1819–95), later Sir, Anglo–German pianist and conductor and founder of the Hallé Orchestra in 1858

[176] The Duke of Cambridge

[177] Kinloch Cooke, Vol II, p 6. The apartment was at Kensington Palace

[178] Silvain Van de Weyer (1802–74), Belgian Minister to UK, m Elizabeth, née Bates (1817–78)

[179] Benjamin Disraeli (1804–81), Earl of Beaconsfield (1876), politician, Prime Minister and novelist

[180] RA VIC/MAIN/D/23/65, Princess of Wales to Queen Victoria, 1868: 26 March

[181] Sir Edwin Henry Landseer (1802–73), painter and sculptor

[182] RA VIC/ADDA/17/265,267, Prince of Wales to Princess Louise, 1868: 6, 13 June

[183] Princess Louise of Sweden and Norway (1851–1926), m the future King Frederick VIII of Denmark

[184] RA VIC/MAIN/Z/449/6, Prince of Wales to Queen Victoria, 1868: 18 April

[185] The Marquess of Abercorn

[186] *Cork Examiner,* 21 April 1868

[187] James Hamilton (1811–85), Marquess and then 1st Duke of Abercorn, statesman, twice Lord Lieutenant of Ireland, m Lady Louisa, née Russell (1812–1905)

[188] RA VIC/MAIN/Z/449/7, Princess of Wales to Queen Victoria, 1868: 19 April

[189] Edmund Burke (1729–97), Anglo–Irish statesman and philosopher

[190] *Enniscorthy News,* 2 May 1868

[191] *The Times,* 27 April 1868

[192] 1833–1868; he at first claimed to be a Fenian but was thought to be insane

[193] Later King Edward II (1284–1327)

[194] Matthew Noble (1817–76), leading portrait sculptor

[195] Adolphe Beau (1828–1910), French photographer and inventor

[196] Frits Hartvigson (1841–1919), Danish pianist and teacher

[197] George Brudenell-Bruce (1804–78), 2nd Marquess of Ailesbury, politician and courtier, m Lady Mary, née Herbert (d 1892)

[198] Albert Bierstadt (1830–1902), German-American landscape painter

[199] With Earl and Countess Vane

[200] Princess Victoria (1868–1935)

[201] Many years later, she wrote to a musician friend, "Music is so <u>wonderful</u> so <u>helpful</u> & I have

longed to be able to play – or produce in some way the sounds I feel & understand." Princess Victoria to Beatrice Harrison, 1918: 6 October, © The Harrison Sisters' Trust

202 RA VIC/MAIN//Z/449/16, Prince of Wales to Queen Victoria, 1868: 6 July

203 RA VIC/MAIN/Z/449/17, Prince of Wales to Queen Victoria, 1868: 24 July

204 John Jackson (1811–85), Bishop of London 1868–1885

205 King George of the Hellenes had married Grand Duchess Olga Constantinovna of Russia (1851–1926) on 27 October 1867

206 Prince Adolphus of Teck (1868–1927), later 2nd Duke of Teck and then 1st Marquess of Cambridge (1917)

207 Between ourselves

208 Constantine (1868–1923), Duke of Sparta, King of the Hellenes, 1913–1917 and 1920–1922

209 The future Emperor Nicholas II (1868–1918), born in May

210 RA VIC/ADDA17/276, Princess of Wales to Princess Louise, 1868: 22 August

211 Alexander Duff (1849–1912), later 6th Earl Fife and 1st Duke of Fife (1889)

212 George Edwin Ewing (1828–84), sculptor

213 RA VIC/MAIN/Z/449/20, 21, Queen Victoria to Prince of Wales, 1868: nd, October; Prince of Wales to Queen Victoria, 1868: 6 October

214 Mark Lemon (1809–84), playwright, author and founding Editor of Punch and The Field

215 RA VIC/MAIN/Z/449/22, 23, Queen Victoria to Prince of Wales, 1868: 22 October; Prince of Wales to Queen Victoria, 1868: 25 October

216 RA VIC/MAIN/Z/449/24, Princess of Wales to Queen Victoria, 1868: 28 October

217 RA VIC/MAIN/Z/449/26, Prince of Wales to Queen Victoria, 1868: 1 November

218 Sir Henry Holland (1788–1873), 1st Baronet, physician and travel writer

219 Sir Charles Locock (1799–1875), 1st Baronet, obstetrician to Queen Victoria

220 RA VIC/MAIN/Z/449/27, Prince of Wales to Queen Victoria, 1868: 5 November

221 RA VIC/ADDY3/p2, the cream contained whale oil, almond oil, white wax, rose water and otto of rose

222 Agnes Zimmermann (1845–1925), German concert pianist and composer who lived in England

223 Eugénie née de Montijo (1826–1920), m Napoleon III, Emperor of the French

224 RA VIC/MAIN/Z/449/28, General Knollys to Queen Victoria, 1868: 3 December

225 RA VIC/MAIN/Z/449/29, Dr Minter to Queen Victoria, 1868: 24 December

226 Mrs Marianne Hull, née Cripps (1811–1888) "Old May", nurse to Queen Victoria's children

227 RA VIC/ADDA17/288,291, Princess of Wales to Princess Louise, 1868: both 14 December

228 RA VIC/MAIN/Z/449/31, Dr Minter to Queen Victoria, 1869: 15 January

229 RA VIC/MAIN/Z/449/32, Princess of Wales to Queen Victoria, 1869: 16 January

230 RA VIC/MAIN/Z/449/38, Dr Minter to Queen Victoria, 1869: 25 January

231 RA VIC/MAIN/Z/449/43, Dr Minter to Queen Victoria, 1869: 5 February

232 RA VIC/MAIN/Z/449/44, Dr Minter to Queen Victoria, 1869: 15 February

233 Tooley, pp 68–69

234 RA VIC/MAIN/Z/449/45, Dr Minter to Queen Victoria, 1869: 19 February

235 Sir Samuel Baker (1821–83), explorer, officer, naturalist, big game hunter engineer and writer

236 RA VIC/MAIN/Z/449/47,48, Susan Martin to Queen Victoria, 1869: 3, 4 March

237 Tooley, p70

238 RA VIC/MAIN/Z/449/49, Dr Minter to Queen Victoria, 1869: 19 March

239 Tooley, p70

240 RA VIC/ADDA3/132, Prince of Wales to Queen Victoria, 1869: 13 April
     Much of the detail relating to the tour comes from press cuttings

241 Tooley, p 71

242 RA VIC/MAIN/Z/449/51, Queen Victoria to Prince of Wales, 1869: 4 May; they did give parties there

243 Tooley, pp 71–2

244 See Dimond, pp 146–152 for more details

245 A captain in the Royal Navy, Frederick Forbes, was sent by the British government to Dahomey in 1848 to negotiate the suppression of the Atlantic slave trade. The King of Dahomey, Ghezo (ruled from 1818 to his death in 1858), refused, but instead gave Forbes a five-year-old girl, Omoba Aina (1843–80), an orphaned Yoruba princess, whom he had enslaved during warfare with the Yoruba people in West Africa. Fearing for the child's safety in Dahomey, Forbes took her back to England on his ship, the *Sally Bonetta*, and introduced her to Queen Victoria who, impressed by the girl's intelligence, sponsored her education and took an interest in her for the rest of her life. Initially called Sally Bonetta Forbes, the girl later adopted the name Sarah Forbes Bonetta. She m James Pinson Labulo Davies, and they had three children, the eldest of whom, Victoria, was the Queen's goddaughter.

246 Duleep Singh (1838–93), last Maharaja of the Sikh Empire, brought to England in 1854, some years after the Anglo–Sikh War. He was befriended by Queen Victoria and Prince Albert and met their children.

247 Princess Gouramma (1841–64) d of the deposed ruler of Coorg, who left her in Queen Victoria's care; the Queen acted as her godmother and she was christened Victoria; she m Lt-Colonel John Campbell.

248 Character in *Oliver Twist* (published as a book in 1838) by Charles Dickens, whose work Alexandra admired. Ali Achmet's portrait was painted by Sir Oswald Brierley on 3 March 1869 (https://www.rct.uk/collection/920363/ali-achmet. See also Battiscombe, p 104; Ridley, p 125;

249 Henry Holmes (1839–1905), concert violin soloist, composer and music educator

250 Teresa Carreño (1853–1917), pianist and composer

251 Wilhelmine (Wilma) Neruda (1838–1911), virtuoso violinist, chamber musician and teacher, m 1) Ludwig Norman, 2) Sir Charles Hallé

252 Henri Vieuxtemps (1820–81), Belgian composer for, and player of, the violin and viola

253 Given by Frances, Countess Waldegrave (1821–79)

254 This may mean GE Ewing; William Ewing had been active as a sculptor some 40 or more years previously

255 Hon Emma, née Bootle-Wilbraham (1805–76), m the 14th Earl of Derby (1799–1869), three times prime minister

256 Frederick Thellusson (1840–1911), 5th Baron Rendlesham, politician, m Lady Egidia, née Montgomerie (c 1843–80)

257 Prince Louis of Battenberg (1854–1921), later First Sea Lord and Marquess of Milford Haven (1917)

258 Lady Mary, née Coventry (1812–89), m Henry Fox, 4th Baron Holland (1802–59)

259 Arthur Wellesley (1807–84) 2nd Duke of Wellington, m Lady Elizabeth, née Hay (1820–1904), Mistress of the Robes to Queen Victoria, 1861–68 and 1874–80

260 Grand Duchess Marie Nicholaievna (1819–76), daughter of Emperor Nicholas I

261 William (1829–1925) and Daniel (1831–81) Downey, brothers, trading as photographers, W & D Downey

262 Francis Egerton (1847–1914), 3rd Earl of Ellesmere, m Lady Katherine, née Phipps (1850–1926)

263 Christopher Sykes (1831–98), politician

264 John Thynne (1831–96), 4th Marquess of Bath, diplomat and public servant, m Hon Frances, née Vesey

265 Danish firm who had a London branch c 1869–80

266 Sarah Angelina Acland (1849–1930), amateur photographer; portraiture and pioneering colour photography

267 Sir Henry Acland (1815–1900), 1st Baronet, physician (accompanied the Prince to USA and Canada in 1860) and educator

268 Dimond, p 102

269 Buxton, an English spa

270 RA VIC/MAIN/Z/449/54–57,59, James Paget to Queen Victoria, 1869: 7, 16, 28 August; 8, 28 September

271 Mary Jane, née Grant (1805–1881), m Edwin Seacole; her autobiography, *Wonderful Adventures of Mrs Seacole in Many Lands,* was published in 1857

272 Prince Edward of Saxe-Weimar (1823–1902) a nephew of Queen Adelaide, who settled in England

273 RA VIC/ADDA8/1897, Princess of Wales to Princess Teck, 1869: 6 October

274 Lady Albertha, née Hamilton (1846–1932) m Marquess of Blandford

275 Lady Maude, née Hamilton (1850–1932) m Henry Petty-Fitzmaurice (1845–1927), 5th Marquess of Lansdowne, statesman, Governor-General of Canada (1883–1888) and Viceroy of India (1888–94)

276 Alfred Tennyson (1809–92), 1st Baron Tennyson, Poet Laureate (1850–92)

277 Alexandra also had several distant ancestors called Matilda (or Maud)

278 May be Prince Albert of Solms-Braunfels (1841–1901)

279 RA VIC/ADDA17/322, Queen Victoria to Prince of Wales, 1869: 24 November

280 Reginald Easton (1807–93), artist

281 Princess Maud (1869–1938) m Prince Carl of Denmark, elected King Haakon VII of Norway in 1905. 26 November was also the birthday of Alexandra's sister Minny; 27 November was Princess Teck's birthday.

282 RA VIC/MAIN/Z/449/60, Dr Arthur Farre to Queen Victoria, 1869: 26 November

283 Established for George I and George II, who did not understand English. A service using the English liturgy, but in German, was performed there but, not being the Lutheran rite, no German wanted to go there in 1869.

284 RA VIC/MAIN/Z/449/62, Queen Victoria to William Ewart Gladstone, 1869: 3 December

285 Beavan, pp 240–241, 242–243

286 RA VIC/MAIN/Z/449/64, Dr Arthur Farre to Queen Victoria, 1869: 8 December

287 Princess Claudine of Teck (1836–94)

Chapter 5

1870–1874

"*When I was in trouble I called upon the Lord and He heard me*"

W

1870 began normally enough; returning to London on 3 February and visiting the Tecks.[1] A theatre visit and a debate in the House of Lords followed, with a duchy meeting and the Honourable Artillery Company's ball on 9 February, and watching Skating Club members on the frozen lake at Regent's Park. The Waleses entertained, dined with the Gladstones[2] on the 23rd and the Queen on the 25th and called on the Dutch queen at Claridges. Albert Edward hunted with the staghounds while Alexandra lunched at home with Louise and later heard Professor Max Müller's[3] lecture at the Royal Institution. But there was trouble.

Sir Charles Mordaunt[4] had started a court case after his wife had confessed intimacy with other men, including the Prince, who, although innocent, was obliged to appear as a witness. There was no alternative, he told the Queen; "altho' my solicitor (Mr. Arnold White) thinks that there is just a chance that at the last moment I shall not be called. Anyhow I am perfectly ready to answer any questions that may be put to me ... Alix has been informed by me of everything concerning this unfortunate case."[5] Some letters[6] "of the most insignificant consequence" were the only evidence against him; however, Sir William Knollys thought that if, inevitably, his name came up in the trial, it would be best if he had the chance "of utterly and emphatically denying everything that could put him in the position of a co-respondent."[7] It would be a warning to be more circumspect in the future, commented the Queen. Alexandra fully supported her husband, who felt he had to appear in court, although all the highest legal authorities agreed it was monstrous. Eleven doctors were evaluating Lady Mordaunt's sanity.[8] The Prince now had to wait while the trial proceeded and Sir Charles mentioned him as often as possible until, on the 23rd, he was summoned, questioned for about seven minutes, "& I think the answers I gave were satisfactory."[9] When asked whether any undue familiarity had ever taken place between him and Lady Mordaunt, he "emphatically answered '<u>never</u>'"[10] and left the court, entirely vindicated.

The Queen had supported him wholeheartedly but thought he would never have been brought into the case if his lifestyle had been irreproachable. They were going to stay with the Manchesters on 14 March, when people were saying the Prince seemed to enjoy constant amusement and frivolous society. The Duchess of Manchester's behaviour was equivocal; the Queen had no proof she actually did anything wrong, but felt impelled to insist to Alexandra that "[She] is not a fit companion for you"; she had done more harm to society by "her tone, her love of admiration & 'fast' style than almost anyone, & what will people say if they see you & Bertie going on a visit to her House, just after all that has happened?" The visit could not be cancelled, "but let it be the last & do not let any intimacy spring up between you & the Duchess."[11] The Waleses, however, chose their own friends. The Duchess, German-born Countess Louise von Alten, was unhappily married and had a longstanding affair with the bachelor Lord Hartington (later 8th Duke of Devonshire) until in 1892[12] they could marry. Alexandra enjoyed the "Double Duchess's" company, and Albert Edward was a friend of the Duke until he died in 1908.

After attending a Monday Popular Concert at St James's Hall on 1 March, Alexandra and the three elder children stayed briefly with the Queen at Windsor, while Albert Edward visited Henry Chaplin[13] at Lincoln until the 5th. He attended the House of Lords again on the 7th and hunted with hounds several times during March and April. Princess Louise and Marguérite d'Orléans[14] called on Alexandra, who, with her husband, later went to the Marlboroughs' dance at St James's Square. On the 9th Alexandra was at the Queen's drawing room; Louise dined, and they went to the Gaiety. For their seventh wedding anniversary the Waleses, after a family lunch and attending Francis of Teck's christening, held a dance. There was a levee on the 11th and later, the couple and Louise went to St James's Theatre. On the 14th they left for a week at Kimbolton Castle,[15] for a hunt meeting (Alexandra in her pony phaeton) and a ball. Back in London on the 21st, they saw the Guards' officers' production at the Holborn Theatre, in aid of the Guards' Institute, on the 24th. The Queen and Louise called the next day; later, the Christians dined and accompanied the Waleses to the Gaiety. By the end of March Albert Edward and Alexandra had lunched with Aunt Cambridge and visited the City of London middle-class schools at Finsbury. General Grey had died and the couple called on his widow[16] at St James's Palace; later they visited the Society of British Artists' exhibition. Alexandra drove on most days and her husband rode or hunted, and chaired a Society of Arts committee meeting.[17] On the 6th, with Prince Teck, Prince Leiningen and Lord Alfred Paget, he watched the boat race from the umpire's boat, (while his wife and sons watched from Chiswick), held a levee and, with Alexandra, later gave a dinner party. After Easter at Osborne with the Queen, and a week at Sandringham, they attended the Royal Academy Exhibition's private view on the 28th and a Society of Arts conversazione at the South Kensington Museum on 4 May. The next day it was the Wandering Minstrels'[18] concert at the Guards' Institute, in aid of All Saints' Convalescent Hospital. On the 9th, Alexandra, with Charlotte Knollys and Lt-Colonel Ellis,[19] saw French and Flemish pictures at the Pall Mall gallery, and the Society of Painters in Watercolours' exhibition. Later, the Waleses attended the philharmonic concert in St James's Hall. After the drawing room on the 10th, it was the Van de Weyers' ball at Arlington Street and the Queen's opening of London University's new premises in Burlington House on the 11th.

On 14 May the couple attended a matinee at the Theatre Royal, to support the Royal Dramatic College fund. Alexandra went to the Royal Italian Opera on 16 May; earlier, JF Boyes[20] had shown them some autotype reproductions of the Sistine Chapel frescoes, and on the 18th Colonel de Szerelmey[21] brought the portrait of Jesus Marie Hodegedria, attributed to St Luke the Evangelist. The next day, Alexandra sat to Mr CE Van Denbosch for the bust intended for the City of London Corporation. The Waleses attended the Italian Opera on 21 May and on the 23rd gave a dinner for King Leopold II; they took him to a flower show at the botanical gardens on the 25th. He had lunch afterwards and went driving with Alexandra, calling several more times before going home on 1 June. On the 26th the Waleses attended a meeting at the Hanover Square Rooms about St George's Hospital's funds and later saw a fan exhibition at the South Kensington Museum. The Manchesters' ball was at Great Stanhope Street on the 27th. The next day Albert Edward's family watched him taking part in the Queen's birthday parade at Horse Guards. Alexandra later went driving with Mary Teck, who came to lunch on the 30th. That evening the Waleses dined with the Sutherlands, and the next day with the Buccleuchs. Ascot Races were approaching and Queen felt obliged to caution her son against having "that set about you whose names inspire no pleasure or confidence in those true and real friends of the throne and family, who have your welfare at heart." She trusted they would attend on Tuesday and Thursday only and, if possible, not both every year. All her true friends hoped they would cultivate "the really good, steady and distinguished people" instead of such as Lord Carrington and Oliver Montagu.[22] Albert Edward assured her that he entirely disapproved of what was bad about racing, but it was the national sport and people enjoyed their participation in it; the carriage procession up the course was regarded as a kind of annual pageant. Tuesdays and Thursdays were of course the great days, but if some of his party also wished to go on the other days, it would be uncivil not to accompany them.[23] However, Alexandra's Ascot attendance, in 37 of the years from 1863 to 1909, was invariably on Tuesdays and Thursdays, with drives, visits or river trips on other days.

On George's birthday, Alexandra asked Mary Teck; "can your little girl come and play with them after luncheon? I am going to Hallé's concert at three o'clock and I should be delighted if you liked to come with me!! and we might drive afterwards!! Try to come if you can, it would be such fun."[24] On the 6th, the Pall

Mall Gallery's Mr Thompson showed the Waleses Sir Noel Paton's[25] picture, *Mors Janua Vitae*. The next day it was Sir Anthony de Rothschild's[26] dinner and ball at Grosvenor Place, and the horse show at the Agricultural Hall on the 8th. Madame Madeleine Graver[27] played the piano to Alexandra on the 9th. On 13 June the whole family left to stay at Cooper's Hill, near Egham, for Ascot week; Alexandra wearing blue and black, while her sons were in sailor suits, with *Ariadne* in gold on the blue ribands round their straw hats. On the 21st the Prince and Princess of Wales visited Dulwich Picture Gallery and Dulwich College, where the Prince gave prizes; the state ball was later. The Mecklenburg-Strelitz couple lunched at Marlborough House on the 22nd and later the Waleses dined at Strawberry Hill. The Queen's garden party at Windsor on the 24th had buffets in St George's Hall and in tents, while music played.[28] The next day Albert Edward and Alexandra gave a garden party at Chiswick. Alexandra went to Henry Holmes'[29] concert at Stafford House on the 27th and on the 28th the Waleses dined with Maria, Marchioness of Ailesbury[30] at Hertford Street.

The Prince's household was changing. Herbert Fisher[31] had been promoted to Vice Warden of the Stanneries in the Duchy of Cornwall, earning more money for his growing family and the new private secretary would be Francis Knollys, "who has got a very good head, & is very hardworking, & acting conjointly with his Father, will be able to take a good deal off the General's hands." Maurice Holzmann would be Alexandra's private secretary.[32] The Waleses opened the new schools for Seamen's Children at Wellclose Square on the 30th; the next day, in the rain, (Alexandra wearing a pink silk dress with a white muslin skirt) they went to Reading, where the Prince laid the New Reading School's foundation stone. On 4 July they gave a ball at Marlborough House; on the 5th they laid the foundation stone of St Saviour's Church for Deaf and Dumb People in Oxford Street[33] and later attended the Austro–Hungarian ambassador's[34] dance at Belgrave Square. They gave a garden party at Chiswick on the 6th before the state concert at Buckingham Palace. After driving together on the 7th Albert Edward later took Alexandra, Eddy, George and little Louise to Dover, en route for Denmark. He was busy with engagements, but there was a problem. Count Bernsdorff,[35] the German Ambassador, had heard that, at the French Ambassador's[36] dinner, the Prince had told the Austro–Hungarian ambassador of his satisfaction that Prussia would lose the coming war with France. Bernsdorff had informed his government.[37] Albert Edward utterly denied saying any such thing, but admitted to the Queen on the 20th; "I am afraid that Alix' feelings are strongly agst Prussia; they have always been so since that unfortunate Danish war, & the war of 1866 has strengthened those feelings. As soon as I see her I shall caution her to be very careful about any opinion she expresses." Nevertheless, he thought Bernsdorff's actions ungentlemanlike and unjustifiable. He wrote again the next day, touched by his sisters' anxiety about the Franco–Prussian war, but reminding them "what the feelings of unfortunate little Denmark must have been when they heard that the Armies of Prussia & Austria were against them. Everybody must confess that that campaign was a war of aggression."

On 19 July Princesses Victoria (two) and Maud (seven months) went to stay with their grandmother at Osborne. Victoria was not happy; her father was sorry she had been naughty, "but everything & everybody is strange to her." He did not wish Maud's diet to be changed until Alexandra, convinced Victoria had been weaned too soon, returned. Later he added; "I daresay you will find Victoria disobedient, but she has rather a peculiar character & requires being treated with great kindness tho' firmness. She has been with Martin[38] more than the others, so that she has become rather <u>too</u> much accustomed to her."[39] Princess Beatrice told Lady Caroline Barrington; "I am sorry to say that Victoria is rather wilful, and very shy, but I hope in time she will like us better."[40] On the 22nd Albert Edward left for Denmark, bringing his family home on 2 August. Alexandra packed her luggage for Scotland and there were more calls and visits until, on the 8th, the family went to stay at Dupplin Castle,[41] continuing to Abergeldie on the 11th. The Queen, with Louise, Beatrice and Arthur, followed by Leopold and the little Wales girls, all arrived at Balmoral on the 18th. Alexandra drove with her several times and they all watched a cricket match between Balmoral and Abergeldie servants on 6 September. At dinner with the Queen on the 24th, the guests included the Earl of Fife, Lady Agnes Duff[42] and Viscount Macduff.[43] On 11 October, the Waleses and four children left for the Douglas Hotel in Edinburgh; they had retrieved Victoria but Maud had remained with the Queen. The Prince laid the foundation stone of the new Royal Infirmary in Edinburgh and joined his family in London (where they had arrived on the 14th) on the 18th.

On the 24th, Princess Louise's engagement to John Campbell, Marquess of Lorne[44] was announced, rather surprisingly as she had earlier turned him down. Albert Edward had been against the match; he liked Lorne personally but knew he was not well off and had heard rumours of his being practically engaged to another lady. Above all he was a commoner. The Queen had been considering a British marriage for her daughter and selected the Duke of Argyll's[45] family, whom Louise also liked. However, the Prince, through his experience of other royalties who had married "out" and their children, understood what difficulties these families, neither completely royal nor completely common, faced: the Duke of Cambridge, Mrs FitzGeorge[46] and their sons; Prince Edward of Saxe-Weimar and Countess Dornburg;[47] the Gleichens[48] and the Tecks and their families; the Battenbergs[49] and others; all had had problems. Albert Edward was not a snob; some of them were his friends, but he knew their status sometimes made life difficult for them and was reluctant for Louise to have the same experience, although he promised his support if she really wanted the marriage. Alexandra agreed, telling Louise, "At <u>last</u> I come to wish you joy of the great event! I must confess it took us rather by surprise as neither of us had thought you had made up your mind. Let me now wish you all possible happiness in your future, and may you never have cause to regret the step you have taken!" She had heard golden opinions everywhere about Lord Lorne, "altho' as my Bertie has already told you, you may have many difficulties to go through but only with <u>true</u> love and the deepest, deepest affection to the one you have chosen, you may look upon these as mere passing trifles." Almost anxiously she wrote "I hope you feel <u>very</u>, <u>very</u> happy!!!" She would always be her true friend "whatever may happen!" Maud was still with the Queen and Alexandra asked after "my darling 'wee baby'?" She missed her awfully, "but now if your Mama likes to keep her till we go to Sandringham she may with pleasure, as this nasty London air can't do her much good."[50]

Alexandra continued her drives until early November; Albert Edward stayed a week with the Londesboroughs,[51] and on the 7th the Christians and the Tecks came to lunch. By the 13th they were at the rebuilt Sandringham, where shooting began at the end of November; the Prince had been shooting at Heveningham, Merton, and Gunton earlier. On 1 December he gave the county ball in the new house, for Alexandra's birthday. Queen Victoria had returned to Windsor and the Waleses attended the mausoleum service on 14 December, reclaiming Maud. Back home on the 23rd there was shooting, Christmas, and skating on Boxing Day.

After the Tecks' brief visit in January 1871, the Wales family returned to London on 7 February. The couple attended the Queen's Opening of Parliament on the 9th, and Albert Edward later heard a debate in the House of Lords. With their three elder children and Arthur, they went to the matinee at Covent Garden on the 11th. Albert Edward attended the Household Brigade's field day at Wimbledon, and the couple gave a dinner party on the 18th. On the 20th, Frank Dillon[52] showed them two pictures of Cairo, painted for him by the Viceroy, and at the Queen's Court next day, Alexandra, like all the other ladies, wore mourning for Victoria's late cousin, Prince Dietrichstein of Nicolsburg.[53]

On 22 February the Waleses lunched with the Queen and the next day saw the art collection at Hertford House[54] with Louise. On the 25th, with their three elder children, they left for two days at Windsor. Alexandra called on Aunt Cambridge on the 28th and on 1 March it was Lord Fife's ball at Cavendish Square. Arthur and other relatives sometimes called at Marlborough House for lunch and on 4 March Albert Edward chaired a meeting there of the almost-completed Albert Hall's provisional committee. He and Alexandra dined later with the Granvilles[55] at the Foreign Office and visited the Old Masters' exhibition at Burlington House on the 6th. While her husband stayed briefly with Henry Chaplin at Lincoln, Alexandra went driving, dined with the Tecks at Kensington and went with Arthur to a philharmonic concert at St James's Hall on the 8th. Coote & Tinney's Quadrille Band played at the Waleses wedding anniversary ball. As usual, Albert Edward carried out many social engagements, while Alexandra, who was pregnant, went driving, received visitors at home and called on the Duchess of Inverness on 17 March. On the 21st the whole family attended Princess Louise's wedding the next day to the Marquess of Lorne in St George's Chapel, Windsor, followed by a dinner party and a concert in St George's Hall. On the 22nd it was the Turkish ambassador's dinner and ball at Bryanston Square, dinner with Aunt Cambridge on the 24th and a drawing room on the 28th.

On 29 March the Queen, with her family, opened the Royal Albert Hall of Arts and Sciences; Alexandra wearing ruby-coloured satin. Sir Michael Costa's[56] specially-composed Cantata was played at this splendid occasion. All went well, despite a noticeable echo, and most of the royalties left after the Cantata but the Waleses stayed for much of the miscellaneous concert that followed. Later they and Arthur visited Frederic Leighton's and John Everett Millais's[57] studios; Alexandra also went to R Pritchett's[58] Gallery of Danish drawings. She and her husband saw the Queen and Ernest II, who had come over for the Albert Hall opening, at Buckingham Palace next day. The Wales couple drove together and received a number of visitors; he also went riding and attended the 10th Hussars Steeplechase meeting, near Southall. As the new baby's birth seemed imminent, the family left for Sandringham on 4 April and Alexandra gave birth prematurely to her third son[59] at 2.45pm on the 6th; her husband was with her. Sadly the tiny baby was very feeble, but beautiful, with perfect little nails; he reminded Mrs Stonor of Prince George. He was in a critical state all day, cold and blue; Alexandra had him in bed with her, trying to keep him warm, but, despite all efforts, he was finally too weak even to swallow. Mr Onslow[60] read the christening service that evening, baptising him Alexander John Charles Albert, with water in a Russian cup, Minny's gift. The little Prince lingered, but died on 7 April, Good Friday. Albert Edward broke the news to Alexandra; they were both terribly upset.

Alexandra had sometimes felt tired and depressed during her pregnancy, but could not think what might have caused the premature birth. There was no real anxiety about her but she could not sleep during the night after the baby's death and the next day her eyes ached from weeping so much. By the 10th Mrs Stonor reported that she had slept better and was recovering her appetite; "I am quite sure that another time she will have to be very careful in the earlier part of the time. She sees her dear children every day, and they are very good, & quiet, when they are with her. She felt much affected when she first saw the two little Princes; she said it reminded her of the one she had lost." Albert Edward had cut off a little of the baby's hair, and placed it in her prayer book. He and Mrs Clarke prepared the body and the coffin; when it was ready, he asked Mrs Stonor "to come with him just to see how he had arranged it with his own hands." The little coffin was on a bed, covered with a white satin pall, with white flowers, mostly camellias, on top. "The poor Prince was so much affected; the tears were rolling down his cheeks – I did feel so much for him!" Several beautiful wreaths of roses, white azaleas and others were brought in. Alexandra had slept badly but was awake at 11.30 on the 11th; she was not going to the funeral at Sandringham Church but particularly wanted Mrs Stonor to do so. She was calmer than expected and asked Mrs Clarke to draw the curtains so that she could see the little procession, with her husband and their three sons, from her bed. Once it was out of sight, she took her prayer book and asked to be left by herself until the mourners came back.[61] It was a dull, chilly day and the sad cortège moved silently from the house to the church, watched by estate workers, cottagers, and school children dressed in the scarlet capes which were Alexandra's New Year's gifts. Albert Edward, Eddy and George walked by the coffin, with the two doctors and a number of servants, including the children's governess, Miss Brown.[62] After the service, the tiny coffin was placed in the vault under the east window, which was at once bricked up; the tombstone would be visible from Sandringham's grounds. The court was already in black for Queen Louise of Sweden and Norway[63] but now there would be deeper mourning for ten days from 10 April.

In eight years of marriage, Alexandra had had six children, perhaps with planning, as there were fairly regular intervals between births. Queen Victoria's first six children had been born in nine years. Alexandra's parents had six children, as, eventually, did her sisters. The Wales children were close enough in age to be good companions; perhaps this was a factor, but despite Alexandra's innate good health, the high birth-rate was exhausting. Her serious illness in 1867–8 may have compromised her daughters' wellbeing; they certainly did not reach a robust old age.[64] Alexandra led an extremely active life and it had caught up with her. On 10 April Dr Farre "had a very long & serious talk with the Prince, about the Future and perfect rest, & he says the Prince quite agreed with him in all he said, in fact Dr Farre said it had been a most satisfactory conversation."[65] There were no more children; Albert Edward cherished his wife. However, frustrated with the trivial official duties which seemed to be his lot, he could not resist the attractions of other women.[66]

By 12 April Alexandra could smile again, had recovered from a cough and eaten a good lunch. The little floral cross which had been on the coffin during the funeral was at the foot of her bed and Albert Edward had arranged for a cruciform flower-bed, planted with lilac, heartsease and white-leaved plants, with primroses and violets round the grave's enclosure. Mrs Stonor told the Queen how affectionately Alexandra spoke of her and how she prized the little locket the Queen had sent her.[67] Albert Edward returned to London on the 25th for levees and the Royal Academy banquet, with Uncle Hans, perhaps one of the baby's sponsors. This kindly, unassuming man quietly offered support by staying with Albert Edward and accompanying him on various engagements and visits. As Freemasons, they attended several Masonic events together. They returned to Sandringham on 2 May but were both back in London on the 8th for the season; Alexandra stayed at Sandringham with the children until the 20th. Arthur, recovering from an accident, then went driving with her several times. She and her uncle visited Madame Jerichau's exhibition at the Danish Galleries in New Bond Street on 26 May. On the 27th Albert Edward and Uncle Hans met Grand Duke Vladimir of Russia[68] at Victoria Station; he accompanied the Wales couple to the Opera Comique on the 30th and Covent Garden Opera on 3 June and on the 5th joined the Ascot party at Titness Park. The Waleses and Uncle Hans visited the Home for Little Boys at Horton Kirby; shortly afterwards the Prince and his uncle-in-law attended a charity dinner for it at the Freemasons' Tavern. On the 13th the Prince and Princess of Wales gave a dinner party for Vladimir and received Napoleon III and Empress Eugénie two days later. Alexandra had resumed attending events such as dinners, a *conversazione* at the South Kensington Museum, a state concert and a flower show. Her uncle left on the 18th; his presence had comforted her, although she never forgot the baby's death. On the 21st, the Wales couple and the Duke of Edinburgh saw the Queen open St Thomas's Hospital; later the couple watched the Household Brigade play the Rifle Brigade at Prince's Cricket Ground in Hans Place. The next day Alexandra heard Hallé's concert at St James's Hall and on the 23rd the Wales family, including their sons, four-year-old Louise and almost-three-year-old Victoria attended a garden party at Buckingham Palace.

On 24 June the couple saw Louis Desange's picture of their wedding procession and his portrait of the late Lord Derby, before visiting the Brownlows[69] at Ashridge for two days. Afterwards they took Vladimir to the Crystal Palace; the next day they visited Edgar Boehm's[70] studio and, later, a state ball. They gave a garden party at Chiswick on 29 June, attended the Queen's Review in Bushey Park the next day and also called on the Emperor and Empress of Brazil[71] at Claridges. After staying with the Queen at Windsor, they, with Louise and Lorne, visited St Bartholomew's Hospital on 4 July; the Prince chaired a meeting of the Court of Governors. Alexandra and Mary Teck visited the Alexandra Institute for the Blind and the International Exhibition of Blind Industries in Bloomsbury on the 5th; the next day the Waleses attended Harrow School's "Speech Day". The Prussians had arrived and called at Marlborough House; in the evening it was the Waverley Ball at Willis's Rooms, raising money to finish the Scott[72] Monument in Edinburgh. Guests came in Scott's-novel-inspired costume; Albert Edward as Lord of the Isles[73] and Alexandra as Mary, Queen of Scots.[74]

The next day they gave another garden party at Chiswick, which the Queen attended. After giving a family lunch and being photographed by Arthur Melhuish[75] on 8 July, the family left on the 10th, for the continent. Alexandra and the children stayed at Bad Kissingen, to restore her health and spirits, and her husband called at Darmstadt before returning to London on the 24th. After Goodwood and Osborne, he travelled to Dublin on the 31st with Arthur, Louise and Lorne, for the Agricultural Show and annual banquet of the Royal Agricultural Society of Ireland, of which he was president. Lord Spencer[76] hoped the Waleses would spend more time in Ireland, deeply regretted Alexandra's current absence and added an extravagant compliment; "her [Royal Highness's] face, her name, her influence always act as a magical spell over those she meets ... and of this I can assure you, no people know better how to appreciate a noble character, especially when God has given it such a beautiful form, as Irishmen."[77] Sycophancy perhaps, but Alexandra often had this effect on people, and not just in Ireland. Later, Albert Edward joined his family at Rumpenheim, including Queen Louise and Princess Thyra, "the grown-up young lady, extremely charming, the eyes very fine";[78] 18-year-old Thyra was on an educational tour in Germany, Italy and Greece. They and Mary Teck walked in the garden and watched the children playing in the courtyard and bowling. On 18 August the Waleses left for the Passion Play at Oberammergau. The Prince then moved on elsewhere, while Alexandra returned to Rumpenheim on the 22nd, so that she and Thyra could celebrate their mother's birthday on 7 September. Thyra and Queen Louise later travelled to Venice and then Greece, arriving there on 10 October.[79]

At Balmoral, Queen Victoria had had a sore throat and an abscess, followed by rheumatism. After returning home, spending two weeks at Aldershot manoeuvres and then being photographed by Bassano[80] the Prince left for Scotland on the 25th, and visited his mother on arrival the next day. Alexandra and her children joined him a few days later. The Hesse family were also at Balmoral and they, with Leopold and Beatrice, went to the ball at Abergeldie on the 4th. On the 17th the Queen gave a ball for tenants and servants on the Balmoral, Abergeldie and Birkhall estates, attending for a short time in an invalid chair. Leaving Balmoral and then staying at Drumlanrig Castle,[81] the Waleses arrived home on 21 October. Alexandra drove, while the Prince shot in Windsor Great Park and Richmond Park; they dined with Alfred at Clarence House on the 27th. They all visited the 19th annual winter exhibition at the French Gallery in Pall Mall, and Messrs H Graves showed the couple two pictures by M M de Zichy,[82] painter to the Russian emperor. Arthur lunched at Marlborough House on the 30th and the next day the couple left for Scarborough, to visit the Londesboroughs.

Back at home on 4 November, the couple invited the Hessians to dinner, and during the next few days saw R Pritchett's portfolio of drawings of Paris in May

1871. Frank Dillon brought a picture of Cairo, commissioned by the Viceroy. On the 5th, the Hessians again dined and accompanied the Waleses to the Globe Theatre. The next day, they all, with Alfred, left for Sandringham, although the Hesse children, who had whooping cough, remained at Buckingham Palace. In Norfolk the three princes went riding and shooting; Uncle George arrived during the afternoon. Alexandra and Alice walked in the grounds and visited the baby's grave. Albert Edward was 30 on 9 November, but because it was the county ball at Swaffham that evening, his birthday ball was held on the 10th instead. On the 13th he felt feverish and Alexandra sent for Dr Gull. She was doing all she could for her husband but her deafness was hampering her and Alice, with sharp ears and nursing experience, decided to stay for the present.[83] Doctors Gull, Clayton[84] and Jenner diagnosed a low typhoid fever, which declared itself on the 20th. Dr Lowe had also arrived. It was a nasty attack but without unfavourable symptoms; the Prince was quietly maintaining his strength. The household became used to the doctors and all liked Gull, who was "serious but not dry, and full of information & philosophy, and a gentleman" while Clayton was "a beast, free and easy to an unbearable extent, & perpetually prating, with or without encouragement." Alexandra and the household all detested him and even Albert Edward was getting irritated, with Clayton going into his bedroom at will and chattering, when he wanted to be quiet. Clayton was "<u>civilly</u> dispensed with" on the 23rd. Alexandra had a bed made up for herself in her husband's dressing room but could not sleep; Lady Macclesfield and Gull wanted her to have a room further away, lest she get ill from lack of rest.[85] Meanwhile the Queen returned to Windsor where, on the 27th, the Wales and Hesse children were sent.

The fever increased; one day Albert Edward told the nurse it would be the turning point and, if he recovered, he would lead a very different life. Sometimes he raved alarmingly and all sorts of revelations and names came out. In his delirium he told Alexandra he was sure she would desert him now, because he had neglected her.[86] She was behaving admirably; "She does not disguise the truth from herself, but her self-control and composure are perfect; she never thinks of herself, but is always with him, excepting when she goes out for air, & meals, or when he is asleep." She was just as gentle and considerate to everybody as usual, but "it goes to one's heart to see her 'going about like a ghost' as they say."[87] Although there still seemed no cause for alarm, the Queen arrived on the 29th. Alexandra had written to Louise in the highest anxiety, "sitting near his bedside while writing as he seems to like to see me about him. To me it seems like a bad dream, having my own darling laid up. I wished it was me instead – I can't <u>bear</u> to see him suffering so, how willingly I would change with him!"[88] On the 29th, the last three days had been terrible "as he was <u>so very</u>, <u>very</u> bad my darling husband! The fever was <u>so high</u> and he was perfectly <u>delirious</u>, at times he did not even know me, and the day before yesterday, I was hardly allowed to nurse him or go to him at all, which was <u>too awful</u>!! He called me his 'good boy' and when once I told him that I was his little wife he said 'that <u>was</u> once but is <u>no more</u> – you have broken your vows!' as he thinks occasionally I have left him altogether." She trusted to God's mercy and Albert Edward's youth and strength, "but I <u>have been</u> – oh! so wretchedly anxious and unhappy!"[89] The Prince did indeed remember her birthday, but a day too late. "What a shame not to have told me" he exclaimed. Alexandra, despite everything, remembered that Lady Macclesfield's birthday was on 2 December and gave her a coloured photograph of herself and a silver-mounted crystal watch. It seemed the Prince was beginning to recover[90] and, writing on the 3rd to her sons to thank them for their good wishes on her birthday, which had been a sad one, as poor Papa was so ill, Alexandra asked them to pray for him every morning and evening, to be good and obedient boys and to work hard at their lessons.[91] She signed herself "your loving Mama"; in other letters it was "your loving Mama Alix". The name "Motherdear", so much associated with her later, had started by 1874, when she used it during a letter.

Lady Macclesfield told her husband on the 7th that really the best thing would be for the couple to be alone together; "He depends on her for his feeding and everything & it is an opportunity not to be lost. But how Princess Alice is to be rooted out is not easy to see. I shall have a great deal to tell you on that subject; suffice it to say for the moment that she is the most <u>awful</u> storyteller I ever encountered, meddling, jealous and mischief-making. For a short time she is everything that is charming, but the less one knows of her the better. I think you will be much entertained by all the stories I shall have to tell you when we meet. Our Princess is so true and so honourable in the middle of it all! But we are all furious at seeing her sat upon and spoken of as if she had not sense enough to act for herself."[92] The Queen returned to Windsor, receiving constant telegrams about her son. They heard of other typhoid cases; the Duke of Beaufort's groom, who had been at Londesborough Lodge during the Waleses visit, and also Alexandra's outrider at Sandringham, Charles Blegg, although he had not been at Londesborough. It was not clear where the Prince could have caught it but he was fluctuating between quiet days and nights, restlessness, rising fever and utter prostration. On the 8th he was struggling for breath; they feared he would die if he did not rally within the next hour. Alexandra telegraphed that news to her parents; she herself kept up heroically. Albert Edward was sleepy but still alive; that evening, Alexandra ran out after dark to pray for him in church.[93] She stayed with him and on the 10th "after hanging over him almost all night has had no sleep today." She had, however, managed to eat some lunch, which bolstered her courage and hope.[94] It was serious; the Queen returned, Alfred and Louise were there and Arthur was expected soon. On the 10th prayers were said for the Prince in St Paul's Cathedral. He seemed quieter that morning and Alexandra, who could hardly be persuaded to leave him, although Alice was also there, told

Mr Onslow; "My husband being, thank God, somewhat better, I am coming to church. I must leave, I fear, before the service is concluded, that I may watch by his bedside. Can you not say a few words in prayer in the early part of the service that I may join with you in prayer for my husband before I return to him?"[95] She left quietly by a side door after the prayer.

By the 11th Albert Edward was very restless; breathless, delirious, talking loudly and incessantly in French, English and German, singing, whistling and laughing wildly. It was "perfectly horrible" and Alexandra was by his side almost constantly, except when she fell asleep from exhaustion. "It is enough to haunt her to her last day, or to kill her outright!" The worst was that there had never been a chance for a prayer or for the Prince to prepare himself for what seemed certain death.[96] His family were gathering; Leopold and Beatrice had arrived on the 10th. Alice had telegraphed to Queen Louise; "my poor brother is very bad, depend on me I shall not leave darling Alix if the worst happens."[97] On the morning of the 11th the household and servants were all called so early that candles had to be lit; Leopold went past a line of attendants in their dressing gowns, to join the family in his brother's dressing room. "It was too dreadful to see the poor Queen sitting in the bedroom behind a screen, listening to his ravings. I can't tell you what a deep impression the scene made on me." In everyone's mind was the Prince Consort's fatal illness, exactly ten years earlier. What struck Leopold particularly "was the noble & truly angelic self[less] devotion of my sister-in-law, she left her husband neither day or night & did everything for him; one evening when I went in for the first time to see him, he was of course still quite unconscious, & she was stroking his hair & bending over him with her lovely pale face, I think I never saw a more beautiful picture, she looked like an angel from heaven."[98] At one point on the 12th, Alexandra was told it would be bad for her husband if she went in at a particular time, so she crawled in, to be near him without him seeing her.[99]

On the 12th Gull pronounced the Prince's breathing easier and his pulse higher; whereupon "this extraordinary family party were all elated – 'So much better' – really likely to turn the corner now! and so on, so they went to bed quite happy." But Lady Macclesfield and Mrs Hardinge awoke, as they had feared, to worse news. Bulletins came every hour, "rather weaker" "upon which Pss Louise says 'No, really? How dreadful', turns round and goes to sleep again! They are wonderful. Pss Alice does feel it dreadfully, but of the brothers poor Prince Leopold seems to be the only one who is [in] the least impressed! The laughing and noise that goes on when the rest get together is very jarring, and all the various comments upon probabilities are so wearing when one's heart is so utterly sick!" If the worst happened, Lady Macclesfield thought the Queen was the only one who would be of any comfort to Alexandra. On the evening of the 13th, Victoria was with her son and he remarked "That lady is very like the Queen – the image of her." Gull told him that it was indeed she, "whereupon the

Prince asked, 'Does she know I have had a very bad fever, but that I am better now'. And then he said to her that it was very kind of her to come & look after him, and said, with his usual civility, 'But it is not right that you should be standing by my bedside.' So she sits holding his hand, and, poor thing, we are so glad, as the recognition will be such a comfort to her! late though it comes." Albert Edward's mind wandered; he was weakening and the end was expected on the 13th or the 14th. Alexandra was wretched, as he had not really been aware of her lately. His brothers were all in low spirits, "having indulged in too much hope last night", while Lady Macclesfield felt as though pendulums were banging inside her head.[100]

But on 14 December, the hallowed, terrible anniversary, there was an almost miraculous change. Albert Edward was less troubled, had slept quietly and his symptoms were abating. However, "the Royal brothers and sisters are the most extraordinary set of beings I ever encountered … Last night Dr Gull sent them all away to ensure perfect quiet and I believe they profited by the opportunity to have a grand quarrel among themselves! when he was lying between life & death." There were squabbles, jealousy and little plots. The house was full but Louis of Hesse was coming, while Lorne did not know whether to come or not.[101] At Windsor, the mausoleum wreaths were ready but all the senior members of the Royal Family were at Sandringham. It thus fell to the children, none of whom had known their grandfather personally, to place the wreaths round his tomb on 14 December. The eldest, Victoria of Hesse, was only eight.

Albert Edward had a peaceful night; recovery would be slow but his appetite was good. Alexandra was cheerful whenever a hopeful change occurred. The others had all been shut out of his dressing room, causing "a grand row". Lady Macclesfield had never seen "such a disunited and unreserved family. Everything that everybody says is repeated all over the house, especially if it is abusive & likely to stir up strife. And the way in which some of them repeat the dreadful things the Prince says in his delirium, is horrible, laughing at it as a good joke! before the servants or anybody!" They had all reacted badly but most of them had gone by 16 December, leaving the house feeling wonderfully quiet; "a welcome calm after the storm, in every sense!" Lady Macclesfield was horrified when Princess Alice, after a conversation about providence, "burst out; 'Providence, there is no providence, no nothing – and I can't think how anybody can talk such rubbish.' Imagine having to struggle through all this, without any trust in God to support one! I am told the Princess Royal is an utter atheist also. Our dear Princess does believe and pray, I am thankful to say! and she finds comfort in so doing."[102] Although very weak, Albert Edward was gaining strength and his mother felt able to return to Windsor on the 19th. A service was held at the mausoleum on the 23rd, in gratitude not only for Prince Albert's life but for his son's recovery. Sadly, Charles Blegg died and was buried on the 21st; he was only twenty and had always performed his duties well. Alexandra and the household, who were represented at the service, watched his funeral procession pass the house. She wrote to her sons on the 23rd, with thanks for their letters, Christmas good wishes and happy thoughts of reunion, as "darling Papa is going to be quite well again."[103] She would shortly tell Dalton that, once at home, the boys would "<u>entirely</u> leave the nursery" for their education and care to advance to a new level.[104] Queen Victoria spent Christmas at Windsor for the first time since 1860 but returned two days later, to find her son much better. Alexandra and Alice went to see another typhoid case at West Newton, a laundress named Mrs Dodman, on the 29th. The Queen sent a message of thanks, on behalf of Alexandra and herself, for universal sympathy during the crisis and a distressful year ended more hopefully than had seemed possible.

As 1872 began, little was happening, apart from a messenger arriving with letters from Minny in Russia. Albert Edward, now cared for just by Alexandra and the professional nurses, was well enough to leave his room by 8 January and by the 14th was so much better that bulletins ceased. By the 23rd the Prince and Princess were taking afternoon drives, once to enquire after Mrs Dodman. The Prince wanted to know how she was, and although unable to leave the carriage, sent her kind messages. She also was recovering. On the 25th Albert Edward walked outside for the first time and went to Park House to see General Knollys, returning by carriage. He was seeing members of his household, receiving congratulations on his recovery and overseeing estate business, instructing his staff to prepare stock from his farm to compete at the forthcoming Norfolk Agricultural Society's exhibition at Lynn. The Queen was sending sermons and articles inspired by his recovery and the Waleses read them together. She was not altogether in favour of the public thanksgiving which had been mooted. Alexandra sympathised; "I <u>do not</u> either like it <u>myself</u>, for it seems to me also to be making too much of an <u>outward show</u> of the most sacred and solemn feelings of one's heart, and I quite agree that a <u>simpler</u> and more private service would be more in accordance with one's <u>own</u> wishes. But then on the other hand the <u>whole Nation</u> has taken such a public share in <u>our</u> sorrow; it has been so entirely <u>one</u> with us in our grief, that it may perhaps feel it <u>has</u> a kind of <u>claim</u> to join with us now in a <u>public</u> and <u>universal</u> thanksgiving."[105]

On 4 February, the couple attended part of the church service and, on horseback, watched part of the West Norfolk Hunt's meet on the 7th, offering hospitality after the hunt. Alexandra could not hide her feelings from Louise; "You can hardly think <u>how</u> happy I am <u>now</u> – everything seems bright and beautiful around me, which only <u>so</u> short ago threatened to become <u>dark for ever</u>!! ... You would hardly <u>know</u> me now in my happiness. We are <u>never</u> apart, and are now enjoying our <u>second</u> 'honeymoon'. <u>Never, never</u> can I ever thank

God enough for all His mercy to me, when He listened to my prayers and gave me back my <u>life's happiness</u>!! My own darling is thank God getting stronger every day, and is looking well tho' pale and thinner, which suits him well." They would join the children at Osborne later, after more than two months.[106] On the 10th they left for Windsor and toured the mausoleum, farms and gardens: Albert Edward's pilgrimage to his father's domain, after surviving the illness which had taken his father away. Hills & Saunders, from Eton, took the first photographs of the couple together since the Prince's illness. They left for Osborne on the 12th; met their sons and Leopold on *Alberta* at Gosport and stayed till the 26th, riding, driving, spending time with the Queen and their family and visiting the scenes of Albert Edward's childhood. The Queen told Vicky; "Dear Bertie looks vy delicate; vy pale & thin & drawn, walks slowly, still a little lame, but is very cheerful & quite himself, only gentler & kinder than ever, & there is something different, wh I can't exactly express. It is like a new life; all the trees & flowers give him pleasure as they never used to do, & he was quite pathetic over his small wheelbarrow & little Tools at the Swiss Cottage. He is constantly with Alix & they seem hardly ever apart! I am sure he is less strong than he likes to appear."[107]

On the 26th they returned to London for the thanksgiving service at St Paul's Cathedral the next day, and general rejoicing. The doctors had agreed the Prince was well enough to attend, despite a slightly swollen leg. People saw him limping but looking healthy, Alexandra was wearing fur-trimmed blue velvet, and their sons were there too. Albert Edward later told his mother how touched he had been at "the feeling that was displayed in those crowded streets" and how glad at being able to take part in the ceremony; although tired, with a painful leg, he was less weary than expected, although Alexandra was exhausted and had a headache.[108] He received more messages, including congratulations from the Lord Mayor and Corporation. The Queen visited the Waleses on the 28th and 1 March and they received more callers and went driving. The doctors recommended spring in southern Europe, as the Prince still needed warmer weather to set him up fully before beginning public duties again. Ponsonby[109] also raised, with the Queen, the question of employment; Albert Edward wanted an occupation, perhaps being attached to government offices and learning departmental business, but not an appointment in Ireland, as had been suggested.[110] Visitors called and on 8 March the couple saw Nash's[111] sketch of the thanksgiving service. While they were away, their children would stay partly with the Queen at Windsor and partly at Chiswick House. They left on the 9th for Paris with their suite, including George Poore,[112] a young doctor who had previously attended Leopold. They arrived on the 10th at the Hotel Bristol, which Poore found very comfortable, with his own bedroom and sitting room. Everyone breakfasted in their own rooms, lunched together (the Waleses lunched alone together) and all met at dinner. Poore did not think his patient would require very close attention. "He is really very well & all I expect to have to do is to stand by in case I am wanted."[113] Everyone was pleasant and kind and the Prince "extraordinary for the amount of consideration he has for others." He was so much better that they were driving, socialising and attending the theatre, but Paris was in a sad state, especially in the Place Vendôme, near the hotel, with burned-out ruins everywhere.[114]

They left on the 13th for Marseilles, "& after our arrival … & after we had had dinner, my Royal patient, to show you of what he is capable, took us all to the Theatre, where we were till past midnight, & when we went to bed we had been up & travelling for 41 hours."[115] In beautiful warm weather they reached Cannes and then Nice, staying at the Hotel Angleterre. The couple attended the English church, full of people wanting to see them, and at the theatre on the 16th there was an ovation, with "God Save the Queen" and the Danish hymn being played. Alexandra had been "literally smothered in flowers. Last night for instance the Prefect came to the box and gave her about 2lbs weight of flowers made into a bouquet, & very beautifully made too, of about 18 inches in diameter, they were Violets, Camellias and Jasmine. This must have been the 9th or 10th bouquet for that day." They wanted to see Rome, but the doctors distrusted its climate; Sir William Gull told Poore on 17 March that marsh fever was very likely if they succumbed to the hot sun and chilly, damp evenings.[116] Undeterred, Albert Edward's party proceeded there briskly via Monaco, Mentone and Genoa. They met King Victor Emmanuel II[117] and Crown Prince Umberto[118] on the 25th and on the 27th, the Pope, "a dear old man", of 80 who looked only 60.[119] They visited studios, galleries and sights, such as the Coliseum and Forum illuminated with bright blue, red and violet lights, but there was typhoid and diphtheria about and on 2 April Poore begged the Prince to leave. King Christian, Queen Louise, Thyra, Waldemar and Prince John had arrived on 17 March and spent Easter week with them; as Mrs Grey told the Queen; "Your Majesty can easily fancy how very happy the dear Princess is to be with her own family again."[120] On 9 April they went to Florence in the pouring rain, Albert Edward extremely well, but Alexandra rather tired, with a sore throat. The Danish party, now at the Hotel Cavour at Milan, planned to go home but by the 16th Thyra was obviously unwell; her parents thought it was just a cold, but Poore was convinced it was typhoid fever, caught in Rome, and he was right.[121]

The rooms at the Hotel Cavour became a temporary hospital and, with the Prince's sanction, Poore became Thyra's doctor, assisted by Dr Sapolini, the court physician. Alexandra had sent for Mrs Jones and, assisted by her recent typhoid-nursing experience, was constantly in her sister's sickroom, but Poore was afraid this might put the Prince at risk from infection and implored him, on the 18th, to leave the hotel. So they left for Venice, while Poore tended Thyra, with ultimate success. Alexandra was unhappy at leaving her[122] but, corresponding with Poore from the Hotel Danielli in Venice, the Prince was glad that the girl's health was improving. They were enjoying Venice but it rained, seemingly every afternoon; they had decided to leave on the 28th for Verona and then return to Milan for two or three nights at the hotel[123] to check on Thyra's progress. Meanwhile, Mrs Jones had arrived; "a great treasure, an excellent nurse but rather inclined to overfeed. HRH I hear had tea and toast every day of his illness!!"[124] wrote Poore. In addition to medical duties, he had to telegraph and write daily about Thyra to the Queen and the Prince. The hotel was now "swarming with Royalty"; the Danes, the Nassaus[125] and the Crown Prince of Hanover[126] and the Waleses were expected back on the 29th. Writing to their children from Venice, Albert Edward was pleased the boys' riding had improved "& I hope that when we come back you will both be able to ride quite alone. You will be glad to hear that dear Aunty Thyra is much better & tomorrow we go to Milan, where she is. Papa misses Eddy & George, & also dear Louise, Victoria and Maud, very much, & hopes to find you all very much grown on our return."[127] Alexandra suggested it "would please dear Apapa and Amama if both Eddy and Georgie were to write a few lines to tell them how sorry you are [about Aunty Thyra]." She had been watching the tame pigeons, which came in at the window "and eat bread and peas from the flour."[128] On 28 April Poore, now "regularly transferred" to the Danes, told his mother the King was "a very nice, kind, quiet man and the Queen is a good-looking, clever, pretty little woman, and although 54 looks more like 34. The whole of the Danish Royal Family are remarkably kind, quiet, homely people and their affection for each other is something really extraordinary. I do not know any private families who always seem so perfectly happy in the society of each other."[129] Alexandra thanked Lady Caroline Barrington for progress reports; the boys' tutor was with them and "I am so glad that you like Mr Dalton,[130] and I am sure he is an excellent man well suited for our little boys, who are really fond of him! I am so glad they are such good obedient boys while we are away. All I meant about them not going sightseeing too much, was, I think, while in the Country, they need not go so much to London etc also, because I think they will otherwise be bored when we return if we don't let them do the same; flower shows or anything like it, they may see with pleasure, also visit their Aunt Cambridge and Kew Gardens."[131]

They had gone next to Cadenabbia but the Prince reported on 9 May that, except for one morning, it had never stopped raining and Alexandra had a stiff neck and rheumatism in the shoulder. Abandoning their plan to visit Lakes Lugano and Maggiore, where it was just as bad, they had "decided on returning to Milan tomorrow for a few days, prior to our departure for Turin, fr whence we propose going to Geneva on our way home." It seemed the best thing to do; they had intended being out all day long, but the weather made this uncomfortable and there was the risk of colds, rheumatism or sore throats.[132] However,

Alexandra seemed better than she had for a long time, probably because of the quiet life and early bed time; Mrs Grey almost fancied she had grown "a <u>little</u> fatter".[133] So, reassured about Thyra's health, they left for Geneva, from where Poore wrote on the 19th, after accompanying the Danes there. Thyra was still convalescing under his watchful eye, but a Danish doctor arrived, freeing him to accompany the Waleses back to England.[134] In gratitude[135] King Christian invested Poore with the Order of the Dannebrog,[136] and the Danish Royal Family always showed him friendship. King Christian and Waldemar returned to Denmark on 25 May, but Queen Louise and Thyra did not get home until 28 June, as the girl needed longer to regain her strength. The Wales couple left on 23 May, arriving in Paris the next day; they received callers, attended the theatre and the Exhibition of Fine Arts in the Palace of Industry on the 25th, gave a grand dinner on the 28th, received the French president, Adolphe Thiers[137] on the 30th and arrived home on 1 June.

The return to public life was immediate; the Waleses and their sons visited the horse show at the Agricultural Hall; Albert Edward presided at the Rifle Brigade's annual dinner on 3 June and left for a few days at Great Yarmouth on the 4th, while Alexandra attended Sir James Lacaita's[138] lecture about Vesuvius at Stafford House and also drove and received visitors. On the 10th the whole family left for Ascot week at Titness Park. On the 17th it was a military concert at the Albert Hall, for the Royal Cambridge Asylum for Soldiers' Widows. On the 18th they left for Sandringham and the Norfolk Agricultural Show, but were back by the 21st for the state ball. On the 24th they opened the Bethnal Green Museum on behalf of the Queen. With their three eldest children, they attended Alfred's garden party at Clarence House, later driving with Aunt Cambridge. They lunched with the Queen at Windsor on the 26th and saw the Hampshire and Berkshire Society's Agricultural Exhibition in the Home Park. Later, it was the state concert. On the evening of the 28th, they saw some of the galleries at the London International Exhibition and witnessed the building being lit up. On 2 and 9 July they gave garden parties at Chiswick and on the 3rd visited a bazaar at Knightsbridge Barracks' Riding School for the Convalescent Hospital at Black Rock, with a state ball later. The Prince and Princess called on the French imperial couple at Chislehurst on the 4th, later holding a concert at Marlborough House. The next day they attended the Queen's Review and Field Day at Aldershot. They went to the Wigans'[139] farewell performance at Drury Lane on the 6th and opened St Bartholomew's Hospital's Convalescent Home at Highgate on 8 July. On the 10th the Prince held a meeting of the Royal Commissioners of the Exhibition of 1851 at Marlborough House; on the 11th Alexandra laid the foundation stone of the new Hospital for Sick Children in Great Ormond Street. After a military concert at the Albert Hall on the 12th, the Eton and Harrow match at Lord's Cricket Ground and more social events, the Marlborough House Ball was held on the 17th. On the 20th, with Arthur, they attended a review at

Wimbledon, where Alexandra also gave prizes to the winners at the National Rifle Association meeting. She received Mr Müller, who showed her some of his miniatures on porcelain and ivory.

In early July Ponsonby had told the Queen that the Prince seemed to be "getting tired of balls and parties and would like any business whatever, which gave him an interest and an excuse to get away from them."[140] She thought he had the power to influence society but tended to be led astray through his good nature and by taking sides.[141] Ponsonby thought his way of life was now becoming ingrained and difficult to throw off, but as he had been forced to abstain from public business, he was almost compelled to fall back upon trivia and should be given the chance to take on more official duties before he lost the impetus to do so. Events were now more public than ever before; everyone could find out what everyone else was doing and scandals had serious political effects when connected with a well-known name.[142] Albert Edward agreed; during his illness he had vowed to live differently and be of use. Society was a treadmill; he and Alexandra were often exhausted by all their activities.

Writing lengthily to the Queen, Alexandra mentioned recent difficult events involving Mrs Clarke, the midwife, and, defending her, noted that Alice, who had had her fourth daughter in June,[143] had appreciated her assistance. Mrs Clarke had no bookings and nothing to do until December. Alexandra felt sorry for her and wanted to help; "I really do wish I could do something for her – but what I don't know!! Unless to please her, I could be confined at once!!! which I am happy to say there is not the slightest chance of as yet!" She was feeling tired after the season; they were longing for a little rest and country air and were looking forward to Osborne. However, the main purport of the letter was to beg permission to go to Denmark, where Minny was staying. Albert Edward would be away and they wondered whether the Queen would lend Alexandra *Osborne*. Just now it was very sultry in London and a tremendous thunderstorm had made it feel "exactly like hot steam". Alexandra could hardly hold her pen, she was so hot.[144] The Queen was not in favour of this visit and her son told her how disappointed Alexandra was. Minny could not, as the Queen had suggested, come to England, as the Emperor had only given her permission to be in Denmark for a short time, and she was there without her husband.[145] On 25 July the Waleses and their sons saw pupils from the Metropolitan District Unions' Training Ships and Pauper Schools, in the Horticultural Gardens, before the Prince gave them banners in the Albert Hall. Calling on Aunt Cambridge and the Tecks[146] and chairing a meeting of the commissioners for the Vienna Exhibition of 1873, Albert Edward later took his family to Osborne Cottage.

By 4 August the Queen had relented about Denmark; thanking her, Alexandra pressed the point further. She would like to take all five children. The couple agreed that, having been so much apart from their parents recently it would not be to the boys' advantage to be left with the tutor again; Dalton should go with them, so that they would not miss any lessons. It was so much easier to take them now than when they were older and less able to interrupt their studies. Another reason for going was that Alexandra wished to consult a doctor in Denmark about her health.[147] Reluctantly, on the 5th, the Queen agreed; she could not approve the journey but, as her daughter-in-law was so bent on it, she would not oppose it, provided that Alexandra would not consult the new doctor without asking the English doctors' opinions; and that she would only leave for Denmark when the Prince left Osborne and was not due to return there. The holiday should only be for two or three weeks, including travelling time. The Queen did not approve of taking all the children; it would unsettle the boys and little Maud was still not completely well, and might suffer. However, she would not refuse her consent, commenting rather tartly, "I perfectly understand your being attached to your own Home, & longing to see your Parents and *Geschwister*,[148] but excepting Minny you have seen all so lately that I had not thought you would expect to go there now."[149] Brought up in the country where she had been born, would later rule, and remained after marriage,[150] the Queen was occasionally impatient of Alexandra's homesickness, finding her own large family rather oppressive and marvelling at Alexandra's utter devotion to hers.

The Queen left for Balmoral, the Prince went for a cruise on the Duke of St Albans' schooner, and later, to Crichel, while Alexandra took the children to Denmark on the royal yacht, commanded by Ernest Leiningen. He told the Queen the Danish Royal Family were very happy at Bernstorff; like Dr Poore he had never seen so large a family where they were all so truly fond of one another.[151] By the 27th they were still enjoying life there; Alexandra had also visited the Copenhagen Exhibition. They returned on 14 September and were met by "Papa" at Charing Cross. On the 16th they left for Scotland, staying at Blair Castle, and reaching Abergeldie on the 23rd, but next day there was sad news; the Queen's half-sister had died. The Queen was grief-stricken when the Waleses saw her on the 25th. There was a memorial service for Feodore in Victoria's private apartments on the 27th and sadness overshadowed the holiday. The couple left in mid-October for a few days at Chillingham Castle,[152] leaving the children at Abergeldie. They all arrived at Marlborough House on the 19th and on the 28th it was announced that the Reverend JN Dalton, MA, of Clare College, Cambridge, had been appointed tutor to Eddy and George. The boys accompanied their parents on a visit to Maharajah Duleep Singh[153] and his wife at Elveden in early November and left for Sandringham on the 8th to join the girls. On the 9th the family toured the gardens and grounds to see all the improvements and there was a gigantic bonfire on Sandringham Height. To mark her husband's birthday and recovery, Alexandra presented a lectern to Sandringham Church; a brass eagle with outstretched wings, a red cross on its breast and an inscription: "To the glory of God. A thank-offering, December 14 1871. Alexandra. 'When I was in trouble I called upon the Lord, and He heard me.' Psalm CXX, Verse 1."

For her own birthday, Louise had sent her a "lovely little chair, which really pleased me beyond everything and is so comfortable and pretty". Remembering December 1871, Alexandra could only "thank God over and over again now we are so happy here again and everything looks bright which then looked, oh! so dark and wretched."[154] She and the children stayed at Sandringham, while for Albert Edward there was shooting and a Duchy of Cornwall meeting. He joined Alexandra on 3 December at Gunton and they went to Derby School's Speech Day. On the 9th they gave lunch at Sandringham to the Japanese ambassadors and returned for the mausoleum service on the 14th. At Chatsworth on the 17th, the Prince gave prizes at the Grammar School and Alexandra gave prizes at the School of Art. There was a ball that evening but very little dancing in the crowded rooms. After more shooting and a visit to Haddon Hall, they returned to London, leaving on the 23rd for Christmas at Sandringham with the children and Alfred, and on the 31st for Holkham.

On 1 January 1873 the Waleses rode over to Sandringham to distribute New Year bounties, returning later to Holkham for shooting and a dance, and going home on the 4th to entertain weekend guests. Albert Edward heard on the 9th that Napoleon III, in exile with his wife and son, had died at Chislehurst. He had admired the imperial couple since visiting Paris with his parents in 1855, and remained friendly with them; he went to the Emperor's lying-in-state on the 14th, returning to Sandringham in time for dinner; Alexandra had been driving in the little cart. There was a dance, a meet, guests departed and the couple returned to London on the 20th, leaving for Savernake next day. While the Prince went shooting there, Alexandra and the ladies lunched at Chisbury Lodge. Back in London on the 25th, they went next day to All Saints' Church in Margaret Street and dined later with Uncle George; on the 27th Alexandra returned to Sandringham, where she drove and walked with her sons. Her husband came back on the 30th for more shooting and she joined the party at the shooters' lodge several times. After the county ball on the 31st and the servants' ball on 3 February, the family moved to London. On the 6th Alexandra listened to a debate in the House of Lords and for the next two evenings, despite colds, the couple saw *Wicked World* and *Babil and Bijou* at the theatre. Alexandra recovered first, calling on Lady Hamilton and the Duchess of Inverness and attending All Saints', but Albert Edward stayed indoors at least until the 12th. Then there were three theatre visits, a lecture on Central Asia on the 15th and three dinner parties. On the 20th, Leitch gave Alexandra a drawing lesson and the family went to the circus for Louise's 6th birthday.

More theatres, a concert at the Albert Hall, art exhibitions, visits to the Duchess of Inverness,[155] a court on the 27th and the Old Masters' exhibition at

Burlington House on 3 March, followed. While the Prince visited Belvoir, Alexandra went driving, sometimes with her sons; she attended a play at Drury Lane on the 4th and a concert at the Albert Hall on the 5th, having supper with Mary Teck afterwards. On the 6th she saw *Man and Wife*, dramatised from Wilkie Collins's novel. She sat for her picture on the 8th and again, to a Danish painter, on the 10th. The Prince returned on the 8th, they drove together in the afternoon and celebrated their tenth wedding anniversary with a ball. Over the next month, Alexandra gave many sittings to artists; six to Richmond[156] and seven to others, as well as driving with her children, paying her usual calls and receiving visitors. There were more plays, five concerts and on 25 March, tableaux at Cromwell House; more dinner parties, prize-giving at the Female School of Art and visits to Leighton's, Prinsep's[157] and Weigall's studios. On 29 March, Albert Edward and his sons watched the boat race from the umpire's boat, while Alexandra and Mary saw it from Chiswick. Cambridge won. During Easter at Sandringham there were the usual occupations and nearly every evening they played bowls in their own Bowling Alley. The Prince and guests left on 21 April: he for Vienna on the 24th, while Alexandra remained till 6 May, driving and visiting poor people. In London, she called on the Belgian queen, who dined with her that evening, and saw Faust at Drury Lane. Dining with Queen Victoria on the 7th, she paid a number of calls and received visitors. Before her husband's return on the 27th she went to Windsor, drove and entertained, had art and music lessons, visited the opera, theatre and concerts, and sat twice to Richmond. Sad news came on the 29th; Alice's haemophiliac second son, Frederick[158] had died after falling from a window. Alexandra had more lessons with Hallé on the 30th and three with Leitch in June. On the 3rd she and her husband began a two-day visit to Wigan. [159] Alexandra went to see Harper's[160] collection of watercolours on the 6th; later, the Christians came to lunch and they all went to the horse show. The Waleses visited Empress Eugénie at Chislehurst on the 8th; the next day it was Cowarth Park for Ascot Week.

On 15 June the couple attended the "Hospital Sunday"[161] service at St Paul's Cathedral and dined at Chiswick House because important guests, the Tsesarevitch, Tsesarevna and their sons[162] were coming to stay there next day. Albert Edward and Alexandra met them at Woolwich and on 21 June they all had lunch with the Queen; "He is vy good looking & kind & Minnie very simple & unaffected but she is not (excepting her eyes) pretty & she has not the distinguished face & appearance of dear Alix, tho' in manner they are much alike."[163] They all embraced the season; some sixteen balls, also dinners, plays and operas, naval and military reviews, a polo match, Aldershot, Goodwood and Cowes Week. In between, Alexandra and Minny, who had decided to dress alike, spent as much time together as they could, driving, visiting and sightseeing. There was also the Shah of Persia's[164] visit, from 18 June to 5 July. Waldemar arrived on 28 June, for a party at Chiswick, and stayed till 1 July, when the

Waleses and their guests stayed overnight at Windsor. There were visits to Greenwich Docks, Richmond, the Tower of London, the Bank and Westminster Abbey, Madame Jerichau's pictures and Goode's china shop. On 14 July some Welsh singers came to Marlborough House and on the 21st Alexandra and Minny visited the Newport Market Refuge and House of Charity. The Duke of Edinburgh's betrothal to Grand Duchess Marie Alexandrovna,[165] Alexander II's daughter, was announced on 11 July; another link between Britain and Russia. Alexandra and Minny, identically clad, sat for a joint picture on the 22nd to Mr Koberwein[166] and after dinner at Chiswick on the 27th they all left for Goodwood and Cowes. Yacht parties were held before the Russians took leave of the Queen on 13 August, gave the Waleses dinner on their yacht and left for Denmark on the 14th, while for Albert Edward and Alexandra there were excursions in *Alberta* to the Needles and Alum Bay and visits. Albert Edward went to Holyhead for a week while Alexandra went for walks and bathed at least nine times.[167] On the 26th [168] there was a dinner for the Osborne labourers.

The family returned to Marlborough House on 1 September. Uncle Hans arrived and after two theatre visits they all left for Scotland on the 4th, finding the Queen, Beatrice, Alfred, the Christians and Leopold. It was raining, which continued for all but six days of the next five and a half weeks; as relentless as the deer-stalking and grouse-driving. Alexandra drove everywhere "in a very small light gig with a pony at full gallop, Miss Knollys and her alone in Bashaliks [sic][169] and no one else with them at all except a big black dog."[170] She went for walks, had tea with various people and occasionally the rain stopped for long enough to have lunch outdoors. Ponsonby dined at Abergeldie on the 18th and described the "very comfortable warm drawing room, the table covered with books, *Revue des D. Monds, Fortnightly* and other magazines, photograph books and everything so different to this cold empty house we shiver in here."[171] On the 25th, when it was fine, Alexandra and her party picnicked at Loch Muick and later had tea at Altnaguithasach. At the ball at Balmoral on 7 October, "The event of the evening was Doyle[172] dancing an Irish jig ... he did wonderfully ... but his partner of course knew nothing of it, was shy and tried to get away till the Princess of Wales gallantly took her place."[173] Ponsonby had also talked to Alexandra on the 10th; she "either listened better or understood better than usual what I was saying." She had asked about Mrs Ponsonby's[174] drawing and what sketches she had done at Balmoral. Ponsonby happily expanded on his wife's taste for scenery, "which the Princess said extended to all things as she believed you had excellent taste." The conversation had pleased him, as it went beyond the usual polite remembrances.[175] On the 13th they all returned to England; the Prince alighting at York to visit the Londesboroughs until the 18th. His family and Prince John arrived at Marlborough House on the 14th; Uncle Hans drove with Alexandra, attended the theatre four times and visited the British and South Kensington Museums before going home on the 19th, after they had attended All

Saints'. Alexandra then set time aside for eleven sittings to Koberwein by 1 November. She also went driving, shopping and theatre-visiting, sometimes with her husband. They gave a small dinner party on the 26th, heard Miss Laurence play the piano on the 29th and saw a photograph exhibition the next day. On 3 November Alexandra and the children went to Sandringham; four days later Albert Edward and the first party of guests joined them.

General Knollys's daughter, Charlotte had been accompanying and helping Alexandra in various ways and now this was to be made more official. On 4 November Knollys thanked the Queen for approving Alexandra's appointment of Charlotte as one of her women of the bedchamber; "Sir W Knollys trusts that Your Majesty may never have reason to regret your kindness in this respect and that his daughter's services may never tend in any direction but to her dear Mistress's interests in the fullest acceptation of the term."[176] Alexandra went to listen to singing practice at church on the 7th and on the 10th drove her husband to the station in the little cart; he returned with weekend guests on the 15th after visiting Lord Walsingham.[177] He went to Marham on the 17th, brought more guests on the 22nd and during the next week there was riding and field sports. The county ball was held at Sandringham on the 28th and among the guests were the Mayor of Norwich, Samuel Gurney Buxton[178] and his wife. They first saw Alexandra at the far end of the hall where the dancing was, and she stayed there the whole evening, only moving for supper. Mrs Buxton thought her dress not "very pretty", it was a satin tunic with deep lace round it, over blue tulle, with pearls and diamonds, some sprinkled over her chignon. "She looked as pale as possible ... It seemed to me that she looked a little dull; there were not many very great swells & she did not dance much." Her deafness rather isolated her in a crowded, noisy room, but she did move a little way out of her corner to talk to some ladies she knew, like Countess Gleichen.[179] The Duchess of Manchester was in primrose satin, "enamelled all over face & neck – I may say back, for like the poor beggars she was 'half naked to behold'"; Lady Blandford was very pretty in pale green and lace, Mrs Grey in yellow. "The Prince looked fat & bald but very smiling and sociable." Mrs Buxton, wandering among the comfortable armchairs and sofas in the beautiful drawing rooms, espied many photograph books, two of which she looked through; "One was very interesting, all of the Princess & her sisters & brothers; very old ones, looking oh so dowdy! in the costumes of, say, nursery governesses, but with such pleasant, simple faces, the little girl 'Thyra' principally attired in checks & plaids."[180]

The guests left on 1 December and Alexandra held her birthday tea for the schoolchildren. There were more field sports, the servants' ball on the 5th, and music and bowls occupied the evenings. The Waleses went to London on the 8th, for Blenheim the next day; Alexandra visited Oxford from there on the 11th, for lunch at Dean Liddell's[181] house and tea with Prince Leopold at Christ Church College. At Blenheim, there were "round games" in the evenings and a ball on the 12th. Returning to Marlborough House, the couple left for the mausoleum service at Windsor, which Ponsonby attended for the first time. It lasted about 45 minutes and all the Royal Family, about a dozen household and a dozen servants were there. There were psalms, prayers and chapters, three hymns sung by ten members of St George's Chapel choir, and a sermon by Dean Stanley. "And we all sat round the Prince's tomb. I believe there are many who complain that it is praying for the dead[182] & who write indignant letters to the Dean about it." Alexandra and the Hessians went afterwards to the governor's house, Norman Tower; "They came to see the Prisons and were delighted."[183] Back in London on the 15th, with the theatre in the evening, they left next day for the Suffields' shooting party at Rendlesham, including playing, dancing and singing and a ball on the 18th. The Waleses returned to London on the 20th and the Hessians dined with them. Alexandra went out shopping in the evening of the 22nd and they were back at Sandringham the next day; presents were distributed and meat given to the poor on the 24th. Mr Onslow preached on Christmas Day, and he, Miss Onslow and the Knollys family dined with the royal couple. There were Christmas tree gifts and games; Major Grey, the Prince's equerry unfortunately broke a rib playing bowls. After more country sports, the year ended with a small dance. Albert Edward was sorry his mother had not liked Richmond's picture of Alexandra, who had also given one to him. It did not do her justice and was too dark, but belonged to a certain school of painting "which I cannot help admiring, though I am afraid that you do not."[184]

The Queen had other matters to consider, including a wife for Arthur. Thyra had been mentioned but Victoria was strongly against it, not through Thyra's fault but because of her relatives. She had never got over her dislike of Queen Louise, fanned by prudish disapproval of the Danish queen's lively manner, which seemed to Victoria to be "a very <u>familiar</u> <u>flirty</u> way with men." Now she saw similar freedom in the behaviour of Alexandra and Minny, especially that there was "<u>no doubt</u> that the Pcess of W & her sister, <u>from</u> <u>no</u> <u>wrong</u> <u>motive</u>, but <u>still</u> from a grievous want of Dignity & of knowledge of the World, have got O Montagu <u>invited</u> to St Petersburg,[185] & <u>not</u> the P of W who <u>dislikes</u> him. <u>This</u> is a <u>fact</u> <u>not</u> to be <u>lost sight of</u>, & wh <u>Pce</u> Arthur shld know, for it points to the gt <u>inadvisability</u> of having another sister married to <u>Arthur</u>. Dean of Windsor,[186] who is <u>very</u> <u>wise</u> about <u>all</u> these things is <u>most</u> <u>anxious</u> that A shld not marry Thyra – 'Oh! don't let that be, unless there is great attachment!' And the Queen owns that the <u>folly</u> of the 2 sisters, wh unfortunately [is] the Mother's also … makes her desirous that A shld not marry T".[187]

Whether or not Albert Edward disliked Montagu, even the Queen knew Alexandra's and Minny's behaviour was not immoral. It was just not the English way, although many of the English seemed to like it. It was Alexandra's "un-English cordiality" that had won over the "City Fathers" at the Guildhall in 1863 and made her so popular. If Thyra had married Arthur and behaved similarly, she would probably have been equally well-liked; it was certainly unfair to condemn her out of hand. At Osborne on 19 December, Ponsonby had heard some gossip from A Paget,[188] who "launched off about Oliver Montagu; said he was convinced there was no truth in the stories about there being any love as to the Pss of Wales, who merely liked to have a good looking fellow near her, but thought it a grievous pity that he always was about there as it was impossible to prevent people from telling lies, therefore he confessed he did not like [Montagu's] going to Russia in the P of Wales's suite."[189] Montagu, a bachelor, was a sociable and trusted family friend; on occasions such as the county ball, described above, Alexandra might well need a dance partner, as her husband was expected to dance with other ladies and it was important she had someone reliable whom she liked; he would sometimes assume this role and might also join the Waleses suite during functions and visits, or be invited to their parties. Alexandra did indeed appreciate male good looks and was fond of Montagu, but was far too circumspect to give way to this and was also in love with her husband. References which she made to Montagu, for example, in letters to George over many years, all show that she saw him as a very dear friend, who had been helpful to her and was part of their intimate family circle. Montagu himself wrote long letters to Albert Edward and, later, George, reporting on events. Alexandra was always loyal to her friends and she and Montagu shared interests, including photography, and also religion, which they both took seriously and would discuss. He was lively, cheery and thoughtful, almost in a brotherly way, and utterly devoted to her.

Alexandra possessed a number of books about religious and other beliefs. They included *Sondagsminder; praedikener* (sermons)[190] by Jakob Paulli (1844–1912), who was the clerical son of her old friend Pastor Paulli; *Eternal Hope*: five sermons preached in Westminster Abbey, November and December 1877, by Revd Frederick W Farrer;[191] and *The Philosophy of Religion, in England and America*, by Alfred Caldecott.[192] She also had *The Bible, designed to be read as literature*, edited and arranged by Ernest Sutherland Bates.[193] In addition were *Synopsis or a synoptical collection of daily prayers, the liturgy and principal offices of the Greek Orthodox Church of the East*, translated and edited by Katherine, Lady Lechmere;[194] *Modern Spiritualism: a history and a criticism*, by Frank Podmore;[195] and *Myths of the Hindus and Buddhists*, by Sister Nivedita (Margaret E Noble) and Ananda K Coomaraswamy, with 32 colour illustrations by Indian artists.[196] Another kind of belief was represented by *Dreamers of the Ghetto*, essays about famous Jewish figures, by Israel Zangwill (1864–1926), a British author at the forefront of cultural Zionism.[197]

There were special plans for January 1874 and the family went to London on the 5th. Albert Edward was installed as Master of the Prince of Wales Lodge on the 7th; stayed overnight with the Queen at Osborne, and unveiled the statue of his father at Holborn Circus on the 9th. Later, the couple and their four elder children went to the Theatre Royal. The next day, with Arthur and their suite, they set off for St Petersburg, leaving the children at Sandringham under Dalton's and Miss Louisa Walkley's care.[198]

At Berlin the Crown Prince received them; they met the Emperor, Empress and others, and were taken to the Thiergarten[199] for ice-skating. There was a grand dinner later. While the gentlemen went out shooting on the 13th, Alexandra and the Empress visited the Augusta Hospital. The party left at 11pm and later were received officially at the Russian border. Further down the line their train stopped at a small station near Luga, where the Tsesarevitch and Tsesarevna were waiting; they travelled together, arriving at St Petersburg on the 16th and going to the Anitchkoff Palace, where they all dined that evening. On the 17th, with Alfred, they all saw *La Traviata* at the Italian Opera; Grand Duchess Marie and Minny both in pink, while Alexandra wore crimson velvet. On the 18th, the annual ceremony of blessing the River Neva took place; it was freezing and the streets were snowed up. Indoors were balls, dinners and other festivities and on the 23rd the Russian wedding service was held in the Winter Palace's private chapel. The English one was held in the palace's Alexander Hall,[200] followed later by a grand ball. On the 24th there was an imperial hunt at Gatchina and on the 26th a grand parade of about 30,000 troops in front of the Winter Palace. A gala performance; one act of *Romeo and Juliet* and a ballet, *Le Papillon*, was held at the Grand Theatre on the 29th. The next day the fire brigade was reviewed on the Champ de Mars and the Cossack bodyguard in the Michael Manège. A grand ball in the Winter Palace's Nicholas Hall was followed next evening by another at the Anitchkoff. Oliver Montagu kept a graphic diary of the visit, with photographs, souvenirs and writing.[201]

Alexandra told Eddy on 1 February; "We are delighted with everything at Petersburg, and very happy to be with Aunt Minny and Uncle Sacha in their lovely palace. Dear little Nicky and Georgy[202] ask a great deal after you all and come in every morning while I dress, and wish to hear all about cousins. The weather is beautifully frosty now, and Aunt Minny and Mama drive in sledges every day and skate too, and then we are driven down some steep icebergs on little chairs and seats which is most amusing. Papa has been out shooting some wolves and soon he is going after some bears." The wedding had been a beautiful sight and Uncle Alfred and the new aunt, Marie, were very happy together. Alexandra was looking forward to hearing Eddy play his new tune and sing all their old songs when she came home.[203] She told George about the Foundling Hospital in Moscow where "I think we must have seen about a thousand babies there together, which was a very curious sight." They had also seen the great

"Tsar Bell", "which you must have read about." It was so cold on the ice that her fingers, nose and cheeks almost froze; she looked like "a great bear out driving, wrapt up in an enormous fur cloak and cap."[204] All festivities ended abruptly when Lent began and, soon afterwards, the English party took its leave. On 2 March the children went to stay with the Queen at Windsor; meanwhile their parents were in Berlin, greeting the Edinburghs at the Eastern Railway Station. They visited Fritz and Vicky, who told her mother; "I thought darling Alix in spite of all fatigues ... looking very well – and lovelier than ever! My children went wild about her, and little Sophie[205] would not leave her side, but followed her about like a little dog, calling her 'pretty Auntie'".[206] After a court dinner in the palace's White Hall, the Wales couple saw a ballet at the Opera House before leaving to call on the Hessians in Darmstadt. They reached Marlborough House and the children on the 5th. Alexandra went driving with her sons; relatives called. After visiting the Russian Ambassador[207] the couple and their sons welcomed the bridal pair at Windsor the next day and later travelled between Windsor and London several times, for more celebrations.

There was a family lunch at Marlborough House on the 12th and Alexandra later dined with the Queen, while Albert Edward dined with officers of the Royal Horse Guards at Albany Street Barracks. On the 13th the couple took the Christians and the Duc d'Aumale to the French play at Holborn Theatre. On the 16th the Waleses and their sons saw the Landseer exhibition at Burlington House and gave a dinner for the Edinburghs, with the band of the Grenadier Guards playing "God Save the Queen", the Russian national anthem and some light music. Hunting and steeplechasing, the Prince also joined his wife and the Edinburghs for a debate in the House of Lords on the 19th. Later the couple heard Arthur Sullivan's[208] Oratorio, *The Light of the World* at the Albert Hall. They visited Empress Eugénie at Chislehurst on the 21st and also Millais's, Leighton's and Prinsep's studios on the 23rd. Albert Edward initiated Arthur as a Freemason into the Prince of Wales Lodge, afterwards presiding at the Lodge dinner at Willis's Rooms on the 24th. On the 26th the Waleses visited Uncle George and, later, the French Gallery in Pall Mall. Adolphus, Hereditary Grand Duke of Mecklenburg-Strelitz called; he and Albert Edward visited the zoo and watched the boat race, while Alexandra drove with her daughters. On 30 March it was the Queen's review, at Windsor, of troops returned from the Gold Coast; later it was Handel's *Messiah* at the Albert Hall. The next day, with Marie,[209] they visited Boehm's studio. After Easter at Sandringham they returned on the 27th and then visited the Edinburghs at Buckingham Palace, and Mary Teck, who had had her youngest child, Alexander[210] on the 14th, at Kensington Palace. There was more riding and driving, socialising with the Edinburghs and with Adolphus, the opera at Drury Lane, a ball at the Mansion House in honour of the Edinburghs and a private view at the Royal Academy. On 1 May, Dalton took Eddy and George to see the Middle-Class School in Cowper Street, Finsbury.

The Christians came to stay on the 4th and accompanied the Wales couple several times. By 12 May Albert Edward and Alexandra had attended a drawing room, the French Embassy ball, the Italian Opera and the Westminsters'[211] ball at Grosvenor House.

Emperor Alexander II, with his son, Grand Duke Alexis[212] arrived at Windsor on 13 May. Alfred had met them at Flushing and Albert Edward, Marie and Arthur were waiting at Dover, to escort them to Windsor, where the Queen, Alexandra and the rest of the Royal Family received them in the Grand Entrance, with dinner later in the Oak Room and a state banquet next day. The Prince and Princess of Wales took the Emperor to Buckingham Palace and he drove, paid calls, dined at Marlborough House and went to the Sutherlands' ball at Stafford House. On the 16th the couple took him to the Crystal Palace for a fête in his honour. He attended the Russian Chapel in Welbeck Street next day; later, he, Alexis and the Edinburghs dined with the Waleses at Chiswick. There were more events in his honour: a state concert at the Albert Hall; a review at Aldershot; a state ball at Buckingham Palace; a Royal Artillery review on Woolwich Common and a dinner at the Foreign Office. The Prince and Princess accompanied him to them all; the Queen had left for Balmoral on 20 May, taking Eddy and George with her. On the 21st, the couple met Alexander II at Charing Cross and saw him off at Gravesend. It must have been an exhausting nine days, yet that evening they went to the Alfred Pagets' ball, and Louise and Lorne's garden party at Argyll Lodge next day.

They continued riding and driving and on the 25th watched a cricket match between the Household Brigade and Sevenoaks Vine Club at Prince's Ground, and dined with the Manchesters at Great Stanhope Street. On the 26th the Prince attended the former Belgian Ambassador, Silvain Van de Weyer's funeral, at Braywood Church. He had been a good friend of the Royal Family; his children and the Queen's had once played together. At Balmoral, Eddy and George went driving with Aunt Beatrice and Mademoiselle Noréle and also attended the Queen's Gillies' Ball on 29 May. The Queen thought their parents had neglected certain things in their upbringing; Alexandra was "rather obstinate" about it, but she won the Queen's full approval in insisting on great simplicity and absence of pride.[213] The little girls, with their mother, meanwhile watched their father taking part in the Queen's birthday parade at Horse Guards. The boys came home on 3 June, George's 9th birthday and Alexandra drove with them on the 5th. She stood sponsor to the d'Otrantes' baby daughter in the Chapel Royal on the 6th; watched a Household Cavalry polo match at Hurlingham, and, with Alfred, heard Hallé's concert at St James's Hall. Albert Edward attended the 10th Hussars Regimental dinner and Epsom Races and, on the 8th, with Alfred, introduced Arthur, now Duke of Connaught, to the House of Lords, while Alexandra and Marie visited the School for Art Needlework in Sloane Street. The Wales couple attended the Sutherlands' dance at Stafford House and on the

9[214], took their sons to the horse show at the Agricultural Hall. There were more dinners, balls and a state concert on the 10th; on the 12th, Alexandra and the Edinburghs attended a bazaar at Knightsbridge Barracks' Riding School, for the Homoeopathic Hospital.[214] Madame Eugénie Devaux[215] came to play the piano, followed by the Swedish Ladies' Vocal Quartet's recital. The Waleses dined with the Brands[216] at the Palace of Westminster and on the 14th attended a service at the Temple Church. On the 15th they left for Ascot week at Armytage Hill.

Returning on the 23rd, they attended the Austro–Hungarian Embassy ball in Belgrave Square and the next day visited the Edinburghs, who were going abroad. Alexandra drove with Helena; Mary Teck called later and the Waleses presided at the state ball that evening. Alexandra went driving with her sons; on 26 June, Mr A Borgen, of the Royal Danish Galleries in New Bond Street, showed her some archaeological gold jewellery from his London manufactory. Later, it was Lady Marian Alford's[217] dance at Alford House and on the 29th dinner with the Shrewsburys[218] at Dover Street. There was a state concert on 1 July and on the 4th the couple took their sons to the Tait's[219] garden party at Lambeth Palace; later they attended the Wellingtons' ball at Apsley House. They visited Aunt Cambridge, still recovering from a stroke in November, at Kew on the 6th. Three days later they attended her grandson, Alexander George of Teck's christening at Kensington Palace, afterwards leaving for Windsor. The Prussians were there too and later stayed at Marlborough House, accompanying their hosts to a number of events over the next week. On the 17th, Princess Charlotte, their eldest daughter, joined them and the next day went driving with Alexandra, her sons and little Louise. Alexandra also collected Mary Teck in her carriage and they both went to Prince's Ground, to see the skating on wheels, "very amusing".[220] On the 20th, the Prussians left for Sandown, Isle of Wight, while Charlotte went to stay at Cumberland Lodge. Later, the Waleses saw a cricket match at Prince's Ground, between Gentlemen of the South and Players of the North. Alexandra called on Aunt Cambridge again; later the couple dined with the Wiltons at Grosvenor Square. The next day Alexandra drove with her sons, and Charlotte came back to Marlborough House, leaving on the 23rd for Sandown. Albert Edward went riding on the 24th while Alexandra drove with her daughters, and that evening they gave a fancy-dress ball. There were six set quadrilles; Venetian, Vandyk, Clubs, Diamonds, Hearts and Spades, appropriately dressed. Alexandra, partnered by Lord Hartington, led in the Venetian Quadrille, attended by her sons, as pages in white satin and gold costumes. She was wearing a ruby velvet and blue satin costume, sewn with jewels, pearls and gold embroidery, with a small ruff round her neck and a close-fitting velvet cap. Albert Edward, in Vandyk costume, partnered by the Duchess of Sutherland, led in the Vandyk Quadrille; the "Card Quadrilles" followed.

On 24 July, the Wellingtons followed suit with a fancy-dress ball at Apsley House. The next day Alexandra presented a cup to the winners of a polo match at Hurlingham. The children left for Osborne Cottage with Dalton on the 28th, and were joined by their parents on 1 August after Goodwood. The next day they attended church with the Queen and family, and Empress Elizabeth[221] visited them later. Cowes Regatta was in full swing and they watched it on the 7th. On the 8th the Queen went to the school feast at Whippingham Rectory, followed later by Princess Beatrice, Charlotte[222] and Victoria[223] of Prussia and Eddy and George of Wales. Alexandra had lunch with her mother-in-law and other relatives and her daughters often visited the Queen, who, with Alexandra and Beatrice, called on Empress Elizabeth on the 12th. Albert Edward had enjoyed Cowes Week and visiting Plymouth on the 13th; he returned to London on the 22nd, while the children left in *Osborne* for Denmark, with the Revd Robinson Duckworth[224] and Dr Poore. Meanwhile Alexandra had gone to stay at the Douglas Hotel in Edinburgh. Her father and youngest brother arrived on *Jylland*, which docked in Leith Roads on the 16th; she met them, stayed two hours on board and then took the King back to Granton. Over the next few days they drove in an open carriage, visiting Dalkeith, Holyroodhouse, Hopetoun, Edinburgh Castle and Mr Steell's[225] studio, where they saw castings for the national monument to the Prince Consort in Edinburgh and a bust of the Prince of Wales. "Dear Papa is quite enchanted with the country, and certainly Edinboro' from the sea, where his ship is lying, is one of the finest views in the world." He was looking very well, younger than ever, and Waldemar was almost his height. Alexandra was missing her husband and children but looked forward to seeing them in Denmark;[226] meanwhile she, her father and brother left on *Jylland*, reaching Copenhagen on the 23rd, two days before the children on *Osborne*. Duckworth acted as tutor until Dalton could join them, and gave the boys lessons for three hours a day.[227]

Albert Edward left on the 26th for his nephew William's confirmation at Potsdam on 1 September. After watching manoeuvres and paying other visits, he reached Copenhagen on the 17th, was welcomed by the Danes, his wife and children, and all drove off to Bernstorff, cheered by large crowds. General Knollys meanwhile had written to the Queen from Bernstorff on the 14th, agreeing that the Waleses should not go to Paris on their way home; "It is the most dangerous place in Europe, and it would be well if it were never revisited." Rumours that the Prince was in debt were not true, but any Continental visit separating the couple, whether the Princess was in Denmark or elsewhere, was most undesirable and should be as short as possible. The General had hoped to speak to the Danish king and queen about this but they had never given him an opportunity to broach any subject concerning their eldest daughter and her husband; apparently the King would not like to have this forced on him unless he himself had led up to it. There was also Sunday observance; the Queen had views about this but the Danish monarchs had different ideas and Alexandra followed their example.[228] On the 22nd the family saw a review of the garrison at

Copenhagen and on the 23rd all had dinner with the Crown Prince at Charlottenlund, dining on *Osborne* next day. The holiday continued cheerfully until October; the Wales family arrived home on the 29th. The Duchess of Edinburgh had recently had her first child, Alfred[229] and her mother had come to be with her; she and the Tsesarevitch[230] (Sacha) were staying at Buckingham Palace. The Waleses visited them all; later they and Sacha went to St James's Theatre. The next day the couple lunched with the Russian Ambassador at Chesham House, and dined with the Edinburghs and Russians at Buckingham Palace. Sacha lunched with them the next day. They called on Aunt Cambridge and her sister at Kew on the 31st and went to the theatre with Sacha and Louis of Battenberg later.

On 2 November, the Waleses left to stay at Packington Hall[231] during an official visit to Birmingham. They saw an exhibition at the Society of Artists' rooms and later visited Elkington's manufactory, where Alexandra gilded a vase and accepted a basket of real flowers, frosted with gold and silver. At Messrs Gillott's, where much of the work was done by women, they saw a steel pen being made from start to finish. Lastly they visited Messrs Ralph Heaton and Sons' coin and metalwork manufactory; some bright white medals had been made to mark the royal visit and the Prince requested some for his children.[232]

They celebrated Albert Edward's birthday at Sandringham but on 23 November the Edinburgh baby was christened at Buckingham Palace and he was one of the sponsors. The Russians left at 8am on the 24th and in the afternoon the Waleses went to visit Panshanger.[233] Alexandra told George how much she was thinking of them, especially "my darling little Harry,[234] whose 4th birthday it is. Give her a great kiss from me and tell her 'Mother dear' has not forgotten her little pet, and that she shall have lots of presents on Sunday. I only wish I could have been with you all today." It had been bitterly cold standing about while Papa and the other gentlemen were shooting but she was glad her sons had been good hosts: "Dear Lady A[235] gave us the last accounts of you and told us you had been very good at her last breakfast at Sandringham, when you two did the waiters to her and Oliver Montagu, and that you accompanied them to the station on your ponies." The christening "went off very well, and he did not scream at all, which he ought to have done for luck's sake." [236]

They returned to Sandringham on the 28th and from 7 December the Prince stayed briefly at Didlington Hall.[237] Meanwhile Lt-Colonel Grey, his equerry, became ill at Sandringham with severe inflammation of the lungs, and, fearing he was dying, sent for Alexandra in the morning of the 10th. She later told "My own darling husband"[238] (in what may be the only letters to him from her that have survived), what happened. She had been frightened as it "recalled to my mind the dreadful time, when I used to be awake during your terrible illness." Grey had told his wife he would like to see the Princess once more, "I promise I won't speak, I only want to take her by the hand!!" Alexandra had found Dr

Lowe still wearing his white necktie and evening coat; he had gone there straight after dinner and stayed all night. Grey's wife was kneeling at his bed, "& then poor Grey stretched out his poor hand to me, & pressed mine … & his poor eyes looked so bright & kindly at me, as if he wished to say so much but <u>could</u> not!" She almost broke down and had had to hurry out of the room. He had seemed to rally but told his wife he thought it was the last time he would see the Princess. He had been so pleased at the Prince's message "& knows all the kind things you said about him … I am so sorry you are not here, my little Man, I am sure he would have liked to see you once more."[239] The next day Alexandra and others waited nearby until the doctor called them in; Grey was struggling for breath and "never can I forget that scene by his bedside … & I hope to God I may <u>never</u> live to go through the same again. This was the first time I ever saw anybody dying or dead & it was heartbreaking to witness."[240] Mrs Grey's kindness to everyone else was too much for Alexandra, who broke down sobbing. The widow and her son later took leave of her, thanking the Prince "for all your kindness & to tell you how devoted he had always been to you." Haunted by Grey's terrible dying expression, she later went for a last look at him; "& I can't tell you <u>how beautiful</u> he looked, with a smile upon his face, as if he was just about to speak." She was so thankful her last sight of him was so much less painful. Albert Edward blamed himself for not being there; he had never thought the apparently strong, healthy man would succumb and felt as sad as if he had lost a close relative. He told the Queen that Alexandra had done everything she could to comfort the widow, but "the trying scenes have quite knocked her up, so that she will not be able to accompany me to Windsor tomorrow." He still could not believe he would never see his equerry again, "a kinder or more generous disposition never existed. He was beloved by all his friends & acquaintances & all my servants were devoted to him."[241] Alexandra arrived in London on the 15th and the couple later went to Windsor. On the 18th the Prince attended Grey's funeral at Embleton Church and placed two wreaths, from himself and Alexandra. On the 21st, they left for Christmas at Sandringham with the children.

The Queen had been concerned for some time about the couple's religious observance. They were regular church-goers, but since at least 1873 this included occasional attendance at All Saints' Church, Margaret Street, London W1, built in 1859. Alexandra enjoyed the superb music there, but the rites were Anglo–Catholic; it was one of the churches inspired by the Oxford Movement,[242] advocating a return to pre-Reformation services, but in English. It was not Roman Catholic, but, given that the Act of Settlement barred members of the Royal Family from being Catholics, the Queen felt rather anxious about All Saints. Towards the end of 1874 she discussed it with the Dean of Windsor, who suggested invoking the Archbishop of Canterbury;[243] "If Your Majesty cannot prevail in any other way you could propose, with kindness, that as the Prince and Princess could not agree with you and you felt strongly upon the subject, you hoped that they would be ruled by the opinion of the Archbishop if privately referred to." He felt; "the Princess is very much set upon the subject of religious music and does not take in the other consequences." But as the Bishop of London had recently made a fresh appointment at All Saints', sanctioning the services, the Archbishop might find it difficult, despite valid grounds, to put the case for the Waleses non-attendance there. If so, the dean would gladly reason with the Prince first, leaving the Archbishop as a last resort.[244] There it seems to have rested; although Alexandra also went to other churches for their music[245] she (and sometimes her husband and children) attended All Saints at least 141 times between 1873 and 1902. She also went to a service there on 1 January 1915.

Notes

[1] Whose second son, Francis (1870–1910), had been born on 9 January

[2] William Ewart Gladstone (1809–98), statesman, four times chancellor of the exchequer and four times prime minister, m Catherine, née Glynne (1812–1900)

[3] Friedrich Max Müller (1823–1900), German-born philologist and orientalist, living in England

[4] Sir Charles Mordaunt, 10th Baronet (1836–97), m Harriet, née Moncrieffe (1848–1906)

[5] RA VIC/MAIN/Z/449/66, Prince of Wales to Queen Victoria, 1870: 10 February

[6] The Prince was good at letter-writing and wrote copiously, often to lady friends and acquaintances. However innocent the letters might be, they invariably got him into trouble if they became public

[7] RA VIC/MAIN/Z/449/69, General Knollys to Queen Victoria, 1870: 12 February

[8] RA VIC/MAIN/Z/449/70, Prince of Wales to Queen Victoria, 1870: 14 February

[9] RA VIC/MAIN/Z/449/83, Prince of Wales to Queen Victoria, 1870: 23 February

[10] RA VIC/MAIN/Z/449/84, General Knollys to Queen Victoria, 1870: 23 February

[11] RA VIC/MAIN/Z/449/94, Queen Victoria to Princess of Wales, 1870: 3 March

[12] RA GV/PRIV/AA/19/33, Prince of Wales to Duke of York, 1892: 16 August; "I called on Dss (Louise) of Manchester in Town, who told me as a profound secret she was going to be married to Duke of Devonshire today! He has also written to Gd Mama and Mama about it. It is I am sure the right thing to do – & they are sure to be very happy." Spencer Cavendish (1833–1908), Lord Hartington, later 8th Duke of Devonshire

[13] Henry Chaplin (1840–1923), later 1st Viscount Chaplin, politician, landowner and race-horse owner

[14] Princess Marguérite d'Orleans (1846–93) later married Prince Wladyslaw Czartoryski

[15] Seat of the Duke of Manchester; the Waleses stayed there for the Grand National Hunt and Cambridgeshire Hunt Steeple meeting at Cottenham.

[16] Mrs Grey, née Caroline Farquhar

[17] To organise the annual International Exhibition's new educational division for 1871

[18] Perhaps inspiring *A Wand'ring Minstrel* I, sung by Nanki-Poo in Gilbert and Sullivan's *The Mikado* (first performed in 1885)

[19] Arthur Ellis (1837–1907), later Major-General Sir, army officer and courtier

[20] Possibly John Frederick Boyes (1811–79), classical scholar

[21] This is probably the Hungarian Colonel Nicholas Charles Szerelmey (1803–75), inventor,

caricaturist, printer, engineer, explorer and academic, who also had a passion for archaeology. His pioneering restoration techniques were used for repairs to the Houses of Parliament in the mid-1850s and the success of this led to the formation of a company which expanded and flourished into the 21st century. http://szerelmey.com/our-history

22 RA VIC/MAIN/Z/449/97, Queen Victoria to Prince of Wales, 1870: 1 June; Montagu, a lively, convivial friend of the Waleses, was a frequent guest who had been part of their suite during the Eastern holiday. He sometimes accompanied the Prince on visits and, for example, sometimes acted as Alexandra's dancing partner.

23 RA VIC/MAIN/Z/449/100, Prince of Wales to Queen Victoria, 1870: 5 June

24 RA VIC/ADDA8/1962, Princess of Wales to Princess Teck, 1870: 3 June

25 Sir Joseph Noel Paton (1821–1901), Scottish artist and sculptor, poet and folklorist

26 Sir Anthony de Rothschild (1810–76), 1st Baron Rothschild, financier, philanthropist and race horse breeder

27 Johanna Magdalena Graver (b 1829), Dutch concert pianist

28 By the 2nd Life Guards' and Scots Fusilier Guards' bands, the Queen's private band and the London Glee and Madrigal Union

29 Henry Holmes (1839–1905), violinist, composer and teacher of the violin

30 Maria, née Tollemache (c 1810–93), second wife of 1st Marquess of Ailesbury

31 Herbert William Fisher (1826–1903), historian, tutor at Oxford and then private secretary to Prince of Wales

32 RA VIC/MAIN/Z/449/104,106, Prince of Wales to Queen Victoria, 1870: 29 June, 2 July

33 This was on the south side of Oxford Street, at the corner with Queen Street (later Lumley Street), facing the site where Selfridge's department store would later be built.

34 Count Rudolf Apponyi (1812–76)

35 Count Albrecht von Bernsdorff (1809–73)

36 Charles, Marquis de la Valette (1806–81)

37 RA VIC/MAIN/Z/449/113, Memorandum by Francis Knollys, 1870:20 July

38 Mrs Susan Martin, the children's nurse

39 RA VIC/MAIN/Z/449/112, 114,115, Prince of Wales to Queen Victoria, 1870: 20–21 July

40 RA VIC/ADDC26/146, Princess Beatrice to Lady Caroline Barrington, 1870: 21 July

41 With the Earl and Countess of Kinnoull, then George Hay-Drummond (1827–97), the 12th Earl, who m Lady Emily, née Somerset (1828–95)

42 Lady Agnes Duff (1852–?), m 1) George Hay-Drummond, 2) Herbert Flower, 3) Alfred Cooper

43 Later, as Earl of Fife, Macduff would become important to the Wales family.

44 ohn Campbell, Marquess of Lorne (1845–1914), 9th Duke of Argyll. Governor-General of Canada, 1878–83

45 George Campbell (1823–1900) 8th Duke of Argyll

46 Louisa (Sarah), née Fairbrother (1814–90) m Duke of Cambridge; their sons were Colonel George FitzGeorge (1843–1907), Rear-Admiral Sir Adolphus FitzGeorge (1846–1922) and Colonel Sir Augustus FitzGeorge (1847–1933)

47 Prince Edward of Saxe-Weimar-Eisenach (1823–1902), a nephew of Queen Adelaide (wife of William IV), army officer, settled in England, m morganatically, Lady Augusta, née Gordon-Lennox (1827–1904), created Countess of Dornburg

48 Prince Victor of Hohenlohe-Langenburg m Laura, née Seymour (1832–1912) morganatically; she was created Countess Gleichen but Queen Victoria later permitted her to be called Princess Victor of Hohenlohe-Langenburg in England

49 Prince Alexander of Hesse and By Rhine (1823–88) m Countess Julia von Hauke (1825–95) morganatically; she was given the title Princess of Battenberg; their five children also used the name Battenberg

50 RA VIC/ADDA17/384, Princess of Wales to Princess Louise, 1870: 14 October
51 William Denison (1834–1900), 1st Earl of Londesborough, m Lady Edith, née Somerset (1838–1915)
52 Frank Dillon (1823–1909), landscape painter
53 Count Alexander von Mensdorff-Pouilly, 1st Prince von Dietrichstein zu Nikolsburg (1813–71) was Queen Victoria's first cousin, as their mothers, Princesses Sophie and Victoria of Saxe-Coburg-Saalfeld were sisters.
54 In Manchester Square; it was later known as the Wallace Collection
55 Granville George Leveson-Gower (1815–91), 2nd Earl Granville, statesman, m Castalia, née Campbell (1847–1938)
56 Sir Michael Costa (1808–84), Italian-born conductor and composer who achieved success in England
57 John Everett Millais (1829–96), 1st Baronet, artist and a founder of the Pre-Raphaelite Brotherhood
58 Robert Taylor Pritchett (1828–1907), gun manufacturer, artist and illustrator
59 Prince Alexander of Wales (6–7 April 1871)
60 Revd William Lake Onslow (1820–77), then rector of Sandringham
61 RA VIC/MAIN/Z/449/127,128,130,131,132, Mrs Elise Stonor to Queen Victoria, 1871: 7–11 April
62 RA VIC/MAIN/Z/449/133, List of household attending the funeral
63 Princess Louise of the Netherlands (1828–71), m King Carl XV and IV of Sweden and Norway; she had died on 30 March. She was the mother of Alexandra's sister-in-law, Crown Princess Louise of Denmark
64 Whereas Alexandra lived to be nearly 81, her daughters were only in their 60s when they died
65 RA VIC/MAIN/Z/449/132, Mrs Stonor to Queen Victoria, 1871: 11 April
66 See *Bertie* by Jane Ridley for more information on this
67 RA VIC/MAIN/Z/449/139, Mrs Stonor to Queen Victoria, 1871: 16 April
68 Grand Duke Vladimir Alexandrovitch (1847–1909), brother of the Tsarevitch
69 Adelbert Wellington Brownlow-Cust (1844–1921), 3rd Earl Brownlow, soldier, courtier and politician, m Lady Adelaide, née Chetwynd-Talbot (c 1844–1917)
70 Joseph Edgar Boehm (1834–90), 1st Baronet, medallist and sculptor
71 Pedro II (1825–91), 2nd and last Emperor of Brazil, m Teresa Cristina of the Two Sicilies (1822–89)
72 Sir Walter Scott (1771–1832), 1st Baronet, Scottish historical novelist, poet, playwright and historian
73 One of his own titles
74 Their mutual ancestress
75 Arthur James Melhuish (1829–95), photographer
76 John Spencer, 5th Earl Spencer (1835–1910), Lord Lieutenant of Ireland from 1868–74 and 1882–5
77 Press report, August 1871
78 Kinloch Cooke, Vol II, p 48
79 *Kongstanken*, by Tor Bomann-Larsen, Norway 2002,Vol I, p 101
80 Alexander Bassano (1829–1913), leading portrait photographer
81 Seat of the Duke of Buccleuch
82 Mihàly (or Mikhail Alexandrovitch) von Zichy (1827–1906), artist
83 RA VIC/ADDC18/62, Lady Macclesfield to her husband, 1871: 22 November
84 Oscar Clayton (1816–92) later Sir, surgeon, courtier and socialite
85 RA VIC/ADDC18/65, Lady Macclesfield to her husband, 1871: 24 November

86   Albert Edward had flirted with a young widow, Lady Susan Vane-Tempest, who became pregnant in March 1871. Fearful, she only informed him when it was too late for a safe termination. She was told to consult Dr Clayton, and the Prince ceased all communication with her. No baby appeared, but Lady Susan lived only four more years. [See Ridley, pp 144–148] This tragic story puts Albert Edward in a thoroughly unfavourable light, but he was not, at heart, cruel, and his behaviour during his illness shows its effect on him; vowing to lead a very different life, rambling about infidelity, calling out names in his delirium and being irked by the garrulous Clayton, whose conversation can only be imagined. The episode would also have contributed to the Prince's underlying pessimism and depression, which grew as he aged.

87   RA VIC/ADDC18/72, Lady Macclesfield to her husband, 1871: 1 December

88   RA VIC/ADDA17/510, Princess of Wales to Princess Louise, Marchioness of Lorne, 1871: 23 November

89   RA VIC/ADDA17/512, Princess of Wales to Princess Louise, Marchioness of Lorne, 1871: 29 November

90   RA VIC/ADDC18/75, Lady Macclesfield to her husband, 1871: [2 December]

91   RA GV/PRIV/AA6/121,122, Princess of Wales to Prince Eddy and Prince George, 1871: 3 December

92   RA VIC/ADDC18/80, Lady Macclesfield to her husband, 1871: 7 December

93   RA VIC/ADDC18/83, Lady Macclesfield to her husband, 1871: 9 December

94   RA VIC/ADDC18/81,84, Lady Macclesfield to her husband, 1871: 8, 10 December

95   Quoted in report in *The Times*, 11 December 1871

96   RA VIC/ADDC18/86, Lady Macclesfield to her husband, 1871: 12 December

97   RA VIC/MAIN/Z/450/5, Queen Louise of Denmark to Queen Victoria, 1872: 10 February

98   RA VIC/ADDA30/366, Prince Leopold to George Stirling, 1872: 16 January

99   RA VIC/ADDA36/401, Henry Ponsonby to his wife, 1871: 13 December

100 RA VIC/ADDC18/87, 88, Lady Macclesfield to her husband, 1871: both 13 December

101 RA VIC/ADDC18/89, Lady Macclesfield to her husband, 14 December; Lorne had so recently joined the royal family that he was uncertain what to do.

102 RA VIC/ADDC18/91, Lady Macclesfield to her husband, 1871: 16 December

103 RA GV/PRIV/AA6/124, 127, Princess of Wales to Prince Eddy and Prince George, 1871: 23 December

104 RA GV/PRIV/AA6/128, Princess of Wales to John Neale Dalton, 1872: 19 January

105 RA VIC/MAIN/Z/451/114, Princess of Wales to Queen Victoria, 1872: 27 January

106 RA VICADDA17/528, Princess of Wales to Princess Louise, Marchioness of Lorne, 1872: 7 February

107 RA VIC/ADDU32/1872:14 February, Queen Victoria to Crown Princess of Prussia

108 RA VIC/MAIN/Z/451/137, Prince of Wales to Queen Victoria, 1872: 27 February

109 Henry Ponsonby (1825–95), Major-General Sir, army officer, Queen Victoria's private secretary and keeper of the privy purse

110 RA VIC/MAIN/Z/450/14, Colonel Henry Ponsonby to Queen Victoria, 1872: 7 March

111 Possibly Joseph Nash (1809–78), watercolour painter and lithographer, although by this time his work was being affected by poor health

112 Dr George Vivian Poore (1843–1904)

113 Hampshire Record Office: 39M85/PC/F30/3/3, Dr George V Poore to his mother, 1872: 11 March

114 In 1871, as a result of the Franco–Prussian War, the Prussians besieged Paris; the French Government retreated to Versailles; and the Communards took over Paris. The government forces then fought the Communards and revolution prevailed in Paris, with many casualties. When the Communards were defeated, a parliamentary republic was set up.

[115] HRO: 39M85/PC/F30/3/6, Dr GV Poore to his mother, 1872: 17 March

[116] HRO: 39M85/PC/F30/3/7, Sir William Gull to Dr GV Poore, 1872: 17 March

[117] Victor Emmanuel II (1820–78), King of Italy from 1861

[118] Umberto (1844–1900), later King Umberto I of Italy

[119] HRO: 39M85/PC/F30/3/11, Dr GV Poore to his mother, 1872: 28 March; the Pope was Pius IX (Giovanni Ferretti) (1792–1878)

[120] RA VIC/MAIN/Z/450/26, Mrs Theresa Grey to Queen Victoria, 1872: 9 April

[121] HRO: 39M85/PC/F30/3/29, Dr GV Poore to Marcus Beck, 1872: 26 April

[122] RA VIC/MAIN/Z/450/32, Mrs Grey to Queen Victoria, 1872: 23 April

[123] HRO: 39M85/PC/F30/3/26, Prince of Wales to Dr GV Poore, 1872: 24 April

[124] HRO: 39M85/PC/F30/3/29, Dr GV Poore to Marcus Beck, 1872: 26 April

[125] Adolf (1817–1905), erstwhile Duke of Nassau who had lost his territory to Prussia in 1866, but became Grand Duke of Luxemburg in 1890. His wife was Princess Adelaide of Anhalt-Dessau (1833–1916)

[126] Ernest Augustus (1845–1923), deprived of his inheritance by Prussia in 1866, he became Duke of Cumberland instead of King of Hanover when his father died in 1878

[127] RA GV/PRIV/AA13/1, Prince of Wales to his children, 1872: 28 April

[128] RA GV/PRIV/AA28/1, Princess of Wales to her sons, 1872: 27 April

[129] HRO: 39M85/PC/F30/3/31, Dr GV Poore to his mother, 1872: 28 April

[130] Revd John Neale Dalton (1839–1931), tutor to Princes Albert Victor and George, chaplain to Queen Victoria and a Canon of Windsor from 1885–1931

[131] RA VIC/ADDC26/66, Princess of Wales to Lady Caroline Barrington, 1872: 2 May

[132] HRO: 39M85/PC/F30/3/35, Prince of Wales to Dr GV Poore, 1872: 9 May

[133] RA VIC/MAIN/Z/450/34, Mrs Grey to Queen Victoria, 1872: 12 May; despite poor weather, Alexandra enjoyed this, her first stay in Italy and at some point the couple decided to learn Italian; Alexandra had *Italian Self-Taught, a new system on the most simple principles for universal self-tuition* (RCIN 1230948) and also Alfred Hoare's *An Italian Dictionary* (RCIN 1036382)

[134] HRO: 39M85/PC/F30/3/36, Dr GV Poore to his mother, 1872: 19 May

[135] As also to Dr Sapolini

[136] HRO:39M85/PC/F30/3/37, Dr GV Poore to his mother, 1872: 21 May

[137] Adolphe Thiers (1797–1877), historian, French president and 1st President of the French Third Republic

[138] Sir James Lacaita (1813–95), Anglo–Italian politician and writer

[139] Alfred Wigan (1814–78), actor manager, who took part in the first royal command performance before Queen Victoria on 28 December 1848. His wife, the actress Leonora Pincott (1805–84) styled herself as Mrs Alfred Wigan.

[140] RA VIC/MAIN/Z/459/33, Colonel Ponsonby to Queen Victoria, 1872: 1 July

[141] RA VIC/MAIN/Z/459/35, Memorandum by Queen Victoria, 1872: 9 July

[142] RA VIC/MAIN/Z/459/36, Colonel Ponsonby to Queen Victoria, 1872: 9 July

[143] Princess Alix of Hesse, later Empress of Russia

[144] RA VIC/MAIN/Z/450/48, Princess of Wales to Queen Victoria, 1872: 23 July

[145] RA VIC/MAIN/Z/450/50, Prince of Wales to Queen Victoria, 1872: 26 July

[146] In September 1871 the King of Württemberg had made Prince Teck a Duke; henceforth the couple were known as the Duke and Duchess of Teck

[147] RA VIC/MAIN/Z/450/51, Princess of Wales to Queen Victoria, 1872: 4 August; Sir Thomas Biddulph had suggested getting the doctors to say the trip was medically desirable, for getting advice available in Denmark but not England, RA VIC/MAIN/Z/450/52, 1872: 4 August

[148] German for siblings

149 RA VIC/MAIN/Z/450/53, Queen Victoria to Princess of Wales, 1872: 5 August
150 Prince Albert might well have understood his daughter-in-law's feelings better
151 RA VIC/MAIN/Z/450/56, Prince Ernest of Leiningen (1830–1904) to Queen Victoria, 1872: 24 August
152 With the Earl and Countess of Tankerville, then Charles Bennet (1810–99), 6th Earl, who m Lady Olivia, née Montagu (1830–1922)
153 Maharaja Duleep Singh (1838–93) later Sir, last Maharaja of the Sikh Empire, m 1) Bamba Müller
154 RA VIC/ADDA17/551, Princess of Wales to Princess Louise, Marchioness of Lorne, 1872: 8 December
155 Who died on 1 August 1873
156 Sir William Blake Richmond (1842–1921), portrait painter, sculptor and designer of stained glass and mosaic. He was influential in the early stages of the Arts and Crafts movement.
157 Valentine Prinsep (1838–1904), painter of the Pre-Raphaelite school
158 Prince Frederick William of Hesse ("Fritty") (1870–73)
159 They opened the new Wigan Infirmary, then later opened the new Town Hall in Bolton and unveiled the statue of Dr Chadwick, a local benefactor, in Southport
160 Henry Andrew Harper (1835–1900), landscape painter
161 This was a Sunday set aside for London churches to receive charitable donations for hospitals
162 Grand Dukes Nicholas and George
163 RA VIC/ADDU32/1873:21 June, Queen Victoria to Crown Princess of Prussia
164 Naser al-Din Shah Qajar (1831–96); reigned from 1848–96
165 Grand Duchess Maria Alexandrovna(1853–1920), later Duchess of Edinburgh and of Saxe-Coburg-Gotha
166 George Koberwein (1820–76), Austrian painter and photographer
167 Probably in the cordoned-off swimming area at Osborne
168 Prince Albert's birthday
169 A Bashlyk is a hood, usually worn with a cloak (burka) and fur hat (papakha) by Circassian tribesmen in the Northern Caucasus region, as travelling costume. As it was exclusively male attire, Alexandra would have felt particularly daring and dashing, galloping around the Balmoral estate in it. The hoods may have been a present from Minny, who owned such an item herself at least by 1888; Catalogue of exhibition, *Kejserinde Dagmar; Maria Feodorovna, Empress of Russia*, at Christiansborg Palace, Copenhagen, 1997, p 428, item 74.
170 RA VIC/ADDA36/666, Colonel Ponsonby to his wife, 1873: 9 October
171 RA VIC/ADDA36/642; Colonel Ponsonby to his wife, 1873:19 September; he is referring to Balmoral
172 General Sir Charles Hastings Doyle (1803–83) then Commander of British Troops in Canada (aged 70)
173 RA VIC/ADDA36/665, Colonel Ponsonby to his wife, 1873: 8 October
174 Hon Mary, née Bulteel (1832–1916)
175 RA VIC/ADDA36/667, Colonel Ponsonby to his wife, 1873: 10 October
176 RA VIC/MAIN/Z/450/68, Sir William Knollys to Queen Victoria, 1873: 4 November. They never did.
177 Thomas de Grey (1843–1919), 6th Baron Walsingham, politician and amateur entomologist
178 Samuel Gurney Buxton (1838–1909), JP, Deputy Lieutenant and Sherriff of Norfolk, m Louisa Caroline, née Hoare (1840–79)
179 Laura, née Seymour (1832–1912) m Prince Victor of Hohenlohe-Langenburg, morganatically, and was created Countess Gleichen (1861); Queen Victoria later permitted her to be called Princess Victor of Hohenlohe-Langenburg in England.

[180] RA VIC/ADDU/224, Louisa Caroline Buxton's memories of the occasion, 1873: 3 December, copy of original document held at the Norfolk Record Office, R155D

[181] Henry George Liddell (1811–98), Dean of Christ Church College, Oxford, from 1855–91

[182] Seen as a Roman Catholic practice

[183] RA VIC/ADDA36/699, Colonel Ponsonby to his wife, 1873: 14 December

[184] RA VIC/ADDZ450/84, Prince of Wales to Queen Victoria, 1873: 31 December

[185] For the Duke of Edinburgh's marriage to Grand Duchess Marie in January 1874

[186] Gerard Wellesley (1809–82), Dean from 1854–82

[187] RA VIC/ADDA25/393, Queen Victoria to Colonel Sir Howard Elphinstone, 1873: 19 December

[188] Probably Lord Alfred Paget (1816–88)

[189] RA VIC/ADDA36/700, Colonel Ponsonby to his wife, 1873: 19 December

[190] RCIN 1033842

[191] RCIN 1037269

[192] RCIN 1231748

[193] RCIN 1056214

[194] RCIN 1054283

[195] RCIN 1232408–9

[196] RCIN 1033744

[197] RCIN 1230738

[198] RA VIC/MAIN/Z/450/90, 91, JN Dalton to Queen Victoria, and Louisa Walkley to Queen Victoria, both in 1874: 31 January. Louisa Walkley (d 1895) was head nurse to the Prince and Princess of Wales's children.

[199] The zoo

[200] It was conducted by Arthur Penrhyn Stanley (1815–81), Dean of Westminster

[201] RCIN 2933773

[202] Grand Duke George Alexandrovitch of Russia (1871–99), second surviving son of Alexander III

[203] RA GV/PRIV/AA6/143, Princess of Wales to Prince Eddy, 1874: 20 January – 1 February

[204] RA GV/PRIV/AA6/145, Princess of Wales to Prince George, 1874: 30 January – 12 February

[205] Princess Sophie of Prussia (1870–1932), later m Constantine I, King of the Hellenes

[206] RA VIC/MAIN/Z/28/11, Crown Princess of Prussia to Queen Victoria, 1874: 4 March

[207] Pyotr Shuvalov (1827–89), Ambassador from 1874–89

[208] Arthur Seymour Sullivan (1842–1900), later Sir, composer, famous for collaborating on 14 operettas with WS Gilbert

[209] The Duchess of Edinburgh

[210] Prince Alexander of Teck (1874–1957), later Earl of Athlone (1917); Governor-General of South Africa and of Canada

[211] Hugh Grosvenor (1825–99) Marquess and then 1st Duke of Westminster, m 1) Lady Constance, née Sutherland-Leveson-Gower (c 1835–80)

[212] Grand Duke Alexis Alexandrovitch (1850–1908)

[213] RA VIC/ADDU32/1874:16 March, Queen Victoria to Crown Princess of Prussia

[214] Which had been founded by Dr Quin

[215] Madame Eugénie Devaux (d 1899), pianist

[216] Henry Brand (1814–92) was Speaker of the House of Commons

[217] Marianne, née Compton, (1817–88), artist, art patron and author, m Viscount Alford, who died before succeeding to his father's title of Earl Brownlow; she was subsequently known as Lady Marian Alford

[218] Charles Chetwynd-Talbot (1830–77), the 19th Earl of Shrewsbury, m Anna, née Cockerell (1836–1912)

219 Archibald Campbell Tait (1811–82), Archbishop of Canterbury, and his wife Catharine (1819–78)

220 Kinloch Cooke, Vol II, p71

221 Elizabeth (1837–98), d of Maximilian, Duke in Bavaria, m Emperor Franz Joseph of Austria, she was staying *incognita* as Countess of Hohenembs at Steephill Castle, Ventnor

222 Princess Charlotte of Prussia (1860–1919), m Bernhard III, Duke of Saxe-Meiningen

223 Princess Victoria of Prussia (1866–1929), m 1) Prince Adolf of Schaumburg-Lippe, 2) Alexander Zoubkoff

224 Revd Robinson Duckworth (1834–1911), instructor and governor to Prince Leopold at Trinity College, Oxford, 1866–70, Canon and Sub-Dean of Westminster

225 John Robert Steell (1804–91) later Sir, Scottish sculptor

226 RA VIC/MAIN/Z/450/107, Princess of Wales to Queen Victoria, 1874: 19 August

227 RA VIC/MAIN/Z/450/115, Robinson Duckworth to Queen Victoria, 1874: 28 August

228 RA VIC/MAIN/Z/450/124, General Knollys to Queen Victoria, 1874: 14 September

229 Prince Alfred of Edinburgh and later of Saxe-Coburg-Gotha (1874–99)

230 Minny did not come, as she was pregnant; Grand Duchess Xenia was born on 6 April 1875

231 Seat of Earl of Aylesford

232 They had gone to Sandringham on the 3rd. Heaton's were busy coining pence for Singapore and elsewhere and had recently coined over 100 tons of silver for the government.

233 Seat of Earl Cowper, then Francis Cowper (1834–1905), 7th Earl, who m Lady Katrine, née Compton

234 Princess Maud's family nickname, supposedly after Admiral Sir Harry Keppel, as she was inclined to be a belligerent little tomboy

235 Maria, Lady Ailesbury

236 RA GV/PRIV/AA28/2, Princess of Wales to Prince George, 1874: 26 November

237 With the Tyssen-Amhursts; William Tyssen-Amherst (1835–1909) later 1st Baron Amherst of Hackney, m Margaret, née Mitford

238 RA VIC/MAIN/Z/450,148, Princess of Wales to Prince of Wales, 1874: 11 December (full account)

239 RA VIC/MAIN/Z/450/142, Princess of Wales to Prince of Wales, 1874: 10 December

240 RA VIC/MAIN/Z/450/147, Princess of Wales to Prince of Wales, 1874: 11 December

241 RA VIC/MAIN/Z/450/144, Prince of Wales to Queen Victoria, 1874: 11 December

242 Alexandra owned *The Secret History of the Oxford Movement*, by Walter Walsh, RCIN 1033649

243 Archibald Campbell Tait (1811–82), Archbishop of Canterbury from 1868–82

244 RA VIC/MAIN/Z/450/159,160, Dean of Windsor to Queen Victoria, 1874: 24, 28 December

245 Such as St Anne's, Soho and the Berkeley Chapel, as well as the churches, chapels, abbeys and cathedrals traditionally associated with the Royal Family

Chapter 6

1875–1879

"When I might have gone [to India] …
he would not let me"

❦

After attending a royal wedding[1] in Brussels on 4 February 1875, Albert Edward rejoined his family in London on the 7th, when Alexandra went to her first 1875 Monday Popular Concert at St James's Hall. She met and entertained friends and relatives; and on the 14th thanked the Tecks for their Christmas presents, including "the puggie on its blue cushion" which was "most comfortably established on my dressing table where it is always eying me and putting me in mind of the dear donor." "Poor Paraquita Milles"[2] had given her an overwhelming present of 40 live parrots which needed re-housing after her father's death in 1874; she had selected Alexandra "to take care of her forsaken pets!"[3]

On little Louise's birthday the family went to Sanger's[4] Amphitheatre and, after several days with the Edinburghs at Eastwell Park, the couple gave a dinner party on 2 March to guests including the Austro–Hungarian ambassador, Count Beust;[5] Josef Horrath,[6] the cymbal virtuoso, played after dinner. The Queen held a court on the 8th; the Waleses gave a wedding anniversary ball on the 10th and attended social events with the Christians. With the King and Queen of Naples,[7] they lunched with the Queen at Windsor on the 15th, visited Louise at Kensington Palace on her birthday and on the 20th, Alexandra attended the Royal Albert Hall Amateur Orchestral Society's concert. On the 25th, Maundy Thursday, she took her sons to watch 112 elderly men and women[8] receiving the Royal Bounty during a service in Whitehall Chapel. Boys of the Chapel Royal led a procession, a service followed, and clothes and money were distributed from the Royal Closet. At Scotland Yard, over 1,000 "aged, disabled and meritorious persons", recommended by London clergy, were given other Royal Bounties.

On Saturday, Alexandra and her children arrived at Windsor for Easter morning service in the private chapel, walking and driving with the Queen and Beatrice. One day the children visited the Christians' family at Cumberland Lodge. Albert Edward (after two weeks in Marseilles and Nice)[9] joined them in

London on the 6th, when the couple opened the Merchant Tailors' School's new building, and visited the Charterhouse. At Chatham on the 7th the Princess named the new ironclad ship, *Alexandra.* The next day they visited Aunt Cambridge, now an invalid with a paralysed left hand, who still liked to see people and took a keen interest in what was going on.[10] The Wales couple regularly visited her at Kew, Kensington Palace and St James's Palace and sometimes took their children.[11]

Meanwhile Albert Edward secretly planned a *fait accompli,* creating a good opportunity for his diplomatic and social skills. It was fifteen years since his successful visit to Canada and America, while his brother Alfred, in the navy, had visited Australia, South Africa and elsewhere. Albert Edward had escaped death in 1871 and nothing was going to stop him justifying this. Ponsonby told his wife, on 6 April, of the Prince's long-held desire to visit India. After securing Lord Salisbury's[12] approval, he "exploded his notion very suddenly so that the Queen hadn't time to say no, the Indian Council, dazzled with the proposal, hastily said yes, and the Prince who said nothing to Pss, who he didn't intend to take with him, got the notice slipped at once into the papers before anyone had time to think of it, or the Cabinet had discussed it. So he has secured it as far as he can by a sort of surprise." The Cabinet grumbled; Northcote[13] counted the cost; the Queen, who did not like it at all but who would not have gone to India herself because of the heat, refused to lend her son the royal yacht. Although reluctantly consenting, she told Lord Salisbury she thought "the <u>risk</u> and responsibility <u>very great</u>, for the Prince of Wales is no longer in his former health and invariably overdoes his powers of endurance and fatigue and the distance from home is enormous!" Politically it might be beneficial but it was very troubling.[14] The War Office, Admiralty and India Office were not keen to set aside "one of the large troop ships to be fitted up as a palace for the voyage" and the Lord Chancellor[15] worried about a regency in case anything happened to the Queen during the Prince's absence.[16]

Alexandra was devastated; her husband would be away for months in a fascinating, exotic place, with an element of risk – and he had not asked her to accompany him. The Queen agreed; "the Princess going too would be out of the question, what would she do with the Native Princes and their wives?"[17] In fact, Alexandra would later be on good terms with several Indian maharanis and had enjoyed meeting local dignitaries during the 1869 eastern tour. The ladies in the Viceroy's harem had liked her and Egyptians generally were charmed by her friendliness and courtesy.[18] The heat might present unfamiliar maladies, but she had survived Egypt; as usual, her qualities and stamina were being underestimated. Most hurtfully, her husband was prepared to do without her, when her supreme wish was to help him. She longed for justification as much as he did, but he was so bent on achieving the coup and proving his own worth that he did not really consider her. Her regret for India was lifelong; "when I might

4 The children of the Prince and Princess of Wales, 1875; left to right: Princess Louise, Princess Maud, Prince Albert Victor (standing), Prince George, Princess Victoria. *Bassano*

RCIN 2509339

have gone, that time with my dear husband, he would not let me, and to this day I do not know why, excepting that he said at that time it was difficult for ladies to move about there – as if that would have mattered to me!"[19]

He would leave in October; meanwhile Alexandra drove and the couple saw an exhibition at the French Gallery in Pall Mall and, after briefly visiting Sandringham, attended the Royal Academy's royal private view on 29 April and Lady Caroline Barrington's funeral at Kensal Green on 3 May. The next day, after a large family lunch at Marlborough House, Madame Hager showed off her performing dog[20] and the Christians stayed for a few days. On the 5th the Prince and Princess of Wales dined with Maharajah Duleep Singh and his wife at Grafton Street, and afterwards attended the Alfred Pagets' dance at Queen Anne Street. On the 6th, the Hessians, on holiday with their family, and Louise called. Alexandra drove with Helena and later the Waleses dined with the Queen; Alexandra and her children spent the day at Windsor with her on the 11th. They returned the next day for a small party; Alexandra, the Christians and the Tecks, all with their children. They met in the Red Drawing Room at 4pm for a dance, with Mr Willoughby playing the piano, and refreshments in the large dining room.

Charlotte, Victoria and Waldemar[21] of Prussia called on the 12th and Alexandra also went driving with her three eldest children and Marie.[22] There was a state concert later. The Dowager Grand Duchess of Mecklenburg-Strelitz[23] (Aunt Cambridge's sister), Louis of Battenberg and Helena also called. On the 14th the Hessians came to stay; there were balls, dinners and Hallé's piano recital at St James's Hall before Alexandra took them briefly to Sandringham. After this, they all visited Boehm's studio and on the 26th, with a party of relatives, Epsom Races. The Waleses took the Hessians to dinner with the Tecks on the 27th and the Bradfords[24] next evening; the Hessians accompanied Alexandra to another Hallé recital at St James's Hall, and the Queen's birthday parade at Horse Guards on the 29th. Later the Hessians and Prince William[25] spent two days with Leopold at Oxford, and the Wales couple and their sons watched a polo match between military and civilian teams at Hurlingham. Aunt Cambridge's sister came to lunch on the 31st and the next day, Albert Edward and Louis of Hesse watched the Royal Thames Yacht Club's cutter race from Mr T Brassey's[26] yacht, at Gravesend. Alexandra and Alice visited the Fitzhardinges[27] at Cranford and they all went to the Duchess of Marlborough's ball.

Driving, concerts, and a state ball followed. Ernest Louis of Hesse[28] (six and a half) joined them for the horse show at the Agricultural Hall on 3 June. On the 4th, the Wales family visited Leopold at Oxford; on the 7th, with the Hessians and William, they began Ascot week at Titness Park. A week later, the Sultan of Zanzibar[29] called at Marlborough House and on the 17th Alexandra and the Hessians visited Westminster Abbey before they left. She heard two more of Hallé's recitals at St James's Hall and, with her husband, attended the Russian

Embassy ball[30] and seven others. They spent a few days at Stratfieldsaye[31] and gave a dinner for the Dutch queen on the 26th. Alexandra drove with her sons and there were lunches for relatives and others, such as Grand Dukes Alexis and Constantine.[32] The Waleses and their sons attended a polo match at Hurlingham on the 26th and a military inspection at Aldershot on the 28th. Garden parties included one at Chiswick on 5 July, to which the Queen and other royalties came. Alexandra and her sons watched pupils of the Association for the Oral Instruction of the Deaf and Dumb taking examinations at Grosvenor House on the 2nd; she was interested in the use of sign language.[33] Boys from the home in Regent's Park Road gave a gymnastic display at Marlborough House and the next day Alexandra took Eddy and George to Mademoiselle Georgina Schubert's[34] matinée musicale at Grosvenor House. On the 12th the couple visited Norbiton and Alexandra opened the Metropolitan Convalescent Institution's new buildings.

Waldemar, whose ship, *Heimdal,* had docked at Southampton on 18 July for two days, accompanied the Waleses to Margate, where Albert Edward opened the new branch of the Asylum for the Deaf and Dumb. The season ended with the Marlborough House Ball on the 23rd and the next day the couple attended the Aylesfords'[35] daughter's christening; Alexandra stood sponsor. On the 26th she visited the Marine Picture Gallery and Royal Danish Galleries before leaving with her husband for Goodwood. They joined their children at Osborne Cottage from 1–13 August, meeting the Queen frequently. On the 17th the couple inspected munitions and cutlery factories in Sheffield, where the Prince presented new colours to their guard of honour, the 19th, 1st Yorkshire Regiment, which, by Alexandra's wish, became "The Princess of Wales's Own Yorkshire Regiment". They stayed at Oakbrook, then at Longshawe,[36] and left on the 20th for Abergeldie, via Retford, where the train bringing the children from London was waiting. In Scotland they saw the Queen, went driving and attended the Braemar Gathering, a ball at Abergeldie and the Gillies' Ball at Balmoral.

A Danish visit was under discussion. Albert Edward would soon leave for India and as Alexandra could not go with him, she wanted to spend some of the time with her family. The Queen had told her on the 16th that she "would honestly have preferred, & I think everyone else would, if you had not gone out of the Country, & above all not the Boys (for I have often been blamed for allowing that) during Bertie's absence, & that is why I wished so much that your Parents, to whom I mentioned this, should come & stay with you, & I had also greatly hoped, that you & the children would have spent Christmas with me." But as Albert Edward wanted his long absence broken up for his wife, she finally consented, providing Alexandra was not away for longer than from mid-December to the end of January, "when I hope you will join me at Osborne." She had written to Queen Louise about this and was also very anxious that, before going to Denmark, they should "come to me at Windsor, as soon as I return, which would be about the 20th of November, I should think. It will be something to look forward to, when I leave this dear place."[37] Disraeli backed Alexandra up, assuring the Queen there was no legal or constitutional objection to the visit; it seemed harsh to keep Alexandra away from her close relatives during her husband's absence.[38]

On 18 September Victoria took leave of the family at Abergeldie and they returned to London the next day, leaving again for Sandringham on the 24th. The Tecks were guests and Mary told her mother on the 3rd October about the service, with special prayers for Albert Edward's voyage, "which of course upset Alix & me." Later, despite pouring rain, they did the "Sunday round", including the new Dairy,[39] and returned to London on the 6th for a large dinner on the 10th and other family meetings. Mary Teck thought Alexandra "a very great darling and I just adore her. Though I am quite in favour of Wales going to India, I grieve for her at the long separation, and wish she could have gone out with him, if only for a part of the time."[40] However, her health might suffer and it would be a terrible wrench to leave her children for so long. Saying goodbye to everyone, Albert Edward left for Paris en route for India on the 11th. Alexandra went with him to Calais and took leave on board *Castalia*. "The parting from Alix was dreadful", he telegraphed to the Queen.[41] Charlotte Knollys told her, "The Princess is extremely unhappy & tired … No words can describe the pain of the last parting scene & it was impossible to say which was the most overcome, the Prince or the Princess." He had stayed on *Castalia* with her until his train left for Paris at 2 o'clock.[42] On the 13th, his family returned to Sandringham but Charlotte heard from her brother Francis that "the Prince is still very low". She herself had never witnessed anything like his grief at the moment of parting; "Saying goodbye to the Children also affected him greatly & they too seemed to feel it very much. They are all very well & good & the Princess devotes herself to them which will I am sure be a great distraction for her during the Prince's absence."[43]

Alexandra always loved being with her children. Although often indulgent and tolerant, she did not let them have everything their own way and always made it clear that she was in charge and had to be obeyed. She took her maternal responsibilities seriously and although she trusted the children's attendants, her influence was paramount. She encouraged the children to be unselfish, considerate to servants and sympathetic to the poor and scolded them severely if their naughtiness hurt other people. Their father was equally devoted and took care to write to them while he was away. Meanwhile, Alexandra delightedly welcomed her parents and Thyra at Dover on 2 November, with theatre visits three evenings running. The Danish minister and Madame Bülow[44] came to dinner on the 3rd and King Christian visited Empress Eugénie at Chislehurst next day; then it was a fortnight at Sandringham. While the weather there was cooler, the Prince was now basking in great heat at Poona, touched that George had written to him on his birthday. He had met "two Maharajahs who are younger than you & Eddy, & they wear beautiful dresses with turbans which are covered with diamonds, pearls and emeralds. Many of the soldiers here, who wear red coats as at home, are black men, & wear turbans."[45]

Queen Louise and her daughters visited the National Gallery on the 19th and on Sunday the 21st, with the King, attended a service at Westminster Abbey. The Scots Fusilier Guards' Band played later in Marlborough House's garden. King Christian went home that evening, while his wife and daughters attended a Monday Popular concert at St James's Hall on the 22nd, visited Empress Eugénie on the 23rd and the French and Doré picture galleries on the 24th. On the 25th it was the Indian Museum, the National Training School of Cookery, the Schools of Science at South Kensington and the Albert Hall. The Queen had invited them to Windsor from the 29th and on 1 December, Alexandra's birthday morning, the Scots Guards' Band played under her windows. Later, at dinner, the Queen's private band played music by Auber,[46] Meyerbeer,[47] Mendelssohn and Rossini.[48] Alexandra and her family returned to London on the 2nd; Queen Victoria called on the 5th and took leave of Queen Louise and Thyra, who left for home that evening. George, who with Eddy had remained at Windsor, wrote to his mother, who had been "very sad saying goodbye to my darling Mother-dear and Aunt Thyra, although this time, thank God, we hope to meet again so soon." There was thick snow everywhere "and the lines to Dover are so blocked up that poor Amama could hardly get through ... I have got some lovely presents from dear Papa for you both which I will bring tomorrow."[49] On the 7th they went for another week with the Queen, for the mausoleum service and the Edinburghs' new daughter, Marie's[50] christening in the private chapel; Alexandra was a sponsor and her sons attended, although the girls had already returned to London. Later they all left for Denmark. The Prince wrote to wish the children a "very merry Xmas, & a happy New Year, & I hope you won't forget poor Papa who is so far away from you all. I shall miss you all very, very much, but trust you will all be very happy, which I do not for a moment doubt ... I wonder if you have snow in Denmark; here it is just like summer."[51]

Albert Edward received their replies at Calcutta; George's and Louise's in French. From the camp at Agra on 28 January 1876, he wrote about his growing animal collection; two young tigers, given by a Maharajah, and a very pretty little pony. "I think the 'Serapis' will be a Noah's Ark when I come home, as I shall bring back so many wild beasts. I don't know where we shall put them all, unless we start a Zoological Garden at Sandringham – would it not be great fun."[52] There was also "a very fine dog ... he is brown with long hair, & seems very good tempered, & he comes from Thibet, which Mr Dalton will show you on the map." While shooting, he had ridden an elephant, as the jungle grass was so high.[53] His family arrived home on the 6th; Alexandra called the next day on Aunt Cambridge and saw other relatives and friends, lunching, driving and dining at least twelve times with the Duchess d'Otrante[54] before the d'Otrantes left on the 24th. On Sundays she went to All Saints'. Mail from India nearly always arrived on a Saturday or Sunday; Indian letters were usually sent on Fridays and on the 11th and the 18th Alexandra wrote all day long. She attended concerts, and saw *Dick Whittington and his Cat* at Drury Lane; *Piff Paff*, with the Edinburghs, at the Criterion; *Tottles and Spelling Bee* at the Gaiety, but fog on the 11th kept her at home. The children had tea at Lady Suffield's[55] house on the 19th and at Clarence House next day.

The Prince's party had brought two little orphaned bears back to camp, to tame, but one later died. With an armadillo, looking "very like a moving artichoke" they were put in boxes in Mr Bartlett,[56] the taxidermist's tent, but "They all got loose in the night, & frightened him so that he did not know what to do, & was afraid of getting out of bed!"[57] A tiger cub was found and Sir Jung Bahadur,[58] with whom they were shooting, presented more wildlife; "There are deer & wild goats, a sheep with his horns grown together, tigers, leopards, a Himalayan bear & wild dogs. The birds chiefly consist of Himalayan pheasants with beautiful plumage – they are accustomed to a cold climate so that it is very doubtful whether they will live during our passage through the Red Sea."[59]

The Waleses were friendly with Lord and Lady Aylesford[60] and the Prince had invited Lord Aylesford (known as Joe) to join his suite in India. Meanwhile, Lady Aylesford was having an affair with the Marquess of Blandford, but as Alexandra had seen him on 23 February in London and knew that "E"[61] was in the country, she told her husband on the 28th that "she knew all about E, but things look a little better. There is a chance. Pray try your utmost to smooth matters with Joe."[62] Meanwhile she dined with the Queen, who was back in London; the Teck children came to tea on the 27th and there were more social events. Now the Duchess of Manchester, Lord Randolph Churchill[63] and Lord Lansdowne,[64] all trying to prevent the Aylesfords separating, begged the Prince to use his influence with Aylesford, who left for England at the end of February.[65] Lord Randolph, trying to protect his brother, Blandford's, reputation, warned the Prince he would be held responsible for whatever line of conduct was adopted. Albert Edward was astonished; he entirely approved of Aylesford's action but had not advised him.[66] Lord Alington[67] and Lady Aylesford called on Alexandra on the 28th; Blandford on the 29th and Lord Randolph on 1 March, all pressing her to get her husband to stop Aylesford seeking a divorce, which she was already trying to do. Hearing of this, the Prince was furious they had tried to coerce her in his absence. Alington had acted thoughtlessly and his sincere apologies were accepted.[68]

In early March Alexandra went to Goode's china shop and Weigall's, Boehm's and Desange's studios, and was busy arranging books all day on the 7th. She spent her wedding anniversary with the Queen at Windsor, driving with her and with Beatrice. The Empress of Austria called on the 12th. Alexandra had lessons in illuminating and thoroughbass on the 13th and the 15th; on the 16th she and her mother-in-law visited the Duchess of Kent's mausoleum, fifteen years after her death. Alexandra was photographed on the 22nd and, after a "Hen Dinner" on the 24th, went back home and attended a Popular Concert on the 25th. From Suez, Albert Edward told George; "You will be glad to hear that all the animals are well – only a few birds as yet have died. We have two tigers who are tolerably tame, at least they are led about by a man once a day. The other day Mr Sydney Hall[69] was drawing one of them, & suddenly [the tiger] made a dash with his paw at him, & tore his trousers from top to bottom! Curious to say he has never attempted to draw him since."[70]

Lord Hardwicke[71] now told the Prince that Lord Randolph would do everything he could to keep the Aylesford affair quiet, but had three supposedly compromising letters from the Prince to Lady Aylesford.[72] These had been submitted to the Solicitor General,[73] who had remarked that, if they were published, the Prince would never sit on the throne of England. If Aylesford went to court, Lord Randolph was determined the Prince should be put in the witness box. Despite anxiety, Alexandra continued as usual; she called at Leighton's, Prinsep's and Harper's studios; she saw *William Tell* and *Ballo in Maschera* and visited the British Home for Incurables on the 29th. After visiting Aunt Cambridge on 1 April, she left for Sandringham for her usual pastimes; letters from her husband arrived on the 8th. One of her main duties at this time was visiting a "poor girl" whom she went to see at least nine times, and also a "boy with fits". Her sons were working very hard at their lessons for five and a half to six hours every day, doing better in some subjects than others and particularly needing to work at modern languages.[74] On 12 April some Indian animals arrived in the snow, which continued on the 13th, when they went to see them. A letter from the Prince came on the 24th and the next day more animals were delivered.

From Malta on 10 April, the Prince had thanked Lord Hardwicke for his help; he could not interfere with Aylesford's decision about a divorce and, personally, "Have never in my life, that I know of, written letters to Lady A which might not be read by the whole world." Copies should be sent to the Queen and Alexandra to prove his point.[75] He was extremely upset; his homecoming was spoiled and he felt like staying abroad indefinitely. However much he tried to prove his worth – currently, with a successful tour – scandal always seemed to ruin it. He just wanted to be with his family. Alexandra had told the Queen he had sent her a very dear letter "from Malta where there seem to have been a good many functions, which at last must be very tedious. He tells me in this letter that he wishes me <u>with all the children</u> to come out as far as '<u>The Needles</u>' to meet him, as he is particularly anxious that we should meet <u>first</u> and <u>alone</u>. He has therefore also written to Alfred that <u>he</u> and Uncle George are not to come further than Portsmouth to welcome him. Might I therefore ask you to be so very kind as to allow me to have one of your yachts for that occasion?"[76] On the 29th Alexandra wrote her husband her last letter before his return, and received one from him on 2 May. On the 8th she and the children made their way to Portsmouth on the 10th, sleeping on board *HMS Enchantress*. *Serapis* arrived the next day and Albert Edward was reunited with his family, all very thankful he was safely home, and showed them over *Serapis*. Back in London, he called on the Queen and her guest, Empress Augusta. Later, it was *Ballo in Maschera* at Covent Garden.

As usual, Albert Edward had been doing too much and had a painful leg, which improved with rest, but there was a drawing room on the 12th, followed inevitably by dinners, balls, concerts, plays, operas and guests, such as the King and Queen of Hanover. The Waleses drove together and on 14 May attended the afternoon service at Westminster Abbey. Princess Charlotte of Prussia, almost sixteen, stayed with them for two days. The Prince relentlessly attended functions, travelled about and, not surprisingly, was laid up for a few days. On 1 June Alexandra dreaded going to the ball without him[77] but by the 5th he was well enough to accompany the family to Sandringham; the Queen had sent him an excellent salmon from Scotland. They toured the estate and one day the Oddfellows' Band went past the house. Alexandra visited the poor girl several times and said goodbye to her on the 11th; Ascot week was imminent and she would not return to Sandringham until 3 November.

Alexandra attended Ascot Races as usual, otherwise driving and lunching in the woods. Albert Edward went to a cricket match on the 17th and on the 19th, back in London, they viewed his presents at the Indian Museum at South Kensington, later seeing *Don Giovanni*. Sir Salar Jung[78] came to dinner on the 20th and there was a party for him at Stafford House two days later. The Waleses attended Disraeli's dinner at the Foreign Office on the 24th and there were more dinners, balls and concerts. The couple visited the horse show at Alexandra Park on the 21st; Empress Eugénie and her son[79] came to lunch on the 27th and on 1 July there was a volunteer review in Hyde Park. The season was exhausting; Alexandra stayed at home on the 2nd and sometimes dined alone. After more festivities, her brother, King George, arrived on the 12th to stay; he and the couple visited the Queen at Windsor. The next day they gave a large dinner for him at Marlborough House and he later drove several times with Alexandra. Patti[80] and Maurel[81] sang in *L'Etoile du Nord* at Covent Garden on the 15th; there was a dinner, and a garden party at Chiswick House on the 16th and the 18th, a dance and theatricals took place at the French Embassy on the 17th and a circus, fountains, dinner and fireworks at Crystal Palace. Queen Olga arrived on the 18th and Alexandra went driving with her. Two days after the Marlborough

House Ball on the 20th, the Waleses saw "Willy and Olga" off to Denmark, from Dover. On the 29th, after Goodwood, the family went to Osborne Cottage, sailing, seeing friends and relatives and going on excursions. Queen Victoria left for Scotland on 15 August and the Prince visited Trouville and Brussels, while Alexandra went out in the steam launch and also bathed at least six times. The family were reunited in London on the 23rd; Alexandra had two lessons with Leitch, and after a promenade concert and *Bull by the Horns,* at the Gaiety they all left for Abergeldie on the 27th.

On 29 June Lord Randolph had offered to apologise to the Prince, who finally accepted this on 18 September.[82] Not only had he accused Albert Edward of making Aylesford go to India so as to facilitate the adulterous affair and provoke a divorce; he had tried to blackmail him and had caused Alexandra distress. The Solicitor General had never seen the three letters; the comment about danger to the Crown was a lie.[83] It was some years before the Prince spoke to Lord Randolph again, while Aylesford remained a friend.[84] Meanwhile, Oliver Montagu arrived at Balmoral with two Indian officers on the 30th. The Braemar Gathering, with Lord Fife's luncheon, the Gillies' Ball and the Aboyne Games followed. On 5 September Alexandra and her children went up Killie Krankie and, while Albert Edward went stalking, she went sea-fishing. There was a picnic at Loch Muick, drives, lunch and tea with the Queen and a walk on the 12th to see Mrs Smith. Uncle Hans arrived at Abergeldie on the 18th, and Alice arrived at Balmoral the next day. On the 21st Albert Edward took his sons out stalking for the first time. The family left on the 27th and stayed at Dunrobin[85] for two balls, a volunteer review and an exhibition at Thurso. Alexandra also drove, walked and watched target practice. There was a picnic at Loch Brora on 5 October and the next day a visit to John O'Groats and lunch at Barrogill Castle.[86] Despite rain there were more outings and on the 10th they saw the Duke of Sutherland's land improvements (including steam ploughs) at Lairg. On the 16th, they went home via Glasgow, for a volunteer review, lunch with the Lord Provost, and the Prince's foundation-stone-laying of the new post office.

Back in London the next day, they visited the great-aunts[87] at St James's Palace, attended a promenade concert at Covent Garden and over the next few days saw Wagner's[88] *Flying Dutchman, Dan'l Druce* and *Peril*. The Prince went to Newmarket on the 23rd and that evening Alexandra saw Bluebeard at the Folly. They socialised with the Hessians, attending All Saints' together on the 22nd. Alexandra and Alice went driving, and had tea with Uncle Hans at his London residence on the 28th. He joined the Sandringham party on 3 November. The labourers' dinner took place on the 9th and the county ball on the 10th. On the 11th the hunt met at Congham. Albert Edward went to Merton on the 13th, bringing more guests on the 18th. Alexandra had thanked the Duchess of Manchester for something which was to be specially ordered, "a petticoat like yr charming black one; I should like it beyond everything only I shld prefer the scent to be either violet or even *poudre de riz*[89] which always smells like a baby!!"[90] Evidently scented petticoats were all the rage. After two days at Gunton, the couple returned with more guests, to whom Alexandra showed the stables and kennels, and celebrated her birthday on 1 December with tea for the schoolchildren, and the servants' ball. The Prince and guests left on the 4th but Alexandra stayed, going for walks round the estate before leaving for London on the 11th with her daughter Louise. She visited Aunt Cambridge next day and sat three times to the artist, James Swinton.[91] After the mausoleum service, the Waleses left for Holkham with Louise on the 18th; she went home en route and her parents arrived on the 22nd for Christmas.

On his thirteenth birthday, 8 January 1877, Eddy went shooting for the first time and got four rabbits. The family left Sandringham on 6 February, in time for the Queen's Opening of Parliament on the 8th, a levee and three theatres. Alexandra drove with the children, who were also taken to see *Robin Crusoe* at Covent Garden and *Forty Thieves* at Drury Lane. Louise's tenth birthday party was on the 20th.

Because of a bad cold, sore throat and swollen glands, Alexandra missed the drawing room on 2 March, but went to church two days later, still weak and depressed. Sir William Gull thought the spring weather might help her recover. By the 7th she was well enough for her first drawing lesson with Mr Harper and in the afternoon of the 9th heard Bach's *St John Passion* at St Anne's Church in Soho. On the 11th Gull advised the Prince, who entirely agreed, that, although Alexandra was getting stronger, she should rest quietly at home. There was a ball at Marlborough House on the 12th but she was still no better and on medical advice did not attend the drawing room on the 14th. Gull recommended a stay in southern Europe, but Alexandra was reluctant to be regarded as an invalid and also wanted to be near her sons, who had an important examination in May. She brushed off Gull's suggestion[92] and continued as usual, taking another drawing lesson with Mr Harper on the 15th and seeing *Artful Cards* at the Gaiety that evening with her husband. She went driving on the 16th, attended the evening service at St Anne's and on the 18th went to church twice. Albert Edward was glad the Queen agreed "that Alix should go abroad for 5 or 6 weeks for her health to a warmer climate." As Gull was their medical adviser, they were really bound to follow his advice; "& Alix is now also quite of that opinion." The Queen had offered to have the girls to stay and also wanted the boys to visit her later at Balmoral but, as their father said, this would depend on their studies and the outcome of their approaching examination. General Knollys, nearly 80, had resigned, but was happy to remain as Honorary Groom of the Stole to the Prince. His successor was General Sir Dighton Probyn,[93] thoroughly straightforward, high-minded, honourable and dependable; the Prince had great respect for him.[94] Probyn remained in his household, and afterwards in Queen Alexandra's, virtually until his death. Thus by 1877 the three stalwart attendants; Francis and Charlotte Knollys and General Probyn, had been recruited.

In the next few days Alexandra visited the Society of British Artists and later, with her husband, studios. They opened new wards at Charing Cross Hospital on the 21st. She attended a charity concert at Grosvenor House for the Ladies' Work Society on the 22nd and called on Aunt Cambridge next day. Gull, at the Queen's request, wrote to King George about Alexandra's need of a recuperative holiday in Athens, leading "as quiet and unexciting a life as possible, availing herself of every means for restoring the nervous power and tone." He recommended quiet drives, gentle horse exercise (limited, to avoid fatigue) and early bed time, to promote "that repose which the depression of strength and exhausted nerves obviously call for."[95] Charlotte Knollys would accompany her and promised the Queen regular reports; "I am convinced that the very best thing for her is complete change as she has been so dreadfully pulled down by her severe cold that she cannot at all rally from it ... I will do my best to take every possible care of the Princess."[96]

The Waleses planned to leave for Paris on 24 March, Alexandra then continuing to Greece, but unfortunately Albert Edward was in agony with an abscess which needed lancing twice. The journey was postponed. Alexandra was very worried about him "God grant he may not have to suffer any more – willingly I wld bear all the pain for him." They spent Easter in London; the boys went to Sandringham with Dalton on 2 April. The couple dined alone together until the 4th, when Alexandra[97] set off, hating leaving her husband and missing him dreadfully.[98] Driving and paying calls in Paris till the 6th, she arrived in Athens on the 10th. In London the Prince rested but on the 8th drove with his sister Louise. His daughters were with him and the next day he "Drove out with little Pss Louise."[99]

Charlotte Knollys told the Queen on the 10th that Alexandra did not seem tired after the long journey, no longer had neuralgia and had felt better ever since leaving London. The palace at Athens was very nice and comfortable, with large, airy rooms and the King and Queen were delighted to see Alexandra again.[100] She drove, walked in the gardens and attended the Te Deum at the cathedral with them as part of the Greek Independence Festival on 12 April; that evening there was a dinner for over 100. There were more dinner parties, but Alexandra also dined alone at least nineteen times. It was a rest cure, but what she embraced most enthusiastically was skating "on wheels". At 32 she still loved ice-skating, and, lacking frozen lakes at Athens, went out roller-skating, mostly with her niece and nephews, about 30 times. So much for quiet drives and repose; Gull might have been rather startled by her energy. On the 19th Charlotte wrote again;

Alexandra was decidedly better, rose early, retired early "& leads the quietest, most healthy life in the world, being out a great deal in the open air." For some reason she did not mention the roller-skating, although she was certainly aware of it.[101] The Greek children were very well; the eldest girl was exactly like her mother and they all spoke English among themselves, having had English nurses from birth. Alexandra had been to see the King's country place at Tatoii, about 14 miles away and 2,000 feet above sea level; the scenery, with fir trees and large rocks, reminded Charlotte of Scotland. "The King is making a little farm there & the Alderney cows seem to thrive remarkably well."[102]

On the 20th, Charlotte again stressed Alexandra's quiet life; "early hours & a total freedom from every kind of excitement. The Princess amuses herself with drawing & walking & driving with the King and Queen." Everything was orderly and well-managed and the servants wore picturesque national dress. The climate, sunny, with cool breezes, was perfection and the palace gardens "are the most beautiful I ever saw, not only orange trees, palms & every description of tropical plants, but the flowers are arranged & kept in the most wonderful manner & the <u>masses</u> of colour are almost startling in their brilliancy."[103] On the same day Alexandra thanked Dalton for looking after her sons. Mathematics were important but so were general behaviour and demeanour; "One thing I must ask you, especially now I am away, to pay great attention to their being obedient and <u>obeying the moment</u> they are told. Also let them be civil to everybody high and low, and not get grand now they are by themselves – and please take particular care they are not <u>toadied</u> by the Keepers or any of those around them."[104]

Alexandra went to see the Acropolis and attended the King's "Name Day" service at the cathedral on 5 May. On the 2nd, she wished her sons good luck in the examination they were to take before becoming naval cadets; "remember that your efforts to do well <u>now</u> will have an influence for the <u>whole</u> of your lives. How constantly I am thinking of you especially at this time and it is grief to me being separated from you now, and I don't know <u>how</u> I shall get through the 14th, which I believe is that of your Examination. God grant that all may pass off well." Papa was expected home from abroad soon; "How pleased you will all be to see him again – I quite envy him and you too." She was enjoying her holiday; "I will certainly get a lot of photos from all the places here, which are so pretty, particularly that <u>lovely</u> garden, which I am sure must have been the original <u>paradise</u>. You would be amused to see Mother dear sleeping in a kind of muslin cot with white curtains buttoned up close all round to keep the nasty gnats out, who at first bit me horribly – then at 7 o'clock out Mother dear hops from her cage and perches herself on the window sill, opens it and breathes the lovely fresh and sweet scented morning air, and this morning in my nightgown, I made a beautiful sketch of the Acropolis. We went up there again the other day and I enjoyed it immensely, the view there is too beautiful, the whole town of Athens at one's feet; the sea and the mountains in the distance and all round the wonderful remains of Temples which have stood for hundreds and thousands of years. They have excavated a lot more since I was here last and it is most interesting to see all these wonders of antiquity. Every day I regret more that you are not here with yr little cousins, as I am sure you wld have such fun together particularly at skating, they get on capitally and hardly ever fall now."[105] On the 12th she promised, during "these anxious days of your examinations ... my spirit will be with you and you will [hear] a little voice whispering in yr ears to encourage my dearest boys, and implore them to do their utmost."[106] Charlotte continued sending the Queen good news of Alexandra's improved health and enjoyment of a quiet life. On the 18th Alexandra learned that her sons had passed a good examination.[107]

On 17 May their father took them and Louise to the Westminster Aquarium to see Zazell.[108] The next day, the boys went to Windsor, to accompany their grandmother to Balmoral. On the 26th Albert Edward took the girls to a charity military concert, for the Royal Military Cambridge Asylum, at the Albert Hall, "which I think they enjoyed very much."[109] Alexandra received her home letters on the 23rd and simultaneously Alfred, on board *HMS Sultan*, arrived; there was a party there next day and she lunched on board on the 27th. There was trouble in Greece and on the 28th a deputation petitioned the King for a change of minister; later, a mob gathered outside the palace, demanding war and a permanent ministry. He finally persuaded them to disperse after three and a half hours. It was now time to go home; Alexandra, Willy and Olga left in *Amphitrite* on the 30th, for Corinth, where she boarded *Osborne* and steamed through the Ionian Islands all the next day. Travelling by train from Brindisi, via Turin, she finally reached the Hotel Bristol in Paris at 6pm on the 2nd and wrote immediately to George for his birthday, "which I am so sorry we cannot spend together – but we will keep it in a few days after our return home." Papa was arriving at 6.45am on the 3rd to join her at the hotel; "I hope I shall be ready in time but it is rather an early hour after so long a journey".[110] "Three cheers for old Motherdear's coming home!!"[111] she added. Albert Edward "found dear Alix looking very well; delighted to be together again."[112] They enjoyed four days in Paris, breakfasting at the Café de Madrid in the Bois de Boulogne on the 3rd, driving, visiting, shopping and theatre-going. They arrived home on the 7th and later went to the Agricultural Hall for a horse show. The next day they attended Sandown Races and *Faust* at the Haymarket. The Ascot party was at Easthampstead Park; after seeing Virginia Water and the Temple, they left on the 18th, visiting Wellington College on the way home.

Gull saw Alexandra on the following day; he thought she looked stronger but was thinner and too pale. Unfortunately she had a cold and sore throat, but was delighted to be with her children. Gull had expected more from the holiday but still thought there was some improvement. He begged her not to over-tax her strength[113] but she could scarcely avoid this. On the 19th she gave medals at the Horticultural Society's Flower Show in South Kensington and, with her husband, visited *Warspite*, off Woolwich on the 21st, to present Marine Society prizes. Later they gave a dinner party for the Emperor and Empress of Brazil. There were balls, theatres, concerts and more dinners; on the 27th Alexandra went to a bazaar at the Horticultural Gardens, for the Eastbourne Convalescent Home. Some Danish ladies sang for her on the 28th and the next day Lady Suffield's children came to tea. On the 30th the family went to Sandringham and Waldemar came to stay while Albert Edward was at Newmarket; they went driving and on 5 July Alexandra took all the children to Hunstanton, where there was a thunderstorm. They left and, collecting Albert Edward, arrived in time for the state concert. They went to the Chapel Royal of the Savoy's Schools and Alexandra presented prizes; they visited the College of Surgeons and Museum, later seeing *Lohengrin* at Covent Garden; on 14 July they unveiled Count Gleichen's[114] statue of King Alfred at Wantage, but Eddy was ill.

He had felt unwell on the 7th, was diagnosed with typhoid fever and stayed in bed for a month; "it is impossible there could be a more patient, gentle, uncomplaining sufferer than Prince Albert Victor"[115] wrote Dalton. There was no cause for great alarm, so, although spending a lot of time with Eddy, Alexandra, with her husband, continued as usual: to the zoo with Waldemar and, after he had left, Sir Richard Wallace's[116] collection of pictures at Hertford House. The usual seasonal balls, dinners and opera (*Lucia di Lammermoor* on the 12th at the Haymarket) continued. Alexandra drove and paid visits, sometimes with the children, and called on Aunt Cambridge, 80 on the 25th. Gull told the Queen on 21 July that he considered Prince Eddy's illness had been contracted at Sandringham; the Princess was very well, but Princess Victoria had been ailing since coming to London; she might also have been infected at Sandringham and, although she seemed much better two days later, Gull had no doubt she had had a mild typhoid-like infection. Albert Edward would have Sandringham's sanitation thoroughly investigated immediately.[117]

On the 21st he took George and Louise to Lady Holland's[118] garden party at Holland House. They had been urged to send the four younger children to stay with the Queen at Osborne, but Alexandra suspected the source of infection was in fact Marlborough House; if the children had imbibed it, they might fall ill at Osborne, far away from her care; on the other hand, as most of them seemed uninfected so far, it was unlikely to happen now. "I trust indeed it may be so", wrote Gull.[119] The Prince returned from Goodwood on 3 August and the next day they saw Zazell and the Gorilla at the London Aquarium. William of Prussia came to lunch and dinner. The Royal Academy's private view was on the 5th, but Eddy had not fully recovered. On the 6th Albert Edward left him with Alexandra and took the others to stay on *Osborne* at Cowes, where she was satisfied they would have lots of fresh air and could "always play on the beach as much as usual, and have their bathing and all, and will be kept as much out of the way of strangers as in a house." While she was writing, Eddy kept interrupting; he was pretty well, although his temperature had gone up. "I am with him all day long and only take a short drive on the evening, and he continues as good a patient as possible, but what a long and dreary time it has been."[120] She had no intention of leaving him but was worried he was losing valuable preparation time for *Britannia* and would be behind all the other boys.[121]

A report had appeared on 3 August. Eddy's fever could have been caught at Marlborough House, as the incubation period had been almost too short for it to have infected him during only six days at Sandringham. The nearby War Office was insanitary and the local drains were in a bad state. Marlborough House's closets and passages were "often little short of poisonous, and nearly always stuffy."[122] This could have aggravated Alexandra's illness; her symptoms improved when she left London and returned when she did. On the 9th it was reported that Marlborough House's drainage was to be entirely reorganised.[123] Ground subsidence, for example, after heavy rain, meant that drain pipes from the house were not level and effluent had filtered backwards under the basement, producing noxious conditions. Repairs in 1877–8 corrected this.[124]

Eddy moved onto the sofa on 8 August but relapsed back into bed on the 11th. His mother spent time with him but also went out driving. She thanked George for his letters "and the beautiful prawns just arrived, which Wright brought me, in triumph, and I of course at once began to eat them, and they are quite excellent – <u>how</u> nice of my little Georgie to think of poor Mother dear; at first I thought they were little crabs! but these are delicious and so beautifully juicy!! I am sure when I show them to poor Eddy he will want some too, but I am afraid they would be very bad for him; he is delighted with your letters and longs to be with you but I fear it will be much longer than you all expect before <u>we</u> are <u>allowed</u> to come to Cowes! Is it not tiresome, we all being separated like this, and we feel very lonely here in this big place! But dear Eddy is the most cheerful of the party and I read to him all day long, all kinds of books. We have finished 'Jack the Lion Killer' and you must read it as it is most exciting and interesting. We also played several games of cards. He has grown very tall, the top of his head comes right up to my eyes, but he is as thin as a <u>stick</u>, and when he tries to take a few steps, his legs are very shaky." She hoped George was being a good boy and working at French; "You seem to have had a great deal of fun going about with Papa and now I hear you are going to Ostend – mind you are very civil to everybody and <u>don't</u> get <u>uppish</u>."[125] Papa had taken them to see the ships at Cowes, especially *Thunderer*; they were going to Ostend on the 13th for a few days, meeting the Prussian family and Charlotte's fiancé, Prince Bernhard of Saxe-Meiningen.[126] After lunch at Osborne with the Queen on 18 August, they went to London. King Christian had arrived and Alexandra took him to see the zoo and Zazell, several theatres and a concert.

By 18 August Eddy was back on the sofa; his father and siblings found him much better and very cheerful and they returned to Cowes on the 20th. Alexandra walked and drove with her father until he left on the 24th; Eddy meanwhile had gone out once or twice in the "garden chair". By the 25th he was almost well and, on medical advice, went with his mother and Charlotte Knollys to Cowes, although he stayed at Osborne House, comfortably settled in the three rooms the Queen had lent them. Alexandra was "living on board as I thought it not right any longer to neglect the other children and my Bertie, and the beautiful air seems to revive me, but I come up here for luncheon and stop all the afternoon with the dear child, who is now gaining ground every day and I hope will pick up quicker than we thought."[127] Gull had advised a quiet regime, with no hurrying or agitation, which might affect Eddy's nerves; Mrs Jones and Fuller, the boys' valet, were looking after him. Alexandra spent the 27th and other days with him; otherwise there was sailing, entertaining, excursions and visiting for the next four weeks. She played on the beach with the other children and lunched at Osborne. Albert Edward had earlier been to Trouville for a week and left for London on the 13th. The *World* had attacked him because of an undefined feeling that he did not treat his wife, who was very popular, fairly. He was also accused of frivolity, but, as Ponsonby wrote "this is hard on him, for what is he to do." Attempts to find him worthwhile employment had been made and Gladstone had tried his best but the Prince had only been sent a few very dull Foreign Office despatches; the more interesting ones were confidential and kept from him, which naturally made him rather sour.[128] As for his relationship with Alexandra, the public, as usual, was reading too much into their times apart which could, especially in 1877, be explained, for example, by illness.

Alexandra and the children stayed another week, driving through Cowes in a little cart, sailing, excursions, picnics and visiting friends; Eddy had moved to the yacht by 16 September. The next day the sailors danced and sang before dinner. On the 21st Alexandra wrote wisely and sensibly to Dalton about her concerns; since Eddy's illness, the boys were "perpetually quarrelling and using strong language to each other." Also, "they are both but more especially Eddy, I am sorry to say, fearfully inquisitive, which for boys at their age too[129] is a dreadful habit, and makes them quite a nuisance for they always break into everybody's conversation, and it becomes impossible to speak to anyone before them." This should be stopped before they left home for naval training and it was too late. On the third point she felt most strongly; "politics of any kind, home or foreign, should be as much as possible kept from them, as they are much too young to form any sound ideas for themselves, therefore it is a pity they should express their opinion on subjects they cannot understand, and which later on, and in their position, will stick to them for life." Above all, they should take a broad view of everything and not be influenced by party spirit either in politics or religion, although she knew Dalton would not try to do this.[130]

Alexandra and the children left on the 21st for Clarence House while Marlborough House was being overhauled and the Edinburghs were abroad, and started for Abergeldie on the 25th. There had been two deaths in the Prince's circle: Mr Onslow, the elderly Sandringham Rector, from dropsy; he was good-natured and unselfish and had not looked after himself. The other was Gillett, the Prince's valet for almost 29 years; "I have lost in him as true a friend as he was a devoted servant."[131] In Scotland, the Prince stalked deer and grouse and there were visits to the people on the Balmoral estate. The Queen and Beatrice came to tea on the 30th and 7 October. The engagement diary, however, was left blank for the rest of the year because Charlotte became ill with typhoid fever on 2 October[132] and was quarantined at Abergeldie, where Alexandra stayed and helped look after her.[133] The boys would soon embark on their training; despite earlier doubts, Eddy was well enough and Gull was satisfied with him. They left Aberdeen with their father on the 15th for London; three days later, he took them to HMS *Britannia* at Dartmouth and stayed overnight. Alexandra told the Queen; "My darlings have just left – it was a great wrench! but must be got through! – though it is terrible for me who is left! I trust to God all may go well for them, and that their first step in the world by themselves won't be a too difficult or hard one – poor little boys, they cried so bitterly!"[134]

She had written; "It was very horrid to see you two dear boys and dear Papa drive off like that and leave us poor things behind … How my thoughts will follow you tomorrow when dear Papa takes you down to Dartmouth to put you on board the 'Britannia'. I hope and trust that all may go well and that you will be two brave little boys when Papa leaves you, and bear in mind that God will ever be near you, and that you must try yr best to get on there, and be an honour and pride to us all."[135] On the 19th the Prince toured the ship, seeing the cadets at their studies, and then Dartmouth, the old castle, naval hospital, gymnasium and cricket ground. After lunch on board, Albert Edward returned to London. Another letter arrived from Alexandra; "Although I wrote yesterday, I must send a few lines to ask you how you are getting on on board the 'Britannia' which is now to be your home for two years. I am afraid it was horrid seeing dear Papa leave and having to stay behind, but I hope the time will soon pass and then you will stop 6 weeks at home."[136]

While her husband was in London and Newmarket, Alexandra remained at Abergeldie with her daughters and Charlotte, and on 22 October told the Queen she would certainly send the girls to a ball at Balmoral; she would have been delighted to come too but had not the heart to leave "poor dear Charlotte". Albert Edward wanted her at Sandringham by 2 November, as Ernest of Hanover was arriving on the 3rd; she would, regretfully, have to forego the Hallowe'en celebrations at Balmoral.[137] From Euston Hall Albert Edward wrote of his pleasure that his sons liked *Britannia* "& have entered with spirit into your studies & recreations, & I trust you will both bear in mind what I said to you both before leaving the ship, & that I shall hear nothing but the best accounts of you both." He hoped Alexandra would arrive in London with Charlotte on the 31st and they could go to Sandringham together on 2 November,[138] but it was not to be; "I felt sure that you would both be very sorry to hear of poor Charlotte's relapse. However, the accounts are more favourable today … It will I fear be very doubtful whether Mama will be able to arrive at Sandringham for my birthday, which will be a great disappointment to me, but I am most anxious (as she is) that she should not leave Charlotte till she is able to travel."[139] He went to Norfolk on the 3rd for the first shooting party; accepting and praising Alexandra's decision to stay at Abergeldie, he had arranged that the shooting parties at Sandringham would be for men only, so that she would not be expected.[140]

During this time Alexandra had felt deeply conflicted and the Queen's support was very reassuring; "It is such a relief to me and a great comfort to know that you so thoroughly understand me. I only wish to do what is right, and my duty, but at present I must remain here! – I feel I could not leave her thus!"[141] Augusta, Grand Duchess of Mecklenburg-Strelitz had caused a flurry by criticising Alexandra to the Queen for staying with Charlotte; something which she hastily withdrew and which possibly originated with Aunt Cambridge. As the Queen told Augusta, she had seen Alexandra's distress between the fear of neglecting Charlotte and displeasing her husband, and had wanted to defend her, though she knew Aunt Cambridge did not value Miss Knollys as she (the Queen) did and had regretted "Alix's not always having Ladies of high rank with her." Victoria's opinion "by experience is, that the strongest & most disinterested friendships are generally not inside one's family, & are irrespective of rank & position; they are, I verily believe, for all eternity."[142] Thus the Queen revealed her own feelings about faithful friends from different ranks, and one in particular. She may well have discussed this with Alexandra, who, in thanking her for her kindness and understanding, took care, in a subsequent letter, to make a sympathetic reference; "One line with a thousand thanks for all yr great kindness to me on this dear day, which certainly was a sad one away from my darling Bertie. I was also so touched by all you did today and it was very good in Brown[143] to have thought of drinking our health today."[144] Also, "I cannot sufficiently tell you dear Mama how very kind my darling Bertie has been about it all – most unselfish and I am so grateful to him for it."[145]

She wrote to George; "My thoughts are always with you and I pray God you are getting on well at your studies. I am sure you must often feel as poor Walter Evson did at first at St Winifred's School! do you remember that charming book I was reading out to you just before you left. I hope you are trying to work as well as he did – and all what may seem hard, difficult and strange to you now will in a short time seem quite easy to you, if once you put your mind to it, and I need not say how happy it will make us to hear only good reports of both our dear boys. I hear from all sides that you have both been very obedient and good. I am delighted to hear this, and hope that you will continue to be so, and that no Master will have to find fault with you." She and the girls were delighted with his letters, sitting together to read them. Charlotte was "really getting better now at last, but what an awful time we have had of anxiety and suspense – poor Francis is worn to a shred & I am sure wants a strong 'pick-me-up' whenever we leave this place." The "dear little Sisters have been <u>very</u>, <u>very</u> good since you left, they really have been a great comfort to me. I really think <u>your</u> nice and dear little letter, with all the good advice to Louise, has had the best possible influence on her, as she has set such a good example ever since to her sisters, is very obedient and <u>never</u> speaks another word but French to Mlle. She really can speak it very nicely now, and you will both be astonished to hear how well they have got on since you left."[146] Ponsonby suspected Alexandra stopped at Abergeldie not just for Charlotte, but also because she liked being there quietly with her daughters, away from "the vortex" of London society life.[147]

The doctors had disagreed about Charlotte's treatment and it had been a difficult time.[148] Leopold had also been ill but "his real delight is a visit from the Princess of Wales who comes here[149] regularly every day at 5."[150] Alexandra, while happy her sons had settled down so well on *Britannia*, was rather mystified, as she told Dalton; "they seem <u>very far</u> behind the other boys in all their work; I cannot quite understand this, as after all they passed, I thought, a very good examination, and for the last year I was under the impression they were devoting all their time in preparing for the kind of work they are doing now!" However, she had never been as sanguine about their performance as Dalton, and realised allowances should be made for their never having had to work in a class of other boys before. "Still I <u>am</u> anxious it shld be impressed upon them <u>most strongly</u> <u>the shame</u> of being at the bottom ... and that they are doing discredit both to themselves and us." Also, 'Altho' I will in no way interfere from so far off, I cannot help thinking that under <u>these circumstances</u> it is most unadvisable they should have all these <u>extra treats</u> and excitements, which you always used to tell me at home <u>disturbed</u> their minds for the next day." She wanted them treated exactly like the other cadets, and any pleasure or late hours which would not have been approved of at home should be stopped; "as you know well that on their return they will have <u>none</u> of these things, and they will then only find their <u>home dull</u> and stupid! <u>Nothing</u> would give me greater pain than to find them changed in this respect and to see them return, instead of the unaffected, innocent boys who left us, turned into little old fashioned stuck up men!" Sending her love, she urged them "to do their utmost to get on."[151]

Charlotte was well enough to travel by the 22nd and when Albert Edward returned from Londesborough on the 23rd he found her at Clarence House. His family were looking well but, although Charlotte had borne the journey, she had been feverish ever since; Gull and Clayton ordered her to be kept perfectly quiet and there was nothing to stop the family leaving for Sandringham on the 26th. On 1 December, Alexandra was greeted by her sons' "very nice photos which smiled at me when I came into the 'birthday room'. I like the one where you are doing the ropes together with the old sailor, whoever he is, very much, and they are all very like." It had been a beautiful day; they had had a splendid run of an hour and a half out hunting.[152] Within ten days they were back in London, and the couple went to Windsor for the mausoleum service. Their sons returned on the 20th and by the 22nd the whole family was ready for a Sandringham Christmas after a hard term's work and an inordinately illness-filled year.

Alexandra's annual birthday tea in 1877 had been cancelled because of a local epidemic and was held in January 1878 instead. The children from Sandringham, Dersingham, West Newton and Wolferton schools lined up and marched to Sandringham, where the Princess and her children, in a tent in front of the house, handed out the customary New Year's Eve cloaks and caps before tea. The Waleses supported elementary education and had funded the establishment of good school-rooms and teachers in the four villages. Alexandra in particular always monitored their welfare and the children's progress. An undated letter to Dalton[153] shows her deep concern for her own children's education too; "I quite approve of the children recommencing their work regularly and at once, so pray let Mr Mariette[154] come every day while we are in London. About the gymnastics they can have them every alternate day at 3.30 and ride the other days at the same hour, instead of in the morning, as they always have a break of a quarter to half an hour with me between the English and French lessons. I am also very anxious that the hour in the evening should be reserved for the preparation only of their work for the next day, including writing exercises for you and learning by heart etc: which must all be done by themselves. They must also begin to prepare for their French lessons; that they can however do in Mlle's rooms."[155] Dalton apparently supervised the young princesses' education too, and as their brothers were about to leave for Dartmouth, at least some of the instructions may relate to them. Alexandra had had lessons in gymnastics as a girl.

The Christians arrived and the tenants' ball was held on 4 January, followed the next day by the West Norfolk Hounds' meet at Gayton. The Prince Imperial came to shoot on the 7th and later accompanied Albert Edward to Scotland, staying at Hamilton Palace. The Waleses and their sons returned to Clarence House on the 25th and Albert Edward saw the boys and Dalton off to Dartmouth next day. The couple met Empress Elizabeth at Claridge's and on the 28th went to stay at Crichel.[156] George's letter had given his mother "the greatest pleasure and all your good thoughts and the nice and kind things you say about me and your home touched me very much. I too miss you both terribly and it was indeed a very sad parting, <u>how</u> I <u>hate</u> partings!!" Lady Knollys had died from bronchitis; she had managed to visit her convalescent daughter but naturally the family, especially Charlotte, to whom Alexandra broke the news personally, were grief-stricken. "I cannot say <u>how</u> deeply I feel it too, as I was very fond of dear Lady Knollys, whom we have known for so many years now, and in fact looked upon her like a member of our family almost. Do both of you write a little line of sympathy to the poor General and Charlotte."[157]

After hunting, shooting and a ball, the couple returned to London, and the Prince exhorted his sons to "apply yourselves vigorously to your studies, so as if possible to excel over the Cadets of your standing at the next Exam".[158] Royal birth was no excuse for slacking and he wanted them to advance through hard work rather than privilege. On 4 February the couple attended a debate in the House of Commons and heard speeches by Gladstone and Gathorne Hardy.[159] There were theatre visits, a ball at the German Embassy on the 6th for Crown Prince Rudolph,[160] and visits to Leighton's and Prinsep's studios; at the latter were the Indian portraits and sketches for his picture of the Queen's proclamation[161] at Delhi on 1 January 1877. Alexandra drove with her daughters on most days and Albert Edward sometimes went stag-hunting. On the 14th the couple took the girls to an amateur production at the Gaiety, and Alexandra attended the Salisbury's ball in honour of Crown Prince Rudolph on 16 February. Albert Edward and Arthur left for a double wedding on the 18th in Berlin; Princess Charlotte married Bernhard, Hereditary Duke of Saxe-Meiningen and Princess Elizabeth of Prussia[162] the Hereditary Grand Duke of Oldenburg. Albert Edward sent his wife a detailed account.[163]

Alexandra reproached George; "I was sorry you two naughty boys forgot poor little Louise's birthday; she however was very nice about it and never complained. She only said she wished you were both here and could have played with all the children who came to tea with them, the Harbords and cousins, and we had a game of lottery, where we missed you so dreadfully. They all got some very nice little presents and Louise ... got a lot of pretty new books, a work box, some china, a little arrow brooch, <u>one</u> pearl, and silver spoons from Grandmama. We all miss dear Papa very much and I don't think he will be back before the 9th or 10th! ... Saturday week I went down to Northamptonshire to Lord and Lady Spencer[164] for a few nights to see the Empress[165] hunt." The Tecks were there too and they all dined one evening with the Empress, who had now gone home; her son was staying a little longer. "Poor little Victoria has not been very well lately and was obliged to stop in bed for three days with a bad cough and cold, but I hope she will soon be all right again; they all three send you both their best love." They were now back in "dear old bright, comfortable Marlborough House."[166] After Berlin, the Prince called at Darmstadt, and Paris[167] and returned on the 10th. "He is looking very well, and brought me a lot of lovely violets, and the Sisters each a box of bonbons." For their fifteenth wedding anniversary, "Papa gave me the charming statue of you two, done by Victor Gleichen, which you kept so <u>beautifully</u> secret when at Sandringham. We see by the papers that Eddy has been christening a ship!! he <u>never told me</u> a <u>word</u> about it, when he wrote yesterday. Why did he not? ask him from me." She had taken the girls to see the Christy Minstrels and asked George about his own singing, "I hope that you at least join the Choir <u>sometimes</u>, it wld be such a pity if you were to forget all you know!" She was delighted he was getting on so well with his work and hoped he was always "a good & obedient boy".[168] The couple saw *Les Cloches de Corneville* at the Folly on the 11th and life continued as usual. Alexandra was touched at the Queen giving her "your Indian Order and wishing me to have it before anybody else." She would wear it shortly.[169]

They visited Empress Eugénie and her son at Chislehurst on the 25th and two days later the Prince, staying at Croxteth Hall,[170] saw the Grand National Steeplechase for the first time. Alexandra attended the Saturday Popular Concert at St James's Hall on the 30th; later, the couple saw Neville Moritz[171] play *Othello* at the Queen's Theatre. The next day Alexandra visited the French Gallery and Vincent Robinson's[172] establishment, where an Eastern apartment, brought from Damascus, was on show. It was the Cork and Orrerys'[173] ball that evening and, two days later, lunch with the Queen at Windsor, before a charity concert at Grosvenor House for the training ship, *Clio*, docked at the Menai Straits. On 4 April Sir Sydney Waterlow[174] showed the Waleses round St Bartholomew's Hospital's medical council, school buildings, and main wards, where they talked to patients and noted special cases pointed out by the surgeons. The patients had not been told they were coming but of course recognised them. Children to whom Alexandra spoke were delighted and struggled to sit up as she said "Good-bye". The couple saw the dispensaries and washing places before leaving over two hours later. The next day, they visited Leighton's and Millais' studios. To Alexandra's pleasure, her brother, Frederick and his wife, Louise arrived for three weeks on 6 April; they all went to the Royal Italian Opera at Covent Garden that evening. It was a debate in the House of Lords on the 7th and a special dinner at Marlborough House, with music by Mademoiselle Redeker,[175] Baron F Orczy,[176] Herr Henschel and the Grenadier Guards Band. On the 9th it was Northampton Races. On the 10th the Christians came to lunch and afterwards the Waleses and their guests saw the Minton ceramics for the Paris Exhibition, later attending the Court Theatre. The next day they toured Windsor Castle, St George's and the Wolsey Chapels before lunching at Cumberland Lodge; they drove and later dined with the Salisburys[177] on the 12th. On the 13th Albert Edward and Frederick watched the boat race, and Empress Eugénie and her son called at Marlborough House. Alexandra took her relatives to the Danish chapel at Poplar's morning service on the 14th; the next day there was more driving, and the Prince of Wales's Theatre, with Arthur. The Waleses spent Easter at Sandringham, from the 16th to the 24th.

That evening Albert Edward took Frederick to the Grand Lodge's annual festival at the Freemasons' Hall. The Universal Exhibition was opening on 1 May and he left for Paris on 25 April. Alexandra and the Danes saw *The Pink Dominoes* at the Criterion and the next day, with the boys, went to the National Gallery, the Society of Painters in Water Colours' Exhibition and, later, the Gaiety. On the 27th they lunched with the Queen at Windsor. They visited the Tower of London on the 29th, after which Frederick left for the Paris Exhibition's opening. On the 30th, Alexandra, her sons and sister-in-law were shown round St Paul's Cathedral by the dean.[178] After seeing the tombs in the crypt, they climbed the main stairs to the galleries, halting in the Upper (or Golden) Gallery and pointing out the landmarks that could be seen. From here, Alexandra, with her sons, negotiated the narrow steps leading to the "ball" despite her stiff knee, which always made stairs difficult for her, and the long skirts trailing around her. They had climbed 600 steps altogether and the boys were thrilled at actually sitting within the "ball". Later they saw the library and the Wellington monument.[179] Alexandra and her sister-in-law left for Paris on 2 May. They all visited the Exhibition on the 4th and saw Mr Wills's splendid display of new plants; he presented bouquets to the two princesses. On the 13th the President and the Duchess of Magenta[180] gave a state dinner at the Elysée Palace, and the next day the British Embassy held a grand banquet for 1,500, followed by a soirée to which the Japanese exhibitors also came. Alexandra, who had no time to write to her sons until after returning home on the 17th, told them she had been "8 times to the Exhibition and saw everything there was to be seen. We had a climb up into the Trocadero, which reminded me of our crawling up into St Paul's Steeple. The English section was splendid and so were the French and Japanese." The boys had not been allowed to interrupt their studies to go to Balmoral with the Queen, seeing their parents briefly in London on the way, but it could not be helped. Instead, the Queen had taken two Wales granddaughters; "So you see we had to make a double sacrifice, and have only kept Louise at home, who is very lonely but still rather pleased to have remained with us. They all three cried floods and little Harry declared at the last moment, 'I won't go', with a stamp of her foot."[181]

The Prussians, with their four younger children, were in London and met the Waleses several times; Alexandra also often took Louise driving, and they went to Hallé's concert at St James's Hall on 24 May; to Horse Guards Parade on the 25th; and to the Royal Horticultural Society's Flower Show on the 28th. Waldemar, whose ship was at Calais, arrived on the 27th for three days, "which we enjoyed immensely together. He was just the same as usual, and ate as much as ever; he used to get up at 7 every morning to drive my four greys, with Westover; in the middle of the day about 11 we rode together." She attended Mario's[182] benefit concert at St James's Hall on the 29th and Hallé's concert on 30 May, when she also went to the afternoon service at Westminster Abbey. "Little

Victoria and Harry are still in Scotland and won't come back till the 7th. Dear Grandmama never lets them go when once she has got them, and poor little Louise misses them dreadfully."[183] Alexandra was sorry to miss George's birthday again but would keep some of his presents until he came home. His father wrote, "Dear Mama has sent you fr us some fruit & cake & a pin which I hope you will like. Grandmama has sent you also some books. I hope that you have both written to her. Remember that you will be 13 tomorrow! Quite a big boy, so I hope that you will continue to work hard at yr studies & pass a good examination."[184] On the 5th the Waleses, the Christians and Arthur went to Epsom Races and on the 6th there was a state concert. Alexandra went to another Hallé's concert on the following day. Victoria and Maud came home and their mother, delighted to have them back, took all three girls to the horse show at the Agricultural Hall on the 12th and to other places later. Albert Edward had brought back "a very pretty 'pudding' dog"[185] from Paris; "He is quite young, & will be trained to run by the carriage. I brought sisters two white Java sparrows & for myself some Chinese nightingales, which are very pretty. I have also got a new kind of terrier, & if you are both very industrious at your studies & have good reports, I will give it to you both when the Term is over."[186] The Queen's cousin, King George V of Hanover, had died and on the 22nd his son, Ernest Augustus, Duke of Cumberland,[187] and daughters, Frederica[188] and Mary,[189] brought his body to England for the funeral on the 24th at St George's Chapel, where he was laid to rest. Before they left, the three dined at Marlborough House; Ernest was engaged to Thyra.

On 28 June the Waleses attended prize-giving at the Infant Orphan Asylum at Wanstead, having first visited it on 28 June 1866. Alexandra presented prizes and toys and Dagmar Petersen, aged about seven, whose father had been Danish, made a little speech in reply. Alexandra talked to her specially afterwards and asked the staff about her. More relatives and friends called and the couple stayed two days at Bestwood Lodge.[190] They also visited Nottingham and the Prince opened the new Fine Art Museum. The Hessians[191] had arrived at Buckingham Palace on 5 July, en route for Eastbourne, where the Prussian children were already staying at the Cavendish Hotel. That evening, the Wales couple went to the Duchess of Manchester's party. "All the Harbords, Stonors, Lady Macclesfield's two girls, Cousins and Colonel Clarke's little girls"[192] came for Victoria's birthday on the 6th, with tea in tents and games. There was a state ball on the 12th and the next day a garden party at Marlborough House, to which the Hessian family came. The Waleses went to Lady Holland's garden party and a review at Aldershot next day and on the 16th attended the wedding of the Suffields' eldest daughter, Cecilia Harbord.

The Hessians returned to Eastbourne on 20 July; later, Mademoiselle Augusta Schou,[193] of the Royal Opera at Copenhagen, sang before Alexandra. On the 22nd the Prince and Princess of Wales called informally at the London Hospital in Whitechapel Road and toured the wards. They left for prize-giving (Alexandra giving the prizes) on *Britannia* on the 24th, and brought their sons home next day; the family saw *HMS Pinafore* at the Opéra Comique on the 27th. While the couple were at Goodwood, the children stayed with the Queen at Osborne, joining their parents on *Osborne* at Portsmouth on 3 August. Alexandra and the children lunched with the Queen on the 10th and the next day the boys and their parents went to see the laying of the dedication stone of the Parish Church of St Mary, Southampton, instigated by Albert Edward's friend, the late Bishop of Winchester.[194] The family watched the Queen's Naval Review on the 13th, from *Victoria and Albert*. Three days later, Alexandra's parents, Thyra and Uncle William of Glücksburg[195] arrived from Copenhagen; Albert Edward brought them to Cowes on the 17th for another two weeks, visiting the Queen several times. On 4 September, with the Danes, they returned to Marlborough House and later attended a promenade concert at Covent Garden. All the guests went home and on the 7th Eddy and George, with Dalton, left for *Britannia*, while their father went to stay at Brantingham Thorpe[196] for Doncaster Races. On the 3rd, shockingly, the Thames passenger paddle-steamer, *Princess Alice*, had sunk after a collision, with great loss of life; the Waleses gave 50 guineas to the disaster fund. It would prove a bad omen.

Alexandra and the girls had been rather abandoned by their relatives, but soon they all left for Rumpenheim. When they returned, on the 24th, it was to leave again on the 25th for Scotland, where, by then, Albert Edward was; he met them at Aberdeen and took them back for a fortnight at Abergeldie. Alexandra wrote; "I went out with Papa deer driving the other day at Invercauld, where he shot one stag, and we had to lie for an hour and a half in pouring rain before a shot was fired. Altogether they killed 5 stags that day. We had to ride our ponies part of the way, they were all very fresh and 'pully', having been kept waiting so long in the cold, and going back to Invercauld, Charlotte and Mr Hall went in Colonel Farquharson's carriage, as it was raining so hard; dear Andrew[197] and Francis were walking, while the rest rode, when all of a sudden, Colonel Farquharson[198] came galloping by, knocking off dear Andrew's hat, which created a great commotion among us all, as the hat rolled under our carriage, which frightened the horses, who immediately began kicking violently over the traces – upon which Francis rushed up, insisted upon our being dragged out, as he thought the whole carriage would be smashed; in the middle of all this, Lord Colville's[199] pony lashed out and began kicking Papa's in a most furious way, who had a narrow escape of having his legs broken, however, all is well that ends well and we got back to the house, where we had a <u>lovely tea</u> of scones and honey, <u>how</u> you wld have enjoyed it."[200]

The rest of the holiday was quieter, partly because of Sir Thomas Biddulph's[201] recent death, and Alexandra suggested her sons might write to his son, Victor, which they did.[202] She expressed her own sympathy to the Queen on

16 October; "I do feel for you so in all yr worries and troubles which indeed seem endless at this present moment. I know also what a fearful loss poor Sir Thomas Biddulph must be and how each day you must feel it more and more and miss your faithful friend's clear head and valuable advice!" Marie had written a rough and hasty letter to the Queen, when she was really angrier with the Admiralty, which had just sent orders to Alfred. Alexandra hoped, soothingly, that the Queen would "have fine weather for yr visit to the Glassalt Shiel where you will enjoy a few days' perfect rest and peace away from all the bothers of yr Country and Family!!!! but I am not sure that the last are not the worst of the two!"[203] Ponsonby had seen Alexandra and her daughters on 8 October, when "she talked away in such a cheerful easy way that it charmed one." At dinner three days later he noticed that she "seems to me often to hear when it is supposed she doesn't. Northcote raised his voice in talking to her, but when the Prince of Wales talked to the Queen about the Duke of Edinburgh going across the Atlantic ... and then whispered to the Queen, the Princess scarcely turned her head towards them, but twice smiled, evidently at the revelations."[204] After lunches and drives with the Queen, the couple and their daughters left for London, where, the next day, the Prince chaired a meeting of the Royal Commission of the Paris International Exhibition's Finance Committee. They went to the theatre in the evening and again on the 15th, when they took Louise to see *HMS Pinafore*.

On the 16th the couple left for Paris; their party included Christopher Sykes and "all the French are much struck by his height & imposing appearance."[205] The Prince attended the distribution of Exhibition prizes on the 21st and the next day it was the Grand Exhibition Fête at Versailles. He had had a good press for his part in the Exhibition; like his father, he took on "opportunities of public usefulness" and was ready "to undertake work, and to persevere till it is finished, and finished with credit." This would be invaluable when he eventually became King.[206] The ball at Versailles was "a terrible crush. There was in fact such a crowd that I don't think anybody enjoyed themselves. The fireworks were rather fine, but the rain had 'damped their ardour' considerably". The Danes and the Waleses went up in the giant balloon which made several ascents daily from the Tuileries' gardens. Also, as Albert Edward told George, they had seen "a play called 'Le Tour du Monde en 80 Jours'.[207] It lasted a long time, but parts of it were rather entertaining, & the scenic effects very good. The attacking of a Railway Train in the Rocky Mountains by Red Indians & the blowing up of a steamer crossing the Atlantic was very well done, & would have delighted you & Eddy."[208]

Alexandra promised to get birthday presents in Paris for her sons to give their father. She was glad George was getting on well with his work and music, "but tell Eddy how sorry I am that he does not go on with his, as he will regret it some day when he grows up, for he has a very good ear and great taste for it." She had seen Monsieur Bidde's wild beast show; he subdued a fierce lioness with a whip, "but ended by kissing her, when she wagged her tail and laid down quietly at his feet, then he let in an Elephant, a bear, 5 hyaenas and dragged in a poor little lamb, who seemed in a dreadful fright among all those wild beasts; he then put its poor little head nearly into the lion's mouth and made them lie down together, when the Elephant stepped over them; he next made the bear and lioness embrace each other, with a loving growl; after this 5 lions rushed in at once and he made them perform all kinds of tricks, also two large tigers came in, who he said were the most difficult of all to tame. It was most exciting but I was in a horrible fright lest at any moment the poor man shld be eaten up." Her father had sent sad news of his eldest brother, Karl, Duke of Glücksburg's, death.[209]

At the end of their trip, the Waleses visited Crystal Palace's Bible Stand Committee's Kiosk, opposite the Trocadero, contributed to the fund and accepted a copy of the smallest Bible in the world, printed at Oxford in minute type, on very thin silky paper. They returned to London on 4 November and, after various engagements, left on the 8th for Sandringham for the Prince's birthday party, and shooting. Alexandra wrote in distress to the Queen about the worsening situation in Greece, now in conflict with Turkey; "if the promises made to Greece by the Great Powers are not speedily fulfilled all must be up. It is but too clear that England is the only country which has it in its power to make Turkey do what she ought, & she now again is the only one who seems disinclined to carry out what all the others are trying their utmost to bring about!"[210]

In Darmstadt, diphtheria had struck the Hesse family. Victoria had recovered and Elizabeth had escaped infection but Irène, Alicky and Marie (known as May) had succumbed. On 16 November, four-year-old May died.[211] The Grand Duke and Ernest Louis were getting better but "poor Aunt Alice is in terrible grief, & is far from well besides, & the strain on her mind & the anxiety she has gone through are most distressing."[212] At Sandringham a ball had been held on the 15th. Alexandra's 34th birthday fell on a Sunday and the couple, their daughters and the Tecks went to church. Alexandra thanked the Queen "for yr most affte letter with all the kind things you say of me, but I feel really quite ashamed of so much praise as I don't deserve a quarter of it, though one thing at least is true, how entirely I return your affection which I value above all things; from the first day of my landing in England you have always shown me such invariable kindness that I should indeed be ungrateful if I did not do my best to show you in every way how much I appreciate it. Thanks a thousand thanks for all your loving kindness – the charming picture of my pets has delighted me beyond measure and I think it is very good. The little brooch is too pretty and is doubly precious in my eyes from yr having picked up the stone yourself. We spent a very happy tho' quiet day and my Bertie quite overloaded me with lovely presents."[213] She also thanked Dalton for contributing to the "lovely silver jug" from the household, which was "the fellow" to the one given to the Prince on 9 November. She had appreciated his frequent letters and reports; George had passed a very good examination in seamanship, although unfortunately poor Eddy had not.[214]

Albert Edward left for London on 2 December and Alexandra joined him on the 9th, when they heard that Alice had diphtheria. Alexandra told Dalton again how disappointed she was at Eddy's lack of progress; in fact Lord Ramsay[215] had as good as advised them to remove him from *Britannia*. This would, she was sure, be a great mistake, as he would then have to be educated at home, quite alone. She was afraid Lord Ramsay might lead her husband into "some hasty conclusion" and as "Lord R's opinion is the most <u>unfavourable</u> of everybody's – will you not therefore speak to him before he comes up, as no one knows better about the boy than yourself, and I feel more trust in yr judgement of him than any others."[216] On the 11th the Waleses received Messrs RS Garrard, bringing a gold inlaid casket from British residents in California, to give to Lord Beaconsfield. Two days later they received the Chinese Minister, Kuo-Ta-Jen, before he went home. Later, they attended the mausoleum service at Windsor. There had been good news from Russia as "dear Aunt Minny and Uncle Sacha have another little boy."[217] Alexandra greatly regretted being unable to attend Thyra's wedding;[218] Waldemar was sad she was leaving home, but was now working hard for the naval lieutenant's examination. All this was overtaken by dreadful news later on the 14th; Alice had died on the anniversary of her father's death.

The Royal Family was overwhelmed with distress. Albert Edward, Leopold and Christian left on the 16th for the funeral and court mourning was decreed for six weeks. Alexandra wrote; "It is indeed <u>too</u>, <u>too</u> dreadful! and I cannot think what poor Uncle Louis and the poor little Children will do without her, who was so devoted to them … Poor Papa is terribly cut up by the loss of such a dear Sister. I am sure you two will never forget yr dear Aunt Alice who loved you fondly, and you will have seen by dear Papa's letter to Eddy, what she was to him and indeed to us all. I gave yr messages to poor Grandmama and Papa, which pleased them much … Dear Papa left last night for Frankfort, to attend the last sad ceremony! which will be <u>too</u> dreadful for him. They are not however going to stay at Darmstadt on account of the infection and will be back again at the end of the week. I shall return to Windsor this afternoon to try and comfort poor Grandmama in her dreadful sorrow, and I shall then come back to take you down to Sandringham. The poor little Sisters are most impatiently awaiting you. Don't you think you had both better write a few lines of condolence to Grandmama, as she feels this terrible blow so much. God bless you both, my darling boys, and may you <u>never know</u> what such sorrow is."[219] The funeral was at Darmstadt on the 18th, when a service was also held in the private chapel at Windsor. The Queen went to Osborne, where her sons saw her on their return.

Alexandra went to Sandringham and Thyra married the Duke of Cumberland on the 21st in the chapel adjoining the Royal Castle of Christiansborg. Albert Edward joined his family at Sandringham. On the 27th, Alexandra thanked Mary Teck for more lovely Christmas presents, including a pin, a tri-coloured pencil and "that darling puggy – I really have no words to express my admiration for it, it is simply an adorable pug and will never leave my dressing table – wherever I go, he will have to come too and keep guard over me like a black faced angel that it is. I really am delighted with it, and never saw one like it." The Cumberlands' wedding had gone off beautifully and they were very happy, but it had been a sombre Christmas; "my poor Bertie still looks very sad and unhappy, but no wonder – he was so fond of poor darling Alice!"[220] At Osborne, the Queen, engulfed by grief and messages of condolence, noted "A very dear kind one from Bertie, speaking of Alix being 'much too good for him', & so delighted at my great praise of her."[221]

⚜

Still in mourning, the family walked to Appleton Water Tower on 2 January 1879 and also heard singing practice in the church. Heavy snow preceded skating and walks, and shooting party guests, including Mr JW Lawless[222] from *HMS Britannia*, started arriving on the 4th. Alexandra drove her small team of ponies, paid calls and went for walks with her daughters. Albert Edward had earlier met the Hessian family at Flushing and brought them back to stay with the Queen at Osborne. On the 25th he saw his sons off to Dartmouth. In the quiet, dull house, Alexandra wrote; "I was so low this morning to have no Georgie to read to me while my hair was done! Cocky hung its head and Dovey would not coo, they all felt sad with poor old Mother dear. Dear Papa came home Saturday night late, he gave me the last accounts of you. I am so glad you enjoyed yourselves at the Pantomime which must have been very amusing, particularly the Vokes family[223] and the Clowns. I am sure dear old Aunt Cambridge was delighted to have seen you both ... I have thought much of you today, the first day of study after the holydays! I do hope and trust you both did yr very best. I dare say it is hard at first, but if you only try to persevere, I am sure you will get on well at last. The ice is pretty good still, but also there we miss you sadly. I and Sisters did not enjoy the skating at all the first day. We have not been reading much yet, as the Sisters had to go to bed early, and we have been disturbed a good deal hitherto."[224] Albert Edward wrote, "It is still freezing here & the ice is now first rate, & much smoother than it was at first. The girls improve daily in their skating ... I am glad you like Hornby & Harbord & hope you have found some other nice cadets. It gives me great pleasure to hear that your Reports this week have been good. Only let them continue so, & try & work very hard."[225]

Leaving the girls at Sandringham, the couple went to London on 7 February, and that evening Arthur dined with them, when "they were both nice & kind as ever." He told his fiancée, "Bertie & Alix seemed <u>happier</u> & more intimate together than usual which I was so glad to see."[226] The next day the Waleses went to Osborne, where, despite pouring rain and high wind, it was as warm as April. They walked to Egypt Point with the Hesse family on the 11th; visited the Swiss Cottage and the church at Newport, where there was a monument to Charles I's daughter, Princess Elizabeth; perhaps they were considering Alice's memorial. Albert Edward told his sons that everyone was well, but the Hesse cousins "were dreadfully sorry not to have seen you. We see a great deal of them, & they are constantly in our rooms, & go out walking with us."[227] On the 12th they took Grand Duke Louis back to London, leaving his family at Osborne, and the girls arrived from Sandringham. Three days later Crown Princess Victoria arrived. The Waleses attended debates in the House of Lords; Louis returned to Osborne; visitors came and calls were paid. On the 16th and the 17th the couple, with Vicky, went to the Royal Academy's Winter Exhibition, the French Gallery and Maclean's Gallery. Alexandra had no time to write to George until the 17th, when she told him how sad it had been "to see poor Uncle Louis and the Cousins in this dreadful way again, without dear Aunt Alice. I cannot tell you <u>how</u> much I missed her, and how sad it made me to see them <u>alone</u>!! Poor little Cousins, theirs is indeed a sad, sad lot and they will feel it more every day." News from the Cape was grave; "we have had such a dreadful defeat and lost so many men. A lot of Regiments are going out at once, and many Officers have applied to go. Lord Downe[228] and Oliver Montagu I think are also going."[229]

They visited the South Kensington Museum and Boehm's studio on the 19th. Albert Edward had a cold and "We had such a dense fog this morning that we had to light all the candles. The sky looks just like chocolate."[230] Nevertheless, Aunt Vicky was looking well and hoping to see her nephews at Windsor soon. On 20 February the Waleses and their daughters lunched there with the Queen and the Hesse family, later dining with the Tecks. The next day they and Vicky visited the Grosvenor Gallery, and Doulton's Pottery Works and the Burlington Fine Arts Club on the 22nd. Vicky then left for Eastwell, Alexandra and the girls for Norfolk and Albert Edward for Paris, hoping to get rid of his cold later at Pau and Biarritz. Eight inches of snow had recently fallen in London, the ground was still covered and there was a thick fog.[231] At Sandringham; "We have had lovely weather the last few days and have been riding every day since I came here, all my <u>5</u> different horses – and one dog. We went about 25 miles. The girls came out every other day, but they really ride very well now, particularly <u>Harry</u> and <u>Victoria</u> who are not the least nervous and go over every sort of bank and ditch. All the dogs at the kennels are very well, and I take them all out occasionally ... I read to [the Sisters] in the evening sometimes, but not often this time, as we always come home rather late from riding."[232] Albert Edward wrote; "Pau is a very pretty place & the view of the Pyrenees remarkably fine. One day I went to

Lourdes where the pilgrimages you may have heard of take place. Our Hotel here is close to the sea, & we can hear the waves of the Atlantic dashing over the beach close under our windows."[233] On 10 March the couple and their daughters celebrated the anniversary at Marlborough House with a big family dinner. The next day, meeting the Belgian sovereigns en route, they went to Windsor. The boys arrived from Dartmouth and on the 13th Arthur, Duke of Connaught married Princess Louise Margaret of Prussia in St George's Chapel, before a large family gathering. After the wedding breakfast in the dining room, the bridal pair left for their honeymoon at Claremont.

On the following day, the Wales couple returned to London, giving a dinner party on the 15th for the Prussians, their son William and Louise Margaret's parents, Prince and Princess Frederick Charles.[234] The Waleses attended morning service at the Berkeley Chapel on the 16th and gave another family dinner. On 17 March there was a levee and a dinner party; on the 18th, while the Prince visited Oxford with the Prussians, Alexandra drove with her daughters. On the 19th she drove with Vicky who, with William, returned to Berlin, while Fritz went to Eastwell. Albert Edward and Alexandra rode together on the 20th and Alexandra also drove with the children but dined alone as her husband was dining with Christopher Sykes at Hill Street. The couple, with Frederica of Hanover, lunched at Windsor with the Queen and other relatives and later gave a dinner for the Belgian couple, while boys from the Chapel Royal sang glees. There was a family dinner on the 23rd but by the next day, when a levee was held and Lord Beaconsfield gave a dinner for the Belgians, both Alexandra and the Belgian queen had colds.

A drawing room was held on the 27th but news came that Waldemar, the Prussians' youngest son, had died of diphtheria. Albert Edward wrote to George at Dartmouth; "I knew you would be sorry for poor dear little Waldy. Aunt Vicky is quite prostrated with grief, as you know how fond she was of him. I remember how happy you were at Ostend playing with him two years ago. There is no objection to your taking part in the Regatta, & I hope your boat will win."[235] Alexandra also wrote; "Poor little boy – he was only just 11 and seemed such a happy bright little fellow. It is hard that he should have been taken away so young from his poor unhappy Parents and brothers and sisters. I hear they are quite inconsolable." The coffin had been placed next to Sigismund's[236] in the family vault at Potsdam. Alexandra apologised for not writing sooner, but had been "quite ill myself with such a bad cold and neuralgia. I fear the weather has been very cold with you too."[237] She felt better in a few days and, usually with her husband, visited nine artists' studios in the next week. On 3 April she went to an amateur Bach concert, and called on Mrs Langtry[238] and Madame de Bülow on the 7th. The boys returned from Dartmouth on the 9th and they all spent Easter at Sandringham, amid heavy snow. Guests arrived and there was Nap and Bowls in the evenings. On the 14th the couple opened a wing of the Convalescent

Hospital at Hunstanton, built by public subscription in 1877 to mark the Prince's recovery from typhoid. Miss Beck, sister of Sandringham's agent, was matron. Alexandra had donated a bed and during one of her visits lay down on it, to make sure the spring mattress was still in good condition.[239]

On the 15th, an American, Dr WF Carver, "Champion Rifle Shot of the World", showed his skill in shooting glass balls with rifle and gun outside Park House. The next day the party hunted with Mr Villebois's Harriers and the couple went riding several more times. Alexandra assured Dalton that his plan for her sons' future would not be shown to the two admirals, who might try to alter it; she had made her husband promise not to mention it to them, as Dalton was the one who truly had the boys' interests at heart and knew them so well.[240] She and her sons went out with the harriers on the 23rd the day before their father was to take them back to London, for Dartmouth. The guests left, Alexandra rode and the next day saw *Beauty and the Beast* at West Newton School. She occupied herself as usual, and returned with her daughters to London on 3 May. There was a charity concert at the Albert Hall on the 5th, for casualties in the recent Hungarian floods. Soon afterwards, Alexandra's brother Frederick arrived; they dined at home but Albert Edward had already agreed to preside at the Cabdrivers' Benevolent Association Festival Dinner. The next day, after the drawing room, the Prince, with his wife, presented a petition in the House of Lords, on behalf of the farmers of Norfolk, in favour of allowing marriage with a deceased wife's sister, a perennial bone of contention in Parliament.

During her brother's visit, till 28 May, Alexandra saw the operas *Lucia di Lammermoor, Faust, Aida, Don Giovanni* and *Les Amants de Verone* as well as six plays and two concerts, often with her husband or brother. There was a charity performance at the Gaiety on the 7th for casualties in the Isandala Disaster.[241] Edison's "Telephone" was demonstrated at Marlborough House on the 10th. They visited the Royal Academy, the Grosvenor Gallery, an Assault of Arms at the Albert Hall on the 12th, a meeting of the Four-in-Hand Club in Hyde Park and an afternoon performance at Olympia. Next were a charity bazaar at Knightsbridge for paralysed children, a flower show at the Royal Botanic Gardens in Regent's Park, and a charity bazaar at the Duke of Wellington's Riding School, for the Consumption Hospital at Ventnor. On the 24th they "freed" five bridges over the Thames[242] and attended the inaugural service of the Guards' Chapel at Wellington Barracks on the 25th. Alexandra had earlier told her sons; "Grandmama has been in London and all the Uncles and Aunts!!! for drawing rooms etc. She is soon going to Scotland and is going to take two of the girls, which is a great loss to us. I hate letting any of you go out of my sight even for [a] week, yet I have to lose my dear boys for all these months, and now we shall be very lonely with only one Chicken left; they will draw lots this time which is to stay at home! ... The Sisters enjoyed their entertainment very much the other day at Lady Dudley's,[243] where they danced and let off balloons – Elephants and Fish & Punches which went flying all over the Park and some stuck on the trees."[244] Louise and Maud went to Scotland with the Queen on the 21st, leaving the one chicken, Victoria, behind. Alexandra had given the Queen a tea-cosy for her birthday.[245]

On 29 May Alexandra thanked George for his letter; "I gave all your kisses to Victoria, which made a <u>great</u> noise, & I am quite sure if we had had a <u>telephone</u> down here you wld have heard them quite distinctly!... Dear Uncle Freddy left last night – I was <u>so</u> sorry to part from him and we did enjoy those three weeks so much together. I am so glad you two saw him still, was he not fun that day in the carriage reading out Eddie's diary! What delightful two days they were you spent here at home with us – how kind of dear Papa to give us such a delightful surprise![246] ... I am so glad you have been doing yr work so well since yr return and I hope you will go on in the same way and pass a good examination." Waldemar, very well and even bigger, had just arrived for two days on his way to Madeira, sorry not to see his nephews and sending them his love. "Yesterday we all went to the Derby, which was great fun and Freddy enjoyed himself very much."[247] On the 30th Victoria and her parents arrived at the Hotel Bristol in Paris, for social visits, drives, walks, theatres, the races, the salon, M d'Epinay's studio, the Hippodrome and Sir Richard Wallace's Hospital.[248] Victoria, nearly eleven, was having the time of her life. The weather was bad "but we don't mind and are out all day long. We have just returned fr some races where one of the stands was on fire, which was most exciting." Albert Edward wrote; "Victoria likes being here with us very much, & went in a carriage driven by an ostrich in the Zoological Gardens yesterday."[249] To George, his mother wrote; "Fancy my writing from Paris to wish you joy on yr dear birthday! yr <u>14th</u> too. Victoria says 'so old and so small'!! Oh my! you will have to make haste to grow." She sent him a box of chocolates, promising to celebrate his birthday when he came home.[250]

They returned home on 9 June and, after seeing M Vereschagin's[251] pictures of the Russo–Turkish War in the French court at South Kensington, all left for Ascot Week at Cowarth Park. The couple lunched at Cumberland Lodge on the 15th and returned the next day for the season, but on the 19th heard that, tragically, the Prince Imperial,[252] serving with the British army in Zululand, had been killed on the 1st. Urging George to do his utmost in the coming examination, Alexandra reminded him how well Napoleon Louis had done as a cadet at Woolwich. She could think of nothing else but "this sad and horrid death – the poor unfortunate Empress cannot get over it at all and no wonder." They had called at Chislehurst but not seen the grieving mother. Visiting the show at the Agricultural Hall at Kilburn, of which the Prince was president that year, they saw "all the horses, fat beasts etc. – and dairies and places where they made butter, and tasted some <u>Danish</u>, which got a prize. We also saw the most absurd Donkey you ever saw in yr life, a huge animal with a very short tail and long legs, and such long ears. We lunched at the place, and sisters came too, and on Sunday we had service in the tent, which all the farmers and shepherds attended."[253] She visited hospitals, the Alexandra Orphanage and fulfilled other engagements but had also started music lessons with Hallé on 27 June, 1 and 4 July. Waldemar stayed overnight on 10/11 July and on the 12th the Waleses joined other royalties and the Bonaparte family at Chislehurst for the Prince Imperial's funeral; "my heart bleeds when I think of that poor Empress who has no longer any dear boy to comfort her in her loneliness. The funeral was too sad."[254]

By the 14th the boys had achieved first class in seamanship and Eddy actually stood higher on the list than George. They had both been working hard, with extremely gratifying results.[255] Dalton had tended his resignation; on the 21st Alexandra begged him to reconsider; the couple were completely satisfied with his performance of his task. "Forgive me for saying, that should any little thing have hurt yr feelings or discouraged you, do not let that come before the devotion which you have hitherto always shown to our dear boys – and the want of which at this critical moment of their existence may have a prejudicial effect over their whole lives. Pray, dear Mr Dalton, think this well over, and do not leave them".[256] Dalton, who was thinking of getting married, was not proof against this appeal and stayed.

There was a family drama; Princess Frederica of Hanover was in love with Baron Alfons von Pawel-Rammingen,[257] formerly her father's equerry. Her mother, Queen Marie,[258] and siblings disapproved, and Frederica ("Lily") was in England, staying with the Duchess of Cambridge. Queen Victoria and Alexandra were sympathetic; the Queen had been "quite a mother" to Lily,[259] but felt she should not interfere, lest she anger Queen Marie. Alexandra suggested Victoria should strongly urge her "to consent to this marriage which in [Lily's] present lonely isolated position wld be the only thing that could secure her happiness and I am sure she is much too fond of this man to give him up for anybody! And what is to become of the poor girl if she does not marry, she cannot remain on for ever with Aunt Cambridge nor cld she possibly return home under the existing circumstances. She will herself let you know as soon as she hears further. Poor thing, she is indeed much to be pitied and seems very low, and is in such a fright of anyone else hearing of it."[260] Alexandra, as usual on the side of true love, was supporting a controversial match; royalties were not supposed to marry their staff. But when, many years later, she was faced with a similar case in her own family, she was much less certain what to do. Lily did marry her baron, in the private chapel at Windsor Castle on 24 April 1880; afterwards they lived mainly in England.

After more functions and briefly visiting Hatfield, the Waleses went on 21 July to stay at Brocklesby,[261] inaugurating the Union Dock at Grimsby on the 22nd and unveiling a statue of Prince Albert. They returned on the 23rd and their sons on the 24th. On 2 August, the whole family left for Cowes, staying on *Osborne* as the Edinburghs were at Osborne Cottage. There was sailing, visiting Osborne House and relatives and on the 6th they went on board *HMS Bacchante*, soon to become important to their sons. After excursions, more yachting and racing, Alexandra and her children returned to London on the 16th and on the 19th left with Waldemar for Denmark. The next day they saw Cologne Cathedral and the zoo, finally reaching Bellevue, and then Bernstorff, on the 22nd. Albert Edward, still on board *Osborne*, was glad George had enjoyed visiting Cologne; "I feel sure that the magnificent Cathedral there must have inspired you very much. The Zoo must have been great fun ... you must ask Apapa to let you & Eddy go sometimes to Copenhagen to see the Museums, which are sure to interest you."[262] Alexandra was going about as usual and also visited the Exhibition in Copenhagen on 6 September. There was an evening party and singing by Trebelli[263] for Queen Louise's birthday. As ever, Alexandra was finding it hard to get time to herself and Charlotte Knollys wrote to Queen Victoria on her behalf. Queen Louise was leaving that day to be with the Duchess of Cumberland, who was expecting a baby at the end of the month. Eddy and George would go as far as Lübeck with her, on their way home. Bernstorff was crammed; every night there were 20 to 30 at dinner. At 9pm everyone met again for tea and stayed together till 11, making the evenings "dreadfully long". The Tsesarevna was looking much the same but her husband had grown very stout and bald. Their children were particularly nice; the eldest, Grand Duke Nicholas, was good looking and clever; they had an English tutor and already spoke several different languages. Charlotte was less impressed with the Crown Prince's children, who were much more like their mother[264] than their father. The weather was very bad. She would write again later "if the Princess is still unable to do so herself. I am sure Your Majesty will understand that her family will never let her out of their sight, so that it makes it extremely difficult for the Princess to do anything."[265]

The boys went home and on 17 September their father took them to Portsmouth and Spithead, for *Bacchante*, in which, as midshipmen, they would tour the world for three years, with occasional holidays at home. He went on to Darmstadt. *Bacchante* left Portland on the 25th and Albert Edward told George on the 30th; "I shall never forget what I felt wishing you goodbye on the 19th & I am glad to hear from you, that you will bear in mind all the advice I gave you on the *Osborne* before we parted & remember all the different points I touched upon." He had enjoyed visiting the Hessians but had missed Aunt Alice dreadfully. After calling at Rumpenheim, he had seen "a very pretty Industrial Exhibition at Offenbach" where "I took some lottery tickets ... & I have one for you & Eddy & also for each of the Sisters, so I hope that you may perhaps win something nice."[266] On the 27th Alexandra, their daughters and most of the Danish Royal Family met him at Copenhagen. She wrote; "It is very nice having dear Papa here too now, and we take our usual long walks and drives altogether."[267] He wrote that everybody was well, including "the Russian Cousins, who are dear children." They were leading "the usual life that is generally lived here" and had, among other things, seen a very pretty Russian ballet at the theatre.[268] Britain and Russia were wrangling about Afghanistan and the route into India and encountering the Tsesarevitch might be politically embarrassing, but "I think it may do good meeting here on neutral ground. I shall of course avoid politics as much as possible, but as he married dear Alix' sister who I am very fond of, I am most anxious that our relations should not be strained. Alix writes that he is wonderfully improved in every way, most amiable, & thought him sensible & by no means violent in politics."[269] Charlotte thought Albert Edward looked well and in excellent spirits, while the Tsesarevitch's manners were much improved; he seemed politically moderate and was certainly a perfect husband and father. The three princesses were well and growing; Victoria was now decidedly taller than Louise.[270]

On 15 October the Waleses, on *Osborne*, the Russians on *Tsarevna* and King Christian on *Slesvig* all left for Hamburg, where *Osborne* returned to Copenhagen, to collect the three Wales princesses and take them home. Their parents, the Russians and King Christian continued to Frankfort; the King went on to Gmunden, where the Queen had been staying for Thyra's confinement,[271] while the Waleses and Russians proceeded to Paris, to enjoy theatres, cafés and hospitality, but heard the girls had only reached England on the 21st after a rough passage. Albert Edward and Alexandra arrived home on the 24th and after theatres, dinners and a visit to Madame Tussaud's,[272] Alexandra took her daughters back to Sandringham on 4 November, missing her sons; "Every evening I expect to see you coming in after tea and every morning on awaking I can almost fancy yr two little voices squeaking into my ear, but instead of that it is only the two white kittens which the Sisters are putting on my pillow." She hoped they had both got over their seasickness; the poor girls had been "horribly ill coming home from Denmark." There was a new organ in the church and a good and pretty medallion of Aunt Alice. She could not finish her letter until after "Papa's birthday – he got a great many beautiful presents", but there was no particular entertainment as it was on Sunday and Victoria and Maud were unwell. She had had a good day's hunting on the 10th, with a 35 minute run and her mare, "Victoria", jumping everything; her sisters-in-law, staying with them, were nowhere.[273] Louise Margaret later wrote to say how much she had enjoyed her visit; Alexandra assured her it had been "an equal pleasure to us to have you here, and I am so glad you have got over yr fright of me, as I noticed that you used to consider me a most formidable personage, and one only to be approached in fear and trembling but now that we know each other I hope we shall always be good friends."[274] Perhaps the Duchess, a Prussian princess, had heard of Alexandra's feelings about that country.

There were more field sports and Albert Edward accompanied guests to and fro; Maud was very disappointed he thus missed being there on her birthday, 26 November. But there were compensations; "You will be pleased to hear that Dovey has laid two eggs! All the other birds and dogs are very well, with the exception of poor Puggy, who has a bad cough! The dear little Indian pony comes out walking with us now, and it came all the way <u>upstairs</u> into my dressing room, & walked down again like a Christian."[275] Alexandra celebrated her own birthday with the schoolchildren's tea party and received many presents, including, from her husband, a watercolour drawing of *Bacchante*, by Algernon Yockney,[276] formerly assistant paymaster on the royal yacht.[277] Everyone enjoyed playing bowls and loo. They left on 8 December for London engagements and the mausoleum service on the 14th. After shooting and skating at Eastwell, they returned on the 19th and left for Sandringham a few days later, before Christmas guests arrived. Alexandra told George about the terrible gales sweeping the country, including Scotland, where "the <u>large</u> railway bridge over the Tay, two miles long, over which we went last year, was blown down into the sea with the train which was crossing at the moment, and every soul in it was drowned – is it not too awful!! It makes me shudder to think of." They all missed the boys, but "the girls were delighted with their presents and they were allowed to come down after dinner the night we had the tree. We very nearly had an accident, as, in taking off the things, Lord Aylesford got on the tree and down it came, right on the gas chandelier, knocking down all the glass shades, and, in raising the tree, they very nearly pulled the whole Chandelier down, which I am sure wld have caused an explosion of gas." She was touched that George had sent them a hymn, "the words are lovely, and Sisters and I have been singing it to the piano. We had such pretty hymns on Xmas day, and I could not help thinking how much you wld have liked them." She thanked God "for all His mercy during the past, and pray for the continuation of it into the coming, year."[278]

Notes

[1] Princess Louise of the Belgians (1858–1924) and Prince Philip of Saxe-Coburg-Gotha (1844–1921)

[2] Anna Maria Maraquita Milles (d 1896); the word-play is obvious. Her father was the 4th Baron Sondes.

[3] RA VIC/ADDA8/2145, Princess of Wales to Duchess of Teck, 1875: 14 February

[4] Sanger's circus

[5] Count Frederick Ferdinand Beust (1809–1886), Austro–Hungarian ambassador in London, 1871–1878

[6] Or Horvath

[7] Francis II, King of The Two Sicilies and Naples (1836–1894), m Maria Sophie (1841–1925), d of Maximilian, Duke in Bavaria, and thus sister to Empress Elizabeth

[8] 56 of each; the Queen was 56 that year.

[9] The Prince was now permanently more susceptible to illness than before typhoid in 1871,

and began regular spring visits to the milder climate of southern Europe, combined later with summer visits to spas, such as Homburg and Marienbad, where clients "drank the waters" in order to control their weight.

10 Kinloch Cooke, Vol II, p73
11 Once, they took their daughters, but as the Duchess found it too tiring to see everyone together, the girls were left with Ella Taylor and asked to see her room. This meant going through a drawing room with a very high ceiling, undergoing repairs, and a gilder who had been re-gilding the cornices had left his ladder there. "The Princesses no sooner spied this ladder when like 3 squirrels they had climbed up to the top." Poor Miss Taylor and a passing footman were horrified, but could only wait calmly for the squirrels to come down. As he left, the Prince remarked; "I fear you found my children very wild." RA VIC/ADDA8/390/Taylor, p 63
12 Robert Gascoigne-Cecil (1830–1903), 3rd Marquess of Salisbury, statesman
13 Sir Stafford Northcote (1818–1887), later Ist Earl of Iddesleigh
14 RA VIC/MAIN/Z/468/3, Queen Victoria to Lord Salisbury, 1875: 17 March
15 Hugh Cairns (1819–1885), 1st Baron Cairns
16 RA VIC/ADDA36/882, General Ponsonby to his wife, 1875: April
17 RA VIC/ADDA36/880, General Ponsonby to his wife, 1875: 6 April
18 Tooley, pp 66, 67
19 Queen Alexandra to Lady Hardinge of Penshurst, 1913: 12 November 1913, *King Edward VII by Sir Philip Magnus*, p 134
20 Madame Hager came from Switzerland and her dog, Minos, performed memory tricks
21 Prince Waldemar of Prussia (1868–1879), 4th son of the Crown Prince and Princess
22 Duchess of Edinburgh
23 Princess Marie of Hesse-Cassel (1796–1880), m George, Grand Duke of Mecklenburg-Strelitz
24 Orlando Bridgeman (1819–1898), 3rd Earl of Bradford, courtier and politician, m Hon Selina Weld-Forester (d 1894)
25 Prince William of Hesse (1845–1900), brother of Prince Louis of Hesse
26 Thomas Brassey (1836–1918), Earl Brassey (1911), politician, keen yachtsman, founded *The Naval Annual*
27 Hon Charles Paget Fitzhardinge Berkeley (1830–1916), 3rd Baron Fitzhardinge, m Louse Lindow (d 1902)
28 Prince Ernest Louis of Hesse (1868–1937), later Grand Duke of Hesse and By Rhine
29 Sayyid Sir Barghash bin Said Al-Busaid (1837–1888), Sultan of Zanzibar from 1870–1888
30 At Chesham House
31 Seat of the Duke of Wellington, then Arthur Wellesley (1807–1884), 2nd Duke, who m Lady Elizabeth, née Hay (1820–1904)
32 Grand Duke Constantine Nicholaievitch of Russia (1827–1892), 2nd son of Emperor Nicholas I
33 RA VIC/ADDCO7/1/0995, Lord Granville to General Knollys, 1876: 19 May
34 Georgina Schubert (1840–1878), opera singer
35 Heneage Finch (1849–1885), 7th Earl of Aylesford, m Edith Peers-Williams (d 1897)
36 The Duke of Rutland's shooting lodge
37 RA VIC/MAIN/Z/450/161, Queen Victoria to Princess of Wales, 1875: 16 September
38 RA VIC/MAIN/Z/468/46, Benjamin Disraeli to Queen Victoria, 1875: September (nd)
39 Kinloch Cooke, Vol II, p73
40 VIC/ADDA8/2185, Duchess of Teck to Duchess of Cambridge, 1875: 3 October
41 RA VIC/MAIN/Z/468/58, Prince of Wales to Queen Victoria, 1875: 12 October
42 RA VIC/MAIN/Z/468/64, Charlotte Knollys to Queen Victoria, 1875: 12 October

43 RA VIC/MAIN/Z/468/71, Charlotte Knollys to Queen Victoria, 1875: 16 October

44 Bernhard Ernst von Bülow (1815–1879), Danish and German statesman, m Louise Victorine Rücker

45 RA GV/PRIV/AA13/4, Prince of Wales to Prince George, 1875: 14 November

46 Daniel Auber (1782–1871), French opera composer

47 Giacomo Meyerbeer (1791–1864), German/Jewish opera composer

48 Gioachino Rossini (1792–1868), Italian composer of operas and other music

49 RA GV/PRIV/AA28/3, Princess of Wales to Prince George, 1875: 4 or 6 December

50 Princess Marie of Edinburgh (1875–1938), later Queen of Romania, w of King Ferdinand of Romania

51 RA GV/PRIV/AA13/9, Prince of Wales to Prince George, 1875: Christmas

52 RA GV/PRIV/AA13/11, Prince of Wales to his sons, 1876: 28 January

53 RA GV/PRIV/AA13/12, Prince of Wales to his sons, 1876:10 February

54 Her friend, the Hon Mrs W Grey, had remarried

55 Cecilia, née Baring (d 1911) m Charles Harbord, 5th Baron Suffield

56 This is almost certainly Abraham Dee Bartlett (1812–1897), taxidermist, expert on captive animals and superintendent of London Zoo, or possibly his son Edward (1836–1908), ornithologist and herpetologist

57 RA GV/PRIV/AA13/13, Prince of Wales to his sons, 1876: 16 February

58 Maharaja Sir Jung Bahadur Kunwar Ranaji (1817–1877), Prime Minister of Nepal

59 RA GV/PRIV/AA13/14, Prince of Wales to his sons, 1876: 23 February

60 Heneage Finch (1849–1885), 7th Earl, m Edith, née Peers-Williams (d 1897)

61 Edith, (Lady Aylesford)

62 RA VIC/ADDCO7/1/1073, Princess of Wales to Prince of Wales, 1876: 23 February; 1074, Prince of Wales to Princess of Wales, 1876: 25 February; 1075, Princess of Wales to Prince of Wales, 1876: 28 February. Some of Alexandra's telegrams to her husband have survived, while letters have not.

63 Lord Randolph Churchill (1849–1895), politician, father of Sir Winston Churchill

64 Henry Petty-Fitzmaurice (1845–1927), 5th Marquess of Lansdowne, distinguished statesman, in 1876 War Minister and Foreign Secretary

65 RA VIC/ADDCO7/1/1078–1083, Duchess of Manchester, Prince of Wales, Lord Randolph Churchill, Lord Lansdowne (2), all 1876: late February

66 RA VIC/ADDCO7/1/1087, Lord Randolph Churchill to Prince of Wales, 1876: 29 February; 1088, Prince of Wales to Lord Randolph Churchill, 1876: 4 March

67 Henry Gerard Sturt (1825–1904), 1st Baron Alington

68 RA VIC/ADDCO7/1/1092A, Lord Alington to Prince of Wales, 1876: 6 April; 1095, Prince of Wales to Lord Alington, 1876: 15 April

69 Sydney Prior Hall (1842–1922), later Sir, portrait painter, illustrator and the artist in the Prince's suite

70 RA GV/PRIV/AA13/15, Prince of Wales to Prince George, 1876: 25 March

71 Charles Yorke (1836–1897), 5th Earl of Hardwicke, politician, also a dandy and gambler

72 She had given them to Blandford, who had passed them to his brother

73 Sir Hardinge Gifford (1823–1921), 1st Earl of Halsbury (1885), later Lord High Chancellor

74 RA VIC/MAIN/Z/450/163, JN Dalton to Queen Victoria, 1876: 10 April

75 RA VIC/ADDCO7/1/1091, Lord Hardwicke to Prince of Wales, 1876: 4 April; 1093. Prince of Wales to Lord Hardwicke, 1876: 10 April; 1094, General Ponsonby, on behalf of the Prince of Wales, to Queen Victoria, 1876: 10 April

76 RA VIC/MAIN/Z/469/73, Princess of Wales to Queen Victoria, 1876: 14 April

77 RA VIC/MAIN/Z/450/172, Princess of Wales to Queen Victoria, 1876: 1 June

78 Prime Minister of Hyderabad

79   Napoleon Louis (1856–1879), Prince Imperial
80   Adelina Patti (1843–1919), Italian coloratura soprano, and billiard player
81   Victor Maurel (1848–1923), French operatic baritone
82   RA VIC/ADDCO7/1/1104, Lord Randolph Churchill to Duke of Marlborough, 1876: 29 June; 1106, Duchess of Marlborough to Prince of Wales, 1876: 4 July; 1108, Lord Randolph Churchill to Prince of Wales, 1876: 12 July; 1124, Lord Randolph Churchill to Prince of Wales, 1876: 26 August; 1126, Prince of Wales to Lord Randolph Churchill, 1876: 18 September
83   RA VIC/ADDCO7/1/1127, Lord Beaconsfield to Prince of Wales, 1876: 26 October
84   Lady Aylesford resumed her affair and died later, in disgrace.
85   Seat of the Duke of Sutherland
86   Seat of the Earl of Caithness, who was James Sinclair (1821–1881), the 14th Earl, politician, scientist and inventor; his wife was Marie de Mariategui (1830–1895) who was interested in spiritualism. Barrogill Castle was later known as the Castle of Mey.
87   Aunt Cambridge and her sister, the Dowager Duchess of Mecklenburg-Strelitz
88   Richard Wagner (1813–1883), German composer, theatre director and conductor
89   Rice powder, perhaps used as talcum powder for babies
90   RA VIC/ADDC2/26, Princess of Wales to Duchess of Manchester, 1876: 17 November
91   James Rannie Swinton (1816–1888), Scottish portrait painter
92   RA VIC/MAIN/Z/452/2, 3, 4, Sir William Gull to Queen Victoria, 1877:4, 11, 14 March
93   General Sir Dighton Macnaghton Probyn, VC (1833–1924), courtier
94   RA VIC/MAIN/Z/452/5, Prince of Wales to Queen Victoria, 1877:16 March; Z/452/22, General Knollys to Queen Victoria, 1877: 7 April
95   RA VIC/MAIN/Z452/8, Sir William Gull to Queen Victoria, enclosing letter to King George of the Hellenes, 1877: 23 March
96   RA VIC/MAIN/Z452/9, Charlotte Knollys to Queen Victoria, 1877: 24 March
97   With Charlotte Knollys and Lt Colonel Teesdale
98   RA VIC/MAIN/Z452/10, 17, 20, Princess of Wales to Queen Victoria, 1877: 26 March, 4, 5 April
99   RA VIC/EVIID/1877: 9 April
100 RA VIC/MAIN/Z450/25, Charlotte Knollys to Queen Victoria, 1877: 10 April
101 She recorded it in the engagement diary
102 RA VIC/MAIN/Z/450/32, Charlotte Knollys to Queen Victoria, 1877: 19 April
103 RA VIC/MAIN/Z/452/36, Charlotte Knollys to Queen Victoria, 1877: 20 April
104 RA GV/PRIV/AA6/165, Princess of Wales to JN Dalton, 1877: 20 April
105 RA GV/PRIV/AA28/5, Princess of Wales to her sons, 1877: 2 May
106 RA GV/PRIV/AA28/6, Princess of Wales to her sons, 1877: 12 May
107 RA VIC/MAIN/Z/452/44, Charlotte Knollys to Queen Victoria, 1877: 18 May
108 Ada Wallett (1865–1929), circus equestrian
109 RA GV/PRIV/AA13/18, Prince of Wales to Prince George, 1877: 27 May
110 52 hours from Greece
111 RA GV/PRIV/AA28/7, Princess of Wales to Prince George, 1877: 2 June
112 RA VIC/MAIN/Z/452/51, Prince of Wales to Queen Victoria, 1877: 3 June
113 RA VIC/MAIN/Z/452/60, Sir William Gull to Queen Victoria, 1877: 3 July
114 Prince Victor of Hohenlohe-Langenburg
115 RA VIC/MAIN/Z/452/65, JN Dalton to Queen Victoria, 1877: 19 July
116 Sir Richard Wallace (1818–1890), 1st Baronet, art collector, illegitimate son of 4th Marquess of Hertford
117 RA VIC/MAIN/Z/452/66–68, Sir William Gull to Queen Victoria, 1877: 21, 23, 25 July
118 Mary Augusta, née Coventry (1812–1889), m 4th Baron Holland

[119] RA VIC/MAIN/Z/452/69, Sir William Gull to Queen Victoria,1877: 28 July

[120] RA VIC/MAIN/Z/452/74, Princess of Wales to Queen Victoria, 1877: 2 August

[121] RA VIC/ADDA36/1284, General Ponsonby to his wife, 1877: 6 August

[122] *The British Medical Journal*/1877: 3 August

[123] *The Medical Examiner*/1877: 9 August

[124] Beavan, pp 243–244

[125] RA GV/PRIV/AA28/8, Princess of Wales to Prince George, 1877: 11 August

[126] Prince Bernhard of Saxe-Meiningen (1851–1928), later Bernhard III, Duke of Saxe-Meiningen

[127] RA VIC/MAIN/Z/452/87, Princess of Wales to Queen Victoria, 1877: 27 August

[128] RA VIC/ADDA36/1314, General Ponsonby to his wife, 1877: 8 September

[129] 13 and 12

[130] RA GV/PRIV/AA6/179, Princess of Wales to JN Dalton, 1877: 21 September

[131] RA VIC/MAIN/Z/452/90, Sir D Probyn to Queen Victoria, 1877: 31 August

[132] RA VIC/MAIN/Z/452/102, Dr Marshall to Queen Victoria, 1877: 5 October

[133] RA VIC/MAIN/Z/452/99, Prince of Wales to Queen Victoria, 1877: 30 September

[134] RA VIC/MAIN/Z/452/108, Princess of Wales to Queen Victoria, 1877: 15 October

[135] RA GV/PRIV/AA28/9, Princess of Wales to Prince George, 1877: 17 October

[136] RA GV/PRIV/AA28/10, Princess of Wales to Prince George, 1877: 18 October

[137] RA VIC/MAIN/Z/452/110, Princess of Wales to Queen Victoria, 1877: 22 October

[138] RA GV/PRIV/AA13/19, Prince of Wales to Prince George, 1877: 26 October

[139] RA GV/PRIV/AA13/20, Prince of Wales to Prince George, 1877: 2 November

[140] RA ADDA36/1354, General Ponsonby to his wife, 1877: 5 November

[141] RA VIC/MAIN/Z/452/113, Princess of Wales to Queen Victoria, 1877: 28 October

[142] RA VIC/MAIN/Z/452/118, Queen Victoria to Grand Duchess of Mecklenburg-Strelitz, 1877: 1 November

[143] John Brown (1826–1883), Queen Victoria's Highland attendant

[144] RA VIC/MAIN/Z/452/121, Princess of Wales to Queen Victoria, 1877: 9 November

[145] RA VIC/MAIN/Z/452/119, Princess of Wales to Queen Victoria, 1877: 1 November

[146] RA GV/PRIV/AA28/11, Princess of Wales to Prince George, 1877: 15 November

[147] RA VIC/ADDA36/1368,1371, General Ponsonby to his wife, 1877: 18, 20 November

[148] RA VIC/ADDA36/1354–5, General Ponsonby to his wife, 1877: 5, 6 November

[149] ie Balmoral

[150] RA VIC/ADDA36/1362, General Ponsonby to his wife, 1877: 12 November

[151] RA GV/PRIV/AA6/183, Princess of Wales to JN Dalton, 1877: 20 November

[152] RA GV/PRIV/AA28/12, Princess of Wales to Prince George, 1877: 7 December

[153] Subsequently dated 1878

[154] Mr Mariette was French tutor to Princes Eddy and George in 1876 and perhaps 1878

[155] RA GV/PRIV/AA6/192, Princess of Wales to JN Dalton, nd, c 1878

[156] Seat of Lord Alington

[157] RA GV/PRIV/AA28/13, Princess of Wales to Prince George, 1878: 30 January

[158] RA GV/PRIV/AA13/26, Prince of Wales to Prince George, 1878: 3 February

[159] William Ewart Gladstone, (1809–1898), at this time leader of the opposition, but prime minister for 4 separate terms between 1868–1898; Gathorne Gathorne-Hardy, later 1st Earl of Cranbrook, at this time secretary of state for war

[160] Archduke Rudolph (1858–1889), Austrian Crown Prince

[161] As Empress of India

[162] Princess Elizabeth of Prussia (1857–1895) m Frederick Augustus (1852–1931), Grand Duke of Oldenburg

[163] RA VIC/MAIN/Z/452/164, Prince of Wales to Queen Victoria, 1878: 20 February

164 John Poyntz Spencer (1835–1910), 5th Earl Spencer, m Charlotte Seymour (1835–1903)

165 Elizabeth, of Austria

166 RA GV/PRIV/AA28/14, Princess of Wales to Prince George, 1878: 26 February

167 In connection with the forthcoming Universal Exhibition

168 RA GV/PRIV/AA28/15, Princess of Wales to Prince George, 1878: 10 March

169 RA VIC/MAIN/N/34/103, Princess of Wales to Queen Victoria, 1878: 19 March

170 Seat of the Earl of Sefton; William Molyneux (1835–97), 4th Earl, who m Hon Cecil, née Jolliffe (1838–99)

171 Hungarian actor of tragic roles

172 Vincent Robinson (1829–1910), collector and dealer in Islamic artefacts; business established in 1840

173 Richard Boyle (1829–1904), 9th Earl of Cork and Orrery, courtier and politician, m Lady Emily, née de Burgh (1828–1912)

174 Sir Sydney Waterlow, 1st Baronet, (1822–1906), philanthropist and politician

175 Auguste Redeker, singer

176 Baron Felix Orczy de Orci (1835–1892), Hungarian composer, father of Baroness Orczy, author of *The Scarlet Pimpernel*

177 3rd Marquess of Salisbury and his wife, Georgina, née Alderson (1827–1899)

178 Richard William Church, (1815–1890), Dean of St Paul's from 1871–1890

179 Information from press cutting

180 Patrice de MacMahon (1808–1893), Duke of Magenta, President, 1873–1879, m Elisabeth, née de la Croix de Castries (1834–1900)

181 RA GV/PRIV/AA28/17, Princess of Wales to Prince George, 1878: 7 May

182 *Giovanni* Matteo Mario (1810–1883), famous Italian operatic tenor

183 RA GV/PRIV/AA28/18, Princess of Wales to Prince George, 1878: 1 June

184 RA GV/PRIV/AA13/33, Prince of Wales to Prince George, 1878: 2 June

185 A Dalmation (with spots, like the pudding "Spotted Dick")

186 RA GV/PRIV/AA13/34, Prince of Wales to Prince George, 1878: 21 June

187 Because Prussia had taken Hanover over in 1866, King George V's only son, Ernest Augustus, did not succeed him as King, but used the English title of his grandfather, who had become King of Hanover in 1837; this loss of status was a source of bitterness against Prussia

188 Princess Frederica of Hanover (1848–1926), m Baron von Pawel-Rammingen

189 Princess Mary of Hanover (1849–1904)

190 With the Duke and Duchess of St Albans

191 Now Grand Duke and Grand Duchess of Hesse

192 RA GV/PRIV/AA28/19, Princess of Wales to Prince George, 1878: 8 July; Colonel Clarke was Sir Stanley de Astel Calvert Clarke (1837–1911), army officer and courtier

193 Augusta Schou (1855–1910), Danish operatic soprano

194 Samuel Wilberforce (1805–1873), Bishop of Winchester from 1869–1873

195 Prince William of Glücksburg (1816–1893)

196 Christopher Sykes's house

197 Andrew Pepys Cockerell (1830–86), groom-in-waiting to the Prince from 1877–86, and friend

198 Probably Lt-Colonel James Ross Farquharson of Invercauld (1834–1888)

199 Charles Colville (1818–1903), Lord Colville of Culross, later 1st Viscount Colville of Culross

200 RA GV/PRIV/AA28/20, Princess of Wales to Prince George, 1878: 7 October

201 Sir Thomas Myddelton Biddulph, (1809–1878), then Keeper of the Privy Purse

202 RA GV/PRIV/AA28/20, Princess of Wales to Prince George, 1878: 7 October

203 RA VIC/MAIN/Z/452/195, Princess of Wales to Queen Victoria, 1878: 16 October

[204] RA VIC/ADDA36/1547,1549, General Ponsonby to his wife, 1878: 9, 12 October

[205] RA GV/PRIV/AA13/40, Prince of Wales to Prince George, 1878: 22 October

[206] Unattributed press cutting, 25/10/1878

[207] "Around the World in 80 Days"

[208] RA GV/PRIV/AA13/41, Prince of Wales to Prince George, 1878: 26 October

[209] RA GV/PRIV/AA28/22, Princess of Wales to Prince George, 1878: 26 November; Karl, Duke of Glücksburg (1813–1878)

[210] RA VIC/MAIN/B/59/21, Princess of Wales to Queen Victoria, 1878: 6 November

[211] Princess Marie of Hesse (1874–1878)

[212] RA GV/PRIV/AA13/44, Prince of Wales to Prince George, 1878: 17 November

[213] RA VIC/MAIN/Z/452/200, Princess of Wales to Queen Victoria, 1878: 3 December

[214] RA GV/PRIV/AA6/210, Princess of Wales to JN Dalton, 1878: 5 December

[215] John William Maule Ramsay, (1847–1887) later the 13th Earl of Dalhousie, styled Lord Ramsay between 1874 and 1880, was a naval commander, politician, and equerry and extra equerry to the Duke of Edinburgh.

[216] RA GV/PRIV/AA6/212, Princess of Wales to JN Dalton, 1878: 11 December

[217] Grand Duke Michael Alexandrovitch (1878–1918)

[218] Unfortunately she had not yet been able to attend any of her siblings' weddings

[219] RA GV/PRIV/AA28/24, Princess of Wales to Prince George, 1878: 16 December

[220] RA VIC/ADDA8/2355, Princess of Wales to Duchess of Teck, 1878: 27 December

[221] RA VIC/QVJ/27 December 1878

[222] John W Lawless, naval instructor to Princes Eddy and George

[223] The Vokes family were a brother, Fred (1846–88) and three sisters, Jessie (1848–84), Rosina (1854–94) and Victoria (1853–94) and another actor, who changed his name from Walter Fawdon to Fawdon Vokes (1844–1904). They were popular in pantomime in London and America.

[224] RA GV/PRIV/AA28/25, Princess of Wales to Prince George, 1879: 27 January

[225] RA GV/PRIV/AA13/46, Prince of Wales to Prince George, 1879: 31 January

[226] RA VIC/ADDA15/6921, Duke of Connaught to Princess Louise Margaret of Prussia (1860–1917), 1879: 8 February

[227] RA GV/PRIV/AA13/47, Prince of Wales to his sons, 1879: 10 February

[228] Major-General Hugh Dawnay (1844–1924), 8th Viscount Downe, army officer, President of the MCC

[229] RA GV/PRIV/AA28/27, Princess of Wales to Prince George, 1879: 17 February

[230] RA GV/PRIV/AA13/48, Prince of Wales to Prince George, 1879: 17 February

[231] RA GV/PRIV/AA13/49, Prince of Wales to Prince George, 1879: 22 February

[232] RA GV/PRIV/AA28/28, Princess of Wales to Prince George, 1879: 6 March

[233] RA GV/PRIV/AA13/50, Prince of Wales to Prince George, 1879: 2 March

[234] Prince Frederick Charles of Prussia (1828–1885), m Princess Maria Anna of Anhalt-Dessau (1837–1906)

[235] RA GV/PRIV/AA13/52, Prince of Wales to Prince George, 1879: 30 March

[236] His brother, who had died in 1866

[237] RA GV/PRIV/AA28/29, Princess of Wales to Prince George, 1879: 30 March

[238] Emilie Charlotte Le Breton (known as Lillie), (1853–1929), m (1) Edward Langtry, (2) Sir Hugo de Bathe, was a "professional beauty" (and later, actress) who had taken London Society by storm and had many admirers, including the Prince of Wales. Alexandra was doing her duty as an understanding, though not rejoicing, wife.

[239] Tooley, p 88

[240] RA GV/PRIV/AA6/219, Princess of Wales to JN Dalton, 1879: 17 April

[241] This was part of the current conflict in South Africa; many British troops had been killed.

242　Declared them open, free of charge
243　Georgina, née Moncrieffe (1846–1929) m William Ward, 1st Earl of Dudley
244　RA GV/PRIV/AA28/30, Princess of Wales to Prince George, 1879: 9 May
245　RA VIC/ADDA36/1639, General Ponsonby to his wife, 1879: 19 June
246　The boys had come up on the 24th and returned to Dartmouth on the 25th
247　RA GV/PRIV/AA28/31, Princess of Wales to Prince George, 1879: 29 May
248　The Hertford British Hospital
249　RA GV/PRIV/AA13/57; Prince of Wales to Prince George, 1879: 3 June
250　RA GV/PRIV/AA28/32, Princess of Wales to Prince George, 1879: 2 June
251　Vasily Vasilyevitch Vereschagin (1842–1904), Russian war artist
252　Napoleon Louis, (1856–1879), Prince Imperial, only child of Napoleon III and Empress Eugénie
253　RA GV/PRIV/AA28/33, Princess of Wales to Prince George, 1879: 26 June
254　RA GV/PRIV/AA28/34, Princess of Wales to Prince George, 1879: 16 July
255　RA VIC/MAIN/ Z/453/30, Prince of Wales to Queen Victoria, 1879: 14 July
256　RA GV/PRIV/AA6/226, Princess of Wales to JN Dalton, 1879: 21 July
257　Baron Alfons von Pawel-Rammingen (1843–1932)
258　Princess Marie of Saxe-Altenburg (1818–1907) m King George V of Hanover
259　RA VIC/MAIN/R/7/22, Princess of Wales to Queen Victoria, 1879: 19 July
260　RA VIC/MAIN/Z/162/4, Princess of Wales to Queen Victoria, 1879: 28 July
261　With Lady Yarborough; Lady Victoria Alexandrina, née Hare (d 1927), widow of Charles Anderson-Pelham (1835–1875),3rd Earl of Yarborough, m (2) John Richardson
262　RA GV/PRIV/AA13/60, Prince of Wales to Prince George, 1879: 24 August
263　Zelia Trebelli-Bettini (or Zelia Gilbert) (1836–1892), French operatic mezzo-soprano
264　Who was considered plain
265　RA VIC/MAIN/Z/453/43, Charlotte Knollys to Queen Victoria, 1879: 10 September
266　RA GV/PRIV/AA13/61, Prince of Wales to Prince George, 1879: 30 September
267　RA GV/PRIV/AA28/36, Princess of Wales to Prince George, 1879: 29 September
268　RA GV/PRIV/AA13/61, Prince of Wales to Prince George, 1879: 30 September
269　RA VIC/MAIN/Z/453/47, Prince of Wales to Queen Victoria, 1879: 17 September
270　RA VIC/MAIN/Z/453/56, Charlotte Knollys to Queen Victoria, 1879: 8 October
271　On 11 October, with Princess Marie Louise, (1879- 1948), m Prince Maximilian of Baden
272　The London waxwork museum, founded by Marie Tussaud, née Anna Maria Grosholz (1761–1850), in 1835; it was situated in Baker Street, then in Marylebone Road, where it still existed in the 21st century.
273　RA GV/PRIV/AA28/37, Princess of Wales to Prince George, 1879: 8–11 November
274　RA VIC/ADDA15/3268, Princess of Wales to Duchess of Connaught, 1879: 22 November
275　RA GV/PRIV/AA28/38, Princess of Wales to Prince George, 1879: 1 December; the pony was called Nawab
276　Algernon Yockney (1843–1912), artist specialising in naval pictures
277　RA GV/PRIV/AA13/66, Prince of Wales to Prince George, 1879: 1 December
278　RA GV/PRIV/AA28/39, Princess of Wales to Prince George, 1879: 31 December

Chapter 7

1880 – 1884

"I think we are bound to try and help those who are so near and dear to us"

❦

Alexandra took her daughters to their first hunt, meeting near Appleton Water Tower, on New Year's Day, 1880. On 5 January they saw *Else of Drusenheim* at Castle Rising School and on the 28th selections from *HMS Pinafore* in the Bowling Alley. After entertaining guests, the Waleses returned to London and on the 20th attended the Lindsay's[1] party at the Grosvenor Gallery for Louise, who was shortly leaving for Canada.[2]

On the 15th Alexandra thanked Dalton for looking after her sons, and the interesting letters, charting *Bacchante's* progress. They still needed to work harder and he was preparing them for confirmation, which they took very seriously. She was also glad extra attention was being paid to the all-important French.[3] A false report that they had had their noses tattooed had appeared. "Well, you stupid Georgie how could you have yr little impudent Snout tattooed – what an <u>object</u> you must look and won't everybody stare at the ridiculous boy with an <u>anchor</u> on his <u>nose</u>! Why on earth not have put it somewhere else!"[4] Alexandra wrote. She was glad they were becoming "first rate sailors and are no more feeding the fishes?"[5] Their father had seen *Gulliver*, a spectacular burlesque at the Gaiety, including, in one scene, "120 children on the stage ... fr 8 to 15 years old. One little girl who takes the part of a Queen is said to be 3½ years old, & she sings and dances. There is also the scene of a ship that goes down, & you see the waves breaking over it."[6] It was so good that he took his wife and daughters on 14 February. They visited the Graphic and Agnew's galleries, and five theatres, before the end of February, also taking the girls to *HMS Pinafore* at the Opéra Comique on the 23rd and to Hengler's Circus,[7] with a carnival on ice, in Argyll Street on the 28th. On the 18th Alexandra had heard Tennyson[8] recite at Mrs Greville's[9] house. After the Opening of Parliament and a debate in the House of Lords on the 5th, the Waleses returned on the 20th for the Duke of Argyll's Afghanistan debate, and Sandown Park Races on the 24th and the 25th.

In March the couple saw the "Old Masters" Exhibition at Burlington House and the studios of M Neuville[10] (to see pictures of Rorke's Drift) and Alma Tadema.[11] They attended five more plays, three concerts, and Alexandra went to a Saturday Popular concert; she also had two music lessons with Hallé. As usual, she heard Bach's Passion music during Lent, *St John Passion* at St Anne's, Soho on 19 March and *St Matthew Passion* at St Paul's Cathedral on the 23rd. She encouraged her sons to "think a great deal of yr confirmation and remember <u>what</u> a serious step it is, when you take all the promises upon yourself which were made for you at your baptism. I trust therefore that you both pay the greatest attention to everything Mr Dalton tells you about it, as the resolutions made now will help you through yr whole life." Less seriously, she really envied the beautiful weather and interesting lands they were experiencing; "I shld so enjoy being with you then we cld talk it all over together afterwards. You will be a real 'travelled Monkey' when you come home! ... I am looking forward quite as much as you do, to the time when you will be back and we certainly will do all kinds of things together. We will read and paint and ride together etc etc."[12] On the 26th the Waleses left for Brussels, meeting relatives and watching actors from the Paris Comédie Française at the Theatre Royal. Alexandra drove to Waterloo after church next day. They left on the 29th for Darmstadt; Queen Victoria arrived, and Victoria and Elizabeth of Hesse were confirmed on the 31st. There were operas; Wagner's *Die Meistersinger von Nürnberg* and Rossini's *William Tell*; and a play, *Der Veilchenfresser* on 2 April. On the 5th the Prince left for Paris and Alexandra for Denmark, to help celebrate her father's birthday on the 8th with a reception and a ball. She saw the ballet, Aditi twice and went to a concert; Hallé, Madame Neruda and her brother[13] gave a recital at the palace on the 11th. Within a week Alexandra left, met her husband at Calais, and they went home together. On the 14th, at Bagshot with the Connaughts, they watched Albert Edward's horse, "Leonidas", win the Military Hunt Steeple Chase at Aldershot. They attended Betty Harbord's[14] wedding to Lord Hastings on the 17th and saw more operas and plays; *Lucia di Lammermoor, The Naval Cadets, Rigoletto, Le Prophête, Faust and Les Huguenots.* Alexandra also heard an amateur Bach concert at St James's Hall on the 21st and saw Tableaux Vivants at Cromwell House on the 28th. She visited the Royal Academy, paid calls, went driving and on 1 May the couple saw *Heartsease*.[15]

On 3 May, *HMS Bacchante* docked at Spithead and the boys were welcomed with open arms. Next evening the whole family saw Gilbert and Sullivan's new operetta, *The Pirates of Penzance* at the Opera Comique. The Waleses gave a large dinner to the new government on the 5th but had lunch with the Queen at Windsor and saw *Lohengrin* in the evening. Next evening Albert Edward was out, so 16-year-old Eddy dined alone with his mother instead. There were more theatres, then on the 10th Louis of Hesse, with his daughters Victoria and Elizabeth, arrived, and they all had dinner with the Queen on the 13th. On the 14th the Wales couple saw the Industrial Arts of India collection at the South

Kensington Museum, followed by Lady Folkestone's[16] Concert at St James's Hall, for Great Ormond Street Children's Hospital; the next day it was *Romeo and Juliet* at Covent Garden. On the 17th they took their sons to Torquay, staying first at Sutherland Lodge[17] and then at Tregothnan.[18] There was shopping and sightseeing and a county ball on the 18th. On the 20th Albert Edward laid the foundation stone of the new Truro Cathedral, followed by a militia and volunteers review at Treliske. They went home on the 21st and Louis of Hesse and Louis of Battenberg joined them; there was a dinner and dance at the Wombwell's[19] house in Portman Square later. Hallé conducted *Faust* at St James's Hall, and a season of French plays at the Gaiety included *Adrienne le Couvreur* and *Frou Frou*, with Sarah Bernhardt. They also saw *Phèdre and Lohengrin*.

The Queen, at Balmoral, was 61 on 24 May and Albert Edward apologised for not sending his main present, because of its size: two large old bronze cranes, excellent examples of their kind, "which I thought would look very well in one of the corridors at Windsor." They could be fired up[20] with gas, if required, through a pipe. The other present was easier; "Alix & I also send you a Gypsy Kettle which we heard you would like to have." They entirely agreed with her that their sons should be kept "simple, pure & childlike as long as it is possible" and away from "fashionable society". "The older they get, the more difficult we see is the problem of their education & it gives us many an anxious thought & care."[21] The Queen added that, apart from religious education, the most important thing was foreign languages, in which the boys were sadly deficient. Her children had spoken German and French at five or six. Eddy and George should spend some months in France or Switzerland, speak almost nothing but French, and later do the same in Germany.[22]

Alexandra drove and rode "Viva" and "Victoria" and the Waleses went to the Derby on the 26th, attending Trooping the Colour on the 29th and a horse show at the Agricultural Hall on the 31st. Lord Fife gave a dinner and dance that day and there were two concerts on 2 June. On George's 15th birthday, the whole family went to Covent Garden for *Il Barbiere de Seviglia* and King George[23] arrived at Marlborough House. The next day he and Albert Edward attended a memorial service at the Russian Chapel in Welbeck Street for the late Empress Marie.[24] At Gravesend on the 5th, Alexandra and her brother boarded Lord Alfred Paget's steam yacht, *Amy*, while Albert Edward and his sons sailed on *Formosa* in the Royal Thames Yacht Club Cutter Match. Ascot Week, at Titness Park, started on the 7th, with racing or visiting during the day and loo or Baccarat in the evening. A week later the Waleses saw *Adrienne le Couvreur and Frou Frou* again at the Gaiety. Alexandra rode "Azeezah" at a field day and march past at Aldershot. Later it was a bazaar at Kensington House for the Kensington Industrial School for Girls. King George received the Freedom of the City at the Guildhall on the 16th and, while Albert Edward was away, he and Alexandra shopped, drove and saw *Faust* at the Haymarket and Sarah Bernhardt's[25] "benefit" at the Gaiety. On the 20th Alexandra attended a flower service at Berkeley Chapel and visited the Victoria Hospital for Children. The next day she was photographed at Downey's studio.

Alexandra and her brother visited Alma Tadema's studio on 22 June; on the 23rd there was the Military Tournament[26] at the Agricultural Hall, and a state ball. Alexandra opened a new recreation ground in Baker's Row, Whitechapel on the 24th. She and her husband went to the Wiltons'[27] dinner and dance, while her brother dined with Lord Granville. The next day there was lunch at Windsor with the Queen, and the Alfred Pagets' dinner and dance. On 26 June the Waleses drove over Wandsworth, Putney and Hammersmith Bridges to "free" them,[28] and later saw *Le Reveillon* at the Gaiety. Alexandra distributed the RSPCA's[29] prizes to essayists from London schools, at St James's Hall on the 28th. There were more balls, drives with her brother and, on 1 July a concert at St James's Hall by the blind pupils of the Institution Nationale des Jeunes Aveugles. Later there was a special "house-warming" ball for new buildings at Knightsbridge Barracks; Albert Edward watched preparations during the morning[30] and at 11.30pm the couple joined the throng at "The Blues Ball", with dancing till 6 in the morning. Some 35 years later, Louisa Sassoon[31] remembered seeing Alexandra in a dark blue dress, trimmed with red roses[32] with the early morning sun streaming in on her. Despite such a late night, the Waleses lunched at Woburn Abbey on 2 July and toured the house and grounds. On the 3rd they attended the Centenary Gathering of some 20,000 Sunday school children at Lambeth Palace, later dining at the Ranelagh Club and watching polo by "lime light",[33] with fireworks afterwards. Alexandra had a last drive with her brother on the 4th and took the children to Sandringham on the 6th, where she rode "Robin Hood" and "Viva". Albert Edward arrived on the 9th from Newmarket, for a cricket match next day, and wrote again to the Queen about his sons; Eddy was to join George for the rest of the *Bacchante* cruise, despite not being destined for a naval career. The Queen, the Prince and others did not entirely agree with this, but accepted Dalton's opinion that it would be best for him; he was rather slow in his studies[34] and needed the stimulus of competition with George. At least he would see distant parts of the world and have French lessons on board from a good teacher, Mr Sceales, and would start military training when he was older.[35]

They returned to London on the 12th and attended Mr Leslie's choir's last concert[36] at St James' Hall. The next day they gave a garden party at Marlborough House, to which the Queen came. On the 14th she reviewed the Aldershot Division and Household Cavalry (the Prince leading) at Windsor. Alexandra went to Mary Teck's bazaar the next day and, with her husband, to Lady Lindsay's Amateur Concert at the Grosvenor Gallery, for the People's Entertainment Society. On the 16th she laid the foundation stone of the new Chelsea Hospital for Women; the next day there was a garden party at Holland

House, with *La Traviata* at Covent Garden later. They had a lawn tennis party in the garden on the 18th and the next day the boys left for Portsmouth. This was not a final farewell; *Bacchante* was joining the Channel Squadron at Bantry Bay before anchoring at Spithead. After three more balls and the Marlborough House Ball on the 23rd, Alexandra presented prizes at Wimbledon on the 24th, at the National Rifle Association's meeting; later, the couple went to a charity fête at Kensington House, for the Mansion House Fund helping victims of the loss of *HMS Atalanta*.

After Goodwood, the family stayed on *Osborne* at Cowes for sailing, racing and sea trips during August. On the 4th they visited Osborne House and saw fireworks being let off from the Royal Yacht Squadron Castle. There was a naval review on the 10th and later, at Portsmouth, a "night attack" with electric light. Alexandra and her children saw the Queen several times, lunching at Osborne on the 22nd, before she left for Scotland on the 25th. They went to Osborne Bay and had tea in the summer house, called unexpectedly on Lady Waterford[37] at Highcliffe in Christchurch Bay on the 26th and later went again for tea, with fruit and ices. "The Princess picked a ripe fig off our tree and ate it and thought it so good, and then all the children fell upon the tree and picked much that was not good."[38] There were more expeditions and seining[39] parties, a visit to the *Sea Flower*, a training ship for boys, and a boat race afterwards. Later, Mr and Mrs Vance gave a comic performance.[40] The family returned to London on 10 September, Uncle Hans arrived and they visited the London Aquarium and the theatre; on the 13th the couple took the children to *Haverley's American United Mastodon Minstrels*.[41] The next day, their father and great-uncle took the boys to *Bacchante* at Spithead, to continue their world voyage, sorry the holiday was over and miserable at saying goodbye. As Alexandra wrote; "none of us could speak, we were all so choky! ... Those partings take indeed a whole bit out of one's life but we must make the best of it ... We <u>miss</u> you <u>terribly</u>, the house is so dull and I <u>have</u> <u>no</u> <u>one</u> to <u>scold</u>."[42]

Still downcast, the couple, the girls[43] and Uncle Hans arrived at Abergeldie on 16 September, but Louis of Hesse and his three youngest children, Irène, Ernest Louis and Alix came to Balmoral and the families met several times. Albert Edward and other gentlemen stalked deer and drove grouse, while Alexandra and others were "all trying hard to catch fish here, but we only succeed in getting baby trout."[44] It was fine and quite warm and she walked with the children, drove with the Queen and paid a number of visits. On the 23rd and 1 October there were cricket matches between the Balmoral and Abergeldie servants and a Gillies' Ball at Abergeldie on the 4th, to which the Queen and her party, as well as people from Birkhall and Glenmuick, came. Five days later Alexandra told George; "We have had a dance at Balmoral the other day, which was a great success. Sisters and Cousins were also present and enjoyed themselves immensely. Grandmama danced with Ernie and Papa." The local people "enquire most kindly after you. Papa has had very good sport I think – one day he killed <u>six</u> stags at Invercauld in two drives ... We drove over there and had tea with them all, where they gave us what you would have liked, <u>excellent</u> scones and honey." Also at Balmoral was Sir Bartle Frere,[45] who "brought us a huge Ostrich egg which we ate – it held as much as 24 hens' eggs."[46] There was a Balmoral Gillies' Ball on 11 October; afterwards, the Waleses stayed at Aboyne Castle[47] till the 16th, returning to London the next day.

Alexandra drove almost daily and there were six more theatre visits. On the 26th the Prince went to Newmarket and later Euston.[48] Alexandra saw *Olivette* at the Strand again and on the 27th invited her old English teacher, Miss Knudsen, to dinner. She took Maud to stay overnight at Eastwell with the Edinburghs; on their return, they found Papa and Uncle Hans, who had been staying at Luton. Later they saw *Rigoletto* at Her Majesty's. Alexandra went to theatres four evenings running; during the day the couple drove, lunched with the Christians at Cumberland Lodge and visited Empress Eugénie at Chislehurst. They then took Aunt Louise and William of Prussia to Sandringham. There was good news; "dear Aunt Thyra has got a little boy[49] the other day, a 'son and heir' – I can't fancy her with two Children!!!" Poor Uncle Willy and Aunt Olga had lost their "dear little baby <u>Olga</u>[50] ... after a <u>few</u> days illness, they are both too miserable and unhappy about it. It was 6 months old and such a little darling." As Alexandra knew only too well, "it is so terrible losing a little child <u>however young</u>."[51] However "All the dogs and Dovey are quite well, the former have been painted in a picture with me to give Papa on his birthday." Guests arrived on 9 November for field sports, with loo and bowls in the evenings and the county ball on the 12th. While Albert Edward was in London, Alexandra stayed, calling first on Mrs Sell,[52] and for the next four days did some drawing; all day on the 16th. She also rode "Viva" and went for walks. Albert Edward returned on the 19th with more guests for a couple of days, then on the 22nd the Waleses went to stay at Melton Constable with the Hastings couple, whose wedding they had attended in April; "We are going to stop with Betty and her little husband today and I am very curious to see their house!"[53] On the 27th they returned to Sandringham for a weekend house party and new guests on the 29th. Alexandra thanked Lord Beaconsfield for his latest book, *Endymion*. Adopting his flattering style, she was "looking forward to spending many most agreeable hours with one of the best Authors of the Century. May I only ask you still further to enhance the value of the book by writing your name in it when we next meet."[54] He was a friend of hers; she had already asked for his help regarding Greece and had sent him a bottle of "Febrifuge", one of the medicines she favoured; "I must however warn you not to take more than a teaspoonful in a wine glass of water, or else it will certainly make you 'Dizzy'."[55] On another occasion, at a banquet, he was trying to cut a hard bread roll and, as he turned to speak to her, the knife slipped and cut his finger. She at once bandaged it with her handkerchief and he

5 Pencil sketch, "A Game of Cards" c early 1880s, with, left to right: Prince Leopold, Prince of Wales, Christopher Sykes, Prince John of Glücksburg. *Alexandra, Princess of Wales*

RCIN 980432.1

said "When I asked for bread they gave me a stone, but I had a Princess to bind my wounds."[56]

On Alexandra's birthday there was a Meet at Anmer; Victoria's pony ran her up against a gate post and she fell off, luckily unhurt.[57] A conjurer, Dr Holden,[58] provided the evening's entertainment. Alexandra told George she had "missed you both dreadfully on my old birthday. How many thousands of miles we were apart on that day, but I know our spirits met many a time which is always a great consolation when apart."[59] She and the girls met Papa at Windsor on the 11th, for dinner with the Queen and tea at the Deanery on the 12th. Alexandra drove and walked with the Queen on the 13th, then, after the mausoleum service, they returned home. The next day there was an unusual diversion; the "American Midgets" called.[60] Alexandra then did a great deal of shopping and the couple saw *Adrienne le Couvreur* and *Olivette* once more, and a burlesque at the Gaiety. Alexandra and her daughters returned to Sandringham on the 22nd and two days later Albert Edward arrived with the three old friends who were to be the only guests over Christmas; Christopher Sykes, Count Jaraczewski[61] (known as "Sherry Whisky") and Andrew Cockerell. Meat was given to the labourers on the 24th; on Christmas Day the family went to church and received Holy Communion. The rector, Mr Hervey,[62] and members of his family were among the dinner guests. More guests arrived on the 28th and the 29th, and the year ended with field sports, "round games" in the evenings, the servants' ball on the 30th and charades on New Year's Eve.

Hoping they liked her little Christmas presents, Alexandra wished her sons "A happy New Year ... and many of them and may <u>1881</u> see you both a <u>bigger, wiser</u> boy!" They would "both be sorry to hear that poor Walkley[63] has left us, as the Sisters are now too big for the nursery ... but we hope to see her very often."[64] The sisters had also outgrown their teacher, Miss Newton,[65] but old loyalties remained. Alexandra told Miss Newton she would have less work than before, only one lesson a week, but they would be quite willing for her to "<u>raise</u> yr <u>terms</u> accordingly" to compensate.[66] Miss Newton must also have been pleased when a colleague[67] mentioned; "Yesterday the Pss told me the English master was making a report about the studies; he said that the children were <u>far above the average</u> in their knowledge of history; the Pss in telling me this added 'Now this is evidently Miss Newton's doing, she has had entire management of this branch, and I love dear Miss Newton, & tell everybody it is owing to her & I hope you will write & tell her this from me.'"[68]

❦

January 1881 was intensely cold and Alexandra told her sons, at the Cape, that "we are literally <u>snowed up</u>, and in some places the snow is 7 foot deep. <u>No post</u> could come today, and we know nothing of the outer world, it is snowing tremendously and the wind is very high. Directly I have finished my letter I am going out with Sisters for a walk, and expect we shall be half buried in the Snow. I only wish you were both here, what fun we should have. It is impossible to skate on account of the mountains of snow."[69] It was the same in London; on the 20th Papa was "nearly snowed up ... I arrived here from Sandringham on the 17th & the following day it blew a gale of wind, & there was such a snow storm that hardly a carriage could move, & even people walking were carried off their legs. Nobody could get cabs or conveyances of any kind, & the streets were impassable almost." People were wading up to their knees in snow and he had driven a sleigh along the Thames Embankment, where it was very strange to see all the ice floating down the river.[70]

At Sandringham, they had had "an excellent Conjurer and another night there was a little dancing, on which occasion Mademoiselle[71] fell flat down on her stomach poor thing, which did look too funny." George's account of the "Crossing the Line" ceremony and other things had amused Alexandra; "You will be as good as 'The book of travels' to listen to on yr return, and you will have to <u>tell</u> instead of my reading to you all in the evening." Two sailors, from *Bacchante* and *Inconstant* had been lost; "It seems so terrible to think that the poor people should have been alive and well in the morning and dead and buried before night."[72] She thanked Dalton again; gratifyingly "Eddy was the one who had been doing best both in conduct and French – it just shows that he himself now sees the importance of it & tries to get on." However, she hoped "they have quite given up that <u>horrid</u> bad habit of always squabbling together, and that Eddy is less absent and Georgie not too full of himself, as all these little failings tell so much against them."[73] In London on 31 January it was quite mild. Alexandra left Sandringham rather despondently and so did the girls; "Sisters have a lot of lessons since this return with all kinds of different Masters, which I don't think they quite appreciate."[74] She had consulted Teignmouth Shore,[75] as he told the Queen. Louise and Victoria were growing up and it was important their thoughts were "wisely guided and habits of life judiciously formed" because of "the immense influence which these children will have in after years upon the coming generation of Englishwomen." Alexandra had told him how helpful a clergyman[76] had been to herself as a young girl and hoped Shore would be a "pastor" to her daughters. "HRH said that she would ask me sometimes to accompany the Princesses when they went out, so that I might have opportunities of guiding & advising them; and that Her Royal Highness herself would see me more frequently along with them." He sincerely wished to be of use to them and worthy of the Queen's confidence.[77]

In London there had only been "a few dinners & a Concert" but the Prince and Princess of Wales did take their daughters to see *Mother Goose* at Drury Lane on 5 February. The Edinburghs also "asked them to join the little Cousins at a Circus, which they enjoyed immensely."[78] The Waleses dined with the

Charles Beresfords[79] at Eaton Square on the 6th and met his youngest brother, "a most ridiculous boy, the living image of Tom Fat!!"[80] Alexandra was so struck by this that "I think I rather affronted Charles Beresford by telling him so, but true it is all the same."[81] Louise's birthday party on the 21st included a conjurer, performing dogs and little people. Alexandra was not sure how long she would stay in London; Papa was leaving on the 24th for "that grand marriage at Berlin".[82] "Dear old Great Uncle George"[83] died on 5 March, then Dowager Queen Caroline of Denmark[84] on the 9th, who "leaves an irreparable blank at home"[85] and there was bad news about "<u>dear</u> old Aunt Line" who was very ill.[86]

Alexandra told her sons on 10 March; "Well, it is <u>18 years</u> today that you have got a Mother!! Now I have been here exactly half my life! I wish you had been here today. Papa also is away so Sisters and I are quite alone."[87] Sadly, they heard on the 11th of their recent guest, Count Jaraczewski's sudden death. Truly shocking was the assassination of Alexander II on the 13th, the day Albert Edward came home. Horrified, Alexandra heard he had been "driving home on Sunday last from a Parade when a bomb was thrown under his carriage, shattering the back of it and killing his Cossack & wounded several of the escort; the Emperor got out to look after the poor wounded, when a second bomb was thrown between his legs <u>smashing</u> <u>them</u> <u>both</u> and nearly killing him and several of the bystanders. Is it not too shocking. In this state the poor man was carried home, dying in less than an hour, he was frightfully injured, both legs hanging by the flesh, one of them being shattered right up to the thigh, his stomach being torn open, his hands and face also badly wounded also one of his eyes forced from its socket – <u>too</u> fearful!" The new emperor and empress were in despair; "<u>What</u> a future for them! And I do not think they are any of them safe while those dreadful Nihilists and secret societies are in existence as their whole aim is to destroy Monarchy, no matter who the individual is. It makes me tremble for my beloved Sister and Sacha – God protect them!" The Edinburghs and Grand Duke Alexis immediately left for St Petersburg; the next day there was a memorial service at the Russian Chapel in Welbeck Street. "And now Papa and I are going next Monday for the Funeral. I could not bear to let Papa go by himself and also I long to be with poor little Minny in this terrible time."[88]

They arrived in St Petersburg on the 24th, staying at the Anitchkoff Palace with the new Emperor Alexander III and Empress Marie Feodorovna. They dined at the Winter Palace with the imperial couple and the Danish and German crown princes, and later attended a service at St Peter and St Paul Cathedral, where Alexander II lay in state. There were more services over the next two days; then on the 27th the funeral, nearly three hours long, was held in the cathedral. The next day Albert Edward invested Alexander III with the Order of the Garter. The families met, walking and sleighing in the Nevsky Prospekt, with teas, suppers, visits and games of whist for Albert Edward in Alfred's rooms at the Winter Palace. He went home on the 31st but Alexandra stayed; the Queen, unable to resist Minny's pleading not to be parted from Alexandra again so soon, having reluctantly given her permission.[89] Minny was still haunted by what she had seen at the palace after the attack: "there he was lying on his bed, apparently dead tho' he still breathed" and was "far from pleased at being Empress now".[90] Alexandra thanked the Queen for letting her stay, Minny too "was so grateful … tho' we both quite understood yr scruples, but never mind dear Mama, I have nearly come to the end now, and through this my poor sister has had a few moments more happiness. It really was very kind in my Bertie also to have let me stop but he knew <u>how</u> much our hearts were set on it – and after all it wld have mattered much less if anything had happened to me than to him! besides I think one is bound to try and help those who are so near and dear to us, in moments of <u>danger</u> and <u>trouble</u> like these, one must put oneself entirely on one side! … It makes one tremble to think of all that may happen to them, but they have indeed both put their whole trust in God, as they know that He alone can save from their foes. God grant them peace and safety as at present they seem to be surrounded by danger from all sides. They <u>are both</u> very <u>calm, courageous and resigned</u>, and one cannot help admiring them for it."[91] By 9 April the imperial couple were at Gatchina, while the assassins' trials took place.

Alexandra came home on the 11th, dining alone with her husband. A peaceful Easter at Sandringham was a relief and Albert Edward told George on the 21st; "all the dogs are well and so are the monkeys. The white rats & mice increase enormously, as you can imagine … On the 18th we went to Norwich to see & inaugurate the 'National Fisheries Exhibition'. It is the first of the kind that has ever been held in England & was very interesting & well arranged."[92] On the 19th Lord Beaconsfield, seriously ill, had died; Albert Edward returned to London for the funeral at Hughendon on the 26th, while Alexandra came back on the 27th. They met the Edinburghs several times as Marie had returned from Russia, still in mourning for her father. Restrictions were less for the Waleses and they attended Gilbert[93] and Sullivan's *Patience, or Bunthorne's Bride* on 2 May and *Faust* on the 3rd, before the Prince left on the 4th for the wedding[94] at Vienna on 10 May. At Marlborough House, Alexandra's beloved nurse, "Jonnie",[95] had inflammation of the lungs. She used to bring Alexandra's coffee in the morning, but now "Sisters have to do it all in her place." She died on the 14th and Alexandra was inconsolable, telling the Queen; "It is indeed hard to lose an old friend, and I am but slow at making real friends, but when I once like a person I cling to them perhaps more so than most, and she was such an excellent, honest, true, kind and unselfish being, whom I loved with my whole heart and placed my entire confidence in. She came to me first when I was so ill and suffering with my knee, and since then has nursed my Bertie, Eddy and Charlotte and <u>Thyra</u> besides many of the servants, who were all devoted to her."[96]

She told George; "Papa has been away over a fortnight and I have been here alone with Sisters and in a terrible state of anxiety & distress about my poor dear

Jonnie, I never left her the last few days, & she died in my arms. Thank God I was with her and she said so many kind & nice things to me up to the last ... I have been nowhere since as I have not the heart to go out excepting last night when I had to be present at a <u>dreadful</u> State Concert, which you know I always hate – and alone too without Papa which made it much worse." May Teck "has grown quite a tall lady since you were away with her hair done up & long petticoats, nearly as tall as I am; the boys have grown too and are much nicer than when you saw them last."[97] Everyone had been vaccinated, as there was smallpox in London. Aunt Louise hardly ever came near Alexandra, who had called on her many times; the Edinburghs were "shut up at Eastwell on account of their deep mourning" and the Queen was going to Scotland. It was dull and lonely without "dear Papa" but he came back early on the 23rd and they went for a ride. There was a levee at St James's Palace that afternoon and a performance of *Dinorah* later. Alexandra enclosed "some new photos of the Sisters, and of myself in all my grandeur done the other day going to the drawingroom." For Ascot Week they stayed at St Leonard's Hill, "a new place ... with a lovely view of Windsor in the distance," with many old friends, including Lord Fife[98] and Oliver Montagu. Alexandra wrote on the 17th, "I am <u>scribbling</u> off two lines by this mail as I have hardly a moment to myself. You know how it always is this week of Ascot ... We have been twice to the races & today is the last day there – tomorrow we go to Virginia Water & on Sunday to Colonel Williams'[99] place, Temple, & on Monday back to London. Our party is a very nice one."[100] There were more operas and plays, a state ball and a state concert. On 9 July they attended the volunteer review at Windsor with many other royalties, including Waldemar.[101]

The Marlborough House Ball (to which the King of the Sandwich Islands[102] came) was held on the 22nd. On the following day Alexandra presented prizes to the volunteers at Wimbledon. During Cowes Week the Waleses often saw the Prussians, who were staying at Norris Castle; on 11 August they were all photographed with the Queen at Osborne. After sailing and social events, the Wales family returned home on 2 September and all left for Liverpool on the 7th; the couple staying at Croxteth,[103] while the girls stayed at Knowsley.[104] Alexandra thanked her sons for sending her a special cart from the Cape; "We saw it in London & I immediately got into it & drove round & round the Court Yard, and think it quite charming. The thought which prompted you to send me this pleases me more than anything – it shows you know my tastes & never forget old Mother-dear! Please also tell Mr Dalton <u>how</u> much obliged I am to him for having taken all the trouble about it – ordering it etc etc. I shall use it often when at Sandringham and think of you my dear boys."[105] In Liverpool the Prince inaugurated the new Langton Dock and the Princess christened the new Alexandra Dock. After lunch, the presentation of an address and a march past of volunteers, the couple left Croxteth at midnight for Scotland and a month's deer-stalking.

6 The Princess of Wales (centre) with Empress Marie Feodorovna of Russia and Princess Marie of Greece, c late 1880s,
attributed to Princess Victoria of Wales

MFV Lobb Album 12   National Library of Wales

They were leading their usual life at Abergeldie but missed the boys dreadfully – "whenever Sisters & I go out on expeditions they always say how they wish you to be here. Thank goodness up till today nearly a fortnight we have had lovely weather, but today it is <u>awful</u>." Uncle George had been staying with them but now had gout in his hand; the Edinburghs had left that morning; the Connaughts were still there, as were Leopold and Beatrice, both unwell.[106] As entertainment, FC Burnand's[107] play, *The Colonel* was performed in the Balmoral Coach House on 4 October. The Waleses and their daughters reached London on the 11th and on the 13th attended the Sandringham Rector's wedding to Miss Lennox,[108] at St Paul's Church, Knightsbridge. "They looked a funny little couple, he just like Cock Robin & she like Jenny Wren – 'Out upon you – fye upon you – bold faced jig' but they gave us no cake & wine after as there was no breakfast."[109]

There were more theatres and then, on 22 October, the three girls returned to Sandringham while their parents left for Paris to see the Electric Exhibition in the Palais d'Industrie, twice. They also met the President and Madame Grévy[110] at the Elysée Palace, paid many calls, shopped, and attended Chantilly Races as well as visiting the studios of Messrs Détaille,[111] Meissonnier,[112] Jacquet[113] and Jerveur. The Prince consulted his dentist, Dr Evans.[114] On several evenings they dined at the Cafés Anglais, Castiglione and Bignon and saw six plays and a ballet. On the 28th they saw M de Munkacsy's[115] picture, *Christ before Pilate* at C Sedelmeyer's[116] in the Rue de la Rochefoucauld, and got home on the 31st after a very enjoyable trip. Everything looked the same at Sandringham on 3 November, "with the exception of a lot of poor trees blown down." Alexandra still missed Jonnie; "I always expect to see her walking into my dressing room in the morning & I don't know at all how to get on here without her, & she will above all be an irreparable loss among the poor people!" The Bishop of Norwich[117] reopened the refurbished West Newton Church on the 6th, and she had called on the Herveys; "It seemed so funny to think of him as being married, but they seem delighted with each other & their little house."[118] Papa's birthday was the best day of shooting at Sandringham ever known, with a bag of 2,244 head. "We had our usual ball on Friday & on Saturday we hunted, which was great fun. The Meet was at Hillington where there are some new people this year – the ffolkes[119] have let it, being hard up, & live themselves in a small cottage in the village. Poor Mr Hamond[120] had the gout & had to hunt on wheels & two crutches!"[121]

One guest, from 12–13 November, was Commander Henry Rose, from *Osborne*, who, with the Charles Beresfords, was staying at Sandringham for the first time. They arrived in the afternoon and found Alexandra, in her riding habit, dispensing tea in the hall, which was very comfortably furnished with sofas and armchairs, a writing table and a piano, while pictures of the Royal Family and the palace in Denmark were interspersed with "magnificent antlers of moose, wapiti, antelope, deer and all sorts of game." Aged, tattered military colours were draped beside the pictures, while the oak-parquet floor was "strewn with innumerable mats, tiger skins etc." At the entrance, holding a card tray, "stands grinning, as if for a hug of anything but friendship, an enormous bear." Alexandra, with her daughters, welcomed the guests with a sweet smile, "while the Prince with his genial face brimming with good-nature shook us all by the hand, & in a moment you felt that you were not only in the presence of two of the most distinguished royal personages in Europe but under as kind a host & hostess's roof as any in England." The next day, Sunday, breakfast was served from 9.30–11; the Waleses having theirs in their own room. After church and lunch, everyone donned "shooting coats & joined the big procession to visit the various gardens, menagerie, horses, cows etc. The Prince has a very large collection of dogs from all parts of the world – bears, monkeys, parrots etc etc. It was very pretty to see the Princess going round with baskets of bread, apples etc feeding all her pets; she didn't miss a single animal, & when I tell you there were something like 80 <u>horses</u> alone, you may imagine it was a long job."[122] Rose was astonished by the game larder, containing over 4,000 head of pheasant and partridge, with 1,000 hares and rabbits in a lower room, all killed in one week. "The Prince sent me back with a large hamper of game for the 'Osborne' – about 16 pheasants, a dozen partridges, some wild duck & some hares! – something like a hamper. He is most generous I believe, & I don't think any of his game finds its way to the market."[123]

Alexandra told George on 1 December; "I am actually writing on my birthday altho' as you may imagine in a fearful hurry as I am overwhelmed with telegrams & letters and we are going out to join Papa & the shooters at luncheon in Wolferton Wood directly." His letter from Japan had arrived the night before, "it was the nicest present I had & it really seemed as if I was hearing you speak. My darling boys I do miss you <u>dreadfully</u> and wld give anything to have you here today. We have a large party as usual in the house ... I have had a table full of most lovely presents but it wld take too long to tell you them all. Papa gave me a lovely little Russian bracelet & a lot of other things, the dear Sisters a very pretty little cushion they worked themselves ... You will be ... astonished to hear of <u>Leopold's</u> engagement to a Princess Hélène of Waldeck!!!![124] He says he is very happy but I don't know when the marriage is to be."[125] A visit to Longleat,[126] the mausoleum service, more theatres, and a large family dinner at Marlborough House on the 18th, when Baron N Rothschild's[127] Vienna Orchestra played, followed. The Herveys, the Probyns,[128] Mrs Greville and the French governess, Mlle Vauthier joined Christmas dinner at Sandringham on the 25th.

✴

"May the remaining months you are still at sea pass very quickly! What joy it will be when you come back"[129] wrote Alexandra on 10 January 1882. Eddy, after all, had proved himself, laying the foundation stone of the Queen's statue at Sydney on 2 August and making a graceful speech to the Japanese Mikado[130] when he visited *Bacchante* in October.[131] He was like his parents; although shy, he instinctively said the right thing, a valuable asset, and his apparent lethargy was diminishing as he found more and more to interest him. Sir John Pope-Hennessy,[132] Governor of Hong Kong, met the princes there and was impressed, especially with Eddy; "I never met a youth of eighteen who talked more sensibly on public affairs; the strength of the Navy, Colonial defence, British commerce in the East, the democracy in Australia, the loyalty & great value of the Irish Constabulary, & many similar questions; to say nothing of Chinese music, Japanese art, public speaking etc. etc."[133] Eddy was inquisitive, had a good memory, and, like his father, learned as much from watching and listening as from lessons. Dalton was pleased with him; "Prince Albert Victor is growing in intelligence every day. Mr Dalton confidently hopes that the Queen will be pleased with His Royal Highness's improvement in every way on return to England."[134] Alexandra had asked Dalton on the 11th, privately, to consider the best course for her sons in the immediate future; "It is very certain that they ought in the first place to make foreign languages their especial study as in that they are so very backward – the question is how & where! It is unfortunate as it turns out that they should be coming back just in the Season, which I fear will be such a bad thing for them, but we must trust to providence and hope for the best."[135]

At Sandringham, she took walks, paid calls, and visited "all our poor people both at West Newton & Dersingham which I cld not do when the house was full". On 9 January she drove in the cart with her daughters before their visiting German governess, Fräulein Charlotte Noedel, returned. Guests went home and on the 16th the Prince brought more from London. There had been several fires but as the girls had already told their brothers about them, Alexandra "would not repeat all that but only say thank goodness I was not made into Guy Faux!"[136] They had all enjoyed hunting "but Louise always sticks to old Euston, she is too frightened to ride Maurice." On 18 January Mr Baskcomb[137] and Company performed Gilbert and Sullivan's *Trial by Jury* in the Bowling Alley and next evening Toole and Company[138] gave *Steeplechase, Our Clerks* and *Ici on parle Français*. Albert Edward hunted and shot with Christopher Sykes, and there were more guests. Alexandra, happy at Sandringham, regretted having to leave so soon,[139] but the couple attended debates in both Houses of Parliament on 7 February, and also saw the Connaughts' new daughter,[140] at Windsor; the Prince told George; "The Baby is a dear little thing & I am sure you would like to see it – Mama was delighted with it."[141]

They attended an Irish Ballad concert, *The Flying Dutchman*, an Assault of

Arms at the Albert Hall, *Ours* at the Haymarket and *Two Roses* at the Lyceum. On the 14th they took the girls to the pantomime, *Bo Peep*, specially performed for poor children, at Covent Garden. A drawing room and dinner with the Queen were followed on the 17th by the Honourable Artillery Company's Ball. On the 18th Alexandra went to a Popular Concert, and later the couple saw *The Squire* at St James's Theatre. Next evening they gave a "theatrical dinner" at Marlborough House, with 36 guests, all connected with the stage. Alexandra was enjoying George's descriptive letters, especially the Egyptian ones; "at the time I was there, it seemed to me the end of the world!! But I did enjoy myself there & thought it an entirely new world. Everything was so very different from Europe & the bronzed and black people so nice & the whole place so quaint. Though we did not live in the palace you are going to stay in, I know quite well where it is & how it looks, and I envy you going up that delightful Nile."[142] The present Khedive[143] had then been "only about your age and took me to see all the Harems – will you remember me kindly to him! I hope you speak lovely French to them all there. You will both have to exert yourselves now or you will appear very uneducated."[144] The boys had recently been greeted with addresses and a guard of honour in Ceylon, which, she noted, "must seem funny to you to be going through what we generally have to do."[145] The Queen had sent round an unflattering picture of Leopold's fiancée but Alexandra met her on the 28th and was "agreeably surprised; she is much prettier than her photograph & seems very nice & friendly." Alexandra called on her again two days later, before she returned to Germany with her father. That day they were all horrified when a man called Maclean[146] fired at the Queen on her way from Windsor Station to the Castle. "Thank God, no harm was done, & she has not felt the shock".[147] It was almost exactly a year since Alexander II had been killed.

On 28 February Albert Edward chaired a meeting at St James's Palace establishing a Royal College of Music, under his immediate control and superintendence. Support had already been offered and nationwide meetings would seek to raise funds to found and endow it. He wanted to create "an institution bearing the same relation to the art of music as that which our great public schools – Eton and Winchester for example – bear to general education … In laying this great national question before you, I have followed the example of my father by offering to place myself at the head of a great social movement."[148] Loving music, the Waleses used their patronage constructively in the future. Prosaically, the weather deteriorated and they all got colds,[149] but there were more theatre visits, parties, balls and a private view of an "Old Masters" exhibition at Burlington House. On 10 March they gave a Children's Ball at Marlborough House. The next day, they attended Margaret of Connaught's christening at Windsor and later visited Count Jaraczewski's and Dr Quin's[150] graves at Kensal Green Cemetery. They saw *Madame Favart* at the Avenue and other performances, including *Patience* at the Savoy on the 24th. On the 22nd they visited the Channel Tunnel workings at Dover and on the 25th the Electric Exhibition at Crystal Palace. But Alexandra's friend, Mrs Greville, died; "I cannot say <u>how</u> sorry I am. I was devoted to her as you know & she was always such fun & so very kind to us all and this year we saw more of her than ever as she was quite established with General Probyn & his wife after her poor Mother's death ... Do both of you write him a line of sympathy if you can."[151]

Alexandra sat to Leslie Ward[152] on the 17th and by the end of March had visited six artists' studios. Between 29 March and 4 April she had six drawing lessons with Henry Harper. As it was Lent, she heard Bach's *St John Passion* at St Anne's on 17 March. Hallé and Neruda played when she had tea with her friend Mrs Baring;[153] that evening it was Madame Schumann's concert at St James's Hall, and on 3 April a Popular Concert. On the 5th the Waleses left for Easter at Sandringham and, after church on the 6th, Alexandra told George; "<u>Today</u> exactly 11 years ago, the poor little baby brother was born, but alas, was taken from us again the next day; it is sad to think that nothing remains here on earth to remind us of him, but his little grave! which I went to see this morning and picked a little flower which I will send you in this letter." The Probyns were away, still mourning their sister's death, as Alexandra also was, but "I have been painting and drawing a great deal lately and you will be pleased to hear that I have finished my little sketch book, where you <u>all</u> are in! I am so glad to hear that you also have been sketching while in Egypt."[154] She and the girls remained at Sandringham while Papa carried out official duties at Portsmouth. "Everything looks lovely here now, & the dogs are delighted to see us; lots of them have puppies, such dear little fox terriers. We have been scampering about all day long, and the other day I gave a grand tea to all the schoolchildren ... & then they had games after – the fête lasted from 4 till 8." There had been 300 children and long tables had been put out in the park in front of the rectory, so that Mrs Hervey, who had been ill, could see it all from her bed. Papa returned on the 12th with guests but "is it not tiresome that the lovely weather we had for a week has turned into wet & now it is awful, and unfortunately we have the house full. Uncle George, Aunt Augusta who has never been here before and is delighted with the place, Mary & Teck, Aunt Louise & some men ... I am going to stop till next Wednesday but I hope all the party goes on Monday so I may still have two days peace before the Season begins." Luckily they did and she rode and drove the Cape cart before returning to London on the 19th.[155]

On 26 April, the couple left for Windsor, where a large family party awaited the Duke of Albany's wedding to Helen of Waldeck-Pyrmont next day; the honeymoon was at Claremont. The Dutch sovereigns[156] attended, as the Queen was the bride's sister. To Alexandra's delight, her brother Frederick came for a month on the 28th, and *La Traviata* next day was followed by more theatres and events. Alexandra, and then, inevitably, her daughters, unfortunately got German measles on 3 May but recovered quite swiftly. Also, as she told George on the 24th, "Fancy poor Oliver Montagu had a <u>dreadful</u> accident the other day, & very nearly killed; he was driving a buggy along Pall Mall when one of the shafts broke & the horse bolted & pitched him out on his head ... he was picked up <u>insensible</u> & carried to Charing Cross Hospital, then to Mr Hewett who bandaged him up & then drove him home to his Barracks. We saw him here the other day & I shall never forget the sight – first of all <u>one side</u> of his face was unrecognisable & swelled out fearfully, his mouth crooked, his nose with a large sore as well as his chin & with a big black eye, then both his knees broken as well & they were both bandaged up so tight that they were quite stiff so that he cld hardly walk. I am afraid I behaved very unfeelingly ... I could not help bursting out laughing in his face, but I must say Papa behaved as badly – but he did look too funny, poor man. Uncle Freddy was the only kind man and was so sorry for him that he took him down in the lift, as he cld hardly get up & downstairs – he is better now, however." She resumed her letter on the 31st, feeling "rather low at this moment as I am alone, dear Papa went to Yarmouth yesterday for a few days – dear Freddy left on Saturday after four charming weeks spent together ... he was just the same as ever with his 'darling little face' as you used to say. We were always together & it was such a pleasure to us both & now it feels horrid without him. He and Aunt Swan[157] are going to Sweden for the Silver Wedding of the King & Queen[158]... next week, and that was why he had to hurry off so! which was a great pity." Louise was still unwell from German measles "& <u>fainted</u> in yr favourite Church the Chapel Royal last Sunday, which was the only time we have been there for a year or so!!"[159]

George's 17th birthday was on 3 June; "A thousand good wishes on this dear day; God bless & protect you, & may you grow up wise & good, but ever remain the same darling boy to yr old Mother-dear, that you are now." They were just back from Trooping the Colour; "they all came here for breakfast & then we sat on the wall to listen to the band." She sent him "a tiny book ... it is called 'Gold Dust' it is such a dear little book, which I am very fond of. You can occasionally read a little verse & try & live according to its precepts, and think of old Mother dear when you read it!"[160] After more concerts, theatres and balls they left on the 5th for Eton, where the Prince unveiled a new screen in the chapel commemorating Old Etonian officers killed in Afghanistan and South Africa. After lunch with the Provost and a cricket match, they unveiled a window in Holy Trinity Church, celebrating the Queen's escape from assassination, and finally drove to Cowarth Park for Ascot Week, although the three girls stayed with Mr and Mrs Welsh[161] near Virginia Water. Guests included Oliver Montagu, apparently sufficiently recovered. Attending races on two days, Alexandra drove or walked and had tea with Lady Lonsdale[162] at The Glen on 7 June. They played loo every evening and returned to London on the 12th.

There they saw *Le Sphinx*, with Sarah and Jeanne[163] Bernhardt, and attended the Russian Embassy ball, Hallé's concert, a symphony concert at St James's Hall, a concert and dance at the Royal Pavilion, Aldershot, and *Tannhäuser* and *Nozze di Figaro* at the opera. There was a charity bazaar at the Horticultural Gardens, for Distressed Irish Ladies; visits to Wellington College, a home for poor girls, and the Military Tournament at the Agricultural Hall. Helena came to stay from 12–29 June. On the 21st it was a charity bazaar at Grosvenor House for the School of Art Needlework; Alexandra had tea at Colonel Ellis' house, where she was entertained with music by Tosti,[164] and Mademoiselle Adler. She later attended the state ball. The next day the Waleses left for two days in Bradford, opening the technical school and a charity bazaar for the Church Institute. After the flower service at Berkeley Chapel on the 25th, Alexandra visited the Women's and Children's Hospital in Waterloo Road. At Hastings and St Leonard's the next day, the couple opened the new People's Park and the Convalescent Home for Poor Children's new building, and received donations. In the evening Alexandra saw *Ruy Blas*. Regretting her sons' absence, she wrote; "God grant it never may be so long again, it really is too much out of our lives ... Take great care of yourselves now, don't get overheated & then get a chill on the top of it as that wld be dreadful, just coming home too." Happily, "dear little Minny Minny had another little girl. They are quite overjoyed at having a second daughter – her name is Olga."[165] Elizabeth and Irène of Hesse had come to lunch and were going to see *Patience* with their Wales cousins. "Last night we had the Court Concert which you know I detest & the heat was quite awful. Thank goodness all those Court affairs are over for the year."[166]

The season had been particularly busy and three more weeks of concerts, operas, plays and balls were still to come, as well as engagements; opening the new wing of the Metropolitan and City Police Orphanage at Twickenham, visiting the boys' home at Fortescue House, opening a charity bazaar for the National Refuges for Homeless and Destitute Children and visiting the Roman Catholic Hospital, Convent and Church of St John of Jerusalem and St Elizabeth of Hungary in Great Ormond Street. A children's party for Victoria's 14th birthday, a garden party for 3,000 guests, including the Queen, and the annual ball on 21 July were held at Marlborough House. Racing at Goodwood followed. Meanwhile Alexandra had written "my last letter before we meet" to George on the 19th. The boys were to be confirmed soon after their return, at Whippingham Church, as many of the family would be on the Isle of Wight. She wanted them to understand confirmation's significance. "I am sure both my dear boys will have thought very seriously on this most important subject & if you read my letter to Eddy you will see all I tell about it and how anxious I am that you shld realize the sacredness of the holy rite & make it a fresh starting point in yr lives. And always pray to God to give you strength to put from you all yr little faults & help you to carry out the promises which you are about to remake. I know you have been reading & preparing for it regularly with Mr Dalton. I am so glad too that you like to read my little book, 'Gold Dust' sometimes." The boys were deep in examinations, hoping for success. She mourned the death toll in the Egyptian Campaign, where the Khedive, whom the boys had recently met, was in great danger. Uncle Alfred had nearly drowned while out fishing; "mind you are <u>most careful</u> whenever you go anywhere on a river & near a weir." She felt very tired, as "We have had more to do here this year than ever, I think, and no end of functions."[167]

On 31 July and 1 August the couple inspected squadrons of the Blues and Life Guards at Regent's Park and Knightsbridge Barracks before they left for Egypt. At Cowes on the 2nd they visited the steam ship *Holland*, with some of the Egypt-bound soldiers on board, and accompanied it in *Osborne* as far as Yarmouth. At last, on the 5th *Osborne* steamed out of Cowes to meet *Bacchante* off St Alban's Head. Prince Albert Victor and Prince George of Wales were confirmed by the Archbishop of Canterbury at Whippingham Church on the 8th, with tea at Osborne House afterwards. The next day they took Holy Communion with their parents. There were visits to the troop ships starting for Egypt, the Corinthian Regatta in Osborne Bay and dinner at Osborne on the 13th, to which the almost-adult princes were invited. On the 14th the family returned to London, stopping for a concert at Portsmouth in aid of the Royal College of Music. The next day the parents took their sons to see Mr Gladstone in Downing Street and Lord Northbrook at the Admiralty. There were theatres, and interesting visitors at Marlborough House; on the 16th Cetewayo,[168] King of the Zulus, and some Zulu chiefs; on the 17th, some Maori chiefs from New Zealand.[169] The family reached Wiesbaden on the 19th and dined with King Christian and Queen Louise at their hotel. On the 20th Albert Edward left for his usual "cure" at Homburg but his family spent the next three weeks with relatives,[170] going on trips to Königstein, Frankfurt, Rumpenheim and Homburg, where they called on him on the 24th. There were also plays, Wagner's operas, a conjurer, a concert and other entertainments. On 11 September Alexandra and children met "Papa" at Darmstadt and all, including the Greeks, left for England on the 13th and for Abergeldie two days later.

King George and Queen Olga left after a week of drives and excursions round the Balmoral estate. After a few days in London, Albert Edward returned to Scotland on the 27th to stay with his family and bring them home on 8 October. On the 9th Alexandra took them all to the Aquarium and that was the end of the boys' holiday; the next day their father took them to Paris and then Lausanne, to be coached in French. Alexandra paid visits, went to Madame Tussaud's and dined alone, already missing her sons. "I miss you both dreadfully ... I am sure you must have felt parting from dear Papa very much." His little dog, Fossy, was somehow left behind, "tho' to you it must have been a consolation". Not for long, however, as she had to be sent back to Papa in Paris. Alexandra supposed; "by now you have quite settled down to yr work and new life, and are getting <u>on well</u> with yr French. Mind you always speak it, & am glad you have made up your

mind to study as hard as possible. I hope I may only hear good reports of you &
mind that you in particular do not <u>quarrel with</u> or <u>irritate</u> yr brother. Remember
Georgie dear this is a <u>dreadfully</u> bad habit & must be got rid of before you
return."[171] Sandringham was full of workmen, so she could not go back yet, but
at least Papa was coming home the next day. They watched troops arriving from
Egypt, and visited the theatre, before he left for Newmarket. Alexandra went
driving and on the 28th heard Neruda, Janotha[172] and Piatti[173] at a Popular
Concert. On the Prince's return, Louis of Battenberg came to stay for a couple of
days, bringing "a most delightful cart from Japan which I am sure you will have
seen; he drove me all round the <u>drawing room</u> and hall. I am going to have some
shafts made so that a pony may draw it." More seriously; "I am so glad, Georgie
dear, that you too promise to remember all the good advice I gave you both in
Eddy's letter, & that you will try for the future not to quarrel with yr brother
from whom, as you say, you will so soon be parted! I hope also you have both
acted on what I said with regard to not contradicting people – it is such a <u>very
rude habit</u> & affronts people more than anything." She added, "How have you
been getting on with your studies and particularly with the French. <u>Do always</u>
speak it whenever you can, or else this tiresome separation will be no use." Sir
Garnet Wolseley[174] had returned from Egypt "and we asked him to dine with us,
but Grandmama had already made him go up to Scotland so we have not seen
him yet."[175] He finally visited Marlborough House on 1 November.

Dalton had reported on the boys' life at Lausanne and on the 7th Alexandra
told him; "I am glad to hear that you think on the whole they are making a very
satisfactory progress, but I cannot help fearing that you are too many English
together & naturally they cannot be expected to speak French to either you or
Mr Lawless, who himself you say is a very bad hand at it. What they really want
is to hear good French continually spoken before them by French people, as it is
very essential that their ear should get accustomed to the language <u>properly</u>
spoken!" It might also be a good idea to invite some of the college boys to meet
them, or for them to attend interesting lectures there. "I am glad they read aloud
in the evening but tho' I have no doubt that Dumas'[176] <u>novels</u> are very
interesting, still I cannot help thinking that <u>Novels</u> are not useful reading & do
the boys no good. In the French literature there are so many useful & most
entertaining books in the shape of *Mémoires* & historical works which wld be far
better for them – Lamartine's[177] *Girondins* for example is most interesting."
Alexandra herself owned a large collection of French literature. She agreed
wholeheartedly that the boys should not attend too many formal luncheons and
dinners.[178]

After more plays and Gounod's[179] *Redemption* at the Albert Hall, they
returned to Sandringham, which looked "quite charming & you will find a great
many improvements since you were last here." Papa's birthday, sports and guests
left no time for writing until 16 November; "While the house was full I cld not

find a spare moment, & since they have left had so much to do both indoors and out, settling & looking after all sorts of things, & then I had to visit the poor people whom I had not yet seen. One poor girl, only 17, is dying of consumption, she is the woodman's daughter & lives near Jocelyn Wood; it is very sad to see her thus."[180] They all went to London on the 17th for the Queen's inspection of the Brigade of Guards, back from Egypt, at Buckingham Palace, and her review of troops at Horse Guards Parade, followed by an evening party at the War Office. At Windsor they saw the Queen present Egyptian Campaign medals; at Merton[181] there was shooting and partridge driving. The Waleses returned to Sandringham on 25 November for more entertaining, with games of loo and bowls. Maud had a birthday table of presents on the 26th.

Alexandra thanked George for "yr dear little birthday card ... I got lots of beautiful presents which I will show you when you come here. Fancy in a <u>fortnight</u> now you will be at home once more & what fun we will have, with Xmas and everything. I am glad you have got most of yr presents ready & that is always a great undertaking, and I am now going up tomorrow about mine. We had such a nice cheery party last week and everybody seemed to pull together so well & enjoy themselves ... Louise has suddenly taken to ride Minny (rather late in the day don't you think so) and will now ride nothing else, while Victoria has given up Alix in disgust as she bucks so & is now riding Euston." Alexandra had several new horses, as well as Lord Castlereagh's[182] present of "a charming little Shetland pony". There had been a schoolchildren's tea party in the Coach House and the tenants' ball later; "great fun and Sisters were allowed to appear as it was my birthday and danced a great deal."[183] They stayed up till 2 in the morning.[184] The review in London had been very successful and enjoyable, as a dense fog had cleared and revealed a cold, bright day. "On our return home I got out of the carriage & stood at the bottom of St James' Street by Papa's horse; here we saw better than anywhere as they passed quite close ... The whole of the Indian Contingent came to Marlborough House, some of them very handsome men."[185] The Alhambra had been gutted by fire and the giantess, Marian Wedde,[186] who had been appearing there, visited Marlborough House. They saw *Iolanthe* and other pieces, there were private views and a visit to Mr Jones' collection[187] at the South Kensington Museum. The couple opened new City of London schools on the Thames Embankment on the 12th and two days later attended the mausoleum service. They received the Madagascan ambassadors on the 19th and the next day the boys arrived from Lausanne. It was Lady Dudley's Children's Christmas Party at Dudley House on the 21st and the Wales family left for Sandringham the next day for their own celebrations, with billiards, sports and walking. On the 30th, Monsieur Hua, the new French master, arrived.

⚜

Albert Edward was going to the Prussians' Silver Wedding celebrations at Berlin on 25 January 1883. The boys were enjoying the last few days of their holiday and accompanied their parents to London on the 11th and Osborne the next day. On the 15th they left for Switzerland and Alexandra went back to Sandringham. Deciding to see her husband off, she returned on the 20th, but Prince Charles of Prussia[188] died and the Berlin festivities were postponed for a month.[189] "I don't know what Papa will do as he had packed up everything. At present I shall stop here with him till I know his plans, & then return to dear Sandringham where the poor Sisters are very angry at being left by themselves." Papa soon decided; "as all his plans were made for going abroad, and as Berlin was knocked on the head at present, he thought he wld go and get a little sun in the South of France."[190]

Meanwhile little Fossy had died at Sandringham and almost simultaneously Tchow, the Chinese dog the boys had brought back and which their father had taken on holiday with him, also died. "Poor Papa is quite cut up about it, how he will miss <u>both</u> those faithful dogs. I think he had much better take back poor old Carlo who is in disgrace, I don't know exactly why excepting that his <u>odour</u> is not very pleasant & he does snore loud." Louise had taken to "<u>jumping</u> lately on 'Minny', actually a hurdle & lots of banks & fences." The widowed Mrs Stonor and her daughter Julia[191] had come to Sandringham for a short break. Another visitor was less welcome; "yr friend Baron <u>Stern</u>!! who quietly came all the way from London, walked up to the house saying he was the Prince of Wales & wished to speak to me, & he was sure I wld see him. They told him however I had gone out hunting. I was playing the piano in the Hall when suddenly, the Sisters called out 'Why there is old <u>Stern</u>' & so it was, there he was, escorted by <u>Walker</u> & in pelting rain with an umbrella being trotted back to the Station, from where he had only just come, poor man. I was quite sorry for him, as he is mad & quite harmless. I wish I had met him out of doors & heard what he had to say." She was glad her sons had met her Aunt Frederike, Duchess of Anhalt-Bernburg,[192] but "curious to know in what language you made conversation. She is Apapa's second sister & is very kind, but I never knew her as much as all the others as she hardly ever came out of Germany."[193] When the boys saw their great-aunt again, their mother was amused "to hear the mixture of languages you cook up together. So you went to attend some French lectures at Lausanne. I hope you understood it all. It is very good practice for you both writing to the Sisters in French; go on doing it, I am sure it is an excellent plan for you all."[194]

After riding and visiting locally, Alexandra took the girls back to London on 14 February, to welcome Papa the next day. The couple attended a charity concert and a play and gave a dinner party on the 18th. They went to Windsor for Arthur of Connaught's[195] christening and visited JM Whistler's[196] exhibition of etchings and dry prints at the Fine Art Gallery. Louise had her 16th birthday party on the 20th and their parents took the girls to Hengler's Circus the next day.

Alexandra heard Gounod's *Redemption* at St Anne's on the 22nd and on the 24th Albert Edward left for Berlin. Alexandra welcomed him back on the 10th in London and, much to her disgust, found that he had been made Honorary Colonel of a Prussian Regiment.[197] They attended an evening party at Burlington House for an "Old Masters" exhibition on 10 March. It was disheartening to learn from Dalton that Eddy had relapsed into indolence and inattention at Lausanne and had seemed rather ungrateful towards him; however, Alexandra was sure this was only temporary and Eddy was not as insensible as he seemed.[198] Meanwhile her multiple activities continued; three drawing lessons with Mr Buckman,[199] a visit to Mrs Amyot's studio, amateur theatricals on the 13th and the 17th and also being present at *Iolanthe*. Alexandra gave prizes to pupils of the Girls' Public Day School Company at the Albert Hall on the 16th and took her daughters to Mrs Baring's party afterwards. She also heard Bach's *St Matthew Passion* at St Paul's Cathedral's evening service and "Bach's beautiful Passion Music of St John, which quite inspires one & does one good!" at St Anne's on the 23rd.

Easter was spent in London, sadly without the boys; "I suppose it is <u>wiser</u> so, as it wld have been a pity to take you away from yr last chance of learning to speak French thoroughly, and I am sure you will feel the necessity of it yr self. Do try <u>both</u> of you to make the <u>most</u> of the short month left you, & work with all yr might & main." She added, "we cannot have all we want in this world & must learn to bear our disappointments manfully." She also hoped "you saw my last long letter to Eddy, for what I said to him, applies generally to you both. Remember also Georgie dear, it is probably yr last time together, therefore be as nice as you can to yr brother or you will be sure to be sorry for it afterwards when you are separated." They were soon going to Sandringham and "Grandmama is actually going to pay us a visit there!!! after all those years. She was coming on Wednesday next, but now unfortunately she has <u>tumbled</u> down stairs & sprained her ankle, so she has put it off till the week after, which is a great pity!" In addition, "poor Aunt Frederike" and "poor Mr Hua" had been unwell; Mrs Stonor had enteric fever; Alexandra herself had had a bad cold and lost her voice. To cap it all, "Poor <u>Polly</u> the green parrot in the hall" had died suddenly, "how we shall miss his talk, singing & laughing! He bit my finger very bad just before we left Sandringham!" But "Papa has got a <u>new dog</u>! a <u>white Tchow</u>; that is to say, he is bigger & comes from Lapland, but I think he is an <u>elderly</u> dog, as he is very quiet in manners, & not at all high spirited like poor Tchow or even Jossy."[200] The dog, "Bertie", was a present from Prince Bariatinsky.[201]

On Easter Monday they went to Windsor for Alice of Albany's[202] christening; as Alexandra put it, "<u>Leopold</u> of all people has become a worthy <u>Father</u>!! fancy that. I can hardly believe that <u>he</u> has become such a responsible person!! how <u>important</u> he will be now!!"[203] Albert Edward was one of the sponsors. Later, the

Waleses and their daughters saw Offenbach's[204] spectacular "operette", *A Trip to the Moon*, with a delightful ballet, at the Haymarket. On 27 March the Queen's Highland attendant, John Brown, died. Whatever he thought of Brown, Albert Edward knew the Queen had valued him as a true friend and it was therefore appropriate for his sons to send condolences; "You have I hope both written to Grandmama in consequence of poor Brown's death. He is to be buried at Balmoral & the body is to leave Windsor tomorrow."[205] Although it was still snowing heavily, the couple and their daughters left for Sandringham on the 28th. Their guests included Mary Teck and May, as well as the Gladstones; he cut down a tree on the 31st.[206] Guests arrived and departed; games of loo and bowls were played in the evening and Alexandra enjoyed her usual outdoor pastimes. The couple were both in London by the 14th and went to see Mrs Stonor, but "we were just in time to see her die! ... I cannot get her last moments out of my head, nor those poor heartbroken Children kneeling round her bed side, & sobbing their hearts out ... I can hardly believe that I shall never see her dear & kind face again & I was so fond of her too. She had been with me ever since I came." Alexandra was especially sorry that "Poor little Julie seems quite alone in the world" and always showed her kindness and friendship. As for herself; "I am going off, by myself to Osborne, to spend two days with poor Grandmama, who has not yet recovered from her sprain & is still very low spirited. Did you write to her when I told you?"[207] The Queen told Vicky, "Dear Alix has been here for 2 nights & nothing could exceed her tender sympathy & complete understanding of all I feel & suffer."[208] Ponsonby had seen them driving together in silence; "HRH made a peculiar smile at us as if to say that it was not lively." Alexandra had found the Queen in much lower spirits than she had expected, but the household thought her visit had "stirred up HM and did her a deal of good as she is busy on dozens of things now."[209]

The young princes were coming home soon and the plan was for Eddy to stay and study and George to go to sea for a year to the North American Station on board *HMS Canada*, a corvette commanded by Captain Durrant,[210] before starting at the Royal Naval College at Greenwich. His father wrote, "We shall be very sorry to part with you so soon ... but as we hope that you will make the Navy yr profession, it is absolutely necessary that you should go to sea again."[211] Alexandra accepted it was settled, hoping for the best, "though it does seem hard to have to part again so soon!!!!"[212] She enjoyed theatres, galleries, concerts and visits before her sons returned from Ouchy on 4 May. Fräulein Noedel was appointed resident German governess to their sisters on the 3rd.[213] On the 7th the couple opened the Royal College of Music at Kensington and later watched the Grand Military Chess Tournament, "with living pieces", at Hengler's Circus, in aid of the Royal Hospital for Women and the West End Hospital for the Nervous System. There were balls, plays and on the 12th the International Fisheries Exhibition opened; the next day some French, Dutch and Belgian fisherwomen, and on the 16th a deputation of fishermen of the United Kingdom and Scottish fisheries, came to Marlborough House. Alexandra paid calls, had a drawing lesson with Corrodi[214] on the 18th and played lawn tennis[215] on the 25th. She held a drawing room on the 21st; there was a large dinner at Marlborough House and a state ball at Buckingham Palace. On 4 June they left for Ascot Week at Cowarth Park. Early on the 13th, Alexandra wrote a loving message to George before his father took him to Spithead later. She knew how hard it would be for him to go away for the first time without his brother, Dalton or Fuller, "but remember darling that when all others are far away God is always there, and He will never forsake you, but bring you safe back to all of us who love you so ... Strive to get on in all that is good, & keep out of temptation as much as you can – don't let anyone lead you astray. Remember to take the Sacrament about every quarter, which will give you fresh strength to do what is right, & also never forget either yr morning or evening Prayer. We must all try & console ourselves by thinking how quickly the year will pass & what delight it will be to meet once more."[216]

When Alexandra wrote again, she had been "very busy & hunted more than ever since you left, & <u>hated</u> that State Concert the night of yr departure; when everybody spoke of you I cld not help crying."[217] The season gave her very little time to herself until their ball closed it on 27 July. Eddy meanwhile had gone to Sandringham on 19 June to work and Alexandra wrote later to Dalton, who had reported on his progress; "We are none of us blind to his faults & I can therefore rely more entirely on yr reports than on those of anyone else. I hope really now he is doing his best, though what you say about the French is not as it ought to be."[218] Eddy was probably missing his brother; however, he had got on well with two other young men at Lausanne. Victoria's birthday party was on 6 July and on the 13th Alexandra took the girls to the zoo. The Waleses gave a garden party on the 23rd and left for Goodwood on the 30th; Alexandra and the girls joined Albert Edward on board *Osborne* at Cowes on 4 August. Louis of Hesse and his three elder daughters were at Osborne and the great excitement was that Victoria of Hesse was engaged to Louis of Battenberg.

Alexandra had enjoyed Goodwood, riding every afternoon after the races and now "We have spent a delightful 10 days on board in spite of the horrid weather; every day wind & rain." She was returning to London the next day, then Papa was going to Homburg, while she and the girls were off to Denmark; "I am looking forward immensely to going home, where I hope to stay till the middle of October. Minny, Thyra & Willy will be going too, so we shall have fun. Eddy will join me later & Papa too after having finished his cure at Homburg."[219] Arriving at Bernstorff on 16 August, Alexandra plunged into everything; theatre, a dance, tea, church and a meeting of the Archaeological Society in the university's hall. On the 29th, "I need hardly tell you <u>how delighted</u> I am here in my dear old home, & now we are <u>all 6</u> together! for the first time since I married

– all of the sisters & brothers have been flocking in gradually … So you may imagine my <u>delight</u> … We are indeed a merry, happy party now. First of all there is darling Amama & Apapa – who look really quite the youngest of us all; then Minny & Sacha with 5 children, Willy & Olga with 2 girls, Freddy & Louise with 6 children, Old Mother dear with 3 girls! <u>Thyra</u> with 3 chicks!! & Waldemar with none at all!!!! then Uncle <u>William</u>, & Hans." With very little chance to write, she continued on 3 September; "I am really in despair at not having had time ever to finish these few lines! But you have no idea what it is here – we are never apart & my room generally crowded as it is next to the breakfast & luncheon room. My poor little Georgie must forgive old Mother dear this time & take the 'will for the deed!'" Eddy was dull and lonely at Balmoral, but was due in Denmark in a couple of weeks.[220] On Queen Olga's birthday[221] the Russian sailors sang a Te Deum for her in the great hall at Fredensborg. Alexandra attended the opening of a Russian Chapel in Copenhagen on the 9th, where, two days later, a service was held for Sasha's "name day". Eddy arrived on the 18th and King Christian's sister, Princess Louise of Glücksburg,[222] came next day for a week. Papa arrived on the 29th and the Waleses sat for their pictures. Alexandra told the Queen, "My Bertie" was looking all the better for his cure. "He evidently has enjoyed being able to wear his <u>German uniform</u>[223] though I have drawn a veil over this subject & have asked no questions. I am so glad he found them all still here, as I am afraid the happy family circle will now soon be broken up, I dread the partings so."[224]

Back in London on 22 October, Alexandra and her daughters felt low; Papa had taken Eddy to Cambridge and had called at Sandringham to check the progress of the new rooms before going to Newmarket for a week. "So it is very dull here all alone, after our delightful & happy family meeting at home, & today I own I have been quite home-sick all day long, & the more so as after all I might have stopped a fortnight longer but had to hurry back thinking I was to start at once for Balmoral, but now I find the House is full & Grandmama cannot receive me till the 29th when it is too late for me to go." The partings had been miserable; "then came that <u>awful</u> moment of <u>tearing</u> ourselves away from each other, not knowing <u>when</u> & <u>how</u> our next meeting may be. Poor little Minny; I can see her now standing on the top of the steps in utter despair, her eyes streaming down with tears & trying to hold me as long as she could. Poor Sacha too felt the parting very much & cried dreadfully & dear Nicky, Georgie & little Xenia also; it was <u>too</u> horrid." Parting from her parents was also "too awful & the cup seemed overflowing." They left on *Dannebrog* which immediately ran aground; consequently they missed the train at Lübeck and had to take a 'special' all the way to Flushing, arriving rather tired next evening and finding *Osborne* waiting. "We had an <u>awful</u> passage, a South Westerly <u>gale</u> sprang up in the night & kept us <u>three hours longer</u> at sea; nearly everybody including the crew were ill, but I am delighted to say I did not feel anything nor was I the least sick altho'

I was nearly pitched out of my bed."[225] In London she went to the theatre, and had lunch and tea with Lady Lonsdale. On 2 November Eddy came for the day from Cambridge; the next day his parents and sisters returned the call and lunched with him on the way to Sandringham. His rooms were charming, "he is very comfortably established & I think on the whole likes it very much. I only hope he will do his best to get on, it is so important for him." Alexandra apologised for her late letter of 14 December, but "when I first went to Sandringham we immediately had the house full of people; when they left I was unfortunately <u>not at all</u> well, having caught cold before I left London! which gradually got worse with an awful cough which went on for a month, so … was shut up for a whole fortnight, it was too tiresome." Papa's birthday house party had been "entre nous rather dull; composed chiefly of distinguished Foreigners, French & German whom I had never seen before & who had never set eyes on each other." There had been a leavening of other people "but they somehow or other did not pull well together I thought, but then, <u>you know</u>, I did not feel well <u>at all</u>, all that week so that may have had something to do with it."[226]

Marie, Duchess of Edinburgh would have agreed with her. She and Alfred were there that week and she relieved her feelings by writing a long, complaining letter to a friend, having been "smiling and talking in this dull atmosphere of so called pleasure, lonely, not understood, longing for something better and being sadly aware that I will never get it." At the shoot the day before "I thought every minute, my head would be blown off and we all took refuge under a tree and were intensely pleased when the beat was over." She took solitary morning walks in the park, as the other ladies did not appear until lunchtime. "The Princess feels still very unwell from her cold and I suppose it augments her deafness; she hears so badly that I can hardly make myself understood. Conversation then is real hard work and I am sorry as she is so nice and kind and wants to talk to me a great deal. But having to speak so loud makes me cough and two days ago I was afraid of being laid up, as I felt fever coming on but I shook myself violently both morally and physically and am really getting better." On 9 November they lunched at home, "dull parties, children, governesses, architects and Arthur Ellis." Ellis puzzled her; he seemed to be trying to flirt with her. There was one ugly and amusing Frenchman, who talked too much and another who was dull "but evidently I have a power of attraction over him, because he always comes up to me, though he has not much to say for himself." She had been driven to reading poetry in her room and had been hoping they could escape on Saturday, but Albert Edward insisted they stay until Monday.[227]

The new ballroom was inaugurated on his birthday. Eddy came for the ball, bringing a college friend, John Baring,[228] "such a nice boy". The second party was slightly more amusing; arriving on the 26th, guests included Prince Christian "who did nothing but <u>eat</u> & shoot other people's pheasants", "Mrs Leigh & Mr Falbe[229] who were <u>engaged then</u> & <u>married</u> the day after they left us", "dear Uncle George", Lord Fife, Mr F Rothschild,[230] Mr Montgomery, "Oliver M, our 'dear friend' who asked a great deal after you" and others. The weather was lovely except on Alexandra's birthday, which was damp and cold. It had been delightful to receive George's letter; "Yes indeed I am getting quite an old Mother Hubbard!!!! & I think it high time to leave off keeping my birthday any longer, as it is getting ridiculous! don't you think so too you dear thing!" New rooms had been built on the ballroom passage upstairs; George would have one of these on his return. She thanked him very much for the fur rug he and Aunt Louise, (then in Canada) had sent her. "I got lots of beautiful presents among others <u>fur</u> enough to cover a whole regiment … & lots of pretty old keepsakes from all our various friends. Sisters had worked very nice things for me, slippers & a bag. Well, I must confess that after dancing all night[231] I found it very difficult to get up in the morning, but I was obliged to bundle up as quick as I could, as before going out hunting, the Meet being at the House, they all came to wish me joy on my birthday, & then we all went into the new ballroom where the Meet breakfast was prepared." Mr Hamond was retiring as master and the Prince made a speech before presenting him with a picture of the Hamonds on horseback. After some emotional cheers, "we all mounted our steeds (don't that sound well or poetical, as you wld say) & drew Dersingham Coverts, but of course never saw a Fox."[232] After a few days in London they came back and "had a very nice Xmas & lots of pretty presents. We had the tree & tables in the new room, which looked so nice, & saved us a great deal of trouble, as none of my poor furniture or piano had to be moved out of the hall this time." Dalton had spent Christmas with them, as had Julie Stonor, who "seemed quite happy here, poor girl, it was her first Xmas without her poor Mother, so I asked her, thinking she wld prefer that to being at Stonor." On the 29th Alexandra sat to M Lacretelle, who had sketched her husband the previous summer. The latest was that "old Mr. Billy Russell,[233] formerly Times correspondent, is going to marry a young Italian Countess whose name I forget now! Papa wrote & told him he thought he must be suffering from softening of the brain, poor old thing, but he seems <u>delighted</u> all the same." Looking back, apart from the deaths of General Knollys[234] and Mrs Stonor, 1883 had been one of her happiest years; "certainly every year has <u>its sorrows</u> as well as <u>blessings</u>, & we must never forget to be prepared for one & grateful for the other!"[235]

George had passed his six-month examination with flying colours, to Alexandra's "<u>great</u> pleasure and we are all delighted to hear it – how glad you must be & what a satisfaction besides. Now you see how important it was to work <u>really hard</u>, and you will not regret the few lawn tennis parties etc you had to give up for its good."[236] Eddy had celebrated his 20th birthday on 8 January

1884, with very successful theatricals in the new ballroom. On the 26th, after visiting Crichel, the family saw "Sir A Sullivan's new piece, 'The Princess Ida' – the music was pretty & dresses beautiful, but we preferred 'Patience' & 'Iolanthe'", Albert Edward told George.[237] They settled down in London again on 5 February and, after Parliament reconvened, Alexandra attended debates in the Commons on the 12th, while her husband observed the vote of censure on the government, moved by Lord Salisbury in the Lords. She noted; "Parliament has begun in a very stormy manner, and the government has been attacked most ferociously for the manner in which they have conducted the Egyptian affairs. Indeed things look very bad there again & we are <u>now</u> – tho' I fear rather late, sending a lot of poor troops out."[238] George was in Barbados, where "those tiresome dinners etc I fear you don't enjoy so much; I certainly think they always are a great bore." She sent him "a story which I think will interest you immensely, it is most exciting, keep it till yr return. I am sure all yr friends on board will like to read it."

On the 19th she took the girls to the pantomime, and Louise had her 17th birthday party. On 10 March Alexandra wrote; "Just fancy my having been married <u>21</u> years already! how old we are all getting. We gave a charming & most successful Children's ball that day, which Sisters enjoyed very much. Poor Eddy I am sorry to say was not allowed to come up for it, as they thought it would disturb too much."[239] It had lasted till 2am. At the two drawing rooms in mid-March, Charlotte Knollys noted, unusually[240] that on the 14th Alexandra wore a "brown velvet dress and train with gold Indian stuff & Indian jewels" and on the 20th a "Crimson broche dress, crimson velvet train." There were more drives, theatres and visits and on the 19th the couple opened the Westminster Training School & Home for Nurses, at Queen Anne's Gate. On the 18th Mlle Mohrenheim[241] dined at Marlborough House and accompanied Alexandra and on the 28th Madame Neruda came to play. However, news came that Leopold, Duke of Albany, who had been suffering from rheumatism, had died at the Villa Nevada in Cannes. He had tripped when going upstairs, hurt his knee badly and died that night after convulsions. "It is indeed <u>too sad</u> & that he should have died out there quite by himself without his poor wife, or any of his own near or with him. Poor Dr Royle[242] & Captain Percival[243] were the only friends there & he died in their arms, & they did all in their power to restore him to life, but alas to no avail."[244] On the 29th the Waleses called on the young, pregnant, widow at Claremont, "terribly unhappy but so good & resigned ... Poor little thing; for her it is indeed her <u>all</u> she has lost, & they were so happy together." The Queen too was resigned, having always known that such a tragedy was possible. Albert Edward set off for Cannes to bring Leopold home on 3 April; two days later the funeral was held at St George's Chapel.

The couple were to attend Victoria of Hesse's wedding to Louis of Battenberg at Darmstadt, but this now had to be postponed. On the 12th they went instead to Sandringham for Easter and Louis, unhappy at the delay, stayed for three days. Alexandra had attended All Saints' on Good Friday, for Bach's *St Matthew Passion* "for <u>3</u> hours in the morning, rather too much of a good thing!!! & in the afternoon for another 2 hours at St Anne's."[245] Adolphus and Francis of Teck spent a week of their Easter holidays at Sandringham, as their family was in Florence.[246] Alexandra went to London with her husband and daughters on the 26th, calling on Helen Albany at Claremont afterwards. Two days later the whole family left for Darmstadt. The wedding, which took place quietly at 5pm on 30 April, "went off very well & was a very pretty one, & they looked both very happy & bright."[247] A banquet for 172 people, including the Queen, followed. Albert Edward told George; "we shall I think remain abroad, till the first fortnight in June as we cannot go out in London at present, or take part in any public functions."[248] Eddy returned to Cambridge on 3 May; "He will have to study hard now as he has been away some time."[249]

On the 6th the Prince went to Potsdam for a few days and then to the spa, Royat les Bains. Alexandra and her daughters stayed six days with the Cumberlands. "I enjoyed my stay at Gmunden so much; first of all it is a lovely spot, a grand kind of Scotland, with the most beautiful hills & views, & then it was so nice seeing dear Thyra & Ernest & their delightful Children in their bright & happy home. We lived in a charming little house opposite theirs & made some delightful expeditions on the mountains & lakes." It was sad saying goodbye but they were going to Rumpenheim, where a large family party was gathering for the wedding of Alexandra's first cousin, Elisabeth of Hesse-Cassel,[250] to the Hereditary Prince of Anhalt on the 26th. Alexandra was delighted to see her parents, Minny, Freddy and Waldemar and various other relatives. On 27 May she apologised to George for her "<u>awfully</u> badly written letter, but you have no idea under what difficulties I am writing; the room more or less full, dear Minny Minny writing at one table, everybody talking & asking questions, which really drives me to distraction & I don't know what I am saying nor can I collect my thoughts at all." The wedding had gone off well; "Elisabeth the bride looked very happy & bright & so did the bridegroom ... who seems a very nice young man. Uncle Fritz Hesse & Aunt Anna, who are very much pleased at their eldest daughter's marriage, had asked the whole world in general & there was a tremendous gathering of all the German Princes they cld find". Two days later they went to Baden to see Empress Augusta, took other excursions and then on 4 June Alexandra, her daughters and her parents left for the Hotel du Parc at Wiesbaden, where the next day Albert Edward joined them.

Meanwhile the Queen was writing to Vicky, who had asked about Teignmouth Shore; "I know him well; he is a clever & a vy plausible man & took me & others of the family vy much in, but he is vy pushing, designing & rather a vulgar minded man, & all the Clergy of different views dislike him. He likes to be with people of rank & title & boasts of never having had to do with the poor! He can preach vy well, & his short services were much liked for children. But both Alix & Mary Teck have seen through him, & the children dislike him, out of the pulpit particularly. I thought it my duty just to warn you, as Louis also found him out abt the Alice Hospital. Of course be civil to him, only beware of him."[251]

Alexandra told George; "Eddy will soon leave Cambridge now, but poor boy is going for a little time to Heidelberg to study <u>German</u>! ... really it is very necessary for him & you too Georgie dear to know <u>German</u>."[252] On 13 June the family returned to London, where Eddy joined them on the 16th. He left for Heidelberg three days later, to be coached by Professor Ihne;[253] meanwhile, as mourning restrictions were lifting, his parents had resumed public life, including attending a lecture on "The Liquefaction of Gasses" by Professor Dewar[254] at the Royal Institution on the 26th. The next day they inspected the Xth Hussars and presented Sudan Campaign medals at Shorncliffe Camp. On the 30th Alexandra laid the foundation stone of Alexandra House[255] next to the Royal College of Music. From 3–26 July she had eight drawing lessons with Mr Harper. On 8 July she opened Sandringham Buildings for the Poor of London, and went with the Prince to lay the foundation stone of St Anne's Society's new schools' chapel on the 9th, and of the new bridge at Putney on the 12th. On the 14th she opened Miss Mary Wardell's[256] Convalescent Home for scarlet fever patients at Brockley Hill and, with Albert Edward, a Bazaar at the Duke of Wellington's Riding School, Knightsbridge, in aid of enlarging Kew Church. On the 21st the couple lunched with the Caringtons[257] at Whitehall Yard and watched demonstrators supporting the "Extension of the Franchise" Bill march past, which took three hours. Meanwhile, George had had great success with his examination, "really nothing could have pleased me more ... fancy out of <u>1,000</u> – Mark 985 seems first rate." Eddy "seems to like his little cottage at Heidelberg very much & above all the dear old Professor Ihne in whose house he is. He is a delightful old man, so clever & most cheery & nice." "Poor old Bentley"[258] in service for 21 years, had recently died; "we shall all miss him & his poor fat cherub-face & form." Louise's confirmation was approaching; "It seems hardly possible to believe as yet, & she is not very tall either."[259] After Goodwood, they left for Cowes on 2 August but, on *Osborne*, called at Yarmouth, where George's ship, *Canada* had docked. On the 4th the Queen gave him the Order of the Garter at Osborne House. Two days later, Louise was confirmed there and the next day took Holy Communion with her parents at Whippingham Church.

The family left on the 18th for London, where Eddy joined them, and saw *Twelfth Night* at the Lyceum that evening. The next day they all left for Northumberland, to stay with the Armstrongs[260] at Cragside. Sir William, a scientist, inventor, industrialist and benefactor in, especially, education and health provision, was also a keen art collector. Lady Armstrong was an enthusiastic and knowledgeable gardener, who directed the garden works at Cragside. Many of Sir William's inventions were in use; with electricity, provided by water power, they included lifts for the servants to get coal up to the bedrooms, gongs to announce meals, automatic turnspits, an internal telephone system, hot and cold running water, lighting, central heating and mechanical aids. These innovations appealed greatly to the Waleses, who described their hosts as "the most charming old couple". The house was "most comfortable with lots of beautiful pictures, and a lovely situation on the side of a hill laid out on rocks planted with heather and ferns."[261] A new drawing room, designed by Norman Shaw,[262] had been completed just in time for the royal visit and a set of rooms, known as the "Owl Suite" because of the carved owls on the bed-posts, was refurbished with distinctive furniture and in-built plumbing, for the royal guests. In the dining room was a stone inglenook and on the lintel over the fire was an inscription, "East or West – Hame's Best".[263] Unique devices to make life more comfortable appealed to Alexandra and at some point her husband designed a sofa for her boudoir at Marlborough House, which could hold books on one side and had a reading desk on the other.[264] While at Cragside, the couple visited Newcastle and opened Armstrong Park, the Natural History Museum, the Public Library's Reference Department and the next day, the new Albert Edward Dock on the Tyne. Proceeding to Edinburgh, Alexandra was delighted with the infirmary, one of the finest and best hospitals she had ever seen. On 23 August the gigantic railway bridge being built over the Firth of Forth was interesting and wonderful, "but whether I shall ever like to go over it is quite another question, & after that fearful calamity of the Tay Bridge[265] I shall always be thinking the same thing will happen to this, altho' all the Engineers declare this will be as safe as a rock."[266]

Two days later they reached Abergeldie, where Alexandra wrote to the Queen about a very sensitive matter. She was touched so much confidence had been placed in her; she knew how lonely the Queen felt, not only as a widow but also because of John Brown's death in 1883 and, more recently, Leopold's. How comforting, then, that Beatrice would always be there. But now Beatrice had fallen in love with Henry of Battenberg,[267] Louis' brother, whom she had met at the Darmstadt wedding, and although her mother had gradually accepted this, she was miserable about it. Alexandra as ever was sympathetic and consoling; "as you have always nursed the hope of keeping yr one little ewe lamb entirely to yrself, I can therefore well understand what a terrible shock it must have been to you, when you heard that she had found a new interest. We must hope however that all will be for the best & that she will continue for many a long year to be the same comfort & help to you, that she has hitherto always been." She had discussed it earlier with "Bertie", who quite understood it all "& is entirely of our opinion, so you will find no difficulties on his side whenever you wish to speak to him about it! At the same time I told him you wld prefer his not mentioning anything at present, & of course he will never say a word on the subject to anybody else."[268]

At Aberdeen on the 28th, in heavy rain, Alexandra presented new colours to the 3rd Battalion, Gordon Highlanders. Vicky and her second daughter[269] were staying at Balmoral and on 9 September Alexandra sat with Vicky while she drew an old woman at the gates. Three days earlier, Albert Edward had taken George to the Royal Naval College. Alexandra wrote; "I am glad you seem to like Greenwich & that yr rooms at the Naval College seem nice & cheery & that you know most of the people there, which will make a great difference to you." Eddy had brought his German tutor to Abergeldie and went "out stalking yesterday & got a stag & the poor old Professor went with him but I think he was rather done up & went to bed directly after dinner."[270] The weather was fine and Eddy had good luck with the stags, shooting eighteen by the 22nd. He and Alexandra had dined six times with the Queen, "so you see we are very much in request this year." Louis of Hesse, his daughter Irène, Helena, Helen Albany with her two children and the Edinburghs were also there, as were friends, including Oliver Montagu, Andrew Cockerell and H Calcraft. George came for a few days, Professor Ihne left on the 29th and Grand Duke Michael Michaelovitch of Russia[271] arrived on 7 October.

At dinner on 29 September, Ponsonby had sat next to Alexandra, "who heard all I said & I heard what she said". They were talking about Lady Lonsdale; Alexandra said she did not much care for her, but was determined she should have fair play. Mrs Gladstone had told the Queen all sorts of stories about her, much of which was untrue. In fact "William"[272] had immediately been captivated by Lady Lonsdale "& could not tear himself away from her and Lady Dalhousie".[273] The Queen disapproved of Alexandra's friendship with "a woman who openly says that her child is not her husband's" but when questioned about Lady Lonsdale and Mrs Gladstone, Alexandra went off to ask Lady Lonsdale, so really "they here force on the friendship as Lady L is posing as the oppressed one and the Pss takes her part."[274] On 9 October Alexandra told Ponsonby "she liked talking high treason sometimes and mixing in politics which she had no business to do and therefore she would say at once she was tired of Egyptian bother. Why don't you take it at once and have done with it. Anybody but dear William would have done this long ago. We don't want it I dare say but we have got it and so we had better declare ourselves at once and have no more bother." She was "very sour agst Mrs G so I suppose there have been more Lonsdale rows."[275] Alexandra continued to champion Lady L (later Marchioness of Ripon and Countess de Grey), who ultimately became one of her best friends; she was a great patron of the arts, especially opera, so they had much in common.

The couple and their daughters left Scotland on 10 October, despite an unexpected heavy snow-fall, and reached London next morning. It was Saturday; George came for the weekend, as he would now do regularly, and Eddy went back to Cambridge on the 13th. The Waleses were attending performances again, *The Iron Master* on the 11th and Gounod's *Redemption* at

Norwich on the 15th, but that day they heard of Alexandra's Uncle, Landgrave Frederick's death. She continued social visits and dinner parties but attended fewer theatres than her husband, although she had seen *Our Boys, Divorçons* and *Romeo and Juliet* by 6 November. She called on Aunt Cambridge[276] several times. Waldemar arrived for a few days on the 26th, and there were visits to the Health Exhibition, the zoo and Madame Tussaud's. On 7 November they returned to Sandringham for Albert Edward's birthday house party. Lady Sophia Macnamara,[277] whom Alexandra found amusing, was one of the guests. On the 17th, "Fancy what a commotion we had yesterday. The old bear, the big one, jumped from his stand or pole right <u>over the rails</u> – he saw a small basket with carrots or biscuits which tempted him so that he took this leap; fancy if we had been there!! how pleasant, & luckily the goats were all in the Park or I am sure he wld have ate a few of them. It seems that he, poor old thing, was rather frightened so remained all night in the enclosure and this morning poor old <u>Elder</u> had the pluck to walk up to him by himself, as no one else wld go, & stroke him & coax him down the steps where he followed him quite quietly – fancy that. Now they have cut his pole lower so that he shld not attempt such a thing again. Fancy if he were to do that on our Sunday visit! that wld be fun indeed."[278] Mr Bertram[279] performed conjuring for Maud's birthday on the 26th. For her own birthday, Alexandra gave a tea in the Coach House to the local school-children, and Louise joined the adults at dinner. On 4 December the Waleses attended the Duke of Albany's[280] christening at Esher Parish Church.

Alexandra hoped Dalton would spend Christmas with them (George, doing very well at Greenwich, would be there too), and that Dalton was "really satisfied with Eddy this time & that he <u>does</u> work harder now. I am <u>so</u> very anxious that when he comes home this time for a long holyday that he shld be made to do a certain amount of work every day, as it becomes such a <u>very</u> <u>bad habit</u> of being so completely <u>idle</u> when at home, & he ends by boring both himself & others as well."[281] The Waleses hated being idle but this had come with maturity; Eddy's faults were not unlike Bertie's at the same age. They stayed at Eastwell with the Edinburghs from 8–13 December, and later with the Dudleys at Witley Court. In London on the 20th, they saw *Diplomacy* at the Haymarket. Oliver Montagu had been staying at Witley, and Sandringham; however, on the 21st; "OM had his eye taken out." As Alexandra wrote to Mary Teck, "I know you will be sorry & horrified to hear that poor dear Oliver M has had his poor eye taken out yesterday or he would have lost the sight in both eyes." He had been in great pain but was now feeling better.[282] The Tecks were still in Italy, but she hoped they were getting on well and would soon be back.[283] Guests, including Julie Stonor, arrived. The labourers received their meat; the house party and the servants their presents; and the girls joined the formal dinner on Christmas Day. Riding and field sports completed the year and on the 31st news came from Osborne that Beatrice was engaged to Henry of Battenberg.

Notes

[1] Sir Coutts Lindsay, 2nd Baronet (1824–1913), artist, watercolourist and playwright, and his wife, Caroline, née Fitzroy (1844–1912), artist, novelist and poet; the couple had founded the Grosvenor Gallery in 1877, for showing work by the Pre-Raphaelite Brotherhood.

[2] Her husband, Lord Lorne, was Governor-General of Canada from 1878–1883.

[3] RA GV/PRIV/AA6/236, Princess of Wales to JN Dalton, 1880: 15 January

[4] RA GV/PRIV/AA28/39, Princess of Wales to Prince George, 1879: 31 December

[5] RA GV/PRIV/AA28/40, Princess of Wales to Prince George, 1880: 15 January

[6] RA GV/PRIV/AA13/67, Prince of Wales to Prince George, 1880: 16 January

[7] Established in 1848 by Charles Hengler (1820–1887) from a circus family; by 1875 it had branches in Glasgow, Edinburgh, Liverpool and London.

[8] Alfred Tennyson, 1st Baron Tennyson (1809–1892), poet laureate

[9] Sabine Thellusson (1823–1882), m Richard Greville; she was a society hostess with many friends and acquaintances, including Henry James. Lady Probyn was her sister.

[10] Alphonse Neuville (1835–1885), French military artist

[11] Sir Lawrence Alma-Tadema (1836–1912), Dutch painter who settled in England

[12] RA GV/PRIV/AA28/42, Princess of Wales to Prince George, 1880: 1 March

[13] Franz Xaver Neruda (1843–1915), cellist and composer, who lived in Copenhagen

[14] Elizabeth, née Harbord (1860–1957) m George Astley, 20th Baron Hastings (1857–1904)

[15] An English version of "La Dame aux Camellias"

[16] Helen, née Chaplin (1846–1929), musician, and sister of Henry Chaplin, m 5th Earl of Radnor (1841–1900), who was styled Viscount Folkestone from 1869–1889

[17] With the Duchess of Sutherland

[18] With the Falmouths; Evelyn Boscawen (1819–1889), 6th Viscount Falmouth, successful breeder of race horses, m Mary, née Stapleton (1822–1891), the 13th Baroness le Despencer

[19] Sir George Orby Wombwell (1832–1913), 4th Baronet, army officer who survived the charge of the Light Brigade, m Lady Julia, née Child-Villiers (d 1921)

[20] Presumably as lamps

[21] RA VIC/MAIN/Z/453/96, Prince of Wales to Queen Victoria, 1880: 22 May

[22] RA VIC/MAIN/Z/453/104, Queen Victoria to Prince of Wales, 1880: 26 May

[23] Alexandra's brother, King George of the Hellenes

[24] Empress Marie Alexandrovna (1824–1880), wife of Alexander II; she had recently died after a long illness.

[25] Sarah (Henriette Rosine) Bernhardt (1844–1923), prominent French actress

[26] In aid of the Friends of the Royal Cambridge Asylum for Soldiers' Widows

[27] Arthur Grey Egerton (1833–1885), 3rd Earl of Wilton, politician, m Lady Elizabeth, née Craven (1836–1919)

[28] Declare them open to free public traffic

[29] Royal Society for the Prevention of Cruelty to Animals; its "Royal" status was granted by Queen Victoria in 1840

[30] RA VIC/MAIN/EVIID/1880: 1 July

[31] Eugenie Louisa Perugia (1854–1943), married Arthur Sassoon (1840–1912), a friend of the Prince of Wales

[32] RA GV/PRIV/AA56/17; Louisa, Mrs Arthur Sassoon, [1915]; red and dark blue are the Regimental colours

[33] Electric light

[34] Which might have been caused by long-term after-effects of typhoid fever three years previously

[35] RA VIC/MAIN/Z/453/121, Prince of Wales to Queen Victoria, 1880: 11 July

36 Henry David Leslie (1822–1896), composer, conductor and founder of choirs and music schools; "Henry Leslie's Choir" started as a madrigal society, which was dissolved in 1880, but later re-formed and he conducted it again from 1885–7.

37 Lady Blanche, née Somerset (c 1854–1897) m John Beresford, 5th Marquess of Waterford

38 Lady Waterford, quoted in Tooley, p 106

39 A seine is a long fishing net, weighted down and dragged horizontally along the sea bed by a line of people

40 Alfred Vance (born Alfred Peek Stevens), (1839–1888), music hall performer of Cockney songs; "Mrs Vance" was perhaps his wife, or stage partner

41 This was a blackface minstrel troupe, created in 1877 by Christopher (better known as JH or "Jack") Haverley, an American theatre manager and promoter of blackface minstrel shows

42 RA GV/PRIV/AA28/43, Princess of Wales to Prince George, 1880: 15 September

43 Maud had ear-ache

44 RA GV/PRIV/AA28/44, Princess of Wales to Prince George, 1880: 28 September

45 Sir Henry Bartle Frere (1815–1884), 1st Baronet, colonial administrator

46 RA GV/PRIV/AA28/45, Princess of Wales to Prince George, 1880: 9 October

47 With Charles Gordon (1847–1937), the 11th Marquis of Huntly, politician, m Amy, née Brooks (d 1920)

48 Seat of the Duke of Grafton; William Fitzroy (1819–1882), politician, m Hon Marie, née Baring

49 Prince George William of Cumberland (1880–1912)

50 Princess Olga of Greece (1880)

51 RA GV/PRIV/AA28/46, Princess of Wales to Prince George, 1880: 3 November

52 Whose son had been killed in the gun room by another boy accidentally letting off a gun

53 RA GV/PRIV/AA28/47, Princess of Wales to Prince George, 1880: 22 November

54 RA VIC/MAIN/S/31/98, Princess of Wales to Lord Beaconsfield, 1880: 29 November

55 RA VIC/MAIN/S/31/30, Princess of Wales to Lord Beaconsfield, c1880: undated

56 Tooley, pp 77–8; as Benjamin Disraeli, Beaconsfield was known popularly as Dizzy

57 RA GV/PRIV.AA13/76, Prince of Wales to Prince George, 1880: 1 December

58 John Watkins (1844-c 1914), "Dr Holden", society conjurer, had worked at the Royal Polytechnic Institution

59 RA GV/PRIV/AA28/48, Princess of Wales to Prince George, 1880: 2 December

60 This was probably Francis Joseph Flynn (1864–1898), known as General Mite, with another little person, either Lucia Zarate (1864–1890), or Emily Edwards (1877–1919), each his stage partner at different times. Mr Flynn's father, EJ Flynn, was his manager.

61 Miecislas Jaraczewski (1838–1881), a charming, enigmatic Polish count, apparently committed suicide later

62 Frederick Hervey (1846–1910), rector of Sandringham, 1878–1907, later Canon

63 Miss Louisa Walkley, Head Nurse from October 1872

64 RA GV/PRIV/AA28/49, Princess of Wales to Prince George, 1880: 31 December

65 This may be Miss Ann Newton, who had also taught the Teck children. She apparently died in 1882.

66 RA VIC/ADDU/404/2, Princess of Wales to Miss Newton, undated, c 1880–1

67 Likely to have been Charlotte Knollys

68 RA VIC/ADDU404/3, [Charlotte Knollys to Miss Newton], undated, c 1880–1

69 RA GV/PRIV/AA28/50, Princess of Wales to Prince George, 1881: 19 January

70 RA GV/PRIV/AA13/79, Prince of Wales to Prince George, 1881: 20 January

71 Léonie Vauthier, French governess to the Wales Princesses

72 RA GV/PRIV/AA28/51, Princess of Wales to Prince George, 1881:3 February

73 RA GV/PRIV/AA6/248, Princess of Wales to JN Dalton, 1881: 18 January

[74] RA GV/PRIV/AA28/51, Princess of Wales to Prince George, 1881: 3 February

[75] Thomas Teignmouth Shore (1841–1912), incumbent of the Berkeley Chapel, Mayfair; Chaplain in Ordinary to Queen Victoria (1878–1901)

[76] Pastor Paulli

[77] RA VIC/MAIN/Z/454/21, Revd T Teignmouth Shore to Queen Victoria, 1881: 7 February

[78] RA GV/PRIV/AA28/52, Princess of Wales to Prince George, 1881: 9 February

[79] Charles Beresford (1846–1919), 1st Baron Beresford, admiral and politician, m Ellen Jeromina (Mina) Gardner

[80] Unidentified but perhaps a comic or fictional character

[81] RA GV/PRIV/AA28/53, Princess of Wales to Prince George, 1881: 19 February

[82] RA GV/PRIV/AA28/51, Princess of Wales to Prince George, 1881: 3 February, about the wedding of Prince William of Prussia and Princess Victoria of Augustenburg

[83] Landgrave George of Hesse-Cassel (1793–1881), brother of the Duchess of Cambridge

[84] Princess Caroline of Schleswig-Holstein-Sonderburg-Augustenburg (1796–1881) m King Christian VIII

[85] RA VIC/MAIN/ Z/454/29, Princess of Wales to Queen Victoria, 1881: 10 March

[86] Probably Princess Caroline of Denmark (1793–1881), daughter of King Frederick VI and wife of Ferdinand, Hereditary Prince of Denmark (who had died in 1863)

[87] RA GV/PRIV/AA28/54, Princess of Wales to her sons, 1881: 10 March

[88] RA GV/PRIV/AA28/55, Princess of Wales to Prince George, 1881:17 March

[89] RA VIC/MAIN/Z/454/65,73, Empress Marie Feodorovna to Queen Victoria, 1881: 29 March; Queen Victoria to Princess of Wales, 1881: 30 March

[90] RA GV/PRIV/AA29/1, Princess of Wales to Prince George, 1881: 21 April

[91] RA VIC/MAIN/H/44/9, Princess of Wales to Queen Victoria, 1881: 6–9 April

[92] RA GV/PRIV/AA13/83, Prince of Wales to Prince George, 1881: 21 April

[93] William Schwenk Gilbert (1836–1911), later Sir, dramatist, librettist, poet and illustrator; collaborated in 14 operettas with Sir Arthur Sullivan

[94] Of Crown Prince Rudolph and Princess Stephanie of Belgium (1864–1945), d of King Leopold II

[95] Mrs Elizabeth Jones

[96] RA VIC/MAIN/Z/454/96, Princess of Wales to Queen Victoria, 1881: 14 May

[97] RA GV/PRIV/AA29/2, Princess of Wales to Prince George, 1881: 20 May

[98] Alexander Duff (Macduff) was now 6th Earl Fife

[99] Lt General Owen Williams (1836–1913), army officer and politician

[100] RA GV//PRIV/AA29/3, Princess of Wales to Prince George, 1881: 17 June

[101] Serving on "Jutland", moored at Southampton

[102] King Kalakaua (1836–91), King from 1874–91

[103] With the Earl and Countess of Sefton; there had been an outbreak of measles at Croxteth, hence the girls staying at Knowsley

[104] Seat of the Earl of Derby, Edward Stanley (1826–93), the 15th Earl, statesman, m Lady Mary, née Sackville-West, widow of the 2nd Marquess of Salisbury

[105] RA GV/PRIV/AA29/4, Princess of Wales to Prince George, 1881: 8 September

[106] RA GV/PRIV/AA29/5, Princess of Wales to Prince George, 1881: 20 September

[107] Sir Francis Cowley Burnand (1836–1917), comic writer, playwright and Arthur Sullivan's collaborator in Cox and Box

[108] Mabel Elizabeth Lennox (d 1939) m Revd Frederick Hervey

[109] RA GV/PRIV/AA29/7, Princess of Wales to Prince George, 1881: 21 October

[110] Jules Grévy (1807–91), President of France from 1879–1887, m [no information]

[111] Edouard Detaille (1848–1912), French military artist

[112] Ernest Meissonier (1815–91), French military painter and sculptor

113 Gustave Jacquet (1846–1909), French portrait and genre painter
114 Thomas W Evans (1823–97), Philadelphia-born surgeon dentist to Napoleon III and to the Prince of Wales
115 Michael Lieb (1844–1900) b in Munkacs, Hungary, and took the name Munkacsy; genre and biblical painter
116 Charles Sedelmayer (1837–1925), Austrian art dealer, collector and publisher, based in Paris
117 Hon John Pelham (1811–94), Bishop of Norwich from 1857–1893, chaplain to Queen Victoria from 1847
118 RA GV/PRIV/AA29/8, Princess of Wales to Prince George, 1881: 3 November
119 Sir William ffolkes (1847–1912), 3rd Baronet, MP for King's Lynn, m Emily, née Elwes (1855–1915) d of Robert Elwes, artist, traveller and explorer
120 Anthony Hamond (1834–95), Master of West Norfolk Foxhounds from 1865–83
121 RA GV/PRIV/AA29/9, Princess of Wales to Prince George, 1881: 17 November
122 Alexandra fully shared her husband's love of dogs; according to Arthur H. Beavan [Beavan, p 80] she was also fond of Persian cats which "abounded" at Sandringham and Marlborough House. In both places there were areas in the grounds for pets' graves.
123 RA VIC/ADDU/344/1881: Commander Rose to Edie (his wife?), 1881: 12–13 November, © The descendants of Commander Rose
124 Princess Helen of Waldeck-Pyrmont (1861–1922), m Prince Leopold, Duke of Albany
125 RA GV/PRIV/AA29/10, Princess of Wales to Prince George, 1881: 1 December
126 Seat of the Marquess of Bath, then John Thynne (1831–96), 4th Marquess, who m Frances, née Vesey
127 Nathaniel Rothschild (1840–1915), 1st Baron Rothschild, banker and politician
128 Sir Dighton Probyn and his wife, Letitia, née Thellusson (d 1900)
129 RA GV/PRIV/AA29/11, Princess of Wales to Prince George, 1882:10 January
130 Meiji (1852–1912), Mikado, or Emperor, of Japan from 1867–1912
131 RA VIC/MAIN/Z/454/180, note enclosed with letter from Lord Clanwilliam, 1881: 31 October
132 Sir John Pope-Hennessy (1834–1891), grandfather of James Pope-Hennessy, biographer of Queen Mary
133 RA VIC/MAIN/Z/454/182, Sir John Pope-Hennessy to Lady Ely, 1882: 2 January
134 RA VIC/MAIN/Z/454/185, JN Dalton to Queen Victoria, 1882: 15 January
135 RA GV/PRIV/AA6/261, Princess of Wales to JN Dalton, 1882: 11 January
136 RA GV/PRIV/AA29/11, Princess of Wales to Prince George, 1882: 10 January
137 William Alfred Baskcomb, joined the Prince's household in1873, became chief clerk and retired in 1894
138 John Lawrence Toole (1830–1906) comic actor, actor-manager and producer
139 RA GV/PRIV/AA29/13, Princess of Wales to Prince George, 1882: 3 February
140 Princess Margaret of Connaught (1882–1920), m Prince Gustaf Adolf of Sweden, later King Gustaf VI Adolf
141 RA GV/PRIV/AA14/5, Prince of Wales to Prince George, 1882: 10 February
142 RA GV/PRIV/AA29/15, Princess of Wales to Prince George, 1882: 24 February
143 Mohamed Tewfik Pasha (1852–1892), eldest son of Khedive Ismail; Khedive from 1879–1892
144 RA GV/PRIV/AA29/16, Princess of Wales to Prince George, 1882: 3 March
145 RA GV/PRIV/AA29/15, Princess of Wales to Prince George, 1882: 24 February
146 Roderick Edward Maclean (c 1854–1921), committed to Broadmoor
147 RA GV/PRIV/AA14/6, Prince of Wales to Prince George, 1882: 3 March
148 RA VIC/MAIN/Z/454/191, Report of meeting at St James's Palace on 28 February 1882

[149] RA GV/PRIV/AA29/16, Princess of Wales to Prince George, 1882: 3 March

[150] Dr Frederick Hervey Foster Quin (1799–1878), first homeopathic doctor in England. He was witty and amusing, very popular in society, and an early friend of the Waleses; the Prince consulted him at Victoria Mansions. Quin founded the London Homeopathic Hospital.

[151] RA GV/PRIV/AA29/18, Princess of Wales to Prince George, 1882: 24 March

[152] Leslie Ward (1851–1922), later Sir, portraitist and caricaturist; drew for *Vanity Fair* as "Spy" and "Drawl"

[153] Louisa (Bulteel), (1839–92), wife of Edward Baring who was created 1st Baron Revelstoke in 1885; they were the parents of John Baring, 2nd Baron Revelstoke

[154] RA GV/PRIV/AA29/19, Princess of Wales to Prince George, 1882: 6 April

[155] RA GV/PRIV/AA29/20, Princess of Wales to Prince George, 1882: 14 April

[156] King William III (1817–90) and Queen Emma (1858–1934), formerly Princess Emma of Waldeck-Pyrmont

[157] His wife, Crown Princess Louise

[158] Oscar II (1829–1907) and Queen Sophie (1836–1913), née Princess Sophie of Nassau

[159] RA GV/PRIV/AA29/21, Princess of Wales to Prince George, 1882: 24/31 May

[160] RA GV/PRIV/AA29/22, Princess of Wales to Prince George, 1882: 3 June

[161] Captain David N Welsh, RN, looked after the Fishing Temple at Virginia Water

[162] Constance Gwladys, née Herbert (1859–1917), patron of the arts, m (1) 4th Earl of Lonsdale; (2) Frederick Robinson (1852–1923), 2nd Marquess of Ripon and Earl de Grey

[163] Jeanne Bernhardt (1851–1900), actress, sister of Sarah Bernhardt

[164] Francesco Paolo Tosti (1846–1916), later Sir; Italian composer and music teacher who settled in England and was singing teacher to the royal family

[165] Grand Duchess Olga Alexandrovna of Russia (1882–1960), m (1) Duke Peter of Oldenburg (1868–1924), (2) Colonel Nicholas Alexandrovitch Kulikovsky (1881–1958)

[166] RA GV/PRIV/AA29/23, Princess of Wales to Prince George, 1882: 29 June

[167] RA GV/PRIV/AA29/24, Princess of Wales to Prince George, 1882: 19 July

[168] Cetshwayo kaMpande (c 1826–84), King of the Zulu Kingdom from 1873–79

[169] Hirini Taiwhanga, Wiremu Parore and Hakena Parore were a delegation seeking redress of grievances relating to the Treaty of Waitangi

[170] Including the King and Queen of the Hellenes

[171] RA GV/PRIV/AA29/25, Princess of Wales to Prince George, 1882: 19 October

[172] Natalia Janotha (1856–1932), Polish pianist and composer

[173] Carlo Alfredo Piatti (1822–1901), Italian cellist, teacher and composer.

[174] Field Marshal Sir Garnet Wolseley, later 1st Viscount Wolseley (1833–1913), an influential and admired military commander who also introduced army reform

[175] RA GV/PRIV/AA29/40, Princess of Wales to Prince George, 1882: 30 October

[176] Alexandre Dumas (1802–70), French writer

[177] Alphonse de Lamartine (1790–1869), French author, poet and statesman

[178] RA GV/PRIV/AA6/282, Princess of Wales to JN Dalton, 1882: 7 November

[179] Charles Gounod (1818–93), French composer of operas and other music

[180] RA GV/PRIV/AA29/26, Princess of Wales to Prince George, 1882: 16 November

[181] Seat of Baron Walsingham, then Thomas de Grey (1843–1919), 3rd Baron, m 3 times

[182] Charles Vane-Tempest-Stewart (1852–1915), styled Viscount Castlereagh between 1872 and 1884, later 6th Marquess of Londonderry, politician, landowner and benefactor

[183] RA GV/PRIV/AA29/27, Princess of Wales to Prince George, 1882: 7 December

[184] RA GV/PRIV/AA14/17, Prince of Wales to Prince George, 1882: 3 December

[185] RA GV/PRIV/AA29/27, Princess of Wales to Prince George, 1882: 7 December

[186] Marian Wedde (or Wehde) was born in Germany in 1866; she grew to over 7' tall

187 John Jones (c 1798/9–1882), a successful London tailor, was an art collector who bequeathed his collection (of, mostly French the 18th century objects and furniture, but also paintings and books) to the museum

188 Prince Charles of Prussia (1801–83), brother of Emperor William I

189 RA GV/PRIV/AA29/28, Princess of Wales to Prince George, 1883: 20 January

190 RA GV/PRIV/AA29/29, Princess of Wales to Prince George, 1883: 25 January

191 Hon Julia Stonor (1862–1950), m Ferdinand, Marquis d'Hautpoul de Seyre (c 1860–1934)

192 Princess Frederike of Schleswig-Holstein-Sonderburg-Glücksburg (1811–1902), m Alexander, Duke of Anhalt-Bernburg

193 RA GV/PRIV/AA29/31, Princess of Wales to Prince George, 1883: 7 February

194 RA GV/PRIV/AA29/30, Princess of Wales to Prince George, 1883: 25 February

195 Prince Arthur of Connaught (1883–1938), son of the Duke and Duchess of Connaught

196 James Abbott McNeill Whistler (1834–1903), American artist, based mostly in England

197 RA GV/PRIV/AA29/33, Princess of Wales to Prince George, 1883: 27 March

198 RA GV/PRIV/AA6/288, Princess of Wales to JN Dalton, 1883: 11 March

199 Edwin Buckman (1841–1930), art teacher to the Princess

200 RA GV/PRIV/AA29/32, Princess of Wales to Prince George, 1883: 23 March

201 RA GV/PRIV/AA14/29, Prince of Wales to Prince George, 1883: 2 April

202 Princess Alice of Albany (1883–1981), m Prince Alexander of Teck (1874–1957), Earl of Athlone (1917)

203 RA GV/PRIV/AA29/30, Princess of Wales to Prince George, 1883: 25 February

204 Jacques Offenbach (1819–80), German-born French composer of operettas

205 RA GV/PRIV/AA14/29, Prince of Wales to Prince George, 1883: 2 April

206 This was an interest of Gladstone's

207 RA GV/PRIV/AA29/34, Princess of Wales to Prince George, 1883: 19 April

208 RA VIC/ADDU32/1883: 21 April, Queen Victoria to Crown Princess of Prussia

209 RA VIC/ADDA36/2166, 2167, General Ponsonby to his wife, 1883: 21, 23 April

210 Francis Durrant, RN (1837–96), later Rear-Admiral, appointed Governor to Prince George in 1883

211 RA GV/PRIV/AA14/31, Prince of Wales to Prince George, 1883: 16 April

212 RA GV/PRIV/AA29/34, Princess of Wales to Prince George, 1883: 19 April

213 RA EB/EB/68, p13, Establishment Book for the Household of Albert Edward, Prince of Wales, 1863–1901

214 Hermann David Salomon Corrodi (1844–1905), Italian painter of landscapes and orientalist scenes

215 She did not really care for tennis; perhaps her stiff knee made it difficult to respond promptly to her opponent's unexpected movements

216 RA GV/PRIV/AA29/35, Princess of Wales to Prince George, 1883: 13 June

217 RA GV/PRIV/AA29/36, Princess of Wales to Prince George, 1883: 15 June

218 RA GV/PRIV/AA6/294, Princess of Wales to JN Dalton, 1883: 13 July

219 RA GV/PRIV/AA29/37, Princess of Wales to Prince George, 1883: 12 August

220 RA GV/PRIV/AA29/38, Princess of Wales to Prince George, 1883: 29 August – 3 September

221 3 September

222 Princess Louise of Scheswig-Holstein-Sonderburg-Glücksburg (1820–94), Abbess of Itzehoe

223 The Prince had attended military manoeuvres in Germany

224 RA VIC/MAIN/Z/162/7, Princess of Wales to Queen Victoria, 1883: 1 October

225 RA GV/PRIV/AA29/39, Princess of Wales to Prince George, 1883: 10–22 October

226 RA GV/PRIV/AA29/41, Princess of Wales to Prince George, 1883: 14 December

227 RA VIC/ADDA20/1072, Duchess of Edinburgh to "My dear General" perhaps Sir Garnet Wolseley, 1883: 9 November

228 John Baring, 2nd Baron Revelstoke (1863–1929), son of Alexandra's friend, Mrs Baring; college friend of Prince Eddy; and object of romantic interest to Princess Victoria

229 Eleanor, née Hawkes (d 1899), m (1) Humble Ward, (2) John Gerard Leigh, (3) Christian Frederick de Falbe (1828–1896), Danish Ambassador to UK

230 Ferdinand Rothschild (1839–98), Baron Ferdinand de Rothschild, banker, art collector and politician

231 The three young princesses had come down for the tenants' ball on 30 November and Oliver Montagu danced with them and took them to supper; it had been great fun. RA GV/PRIV/AA47/29, Oliver Montagu to Prince George, 1883: 10 December

232 RA GV/PRIV/AA29/41, Princess of Wales to Prince George, 1883:14 December

233 William Howard Russell (1820–1907), Sir; Irish reporter with The Times; m Countess Antoinette Malvezzi

234 General Knollys died on 23 June 1883

235 RA GV/PRIV/AA29/42, Princess of Wales to Prince George, 1883: 31 December

236 RA GV/PRIV/AA29/43, Princess of Wales to Prince George, 1884: 14 January

237 RA GV/PRIV/AA14/51, Prince of Wales to Prince George, 1884: 31 January

238 RA GV/PRIV/AA29/44, Princess of Wales to Prince George, 1884: 14 February

239 Interfere with his studies at Cambridge; RA GV/PRIV/AA29/46, Princess of Wales to Prince George, 1884: 10 March

240 RA VIC/MAIN/QAD/1884: 14, 20 March

241 This may be Louise Mohrenheim (b1859), d of Baron Arthur Mohrenheim (1824–1906), Russian ambassador in UK from 1882–4; she was maid of honour to the Russian Empress and m, 1890, Edouard, General de Sèze

242 Dr Arnold Royle, Surgeon-in-Ordinary to the Duke of Albany

243 Captain Clifton Perceval, friend and equerry to the Duke of Albany

244 RA GV/PRIV/AA30/1, Princess of Wales to Prince George, 1884: 1 April

245 RA GV/PRIV/AA30/2, Princess of Wales to Prince George, 1884: 15 April

246 Where they were staying, for economic reasons

247 RA GV/PRIV/AA30/3, Princess of Wales to Prince George, 1884: 13 May

248 RA GV/PRIV/AA14/57, Prince of Wales to Prince George, 1884: 25 April. Mourning hampered activities.

249 RA GV/PRIV/AA30/3, Princess of Wales to Prince George, 1884: 13 May

250 Princess Elisabeth of Hesse-Cassel (1861–1955), m Leopold, Hereditary Prince of Anhalt (1855–86)

251 RA VIC/ADDU32/1884: 30 May, Queen Victoria to Crown Princess of Prussia

252 RA GV/PRIV/AA30/4, Princess of Wales to Prince George, 1884: 27 May

253 Professor Wilhelm Ihne (1821–1902), historian and philologist, who taught English at Heidelberg University from 1873

254 Sir James Dewar (1842–1923), Scottish chemist and physicist who invented the vacuum flask, researched the liquefaction of gases and studied atomic and molecular spectroscopy

255 Hostel for students

256 Miss Mary L Wardell founded the Convalescent Home at Verulam House in 1884; Alexandra became the Home's patroness

257 Charles Robert Wynn-Carington (1843–1928), 3rd Baron, then 1st Earl (1905) Carrington, Marquess of Lincolnshire (1912), m Hon Cecilia, née Harbord (1856–1934)

258 James Bentley, joined the Prince's household in 1864, became upholsterer, d 1884

259 RA GV/PRIV/AA30/5, Princess of Wales to Prince George, 1884: 28 June

[260] William Armstrong (1810–1900), Sir, then 1ˢᵗ Baron Armstrong (1887), m Margaret Ramshaw (c 1804–93)

[261] RA VIC/MAIN/Z/162/11, Princess of Wales to Queen Victoria, 1884: 24 August

[262] Richard Norman Shaw (1831–1912), architect

[263] *Cragside*, by Hugh Dixon and Andrew Saint © 2007 The National Trust, pp 2, 3, 9, 10, 18, 29, 31
ISBN 978-1-84359-322-5

[264] Tooley, p 75

[265] During a violent storm on 28 December 1879, the first Tay Rail Bridge collapsed as a train went over it, killing all 75 people on board.

[266] RA VIC/MAIN/Z/162/11, Princess of Wales to Queen Victoria, 1884: 24 August

[267] Prince Henry of Battenberg (1858–96)

[268] RA VIC/MAIN/Z/162/11, Prince of Wales to Queen Victoria, 1884: 24 August

[269] Princess Victoria, also known as "Moretta"

[270] RA GV/PRIV/AA30/6, Princess of Wales to Prince George, 1884: 10 September

[271] Grand Duke Michael Michaelovitch of Russia (1861–1929)

[272] Gladstone

[273] Lady Ida, née Bennet (c 1857–87), m the 13ᵗʰ Earl of Dalhousie

[274] RA VIC/ADDA36/2373,2375, General Ponsonby to his wife, 1884: 30 September, 2 October

[275] RA VIC/ADDA36/2381, General Ponsonby to his wife, 1884: 10 October

[276] Also Aunt to the late Landgrave

[277] Lady Sophia, née Hare (1835–1912), m Arthur Macnamara

[278] RA GV/PRIV/AA30/8, Princess of Wales to Prince George, 1884: 18 November

[279] Charles Bertram (1853–1907), conjurer who performed for the royal family

[280] Prince Charles Edward (1884–1954) inherited his late father's title at birth; later Duke of Saxe-Coburg-Gotha

[281] RA GV/PRIV/AA6/338, Princess of Wales to JN Dalton, 1884: 7 December

[282] Oliver Montagu had once been wounded in an eye in Malta and in November 1875 he had been accidentally shot in the eyelid while staying at Wimpole; RA VIC/ADDA36/1007, 1008, 1010, General Ponsonby to his wife, 1875: 14, 15, 16 November

[283] RA VIC/ADDA8/2600, Princess of Wales to Duchess of Teck, 1884: 22 December

Chapter 8

1885–1889

"Yes indeed we are a most happy family"

〜〰〜

E ddy, 21 on 8 January 1885, was congratulated by tenants and officials in the ballroom, while labourers and schoolchildren outside gave "Three Cheers". Sanger's Circus[1] was in a large tent in the field behind the kitchen garden; there were celebratory meals for labourers and women, the county ball and, the next day, the tenants' ball. The West Norfolk Hounds met on the 10th, and the German ambassador,[2] representing Emperor William, invested Eddy with the Order of the Black Eagle. Eddy left on the 16th and by the 30th his parents were in London, where they saw *Frou Frou* at the Royalty and, at the weekend, with their sons, *Dick Whittington and His Cat* at Drury Lane.

On 1 February Albert Edward left for Cannes and the boys for Cambridge and Greenwich. The girls were still at Sandringham and Alexandra, in London, was desolate. During the afternoon of the 2nd, without telling anyone where she was going, she went out alone and did not return till late. Her household were frantic with worry, but she turned up again, quite calmly and said she had been riding on the London Underground. The story goes that she added "I had to get away from Charlotte!"[3] Royal life could be claustrophobic; in Denmark Alexandra often went for walks, alone or accompanied. She owned a London guidebook, Herbert Fry's *London in 1881* and other books about London. Fond though she was of Miss Knollys, she simply had to escape sometimes. The devoted and indispensable Charlotte hardly ever went on holiday and when she was ill on duty, Alexandra looked after her. She was almost more like a sister than a servant, but perhaps her greatest service was to outlive Alexandra, sparing her another sad loss.

On 3 February[4] Alexandra told George; "I was so sorry when you had to leave me the other night, & there I was all by myself, feeling rather low, I confess, having been deserted by all my dear ones ... I am going back at 2 o'clock to the three little old hags,[5] when I shall read about that beast Quilp[6] to them tonight – how we shall miss you & Eddy."[7] On the 12th, she sent bad news: the Mahdi's[8] forces had captured Khartoum "and our poor brave Gordon,[9] the greatest hero of our time, most probably killed & when his release seemed so near! – if only we had gone out there long ago, all this might have been spared!" Gordon and many other officers had indeed been killed and more troops were going out, including Charlotte's brother, Cyprian.[10] Alexandra had had "good accounts of dear Papa" but was shocked at his involvement in a minor train crash and a carriage accident, although he was quite safe.[11] She and the girls went back to London on the 17th; Papa returned two days later, in time for Louise's 18th birthday and a family dinner. Early the next day the couple went to Wellington Barracks and Westminster Bridge steps, and saw the Scots Guards off for Suakim. Later, it was an amateur performance of *Saul* by the Handel Society at St James' Hall, and *As You Like It, Junius in the Household* [12] and a circus at Covent Garden during the week. There was also an afternoon performance of Lady Arthur Hill's[13] operetta, *A Lost Husband*, at the Criterion on the 28th, raising money to restore Wolferton Church.

At Lansdowne House on 24 February, Alexandra attended the first of six meetings of her Branch of the National Aid Society, of which she was president. The Society organised sending stores to troops fighting in the Sudan and Egypt and had a number of sub-committees in England and Egypt. Alexandra had thrown herself enthusiastically into the work and asked the Queen to become patron of her branch; "I have the matter very much at heart & take the greatest interest in trying to carry it out efficiently, and yr advice & Assistance would be of the greatest help to us all. I am sure you will agree with me that we could not have a better cause than try & relieve in some degree the fearful suffering of our poor, brave, sick & wounded soldiers in a far off land."[14] The Queen entirely agreed, consented to be patron and sent £50 and some tobacco and flannel.[15] Alexandra was delighted, assuring her; "You have no idea how I have gone in heart & soul [into] this first work in which I have ever taken an active & personal part. I have given some work to the children to do, & of course shall be delighted if anyone will help us. We are getting on so well & have sent out numbers of stores of all kinds."[16] She was just as keen as her husband to contribute to good, national causes, including foreign policy. Britain and Russia were vying for influence in Afghanistan and she was horrified that this rivalry could cause war. Could Minny do something to prevent this, she asked on 12 March, although Russia had got rather close to India, "which we must naturally defend". Alexandra was being blunt "but naturally just for you!!!"[17]

She sat to a Danish painter on 2 March; there were more theatres, a small family dinner and dance on the 10th and Waldemar arrived. On the 18th Louise attended her first drawing room. Later, Albert Edward and Eddy set off for the German emperor's 88th birthday celebrations at Berlin on the 22nd; they also visited Darmstadt, returning on the 27th for a family Easter at Sandringham. The couple and Eddy left for Ireland on 7 April; writing to George from Dublin Castle and insisting "I am an excellent sailor & tho' we rolled about a great deal I felt very comfortable all the time", Alexandra reported that they had been well received, the Irish people were friendly and they had the same nice rooms at

Dublin Castle as before. They had started with a cattle and horse show and then on the 9th Papa held a levee, while "I visited the Alexandra College".18 That evening she held a "drawingroom which began at 9.30, & ended at 1¼; good, that, was it not, but oh my poor feet & legs. It all ended with a procession & then supper, but I went straight to my room instead, I was so tired." On the 10th, at the Royal University of Ireland, "I have just taken my degree as a Doctor of Music – I feel very proud indeed!!! but it was an awful shy undertaking! Fancy poor old Mother dear had to put on … most magnificent white and red satin Doctor's Robes & carried my Hat or cap in my hand, & two women students dressed me up & I had to take off my bonnet & all … Then I was escorted by the Duke of Abercorn into an enormous hall or theatre & took my place by his side on a very high platform & here I was made a Doctor. Imagine my feelings when they called out my name & I had to get up & bow; I did feel such a fool … Papa was also made a Doctor but only of Laws, not such a grand one as me!!! And after all this was over we had to sign our names as Doctors in a huge book & then I & the Chancellor, the Duke of Abercorn hobbled down those horrid steep steps together amidst the shouts, applause & I am sure, laughter of the Students. Tonight there will be a huge state ball so I will finish now & try & rest a bit." She hoped George would enjoy his evening with Oliver Montagu "whom you may show this letter to if you like."19 After a state dinner on the 11th and a military event, the official part of the visit was practically over and they visited Convamore, Curraghmore, Cork, Killarney, Phoenix Park, Punchestown Races, Belfast, Donegal and Baronscourt. However, there had been some dissension, and trouble at Cork.

Alexandra saw Lady L Egerton20 about the National Aid Society on 29 April and during May attended three more committee meetings. There were also plays, concerts, a private view and the opening of the Inventions Exhibition at South Kensington, perhaps recalling Cragside. Eddy was now at Great Yarmouth with the Prince of Wales's Own 2nd Brigade, Eastern Division, Royal Artillery, but was later gazetted a lieutenant in the 10th Royal Hussars. George was working hard at Portsmouth, which was less arduous than Greenwich.21 They joined their parents at Sandringham on the 23rd for the weekend. The Waleses returned to London on the 29th for the season and spent Ascot week at Easthampstead Park with old friends. Alexandra had another NAS meeting on 23 June, opened a convalescent home at Swanley on 10 July and attended functions at Leeds and at Regent's Park Barracks. She chaired a general meeting of the NAS on 20 July and on the 22nd the whole family crossed the Solent for Beatrice's wedding to Henry of Battenberg the next day, at Whippingham Church. There was a family lunch in a tent and a reception, before the bridal pair left for Quarr Abbey. The Queen gave a large dinner in a tent, followed by an evening party and illuminations. After breakfast with her next morning, the couple went back for the Marlborough House Ball. The next day, a society wedding at Coombe Wood was followed by Lady Archibald Campbell's[22] pastoral play, *The Faithful Shepherdess*, in Coombe House grounds. Later, Alexandra went to see *The Mikado*.

After Goodwood, Cowes Week and sailing expeditions, Alexandra and the girls went on 19 August to stay with the Cumberlands at Gmunden, while Albert Edward was in Norway. There were theatres, tea parties and excursions; it was "such a lovely place, & we walk & climb about a great deal. Yesterday we all made a delightful expedition down the river down the rapids in large flat-bottomed boats[23] which was splendid fun; it wants a very cool-headed man to steer or the boat must get smashed", wrote Alexandra. She rather enjoyed slightly dangerous activities. Her parents were also there and "Dear Aunt Thyra & Uncle Ernest are so pleased at having … us all here; their 5 dear little children[24] are such ducks, particularly my sweet fat Plumpy, who is such a dear & affectionate little man. The second little girl, Alix, my Godchild is like a lovely wax doll with flaxen coloured silky curls … a tiny little dear; the baby is like a sparrow at present but I like to carry him about & cuddle him. I washed him last night, he looked so funny struggling about like a big spider & rather like the chickens just coming out of their eggs at Sandringham!" She and the girls were going to Denmark, and "From dear Papa I have very good accounts from Norway where he seems to enjoy himself in spite of the cold, as he says it is winter weather."[25]

On 7 September the family, congregated at Fredensborg, celebrated Queen Louise's birthday. Albert Edward arrived on the 14th, as did the Duc and Duchesse de Chartres[26] with their son and daughter Marie, who was engaged to Waldemar. Alexandra had a new project; Anglican services were held in Copenhagen, but there was no English church and she had been urging for one to be built, to be dedicated to St Alban,[27] England's first Christian martyr, who was also venerated in Denmark; King Canute[28] had taken his relics to a special shrine at Odense.[29] On the 19th the whole family watched her lay the foundation stone, flanked by a bodyguard of men from *Osborne*, where the Waleses gave a large lunch afterwards. Later they saw the opera, *Mephistopheles*, with supper on the Russian yacht, *Derjava*. The couple spent the night alone on *Osborne*, lunching on *Derjava* next day. At Landskrona on the 22nd, they saw Mr Nordenfeldt's[30] submarine boat trials. Albert Edward left for Hungary that night but Alexandra remained, walking, visiting and on 8 October attending Nilsson's[31] concert in Copenhagen. She had arranged for George[32] to "go with us all on to Paris! think of that! & to be present at dear old Waldemar's wedding with Marie d'Orléans á Eu! I think it will simply be lovely! What do you think??? My only regret is poor Eddy who cannot come too." She was having "a lovely time here with all my dear people. Dear Papa spent a charming 10 days here but unfortunately had to leave already two days ago for Hungary … He was in excellent spirits & humour! & seems to have enjoyed his visit in Norway & Sweden." She concluded, "Alas! I must close now as everybody has come in and are in <u>a frantic</u> state of hunger, and luncheon is ready ... dear Waldemario is so happy & delighted with his girl, who really is nice & cheery."[33]

They left on 18 October, meeting Papa at the Château d'Eu on the 21st. Waldemar and Marie had had a civil ceremony in Paris on the 20th but on the 22nd were married in a Roman Catholic service in the chapel at Eu, followed by a Danish Protestant one. This was the only wedding of a sibling that Alexandra attended.[34] The Wales family reached the Hotel Bristol in Paris on the 24th and, writing to the Queen, Charlotte Knollys mentioned the French princesses, especially the charming Amélie d'Orléans.[35] Prince George and his sisters had also made a very favourable impression; they were less shy and had nice, civil manners. Their mother looked remarkably well and did not seem at all tired despite all her travelling.[36] In Paris, they visited the theatre and Chantilly but had all returned home by the 29th. On the 31st the couple opened the Working Lads' Institute at Whitechapel and later, Alexandra had a drawing lesson with Mr Harper. Returning to Sandringham on 4 November, the Waleses were joined later by their sons and guests, for the Prince's birthday. However, Andrew Cockerell became ill and Sir Oscar Clayton was summoned from London. Field sports continued until the 16th, when the Prince and Princess went to stay briefly with the Edinburghs at Eastwell. Cockerell was too unwell to leave until the 25th and was taken away in an invalid carriage. More guests came for Alexandra's birthday; on 10 December she went to London with Louise, then to Windsor for the mausoleum service. Later, the couple, their sons and Louise spent four days at Holkham. Julie and Harry Stonor[37] were again invited for a Sandringham Christmas and it was all very jolly but on the 27th Alexandra felt unwell; Clayton was sent for, and she finished 1885 seriously ill, in bed with diphtheria.

Alexandra had always suffered from throat infections but she was luckier than Alice in 1878. The servants' ball was on New Year's Day 1886 and her daughters and, eventually, eight servants went down with diphtheria. Alexandra felt better by 3 January, returned to London with her family on the 18th, visited the Queen on the 20th and went driving. On the 27th she saw Millais' pictures at the Grosvenor Gallery and later attended a wedding, a Popular Concert and the circus at Covent Garden. She continued her drives, even on 8 February, when "a mob of unemployed working men and socialists broke windows and looted shops."[38] The couple saw *Faust* the next day and Alexandra went again on the 15th; she often enjoyed seeing performances several times, perhaps to make sure she had heard correctly. On the 10th the Waleses gave a large dinner party[39] for Alfred, now commander of the Mediterranean Station. On the 21st Albert

Edward left for Cannes with George, who was joining *Thunderer* in the Mediterranean Squadron. Eddy went to Cambridge on the 23rd but by then Alexandra had to stay indoors.

She told George that her misery at parting from her dear ones had made her quite ill, "as first of all my wretched eyes got so inflamed & then my foot has been bad and yesterday it began with a stupid little scratch which gradually gathered & swelled out dreadfully, so that I was quite unable to walk & wheeled myself about in my old arm chair quite like a decrepit old Hag." It had been worse because "We seem to have grown so much nearer to each other & I feel I have all yr confidence as well as yr affection." She was "always yr best & truest friend, & [feel] a greater interest in you than it is possible for anyone else to do! ... it was indeed dreadful for me to see you go off like that & for so long too! though, thank God, the time flies much quicker than one imagines." George had been very low, not just at leaving home but also because he was in love with Julie Stonor, a Roman Catholic and therefore barred to him. Alexandra, always sympathetic to romance, was tactful and understanding; "Cheer up now & work like a man, then you will see everything in a brighter light. I have not seen Julie since as she left last Monday, but the girls have heard from her, also there was a letter enclosed to you!!! & you sent one to her, which I also saw! but of course only the outside! but dear Georgie, I think it wiser not to write through the Sisters but if you write send them direct! I only say it for their sakes, as they are really too young to get all these kind of thoughts into their heads." She herself had spent a very dull time "alone with my horrid foot tied up, bad eyes & a bunion on my nose! a lovely sight indeed! I hope however to get away on Monday as soon as I can get a boot on."[40] On 1 March they left for a month at Sutherland Tower in Torquay.[41]

Louise (nineteen), Victoria (seventeen and a half) and Maud (sixteen) were certainly young, but Alexandra herself had been married at eighteen; did she ever feel this might have been too early? As for "these kind of thoughts", she had been thinking romantically at least since her engagement in September 1862, although her romance was sanctioned and led very soon to marriage. Her sister Minny had initially been very unlucky; her first engagement, at nearly seventeen, ended with her fiancé's death seven months later. When she married his brother in 1866, she was barely nineteen. Thus, although early marriages for princesses were normal, Alexandra may have felt she should not encourage her daughters to become romantically involved too young, especially considering their frequent ailments. Other problems arose from this but she was acting for the best. Like her own mother, she was careful and quite strict with them and only allowed them to enter court life gradually.

The Duchess of Sutherland reported to the Queen that Alexandra looked much better, "it is a real happiness to have this visit from her, as she is so sweet & kind, & so easily amused; in the house she really needs nothing but her piano, at which she is constantly seated." The Princess "so enjoys the quiet country life, & has such very simple tastes, & the three Princesses are like her in this, & all so <u>very</u> nice." She hoped Alexandra would return home quite strong and well; her foot seemed to be making good progress.[42] Alexandra did not write to George again until 17 April; "Thank God I am at last really well again & hope now quite to have done with feeling ill, illness etc etc. <u>Torquay</u> was very nice & we led a very pleasant life altho' I was far from well there, & it was very cold even there excepting a few days when the sun was shining brightly, & then the girls will have told you how much we enjoyed ourselves."[43] Papa had visited and found them looking much better, although Alexandra had a cold and Louise was still pale.[44] They returned home on 3 April and afterwards heard Liszt's[45] Oratorio, *St Elizabeth*, at St James's Hall, in his presence; "he got a tremendous ovation – also at the Smoking concert the day before yesterday when several of his pieces were played. He dined with us tonight, & played beautifully on the piano afterwards. He is 75 years of age."[46]

After Easter at Sandringham, Alexandra had "had so much to do & with dear Toria's confirmation & with one thing & another I never have been able to write, & have treated my poor Georgie really in a brutal way!" The Great Powers were trying to blockade all the Greek ports, "which under existing circumstances I suppose is the only way in making that obstinate Greek Government give in & disarm! Poor Uncle Willy you may well imagine is placed in a terribly awkward position, & is powerless to do anything! I only hope & trust when they see that the Great Powers really are <u>in earnest</u> this time that they will disarm at once and peace be once more restored in the East." She had seen Julie Stonor in London "& we had a little talk together. She told me she had heard from you pretty often?? She is looking much better now! I hope my poor Georgie <u>you</u> are feeling much better now! I am sure, though one <u>cannot forget</u>! yet change of scene & plenty of work is the best thing in such cases for one!! don't you think so too? I am so glad you have such a charming, kind, sensible & trustworthy Captain, as dear Captain Stephenson[47] is, who I look upon as one [of] my best friends; in him you have the best companion possible & one who reminds you of home too, as he belongs to us, & to whom you can talk openly! Please thank him for a very kind letter I got today from him."

The Archbishop of Canterbury[48] confirmed Victoria in Sandringham Church on 22 April; she looked "very nice in her simple white dress, & it was a very pretty & solemn ceremony! I was so glad it took place here in our dear little Church." Mary of Teck and May had attended. Alexandra returned reluctantly to London on 3 May; quite recovered but dreading "all the noise, bustle & fatigue."[49] Much was happening; the Colonial Exhibition, opened by the Queen on the 4th, drawing rooms, concerts, plays, operas, opening Putney Bridge, dinners and balls. They saw Professor Warr's[50] *The Story of Orestes*, based on Aeschylus's Orestean Trilogy, performed by amateurs at the Prince's Hall on the

13th. Earlier, Alexandra had had the first of at least four lessons with Francesco Paolo Tosti, popular composer and royal singing teacher; "I have just been having a lovely singing lesson, with Tosti – what do you think of that! & now Louise is having hers & shouting away behind me, & then Victoria will have hers. It is great fun & we all mean to sing beautifully when you come back." [51] There was another Greek play at the Greek Theatre in Argyll Street on the 17th; J Todhunter's[52] *Helena in Troas*, for the British School of Archaeology at Athens. Alexandra also attended "Ambulance"[53] lectures on 14 and 19 May.

As George was stationed in the Mediterranean, he represented the family at Crown Prince Carlos of Portugal's[54] wedding to Princess Amélie d'Orléans on 22 May; "yr dear & pretty friend Amélie! I wonder whether you will be pleased or not, or whether yr feelings will be too much for you, seeing her marry that conceited little curly head!!" Alexandra had chosen "a very pretty snake brooch" as George had wanted to give Amélie a present.[55] She added "I am so sorry she cld not wait & marry one of you, that lovely girl, tho' she is a Roman Catholic!!" The Waleses had long been on friendly terms with her family. Alexandra had been touched by George's letter; "Indeed, it is an ample reward for everything I have tried to do for the welfare & happiness of my darling Georgie. I must say it is good of you to have resisted all temptation so far, & it is the greatest proof you could possibly give of how much you wish to please me, that you should have done it for my sake, & the promise you gave me of yr own accord a few nights before you left – no words can express how grateful I feel to God for having given me such a good son, in every way." She had seen Julie several times "& we often talked about you together, & she is a dear, good little girl; she sends you her very best love & is going to write soon again."[56] On 3 June George was 21; his mother sent him a tiny pin and an affectionate letter, which was left by mistake in her blotting book and discovered, with horror, more than a month later.[57] On 7 June she told Dalton she would be delighted to accept a copy of his book, *The Voyage of HMS Bacchante*, "which I must tell you Eddy has not yet deigned to show me!! I have read all the reviews of it in the papers which are certainly most complimentary. It must indeed be a great satisfaction to you after all the trouble you have taken about it."[58]

This year the Ascot party, including Julie Stonor, Lord Fife and Oliver Montagu, was at Harewood Lodge at Sunninghill, but on the 9th they heard that Andrew Cockerell, groom in waiting to the Prince for 30 years, who had collapsed at Sandringham in November, had died. After taking Louise with them on a visit to Easton Lodge, the Waleses continued their public duties, including laying the foundation stone of the new Tower Bridge on 21 June. Alexandra opened the new wing of Queen Charlotte's Lying-in Hospital in Marylebone Road on the 25th and the couple subsequently opened the People's Palace in the Mile End Road, the new outpatients' wing of the Royal Victoria Hospital for Children in Chelsea and Bleyton's[59] Industrial Dwellings in Hoxton. They also attended a matinée of Cherubini's[60] opera *The Water Carrier,* by pupils of the Royal College of Music, at the Savoy on the 24th, and a concert, dinner and fireworks at the Crystal Palace two days later. The Comte de Paris,[61] Duc de Chartres and their sons came to lunch on 3 July, entertained by M Slaviansky-d'Agreneff's[62] Russian Choir. On the 4th the Waleses had tea with Lord Fife at Sheen Lodge, playing lawn tennis and later dining outside, as it was so warm.[63] They took Louise to Newmarket on the 6th; she and Alexandra stayed "with the Cadogans[64] which was real fun, & we rode every day & altogether the life there was very pleasant & independent."[65] The couple gave a garden party on the 10th, to which the Queen came, as did the Paris couple with their daughter, Hélène,[66] "who has grown so pretty".[67]

After briefly visiting Sandringham for a livestock sale, they held the Marlborough House Ball on the 21st. Earlier they had seen amateur theatricals at the Novelty, in aid of the Home for British and American Governesses at Berlin. Goodwood was followed by Cowes, where, on *Osborne,* they "again spent a delightful time … this year, & have been out sailing every day almost, with nice people & our old friends."[68] They were back in London on 11 August and "Tomorrow we are off to tiresome old Germany! I & the girls … We are going to Schwalbach for a fortnight to take iron bathes which are to give us all renewed strength & vigour after our tiresome Diphtheria last winter. I must say I am now feeling perfectly well again but it was a very long time before I got quite right. I think it will be a very good thing for Louise taking those bathes as she is always so pale & suffers from headaches & neuralgia. Do you remember you used to chaff her always having an ailment or other whenever you came back!!" Papa would take the waters at Homburg; they would go together to Schlangenbad "to see the old Empress of Germany & then drive on to Schwalbach where Papa will spend one night with us." As for "my own people, no one came this year excepting little Carl,[69] who was on his first sea [voyage]. He is very much improved & poor little boy was quite delighted here & enjoyed it all so much; he cried floods when he left us; he has grown quite a big boy already."[70] Oliver Montagu had been kicked by a horse, but although lame and on crutches, he was in good spirits at Goodwood[71] and Cowes. Poor Julie had fallen and hurt her head at a dance but was recovering. At Aldershot, Eddy "is going to study French hard now, & lots of military things besides till we all go up to Scotland together."[72]

From Schwalbach, Alexandra lamented; "I was so well in England & particularly so at Cowes on board the dear old *Osborne* & the moment I got here I was taken ill with a really bad throat again, so much so, that I had to go to bed; what it was or why I got it I cannot tell, but I do not think it was a cold! Consequently I lost a whole week's baths and cure & have only begun a week ago. The water tho' not very bad tastes like rotten eggs or ink but the baths are lovely, you are bubbles all over like [a foaming] bottle of Champagne." The

German empress had looked "awful, like an old painted doll with shaky hands, poor old lady, I am so sorry for her, but I do … think her maid or hairdresser or whoever <u>paints</u> her <u>face</u> for her might make a prettier or more fascinating picture than is now the case, but she was very kind to us all & asked endless questions! I was so glad Papa came with us or it wld have been still more alarming alone, as it was fearfully stiff & formidable." Schwalbach was very quiet and nice, "not to say dull exactly, but we don't mind & have plenty to do, with drinking, bathing, walking, drawing, writing, reading & playing the piano. Dear Papa is at Homburg drinking away there & we have only seen each other twice since we came here, but I hope may meet once more before leaving old Germany!" Amusingly, the bachelor Bobby Spencer[73] "walks about here with three wives, Lady Ormonde,[74] Mrs Mills & Mrs Grosvenor, & we all meet several times a day walking about, drinking or listening to the band." Bulgarian affairs were critical, "with that wretched Sandro driven away in this cruel ungrateful way; they say it is a Russian plot, but <u>who</u> knows if it is not the work of Mr Bismark himself; he put him there & finding he did not do exactly as he wished may have whisked him off now!!! & cleverly put the whole thing apparently on Russian shoulders!!! – *qui vire verra*!" They met Albert Edward at Frankfort and the next day Alexandra and the girls left, arriving at Bernstorff on the 5th "just for a <u>peep</u> at them all, as I can't spare more than a week, being due in Scotland on the 18th of Sep, where Papa will join me fr Doncaster."[75]

At Abergeldie, the men went deer-stalking as usual, while Alexandra drove and lunched with the Queen and with Beatrice, and had tea with Helen Albany. There were guests, picnics, outings and a Gillies' Ball. Albert Edward stayed at Mar Lodge,[76] Lord Fife's place, for a week, and his family joined him there for a couple of days; it was all very pleasant. Alexandra had enjoyed reading about George's recent visit to Constantinople, which she "remembered so well & all its many beautiful points & places of interest, but I always admired it most from the Bosphorus, as the town itself is rather dirty to live in & the pavement too atrocious for words. I wonder if the streets still swarm with those poor unfortunate dogs." She had been shocked at their plight in 1869. She continued; "You are really a dear thing writing so often when yr wicked old Mother dear treats you so rarely to a letter." He had asked for some music scored for the ship's band to play, which she had ordered. Meanwhile she sent "an exciting book for you which I am sure you will like & some <u>awful</u> photos done at Schwalbach but which will remind you of us all the same."[77] Albert Edward hoped George was not forgetting his French and could speak it sometimes. "You should also read it. I will send you out 'Les Misérables' by Victor Hugo. It is very long, but I read it when I was 20 & could not put the book down."[78]

Now on board *HMS Dreadnought* at Corfu, George wrote, hoping his mother was really well and strong again and sympathising, as a fellow-sufferer, with Louise's neuralgia. Prompted by a *Vanity Fair* article of 9 October, headed "An

English Queen-Consort" and perhaps also by his own feelings for Julie Stonor, he had been thinking hard. "Have you read that article ... if you have not, you must get it & read it. I think it is one of the best I ever read, & I am sure you will agree with me. Of course the first part is <u>stuff</u> (as you would say) but what it says is that all English people hope that dear Eddy will not marry a <u>German</u> but that he will marry some <u>English</u> woman, of course there is plenty of time to think of that. When I read it, it struck me as being so sensible & so true, & the more I have thought over it the stronger I feel that it would be so much nicer if he married an English person, I think, darling Mother dear, that you think the same as I do, but I am afraid that both Grandmama & dear Papa wish him to marry a German, but I don't know ... There are hundreds of things like that, that I should like to talk to you about. Do you remember all our little talks we used to have together before I left? And now that I am away from home I think of all these things much more than I did, & I suppose that is because I am getting older too." He also sent an article from "a stupid little paper called the '*Bat*' which was sent to me, it is great nonsense but rather amusing: 'Prince Edward of Wales is reported to be going to be married to the daughter of a tenth rate German Duchy. This is indeed a new matrimonial departure. There is some compensation in the fact that the Prince of Wales' daughters will probably marry some decent European royalties, and that jolly looking lad Prince George Frederick may possibly pick up a millionairess while sailing from port to port in foreign climes'"[79] Alexandra replied; "I quite agree with you about that article about Eddy – but wld others & Papa??"[80] However, this was the beginning of changing attitudes which would particularly influence the marriages of George's own descendants.

Papa got, as usual, an enormous lot of birthday presents "& in the evening we had a very good conjurer with a vanishing Lady which was first rate I must say & which highly delighted our guests & neighbours." Out shooting, the Comtesse de Paris "was very proud of having killed, herself, 64 pheasants & two Woodcock; not bad for a Lady! tho' I cannot say I admire a lady doing that sort of thing, & I for my part could not kill a poor wretched animal." Nevertheless it was great fun to watch her, "in a most extraordinary get up with very short petticoats. She is such a dear & I do like her very much & Hélène is also a dear & pretty girl who has grown immensely & is nearly as tall as Amélie." The guests were all cheerful and the party had gone off well, despite atrocious weather the last two days, cancelling shooting, but there was hunting on the 13th. Alexandra's horse, Viva, was unwell, so she decided to try "a lovely chestnut, but which I had <u>never tried</u> yet, so did not much like getting on him at first till I found how beautifully he went without pulling the least, & he jumped banks beautifully too so that finding this & that I cld stick on I simply was delighted & flew along & left old grumbling Probyn miles behind. I was so glad, & you wld have laughed if you cld have seen him scrambling after but never catching me up till a check came on, it was so nice, & that showed those fools that it only was the horse's fault & not mine that I did not seem to ride so well last year! ha ha!" She was amused by photographs of a bearded George; "Really quite a fine beard too!! Eddy will be quite jealous when he sees it as he has none nor any sign of it either yet, tho' he twiddles about at his little wee moustache in a most ferocious way, thinking that will make it grow better & help it on!!!" She had met Captain Bedford,[81] George's late captain on *Dreadnought*, but had not known he had a "smashed hand". "It was a <u>horrid</u> feeling shaking hands with him & that naughty Harry[82] immediately said 'Oh it felt like a great <u>purse</u> in my hand.'"[83] She was glad George had "got my music all right for yr band & I hope they were tunes you had not yet had. Do you play at all now, I wish you wld keep it up! as I know how you will regret it some day."

There had been a devastating fire at the Berystede, the Standish's[84] house, although they had escaped. Alexandra sent her love to George and the Edinburghs; "Tell her I hope <u>some</u> day to get a line from her as I am longing to hear from her, but beginning to think she has quite forgotten poor me."[85] There were more guests for her birthday and a tenants' ball on 3 December. Next, they had "another lovely & cheery week" at Luton Hoo. "Both Mr & Mme de Falbe were most kind – there was some shooting every day & in the evening a round game & once some French acting, which was very good." On the 13th they went to Windsor for "the 14th, <u>Mausoleum day</u> to pray! and spent the rest of the week in London choosing our innumerable presents." Princess Beatrice had recently had a son[86] and Alexandra commented wickedly; "On the Sat we again went to Windsor for the <u>BB</u> Xning! The old girl is very proud of her child tho' she looked a hundred, the baby very small & he ten years younger.[87] Prince Alexander[88] & poor Sandro were also there but on the whole wonderfully cheery I must say!" She had returned to Sandringham "to my dear three old Hags last night and found them well & delighted to have me back again; they were skating when I came but alas today is a beastly thaw."[89] She thanked George for his nice letter and pretty cards; "Thank God everything went off well Xmas & I was all right this time & not knocked up. Do you remember last year, when I was ill just now with that horrid diphtheria & the night of the tree & <u>squirts</u> when we two fought, I with the hunting whip & you with the squirt?[90] It hardly seems like a year ago does it?" She deeply regretted he had not been able to spend Greek Christmas at Athens, as hoped, but at least he would see his father at Cannes in February, & also perhaps!!! ... finding dear <u>Julie</u> at Cannes – what a bit of luck her being there & won't you be pleased!"[91]

✿

1887, Golden Jubilee year, opened at Sandringham with shooting, frost and skating; on 5 January they made a snow man and had snow-balling.[92]

Wyndham's[93] Company performed *David Garrick* in the ballroom on the 7th. One of the guests, the explorer Henry Morton Stanley,[94] was joining the Emin Pasha relief expedition[95] in Central Africa; "a long, arduous & dangerous journey. He gave us a short & most interesting lecture of what he intended doing."[96] In London on 3 February, they saw *The Noble Vagabond* and *The Rivals,* before Albert Edward went to Paris and Cannes and Alexandra returned to Sandringham, for drawing lessons with Mr Harper, riding, driving, visiting, and hunting on the 24th. George had heard some gossip; "So you have been told some <u>unkind</u> stories about poor Lady de Grey – of course I do not know what you have heard, but I can tell you whatever <u>ill-natured</u> thing it is, it is a <u>lie</u>, as she is perfectly happy & contented with her little Lord & Master & they are travelling together in Spain paying a visit to the Paris's, after having just nursed her brother who was very ill at Monte Carlo. You may tell all this <u>as a fact</u> to <u>whoever was</u> yr informer! And tell me next time what it was you <u>did</u> hear. How ill-natured people always are about her poor thing, it really is too bad."[97] Meanwhile some letters had arrived; one from Julie "telling me about you & everything down there" and several from George; "so your joy was great, you say, on seeing her again. I can well understand my poor dear boy! & you think you are as much in love with her as ever! She & I, as she will have told you, had long talks about you & it all; but there it is & alas! rather a sad case I think for you both, my <u>two</u> poor children! <u>I</u> only wish you could marry & be happy but alas alas I fear that cannot be!" Julie was "such a dear good sweet girl & always the same and comes to me, old Motherdear, for everything – she is, as you say, such a pretty, simple, unaffected dear. She knows quite well that I too am very fond of her, & we have grown to know each other so well too this winter; thank her for her letter & tell her I am going to write very soon, but am very busy now <u>painting</u> all the morning ... [&] ... sometimes rather late in the afternoon as the days are so much brighter now."[98] Julie's heart had been touched but she had accepted the situation as best she could and remained a lifelong family friend.

The Prince returned from Cannes on 1 March, pleased to find his family well, although Louise still had neuralgia. They went to the theatre and dined with the Queen; on the 3rd Victoria attended her first drawing room "& looked very well."[99] On the 5th they saw the new Gilbert and Sullivan operetta, *Ruddigore*; "though it is not as good as some of [their] other pieces, the music is pretty & there are some very amusing scenes in it."[100] Alexandra had been to a Saturday Popular Concert earlier. The usual enjoyable "Juvenile Ball" was held on the 10th. "Juveniles" perhaps meant the age group later called teenagers; young people were regarded as children until they reached eighteen, when, in the Royal Family, an heir could succeed to the throne. The Prince had gone abroad, to congratulate the German emperor on his 90th birthday, but a shocking story suddenly broke on the 25th. Alexandra, with toothache and the remains of a cold, read in a newspaper that her sister Thyra had gone mad. Although acutely distressed, she still had an engagement at the Brompton Consumption Hospital later that day. Oliver Montagu, having heard the news, joined her party, with her daughters, Charlotte and others, later telling George; "we gave the poor patients a concert, your Mama accompanied us in songs, & then she & Charlotte played duets & your sisters played also & it all did capitally; the poor people were most delighted & then after we went round the wards & saw the worse cases who were not able to get up, & your Mama gave them flowers. Your Mama was a little shy at first but soon got all right, & your sisters enjoyed it all immensely."[101] It was probably his idea, to rally Alexandra as well as the patients.

The report about the Duchess of Cumberland was grossly exaggerated. As Albert Edward told George; "Her nerves & spirits had got depressed to such an alarming extent & she was suffering fr 'anaemia' ... & articular rheumatism, that it was considered necessary that she should be placed under the care of Dr Leichsdorf, in his house near Vienna & for a time to be separated fr her husband, children & belongings."[102] There was every hope of her recovery, as Alexandra reported, "dear little Thyra is so much better now that she has been told she is at some bath[103] for her health and as soon as she is better she will go home! It all arose from <u>weakness</u> as it seems she has been ailing all the winter from rheumatism etc but her terrible melancholia only showed itself quite suddenly, so pray God with rest & proper nursing too, she will regain her strength." It was agonising for her relatives, who were not allowed to visit her, but she had a friend with her, a nice deaconess, who sent them regular reports. The worst thing was that a garbled version had got into the press; "the darling <u>never</u> was <u>mad</u>!! simply worn out & her poor brain tired & weak, nothing else! You may tell this to anyone who asks." In fact Thyra was pregnant; she made a good recovery and had her youngest child, Ernest Augustus,[104] on 17 November, but after her illness her hair turned white.

Maud was confirmed by the Archbishop of Canterbury at Sandringham Church on 7 April. Alexandra told George how she had "looked so sweet in her little white <u>long</u> frock & veil, with coiffure turned <u>up</u>, (which you don't like) but which suits them all three. She answered all questions at her examination <u>so</u> well & <u>had more</u> than any of you. She <u>never</u> <u>hesitated</u>." The other two were also flourishing. "Thank God Louise seems much better now & is looking ... quite bright & cheery again. We are having our lovely rides every afternoon & the girls ride <u>very</u> well I must say, particularly the two little ones – tho' Toria is <u>much</u> taller than you now!! She really is a <u>tall</u> young person!!"[105] Louise's revived spirits might have had something to do with Lord Fife's recent return from India;[106] he visited Sandringham on the 9th. The Waleses had hoped George could go to Athens while serving in the Mediterranean; this had not yet been possible and it seemed the naval authorities had continually made excuses about it. Now, however "at <u>last</u> my Georgie is going to Athens to see my dear Willy, Olga & Cousins. I am so glad, as poor Uncle Willy was rather hurt – he has been

<u>badly</u> treated so often lately. How I wish I could go & meet you there!!" Sadly, due to a misunderstanding, the King and Queen were away when George's ship arrived at Athens. Alexandra feared she would have to leave Sandringham soon; "I <u>shall</u> be sorry & rather dread this season with all its Jubilee & stuff!!! ... Papa is in London but has dinners & <u>races</u> every day so I stayed on a little longer to get well again." They were all looking forward to George's home leave in June for the celebrations.[107] Mr Harper came back towards the end of April to draw with Alexandra and she went to London with the girls on the 30th. On 2 May the Prince and Princess opened the Jubilee Exhibition at Manchester. When they returned, Alexandra's brother Frederick arrived on a visit and there were entertainments, including Buffalo Bill's[108] Wild West Show, and functions, such as the Queen's opening of the Queen's Hall at the People's Palace in the East End, where she laid the first stone of the technical and handicraft schools, on the 14th.

On 21 May the Waleses opened the London Hospital and Medical College's new library and other buildings in Whitechapel Road; the matron, Miss Eva Luckes[109] and her staff received them at the new nurses' home. After a short religious service, the Duke of Cambridge, as president of the hospital, asked the Princess to declare the Alexandra Home open. The Prince was to open the new medical college buildings and, on the way, they visited several wards, Alexandra tearing up her bouquet and giving a flower to each sick woman and child. They had heard about another patient and wanted to meet him, so were taken to the east wing basements where, for about a year, in his own rooms, had lived Joseph Merrick,[110] more for his comfort and protection than because he could be cured there. Frederick Treves,[111] who was particularly interested in his case, accompanied them. Alexandra had been warned of his shocking appearance and saw, as Lady Geraldine Somerset described, "a sad spectacle! <u>enormous</u>, with two great bosses on the forehead really like an elephant's head, & a protruding face like a snout, one <u>enormous</u> hand like the foot of an elephant, the other, the left hand, extraordinarily, exceptionally <u>small</u>! He can never go out, he is mobbed so, & lives therefore a prisoner; he is less disgusting to see than might be, because he is such a gentle, kindly man, poor thing."[112] He was known as "the Elephant Man", and was, according to the Duke of Cambridge, "a painful sight to look at, though intelligent in himself."[113] With great compassion and aplomb, Alexandra went forward smiling, took Merrick's hand and sat down beside his chair to talk to him. Albert Edward also spoke to him. Merrick had a collection of curios, presents and photographs given him by well-wishers and Alexandra looked at them with interest. She gave him some of her flowers and then the party withdrew, leaving him quite overcome. Later he received a small parcel containing Alexandra's signed photograph, for his collection. He broke down and wept. The picture was framed and hung in his room; Treves suggested writing a letter of thanks, which he did. She went again and at Christmas sent him three cards with personal messages on the back. She encouraged her friends

to visit him and the Prince would sometimes have a bag of game sent to him after a shoot. Alexandra sent more Christmas cards in 1888 and 1889; on 11 April 1890 Merrick died.[114] As for Treves, he became a leading authority in the treatment of chronic relapsing appendicitis and would be of great help to the Royal Family in the future.

Alexandra visited Wormwood Scrubs prison on 23 May. Despite many commitments she managed to fit in another drawing lesson with Mr Harper on the 31st. The Ascot party met at Sunningdale Park and on 16 June George came home after his mother had presented prizes at the Royal Victoria Patriotic Asylum for Girls at Wandsworth Common. On the 17th, guests, including the Danish and Greek kings and the Greek crown prince, arrived; there were large family dinners at Marlborough House and Buckingham Palace. The Queen's Jubilee procession and service in Westminster Abbey were held on the 21st, with a state dinner and reception later. The Queen presented a cup to the most deserving child at the Children's Jubilee Fête in Hyde Park on the 22nd; there was a state ball on the 24th and a state dinner in St George's Hall at Windsor the next day, with an evening party in the Waterloo Gallery and a concert by pupils of the Royal College of Music. Eddy and George left on the 27th for jubilee festivities in Dublin, returning on 1 July. Two days later, the Prince and Princess attended a garden party at Buckingham Palace and on the 30th a dinner, followed by fireworks and an open air ballet at Crystal Palace. On1 July was Henley Regatta; the Waleses proceeded up river in a steam launch. There was still little chance of rest but they managed to escape to Sandringham on the 16th for the weekend. Back in London, it was the shooting competition for the Queen's Prize at Wimbledon, visiting the Girls' Friendly Society's Lodge at Brixton Rise and on the 23rd attending the naval review at Portsmouth. On the 27th Alexandra had a drawing lesson with Mr Thomas[115] and the next day the family converged on *Osborne* in Portsmouth Harbour. There were fireworks at the Royal Yacht Squadron Castle and their jubilee ball the next day at Northwood House. The RYS Jubilee Channel Race to Cherbourg and back was held on 8 August. Eddy left for Scotland, and George, with Louis of Battenberg, for Gibraltar, to join *HMS Dreadnought* on the 11th. The Waleses returned on 10th for the National Eisteddfod of Wales at the Albert Hall. Albert Edward, Victoria and Maud saw Louise off from Charing Cross on the 13th for Switzerland, with Mary Teck and her family. Charlotte, who, incidentally, would be getting a long holiday, accompanied her. Louise "was very low at parting" but her father felt sure the trip would do her good. Later, he saw Alexandra, Victoria and Maud off for Denmark; "they started at 2.15 with every prospect of a fine passage. I am now 'the last of the Mohicans'![116] & leave at 8 tonight, & hope to reach Homburg between 6 & 7 tomorrow evening."[117]

At Bernstorff, Alexandra had no time to write to George until 21 August; it was comforting they understood one another so well, "Though at first, owing to this blessed Jubilee year, we did not have so many 'talks' as usual, yet we had some very nice & cosy ones before you left." She was glad he had had a good passage back to Gibraltar; "We had the most awful one I think we ever had; blowing a gale for three nights & 4 days was simply <u>beastly</u>. Although I was very <u>little</u> sick once or twice, it was too horrid rolling about & pitching about like that for so long. The poor Sisters were very bad & the sailors too. One day I had to remain in bed all day long because it was simply impossible to stand in my cabin where everything was rolling about the floor, & I cld find no clothes to wear. My poor Maid was very ill all the time & I never saw her till the last day." They soon forgot their trials on arrival; there were two new babies, one the Waldemars' son, "charming & something like dear old Waldemar himself".[118] The other belonged to "Freddy & Aunt Swan" and was "also a <u>great fat</u> beauty, a regular prize pig, with which she is perfectly delighted & very proud of."[119] Queen Louise was just the same but sometimes looked anxious about "poor dear Aunt Thyra", slowly recovering and much missed. Alexandra also missed Louise; "it seems so strange to be without her. I always fancy she must be there hidden somewhere. I do hope St Moritz will do her good & that she at last may get rid of all her ailments, she really has <u>suffered</u> a lot of <u>pain</u> & discomfort for so long now, poor child." Eddy was having good sport in Scotland but had only sent a telegram, not a letter and "from dear Papa I have good accounts but the weather seems horrid at Homburg & he feels rather depressed, I think; he drinks the waters regularly & I hope will feel all the better after the cure." She was horrified that cholera was rife in Malta and hoped every precaution would be taken against it.[120]

Louise and her party reached St Moritz, which she found very beneficial, on 17 August.[121] They moved to Cadenabbia and Baveno; the Tecks were home by 19 September, while Louise, with Charlotte and Doctor Laking,[122] moved to Milan and then Venice, where she was delighted with everything and seemed much better, which her mother only hoped would continue when she came home. At Vienna, Louise met King George, Queen Olga and their two daughters, who had just left Denmark; "The poor Sisters are quite low about it still as those darling girls Alix[123] and <u>my</u> <u>sweet</u> little <u>Minny</u>,[124] whom I wish <u>you</u> could marry some day, were always with them all day long."[125] Albert Edward had enjoyed a fortnight in Denmark, telling George; "All here are wonderfully well & in excellent spirits, & one would hardly believe dear Amama was 70. You can picture our life here, & all the noise & racket, but we are 'a very happy family <u>we</u> <u>are</u>'!"[126] Danish holidays were lively and energetic. Among others, Alexander III, tall and heavily built, would go for long walks with the children and join in, or lead, all their fun, games and mischief. The family was very agile and King Christian used to say that if, one day, they were all in need, or were turned out of their countries, he would start a circus with them. Everyone had a role except Queen Olga and Crown Princess Louise, who were not gifted as acrobats or equestrians and would have to be programme sellers. At Fredensborg there was a low, flat sofa in the small drawing room, where the children would turn somersaults. Sometimes the adults would join in and Alexandra was best at it; she somehow managed to turn over without her head touching the sofa. This might all be done in evening dress with jewels and flowers in the hair.[127] Eddy stayed until the 12th, when he had to join the Lancers at York. "He is very happy here & enjoys it all very much; the Greek cousins & Uncle Sacha chaff him a good deal which is great fun & does him a world of good." Nicky of Russia "is a charming boy & reminds me of my Georgie & is yr height too." On the 17th St Alban's Church was consecrated and they attended morning service there the next day. It was still mostly fine, and picturesque, with autumnal reds and yellows. Alexandra had decorated her letter with two hand-painted rose petals. She was not sure how long she would stay, but at least as long as Minny and until her parents went to Gmunden. "Thank God darling Thyra is getting quite well now altho' gradually so; she wrote a most touching letter to Mama on her birthday, the first since her illness, which was the best proof of her recovery." Waldemar was very proud of his new baby. He, his wife and Uncle Sacha had just come back "from a chase in the woods; they started soon after 4 this morning, saw a few deer, missed them & came home empty handed!! What fun!!"[128]

Albert Edward left on the 20th and, via Dresden and Berlin, Louise arrived at Fredensborg on 8 October and found that an unwelcome guest had joined the happy family. On the 12th "Russian Georgie" went down with measles; on the 14th Louise,[129] Ingeborg[130] and Harald[131] of Denmark, as well as Olga of Russia, followed. The next day, Maud fell ill and so, on the 17th, did Victoria. Nicky of Russia and "Greek Georgie"[132] succumbed as did, on the 18th, Uncle Hans. Alexandra and her daughters had intended to go home on about the 21st but this was now out of the question. On the 27th Louise became ill. As her father wrote; "Fancy, what bad luck; now Louise has got the measles, fortunately in a mild form, but it is certain that Mama will have in consequence to remain another three weeks in Denmark. It is really too unlucky. I shall have to spend my birthday alone at Sandringham, wh will be very sad for me."[133] There was bad news from San Remo; the German crown prince, who had already been treated for a growth in his throat, had developed another, possibly cancerous; the doctors all agreed that no external operation should take place yet. "It is most sad, as U Fritz's life is of such value, & the old Emperor's is very precarious now."[134] Alexandra and the girls arrived in London on the 19th "all looking wonderfully well & have grown fatter. In fact I never saw Sisters looking better." George had finally visited his uncle and aunt in Greece and it had all gone off very well. Queen Louise was with Thyra, now recovered from her confinement. Alexandra and the girls went to Sandringham on 23 November and Papa joined them on the 26th, Maud's eighteenth birthday. They heard Uncle Fritz almost certainly had throat cancer, although his general health was good and his "courage & fortitude ... magnificent."[135]

Guests arrived at Sandringham for shooting and, on 2 December, the county ball. Lord Fife was staying at Castle Rising and Alexandra had lunch and tea with him there on the 6th. She and the girls left for London on the 10th and then, with the Prince, Windsor, for the 14th. The couple went to stay at Ashridge,[136] while the girls returned to Sandringham. George had sent a Christmas letter, and had enjoyed a picnic with his Aunt Marie[137] and cousins at St Paul's Bay in Malta. He had heard from his sisters, delighted to be back at "dear old Sandringham, especially Toria, who is so pleased to be able to ride again," and wished he could be there too.[138] Alexandra wrote to him again; "At last! you will say – that horrid old hard-hearted Mother dear can find time to write to her poor absent boy! I know it is too bad & I am miserable about it too ... but alas since I have been back only 4 weeks now, I really have not had, so to speak, one second to myself, really been hunted to death as usual during all this blessed Xmas time ... Please forgive me is all I can say!" Captain Stephenson was there for Christmas; he too missed George but said there was no objection to his going to Athens again, for Greek Christmas, "& you may ask for leave to go there with our full sanction." Everything at Sandringham was the same, although "our dear old faithful Downie",[139] the butler, had died in their absence; "it is too sad without him; I was so fond of the dear old man." She was sorry for her disjointed letter, already several days old, "but I have been interrupted so often & every time I am trying to write the girls will thump the piano which disturbs me dreadfully & I write awfully badly & stupid nonsense in consequence – at this moment it is Victoria & Julie grinding away sweetly at some old waltzes of theirs." Eddy appeared happy to be there, although on the whole he seemed to like York and the 9th Lancers. At Windsor the Queen had been "in excellent spirits tho' a little aged. She is delighted with her two Indian Servants[140] who are always in attendance. Beatrice's two babies are supposed to be the greatest beauties there ever were seen before; that I can't see! – but the eldest cherub has a devil of a little temper already!"[141] Albert Edward wrote that 1887 had been very eventful and in many respects very happy – "Let us hope that 1888 will be equally so."[142]

In the bitterly cold January 1888, snow-roughened ice on the lake made skating difficult. The tenants' ball was held on the 6th and, after the Prince had gone to London, Alexandra and the girls stayed three days with a recent guest, the Duchess of Manchester, at Kimbolton (the Duke was in Australia) and "had real fun & went on our own hook."[143] Back at Sandringham new guests included the Portuguese Marquis de Soveral,[144] "alias the blue monkey",[145] a recent acquaintance who became a valued family friend. After the guests left on 6 February, Albert Edward went to London and, later, Paris and Cannes but Alexandra stayed, visiting locally; there was "a poor boy only

17, at Babingley dying of heart complaint & suffering tortures, poor boy & his legs & feet are so swelled it is sad to see." The animals were well but some horses were to go "as Papa is very hard up!!! I fear our new Mares etc involve a good deal." She was delighted with George's letters, especially as Aunt Olga had painted little flowers and birds on the paper. He had loved staying at Athens and wrote; "Uncle Willy wants to know if you continue to receive all his letters, which he writes every week. He says 'she always telegraphs 'Am writing', 'Have written', 'Shall write' but never a letter comes', and then he laughs & says it is a sort of joke now!" Aunt Olga had just written to Alexandra "but I can't read it, the only thing I can see is that she calls you <u>old</u> <u>Coldcream</u> or something, whatever that means but I don't see where the joke is, unless she means that you always smother your face with it before dinner, perhaps that is it."[146] Alexandra, the girls and Julie were "having a lovely time of it here alone just as we used in <u>old times</u> and it is so snug & cosy in the dear old Hall in the evening when I read by the hour to them." They were "again plunged into the depths of winter & it is now snowing as hard as ever it can, a regular '<u>blizzard</u>' and if this goes on we shall be snowed up." She had to leave on 23 February for "a beastly Drawingroom on the 24th."

The old German emperor was dying and his son's health was compromised; a breathing tube had been inserted into his surgically-opened windpipe. "I only trust to God he now may get better, but who knows!"[147] Alexandra wrote. It overshadowed the couple's approaching silver wedding celebrations, for which George had permission to come home. On 6 March Albert Edward returned from visited Vicky and Fritz at San Remo. Eddy and George arrived later; there was a theatre visit that evening and a levee next day, but on the 9th Emperor William died. Alexandra's response to such timing can only be imagined; a drawing room was postponed but as guests and deputations for the silver wedding were already approaching, celebrations were barely affected by mourning. Congratulations and presents were arriving and on the 10th there was a grand dinner at Marlborough House; the Queen, King Leopold II, Frederick and Louise of Denmark and over twenty more royalties attended. It was the first time the Queen had dined out since Prince Albert's death; they had not achieved a silver wedding. Albert Edward gave his wife jewels and a bespoke travelling clock, inscribed "In memory of March 10, 1863–1888, from AE."[148] There was a special evening service at the Chapel Royal in Whitehall the next day and another large dinner party at Marlborough House, but on the 13th Albert Edward, Eddy and Frederick left for the Emperor's funeral at Berlin on the 16th, returning four days later. Alexandra visited the Danish Home at London Docks and a plain needlework exhibition, and later the Waleses attended the 19th annual concert, at St James's Hall, for the Metropolitan and City Police Orphanage. On the 22nd Alexandra saw *The Pirates of Penzance* and there were other theatres and dinner parties until Good Friday, with Handel's *Messiah* at the Albert Hall before they left for Easter at Sandringham. The Danes departed and George left on 11 April for his ship at Malta.

Victoria had a chill and two servants, Mary[149] and Harriet, were unwell. Alexandra sat with her daughter and read a little to Mary, but Harriet[150] died on the 18th. Meanwhile Albert Edward had seen how ill the new German emperor, Frederick III was and admitted being "in constant fear & trembling whenever a telegram arrives."[151] All future plans depended on news of him. On the 23rd Albert Edward left for several dinners and other events in London "for himself alone", so Alexandra stayed at Sandringham, feeling rather sad. She responded to a remark of George's; "Yes indeed we are a most happy family & I thank God for having given me such good & affectionate Children who are my real comfort in this world." "Dear Papa" was not mentioned, but they had all taken Holy Communion together; "May it keep us all free from temptation & give us strength to bear all trials which come to each of us." Victoria was better and "the other Hags too [are] minus their various little ailments." Alexandra was having great fun doing leather work[152] but "old Fräulein jumping about & fidgeting in all directions" was nearly driving her wild. "The Girls say they are so glad; this is what they have had to go through all these years & never got any pity, & now I can feel it for myself!"[153]

The Waleses were sponsors to Sir Francis and Lady Knollys'[154] baby,[155] christened Alexandra Louvima Elizabeth at the Chapel Royal, St James's on 5 May; the middle name combined Lou[ise], Vi[ctoria] and Ma[ud]. "It is a fine child & it just cried sufficiently for luck whilst the water was put on its head"[156] the Prince wrote. Louvima or Baba, as she was called, became a much-loved member of the Princess's circle, but just now, Alexandra felt very cross; she had been reluctant to leave Sandringham "& at present hate everything here, even the beastly electric light in my rooms, which everybody tries to persuade me is perfectly charming. It is hidden by vulgar shells! which I have the pleasure of looking at all day long empty & hideous!!! I & Papa have to race up to Scotland for three days pleasures, in the train & at an Exhibition at Glasgow & Blackburn. On my return here, to make things pleasanter, Grandmama wishes to take away two of the girls from Thursday till Monday, & you know how I hate to let them go anywhere alone without me! Next, I have to open two detestable Bazaars with all their botherations staring me in the face. If people only wld let me go privately to their various houses & places – but to make these 'wild beast' shows & advertisement of one is what I loathe."[157]

The Queen commented to Beatrice; "Victoria & Maud are quite charming girls & Victoria is so sociable & has so much to say. They are delighted with the country & everything; Maud draws so very well."[158] The Queen had driven with Alexandra to Cumberland Lodge for tea; the Christians' younger daughter, Louise,[159] was "becoming a handsome girl, & will be really so when she fines down. Alix was much struck by her & also thinks Abby[160] will not later be plain.

I think Christle improved tho' not in looks." The Queen had been speaking "by Bertie's wish" to Alexandra about "Fritz Leop[161] ... & I found her quite reasonable. The girls are so happy at home that I don't think they will readily marry."[162] Nevertheless she was considering the options. The season had begun and mourning was ending. There were plays and operas and Alexandra opened the Anglo–Danish Exhibition at South Kensington, in aid of rebuilding the British Home for Incurables, the first institution in England of which she had become patroness. The Prince went briefly to Berlin again, for a wedding[163] on 24 May. In a birthday letter, Alexandra told George, "We have had three balls running this week, and I feel quite idiotic. Tonight we give a great dinner for the King of Sweden ... then go to a ball at the Wimbornes. Tomorrow we go all day long from 10 o'clock to Cambridge to see Eddy being made a Doctor – in the evening we dine with the Staals,[164] so you see how we are hunted about." She sent him "a crystal ball clock which I believe goes very well & is something new, & [is a] rather nice fat thing."[165]

The Ascot party was at Sunningdale Park, but on 15 June news of Frederick III's death came at last. The couple, Eddy and a large suite including Oliver Montagu left for the funeral at Berlin on the 18th. They returned on the 25th and the girls, who had stayed at Windsor, joined them. Alexandra had been very upset; "poor Aunt Vicky is to be pitied more than words can say as by his death she has not only lost the very best of husbands, but everything & her position is anything but pleasant in that dreadful country surrounded by brutes of all shades; hers is now a lonely life & her future [a] terribly sad one! All her plans & ambitions crushed & nothing remains but the remembrance of the past. Instead of William being a comfort & support to her, he has quite gone over to Bismark & Co who entirely overlook or crush her! which is too infamous."

Eddy was "laid up with the gout (like an elderly gentleman) in his big toe!! poor boy, is it not too bad & why he shld have that being quite thin & slight. Papa is rather crowing over him I think, never having been bothered with it himself!" Their mourning had made it a quiet season, and leaving for Cowes had been delayed by Marie, Duchess Paul of Mecklenburg-Schwerin's[166] illness; she and her husband, friends of the Waleses, were in London when she was taken ill, fortunately near Dr Laking's house. Alexandra stayed with her there for fourteen hours, as she nearly died of "some internal complications which four Doctors were unable to understand".[167] The Mecklenburgs stayed four days at Marlborough House until she was well enough to go home on 30 July. Albert Edward told George; "Mama was of the greatest comfort & solace to her."[168] Returning from Cowes on 13 August, the couple travelled together on the 14th to Coblenz "from where Papa goes to Homburg & I to Wiesbaden to see dear Apapa[169] for a few days, then on to Gmunden to spend a few weeks with dear little Thyra whom I have not seen since her serious illness last year." Queen Olga had recently had her fifth son, Christopher; "So there will be a little Andrew &

Christopher, how funny."[170] On 16 August Albert Edward came over from Homburg to lunch; that evening Alexandra saw the opera, *Marta* at Wiesbaden. Stewart Cumberland[171] demonstrated thought-reading on the 17th and on the 18th it was the circus. The Prince met his family again at Frankfort on the 19th; he then returned to Homburg and they continued to Gmunden. At Wiesbaden they had seen the Duke of Sparta, who had been studying German at Heidelberg, and "What do you think he has been doing since – Why! 'gone & got engaged' to be married to little cousin Sophie!!![172] This is all very well & delightful but really he is much too young only just 20 & looks such a boy altho' he is a very clever one." Alexandra thought, wisely, that he should have travelled first and seen a little more of the world in general "& then in a year [or] two he might have thought of marrying. I told him as much myself the other day & he quite agreed! but I believe *entre nous* her dear brothers, William & Henry[173] have somehow interfered & hastened it on!! by what I can make out, but don't mention this to anybody! Tino went straight to Berlin for those ridiculous old Manoeuvres, & it was settled almost directly he got there! ... Anyhow I hear they are all delighted, & little Sophie is a dear little thing if she only were not a Prussian!"

Thyra was "looking better than I have ever seen her; quite blooming with health, & so happy with her dear old Ernest & their 6 darling lovely little Cherubs!" Their new house in the hills, Villa Cumberland,[174] was charming and very comfortable, with beautiful views and fresh air.[175] Minny arrived, with Nicholas and Xenia; "Oh it was so nice having her here & as you can imagine we three Sisters were never apart. She was looking so well. We made some delightful expeditions up on the hills to their various shooting lodges, which was great fun as we were all on ponies. One day it unfortunately poured but it did not matter, we liked it all the same." In the evenings Herr Döme sang twice and Lucca[176] once. Albert Edward arrived on 7 September for two days; "Dear Papa is looking pretty well, I think – the cure has rather pulled him down & he has suffered so much from his wretched teeth lately."[177] After more excursions, parties, and a great dinner for Ernest's birthday on the 21st, the holiday was over. Alexandra and the girls left, and, via Munich's galleries and Cologne Cathedral, reached Flushing on the 24th en route for England, where, almost immediately, they set off for Scotland. Papa meanwhile was hunting fur and feather in Hungary and visiting Austria. He told George; "I always wear tennis shoes with spats stalking in Hungary, as the ground is so dry & the least noise is heard."[178]

At Balmoral, *Tableaux Vivants* were acted for the Queen's amusement on 5 and 6 October. The words were H E N R Y M A U R I C E, Henry of Battenberg's names, with a tableau for each letter; Eddy and his sisters were in seven of them. Alexandra watched the rehearsal approvingly on the 3rd. Staying at Balmoral was Alix of Hesse, who also took part and in whom Eddy had a romantic interest. Alexandra painted, sketched and had more lessons with Mr Harper, who was at

Balmoral for a week. She and the girls returned to London on the 18th, "to get my winter clothes & await Papa's arrival from abroad." The boys were undertaking official duties; George in Athens again for his uncle's Silver Jubilee later in October and Eddy in Copenhagen for his grandfather's silver jubilee in November. William II was behaving appallingly to his mother and now "has been personally most frightfully rude & impertinent towards Papa, & actually refused to meet him at Vienna!! He is perfectly infuriated against <u>England</u> … and all about the publication of his Father's diary etc etc, he puts it down to his Mother & England. Oh he is mad and a conceited ass, who also says that Papa and Grandmama don't treat him with proper respect as the <u>Emperor</u> of <u>all</u> & <u>mighty</u> <u>Germany</u>! But my hope is that <u>pride</u> will have a fall some day!! & won't we rejoice then." Landgrave Frederick William,[179] whom the naughty Wales children had called "Mutton Hair", had drowned on his way to Singapore on 14 October, the day before his 34th birthday. "I am really <u>so</u> dreadfully shocked & sorry about it, & the poor boy was so far away from all his belongings & home – it is too sad."[180] It was feared he had jumped overboard while mentally disturbed.[181]

Alexandra attended an organ recital at Westminster Abbey on the 26th and on the 30th went to Alexandra Palace with her husband and daughters to see Professor Baldwin[182] ascend 5,000 feet in a balloon and descend by parachute. He told them it had been one of the most successful of his 45 performances.[183] There was bad news on the 31st from Russia; the Emperor, Empress and some of their family had been involved in a terrible railway accident at Borki. In all, 6 carriages were smashed, 21 servants and officials killed and 36 wounded. The Imperial Family escaped serious injury but were profoundly shocked, not least because the cause was hard to determine.[184] At Sandringham, there were shooting parties and George was expected home on 19 November but Alexandra had made a sudden decision and on the 12th she, Eddy and Victoria left for Denmark. As she told George; "Yes, was I not a <u>beast</u> to go away just when my poor Georgie boy was coming home! but I could not resist having been here on this occasion … & dear Apapa & Amama were so pleased to have had me, Toria & Eddy for their 25th Jubilee. All the fêtes & festivities went off beautifully & the whole town & country were most enthusiastic, & it was <u>all lovely</u> – but the amount we have done is something wonderful. Thank God Mama & Papa have stood it all so well. I have no time for more, so many people to see & Amama wants me."[185] Feeling loved and useful in Denmark was a tonic after a slightly tarnished silver year. Back at Sandringham on the 24th, guests arrived and Alexandra celebrated her birthday with the schoolchildren's tea party. She was touched at Dalton's contributing to her present (a sofa) from the household and looked forward to seeing him[186] and meeting his wife and baby.[187] The usual Windsor visit was paid and on 13 December the Prince placed some returned relics of Charles I[188] in his coffin in the vault in the nave of St George's Chapel.

Empress Frederick and three daughters lunched at Marlborough House on the 16th, later spending Christmas with the Queen at Osborne. By the 22nd the Wales family was at Sandringham.

The couple came to London for a wedding[189] on 5 January 1889, attending two church services, the circus and a pantomime, before returning to Sandringham on the 7th. On the 12th Vicky and her daughters arrived and all planted oak trees in the grounds on the 18th. As they were in mourning, the only entertainment was a demonstration of Edison's[190] phonograph by a Mr Hamilton on the 19th, when one of the dinner guests was Sir Arthur Sullivan. Afterwards the Waleses stayed at Aske[191] during a visit to Middlesbrough; they inspected the Middlesbrough and Cleveland Centre of the St John Ambulance Association, visited the Cleveland Club and attended the Mayor's banquet in the Exchange Rooms. The Prince left on the 25th for London; Alexandra remained until the next day, but that evening they were both back at Sandringham. On the 30th news broke that Crown Prince Rudolph, only son and heir of Emperor Franz Joseph of Austria, had suddenly died; shockingly, Rudolph and his mistress, Marie Vetsera[192] had been found dead at a hunting lodge at Mayerling.[193] Albert Edward and his sons attended a Requiem Mass for him at the Roman Catholic chapel in Farm Street on 5 February. Alexandra and her daughters came to London on the 9th, for another wedding on the 12th. Later the Prince left for Paris and Cannes; Eddy had already returned to York and three days later George left to join his ship at Gibraltar.

At Sandringham Alexandra and the girls "as you may imagine take life easy at present, though I have such a lot to do ... Sisters are now all seated in their usual old corners & only yr poor 'Grand Mother Chair' is empty! I have even been smoking my solitary pipe!! with Papa's head on, to make it brown when you come back!!"[194] Returning on the 23rd, they saw *Macbeth* at the Lyceum and dined with the Queen, Empress Frederick and others on the 25th; "Grandmama was in very good spirits, poor Aunt Vicky less so, particularly on the eve of her departure." On the 26th there was a "tiresome Drawingroom", but this time it was different; "everything was going on in the usual way, when suddenly Grandmama said it was hot & told the Dss of Buccleuch[195] to take off her shawl; the latter being rather fidgety & fussy or over-anxious, poor thing, caught it in the veil at the same time as Grandmama turned her head upwards towards Lord Lathom,[196] so lo & behold, the whole head edifice, veil, cap, crown & all, were flying off in a jiffy, & there stood poor little Grandmama with her bare head & nothing on but her little twisted pigtail as big as a shilling at the back of her head. I thought I should have died, but thank goodness I behaved beautifully & never laughed till Grandmama roared, when the tears ran down my cheeks. We clapped it on as quickly as we cld after having recovered from the first shock, I in an awful fright of having put it on the wrong way up. In the meantime the Ladies were waiting to be presented, & cld not make out what all this shuffling was about, & when at last they were let loose with a rush, Grandmama was in fits of laughter in their faces!! Oh it was killing & I shall never forget the sight, it was as good as a Pantomime. Then the ladies went by extra badly, so slow that they were told every moment to hurry up & go forward. One refused to take the least notice of Grandmama & only gave me a familiar nod, so altho' she was nearly down the line she was bodily taken back, when she merely said 'beg pardon Ma'am' & walked on; another deliberately put her hand on Gd Mama's & kissed it with a great smack. As a finishing touch to this undignified state ceremony, one of the little pages was led out in a faint."[197]

Back at Sandringham, Alexandra developed "a most beastly cold & am feeling more wretched than I can say! ... I caught it from all those old Hags & Charlotte who has been decrepit ever since the drawingroom. I flattered myself that I had escaped but now I have got it with a vengeance." She even doubted she would be well enough to meet Papa in London on his return from France. A lot of George's new photographs by Downey had arrived, "all very good, excepting a profile one which gives you a kind of lemon shaped head." Despite horrible weather she had visited all the poor people and distributed clothes, food and money.[198] She and the girls did go to London and the Waleses celebrated their anniversary on 10 March with a large family dinner. They attended plays, parties and the Royal Institute of Painters in Watercolours' annual exhibition. Alexandra heard Bach's[199] passion music at St Anne's and then on the 20th saw a musical gymnastics display at Alexandra House. On the 27th Master Otto Hegner, (twelve), came to play[200] and the composer Edvard Grieg[201] and his wife called later. William Cave Thomas, who had given Alexandra three painting lessons, came six more times and apparently brought a model, "ED" on 9 and 10 April, but the second time it was "too dark to paint ED."[202]

Aunt Cambridge, aged 91, died on 6 April. Alexandra and Lady Geraldine were the only ones there "when she died which was terribly sad, tho' for her a relief as she suffered to the last, & did not speak a word before she died ... Poor dear Aunt – how we shall miss her!" After memorial services and the funeral at Kew Church on the 13th, the couple returned to Sandringham to prepare for an historic event on the 23rd. The Queen was "actually coming here tomorrow with Louise![203] I wish Grandmother had come by herself!! The place is gone mad with interminable arches springing up here & there & everywhere, Militia lying about in the fields in tents airing themselves in the rain, poor things, 150 hunting men to escort H Majesty's carriage etc etc." "I must go & see the pretty soldiers now in Camp",[204] Alexandra added, ironically. George came home on leave and on the 26th extracts from *The Bells* and the final scene from *The Merchant of Venice*, with Henry Irving,[205] Ellen Terry[206] and the Lyceum Company were performed. The Queen left the next day, greatly touched by "Bertie and Alix's" kindness and affection and having much enjoyed her visit. She had toured the grounds and gardens and, after visiting the church, went to "The Girls' needlework school, where they are taught plain sewing, which is very useful, & was started by Alix." Two days later, she inspected "a Working Men's Industrial School, which Alix established & where they are taught to carve in wood & stamp or hammer brass. Here, as well as at the Needlework School, Fräulein Nödel teaches."[207]

These two institutions, known as the technical school, were started through Alexandra's interest in the Arts and Crafts movement; fortuitously, her daughters' German governess was an accomplished craftswoman. The revival of traditional arts and crafts, linked with education, philanthropy and self-fulfilment, began in England in the 1870s. John Ruskin[208] promoted redeveloping rural industries, in *Fors Clavigera: Letters to the Workmen and Labourers of Great Britain* in 1871. In America in 1880, Charles G Leland[209] favoured starting classes in rural areas so that people could earn money by selling their handiwork. In Britain in the 1870s, Mrs Eglantyne Jebb[210] had set up woodcarving classes to discourage idleness and foster artistic appreciation and a sense of community and formed the "Cottage Arts Association". Similar projects were started across Britain, becoming part of a larger, London-based organisation, formally constituted in 1884 as the Home Arts and Industries Association, with an office in Langham Place, W1. Mrs Jebb, Mr Leland and Mrs Watts[211] were on the committee; Earl and Countess Brownlow were also involved and he became president of the HAIA. The movement appealed to ladies, like Alexandra, who cared about the welfare of tenants and villagers on their family estates. The Association did not offer funding; Alexandra paid for her school out of her own allowance. By 1885, when the HAIA held its first exhibition at the Albert Hall, it had 40 groups throughout England and Ireland, with 320 students. Whether they then included a Sandringham group is unclear but evidently one had started at least by 1889, when there were between 291 and 450 groups, with 4,000 or 5,000 students and some 1,000 teachers.[212]

Alexandra received, on 6 May, a silver casket with a gold and ruby necklace and bracelets as a silver-wedding present from the ladies of South Australia. The play that evening was *Wealth* at the Haymarket. The next day she laid the foundation stone of a new Women's Hospital in Euston Road. George had to return to Portsmouth on the 12th but would soon be visiting again. In addition to the usual seasonal activities, Carl of Denmark and George of Greece arrived for a week on the 26th and on the 30th the Paris couple[213] held their silver wedding garden party at Sheen House. On 8 June, the Wales family left for Paris, partly to see the International Exhibition,[214] which the Prince had helped to organise, but also as a special treat at the end of an era; it was the last holiday they took together as parents with five unmarried children. They stayed at the Hotel

Bristol, visited friends and acquaintances, went to theatres and dined at cafés and restaurants. On the 9[215] they saw panoramas and paid their first visit to the Exhibition on the Champs de Mars, where they later saw illuminations of the fountains, gardens and Eiffel Tower.[215] The next day they saw the English section and rode up to the very top of the Eiffel Tower in *ascenseurs.* Unfortunately George had to return to Portsmouth later, but the others went on the 11th and the 12th and saw picture galleries, watercolours, French jewellery and *orfèvrerie.* There was racing at Auteuil and on the 13th it was Buffalo Bill's Wild West Show at Neuilly, visits and shopping. The next day at the Exhibition they saw the English, Colonial, Indian, Russian, Italian and American sections. On the last day they visited the Institut Pasteur, met Louis Pasteur[216] and his sons and saw inoculations being administered, before a last visit to the Exhibition, to see the Austrian, Belgian and French sections. They lunched in a Russian restaurant and saw the eastern kiosks and bazaars at the War Office exhibition afterwards. At midnight they left by special train and arrived home on the 16th. Ascot week was spent at Sunningdale Park; races were run, prizes were won and then, on the 20th, Louise became engaged to Lord Fife.

Alexander Duff, 6th Earl Fife, a grandson of the 18th Earl of Errol and his wife,[217] Elizabeth FitzClarence, the illegitimate sixth child of the Duke of Clarence (later William IV) and the actress, Mrs Dora Jordan, was thus descended, like his fiancée, from George III,[218] whose great-great-grandchildren they both were, although Fife was over seventeen years older than Louise. As a young man, Macduff,[219] as he was known, became friendly with Albert Edward, who, being eight years older, to some extent took him under his wing. Macduff was one of the Waleses' inner circle. He came to their parties, entertained them at Mar Lodge, Castle Rising and East Sheen Lodge and was a familiar face to their children; Louise had known him most of her life and, at nearly 40, he was unmarried and apparently unattached. Louise had always been frail and shy, preferring a private country life to a cosmopolitan one, but, like her mother, she could be very determined; in about 1887 she had fallen in love with Macduff and no one else would do; he too was fond of her, although he might well have discounted any hopes for the future. The Prince and Princess perhaps expected their eldest daughter to make a grander match but knowing her character and knowing Macduff, who could offer her a very comfortable home, they agreed. He was, after all, a distant cousin. His journey to India and Louise's European tour in 1887 may at least partly have been made so that they could spend time apart and make sure their feelings for one another were real. Macduff had a number of talks with the Waleses in the months before the engagement and perhaps it was resolved then. On 26 June he asked the Queen for "your gracious favour and approval of my proposed engagement to Your Majesty's granddaughter, Princess Louise of Wales. I am very anxious that Your Majesty should know how much attached I am to Princess Louise, who has also told me of her long affection for myself, which has touched me deeply. I feel that our ideas and tastes are so entirely united that I am sure we shall live very happily together; should we be fortunate enough to receive Your Majesty's gracious consent to our marriage. I fear that I can only feebly express my great appreciation of Princess Louise's inestimable qualities and my daily increasing love for her." The Prince had offered to give the letter to the Queen "and he will I know say much that I feel it is difficult to write."[220]

That day the family went to London and saw, appropriately, *Macbeth*[221] at the Lyceum. With the Queen's sanction, the engagement was announced officially the next day and Louise, her parents and Macduff dined with her at Windsor that evening. Albert Edward hastened to tell Vicky; "Now I have a great piece of news to announce to you; Lord Fife has asked to marry our Louise & we have given our consent! It seems that they have been devoted to one another for two years, but he was too shy to propose till a few days ago; they are so happy together, & we have always been so fond of him that I am sure we have done right in giving our consent." The Queen too had always liked him and he was an excellent neighbour to Balmoral.[222] Later, Albert Edward added; "It would please you to see how happy Louise & Fife are, & I never saw anybody more in love than he is."[223] On the 29th they were photographed together at Downey's studio and there was a party at Sheen the next day. Amid the grand seasonal events, Louise, intensely happy, had lunch with her fiancé at his house on 2 July. The Shah of Persia[224] was visiting England and he, as well as the Queen, attended the garden party at Marlborough House on the 4th; the Waleses attended a garden party at Hatfield for him on the 8th. From 16–19 July there were four balls and more to follow and wedding preparations were already under way. Royal guests started to arrive and on 27 July Louise and Macduff (created Duke of Fife) were married by the Archbishop of Canterbury in the private chapel of Buckingham Palace; the Queen gave the wedding breakfast. The groom had balked at her wish that he should wear his kilt.[225] Afterwards everyone returned to Marlborough House for a reception and garden party, and the happy couple left for their honeymoon at East Sheen Lodge. The marriage was popular[226] despite her being 22 to his 39; she had evidently chosen him for love and he was British. One paper noted he was a Guelph on his mother's side. Albert Edward admitted to Vicky; "the parting with our first child was a great pang to us, but as we know how happy she is & has every prospect of always being so, & above all remains in the country, we have every reason to be content."[227]

There were, inevitably, thoughts and discussions about Eddy's marriage prospects; although he yearned for Alix of Hesse (seventeen),[228] she had other ideas. The Waleses, with their four remaining children, boarded *Osborne* for Cowes Week, on 2 August. The German emperor had come for a week and there were several events in his honour[229] before he went home. On the 12th the Wales family returned to London; the Fifes called at 4.00 and later for dinner, after which they all went to the Savoy for *The Yeomen of the Guard.* The Fifes left for Scotland the next day.[230] The Prince, with a bad leg, left for Homburg on the 14th but Alexandra, Victoria and Maud returned to *Osborne* for another week. Before leaving for Denmark on the 23rd, Alexandra told George; "Papa is much better now, but he must take more care of himself & rest." She had been so busy at Cowes, visiting the Queen every day and going on expeditions, that it had been impossible to write sooner. Alicky was at Osborne; "She was rather shy with me but has grown much slighter & prettier! You & Eddy will see her in Scotland later on."[231]

Alexandra reached Fredensborg on the 25th. Greek, Russian and Cumberland relatives arrived; on Queen Louise's birthday 88 people dined. On Alexander III's name day, 11 September, there were 90. Alexandra told George, (who, during manoeuvres in *Torpedo Boat 79*, had acted with great responsibility when another torpedo boat got into difficulties) how proud she was of him. He, like his father and brother, was now going north. "How you will enjoy going up to dear old Scotland now & to darling Louise's new home! I wish I cld have been there too, but never mind, perhaps it is wiser so, and that old Mother in law keeps out of the way at present, which I have begged the rest of the <u>August</u> family to do likewise." She was sure Papa would feel better there and his leg would consequently improve "but he must be <u>careful</u> & not stand or walk too much at present at least."[232] On the 18th Vicky, with three daughters, came for three days and on the 19th the King of Sweden and two sons came to luncheon. Christian IX's sister, Louise of Glücksburg arrived on the 24th, leaving on 1 October for Itzehoe, where she was Abbess. Albert Edward and his sons arrived on the 30th. Edison's phonograph had been demonstrated on the 28th and on 3 October Sasha and Minny gave a tea party at their new house, a "Russian pavilion" in the park. On the 12th, the Wales family left, and, via Munich and the Brenner Pass, reached Venice and boarded *Osborne*, anchored opposite the Doge's Palace. For the next three days they visited churches, curiosity shops, St Mark's, the Doge's Palace, dungeons and the Armenian Convent. At night on the 17th there was a Band and a gondola procession on the Grand Canal. At Corfu on the 19th, they visited the King's Town Palace, landed the next day at Navarino and on the 23rd, with the Mediterranean Fleet of seven vessels, entered the Piraeus, and reached Athens by train.

This pleasant trip gave the family another chance to be together for a while. There was also a wedding. Empress Frederick and her family arrived, and on 27 October Sophie of Prussia married Constantine, Duke of Sparta. There were 250 to dinner.[233] On the 28th, Alexandra and her daughters, with Vicky and hers, went to the Piraeus to see Papa off to Egypt and Eddy off to India. At Athens, a ball for 3,800 was held on the 29th and on the 30th a firework display at the Champ de Mars. Albert Edward returned on 7 November; there was a concert and later a view of the Acropolis by moonlight. Leaving Athens on the 11th they reached Brindisi the next day, after a very rough passage, and Paris on the 15th. The couple later saw *La Lutte pour la Vie*, while their daughters went to the circus. Next evening it was Offenbach's *La Vie Parisienne*. Back home on the 18th, the Fifes dined and then lunched for the next two days; returning to Sandringham on the 22nd, Albert Edward, between house parties, stayed with them at Castle Rising for the shooting and, despite thick snow, Alexandra and her daughters went for meals there for the next three days. More guests arrived, including the Paris couple and Hélène. Frost prevented hunting, so the Waleses went in sleighs to Hillington to present a gold watch and purse of £240 to the Huntsman, Bob Clayton, on 7 December. After London and Windsor, they stayed at Luton Hoo[234] but all returned to Sandringham on the 23rd, for Christmas.

Notes

1	Run by "Lord" George Sanger (1825–1911), showman, and his brother John (1816–89), circus proprietors
2	George Herbert Münster (1820–1902), ambassador from 1873–85
3	Information given to the author by Lt Commander CH Knollys
4	The note is undated regarding day and month but its position in the file and evidence in it which tallies with other sources make it very likely that it was written on 3 February
5	Family nickname for her daughters
6	She was reading Charles Dickens' *The Old Curiosity Shop*
7	RA GV/PRIV/AA30/10, Princess of Wales to Prince George, 1885: undated, perhaps 3 February
8	Muhammed Ahmad (1844–85), Nubian religious leader and ruler of Sudan, proclaimed "Mahdi", or messianic redeemer of the Islamic faith, by his supporters
9	General Charles George Gordon (1833–1885), army officer, administrator and Governor-General of the Sudan
10	Captain Arthur Cyprian Knollys (1850–90)
11	RA GV/PRIV/AA30/9, Princess of Wales to Prince George, 1885: 12 February
12	The first night of Lord Lytton's posthumous play; Edward Bulwer-Lytton (1803–1873), 1st Baron Lytton, was a writer and politician
13	Annie Fortescue Harrison (1851–1944), composer of songs, m Colonel Lord Arthur Hill (1846–1931), politician
14	RA VIC/MAIN/Z/455/3, Princess of Wales to Queen Victoria, 1885: 20 March
15	Tobacco was regarded as a treat, not, at that time, as a serious health risk. The flannel cloth would have been used for bandages and clothing.
16	RA VIC/MAIN/Z/455/5, Princess of Wales to Queen Victoria, 1885: 26 March
17	Copy held in the Royal Library, Copenhagen, of a document in the State Archives of the Russian Federation, (GARF) Collection 642, quoted by Preben Ulstrup in *Kejserinde Dagmar*, p 188
18	This was a private girls' school founded in 1866 by a Quaker, Anne Jellicoe and named after the Princess, adopting the Danish colours, red and white, as its own. Its curriculum was made equivalent to that in boys' schools, ultimately enabling its girls to gain university degrees from 1891.

19 RA GV/PRIV/AA30/11, Princess of Wales to Prince George, 1885: 10 April
20 Perhaps Lady Louisa, née Cavendish (1835–1907), m Hon Francis Egerton; sister of the 8th Duke of Devonshire
21 RA GV/PRIV/AA15/21, Prince of Wales to Prince George, 1885: 17 April
22 Janey Sevilla, née Callander (1846–1923), society hostess and theatre producer, m Lord Archibald Campbell
23 These were salt boats going down the River Traun
24 The three children mentioned were Prince George William (1880–1912), Princess Alexandra (1882–1963), m Frederick Francis IV, Grand Duke of Mecklenburg-Schwerin, and Prince Christian (1885–1901)
25 RA GV/PRIV/AA30/12, Princess of Wales to Prince George, 1885: 29 August
26 Robert d'Orléans (1840–1910), Duc de Chartres, m Princess Françoise d'Orléans (1844–1925; they had three sons and a daughter, Marie (1865–1909), who m Prince Waldemar of Denmark
27 St Alban, by tradition, was beheaded in the Roman city of Verulamium (now known as St Albans) at some time between 209 and 304 AD
28 Canute the Great (994–1035), King of Denmark, England and Norway
29 Tooley, p125
30 Thorsten Nordenfelt [sic] (1842–1920), Swedish inventor and industrialist
31 Christina Nilsson (1843–1921), Swedish opera singer, m the Count of Casa Miranda
32 Who arrived on 10th
33 RA GV/PRIV/AA30/13, Princess of Wales to Prince George, 1885: 18 September
34 She had been prevented from attending the earlier weddings because of pregnancy and other reasons
35 Princess Amélie d'Orléans, (1865–1951) d of the Comte de Paris, m Crown Prince, later King, Carlos of Portugal
36 RA VIC/MAIN/Z/460/103, Charlotte Knollys to Queen Victoria, 1885: undated, October
37 Sir Harry Julian Stonor (1859–1939), courtier, brother of Julie
38 RA VIC/MAIN/QAD/1886: 8 February
39 At which the Ladies' Viennese Orchestra played
40 RA GV/PRIV/AA30/15, Princess of Wales to Prince George, 1886: 26 February
41 Staying with Anne, née Hay-Mackenzie (1829–88) w of 3rd Duke of Sutherland; she had been Mistress of the Robes to Queen Victoria from 1870–1874
42 RA VIC/MAIN/Z/460/110, Duchess of Sutherland to Queen Victoria, 1886: 13 March
43 RA GV/PRIV/AA30/16, Princess of Wales to Prince George, 1886: 17 April
44 RA GV/PRIV/AA15/43, Prince of Wales to Prince George, 1886: 17 March
45 Franz Liszt, composer and musician, (1811–86)
46 RA GV/PRIV/AA15/46, Prince of Wales to Prince George, 1886: 11 April
47 Sir Henry Frederick Stephenson (1842–1919), RN officer, equerry to the Prince of Wales, and Arctic explorer
48 Edward White Benson (1829–96), Archbishop of Canterbury from 1883–96
49 RA GV/PRIV/AA30/16, Princess of Wales to Prince George, 1886: 17 April
50 George Warr (1845–1901), professor of the classics who translated parts of the *Iliad* and *Odyssey* into verse
51 RA GV/PRIV/AA30/18, Princess of Wales to Prince George, 1886: 15 May
52 John Todhunter (1839–1916), Irish poet and playwright
53 St John Ambulance Association
54 Crown Prince Carlos of Portugal (1863–1908), later King Carlos I; he was a distant cousin of the Prince of Wales
55 RA GV/PRIV/AA30/18, Princess of Wales to Prince George, 1886: 15 May

[56] RA GV/PRIV/AA30/17, Princess of Wales to Prince George, 1886: 10 May

[57] RA GV/PRIV/AA30/19,20, Princess of Wales to Prince George, 1886: 3 June, 25 July

[58] RA GV/PRIV/AA6/359, Princess of Wales to JN Dalton, 1886: 7 June

[59] Charitable foundation based on a gift from William Bleyton (died 1591) to the poor of his parish

[60] Luigi Cherubini (1760–1842), Italian romantic and classical composer of operas and sacred music

[61] Philippe d'Orléans, Comte de Paris (1838–94) m Princess Marie Isabelle 1848–1919), d of Duc de Montpensier

[62] Dmitri Slaviansky-d'Agreneff, Russian choir master, whose choir performed several times to the royal family

[63] RA GV/PRIV/AA15/59, Prince of Wales to Prince George, 1886: 11 July

[64] George Cadogan (1840–1915), 5th Earl Cadogan, politician, m Lady Beatrix, née Craven (1844–1907)

[65] RA GV/PRIV/AA30/21, Princess of Wales to Prince George, 1886: 11 August

[66] Princess Hélène d'Orléans (1871–1951), m (1) Emanuel Filibert (1869–1931), 2nd Duke of Aosta, (2) Colonel Otto Campini

[67] RA GV/PRIV/AA15/59, Prince of Wales to Prince George, 1886: 11 July

[68] RA GV/PRIV/AA30/21, Princess of Wales to Prince George, 1886: 11 August

[69] Prince Carl of Denmark (1872–1957) elected King (Haakon VII) of Norway in 1905, m Princess Maud of Wales

[70] Prince Carl of Denmark was then 14; he stayed from 20–23 July. RA GV/PRIV/AA15/61, Prince of Wales to Prince George, 1886: 26 July

[71] RA GV/PRIV/AA47/66, Oliver Montagu to Prince George, 1886: 16 August; Alexandra had lent him her wheel-chair at Goodwood

[72] RA GV/PRIV/AA30/21, Princess of Wales to Prince George, 1886: 11 August

[73] Charles Robert Spencer, (1857–1922) later 6th Earl Spencer

[74] Lady Elizabeth Grosvenor (1856–1928), m James Butler, 3rd Marquess of Ormonde (1844–1919)

[75] RA GV/PRIV/AA30/22, Princess of Wales to Prince George, 1886: 28 August. Prince Alexander of Battenberg (1857–93) had been elected as Prince of Bulgaria (served from 1879–86); he m Johanna Loisinger (1865–1951)

[76] Lord Fife's place

[77] RA GV/PRIV/AA30/23, Princess of Wales to Prince George, 1886: 10 October

[78] RA GV/PRIV/AA15/11, Prince of Wales to Prince George, 1886: 16 October

[79] RA GV/PRIV/AA36/13, Prince George to Princess of Wales, 1886: 21/23 October

[80] RA GV/PRIV/AA30/24, Princess of Wales to Prince George, 1886: 10 November

[81] Frederick Bedford (1838–1913), later Admiral Sir, RN officer, later Governor of W Australia (1903–1909)

[82] Princess Maud's nickname

[83] RA GV/PRIV/AA30/25, Princess of Wales to Prince George, 1886: 23 November

[84] The Standishes were friends of the Waleses; Henry Standish (1847–1933) was the last Lord of the Manor of Standish in Lancashire. His wife, Hélène, née de Perusse des Cars (1847–1933) was a society figure

[85] RA GV/PRIV/AA30/24, Princess of Wales to Prince George, 1886: 10 November

[86] Prince Alexander of Battenberg (1886–1960), Marquess of Carisbrooke (1917), m Lady Irene, née Denison (1890–1956)

[87] Prince Henry was only a year younger than his wife

[88] Prince Alexander of Hesse, morganatically married to Countess Julie von Hauke; they were the parents of the Battenberg family. Sandro was his son, Alexander, back from Bulgaria.

89 RA GV/PRIV/AA30/26, Princess of Wales to Prince George, 1886: 22 December

90 She added, in another letter (RA GV/PRIV/AA30/26) "and you nearly put out my eye with scent", which might explain her subsequent eye trouble. The squirts were Christmas novelties that contained scent.

91 RA GV/PRIV/AA31/3, Princess of Wales to Prince George, 1886: 31 December

92 RA GV/PRIV/AA16/25, Prince of Wales to Prince George, 1887: 10 January

93 Sir Charles Wyndham (born Charles Culverwell) (1837–1919), actor and theatre proprietor who specialised in comedy and farce

94 He had changed his name from John Rowlands (1841–1904) and was a Welsh/American journalist, explorer, soldier, colonial administrator, author and politician

95 The expedition (1886–89) was intended to relieve Mehmed Emin Pasha (1849–92), born Eduard Schnitzer, an Ottoman physician and naturalist of German/Jewish origin, who was governor of the Egyptian province of Equatoria on the upper Nile, and was being threatened by Mahdist forces

96 RA GV/PRIV/AA16/27, Prince of Wales to Prince George, 1887: 23 January

97 The widowed Lady Lonsdale had married the Marquess of Ripon (and Earl de Grey) on 7 May 1885

98 RA GV/PRIV/AA30/27, Princess of Wales to Prince George, 1887: 16 February

99 RA GV/PRIV/AA16/29, Prince of Wales to Prince George, 1887: 5 March

100 RA GV/PRIV/AA16/30, Prince of Wales to Prince George, 1887: 12 March

101 RA GV/PRIV/AA47/79, Oliver Montagu to Prince George, 1887: 26 March

102 RA GV/PRIV/AA16/33, Prince of Wales to Prince George, 1887: 3 April

103 ie. spa

104 Prince Ernest Augustus of Cumberland (1887–1953), m Princess Victoria Louise (1892–1980), only daughter of the German Emperor William II; Prince Ernest Augustus was then allowed to reclaim the title of Duke of Brunswick, one of his father's subsidiary titles, the kingdom of Hanover having been taken over by Prussia in 1866

105 RA GV/PRIV/AA30/30, Princess of Wales to Prince George, 1887: 22 April

106 RA GV/PRIV/AA16/33, Prince of Wales to Prince George, 1887: 3 April

107 RA GV/PRIV/AA30/30, Princess of Wales to Prince George, 1887: 22 April

108 William Frederick Cody (1846–1917), known as "Buffalo Bill", American soldier, bison hunter and showman

109 Eva Luckes (1854–1919), Matron of the London Hospital from 1880–1919

110 Joseph Merrick (1862–90)

111 Frederick Treves (1853–1923), later Sir and 1st Baronet, surgeon and anatomist

112 RA VIC/ADDC6/3/1887: 22 May, Lady Geraldine Somerset's diary, kept for the Duchess of Cambridge. Lady Geraldine had heard about Merrick from the Duke of Cambridge

113 RA VIC/ADDC6/3/1887: 21 May, the Duke's comment was reported by Lady Geraldine Somerset

114 See *The History of the Elephant Man*, by Michael Howell and Peter Ford, 1980, for more information about Joseph Merrick's life and medical condition.

115 William Cave Thomas (1820–1906), Painter, sculptor, author and one of the Princess of Wales's art teachers

116 Historical novel, written by James Fenimore Cooper (1789–1851) in 1826 and set in 1757, during the Seven Years War between Britain and France, which had a front in N America; both sides relied on native American allies

117 RA GV/PRIV/AA16/43, Prince of Wales to Prince George, 1887:13 August

118 Prince Aage of Denmark, later Count of Rosenborg (1887–1940)

119 Prince Gustav of Denmark, (1887–1944). Unusually for a member of the Danish Royal Family, he was significantly overweight until his 20s, when he went into the army

[120] RA GV/PRIV/AA30/31, Princess of Wales to Prince George, 1887: 21 August

[121] RA GV/PRIV/AA16/46, Prince of Wales to Prince George, 1887: 2 September

[122] Francis Laking (1847–1914), Sir and 1st Baronet, physician and surgeon-in-ordinary to King Edward VII and King George V

[123] Princess Alexandra of Greece (1870–91) m Grand Duke Paul Alexandrovitch of Russia (1860–1919)

[124] Princess Marie of Greece (1876–1940) m (1) Grand Duke George Michaelovitch of Russia (1863–1919) and (2) Admiral Pericles Joannides (1881–1965)

[125] RA GV/PRIV/AA30/32, Princess of Wales to Prince George, 1887: 30 Sepember

[126] RA GV/PRIV/AA16/47, Prince of Wales to Prince George, 1887: 9 September; the quip seems to have been a popular catch-phrase

[127] *A Romanov Diary*, the autobiography of Grand Duchess George of Russia, p 22

[128] RA GV/PRIV/AA30/32, Princess of Wales to Prince George, 1887: 30 September

[129] Princess Louise of Denmark (1875–1906), m Prince Frederick of Schaumburg-Lippe

[130] Princess Ingeborg of Denmark (1878–1958).m Prince Carl of Sweden (1861–1951)

[131] Prince Harald of Denmark (1876–1949), m Princess Helena of Glücksburg (1888–1962)

[132] Prince George of Greece (1869–1957), High Commissioner in Crete, 1898–1906, m Princess Marie Bonaparte (1882–1962)

[133] RA GV/PRIV/AA16/54, Prince of Wales to Prince George, 1887: 30 October

[134] RA GV/PRIV/AA16/56, Prince of Wales to Prince George, 1887: 13 November

[135] RA GV/PRIV/AA17/1, Prince of Wales to Prince George, 1887: 20 November

[136] With the Brownlows; Adelbert Brownlow-Cust (1844–1921), 3rd Baron Brownlow, army officer, courtier and politician, m Lady Adelaide, née Chetwynd-Talbot (1844–1917)

[137] Duchess of Edinburgh

[138] RA GV/PRIV/AA36/14, Prince George to Princess of Wales, 1887: 18 December

[139] Robert Downie, d 1887; entered royal service as footman in 1858, page from 1869, wine butler from 1877

[140] Abdul Karim (1863–1909), later the Munshi; Mohammed Bukhsh

[141] RA GV/PRIV/AA30/33, Princess of Wales to Prince George, 1887: 24/28 December; the other baby was Princess Victoria Eugénie (Ena) of Battenberg (1887–1969), m King Alfonso XIII of Spain (1886–1941)

[142] RA GV/PRIV/AA17/6, Prince of Wales to Prince George, 1887: 25 December

[143] RA GV/PRIV/AA30/34, Princess of Wales to Prince George, 1888: 10 February

[144] Luis Pinto de Soveral, Marquis de Soveral (1851–1922), diplomat, Portuguese Minister in London, 1897–1910

[145] RA GV/PRIV/AA17/10, Prince of Wales to Prince George, 1888: 22 January

[146] RA GV/PRIV/AA37/17, Prince George to Princess of Wales, 1888: 24 January

[147] RA GV/PRIV/AA30/34, Princess of Wales to Prince George, 1888: 10 February

[148] Tooley, p106

[149] Mary Hughes, housemaid since 1863, d in June 1888

[150] Harriet Hammond, housemaid from 1877 then linen room maid from 1886–88

[151] RA GV/PRIV/AA17/16, Prince of Wales to Prince George, 1888: 22 April

[152] Probably learnt from Fräulein Noedel

[153] RA GV/PRIV/AA30/36, Princess of Wales to Prince George, 1888: 22 April

[154] Ardyn Mary, née Tyrwhitt (1860–1922), m Francis Knollys, later 1st Viscount

[155] Louvima Knollys (1888–1958), m (1) Allan Mackenzie, (2) Richard Checkley

[156] RA GV/PRIV/AA17/18, Prince of Wales to Prince George, 1888: 5 May

[157] RA GV/PRIV/AA30/37, Princess of Wales to Prince George, 1888: 5 May

[158] RA VIC/ADDA23/23, Queen Victoria to Beatrice, Princess Henry of Battenberg, 1888: 7 May

159 Princess Louise, later known as Marie Louise, of Schleswig-Holstein (1872–1956), m Prince Aribert of Anhalt

160 Prince Albert of Schleswig-Holstein (1869–1931) younger son of Prince and Princess Christian, who became Duke of Schleswig-Holstein-Sonderburg-Augustenburg

161 Unidentified but possibly Prince Frederick Leopold of Prussia (1865–1931), (a great-grandson of King Frederick William III) of suitable age; however, he married Princess Louise Sophie of Augustenburg in 1889.

162 RA VIC/ADDA23/24, Queen Victoria to Princess Beatrice, 1888: 18 May

163 Prince Henry of Prussia married his cousin, Princess Irène of Hesse

164 Baron Egor Egorovitch Staal (1822–1907), Russian Ambassador to the UK, 1884–1902. His wife was a daughter of Prince Michael Gortschakoff.

165 RA GV/PRIV/AA30/38, Princess of Wales to Prince George, 1888: 3 June

166 Princess Marie Windisch-Grätz (1856–1929), m Duke Paul of Mecklenburg-Schwerin (1852–1923)

167 RA GV/PRIV/AA30/39, Princess of Wales to Prince George, 1888: 12 August

168 RA GV/PRIV/AA17/30, Prince of Wales to Prince George, 1888: 29 August

169 He and his brother, Prince John, were taking a course of baths there

170 Prince Andrew of Greece (1882–1944) and Prince Christopher of Greece (1888–1940); coincidentally, the two little boys had the names of the Waleses' friends, Andrew Cockerell and Christopher Sykes.

171 Stewart Cumberland (1857–1922) used a technique based on interpreting people's subconscious movements and "body language" to reveal what they were thinking

172 Princess Sophie of Prussia, third daughter of Empress Frederick

173 Prince Henry of Prussia (1862–1929), m Princess Irène of Hesse (1866–1953)

174 Reputedly a copy of the Marienburg, near Nordstemmen in Hanover

175 RA VIC/MAIN/Z/455/173, note

176 Pauline Lucca (1841–1908), operatic soprano, born in Vienna

177 RA GV/PRIV/AA30/40, Princess of Wales to Prince George, 1888: 6,7 September

178 RA GV/PRIV/AA17/38, Prince of Wales to Prince George, 1888: 22 September

179 Alexandra's cousin, Landgrave Frederick William of Hesse-Cassel (1854–88)

180 RA GV/PRIV/AA31/1, Princess of Wales to Prince George, 1888:17 October

181 RA GV/PRIV/AA36/23, Prince George to Princess of Wales, 1888: 29 October

182 Thomas Scott Baldwin (1854–1923), American balloonist, army officer and designer of dirigibles and airships

183 RA GV/PRIV/AA17/44, Prince of Wales to Prince George, 1888: 31 October

184 RA VIC/MAIN/Z/455/180, Princess of Wales to Queen Victoria, 1888: 31 October

185 RA GV/PRIV/AA31/2, Princess of Wales to Prince George, 1888: 21 November

186 Now a Canon of St George's Chapel (1885–1931)

187 RA GV/PRIV/AA6/378, Princess of Wales to JN Dalton, 1888: 5 December

188 King Charles I (1600–49)

189 The Manchesters' daughter, Lady Alice Montagu (1862–1957), married Edward Stanley (1865–1948), later the 17th Earl of Derby

190 Thomas Alva Edison (1847–1931), American inventor and businessman

191 Seat of Lawrence Dundas (1844–1929), 3rd Earl and later 1st Marquess of Zetland, statesman; he m Lady Lilian, née Lumley (1851–1943)

192 Baroness Marie Vetsera (1871–89)

193 It was later suggested that, in a death pact, Rudolph had shot Marie and then turned the gun on himself

194 RA GV/PRIV/AA31/4, Princess of Wales to Prince George, 1889: 18 February

195 Lady Louisa, née Hamilton (1836–1912), courtier, m William Montagu-Douglas-Scott, 6th Duke of Buccleuch (1831–1914)

196 Edward Bootle-Wilbraham (1837–98), 1st Earl of Lathom, courtier and politician

197 RA GV/PRIV/AA31/5, Princess of Wales to Prince George, 1889: 28 February

198 RA GV/PRIV/AA31/6, Princess of Wales to Prince George, 1889: 6 March

199 Johann Sebastian Bach (1685–1750), prominent German composer and musician

200 Otto Hegner (1876–1907), Swiss pianist

201 Edvard Grieg (1843–1907), Norwegian composer and pianist, m his first cousin, Nina, née Hagerup (1845–1935), lyric soprano

202 RA VIC/MAIN/QAD/1889: 9, 10 April; ED seems to have been a life model and, coincidentally, Alexandra would, in 1904, become the first patron of Bedford College, whose original premises in Bedford Square included a very successful art school. This had the first studio in England in which, from 1849, women could work from the life. It was discontinued in 1914 for lack of space after the college moved to new premises in Regent's Park. See Margaret J Tuke, *A History of Bedford College for Women, 1849–1937*, p 87.

203 Princess Louise, Marchioness of Lorne. She had a reputation for trouble-making

204 RA GV/PRIV/AA31/7, Princess of Wales to Prince George, 1889: 7 April

205 John Henry Brodribb (1838–1905) changed his name to Henry Irving; famous actor and actor-manager

206 (Alice) Ellen Terry (1847–1928), later Dame, was a renowned actress

207 RA VIC/MAIN/QVJ/1889: 24–27 April

208 John Ruskin (1819–1900), leading art critic, art patron, artist, philosopher, social thinker and philanthropist

209 Charles Godfrey Leland (1824–1903), American journalist and humourist who became interested in folklore and folk linguistics; he was also a pioneer of art and design and founded the Public School of Industrial Art in Philadelphia

210 Eglantyne Louisa, née Jebb (1845–1925), Irish social reformer and keen supporter of the arts and crafts movement, m her first cousin, Arthur Jebb

211 Mary Seton, née Fraser-Tytler (1849–1938), painter, craftswoman, designer and social reformer, m the distinguished artist, George Frederic Watts (1817–1904)

212 *See International Arts and Crafts*, edited by Karen Livingstone and Linda Parry; essay, *Nature and the Rural Idyll* by Mary Greensted, p 96, V & A Publications, 2005; Melanie Unwin's *A Woman's Work?: Gender and Authorship, the Watts' Chapel and the Home Arts and Industries Association*, unpublished PhD thesis, Royal College of Art, 1997, held in the National Art Library and the RCA

213 Comte and Comtesse de Paris

214 Marking the centenary of the French Revolution

215 Built as the entrance to the Exhibition

216 Louis Pasteur (1822–95), French biologist, microbiologist and chemist who discovered the principles of vaccination, microbial fermentation and pasteurisation

217 William Hay (1801–46), the 18th Earl of Errol, m Lady Elizabeth, née FitzClarence (1801–56)

218 King George III (1738–1820)

219 "Viscount Macduff" was his courtesy title as eldest son of the 5th Earl Fife

220 RA VIC/MAIN/Z/456/28, Lord Fife to Queen Victoria, 1889: 26 June

221 Containing three hags and a Macduff

222 RA VIC/ADDA4/15, Prince of Wales to Empress Frederick, 1889: 27 June

223 RA VIC/ADDA4/16, Prince of Wales to Empress Frederick, 1889: 10 July

224 Naser al-Din Shah Qajar (1831–96), Shah from 1848–96

225 RA VIC/MAIN/Z/456/54, Prince of Wales to Queen Victoria, 1889: 23 July

226 "Duchess of Fife" became Cockney rhyming slang for "wife", hence "My old Duch".

227 RA VIC/ADDA4/17, Prince of Wales to Empress Frederick, 1889: 30 July

228 Known as Alicky

229 Including dinner at Osborne House, a naval review at Spithead and a military review at Aldershot

230 RA GV/PRIV/AA18/5, Prince of Wales to Prince George, 1889: 11 August

231 RA GV/PRIV/AA31/8, Princess of Wales to Prince George, 1889: 23 August

232 RA GV/PRIV/AA31/9, Princess of Wales to Prince George, 1889: 2 September

233 When the German Emperor left after the wedding, he forgot to say goodbye to his sister, the bride. Princess Marie of Greece remembered "the Princess of Wales being extremely put out by this, and calling him back." (*A Romanov Diary*, the autobiography of Grand Duchess George of Russia, p 42)

234 With the de Falbes

Chapter 9

1890–1894

"My darling Eddy"

W

hen his former valet, Macdonald,[1] died on 6 January 1890, the Prince was away. He asked Alexandra to attend the funeral but she had influenza; "My <u>back</u>, head & <u>limbs</u> ache so that I can only just manage to crawl into my sitting room, where I stayed all yesterday & slept most of the day – one <u>must</u> sleep … Oh it is such a bore just when I was so well & this week too when I had such lots to do here."[2] She managed to get to London on the 13th and theatre-visiting started again. Alexandra particularly liked *A Man's Shadow*[3] and *The Gondoliers*, which by 15 March she had seen three times. They saw other shows, generally several times a week, especially during her brother Waldemar's visit, from 8 February. On the 16th the Waleses saw the "Exhibition of the Royal House of Tudor" at the New Gallery in Regent's Street; the next day, Boz, a collie belonging to an American, Mr Harris,[4] performed tricks at Marlborough House. Alexandra visited Louise at 15 Portman Square[5] on her birthday and the Fifes and Waleses later lunched and dined together. After a weekend at Windsor with the Queen, Alexandra and her daughters returned to Sandringham, but had to be back for a drawing room and more theatres and exhibitions. Alexandra attended a service at St Paul's; the next day, 10 March, the anniversary ball was held at Marlborough House. In the evening of the 15th they viewed the electric lighting in the British Museum. After learning how to varnish pictures on the 17th, Alexandra returned Lord Rosebery's[6] "picture of Her Most Gracious Majesty the Queen, 'beautiful for ever' and varnished by my own skilful hands, & I hope to the complete satisfaction of its owner. Picture-cleaner and varnisher – Alexandra."[7]

On the 19th Albert Edward and George left for a German state visit and Alfred of Edinburgh's confirmation at Coburg on the 30th. George, who rather hoped he might eventually marry his cousin, Marie of Edinburgh, stayed behind after his father left for Paris and Cannes on the 31st. Alexandra had been visiting art galleries, dining with the Tecks at White Lodge and receiving Mrs Gladstone. She heard Bach's *St Matthew Passion* at St Paul's on 1 April and went the next day to Alma Tadema's studio and an evening party, where the Hallés and Signor Piatti played and Signor Onofroff[8] gave a "thought-reading" demonstration. April 4th was Good Friday but Alexandra could not attend Bach's *St John Passion*, as planned. She had been anxious about Uncle Hans, who had been dangerously ill but now she herself had "a very nasty painful ulcerated throat with high fever, which at first made Laking think I had <u>scarlet</u> fever!! just think how jolly – but how & where I cld have caught it wld have been a marvel." She felt better after returning to Sandringham on the 10th but had hated having to stay in bed over Easter and commented, archly, that George, whom she wished was there, "seems however quite happy where he is!!! & won't hurry back till the 18th."

Alexandra was feeling even more irritated than usual about Germany. William II had given George the Order of the Black Eagle; "And so my Georgie boy has become a real live <u>filthy blue</u> coated <u>Pikkelhaube German</u> soldier!! Well I never thought to have lived to see <u>that</u>! but never mind, as you say it could not be helped, it was yr misfortune & not yr fault, & everything was better, even <u>my</u> two boys being sacrificed,!!! than Papa being a <u>German Admiral</u> – <u>that</u> I cld not <u>have survived</u>, you wld have had to look for poor old Mother dear at the bottom of the sea the first time he adorned himself with it." She was glad all had gone well and William had been amiable, although the pomp and circumstance had doubtless been to distract England from German ambitions in Africa. George's report was interesting, nevertheless. "Poor boy, what a lot you had to drink." She was glad he had called on "my <u>old Nurse</u> who was so delighted with Papa's & yr visit" but could not understand why Alfred had taken Holy Communion directly after his confirmation "before all those people" and was rather shocked that Papa and especially George had followed, "as with you it must have been a <u>perfect farce</u>, as you have often told me you did not understand a word of German." It was wrong to take part in a religious ceremony without fully understanding it. But "I am glad you found dear little Missy so much improved, & that she paints & draws flowers so well."[9]

Alexandra attended a wedding[10] at St Paul's, Knightsbridge on the 16th, but returned to Sandringham on the 18th, as her husband and son were back. Among the guests arriving on the 26th was Stanley, who gave a lecture on his travels. In London on 1 May, Alexandra opened the "Flower Girls' Guild" in Bayswater and next evening went to St James's Hall, where the Emin Pasha Relief Committee (chaired by the Prince) officially welcomed Stanley, who delivered an address. The couple went to the Albert Hall on the 5th for a special Royal Geographical Society meeting in honour of Stanley, who spoke once again. Travellers' tales always fascinated Alexandra and attending three similar talks perhaps ensured she had heard correctly. They visited the Albert Hall again on the 10th for a concert by 500 Guildhall School of Music students and the Royal Artillery Band, in aid of Morley House Convalescent Home for Working Men, later seeing Lillie Langtry[11] in *Esther Sandroz* at the St James's.

Eddy had returned from hunting and shooting in India, having told Uncle

George; "I don't think people can possibly realise without coming out here how vastly interesting a country this is. I always thought it was a magnificent country but find it far above my expectations, both in the numberless tribes and races, and in the beauty and variety of its scenery." The cavalry force of British and Indian troops at Muridki deeply impressed him, and he was honoured and touched when the 1st Punjab Cavalry regiment was named after him.[12] Eddy enjoyed society, but, at 26, everyone wanted him to settle down; his father and grandmother regretted Alix of Hesse's refusal to consider him as a husband and the list of other princesses was not very encouraging.[13] Ponsonby had heard Eddy was interested in Hélène d'Orléans, who was, as a Roman Catholic, impossible, and "altho' he privately believes the Prince of Wales would not dislike Princess Margaret of Prussia[14] he feels convinced that the Princess would object most strongly and indeed has already done so."[15] Nevertheless the Queen wrote to Eddy, repeating the ban on Hélène and advancing "Mossy's" claims.[16]

The Queen unveiled "The Women's Jubilee Offering": a statue of Prince Albert, at Smith's Lawn in Windsor Great Park on 12 May. On the 19th a despondent George left for the North American and West Indian Station, to command *HMS Thrush*, but Alexandra felt sure he would feel much better once he was well away and, as a commander, would have plenty to do. She hoped "our new remedy[17] which we found advertised in the papers" would combat seasickness. "You must let me know if it really is of any use." They had all been busy since he left. At the "very tiresome" court ball on the 20th, "Papa took in the delightful fat old Queen Isabelle of Spain[18] & I went in with the King of the Belgians, a <u>pretty</u> <u>sight</u> indeed! We all <u>waddled</u> & <u>limped</u> together. You wld have laughed to have seen me sitting with her on the haut pas, she looking like a fat pâté, but she is very amusing & good-natured."[19]

George thanked his mother for her understanding and good advice. They had arranged a "Unicode" for telegrams in connection with a certain event.[20] He had just seen in the papers that "Eddy has been made the Duke of Clarence & Avondale, how funny it sounds. I just got a telegram from him, signed 'Clarence & Avondale' & at first I couldn't make out who it was from. You ought to be proud of your son and heir having such beautiful names." He was feeling much more cheerful, settling down in his new command[21] and had sent his mother a book, to her "surprise & delight, it certainly looks an exciting story & I have already begun it & will read it tomorrow in the train going back to London. How nice of you thinking old Mother dear might like it too!" All the chestnuts, lilacs, laburnum and may at Sandringham were out; she had been unwell in London but had soon recovered. Eddy, who was with her, "is also looking much better now I think & the rest here has done him a lot of good … & he enjoyed his quiet peaceful life so much after all the bustle & travelling he has had for six whole months." She added, "Yes, is it not funny <u>Eddy</u> as <u>Duke</u> of <u>Clarence</u> – I am not sure I appreciate it much."[22] They had to leave next day for Horace Farquhar's[23] dinner party in London, which the Fifes were attending; "it really seems a shame to leave [here] but poor dear little Louise wld never forgive me if I were to throw over the <u>brother-in-law</u>!!!"[24] Her maid Lizzie had come back from a Brighton holiday engaged to the Sandringham telegraph clerk, who had followed her there; Alexandra despaired to think of losing her after sixteen years.[25] The season was busier than ever. *Die Meistersinger* at Covent Garden, "was beautifully given but very long."[26] Ascot week began on the 17th but on the 16th Louise miscarried a son. Alexandra visited her several times and she made a good recovery; "Of course poor Macduff is very unhappy about it all, but he is most sensible & does all he can to cheer her up, and was with her all the time & has never left her for a moment since; he really is most touching in his devotion."[27]

Meanwhile Britain was to establish a protectorate in Zanzibar, a German sphere of influence, in exchange for Heligoland, formerly Danish but British since 1814. Alexandra strongly disapproved, denouncing it as a knuckledown to Germany and most detrimental to Danish interests. The Danish-speaking inhabitants' liberties were protected, but she pitied them; was this sacrifice of British naval interests, for some acres of African land, actually concluded? Ponsonby was not sure. "The Prince of Wales did not say much except that he agreed with the Princess."[28] However, on 15 June it was confirmed that the Sultan of Zanzibar had accepted the Queen's protectorate. During June, Alexandra wrote a memorandum[29] about Heligoland's strategic importance as a British naval base and the danger of it becoming German, which she sent to Lord Rosebery, who, impressed, passed it to Gladstone and others.

The Waleses visited the Cheyne Hospital for Sick and Incurable Children on the 25th, with a state concert later. Fräulein Tschetschen played the violin and Mademoiselle Römer sang before Alexandra on the 28th. On the 30th it was Lady de Ramsay's[30] children's tea, and in Marlborough House gardens on 4 July Alexandra, as President of the National Pension Fund for Nurses, presented certificates to some of the first 1,000 nurses who had joined; she also received purses for the JS Morgan Memorial Benevolent Fund.[31] The following week was particularly busy; on the 7th there was a levee and the Prince and Princess opened Vauxhall Park in Lambeth. On the 8th they laid the foundation stone of the Royal College of Music's new building at South Kensington. On the 9th they were at the Cycling and Athletic Meeting at Paddington Recreation Ground. The next day it was lunch in the Painted Hall at Greenwich and prize-giving to the Royal Hospital School boys. Operas or balls filled the evenings. On the 12th they opened the National Rifle Association's new ranges at Bisley; Alexandra fired the first shot at 500 yards. The Marlborough House garden party was on the 14th and there were more seasonal events. The family attended Mademoiselle Léonie Vauthier's[32] wedding to Edward Johnson, at St George's, Hanover Square on the 26th. Alexandra sat to the sculptor Count Gleichen[33] on 6 June and 27 July; then it was Goodwood, and then Cowes Week in early August. Eddy had been unwell, but was benefiting from Scarborough's sea air and going to Scotland later.[34]

Alexandra was completely exhausted, with headaches;[35] after Cowes, Albert Edward left for Homburg and she, with her daughters, went to Mar Lodge. She apologised to George; "What can I say in self defence for my horrible long silence – which you might easily put down as if I wished to have done with you for ever!" It was "merely the old, old story"; no time and too tired to write. "I think it must all be owing to that horrid Influenza which I had so many times, or age creeping over me,[36] which has succeeded in making the utter idiot of me that I have become." After all, "the Sisters, Papa & Eddy have given you continual news, so that I hope you will hardly have missed my poor little letters. Did you?" Now she had such exciting news she hardly knew where to begin; "Well, what do you think – dear Eddy & sweet lovely Hélène are engaged to each other! tho' still a dead secret, so mind you hold yr tongue! & if you must give vent to yr feelings then write to me about it ... They were all here for a few days, & Eddy by chance through being ill came up here much sooner than he wld have done otherwise ... Well, providence put him here & did the rest! She, dear child, consented for his sake to make that terrible sacrifice of changing her religion, & so they both went together to Grandmama & appealed to her for her help & consent, which she gave being much touched by their confidence in coming to her straight – fancy that! How delighted & happy we were you may easily imagine, but now comes the worst part; the Comte de Paris will not give his consent on those conditions! So there we are at a standstill!! & must have patience & trust to God that it may all come right at the end yet. Poor Eddy & she ... say they will never give each other up, they are very much in love ... & I shld be in utter despair if they were not allowed to marry. She is a perfect angel & so pretty & devoted to Eddy, & the whole of England wld be delighted. I am sure she wld take them all by storm."

In fact, appealing to the Queen had been Alexandra's idea; it had rather startled Eddy, although he was so anxious for the engagement to prosper. He and Hélène had driven off nervously to Balmoral in the carriage, eating their lunch on the way; "You can imagine what a thing to go through", Eddy told George. He expected Grandmama to be furious but, surprisingly, "she was very nice about it and promised to help us as much as possible, which she is now doing." As Alexandra had foreseen, she appreciated their appealing directly to her, apparently without consulting their parents. "This as you know was not quite true", confided Eddy, "but she believed it all and was quite pleased." [37]

It was an utterly doomed relationship; all the sadder because it seemed so perfect. Princess Hélène, whose father was pretender to the French throne in exile, had spent much of her life in England, where she felt at home, while still indubitably French and Roman Catholic. Her family and the Waleses were on friendly terms; Alexandra had already hinted she would have liked one of the daughters to marry one of her sons, but however predictable her preference for

French princesses over German ones, even a light-hearted quip was tempting fate. George had indeed fallen in love with the Roman Catholic Julie Stonor; ironically the Protestants (Alix of Hesse and Marie of Edinburgh), whom the Wales princes would have been happy to marry, rejected them, while the Catholics who loved them were barred. No member of the Royal Family could marry a Catholic without losing all their rights; challenging the Act of Settlement could threaten the foundations of the Protestant Hanoverian dynasty, chosen in preference to its exiled Roman Catholic Stuart cousins, who had a better claim. Alexandra knew this but as she and her siblings had married Anglican, Russian Orthodox, Lutheran and Roman Catholic spouses, the religious question, although important, perhaps seemed less intransigent to her.

Alexandra's response to Eddy's poignant romance contrasts with her attitude to Louise's nuptials the year before, which, to judge merely from the unavailability of any surviving written evidence, seemed lukewarm. She may have worried whether her delicate daughters would ever find understanding and caring husbands, or whether they would in fact be better off at home. She may have been slightly mystified by Louise's devotion to a pleasant but apparently unexciting middle-aged man, but she accepted her decision. Now, at Mar, she reflected; "It is so nice up here in dear Louise's lovely Highland Home where they both seem so happy together. Indeed that is a pleasure to see how well that marriage answered in every way!" Losing the baby had been very sad; "Poor child, it was a great disappointment her having that unfortunate mishap!!! & you had marked what we were to telegraph to each other, either boy or girl! & after all it was neither!" "Better luck next time" George had written.[38] Apologising for her short letter, Alexandra sent it anyway, as she could think of nothing else but "Poor Hélène & Eddy". Maud, with digestive problems, had gone on 23 August to Vichy for treatment, with Fräulein Noedel as companion and courier.[39] The holiday continued pleasantly at Mar but on 11 September Charlotte Knollys had to go to London because her brother Cyprian was terminally ill with a brain tumour; naturally she was allowed time off and had to leave the engagement diary until 16 October.

Albert Edward had returned from Homburg on 5 September. Travelling north three days later, he stayed with the Wilsons at Tranby Croft,[40] during the Doncaster races. On the 11th the party broke up when Mrs Wilson's brother died, and the Prince transferred to the cavalry barracks at York (X Royal Hussars) before leaving for Scotland and arriving at Abergeldie on the 13th to stay with Alexandra. Tranby Croft would have serious repercussions later but meanwhile they led their usual life in Scotland until he left on 2 October for Austria. She stayed until the 10th, after four weeks at Abergeldie, living "entirely on the high road between there & Balmoral,[41] that I really never had a moment to myself. We had on the whole lovely weather, & sometimes very hot & the dear old garden at Abergeldie was too lovely for words, with every kind of sweet scented bright coloured flower & strawberries, gooseberries & every berry under the sun! Altogether it was very nice this year." Eddy was nearly well but very low, as his love-affair had stalled; Alexandra feared the match would never come off "which wld indeed be <u>too great</u> a pity for words, & <u>very</u> hard on both." Hélène's parents refused to let her change her religion in order to marry; the Queen had been very kind but there was little she could do. "God grant all may still come right in time; in the meantime they go on writing the most affectionate letters to each other. We too, as you say, look upon her as a child of ours already." Alexandra, Eddy and Victoria were still in Scotland because the Queen wanted them there for her annual tableaux vivants. "Some were very pretty & Toria looked very nice as Lady Macbeth's Lady-in-Waiting, while Eddy was the King & looked exactly like the old pictures of the Kings of England." There was great excitement at the visit of Queen Elizabeth of Roumania, the poetess, "Carmen Sylva". "She really was charming & most taking & clever – she read some of her poetry to us one evening after dinner."[42]

Alexandra hurried back to London on 10 October to see Maud, generally much better after an unexpectedly long stay of six weeks at Vichy. They and Victoria returned to Sandringham on the 16th, where Maud was soon riding, walking and driving again. The gardener, "poor <u>old Penny</u>[43] has left & is pensioned, one misses his important figure very much I must say, altho' he never wld get any of my poor inexpensive little flowers!!!"[44] On the 27th, the Waleses went to stay at Wynyard Park[45] and saw the railway engine works and workshop at Seaham Harbour as well as Lord Londonderry's 2nd Division Artillery Volunteers. On 2 November Alexandra went to Durham Cathedral. They planted trees and returned to London on the 3rd, seeing French plays at St James's Theatre later. By the 7th they were all at Sandringham. On Albert Edward's birthday, a Sunday, the enlarged Sandringham Church was reopened. Guests arrived and the county ball was held on the 14th. Unfortunately, Maud "cut a voluntary"[46] out hunting on the 15th, as her horse shied and she was unprepared. "She was rather stunned at the time & has kept quiet since, but is really not much the worse", her father wrote.[47] Eddy had gone to Berlin on the 15th for a cousin's wedding[48] but his own prospects were abysmal. George told Alexandra that the Queen had written "a great deal about poor Eddy, everything seems to be as bad as can be; the only thing to be done now, as the Comte de Paris will not give his consent, is for them to wait until Hélène comes of age[49] & then nobody can prevent her changing her religion & then they can marry, only of course it will be horrible for them to wait all this time. I am afraid poor Eddy must be very wretched about it all but I don't know much as he has not written to me for over three months. Grandmama also appears to be very anxious for both of us to marry as soon as possible, I am in no hurry at all & I told her that I thought it was very bad for men to marry too young, don't you agree with me."[50] They visited Castle Rising, Melton Constable, Crichel and finally Windsor for the mausoleum service before returning to London, where Alexandra spent three days shopping. They were all back at Sandringham by the 22nd; Alexandra prepared the presents on the 23rd and the Christmas guests arrived the next day. On the 31st there was skating and ice hockey all day long.

1891 began with heavy snow and the Prince went shooting briefly at Wretham Hall.[51] Eddy went to Osborne on 2 January for Henry of Battenberg's ball at Northwood, celebrating his governorship of Carisbrooke Castle[52] but returned for his birthday and the amusing play, *A Pair of Spectacles* by Hare's Company.[53] Ironically, Alexandra's eye became inflamed and she consulted Mr Critchett[54] on the 16th. The best news, which she told George on the 15th, was that "dear Louise … is again <u>expecting</u>! Thank God! & this time we hope all will be right as she is taking extra care of herself, poor child, & does exactly what the Doctors tell her. We are all delighted about it, & thank God she is really very well on the whole. Mind & not tell Sisters anything about this as they of course know nothing."[55] She felt guilty for not writing sooner "but you better than anybody know <u>how</u> difficult it is for me to find a quiet moment, particularly when we have the house full, and at <u>Xmas</u> time & up to New Year; it really is too much for me, & this year I seemed to have more to do than ever, & quite collapsed at the end, as unfortunately during my visit to Crichel I got one of my bad throats … and <u>Windsor</u> certainly did not improve it, on the contrary I thought one night I shld have died, as I cld neither swallow nor speak, on top of that I caught a bad cold with which I had to drag myself about to do everything for Xmas etc." The girls had enjoyed skating and hockey; everyone skated because the heavy snow prevented shooting. Unluckily Charlotte fell, was concussed, developed pleurisy and was quite ill.

Alexandra commented, "so Grandmama has told you all about poor Eddy's affairs up to date. Yes it is <u>sad indeed</u> – but not quite as has been represented to you, as the poor Comte de Paris is as anxious about it as we are, but simply cannot sanction her changing her religion, but now the dear <u>girl herself</u> has put the real stumbling block in the way by going all the way to Rome to see the Pope![56] who of course cld not advise her to change, on the contrary has pointed out to her the wickedness of such a step from the Catholic point of view." All they could do now was "to wait & see what time can do for us & trust <u>to God</u> to help us. In the meantime they go on corresponding & loving each other from a <u>distance</u> and strange to say her Parents have not yet put a stop to it, which looks as if they also hope for the best." The Queen thought George should marry and get an heir, "but I quite agree with you it certainly wld be <u>too soon</u> in every way!! particularly as the bride elect is not in long petticoats yet!!![57] *Entre nous*, talking about <u>her</u>![58] it is a pity those Children shld be entirely brought up as Germans.

Last time I saw them they spoke with a very strong foreign accent, which I think is a great pity, as after all they are English." Barings Bank's acute recession was very sad; "Poor John[59] was here last week, & he bears it wonderfully well, but it must be a terrible comedown for them all." Sir Edgar Boehm, the sculptor, had died; "an irreparable loss to art."[60] The sculptor, Princess Louise, a close friend, had been there at the time and it had been a great shock.

On the 31st the New English Opera House opened with the first performance of Sullivan's new opera, *Ivanhoe*, in the Waleses presence; "The music is really very fine & most beautifully put on the stage."[61] Alexandra attended a Monday Popular Concert on 2 February, returning to Sandringham the next day. More guests, including Sullivan, came on the 6th; after they had left, Alexandra stayed mostly at Sandringham until 3 March, when she and the girls went to London for the first drawing room, a horse show and other functions, returning to Norfolk on the 14th for a week. Meanwhile, perhaps because of illnesses, ailments and Charlotte's accident, from which she was still recovering, Alexandra's thoughts turned to first aid and Dr Manby[62] held a course of lectures at the local school. She told George; "the reason I have had <u>so</u> little time to myself this winter was principally poor Charlotte's <u>long</u> illness, which Sisters I am sure have told you about and who I nursed entirely myself, which naturally took up a great deal of my time, & before that we had so <u>many visitors</u>[63] this winter <u>continually</u> ... & then I managed to get an Inflammation in one of my eyes,[64] which prevented my doing anything for a time!" The six "ambulance classes", held from 20 March to 18 April were a new interest; "We have had a nice tho' very busy little time here now & we have all attended classes & lectures on First Aid – St John's Ambulance Society, & passed our examination, thank goodness, which was <u>alarming</u>. You ought to have the same on board yr Thrush for yr Men & yr self, it is so useful & most interesting."[65] She had achieved the highest marks, noted Charlotte, who fully appreciated her nursing skills.[66]

Tranby Croft had become notorious. They had been playing baccarat[67] and one guest, Sir William Gordon Cumming,[68] had cheated. The others made him promise not to play cards again, but news had leaked out. George had asked his mother about "that <u>horrid Cumming</u> business you read about in the papers. You were quite right to think that as usual, Papa, through his good nature, was dragged into it & made to suffer – for trying to save, with the others together, this worthless creature, who since then has behaved <u>too abominably</u> to him & all. As Papa has, I know, himself also written, I won't repeat all but merely say <u>what</u> a <u>terrible worry</u> & bother & anxiety it has been to us both, and that poor Papa has been <u>quite ill</u> from it all & made me very anxious & unhappy and even <u>now</u> he is <u>not</u> himself yet – looks very depressed and out of sorts & cannot shake off the cold he has had on his chest. The <u>beastly</u> trial was to have come on <u>today</u> when Papa & all the other unfortunate people who <u>were present</u> on the occasion when that <u>brute</u> cheated were summoned from far & near, & now at the <u>last</u> moment it has been put off for <u>another</u> <u>Month</u>". This was a terrible nuisance and made everything very awkward for the rest of the season. "Is it <u>not too</u> bad; but enough about this beastly thing – and that vile <u>Snob</u> I never cld bear & always thought him false & sneaky & conceited & full of himself beyond words."[69] Albert Edward had not gone abroad as usual and told George; "No wonder you are surprised at the accounts you have read about Sir WG C & the outrageous way in wh he has done his utmost to mix my name up in the matter in endeavouring to cloak his iniquities ... The whole thing has caused me the most serious annoyance & vexation & that is one of the reasons why I thought it best not to go abroad, not knowing what might turn up."[70] Later he noted; "Tomorrow I go to ... Town as I am afraid the G Cumming Trial comes on at the end of the week, & I fear I shall have to appear as a witness wh is a great bore."[71] The trial's postponement was very regrettable.[72]

George's future was again under review; "Well & now about yr matrimonial prospects!!! ha ha ha!" wrote Alexandra. "You are <u>quite</u> right to think Grandmama has gone mad on the subject; it <u>is too</u> ridiculous & it will be a very bad plan both for you in yr position & the girl being a <u>perfect baby</u> yet, altho' Aunt Marie, begging her pardon, does <u>all</u> she can to make her <u>old</u> <u>before</u> <u>her</u> <u>time</u>, which I think the greatest mistake & <u>pity</u> in the world, which I know you think also and what do you say [to] Aunt Marie having <u>hurried</u> on the <u>two girls'</u> confirmation, & in <u>Germany</u> too, so that now they won't <u>even know</u> that they have <u>ever been</u> English, particularly as they have been confirmed in the <u>German</u> <u>Church</u> which was quite a different matter for their brother, the <u>heir</u> of Coburg!!! Even Aunt Vicky was furious about it & wondered how Alfred could allow it, and now Marie's ambition is to bring them <u>out</u> at once." That and their German accent were such a pity. Eddy's prospects were no brighter, although he and Hélène were still in love. Poor Beck, Sandringham's agent for 25 years, had died and was much missed. Alexandra was looking forward to being a grandmother very soon and would send a coded message when the time came. Charlotte was much better although "her head is still very weak" and her little niece, Baba, had been to Sandringham. "Such a little tootsums – calls me <u>Tiny</u> <u>Mama</u>." Victoria had photographed them together and Alexandra sent "two funny ... books for you, some little photo's I took & a tiny little pocket prayer book".[73] She had begun taking photographs and decided to have her snapshots used as decorations on a china tea service, made by Brown-Westhead, Moore & Co., of Cauldon Place, Hanley, as "Cauldon Ware". It was designed by Mortlock's Ltd, one of the principal London china dealers, who sold it to her from their pottery galleries in Oxford Street and Orchard Street.[74]

Joining her husband in London, Alexandra started visiting Louise at Sheen almost daily, while also attending operas between 21 April and 16 May; *Rigoletto*, *Romeo and Juliet* (three times), *Lohengrin*, *Faust* (twice), *Le Prophête*, *The Gondoliers*, *Mefistofele* (twice), *Tannhäuser*, *The Corsican Brothers* and *L'Enfant*

Prodigue. After a late night at *Faust* on the 16th, she was awoken "at <u>3 am</u> by a light being held in my eyes & a note thrust into my hand, from Macduff dated <u>12</u> o'clock, begging me to come at once! Up I jumped into my bath, into my clothes, & into my carriage, <u>quite</u> by myself, & Osborne drove me down at full gallop & I was there <u>within the hour</u> if you please! – a wonderful feat I consider, & at <u>4</u> o'clock I was by poor Louise's bedside & at 5 <u>thank</u> God I was a happy Grand-Mother & held my little naked grandchild[75] in my arms!! It squeaked like a little sucking pig, but it is such a sweet little thing … Dear Louise & Macduff are delighted with it. I was sorry not to have been able to send you a telegram in <u>our</u> cypher but unfortunately I had not brought yr little book with me. I sat down after all was well over & she asleep at 7o'clock & wrote all my telegrams & letters till 10 when I collapsed & was ready to drop, so laid down for 2 hours & had a sleep. By 2 o'clock Papa & Sisters & Eddy arrived to inspect the Infant, & dear little Louise showed it them herself & they were all delighted with it. I must say it looks just like all of you – a nice small child weighing 7 lbs. How funny it will seem to you seeing <u>Louise's</u> daughter". It was quite extraordinary, but she was absolutely thrilled to be "an 'Old Granny' ha ha ha!! and a real <u>rum'n too</u>!"[76]

The perennial problem of William II had sprung up again; he disapproved of his sister Sophie converting to Greek Orthodoxy. It was none of his business, but "that brute has forbidden her to enter Prussia for 3 years, as a punishment, when he says she can think matters over! Grandmama & poor Aunt Vicky are furious with him but alas all the same we shall have to receive him here next month & Madame[77] too!! which will be an awful bore." Poor Eddy's hopes had been crushed; Hélène had sadly ended the engagement, saying she could never change her religion now. "It is indeed <u>too</u> sad & that both their lives shld be made miserable for such a reason … To me too it is a <u>horrible grief</u> I own as she wld have made the most perfect wife for Eddy in every way & they were so fond of each other." He had declared he would not give her up, but it was all no use.[78] The Gordon Cumming trial was "not yet decided, tho' I suppose he is doomed, poor man. It is a horrible thing & scandal."[79] The Prince, in court on six days, was cross-examined by Sir C Russell[80] on 1 June. "How it will end it is impossible to say, but I expect it will go on two days longer. To everybody it will be a great blessing when it is over"[81] he wrote. It finally ended on the 9th, in favour of the defendants; "This has been a great relief to my mind, after the spiteful way in wh the Solicitor General (Sir E Clarke)[82] attacked me. The Newspapers in their articles (many of them) have been very unpleasant & spiteful but I must 'grin & bear it' as at any rate I have the implicit conviction that I have acted perfectly straightforwardly & honourably in the matter. Thank God! the Army & Society are now well rid of such a d-d blackguard" who compounded his infamy by immediately marrying a young American heiress.[83]

Meanwhile Alexandra continued visiting Louise and fulfilling engagements, such as opening the HAIA's Exhibition at the Albert Hall on 2 June, attending

Lady de Grey's afternoon musical party on the 5th and watching a French fencing display at Marlborough House next day. Opera still figured strongly, and on the 8th the Ascot party went to St Leonard's Hill, after a very stressful time. The Prince received "a tremendous ovation fr the public" when his horse, "The Imp" won the Ascot High Weight Plate, "wh was most gratifying especially after the way the Papers have abused & vilified me after the Cumming Trial". The couple returned on the 15th and later saw *Mariage Blanc* at the Royalty. On the 16th they bade farewell to the Fifes, who were going to Brighton, and later attended the Tecks' silver wedding garden party at White Lodge. On the 17th, Christian Victor,[84] "Christle", just back from military duties, lunched at Marlborough House, "looking very well, lost a stone in weight, & has been under fire in two separate actions."[85] On 20 June Victoria, Maud and their parents went to Eastbourne, where Alexandra opened the new wing of All Saints' Children's Convalescent Home. They all lunched at Compton Place, where the princesses stayed for two days while the Prince returned to London. News that George may have heard with mixed feelings was that Julie Stonor was engaged to the Marquis d'Hautpoul,[86] a widower with a little boy of six, whom she had met while in Egypt for her health.[87] They were married on 18 July.

The Fifes' daughter, Alexandra, was christened on 29 June in the Chapel Royal, St James's; the Queen, as godmother, came from Windsor to hold her but went straight back afterwards without partaking of the large lunch at Marlborough House.[88] George's ship was due shortly, but meanwhile there were more balls, operas and festivities. Alexandra saw *L'Enfant Prodigue* for the fourth time on the 30th. On 4 July the German imperial couple arrived, staying at Windsor, where the Wales family visited them. On the 5th the Christians celebrated their silver wedding; the next day their daughter, Louise, married Aribert of Anhalt[89] in St George's Chapel. A state banquet at Windsor followed on the 7th, then an opera gala at Covent Garden. On the 9th there was lunch at Lord Londonderry's house, "to meet the Emperor and Empress" but Alexandra was too tired to attend the evening performance at the Albert Hall. After luncheon at the Guildhall and a state ball on the 10th, the Germans finally left on the 13th and the Waleses and their daughters went to Newmarket for three days. More official functions, operas and balls followed; Alexandra presented certificates to 600 Pension Fund nurses on the 25th. After a weekend at Luton Hoo the couple went to Goodwood, happy that George, on *Thrush* had arrived a week early; he joined them at Cowes on 1 August. As usual, they enjoyed sailing, trips and visiting Osborne; unfortunately Mr Tyrwhitt,[90] who was with them, became ill and was moved to Portsmouth, where he died on the 9th. Albert Edward went to London on the 10th and Alexandra enjoyed cruising about in torpedo boats, visiting Porchester Castle and touring *HMS Victory*. They left on the 17th and on the 19th Alexandra, her daughters and son-in-law left for Denmark, arriving on the 22nd, while Albert Edward went to Homburg for his cure.

The Queen and her son had been discussing Eddy's future. Apart from Denmark, he and his brother had really only ever been to English-speaking colonies; lacking fluent French and German, they were in danger of becoming very exclusively English. "To be 'insular' for a private individual is a disadvantage but, for a Prince, it is in these days a real misfortune" she stated.[91] They, particularly Eddy, needed to travel widely in Europe, not just to courts and capitals. Albert Edward, while not disagreeing, still felt that being English would make his sons popular at home. The couple had thought carefully and anxiously about Eddy's education and future, especially "the difficulty in rousing him". "A good sensible Wife, with some considerable character is what he needs most, but where is she to be found?"[92] The Queen insisted that, while "one can never be too fond of one's Country, a Prince ought to be cosmopolitan, ought to have seen with his own eyes, the difference in other countries to his own." The lack of this had made William II "what he is".[93]

If Prince Eddy had lived long enough to broaden his abilities and interests, he might not have disappointed his relatives. He was maturing slowly as, in some ways, his father had; he had been set back by serious illness in 1877, and his mother thought the Indian trip had affected his health. He was peace-loving and good-natured like his Danish relatives. Albert Edward, while loving them all dearly, was frequently irritated by the indecisiveness and easy-going attitudes at the Danish Court, which he could recognise all too clearly in his son, just as Alexandra's affection for Eddy would have been increased by the likeness. Eddy enjoyed amusement[94] but had impressed Sir John Pope-Hennessy in Hong Kong by his wide knowledge in January 1882, and was fascinated by India; he would have benefited from all kinds of cultural influences and gained confidence, if there had been time, and his emotional stability could have developed and flourished in a happy domestic life.

The Russian family arrived on 24 August, and two days later George arrived from England. The relatives assembled, visited Copenhagen and the theatre and celebrated family anniversaries. Macduff had left on the 29th; his wife and George on 9 September. On the 18th news came that Grand Duchess Paul,[95] in Russia, had had her second child[96] but was seriously ill. When her parents arrived the next day, she was alive but unconscious. Everyone was in a state of dread until, on the 24th, news came that she had died. Sacha, Minny, their two eldest children, and George, Nicholas[97] and Marie of Greece all left next day for Moscow. Alexandra was doing all she could to support her parents but her thoughts were with the family in Russia, "Poor dear Willy & little darling Olga ... Poor Willy said to me 'Oh if she dies I shall go mad' – he loved her so! ... Poor Paul[98] is quite in despair at his cruel and irreparable loss."[99] The Grand Duchess was buried at St Petersburg on the 30th and all those who had left Denmark for the funeral returned on 6 October and tried to resume their tragically-interrupted holiday. The Russians were going home on the 29th and Alexandra had decided that, having been unable to attend Minny and Sacha's marriage in 1866, she would be there for their silver wedding instead.[100] Telling her husband of her plans, she embarked with her daughters and other relatives on *Polar Star*, arriving at the Russian frontier on the 31st. Travelling all day and the next night by train, she heard there had been a serious fire at Sandringham, destroying fourteen rooms and damaging twelve more. Albert Edward had wanted to surprise her by altering the flower-beds in the gardens, but he had been somewhat pre-empted.[101]

The area affected included the girls' former schoolroom,[102] their bedroom and rooms used by governesses, dressers, housemaids and Charlotte Knollys. The house was fully insured, but this would not compensate for the loss of precious possessions. The young princesses' "little things" were all burned or damaged. Charlotte had lost her late parents' valuable books, drawings and pictures.[103] All the rooms on the floor beneath had been badly damaged by water. But, as Sir Dighton Probyn told the Queen, "Notwithstanding all this, the Prince of Wales, with his usual resolution and determination to carry out any plan he has ordered, still says that his party will come here on Saturday next. It seems impossible, but one should not allow (the Prince always thinks) that anything is impossible, so the order has gone forth and night & day till Saturday, all will endeavour to do their utmost to carry out the Prince's wishes, and get the house ready for the guests. The walls of course cannot be papered, nor the walls of those bedrooms damaged by water."[104] Thus grimly Albert Edward prepared to celebrate his 50th birthday and he informed the Queen of his arrival at Sandringham, "with Eddy, George, Louise, Macduff and Baby – found house comfortable and tidy."[105] Far away in Russia, Alexandra was "in despair about dreadful fire at S cannot conceive the cause."[106]

It seems, understandably in view of events, that no further letters between the Waleses and George were written, or kept, until May and June 1892. Alexandra's Engagement Diary for 1891 (the Prince's has not survived) notes that they arrived in the Crimea on 3 November and she saw churches, war cemeteries and battlefields at Sevastopol. Reaching Livadia on the 4th, she visited other nearby villas, including Massandra, Aloupka and Orianda; it was a beautiful spot, with magnificent scenery. The silver wedding day was celebrated with a Te Deum at midday on the 9th. It was also Albert Edward's birthday and the couple's thoughts were doubtless with each other. On the 11th Alexandra visited a Tartar village and had coffee in one of the houses. She had told her husband she expected to stay until the 19th and then come home;[107] meanwhile she enjoyed sightseeing. This was shattered on the 15th by a telegram reporting that George had typhoid fever. He had become ill after returning to Marlborough House, relatively mildly, but there was still cause for anxiety and, leaving as soon as she could, on the 17th, Alexandra raced across Europe, travelling day and night, but could not get home until 11.30 am on the 22nd. Reassuring herself about George's condition, she later went to church. The illness took its course and George slowly began to recover. Christmas at Sandringham was impossible but life went on fairly normally at Marlborough House; Alexandra of course looked after her son but still managed some visits, exhibitions and *Cavalleria Rusticana* twice. On the 24th the Prince went to Luton Hoo for a few days. Eddy's future had been settled and Albert Edward assured the Queen that he would propose to Princess May of Teck, "but we thought it best '*de ne pas brusqué les choses*' & as she is coming to us with her Parents after Xmas to Sandringham, everything will I am sure be satisfactorily settled then."[108]

They wanted to protect Hélène; she and her family were going away in mid-December and would be far off when the news was announced. But on 3 December Eddy was at Luton Hoo for a ball; so, it happened, were May and her mother. He proposed to May and she accepted him. "What joy is this that after all these years our dear children shld be united, & what I hope will be to their mutual happiness & a blessing for the Country!" Alexandra told her cousin, "I do pity you with all my heart losing yr <u>May</u>, yr right hand, yr all, but still you keep her near you! I do hope to see you all on <u>Monday</u>! that I may give my future daughter-in-law my blessing."[109] She told May that she was "so delighted at the good news, & trust that you & Eddy may have a long & happy life together in store. You may be sure that you will always find a true friend in me."[110] The Queen expressed "joy & thankfulness at our darling Eddy's engagement to dear May Teck, which he announced to me this evening, on our return from Farnborough. May God bless the dear young people who have, I fully believe, every prospect of being happy, both being very good, unselfish, & having a strong sense of duty." She would announce her assent at the Privy Council meeting on the 12th.[111]

Victoria, who had kept up a cousinly correspondence with May since at least 1883, wrote to congratulate her. "I must just send you a few lines to tell you how happy I am to think you are engaged to dear Eddy. It does indeed seem like a dream to think you will now be our sister! a <u>dearer</u> one we certainly could not wish for."[112] There were other thoughts in her mind but she was doing her best to focus on her affection for May. Alexandra told the Queen; "<u>This time</u>! I do hope that dear Eddy has found the <u>right</u> <u>Bride</u> at last and that nothing will prevent him & dear May from spending a very happy future together, a blessing to themselves & the whole Country, which I know will rejoice at this marriage! & I only wish it cld have been some years ago when <u>I</u> <u>first mentioned</u> it, & so have spared the sad tragedy & blighted life of that sweet dear Hélène." They all knew and loved May; she would be "one of us at once, and the fact of her being English will make all the difference & carry the whole Nation with them, particularly as dear May has always been one of the most popular members of the family."[113] It looks as though George was right about his mother's opinion of English marriages in 1886. While she was fond of the French princesses and may also have considered her Greek nieces, Alexandra knew well that an English match would be the most popular, certainly more than a German one, and an English bride would not have to leave her own country or have the conflicted loyalties of which she herself was only too aware. There was general satisfaction, the Queen came to tea on 7 December and the future looked bright. Nevertheless there was private sadness; Eddy, although willing to do his duty, could not forget Hélène and his mother and sisters understood how he felt. London was shrouded in dense fog as the family celebrated Christmas Day; the Chapel Royal in the morning, Westminster Abbey in the afternoon and dinner with the Fifes. As George was clearly recovering, they decided to go to Sandringham, where enough rooms were habitable and accordingly did so on the 30th, at the end of a very difficult year.

Prince Victor of Hohenlohe-Langenburg's[114] funeral took place in London on a cold and chilly 3 January 1892, attended by Albert Edward and Eddy, who returned to Sandringham the next day with guests, including the Teck family, Uncle George, Major Arthur Davidson[115] and Oliver Montagu. Victoria had influenza and on the 7th Eddy succumbed, only coming down in the afternoon of 8th to see his birthday presents. The next day he had inflammation of the lungs. Laking was called and, as Eddy's condition rapidly deteriorated, Dr Broadbent,[116] Sister Victoria and Nurse Ward arrived. He was delirious, talking French and calling "Hélène! Hélène!" Charlotte Knollys told the Queen; "The Prince & Princess are, thank God, not ill themselves but dreadfully overcome with the deepest anxiety & sorrow & are in utter despair at the idea of what <u>may</u> be before them ... the gloom & sadness of the whole house ... puts me so in mind of that fearful time when the Prince was so ill, but he was spared to us then & we must trust & hope that this precious life will be so also."[117] It was not to be; Eddy died at 9.10am on 14 January and at 11pm the rectors of Sandringham and Wolferton conducted a service in his room.

Albert Edward told his mother; "Poor dear Alix is well in health, but terribly restless & cries all day poor thing. In fact we feel even more miserable today than we did yesterday, if it is possible."[118] May wrote; "Darling Aunt Alix never left Him a moment and when, a few minutes before the end, she turned to Dr Laking & said 'Can you do nothing more to save him?' & he shook his head, the despairing look on her face was the most heart-rending thing I have ever seen."[119] Eddy's parents followed his coffin to Sandringham Church at 11pm on the 15th. Alexandra told the Queen on the 17th; "the pain is too awful for words and the loss of my darling Eddy, my first born, I shall never get over ... Today we all took the Holy Sacrament with him still near us, God help us on, His will be done! poor darling May, my heart bleeds for her too."[120] Services continued for five days; Alexandra went to church twice on the 19th. On the 20th a gun carriage took the coffin to the station and it was conveyed in a violet velvet-lined compartment to Windsor, with the family, May and suite. Oliver Montagu had written to George, just before going to All Saints', which, only three Sundays before, Eddy had attended. London was like a city of the dead, with empty theatres and everyone in a state of shock. There was only one topic of conversation and he was astonished that "amongst a cold, undemonstrative people as ours is, there could have been anything like the extraordinary sympathy shown by all classes". There was deep regret at there being no procession through London, as millions would have turned out in support. Montagu would always be grateful "to your Papa & Mama for letting me come down last Friday, & I shall never forget all your kindnesses to me when there, when perhaps you would all sooner have been left alone in your grief." Urging George to take great care of himself, he prayed "God bless & preserve you all, & may He give you that comfort in this terrible hour, that the world cannot give, & may He give you all strength to bear the fearful strain that has been so suddenly & under such sad circumstances forced upon you." Don't dream of answering this, he concluded, with dutiful messages from "your faithful friend."[121]

It was cold, there were infections about and the Waleses feared the 72-year-old Queen would endanger her health if she left Osborne's milder climate for the funeral at Windsor. In fact she was feeling perfectly well but was anxious that they should not exhaust themselves; she would, reluctantly, stay away but would be consoled if Alexandra did not go either, as the strain on her would be so great.[122] But Alexandra wanted to arrange the music herself and, as Albert Edward told his mother; "Alix is perfectly able to undergo whatever she feels it is her duty as a mother to go through. You wish my sisters should attend. We perfectly understand and appreciate. Alix only hopes our portion of the Royal Closet may be reserved for her and the girls."[123] Alexandra added; "I feel I cannot stay away. My darling Eddy would have wished me to take him to his last resting place, so I shall hide upon the staircase in a corner, unknown to the world."[124] On the 20th she waited until the funeral cortège had left the castle, and drove unobserved via the Slopes to the Deanery, from where Harry Stonor accompanied her to the Queen's Closet.[125] When St George's Chapel had cleared after the service, she went down into the quire with her daughters, Mary Teck and May, for a last close look at the coffin before, to the music of the *Dead March* in Saul and accompanied by his father, Eddy was taken to the Albert Memorial Chapel. Alexandra then returned privately to the castle, but Sir Francis Knollys feared "her really sad time is now about to come and ... she will feel her loss more and more."[126] The family, including her brother Frederick, stayed at Windsor, visiting the chapel again on the 21st. The Christians came to lunch; Helena saw that Albert Edward was "very brave & does his best but his heart is well-nigh broken. He said to me, 'I am becoming like a stone'". Alexandra looked very tired and sad but seemed to find comfort in talking about Eddy; George was miserable and they all kept referring to Eddy as if he were still alive.[127] After more services, they visited the chapel on the 23rd before returning to Sandringham where, the next day, Canon Fleming preached a funeral sermon. "It is I know of no use repining & we must bow to the will of One who does all for the best – still such calamities embitter one's life, which at the best is full of sorrows & worries"[128] wrote the Prince to his mother.

Eddy's sisters had all written affectionately to Hélène. Maud wrote, "you were really the one he loved. And now he is yours still and nobody can take him away from you." Victoria wrote, "Do you know that as I watched them carrying him into the very same church where a month later he was to be married, I felt I could bear this indeed ten thousand times more than that he should belong to another but you! ... He was meant for you." Louise wrote, "God had been merciful and done all for the best instead of him belonging to another ... yours in life, he is yours in death." They and their mother knew the truth; "that he was fond of M, but you are the one he loved, & he told me so, & wore your little coin always, & has it on even now."[129] Their misery was heightened by romantic feelings about doomed love, but May was in a very awkward position. She had only been engaged for a month and, despite mutual affection, must have known of Eddy's feelings about Hélène. Being bereaved was sad enough but sensing one had only been second best was rather demeaning, especially for a shy person like May. How were they all to regard her now? As Eddy's fiancée, she had been kindly welcomed into the family, whom she had known all her life. The girls liked her well enough but their interests were not hers[130] and for them she was not quite as *sympathique* as Hélène. However, Alexandra wrote, "as you say, our trial seems to get worse & harder to bear every day. The blank is too awful & every moment I expect the Dear One to come in, or to hear his dear voice calling me & then I realize with the sharpest pain that he has gone for ever & that we shall never see him again on earth!" As "a poor old broken-hearted Mother who clung to her Firstborn!!" she chided herself for selfishness; "Indeed you, my sweet May are never out of my thoughts & I mourn for the loss <u>you have</u> sustained, who only learnt to love him! to lose him so soon for ever! We all do miss you here so much & hope to see more of you."[131] The other person with whom May could grieve was George; they had always been friends.

From Sandringham, Alexandra told the Queen; "It was a great consolation and comfort to us to have those beautiful touching services both in the lovely Memorial Chapel & in St George's itself, & I cannot tell you how much those <u>angel voices</u> soothed my broken wounded spirit ... It is <u>too</u> kind & touching in you, dearest Mama, to say that you wld help me to have him near us here but as he, the <u>dear</u> one, now lies so <u>peacefully</u> in that lovely bright Memorial Chapel and Bertie seems to wish him to be left there, I must not be selfish, & leave him to <u>rest there in perfect peace</u>! where I can go & see him occasionally ... Poor dear

May bears up wonderfully in her trying & sore affliction & clings very much to us still … It has been a <u>great</u> tho' sad comfort to us to come back here among the scenes of his happy childhood, his alas! too short life & his heart-rending last moments! I continually fancy I hear his dear voice calling me 'Ma' as he did for fun so often. Oh it is a terrible grief to miss his daily presence & all his dear affectionate ways … my dear, <u>dear</u> Eddy – my <u>Firstborn</u>! who first taught me the blessed name of 'Mother.'"[132]

The widowed Princess Victor of Hohenlohe-Langenburg with her daughter Victoria (Valda) Gleichen[133] came to lunch on 25 January. Alexandra's brother left and she remained at Sandringham until 1 February, when the Waleses went to London and, the next day, Osborne; the Queen wanted a quiet talk with them, as there was a lot to say and it would be best to see the Tecks another time.[134] Alexandra drove with her nearly every day until the 9th, when they returned to London. Victoria had a sore throat and Alexandra was restless, with aching limbs, inflamed throat and swollen glands, but her temperature was, if anything, below normal. On the 10th she still felt wretched, although she could swallow more easily. Advised by the doctor to keep quiet and lie down, she tried to recover from the strain of the past two months. On the 11th she looked no better, but Laking thought she was well enough to go to Eastbourne, as arranged.[135] The Duke of Devonshire[136] had lent them Compton Place and the family went there that day, with Lady Knollys and Baba. It was a charming house and the fresh air would do them all good, although it could not mend their grieving hearts.[137] Lord Rosebery arrived on the 13th, still mourning his late wife, Hannah, and, as Alexandra wrote, "Poor man, he looks indeed as if the shadow of death had passed over him & he is very much altered, & miserable. We had a long talk together about all our sorrows."[138]

On the three Sundays they attended church at All Saints' Convalescent Home. Albert Edward had to go to London on the 17th and the 24th but returned; he and Alexandra wanted to be together. The Fifes, Uncle George and Major Davidson arrived on the 20th. Other relatives and friends called and on the 24th, May and her father arrived; 27 February would have been her wedding day. Albert Edward left on the 29th but Alexandra stayed, visiting the Children's Convalescent Hospital on 1 March and perhaps comforted by seeing young patients who were going to recover. She attended services at two other churches the next day before returning to London on the 3rd. There were more visitors; they went to the Albert Memorial Chapel on the 6th and three days later left London, reaching Cap Martin early on the 11th. It had been a profoundly shocking and distressing time, so soon after Grand Duchess Paul's death, the fire at Sandringham and George's serious illness. Just when Eddy's future seemed secure, Fate had snatched him away. What were their thoughts? Had his grief at parting from Hélène lowered his resistance to illness and had he, in effect, died of a broken heart? That would have made his death, if possible, even sadder.

Meanwhile there were walks, drives, excursions, visits and some peace in the South of France; they would not see Marlborough House again until 2 May. Their hotel stood on a cape covered with pine woods, near the sea, with a fine, bracing climate and comforting privacy. However, there was more sadness; Louis IV, Grand Duke of Hesse, died on 13 March.[139]

On their return and after visiting Windsor again, the Prince and his son inspected fire reparations and other works at Sandringham. George stayed and told his mother; "We went all over the house which looks charming, the roof & the rooms upstairs are finished, but of course there is nothing in them yet. And all the other rooms below them are quite dry, your boudoir & the bamboo rooms look exactly the same, & I am sure you will like the bow window in the drawing room, which is built where the conservatory was, & there is so much more room now. They are getting on well with the bachelors' rooms but there is not much to see yet. The Cottage when finished I think will be charming & also the improvements in the grounds round it ... Papa & I went into darling Eddy's room yesterday, it looks just the same & we haven't touched anything, except that the new cupboards are in & I think they will do very well. I must say I agree with you Motherdear in thinking that it would be better to take the bed away."[140] His parents and sisters arrived on 14 May but were back in London again on the 22nd, leaving later and arriving in Denmark on the 24th. George was made Duke of York that day. His father hoped he could get a ship for the summer manoeuvres; it would be popular with the navy and nation, and good for him. Naturally he needed time to recover but Albert Edward thought it would be bad if he gave way to lethargy "& led a life of ease".[141]

Alexandra's parents celebrated their golden wedding on 26 May, but the Waleses, in deep mourning, just went to the thanksgiving service; as it was, Alexandra "was very much affected & at one moment I feared she would break down altogether, it is very painful to her seeing so many people for the first time after all her misery", wrote Charlotte.[142] On the 30th, 132 lunched on board *Polar Star* and 101 had lunch at Fredensborg on 3 June. The next day Albert Edward and George left for Homburg to visit Empress Frederick en route for England. Back in London, Albert Edward told George that, despite Uncle Alfred's delight at the idea of his eldest daughter being considered for George's wife, Aunt Marie had taken it out of his hands and negotiated a marriage for her with Crown Prince Ferdinand of Roumania.[143] Albert Edward had not yet heard from Mama; "evidently the Danish air is not conducive to letter writing!"[144] but by the time he finished his next letter she had contacted him. She was now looking brighter and enjoying her relatives' company; Marie Louise of Cumberland had measles but luckily no one else seemed to have caught it. Alexandra saw the golden wedding presents on display at Copenhagen and took a short trip on *Tsarevna*. On Victoria's birthday there was "*chocolade* & congratulations". Alexandra had only just managed to write to George (on board his new ship,

HMS Melampus) "as naturally I always am with my dear ones & really have not a minute of the day I can call my own. I do write sometimes to Papa at night but that tires me so & prevents my sleeping all night long which is such a bore, particularly as ... such a lot of thoughts will crowd down upon one & I see my darling Eddy ever before me & all his dreadful fatal illness & his last days pass through my mind like a whole panorama. Oh Georgie dear I shall <u>never, never</u> get over that <u>terrible</u> <u>sorrow</u>. How one misses that dear boy and I do not see <u>how</u> this ever can get better or his loss less bitter and I know you too will always feel this. Oh it is indeed a <u>life-long</u> sorrow & a fearful trial to bear! as we ought to! & without a murmur to say 'Thy will be done'." She was feeling better in health and "this dear old place is so bright & cheery & I have a dear little room, which used to be the nursery, with a partition, which makes it look like two rooms, & it is next to Sacha & Minny's so we live all together & Minny & I paint in my room, & now the roses are in full bloom so we have filled it with lovely flowers which makes it look so bright & pretty." She was glad that, on meeting Aunt Marie recently, George had found her just the same "& that Missy seemed to know nothing at all about that tiresome & for us all most disagreeable business, & episode! Evidently she never cared one bit really about you or she wld not now be so happy with her Ferdinand." George and Papa had stayed at Warwick Castle and Alexandra smiled quietly; "So you liked yr visit to Warwick which is such a beautiful place, something like Windsor I have always heard, but what amused me *entre nous* was that neither you nor Papa mentioned Lady Brooke[145] altho' we all know what a beauty she is, but merely described the pigs & how the cows were milked by machinery!! all I can say is '*honi soit qui mal y pense*'!!"[146] Her hurt and fury had evolved into derisive tolerance, now habitual but never fundamentally changing her affection for her husband.

On 10 July Alexandra and her daughters left Denmark, meeting Vicky and hers at Frankfort next day and dining at the station before continuing their journey. They arrived in London on the 12th and, with Albert Edward, went on the 18th to Sandringham, which was looking "very pretty, & Mama is I think pleased with everything inside & outside. The Drawing rooms look very nice now."[147] George was going to study at Heidelberg with Professor Ihne; his mother thought it "<u>quite right</u> & very <u>wise</u> of you at last to have made up yr mind to study <u>German</u> thoroughly, which as well as <u>French</u> ought to be known by everybody. And you know <u>how</u> anxious I have <u>always</u> been for you to keep up yr languages, which you were taught when quite a child." She had been relieved to find him unchanged, having feared at Eastbourne that his "head was a little turned", but made allowances for his frailer state of health and sorrow for his beloved brother. Just how important his affection was is clear in her letter; "You know my Georgie that you are everything to us now, & must give us double affection for the one that has gone before us!" Even for a loving and dutiful son this was quite a heavy burden.

Alexandra planned going to Cowes later, once "William the Great", who unfortunately seemed to be making annual visits, had left. Baba Knollys was at Sandringham "as sweet & dear as ever, enjoying herself immensely & looking the picture of health. She cheers us all up & gives us plenty to do running after [her] but she is such a dear good little child & she often asks after Georgie & hopes to see you soon." Frank Beck,[148] having succeeded his father as agent, was now a father himself and Alexandra was to be the baby's godmother.[149] Signor Corrodi came on 27–29 July to give her painting lessons; she painted all day on the 28th and part of the 29th. She visited everyone on the estate, walked, drove and, on 5 August, fished in the lake, a sport which appealed to her. On the 8th she left for Osborne, drove with the Queen and went sailing, returning to London on the 17th; the next day Albert Edward went to Homburg, from where he suggested George "might on Sunday go to White Lodge to pay Aunt Mary a visit, say for luncheon, if you wrote to propose yourself. I think it would be a good thing to do, & quite natural. Nobody need know anything about it."[150]

On 2 September, Alexandra and her daughters left, reaching Mar Lodge in the pouring rain the next day. Oliver Montagu came to teach her about fishing, from the 5th to the 22nd. Albert Edward arrived on the 15th and Alexandra and the girls went fishing nearly every day, despite continual rain. On 3 October it was "quite atrociously bad, pouring all day long with mixtures of <u>sleet</u> & <u>snow</u> & all the hills around us white, it has quite put a stop to my <u>frantic</u> <u>fishing</u>! Every day for 4 weeks I have been hard at it trying to catch a salmon and am happy to say at last I caught <u>four</u> & one of the biggest of the season, weighed 16½ lbs, so you may imagine <u>my</u> delight! Oliver taught me first how to cast the line & hold the rod, & lately I have been out from morning till night with poor old Stephenson, Cameron & a first rate fisherman, Grant, at Invercauld, as I was so anxious & determined to get <u>one</u>, at any rate." The rest, bracing air and an absorbing occupation had done her good, although she and Victoria had both had toothache. Louise was "beginning again[151] & <u>very</u> sorry for herself! <u>Baby</u> is too sweet now & likes me very much, is beginning to stand & tries to walk & can say some words. We were photographed together <u>she & her Granny</u>, as soon as I get it I will send it to you." She was not sure how long she would stay there; "unfortunately dear old Sandringham is again being pulled to pieces & rebuilt, that we can't go there just yet which is <u>such</u> a pity ... Grandmama thank God is well & walks better again & rides her pony, which is a good thing as it <u>shakes</u> her up a bit." She was amused that George was being linked with Victoria of Schleswig-Holstein; "So the <u>Xtians</u> have been following you about with their lovely Snipe! Well it <u>will</u> be a pleasure to welcome the beauty as yr bride, when may we expect the news?"[152]

The Prince left on 7 October; his wife and daughters on the 13th. It was raining, as Charlotte noted; "having rained 33 days out of the 41 we were at Mar Lodge." They reached home on the 14th and two days later attended Tennyson's funeral in Westminster Abbey. Alexandra wrote; "he will be greatly missed by the Whole Nation, dear old man, I liked him so much personally & he was so very original, do you remember his book or play 'Queen Mary' we read together!! rather <u>strong</u> language we thought!"[153] The Tecks and three elder children dined on the 17th and Alexandra, Victoria and Maud, not unnaturally, had lunch at White Lodge on the 20th. They also visited the Paris couple at Stowe on the 26th; "whom we had not seen since all our sorrow, poor dear Hélène was too sweet & touching for words, & prettier than ever." On the 29th Alexandra was distressed to find the Albert Memorial Chapel "all in a state of untidiness as the workmen had to do something to it, which made it all the more painful. Oh it is all <u>too</u> dreadful."[154] After entertaining the Waldemarias,[155] visiting galleries, driving, walking in Regent's Park and the zoo, Alexandra and the girls finally left for Sandringham on 3 November. The Fifes came several times; there were the usual parties and guests, including the Tecks, May and Frank. Alexandra thanked Dalton for his kind letter and contribution to her birthday present but "You will readily understand <u>what</u> a trying day this was to me, the <u>first</u> without my darling Eddy." But his spirit seemed present, and "I wld not recall him to this world of pain & sorrow."[156] There was more entertaining and field sports until, on the 12th, she, George and Maud came to London, attending the mausoleum service on the 14th; two days later, Alexandra and Maud, with Admiral Stephenson, went to the stores. They returned to Sandringham and Christmas went ahead, although changed forever.

January 1893 was cold and frosty and everyone who could skate did so, Alexandra until the 23rd. The couple and George went to the Albert Memorial Chapel on the 14th, Eddy's first sad anniversary; Victoria and Maud wrote to May to mark the date.[157] Guests arrived over the next fortnight, by which point nine people Albert Edward knew had died. Saddest of all, Oliver Montagu died at Cairo, as they heard on the 24th. Alexandra told George; "it has been a terrible time of anxiety & then misery at losing our dear, dear old friend, who was so much to us for so many years, & whose loss is <u>quite</u> irreparable to <u>me</u> & whom we shall never cease to miss & regret; one cannot realize it yet, it seems impossible that we shall never see his dear face again or hear his cheery voice."[158] His brother[159] came to lunch on the 10th and on the 22nd Alexandra and Maud went to Hinchingbrooke, where Oliver's body lay. They attended the service at Sandringham on the 23rd, the day of the funeral at Brompton, at which the Prince was present.

Thinking continually of May, Alexandra wrote; "I am sure that you also felt yr <u>dear Godpapa's</u> sad death, very much, you had already learnt to appreciate him as one of us, the dear old family friend. Indeed he will be terribly missed by us all."[160] It was a heavy blow for Alexandra, still grieving for Eddy and worrying incessantly about George and his prospects. Many people, the Queen included, thought the perfect solution would be for him to marry his brother's fiancée. Alexandra too could see this; they knew May well, she was Protestant, royal,[161] born and brought up in England. She was rather shy but dutiful, healthy, good-humoured, intelligent and of a serious frame of mind. Alexandra, who had always loved her cousin Mary, was fond of May too. Why should not May, considered ideal for Eddy in his future position, also suit his brother? Logically perhaps, but Alexandra was 'all for love' and knew George was mourning his brother and worrying about his future. He had lost Julie Stonor, been rejected by Marie of Edinburgh and now felt he was being pushed too quickly into something he was not sure about; of course he and May liked each other but did they really want to be together? Indeed, was it fair to expect May simply to exchange one brother for another? Alexandra, determined to secure him some leeway, told him of her conversation with the Queen; George "required a complete change & rest before settling down in life, & that I intended & proposed to take you with me on the Yacht for a short time, & you wd come back fresh & less worried & ready to settle yr own affairs, & I also mentioned that a long engagement was a great mistake under the circumstances & the marriage I thought cld not be till June, as I shld be away on account of Victoria[162] in April & she in Scotland in May, therefore the earliest seemed to me the month of June, & I added that if she were to see you a day or two before our going abroad you cld explain things yourself. This is all I have said & that I hoped with her usual kindness she wld help us now, so you see my Georgie boy I hope that things will be made a little easier for you now, & less irksome, & that in the end it all will be crowned with happiness for you both. I too am worried to death about it, & can so well enter into all yr poor feelings."[163] Alexandra was at her best, decisive, reasonable and eloquent. It was a delicate situation, but a familiar one; Minny had married her dead fiancé's brother, to their mutual happiness. Why not this time?

It is clear that Alexandra did not see May's morganatic heritage as a disadvantage in her union with Eddy or, later, George. The idea that she and her daughters were unkind to May on this count[164] completely contradicts Alexandra's documented opinions and her belief in cultivating a spirit of harmony in the home. The Waleses had initially invited Prince Teck to England at a time when a husband for Princess Mary was being sought, and they offered the couple friendship. The children all played together and Alexandra saw May's potential as a possible daughter-in-law. Morganatic marriages mattered a great deal abroad, but the "unequal" concept was not part of British tradition,[165] although the monarch's necessary permission for any British royal marriage was; for example, Queen Victoria allowed Louise to marry Lord Fife, whose own ancestry would have been regarded as morganatic abroad.

Alexandra congratulated George on making his maiden speech when receiving the Freedom of the Merchant Tailors' Company. "I did pity you so, & it must have been too awful, & I am sure you did not eat much at that dinner." While appreciating the honour, he must have been delighted when it was over. He was going to talk to Grandmama at Osborne; meanwhile Alexandra was "glad you & Papa went to White Lodge & that you found dear May looking well & pretty." Lord Sandwich and Lady Emily Dyke[166] were coming to Sandringham to give her "all the last sad details about our dear, dear Oliver."[167] All went well at Osborne but the newspapers were annoying; "Did you among other announcements see yr self <u>arm in arm</u> (walking in Richmond Park) with poor May!!"[168] On 2 March they went to see Eddy's coffin laid in the marble sarcophagus built by Alfred Gilbert[169] in the Albert Memorial Chapel, and visited Louise at Portman Square afterwards. The Tecks, with May, followed by the Fife's, dined at Marlborough House on two evenings, and on the 4th, Alexandra, George, Victoria and Maud left for *Osborne*, moored at Genoa.

This was Alexandra's first Mediterranean cruise, (although she had already visited Italy and Greece), which was to give respite from the distress of the last eighteen months. Alexandra had always enjoyed sightseeing and the tour began with art galleries, churches and archives. She was interested in the Jesuits' church[170] at Genoa and also "Byron's Cave" at Venere and Shelley's house at Terenze. Meanwhile, in a letter to George, his father reported lunching with the Tecks, when Aunt Mary told him May "was much pleased" with George's letter to her.[171] The holiday continued in Livorno, Pisa and Florence; all the sights as well as two visits to Doney, the chocolate shop. As there was so much to see, Alexandra, unusually, got up at 7am on the 16th. They spent two days on Elba; the Waleses were interested in Napoleon[172] and Alexandra had a collection of items relating to him.[173] The next day it was Rome: St Peter's and its treasures, churches, galleries, studios, the Colosseum and other landmarks. They met the English Consul, Sir Dominic Colnaghi,[174] and a Mr Moriarty demonstrated the phonograph. They visited Corrodi's studio, met the King and Queen of Italy[175] and had an audience with Pope Leo XIII on the 23rd. In Naples, they saw the National Museum and other sights; at Portici on the 25th they drove in carriages for two hours up Mount Vesuvius. After lunch at a hotel they ascended the volcano by train, then walked about and down to where the red hot lava was flowing; Alexandra telegraphed to her husband to say how much she was enjoying it.[176]

Over the following days they saw the blue cave at Capri, an excavation at Pompeii and Sorrento and a troupe of performers played, sang and danced the tarantella for them on the yacht at Castellamare. Back in Naples they visited the museum, lunched at a café, shopped and drove on the Corso. Staying nearby were the Saxe-Meiningens[177] and Princess Aribert of Anhalt. Albert Edward wrote; "What a pleasant surprise to have found Charlotte ... Bernhard was less so. I hope my niece Louie (as she is called) was looking better."[178] Poor Louie's marriage, which she had begun so happily in 1891, was proving difficult. They and Countess Hohenau[179] dined with Alexandra and her party on the 28th, while a Neapolitan band played for them. Visiting several churches, driving to Capodimonte, and moving on to Castellamare, Positano and Amalfi, they started for Sicily. On 31 March, Good Friday, they attended the English Church at Palermo, later visiting the Duc d'Aumale's villa and garden, which he wanted Alexandra to see. She also saw the church and cloisters of Monreale, with wonderful mosaics. The next day they toured Palermo, despite Maud's feverish cold.

At Messina on Easter Sunday, they attended Vespers in the cathedral, and on 3 April a telegram announced the birth of Louise's second daughter, Maud.[180] Albert Edward, at Easton with the Brookes for a few days wished it had been a son but "The Baby is a dear little thing, & the 'Old' Baby is delighted with her & calls her Sister." Macduff was quite content, although Louise would have preferred a boy.[181] It was too rough to land at Taormina, so they moved on to Catania, for the cathedral and monastery of St Niccola and the gardens of Bellini, then steamed through night and day, reaching Corfu late on the 6th. After lunch at the palace, they drove to Mon Repos and the Empress Elizabeth's Villa Achilleion, where she received them the next day. They landed at the new Corinth Canal works on the 9th, taking the train to Athens the next day. There was a Te Deum in the cathedral on 12 April, Greece's "Day of Independence". They went to the Acropolis, lunched at the British Legation, and on the 16th attended a service at the English church; later there was a dinner for 60. George, as the Queen's representative, left for Rome on 17 April for the Italian sovereigns' silver wedding celebrations on the 22nd. Alexandra and the Greek sovereigns accompanied him to the Piraeus, taking steam-launch excursions afterwards. The next day Alexandra received Mademoiselle Tricoupi[182] and visited the English School of Archaeology, going to Phalerum by steam train on the 19th. On the 20th Victoria and Maud visited the Central Museum; Alexandra went to the Piraeus for a steam-launch trip and the next day accompanied Willy and Olga round Salamis and Eleusio Bays. On the 22nd there was an English service at St Paul's Church, and lunch and tea at Tatoii. Alexandra painted all the next day and for part of the following one; she went to Phalerum over two days and was photographed on 27 April. There were family lunches, more trips and on the 30th, dinner at Themistocles'[183] house.

George was much missed, wrote Alexandra, and she was longing to hear all about his visit to Rome. They were going to "cruise about a little longer, which I am certain will do Toria a lot of good, & then come home slowly for Whitsuntide. I shall naturally be very sorry to leave all the dear ones here next Monday or Tuesday but I am only too thankful we came for a bit even & have seen them all, it does one good to meet & exchange thoughts with those one loves." She and Aunt Olga had been "painting away like mad every morning; did you like the little Easter eggs she did all over her letter to you, did not they look nice! Willy & I walk every morning after breakfast in the lovely garden, & talk politics. I do hope things will still come all right about this loan, as it worries poor Uncle Willy dreadfully." Her thoughts were continually with George; "& how I shall pray that the step you are about to take will be for yr mutual happiness!! Indeed it is sad to think that we shall never be able to be together & travel in the same way but yet there is a bond of love between us, that of Mother & Child, which nothing can ever diminish or render less binding, & nothing & nobody can or shall ever come between me & my darling Georgie boy."[184] They left Athens on 2 May, with all the Greek relatives, who dined on *Osborne*. The ship put in to Cerigo on the 3rd, so that Alexandra could send telegrams and on the same day in England Prince George proposed to Princess May of Teck and was accepted.

Alexandra's party had intended to visit Olympia but "the fresh water pipes under the ship burst" so they had to go straight to Malta instead, which she found delightful. "We have been everywhere, Government House ... had tea[185] at that lovely San Antonio, & visited the Cathedral here & at Civita Vecchia, today we have been walking in Town all the morning & are now going to pay the Admiral & his wife a visit & then see other sights!!!" Her letter began more seriously and the change in her writing, tidy and formal, showed a struggle with her emotions: "I got yr news yesterday and you will believe and know with what mixed feelings I read yr telegram. Well all I can say is that I pray God to bless you both and give you both a long and happy life together and that you will make up to dear May all she lost in darling Eddy and that you will be a mutual happiness to each other, a comfort to us and a blessing to the Nation! My thoughts & prayers have never left you and I am longing to hear details about it all and how you made up yr mind so quickly after yr return."[186] Of course she was delighted and was doing her best to welcome the future. They left Malta for Syracuse and Cotrone on the 7th, visiting interesting places on the way. After Brindisi, Spoleto and more sightseeing, they reached Venice in the late afternoon of the 12th; next morning, Alexandra went to St Mark's Place, visited Aunt Frederick[187] and rode in gondolas all day until evening, later ascending the Campanile to see the sunset. The next day it was St Mark's Cathedral, the public gardens and churches, and the equestrian statue of Il Coliogno. On the 15th they climbed the Campanile again and visited churches, the Doge's Palace and the shops. Eventually they left for Milan and then Paris, arriving on the 18th. They saw Mrs Standish and the d'Hautpouls, and attended the salon. They reached London at 5am on the 20th, after exactly eleven weeks' absence and 2,543 miles of travelling in *Osborne*.

Alexandra's hopes for George struggled with sorrow for Eddy, now supplanted privately as well as publicly by his brother; his life seemingly irrelevant and his death more final. However, she did not expect, selfishly, to keep George perpetually by her side and was delighted he was going to marry her beloved cousin's daughter. May had written to her and she had welcomed her back "once more as my dear daughter", wishing her the happy future with George that had been denied her with Eddy; "For my own self I need hardly speak as you know <u>how</u> much I have always loved you and how glad I am that you will still belong to us. And I know too that we two will always understand each other and I hope that my sweet May will always come straight to me for everything."[188] She did achieve a good relationship with May, although the two were inherently different and there would be misunderstandings.

After a service at the Chapel Royal on the 21st, they called on the Fifes and then White Lodge for a family dinner party. The next day the Waleses watched the eighth annual parade of the London Cart Horse Society in Regent's Park's inner circle. The Tecks came to lunch on the 23rd and then Alexandra and her daughters left for Sandringham on the 25th, followed two days later by Albert Edward and George, but by 2 June they were all back in London for Trooping the Colour on the 3rd. Two days later the couple attended a special service marking the restoration of the ancient Priory Church of St Bartholomew the Great in West Smithfield; the next day the Prince laid the memorial stone of the United Services Institution in Whitehall and opened the Naval and Military Bazaar in the Banqueting Room. Alexandra left on the 7th for Balmoral to confer with the Queen and watch the Tableaux Vivants. Travelling overnight on the 10th, she crossed the Tay and Forth Bridges, reached London on the morning of the 11th and dined at White Lodge later. She saw *Carmen* on the 12th, apparently her first opera since Eddy's death, heralding more theatre visits. She gave Luke Fildes[189] four sittings for the household's wedding present picture to George and was also photographed by Lafayette[190] on the 14th. There were more visits to White Lodge and on the 19th a concert at Bridgewater House for the Chapel Royal, St James's' Choir. The Fifes' second daughter was christened on the 22nd at Marlborough House Chapel and the next day Hélène and her parents came to lunch. The Waleses opened Great Ormond Street Children's Hospital's new wing on the 24th and called to congratulate the Mecklenburg-Strelitzes on their golden wedding on the 28th. Later, they attended the unveiling of Louise's statue of the Queen in Kensington Gardens.

On 30 June wedding guests, the King, Queen and Prince Waldemar of Denmark and the Tsesarevitch, arrived but Alexandra did not attend that evening's state ball. Nicholas noted; "Aunt Alix is as sweet and wonderful as ever, but sorrow has left its mark on her; she is always dressed in black. Victoria has got much thinner and unfortunately does not look well; Maud on the other hand has put on weight."[191] The Waleses had earlier opened the National Workmen's Exhibition at the Royal Agricultural Hall, and on 3 July a charity bazaar for the Alexandra Hospital for Children with Hip Disease. The Gala Performance at

Covent Garden on the 4th was of course *Romeo and Juliet;* the next day the Queen was one of 5,000 guests at a garden party at Marlborough House, with a large dinner at Buckingham Palace later. On 6 July, Prince George, Duke of York and Princess Victoria Mary of Teck were married at the Chapel Royal, St James's. After the wedding breakfast at Buckingham Palace, they left for their honeymoon at their new home, York Cottage,[192] Sandringham. In response to George's letter Alexandra replied; "you have still been thinking of yr old Mother-dear, to whom I know you will always remain the same! and that I have gained a daughter as you say instead of losing a son! & indeed I love sweet May so much as she knows well, & I am sure that she will make you as happy as I know my Georgie boy will make her." She was delighted it had all gone off so well but feared they must have been very tired on their arrival at Sandringham, "but I hope you will have plenty of time to get peace & quiet, which you both poor dears were in such need of."[193] Victoria hoped they were well and settling down, in what she described as "the first letter to 'Sister May' & 'Duchess of York'!!!!"[194] Alexandra, although rather weary,[195] had now resumed the social life which mourning had curtailed for 18 months. She visited galleries, fulfilled engagements, called on friends and attended plays and operas; on the 11th, *Cavalleria Rusticana* conducted by the composer, Mascagni.[196] On the 17th she and her mother went to Alfred Gilbert's studio to see his sculpture of Eddy. The next day she, three daughters, parents and brother all left for Sandringham, where she visited the technical school on the 20th. Albert Edward joined them on the 21st and guests arrived. They had tea at York Cottage on the 23rd but by the 25th were all back in London. They visited the South Kensington Museum and the next day, Alexandra took leave of her parents at Tilbury. From 28–31 July she sat again to Luke Fildes. The Yorks arrived at York House[197] on the 28th and she had tea with them; on such occasions she would nearly always walk there, sometimes alone, followed by a private detective. When driving informally she used a plain brougham, with no insignia.[198]

Meanwhile Lord Rosebery told the Queen that "he had an opportunity last night of ascertaining on what he considers the very best authority (though not that of the Prince of Wales himself) that His Royal Highness was entirely opposed to the marriage in question and would never under any circumstances give his sanction to it. Nevertheless Lord Rosebery will hope to have a favourable occasion for discussing the matter with His Royal Highness, in obedience to Your Majesty's wishes."[199] This apparently concerned Victoria or Maud, as they were the only ones over whose marriages the Prince would have such influence. "The very best authority" is likely to have been Alexandra, but the bridegroom's identity is not revealed. Victoria apparently favoured John Baring, later Lord Revelstoke, Eddy's college friend, whom the Wales family liked very much; Maud, many years later, said Victoria had been in love with Lord Revelstoke.[200] However, Baring's Bank's financial problems would have made permission for a royal alliance unlikely, even if John Baring reciprocated Victoria's feelings. Perhaps this was one reason for her ill health and need for a change of air. Maud herself was rather interested in Frank of Teck, who, in the end, proved unreliable. But how could all this have been Lord Rosebery's business? Time would tell.

On 1 August Alexandra and her daughters left to join Albert Edward at Cowes. It was impossible to avoid William but he sailed off on the 6th and they enjoyed socialising, yachting and visiting Osborne House. They returned to London on the 14th, entertaining the Yorks to dinner. Two days later, Alexandra and the girls set off for Norway, on *Osborne*. This cruise perhaps gave Alexandra her first chance of compiling a holiday album of her own paintings and her own and other photographs, enlivened by her own descriptive narrative.[201] It was a "really delightful & pleasant cruise ... The weather has been perfect except two days & we have enjoyed our lovely steams up those beautiful grand old Fjords more than I can say." At Christiania "we have been running about all day long like mad, seen all the sights, which were not much, a very big, not beautiful palace of the King's, from top to bottom, but what really was very interesting was the wonderful old Vikings' ship, which is about 1,100 years old." Victoria had been wonderfully well the whole time, the continual bracing sea air had "done her a lot of good & the quiet rest as well."[202] They left for Denmark the next day and Alexandra could not write again until 4/7 October, as her room had been "a perfect club, & everybody, old, young, big & small come tumbling in at all hours of the day!" She, her mother and Minny sat there in the morning, drawing, painting or working, while "the girls" were next door.[203] On 5 September Uncle William of Glücksburg had died, which had brought back all her misery; "I cannot tell you how dreadful it was to me & recalled all the terrible time when our poor darling Eddy was taken from us. Thank God I still found him alive & he was so pleased to see me and asked after you all ... at last he said 'now I can bear it no longer & I must be left alone' & then said Goodbye & sent his love to everybody, & when we left his room he waved his hand to us." He died later; his funeral was on the 13th and the next day his coffin was laid in the family vault at Roskilde.

Alexandra paid calls and went for walks, although on the 24th there was a gale with thunder, lightning, rain and, the next day, hail. On the 30th she and Minny watched a review at Copenhagen; "It has been rather stormy & rainy of late but not at all cold, quite summer-like still. I shall come home by sea, & pick out a fine day to start on."[204] It improved on 18 October and they finally arrived in London on the 21st. Alexandra sat twice to Fildes on the 26th and the 27th and received Mr Sainton,[205] with his silver point drawings, the next day. On the 30th she and her daughters went to Sandringham. Two days later they heard that General Teesdale,[206] a true friend to the Prince for over 36 years, had died. "Bena" Hardinge came into her first waiting[207] on 3 November and the first house party arrived. Mr Rolfe,[208] helpful as a *cicerone* in Italy, arrived on the 9th; the labourers' dinner was held and Bertram the conjurer performed in the ballroom. On the 19th a fearful three-day gale began, and the willow tree in front of the house was blown down. Alexandra got influenza and could barely look at her birthday presents on 1 December; on the 9th she visited the Wolferton Stud but three days later was back in bed. Dr Broadbent was called and arrived in the middle of the night. Her worried son wrote sympathetically from Windsor; "Toria has been a real Angel & has telegraphed & written to me every day to tell me how you are, & I am glad to hear that you are going on well, but I am sure you feel wretched still & your poor throat gives you so much pain. I am so sorry but trust in a few days that it will have passed."[209] She had to stay in her room, dine upstairs and only go down for tea on the 29th. Charlotte and Maud also succumbed; altogether not a very happy Christmas.

The patients began improving and 1894 looked hopeful. George and May were happily married, with a baby expected; Louise, though still ailing, was comfortably settled with her family; Victoria (26) and Maud (25), despite poor health, got on well together and were good companions for their mother. There was still plenty of time to find husbands. May came to lunch and tea twice during the first week of January and on the 11th Alexandra, Maud and Charlotte went out after nearly six weeks indoors. There had been unhelpful press reports about Alexandra's health; she was better but it was decided not to issue rebuttals, although "not unnaturally a certain number of people believe what is written about the Royal Family ... in these papers."[210] There were the usual house parties, with Gottlieb's Band playing in the evenings. Ernest Louis, Grand Duke of Hesse, got engaged to his cousin, Victoria Melita of Saxe-Coburg-Gotha;[211] Albert Edward "was not surprised at Ernie's engagement as I knew Aunt Marie had 'booked him' long ago! It will I am sure turn out a happy marriage."[212] On 3 February Alexandra and her daughters, joined en route by Albert Edward, left briefly for Osborne, where Vicky was staying. On the 8th they dined at Olympia and saw *Arabian Nights* tableaux, the ballet *Constantinople*, shops, and caiques to ride in. The next day it was *Cinderella* at the Lyceum. Returning to Sandringham, they dined several times with the Yorks; Alexandra and the girls joined Papa in London on the 19th and on the 21st Ernest Louis, with Alix and the Louis Battenbergs, came to lunch. Albert Edward took "Ernie" to the theatre and a smoking concert.[213]

On 23 February Alexandra heard Gounod's *Redemption* at evening service in St Peter's, Eaton Square. The next day the Waleses opened the Polytechnic Institute at Battersea and later took Vicky to Sandringham for two days. Albert Edward left for Cannes and Alexandra sat to Feodore Gleichen[214] on 1 March.

Then followed Bach's *St John Passion* at St Anne's; an exhibition of portraits by Old Masters; morning service at St Paul's Cathedral and then, with Vicky, visiting Luke Fildes' and Sir Frederic Leighton's studios on the 5th. Alexandra still had her 1884 brown velvet dress with "gold Indian stuff & Indian jewels", perhaps a favourite because of the Indian connection. By now it looked tarnished and she offered it to Leighton, "hoping very much some day to see it made new again in one of yr lovely pictures." Its delivery was hampered by the "bustle & confusion with the Empress etc" but they had all been "so delighted with all yr beautiful pictures the other day."[215]

Alexandra attended the Hunters and Hackney Show at the Agricultural Hall on the 7th, lunched at Windsor the next day, and visited Eddy's tomb. After a service at St Paul's on the 9th she inspected the mosaics. She and three daughters went to Sandringham on the 10th, Louise leaving on the 15th. It had been "so nice having dear little Louise here for a little & she too enjoyed it so much & was in the highest spirits, being chaffed mercilessly by us all, which does her a lot of good!! She really is too funny sometimes." Alexandra had called on Mr Taylor, landlord of "The Feathers" at Dersingham, dying of cancer. Mr Dormer, porter at Marlborough House, had died suddenly and "poor Gwilliam"[216] was very ill. "It is so sad to think of so many of our nice people dying." The Yorks had been busy in London and she was sure George "enjoyed seeing the Manufactory of stamps in which you always take so great an interest." Papa at present had won every race on the French coast with *Britannia*. The Queen was also abroad; it seemed "very strange that the Sovereign and Heir can both be absent together & particularly at such a critical moment for the country with a new Prime Minister!!!"[217]

The Yorks arrived on 22 March for Easter, much to Alexandra's delight. She and the girls stayed as usual until 30 April; the Prince had arrived on the 6th and, after travelling between residences, finally left on the 16th for the marriage at Coburg.[218] It was an interesting event; guests had gathered for one wedding, only to witness the dawning of a much grander one. As Alexandra wrote to George on the 20th; "And what do you say to our dear Nicky actually being engaged after all to Alicky, who only the other day boasted of having refused him on account of religion & two days after telling him she accepts him willingly!!! Well all I can say is that I hope she will make him happy as he is the best & kindest boy in the world & next to you & darling Eddy I like him best." Although fond of her, Alexandra had been a little hurt on Eddy's behalf when Alicky turned him down. Religion had influenced the later love lives of both; Eddy had lost his Roman Catholic fiancée and Alicky had finally embraced Russian orthodoxy. Alexandra wondered "what Grd Mama says now?! to that wonderful decided character?? of Alicky's, of whom she only again the other day said 'She will never change her religion & she promised it to her Father!!!'"[219] Did Alexandra therefore respect Alicky less than Hélène, or was the triumph of love paramount? Albert Edward wrote to George; "I was sure you would be pleased at Nicky's engagement & they seem so happy together. There is no doubt he has been in love with her for 5 years, & I believe she has also liked him very much but the religious scruples were the difficulty. Ernie's marriage however resolved her to accept Nicky ... William had no more to do with the matter than you or I had but he & Aunt Vicky & all of us at Coburg were most anxious that there should be no refusal. Gd Mama quite approves & is very fond of & kind to dear little Nicky."[220]

Grandmama and Aunt Vicky had also been discussing other marriages. Vicky wrote; "With regard to the sweet Wales girls, I do so wish Max of Baden[221] might still be thought of for <u>one</u>, but alas it has so got about that they will not look at the Princes that come from Germany or indeed at any Princes, that the latter are afraid and shy of going! I do <u>not</u> think anything <u>is</u> settled about Württemberg; & if you & Bertie were to invite Max to England there might be a chance! ... Then there is the <u>very</u> nice <u>second</u> son[222] of Bathildis of Lippe ... he admires Maud so much. Why could he not show himself in England; Alix would not mind him because he is her cousin's son, I am sure ... It really makes me unhappy to think those 2 <u>most</u> charming & sweet girls, our own dear Bertie's daughters, should not have homes of their <u>own</u>! It <u>looks</u> <u>so</u> <u>strange</u> too, all the other cousins are marrying off! Will you think about it?"[223] Dolly Teck and Ernie Hohenlohe[224] would not do but the widowed Grand Duke Paul might. "Max of Baden wld <u>have</u> to be <u>invited</u> because he would not come of his own accord, having heard that <u>Germans</u> are at a discount in our dear Alix's favour!" She would gladly write to Bertie but was "so afraid of displeasing dearest Alix, who has always been <u>so</u> exceedingly kind & good & dear to me, or of appearing to meddle in her family affairs, but it really is <u>not</u> wise to leave the fate of those dear girls 'dans la vague' for years longer, or marriages will be made wh will not please & wh will create difficulties."[225] In fact, royal marriages were changing. Historically, older relatives had sought out suitable partners for their young people, introduced them and trusted affection would develop. But "Cousin Lily" of Hanover, Beatrice, Louise of Wales, Louise of Schleswig-Holstein and now Alix of Hesse had all decided on their husbands without really involving their parents. Hélène d'Orléans had chosen Eddy against all advice and would have married him if she could. Victoria and Maud may well have thought they could do the same (after all, their sister had got what she wanted). Like their mother, they did not want "an arranged thing"; they were happy at home in England and there was the comforting thought of John Baring, or Frank of Teck or others quite nearby, and who knew what might happen?

Alexandra's knee had been painful but now she could ride a little. "The Masseuse answers well for both me & Victoria who seems really much better now I am happy to say." Baba Knollys was coming on the 21st, to her great delight, "as I am not allowed to see my little Grd Children as both my dear <u>Son</u>

<u>in law & daughter</u> do not think I am capable of taking care of them, I have to borrow other people's children until <u>yours arrive</u> whom I know you & dear May will trust to my care occasionally!!!"[226] She stayed at Sandringham, riding, driving, visiting and entertaining until the 30th, when she joined her husband in London on his return. Then there was the state opening of the Royal College of Music's new building on 2 May; galleries, exhibitions and the third drawing room, held by Alexandra on the 4th. She visited the National Silk Textile Exhibition at Stafford House on the 8th and the couple saw Eleonora Duse[227] in *La Dame aux Camellias* at Daly's three days later. Alexandra and the girls returned to Sandringham on the 12th; she gave prizes at the Dersingham "Sports" on the 15th. In London, she watched her husband invest George with the Spanish Order of the Golden Fleece, on behalf of the Queen Regent,[228] on the 22nd. Queen Victoria received an unusual birthday present from her Wales granddaughters on the 24th; a small wooden stand "which we thought might be useful for holding your papers, it came from Mama's carving school at Sandringham."[229]

Seasonal and other events proceeded; Fräulein Eibenschütz[230] played the piano and Herr Döme's "Bullet-proof Cuirass" tested Captain Martin's and Mr Western's skill in rifle and pistol shooting. Alexandra watched a dancing class at Dorchester House on 1 June and inspected Tuxen's[231] picture of the Yorks' wedding. On George's birthday there was a large family dinner, with Gottlieb's Band and the dancer "Little Ruby" afterwards. The Princess visited Alexandra House on the 9th and two days later opened Poplar Hospital, while the Prince opened a new Institute, affiliated to the Missions to Seamen, for mariners in the Port of London. That evening, Jean de Reszke[232] made his first appearance at the opera in *Werther*. On the 13th the Waleses, their daughters and Christian of Denmark,[233] staying until the 22nd, went to Aldershot, where Albert Edward presented colours to the 2nd Battalion, the Worcester Regiment. On 16 June Neruda played the piano with Alexandra. Ascot Week was spent at Cowarth Park, then, on the 23rd, Alexandra went to White Lodge and later telegraphed to Charlotte at Marlborough House; "Thank God all well over a son[234] was born big strong child dear May bore up well Georgie and we all overjoyed I with her all the time just come back here A."[235] She had witnessed the birth, as at Sheen in 1891. They called at White Lodge again on the 25th, before Alexandra presented challenge banners to London School Board children, for drill and exercise competitions, at the Albert Hall.

On 23 June, Tsesarevitch Nicholas arrived at Windsor, where his fiancée was staying with her grandmother. He went to Sandringham on the 28th, enjoying the refreshing drive through the woods to the house. They had all hurried off to a horse sale near King's Lynn; "Uncle Bertie was as funny as usual and in the carriage there were two or three misunderstandings between him and Aunt Alix. That always happens, because she does not hear what he says and he hates to repeat his own words."[236] Nicholas returned to Windsor when the family went to London for the Prince's state opening of the new Tower of London bridge, in the Queen's name, on the 30th. Archduke Francis Ferdinand of Austria[237] arrived at Buckingham Palace, where the Waleses gave a large luncheon on 2 July for him and Nicholas; later there was the second state ball. On the 3rd Alexandra opened the Hospital for Incurables at Streatham. Nicholas and Alicky arrived and stayed for lunch next day. Alexandra gave prizes at Harrow School's Speech Day on the 7th; on the 9th she heard Mademoiselle Brönnum sing and also visited her art teacher, Henry Harper's exhibition. From 10–13 July the couple and the girls stayed at Penrhyn Castle, watching an Eisteddfod and a Gorsedd, visiting Lord Penrhyn's slate quarries and steam-yachting through the Menai Straits. On the 13th Alexandra laid the first stone of the Royal Alexandra Children's Hospital and Convalescent Home at Rhyl. They returned in time to see *L'Attaque du Moulin* at Covent Garden, and the next day Alexandra watched the Eton and Harrow cricket match at Lord's.

At White Lodge on 16 July the Yorks' son was christened Edward Albert Christian George Andrew Patrick David; his family would always call him by the last name. Alexandra sat for her bust on the 23rd and also played the piano with Neruda; on the 30th the Waleses saw *Die Meistersinger* (with supper) at Covent Garden. The next day Alexandra, Victoria and Maud left for Russia; Xenia was to marry her second cousin, Alexander Michaelovitch[238] and Minny needed her sister's support at a trying time. They reached Peterhof on 3 August and on the 4th inspected the military camp at Krasnoe Selo, with a grand tattoo at sunset. There was a mass in the chapel on the 5th and the marriage took place the next day at 3pm, followed by a large dinner and a concert. A gala theatre performance and a concert in the "Salle des Marchands" by a Roumanian band took place on subsequent days. Exquisite toilettes were essential and when Alexandra looked through the clothes she had brought, they were all wrong. She begged Charlotte, "I am in despair about all my rotten things, gown, head etc – nothing does – do come a minute 11.30 or 12. A" [239] Even so, the admiring Grand Duke Constantine Constantinovitch[240] thought that, at 49, she looked only 30; "She is marvellously slim and her bright kind smile creates an enchanting impression."[241]

They left Peterhof for a grand review on the 16th at Krasnoe Selo, with lunch in a tent and the theatre later. Alexandra wrote lengthily to George; "I am so glad that you & Papa miss us a little! on board the dear old Osborne, & I myself am also very sorry not to have been there with you both this time but it cld not be helped, as dear little Minny Minny wanted me so much for Xenia's marriage! and now I must say I am very glad I came as I really was of some little comfort & help to her during that for her dreadfully trying time, also for dear Sacha's sake I am glad we are all here as well as little Minny of Greece, as so many in the house help to cheer them up when I know they both would be low & unhappy after dear

Xenia's departure." Sacha had been seriously ill and still looked unwell and exhausted; she wished he could have a proper rest in the refreshing Scottish air. "Today for instance was a most tiring day for him – at 12 o'clock there was a tremendous parade of the Preobrajenski Regiment & all the Guards ... first he had to walk down the lines, then there was a short service & blessing & sprinkling of holy water, then a long March past and all the time poor Uncle Sacha had to stand in the sun & several times without his hat; after that we visited the various regiments' Mess rooms where the men had their dinners & Minny & Sacha had to taste the soups & dishes, & Sacha drank their health & they all cheered tremendously." It had been very interesting but it was extremely hot, they did not get to the large house where the big military lunch was served until after 2pm, and then there were a lot of people to talk to. On returning home at about 4.00 "poor Uncle Sacha very nearly fainted & looked quite green! It really distressed me dreadfully & poor Minny Minny is getting so anxious too." They persuaded him to consult the Moscow doctor who had treated him in the winter.

Alexandra was fascinated by the camp and wished "we could go [to Aldershot] like that for a week's stay every year. Every morning early ... we drive out to see the troops & the first day's manoeuvre was most exciting & lasted till one, the girls & little Minny rode each time with Sacha, Minny & I & dear Aunt Olga drove, & yesterday afternoon Minny was on horseback too & inspected her own regiment. She alone without Sacha! She just cantered along the whole line of her regiment by herself, followed by four Cossacks & two Trumpeters, her bodyguard, & then a whole staff ... came next; it was [a] very pretty sight indeed & I was very proud of my little sister I must say." Camp life was great fun; they were out all day long, then had a "high tea with meat etc" at 7pm and went see a play or ballet at the theatre at 8pm "& the acting first rate altho' in Russian". Many members of the Imperial Family attended, including Grand Duke Vladimir, his wife[242] and children; their sons' tutor, Mr Gordon-Ross, was Captain Holford's[243] first cousin. After an inspection and march past of 40,000 men, the camp broke up on the 20th and the party returned to Peterhof. Alexandra and the girls stayed, attending functions and going driving,[244] until 29 August. Visiting Hamburg Zoo two days later, they reached Bernstorff the next day in time for Queen Louise's birthday, when her granddaughter, Louise,[245] became engaged to Frederick of Schaumburg-Lippe. On 22 September Alexandra and her daughters left, joining their relatives, the d'Hautpouls and others at Mar Lodge on the 25th. Over three weeks they visited the Queen, walked and had picnics, despite rain. Albert Edward left on 6 October, Alexandra and the girls on the 15th.

Grave news came from Russia and on 21 October there were prayers for the Emperor in Sandringham Church. They returned to London on the 29th but the next day Minny telegraphed, begging Alexandra to come to Livadia. The Waleses set off; travelling day and night they were met at Wels in Austria by the Cumberlands, who accompanied them as far as Vienna, where, at the British Embassy, they heard the Emperor had died. Alexandra was terribly upset and her husband feared she would collapse from grief. At Odessa they boarded the armed cruiser, *Orel*[246] but did not reach Livadia until 4 November, where a funeral service was held at 9pm. "There are 1,000 persons lodged & fed at Livadia at present," noted Charlotte Knollys.[247] Albert Edward told George; "the consolation wh dear Mama is to A Minny is enormous & she slept in her room last night, & [A Minny] was in consequence able to sleep better than she has done for a long time."[248] After five more services, and another at 8.30pm on the 8th, the procession set off. At Yalta they embarked on a cruiser for Sevastopol and travelled all night in four trains, with 1,729 pieces of luggage.[249] Pausing to hold services at railway stations, they finally arrived at Moscow on the 11th, reaching the Kremlin at midday; a service was held at the Archangel Cathedral. After another service, the journey resumed the next day, culminating at St Petersburg at 10.15; a service was held, with another at the St Peter and St Paul Cathedral at 2pm. Services continued over the next five days, although on the 14th the Empress and Princess did not attend, as "poor Minny does not feel very well, her back is bad & she nearly fainted a moment ago." Alexandra had made her lie down on the sofa but she cried so bitterly that Alexandra could not leave her.[250] George arrived and on the 19th Alexander III was finally laid to rest after a three-hour service at the cathedral. A mass for the dead was held there next day, the twentieth after death.

On 21 November the new Emperor, Nicholas II, gave a banquet for 300 members of the Imperial Family and foreign royalty in the Winter Palace. Alexandra visited Fabergé's shop on the 22nd, and lunched with Grand Duke[251] and Grand Duchess Serge on the 23rd. A bad cold kept her from church on the 25th but on the 26th, Nicholas II married Princess Alix of Hesse (henceforth Empress Alexandra Feodorovna) in the Imperial Chapel of the Winter Palace. The wedding breakfast was at the palace and afterwards the young couple took up residence at Minny's palace, the Anitchkoff. Alexandra drove on the 27th with her father. She was 50 on 1 December; curiously she celebrated both her own and her husband's half century (in 1891) in Russia. The mayor of St Petersburg and a deputation presented an album of photographs; there was lunch with Nicholas, Alicky and Minny, congratulations from the Imperial Family and later a dinner at Anitchkoff. The next day Albert Edward, George, King Christian, King George and Queen Olga and others left but Alexandra stayed a little longer. She thanked Queen Victoria for two birthday presents; a little enamelled watch and the recent "Four Generations" photograph, framed.[252] Recalling recent events, "the saddest thing of all" had been when Sasha was carried from Livadia by his sons, brothers and kinsmen, then borne by Cossacks in torchlight up to the church on the hill; "the Moon shining & the path strewn with evergreens." She had walked immediately behind the coffin, supporting her heartbroken sister. Later they had all accompanied the body on foot down the mountain path, taking two and a half hours, while "the sun shone gloriously and the sea was sparkling in its rays." The road was lined by thousands of weeping people, who fell on their knees and crossed themselves as their Emperor was carried past. She marvelled that Minny got through the constant, terrible ordeal of daily funeral services and processions; she was "so wonderfully <u>good</u> & <u>brave</u> & an example to all. She tries <u>so</u> hard to bear up but she constantly breaks down & every morning when she gets up I find her in floods of tears!" It was impossible to leave her yet, although Alexandra hated being parted from her family and home in England.

The wedding had been "a brilliant sight & dear [Alicky] looked <u>lovely</u> & most dignified. I did so wish you cld have seen her." Nicholas was the most charming son in the world and full of consideration for his mother, who had told Alexandra, "thank God for having given me such an Angel for a son, and not like poor <u>Vicky's</u>!" The young couple were very happy indeed together; the new Empress was a comfort to her mother-in-law and they got on well. Alexandra was "so thankful that Bertie came out with me here during this terribly trying time and people are all so glad that he shld have shared our sorrow." Her father was going straight to another funeral; his youngest and favourite sister, Louise, Abbess of Itzehoe, had died there on 30 November; "She was such a dear & we all were devoted to her."[253] The bridal couple began a short honeymoon at Tsarskoe Selo on 4 December; meanwhile Alexandra received officials, walked in the garden, drove with Minny and helped her in various ways. Minny told her mother on the 6th; "In the evenings we two sit quite alone when Micha goes to bed, and Nicky naturally would rather sit downstairs with his Alicky. And I would not like to bother them either, the poor things, for the whole day he is busy and has to see people as well, so that one must let them have a <u>little</u> time to sit <u>alone</u> together in the evening!"[254] Alexander III had been colonel of eighteen regiments and his uniforms were brought to Anitchkoff Palace on the 14th. Alexandra paid calls and went sledging with Grand Duchesses Elizabeth and Xenia. Not everyone was prepared for the extreme cold, but she offered kind and practical help: "My dearest old Char, I send you by bearer a nice <u>cheap</u> fur coat but delightfully warm and as you won't wear it for show in England but only for warmth here it won't matter what fur it is made of. So here it is and you must wear it at once today. Yrs A."[255] She was also being careful not to embarrass Charlotte by choosing something too expensive.

On the 25th Alexandra went to the English church; Russian Christmas would not be celebrated until 6 January, which was sad for the 2 or 3,000-strong English community in St Petersburg. The 25th was an ordinary day and, being mostly merchants or tradesmen, they were expected to work as usual; only about 60 had attended the English service. As traders, they were "not admitted into any <u>good</u> Russian society, or received at Court", however large their businesses might be.[256] Alexandra told her son on the 21st how she missed her English relatives after they had left. "We are as you know leading the most quiet of lives now – darling Aunt Minny Minny & I & her Children of course but as I am only here for her sake I am only too thankful to be able to spend her first lonely Christmas with her & help her with her many things. Of course I am *au fond* terribly sad at spending Xmas so far away from you all, but you will know how near you all my spirit is!!! I hope you will all like the little Russian things I sent, & that you will often use my red cigarette case. And now let me congratulate you on our sweet & precious little David's first tooth, which is quite an event in the family! I do hope he is well & happier in consequence! but I feel so unhappy at hardly knowing him at all, which really seems inconceivable!! ... Give me one thought & breathe a little prayer on Xmas day in our dear little Church when you sit next to my vacant place, & my poor Eddy!"[257] It was milder, which made sleighing rough and uncomfortable but as the wheels had been taken off carts and carriages for the winter, it would be a nuisance to put them on again prematurely.[258] On the 29th Alexandra and Minny visited Tsarskoe Selo, for lunch at the Alexander Palace with the young couple and a tour of the Catherine Palace. Alexandra spent the last two days of the year visiting the English church, walking in the garden with Minny and lunching in her own room with Charlotte Knollys.

Notes

[1] Archibald Macdonald, appointed brusher in 1861, jäger in 1864 and valet in 1880 to the Prince; retired in 1887

[2] RA GV/PRIV/AA31/10, Princess of Wales to Prince George, 1890: 9 January

[3] RA GV/PRIV/AA18/12, Prince of Wales to Prince George, 1890: 12 February

[4] Boz (c1883–97) performed memory tricks. His owner, Mr DH Harris, was a stock breeder.

[5] The Fifes' London residence

[6] Archibald Philip Primrose (1847–1929), 5th Earl of Rosebery, politician, PM from March 1894-June 1895, m Hannah, née de Rothschild (1851–90)

[7] Battiscombe, p177

[8] "Signor Onofroff", Belgian magician (dates unknown), who specialised in hypnotism and mind-reading.

[9] RA GV/PRIV/AA31/11, Princess of Wales to Prince George, 1890: 4 April

[10] Hon Winifred (Bena) Sturt (1868–1914) to Charles Hardinge, (1858–1944), 1st Baron Hardinge of Penshurst, Viceroy and Governor-General of India, 1910–1916

[11] Emilie (Lillie), née Le Breton (1853–1929), socialite, actress and producer, m (1) Edward Langtry, (2) Sir Hugo de Bathe, 5th Baronet

[12] RA VIC/MAIN/Z/456/137, Duke of Clarence and Avondale to Duke of Cambridge, 1890: 30 January

[13] RA VIC/MAIN/Z/456/160, Prince of Wales to Queen Victoria, 1890: 31 March

[14] Princess Margaret of Prussia (1872–1954), m Frederick Charles, Landgrave of Hesse-Cassel (1868–1940)

[15] RA VIC/MAIN/Z/475/2, Sir Henry Ponsonby to Queen Victoria (?), 1890: 19 May

[16] RA VIC/MAIN/Z/475/3, Queen Victoria to Duke of Clarence and Avondale, 1890: 19 May; Princess Margaret of Prussia was known as "Mossy"

17 RA GV/PRIV/AA36/26, Prince George to Princess of Wales, 1890: 8 June; it was a Kola nut, but sadly had not worked

18 Queen Isabella II of Spain (1830–1904), m Infant Don Francisco de Asis (1822–1902), granted title of King

19 RA GV/PRIV/AA31/12, Princess of Wales to Prince George, 1890: 22 May

20 Louise was expecting a baby

21 RA GV/PRIV/AA36/24, Prince George to Princess of Wales, 1890: 24 May

22 George, 1st Duke of Clarence (1449–78), had reputedly been executed by drowning in a butt of Malmsey wine. The title had also been borne by the future King William IV, whose earlier long liaison and large family with Dora Jordan had been a fruitful source of gossip.

23 Horace Farquhar (1844–1923), Baron, Viscount, and 1st Earl Farquhar (1922), politician, courtier, m Emilie Packe (d 1922)

24 ie, George's brother-in-law, the Duke of Fife

25 RA GV/PRIV/AA31/13, Princess of Wales to Prince George, 189: 27 May

26 RA GV/PRIV/AA18/18, Prince of Wales to Prince George, 1890: 9 June

27 RA VIC/MAIN/Z/456/171, Princess of Wales to Queen Victoria, 1890: 18 June

28 RA VIC/MAIN/P/20/34, Ponsonby to [Sir Fleetwood] Edwards, 1890: 14 June; 35, Lord Salisbury to Queen Victoria, 1890:15 June

29 Published in full in Battiscombe, 1969, pp 176–179

30 Lady Rosamund, née Spencer-Churchill (1851–1920) m William Fellowes (1848–1925), 2nd Baron de Ramsay

31 Junius Spencer Morgan (1813–90), American financier who founded the merchant banking firm, with branches in London and New York City

32 The girls' French governess

33 Prince Victor of Hohenlohe-Langenburg's professional name

34 RA VIC/MAIN/Z/456/177, Prince of Wales to Queen Victoria, 1890: 28 July

35 RA GV/PRIV/AA36/29, Prince George to Princess of Wales, 1890: 22 July

36 She was only 45

37 RA GV/PRIV/AA39/62, Duke of Clarence and Avondale to Prince George, 1890: 11 September

38 RA GV/PRIV/AA36/29, Prince George to Princess of Wales, 1890: 22 July

39 RA GV/AA31/14, Princess of Wales to Prince George, 1890: 30 August

40 Arthur Wilson (1836–1909), prominent ship owner, m Mary Emma, née Smith (1843–1927)

41 For frequent discussions with the Queen, probably about Eddy's romance

42 RA GV/PRIV/AA31/15, Princess of Wales to Prince George, 1890: 23 October; the Roumanian queen was the former Princess Elizabeth of Wied

43 Charles Penny (d 1903), head gardener at Sandringham c 1873–1890

44 RA GV/PRIV/AA31/15, Princess of Wales to Prince George, 1890: 23 October

45 Seat of the Marquess of Londonderry, then Charles Vane-Tempest-Stewart (1852–1915), 6th Marquess, politician, landowner and benefactor, m Lady Theresa, née Chetwynd-Talbot (d 1919)

46 Military term, meaning to dismount, but in this case she fell off

47 RA GV/PRIV/AA18/37, Prince of Wales to Prince George, 1890: 17 November

48 Princess Victoria of Prussia married Prince Adolph of Schaumburg-Lippe

49 At 25, in 1896

50 RA GV/PRIV/AA36/31, Prince George to Princess of Wales, 1890: 23 December

51 With Baron Moritz von Hirsch (1831–96), German/Jewish financier and philanthropist

52 RA GV/PRIV/AA18/44, Prince of Wales to Prince George, 1891: 6 January; the Prince, who thought his brother-in-law was rather "above himself" referred to him as "Cocky Leeky", a

joke based on Prince Henry's nickname of Liko (and of course a reference to cockie-leekie soup)

53 John Hare (1844–1921) (b John Fairs), later Sir, actor and theatre manager, specialising in comedies

54 George Anderson Critchett (1845–1925), 1st Baronet, surgeon-oculist to King Edward VII and King George V

55 RA GV/PRIV/AA31/16, Princess of Wales to Prince George, 1891: 15 January. Unmarried girls were not supposed to hear discussions about pregnancy, although unmarried men could.

56 Pope Leo XIII (1810–1903), pope from 1878–1903, b Vincenzo Giacchino Raffaele Luigi Pecci

57 Princess Marie of Edinburgh was still only fifteen

58 The Duchess of Edinburgh

59 John Baring (1863–1929), 2nd Baron Revelstoke, senior partner of Baring's Bank from 1890s till his death. He was not implicated in the bank's acute recession in 1890.

60 RA GV/PRIV/AA31/16, Princess of Wales to Prince George, 1891: 15 January

61 RA GV/PRIV/AA18/48, Prince of Wales to Prince George, 1891: 1 February

62 Alan Reeve Manby (1848–1925), later Sir, Surgeon-Apothecary to the Royal Household, 1885–1924

63 Including Vicky and her youngest daughter, Margaret, whom Queen Victoria hoped would interest Eddy

64 RA GV/PRIV/AA18/46, Princess of Wales to Prince George, 1891: 18 February; she had had to wear a patch over her eye

65 RA GV/PRIV/AA31/17, Princess of Wales to Prince George, 1891: 18 April; she owned at least two medical books, SFA Caulfield's *The Home Nurse: a Handbook for Sickness and Emergencies* RCIN 1037378, and *A Dictionary of Medicine, including Diseases Peculiar to Women and Children*, in 2 parts, ed Richard Quain; RCIN 1231217–8

66 RA VIC/MAIN/QAD/1891: 25 May

67 Baccarat was then illegal in England if played for money

68 Sir William Gordon-Cumming (1848–1930), 4th Baronet, army officer, m Florence Garner (d 1922)

69 RA GV/PRIV/AA31/17, Princess of Wales to Prince George, 1891: 18 April

70 RA GV/PRIV/AA18/55, Prince of Wales to Prince George, 1891: 29 March

71 RA GV/PRIV/AA19/2, Prince of Wales to Prince George, 1891: 13 April

72 RA GV/PRIV/AA19/3, Prince of Wales to Prince George, 1891: 19 April

73 RA GV/PRIV/AA31/17, Princess of Wales to Prince George, 1891:18 April

74 Dimond, p 65

75 Lady Alexandra Duff (1891–1959), later Princess Alexandra of Fife and 2nd Duchess of Fife in her own right, m Prince Arthur of Connaught (1883–1938)

76 RA GV/PRIV/AA31/18, Princess of Wales to Prince George, 1891: 3 June

77 Empress Augusta Victoria, his wife (an Augustenburg)

78 Prince Michael of Greece, *Eddy & Hélène, an impossible match*, 2013

79 RA GV/PRIV/AA31/18, Princess of Wales to Prince George, 1891: 3 June

80 Charles Russell (1832–1900), Baron Russell of Killowen, lawyer and politician, Lord Chief Justice

81 RA GV/PRIV/AA19/9, Prince of Wales to Prince George, 1891: 2 June

82 Sir Edward Clarke (1841–1931), barrister, politician and Solicitor-General from 1886–92

83 RA GV/PRIV/AA19/10, Prince of Wales to Prince George, 1891: 10 June

84 Elder son of Prince and Princess Christian

85 RA GV/PRIV/AA19/11, Prince of Wales to Prince George, 1891: 17 June

86 Ferdinand, Marquis d'Hautpoul de Seyre (c 1860–1934)

87 RA GV/PRIV/AA19/12, Prince of Wales to Prince George, 1891: 24 June

88 RA GV/PRIV/AA19/13, Prince of Wales to Prince George, 1891: 1 July

89 Prince Aribert of Anhalt-Dessau (1864–1933)

90 This is probably Henry Tyrwhitt-Wilson (1854–91)

91 RA VIC/MAIN/Z/475/16,17, Queen Victoria to Prince of Wales, 1891: August; 4 August

92 RA VIC/MAIN/Z/475/18, Prince of Wales to Queen Victoria, 1891: 5 August

93 RA VIC/MAIN/Z/475/ 19, Queen Victoria to Prince of Wales, 1891: 5 August

94 Perhaps rather too much; like his father, being given greater responsibility could have been advantageous

95 Formerly Princess Alexandra of Greece

96 Grand Duke Dmitri Pavlovitch of Russia (1891–1942)

97 Prince Nicholas of Greece (1872–1938), m Grand Duchess Elena Vladimirovna of Russia (1882–1957)

98 Grand Duke Paul Alexandrovitch of Russia (1860–1919), m (1) Princess Alexandra of Greece, (2) Olga Karnovitch (1866–1929)

99 RA GV/PRIV/AA31/20, Princess of Wales to Prince George, 1891: 26 September

100 Her decision may partly have been taken as a result of her anger at her husband's current affair with Lady Brooke and his quarrel with Lord Charles Beresford, another of Lady Brooke's lovers

101 RA GV/PRIV/AA19/17, Prince of Wales to Prince George, 1891: 31 August

102 The myth that they were poorly educated could have arisen from the destruction of lesson books in the fire

103 RA VIC/MAIN/Z/457/37, Charlotte Knollys to Queen Victoria, 1891: 8 November

104 RA VIC/MAIN/Z/457/31, Sir Dighton Probyn to Queen Victoria, 1891: 2 November

105 RA VIC/MAIN/Z/457/36, Prince of Wales to Queen Victoria, 1891: 7 November

106 RA VIC/MAIN/Z/457/32, Princess of Wales to Queen Victoria, 1891: 4 November

107 RA VIC/ADDA4/37, Prince of Wales to Empress Frederick, 1891: 11 November

108 RA VIC/MAIN/Z/4/75/23, Prince of Wales to Queen Victoria,1891: 3 December

109 RA VIC/ADDA8/2750, Princess of Wales to Duchess of Teck, 1891: 5 December

110 RA GV/QM/PRIV/CC42/32, Princess of Wales to Princess May of Teck, 1891: 5 December

111 RA VIC/MAIN/Z/475/27, Queen Victoria to Princess of Wales, 1891: 5 December

112 RA GV/QM/PRIV/CC45/99, Princess Victoria of Wales to Princess May of Teck, 1891: December (nd)

113 RA VIC/MAIN/Z/475/49, Princess of Wales to Queen Victoria, 1891: 6 December

114 The sculptor, Count Gleichen, nephew of the Queen, who had resumed his former title

115 Arthur Davidson (1856–1922), later Colonel Sir, soldier and courtier (in 1892 ADC to Duke of Cambridge)

116 William Broadbent (1835–1907), later 1st Baronet, physician to Queen Victoria, Edward VII and George V

117 RA VIC/MAIN/Z/475/165, Charlotte Knollys to Queen Victoria, 1892: 13 January

118 RA VIC/MAIN/Z/95/8, Prince of Wales to Queen Victoria, 1892: 15 January

119 RA VIC/MAIN/Z/95/9, Princess May of Teck to Queen Victoria, 1892: 16 January

120 RA VIC/MAIN/Z/475/194, Princess of Wales to Queen Victoria, 1892: 17 January

121 RA GV/PRIV/AA69/81, Oliver Montagu to Prince George, 1892: 18 January

122 RA VIC/MAIN/Z/475/195, Queen Victoria to Princess of Wales, 1892: 17 January

123 RA VIC/MAIN/Z/475/199, Prince of Wales to Queen Victoria, 1892: 18 January

124 RA VIC/MAIN/Z/475/200, Princess of Wales to Queen Victoria, 1892: 18 January

125 The place from where Queen Victoria had watched the wedding of the Prince and Princess of Wales in 1863

126 RA VIC/MAIN/Z/475/224, Sir Francis Knollys to Sir Henry Ponsonby, 1892: 20 January
127 RA VIC/MAIN/Z/475/229, 238, Helena, Princess Christian to Queen Victoria, 1892: 21, 24 January
128 RA VIC/MAIN/Z/95/15, Prince of Wales to Queen Victoria, 1892: 20 January
129 Prince Michael of Greece, pp 79–83
130 For example, unlike Princess May, the Wales princesses were enthusiastic horsewomen
131 RA QM/PRIV/CC42/33, Princess of Wales to Princess May of Teck, 1892: 19 January
132 RA VIC/MAIN/Z/95/18, Princess of Wales to Queen Victoria, 1892: 28 January
133 Victoria, née Gleichen (1868–1951), m Lt-Colonel Percy Machell
134 RA VIC/MAIN/Z/457/51, Queen Victoria to Prince of Wales, 1892: 24 January
135 RA VIC/MAIN/Z/457/59,60,61, Dr Laking to Queen Victoria, 1892: 10, 11, 11 February
136 Spencer Cavendish (1833–1908), 8th Duke of Devonshire, statesman, m Countess Louise von Alten (1832–1911), who previously m 7th Duke of Manchester
137 RA VIC/MAIN/Z/457/62, Princess of Wales to Queen Victoria, 1892: 12 February
138 RA VIC/MAIN/Z/95/22, Princess of Wales to Queen Victoria, 1892: 14 February
139 RA VIC/MAIN/Z/457/68, Charlotte Knollys to Queen Victoria, 1892: 13 March
140 RA GV/PRIV/AA36/32, Prince George to Princess of Wales, 1892: 11 May
141 RA VIC/MAIN/Z/457/69, Prince of Wales to Queen Victoria, 1892: 6 May
142 RA VIC/MAIN/Z/457/75, Charlotte Knollys to Queen Victoria, 1892: 26 May
143 Prince Ferdinand of Hohenzollern-Sigmaringen (1865–1927) became his uncle, King Carol I's heir to the throne of Roumania, m Princess Marie of Edinburgh (1875–1938)
144 RA GV/PRIV/AA19/23, Prince of Wales to Duke of York, 1892: 12 June
145 Frances Evelyn ("Daisy"), née Maynard (1861–1938), m Francis Greville (1853–1924), Lord Brooke, who became 5th Earl of Warwick in 1893
146 RA GV/PRIV/AA31/21, Princess of Wales to Duke of York, 1892: 28 June
147 RA GV/PRIV/AA19/27, Prince of Wales to Duke of York, 1892: 20 July
148 Frank Beck (1861–1915), land agent from 1891–1914, when, as Captain, he volunteered for service in the war, m Mary Plumpton Wilson
149 RA GV/PRIV/AA31/22, Princess of Wales to Duke of York, 1892: [July]
150 RA GV/PRIV/AA19/37, Prince of Wales to Duke of York, 1892: 30 July
151 She was pregnant
152 RA GV/PRIV/AA31/23, Princess of Wales to Duke of York, 1892: 3 October; Princess Victoria (1870–1948) of Schleswig-Holstein's rather long, thin nose reminded Alexandra of a snipe's bill. The comment seems harsh but was a private family joke; Alexandra would never have repeated it to the girl herself. In fact, Princess Maud, also with a long thin nose, was nicknamed "Snipey" too. Her sister Louise, writing to Francis Knollys in 1885, enclosed drawings of the three sisters as animals, calling them Toots (Louise), Gawks (Victoria) and Snipey (Maud). Ridley, p 241, quoting the letter, published in Giles St Aubyn's *Edward VII*, p 103
153 RA GV/PRIV/AA31/24, Princess of Wales to Duke of York, 1892: 10 October
154 RA GV/PRIV/AA31/26, Princess of Wales to Duke of York, 1892: 29 October
155 Alexandra's name for her brother and his wife
156 RA GV/PRIV/AA6/429, Princess of Wales to JN Dalton, 1892: 9 December
157 RA QM/PRIV/CC45/127,128, Princess Victoria, 1893: 16 January; Princess Maud, 1893: 20 January; both to Princess May of Teck
158 RA GV/PRIV/AA31/27, Princess of Wales to Duke of York, 1893: 1 February
159 Edward Montagu (1839–1916), 8th Earl Sandwich, politician and author
160 RA QM/PRIV/CC42/34, Princess of Wales to Princess May of Teck, 1893: 12 February
161 Her mother was a British princess and her father, although the result of a morganatic marriage (a royal person marrying a commoner), came from the Württemberg royal family on his father's side.

162 She had been ailing for some time and needed a change; she may well have anguished over the possibility that Eddy had caught the fatal influenza from her.

163 RA GV/PRIV/AA31/27, Princess of Wales to Duke of York, 1893: 1 February

164 Pope-Hennessy/Vickers, p 132 etc

165 For example, the founders of the Tudor and Stuart dynasties had not been royal and only two of Henry VIII's six wives had been from royal families. James II's first wife had been Anne Hyde, making their two daughters, who both succeeded to the throne (Queen Mary II and Queen Anne) of "morganatic" heritage.

166 Sister of Oliver Montagu and Lord Sandwich, Lady Emily, née Montagu (1846–1931) m Sir William Hart Dyke, (1837–1931), 7th Baronet, politician and tennis pioneer.

167 RA GV/AA31/28, Princess of Wales to Duke of York, 1893: 7 February

168 RA GV/AA31/29, Princess of Wales to Duke of York, 1893: 13 February

169 Alfred Gilbert (1854–1934), later Sir, sculptor; he finished Prince Eddy's tomb in the 1920s and also made Queen Alexandra's memorial at Marlborough House after 1925.

170 Alexandra had become interested in the Jesuits after reading Joseph Henry Shorthouse's *John Inglesant* (published in 1881); she visited several of their churches during this holiday

171 RA GV/PRIV/AA19/53, Prince of Wales to Duke of York, 1893: 8 March

172 Napoleon Bonaparte (1769–1821), Corsican-born statesman and military leader who was Napoleon I, Emperor of the French, from 1804–14 and briefly again in 1815; his rise to power was not propelled by royal ancestry

173 Dimond, pages 78, 79

174 Sir Dominic Colnaghi (1834–1908), diplomat and art historian

175 King Umberto I (1844–1900), m Princess Margherita of Savoy (1851–1926) Queen Margherita

176 RA GV/PRIV/AA20/1, Prince of Wales to Duke of York, 1893: 29 March

177 Prince and Princess Bernhard of Saxe-Meiningen

178 RA GV/PRIV/AA20/1, Prince of Wales to Duke of York, 1893: 29 March

179 Charlotte, née von der Decken (1863–1933) m Count Frederick of Hohenau (1857–1914), s of Prince Albert of Prussia and Rosalie von Rauch, created Countess of Hohenau

180 Lady Maud Duff (1893–1945), later Princess Maud of Fife, m Charles Carnegie (1893–1992), the 11th Earl of Southesk

181 RA GV/PRIV/AA20/3, Prince of Wales to Duke of York, 1893: 7 April

182 Perhaps Mademoiselle Trikoupis, sister of Charilaos Trikoupis (1832–96), Greek prime minister

183 Themistocles (c 524 – 459 BC), Athenian politician and general

184 RA GV/PRIV/AA31/30, Princess of Wales to Duke of York, 1893: 28 April

185 With the Governor, General Sir Henry Smyth (1825–1906) and his wife

186 RA GV/PRIV/AA31/31, Princess of Wales to Duke of York, 1893: 6 May

187 Landgravine Anna, widow of Alexandra's Uncle Frederick of Hesse-Cassel

188 RA QM/PRIV/CC42/35, Princess of Wales to Princess May of Teck, 1893: 12 May

189 Sir Luke Fildes (1843–1927), artist

190 James Stack Lauder (1853–1923) used the pseudonym Lafayette for his portrait photography business

191 Andrei Maylunas and Serge Mironenko, *A Lifelong Passion*, p 27

192 Earlier known as the Bachelors' Cottage, as single male guests would stay there during house-parties.

193 RA GV/PRIV/AA31/32, Princess of Wales to Duke of York, 1893: 8 July

194 RA QM/PRIV/CC45/140, Princess Victoria to Duchess of York, 1893: undated

[195] RA VIC/MAIN/Z/457/148, Princess of Wales to Queen Victoria, 1893: 10 July

[196] Pietro Mascagni (1863–1945), Italian composer, mostly of operas.

[197] The apartment formerly used by the Duchess of Cambridge in St James's Palace

[198] Beavan, pp 1, 121

[199] RA VIC/MAIN/Z/457/149, Lord Rosebery to Queen Victoria, 1893: 13 July

[200] Author's conversation with the late Mr Leslie ("HRH") Everest, Queen Maud's trichologist

[201] Dimond, pp 70–6

[202] RA GV/PRIV/AA31/33, Princess of Wales to Duke of York,1893: 31 August

[203] RA QM/PRIV/CC42/38, Princess of Wales to Duchess of York, 1893: 13 October

[204] RA GV/PRIV/AA31/34, Princess of Wales to Duke of York, 1893: 4–7 October

[205] Charles Prosper Sainton (1861–1914), artist, made drawings with a "pencil" of silver metal instead of graphite, leaving a silvery line. Alexandra seems to have admired the technique

[206] Major General Sir Christopher Teesdale (1833–1893) equerry and then extra equerry to the Prince

[207] Began her duties as lady-in-waiting

[208] A member of the Rolfe family of Heacham, most likely Eustace Neville-Rolfe (1845–1908), Consul-General at Naples and author; Alexandra later had a copy of his book, *Pompeii: popular and practical, an easy book on a difficult subject*; RCIN 1037372

[209] RA GV/AA36/34, Duke of York to Princess of Wales, 1893: 14 December

[210] RA VIC/MAIN/I/60/51, Francis Knollys to Sir Henry Ponsonby, 1894: 26 January

[211] Princess Victoria Melita of Saxe-Coburg-Gotha (1876–1936), m (1)Ernest Louis, Grand Duke of Hesse, (2) Grand Duke Kirill Vladimirovitch of Russia (1876–1938)

[212] RA GV/PRIV/AA20/24, Prince of Wales to Duke of York, 1894: 11 January; it did not

[213] RA GV/PRIV/AA20/26, Prince of Wales to Duke of York, 1894: 18 February

[214] Feodore Gleichen (1861–1922), sculptress daughter of Prince Victor of Hohenlohe-Langenburg

[215] Quoted from Alexandra's letter to Leighton, undated, but, due to circumstantial evidence, probably written on 7 March 1894; it is not known whether he did use the dress in a picture. Leighton House Museum, LH/1/1/2/31, © The Royal Borough of Kensington and Chelsea

[216] John Gwillim, messenger in the Comptroller's Office

[217] RA GV/PRIV/AA31/35, Princess of Wales to Duke of York, 1894: 15 March; Lord Rosebery was in office from March 1894 until June 1895

[218] Of the Grand Duke of Hesse and Princess Victoria Melita

[219] RA GV/PRIV/AA31/36, Princess of Wales to Duke of York, 1894: 20 April

[220] RA GV/PRIV/AA20/33, Prince of Wales to Duke of York, 1894: 25 April

[221] Prince Maximilian of Baden (1867–1929), Chancellor of the German Empire in October-November 1918

[222] Perhaps Prince Frederick of Schaumburg-Lippe (1868–1945); he m Princess Louise of Denmark in 1896. His mother, Princess Bathildis of Anhalt-Dessau (1837–1902), m Prince William of Schaumburg-Lippe (1834–1906)

[223] RA VIC/MAIN/Z/55/71, Empress Frederick to Queen Victoria, 1894: 23 April

[224] Ernest II, Prince of Hohenlohe-Langenburg (1863–1950) m Princess Alexandra of Saxe-Coburg-Gotha (1878–1942)

[225] RA VIC/MAIN/Z/55/73, Empress Frederick to Queen Victoria, 1894: 26 April

[226] RA GV/PRIV/AA31/36, Princess of Wales to Duke of York, 1894: 20 April

[227] Eleonore Duse (1858–1924), famous Italian actress

[228] Archduchess Maria Cristina of Austria (1858–1929), m King Alfonso XII of Spain (1857–85). Their son, Alfonso XIII (1886–1941) was born posthumously and his mother acted as regent until he was of age.

229 RA VIC/MAIN/Z/85/6, Princess Maud to Queen Victoria, 1894: 23 May

230 Ilona Eibenschütz (1871–1967), Hungarian pianist

231 Laurits Tuxen (1853–1927), Danish painter and sculptor, specialising in figure painting

232 Jan, or Jean de Reszke (1850–1925), Polish operatic tenor

233 Prince Christian of Denmark (1870–1947), later King Christian X, eldest son of Crown Prince Frederick

234 Prince Edward of York (1894–1972), later Prince of Wales, King Edward VIII and Duke of Windsor, m Wallis Warfield (1896–1986), created Duchess of Windsor

235 RA VIC/MAIN/QAD/1894: 24 June

236 Maylunas and Mironenko, p 76

237 Archduke Franz Ferdinand of Austria (1863–1914), heir to Emperor Franz Josef, m Sophie, née Chotek (1868–1914), created Princess of Hohenburg

238 Grand Duke Alexander Michaelovitch of Russia (1866–1933)

239 RA VIC/MAIN/QAD/1894: August

240 Grand Duke Constantine Constantinovitch of Russia (1858–1915), m Princess Elizabeth of Saxe-Altenburg (1865–1927)

241 Maylunas and Mironenko, p 88

242 Duchess Marie of Mecklenburg-Schwerin (1854–1920), m Grand Duke Vladimr Alexandrovitch of Russia

243 Lt-Colonel Sir George Holford (1860–1926), equerry to Duke of Clarence and Avondale and later to King Edward VII, Queen Alexandra, and extra equerry to King George V

244 RA GV/PRIV/AA31/37, Princess of Wales to Duke of York, 1894: 16 August

245 Eldest daughter of Crown Prince Frederick

246 RA GV/PRIV/AA20/43, Prince of Wales to Duke of York, 1894: 5 November

247 RA VIC/MAIN/QAD/1894: 4 November

248 RA GV/PRIV/AA20/43, Prince of Wales to Duke of York, 1894: 5 November

249 RA VIC/MAIN/QAD/1894: 8 November

250 RA VIC/MAIN/QAD/1894: 14 November,, note from Princess of Wales to Charlotte Knollys

251 Grand Duke Serge Alexandrovitch of Russia (1857–1905), m Princess Elizabeth of Hesse (1864–1918)

252 Several of these were taken at White Lodge after the christening of Prince Edward of York.

253 RA VIC/MAIN/Z/499/163, Princess of Wales to Queen Victoria, 1894: 3 December

254 *Kejserinde Dagmar. Maria Feodorovna, Empress of Russia*, Ulstrup p166, © GARF, Maria Feodorovna to Queen Louise of Denmark, 1894: 24 November/6 December

255 RA VIC/MAIN/QAD/1894: 15 December, note from Princess of Wales to Charlotte Knollys

256 RA VIC/MAIN/Z/457/207 Charlotte Knollys to Queen Victoria, 1894: 26 December

257 RA GV/PRIV/AA31/38 Princess of Wales to Duke of York, 1894: 21 December

258 RA VIC/MAIN/Z/457/207 Charlotte Knollys to Queen Victoria, 1894: 26 December

Chapter 10

1895–1899

"I am going to make my will ... and begin tearing my letters!"

ᐯ

On 5 January 1895 there was a Christmas tree, presents, an evening service, and on the 6th, Russian Christmas Day, a service was held at 11pm in the private chapel. Alexandra watched the Cossacks of the Guard receiving gifts from the tree on the 7th and on the 13th the sisters drove to the Peter and Paul Fortress, "where all was so peaceful and nice, the Cathedral all in semi darkness with only a few soldiers on guard." They were going to Gatchina the next day and there was better news of Queen Louise, who had been too ill to come to Russia.[1] Alexandra had done her best to comfort Minny and fully intended leaving on the 8th; she was longing to get home, but her sister begged her to stay until Russian New Year.[2] Alexandra was worried about her mother but her husband was astonished when she told him she was going to Copenhagen; "I think she is quite right to see Amama who has been so ill, & it will cheer her up, but these continued & somewhat sudden changes of plans are excessively inconvenient."[3] Parting from Minny was dreadful but Alexandra left on the 16th in the imperial train; transferred to a German train at Wirballen the next day and made her way to Denmark. She explained to Queen Victoria; "No one can wish more than I do, nor long more for my home, but was most urgently pressed by my Brother and Doctors to come here, as though my dear mother [is] better after her very <u>painful</u> serious illness, [she] is still so weak and pulled down that I cannot help being anxious; wants great care and cheering up now, my dear Father too."[4] She stayed with her mother all day on the 25th and on 2 February a boy musician played to Queen Louise. Satisfied with her progress, Alexandra left the next day, reaching home just after midnight on the 5th; "so delighted to be back with all my dear ones."[5]

There was skating and a hockey match between Sandringham staff and the Household Brigade on Buckingham Palace's frozen lake. After skating there on 8 February, the Waleses visited the General Post Office, including the Central Telegraph Office and sorting offices.[6] Subsequently Alexandra skated every day, saw relatives and friends and went to a Monday Popular Concert. There were more hockey matches but mourning for Alexander III limited social activities. On the 17th Albert Edward was laid up with a bad cold and Alexandra stayed with him all day, but he felt well enough to leave on the 23rd for Cannes, while his wife, daughters and Baba Knollys went to Sandringham. Two days later, Alexandra attended her dresser Bessie Temple's marriage to Sinclair,[7] master at arms on *Osborne*. The Yorks, at York Cottage with their son and the Duke of Teck, went to London, leaving the baby and his grandfather at Sandringham House. George was delighted to hear that "Baby 'David' has just got his 4th tooth, I hope he has been behaving himself & is nice to his Granny & his aunts, who I am afraid spoil him with kindness." He could not be in better hands and now, they hoped, "he will always know you quite well & be pleased to see you … we both miss the sweet child horribly, but it would have been very stupid of us to have brought him up to London, when all this Influenza is about, & it is not much better than it was." They would visit St Mary's Hospital to see Dr Broadbent and perhaps Sister Victoria.[8] He hoped "your fish dinners for the children were a success, May & I are giving some too."[9]

Alexandra drove, walked, paid calls and on the 16th lunched on the seashore at Heacham. She was delighted to be trusted with the baby and told May; "He takes such notice now & is very forward for his age, he boxes my ears occasionally and has lately taken to pulling <u>my hair</u> which might lead to disastrous consequences,[10] & annoys Toria & Harry extremely when he makes a sudden dash at the invisible nets."[11] On the 19th she heard that Hélène was engaged to the Duke of Aosta.[12] By the time she replied to George's letter, he had influenza, "but am glad you took it in time & kept yr bed. <u>Promise</u> me to stay <u>in it</u> till you <u>really</u> feel <u>all right</u> again as otherwise one begins it all over again & it makes one so horribly weak & the second attack generally goes on yr chest."[13] They had escaped infection at Sandringham but she dreaded going to London when Papa returned. On the afternoon of the 24th, a great gale sprang up and felled more than 2,500 trees[14] on the estate; twenty in the garden and part of the kitchen garden wall came down.[15] Alexandra and her daughters went to London on the 27th and met Albert Edward the next day. They visited Leighton's and Prinsep's studios on the 29th and later, Alexandra heard Bach's *St John Passion* at St Anne's. The Prince had expected to stay in London till the week of 8 April[16] but on 30 March they went back to see the gale damage. He stayed until the 2nd, walking about, touring the estate and, that morning, planting trees before returning to London. The Comtesse de Paris and Hélène stayed for a few days and on the 5th Alexandra walked around and planted more trees. Albert Edward returned on the 10th and the next day the family took Holy Communion at Wolferton Church. The Fifes, Uncle George and others came for Easter and on Easter Monday, Alexandra and all except Albert Edward, who had a cold, joined the West Norfolk Hunt Steeplechases at East Winch.

Alexandra stayed for three weeks while her husband ferried guests back and forth; she and the girls returned on 6 May, as Queen Wilhelmina of the Netherlands[17] (14) and her mother, Queen Regent Emma, were in London. There was a large dinner at Marlborough House to honour Emma; both queens lunched the next day. Alexandra went to theatres, and the couple heard the Vienna Orchestra at the Imperial Institute on the 11th, when Alexandra also sat to Josefine Swoboda,[18] with six more sittings by the end of May. She attended the horse show at the Agricultural Hall on the 14th and the next day held a drawing room. On the 16th the Prince went to Warwick Castle, while his wife and daughters visited Windsor and then Sandringham before returning on the 23rd. On the 25th the Emir of Afghanistan's second son, Shazadah Nasrulla Khan,[19] called at Marlborough House; later the Waleses inspected the Civil Service Volunteer Corps and distributed long service medals at Chelsea Barracks. There was a levee on the 27th, the first state ball, and several theatre visits, including *Lohengrin* on the 31st.

Next week Alexandra was at Sandringham for the Dersingham Sports on 4 June. On the 8th the couple went to the Ladies' Kennel Association's Dog Show at Ranelagh, where she presented the champion prize. There were more theatres, and another portrait sitting on the 10th. The next day the Siamese crown prince[20] and his younger brother came to lunch. On the 12th Alexandra saw the Children's Floral Parade and Floral Fête in the Botanic Society's gardens in Regent's Park; on 13 June it was the HAIA's 11th annual exhibition at the Albert Hall. The Waleses always encouraged "home manufactures" of all kinds; not only had Alexandra started the technical school at Sandringham but, apart from some Eastern art-work, tapestry and Sèvres china, almost everything in Marlborough House was British-made: furniture, woven silk, Axminster carpets and upholstery; the couple also habitually dealt with London tradesmen.[21] The exhibition included crafts using wood, metal, pottery, leather and cloth, with needlework, knitting, lace-making, weaving and bookbinding, all sent by classes belonging to the Association, with a loan collection of cut leather work from the South Kensington Museum. People from the classes gave demonstrations, while a potter from Aller Vale "threw" vases and pottery on a primitive "kicking wheel". This year Alexandra showed some iron fire-wood stands which she had designed; one was in her boudoir at Marlborough House.[22] She also enjoyed needlework and embossed leather work, learned how to spin, showed an interest in mosaics and admired metalwork.[23] Victoria favoured bookbinding.

Ascot week was at St Leonard's Hill; on 8 June they drove up the course in state and the Prince won the Coventry Stakes and the Queen's Gold Vase with "Persimmon" and "Florizel II". On the 14th they heard that Mar Lodge had burned down, fortunately in the family's absence. After tea with the Queen in Frogmore House garden on the 23rd, they returned home and Alexandra's brother Frederick came to stay until 1 August. There were two bazaars to open, a hospital to visit, dinners to attend and on the 28th Lady de Grey brought Cécile

Chaminade[24] to play the piano. Prince Maximilian of Baden called on 1 July. The next day Alexandra visited the Indian Exhibition at Earl's Court and rode on the "Great Wheel". She went to Olympia on 4 July and the zoo on the 7th; later, they gave a large party for Archduchess Stéphanie of Austria.[25] For her 27th birthday, Victoria's parents gave her a dark mahogany Bechstein upright piano, with gilt fittings, selected by Tosti.[26]

On the 8th, at Epsom, the Waleses laid the foundation stone of new Lower School building of Epsom College and opened the Royal Medical College's new building. On the 10th, they, their daughters and guests, including Frederick and Constantine,[27] attended the sale of 53 of the Prince's Hackney horses at Wolferton. He and most guests left on the 12th but Alexandra did not return until the 15th, for the state ball; she, her daughters, brother and nephew visited the African Exhibition[28] at the Crystal Palace on the 17th. The season was nearly over but there was a wedding on the 20th, an Aldershot review on the 25th and a presentation of certificates to nurses in Marlborough House gardens on the 26th. They had tea in a large tent, with florally-decorated tables; afterwards, Alexandra gave a spray of roses to one nurse and invited all the others to help themselves.[29] She visited Alexandra House and the Hospital for Incurable Children on the 31st and was photographed by Alice Hughes[30] on 1 August. The next day the family boarded *Osborne*, opening the London and South Western Company's new graving dock at Southampton on the 3rd on the way to Cowes. Albert Edward raced in Britannia and on the 5th Alexandra and the girls lunched on board John Baring's yacht, *Gabrielle*, while William II arrived for his usual week on *Hohenzollern*. They watched Brenner Torpedo experiments at Yarmouth on the 12th.[31] On the 13th Alexandra sailed with Archduchess Stéphanie on *Britannia*, which won "Her Majesty's Cup". Back in London, Alexandra sat to Edward Hughes[32] and on the 19th she and her daughters left for two months in Denmark. At sea, just before arriving on the 22nd, she reproached George; "How I wish you & dear May cld have come with us, and it really was too great a pity yr not having followed my advice two years ago! when you both might, could, & ought to have done so. Who can tell now whether May will ever see my dear old home with all the family together! Alas, dear Sacha she never saw! and with him and all together you know best yourself how bright & jolly it all used to be." They had had a good passage with heavenly weather and "We have all rested & taken life easy for once, there is no hurrying about this time! real quiet and peace." She had "nothing of interest to tell you from here. Altho' I have been watching the sea every day with the greatest care I have not yet discovered anything very startling – no sea serpent – nor whales – or any other monster – which is a pity, as I shld then have been able to give you a full & lovely description of each individual. I hope you all enjoyed the play you went to with Papa, & that you saw him off yesterday on his way to Homburg."[33]

Queen Louise was almost well again, although unfortunately the King was not, and neither was "Russian Georgy"; Dr Leyden[34] saw him on the 5th and on the 12th he returned to the Caucasus.[35] Charlotte Knollys thought the family had not noticed how ill he looked and would probably be angry if they knew she had told Queen Victoria.[36] The Prince arrived on the 14th and went to stay with Freddy and Swan at Charlottenlund, because Bernstorff was full. They were all well, he told George, "including Apapa & Amama. The former looking thin & the latter rather aged, but really looking well. So is poor A Minny. Poor little Georgy with Xenia & Sandro I passed in 'Polar Star' & we waved our caps to one another. They had been on board since Thursday but weather being stormy didn't start till yesterday – the accounts of the poor boy are I fear not favourable!"[37] He later described the large family lunch they had given on *Osborne* on the 23rd and the visit to *Standard*, "the new Yacht building at Copenhagen wh poor U Sacha ordered. It is 75 feet longer! than 'Polar Star' but won't be ready till April! It is to cost over £300,000! What waste!"[38] Charlotte thought Grand Duke George very quiet and reserved and unlike his brothers in face and disposition, "but he is most patient & gentle in all his sufferings & very much attached to his family." His brother Michael was "one of the nicest, best boys in the world", straightforward and truthful with a pleasant face and charming manners, universally beloved and a great comfort to his mother. Their sister Olga was "just like a little English girl & all her family have to talk to her in English as she does not know her own language properly. She is not pretty but very bright & clever looking."[39] Olga was still much with her beloved English nurse, Mrs Francklin.[40]

Alexandra was finding writing impossible; "I am <u>never</u> alone, and <u>always</u> downstairs with Mama & Minny! All the morning we paint together & after luncheon the whole family is together & we walk or drive or do something together – dinner at 7 & the whole evening spent together till 11, when I am too tired to write." Her parents were well, "Tho' dear Apapa looks still rather pulled & worn ... Dear Amama ... walks wonderfully well again." They had seen Papa most days and he had much enjoyed himself at Charlottenlund, where he had been very welcome. The children had cried when he left.[41] Princess Waldemar had had a daughter[42] on the 17th, to their delight, although it was "rather <u>unfortunate</u> its taking place just when all these <u>children</u> were here together!!!! and she certainly was not a pretty sight to behold beforehand!!!"[43] Her daughter would be brought up as a Roman Catholic (her four sons were Lutherans, like their father) "but Waldemar takes it, as he does everything else, with the <u>most</u> profound equanimity."[44] The Yorks were in Scotland; "So now you are <u>after all</u> <u>with</u> somebody else at Dunrobin. <u>I</u> cannot help feeling <u>sorry</u> <u>for that</u> as I thought it wld have been wiser in every way to have avoided!!! although I know it was not yr fault, they being asked at the same time as you two!"[45] On 24 September Alexandra walked, shopped, called on Miss Knudsen and visited the Deaconesses Establishment. Albert Edward planned to leave on the 27th but

Osborne was fog-bound and he had to go by train the next day. All, including Victoria and King Christian, seemed well and in good spirits. Grand Duke George was happy at Abas-tuman, in a nice house with well laid-out grounds, where cousins and friends often stayed with him.[46] Princess Margrethe was christened by a Roman Catholic Bishop in the drawing room at Bernstorffs Höj on 15 October. Madame Neruda, her brother, sister and Herr Hansen, gave a "repetition" at Bernstorff. Alexandra and the girls arrived home with momentous news on the 26th. As Queen Victoria told Maud; "Many thanks for dear letter, most heartily approve your engagement and send you my blessing and every wish for your happiness. Hope shortly to make the acquaintance of my future grandson."[47] Maud was engaged to her cousin, Carl. Charlotte told the Queen "how very happy Princess Maud is, it is a regular 'love match' on both sides & he says he has cared for her for three years & she certainly seems extremely fond of him. Prince Carl is good looking, with pleasing manners & rather like an Englishman in appearance, in fact very taking altogether … Everybody in Denmark seems delighted & the Prince and Princess are very much pleased also, though of course they will miss Princess Maud dreadfully."[48]

The Waleses saw Mrs Patrick Campbell[49] in *Romeo and Juliet* and Alexandra, Victoria and Maud returned to Sandringham on the 31st; Albert Edward arrived on 2 November and shooting parties began. Carl arrived on the 7th for five days, and 400 labourers were given a dinner on the 9th. In Russia on the 15th, Empress Alexandra gave birth to a daughter.[50] A servants' dance celebrated Maud's birthday; new guests, including Louise, arrived for Alexandra's birthday, a Sunday, and the family all took Holy Communion. Albert Edward left on 9 December with all guests except Lady de Grey. She stayed a little longer and drove with Alexandra, who, with her daughters, left for Windsor and the service on the 14th – when May had a second son.[51] As Albert Edward hinted broadly to George; "I am quite delighted … You must not be in a hurry about names & sponsors, as we must talk that over together, & I hope you will not be bothered about it fr here. Grandmama was rather distressed that this happy event should have taken place on a doubly sad anniversary for us, but I think, as well as most of us in the family here, that it will 'break the spell' of this unlucky date."[52] Alexandra too sent congratulations; "Oh what joy!! Fancy yr having a second son now! And thank God all is well over and our sweet May well through her troubles and in fact quite herself already … I was sorry not to have been with you, but as everything went so quick & well I daresay you were both rather relieved to be by yourselves. We were all so delighted that it was another boy altho' I know you wished very much for a little girl, but better luck next time!!!"[53] She was in the "midst of that gruesome present choosing & tired to death"; she went to Maple's the next day. They were all at Sandringham by the 24th, with 30 dining on Christmas Day.

❦

As 1896 began, the burning topic was the York baby's name. "Grandmama I find is most anxious that he should be called <u>Albert</u>, & begged me to tell you so, as an urgent appeal fr her" the Prince told George. "As the little boy was born on the day of my Father's death, I think there is a strong reason for giving him that name & I should imagine that people would rather expect it. It has also become a much more English name, & you might like to call him later <u>Bertie</u>, the name I have always gone by in my Family. So you can think it well over."[54] It would be tactful and gratifying to Grandmama if George suggested the name to her himself. "You may have preferred some other name but you must remember it was yr Grandfather's & is mine, & he has left so great a name in our Country, that it is one which anyone would be proud to bear."[55] There was really nothing more to say and George had always been dutiful. The family attended a service at Windsor marking Eddy's death but on 22 January heard that, tragically, Henry of Battenberg, in Ashanti on military duties, had caught fever and died at sea on the way home. Alexandra and her family left Sandringham on 3 February, met Albert Edward at Haverstock Hill, and joined the Queen at Osborne. The next day the Prince, his son and Ernest Louis of Hesse took a steam launch to meet *Alberta*, bearing Henry's coffin, (conveyed on board *HMS Blenheim* from Madeira), for a military funeral at Whippingham Church on the 5th. Albert Edward and George walked along the sea wall on the 6th with Beatrice, a widow with four children at 38. Despite mourning, the Waleses attended the Opening of Parliament on the 11th and later heard a debate.

On the 10th Alexandra had driven in the park and watched people riding bicycles, the latest craze. She told George; "I am sorry you give up yr bicycling in London – why not send it on to Battersea Park where I shd think it is quite quiet now, as most of the people go in the park to make an exhibition of themselves."[56] The new baby was christened Albert Frederick Arthur George at Sandringham Church on the 17th and the Yorks took both children to Windsor to see the Queen. Alexandra "was sure [Grandmama] wld be pleased with the sweet babies. I hope 'David' did not say his name was 'damn' when she asked him!" The Jameson Raid was in the news[57] and she wrote "So Papa saw poor Dr Jameson – I wish I had – poor man I am <u>so</u> sorry for him & think he must be so humiliated now. I do hope they will all be let off." Lord Leighton died on the 25th January. The Waleses had often visited his studio and were friendly with him; in June 1895 Alexandra had given him a chair, furnished with old Italian-style coloured silk embroidery, on which she had worked while with her sister in Russia,[58] writing "I only hope you will like it – and use it please at yr writing table in your beautiful studio."[59] He responded by drawing a picture for her.[60]

Alexandra's sister-in-law Louise had recently stayed at Sandringham; she had developed her artistic skills and was still fond of her husband, but the marriage had been disappointing and they were often apart.[61] She was regarded as a mischief-maker, but Alexandra was prepared to overlook many things, "Yes indeed <u>how</u> well I remember & <u>often</u> I think of that time when I was so ill & suffering from my leg & you dear little girl used to come & sit with me & cheer me up! Yes I have <u>never</u> forgotten that or ever changed. Indeed I do not think it is in my nature, & when I like a person once – I always do. You tell me how pleased you were to see such a good spirit of harmony in our home – that indeed has been my one object in life and to bring up my children <u>never</u> to speak or even <u>think</u> evil of each other, as '<u>Jealousy</u>' is at the bottom of all mischief & misfortune in the world."[62]

On 1 March Prince Carl arrived at Sandringham, accompanying Alexandra and her daughters to London the next day and Windsor on the 5th. Subsequently they visited the Grafton Gallery, a Spanish exhibition at the New Gallery, the London Aquarium, the Alexandra Children's Hospital and a musical ride for bicycles at Brighton. Alexandra had to attend the first drawing room on the 11th but visited the Hunters' Show at the Agricultural Hall and also watched skating at "Niagara"[63] on the 12th. That afternoon a nurses' deputation gave Maud a tea table as a wedding present. They returned to Sandringham on the 14th; news came of the death of Mrs Warren, (Bessie Lockyer). On the 19th, Alexandra toured Appleton Farm and garden; Appleton Manor was to be a wedding present to Maud, giving the couple a house in England. When Carl (now known as Charles) went home on the 23rd, "Poor Charles & Harry were both very sad at parting but I hope later on he may be allowed to come again." Albert Edward was at Cannes; unluckily *Britannia* had only won one race. Alexandra had invited the Coburgs, their daughter, Alexandra, her fiancé, Ernest of Hohenlohe-Langenburg[64] and Lord Lorne for two days. "The <u>Edinburgh</u>[65] visit went off very well & I think they were delighted with all they saw ... We played <u>Whist</u> every night after dinner!" Louise was away and Lorne "<u>poor man</u> actually spent his <u>Silver Wedding day</u>!!![66] with <u>me</u> here instead of his <u>Silver bride</u>! who preferred basking in the Southern sun – rather <u>unkind</u> ... to say the least of it. I gave him our joint present, a large silver bowl, with which he seemed much pleased." Poor Poetry, one of the best mares, and "one of those sweet little black Kerry cows" had died. In York Cottage's garden "They have been <u>planting</u> some nice bushes & shrubs near the Cottage which is a great improvement, thank goodness it was <u>not</u> cutting down or <u>pulling out</u> as usual!!"[67]

While the Yorks were at Coburg, Alexandra looked after their children; "And now I must tell you <u>how</u> sweet the two dear little babies were when I had them with me, & I was <u>so</u> sorry when we had to part. The first day after yr departure poor little David was really very unhappy & cried for Papa & looked for you everywhere! really <u>quite touching</u> but after that he ... really was <u>very</u> good & never <u>cried</u> once all the time, <u>nor cried</u> for <u>Nana</u>[68] which I was very pleased about. I made both children come down in the afternoon, the nursery maid went away & Nana stayed with baby while little David played about quite happy & never even minded when Nana went away with baby. I was very strict with him but always made him quite happy & feel confidence in me, & one ought <u>not</u> always to check them when so small, it all comes in time, nor always when they naturally sometimes will cry for their Nurse – take no notice of it at <u>first</u> & then they gradually get out of the habit, as otherwise they always dread coming down for fear of Nana being sent away or their being scolded. He actually, when I came into their room, wanted me to carry him away & said Good<u>bye</u> Nana – too funny. Poor Nana herself was <u>so</u> delighted at this change & with tears in her eyes she said 'if only the Duke & Duchess cld. see him <u>now</u> & what good manners he has got' & she begged me to write & tell you both. I must say she was <u>very sensible</u> all the time & she looked well after both those precious little ones."[69]

An adult's tricycle had been acquired and Alexandra rode it for several days. She attended the christening of Bessie's child, Alexander Temple Sinclair.[70] The family spent Easter at Sandringham and when Albert Edward returned from abroad he too rode the tricycle, to Appleton. They left for London on 20 April and saw *The Prisoner of Zenda* the next evening and then *The Grand Duke*, Gilbert and Sullivan's latest operetta. Alexandra had made one of her impulsive decisions, as she told George (the Yorks were in Copenhagen) from La Turbie, where Minny was visiting her son Georgy; "You must have been surprised to hear of my sudden visit here! So was <u>I</u>! – it all came so very suddenly, & unexpectedly. Poor darling Minny wrote & entreated me to come if possible even for 10–12 days, & as I had luckily no fixed engagements or any functions at this moment, & Papa had a lot of <u>public dinners</u> & Newmarket coming on, I & the girls started off at a moment's notice, the day after the drawing room. Luckily it was <u>not</u> a great scramble, & I took it all very calmly & have hardly taken anything with me, & this time our luggage is quite small, I have only <u>three small</u> boxes. We really did not miss our dear old comfortable carriage very much after all – the coupé lits are very comfortable & besides the journey was <u>so</u> short." Grand Duke George was much better than expected; the doctors said one of his lungs had healed and he was no worse than after his severe attack in the autumn. When he was strong enough he would return to the Caucasus by sea on his yacht, *Zarnitsa*, in which Alexandra had sailed from Monaco to Villefranche; "She is built in England & most comfortable & beautifully fitted up." She was delighted to see Minny looking well, and they all went for local trips, twice visiting Queen Victoria at Cimiez. On 5 May Alexandra and the girls shopped and lunched at the Restaurant de la Régence in Nice. George, with Charles, was due in Paris and she told him on the 10th; "We shall arrive in Paris at 5.45 in the afternoon on Wednesday. Shall we drive together & can you arrange something for us in the evening. It <u>must</u> be a proper play for <u>the girls</u> – or we can divide some of us. We three & a gentleman for instance to some amusing play & they to something else, or <u>all</u> of us to the Hippodrome, or <u>Opéra Comique</u> which I hear is good, but the latter <u>only if we</u> can wear <u>bonnets</u> because there wld be no time to do one's hair!!! *comprenez vous*. So do find out all about it & arrange something. <u>How</u> nice just to meet there, & that you were allowed to bring Charles with you."[71] Propriety and etiquette were tricky things, but in the end they saw *Les Deux Gosses* at the Ambigu, the Nouveau Cirque and *Dindon* at the Palais Royal and also enjoyed seeing friends, visiting the salon and eating at cafés. They arrived home on the 16th and Alexandra was soon opening new municipal buildings at Croydon, visiting a flower show in the Temple Gardens, watching Trooping the Colour, chairing the SSFA's[72] annual meeting at the Royal United Services Institution and viewing an exhibition of old Spanish, Italian, French, Polish and Indo–Spanish embroideries and brocades at Messrs Debenham & Freebody's[73] galleries in Wigmore Street.

On 21 May she opened a charity bazaar and fête for the West London Hospital at Hammersmith and visited the Queen at Windsor, returning there on the 22nd with her daughters and Charles. Back at Sandringham the next day, they inspected Appleton Manor on the 25th. After London again and a visit to Hatfield, "Persimmon" won the Derby on 3 June in the shortest recorded time, causing jubilations at the Jockey Club's Derby Dinner that evening at Marlborough House and at Lady Derby's dinner and dance. The next day Lord Rothschild's[74] team of zebras called at Marlborough House and Charles returned to Denmark. The Waleses opened the East London Trades, Industries and Arts Exhibition at the People's Palace on the 6th and the next day had tea with Uncle George and dinner with the Tecks at White Lodge. On the 9th Alexandra opened a bazaar in Hackney, for the Hackney and East Middlesex Band of Hope Union. At the theatre she saw Wagner's operas, as well as *The Geisha* at Daly's on 2 June. Another drawing room was held on the 10th; the next day included visits to Alexandra House and a concert at the Queen's Hall for the Great Northern Hospital's Ladies' Association's Endowment Fund. On the 12th it was a dog show at Holland Park, followed by Ascot week at Silwood Park. Alexandra had visited the HAIA's exhibition at the Albert Hall on the 11th. Several noble ladies had their own classes, but "above all the Association has for an active patron and kind friend her Royal Highness the Princess of Wales." She showed a spinning chair and a corner chair carved by the boys of her school, decorated with incised gilt leather, cut and gilt by her. Her forged iron log-stand appeared again and she had woven a length of brown homespun cloth, using wool from Albert Edward's Southdown flock. Her daughters and May also showed work. Touring the gallery, Alexandra was given a letterfrack bicycle basket full of roses. She bought a chair, a roll of silk from Cork, embroidery from West Meath and a length of Nottinghamshire Torchon lace, made by Stephen Wallinger (92).[75]

After visiting Guy's Hospital, and the Albert Hall, celebrating the 30th anniversary of Dr Barnardo's[76] Homes for Orphan Waifs, the Waleses and their daughters left on the 25th for Aberystwyth, where the Prince was installed as Chancellor of the University of Wales. Alexandra received the degree of a Doctor of Music and also opened Alexandra Hall.[77] The next day at Cardiff they visited an exhibition; the Prince received the Freedom of the Borough and opened the Free Library. After returning to London on the 27th, they attended a cattle and sheep sale back at Wolferton on 3 July, but returned on the 6th for the Levee, and *Mefistofele* that evening at Covent Garden; more theatres followed. Christian and Charles of Denmark arrived and there was a garden party at Buckingham Palace on the 13th. Among her wedding gifts, Maud received a Bible from the Young Women's Christian Association and a diamond and pearl necklace from Royal Warrant Holders. Danish royalty and Nicholas of Greece arrived on the 18th and two days later a deputation presented a Welsh gold wedding ring. The Queen came to tea on the 21st and there were visitors all day long. After a family dinner at Marlborough House, there was a "Cinematoscope" of moving photographs. The wedding, on the 22nd in Buckingham Palace's private chapel, was followed by the breakfast and a reception and garden party at Marlborough House; Prince and Princess Charles of Denmark left for their honeymoon at Appleton Manor. On the 29th Alexandra went briefly to Sandringham and called on them but left Appleton early on the 31st for Cowes, meeting her husband on the way. She had tea with the Queen the next day; there was sailing on *Britannia* and meetings with Empress Eugénie. On 5 August the Queen received Li Hongzhang[78] before he came on board *Osborne*; later Herr Wingard performed conjuring tricks.

Alexandra admired Wagner's music and on the 7th she and Victoria left for Bayreuth, staying at 32, Markgrafen Allee. They walked, shopped, lunched at the Royal Restaurant and on the 12th called on Wagner's widow. They saw *Rheingold, Die Walküre, Siegfried* and *Götterdämmerung* and dined at the theatre restaurant; Alexandra told George, "Toria, Charlotte & I, thoroughly enjoyed the beautiful Wagner music!! which you think horrid & hate!! so!! Our five days stay there incognito was really most successful and delightful – and the 'Niebelungen Ring' as that series of 4 Operas are called, surpassed all one's imagination and the beauty of the Music, the poetry of the whole representation & the excellence of the whole Performance cannot be described, only felt & appreciated when there at Bayreuth in that most wonderful place, & unique Opera House, in the world – it is enormous, the Stage very high & of great breadth and width, unlike any other – there are only Stalls, each row a step higher than the first. We sat in the 8th row, there are only 4 boxes, I think quite at the back." Lady de Grey and friends were there and "we took all our meals at a restaurant – great fun, and our tea & dinner & supper between the acts close to the Theatre & then rushed back to our places, we ladies having to tear off our hats the moment the curtain went up, & put them on again when the curtain dropped; an awful nuisance but part of the play!! There were lots of English I knew and people from all parts of the globe – luckily nobody bothered us. Serge was there & Ella came one day from Francis Bad. We had a charming little house in the country all to ourselves & not far from the town which made it much pleasanter." They left for Nuremberg on the 13th, visited the old castle and stayed overnight in the Hotel Bellevue at Munich. The next day they saw an exhibition and Herr Lembach's[79] studio, went by steamer to Herrenchiemsee and reached Gmunden at 9.30pm.

Alexandra had wanted to visit the Cumberlands because their eldest son had been seriously ill with typhus; he was recovering but "I much fear he will be lame for life." Thyra was well despite all the anxiety and "Poor Uncle Ernest was miserable too about his poor boy & quite touching in the way he looked after him." Reassured, Alexandra and her party left on 17 August, met Albert Edward the next day at Frankfort and travelled together to see Vicky at Friedrichshof. Albert Edward returned to Homburg after dinner but next day came and drove with his wife and sister to Villa Rothschild at Königstein. He met Alexandra, Victoria and others at Homburg the next day for lunch and tea at Ritter's Hotel, and dined at Friedrichshof again. Alexandra commented, "We … paid a visit to dear Papa in his pretty little rooms at Homburg; the first day he was looking well but he caught cold & was coughing & complained of his throat again … I do wish he wld be more careful there particularly during his cure." She and Victoria left on the 21st for Denmark; one of the first things they did was to watch the bicycle competition on the 23rd and Albert Schumann's Circus.[80] On the 31st Alexandra went to see "The Charleses'"[81] future residence in Copenhagen; they were not coming back until it was ready, "which is a <u>wise</u> arrangement". The Waleses had discussed it at Homburg and agreed the young couple should go to Copenhagen in *Osborne* in time for Queen Louise's birthday, but when Alexandra arrived at Bernstorff she found there would be no room for them there as the Russian emperor and empress were coming. Her parents and Frederick were going away and the only space would be at Charlottenlund, with the eccentric Crown Princess, for a month or two "which Freddy himself said would be a <u>mistake</u> the first time of Harry's coming [home], to which I <u>quite</u> agree and <u>no one</u> in Denmark expects them till their house is ready! So now they have still got a <u>nice</u> time to themselves in their dear little English house & home where I hope still to find them." Albert Edward however was furious; it would not look good if they did not return for the family gathering. "I know their rooms in Copenhagen are not ready yet – but what does that matter, 'where there's a will there's a way' & room I am sure could have been found for them. However I now wash my hands of the whole affair, & only hope the 'happy couple' will remain on in England as long as possible … & be in <u>no</u> hurry now about going to Denmark."[82] As Alexandra told George; "Papa & Mama go to Gmunden, & Freddy later on to his daughter, so then <u>Harry</u> & Charles might have remained <u>alone</u> with dear Swan!! Tell Papa so if he mentions this to you."[83]

7 Group taken in Denmark on Queen Louise's 80th birthday, 7 September 1898, left to right: King George I of the Hellenes, Dowager Empress Marie Feodorovna of Russia; Alexandra, Princess of Wales; Grand Duke Michael Alexandrovitch of Russia; Queen Louise of Denmark (in chair); Grand Duchess Olga Alexandrovna of Russia; Princess Marie Louise of Cumberland; Thyra, Duchess of Cumberland; Princess Olga of Cumberland (background); Princess Olga of Cumberland; Prince Christian of Denmark; Victoria Mary, Duchess of York; Alexandrine, Princess Christian of Denmark; George, Duke of York; *private collection*

News came that "Persimmon" had won the "St Leger" on 8 September; on the 9th the Russian couple and on the 12th Uncle Willy and his son, George, arrived at Copenhagen. Alexandra went there to see *Standard*, in which the Russians left for Scotland on the 20th; she and Victoria followed the next day, reaching the new Mar Lodge, where the Charleses were staying, on the 24th. Alexandra went for a rainy walk to see the burned ruins of the old Lodge. Nicholas II, Alexandra Feodorovna and baby, Olga, were staying at Balmoral; the Mar party lunched there on the 29th and the next day the Queen and her party lunched at Mar Lodge. After wishing the Russians goodbye at Balmoral, Alexandra, Victoria and the Charleses spent a few days there before returning to London on 14 October. Albert Edward stayed at Wynyard Park[84] from the 19th to the 24th before returning to London and Alexandra and Victoria went back to Sandringham. The Charleses remained at Appleton until 19 December. Guests began arriving and Gottlieb's Band came for the week of 2 November; after the Prince's birthday, the family stayed at West Dean Park[85] until the 14th. Meanwhile, on the 12th the Revd John Mitchell, rector of Wolferton, resigned; "It is quite as much on account of his own as for his sister's health that he has gone. In fact the madness in his family has quite developed itself in his case."[86] They were a sad loss, having been there some time. Alexandra had often visited Miss Mitchell. Alexandra and Victoria returned to Sandringham but on the 23rd went with Albert Edward and the Charleses to Blenheim. Back at Sandringham, more guests arrived; Gottlieb's Band returned, Ivanoff's Russian troupe of singers and dancers performed on Alexandra's birthday and there was informal dancing in the ballroom on 3 December. After London and Windsor, they returned for Christmas. "Poor Gwillem" had died of typhoid fever on the 13th, as had Maraquita Milles on the 21st. On the 29th Mr Bancroft[87] read Dickens'[88] *A Christmas Carol* in the ballroom after dinner and 1896 ended with a visit to the Hackney and thoroughbred studs.

Edward Terry's[89] Company performed Dickens' *Holly Tree Inn* and *Love in Idleness* on 1 January 1897. On the 4th, the Waleses and Victoria went to Trentham and opened a Grand Victorian Bazaar for the Parish Church at Fenton; the vicar, Revd L Tyrwhitt, officiated at Sandringham Church on the 31st. Alexandra visited Copeland and Minton's pottery works at Stoke on Trent on the 6th, the Prince laid the foundation stone of the Sutherland Institute at Longton on the 7th and they attended a concert, Dr S Heap's[90] *The Maid of Astolat,* at Hornby. Albert Edward went to London briefly, while the others returned to Sandringham; on the 21st Alexandra gave presents to children at West Newton School. Guests arrived and Gottlieb's Band was recalled to play in the evenings, with sleighing, skating and hockey by day. The Prince and guests left on 1 February and on the 6th Victoria's friend, Nora Musgrave[91] and her baby arrived. Alexandra visited the hospital and "Commemoration Exhibition" at St James's Hall in King's Lynn; two days later Empress Frederick and more guests arrived for a week. After this, Alexandra, with Victoria, went to London on the 18th. Greek politics were unsettled and she confided a great weight on her mind to George; "As you can imagine I am in an awful state about dear Willy & the dreadful position he is placed in. It was utterly impossible for him to go on longer under the present state of things, so had to risk all. God grant that things may still be turned, & that good may come out of evil."[92]

Attending theatres throughout February, Alexandra also saw exhibitions of Leighton's and Watts' work with Vicky and dined with the Queen on the 23rd. The first drawing room was on the 24th, and on the 27th she watched bicycle drill at Alexandra House. Albert Edward left for Cannes on 1 March and she had plenty to do but, feeling utterly miserable, returned to Sandringham on the 11th for a quiet time, driving and visiting the poor. Victoria had told George that their mother would be coming up to London early next week before starting for Denmark, and he wrote; "How delighted darling Harry & Amama & Apapa will be to see you again & you will be able to cheer one another up. I do indeed feel for you darling Motherdear, because I know what you are going through & what your feelings are, we must only put our trust in God & pray to him to take us all out of our dangers & difficulties, I can't say more."[93] Back in London on the 22nd, Alexandra attended Lamoureux's[94] concert at the Queen's Hall and the next day left for Denmark with Victoria and Louise.[95]

Albert Edward contacted George from Monte Carlo; "You will I am sure have been as surprised to hear, as I was, of Mama [having] arranged to go to Denmark tomorrow but I think it is a very wise decision on her part. She wrote to me in such low spirits & feeling so utterly depressed at Sandringham that I think it is far better for her to go to her old home for a few weeks, & stay with her Parents besides seeing Maud, as I believe Charles is going to sea for a short time ... I quite agree with you that it is useless discussing the Greek question with dear Mama, as she is so biased on one side that she will not listen to reason & becomes so violent & bitter in her arguments, that she considers poor dear U Willy & the Greeks can do no wrong, & the Gt Powers no right! However the latter have put their 'foot down' & will stand no more nonsense from that courageous but foolish little country, wh for its own interests wishes to set fire to the whole of Europe! I hear Ld Salisbury told Mama that Greece was a tiresome & troublesome Country, or words to that effect, & I cannot help thinking that the conclusion he has arrived at is a very just one!"[96] By the 30th he had had one letter from her; she was happy with her relatives, "but has alas! still got Greece on her brain!"[97] Admiral Stephenson had told him, "Apapa views the Greek question with the greatest calmness wh is having a good effect on Mama."[98] Walks with her father, relatives, parties, the theatre and church helped

Alexandra. She also wrote to Infanta Eulalia of Spain,[99] who had asked her a personal question. After apologising for the long-delayed reply, she assured Eulalie; "do not for one moment imagine that I was annoyed by yr question – on the contrary I was very <u>much</u> flattered that you shld think poor old me & my complexion good. I cld hardly help laughing though when you asked <u>what</u> I did for it, or whom I had seen about it!!! I have <u>never</u> seen anybody or <u>done anything</u> for it – all I ever do is to wash every night in <u>warm</u> water & <u>soap</u> my face with <u>unscented</u> soap called Cameo, & always put cold cream on after to keep it soft. *Voila tout* – and I <u>strongly</u> advise you <u>not</u> to try or consult any specialist for the skin, as they very often <u>spoil</u> the complexion instead of improving it, and you, who have such a <u>pretty, fresh</u> face & <u>white</u> skin really do not require anything to improve it, beyond these simple remedies I have mentioned."[100] She also mentioned how anxious they all were about Greece. On 18 April war was declared between Turkey and Greece and a newspaper cutting of a war map, from *The Standard* of the 20th, was kept in Alexandra's engagement diary.

Victoria was getting out on her own. It was Lent and she disliked taking part in social events, although her mother felt she must follow the Danish custom of carrying on as usual and wanted her to join her. Victoria told May, "<u>You</u> would have laughed at seeing me quite <u>independent</u>! Well, as it is <u>for once</u> in my life, I am profiting. No doubt Mama knows that the <u>Danes</u> can't possibly have any <u>attraction</u> for me!! I even went <u>alone</u> to Church last Sunday as Harry was seedy, & every day walk over to the other Palace. Louise can <u>never</u> go out <u>alone</u> & one of us has always to fetch & take her back, which makes us smile. Let us <u>hope</u> after this I may be <u>allowed</u> sometimes to go to some <u>amusing things</u> with you two. Never mind the words we had[101] after the Portlands' Ball. I <u>did</u> enjoy that tremendously & shall <u>always</u> be <u>grateful</u> to you for having taken me."[102] Victoria was a sheltered young woman who, when well, was attractive, sociable (possibly with her Danish grandmother's so-called "familiar, flirty way with men") and also perhaps rather susceptible, like her father. Alexandra may have worried about her accidentally getting into the wrong company if she went out alone in London. Perhaps this was over-cautious; Victoria was nearly 29, but Alexandra had had a ring-side view of society's ways.

Writing to George, Alexandra was glad the problems with the children's nurse had been resolved and "<u>so</u> delighted to hear such excellent accounts of yr blessed little 'David', & that he is <u>now</u> <u>thriving</u> so <u>well</u> in every way, in fact seems a different child since poor dear Peters left! I was sure he was a strong little fellow *au fond* & not the least more nervous than any other child. He simply wanted encouragement & to be treated like any other little child of his age, her over-anxiety made him a nervous & frightened child; that was all. And thank God that this new Nurse[103] seems to manage & understand the children so well, & I am sure now they will be again just what they were formerly & a real delight to you both. Poor May, she certainly has been terribly bothered about it all, & so were <u>you</u>. I was quite sorry & all this winter to see how uncomfortable it all was & how estranged the children got from you & how little pleasure you had from them." They were all happy together in Denmark, although very anxious about "dear Uncle Willy & the Greek question, which <u>naturally</u> gets worse & worse every day & for him an impossible state to be kept up any longer. Thank God that <u>you</u> quite <u>understand</u> me – tho' I expect <u>few</u> at home do the same. I have lots to tell you when I come home. Oh! if only I had the power I might have told them <u>secret</u> things I have just heard, which wld astonish a few but as I have been so <u>snubbed</u> I will say no more. Altho' I am so sorry not to be with you all at home for Easter yet I am glad <u>not</u> to be there with Uncle <u>George</u> etc at this moment who I know wld drive me wild with their stick in the mud politics & views on <u>this</u>, to me, most <u>alarming question</u>. Don't tell all this, it is <u>private</u>. Darling Minny & I quite agree about all & here everybody too, poor Amama & Apapa are so unhappy but very calm, thank God, & have implicit faith in dear Willy's judgement & know & feel God will help him." They had all taken Holy Communion on 15 April, "in the same church, Slotskirken where I was confirmed & where I took it for the first time in my life!"[104]

Minny left on the 20th; Alexandra spent time with her mother and lunched with Maud on the 23rd. On the 27th she, Louise and Victoria left for England. May had had a daughter on the 25th [105] and Albert Edward reminded George it had been Alice's birthday; "As you know I am the last person to press you about names ... but as dear A Alice was my favourite sister, nothing would give me greater pleasure if you would give your little girl that name."[106] Alexandra and Victoria came back from Sandringham on 7 May to join him for a weekend at Eaton.[107] They called on the Gladstones at Hawarden on the 10th and later saw *Faust* at Covent Garden. The next day there was a drawing room and later that week Alexandra went to Helena's sale of work and an amateur art exhibition. They opened the Yachting and Fisheries Exhibition at the Imperial Institute on the 17th; on the 20th Alexandra went to the HAIA's exhibition at the Albert Hall and then on the 22nd, with her husband, to open the new Blackwall Tunnel. The next week included Guard Mounting Parade at Horse Guards, the Military Tournament at the Agricultural Hall, laying the foundation stone of the Royal Ophthalmic Hospital in City Road and opening the restored chapter house at Canterbury Cathedral. Alexandra also went to Helen Albany's[108] bazaar at the Imperial Institute and on the 31st Mademoiselle Kleeberg[109] played the piano for her at Marlborough House. Receptions, theatres and concerts often filled the evenings. On 5 June the family attended Victoria Alexandra Alice Mary of York's christening at Sandringham Church. Guests arrived and on the 10th some of the Prince's horses were sold at Wolferton. Alexandra was still worried about Greece and in May and June begged the Queen to put pressure on Turkey by having British ships sent to Salonika.[110]

The Queen's diamond jubilee was approaching and the family returned to London. On 17 June "Persimmon" won the Queen's Cup at Ascot; this was extremely gratifying but perhaps a letter from his mother the next day touched Albert Edward even more. Prince Albert had been the last Grand Master of the Order of the Bath, and the idea of someone taking his place still upset her. However, she wished to do something for Bertie, and he already had all the other honours; "I accordingly appoint you to the Office, which has hardly any duties, hoping that you may look upon it as a proof of my affection for you."[111] Madame Albani[112] sang at a grand diamond jubilee festival concert at the Albert Hall on the 19th and later there was a military tattoo with massed bands in the quadrangle at Windsor Castle. The next day, the 60th anniversary of the Queen's accession, a state service was held at St Paul's Cathedral and later the Waleses gave a large family dinner. After lunch, a state banquet and two receptions at Buckingham Palace on the 21st, a state procession left for an outdoor service at St Paul's on the 22nd; the Queen, Alexandra and Helena sitting in a carriage. A state banquet followed and the next day a gala performance at Covent Garden of acts from *Tannhäuser, Romeo and Juliet* and *Les Huguenots*. Alexandra had headed the organisation of a special jubilee fund, providing dinners for the poorest people, and on 24 June, between 11.30 and 1.30, she and her husband went to the People's Palace to see crippled children from Ragged Schools; to Central Hall, Holborn; and to Clerkenwell, to greet the guests at their dinner. She would have found this far more worthwhile than the state ball that evening. On the 26th a Royal Naval review took place at Spithead, which the couple attended on board *Victoria and Albert*; two days later the Queen held a garden party at Buckingham Palace and on 1 July reviewed 25,000 men on Laffan's Plain, Aldershot. On the 2nd, at the Devonshire House fancy-dress ball, Alexandra, as Queen Marguerite de Valois,[113] had Baba Knollys as her page. The Prince appeared as Grand Master of the Knights Hospitaller of Malta.

Albert Edward presented jubilee medals to colonial troops at Buckingham Palace on the 3rd and on the 5th the Waleses attended an SSFA fête at Chelsea Hospital, where he also inspected Chelsea Pensioners and Armed Forces veterans. Victoria's birthday on the 6th was celebrated with a large family lunch and *Die Meistersinger* later. They opened public baths and washhouses at Lambeth, and Park Hospital at Lewisham, and attended Captain Holford's Ball. On the 16th, "Persimmon" won the "Eclipse Stakes" at Sandown. After more functions, they opened the National Gallery of British Art at Millbank, funded and given to the nation by Henry Tate,[114] on the 21st. Alexandra gave prizes to the Royal Academy of Music's pupils at St James's Hall the next day. After Goodwood, Cowes and Osborne, they left on the 10th August for the third cycle of Wagner's "Ring" at Bayreuth, arriving, after a hot and dusty journey, with two hours to spare before *Parsifal*, which began at 4pm and lasted till 10pm, with two entr'actes of over half an hour. Albert Edward wrote; "The representation was

8 Queen Victoria as she appeared at the time of her Diamond Jubilee, 22 June 1897, *Gustav Mullins*. According to a note on the back by "M.E.D.S." "The bonnet worn by the Queen in this picture was made over for her when it came from the milliner's by the Princess of Wales"; *private collection*

simply magnificent & most impressive, but could be given nowhere but here; the stage is dark the whole time, & not a sound is heard. The orchestra is invisible as it plays under the stage. We have since heard 'Das Rheingold' & 'Die Walküre' & I have still to hear 'Siegfried' & 'Götterdämmerung' but on Wednesday I leave for Marienbad so as to begin my 'cure' as soon as possible … We are quite comfortably lodged in the same house Mama occupied last year. The weather is terribly hot & stuffy. We have found a good many people we know."[115] They visited Frau Wagner[116] on the 14th and on the 16th dined at the theatre with her after the second entr'acte in *Siegfried*. All the operas except *Parsifal* were directed by the composer's son, Siegfried.[117] They had called on Lady de Grey at Schloss Plaisanterie and visited Nuremburg on the 13th, "a wonderfully interesting town"; touring the castle and seeing Albrecht Dürer's[118] house.

Albert Edward left for Marienbad on the 18th but Alexandra remained and saw *Parsifal* again. She reached Hotel Victoria at Wörishofen on the 20th for a short "cure", taking two douches on the 21st, walking barefoot in the fields for two days, visiting the cloister and attending a service. She left for Hohenburg and then Munich, for a concert at the opera house on the 23rd. Leaving on the 24th she reached Denmark the next day. Two days later, her niece Ingeborg[119] married Carl of Sweden at Christiansborg Church. Alexandra walked and drove and on 5 September met Victoria and Maud, who had arrived at Copenhagen in *Osborne* after staying at Appleton. The Prince arrived from Marienbad and most of the family were there for the 7th. Alexandra told George; "Thank God the Sisters arrived safely & _ever_ so _much better_ & Toria dear does just what she likes & feels inclined to and rests whenever she can – that _quiet_ peaceful 3 weeks at Appleton did her worlds of good, just what she wanted … Beloved Amama's birthday _80th_ alas!! went off beautifully & both blessed Parents are wonderfully well & happy. We were all so pleased to have dear Papa here & he is at this moment looking the picture of health, _thinner, rested_ & _younger_ and in excellent spirits." They all missed "poor Uncle Willy & Aunt Olga", for whose absence she blamed the German emperor, apparently hindering the signing of peace between Greece and Turkey; "it is not alone hatred against poor Willy & Greece but specially directed _against England_." She feared William was determined to establish a foothold and a fleet in the East "& Turkey in his pocket" which could ultimately threaten England's position in Egypt (and India); Lord Salisbury was not being firm enough, whereas Lord Beaconsfield would have "carried through his wishes & made England stronger than ever in the East … but as to Lord S he wld give way in this as in other things!! You may tell Grd Mama so." Willy was in a very difficult position and she feared one day it would be the same for England, with a German fleet and power in the east as well as the north, where England had let them annex Kiel in 1864.[120] Understandably, she saw Greece, like Denmark, as a small country threatened by a bigger one and cannot be blamed for her concern or her frustration with governmental caution.

However, she was enjoying her holiday, with ballet, excursions and the Harvest Festival service at St Alban's on the 19th. On their "engagement day", 9 September, the Waleses had given a family lunch party on *Osborne* and afterwards cruised round the Swedish island of Hoen.[121] On the 20th the Prince left for his regular visit to Friedrichshof, but Alexandra remained, visiting Miss Knudsen, Tuxen and an art exhibition. She went for a number of walks with her father or Victoria, or alone. Queen Louise was unwell but recovered and Alexandra often drove with her. Meanwhile, back in England, the Prince had seen "a remarkable but very violent Article on Greece in today's '*Observer*'!"[122] The editor of the newspaper at this time was Mrs Rachel Beer,[123] respected as an intelligent woman in a male sphere, who had strong views about current affairs. She was known to Albert Edward and probably Alexandra too. Had Alexandra asked her to champion Greece? Or had the Princess written or planned the article herself – and did her husband know, or suspect?

She and the ailing Victoria[124] arrived home at midnight on 20 October. Alexandra remained in London on the 23rd to see *Diarmed* (with Lord Lorne's libretto) at Covent Garden; the Prince was away and Alexandra joined Victoria at Sandringham the next day. On the 27th she had only just woken up when her maid brought a telegram from the Duke of Teck; Mary was very ill and in some danger and would Alexandra come to White Lodge? But before she could leave, a message came "from poor May saying all was over!" It was a terrible shock. Mary had been unwell and depressed about her husband's failing mental health but had recently seemed more cheerful. Alexandra went straight to White Lodge and found her husband and the Yorks with the grief-stricken Duke. Her cousin looked "so beautiful, calm and peaceful, with such a happy expression on her dear face" but the thought of never again hearing her cheery voice and laugh, or meeting the gaze of her beautiful eyes, was agony.[125] Alexandra returned to Sandringham but came back on the 30th for a private service at White Lodge the next day, calling again on 1 November. On the 3rd the Waleses attended the funeral in St George's Chapel. Alexandra told Queen Victoria that Mary had been "ever a real friend in the best sense of the word." The funeral had been doubly hard to bear because of memories of Eddy, "but I was there for poor dear May's sake & tried to be a help & comfort to her in her overwhelming sorrow for her loving & beloved Mother – what she has lost in her I feel she will but feel more & more every day, & nothing and nobody can ever replace her." May was bearing up bravely; she and George were still at White Lodge, comforting her heartbroken father.[126]

Shooting parties and Gottlieb's Band occupied the following week at Sandringham but Alexandra's thoughts were "always with you all at White Lodge. It all must be too sad for words, & I fear worse & worse every day!! also for poor darling May she must realize her terrible & irreparable loss more and more ... How is poor Uncle Teck now – he must feel so lonely & wretched without that beloved Aunt Mary – what has he thought of doing? is he going to Württemberg first as the King wished, & <u>who</u> with! – as he ought to have someone with him." Papa's birthday had been sad and quiet and the Yorks had been terribly missed. Mary's death had prompted thoughts of mortality and "I am going to make <u>my will</u> as soon as possible and begin tearing my letters!!!" The children, at York Cottage, were well and had brought their grandfather nosegays on his birthday; "They are really such darlings ... sweet little David talks away quite happy, little Bertie also says a few words & quite well but I think is shy about talking, little baby is so sweet & always smiling – I think she now has two teeth." The shooting parties were tiresome; "when one is <u>low</u> & <u>unhappy</u> one hates seeing anybody – thank goodness we have got the band which I always think <u>soothes</u> one's troubled spirit." Alexandra was only rarely allowed to see the Fifes' daughters and was glad to have shown "Louise & <u>Macduff</u> how fully you trust yr precious children into <u>my care</u> – and how fondly I <u>look after them</u>."[127] She and Victoria stayed at Windsor with the Queen from 19–23 November, returning to Sandringham on the 24th; the Charleses were now at Appleton. There were more guests, the mausoleum pilgrimage, then Welbeck Abbey[128] until 18 December. The next day, Alexandra visited Burne-Jones's[129] studio, returning to Sandringham on the 21st. Albert Edward joined her on the 23rd and Baba Knollys arrived. They celebrated Christmas with a large dinner party for relatives, staff and friends, and on the 30th a performance from the Empire Theatre, with music, variety acts and Professor Jolly's four cinematograph shows.

After about nine years, the Prince and "Daisy" Brooke's[130] affair came to a head in 1897/8, and they tried to conciliate Alexandra. Daisy wrote to them both and Albert Edward told her that Alexandra had declared "she felt <u>very</u> sorry for you and that 'out of evil good would come'"; none of her friends were Daisy's enemies, or talked about her. He felt a corner had been turned; Alexandra would now meet Daisy with pleasure, and perhaps they could get up some kind of philanthropic venture together; "she really quite forgives and condones the past, as I have corroborated what you wrote about our friendship having been platonic for some years". This was fantastic optimism; Alexandra had no intention of befriending Daisy and also knew very well it would not be the last time her husband strayed. As he admitted, she had been "an angel of goodness throughout all this, but then she is a lady! and never could do anything that was mean or small!"[131] His feelings for Daisy were cooling, but soon he would make a new friend.

On 3 January 1898 the Waleses and Victoria went to Chatsworth, for shooting and amateur theatricals. Returning on the 8th they saw *The Babes in the Wood* at

Drury Lane, before dispensing hospitality at Sandringham until 7 February. Victoria had longstanding digestive troubles and on the 10th was prescribed a "rest cure" in bed; although Alexandra visited London briefly, she spent most of the next six weeks at Sandringham. On the 26th they heard that King George had been fired at on his way home from Phalerum but was unhurt. Alexandra thanked God for saving "his precious life & also dear little Minny's,[132] but it was indeed a miraculous & providential escape. It gave me a terrible shock when I first heard it just as I was going to church. The accounts in the Times are most graphic as related by himself."[133] She had visited *HMS Thunderer* in 1897 and now thanked Lord Charles Beresford warmly for "that beautiful Telephone made on board the Thunderer ... as I have been longing to have one, only did not know where was the best place to get it. It is great fun sending an unexpected voice into the upper regions and frightening the Family with a <u>clap</u> of <u>thunder</u>!"[134]

Still in mourning, May and her Aunt Augusta had gone to Mentone, with Augusta's granddaughter, Duchess Marie,[135] nearly twenty, who had recently suffered a dreadful experience. She had been raped by a footman, become pregnant, horrified her parents and been forced to give up the child. Augusta and May believed in her fundamental innocence and Albert Edward, then at Cannes, was also sympathetic; Alexandra was "glad Papa has been over there & made them <u>all</u> come over to Cannes where he took them about to various places & people, which I am sure will have done them <u>all</u> good. That poor little girl I am <u>so</u> sorry about. She evidently is quite innocent still in spite of all, but I wish you wld send me sweet May's account about it all ... I will return it to you <u>at once</u>! Please do."[136] Papa had found "A Augusta much aged & grown thin. Poor Marie looks the personification of innocence! The whole story is simply incomprehensible to me. They are all coming over to lunch with U George tomorrow when I shall meet them."[137] He later talked at length about Marie to the Queen, who was very kind and declared she would see Augusta.[138]

Victoria was much better, having walked and driven during the week, and her mother hoped and trusted "she will now gradually get quite strong once again though of course for the present she must be very, <u>very</u> careful – particularly keep a strict diet – and then I hope she will not in vain have taken this long & tedious rest, poor thing."[139] On 25 March Alexandra left for Denmark, while Victoria stayed with the Musgraves at Cromer. Christian IX's 80th birthday fell on Good Friday, so the family celebrations were fairly quiet, with a dinner at Frederick's house. Alexandra attended the Danish church that day and Easter Day and the Russian church with Minny on Saturday. There had been public celebrations and thousands gathered outside the palace to cheer the King. Great advances in agriculture, education, the Navy, industry, science, literature and other matters had been made during his reign; the Danes never forgot their defeat in war but it had not hampered their progress and the Royal Family were greatly loved and respected. Alexandra and Maud left on the 14th and were joined at Sandringham on the 16th by Victoria, who then took Maud to Cromer till the end of April, briefly returning to Sandringham to see their father and the Fifes. They all went to London on 3 May and on the 8th the Waleses inspected Eddy's monument in the Albert Memorial Chapel, still lacking the recumbent statue.[140] The season was beginning; Maud returned to Denmark on the 11th and Alexandra had to stay indoors the next day with an inflamed eye. The 17th was Alexandra Duff's seventh birthday and her grandmother helped celebrate with tea at 15 Portman Square.

Alexandra attended the HAIA's Exhibition[141] on the 19th and Victoria left next day for Windsor, to accompany the Queen to Balmoral, while Alexandra went to a levee, the Military Tournament, the zoo and the opera. Gladstone had died on the 19th and the couple attended his funeral in Westminster Abbey on the 28th, Albert Edward and George acting as pall-bearers. George was to command HMS *Crescent* on a short cruise that summer; the Yorks left on 5 June and he commissioned the ship at Portsmouth on the 7th. Alexandra presented prizes to pupils of the Royal Masonic Institution for Boys at the Albert Hall on the 7th and looked forward to the advent of Wagner's Ring Cycle and other operas at Covent Garden. As the Prince told George on the 13th; "Since you left, we have been very busy. We missed you & May, & the younger generation, very much at the Ball on Tuesday. Mama found it very dull and tiresome, but I fear she finds every evening entertainment so, excepting going to the Opera! & she rarely misses a night or afternoon! in going to C[ovent] Garden. I saw the whole of 'Siegfried' on [Thursday], though it began at 5! but I must say I enjoyed it very much & the Performance was admirably given."[142] Alexandra's understanding of stage dialogue was now hampered by deafness but music was paramount in opera; she could hear it and see what was going on, regardless of the words, and often knew the story already.

Victoria returned from Balmoral on 18 June, after Ascot week. The Waleses attended two weddings on the 20th and the 23rd [143] and Alexandra also visited the Ladies' Kennel Association Show at the Botanic Gardens, and the Royal Academy. Victoria spent the weekend of the 25th at Cowarth with Alice Stanley. On the 27th Alexandra attended the Duchess of Sutherland's[144] charity concert, with well-known performers, for building a church in a poor district of the Potteries. With May, she opened "The Press Bazaar" at the Hotel Cecil the next day. The couple laid the foundation stone of the Deptford Fund House's new buildings at Deptford on 2 July; there were more seasonal events and on the 11th Alexandra opened the Pfeiffer Wing of the London School of Medicine for Women,[145] when her husband paid tribute to her; "It is needless to say how great an interest [the Princess] takes in all that concerns the education of women and in the great strides that have taken place during the last 25 or 30 years in the special education of women as regards medicine."[146] The last state ball had been on the 8th, when Victoria and her Uncle Arthur "valsed a good deal".[147] The next day she went to Cromer with Mrs Hardinge.

On 16 July Albert Edward left for a weekend with Baron Ferdinand Rothschild at Waddesdon, touring the grounds and inspecting the hot houses, gardens and farm. Coming downstairs on the 18th, he slipped and fell, fracturing his kneecap and suffering excruciating pain. He left at 3.30pm by special train for London, and was confined to his own rooms. Alexandra told George that she had spent much of the last ten days there; "It was really a dreadful accident & I only hope to God he may not get a stiff leg like me, which is I confess an <u>awful bore</u> & <u>nuisance</u> and one's wretched leg seems always in the way, & makes everything one wld like to do <u>so awkward</u> – such as <u>riding</u>, running & bicycling etc. <u>Stairs</u> are always detestable & before a lot of people it is odious – simply." She rarely complained about this constant annoyance; luckily Papa was "getting on <u>wonderfully</u> <u>well</u> and so <u>far</u> without a drawback of any kind, he has never had any pain since he came back to London, it was only when the accident happened that he <u>suffered</u> <u>tortures</u>, poor thing." The kneecap had now re-joined and was recovering; "He has been very patient I must say and is quite cheery".[148] Albert Edward thought it "a gt bore being 'tied by the leg' as I now am, as I am feeling so well otherwise, but one must have patience."[149] His leg was strapped up in a splint and cradle; as usual, he still saw a great many people, wrote a lot and read all the papers. Alexandra sat "with him all the evening from 9 till we put him to bed at 11.30. He has every kind of Doctor and Surgeon imaginable and they all put a finger in the pie!!! & say to themselves 'this kneecap we truly laid'!!! (as they do with a foundation stone!)"[150] She was happy as part of the medical team, which also included Victoria's nurse.

Alexandra had received a deputation on 27 July, headed by Sir Thomas Lipton,[151] who gave her £100,000 to found the "Alexandra Trust", providing cheap dinners for poor people.[152] Then it was driving, the zoo, art galleries and visitors. Nicholas and Marie of Greece had arrived; Marie's first visit to London and a dream come true. "Besides all this, I had a special love for … my Aunt Alix. From my very earliest memories she was always a kind of fairy godmother to me, and we loved each other dearly. As a child in Denmark, whenever I was in trouble, I always went to her and she always understood. When I behaved badly, she was the one I asked to go to my father and plead for me; and many a time she got me out of a scrape or saved me from punishment. I was always allowed to go to her rooms whenever I chose. She too was delighted to be able to show me her lovely home and have me stay with her."[153]

On the 30th the Prince was taken by ambulance to Portsmouth and then *Osborne*, with his wife, daughter, and Greek relatives, and stayed there until 8 September. Alexandra was looking forward to nursing and helping him recover, but on 2 August received an urgent message from Denmark; her mother was seriously ill. As Albert Edward told Vicky; "poor Alix was terribly upset, as she didn't want to leave me just now, but she had to hurry out to her Mother, to whom she is so devoted."[154] Alexandra left, with Laking, for Denmark on the 3rd, arrived at Bernstorff in the evening of the 4th and found Queen Louise a great deal better. She drove with her over the next few days and Laking saw her on the 9th before going home the next day. From Cowes, George had sympathised with Alexandra for having had to "rush away like that … & leave dear Papa & all of us just when you hoped to have a nice quiet time & to be able to look after him & then besides that your great anxiety for darling little Amama. Thank God you found her better than you expected, although of course very weak." Laking "has an enormous [amount] of tact & I have the greatest faith in him as a doctor. I trust that now with careful nursing beloved Amama will gradually get back her strength." Papa was doing well; "old McCormac[155] came on Friday evening & left again today, he examined the knee most carefully & said nothing could possibly be going on better." They had given him a more comfortable splint; "Dear Papa is still in excellent spirits & most cheery, I never saw a better patient. I trust he will continue so, whatever happens we must try & not let him get bored."[156] Victoria was very well, resting twice a day; she was in her mother's large, comfortable cabin and had put up all her photographs there. By the 20th, "Every day now [Papa] puts his good leg down & uses your chair with the leg rest which you used 31 years ago & is delighted with it. The 'Osborne' has been for several little cruises which he much enjoys, he is moved up on to the bridge, where he gets more air & sees everything that is going on."[157]

On 12 August, Fräulein Noedel[158] died in London. Alexandra and her daughters sent wreaths for the funeral on the 16th. Fräulein had worked hard to develop the Sandringham technical schools, which were now flourishing. The girls' school, in a low, ivy-covered building near Sandringham Church, provided needlework, cookery and housework classes for girls on the estate. Fräulein had also started a spinning class; spinning was an important Danish industry and Alexandra had set an example by becoming the first pupil; she had a black ebony spinning wheel, tied with the Danish colours of red and white. Her chief intention at the school was to provide different types of education to suit the pupils' needs; the stronger ones could be trained for domestic service, while the delicate ones could work from home and sell their manufactures to earn a living, or become ladies' maids.[159]

At Bernstorff Queen Louise's health fluctuated; sometimes she was not so well but sometimes could sit outside in her rose garden, where Alexandra sat with her. "Naturally Alix can make no plans, as she is afraid of leaving her mother" wrote Albert Edward.[160] The Queen's decline was heartbreaking; "It is indeed the saddest case possible as with a weak heart and at her age alas, it is difficult to know what to expect, there are a great many ups and downs and some days she really seems much better and brighter and cheery, but then comes some slight drawback such as a bad night, when she seems so weak, low and depressed, which makes it dreadful for us all, particularly poor dear Papa." Queen Louise liked having relatives round her and was much looking forward to seeing the Yorks and David in early September. Alexandra was pleased with the latest news of her husband; the doctor was confident "he will be able to bend the knee – altho' it must take a long time ... before getting quite well and straight. What a blessing he is such a first rate patient and of such good <u>health</u> & <u>spirits</u> just now as of course that naturally helps him on wonderfully." She had hated going away; "It was a great wrench for me having to <u>leave him</u> like that and you all just when I might have been of some use to comfort him, but fate is against me and I have no chance! The only time he <u>must</u> remain at home I am <u>compelled</u> by <u>duty</u> to leave him & help to nurse my darling precious Mother. I was also terribly low at leaving you all my blessed Children and the dear old Osborne where we all seemed so happy together."[161]

Something else was worrying her; although Maud loved her husband, she much preferred Appleton to Denmark. Charles was often away at sea and she made herself unwell in fretting for him. As yet she had no children. On 1 September Alexandra wrote hurriedly to George; "In case I shall have no opportunity of speaking to you <u>before</u> you <u>see</u> <u>Harry</u> and Charles, I must beg <u>you</u> <u>both</u> to <u>encourage</u> her as much as possible about <u>everything here</u>, as she is <u>inclined</u> to <u>complain</u> & *raisonné* a good deal, which does her and <u>him</u> so much harm, <u>and she is</u> <u>very</u> happy in her charming home with him as you will see for yr own self. For indeed she <u>must</u> on <u>no</u> account forget that she married a <u>Danish</u> Prince and a naval man and he <u>owes</u> his first duty <u>both</u> to <u>his country</u> and <u>profession</u>." Maud was particularly aggrieved just now because Charles' work obliged him to stay in Denmark over the winter and she would have to remain there instead of going back to England, "So please talk sense to her shld she say anything and tell her it wld be much nicer to come home in the spring etc and <u>above</u> all <u>let</u> her see where her <u>duty</u> and indeed her future happiness lies."[162]

Ironically, Maud was as reluctant to give up England as her mother was Denmark, although Alexandra genuinely loved England and ultimately regarded it as her true home. It was sad that her husband and children were never really comfortable in Denmark, and now Victoria was in a quandary about it. The climate did not suit her and, having been ill, she had not gone there this time, although Alexandra wanted her for emotional support and to see her grandmother, perhaps for the last time. Albert Edward, however, put his foot down; "Mama keeps harping on Victoria's coming out but for her health's sake I am strenuously opposing it. The long journey, the life, climate etc are so bad for her & she is already beginning to fret herself about it, wh gives her bad nights."[163] He added; "How strange that dear Mama won't understand about Toria, when she knows how ill she has been. I cannot and will not be a party to her undertaking that long journey & the life at Bernstorff to the detriment of her health. I have written & said it over & over again, but then comes in that old argument – if I can spare her? If it were not for her health I should have sent her with Nicky & Minny who left for Denmark today." He himself disliked the Danish climate and, despite his affection for the family, was restless there; the meals were at different times and the way of life seemed dilatory, unfocussed and rowdy. In the end, Victoria went to Scotland with him instead.

The Battle of Omdurman, under Major-general Kitchener's[164] command, had been won on 1 September, but on the 10th came shocking news; Empress Elizabeth had been assassinated at Geneva by an anarchist, Lucheni;[165] "That poor charming inoffensive woman – then the poor Emperor after all he has gone through. It is the 'last straw.'"[166] Queen Louise celebrated her 81st birthday; the band played and she received her family in the garden. It was a happy occasion but Alexandra had had to sit up with her mother a few days earlier and on 8–9 September stayed up with her all night. Nearly every evening over 30 sat down to dinner; normality continued although the Queen's life was ebbing slowly away. She was however delighted to see the Yorks and "David", who had stayed from 2–15 September, and her other grandchildren did what they could; George of Greece was "so <u>wonderful</u> in his devotion & <u>praiseworthy</u> patience & <u>remarkable</u> <u>unselfishness</u>, which surpasses all I have <u>ever seen</u> in anybody, much less a young man like him, generally so full of life and go. He knows she likes to have him and he is the only one she trusts in carrying her from chair to couch or bed, so he sits there all day waiting, so as to be ready at any moment she wants him. It really is touching to see." Alexandra, worried about her mother and with a bad finger and sore throat was feeling wretched enough, when, catastrophically, "Uncle Willy very nearly killed my darling little Punchy – with his beastly bicycle, & knocked him down before my very eyes, & I was too late to save him." The little dog was lucky to survive the severe blow on the side of his head. Queen Louise continued going out but during the night of the 25th became weak and breathless and sent for the King. He was "so miserable, & so good & brave, & never leaves her." The next day she went to the rose garden for the last time and that night Minny sat with her. She did not leave her room on the 27th; Alexandra sat with her for 17 hours and Minny and Thyra took turns at the vigil. On the 28th she stayed in bed all day; "God grant she may yet get over this <u>cruel</u> attack, and yet if she is to go on like <u>this in this</u> misery, it wld be a blessing for her, darling Amama, were she relieved from all her sufferings … we can but leave it all to our good God."[167] Queen Louise died early in the morning of the 29th.

For her family, especially her husband, it was an irreparable loss, "as she was so clever & bright & quite the presiding genius of the Family!" Poor Alexandra was heartbroken; she had nursed her mother more or less day and night for eight weeks and Albert Edward dreaded the effect on her health. He hoped she could come home with George, who was going to the funeral, "should her kind, dear Father not require her, as she wants complete change of air & scene, & we have besides been separated for so long."[168] May had written at once, expressing "warm, deep sympathy". She could "only too well imagine what you are going thro' now, the awful sense of desolation when for the first time one's adored Mother cannot answer one, the one Being in the world who was always the same in all one's joys & sorrows, the blank is so agonising and gets more & more so. God help you, darling Mother dear is all I can say." She was thankful they had seen Queen Louise and she had met David, and would always remember her as she had been on her birthday, "so bright and her lovely eyes so clear."[169]

The funeral was held at Roskilde Cathedral on 15 October. In a note to Charlotte, Alexandra wrote, "it was too awful but beautiful. Now all is dark & sad. Last night too sad & heavenly all by torchlight."[170] The mourners departed; Minny and the Greek sovereigns left on the 24th. Albert Edward wanted to go to Sandringham and needed to know Alexandra's plans.[171] Frustratingly, she remained a little longer with her father, but left on the 31st, arriving in London with George next day. Her husband was relieved; "though of course she is dreadfully sad, I was glad to see her looking better than I expected, but a week ago she was really very poorly & quite 'run down'". Alexandra was "thankful to be back once more & to find dear Bertie so much better even than I could have anticipated, in good spirits & health, & his knee very nearly right again. It really was a marvel to me to see him walking about without a stick even, after having left him so helpless."[172] On 3 November they went to Sandringham; after Albert Edward's birthday shooting party, Alexandra and Victoria visited Windsor, drove with the Queen, walked in the town, and saw Eddy's monument, returning to Sandringham on the 18th. Lord Kitchener and other guests arrived on the 27th and Vicky on 7 December. The Waleses attended the mausoleum service on the 14th, with a special prayer for those departed, implying, among others, Queen Louise.[173] The next day, they heard Christopher Sykes had died, after a stroke; Alexandra called to pay her respects at his house. News of Baron Ferdinand Rothschild's death also came. The Prince attended Sykes's funeral on the 20th and the Baron's at the Central Synagogue on the 22nd. He had lost two irreplaceable old friends and told Vicky; "It is all too sad & makes this time of the year, wh to me is always gloomy & depressing (I mean Xmas), worse than ever."[174] On Christmas Eve, "'Father Xmas' came at tea time, after which Tree and Tables".[175] The next day they attended the Christmas service at Sandringham Church.

⚜

Albert Edward was hoping for a peaceful New Year "& that all the Countries who are jealous of one another will 'bury the hatchet'".[176] Alexandra, in mourning, began 1899 quietly, walking, driving and paying calls. Victoria went on 23 January to stay with the Fifes at Brighton and brought Louise back to Sandringham on 4 February. Two days later came news of Alfred of

Saxe-Coburg-Gotha's death, at only 24. "That poor, poor boy! actually dying like that! & from such a terrible, horrible illness & disease too. Poor, poor thing! ... his young life blighted & wasted & in a way misunderstood. How I pity those miserable unfortunate Parents – one's heart bleeds for them & for all the agony they must be going through now! Their only son too!"[177] They had criticised his lack of energy, not realising how ill he was.[178]

Alexandra enjoyed Louise's brief visit; she herself now had a cold, but by the 7th could go out and pay calls, one to Miss Edith Lyne Wolfe,[179] who, with her sister, Mabel Stuart Wolfe,[180] had succeeded Fräulein Noedel at the technical school, with salary, expenses and housing.[181] Although born in Cheshire, they had lived in America. The Charleses arrived on the 18th and Louise later returned; all three sisters were together until she left on the 28th. Alexandra, Victoria and the Charleses spent three days at Windsor before returning to London. Albert Edward left for Paris and Cannes on 2 March, Charles went home on the 8th and on the 11th Alexandra and her daughters left for Marseilles, where *Osborne* was moored. They reached Villefranche on the 17th, and met Albert Edward and his brothers: Alfred devastated by his son's death; Arthur just back from Egypt.

They visited Queen Victoria at Cimiez the next day. Her extra woman of the bedchamber, Mrs Marie Mallet,[182] eyed Alexandra and her daughters with unkindly interest; they looked "very seedy"[183] "and Princess Maud has dyed her hair canary colour which makes her look quite improper and more like a little milliner than ever."[184] Maud enjoyed fashion and cultivated the desirable "wasp waist". Snapshots (which were not over-painted in the way that studio photographs often were) show her almost impossibly small waist; her mother took one, later in the holiday, of Maud with a normal-sized peasant woman in Corfu, "to show the difference in waists!"[185] Although this could be physically damaging, fashion was all. Mrs Mallet found Alexandra's restlessness alarming; "her one idea is to be constantly travelling, she looks ill, so do her daughters and I hear she dreads the possibility of reigning."[186] At present that was unlikely, as the Queen was in good health, but, after her mother's death, Alexandra, as in 1892–3, was filling her time with new places and experiences to assuage her grief. May, and Victoria of Schleswig-Holstein were also at Cimiez, as was Vicky, who was staying at Bordighera. The Waleses and their daughters visited Nice, and had tea at Rumpelmeyer's. Albert Edward returned to Cannes and his wife and daughters went back to Nice, saw Miss Alice Rothschild[187] at Grasse, visited Monte Carlo, Mentone and Bordighera and were shown over *HMS Venus* by Captain Milne.[188]

They had a rough passage to Genoa on 23 March, as Alexandra told George, who was in Scotland, on the 26th; "I do not think you can be much worse off than we are here in a biting icy cold North Easterly wind with snow and hail and all the mountains white with thick snow, simply disgusting, and I do regret

9 Group in Denmark, c 1899, with, left to right: *front row, foreground*, Grand Duke Alexander Michaelovitch of Russia with his son, Prince Andrew; Grand Duchess Olga Alexandrovna of Russia; Prince Axel and Prince Erik of Denmark; *second row, foreground*, Empress Alexandra Feodorovna of Russia, Xenia Alexandrovna, Grand Duchess Alexander Michaelovitch of Russia; Prince Aage of Denmark; Alexandra, Princess of Wales; Princess Margrethe and King Christian IX of Denmark; Dowager Empress Marie Feodorovna of Russia. *Back row*, left to right: Grand Duke Michael Alexandrovitch of Russia holding his niece, Princess Irina; Prince Nicholas of Greece; Emperor Nicholas II of Russia; Princess Victoria of Wales holding Prince Viggo of Denmark; King George I of the Hellenes; Prince Waldemar of Denmark.

RCIN 2923660.d

having left England where it never was so cold & disagreeable as this all through the winter." Gales had already delayed them for four days in Paris and en route to Genoa it was too rough to visit Corsica. Genoa itself was very dull but they were delighted to see Hélène, Duchess of Aosta, before leaving on the evening of the 26th. The next day Alexandra and her daughters reached Elba and had lunch at Napoleon's house, San Martino, before leaving for Civita Vecchia. In Rome the next day, they quickly toured the sights, had tea at a restaurant, shopped, walked round the streets and, after dinner at the Grand Hotel, returned to *Osborne* at 11pm, starting again almost immediately. Calling at Gaëta and Naples on the 29th, they lunched at "Mr Cook's Hotel"[189] on Mount Vesuvius the next day and rode to the top on the Fenicular Railway, walking the last part. Having tea at the observatory on the way down, they got back to the ship just after 7pm; a Neapolitan troupe sang and danced on deck. The next day, Good Friday, they went to the English church, St Mark's, and in the afternoon had tea at Lord Rosebery's villa at Posillipo. On 1 April they landed and shopped before going to Pompeii. There was an Easter Sunday service on board and they also went ashore to the Jesuits' and Santa Chiara churches. After steaming round Capri on Lord Rosebery's yacht, *Catania*, they drove in the Chiaja.

Returning to Rome by train, Alexandra stayed overnight at the Grand Hotel and the next day, 4 April, travelled, via Genoa, all night through the St Gothard Pass; her daughters stayed on *Osborne*, to "go slowly round the coast of Italy in the meantime & meet me somewhere on the other side on my return to the ship." Their former French governess, Mrs Johnson, was with them as a companion.[190] Victoria told Lord Rosebery how much she had enjoyed the last two days and how kind he had been to her.[191] On the 5th Alexandra breakfasted at Basle, lunched at Carlsruhe, arrived at Frankfort, drove in the Palmen Garten and visited Aunt Anna; after dinner at the Hotel d'Angleterre, she left for Copenhagen. The purpose of this journey, which her husband considered very expensive in energy and money,[192] was to see her father on his birthday and attend the christening of Prince Christian's[193] first child, the future Frederick IX, on 9 April; there were now three generations of heirs to the throne. Alexandra left Copenhagen on the 15th and, after breakfast with her aunt at Frankfort, travelled all night through the Brenner Pass, rejoining *Osborne* at Venice on the 17th. Serenaders played and sang that evening. Alexandra's party spent four days touring Venice, meeting Vicky, shopping and enjoying chocolate in the Piazza.

They arrived at Corfu on the 22nd, met King George, went sightseeing and watched the procession of St Spiridion on the 23rd. The yacht steamed to Zanthe on the 26th and the next day to Crete, where the governor, Prince George, met them. Alexandra gave Distinguished Service Medals to British officials and received Russian and French captains. She and her daughters drove to Haleppa and to Mustapha Pasha's old castle and Sainte Trinité de Monte Sina, called on the Lindsays, who had saved 500 refugees, and walked to the Seaforth

Highlanders' cemetery. *Osborne* left Suda Bay on 30 April and arrived at Phalerum the next day. Alexandra and her daughters went to the palace at Athens on 2 May, drove to Phalerum, visited Queen Olga's hospital with her and attended the King's "name day" Te Deum in the cathedral on the 5th, lunching at Tatoii and staying overnight. Leaving the palace on the 7th, they went to Phalerum, then through the Corinth Canal to Patras and, via Zanthe and Messina, to the Port of Goletta on the 12th. The next day a launch took them up the Canal to Tunis; they walked about, visiting bazaars, the Bey's[194] Palace, the museum, the Arab quarter and watching snake-charming, before returning to the yacht at 6.45pm. The next day it was Carthage, to see the ruins, museum and cathedral. Lunching at the Consul's house and visiting the Bey and his harem, they had tea with Madame Millet,[195] the French minister resident's wife. After more sightseeing and shopping, they left on the 16th, anchoring at Cagliari in Sardinia, which they explored the next day, touring Napoleon's house, the cathedral and museum at Ajaccio on the 19th. At Marseilles on the 20th, the British consul, Mr Gurney,[196] showed them round. Via Paris on the 22nd, they reached Marlborough House and Albert Edward joined them the next day after a harness and horse sale at Sandringham.

After this exciting, exhausting holiday, it was Queen Victoria's 80th birthday lunch at Windsor Castle on the 24th. That evening Alexandra attended an opera for the first time since her mother's death, *Lohengrin,* by the Royal Opera Company, with Jean and Edouard de Reszke[197] and Madame Nordica,[198] in the Waterloo Gallery. Her mourning relaxed, Alexandra could attend most of the season's events, including the Queen's birthday parade on 3 June, giving the family breakfast at Marlborough House afterwards. On such occasions they would sit on chairs and benches on top of an artificial hill, "The Princess's Mound", by the garden wall facing St James's Palace, and listen to the Guards' bands playing in Friary Court.[199] At the opera, Alexandra saw *Die Meistersinger, Faust, Romeo and Juliet,* then *Tristan und Isolde, Don Giovanni, La Bohême, Pagliacci* and *Messaline.* She met friends and attended the drawing room on 9 June, but a cold the next day put her temporarily out of action and, taking Victoria and Maud back to Sandringham on the 14th, she avoided Ascot week. The next day the Fife family arrived for four days, to her great pleasure. She returned to London (Victoria and Maud went to Appleton) on the 20th; three days later, Louise and little David, whose fifth birthday it was, came to lunch. Later, the Waleses laid the foundation stone of the Royal School of Art Needlework at South Kensington and, the next day, that of the new buildings of the Post Office Savings Bank at West Kensington.

Meanwhile, Victoria, who was proud of her friendship with Lord Rosebery but could hardly understand why he deigned to speak to her at all, continued to write to him. She felt he was a true friend, to whom she could talk openly, like her uncle, Alexander III. Rosebery had told her about a letter he had written her from Elba, and not sent. She was curious to see it but "if it in any way were to interfere with our 'friendship' I should regret it."[200] On the 27th the Prince went to Newmarket, while Alexandra, with Louise, saw pictures by Benjamin Constant[201] and Henry Harper[202] at the Fine Art Gallery. Alexandra visited the Home for Incurable Children in Cheyne Walk on the 29th and also called on Mrs Johnson.[203] The next day she went to Christie's, the Goupil Gallery and the dog show in Regent's Park and on 1 July to Tiffany's exhibition at the Burlington Club Gallery and the studios of Walter Ouless[204] (where the Prince was sitting for his portrait) and William Orchardson.[205] She also met friends on most days. On the 3rd she returned to Sandringham, driving straight to Appleton to see "the girls". For four days she had lunch and tea there, but on the 8th returned to London for the Review of 30,000 volunteers at Horse Guards. Over the next three days she sat to Benjamin Constant but meanwhile heard of her nephew Georgy's death at Abas-tuman. He had gone out bicycling as usual "when a short distance from the stables he had a fit of coughing and blood spitting, so he got off, when a passing dairy woman came to his assistance. The loss of blood continued so violently that he sank to the ground, lost consciousness and died before his servants could reach him, ten minutes after … poor Minny is indeed to be pitied."[206] He had tuberculosis and the outlook was poor but his death was unexpected and very upsetting.

Alexandra returned to Sandringham on 12 July for a week, visited Appleton, paid her usual round of calls and had Miss Alice Rothschild, Lady de Grey and Lady Gosford[207] to stay overnight. Back in London, she opened the new buildings of the Alexandra Hospital for Children with Hip Disease, in Queen's Square. On the 21st she gave certificates to 1,200 nurses belonging to the Royal National Pension Fund, and the next day visited the London Hospital. She sat three more times to Benjamin Constant, returning to Sandringham on the 24th. She told Sydney Holland[208] how much she had enjoyed visiting the London Hospital; while there, she had offered to pay for some equipment using light to cure lupus, invented by the Danish Doctor Finsen;[209] she and her sister had seen this in Copenhagen in April and been very impressed. She wanted it to be introduced in England and Dr Mackenzie,[210] head physician at the hospital, was going to Copenhagen to inspect it, with two nurses who would learn the system thoroughly. In due course the equipment was installed in a "light cure" ward at the Hospital, and was of great benefit to many patients.[211]

After more calls, tea at Appleton and a memorial service for Grand Duke George at Sandringham Church on 26 July, Alexandra and Victoria left for Portsmouth and Cowes, to join the Prince. Alexandra was on *Britannia* when she raced for "The Queen's Cup" (won by the German emperor's yacht, *Meteor*) and also, with Victoria, when *Britannia* raced again on 3 August. On three occasions, a troupe called "The Jolly Japs" performed in the evening. There were trips and visits to the Queen before returning on the 8th to London and then

Sandringham. The Prince left for Marienbad and on the 14th Alexandra and Victoria for Bavaria, reaching Wörishofen the next day, for a week. Alexandra was there *incognita*, as "Mrs G Smith". "I wonder how long she will be able to maintain her incog!" wrote Albert Edward.[212] She wrote; "We reached this <u>tiny</u> village on Tuesday after a <u>fearful</u>, <u>hot</u>, dusty journey. Here we hoped to find very bracing weather, but at first it was very hot too, but <u>now</u> thank God <u>much</u> cooler & I take two cold water dousche baths every day in the morning when I get up, & one before dinner, which is most refreshing & I hope will be a kind of <u>nerve tonic</u> for me. Toria likes the place also & bicycles every afternoon. We are out all day long, in the morning, directly after my cold dousches, we walk out bare-footed on sandals, Clarke & all & it is a funny sight to see everybody here, fat & thin, old & young bare-footed & such feet too!!! Sight for the Gods indeed." Lady de Grey, Lady Gosford and "poor Aleck"[213] were there.

After leaving on 23 August for Munich, Alexandra saw *Lohengrin* with Prince and Princess Paul of Mecklenburg-Schwerin. The next day her cousins, Adelaide, Grand Duchess of Luxemburg and Princess Hilda of Anhalt spent the day with her, looking at pictures, driving and shopping. Alexandra and Victoria left Munich the next day and, via Frankfort, called on Vicky at Friedrichshof. They reached Denmark on the 26th, staying at Bernstorff. This time there were two anniversaries to remember; Queen Louise's birthday and the day of her death; the family placed wreaths at Roskilde Cathedral on the 7th and took Holy Communion there on the 29th. "Amama" was greatly missed and everything seemed changed but her family gathered as usual, including the Russian imperial couple, with their daughters, Olga, Tatiana[214] and Marie.[215] Alexandra visited the lupus hospital, (meeting Dr Mackenzie and the two nurses) on 9 September and the China Manufactory on the 16th. On the 12th, a statue commemorating the wars of 1848–50 and 1864 was unveiled in Copenhagen. Alexandra spent a lot of time walking, sometimes with her father and Minny. Victoria left for Scotland on the 21st and the Cumberland family arrived on the 27th. Alexandra stayed overnight on *Polar Star* with Minny on 1–2 October and on the 5th there was a cinematograph show.

The three sisters had agreed to take turns to stay with their elderly father and it was difficult for Alexandra to make plans, which depended on his arrangements and their commitments. It was also a struggle, as ever, to tear herself away from her old home, when her relatives, especially her father, begged her to stay a little longer. Fortunately, while Albert Edward liked things organised, he made allowances for her other priorities; by late September he had not heard when she was coming home but realised the pressure she was under. He had been visiting Vicky at Friedrichshof, and one of the guests had been Prince Maximilian of Baden (32). "He has grown a beard" Albert Edward told George, "& is better looking and more charming than ever. Ah! how I wish he was yr brother in law, as to me he would be an ideal son in law."[216] He would have liked this eligible bachelor for Victoria (31); perhaps it might have worked, if Alexandra could have been induced to let her marry a German and if Victoria had liked him enough to leave England, but, in view of events in 1914, he fortunately married her cousin, Marie Louise of Cumberland, instead. Nevertheless, Albert Edward was still hoping Victoria would marry a Prince. He had accepted Louise's choice of Macduff, an old friend and distant relative, but there was little likelihood he would welcome Victoria also marrying a British commoner; he had opposed whatever idea Lord Rosebery put forward and his fears about Louise's marriage to Lorne had been justified.

On 9 October Alexandra left for England; on the same day the Boers gave the British an ultimatum in South Africa. She reached London on the 10th and the next day the South African War began, with the Boers entering Natal. Alexandra went to see alterations at Sandringham on the 12th and stayed overnight; "Mama seems to have enjoyed very much sleeping in the Bachelors' Wing at Sandringham! & I am glad she had time to see everything", wrote the Prince on the 16th.[217] She took her meals at York Cottage and left for Mar Lodge in the evening of the 13th, arriving the next day. The Fifes, Victoria and the Charleses were already there; the latter until the 21st, and Alexandra's nephew Michael was there until 23 October. Meanwhile war news was arriving and Charlotte Knollys began noting casualties and victories and keeping newspaper cuttings in the engagement diary. Alexandra was already thinking about assisting the war effort and asked Sydney Holland to help her organise a hospital ship, to bring back the sick and wounded. He found one, rather old but perfectly seaworthy, although its use was controversial and many, notably the War Office, opposed it. Accepting it enthusiastically, Alexandra interested herself in all the details, recommended a special kind of mattress and received financial donations, Röntgen Ray[218] apparatus and other supplies.[219] After her husband's illness in 1871, a disused farmhouse along the Lynn road from Babingley had, at her suggestion, become a hospital for Sandringham servants. At the outbreak of the Boer War she had it reorganised as a convalescent home for four or five officers. She superintended the furnishing, chose cheerful wallpaper, chintzes and Chippendale furniture and provided recreational facilities, including tennis, a smoking lounge and a veranda.[220]

The Queen, with Beatrice and Prince and Princess Francis Joseph of Battenberg[221] came to lunch on 16 October; after visiting her at Balmoral, Alexandra and Victoria returned to London and on the 28th, with Lady de Grey and Lady Musgrave, attended a symphony concert at the Queen's Hall. On the 30th it was a wedding at Kingston.[222] Writing to Empress Frederick at the end of October, Alexandra was deep in war work; thanking Vicky for a kind donation to her fund for the SSFA, she deplored the loss of life and the problems in the South African campaign. Nevertheless, "We are all doing our <u>little</u> best to help our poor sick & wounded soldiers and <u>my</u> branch of the National Aid Society

<u>under</u> the <u>Red Cross</u> are sending out a Hospital Ship which will be ready to start in about a fortnight's time." She was concerned about Vicky, who was in great pain with what was called lumbago and hoping to stay somewhere warm, perhaps Athens, where her daughter, the Duchess of Sparta, lived.[223]

It was two years since Mary Teck's death and Alexandra wrote in sympathy to May; "Yes indeed I too alas know now too well <u>what</u> that means to have to give up <u>that</u> precious blessed being who was everything to one. Day by day & year by year one feels that <u>terrible</u> <u>irreparable</u> loss more & more & <u>nothing</u> can replace her in one's life or heart, or fill up the awful blank & aching pain which must last as long as life itself. God comfort you, my poor darling May, you know how fully I share yr great trials & do hope you found the poor Father rather better."[224] Alexandra regarded the parental bond as sacrosanct and one of the most important relationships possible between human beings. Combined with love for husband and siblings, devoted allegiance to her parents and children defined her character.

She attended a meeting of the National Aid Society, chaired by Sydney Holland, on 1 November. There would be more meetings in the future. Meanwhile, on the 3rd she went to Sandringham, with Victoria and the Charleses. Albert Edward's birthday shooting party was held and guests arrived, including Lord Rosebery, who on the 12th made some sort of declaration to Victoria. She was astounded; "Of course I wasn't annoyed at anything you said last night – though I own [I] was greatly taken aback! Honestly I never for one moment dreamt of such a thing, & I simply grieve to think <u>I</u> should be the cause of giving you pain etc. I hope you do not regret coming here, & that <u>I</u> did not annoy <u>you</u> in any way. I shall never forget anything of what you said. You must have thought me a fool but I <u>could not</u> answer." On the 29th she wrote again; "I am <u>proud</u> of the devotion & true friendship you have shown me, and I do pray that <u>nothing</u> may change it. <u>You have</u> certainly not added to my troubles & worries. On the contrary it has been a <u>blessing</u> & help to me, to feel I have <u>such a</u> friend."[225] Had Lord Rosebery had been nurturing a hope that they might become more than friends and was this in his mind when he mentioned a possible marriage in 1893? If so, Albert Edward had been dead against it; Rosebery was 21 years older than Victoria; a depressed, still-grieving widower, and, above all, a party politician. Although sometimes a guest, he was not royal, which, for the Prince, would have seriously disadvantaged him as a son-in-law. This might have been overcome had Victoria been as determined to marry him as Louise had been with Macduff. She wrote friendly, affectionate letters to him over some 25 years; was flattered such a great man should be interested in her and remembered some of their early meetings with sentimental pleasure, but seems to have wanted friendship, even if perhaps, at one time, romantic friendship, rather than marriage. She loved him as a friend but was not in love with him as a suitor. Alexandra must have known about this and, as with Julie Stonor, gladly accepted him as a family friend.

Alexandra often visited Appleton but would soon have to leave for Windsor, where the German imperial couple were expected on a state visit; she and Victoria arrived just before them on the 20th. That evening there was a family dinner in the Oak Room, the next day a state banquet for 140 in St George's Hall. Alexandra wanted to inspect her ship privately; "when I am surrounded by <u>so many</u> people I never can see everything thoroughly."[226] On the 22nd she, her husband, Victoria, May and Louise went to Tilbury Docks to see the *Princess of Wales*. They went all over it; the boilers were not yet working but Alexandra was delighted with the arrangements for the patients' comfort and was glad to meet Major Morgan[227] (Senior Medical Officer), Miss Chadwick[228] (army nurse) and three other nurses.[229] Sending birthday greetings to Vicky, she told her the war was gathering momentum and losses were affecting "every family in England". She was "<u>boiling</u> over with fury & indignation at the vile <u>lies</u> & insults that contemptible foreign press heaps upon us and our <u>brave Army</u> [which] has done <u>wonders</u> both in fighting & in <u>organising</u> the enormous <u>transport</u> of all war materials & appliances across such an immense tract of sea." Her hospital ship was about to leave for the Cape; it could hold 200 sick and wounded and would make at least two journeys to bring them back to England. "We have 4 nurses and 20 orderlies & several Surgeons & Doctors & the whole thing most perfectly fitted out in every way ... We have all given everything we can think of for their comfort, and I do hope it will [be] of the greatest help."[230]

They now had to return to Sandringham, where Albert Edward would be bringing the Germans on the 25th, to stay until the 28th. Alexandra showed the Empress round the stables, kennels and Appleton and there was covert shooting and lunch at Wolferton Wood. After more guests, Alexandra spent time with her family until 13 December, when she went to Windsor with Victoria for the next day's service; on the 15th the Waleses presented Sudan Campaign medals to the 1st Battalion, Grenadier Guards at Victoria Barracks. In London there was a variety show at Olympia in aid of Alexandra's hospital ship and an American one, and a League of Mercy meeting at Marlborough House on the 18th. On the 21st Alexandra received six nurses from the London Hospital who were leaving for the war as "Princess of Wales Nurses", and six more, selected by Sir Henry Burdett,[231] the next day. Back at Sandringham, the Christmas tree and tables were set up in the ballroom on the 24th for the first time since Eddy's death.

Meanwhile Albert Edward had met a young couple, the Hon. George Keppel[232] and his wife, Alice, and by 1898 knew them well enough to dine at their house on 27 February and 6 December. In 1899 he met them on five occasions, at home or elsewhere, until September, when Mrs Keppel began to appear alone. This increased over the rest of his life. She was attractive, sociable and flirtatious, and her husband was compliant. It is not impossible that Albert Edward felt comfortable with her for another reason; she had the same name as his late, favourite sister, a birthday at the end of April, and a beloved, slightly older brother, Archibald Edmonstone,[233] from whom, (like the young Bertie and sister Alice), she had been inseparable as a child. Also like Princess Alice, Mrs Keppel, although wholly benign, could be slightly bossy.[234] Their relationship was hardly a quasi-sibling one; however, now aging, often unwell, and reputedly impotent,[235] Albert Edward might well have lacked the energy for a passionate affair, as once with Lady Brooke. The friendship with Mrs Keppel was perhaps more companionable than sexual, although it has always raised scandalous conjecture. She kept him from feeling bored, amused him with gossip and used her influence with her large circle of friends and acquaintances to his advantage. She was shrewd, capable and proud of the relationship, but many in the household – above all, Alexandra – found her over-proprietorial, muscling in where she had no business to be. Albert Edward's enjoyment of shooting parties facilitated this; they were not Alexandra's favourite pastime and, while tolerating men's enthusiasm for blood sports, she was glad when the livestock escaped. Hostesses knew of the Prince's friendship, and Alexandra's absence at some such parties began to create a place for Mrs Keppel as his companion.

Notes

[1]　RA VIC/MAIN/QAD/1895: 13 January

[2]　RA VIC/MAIN/Z/457/208, Charlotte Knollys to Queen Victoria, 1895: 7 January

[3]　RA GV/PRIV/AA20/44, Prince of Wales to Duke of York, 1895: 16 January

[4]　RA VIC/MAIN/Z/457/213, Princess of Wales to Queen Victoria, 1895: 20 January. Alexandra's relatives all relied on her in times of trouble, and she never failed them.

[5]　RA VIC/MAIN/Z/457/218, Princess of Wales to Queen Victoria, 1895: 6 February

[6]　RA VIC/MAIN/QAD/1895: 8 February

[7]　Bessie, née Temple (1869–1952) m Harry Sinclair (1855–1930)

[8]　Who had helped nurse Prince Eddy in his final illness

[9]　RA GV/PRIV/AA36/35, Duke of York to Princess of Wales, 1895: 15 March. No information has yet been found about the fish dinners, but they were clearly a charitable enterprise of some sort.

[10]　Her false toupée might have come adrift, while her daughters' "invisible nets" kept their hair in place

[11]　RA QM/PRIV/CC42/41, Princess of Wales to Duchess of York, 1895: 21 March

[12]　Princess Hélène m Emanuel Filibert (1869–1931), 2nd Duke of Aosta at Kingston on 25 June.

[13]　RA GV/PRIV/AA31/39, Princess of Wales to Duke of York, 1895: 21 March

[14]　RA VIC/MAIN/Z/457/223, Prince of Wales to Queen Victoria, 1895: 28 March

[15]　RA VIC/MAIN/QAD/1895: 24 March

[16]　RA GV/PRIV/AA20/49, Prince of Wales to Duke of York, 1895: 15 March

[17]　Queen Wilhelmina of the Netherlands (1880–1962) succeeded her father William III in 1890 and reigned under the regency of her mother till 1898. She m Duke Henry of Mecklenburg-Schwerin (1876–1934).

[18]　Josefine Swoboda (1861–1924), Austrian portrait painter

[19]　Crown Prince Nasrullah Khan (1874–1920), second s of Emir Abdur Rahman Khan, became Emir himself for one week in 1919.

20 Crown Prince Maha Vajiravudh (1878–1925), trained at Sandhurst. He later became King Rama VI.

21 Beavan, pp 55–56

22 Beavan, pp 76–77

23 Author's conversation with Alexandra's great-grandson, the 3rd Duke of Fife; he remembered being told that she had had "Communistic ideas and a love of metal work." One of Alexandra's books was J Starkie Gardner's *English Ironwork of the 17th and the 18th Centuries: an Historical and Analytical Account of the Development of Exterior Smithcraft* RCIN 1231230

24 Cécile Chaminade, (1857–1944), French composer and pianist

25 Archduchess Stephanie of Austria (1864–1945), widow of Archduke Rudolph, m (2) Elemér, Prince Lónyay de Nagy-Lónya et Vásaros-Namény (d 1946)

26 Beavan, pp 97–98

27 Duke of Sparta, Alexandra's nephew and Godson

28 This was organised by Carl Hagenbeck and included a reconstructed Somali village, with Somali people, and a large number of animals, from May till early October 1895. https://jeffreygreen.co.uk/217-somalis-in-london/ Also in 1895 there was an Indian Exhibition at Earl's Court, organised by Imre Kiralfy and including Indian performers.

29 Beavan, pp 22–23

30 Alice Hughes (1857–1939), leading London portrait photographer, especially of fashionable women and children; she was the eldest d of Edward Hughes

31 RA VIC/MAIN/QAD/1895: 12 August

32 Edward Hughes (1832–1908), portrait painter

33 RA GV/PRIV/AA31/40, Princess of Wales to Duke of York, 1895: 22 August

34 Ernst Viktor von Leyden (1832–1910), German medical professor and physician, including to Emperor Alexander III

35 Grand Duke George Alexandrovitch, (1871–99); he suffered from tuberculosis

36 RA VIC/MAIN/Z/457/229, Charlotte Knollys to Queen Victoria, 1895: 27 August

37 RA GV/PRIV/AA20/58, Prince of Wales to Duke of York, 1895: 15 August

38 RA GV/PRIV/AA20/59, Prince of Wales to Duke of York, 1895: 23 September

39 RA VIC/MAIN/Z/457/230, Charlotte Knollys to Queen Victoria, 1895: 12 September

40 Elizabeth Sophia, née Cook (1834–1913), m Thomas Francklin.

41 RA VIC/MAIN/Z/457/231, Charlotte Knollys to Queen Victoria, 1895: 30 September

42 Princess Margrethe of Denmark (1895–1992), m Prince René of Bourbon-Parma (1894–1962)

43 RA GV/PRIV/AA31/41, Princess of Wales to Duke of York, 1895: 30 September

44 RA GV/AA20/59, Prince of Wales to Duke of York, 1895: 23 September

45 RA GV/AA31/41, Princess of Wales to Duke of York, 1895: 30 September; the other guests were Lord and Lady Brooke

46 RA VIC/MAIN/Z/457/231, Charlotte Knollys to Queen Victoria, 1895: 30 September

47 RA VIC/MAIN/Z/457/238, Queen Victoria to Princess Maud, 1895: 28 October

48 RA VIC/MAIN/Z/457/252, Charlotte Knollys to Queen Victoria, 1895: 29 October

49 Beatrice, née Tanner (1865–1940), famous actress, m (1) Patrick Campbell, (2) George Cornwallis-West

50 Grand Duchess Olga Nicholaievna of Russia (1895–1918)

51 Prince Albert of York (1895–1952), later Duke of York and King George VI, m Lady Elizabeth, née Bowes Lyon (1900–2002), Queen Elizabeth, later The Queen Mother

52 RA GV/PRIV/AA20/64, Prince of Wales to Duke of York, 1895: 14 December

53 RA GV/PRIV/AA31/42, Princess of Wales to Duke of York, 1895: 16 December

54 RA GV/PRIV/AA20/65, Prince of Wales to Duke of York, 1895: 16 December

55 RA GV/PRIV/AA20/66, Prince of Wales to Duke of York, 1896: 19 December

56 RA GV/PRIV/AA32/1, Princess of Wales to Duke of York, 1896: 27 February

57 Leander Starr Jameson (1853–1917), Scottish doctor and colonial politician, led a failed attempt to overthrow Paul Kruger's Boer republic in South Africa between 29 December 1895 and 2 January 1896. He was sentenced to fifteen months in gaol but pardoned, and went on to a successful career in British colonial politics, later being created a baronet

58 Tooley, pp 163, 166

59 Leighton House Museum;LH/1/1/2/26, Princess of Wales to Lord Leighton, 1895: 30 June; © The Royal Borough of Kensington and Chelsea

60 Leighton House Museum; LH/1/1/2/28, Princess of Wales to Lord Leighton, 1895: 5 September, © The Royal Borough of Kensington and Chelsea

61 Lord Lorne is believed to have been homosexual, and the couple had no children

62 RA VIC/ADDA17/882, Princess of Wales to Princess Louise, Marchioness of Lorne, 1896: 26 February

63 A hall in Westminster, where a panorama of "Niagara in Winter" had been displayed, was converted into an ice-rink. https://www.museumoflondon.org.uk/discover/ice-skating-fashion-craze

64 The Yorks were to represent the Queen at their wedding

65 Alfred became Duke of Saxe-Coburg-Gotha in 1893, but Alexandra still used his earlier title

66 21 March

67 RA GV/PRIV/AA32/2, Princess of Wales to Duke of York, 1896: 27 March

68 Mrs Elizabeth Peters was nurse to the children from 1894-April 1897

69 RA GV/PRIV/AA32/3, Princess of Wales to Duke of York, 1896: 2 May

70 Alexander Temple Sinclair (1896-c1989)

71 RA GV/PRIV/AA32/4, Princess of Wales to Duke of York, 1896: 10 May

72 Soldiers' and Sailors' Families' Association, which later became SSAFA, to include the Royal Air Force

73 Draper's business started in 1778 by William Clark; William Debenham became a partner in 1813 and took his son and brother-in-law Clement Freebody into partnership in 1851. The business was incorporated as Debenhams Limited in 1905; with other shops, it evolved into the Debenhams Group, which lasted into the 21st century.

74 Lionel Walter Rothschild (1868–1937), 2nd Baron Rothschild, was a banker, politician and zoologist

75 *Daily Telegraph*, 12 June 1896; Alexandra was fond of lace and had a collection of it; she also had a book, Thomas Wright's *The Romance of the Lace Pillow, being the History of Lace-making*. RCIN 1230799

76 Dr Thomas John Barnardo (1845–1905), Irish philanthropist who founded and directed homes for poor and deprived children

77 Student accommodation for women

78 (1823–1901), a leading, progressive Chinese statesman; Queen Victoria made him GCVO on this visit.

79 Franz von Lembach (1836–1904), German painter of prominent people

80 Albert Schumann (1858–1939), German equestrian and circus director

81 Her name for Prince and Princess Charles of Denmark

82 RA GV/PRIV/AA21/6, Prince of Wales to Duke of York, 1896: 30 August

83 RA GV/PRIV/AA32/5, Princess of Wales to Duke of York, 1896:26 August

84 Seat of Lord Londonderry

85 House belonging to the James'; Evelyn, née Forbes (1867–1929), society hostess, m William Dodge James (1854–1912), s of a wealthy American merchant, who was brought up in England

86 RA GV/PRIV/AA21/17, Prince of Wales to Duke of York, 1896: 23 November; the Revd John Francis Mitchell had been rector since c 1883

87 Squire Bancroft (1841–1926) and his wife, Effie Bancroft (1839–1921) were both actor-managers. He was knighted in 1897. They retired from management in 1885, but he continued acting till 1918.

88 Charles Dickens (1812–70), famous writer and social critic

89 Edward O'Connor Terry (1844–1912), actor-manager

90 Charles Swinnerton Heap (1847–1900), organist, pianist, composer and conductor

91 Hon Eleanor, née Harbord (1868–1936); m Sir Richard Musgrave (1872–1926), the 12th Baronet; the baby became Sir Nigel Musgrave, the 13th Baronet. Lady Musgrave was Princess Victoria's lady-in-waiting.

92 RA GV/PRIV/AA32/6 undated but filed in sequence; Princess of Wales to Duke of York, [1897]

93 RA GV/PRIV/AA36/37, Duke of York to Princess of Wales, 1897: 10 March

94 Charles Lamoureux (1834–99), French conductor and violinist

95 With Maud already in Denmark, this meant a reunion for the three sisters

96 RA GV/PRIV/AA21/23, Prince of Wales to Duke of York, 1897: 22 March

97 RA GV/PRIV/AA21/24, Prince of Wales to Duke of York, 1897: 30 March

98 RA GV/PRIV/AA21/25, Prince of Wales to Duke of York, 1897: 5 April

99 Infanta Eulalia (1864–1958), youngest d of Queen Isabella II of Spain, m Infant Don Antonio (1866–1930), 4th Duke of Galliera

100 Archivo General de Palacio (Madrid), Archivo de la Infanta Eulalia de Borbón, box 13, 554, file 5, letter no 5, Princess of Wales to Infanta Eulalie of Spain, 1897: 28 March

101 This hints at a disagreement and may reflect Victoria's sometimes difficult character

102 RA QM/PRIV/CC45/182, Princess Victoria to Duchess of York, 1897: 13 April

103 Charlotte Bill (1875–1964), "Lalla", employed as under nurse from 1896, did not become head nurse until 1900; there may have been another head nurse in 1897

104 RA GV/PRIV/AA32/7, Princess of Wales to Duke of York, 1897: 12–16 April

105 Princess Mary (1897–1965), later Princess Royal, m Henry Lascelles (1882–1947), 6th Earl of Harewood

106 RA GV/PRIV/AA21/27, Prince of Wales to Duke of York, 1897: 25 April

107 Seat of the Duke of Westminster

108 Helen, Duchess of Albany, widow of Prince Leopold

109 Clotilde Kleeberg (1866–1909), French pianist of German ancestry

110 RA VIC/MAIN/H/40/16,18,28,92, Princess of Wales to Queen Victoria, 1897: May, June

111 RA VIC/MAIN/Z/458/28, Queen Victoria to Prince of Wales, 1897: 18 June

112 Emma Albani (1847–1930), later Dame, leading operatic soprano, m Ernest Gye (d 1925)

113 Princess Marguérite (1553–1615), d of King Henry II of France, m Henry IV, King of France and Navarre (1553–1610); the marriage was annulled but she retained the title of Queen of Navarre and Duchesse de Valois.

114 Sir Henry Tate, 1st Baronet (1819–99), sugar merchant, philanthropist and art collector

115 RA GV/PRIV/AA21/32, Prince of Wales to Duke of York, 1897: 16 August

116 Cosima, née Liszt (1837–1930) m (1) Hans von Bülow, (2) Richard Wagner, whose music and philosophy she promoted

117 Siegfried Wagner (1869–1930), German composer and conductor; directed the Bayreuth Festival,1908–1930

118 Albrecht Dürer (1471–1528), German painter, print-maker and theorist of the German renaissance

119 Second daughter of Crown Prince Frederick

120 RA GV/PRIV/AA32/8, Princess of Wales to Duke of York, 1897: 10 September

[121] RA GV/PRIV/AA21/37, Prince of Wales to Duke of York, 1897: 17 September

[122] RA GV/PRIV/AA21/38, Prince of Wales to Duke of York, 1897: 26 September; The Observer, 26 September 1897

[123] Rachel Beer, née Sassoon (1855–1927), wife of Frederick Beer, who owned *The Observer* and *The Sunday Times*. She became editor of both papers.

[124] RA GV/PRIV/AA21/41, Prince of Wales to Duke of York, 1897: 17 October

[125] RA VIC/ADDA8/55, Princess of Wales to Grand Duchess of Mecklenburg-Strelitz, 1897: 29 October

[126] RA VIC/ADDA8/3396, Princess of Wales to Queen Victoria, 1897: undated

[127] RA GV/PRIV/AA32/9, Princess of Wales to Duke of York, 1897: 13 November

[128] Seat of the Duke of Portland

[129] Sir Edward Coley Burne-Jones (1833–98), 1st Baronet, artist and designer associated with the Pre-Raphaelite movement

[130] Known as Daisy and now Countess of Warwick; her husband had succeeded to the title in 1893

[131] RA PS/PSO/GV/C/O/479B/23B/2

[132] His daughter, Princess Marie, was with him

[133] RA GV/PRIV/AA32/10, Princess of Wales to Duke of York, 1898: 28 February

[134] RA VIC/ADDA7/346, Princess of Wales to Lord Charles Beresford, 1898: 2 March

[135] Duchess Marie of Mecklenburg-Strelitz (1878–1948), m (1) Georges, Count Jametal, (2) Prince Julius Ernest of Lippe-Biesterfeld (1873–1952)

[136] RA GV/PRIV/AA32/11, Princess of Wales to Duke of York, 1898: 19 March

[137] RA GV/PRIV/AA21/51, Prince of Wales to Duke of York, 1898: 10 March

[138] RA GV/PRIV/AA21/52, Prince of Wales to Duke of York, 1898: 16 March

[139] RA GV/PRIV/AA32/11, Princess of Wales to Duke of York, 1898: 19 March

[140] The monument, by Alfred Gilbert (1854–1934) was finally completed in the 1920s; he also produced the memorial to Queen Alexandra on the outside wall of Marlborough House's garden, after her death in 1925

[141] This was the Home Arts and Industries Association's 14th annual exhibition, at the Royal Albert Hall. Among the exhibits was a large embossed leather settee, worked on by Alexandra after her own designs. The Times, 19 May 1898, p 9

[142] RA GV/PRIV/AA21/59, Prince of Wales to Duke of York, 1898: 13 June

[143] Hon Bridget Harbord (1870–1951) and Hon Derek Keppel (1863–1944), later Lt-Colonel Sir, courtier (at this time equerry to the Duke of York) at St George's, Hanover Square; and Lady Mary "Tooka", née Byng (d 1946), (her mother was half-Danish); maid-of-honour to Queen Victoria, m Maurice Talvande (1866–1941), self-styled Comte de Mauny Talvande, landscaper and furniture-maker, at St James's, Spanish Place.

[144] Millicent, née St Clair-Erskine (1867–1955), m Cromartie Sutherland-Leveson-Gower, 4th Duke of Sutherland; she was a society hostess, social reformer and writer.

[145] The new science laboratory of the Royal Free Hospital

[146] Press cutting, 11 July 1898

[147] RA GV/PRIV/AA21/62, Prince of Wales to Duke of York, 1898: 9 July

[148] RA GV/PRIV/AA32/12, Princess of Wales to Duke of York, 1898: 28 July

[149] RA GV/PRIV/AA21/64, Prince of Wales to Duke of York, 1898: 27 July

[150] RA GV/PRIV/AA32/12, Princess of Wales to Duke of York, 1898: 28 July

[151] Sir Thomas Johnstone Lipton, 1st Baronet (1848–1931), self-made man; tea merchant, grocer and yachtsman

[152] The Alexandra Trust Dining Rooms were built in Old Street, London, offering very cheap meals to the poor working classes

[153] Grand Duchess George, p 61

154 RA VIC/ADDA4/70, Prince of Wales to Empress Frederick, 1898: 3 August

155 Sir William MacCormac (1836–1901), 1st Baronet, surgeon, and Sergeant-Surgeon to King Edward VII

156 RA GV/PRIV/AA36/39, Duke of York to Princess of Wales, 1898: 7 August

157 RA GV/PRIV/AA36/40, Duke of York to Princess of Wales, 1898: 20 August

158 Resident German Governess to the Wales Princesses since 1883 and latterly superintendent of the Sandringham Technical School

159 Sarah A. Tooley, *The Girls' Realm Annual, 1901; Queen Alexandra's Hobby: the Royal Spinning School at Sandringham*

160 RA VIC/ADDA4/74, Prince of Wales to Empress Frederick, 1898: 30 August

161 RA GV/PRIV/AA32/13, Princess of Wales to Duke of York, 1898: 25 August

162 RA GV/PRIV/AA32/15, Princess of Wales to Duke of York, 1898: 1 September

163 RA GV/PRIV/AA22/2, Prince of Wales to Duke of York, 1898: 8 September

164 Horatio Herbert Kitchener (1850–1916), senior army officer and colonial administrator, later Field Marshal Earl Kitchener of Khartoum

165 Luigi Lucheni (1873–1910), Italian anarchist

166 RA GV/PRIV/AA22/3, Prince of Wales to Duke of York, 1898: 13 September

167 RA GV/PRIV/AA32/14, Princess of Wales to Duke of York, 1898: 24–27 September

168 RA VIC/ADDA4/78, Prince of Wales to Empress Frederick, 1898: 1 October

169 RA GV/O2548/1, Duchess of York to Princess of Wales, 1898: 29 September

170 RA VIC/MAIN/QAD/1898: 15 October; note enclosed in the Princess of Wales's engagement diary

171 RA GV/PRIV/AA22/7,Prince of Wales to Duke of York, 1898: 25 October

172 RA VIC/ADDA4/82, 83, Prince of Wales to Empress Frederick, 1898: 2 November; Princess of Wales to Empress Frederick, 1898: 8 November

173 RA VIC/MAIN/QAD/1898: 14 December

174 RA VIC/ADDA4/88, Prince of Wales to Empress Frederick, 1898: 18 December

175 RA VIC/MAIN/QAD/1898: 24 December

176 RA VIC/ADDA4/92, Prince of Wales to Empress Frederick, 1899: 1 January

177 RA GV/PRIV/AA32/16, Princess of Wales to Duke of York, 1899: 9 February

178 He is believed to have had syphilis

179 Edith Lyne Wolfe (1863–1946)

180 Mabel Stuart Wolfe (1871–1953)

181 RA EB/EB/69/p82, Establishment List for the Household of Queen Alexandra

182 Marie, née Adeane (d 1934), m Bernard Mallet (1859–1932), later Sir, civil servant

183 Unwell

184 Victor Mallet (editor), *Life with Queen Victoria*, p 156

185 Mediterranean Cruise album, 1899, RCIN 2923470, p36h; see Dimond, p 80

186 Mallet, p 159

187 Miss Alice de Rothschild (1847–1922), Baron Ferdinand's sister

188 Captain Sir Archibald Berkeley Milne (1855–1938), 2nd Baronet, later Admiral

189 Thomas Cook had started a travel and holiday business in 1841, which, with many changes, lasted into the 21st century

190 RA GV/PRIV/AA32/18, Princess of Wales to Duke of York, 1899: 26 March

191 RA GV/ADD/COPY/140/8 Rosebery Papers, Princess Victoria to Lord Rosebery, 1899: 5 April

192 RA GV/PRIV/AA22/14, Prince of Wales to Duke of York, 1899: 30 March

193 Who had married Duchess Alexandrine of Mecklenburg-Schwerin (1879–1952); their elder son (1899–1972) was later King Frederick IX of Denmark; he m Princess Ingrid of Sweden (1910–2000)

[194] Ali III ibn al-Husayn (1817–1902), Bey of Tunisia from 1882–1902

[195] Louise, née Urbain, m René Millet (1849–1919), French Resident-General at Tunis from 1894–1900

[196] Martyn Cecil Gurney (1861–1930), British Consul-General at Marseilles

[197] Edouard de Reszke (1853–1917), Polish operatic bass singer; brother of Jean de Reszke

[198] Lillian Allen Norton (1857–1914), noted American opera singer using the pseudonym Madame Nordica

[199] Beavan, p 16

[200] RA GV/ADD/COPY/140/12, 13; Rosebery Papers, Princess Victoria to Lord Rosebery, 1899: 21, 25 June

[201] Jean-Joseph Benjamin-Constant (1845–1902), French etcher and painter of portraits and Oriental subjects

[202] Henry Harper (1835–1900), landscape painter who gave Alexandra lessons

[203] Formerly Mademoiselle Vauthier, the Wales Princesses' French governess

[204] Walter William Ouless (1848–1933), portrait painter

[205] William Orchardson (1832–1910), portrait and genre painter, who was later knighted

[206] RA VIC/MAIN/H/48/77, Princess of Wales to Queen Victoria, 1899: 14 July

[207] Lady Louisa, née Montagu (1856–1944), lady of the bedchamber to Queen Alexandra from 1901–1925), m Archibald Acheson, 4th Earl of Gosford (1841–1922)

[208] Sydney Holland, later 2nd Viscount Knutsford (1855–1931), at this time Chairman of the London Hospital house committee

[209] Dr Niels Ryberg Finsen (1860–1904), Danish-Faroese physician and scientist

[210] Sir Stephen Mackenzie (1844–1909) physician specializing in skin diseases and ophthalmology

[211] RA VIC/ADDA21/233/59, Princess of Wales to Sydney Holland, 1899: 28 July

[212] RA GV/PRIV/AA22/20, Prince of Wales to Duke of York, 1899: 16 August

[213] RA GV/AA32/19, Princess of Wales to Duke of York, 1899: 20 August; Poor Aleck was the blind Alexander Frederick, Landgrave of Hesse (1863–1925), brother of the late "Mutton Hair". He was a talented musician.

[214] Grand Duchess Tatiana Nicholaievna of Russia (1897–1918)

[215] Grand Duchess Marie Nicholaievna of Russia (1899–1918)

[216] RA GV/PRIV/AA22/24, Prince of Wales to Duke of York, 1899: 6 September

[217] RA GV/PRIV/AA22/28, Prince of Wales to Duke of York, 1899: 16 October

[218] X-ray

[219] RA VIC/ADDA21/233/16, Princess of Wales to Sydney Holland, 1899: 14 November

[220] Tooley, p 86

[221] Prince Francis Joseph of Battenberg (1861–1923), younger brother of Princes Louis, Alexander and Henry, m Princess Anna of Montenegro (1874–1971)

[222] Prince Jean d'Orléans married his cousin, Princess Isabelle d'Orléans

[223] RA VIC/ADDA4/129, Princess of Wales to Empress Frederick, 1899: 30 October

[224] RA QM/PRIV/CC42/47, Princess of Wales to Duchess of York, 1899: 27 October

[225] RA GV/ADD/COPY/140/18,19; Rosebery Papers, Princess Victoria to Lord Rosebery,1899: 13, 29 November

[226] RA VIC/ADDA21/233/8, Princess of Wales to Sydney Holland, 1899: 9 November

[227] Major (later Colonel) Anthony Hickman-Morgan (1858–1924)

[228] Probably Miss Mabel E Chadwick, of QAIMNS Reserve, who died in 1915 in Egypt of fever contracted while on duty there

[229] RA VIC/ADDA21/233/12, Princess of Wales to Sydney Holland, 1899: 30 November

[230] RA VIC/ADDA4/134, Princess of Wales to Empress Frederick, 1899: 19 November

[231] Sir Henry Burdett (1847–1920), financier and philanthropist

232 Lt-Colonel Hon George Keppel (1865–1947), m Alice, née Edmonstone (1868–1947), society hostess and companion of King Edward VII. The Keppel family was well-known to the Waleses. Colonel Frederick Keppel had been in the Prince's household; Admiral Hon Sir Henry Keppel (1809–1904) was a friend; Hon Derek Keppel (George's brother) was in the Duke of York's household and was married to Bridget Harbord, one of Lord and Lady Suffield's daughters.

233 Sir Archibald Edmonstone (1867–1954) of Duntreath, 5th Baronet

234 Less positively, both women were accused of "telling stories". Ridley, p 457, quoting from *Chips*, p 32, by Robert Rhodes James

235 In 1910 the famous London courtesan, trend-setter and horsewoman, Catherine Walters ("Skittles") (1839–1920), who claimed long-standing friendship with King Edward, averred that "The King has been impotent for the last 15 years [ie, since 1895]. [The women] amused him and that was all. He liked having them with him to talk nonsense." Fitzwilliam Museum, *Wilfred Scawen Blunt Papers, MS10, 13 May 1910.*

Chapter 11

1900–1904

"Nothing like Perseverance"

The year 1900 opened ominously. The Prince, who had already lost acquaintances in the war, wrote; "the news from S Africa is no better, & I own I am very despondent & can think of nothing else." Additionally, his brother Alfred was in poor health; his sister Vicky was seriously ill; his mother was nearly 81 and when she died, perhaps soon, his life would change utterly. His daughter Victoria was again unwell; "It is the inevitable result of Xmas festivities (?) Every year it has been the same thing. Laking has been out of Town but I will try & get hold of him, & see if he can come down tomorrow."[1] Alexandra's old doctor, Sir James Paget, had died; after his kindness during her illness of 1867, she would always miss him.[2] George had influenza and on her birthday, the 17th, Lady Probyn died. On the 21st, the Duke of Teck died at White Lodge; he had never recovered from his wife's death but it was very sad. The Waleses attended the funeral at St George's Chapel on the 27th.

Alexandra went to London on 12 February, visited Louise, who was "making an excellent recovery",[3] and also attended plays and money-raising events for war charities, including *Grand Tableaux* at the Haymarket and Adelina Patti's[4] concert at the Opera House on the 22nd. Miss Lowther[5] demonstrated her fencing skills at Marlborough House. On the 26th, the Prince, Princess and their son inspected Alexandra's hospital ship, back with 176 patients at Southampton, and visited wounded soldiers at Netley Hospital. War news was better; General Cronje[6] and his army surrendered to Lord Roberts;[7] Lord Dundonald[8] with an advance guard of the relief army ended the siege of Ladysmith on the 28th, and Sir Redvers Buller[9] arrived the next day. On 3 March the Waleses opened the LCC Boundary Street Estate at Bethnal Green, and on the 7th Lord Rowton[10] showed Alexandra one of his model lodging houses. On the 11th she, Charlotte and Soveral went to see the Fifes and Victoria, staying at Brighton. Alexandra held drawing rooms on the 13th and the 15th and the couple inspected the Alexandra Trust's building in City Road with Sir Thomas Lipton[11] on the 14th. On the 16th they opened the Irish industries sale at the Mansion House, but influenza delayed Alexandra's return to Sandringham.

By the 24th she felt better and told the Queen her niece was engaged; "I hope poor Max and that charming girl of Thyra's will have a happy future."[12] On the 30th the Prince's horse, "Ambush II" won the Grand National; "It really was a splendid sight & no horse could have run better ... The enthusiasm was tremendous – quite 'Persimmon's' 'Derby' over again."[13] Then on the 31st; "Oh my Georgie dear how delightful! Thank God it is all <u>over</u> & darling May has presented you with a <u>third son</u>,[14] <u>just what</u> she wanted. I am <u>so</u> delighted and only hope she did not suffer much. What a surprise; when I got up at 8 these beautiful news greeted me, a <u>son just born</u>! The joy of it all has made me quite well again." Alexandra hoped "Bobs" would grow up "as great a general as his future <u>Godfather</u> I hope! That <u>wld</u> be nice! – the same as the Duke of Wellington[15] was to Arthur."[16] On 3 April the couple met the nurses and staff of the Welch Hospital who were going to South Africa; they later visited The Gables, Surbiton, where Alfred Cooper[17] had offered his private theatre[18] as a convalescent home for wounded soldiers returning on the *Princess of Wales*. The War Office had reluctantly agreed, and it was a great success.[19]

The Waleses left for Denmark on 4 April. As the 5.35pm train prepared to leave Brussels and they were sitting together, having tea, Alexandra noticed "a hand thrust in at the open window opposite, holding some small black object, which I thought someone wished to give us. Nobody else saw it. And suddenly I saw the hand was raised."[20] A Belgian youth[21] had jumped on the carriage's footboard and aimed at the Prince. "As the man fired at me at 2 yards distance it is inconceivable that he missed me. It is fortunate that Anarchists are bad shots; we thought at first it might have been pro-Boer, but apparently not."[22] The bullet had hit the window frame just over their heads, ricocheted and plunged into the seat opposite, between Charlotte and Sir Stanley Clarke.[23] It was small but potentially damaging "if it had hit a vital part". Alexandra wrote; "Well thank God beloved Papa & I escaped from the wld be assassin on our way here!!! ... but it <u>was</u> a narrow shave indeed, which God alone mercifully averted. Thank God I was with Papa & shared the danger in full. It wld have been much, much worse hearing of it afterwards."[24]

The next day they met the Royal Family at Amalienborg and were then so overwhelmed with telegrams and letters that "we have not known which way to turn."[25] Christian IX celebrated his 82nd birthday, looking more like 62, and there was an official reception and dinner at Crown Prince Frederick's house. The Waleses took Holy Communion in the church at Christiansborg on the 12th; on Good Friday and Easter Sunday, they attended St Alban's. The family went to Roskilde on the 19th and Albert Edward then left after a pleasant, quiet fortnight, "& am always sorry to part from Alix' kind & sympathetic relations. My Father-in-law is really a wonderful man in every way."[26] At Marlborough House, he got "a tremendous reception from large crowds in the streets, which pleased him very much. Good sometimes comes out of evil, & I am certain that the affair at Brussels will if possible make you two more popular than ever." George had met Papa at Wolferton Station, where all the tenants received him. All the keepers, schoolchildren and labourers had assembled at the Norwich Gates, "at least 1,000 people, & some of them took the horses out of the carriage & pulled us up to the Cottage, which was very nice of them." George was to attend the Crown Prince's[27] coming of age in Berlin, but was not looking forward to going there, or indeed anywhere abroad, "as they apparently all hate us like poison."[28] William II alone had appeared friendly to England and was delighted to be the new baby's godfather; George told Alexandra he was quite ready to be friends with his cousin.[29] She feared William's civility "is only to suit his own purpose & to throw dust in our eyes, his <u>country</u> cannot disguise its <u>true</u> feelings against us, and all his <u>future</u> will show it with a vengeance."[30] She visited the zoo and the lupus hospital, and arrived home on 1 May. Victoria had returned from Edenhall.

On 7 May the Waleses inspected the officers and crew of *HMS Powerful* at Horse Guards Parade. On the 10th Alexandra gave prizes to pupils from the Girls' Public Day School Company schools at the Albert Hall. The couple attended a charity matinée later that day at St James's Theatre, for the Officers' Families' Fund. There were drawing rooms, and an exhibition of watercolours by Ella Du Cane[31] at the Graves Galleries on the 12th. On the 14th Alexandra saw *Faust* on the first night of the Covent Garden season and many other operas subsequently. News arrived of the relief of Mafeking on 17 May, when Henry William Frederick Albert of York was christened in Windsor Castle's private chapel. Albert Edward's horse, "Diamond Jubilee", won the Newmarket Stakes and, on the 30th, the Derby. The Waleses opened the Military Tournament at Islington; the Prince inspected Scots Guards leaving for South Africa; Alexandra opened the National Bazaar in aid of war funds, visited the HAIA's exhibition at the Albert Hall and watched polo and the Ladies' Driving Competition at Ranelagh on the 26th. On the 28th it was a concert at Bridgwater House for the Chapel Royal's Choir and an exhibition of Welsh Industries at Lord Aberdare's[32] house. News came that Johannesburg had been taken, and Lord Roberts entered Pretoria unopposed.

When they reached Sandringham on 2 June, Albert Edward was astonished to find Alexandra's present of a Venetian red marble fountain, looking remarkably well in the kitchen garden.[33] They watched the Dersingham Sports on the 4th and returned to London on the 5th for *Rheingold*. Back at Sandringham the next day, Alexandra visited the cottage hospital several times, called on the Misses Wolfe on the 8th and returned to London on the 12th for *Romeo and Juliet*. On the 16th the couple gave prizes at the Royal Naval School at Eltham. On the 19th Alexandra and Victoria joined Albert Edward at York, for the Royal Agricultural Society's Show, and all stayed at the treasurer's house. The next day they visited Newcastle, where the Prince laid the foundation stone of the Royal Victoria Infirmary. Back in London, they attended the Wallace Museum's[34] opening on the 22nd and the next day gave David a 6th birthday party at Marlborough House. At the Queen's Hall on the 25th Alexandra presented prizes to pupils of the North London Collegiate and Camden Schools and the next day chaired the fifteenth annual meeting of the SSFA at Chelsea Hospital. On the 28th, the Khedive[35] paid his official visit to Marlborough House. Alexandra opened the Jenny Lind Infirmary near Norwich on the 30th, then, among other events, gave a small children's tea party for Victoria's birthday on 6 July, visited a students' exhibition at Alexandra House and a Scottish industries sale at Stafford House. She wanted to get more nurses out to South Africa and, grudgingly, the War Office had finally let her send 20, selected by Sydney Holland,[36] at her expense, as the "Princess of Wales's Military Nurses". They objected to one because she was over 35; Alexandra (55) insisted she go and eventually the War Office capitulated. "Nothing like Perseverance", she told Holland triumphantly, and it became her catch-phrase at this time.[37] He later declared the country could not have done without these invaluable nurses.[38]

Alexandra went to Southampton with Victoria on 9 July to welcome troops returning on her ship, later telling Vicky it was starting on its third voyage out. Having already sent out twelve nurses, it was good news about her "<u>20</u> extra nurses, they were badly wanted & they are all the very <u>best</u> Sisters from the London Hospital." Mysteriously, she added, "I must tell you privately that I am rather handicapped about my nurses!! & that is the one thing I love to look after."[39] She also mentioned the hospital at Surbiton.[40] On the 12th the Waleses opened St Olave's Union workhouse's new buildings at Ladywell. Waldemar arrived for two days on the 15th. Victoria left for Edenhall with Nora Musgrave on the 17th and the couple saw "Diamond Jubilee" win the "Eclipse Stakes" at Sandown Park on the 20th. Alexandra's evenings were usually spent at the theatre. On the 24th the Prince and Princess visited the Guards' Convalescent Home at Golders Hill. Alexandra and her nephew Constantine[41] had tea with Miss Alice Rothschild at Eythrope on the 26th; the next day Presidents of the League of Mercy had a reception in Marlborough House's garden. A busy season was ending; it was time to relax and take stock but on the 29th the King of Italy was assassinated at Monza,[42] and on the 30th Duke Alfred of Saxe-Coburg-Gotha died of cancer in his sleep, a week before his 56th birthday.

Losing his beloved brother was a tragedy for Albert Edward. Victoria returned from Edenhall on the 31st, and he went to Osborne on 1 August to comfort his grieving mother. The next day he, George and Constantine left for Alfred's funeral at Coburg on the 4th; Alexandra attended the memorial service at the Chapel Royal and on the 5th took Holy Communion at St Paul's, later visiting the Surbiton hospital again. She and Victoria went to Cowes, lunched the next day with the Queen and met Albert Edward at Portsmouth on the 8th. They had tea at Osborne and two days later visited Empress Eugénie on *Thistle*. They and Victoria reached Friedrichshof on the 17th; the Prince later went to

Homburg but visited Friedrichshof over the next four days, while Alexandra and Victoria stayed there. "Poor dear Aunt Vicky" had cancer. Although she looked well in the face and enjoyed talking, she was in a great deal of pain, but "wonderfully resigned."[43] She had no choice, but at least her two youngest daughters and their families were with her and Alexandra's two brothers, Freddy and Willy also came over. Some of them also called at Rumpenheim. Alexandra was glad to have seen Vicky, who "was so kind to Toria & me & we both enjoyed our stay so much."[44] Alexandra and Willy then left for Denmark, while Victoria went to Switzerland.

It was an emotional first visit to Fredensborg since Queen Louise's death, but King Christian was "wonderfully well" and went for walks with them several times a day, as well as riding daily for an hour or two before dinner. Thankfully Maud, although still ailing, was cheerful and looking much brighter. "They are so comfortably established in town & she says she loves her home, which makes me very happy." Alexandra and Minny used the blue sitting room previously occupied by Minny and Sacha and were at that moment both writing to their sons. The Cumberlands and two daughters had arrived, "all looking very well, & he is as funny as ever. Mr Greville cld not get over his looks – certainly one must admit that poor dear Ernest is the ugliest man there ever was made!!! but I like him so much." Sidney Greville[45] was enjoying his visit and was "not at all dull as you imagined, it is alas only my dear Children who are so spoilt that they think everything dull where there is no shooting or where they can't exactly do as they do at home. Voila tout!!! and it distresses me sometimes, as it is apt to make one become selfish at last! when one never goes out of the way to do what others like & only what suits oneself best. Naturally it wld have pleased poor Apapa just to have seen you & dear May, whom he likes so much, for a little here! & I as well; the whole family flattered themselves that it wld also have pleased you to have seen them once again, which you have not done since beloved Amama was taken from us."[46] She had excellent reports of Victoria, who, Albert Edward told George, had gone to Mürren with Mrs Johnson "in the strictest incog! She writes that she likes the place & the air & scenery is splendid. May it only do her good, & that she is not made to go to Denmark too soon?"[47] On the 30th, Alexandra thanked Sydney Holland for all his help; it was so satisfying "that our good ship has gone out once more & that everything now seems in such perfect order."[48]

The September anniversaries were remembered but on the 12th good news came; "Diamond Jubilee" had won the St Leger. Prince Christian's second son, Knud,[49] was christened on the 14th in the Fredensborg Chapel. On the 20th the Russian Band played at dinner for the Duke of Cumberland's birthday and on the 25th Victoria arrived from Switzerland. The Yorks were to visit Australia in 1901 and Alexandra commented; "I quite agree with every condition Grand Mama has made & am so glad that they were announced in the papers at the same time ... You say you know that I don't approve of yr going away so far & for so long! Of course I <u>hate</u> yr going from me!! altho' naturally I think politically it may be a very good thing that one of the family shld represent <u>Grand Mama</u> at the opening of the first Federal Parliament, which marks such an important era in her reign. Still it does not alter the fact that alas we have but <u>one son</u> left! that we can ill spare him or let him run the slightest risk, whereas if we had several sons it would be quite a different thing to send you to any part of the Empire! – <u>there</u> you silly boy now I hope you understand my reasons for not liking yr & dear May's going so far away from yr poor old Mother dear. At any rate you must promise me to leave the children partly under my charge, as it will be very sad for us alone."[50] The supply of princes was indeed dwindling; official duties abroad were not usually required of princesses. Queen Victoria's four sons had all had sons but Albert Edward had only one surviving; Duke Alfred and his only son were dead and the late Leopold, Duke of Albany's only son was to succeed them in Coburg. Arthur, Duke of Connaught and soon, his only son fulfilled engagements when required. Most of Queen Victoria's daughters' sons either lived abroad, or were too young, except for Christian Victor and Albert of Schleswig-Holstein.[51] Visiting the far-flung Empire was now expected; more distant relatives, such as May's brothers, had to play their part. The eventual birth of five sons to George and May seemed fortuitous.

Alexandra was feeling a little hurt; May "evidently thinks I <u>forget everything</u>", whereas "when once I promise a thing I generally stick to it. I now find that she has been asking Charlotte to get her the names or <u>genealogy</u> of my Ancestors, which according to her wish I <u>had</u> previously done & procured last Spring with a good deal of trouble." Alexandra had told May this but had been waiting for the delayed return of Lady Mary Lygon,[52] to whom she was giving the details. "Voila tout, & I hope you will explain this to dear May."[53] This episode is intriguing: May's great interest in, and knowledge of, Royal Family history became legendary. Was she just extending her range – or might this have been a secret morganatic quest? If so, she would have discovered that Alexandra's paternal great-grandmother[54] had been a countess rather than a princess, her Glücksburg ancestors had been addressed as "Highness" or "Serene Highness" rather than "Royal Highness", and that both Alexandra and May were descended from the originally-un-royal Tudors and Stuarts. Alexandra had had no intention of withholding this information. Meanwhile the Prince had visited Mar Lodge and found Louise "looking much better & fatter in the face, he also well … The Children had quite rosy cheeks, but quite treated like little old women!"[55]

More relatives arrived in Denmark, including George of Greece and the Maximilians of Baden. After more walks with her father and family trips, Alexandra left with Victoria on the 24th for the Paris "Exposition Universelle". Her husband had chaired executive committee meetings of the Royal Commission for the Exhibition and helped to obtain loans for the British Pavilion. Alexandra devoted four days to this, the largest international show of contemporary art ever held, including an historic survey of art in France and a retrospective exhibition of French art from 1800–1889; chronophotography by Etienne-Jules Marey;[56] Georges Mélié's[57] films, *Cinderella, Red Riding Hood* and *Bluebeard*; examples of Röntgen rays, and Auguste and Louis Lumière's[58] Kinora viewer, an example of which she acquired.[59] She also shopped, met relatives and friends, dined in restaurants, saw plays and went to Versailles on Mr Singer's[60] "Automobile". It was the kind of holiday she loved; sadly it was interrupted by bad news. On the 29th they heard that Christian Victor (33) had died of enteric fever while on active service in South Africa. He had been a good soldier, popular and respected and knew the Wales family well. On very slender evidence, he may have been fond of Victoria; he kept a photograph of her among his possessions.[61] She would certainly have mourned him, even if just as a cousin.

They returned home on the 30th and on 1 November the Waleses attended "Christle's" memorial service at St George's Chapel, afterwards visiting his parents at Cumberland Lodge. He was buried at Pretoria on the same day. His parents suggested that no one should give up engagements while mourning for him, "as there is nothing Christle would have disliked more."[62] Alexandra and Victoria went to Sandringham on the 2nd; Albert Edward arrived the next day. The Charleses reached London on the 12th and Alexandra and Victoria joined them, all returning to Sandringham on the 17th with Louise (who stayed for the weekend). Alexandra sent kind words and prayers on Vicky's birthday, for the alleviation of the agony she was enduring. The Queen was now much better but shocked by Christle's death; "I was horrified to see her so thin, pale & in such a low state, which I have never seen before."[63]

There were guests and, as in 1899, Mrs Keppel had been invited. Alexandra gave a birthday tea party for 450 children, aged 5–12, in the ballroom, including the children of Tupper[64] who worked for Victoria. Years later, Grace Tupper remembered them all being lined up in queues and filing into the ballroom, where long tables were covered with damask cloths, plates of bread and butter and cakes. Each child was given a slice of a cake made to Alexandra's birthday cake recipe, but without the marzipan or icing[65] and the footmen, the Waleses and their guests waited on them. Alexandra used to send Tupper's four children some of her own chocolates at Christmas, in wooden boxes tied up with double satin ribbon.[66] "She loved vanilla creams flavoured with jam. So did we! They were delicious. She also sent us large round boxes of glacé plums, the boxes were at least 12" in diameter, all tied up with red ribbon. Her chocolates were kept in velvet bags." After Alexandra's death, the Tuppers were given two of these bags, one red and one blue; "they were rather large, and after hoarding them for years we made them into cushions."[67]

On the 10th Alexandra inspected her hospital ship at Southampton, bringing 173 patients back on its last trip. They were sad to take leave of "our poor little ship, which was maligned by the world in general but proved herself superior to many."[68] There were theatres, the Irish industries sale and drives with the Queen at Windsor and the mausoleum service. Alexandra and Victoria returned to Sandringham on the 20th; the Charleses were at Appleton and there was a magic lantern show at York Cottage on the 27th. The Christmas tree held numbered presents, matching numbered tickets; the royal party distributed gifts to staff and tenants, with Alexandra, in a sparkling, sequin-covered dress, bowing as she handed them out.[69]

On 3 January 1901, the hero, Lord Roberts, arrived in London and was taken by the Waleses to Buckingham Palace for a large lunch. Later the Prince dined with him at Mr Brodrick's[70] house, while Alexandra saw *Alice in Wonderland* and the next evening, *Beauty and the Beast*. Returning to Sandringham, she visited the Misses Wolfe on the 8th; the school now taught art needlework and tapestry making. Sewing included babies' clothes, ladies' underlinen and plain dress-making; pupils designed clothes and did fine embroidery, spinning, weaving, crochet, knitting and other crafts, such as woven and drawn-thread linen work.[71] Alexandra had her own hand-loom. At her wish, the spinning wool came from the Sandringham estate flock and was also knitted into socks for the Seamen's Mission, which she supported. Hand-made articles could be ordered and made up for a moderate charge; tuition was free and the girls received wages once their work was saleable; they could sell it at the annual HAIA exhibition but received orders all year round. The school aimed to be partly self-supporting, so as not to over-depend on Alexandra's generosity.[72] The boys' school, now managed by a Mr Swan,[73] was near the stables and the boys learned metalwork, woodcarving and cabinet-making, to qualify them for work in the towns.[74] Alexandra also supported other proponents of arts and crafts and became aware of the work of Annie Garnett, who had set up a studio, "the Spinnery", in the Lake District, where she created dyes based on the local flowers and inspired by the landscape, which were used on the fabric she wove. Her work gained national and international recognition, and Alexandra commissioned a handwoven silk fabric design called "Fritillary".[75]

On the 10th Alexandra attended an entertainment in aid of SSFA and gave presents to the local schoolchildren on the 18th but the next day the couple were summoned to Osborne; the Queen's health was failing. Albert Edward later met his brother Arthur and William in London, and took them back to Osborne on the 21st. The Queen rallied slightly and the Prince saw her frequently during the day on the 22nd, but she was slowly sinking; her relatives gathered around her and she died at 6.30 in the evening. In Russia, Grand Duchess Xenia noted; "Mama received two telegrams from Aunt Alix, one after the other; the first one said [the Queen] seemed a little better, the second informed us of her death. Poor Aunt Alix is in despair."[76] Albert Edward left for a Privy Council meeting at St James's Palace and was proclaimed King Edward VII, dropping his first name, which he considered uniquely his father's. The next day he held a small Privy Council meeting at Marlborough House and returned to Osborne to receive the household's homage. Services were held in Queen Victoria's room for three days; on the 25th her body was taken to the dining room, now a *chapelle ardente*, for another service. The German crown prince, Victoria, the Charleses, Lord Roberts, the Duke of Norfolk[77] and Mr Brodrick arrived on the 26th and on the 27th the Royal Family attended a service at Whippingham Church. It was William II's birthday and he was made a British field marshal; the next day his son was created a Knight of the Garter. Foreign representatives were arriving, one, Grand Duke Michael,[78] with a letter from Nicholas II; "My thoughts are so much with you and dear Aunt Alix now, I can so well understand how hard this change in your life must be, having undergone the same six years ago. I shall never forget your kindness and tender compassion you showed Mama and me then during your stay here."[79] On 1 February, the coffin was drawn on a gun carriage to *Alberta* and, followed by the Royal Family on *Victoria and Albert,* to Portsmouth. On the 2nd the funeral was held in St George's Chapel; the coffin being placed later in the Albert Memorial Chapel, for a short evening service next day. On the 4th it was taken to the mausoleum, where the Queen was laid to rest beside her husband.

King Edward had written to Empress Frederick about their mother's great qualities; "I know full well how yr thoughts will be with us & how as my eldest sister you will give me your blessing, to fulfil my arduous & onerous duties which I have now inherited from such a Sovereign & Mother". William had been "kindness itself & touching in his devotion, without a sign of *brusquérie* or selfishness."[80] On the 6th, in St George's Hall, the King presented Victorian medals to the Queen's Company, 1st Battalion Grenadier Guards, who had been on duty throughout the obsequies. He and Alexandra returned to Marlborough House on the 7th. She had refused to be called Queen until after the funeral and Lord Esher[81] had heard she objected to being called Queen Consort. "She means to be The Queen, although she says pathetically she would prefer a peaceful and quiet station."[82] They opened Parliament for the first time as King and Queen on the 14th; unluckily George was ill and Victoria could not attend either.[83] She told Lord Rosebery; "I am one of those who are only allowed snatches as it were of health & happiness, perhaps just as well; one might like it too much, & forget." Perhaps she was regretting Prince Max of Baden; she was sorry Rosebery "did not see Max. I should have liked to [have] heard your impression – and if he would have suited."[84] As a member of the Royal Family (to which, she later admitted to Rosebery, she never remembered belonging)[85] her choices were limited. Her father hoped she would marry a prince and certainly not a British commoner; her mother, convinced that conflict between England and Germany was inevitable,[86] was against her marrying a German. Victoria herself, a worrier and often a pessimist, had no wish for a high position; she preferred a more private life. It was stalemate.

The next day the couple inspected "Strathcona's Horse", a Canadian regiment returning from South Africa. Alexandra thanked Canon Dalton for condolences; "May God give us strength to fulfil all the many duties & responsibilities which have devolved upon us & enable us to walk in the footsteps of one who set an example to the whole world."[87] Over the weekend at Windsor they toured the rooms with Lord Esher and May. Alexandra wanted to live in the state rooms but the King insisted on occupying his mother's suite and using his father's rooms himself. They disagreed sharply, but discussed every detail and the Queen showed "excellent taste".[88] They lunched with Louise on her birthday; Alexandra sat to the sculptor, Emil Fuchs,[89] on the 22nd and the next day she and Victoria went by special train to Sandringham, while the King went to Germany to see Vicky.

There was keen anticipation about the King and Queen. Alexandra had always been beloved but what was she really like? Eager authors saw an opportunity; Sarah A Tooley had already written a "personal" life of Queen Victoria, now in its third edition. While some biographers prefer waiting until the dust has settled round their subject, there is much to be said for entering the fray while it is still being raised. Mrs Tooley could consult people who had known the Queen since her youth, like Miss Knudsen, and talk to her staff; Alexandra even allowed her to have photographs taken and to study her interests and concerns at Sandringham. At 56 Alexandra still looked youthful and beautiful without artifice, despite unkind rumours.[90] Her voice was deep and clear, with a slightly foreign accent, and she would gesture and nod for emphasis. Her charming smile and expressive eyes were as attractive as ever. Fairly tall, graceful, calm and relaxed, she was always appropriately dressed. Grace Tupper remembered her wearing fawn-coloured tweed costumes when visiting the Tuppers at their house on the Sandringham estate.[91] Alexandra now had her "signature" hair style; a full toupée covering the top of her head and upper forehead and her "back hair" pinned up. She liked high collars and ruffles, hiding the infamous scar and flattering her long neck. Blue and red had been favoured colours, but after Eddy's death she often dressed in silver grey, heliotropes and mauves and combined colours skilfully, using black for dramatic effect as well as mourning. She liked tailor-made costumes, was particular about the fit, favoured non-creasing cloth, preferred velvet to silk evening dresses,[92] and was partial to knitted fabric. She also liked sparkling dresses of metallic-woven cloth, or sequinned and beaded. Later research has revealed[93] an imbalance in some bodice backs, implying curvature of the spine. This could have resulted from uneven gait after her illness of 1867–8 but photographs suggest that her grandmother Landgravine Charlotte, her mother Queen Louise and her sister Thyra (in later life) all had some degree of spinal curvature. In Alexandra's case, it was barely noticeable.

Men had always admired Alexandra but women liked her too, as she was friendly and unaffected,[94] thoughtful and considerate and put people at their ease, always managing to say the right thing.[95] Her niece, Marie of Greece, remembered her hands, with long fingers and almond-shaped nails. In public, she perhaps started "the Royal wave"; "the way she bowed and smiled to everyone was quite unique. Each person in a crowd felt that he or she was being singled out."[96] She was noted for kindness to the staff. Once, when Mr Tupper's family were in London, he took their Aberdeen terrier, Jock, for a run, but he disappeared. The children were very upset but the Queen said "He must be found and you are to say he is my dog." Scotland Yard were informed and about a week later, Jock was discovered at Sevenoaks. His astonished family were full of admiration for the London police, but, as Alexandra well knew, Jock was more likely to be found as "a Royal dog".[97]

Paris Singer brought an electric car to Sandringham and the Queen drove in it twice in late February. A black and red-painted four-wheeled two-seater with a hood was obtained for her and in due course, Pugh, her "phaeton boy" drove it for her. She gradually took to motors, but really preferred horses to mechanical vehicles, even the silver-mounted tricycle that had been made for her.[98] After lunching several times at Appleton, she and Victoria returned to London on 4 March. The King was back from Germany on the 7th and Downey photographed them in state robes at Marlborough House. Victoria mischievously took another shot from the side, revealing the props which steadied them during the long exposure. King Edward went to Hampton Court next day, while Alexandra showed Lady de Grey Buckingham Palace's rooms; she spent the morning there again on the 12th with Lord Esher, "in tearing spirits and will enjoy her new home, when once she begins to arrange her rooms." They toured her suite at Marlborough House on the 18th; "She has some beautiful things, and is in sore distress, because she has so many, and nowhere to put them" without exceeding her allocation of rooms in Buckingham Palace.[99] On the 15th Alexandra and relatives inspected the Yorks' ship, *HMS Ophir*, at Portsmouth and the next day the King presented Victorian and South African War medals to the sailors who had drawn Queen Victoria's gun carriage at Windsor. After a large luncheon on *Ophir*, George and May, temporarily styled Duke and Duchess of Cornwall and York before becoming Prince and Princess of Wales,[100] set off for Australia on 16 March.

Alexandra's planned Danish visit was delayed by "heavy seas". After two sleepless nights worrying about the Yorks and the weather, she wrote that they were longing for details of the cruise so far and missed them both constantly. It was consoling to have the children at Marlborough House; "I am in & out every moment & it makes me feel quite young again having my second batch of chicks near me. I have washed sweet baby several times & he is so good & likes me altho' he occasionally grunts a bit, but I think it is only on account of his teeth. Dear little David does his lessons very well & they are all <u>so obedient</u> & good, & we have good Games in those rooms where there is lots of space. They will stay on with Papa & go with him to Windsor & I hope all come back when I return from Denmark." The Charleses were going to Mentone and Victoria to Wales with Nora Musgrave, via Hampshire. "It is sad all to be parted but it can't be helped." Augusta and her granddaughter, Marie, were in London; Alexandra had taken her to Buckingham Palace and they had dined at Marlborough House. She finished her letter the next day, "as my time is so short & Louise is coming to dinner. Papa dines with the <u>old girls</u> & <u>their Hospital</u>.[101] Toria says 'is that a proper thing for a King to do'!!!"[102] On the 22nd she left him alone with the grandchildren, "who ... make my solitude more lively!"[103] An English Mission announced his accession to King Christian on the 25th and Alexandra saw them privately. Her sisters were there; she drove with Minny and shopped; there were several large dinner parties and, on 8 April, their father's birthday.

Alexandra left on the 9th to see Vicky at Friedrichshof; a sad sight, "although her poor face is not much altered, but she is in such <u>constant</u> <u>terrible agonies</u> that it simply made me miserable to see her. We had long talks about everything & I sat for hours with her. She takes an interest in everything when the pain is not too great, but she is always in bed now & her left arm & hand quite useless. She is driven about in a bath chair once a day but looks <u>so</u> dreadfully tired when she comes in." Two of her daughters were there; "Young Vicky" and a pregnant "Mossy Possy", who came for the day "and looks like a small tub." Alexandra left on the 13th, had tea with her Aunt Anna[104] and reached London on the 14th, ill with something caught at Friedrichshof (which the King suspected was influenza, caught in Copenhagen, "though she would not own to it"). Her throat was so sore she had to stay in bed before leaving for Sandringham on the 18th with her husband, daughter and grandchildren. A "state reception" met them at Wolferton; a guard of honour of Lynn & Hunstanton Volunteers. "We were escorted by a troop of the 'Loyal Suffolk Hussars' commanded by Prince Frederick Duleep Singh[105] & I conferred the MVO on him, as it is the first Yeomanry Regmt that has escorted me since my Accession. There were great crowds all the way & we were received here by the Clergy, Tenantry & School Children. The two latter filed past afterwards."[106]

Alexandra and May, now seasick on *Ophir*, wrote regularly. Alexandra sympathised; "It is indeed a horrid nuisance & makes one feel utterly wretched & miserable while it lasts. Thank God you were able to pull yr self together when you had to land." She wanted to hear everything, especially about Egypt, "which enchanted me so much, it was like a whole new world to me – all those <u>bronzed</u> & <u>black</u> people half naked & the Camels etc etc & the heavenly climate over all.

How I long to go back there some day." Ceylon and Singapore "must also have been most exciting & interesting places to see & I own I envy you much, seeing all those new <u>worlds</u>, people & countries." She also envied their having seen "the new Comet ... We unfortunately cannot see it yet but hope to get a glimpse of it later on."[107] Guests came and went and she decided to try golf, playing several times with Victoria; a boy from the technical school acted as caddy. She liked croquet but not tennis (which her husband enjoyed); the Sandringham courts were now a rose garden with a rustic summerhouse, for taking tea in hot weather.[108] But on 30 April; "We have all been trying hard to play Golf, every day we are at it & Francis is one of the most eager players. I cannot say exactly that any of us in particular are making very great progress, but any how we do our little [best]." The King had a professional golfer from Hunstanton to teach him; "It is certainly excellent exercise, but at present I am not a gt proficient at it."[109] The children were looking "<u>so</u> well & are so bright & happy, they never cry & are <u>most</u> obedient & <u>no one</u> spoils them. I treat them the same as I did you all, so you may be quite happy about them as far as that goes, though I fear you must miss the darlings dreadfully." She worried that "the dreadful war is still going on & altho' we keep on taking prisoners, ammunition, cattle & horses, <u>nothing</u> seems to have a lasting effect upon those Boers! They are a set of regular <u>Brigands</u> & nothing more or less."[110] Her health and spirits had improved, although her throat still troubled her.[111] New motor cars arrived; Paris Singer had sent an engineer and Charlotte petitioned "I think the Queen as well as myself will be most grateful for some instruction in driving."[112]

After the earlier difficulties, Alexandra fully supported Sydney Holland's new plan to form a military nursing corps. Lady Roberts was also involved. It was to be a national scheme and by 24 April Alexandra had approached Brodrick for his support. She hoped they could all agree on the selection of committee members.[113] General Clarke and "Young Ponsonby"[114] had come into waiting and "next month Carrington (whom you have taken!!) & Davidson, whom you <u>might</u> have taken instead!!!" are coming together" as Alexandra told George,[115] rather obliquely. Arthur Davidson,[116] a gentleman although not an aristocrat, educated privately and at Petersham, had started his military career in the 60th Rifles. After distinguished service in several campaigns, he became ADC to the Duke of Cambridge (1890-95), then groom in waiting (1895-6) and equerry (1896–1901) to Queen Victoria. He was conscientious, kind and amiable and the Royal Family liked him; he was thus appointed equerry, assistant keeper of the privy purse and assistant private secretary to Edward VII in 1901. Naturally he met the King's family, including when Eddy died in 1892, and Victoria had noticed him at least by 1901, because she photographed him on the yacht. They got on well and Alexandra, observant and instinctive, would have picked this up very quickly.

The King left for London and the next day Victoria got severe influenza; "she

& Mama have never been able to leave Sandringham since I left there on the 2nd"
the King wrote; "It is doubly unfortunate for V as she was so particularly well,
but the quiet & fresh air for Mama is of great advantage to her."[117] Regarding
Victoria's influenza and Maud's internal troubles, the King mused; "It is so
strange, that notwithstanding that Alix & I are (*unberufen*) very strong, none of
our children are, they are always ailing & complaining."[118] George wrote
regularly about the tour, which was going well, despite intensely hot weather and
occasional seasickness. At home, Sandringham looked its best, especially the
Queen's wildflower garden, winding along near the avenue of Scots firs known as
"Church Walk". Bluebells, pimpernels, bird's-eye, violets, primroses, forget-
me-nots, daisies, buttercups, nettles and flowering weeds grew among the grass
and shrubs, like a natural meadow. In spring, everything burst into bloom and
there were quantities of birds; nightingales' voices filled the air on June evenings.
Alexandra had a rustic table and seats there, where she sometimes had tea. She
also enjoyed tea at the Dairy, built in 1875; she had introduced the Danish
butter-making method and, in the time of Mrs Barker, the old dairywoman, the
princesses would amuse themselves churning the butter. In 1901 the Dairy was
decorated with blue Indian tiles; silver cream pans, lined with eggshell china,
were fixed to a marble counter. Round the walls were marble, terra-cotta, silver
and alabaster models of prize animals bred on the estate and the tea room was
full of presents from family and friends.[119] Other favourite retreats were the
Rosary and summer house beyond the terrace gardens and the cool Alpine
garden near a stream banked by ferns. Primroses were grown elsewhere on the
estate and masses were sent to hospitals and infirmaries. Alexandra loved having
flowers indoors, such as pink Malmaison roses for her own rooms. She had
ferns, plants and flowers everywhere, as well as pet animals, and caged birds in
her dressing room.[120] In the grounds were statuary and items such as an ancient
Greek well from Crete.[121] Alexandra's books relating to gardens and gardening
included picture books and others such as *Twixt Town and Country: a book of
suburban gardening*, by Roma White[122] and Gertrude Jekyll's *Home and Garden,
Notes and Thoughts, Practical and Critical, of a Worker in Both*.[123] She described
the "truly <u>rural</u> life here in this beloved place which is looking so <u>lovely</u> now,
lilacs in full bloom & everything coming out so fresh & lovely, the Children & I
are out <u>all day</u> long, they are <u>so</u> sweet & enjoying themselves thoroughly. Thank
God Toria dear is getting on now tho' slowly, she is out again but her legs are still
weak. Next week we must go back to poor Papa who is alone in London working
away busily, & I do <u>hope</u> she will be much better then." She had been riding
again, alone or with Julie d'Hautpoul, and spending an evening upstairs, "& am
very busy indeed."[124]

She sent Vicky loving thoughts and news: her daughters' health; the King's
regrettable re-arrangement of Queen Victoria's rooms; the future of the military
nurses and a new scheme; and the present beauty of Sandringham's grounds;

"My little dairy garden too, an old fashioned Dutch style, with clipped yew trees, birds etc., with borders of various coloured tulips & wallflowers, is looking its best at this moment." They had tea there with the children, who were her joy while their parents were away. Sandringham's rooms were filled with Vicky's gifts; a little bronze figure, (now standing on a white marble Greek column, given her by her brother); and lovely vases on the library bookcases (the library having recently "been arranged & organised by Hatchard's[125] man & looks twice as well"). The paintings of Windsor and Kronborg that had been Vicky's silver wedding present were now displayed prominently at Windsor. While writing, Alexandra heard that Mossy "has just astonished the world with a second set of twins! Well done, I must say! only I wish for her sake they had been girls this time!"[126] Back in London, they drove in the park on 21 May for the first time since Queen Victoria's death. Alexandra received the Spanish ambassadors and the Duchess de Mandas,[127] and on the 24th accompanied the King when he presented colours to the 3rd Battalion Scots Guards at Horse Guards. She thanked Alfred de Rothschild[128] "for that darling little dog! – with that lovely collar on. I really do not think I can resist it altho' I must confess I have already got 4 of them, one of them is dear little 'Punch' you gave me 8 years ago who is still quite young & lively. I must thank you a thousand times for it & am sure she will be a great pet with us all. Sewell[129] brought her in triumph this morning & assured us she was a perfect little 'Marvel of beauty'".[130]

King Edward had inspected Windsor Castle and grounds several times, on the 25th with his wife and Victoria. Alexandra wrote; "We have had a lot to do since last I wrote & been to Windsor where I missed beloved Grd Mama beyond words, in every nook & corner; otherwise, the weather being fine, it was splendid there, and thank [God] not stiff as in former times & the big drawing rooms already begin to look quite comfortable with plenty of flowers etc. We always dine together in the big White & Gold dining room & Cards etc are played after dinner in the Green & White drawing rooms. The red one is the music room. Our own rooms will be beautiful when finished, with all the splendid, fabulous furniture from the Castle. I have been fishing out beauties from every corner imaginable & I do not think even the Rothschilds cld boast of anything better or more valuable. The pictures too will look splendid in my room. Papa also will have magnificently fitted-up rooms, his father's, but one thing I cld not have done, is dismantling the room where he died & which poor darling Grd Mama had made into her sanctum; she always said her prayers there even the last day she spent at Windsor, she was wheeled in there before going to Osborne!" The children were well and cheerful, David had lost a front tooth, "but it does not show too much"; he and Victoria had had hay fever at Sandringham.[131] There were guests at the castle and sometimes tea parties at Virginia Water. Lord Esher saw the Queen in "a most extraordinary hat, like a squashed mushroom,[132] and yet she looked perfectly regal as usual."[133] Johann

Kubelik, (21),[134] played the violin after dinner on the 31st. Alterations at Windsor included many more bathrooms and water closets, which meant reconstructing some walls; a new bathroom for Alexandra had to be built out in the wall adjacent to her rooms. A studio, fitted with cupboards and shelves for arts and crafts was also provided for her.[135] During reconstruction, the couple lived at Frogmore. King Edward took a great interest in the castle and surveyed it thoroughly, sometimes with the Queen but usually with Sir Arthur Ellis, Sir Horace Farquhar, Lord Esher, Lionel Cust,[136] sometimes Guy Laking,[137] and the new inspector of the castle, Mr GE Miles.[138] To allow more public access, the King had the east terrace opened on a bank holiday, when, naturally, it poured with rain. As they looked out of a window in the Green Drawing Room, he remarked to Alexandra how sad it was that, whatever they tried to do to make the people happy, they could not control the weather.[139]

Mourning for Queen Victoria curtailed social but not official events; on 1 June the couple received a deputation from the American Chambers of Commerce on the Terrace at Windsor. Kubelik played again after a dinner on the 7th and they had tea and croquet in the garden several times. On the 10th they received a special Moroccan embassy at St James's Palace. The King presented South African War medals to 3,000 men and 200 officers at Horse Guards Parade on the 12th. Alexandra suggested a seasickness remedy to May; a lump of ice in a rubber bag, placed "just under yr chest tied on for a short time occasionally while lying flat down." They had taken the children to Virginia Water, where "little David caught his first fish, & danced about with joy shouting all the time 'This is the first fish I ever caught in my life.'" He had asked for the still-living fish to be thrown back into the water "which I thought so nice of him."[140] His parents were approaching South Africa and Alexandra wrote; "If only that horrid war was over; it seems to me so sad, that you shld be received in State & rejoicing in one part of the country when the other is still plunged in the midst of misery & fighting! & just lately we have had so many misfortunes again & lost a lot of good officers & men."

Officers received medals at Marlborough House on the 17th and later Edward and Alexandra returned to Sandringham, where something dreadful had happened; "One thing Papa has had done, which I am more sorry about than I can say! & I am quite sure you also will be, & that is he has done away with our beloved old Bowling Alley we have had all our lives & which is quite an institution here & everybody liked it, particularly as there are very few others left anywhere now. I can cry about it – if he at least just told me of it before or asked me what I thought about it, but no, has it all done without one word & arranged into a kind of library. Of course there are so many books that one must have some more rooms, but we might by & by have added to the end of the house where the three other libraries are, but not remove this dear old thing all you children & I have been so fond of all our lives; with it goes quite a bit out of our former lives. I hope you will say so too when you see it is gone!!!"[141] The King thought it a great improvement; "Mama did not much fancy the change but will I think be ultimately reconciled to it. Hardly anybody played bowls, & the space was really wasted." Now there was a library, sitting and smoking room instead.[142] Alexandra, anxious in her new position, clung desperately to the past, while the King simply wanted to make better use of space and save money; as usual it would be resolved and their mutual affection restored.

Alexandra loved Marlborough House too; their first home, where four of their children had been born. Her rooms were arranged exactly as she liked, including her downstairs sitting room (the tapestry room), where she had some pretty furniture, like the mahogany and gold bookcases holding the Mitchell bequest,[143] and her painting room, originally a passage leading to the garden. Upstairs, her white and gold boudoir, with Indian red silk damask curtains, contained antique and modern furniture, some from Denmark; much was decorated with marquetry, some was covered in red silk slips, with frills, and there was a comfortable sofa, with lots of cushions, facing the fireplace. There was also a bonbonnière, full of sweets, and a large rag doll.[144] As at Sandringham, Alexandra had caged birds: canaries, bullfinches and others, and at one time a blue pigeon that flew freely round her rooms. She had an easel in her private rooms upstairs and often drew there, although painting was only done in the studio below. She had her music lessons upstairs but there were pianos all over the house; she also played well on the zither and occasionally on the harp and dulcimer.[145]

The couple wanted to monitor the running of their household and Alexandra, sometimes with Victoria, started paying friendly, informal visits to the Sandringham kitchens, appearing, unannounced, at about 11am, strolling round watching the staff at work and asking them about what they were doing. The chef, Gabriel Tschumi,[146] felt she would have enjoyed learning to cook and prepare meals herself[147] as most of her questions showed a sound knowledge of kitchen management. As she liked birthdays so much, they began making her a different surprise cake every year; a rich fruit mixture, using 40 eggs and half bottles of brandy and rum, which usually weighed 36lbs. One year it had three tiers, encrusted with sugar pansies, violets, carnations and roses in pastel colours. Another year it was a model of Sandringham Church, with porch, steeple and stained-glass windows. These cakes were the highlight of Alexandra's birthday tea and were made throughout the King's reign and afterwards, although First World War rationing reduced the elaborate sugar decorations.

On waking, Alexandra would take a *chota hazri*[148] at about 9am, with a proper breakfast later, although she ate very little, as Tschumi remembered. From a choice of fish, eggs, meat or game she rarely ate more than an *oeuf en cocotte* (she liked plovers' eggs) and perhaps some jellied meat. She was often slightly late for meals, which could be inconvenient, as some food needed serving at once. It was a long walk from Buckingham Palace kitchens to the Chinese room, where they had small dinners, and Alexandra suggested building a small Chinese kitchen nearby, for preparing after-theatre suppers for guests. This was partially successful but, even so, some food was spoiled when she was late. She was always very apologetic but somehow could not cure this fault.[149]

There had been news from Russia; "Fancy poor Alicky had a fourth daughter, what a disappointment, poor thing, & I am sorry for poor Nicky too, altho' he is so kind about it. It really is <u>too unfortunate</u> & the Russians are so disappointed about it."[150] Returning to London on 27 June, Alexandra, delighted at their excellent reception during their tour, told George; "We too have been leading a very busy life lately & there is always a lot to be done." They had enjoyed ten days at Sandringham and the alterations to York Cottage were going well. There was now "a splendid Motor Car ... & I did enjoy being driven about in the cool of the evening at <u>50</u> <u>miles</u>!! an hour! – when <u>nothing</u> in the way, of course only! & I must say I have the greatest confidence in our driver. I poke him violently in the back at every <u>corner</u> to go gently & whenever a <u>dog</u>, <u>child</u> or anything else comes in our way!" She had motored to Houghton Hall, which George, and especially May, had thought about renting, and had gone all over it, as she liked to do; it was "certainly a very fine old place which might be made beautiful, but take <u>my good advice</u> and <u>do not</u> be <u>in a hurry</u> to bind yr self in any way this first year at any rate. Wait quietly & see how things will turn out & you will find plenty to do with yr money by & by & <u>this next</u> year of all, with so much moving about, & additions in every way! & also let us be <u>near each other</u> this winter at least. We have been separated from each other long enough & yr cottage will be charming!"[151] This sensible advice unknowingly frustrated May's ambition to escape from Sandringham and her husband's family. Fond of them as she was, she had her own ideas and her own confidante, Aunt Augusta. Writing from New Zealand, she noted Augusta's visit to the Royal Academy and regretted Alexandra's not going too; "alas, when she once gets <u>stuck</u> at Sandringham, it is difficult to move her, I had so hoped that in her new position as Queen all this would have improved, & I do feel that it is very important that one should take a lively interest in Art or in anything connected with the good of one's Country, a sentiment in which I know you fully agree. It does not look well either for her so constantly to leave <u>him</u> alone as she does."[152]

It seems that May, at least in 1901, did not really understand Alexandra, or she could never have accused her in this way. In fact both women had a whole-hearted commitment to the nation and the arts; Alexandra had been involved with art since childhood and, throughout all but the last two years of her life regularly and frequently visited galleries, museums, exhibitions and studios, at home and abroad. She saw work by male and female artists, sculptors, painters, draughtsmen and amateurs, including students. She met artists, was shown their work; entertained them at parties; purchased paintings to keep or as presents;[153] gave many portrait sittings; took lessons, showed her own work in amateur exhibitions; and became absorbed in photography, home arts and industries. She owned many art books,[154] subscribed to magazines such as *The Connoisseur*, and was president of the Royal Amateur Art Exhibition, started in 1894 in aid of, largely medical, charities, for many years. Alexandra visited the Royal Academy at least 25 times and saw other exhibitions at Burlington House. In all, she saw work ranging from Old Masters to Jacob Epstein,[155] portraits to landscapes and caricatures to war pictures. Her husband, a keen art connoisseur, often accompanied her but she also went with relatives, friends or household. The couple lived in a part of London renowned for extraordinary wealth in galleries and exhibitions, including many small businesses. The National Gallery, the National Portrait Gallery, the Royal Academy, the Royal Society of Painters in Watercolours and the Royal Institute of Painters in Watercolours were also easily accessible, even on foot, if desired. The Wallace Collection, the Tate Gallery and the South Kensington Museum were not far away; the couple knew Sir Richard Wallace and visited his house before it became a public museum; the Prince opened the Tate Gallery in 1897 and, as King, the Aston Webb building of the Victoria and Albert Museum (formerly the South Kensington Museum) in 1909.

As an amateur artist herself, Alexandra was inquisitive, perceptive and had a keen eye for detail. These skills would have helped her in her royal duties, for example in remembering the many people whom she met. Preferring figure drawing to landscape as a girl, she always noticed how people looked and often, although usually privately, mentioned it frankly, dispassionately, and as though making mental notes. Her letters are sprinkled with such comments as "like a fat dairy maid"; "a kind of lemon-shaped head"; "looks a little like an Italian"; "so like his father, luckily", or "his poor fat cherub face and form". She enjoyed the art of caricature and understood that depicting people's salient features made them instantly recognisable. In her little sketch "A Game of Cards", c 1880–1,[156] the drawing is slight and naïve but the faces – the Prince's lovingly-drawn fine features; Prince Leopold's receding chin; Christopher Sykes's downward-sloping eyes and eyebrows; and Prince John's oval-trimmed beard and "sad" eyebrows – identify the four men perfectly.

Alexandra also cared deeply about charities, education and nursing. In 1901 her husband had only just become King, after a difficult year; she was still uncertain as Queen and had yet to establish her new role. In a letter which the old Grand Duchess wrote to her niece (which crossed with May's), she mentioned something of great relevance. "I had a long talk to Alix about her position as Queen; she says <u>he</u> does not permit her taking it, as he takes everything to himself, lets her do nothing in the way of carrying out her duties; for instance he did not even let her give the Prizes for the Red Cross which she has done hitherto; he says he is in an exceptional position and must take all the honours to himself! She asked me to write down all I remember of the old Court (1837). I will do so, Uncle G and Prince Edward[157] (we three <u>last</u> survivors of that time) assisting me; better <u>three</u> than me <u>alone</u>, as he might think I wanted to <u>meddle</u>."[158] As with the Indian visit in 1875–6, the King, who had waited so long for his kingdom, wanted it all, at least to begin with. While appreciating his wife's support, he was not quite ready to share it with her. His mother, who, in 1840, regarded Prince Albert as just her husband, while she was the Queen, had felt the same. Albert proved himself more than capable of political and public duties, and Victoria came to accept, welcome and depend on him. So with Alexandra; while sometimes she had no choice but to "leave <u>him</u> alone" with state business, the King would soon be too ill to carry out some of his duties and she would prove an excellent deputy. He acknowledged her contribution and fully appreciated her charm and devotion, knowing all too well how much of the hearty national welcome on his accession was because of her. He paid special deference to her as Queen and expected the same from everyone at court.[159] On 12 February 1901 he invested her as a Lady of the Order of the Garter, the first one since the 14th and the 15th centuries, when royal and aristocratic women had been designated "Dames de la Fraternité de St Georges".[160] This honour meant, among other things, that Alexandra had a new sealing wax stamp, with an image of the Collar of the Order of the Garter, to endorse her letters.[161] She herself prompted recognition for Charlotte Knollys, subsequently styled "Honourable", as for a Baron's daughter.[162]

The Queen had been thinking about her coronation dress. She liked Lady Curzon,[163] the Viceroy of India's wife, and respected her fashion sense; she would be the perfect accomplice. Deprived of seeing India for herself, Alexandra took great pleasure in Indian manufactures; in 1882 Maharani Sakwar Bai of Kolhapur had hand-embroidered a cushion for her.[164] Alexandra was now considering an Indian-inspired dress. Lady Curzon obtained a selection of fabrics and on 14 June Charlotte Knollys told her; "[The Queen] thinks the dress for the Coronation would look very well – net embroidered in gold & silver, with rose, shamrock & thistle. Could you therefore have a design made & send it to Her Majesty to look at. It must not be too 'conventional' or stiff but something in the 'flowing' style of your dress & the Queen says it could be made to <u>your</u> measurements". She hoped to talk it over with Lady Curzon when the latter was in England on 30 July.[165] Alexandra had been seeing a great deal of "dear Aunt Augusta" and "poor Marie" lately.[166] The latter had now joined her husband[167] in Paris, while Augusta was being "of the greatest help <u>to me</u>, such an <u>authority</u> on <u>everything</u>, which <u>none</u> of the new generation knows anything about here."[168] The last king and queen to be crowned together had been William IV and Adelaide[169] in 1831; Queen Victoria's coronation had been in 1838. Hardly anyone remembered how things had been done; Augusta had just been an observant young girl. This shortness of court memory, however, made it easier for Alexandra to devise a dress to her own taste.

10 Queen Alexandra in Coronation robes, 1902. *W & D Downey*
RCIN 2106314

On 28 June a herald proclaimed the forthcoming coronation from St James's Palace. In Marlborough House garden on 3 July, "we had an enormous reception of Queen's Jubilee Nurses,[170] whom I gave badges & certificates to. They are now mine by Charter." Alexandra made a speech: "It gives me great pleasure to receive you all here today and it is most gratifying to me to be able to carry on the noble work founded by our dearly beloved and never to be forgotten Queen Victoria. I have always taken the most sincere interest in Nurses and Nursing and it affords me heartfelt satisfaction to be associated with you in your labour of love and charity. I can indeed imagine no better or holier calling than that in which you are engaged, of tending the poor and suffering in their own homes in the hour of their greatest need. I shall follow with interest the reports of the Institute and shall anxiously note the progress which you are making from year to year. I pray that God's blessing may rest upon your devoted and unselfish work and that He will have you all in His Holy Keeping."[171] Sydney Holland had organised this event, prepared the address and offered to read it for her but "Not a bit of it, she would speak 'my own speech' & she did, I am bound to say rather low for 400 women to hear." She was an excellent and fluent speaker,[172] but had been very nervous, although glad everyone enjoyed the tea and garden party. She had not yet had a single word from the War Office about the scheme for military nurses; "but the usual thing from that quarter I suppose." Eventually, however, after a great deal of work, the nursing of the Army was reorganised under the Imperial Army Nursing Board, of which the Queen was president.[173] It ran Queen Alexandra's Imperial Military Nursing Service (QAIMNS), the forerunner of Queen Alexandra's Royal Army Nursing Corps (QARANC).

Victoria celebrated her birthday with a children's party in Marlborough House garden and on 8 July left for Edenhall with Lady Musgrave. The Queen received visitors,[174] drove with the children and on the 11th dined in the garden with the King, "owing to intense hot weather"[175] when "electric fans are an absolute necessity in the rooms."[176] On the 12th a deputation from the Duke of York's School presented David (7) with an album marking the School's centenary. Later, the children left for Sandringham with their grandmother. She took them driving and went herself to Babingley Hospital. They returned to London on the 17th and Victoria joined them the next day; the King, Queen, Victoria and the Fifes all dined in the garden that evening. On the 19th Alexandra received 1,100 nurses belonging to the National Pension Fund. The next day she drove to Coombe Court[177] and the party motored about 50 miles through Dorking, Guildford and Leatherhead. On the 21st the couple motored to Coombe, Kingston, Hampton Court and Esher. Alexandra received many visitors over the next ten days and also watched 3,000 war medals being distributed to the Imperial Yeomanry at Horse Guards. It was a tiring day, although cooler after several heavy thunderstorms. The men were in their grubby, ill-cut khaki uniforms, but the King was "glad personally to meet all those gallant fellows who had served their Country so splendidly in S. Africa."[178] Alexandra received Lady Aberdeen[179] and a deputation, with two albums from the Women of Canada. Victoria went twice to the opera; it was six months since Queen Victoria's death and, as a granddaughter, she could relinquish mourning sooner than her parents. The King presented more South African War medals on the 29th and the three left for Cowes on 1 August.

They sailed in *Britannia*, which the King had sold to Dick Bulkeley[180] but hired back for two weeks, and on 3 August saw the new yacht, *Victoria and Albert*. They toured the National Antarctic Expedition's vessel, *Discovery*, commanded by Robert Falcon Scott,[181] RN, but could not enjoy their holiday for long; Empress Frederick had died. King Edward had intended visiting her later while at Homburg but had been dreading it; "I could hardly have borne seeing her again as she was, I hear, so dreadfully altered."[182] He had written to her every week for many years, the last time on 31 July, and, missing his letters to Vicky, he wrote copiously to Mrs Keppel; some 554 times between 1899 and May 1910. In the same period he wrote to Alexandra some 309 times, but then they were more often together.[183]

George told Alexandra; "I fear dear Papa will feel (Aunt Vicky's death) very much, as really she was his favourite sister … He has indeed had his share of sorrow, as practically in the short space of a year, he has lost his brother, his Mother & his sister … This extra sorrow added to the many worries & anxieties of his new position will be bad for him, you must do all you can to help him & insist on his having a rest this autumn, I suppose he will not now go to Homburg; but Balmoral will do him good & he will be more or less quiet there."[184] In her reply, Alexandra thanked God that Vicky had been released from terrible suffering, but her poor children were much to be pitied "& how <u>we</u> all shall miss <u>her</u> <u>bright</u>, <u>dear</u> & wonderfully gifted self!" She was thankful Papa had not been there at the end, "as he really has gone through <u>so much</u> this year that I am sure it wld have been too much for him." She felt miserable; not only had they lost "darling Aunt Vicky" but had to give up *Osborne*, in favour of *Victoria and Albert*; they had all cried at leaving the old ship. "It is like breaking with <u>all one's</u> youth & <u>former life</u>, both that & tearing oneself away from the <u>old Home</u> here, Marlborough House! That I <u>feel</u> will finish me! All my happiness & sorrows were here, very nearly all you Children born here, all my reminiscences of my whole life are here & I feel as if by taking me away from it a chord will be torn in my heart which <u>can</u> never, never be mended again!! but I dare not think of it even."[185]

The Indian fabric samples had arrived in July and she had chosen several; for a black tulle net dress embroidered with silver lilies and a full train, a mauve net dress embroidered in gold, with a full train, and for the coronation itself, a white net dress embroidered in silver and gold with rose, thistle, shamrock and lotus. She had also been unable to resist some white muslin with gold spots, mauve muslin with gold spots, white and gold silk and a red and gold table cloth with a flower pattern.[186] On 3 August Miss Knollys told Lady Curzon; "the Queen wishes me to write & ask you not to tell anyone in <u>England</u> about the Dresses ordered in India, or else they will be wanting to have some also, whereas HM would like to have something <u>original</u> for her Coronation dress ... The Queen has just told me to send you the enclosed pattern 'just to look at' in case you might be able to take any ideas from it." Later; "I do not think the Queen has the slightest objection to letting it be known in <u>India</u> that her Coronation dress is to be made there, she only thought (*entre nous*) that if the London Ladies got hold of it, they would be wanting to copy hers!"[187]

On the 9th, leaving the grandchildren at Osborne, the King, Queen, Victoria, Nicholas of Greece and Frank of Teck left on *Victoria and Albert* for Germany; "I must say she is <u>beautifully</u> fitted up inside & very comfortable & she was <u>very steady</u>, no vibration whatsoever." On the 11th they were met by the Emperor and Empress, lunched at the old castle at Homburg and met other guests before driving to Cronberg Church for Vicky's funeral. The flower-covered coffin, impressive service and beautiful music were heartrending. The King and Queen had placed a large white cross at the foot of the coffin and a wreath of heather, all flowers from Windsor, with a card from them and their children. Afterwards they went to Friedrichshof; Alexandra "drove all that day with the Empress & wondered all the time what poor Aunt Vicky wld have said, cld she have seen us!" She had never really warmed to Augusta Victoria (an Augustenburg) and neither had Vicky. Alexandra and Victoria felt too depressed to attend the family dinner at Homburg Schloss; next morning they left for Potsdam and a grand reception in the evening and on the 13th Empress Frederick was interred near her husband in the mausoleum at the Friedenkirche, in a three-hour-long ceremony. After a huge dinner they stayed two more days, visiting relatives; on the 16th the King went for his cure and the Queen and Princess to Denmark. *Osborne* was apparently still available; Alexandra had arranged for it to meet them at Hamburg and, "needing a little more sea <u>air & rest</u>" they cruised about for four days before reaching Bernstorff on the 20th. Happily her father looked healthy and unchanged; Maud was well but rather thin and Waldemar's children had just had whooping cough. They were all transferring to the more spacious Fredensborg, as more relatives were coming, including Minny, Willy,[188] and, on 2 September, Nicholas II with his wife and four little girls, but there would be no chance of seeing the Cumberlands; on the 3rd the tragic news came that their second son, Christian, only sixteen, had died from appendicitis, after having unwittingly swallowed a cherry stone.[189] Other news was disturbing; on the 6th the American president, McKinley, was shot and died a week later from his injuries.[190]

The King had written to George about the delicate question of housing; "you allude as to when you will be able to get into Marlbro' House. Of course that is not an easy question to answer as naturally dear Mama, who is miserable at the idea of leaving, will remain on as long as possible. Anyhow I shall do my utmost to get my things removed fr there to Buck: Palace by end of the year. Even if our rooms there are not ready, I have arranged that we can live in the so called Belgian Rooms ... & superintend the arrangement of our permanent rooms upstairs. When you return, wh I hope may be in 2 months fr today! we shall hasten proceedings. It will I am sure not take you 6 months to move fr Y House to M House & you ought to be comfortably established there before Easter!"[191] He reached Denmark on the 8th; dinners at the English and Russian legations followed and the English Biograph & Mutoscope Company put on a show after dinner on the 9th. On the 17th the Danish Biograph Company performed. The King told his son; "We have not yet settled when we leave here, but I am most anxious not to arrive too late at Balmoral, but you know the annual pressure put on Mama to prevent her leaving here!"[192] He had taken his motor to Denmark and terrified the population; "Motors are hardly known here, & not much approved of at present. The inmates of the carriages & carts we pass are certainly so frightened that they generally jump out first. Everything as you know is inclined to old fashioned ideas here, but I feel sure that in time they will become the fashion like in other Countries." He was pleased to find his visit was the first a King of England had ever paid to Denmark. On the 13th he, Alexandra and Minny visited Dr Finsen's Institute for treating lupus with electricity; a wonderful invention which had already produced excellent results.[193]

There were walks, drives and excursions until, on 23 September, they left on *Osborne*, later transferred to *Victoria and Albert*, and reached home two days later. Leaving on the 27th, they arrived at Balmoral on the 28th, Alexandra rather reluctantly. "I think it will be most sad going back there like this, without beloved darling Grandmama! particularly as I have to live in her rooms!"[194] On 4 October, she was writing at Queen Victoria's writing table; "it all seems so strange & unnatural. Papa lives in his Father's rooms next door & we are in & out of each other's rooms constantly. Unfortunately he had a sudden attack of lumbago after having sat in his kilt in the wet, & no wonder, I say, but he is much better today & walks about." Victoria had a chill and Louise was in bed with sciatica, although her children were delighted to see their grandparents and looked the picture of health. There was driving, walking and visiting "all the nice people here, they all miss darling Grd Mama so much" after everything she had done for them.[195] A violinist, Wolff,[196] played on the 10th and on the 14th there was Fraser & Elrick's cinematograph show. On 21 October the royal party left for London. The Charleses arrived on the 25th and on the 31st the King, Queen and family welcomed George and May at Portsmouth on *HMS Ophir* after their successful colonial tour, "where you both did yr duties so well & derived at the same time so much pleasure & interest from all the wonderful sights, countries & people you have seen!" They would miss the children, who had been "the very sunshine in the house, but thank God at Sandringham we are so close."[197]

After a grand reception on 3 November, they left the next day for Sandringham. On the King's birthday, as usual, there was shooting in the woods nearest the house, with beaters wearing their red and blue suits. Lunch was served in a tent near the cover, where the ladies joined the sportsmen. Everyone returned to the house for tea at 5pm, served in the saloon at a set table. Alexandra made and poured out the tea, chatting and laughing with the guests.[198] On that day George was created Prince of Wales; the timing being partly in recognition of the successful tour. There was a cinematograph performance in the evening. Alexandra wrote gleefully to Arthur Ellis about the coronation; "I know better than all the milliners and antiquaries. I shall wear exactly what I like, and so shall all my ladies – Basta!"[199] Sousa's[200] band played on her birthday and shooting parties continued until 16 December, when the couple, Victoria, Maud and Charles went to London. Charlotte had gone there on the 3rd for her nephew's funeral but was unexpectedly kept for two months at Marlborough House with pleurisy, shingles and neuritis. Perhaps through contact with her, Alexandra became ill with chicken pox on the 19th and reluctantly conceded the loss of Christmas at Sandringham. The presents were sent there on the 24th but the couple could not return until the 30th. George and May had gone to York Cottage, but would keep their presents and celebrate Christmas when their parents returned.[201]

⚜

8 January 1902 was the tenth anniversary of Eddy's last birthday; Alexandra, still unwell, was desolate. She had not seen George as often as she would have liked after his long absence, although "I know quite well you do not mean to neglect me ... I know how difficult it sometimes is to meet here."[202] Guests had included the George Keppels. On the 11th, *The Cigarette Maker's Romance*, with Mr and Mrs Martin Harvey,[203] was performed in the ballroom. The King and Queen returned to London on the 13th, visiting Windsor Castle and the Albert Memorial Chapel the next day. On the 16th they opened Parliament but soon afterwards Alexandra returned to Windsor with a bad cold. The King, who had been staying at Penn House,[204] joined her on the 21st. This year, the mausoleum service was held on 22 January, the first anniversary of Queen Victoria's death, replacing 14 December. The next day Patricia of Connaught,[205] Alexander and Victoria Eugénie of Battenberg were all confirmed in the private chapel. There were more guests and Alexandra showed Lady de Grey and Lady Gosford round on the 28th. Official mourning was over and, back in London on the 30th, they saw *Mice and Men* at the Lyric,[206] and the next day *A Country Girl* at Daly's.

After the Sunday Concert Society's concert, conducted by Henry Wood[207] at the Queen's Hall, Alexandra and Victoria spent a week at Sandringham, bringing the Charleses back to London with them. The King, not particularly well, saw doctors almost daily, but still dealt with audiences, visits and official functions. On 11 February the couple saw *The Importance of Being Earnest* at St James's, followed by more plays. Alexandra received Sir Edward Poynter,[208] with 67 sketches from the Members of the Royal Academy, on the 14th. On the 16th the royal couple saw a loan exhibition, "The Monarchs of Great Britain and Ireland", at the New Gallery. Victoria took the Musgraves to Sandringham on the 18th and Alexandra, with Probyn and Charlotte, joined them on the 20th. She went for walks with Charlotte, visited Appleton and called on the Misses Wolfe and others. On returning to London four days later, the royal couple and Victoria saw *Iolanthe* at the Savoy. Alexandra was looking forward to seeing the "stuffs" from India; using them for the coronation was likely to encourage more orders for the Indian workers. Charlotte noted; "All the Peeresses have been holding forth & disputing about their robes & made such a fuss that the strictly regulation Dress had to be abandoned & they were told that they might indulge up to a certain point their individual taste! So now they are pacified."[209]

The King and Queen left on 7 March to lay the foundation stone of the Britannia Royal Naval College at Dartmouth, driving through Plymouth, Stonehaven and Devonport and giving a dinner on board *Victoria and Albert*. The next day it was watching a parade of blue jackets and marines at the Royal Naval Barracks and presenting South African and China War medals to 350 officers and men. Alexandra gave certificates and badges to naval nurses and later launched *HMS Queen*, a first class battleship, while the King laid the first plate of *HMS Edward VII*. On the 9th they attended morning service at the dockyard chapel before steaming to Mount Edgcumbe, for tea and drives round the park and grounds. After another large dinner on the yacht, they went home on the 10th. Alexandra inspected Buckingham Palace the next day, returning later with the King to see the state apartments lit up. There were theatres, and the first court, and the couple planted two copper beech trees in Buckingham Palace gardens on the 15th. Frank of Teck came on the 17th to say goodbye before going to South Africa. They saw a special matinee of *Caste* at the Haymarket on the 18th; Alexandra called on Julie d'Hautpoul and Marcia Dalrymple[210] and on the 23rd visited the Alexandra Hospital for Hip Disease.

Victoria left for Overstrand Hall at Cromer on 24 March; the King prepared for a short cruise; and Alexandra was going to Denmark on the 25th but was kept in London by a violent storm. Reaching Copenhagen on the 27th, just before Easter, she attended services at the Danish church and St Alban's. On 3 April, to her delight, the Waleses arrived for two weeks. King Edward told George he was "glad that you are enjoying yr stay at Copenhagen. Dining at 6.30 is no doubt a bore, but I am sure it is best for Apapa at his age. What a mercy (*unberufen*)[211] that he is so strong & well. You are indeed a large family party wh at times is decidedly fatiguing, especially on account of the dawdling unpunctuality & never settling what to do till 5 minutes before!"[212] The Charleses gave a ball on the 4th; Alexandra drove with her sister, visited the cripples' hospital with her father, and also Finsen's Lupus Hospital. A reception on the 8th, a dinner at Frederick's house, and a concert in Christian VII's palace followed. Alexandra saw plays, and *Die Walküre* on the 12th. She visited Roskilde, Rosenborg and the zoo, toured Thorwaldsen's Museum with Professor Mehldahl,[213] saw some cows at Christiansborg and, with Waldemar, a collection of old pictures. She left on the 21st.

The couple's rooms in Buckingham Palace were not yet ready and they were staying in the Belgian Suite. The King had packed and sorted papers and other things to be brought from Marlborough House on the 27th and had decided to move into the palace after his cruise, on 12 April. He spent several days hanging pictures. Mr Church,[214] who had an astounding memory for all the couple's possessions, organised the move. Alexandra played little part in the arrangement of the palace as a whole but she did take entire responsibility for her own rooms. The King liked to supervise everything in the private apartments but left the actual work in Lionel Cust's hands, including hanging portraits of Queen Victoria, Empress Frederick and Prince Eddy, with which he took special care, in his rooms. Cust sometimes wondered what he really thought about his eldest son, whom he obviously remembered with affection. Visiting Trinity College, Cambridge, in 1884, Cust had happened to spend some time with Eddy. They had become quite confidential and started discussing their families; Eddy was devoted to his mother but rather afraid of his father and aware he was not quite up to his expectations.[215] This would have saddened Albert Edward; it was distressingly like his feelings about his own father, which he had tried so hard to avoid with his own sons.

Meanwhile Alexandra went to Cromer to see Victoria on 26 April, returning with her two days later. She attended a meeting of the Imperial Army Nursing Board[216] at Horse Guards on the 30th and the opening the next day of the Royal Academy's exhibition, with the second court on 2 May. Alexandra heard Newman's[217] concert at the Queen's Hall and, with the King, saw *The President* at the Prince of Wales's Theatre; on the 5th it was *Ben Hur* at Drury Lane. When the opera season began, she went nearly every evening; *Faust, Paolo and Francesca, Lohengrin, Romeo and Juliet, Tannhäuser, Rigoletto*, then *Tristan and Isolde* and *Die Meistersinger*, as well as several plays. An exhibition at Alexandra House on the 8th; receiving some Danish nuns on the 12th; and attending Joachim's[218] last concert at St James's Hall on the 15th followed. The King, Queen and Princess went to Windsor on the 17th, where Alexandra entertained guests and played golf. They visited the mausoleum on the 21st, returned on the 22nd, opened the Military Tournament and saw operas and plays. A flower show at the Temple, the HAIA's exhibition at the Albert Hall, the King's birthday parade and an investiture of the Order of the Garter dominated the last week of May.

Alexandra was enchanted with her Indian dresses, which were being made up and were "a glorious success". She telegraphed to Lady Curzon; "All dresses do beautifully, gold one will be perfect when arranged, thousand thanks for all trouble."[219] Coronation preparations continued and Alexandra, with Lord Esher and Charlotte, privately toured Westminster Abbey on 5 June. No public were about, but the workmen were very interested to see the Queen. Word soon spread and, as they left, Westminster School boys, clergy and servants cheered her for about five minutes. "Such a row. The Queen was <u>delighted</u>. In that respect she is unlike the King, who dislikes a 'reception.'"[220] Peace had been declared[221] and a thanksgiving service was held at St Paul's Cathedral on the 8th. The couple saw an Austrian decorative and fine arts exhibition at Prince's Skating Club on the 9th and Alexandra visited Benjamin Constant's exhibition. They watched the Ranelagh team beat an American team at polo, and on the 12th had a coronation rehearsal in Westminster Abbey. Despite feeling unwell, the King held receptions and another court and visited Aldershot, where, on the 15th, he was taken ill; on the 16th the Queen reviewed 31,000 troops in his stead and presented colours to the Highland Light Infantry. They drove in a brougham to Windsor for Ascot Week but he was not well enough to accompany her in state on the 17th and the 19th, although they drove together on the 18th as he felt slightly better. A ball planned for the 20th was cancelled, but the King received several people and went for drives. Back in London on the 23rd, he received some of the coronation guests who had been arriving. He had borne the journey from Windsor fairly well but was on the verge of collapse and, despite his determination to go ahead with the coronation on the 26th, was forced to accept defeat. By 24 June an operation was unavoidable.

It took place on an operating table in the King's dressing room; Queen Alexandra watched as Dr Frederic Hewitt[222] administered the anaesthetic. The King reacted normally but his changed colour and expression upset her. Sir Francis Laking tried to reassure her and she was persuaded to leave. Nurse Haines,[223] one of the two nurses in attendance, saw her in tears outside the temporary operating theatre, while Sir Frederick Treves performed the operation for perityphlitis.[224] Afterwards, when the King was wheeled back on the table to his bedroom and lifted onto the bed, she came in.[225] He was breathing shallowly through his nose and, to Alexandra's alarm, was still deeply asleep. Dr Hewitt explained that he needed to breathe through his mouth to get more air and that applying a little iced water would probably help. It did; the King immediately woke up, heard all was satisfactorily over "& expressed himself as very pleased."[226] George came in and later the King felt well enough to read and smoke a cigar.[227] The operation had been successful, the wound healed well, he made good progress and was pronounced out of danger on 28 June.

Other matters temporarily assumed less importance but the banquet, in preparation for the 26th, presented a considerable problem. The coronation was only postponed and a banquet would be required later, so the kitchen staff made plans. Some food could be kept in ice-boxes but jellies were difficult to store, so the clerk of the kitchens suggested melting them down and keeping them in bottles until required, when they could be re-melted and returned to jelly moulds. A total of 250 magnum champagne bottles, full of claret and liqueur jelly, were ranged along the wall in a corner of the kitchen. The caviar could be kept on ice and the 2,500 quail preserved, but there was a huge amount of perishable food: cooked chicken, partridge, sturgeon and cutlets, not to mention all the fruit and cream desserts. The staff could use some but the rest would go to charity.[228] The food was put in hampers and, without explaining why it was available, the Sisters of the Poor were asked to distribute it to poor families round Whitechapel and the East End.[229]

Some coronation events were postponed; others, such as inspections of colonial and Indian troops, were carried out by the Prince of Wales, attended by the Queen and Royal Family. Alexandra had blossomed as Queen and was fulfilling engagements and receiving guests, including, on 7 July, the Rani of Partabgarh, (who had had to break caste rules in order to be present and was understandably reluctant to go home without seeing her) and an Australian trooper, Williams, from Thorneycroft's Horse, who had lost his leg in the war. She also attended the Great Ormond Street fête for the children's hospital; on the 5th Victoria and the Charleses visited some of the coronation dinners for poor people. Victoria told Lord Rosebery; "We have indeed been through a dreadful time of anxiety – Ascot too was awful. I knew only too well how ill He[230] was then & yet one had to go about grinning as if nothing was the matter ... You have no idea how wonderful He has been all the time during his fearful sufferings."[231] Foreign guests were going home. Lord Kitchener arrived from South Africa on the 12th to a public welcome; the King received him later. Now for convalescence: on the 15th the royal couple, Victoria and the Charleses, on *Victoria and Albert*, anchored at Cowes, and spent the next three weeks visiting Osborne and gently cruising in the Solent and along the coast to Brighton and Bournemouth. King Edward was on a special diet of chicken mousse and lightly boiled fish, while the others were offered the usual twelve-course meals every day. Alexandra insisted on having vases of roses on the royal table.[232]

During the cruise, she told Lady Curzon about the Indian dresses; "I have had the white & gold embroidered net made up over a cloth of gold which makes a brilliant effect, & the velvet mantle & train have been embroidered in gold to match in England, of English material. I am so proud of wearing an Indian dress for that great occasion & hope you will make this known in India. The mauve is also perfect & I wore it at one of the Courts – the black & silver I have not yet worn but I like it ... How I should love to come this winter for the great Durbar at Delhi! which I am sure will surpass anything in beauty & splendour there ever was seen." She hoped Lady Curzon would help unite the Indian Nursing Service with "my new scheme of Army Nurses which I have so much at heart – it will not

<u>interfere</u> in any way with their present system."[233] The King told George that a warrant, under which he would enter into possession of Marlborough House, had been prepared, and reminded him of their understanding that he would, after his father's death, "give it over to dear Mama as you would naturally occupy Buckingham Palace."[234]

Normally they would now have gone to Goodwood; Alexandra therefore wrote to wish Lady Algernon Gordon-Lennox [235] a pleasant week. Lord Algernon had had a similar operation to the King's and, remembering this, she reported that the King "thank God now is getting on so wonderfully well & the rest & total quiet here on board is doing him all the good in the world, & I trust to God he will be strong enough to stand all the fatigues of the Coronation on the 9th of August."[236] On the 26th the King held his first council since his illness and on 2 August an investiture of KCBs on board the yacht. He thanked George for his devotion and help; "I shall always be most grateful to you for having done so much for me during that time in London, as so much of it was irksome & tiring." He had started walking again and, when his tailor measured him, found he was much smaller round the waist and back;[237] he was daily recovering, with a simple regime and bed at 10.30pm. They had seen Empress Eugénie and a Japanese admiral "& Mama has since gone to Netley, a surprise visit!"[238] Nurse Haines had a long talk to her about Netley Hospital on the 5th; Alexandra had been horrified at how dirty it was.[239] Lord Esher often sat beside her at meals and managed to make her hear. He enjoyed her "ragging moods", feeling that "Her cleverness has always been underrated, partly because of her deafness. In point of fact she says more original things and has more unexpected ideas than any of the family." He watched her charm the Bishop of Winchester[240] into smoking a cigarette with her but later she took him to Queen Victoria's room at Osborne and they conducted a little service by the deathbed. "It is this mixture of ragging and real feeling which is so attractive about the Queen."[241]

On the 6th they returned to London; coronation guests arrived; Alexandra chaired a meeting of the SSFA at Queen's Hall on the 8th, while the King held an investiture in the Throne Room. On 9 August they left the palace at 11.00, for Westminster Abbey. The coronation service had been shortened for the King's comfort but still it lasted 2½ hours. It was a dark day for August and when, at the actual crowning, the electric light was suddenly turned on, the effect was somewhat startling.[242] Later, at the banquet, the quail had come out of storage, the jellies had been re-set and all the other dishes had been prepared afresh, but for a smaller number of guests. There were sugar table decorations: ribbons, flowers, a large plaque with the royal crest on it, and a small sugar crown for each guest.[243] The King held a Privy Council and an investiture on the 11th and, at Devonshire House, Alexandra gave medals to the staff of the Yeomanry Hospital in South Africa. The King inspected and gave coronation medals to the Indian and colonial contingents in Buckingham Palace gardens on the 12th and the 13th. The next day he and Alexandra returned to Cowes, and he held an investiture on board the yacht on the 15th. On the 16th there was a great naval review at Spithead and later, illuminations. On the 17th he received Generals Botha, De la Rey and de Wet,[244] with Lord Roberts and Lord Kitchener, then, with Alexandra, watched the fleet disperse at the Nab. The Shah of Persia[245] had arrived, and on the 20th lunched with them on the yacht at Portsmouth. Alexandra took his photograph.

After the couple had visited St Cecilia's convent and Osborne, a longer cruise began; *Victoria and Albert* left on the 21st for Weymouth, Milford Haven and Pembroke, where they saw the castle on the 23rd, paid calls and the next day anchored at Ramsey. Alexandra later told George; "Our visit to the Isle of Man was most interesting & we drove right across & round the Island – began at Ramsey & ended at Douglas which was <u>crammed</u>, a sea side place like Margate. We paid a visit to the Bishop,[246] lunched [at] an old ruin, Castle Peel, & met Hall Caine,[247] a curious looking man, the same as his books. All our party is getting on well together."[248] The island was hilly, with pretty scenery; after returning to Ramsey by the electric tramway, they left on the 26th and approached Arran slowly, so that *Crescent*, as part of the escort, could fire a shell at Ailsa Craig. "There were thousands of birds, but they did not seem to mind the missile, as many remained sitting with the greatest equanimity."[249] Before leaving Arran, the King managed to shoot a stag weighing over 24 stone.

As Charlotte Knollys told Lady Curzon on the 31st, the Queen kept expressing gratitude for the trouble she had taken, "& only regrets you could not have seen the Coronation dress made up; it really was quite lovely & so superior to <u>any</u> other embroidery of either France or England." The King had got through the coronation ceremony without undue fatigue and was now looking "better & stronger than he has done for many a year."[250] The yacht steamed to Colonsay, Ballachulish, Fort William (with a splendid view of Ben Nevis) and Mull, where they saw Sydney Holland. Next came Skye, Stornaway, Thurso and Dunrobin Bay, where they landed, for tea at the castle and a motor drive with the Duchess of Sutherland for Alexandra. The next day they watched a swimming competition and the Queen also visited a convalescent home and called on the former agent, Mr Wright.[251] She wished George had been on the cruise; chances of meeting were now fewer and it was sad "for a Mother who is as much attached to her beloved Children as I am" to be parted from them so often.[252] Leaving on 8 September, they landed at Invergordon, went by special train to Ballater, and drove to Balmoral, where the Wales family greeted them. Alexandra had given "a lovely Coronation Prayer book" to Nurse Haines, who asked Victoria if her mother could kindly write in it. Victoria was upset and edgy and did not want to go on the coming visit to Denmark. Alexandra sent for Nurse Haines later "& was awfully nice, gave me two photos etc & said I was to take the <u>greatest</u> care of the King <u>while</u> she was away. None of them want to go to Denmark but the King seems to think they ought to." Later, after picnics, tea parties, the Braemar Gathering and a cinematograph show, he saw them off[253] for a month.

Alexandra was, as always, glad to be back in her old home but revealed her confused emotions to George. Although unable to write sooner, because of the surrounding distractions, her thoughts were always with them "& I do long to be near all my dear children & husband many a time, but of course I am happy to be with beloved Apapa & Aunt Minny Minny too. One's life is made up by feeling torn in two, & I feel it a <u>duty</u> too to be with my dear beloved Father as often as I can!!!"[254] She had taken *Victoria and Albert* to her heart; it was supposed to go home now but she kept it until 4 October; "Mama at last allowed the Yacht to leave Copenhagen on Sat: (wh she used as a floating Hotel – or rather Palace!)", the King told George.[255] Alexandra went for walks, visited the theatre and saw an Oriental exhibition near the Tivoli Gardens, as well as attending a review held by her father. Herr Hegner[256] played the cello and Mr and Miss Bramsen[257] played the cello and viola on the 14th. She heard that Maud, who had had a "rest cure" in London, was really much better and impatient to see her husband again. Laking had allowed him to go back to her. The nature of the cure was "a profound secret"[258] but the problem had been treated successfully.

Alexandra was looking forward to returning to Sandringham, delighted that the new gardener there "at least tries to please me too & takes notice of my wishes, which <u>Mackellar</u>[259] always <u>ignored</u> in toto. I am so glad we got this nice new man, Cook,[260] at S & that the other went to Windsor, where he may do what he likes as far as I am concerned."[261] On 20 October she and Victoria went home and Maud arrived at Buckingham Palace on the 22nd. There were theatres, gallery visits and the postponed "coronation luncheon" at the Guildhall on the 25th; the couple drove there in state and returned via London Bridge and Westminster Bridge. A service of thanksgiving for the King's recovery was held at St Paul's Cathedral on the 26th, a dark and miserable foggy day. The red carpet which should have been laid outside had been forgotten; a young man dashed out with a small rug for Queen Alexandra to step on.[262] There was a large royal dinner at the palace later. The King inspected a Guards' parade at Horse Guards on the 27th, having refused to let Alexandra drive with him. She agreed to watch from a window, with Uncle George, but instead drove out of the palace, followed in her carriage "and went all round in the procession!"[263] On the 29th she received Colonel Gildea;[264] later she saw Hall Caine's *The Eternal City*. She and Victoria went to Sandringham on the 31st. The King joined them on 6 November and William II arrived on the 8th, staying till the 15th. The usual shooting followed, and on the 10th tree-planting formed a "Coronation Avenue" to Anmer. In the evenings, the comic singer, Albert Chevalier[265] and the illusionist, Horace Goldin[266] performed; on the 14th Henry Irving acted in *Waterloo* and the Bourchiers[267] in *Dr. Johnson*.

Probyn had told Lady Curzon of the Queen's gratitude to her, "and <u>laughing</u>, but I am sure Her Majesty meant in earnest, said, 'Be sure and tell Lady Curzon to see that the Natives to whom I am going to give my Warrants, do not let the Duchess of Connaught, or any of the ladies now going out to India, copy my Dresses'!! How this is to be managed quietly I cannot think!"[268] Meanwhile, a Miss Bourne visited the technical school and bought four white tea cloths, embroidered with the Queen's monogram, for 12/6 each. Had she wished, she could also have purchased a clock for a guinea, a length of homespun cloth at £3 a yard, a hand-made nightgown, from her own material and pattern, if desired, for 3/- and many other goods as well. The school was thriving; the Royal Family had, apparently for the first time, gone into business. Queen Alexandra had anticipated, albeit in embryo, Duchy Organics and Royal Collection Enterprises, both of which appeared later in the century.[269]

The new reign introduced the holding of November state visits at Windsor. In 1902, the King of Portugal was invited. King Edward went to Windsor on the 17th, followed two days later by Alexandra, who had had a chill. After a theatrical performance in the Waterloo Gallery, a musical ride by the Life Guards in the riding school and other events, King Carlos left on the 24th, when Alexandra returned to Sandringham and later joined them there for a brief visit. The Queen invited 470 schoolchildren to her birthday tea in the ballroom. Back in London on the 8th, the couple attended theatres and stayed briefly at Gopsall;[270] Alexandra also heard Fritz Kreisler[271] play the violin. Back at Sandringham on the 20th, she told George; "How much my thoughts are with you & yr dear May at this moment you will know. I only wish I cld be with you & share all yr trouble & anxiety, but I quite understand dear May does not want me, altho' she need not mind old me, particularly as I was with her the first time. I do hope all will soon be well over now & that she is now under chloroform. It is always worse for those who look on – God bless you both."[272] A little boy[273] was born later; in fact, as the King wrote, "Mama arrived just in time & it looks almost as if May waited for her arrival."[274] With even more to celebrate Christmas went ahead, meat for poor families on the 25th and on the 27th, with music playing, the Queen's Christmas dinner, a traditional meal ending with fruit, crackers, toys and chocolates, at City Road in London, through the Alexandra Trust, headed by Colonel James Gildea, for 1,500 South African War widows and orphans. Estate workers at Sandringham received the King's gifts of beef and there was a Christmas tree for the staff, holding cutlery, so that, eventually, they could collect a whole canteen. Alexandra had also decided they should have a fancy-dress ball on New Year's Eve, which she would attend.[275]

1901 had been overshadowed by mourning, 1902 by the end of the war and the King's illness. 1903 began the Edwardian age in earnest, with a large shooting party and plans for the installation, in St George's Chapel, of the Queen's Garter

HER MAJESTY QUEEN ALEXANDRA'S
TECHNICAL SCHOOL,
SANDRINGHAM, NORFOLK.

❖ BRASS & COPPER WORK. ❖

ASH TRAYS	–	–	–	–	–	from 1 –
TEA TRAYS	–	–	–	–	–	„ 5/-
STRING BOX	–	–	–	–	–	„ 15 –
CIGARETTE BOX	–	–	–	–	–	„ 15 –
„ CUP	–	–	–	–	–	„ 4 –
FLOWER CUPS	–	–	–	–	–	„ 6 –
CLOCKS	–	–	–	–	–	£1 1 0
STRIKING CLOCKS	–	–	–	–		£1 15 0
PHOTO. FRAMES	–	–	–	–		7/6

etc., etc.

Tapestry, Rugs, Curtains, etc.   Embroidered Tea Cloths.   All Executed to Order.

❖ WEAVING, SPINNING. ❖

Homespuns Spun and Woven in the School from the Wool of His Majesty the King's
South Down Sheep.

Per Yard — — 5 – Machine-made — Per Yard

BLANKETS, RUGS, GOLF CAPES, ETC.,
Made to Order from the same Wool.

ORDERS RECEIVED FOR UNDER-LINEN.

Materials Supplied or Ladies' Own Materials Made up and Patterns Copied.

HAND-MADE.						MACHINE-MADE.
From 1/6	–	–	CHEMISES	–	–	from 1 –
„ 1/6	–	–	DRAWERS	–	–	„ 1/-
„ 3/-	–	–	NIGHTGOWNS	–	–	„ 2/-
„ 3/6	–	–	COMBINATIONS	–	–	„ 3/-
„ 3/-	–	–	GENTS' NIGHT SHIRTS	–	–	„ 2/-

Guild work at moderate prices.

Lady Superintendent. EDITH L. WOLFE.

11 List of wares on sale at Queen Alexandra's Technical School, Sandringham; *private collection* banner,[276] embroidered with her arms by the Royal School of Art Needlework[277] and later hung over her quire stall.

On 15 January, Punchy, felled by Uncle Willy's beastly bicycle in 1898, died. The January court was held at Windsor and the mausoleum service took place on the 22nd; the next day Lady Hallé played and St George's Chapel choir boys sang after dinner. On the 26th the Waleses' fourth son was christened George Edward Alexander Edmund in the private chapel; later, a dinner was held in the Waterloo Gallery and the state apartments were used for the first time since Catherine of Braganza.[278] Sousa's Band played in the Waterloo Gallery on the 31st. But by 4 February the King had influenza and felt "low & depressed, & fit for nothing."[279] The Chatsworth visit was put off but Alexandra went driving with him on the 6th. Baba Knollys celebrated her 15th birthday; "Miss Baba Knollys writes to say she will be most happy to see all those who are named in Miss Charlotte Knollys's letter who are fishing for invitations and anyone else who likes to come. Tea at 5 o'clock." Of course they went.[280]

This year Alexandra would again have to endure Mrs Keppel's presence in her home on four occasions: at the Sandringham January house party; dinner at Buckingham Palace on 15 March; dinner on the royal yacht on 7 August and for the King's birthday house party at Sandringham. George Keppel also attended three of these. The King had always been easily influenced by people he liked and, whatever kind of friendship he had with Mrs Keppel, seems to have discounted its effect on his wife, feeling, as he did, that his relationship with her was unassailable. He may genuinely have hoped the two women could become friends, as he had with Lady Warwick – and that bringing Mrs Keppel into Alexandra's circle would facilitate this. Alexandra saw it rather differently. Meanwhile Lord Esher sat next to her at dinner on the 9th; "she talked all dinner time and was in great spirits." He was intrigued by her determination to have her own way; "As Princess of Wales she was never, so she says, allowed to do as she chose. 'Now I do as I like' is the sort of attitude. And among her likes is a fixed resolve to go to India and 'see the natives'. I wonder if she will ever succeed."[281] At the Opening of Parliament on the 17th, Lionel Cust was struck by the beauty of Alexandra's slender figure in a black dress, the blue Garter ribbon making a vivid patch of colour, while her pearls and diamonds sparkled and glistened in the light which fell on her from above.[282] Her pearls could also cause problems. The King was meticulous about punctuality and while she was less so, she had never been known to fail him for an important event. However, a procession from Buckingham Palace was once delayed for about 15 minutes because, as Alexandra was getting into the state coach, one of her strings of pearls caught on something and broke. They scattered everywhere, among carriage wheels and horses' hooves and, as they were so valuable, every single one had to be found.[283]

On 18 February the royal couple visited LCC[284] dwellings on the Millbank

Estate. Returning to Sandringham, Alexandra called on the 21st at York Cottage; her grandchildren were all well and happy except the baby, who "has a very bad arm, & looks pale & fretful after that tiresome vaccination." The spring weather had vanished and "since yesterday it is blowing a gale with alternate showers of sleet & hail. Several poor trees have been uprooted too, which is sad." She had had "so much to do trying to make my rooms straight & less crowded, but don't know where on earth to put the things."[285] She and Victoria returned to London and on 10 March the 40th wedding anniversary was celebrated with a dance for about 400 in the Bow Room. Lord Esher sent the Queen some of "those new daffodils" in congratulation.[286] About 1,000 people attended the second court, on the 20th, and there were theatres and grand dinners almost every evening; the couple had always been generous hosts and wanted their meals to be the best in the world. The King liked classic cuisine and fancy French dishes for state banquets but personally also relished good English cooking; roast beef and Yorkshire pudding, or salt beef with dumplings, carrots, roast potatoes and horseradish sauce.[287] Alexandra reputedly enjoyed Yorkshire pudding too,[288] but also liked prawns, and fresh-water crayfish cooked in Chablis. She preferred a simple chicken casserole, *Poulet Danoise*, to game or venison. She loved *Rødgrød*, a Danish pudding made with raspberries, currants (red, white or black), sago and potato flour, sugar and claret, served with cream and tiny sweet biscuits.[289] She also enjoyed other fruit and was partial to rich fruit cake, not to mention chocolate.

Between 17 and 28 March the Queen visited Alma Tadema's and Prinsep's studios and received three pianists: Miss Grace Smith, Mademoiselle Endom and Miss Jerningham. She also sat nine times to Gilbert for a bust and once to Hughes for a portrait. She left on the 30th for Denmark, the King for Portugal on the 31st and Victoria for a cruise. The Danish visit, as usual, included her father's birthday, Easter, walks, visits, family and friends. One difference was the four-day presence of the German emperor; another was the weather. "After delightful spring weather with nearly everything out, we have been plunged into the very <u>depths</u> of winter; it snowed hard for two days & nights, a regular <u>Blizzard</u>; the snow lying <u>feet</u> deep everywhere!; railways blocked, no traffic whatever, all telegraph wires broken, no ships could go, it was blowing a hurricane; poor Fehr,[290] who was on his way to Naples to join Papa was snowed up somewhere here. Even the ships in the harbour dragged their anchors & there were many casualties; sledges were used everywhere in the country. I even saw some here in town. I have never seen anything like it. All the poor flowers & green trees & bushes disappeared, but now they have come out again apparently not much the worse for it."[291] On the 15th she heard Madame Giers recite, gave K Herr Mehldal the medal for Arts on the 21st, was photographed by Mary Steen[292] and received the architect Glaesel.[293] On the 24th she arrived in London but went to Sandringham the next day for a rest before the season began.

She returned on 4 May and the King, who had been to Portugal, Gibraltar, Malta, Naples, Rome and Paris, the next day. Immediately, Wagner's *Ring Cycle* opened at the opera and they attended on four evenings. On the 10th they dined at the Waleses' house-warming party at Marlborough House. From 11–15 May the King and Queen were at Dalkeith House, holding a court at Holyroodhouse on the 12th, presenting medals, inspecting the Company of Archers, visiting Edinburgh Castle and St Giles's Cathedral and later opening a hospital at Colinton. At Glasgow they laid the first stone of the technical school, lunched at the Guildhall and visited art galleries before going back to London. Victoria returned on the 16th, there were more operas and on the 20th the couple opened the new Kew Bridge. The next day Alexandra spent an hour at the HAIA's exhibition at the Albert Hall and made purchases. Her granddaughter Mary (six) was the youngest exhibitor this year; she had knitted a pair of grey mittens, while May had worked a screen with a floral design in cross-stitch.[294] Alexandra also accepted a cheque for the Jubilee Nurses Fund on the 21st and gave badges to 25 naval nurses on the 29th; later, her cousin, Landgrave Aleck, came to tea. On the 30th the court moved to Windsor; the next day there was sad news of Alexandra's Uncle Julius of Glücksburg's[295] death, but also shocking local news: two Eton boys, Horne and Lawson, had died in a fire at Mr Kindersley's House. For the rest of the week Alexandra drove, rode her horse, Robin, paid calls and played golf. The couple returned to London on 6 June and drove in procession the next day to St Paul's for "Hospital Sunday". Lady de Grey's daughter Juliet was engaged and Alexandra went to see her presents on the 8th, the day before her wedding[296] at St Peter's, Eaton Square. On the 11th the royal couple opened the new outpatients' department at London Hospital and the Queen opened the new lupus light rooms for Finsen's light treatment.

The court spent Ascot week at Windsor; Alexandra played more golf before returning to London on the 22nd for theatres and David's birthday garden party. The Agricultural Show was on the 24th and Trooping the Colour celebrated the King's official birthday at Horse Guards. Miss Marie Hall[297] played the violin to the Queen on the 25th. Earlier in June, Miss Acland had sent her father's memoir and on the 26th Charlotte Knollys told her the Queen "has already begun to read it & finds it contains matter of the greatest interest & reminds her of many interesting people & events connected with her past life."[298] A happy event was expected at Appleton and Alexandra, Victoria and Charlotte went to Sandringham on the 29th, staying in the agent Frank Beck's house because the big house was undergoing works. On 2 July Maud gave birth to a son.[299] The King and the Waleses lunched at Sandringham on the 5th, before returning to London, followed the next day by Alexandra and Victoria, for the French president Loubet's state visit,[300] celebrated with a large dinner and concert, a Gala performance at Covent Garden, a review of 15,000 at Aldershot and a state ball. Alexandra also attended a children's fête at the botanical gardens and on the

9th, a large dinner for the officers of the American Squadron. The next day the couple inspected the City of London Artillery at Horse Guards and attended a ball at Marlborough House on the 13th. Alexandra sat three more times to Gilbert, but on 15/16 July briefly visited Sandringham, where Maud and the baby were both flourishing.

On 21 July the King, Queen and Princess Victoria arrived in Ireland for an official twelve-day visit, spending four days at Viceregal Lodge in Dublin and visiting the Connaughts at the Royal Hospital. Alexandra, who presented badges to Jubilee Nurses at Dublin Castle on the 22nd, later attended the King's levee at Alexandra College, followed by tea at Trinity College. The next day, colours were presented to the Hibernian Military School; there was a review, then races, at Phoenix Park, and a court was held at the castle. On the 24th Alexandra visited the Home for the Dying at Harold's Cross and the Royal Hospital for Incurables. They inspected the Royal Irish Constabulary and visited St Patrick's College at Maynooth. The King had brought his beloved Irish terrier, Jack, but the dog unexpectedly died on the 21st and was buried in the grounds of Viceregal Lodge. Lord Dudley[301] later gave the King a seven-month-old Irish terrier puppy, "& I hope he will grow up a nice dog. I call him 'Pat'!"[302] After a large dinner and evening party on the 24th, the King and Queen spent two days at Mount Stewart[303] and at Belfast on the 27th unveiled Queen Victoria's statue and visited the Hospital, Agricultural Show and a function at the Town Hall. At Buncrana on the 28th they travelled to Londonderry for a procession, addresses and lunch at the Guildhall. They visited the infirmary, laid a foundation stone, planted trees in Brooke Park and presented medals to 300 soldiers. At Killary the next day, they met Lady Dudley, visited three cottages and had tea at the hotel before returning to the yacht. On the 30th they landed and drove 30 miles in motor cars to Recess, for lunch and the Connemara Marble Quarries. They drove in procession through Galway, and the next day went by train to Kenmare, motored to Doreen, Lord Lansdowne's place, and back from there to the yacht at Berehaven. Leaving next morning for Kingstown, they embarked on *Vivid* for Cork, with a military review and presentation of colours, a procession through the streets, lunch with the Lord Mayor, and the Cork Exhibition. They left on 1 August.

After such an exhausting time it was a relief to relax at Cowes, sailing in *Britannia* and going for trips and visits. King Edward had, regretfully, decided he could no longer maintain Osborne as well as Buckingham Palace, Windsor, Balmoral and Sandringham, but hoped his son would take it on.[304] George did not feel able to do this, so it was given to the nation, provided Queen Victoria's rooms were closed to the public. Part of the house would be a convalescent home and there would be a naval college nearby for cadets. The couple left for London on the 10th and for Sandringham the next day, for Prince Alexander Edward Christian Frederick of Denmark's christening. "I give you no account of the

Xtning at Sandringham as no doubt Toria or Maud will have done so, but nothing could have gone off better. The latter is looking very pretty & well & it is a nice, healthy little baby", the King told George. He left for his cure at Marienbad, and Alexandra for Balmoral.

Although missing George, Alexandra was delighted his three younger children were at the castle with her; "I cannot tell you <u>how</u> I love & enjoy having them, they cheer me up & are so bright & delightful. <u>Bobsy</u> is still my heart's delight, but the baby is <u>too</u> sweet for words & a <u>beauty</u> – little Mary also so dear & cheery. The two beloved boys come every afternoon & are looking so well & jolly, only the last few days poor little Bertie had rather an indigestion so had to stay quietly at home."[305] Some cheerful people were with her; Soveral, the Derek Keppels and others and there were drives, tea outdoors and visits to Mar Lodge and other places nearby. The Waleses were away; he at Bolton Abbey and she in Switzerland. Writing to May, George made excuses for not having asked her first before letting the children go to Balmoral with their grandmother. He thought she would not have been so selfish as to refuse, as she was away and they would be well looked after. "Mama as I have always said, is one of the most selfish people I know."[306] Queen Victoria had once said something similar, but was it justified? Alexandra certainly liked her own way and could be headstrong but was also prepared to take a lot of trouble with other people, looking after them or visiting them when they were sick, recently bereaved, or simply alone. Was it her treatment of Victoria, whom she liked to have with her, especially when the King was away? Possibly, but in Alexandra's own experience, adult children stayed with their parents when required; for example, she had nursed her mother in her final illness and she and her sisters had arranged to stay regularly with their lonely widowed father. It was a family duty and of course she hoped her own children would do the same, unless there was a very good reason why not. After all, she respected Victoria's wish to stay with friends sometimes or take holidays without her.

Alexandra went back to London on 3 September and her husband returned the next day. On the 6th she gave a small dinner party then, with Victoria, left on the 7th in *Victoria and Albert* for Denmark. On the 8th a storm began, delaying their arrival at Fredensborg until the 13th. Happily her father was as well and active as ever and Alexandra walked and drove with her sister and other relatives. *Victoria and Albert's* band played on several occasions; Alexandra went to the theatre on the 30th, shopped and paid calls; by 2 October she had a bad cold and stayed in bed but was "better & up"[307] the next day. On the 4th she and Victoria left for Darmstadt, as Alice of Battenberg was to marry Andrew of Greece. The civil marriage was on the 6th, and the religious ceremonies the next day in the Russian and German churches, with dinners and receptions at the Residenz Schloss and the Alte Schloss. On the 8th Alexandra went shopping and took a long country drive, seeing *Aida* later. The next day, after visiting the cavalry barracks, she returned to Denmark with the Greek sovereigns and their son, George, while Victoria left for London at midnight. The family reassembled at Fredensborg for another two weeks, walking, driving, having large dinners, being photographed on the 16th and watching a cinematograph on the 20th. Alexandra took several walks with her father before going home on the 23rd. In London there were theatres and visitors but she left for Sandringham on the 28th and lunched nearly every day with Maud at Appleton. Shooting parties began, the first on the King's birthday, but on 16 November the couple returned to Windsor for the Italian state visit; a banquet in St George's Hall and Sir Charles Wyndham's performance of *David Garrick*. On the 20th another banquet was followed by a concert by Ben Davies,[308] Muriel Foster[309] and Mr Borwick.[310] The Italian sovereigns[311] left on the 21st; later, Grand Duke Vladimir and his wife arrived for a short visit.

Alfred Nutt,[312] Clerk of the Works at Windsor and a talented artist, was helping the King and Queen with memorials to Queen Victoria, one being a statue. Alexandra had thanked him "for all the trouble you have taken about my beautiful Thorwaldsen statue of Christ,[313] and for having it placed exactly on the spot I chose, which the King and I both think does admirably as it harmonizes so well with its background. The Statue itself wld have been far too large on the steps and entirely overpowered the Angels, and if it had been further off on the green it wld not have looked as having any connection with the Mausoleum. Thank you also for letting me see the print of the Memorial over the Queen's bed at Osborne, which is going to be published for Xmas. I think it has come out beautifully [and] your work is seen to advantage."[314] This bronze plaque had been her idea and original design. Alfred Nutt and Ion Pace[315] had helped her realise it; she supervised the work throughout and it was cast at the Gunthorp Foundry. It showed two angels carrying a crown, with "the sacred monogram with rays and winged seraphs amid conventional clouds" above; below were views of Westminster Abbey and Frogmore Mausoleum. Alexandra had suggested the inscription.[316] She admired bronze work and enjoyed designing; the plaque had something in common with the personal bookplate she also designed. This, executed by a Mr Scott, included the opening bars of Gounod's *Romeo and Juliet*; Windsor and Kronborg Castles; three dogs; music scores by Schumann,[317] Rubinstein,[318] Wagner, Brahms[319] and Niels Gade;[320] books by Byron,[321] Shakespeare,[322] Shelley,[323] MacCarthy[324] and Joseph Henry Shorthouse's[325] *John Inglesant*. A dove, a Danish flag, the Prince of Wales's feathers, oak leaves, acorns and roses, a wooden cross and the motto "Faithful unto Death" completed it.[326]

Works had been carried out at Sandringham under the auspices of Paris Singer, including installing new electric lighting and decorating Charlotte Knollys's rooms.[327] Alexandra and Victoria returned there on 23 November but the Queen had to stay in bed with a chill. By the time the King returned on the

28th she was feeling slightly better. A large shooting party arrived; she celebrated her birthday on 1 December and there was a variety entertainment from the Empire Theatre on the 4th. The King and guests left on the 7th and Alexandra subsided back into bed, falling asleep on the 9th with, as usual, her dogs lying nearby. She was awoken in the middle of the night by "a horrible smoke which hurt my eyes & throat, but as my room is always dark I cld not see the intensity of it, & as it made me feel very drowsy too, I merely thought the chimney smoked & put my head under the bed cover & went on sleeping till in a dream I thought I felt the dogs moving about on my feet, when suddenly I was awoke by hearing Charlotte's voice shouting at me & nearly pulling me out of bed – 'get up at once, yr room is on fire!' – so I woke with a start, but could hardly see across the room, where Harriet had also rushed in with my clothes – by this time we nearly suffocated & I had hardly time to save my dogs ... & off we bundled into my dressing room, when with a crash, down came half my <u>ceiling</u> with Charlotte's <u>floor</u>, which at once began to burn my poor things in the middle of the room – table & sopha ... Poor Charlotte was the first to wake by that awful suffocating smoke. She flew out of her room, yelled for her maid, called the policeman outside, who in a few moments had got the whole staff together & both inside & outside the house they worked like slaves & directed the hose so well that really they spoilt very little else but the two rooms & what it contained, & the footmen & housemaids dragged out everything they cld lay hands on. No one lost their head & hardly a word was spoken, while Probyn directed all upstairs in Charlotte's room. It was wonderful <u>what</u> an escape we really had, had we not left the rooms then, we must have been doomed. No one on earth cld have heard us, me certainly not as I sleep quite alone on that floor & no one cld have got into that burning room once the furniture was burning. How wonderfully God saved us, one <u>must never forget</u>! Curiously enough I was not at all frightened but remained quite calm all the time & helped to get all my poor things out; thank God so far the shock has done no harm to poor Charlotte who really was awfully alarmed at first. Many thanks for yr dear letter, I telegraphed at once both to you & Papa. He is coming down here tomorrow for a few hours on his way to London. I wonder what he will say when he sees the awful havoc the fire has made in my dear old bed room; half the ceiling has utterly disappeared & you see right into Charlotte's [room], all the woodwork is coal black. The fire must have been burning for days <u>in her room</u> where it seems a large <u>beam</u> was <u>under</u> her fireplace on my ceiling, it burnt right round her room as far as the bed & that lovely little new room of hers has entirely disappeared. Luckily neither her sitting room nor my dressing room were touched either by fire or water, nor Papa's either & I do hope the smell will have gone by the time he comes back. What a mercy that all the guests were out of the house or I shd have had <u>no</u> room to go to. Now I am in the Bamboo room & my poor things all over the place. Too provoking as you say, just when the house was so clean &

tidy. Luckily it has <u>nothing</u> whatever to do with the Electric light which is <u>perfect.</u> Luckily the dining room has not suffered very much from the water altho' they had to remove the tapestry. We are going to get it all straight for Papa tomorrow tho'. It is very unfortunate for me here just now when I had <u>so</u> much to do for Xmas, & now I have not been able to do a thing in consequence. However we must not complain & only thank God for our really miraculous escape! My poor little house maid had a narrow escape as a bit of ceiling fell on her head & set fire to it, but the men <u>beat</u> it out. I fear a good many of my precious Souvenirs & things, books & photos etc. were both burnt or spoilt by water. The darling Children were most anxious to hear, next morning, whether Granny was burnt, they all came at various times. Poor dear little 'Bobsy' was awfully frightened tho' I think he is a nervous little dear, so he did not come this evening, which was better for him … Thank God dear <u>Toria</u> is all right & her rooms not touched."[328]

Alexandra was fully aware of how serious it had been but had quickly come to a resolution. She had never really been frightened; everyone was safe and had helped; they must not complain and just thank God for saving them. The worst outcome was the King's possible consternation at the damage. In fact Charlotte had saved her life and she herself had shown considerable bravery and presence of mind. Probyn told Singer that "The fire was a very great nuisance" but luckily only affected the Queen's and Miss Knollys' bedrooms. Thanks to Charlotte's swift action, lives had been saved and the staff had extinguished the fire. Despite rumours, the electric lighting had not fused; it had actually been a blessing, as they would otherwise have had to grope their way about in the dark.[329] Augusta was "horrified hearing of dear Alix's danger, too awful to think of! We must give credit to old Charlotte for really saving her life; what Order will the King decorate C with to reward such readiness of thought and action! Though he was in no hurry to hasten to see Alix after her merciful escape", she added, nastily.[330] [331] A conjurer[332] came on the 14th for Bertie's birthday; the next day Alexandra, Victoria, Probyn and Charlotte went to London. Friends called; Alexandra saw *The Cricket on the Hearth* and *The School Girl* at the theatre. Charles arrived from Denmark and Landgrave Aleck came to tea again. Then it was Christmas at Sandringham, with guests and festivities until the end of the year.

On 4 January 1904 the King, Queen and Princess went to Chatsworth, for a Twelfth Cake, amateur dramatics and Carl Herbert's Viennese Band. Mrs Keppel joined the house party for the first time. It was pouring with rain on the 7th but Alexandra visited the Bakewell workhouse and the party motored to Hardwick Hall on the 9th. She and Victoria returned to Sandringham on the 11th; the King brought a shooting party the next day and left with them on the 18th, while Alexandra and her daughters met for tea and lunch. The whole Royal

Family gathered for the mausoleum service at Frogmore on the 22nd. On the 25th the couple visited the Gordon Boys' Home, in aid of which the Bishop of Thetford[333] had preached the regular sermon at Sandringham Church. They opened Parliament on 2 February and later heard Richter's[334] concert at the Queen's Hall. They saw *Humpty Dumpty* the next evening, eating their dinner in the box, and attended a grand Skating Fête at Hengler's Circus, for the Union Jack Club, on the 4th. The next day Alexandra visited Uncle George, who was in failing health.

The War Office had read but not accepted a memorandum, sent by Alexandra, about military nurses, to whom they proposed paying less than civilian nurses. When HO Arnold-Forster[335] became War Minister, Alexandra, determined to strike while the iron was hot, saw him and told Sydney Holland, "he has promised to add to the salary of our 340 Military Nurses, appointed at our first start, so as to be equal to the pay of our civil nurses, as you always said from the very beginning. So now you must be on the look out to see that this Promise is carried out. It is too disappointing to think that we are at a standstill & actually lost 3 Nurses, & only two Military Hospitals are working on our scheme – and Netley above all left in its old disgraceful state. I told Mr Forster to go & see it for himself."[336] On the 6th she received Sir James Gildea and Lady de Grey and saw *The Duke of Killie Krankie* at the theatre. The Sunday service on the 7th was the first in the reign to be held in Buckingham Palace chapel. The court returned to Windsor on the 8th for Alexander of Teck's marriage to Alice of Albany in St George's Chapel on the 10th, followed by a dinner in St George's Hall. Back in London there were more theatres and another concert by Richter. Alexandra sat to Mr Williams[337] for her miniature on the 13th and while the King was in Portsmouth on the 19th, she visited Alexandra House and an exhibition by women artists. On the 23rd she and Victoria went to Sandringham and Mr Staveley, the curate[338] gave a magic lantern show on the 27th. The royal couple visited Cambridge on 1 March, opening the medical and law schools, the botanical laboratory and the geological museum, and unveiling Professor Sidgwick's[339] statue. Alexandra attended a philharmonic concert at the Queen's Hall on the 2nd and the next day visited the Hackney Show at the Agricultural Hall. On the 4th, two pupils from the College of Music sang music composed by Landgrave Aleck. The next day she called again on Uncle George. She and Victoria attended a service at St Paul's for the Bible Society on the 6th and drove together several times. There was a horse show at the Agricultural Hall and theatre visits. On the 11th it was Bach's *St John Passion* at St Anne's, Soho and from 14–16 March an Elgar[340] festival at Covent Garden, with *The Dream of Gerontius* and *Apostles*. Alexandra attended Elgar's vocal and instrumental concert alone; the King told George the music at Covent Garden had been very fine, "& the Orchestra & Chorus quite excellent – but very solemn & I hardly think that you & May would have cared for it."[341] On the 15th Alexandra had also attended a concert in aid of "reclaiming" drunkards, at Stafford House.

On the 17th George, Duke of Cambridge, died, aged 85; a great loss, having been a lifelong presence for Edward and Alexandra. After his funeral in Westminster Abbey on the 22nd, he was buried at Kensal Green. Alexandra wrote in condolence to Augusta. She had seen him a fortnight earlier, in his sitting room, "quite his dear self, in mind, only <u>weak</u> & his sight & hearing had got so bad of late, but he was always so <u>touching</u> & kind to me whenever I came." Augusta, at home, looking after her ailing husband, had now missed her brother's death as well as her mother's and sister's. Her granddaughter Marie, married to Count Jametel, seemed much happier since the birth of their child; Alexandra wondered whether Augusta had seen her since then. As for Uncle George, she "always felt nearer to him than I am sure any of his other relatives here, and he was never failing in his kindness to me. The three poor sons are terribly cut up & I do indeed feel sorry for them, as it must be an irreparable loss to them in <u>every</u> way. I must say they were all very attentive & devoted to him in his last sad illness, & he told me <u>himself</u> how kind & nice they all were to him."[342]

Alexandra sat to Weigall on the 18th and the 19th and received Edward Hughes and his daughter, Alice, now a fashionable photographer; the Queen and princesses had already sat to her. The King and Queen opened the new Law Society's hall in Chancery Lane on the 23rd; the next day, while he was at Knowsley, she attended the People's 4½d Dinner at the Alexandra Trust.[343] On the 25th she received two FitzGeorges.[344] The Charleses and their baby went home; the King and Queen later followed them on *Victoria and Albert,* arriving on the 30th, to celebrate Easter at the Danish church and St Alban's. Alexandra missed her absent sisters but found her father very well; "His dear <u>the 86th</u> birthday went off beautifully ... & we had a lovely bright & mild day for it, <u>crowds</u> of people waiting about the Plads for him as usual & cheering tremendously whenever he showed himself for a second. I had breakfast with him alone at 9.30 & gave him all our presents, he was delighted with the clock you & May sent him & sent you a telegram to thank you." His energy was impressive; "He was a <u>perfect wonder</u> on his birthday; congratulations, receptions, deputations etc etc ... from 9.30 till 1 – then a drive till 4.30, tea at 5 & a huge dinner at 7 at Uncle Freddy's & another tea here at 9.30 till 11. I was half dead but he seemed quite fresh."[345] Papa was well and enjoying himself, spending a lot of time with Uncle Hans, who was in excellent spirits.[346] Irritatingly, the German crown prince had been "sent by his <u>Father</u> – <u>tiresome</u> that every year now he seems to think that either he or his family must come over for [Apapa's birthday];[347] rather a bore, tho' I like this <u>young William</u> <u>very much personally</u>, they are no relation & cost an <u>extra exertion</u> to dear Apapa naturally, as he takes extra pains to do the honours for them & receives them at the Station etc etc & at <u>his age</u> it really is too much."[348]

Alexandra drove with her father, shopped with Maud, saw friends and on the 7th inspected the steamer *Pacific*, about to take a cable out to China. The couple visited Finsen's Institute, the Raadhus, the Northern Museum, the Trifoleram Dairy at Haslev and the Serum Institute; there were also theatres, circus gymnastics, and a ball on the 11th; "Mama danced, but I did not, & contented myself with looking on & playing Bridge. It was frightfully hot", wrote King Edward.[349] On the 12th Alexandra received Mr Bertram, the explorer. The "Entente Cordiale", owing much to the King's affinity with France, had been signed.[350] As he told George, "The Anglo-French agreement is a splendid thing … We have really the best of the bargain & as regards the concessions about Morocco – if we had not made them they would have [taken] them, & our position in Egypt is more assured than ever!" Russia and Japan were at war and "There has been a severe Naval engagement at Port Arthur; a large Russian battleship torpedoed & blown up, & Kiril[351] wounded! but it is not officially confirmed."[352]

At home in London on the 19th there were more theatres and the first court; they saw work by Ella Du Cane and Baragwaneth King[353] at the Graves Gallery, received visitors and paid calls. On the 25th, with Victoria, they left for another hectic Irish visit, going immediately on arrival on the 26th to Punchestown Races, and staying at Viceregal Lodge. On the 28th the King laid the foundation stone of the School of Science; then it was Phoenix Park Races, and a gala performance at Dublin Theatre. The next day they went to Leopardstown Races and left on the 30th for Kilkenny Castle, an Agricultural Show followed by a large party and fireworks. Attending a service at Kilkenny Cathedral on 1 May, they visited an Agricultural Show at Waterford on the 2nd. Relaxing afterwards at Lismore Castle,[354] they walked and drove in five motors to Shambally Castle, about 50 miles away. Returning to London on the 5th, they saw the opera *Romeo and Juliet*, which seems to have been rather a favourite, that evening.

Alexandra attended Joachim's concert at Lord Leighton's house on the 6th, received Count Albert Mensdorff,[355] now the Austrian ambassador, and called on Augusta; the King had earlier told George; "It will be amusing to see her disputing with the FitzGeorges about certain articles of crockery! at the Cottage at Kew!"[356] Seasonal events proceeded until the court moved to Windsor on the 21st. Alexandra visited the HAIA's exhibition on the 12th; while constantly occupied with guests, calls and official engagements, she also heard several musicians. Franz Vecsey (11) played the violin on the 13th and Herold, the Danish tenor, sang the next day. Dr Joachim, Lady Hallé and Mr Borwick played and stayed for tea on the 16th and on the 20th Fröken Stockman played with Alexandra, who also visited the students' art exhibition at Alexandra House. On the terrace at Windsor on the 25th, the couple received 300 delegates from the

Christian Endeavour Convention, and foreign delegates of the Congress of Academics, the Royal Society and the British Academy. Briefly in London on the 26th for the Military Tournament, they returned to Windsor; Augusta came to lunch and the couple motored to Kneller Hall to hear the bands play. There was a levee on the 30th, but on the same day came sad news that the Grand Duke of Mecklenburg-Strelitz (84) had died, as fate would have it, while his wife was in England.

On 3 June Victoria left for Altnaguithasach with the Derek Keppels, until 10 July. In London, the season continued; at Covent Garden, cold suppers would be served for the King, Queen and guests in a private room, between 8.30pm and 9.30pm. About a dozen hampers were prepared at Buckingham Palace and driven to the theatre in the old horse brake. Sometimes there were up to twelve courses, for up to 30, with enough food for the staff too. It would begin with cold consommé, then lobster mayonnaise, cold trout, duck, lamb cutlets, plovers' eggs, chicken, tongue and ham jelly and mixed sandwiches, followed by patisserie and dishes made with strawberries or other fresh fruit.[357] On 4 June Alexandra sat to Mr Abbey,[358] for his coronation picture. Uncle Hans arrived on the 6th for three weeks and on the 9th there was a concert in the Bow Room, at which Melba,[359] Caruso[360] and Gilibert[361] sang and Franz Vecsey played the violin. The court moved to Windsor for Ascot week on the 13th; Alexandra drove with her uncle and showed him St George's and the Albert Memorial Chapel, and, later, in London, Dorchester House. There were more operas, another court, and a charity bazaar on the 21st for the Victoria Hospital for Children. David's tenth birthday party was at Marlborough House on the 23rd and his father held Trooping the Colour the next day.[362] Franz Vecsey[363] and Florizel von Reuter[364] both played the violin at Buckingham Palace; each later had his own London concert, which the Queen attended on 29 June and 2 July. Franz Vecsey played again and the de Reszke brothers sang during Alexandra's visit to Coombe on 3 July. She sat to Tuxen on the 5th and later attended an entertainment at His Majesty's, in aid of the British Ophthalmic Hospital at Jerusalem. On the 6th the King and Queen laid the foundation stone of the new wing of St Bartholomew's Hospital; Alexandra drove with her Fife grand-daughters, unusually but enjoyably, on the 8th. She attended a flower show at St George's in the East and visited the People's Palace on the 14th. From 9–16 July she sat to Edward Hughes, Laurits Tuxen and Abbey. The de Rezskes sang at Buckingham Palace on the 6th and the 11th and Fröken Stockman played again with her on the 15th.

They left on the 19th for Liverpool, where the King laid the first stone of the new cathedral. Reaching Swansea the next day on *Victoria and Albert* they laid the first stone of the new docks, later driving four miles round the town. On the 21st they opened the new Water Works at Rhayader, serving Birmingham. In London on the 22nd, they opened the Royal Horticultural Hall in Vincent

Square, celebrating the Society's centenary; Alexandra later held a reception for 1,400 pension fund nurses. The next day she received General Booth,[365] founder of the Salvation Army. After Goodwood and Cowes, the couple toured Osborne, the private apartments, the new convalescent home and, on 2 August, the new naval college. They sailed in *Britannia* and took trips in *Osborne*, notably to Netley Hospital on the 4th. On the 6th they dined with Princess Beatrice and watched a tattoo at Carisbrooke Castle. After returning to London on the 8th, the King left for Marienbad and Alexandra and Victoria for Sandringham. Finally there was wonderful news from Russia; Empress Alexandra had had a son[366] on the 12th; "the only ray of sunshine during the dark days [Nicky] is passing through. I am to be Godfather. The Xtning is on the 24th & I am sending Louis Battenberg out as my representative."[367] Edward had proposed himself as godfather, thinking that, for various reasons, it might be a good thing to do; Nicholas had gladly assented.[368]

Sandringham looked lovely, with "flowers in masses all over the dear old garden too, where formerly there never was one under <u>Mackellar</u>. <u>Cook</u>, our excellent new man has really done wonders, & made some very pretty new paths etc etc & does all he can to please <u>even me</u>!! & I appreciate it very much. The house is getting on too & the tower will be charming when finished, & Appleton will be quite a mansion. I came here just in time to improve the look of it here & there, with an extra gable to some windows, a small balcony & verandah." She drove her ponies, motored and paid her usual visits. On 20 August she and Victoria reached Mar Lodge, via Abergeldie and Balmoral; at Abergeldie the grandchildren "gave us a most warm & charming welcome, which pleased & touched me very much, they had decorated the whole house, even the tower, with flags. Thank God one & all looked the picture of health, the Highland air has quite set [them] up again, & they seemed all very happy & contented with their 'entente cordiale' between the <u>English</u> & <u>French</u> tutor, governess & nurses both English and German. They all looked a happy family, which pleased me much. I was sorry to part so soon from them again but the kind people at Balmoral wished to give me a reception there too, so off we started & found the whole of our Scotch bodyguard drawn up in front of the house ... We arrived [at Mar] at 2 & found dear Louise, Macduff & 2 sweet girls very well & pleased to see us. Poor Louise is only fairly well, but quite cheery all the same. Unfortunately the weather is <u>cold</u> & they have already fires in the house. We had service in their pretty little Chapel, and now 4 o'clock we are going out for a walk."[369] After two weeks there, driving, fishing, golfing, walking and visiting places nearby, Alexandra and Victoria arrived in London on 3 September, when the King returned from Marienbad. They went to the theatre later and the next day visited Agnes Keyser's King Edward VII Hospital.[370]

On the 5th, Alexandra and Victoria left for Stavanger in Norway, arriving on the 7th, for ten days. They called at Bergen, Aalesund, Merok, Langvingen and

Bergen again, walking about and shopping. "We all did enjoy our cruise & visit to Norway so much, & it was such peace and a real rest at sea, and our various visits on shore ... were delightful. Merok is a beautiful spot & the Fjörds we went through quite lovely; the mountains and cliffs are very grand & imposing, some are 6,000 feet above the sea. We made some charming expeditions in various carioles up the, & across the, mountains, through beautiful scenery & lunched under the snow covered hills; it was great fun & I enjoyed driving the carioles. You will have seen my picture in a kind of gig with the Captain by my side – that was at Bergen." They reached Malö on the 17th and, stopping briefly at Skagum, were joined later by the Charleses. At Copenhagen, they drove to Bernstorff on the 18th, all was well and Alexandra walked and drove with her father. This time Minny was there, fairly well and cheery despite the war, but unfortunately going down with lumbago two days after arriving, "& has been in bed ever since, a terrible nuisance, particularly as we have so little time to spare!! She can hardly move, poor thing, & <u>yells</u> when she is touched. Our dear fat <u>handy</u> Georgie[371] who also is here now, is as <u>usual</u> of the greatest use & help & has to turn her in bed & assist in every way, & he is so funny about it all & makes us go into fits of laughter every moment. That dear old boy, he is quite the <u>nurse</u> of the family as he was when poor darling Amama was so ill."[372]

On the 25th, Dr Niels Finsen died at only 43. Alexandra attended his funeral on the 29th in the Marmor Kirke; she and the family went later to Roskilde. She had received the officers of King Edward's Danish Hussar Regiment on the 28th. The family moved to Copenhagen on 11 October and Alexandra went for walks with her daughters and drives with her convalescent sister. As May told her aunt, "For a wonder in this war, 'Mother dear' is for the Japs! She is not half as Russian as she was & I don't think Aunt Minny can do much harm now in this way."[373] Alexandra called on friends, shopped and walked; on the 19th there was a cinematograph after dinner. In the long letter she had been writing to George, she noted a particularly riling speech by the German emperor, who had linked his wife's name to the "stolen" provinces of Schleswig and Holstein "as <u>hers</u>! – where she <u>never</u> put a foot before she <u>married him</u> – as her Grd Father, & Father, was <u>exiled</u> having been a traitor!! Voila tout, & the <u>vulgarity</u> of praising his wife up to the skies in <u>public</u> sickens one as you say, but he always behaves like a 'parvenu'!" Maud was miserable because Charles had gone to sea for the whole winter; "She & baby will be coming home with me."[374] They arrived on the 23rd.

After drives and receptions in London, Alexandra and her daughters went to Sandringham on the 28th. Guests arrived, including, from 3–12 November, Prince George of Greece. The court moved on the 14th to Windsor for the Portuguese state visit,[375] with two banquets in St George's Hall; performances, on two days, of plays in the Waterloo Gallery; and a concert by Clara Butt[376] and her husband, Kennerley Rumford, on the 18th. Alexandra went for walks and shopped in Windsor; there was shooting and lunch in the park and tea at

Frogmore on the 19th. On Sunday they drove to the gardens in the Home Park. They returned to London on the 21st and King Edward went to stay at West Dean. Alexandra received Judge and Mrs Arunachalam[377] from Ceylon and the next day she and Victoria returned to Sandringham. Snow kept them indoors but Maud came to lunch several times and Louise arrived for the weekend on the 25th. Alexandra was missing her talks with May, as both had been fully occupied and had "not really met or seen each other to <u>talk</u> to for months!! – which makes me <u>quite low</u> at times, as you know well <u>how</u> fond I am of you my dear child."[378] On the 28th the King returned and more guests arrived. Alexandra was 60 on 1 December; she had some wonderful presents but no particular jollification; "really to look at her one cannot imagine her age, for she looks too marvellously young" wrote her daughter-in-law.[379] Alexandra and her daughters had tea at Appleton several times before returning on the 10th to London, where she and the King lunched with Soveral at the Portuguese legation and took leave of the Portuguese sovereigns. More theatres and a stay at Culford Hall[380] followed. They were all back at Sandringham by the 23rd.

Notes

1 RA GV/PRIV/AA22/31, Prince of Wales to Duke of York, 1900: 8 January
2 RA VIC/ADDX/193, Princess of Wales to Miss MM Paget, 1900: 3 January
3 RA GV/PRIV/AA22/32, Prince of Wales to Duke of York, 1900: 15 February
4 Adelina Patti (1843–1919), famous Italian opera singer
5 May "Toupie" Lowther (1874–1944), tennis player and fencer
6 General Piet Cronje (1836–1911), South African Boer commander
7 Frederick Sleigh Roberts (1832–1914), Field Marshal, created 1st Earl Roberts, m Nora Henrietta, née Bews
8 Douglas Cochrane (1852–1935), the 12th Earl of Dundonald, Lieutenant-General
9 Sir Redvers Buller (1839–1908), General
10 Montagu Lowry-Corry (1838–1903), 1st Baron Rowton, philanthropist and public servant
11 Sir Thomas Lipton (1848–1931), 1st Baronet, tea merchant, self-made man, philanthropist, and yachtsman
12 RA VIC/MAIN/S/25/87, Princess of Wales to Queen Victoria, 1900: 24 March
13 RA GV/PRIV/AA22/36, Prince of Wales to Duke of York, 1900: 31 March
14 Prince Henry (1900–74), later Duke of Gloucester, Governor-General of Australia, 1945–47, m Lady Alice, née Montagu-Douglas-Scott (1901–2004), later given the title of Princess Alice, Duchess of Gloucester
15 Arthur Wellesley (1769–1852) 1st Duke of Wellington, leading 19th century military and political figure
16 RA GV/PRIV/AA32/20, Princess of Wales to Duke of York, 1900: 31 March; Lord Roberts (popularly known as "Bobs") was indeed chosen as a sponsor
17 Alfred Cooper owned The Gables Estate and in 1882 had built a small theatre, which was converted to a military hospital during the Boer War, as The Princess of Wales's Private Military Hospital. Mr Cooper was knighted in 1901. The hospital later reverted to a theatre, until 1937. https://database.theatrestrust.org.uk
18 RA GV/PRIV/AA22/38, Prince of Wales to Duke of York, 1900: 3 April

19   RA VIC/ADDA21/233/20, pencil note by Sydney Holland, [1900]

20   RA VIC/ADDA21/233/26, Princess of Wales to Sydney Holland, 1900: 9 April

21   Jean-Baptiste Sipido (1884–1959); he was not prosecuted for the attempt because he was only fifteen

22   RA GV/PRIV/AA22/39, Prince of Wales to Duke of York, 1900: 6 April

23   RA VIC/MAIN/QAD/1900: 4 April

24   RA GV/PRIV/AA32/21, Princess of Wales to Duke of York, 1900: 28 April

25   RA GV/PRIV/AA22/40, Prince of Wales to Duke of York, 1900: 9 April

26   RA VIC/ADDA4/157, Prince of Wales to Empress Frederick, 1900: 18 April

27   Crown Prince William (1882–1951), eldest son of Emperor William II, m Duchess Cecilie of Mecklenburg-Schwerin (1886–1954)

28   Many countries sided with the Boers

29   RA GV/PRIV/AA36/47, Duke of York to Princess of Wales, 1900: 23 April

30   RA GV/PRIV/AA32/21, Princess of Wales to Duke of York, 1900: 28 April

31   Ella Du Cane (1874–1943), British watercolour artist

32   Henry Campbell Bruce (1851–1929), 2nd Baron Aberdare, army officer, m Constance, née Beckett

33   RA GV/PRIV/AA22/44, Prince of Wales to Duke of York, 1900: 2 June

34   Later known as the Wallace Collection

35   Abbas II Helmy Bey (1874–1944), last Khedive of Egypt and the Sudan (ruled from 1892–1914)

36   Sydney Holland (1855–1931), 2nd Viscount Knutsford, barrister

37   RA VIC/ADDA21/233/30–32, pencil note by Sydney Holland; Princess of Wales to Sydney Holland, 1900: 6 July; pencil note by Sydney Holland

38   RA VIC/ADDA21/233/52, pencil note by Sydney Holland

39   Perhaps this refers to differences with Princess Helena, who regarded nursing patronage as her own preserve

40   RA VIC/ADDA4/171, Princess of Wales to Empress Frederick, 1900: 29 July

41   Duke of Sparta, Crown Prince of the Hellenes

42   By an anarchist, Gaetano Bressi (b 1869)

43   RA GV/PRIV/AA22/47, Prince of Wales to Duke of York, 1900: 20 August

44   RA GV/PRIV/AA32/22, Princess of Wales to Duke of York, 1900: 30 August

45   Hon Sir Sidney Greville (1866–1927) courtier, including as Queen Alexandra's private secretary, 1901–11

46   RA GV/PRIV/AA32/22, Princess of Wales to Duke of York, 1900: 30 August

47   RA GV/PRIV//AA22/48, Prince of Wales to Duke of York, 1900: 29 August

48   RA VIC/ADDA21/233/33, Princess of Wales to Sydney Holland, 1900: 30 August

49   Prince Knud of Denmark (1900–76), m Princess Caroline-Mathilde of Denmark (1912–95)

50   RA GV/PRIV/AA32/23, Princess of Wales to Duke of York, 1900: 27 September

51   However, Christian Victor died on active service and his brother Albert became Duke of Schleswig-Holstein-Sonderburg-Augustenburg

52   Lady Mary, née Lygon (1869–1927), m Lt-Col Henry Hepburn-Stuart-Forbes-Trefusis; she was a lady of the bedchamber to the Duchess of York; a hymn writer, who was a friend and promoter of Elgar; and first secretary of the English Folk Dance Society

53   RA GV/PRIV/AA32/23 Princess of Wales to Duke of York, 1900: 27September

54   Countess Frederica of Schlieben (1757–1827), m Frederick (1757–1816), Duke of Schleswig-Holstein-Sonderburg-Beck; their son Frederick William (1785–1831), Duke of Schleswig-Holstein-Sonderburg-Beck, later Glücksburg, became the father of the future King Christian IX of Denmark. On the King's accession in 1863, his brothers' title changed to "His Highness", having been styled "His Serene Highness" earlier.

55 RA GV/PRIV/AA22/53, Prince of Wales to Duke of York, 1900: 4 October

56 Etienne-Jules Marey (1830–1904), French scientist, physiologist and chronophotographer

57 Georges Méliés (1861–1935), French illusionist and film director

58 Brothers Auguste (1862–1954) and Louis (1864–84) Lumiére, made photographic equipment, especially the "Cinematograph" motion picture system, and later the first practical colour process, the Lumiére Autochrome.

59 Dimond, pp 86–7, 160–1

60 Paris Singer (1867–1932), one of the 24 children of Isaac Singer, inventor and industrialist, from whom he inherited money. Among other things Paris built a number of hospitals for the wounded of the First World War.

61 Found among his papers in the Royal Archives.

62 RA GV PRIV/AA22/56, Prince of Wales to Duke of York, 1900:1 November

63 RA VIC/ADDA4/189, Princess of Wales to Empress Frederick, 1900: 21 November

64 William Tupper had first been appointed footman to the three young Wales Princesses in 1882

65 Perhaps regarded as indigestible or unwholesome for children

66 Made especially for her by a firm in Bond Street, likely to have been Charbonnel et Walker

67 RA AEC/GG/8/17, *Memoirs of Miss Grace Victoria Tupper*

68 RA VIC/ADDA21/233/35, Princess of Wales to Sydney Holland, 1900: 7 December

69 RA AEC/GG/8/17, *Memoirs of Miss Grace Victoria Tupper*

70 William St John Brodrick (1856–1942), later 1st Earl of Midleton. A Conservative and Irish Unionist alliance politician, he was Secretary of State for War from 1900–03

71 For example, for bedspreads and tea-cloths

72 *The Girls' Realm Annual, 1901*

73 Or Schwan

74 Tooley, p 85

75 *William Shipley Group for RSA History*, Bulletin 64, March 2020, article by Susan Bennett. An example of the design can be seen at the Victoria and Albert Museum in London.

76 Maylunas & Mironenko, p 204

77 Henry Fitz-Alan-Howard (1847–1917), the 15th Duke of Norfolk, by tradition held the position of Earl Marshal

78 Nicholas II's brother

79 Maylunas & Mironenko, p 204

80 RA VIC/ADDA4/198, King Edward VII to Empress Frederick, 1901: 1 February

81 Reginald Baliol Brett (1852–1930), 2nd Viscount Esher, historian, politician, courtier and "*éminence grise*"

82 Journals and Letters of Reginald, Viscount Esher, Volume I, p 279

83 RA GV/PRIV/AA22/58, King Edward VII to Duke of York, 1901: 14 February

84 RA GV/ADD/COPY/140/30, Princess Victoria to Lord Rosebery, 1901: undated

85 RA GV/ADD/COPY/140/78, Princess Victoria to Lord Rosebery, 1901: 31 January

86 In which she was proved correct

87 RA GV/PRIV/AA6/502, Queen Alexandra to Canon Dalton, 1901:17 February

88 Esher, Vol I, p 288

89 Emil Fuchs (1866–1929), Austrian and American sculptor, medallist, painter and author

90 Cust, p 35

91 Tupper

92 Tooley, pp160–1

93 Kate Strasdin, *Inside the Royal Wardrobe, a Dress History of Queen Alexandra*, p 46

94 Tooley, pp 162–3

95 Tooley, pp77–8

96   Grand Duchess George, p 166
97   Tupper
98   Tooley, pp 163–4
99   Esher, Vol I, pp 288, 290
100 To avoid immediate confusion after his parents' long association with the titles
101 Agnes Keyser, "Sister Agnes" (1852–1941) and her sister, Fanny Keyser had started a private hospital, in which they had interested the King, which was called King Edward VII's Hospital for Officers
102 RA GV/PRIV/AA32/24, Queen Alexandra to Duke of Cornwall and York, 1901: 20/21 March
103 RA VIC/ADDA4/207, King Edward VII to Empress Frederick, 1901: 27 March
104 Dowager Landgravine of Hesse
105 Prince Frederick Duleep Singh (1868–1926), army officer, second son of Maharajah Sir Duleep Singh
106 RA GV/PRIV/AA22/62, King Edward VII to Duke of Cornwall and York, 1901: 18 April
107 RA QM/PRIV/CC42/49, Queen Alexandra to Duchess of Cornwall and York, 1901: 29 April; this was "The Great Comet of 1901" or Comet Viscara
108 Tooley, p 164
109 RA GV/PRIV/AA22/63, King Edward VII to Duke of Cornwall and York, 1901: 2 May
110 RA GV/PRIV/AA32/26, Queen Alexandra to Duke of Cornwall and York, 1901: 30 April – 1 May
111 RA GV/PRIV/AA22/63, King Edward VII to Duke of Cornwall and York, 1901: 2 May
112 RA VIC/ADDU280/5, Charlotte Knollys to Paris Singer, 1901: 16 April
113 RA VIC/ADDA21/233/54, Queen Alexandra to Sydney Holland, 1901: 24 April
114 Frederick Ponsonby (1867–1935), Sir, army officer and courtier, later created 1st Baron Sysonby
115 RA GV/PRIV/AA32/26, Queen Alexandra to Duke of Cornwall and York,1901: 30 April – 1 May
116 Lt-Colonel Arthur Davidson (1856–1922), later knighted
117 RA GV/PRIV/AA22/64, King Edward VII to Duke of Cornwall and York, 1901: 18 May
118 RA VIC/ADDA4/212, King Edward VII to Empress Frederick, 1901: 8 May
119 Tooley, p 81
120 Tooley, p 76
121 Tooley, p 165
122 RCIN 1037371
123 RCIN 1231504
124 RA GV/PRIV/AA32/27, Queen Alexandra to Duke of Cornwall and York, 1901: 17 May
125 Hatchard's, bookshop in Piccadilly, founded in1797 by John Hatchard (1769–1849), publisher and bookseller
126 RA VIC/ADDA4/213, Queen Alexandra to Empress Frederick, 1901: 14 May; Mossy now had six sons
127 Maria Cristina Brunetti y Gayosa de los Corbos (1884–1914), the 13th Duchess of Mandas
128 Alfred de Rothschild (1842–1918), financier, patron of the arts and formerly a college friend of King Edward at Cambridge
129 RA LC/LCO/TRADESWARR/QA/87, Sewell & Cousens were canine surgeons by appointment to the Queen
130 RA AEC/GG/1/8, Queen Alexandra to Alfred de Rothschild, 1901: 25 May. The dog was named Marvel
131 RA GV/PRIV/AA32/28, Queen Alexandra to Duke of Cornwall and York, 1901: 3–14 June
132 The latest fashion; a large flat cap with a peak

133 Esher, Vol I, p 298

134 Jan Kubelik (1880–1940), Czech violinist and composer

135 This was later reassembled for her at Marlborough House

136 Lionel Cust (1859–1929), later Sir, art historian, Director of the National Portrait Gallery (1895–1909), Surveyor of The King's Pictures (1901–27).

137 Sir Guy Laking, 2nd Baronet (1875–1919), historian of armour, keeper of the King's Armoury and first keeper of the London Museum

138 Sir Lionel Cust, *King Edward VII and his Court*, 1930, pp 13–17; the inspector was George E Miles (1853–1942) who was also Chief Officer of the Windsor Castle Salvage corps

139 Cust, p21; as the King raised his voice for the Queen to hear, Cust, nearby, heard every word

140 RA QM/PRIV/CC42/50, Queen Alexandra to Duchess of Cornwall and York, 1901: 12 June

141 RA GV/PRIV/AA32/29, Queen Alexandra to Duke of Cornwall and York, 1901: 19 June

142 RA GV/PRIV/AA23/1, King Edward VII to Duke of Cornwall and York, 1901: 21 June

143 George Mitchell bequeathed his library of 1,500 books (except Boccaccio's *Decameron*) to Alexandra in 1878. RL Catalogue of the Library of George Mitchell, Esquire, RCIN 1028983a; had Alexandra known about the *Decameron's* absence, she might have been disappointed; she certainly had one or two slightly controversial books, such as Jules Lemaitre's *Mariage Blanc* (RCIN 1231239), Count Leo Tolstoy's *Anna Karenina* (RCIN 123066–7), and Grant Allen's *The Woman who Did* (RCIN 1230565) and might not have appreciated her reading being "censored".

144 Tooley, p 75

145 Beavan, pp 35, 36, 78, 79, 85, 88

146 Gabriel Tschumi (1883–1957), Swiss chef, became master chef to Queen Victoria, Edward VII and George V between 1899–1932, and later to Queen Mary from 1948–52

147 Alexandra possessed several cookery books; one was *A noble Boke of Cookry ffor a prince Houssolde or eny other stately Houssolde*, from a rare manuscript in the Holkham Collection; RCIN 1001368

148 A light snack, such as morning coffee

149 Tschumi, pp 98–105

150 RA GV/AA32/29, Queen Alexandra to Duke of Cornwall and York, 1901: 19 June; the child was Grand Duchess Anastasia Nicholaievna of Russia (1901–18)

151 RA GV/PRIV/AA32/30, Queen Alexandra to Duke of Cornwall and York, 1901: 28 June

152 RA QM/PRIV/CC22/71, Duchess of Cornwall and York to Grand Duchess of Mecklenburg-Strelitz, 1901: 14 June

153 See RA VIC/ADDA21/218/107, 32, 60

154 Including Adeline's *Art Dictionary, containing a complete index of all terms used in art, architecture, heraldry and archaeology* (RCIN 1126553) as well as books containing reproductions of art

155 Jacob Epstein (1880–1959), Sir; Jewish American-British pioneer of controversial modern sculpture

156 RL.K432,f 11

157 Prince Edward of Saxe-Weimar Eisenach (1823–1902), Field Marshal, a nephew of Queen Adelaide. He was born in England and became a naturalised British subject; m, morganatically, Lady Augusta Gordon-Lennox.

158 RA QM/PRIV/CC29/17, Grand Duchess of Mecklenburg-Strelitz to Duchess of Cornwall and York, 1901: 18 June

159 Cust, p 33

160 Sir Sidney Lee, *King Edward VII, a Biography*, Vol I, p 54

161 RA VIC/ADDA21/228/236, Queen Alexandra's note, undated

162 Tooley, p 92

163 Mary, née Leiter (1870–1906), m George Curzon (1859–1925), 1st Marquess Curzon of Kedleston, statesman

164 RA VIC/MAIN/N/40/53, Hon C Gonne (Chief Secretary to Government of Bombay) to C Grant (Secretary to Government of India, Foreign Department), 1882: 29 September

165 RA VIC/ADDX13/21, 23, Charlotte Knollys to Lady Curzon, 1901: 14 June

166 RA GV/O2548/5, Duchess of Cornwall and York to Queen Alexandra, 1901: 17 August; Alexandra had given Marie a brooch

167 She had married Count Jametel in 1899

168 RA QM/PRIV/CC42/51, Queen Alexandra to Duchess of Cornwall and York, 1901: 5 July

169 King William IV (1765–1837) m Princess Adelaide of Saxe-Meiningen (1792–1849)

170 The Jubilee Nurses worked as "district nurses".

171 RA VIC//MAIN/QAD/1901: 3 July

172 Beavan, p 196

173 RA VIC/ADDA/21/233/55, Sydney Holland (note), 60, Queen Alexandra to Sydney Holland, 1901: 4 July, 61, Sydney Holland (note)

174 Including Mrs Keppel, invited to join a dinner party on 10th

175 RA VIC/MAIN/EVIID/1901: 11 July

176 RA GV/PRIV/AA23/3, King Edward VII to Duke of Cornwall and York, 1901: 18 July

177 The de Greys' house

178 RA GV/PRIV/AA23/4, King Edward VII to Duke of Cornwall and York, 1901: 26 July

179 Ishbel, née Marjoribanks (1857–1939), President of the International Council of Women, 1893–1899, m John Campbell Hamilton-Gordon, (1847–1934) 7th Earl and then 1st Marquess of Aberdeen and Temair

180 Probably Commodore Sir Richard Williams-Bulkeley, the 12th Baronet (1862–1942)

181 Robert Falcon Scott (1868–1912) RN officer and explorer who led two Antarctic expeditions, m Kathleen, née Bruce (1878–1947), sculptor and socialite

182 RA GV/PRIV.AA23/5, King Edward VII to Duke of Cornwall and York, 1901: 7 August

183 None of these letters survive but their former existence is suggested by hieroglyphs in the King's engagement diary as well as comments in other documents. A short thick line apparently signifies writing to Alexandra, as it only appears when the couple were apart. "Ec" apparently means Mrs Keppel; her name, Alice, backwards was Ecila and he gave that name to one of his horses.

184 RA GV/PRIV/AA37/1, Duke of Cornwall and York to Queen Alexandra, 1901: 11 August

185 RA GV/PRIV/AA32/31, Queen Alexandra to Duke of Cornwall and York, 1901: 7 August

186 RA VIC/ADDX13/26, 44, note by Queen Alexandra, 1901: July; List of Indian Stuffs kept by the Queen

187 RA VIC/ADDX13/25, 27, Charlotte Knollys to Lady Curzon, 1901: 3, 9 August

188 RA GV/PRIV/AA32/32, Queen Alexandra to Duke of Cornwall and York, 1901: 20 August

189 RA GV/PRIV/AA32/34, Queen Alexandra to Duke of Cornwall and York, 1901: 18 September

190 RA GV/PRIV/AA32/33, Queen Alexandra to Duke of Cornwall and York, 1901: 20 September; William McKinley (1843–1901), the 25th American President

191 RA GV/PRIV/AA23/7, King Edward VII to Duke of Cornwall and York, 1901: 1 September

192 RA GV/PRIV/AA23/8, King Edward VII to Duke of Cornwall and York,1901: 12 September

193 RA GV/PRIV/AA23/9, King Edward VII to Duke of Cornwall and York, 1901: 15 September

194 RA GV/PRIV/AA32/35, Queen Alexandra to Duke of Cornwall and York, 1901: 27 September

195 RA GV/PRIV/AA32/36, Queen Alexandra to Duke of Cornwall and York, 1901: 4 October

196 Perhaps Johannes Wolff (1861–1931), Dutch violinist

197 RA GV/PRIV/AA32/37, Queen Alexandra to Duke of Cornwall and York, 1901: 29 October

[198] Tooley, pp 89–90

[199] Esher, Vol I, p18

[200] John Philip Sousa (1854–1932), American conductor and composer known chiefly for military marches

[201] RA GV/PRIV/AA37/5, Prince of Wales to Queen Alexandra, 1901: 24 December

[202] RA GV/PRIV/AA32/38, Queen Alexandra to Prince of Wales, 1902: 8 January

[203] John Martin Harvey (1863–1944), Sir, actor, m Angelita Helena Maria de Silva Ferro (1867–1949), actress

[204] With the Howes: Richard Penn Curzon (1861–1929), 4th Earl Howe, politician and courtier, including being Queen Alexandra's Lord Chamberlain from 1903–25, m Lady Georgiana, née Spencer-Churchill (1860–1906)

[205] Princess Patricia of Connaught (1886–1974), styled Lady Patricia Ramsay after marrying Admiral Sir Alexander Ramsay (1881–1972) in 1919.

[206] The first theatre visit since Queen Victoria's death

[207] Henry Wood (1869–1944), later Sir, conductor, best known for promenade concerts in London

[208] Sir Edward Poynter (1836–1919), 1st Baronet, painter, designer and draughtsman

[209] RA VIC/ADDX13/29, Charlotte Knollys to Lady Curzon, 1902: 14 February

[210] Marcia, née Liddell m Hon North Dalrymple-Hamilton (1853–1906); she was a family friend who was privileged to be nicknamed "Hag" like the Wales Princesses

[211] Mention quietly so as not to tempt fate. Literally: "un-shouted".

[212] RA GV/PRIV/AA23/22, King Edward VII to Prince of Wales, 1902: 10 April; ironically, as King, George was known for "postponing actual details of arrangements until the eleventh hour"; RA GV/BOX21/21, Lord Cromer to Dean of Windsor, 1925: 1 December

[213] Ferdinand Mehldahl (1827–1908), Danish architect, particularly known for the reconstruction of Frederiksborg Castle after the fire in 1859; he was also chamberlain to King Christian IX

[214] W Church, Tapissier at Marlborough House since 1878

[215] Cust, pp 31–36

[216] To which Sydney Holland and Miss Mabel Helen Cave (Matron of Westminster Hospital) had recently been recruited: RA.ADDA21/233/65

[217] Robert Newman (1858–1926), businessman and musical impresario, founded the series of concerts, starting at the Queen's Hall and continuing at the Royal Albert Hall, which became known as "The Proms". He hired Henry Wood as conductor.

[218] Joseph Joachim (1831–1907), famous Hungarian violinist, conductor, composer and teacher

[219] RA VIC/ADDX13/31, 33, Charlotte Knollys to Lady Curzon, 1902: 20 May; Queen Alexandra to Lady Curzon, 1902: 5 May

[220] Esher, Vol I, p 331

[221] The Treaty of Vereeniging was signed on 31 May 1902

[222] Frederick William Hewitt (1857–1916), later Sir, noted anaesthesiologist

[223] Georgina P. Herbert-Haines

[224] Inflammation of the connective tissue around the caecum and vermiform appendix

[225] RA VIC/ADDC13, Nurse Haines' Diary, 1902: 24 June

[226] RA VIC/ADDU383/2; copy of original document, reproduced by kind permission of James Page-Roberts

[227] RA VIC/ADDC13, Nurse Haines' Diary, 1902: 24 June

[228] This was usual with spare food from the royal kitchens, which was also given to hospitals.

[229] Royal Chef, by Gabriel Tschumi, 1954, pp 94–5

[230] The King

231 RA GV/ADD/COPY/140/37, Rosebery Papers, Princess Victoria to Lord Rosebery, 1902: 7 July

232 Tschumi, pp 88–9

233 RA VIC/ADDX13/35, Queen Alexandra to Lady Curzon, 1902: 23 July

234 RA GV/PRIV/AA23/24, King Edward VII to Prince of Wales, 1902: 21 July

235 Blanche, née Maynard (1864–1945) (a sister of "Daisy" Warwick) m Lord Algernon Gordon-Lennox (1847–1921), popular society figure and brother of 7th Duke of Richmond

236 Queen Alexandra to Lady Algernon Gordon-Lennox, 1902: 26 July; private collection

237 RA VIC/ADDC13, Nurse Haines' Diary, 1902:29July

238 RA GV/AA23/25 King Edward VII to Prince of Wales, 1902: 4 August

239 RA VIC/ADDC13, Nurse Haines' Diary, 1902:5 August

240 Randall Thomas Davidson (1848–1930), Bishop of Winchester, 1895–1903; later Archbishop of Canterbury, 1903–28, and 1st Baron Davidson of Lambeth

241 Esher, Vol I, pp 345–346

242 Cust, p 127

243 Tschumi, pp 96–7

244 Boer Generals, who were also politicians; Louis Botha (1862–1919), 1st Prime Minister of the Union of South Africa; Jacobus de la Rey (1847–1914), and Christiaan De Wet (1854–1922)

245 Mozaffar ad-Din Shah Qajar (1853–1907); the Prince of Wales had received him in London first.

246 Norman Straton (1840–1918), Bishop of Sodor and Man from 1892–1907

247 Thomas Henry Hall Caine (1853–1931), later Sir, was a popular novelist, dramatist, writer, poet and critic; m Mary, née Chandler (d 1932). Hall Caine would be of help to Alexandra within a few years.

248 RA GV/PRIV/AA32/39, Queen Alexandra to Prince of Wales, 1902: 1 September

249 RA GV/PRIV/AA23/26, King Edward VII to Prince of Wales, 1902: 27 August

250 RA VIC/ADDX13/36, Charlotte Knollys to Lady Curzon, 1902: 31 August

251 One Henry Wright, as secretary to the then Duke of Sutherland, had compiled game books and a list of dogs at Dunrobin in the 1850s-1870s.
https://search.sutherlandcollection.org.uk

252 RA GV/PRIV/AA32/39, Queen Alexandra to Prince of Wales, 1902: 1 September

253 RA VIC/ADDC13/15 September 1902, Nurse Haines' diary

254 RA GV/PRIV/AA32/40, Queen Alexandra to Prince of Wales, 1902: 13 October

255 RA GV/PRIV/AA23/29, King Edward VII to Prince of Wales, 1902: 7 October

256 Anton Hegner (1861–1915), Danish cellist and composer

257 Henry Bramsen (1875–1919), Danish cellist, with a female relative

258 RA GV/PRIV/AA23/27, King Edward VII to Prince of Wales, 1902: 2 September

259 Archibald Mackellar, formerly head gardener to the Duke of Roxburgh at Floors Castle

260 Thomas Henderson Cook (1869–1947)

261 RA GV/PRIV/AA32/40, Queen Alexandra to Prince of Wales, 1902: 13 October

262 Cust, p 133

263 Esher, Vol I, pp 357–358

264 Colonel Sir James Gildea (1838–1920), army officer and philanthropist who, among other things, founded SSFA, and worked on behalf of Queen Victoria's Jubilee Institute for Nurses, the Alexandra Trust and the St John Ambulance Association

265 Albert Chevalier (1861–1923), music hall comedian and singer of Cockney songs

266 Horace Goldin (1873–1939), stage magician, famous for "sawing a woman in half"

267 Arthur Bourchier (1863–1927), actor and theatre manager, m Violet, née Barnes (1867–1942), actress under the name of Violet Vanbrugh. The couple divorced in 1918.

268 RA VIC/ADDX13/38, Sir Dighton Probyn to Lady Curzon, 1902: 6 December
269 List of goods and prices at the technical schools; private collection
270 With Lord and Lady Howe
271 Friedrich-Max "Fritz" Kreisler (1875–1962), Austrian-born violinist and composer
272 RA GV/PRIV/AA32/41, Queen Alexandra to Prince of Wales, 1902: 20 December
273 Prince George (1902–1942), later Duke of Kent
274 RA GV/PRIV/AA23/35, King Edward VII to Prince of Wales, 1902: 21 December
275 Tschumi, pages 102–3
276 RA VIC/MAIN/W/62/108
277 *The Graphic*, "The Court", 27 June 1903
278 Catherine of Braganza (1638–1705) m King Charles II in 1662; their apartments at Windsor Castle were redesigned between 1675 and 1678
279 RA GV/PRIV/AA23/36, King Edward VII to Prince of Wales, 1903: 4 February
280 RA VIC/MAIN/QAD/1903: 6 February
281 Esher, Vol I, p 373
282 Cust, pp 135–9
283 Cust, p 40
284 London County Council
285 RA GV/PRIV/AA32/42, Queen Alexandra to Prince of Wales, 1903: 23 February
286 Esher, Vol I, p 386
287 Tschumi, pp 82–3
288 Beavan, p 65
289 Tschumi, p 117
290 The royal couple's courier since 1899, Jean Jacques Fehr, appointed Director of Continental Journeys in 1901. Fehr (d 1920) was Swiss and later became a British citizen.
291 RA GV/PRIV/AA32/43, Queen Alexandra to Prince of Wales, 1903: 21 April
292 Mary Steen (1856–1939), Danish photographer and feminist; the first female Danish court photographer and Alexandra's first female court photographer from 1888; like Alexandra, Mary Steen became deaf
293 Henri Glaesel (1853–1921), Danish architect
294 *The Graphic*, "The Court", 30 May 1903
295 rince Julius of Schleswig-Holstein-Sonderburg-Glücksburg (1824–1903) m Elisabeth, née von Ziegesar (1856–1887), created Countess von Roest on her marriage
296 Lady Gladys Mary Juliet Lowther (1881–1965) married Robert George Vivian Duff (1876–1914)
297 Marie Hall (1884–1956), noted violinist
298 Bodleian Library, Acland MSS, d.177/132 2054/26 June 1903
299 Prince Alexander of Denmark, later King Olav V of Norway (1903–1991)
300 Emile Loubet (1838–1929), President from 1899–1906, m Marie-Louise née Picard (1843–1925)
301 William Humble Ward (1867–1932), 2nd Earl of Dudley, Lord-Lieutenant of Ireland, 1902–05, m Rachel, née Gurney (1868–1920)
302 RA GV/PRIV/AA23/43, King Edward VII to Prince of Wales, 1903: 26 July
303 With Lord Londonderry
304 RA GV/PRIV/AA23/16, King Edward VII to Prince of Wales, 1901: 3 December
305 RA GV/PRIV/AA32/44, Queen Alexandra to Prince of Wales, 1903: 26 August
306 RA QM/PRIV/CC3/73, Prince of Wales to Princess of Wales, 1903: 13 August; ironically, Queen Mary was remembered years later by Lord Claud Hamilton, a member of her household, as "one of the most selfish human beings I have ever known." James Pope-Hennessy, ed Hugo Vickers, *The Quest for Queen Mary*, p 141

[307] RA VIC/MAIN/QAD/1903: 3 October

[308] Ben Davies (1858–1943), Welsh tenor

[309] Muriel Foster (1877–1937), contralto; she had studied at the Royal College of Music

[310] Leonard Borwick (1868–1925), concert pianist

[311] King Victor Emanuel III (1869–1947) and Queen Elena (1873–1952)

[312] Alfred Young Nutt (1847–1924), architect and artist; one of his achievements was designing and constructing annexes at Westminster Abbey for the Coronations of Edward VII and George V

[313] A copy of one in Copenhagen

[314] Queen Alexandra to AY Nutt, 1903: 21 November; private collection

[315] Ion Pace (1846–1928), craftsman associated with metal and stained-glass work, including the stained glass in the mausoleum at Frogmore

[316] "Thy Saviour called thee, Beloved, now thy work is done. Thou art weary; come rest in thy Eternal Father's Home. In loving memory from her sorrowing children, grandchildren and great-grandchildren to their ever-beloved Mother and Queen. Victoria. Jan. 22 1901." RCIN 34161. Also see Dimond, p 88; The Sphere, 7 November 1903.

[317] Robert Schumann (1810–56), famous German composer, pianist and influential music critic

[318] Anton Rubinstein (1829–94), famous Russian pianist, composer and conductor

[319] Johannes Brahms (1833–97), famous German composer, pianist and conductor

[320] Niels Gade (1817–90), important Danish composer, conductor, violinist, organist and teacher

[321] George Byron (1788–1824), 6th Baron Byron, famous poet

[322] William Shakespeare (1564–1616), playwright, poet and actor; perhaps the greatest writer in the English language

[323] Percy Bysshe Shelley (1792–1822), famous lyric and philosophical poet

[324] Perhaps Denis Florence MacCarthy (1817–82), Irish poet, translator and biographer

[325] Joseph Henry Shorthouse (1834–1903), novelist who identified with the Oxford Movement's high church Anglicanism; *John Inglesant* was a long "quest" novel about the Jesuits

[326] Dimond, p 95

[327] RA VIC/ADDU280/19, Charlotte Knollys to Paris Singer, 1903: 18 November

[328] RA GV/PRIV/AA32/46, Queen Alexandra to Prince of Wales, 1903: 11 December. The King was at Elveden; hearing of the fire on 10th he left at 9.45am on the 12th for Sandringham. He did not hurry back as his wife had telegraphed herself and he was thus reassured about her safety.

[329] RA VIC/ADDU280/22, Sir Dighton Probyn to Paris Singer, 1903: 19 December

[330] RA QM/PRIV/CC30/68, Grand Duchess of Mecklenburg-Strelitz to Princess of Wales, 1903: 17 December

[331] After Charlotte's death in 1930, The Times, 26 April 1930, p 10, carried an article noting that, after the fire, she had been presented with a gold medal, inscribed "To our dear Charlotte".

[332] Charles Bertram (1853–1907), born James Bassett, magician, known as "The Royal Conjurer" as he performed for royalty

[333] John Bowers (1854–1926), Bishop of Thetford from 1903–26

[334] Hans Richter (1843–1916), Austro–Hungarian conductor

[335] Hugh Oakeley Arnold-Forster (1855–1909), Secretary of State for War, 1903–05

[336] RA VIC/ADDA21/233/68,72, pencil note by Sydney Holland; Queen Alexandra to Sydney Holland, 1904: 29 January

[337] Alyn Williams (1866–1955), successful miniature painter, 1st President of the Royal Miniature Society; also painted King Edward VII

338 Revd HC Staveley

339 Henry Sidgwick (1838–1900), utilitarian philosopher and economist, Professor of Moral Philosophy at Cambridge, 1883–1900

340 Edward Elgar (1857–1934), Sir, renowned composer

341 RA GV/PRIV/AA23/52, King Edward VII to Prince of Wales, 1904: 15 March

342 RA VIC/ADDA8/2939, Queen Alexandra to Grand Duchess of Mecklenburg-Strelitz, 1904: 20 March

343 At the dining rooms near Old Street in London

344 The Duke of Cambridge's sons were Colonel George FitzGeorge (1843–1907), Rear Admiral Sir Adolphus FitzGeorge (1846–1922) and Sir Augustus FitzGeorge (1847–1933)

345 RA QM/PRIV/CC42/60, Queen Alexandra to Princess of Wales, 1904: 12 April

346 RA GV/PRIV/AA23/54, King Edward VII to Prince of Wales, 1904: 3 April

347 Perhaps William II was just trying to mend fences and build bridges, but to Alexandra it looked like bossy encroachment

348 RA GV/PRIV/AA32/47, Queen Alexandra to Prince of Wales, 1904: 9 April

349 RA GV/PRIV/AA23/56, King Edward VII to Prince of Wales, 1904: 13 April

350 This was a series of formal agreements between Britain and France, resolving various disputes. It was signed on 8 April 1904.

351 Grand Duke Kirill of Russia, first cousin of Nicholas II

352 RA GV/PRIV/AA23/56, King Edward VII to Prince of Wales, 1904: 13 April

353 John Baragwaneth King (1864–1939), landscape painter specialising in watercolour

354 Seat of the Duke of Devonshire

355 Count Albert von Mensdorff-Pouilly-Dietrichstein (1861–1945), Austro–Hungarian diplomat, Ambassador to London 1904–1914 and an anglophile; his grandfather had married Queen Victoria's aunt, Sophie of Saxe-Coburg-Saalfeld, and he was thus a second cousin to King Edward VII.

356 RA GV/PRIV/AA23/59, King Edward VII to Prince of Wales, 1904: 2 May

357 Tschumi, p 84

358 Edwin Austin Abbey (1852–1911), American muralist, illustrator and painter, commissioned to paint the official Coronation picture in 1902.

359 Helen Porter Mitchell (1861–1931), known as Nellie Melba, later Dame, famous Australian operatic soprano

360 Enrico Caruso (1873–1921), acclaimed Italian operatic tenor

361 Charles Gilibert (1866–1910), French operatic baritone

362 The King was at Kiel from 23–30 June

363 Franz von Vecsey/Ferenc Vecsey (1893–1935), Hungarian child prodigy/violinist and composer

364 Florizel von Reuter (1890–1985), American-German child prodigy/violinist and composer

365 William Booth (1829–1912), a Methodist preacher who, with his wife Catherine, founded the Salvation Army and became its first General (1878–1912); it was a Christian humanitarian organisation which spread worldwide and continued into the 21st century

366 Tsesarevitch Alexis Nicholaievitch (1904–18)

367 RA GV/PRIV/AA23/60, King Edward VII to Prince of Wales, 1904: 17 August

368 RA GV/PRIV/AA23/61, King Edward VII to Prince of Wales, 1904: 25 August

369 RA GV/PRIV/AA32/49, Queen Alexandra to Prince of Wales, 1904: 20 August

370 At 9 Grosvenor Gardens

371 Prince George of Greece

372 RA GV/PRIV/AA33/1, Queen Alexandra to Prince of Wales, 1904: 30 September

373 RA QM/PRIV/CC/23/12, Princess of Wales to Dowager Grand Duchess of Mecklenburg-Strelitz, 1904: 9 October

[374] RA GV/PRIV/AA33/1, Queen Alexandra to Prince of Wales, 1904: 30 September

[375] King Carlos and Queen Amélie

[376] Clara Butt (1872–1936), later Dame, famous contralto singer, m Robert Henry Kennerley Rumford (1870–1957), baritone singer

[377] Ponnambalam Arunachalam, (1853–1924), Ceylon Tamil civil servant and member of Ceylon's Executive Council and Legislative Council; his wife was Svarnambal, daughter of Namasivayam

[378] RA QM/PRIV/CC42/62, Queen Alexandra to Princess of Wales, 1904: 28 November

[379] RA QM/PRIV/CC24/15, Princess of Wales to Dowager Grand Duchess of Mecklenburg-Strelitz, 1904:4 December

[380] Seat of Earl and Countess Cadogan, then the 5th Earl and his first wife

Chapter 12

1905–1909

"I think we all learn to be Diplomats from experience"

❦

Despite bad weather and influenza at Chatsworth in January 1905, the King was happy playing bridge, but the house was too warm and he was worried about Victoria.[1] Alexandra was enjoying dancing, especially with Admiral Fisher,[2] who had drunk too much champagne, and she also motored to Welbeck and Rufford Abbeys.[3] The Windsor court included a shooting party and the mausoleum service and on the 23rd the King unveiled a Household Brigade memorial at Holy Trinity Church to South African War casualties. The royal couple toured the castle precincts and called at Henry III Tower.[4]

They returned to Buckingham Palace with Victoria and Maud on the 30th and the next day Sir Frederick Treves, with Laking, operated on Victoria for appendicitis. Laking told the King "that Treves never operated better. There were no complications but the appendix was very long and inflamed – so that it was high time it was done". The King sat with Victoria for much of the day;[5] Alexandra, haunted by memories of his 1902 operation, felt overwhelming "gratitude to God that all is well over." Victoria "took the chloroform very well & held mine & Laking's hands, while Nurse Fletcher[6] supported her head – as soon as she was quite off we wheeled her into the next room, where Treves awaited her & the table & everything was prepared, & Miss McCaul[7] & a third nurse were assisting, then I had to let go her hand and shut the door, and my darling Child vanished before my eyes!! and I felt utterly miserable & crushed. Here I waited in the next room, from 5 minutes past 10, till a quarter to 11 when Laking kindly peeped in to tell me, 'operation over, Treves is now stitching it up!!' at 11 Treves himself came out, to tell me all was well over & she bore it well & never moved." Even so, it had been "like some dreadful nightmare" for Victoria, who had wanted to die, but feared this was wrong "as there is One who always knows best, & perhaps has more work for me to do yet! Everyone has been so touchingly kind in every way & that does help one to 'buck up' once more."[8]

Scarcely had Victoria begun to recover than Maud also went under the surgeon's knife. On 7 February Treves carefully performed an excruciating operation on a nasal abscess. Alexandra was "so sorry, poor child; in consequence <u>all</u> the Nurses & Doctors are neglecting my poor Toria, as they all love cutting one about & revelling in one's blood. Come tomorrow & hear all about it."[9] The patients convalesced under her watchful eye and she managed a quick visit to Sandringham on 11/12 March. Victoria was well enough to attend morning service in the private chapel[10] on the 12th. Alexandra had written sympathetically to Lady Curzon about a recent illness and was still thinking about India; "If only it could be managed that the King wld take me out to that beautiful Country which all my life I have <u>so</u> longed to see." She had been terribly anxious about Victoria and longed to see her fit and well, which she badly needed, but trusted now she was "on the real road to perfect & restored health".[11]

An official visit to Portugal was imminent but by 16 March King Edward had a bad cold, with bronchitis. The next day, attended by a doctor, he received Señor Manuel Garcia (100),[12] making him CVO. Alexandra, with Victoria, the Charleses, their son, the suite, (including Lord Farquhar, who had been ill), Treves and Nurse Fletcher, both keeping an eye on Victoria, were already on board *Victoria and Albert*. Gales delayed them and, had the King recovered, he could have joined them at Portland, where they still were on the 17th. As it was, the Queen had to conduct the four-day visit without him. Arriving at Lisbon on the 22nd they drove to the Necessidades Palace, with a large state banquet in the Ajuda Palace later. Alexandra drove in procession round the new park and through the town the next day, with a gala opera performance of *Manon Lescaut* later; on the 24th it was *La Bohême*. They visited Cintra, to Alexandra's delight,[13] and lunched with the Dowager Queen Maria Pia.[14] Alexandra found the visit "charming altho' rather alarming for me <u>alone</u> in State, but both Amélie and Carlos made it quite easy."[15] As usual, she was being modest; the event had been a great success – and she had accomplished it "alone"; something even Queen Victoria had never done. M de Bunsen[16] told Lord Knollys that the visit, intended to be in semi-state but treated much more officially, had been "a most remarkable event". He had never seen anything like Alexandra's exceptionally enthusiastic reception; by contrast, "the spontaneous outburst is conspicuously absent" during William II's current visit.[17] *Victoria and Albert* left for Cadiz on the 25th and they called on the Comtesse de Paris twice; "My visit to Villa Maurique near Seville was delightful and dear Granny Isabel pleased to have us in her own home, where she leads the life of <u>Buffalo Bill</u>[18] – her youngest son Ferdinand[19] and daughter Louise[20] were with her."[21]

At Gibraltar on the 28th they drove through the town in state, had tea with the Governor,[22] and began three delightful and interesting days. "I rode right up to the top of the rock & inside the Galleries & visited the Docks & Ships, among others the 'King Edward VII' and the 'Drake'. Louis and Drino[23] were very flourishing, I saw them every day. Sir G White & all the officers dined here twice & some of them with their wives & daughters lunched." On the battleship, *King*

Edward VII, Alexandra sent her husband a wireless telegraph message; "I am on board the ship named after you and send you my fondest love."[24] She rode on donkeys to all the sights and drove through a tunnel to see the stalactite cave. Leaving on the 31st, they saw the Duchess of Aosta at Genoa on the 3rd; on the 4th "Little Minny"[25] joined them for four days. The yacht docked at Marseilles on the 5th and the King arrived on the 7th. Despite sacrificing her Danish visit for her father's birthday, Alexandra was "very glad to be on board to welcome dear Papa ... who I am sorry to say I [thought] looking very <u>unwell</u> <u>still</u> & dreadfully <u>pulled</u> <u>down</u>, & pale & worn, [but] he is <u>much</u> better <u>today</u> after an excellent night on board & looks better already. I do hope the quiet on the sea will soon set him up again." Always solicitous about illness, she was usually optimistic. Little Minny, who had not seen her uncle for six years, was shocked at his changed appearance. The King noted; "though Toria is still thin, she is in excellent spirits about herself."[26]

The cruise so far had been very successful despite windy weather and Alexandra "never felt better."[27] The King stayed for three weeks, telling George; "we are having delightful weather, quite like summer & it has of course entirely taken away my cold & cough wh at home would have been impossible. We had a first rate passage fr Marseilles ... to Port Mahon. The Balearic Islands are very pretty & we took a drive in Motor Cars here over considerable heights in very twisty roads but lovely scenery. All the people are particularly kind & civil, & when the first curiosity is over, leave one in peace."[28] After a rough passage, they arrived at Algiers on the 16th in the rain; "a striking town but more European than African in appearance."[29] On the 17th they visited a mosque and an exhibition of native work and drove 60 miles to Blidah, where Turkos, Zouaves and Arabs gave a military display. At Bougie, they travelled on the 21st to a small Arab village, Kerrata, "where some Chiefs & a lot of men on horseback[30] recd us. I never saw more beautiful [or] wilder scenery, & I never saw a road better engineered." Leaving on the 22nd for Philippeville, they travelled the next day to Constantine, a fortification on a steep hill, captured by the French in 1837. On the 24th they saw gardens, the museum and a Roman mosaic, before leaving for Alghero in Sardinia, "a quiet little place but we took a long drive and walk." On the 26th they reached Ajaccio in Corsica; "such a pretty place. We went to see the house where Napoleon was born & spent his youth. It belongs to Empress Eugénie & is in a fair state of repair." King Edward was looking forward to going home the next day but Queen Alexandra had other ideas; "It is a great undertaking Mama going the whole way to the Piraeus but she is certainly not in any hurry to get home, so I had to put the 'Courts' as late as possible."[31] At Marseilles he was still marvelling; "Mama & Sisters leave tomorrow afternoon (after coaling) – direct for the Piraeus. A frightfully long sea voyage but ladies never seem to understand distances!"[32]

Alexandra and her party arrived at Athens on 2 May for an eventful week;

Lady Egerton's[33] art school on the 4th, Tatoï the next day and the Te Deum in the cathedral on the 6th. After a service in the English church on the 7th there was a gymnastics display and prize-giving at the stadium. Alexandra attended the Greek theatre on the 8th but the next day went with Queen Olga and Nurse Fletcher to a hospital of which Olga was patron, and saw "a most terrible operation performed on a poor Woman. It was most interesting & wonderfully well & quickly done by a Greek Surgeon of great skill. The poor patient however died three days after." In Malta on the 11th, they visited the palace, cathedral and governor's house and beautiful garden at San Anton. After touring the British ships there, they left on the 14th for Oran, where on the 16th they saw an Arab "Fantasia" for the Feast of Ramadan. At Gibraltar the next day it was the soldiers' hospital; at Algeciras on the 19th it was the Almorainia Convent, the Cork Woods and a military tattoo. Back in Gibraltar for garrison races on the 20th, they set off for Arosa Bay. Alexandra and others went ashore but, while driving, a hurricane blew up; "we positively saw nothing of the country as the dust was so intense – we struggled with our hats & had to tie handkerchiefs over our faces." They returned by train but the sea was so rough the yacht had to wait a mile and a half offshore, and the wind was so strong they could hardly walk along the pier. The nearby *HMS Aboukir* supplied a picket boat, safer than a small launch, and somehow they reached *Victoria and Albert*, where "the whole crew & poor Victoria were anxiously watching our arrival & were wondering how we shd get on board without the boat being dashed to pieces against the ship – they poured gallons of oil on the sea, & luckily a big wave carried us high, when we four ladies leapt out & were saved, while the poor gentlemen were inundated by oil."[34] Alexandra was agile but she was wearing a tailored full-length costume, with a hat; she was lame and 60 years old. It was a close call. They could not leave Arosa Bay till the 24th but the Bay of Biscay luckily was smooth and they finally got home on 27 May. She had enjoyed the cruise, but Alexandra's main feeling was "all is well that ends well." [35]

Waiting for her was a new little friend who might have agreed. Alexandra had always owned dogs; as Probyn put it, "No human being was ever fonder of a dog than our Queen Alexandra is."[36] She liked "all Dogs – Dogs of any breed or description. Her Majesty thinks more however of a Dog's nature and education, than of strict 'show beauty.'"[37] She was good at controlling dogs; perhaps they responded to her low voice and fearlessness. Japanese *Chin*[38] were favourites, so the Empress of Japan[39] decided to offer some as a present. Two pairs of yellow and brown, and two pairs of black and white dogs, with Japanese flower-shaped collars,[40] were chosen and left from Yokahama on 1 April on the North German Lloyd mail steamer, *Prinz Heinrich*, attended by Mr A Yamashita. Eight dogs was a generous gift, but Viscount Hayashi[41] had warned that they were very delicate, "but I hope some of them will arrive safely".[42] They were due on about 19 May and Alexandra, in eager anticipation, sent instructions about their care until her return. Customs would allow them through, apart from checking them for rabies, but alas, when the ship docked, only one had survived. The Queen telegraphed from Gibraltar, "Dreadfully disappointed but so glad one was saved."[43] Her large signed photograph was sent to the Empress and Mr Yamashita received a decorative pin.

One of the kitchen staff's duties was to provide food for the Queen's dogs, including milk for the Borzois, which a footman collected twice a day. The Japanese dogs sometimes tried to follow Alexandra when she visited the kitchens but were sternly checked, lest the staff gave them titbits. Most of the servants privately considered them a dreadful nuisance; they had to have the best food and two of Alexandra's footmen had to groom them every day. Soon after she acquired her Japanese dogs, the staff were told that a night tray should be prepared for her every evening and sent up to her rooms at about 9pm. This was done for about eight years; a cup of soup, some cold chicken, quail or cutlet, and a plate of sandwiches. No-one else asked for this; dinner finished well after 9pm and supper was available, but the tray was usually returned empty next morning. They never found out whether Alexandra enjoyed a nightly snack but strongly suspected it was eaten by her little dogs, which slept in her room.[44]

Charles, Maud and their son went home on 31 May, and the season began as usual. King Alfonso XIII of Spain[45] was in London and a large banquet was held in the Picture Gallery at Buckingham Palace on 6 June. On the 8th Alfonso attended a review at Aldershot, and later, an opera gala at Covent Garden with the royal couple, and was shown over Windsor Castle and grounds the next day. The court moved to Windsor for Margaret of Connaught's wedding to Gustaf Adolf of Sweden[46] on the 15th in St George's Chapel, with large dinners in the Waterloo Gallery on the 13th and the 14th and the wedding banquet in St George's Hall. On the last day of Ascot week there was a cricket match in the home park between David's and Bertie's teams. The next day the royal party travelled by electric launch to Monkey Island, for tea. On 10 July they saw Puccini's new opera, *Madama Butterfly* at Covent Garden, which the King thought "very pretty music, with charming (Japanese) mise en scène & well sung."[47] The next day a double wedding took place in the private chapel at Buckingham Palace.[48]

From 12–14 July the royal couple stayed at Knowsley,[49] opening the new Sheffield University buildings, presenting new colours to the 2nd Battalion, the King's Own Yorkshire Light Infantry, and unveiling a monument to Yorkshire regimental casualties of the South African War. Later, they saw the big guns at Messrs Vickers & Sons' munitions works. On the 13th they opened a new dock at the Manchester ship canal, drove through Salford's Peel Park and unveiled the war memorial, presenting colours to the King's Own Royal Lancaster Regiment the next day before leaving. Alexandra opened the Homes for Officers' Widows and Daughters at Queen Alexandra's court, Wimbledon, on the 15th and finally wrote to George on the 12th; "Thank God all is well over & darling May has her 5th son!!! though I fear it is a disappointment to you, as you wanted a little girl so much, which wld also have been so nice for dear little Mary, but never mind, you will have one next time!! Many thanks for yr dear letter telling me all about it, & how quick it all was & how well she is now in every way & baby 'Johnnie'[50] a beauty & strong & healthy. Yr dear 2nd letter received yesterday also gave me great pleasure, & telling me all about the various names you wish to give the baby. I think they are charming & told Victoria to ask you to let Uncle Hans be one of the Godfathers as his name is John and he wld be so flattered & pleased." Alexandra feared she could not attend the christening at Sandringham, but "I am dying to run down for a day or two to see you all & the new baby! I am trying hard to arrange it, but I am worked very hard now as you will see by the papers, and I had a tremendous meeting here yesterday for our Red Cross, when I had to read out my address – which frightened me to death, which you will understand, & I felt ready to sink under the table, but thank God it all ended well, & they were very kind about it." The visits had gone off well "but the heat was tremendous & I must say I was rather tired on coming home."[51]

She managed two days at Sandringham, then the couple went to Goodwood, before Cowes on 5 August. On the 9th there was a review of the English and French fleets, apropos the "Entente Cordiale". On the 12th they returned to London; the King left for Marienbad on the 14th and the Queen, Princess and party for just over three weeks at Balmoral, seeing May, her children and the Fifes and visiting Loch Muick, Mar Lodge and the local area. On 7 September Alexandra and Victoria left for Denmark, finding King Christian (87) very well and still very active; "He & all the others went the other day to the annual feast at the Skydeban – we were all invited too but declined the honour. I really thought it was too much of the good to begin at 9!! in the morning with a public function, speeches etc."[52] She was delighted to see Minny, thankful for peace between Russia and Japan. Alexandra rather supported Japan, a small nation fighting a big one and felt they had come off worst in the peace settlement, despite winning. Minny probably knew this, but was still looking much better than last year.

Alexandra was taking a great interest in Norway, now independent from Sweden. Charles of Denmark had been invited to be King and negotiations were taking place. Alexandra had explained the situation to Francis Knollys; "how things were here & all facts about Norway, & how impossible it wld have been for Charles to have acted differently in his position here, & that it wld have led to war between the three countries at once! It was very strained between the Swedes & Norway last week, & they very nearly came to blows. Even we here in Denmark knew very little about it, but when I asked Daisy[53] to pay me a visit she answered 'under the present circumstances we cannot leave the country'!!! Very likely he expected to go with his regiment. I hope however now things are getting better, & that I shall see them before long." She was enjoying her Danish visit and sympathised with George for having "lost his 'May' who has fled to London town to look at her gown!! What a bore & nuisance, but I cannot understand why she shld have gone so soon! as the dresses for India cannot take quite such a long time to do!! & try on either. Anyhow I am too sorry for you, as it must be dull & lonely for you in dear old Abergeldie without her. Thank God you kept the Children, as they will cheer you up."[54] They left Denmark on 13 October and the King joined them in London from Scotland, where he had gone after Marienbad. On the 16th the couple laid the foundation stone of "King Edward's Building", the new General Post Office, on the site of Christ's Hospital.[55] They saw Hall Caine's *The Prodigal Son* later and *On the Quiet* at the Comedy on the 17th. The next day they opened Kingsway and Aldwych, the LCC's construction on the "Holborn to Strand improvement" and later saw *The White Chrysanthemum* at the Criterion. The Waleses were going to India to complete the 1901 Empire tour; taking leave on the 19th, Alexandra's feelings were mixed; "Those dreadful partings always seem to take a bit out of one's life, & it is doubly hard when it is for so long a time – nearly 8 months & so far away! but let us hope at least for us here at home, that time will pass quicker than we now anticipate. At any rate I am quite sure that you two will enjoy every moment of your beautiful & interesting visiting in India! which I do envy you dreadfully & never shall cease regretting having been left behind when Papa went alone! I shall never forget nor forgive it." All the children were upset at their parents' departure "& David said he cried a lot, '& so did Mama when she kissed the baby first. She began & then she cld not stop & cried quite loud!'"[56]

Alexandra and Victoria were still in London on the 26th, as Victoria had a cold and lost her voice. The King was away but Alexandra had had a lot to do "so in one way I was rather glad to be left here. One night I went to the Opera to see Mme Butterfly & the Composer Puccini[57] came to see me here. I also went to several Picture Galleries & saw lots of people." Norwegian matters had stalled but Maud had told her "Charles had to make a spontaneous speech the other day at Papa's[58] Privy Council before all the Ministers, when he stated in a very manly & clear way the conditions he made before accepting the Norwegian Crown. He is right to ask for the people's vote besides the Storthing, & I think it will be appreciated in Norway." Russian news was alarming; railway strikes had cut off St Petersburg and Moscow. Minny, still in Denmark, was frantic because she could not get home and all her family were in different parts of Russia. "It is too awful & how & where will it end? God help them all."[59]

Alexandra and Victoria went to Sandringham on 28 October and saw the children at York Cottage; "all 6 looking the picture of health & baby so fat & plump, very like Algy.[60] I visited them all in their snug little rooms & washed 4 of them! Mary is very proud of her room – quite by herself next to Mademoiselle." Their attendants, Mr Hansell,[61] M Hua and Mademoiselle Dussau[62] were really excellent, "always bright & cheery & make the children perfectly happy." Charlotte Bill (Lalla) was a treasure and Elsa also was an excellent nurse. In Russia, "all over the country they are rising en masse! And though at the last moment poor Nicky has been forced into giving a Constitution, & de Witte has been made Premier ... only the near future will show if it was not too late."[63] She told George; "I went to a very interesting lecture at the Cottage, given by a Colonel Patterson[64] who made the Railway through Uganda – the children were most delighted at all his thrilling stories of his attacks by lions & tigers of which he shot any number." She assured him; "we take the greatest care of [the children]. And you may be sure that I interfere in nothing & everything goes on as you & May settled. At present being alone here I have seen them every day, & have been reading to them all in the evening – one dear old book, 'Froggy & its brother Benny', which you all used to like so much when I read it to you! – actually on the same spot where we sat then, & all of these children painting pictures too, just as you all did. I always fancy it must still be all of you 5 sitting round me. When I look up it is hard to realise that these are my Grandchildren." Victoria was improving but not recovered and Alexandra regretted not having another week's peace, as guests were coming the next day and they had to go to Windsor on the 13th for the state visit, although this time it was Uncle Willy with Prince and Princess Nicholas. Russian affairs were now critical; she feared the constitution might have come too late.[65] The King was more forthright; "I much fear it has come too late – but we must hope for the best. Meanwhile strikes continue in all the great Towns. They have got completely out of hand & alas! blood is flowing freely on all sides. Poor Nicky has much to answer for. His weakness & indecision is the sole cause of the terrible state of confusion & lawlessness ... which his Country has got into!"[66]

King Edward enjoyed his birthday but it was slightly marred for Alexandra. "Papa was very well & seemed quite happy surrounded by all his particular friends!! & he got loads of some really beautiful presents." The three elder grandchildren recited "their La Fontaine fables to perfection, without a mistake! & David was overheard telling M Hua 'c'etait un grand succès'!! Then we had an enormous shoot to which I believe the whole of Norfolk came in motors etc to witness the last stand! where they got a 1,000 birds in half an hour even without you!!! ... Mensdorff made a very pretty & touching speech at dinner when proposing Papa's health & we finished up the evening with some very successful theatricals." She continued, meaningfully, "We have the house full of all kinds of people. Young Lord Brooke[67] I must say a very nice & good looking young man, so like his Father[68] luckily ... Old Jane,[69] & Mme K[70] – who had a tommy ache & was sick all night long, which was mighty sad!!!" Alexandra begged George not to overdo things in India; "I fear all the speeches & emotions you will have to go through, in the heat, too, will make you quite thin. All I pray is that you take care of yr self occasionally and not overtire yourself; think of poor darling Eddy! – he never got right again after India!" Charles and Maud expected to be called to Norway on about 20 November. She was in despair at the fearful accounts from Russia, "Poor unfortunate Nicky & poor Aunt Minny, so far away from all her children!" Louise, as the King's eldest daughter, had been created Princess Royal, "which is right & follows History!" Her daughters, Ladies Alexandra and Maud Duff, would become Princesses of Fife. "I do hope it will induce her to let them come out a little more! We are going to try to make them come for Xmas! as a beginning!!!"[71] On the 13th the court moved to Windsor for the Greek state visit; "They had a beautiful reception everywhere & he is delighted with it all; the streets here were charmingly decorated." Ever since their arrival "we have lived in constant excitement ... every night theatre or concert & shooting & sightseeing all day." On the 16th the shooting party bagged about 1,000, mostly rabbits, but the rabbits had their revenge; "Unfortunately Papa had a nasty accident by putting his foot in a rabbit hole, which made him fall forward on his gun, which he broke in two – mercifully it did not go off or he might have killed himself & others, but he broke the tendon at the back of his ankle; it was most painful at first but now does not hurt but has to be bound up tightly like a broken leg, but he hopes to walk about with a stick. He certainly is unlucky with his legs!"[72]

Alexandra had been unwell and it was cold, raw & foggy at Windsor. Thankfully, the Norwegian question was almost settled. She had started "The Queen's Unemployed Fund", "as nobody seemed to stir in the matter & things were getting worse & worse every day; thousands were starving. I am thankful to say we have already got over £24,000 in three or four days." She appealed publicly on 13 November for "all charitably disposed people in the Empire, both men and women, to assist me in alleviating the suffering of the poor starving unemployed this winter" and headed the list with £2,000; the King and other royalties also contributed. *The Queen's Carol*, an anthology by British authors, artists and composers, was published in aid of the fund by the *Daily Mail*. The court returned to London on the 20th, Alexandra very tired after entertaining her brother and seeing a great many people. They went to Sandringham on the 24th; "Thank God Papa's leg is getting all right, but instead of staying here quietly, he went to Castle Rising, & shot out of a small carriage. Toria is much better now thank God tho' I am always afraid of her catching another cold." Importantly, "our darling Harry & Charles have actually started for their new Kingdom in Norway, where they are due tomorrow!! Beloved Apapa made a most touching & beautiful speech both to the Norwegian Deputation & to Charles & Maud! Everybody present was in tears. I am glad I was not present on account of that & at the sad leave-taking!! Otherwise I am so sorry not to have been present at this Historical incident."[73] Charles was now King Haakon VII and their son was Crown Prince Olaf, adopting old Norwegian names.

Alexandra received her birthday presents – "which are very pretty & virtually the whole of Fabergé's shop!"[74] The grandchildren recited French fables to her, despite colds. King Edward's leg was improving but would still take about six weeks to mend. "From Norway we hear [excellent] accounts, their entry & reception was grand & they & baby Olaf received with open arms everywhere … they made a very good impression & so far performed their duties well."[75] The Queen and Victoria went to stay at Welbeck[76] on 11 December; the King joined them the next day. Alexandra was still envious about India; "What a lovely & delightful time you are having in that most beautiful & fairy-like Country – the one wish of my heart to see! I am glad you sometimes think of old me & how I wld have enjoyed it all! Ah, if only I could go once before I die or before I am too old to enjoy it all thoroughly." They would leave for London shortly "to do our dreadful Xmas choosing & shopping. I only hope the fogs won't make everything impossible for one or keep me there; these fogs are very bad for Papa, who nearly chokes, it frightens me dreadfully I must say!"[77] After shooting and motoring they left on the 16th and the King became much "brighter again himself, which makes, as you know, all the difference to me".[78] Triumphantly she told Holland that she had attacked the new War Minister, Haldane,[79] about providing better quarters for the military nurses, which Arnold-Forster and Brodrick had refused to do. Now; "I have made a coup d'état, & taken the bull by the horns at once, by seeing Mr Haldane today." Telling him about the problem, she offered to send Holland to explain. Haldane had been very nice "& had evidently heard something about it already, & seemed quite anxious to be of use to us, & will be quite ready to see you tomorrow (Monday)." Nothing like perseverance and striking the iron while hot, she added. The nurses finally got good accommodation everywhere.[80]

Alexandra was very busy preparing for Christmas; "I have only really had from Monday to do it all in, so I have worked like a slave all day long & half the night too. Today [the 22nd] Toria & I go back to S at 6 o'clock & dine in the train & we shall go to bed at once when we get back & hope to have a good rest so as to begin again tomorrow, when I have to arrange the tables & every [room] in the house."[81] Surprisingly, "dear Nicky & Alicky sent us Xmas presents in spite of all, by a messenger, & I also had a Xmas card from poor dear Ella from Moscow,[82] so I do hope things are much exaggerated in our English papers. Poor dear Aunt Minny is still at Copenhagen & I hope dear Apapa will not let her go – it really wld be madness!" "Harry, Charles & little Hamlet, now Olaf" seemed happily settled in Norway, which augured well for the future.[83]

The Indian Christmas presents "were much admired by all & the children showed them off in great glee." Even baby John "looked at the Xmas tree with large open eyes, staring & smiling at everything." Little George had been delighted with a musical carriage Alexandra gave him, and sat or drove about all evening in it. There were electric boats, trains and a magic lantern for the older boys, "as David had informed me he did not wish for baby toys on his table as it

12 Christmas tree and present tables at Sandringham, published in December 1905
in The Woman's Home Companion, p 9; private collection

looked so childish before all the other people & he was already nearly 12 so did not wish to have any!! So I was very much amused & cld not help chaffing him when the <u>first thing</u> <u>he did</u> & does every evening was to tear round the rooms with a <u>long train</u> belonging to his younger brothers! So I cld not help saying 'Oh I am glad to see you <u>are</u> not too old yet or above playing with other people's toys!!' he was obliged to laugh himself." At the servants' ball "there were some very funny dresses & get ups, particularly some of the men dressed up as women." They were going to Chatsworth for New Year, although Alexandra would rather have stayed quietly at Sandringham.[84] Chatsworth was now a regular engagement for Mrs Keppel too.

⚜

They left on 1 January 1906, after church. Most guests, (including the Fifes, "but alas! still without the Children") had gone; Soveral was coming to Chatsworth. The King was annoyed at having to go "as a cripple … !" still wearing an iron splint after accidentally wrenching another tendon.[85] A torchlight procession and an enormous house party greeted them, with shooting, motor drives and private theatricals to come. On the 8th the King left for London; Alexandra and Victoria for Sandringham. Sadly, on the 4th, Temple[86] had been injured in a cart accident and died on the 8th, to the Queen's distress; "I cannot tell you how sorry I am about it as I have known him for <u>43</u> years ever since I came." She had called on her way back from the station and, although frail, he had seemed quite cheerful. She, Victoria and everyone on the estate attended the funeral and he was buried in Sandringham churchyard.

Alexandra was fascinated by the Waleses' Indian letters and yearned after "that <u>Marble</u> Taj" which must surpass "everything human & heavenly!! Oh how I wish I cld have been there too & seen the moon shining on it." The children were well, "sweet Harry (my Bobsy) always in good spirits & as funny as ever", baby John with "a beautiful colour like a red apple". George had come out in a rash, but was having treatment. Mary loved her riding "and goes very well. She is much fonder of it than the boys, but so it was <u>here</u> just the same formerly, my girls liked it – & Eddy & Georgie were frightened."[87] Alexandra was pleased they had seen the Munshi[88] at Agra "as he wrote most <u>enthusiastically</u> about yr visit to his own Country & that he had seen both you and May once more in his life … poor man, I am so glad." Norwegian news was excellent; "The success … at Christiania is little <u>Olaf</u> (my little Hamlet)[89] who took them all by <u>storm</u> – he liked the saluting & firing of guns & cheers of the crowd, to which he waved his little hand & a Norwegian flag which they had given him as they landed. Harry also says that <u>now</u> she likes the keen invigorating air – it is much colder & dryer now which suits her, but they feel the cold out of doors terribly on their hands & feet." King Edward was slowly improving and very busy, with a new ministry and elections.[90]

On 13 January he returned to Sandringham with more guests, more shooting and hunting, in which Victoria, David and Bertie took part; Alexandra only rarely rode now. After paying visits round the estate, they joined the King at Windsor on the 20th. Alexandra was glad May had seen "my little friend the Rani of Partabhghar & that she remembered me. I saw her several times in London & gave her places at Westminster Abbey for the Coronation & thought her so pretty & nice."[91] She had told George about "that charming Lady Warwick"[92] standing on a wagon in the street, addressing her "comrades", the labourers and "then taking off her glove to shake & feel their horny hands! What a come down for that Kingly Lady!!! Mr Greville[93] & the family are furious." Russian news was better and Norwegian news good. She had been "so touched by yr kind telegram on beloved Eddy's sad 14th – it came while I was sitting doing my hair in my dressing room; it was like a voice from far off & gladdened my sad heart, as that day must ever remain the saddest of my life!"[94]

The mausoleum service was held on the 22nd and there were many guests during the week. Alexandra was a happy grandmother; "Thank God we have yr darling children in the house, which makes all the difference to us all, & they are so good, cheery & very obedient & I scold them all round, if they don't do what Granny says at once, & point out to them 'What will Papa & Mama say when they come home; they will scold Granny & say I spoilt you' – which has a great effect upon them at once."[95] They played games with the children in the corridor and sometimes in St George's Hall "they play charades & we have to guess the words & occasionally they invite Granny to act too." They had taken "Mary & little Harry out for a motor drive with which they were delighted."[96] On the 29th the couple and Victoria motored to Claremont, to see Helen Albany and the Alexanders of Teck, with a new baby.[97] During lunch, Alexandra began feeling faint and unwell and Helen exclaimed "Oh, you look so bad, that motor drive did you no good". She gradually recovered "but somehow could not cast off that dreadful feeling of oppression & melancholy which came over me suddenly! Well, on our return at 4.30 I found a dreadful telegram from Aunt Minny, which I confess frightened me very much, tho' I tried not to think the worst. It said 'darling Apapa has suddenly been taken ill with pain on his chest but he is resting now in bed I will telegraph again. God grant he will be better.' Then Toria came in & I showed her this & said 'oh I hope it was only what I had at lunch & I am sure we both must have had a kind of indigestion,' then we had to go to tea where Lady de Grey & Juliet were waiting for us. Then Papa suddenly sent for Toria, which frightened me again! & when she came back I thought she looked pale & upset, so I said 'Oh tell me at once, what is it', & she wld not answer before the others. So then I felt the worst was coming! & I only said 'Quick, have tea' but I nearly choked with fright & apprehension. She also said 'Papa wants to speak to you' – so after a minute trying still to put it off as long as possible, I went, but alas saw by his face what had happened & then he showed me that awful telegram of

Reuter's; 'King of Denmark died this afternoon 3.30'!" She had blamed her indisposition on Claremont's "dreadful <u>gloomy</u> dining room ... but darling <u>Apapa died</u> at <u>that</u> <u>moment</u> – by the time we made out! is it not curious ... I felt [ready] to collapse altogether & poor Papa was so kind & sympathising. We all left next day. He had to go to London, which I <u>ought by rights</u> to have done too, & then rushed home to poor Aunt Minny, but somehow I was so unhappy that I lost my head & let them settle things for me, so Papa & Toria thought I ought first to rest a few days at Sandringham, & so we went there but I cld <u>not rest</u> & came up the next day & left today the following day – that means this morning at 9.30. I was miserable at leaving dear Papa & Toria & yr blessed Children ... Papa wished to go but really I & the Doctors wld not let him, as his leg is <u>not</u> right yet, & he might catch cold on his chest, & also dear Toria I was afraid of taking as she might catch cold. So I am quite alone and <u>very sad</u>, but God will help me through it all."[98]

She reached Copenhagen on 3 February, missing her father's welcome terribly. Her sisters and Waldemar were there; her brother, now Frederick VIII, was kind but also desperately anxious about his daughter, Louise, Princess Frederick of Schaumburg-Lippe[99] who was critically ill and whom he could not visit, because of events. On the 4th a service was held in the big drawing room, full of flowers, where Christian IX lay in state, with his helmet, sword and spurs of the Life Guard Regiment resting on the coffin and "the Altar with crucifix & large silver candelabras at his head, with the old Standards by his side! It is all <u>beautiful,</u> <u>bright</u> & <u>holy</u> – but Oh <u>so sad</u>. Every morning we have short prayers by his side, but <u>how</u> we miss him no words can possibly describe." Many relatives had assembled; poor Uncle Hans, the last Glücksburg sibling, sad and worried about his future.[100] Alexandra was wishing desperately that one of her own family was there; perhaps Harry and Charles would be able to get away. She saw friends and acquaintances, including the actress, Fru Phister (90),[101] and went for drives; on the 8th she met her brother Willy at the station but developed a cold soon afterwards.

On 13 February Christian IX's body was taken to Christiansborg Church, which his three daughters visited daily until, on the 16th, the family accompanied the coffin to Roskilde. "It was a most <u>wonderful</u> sight to see how <u>deeply</u> & touchingly the people high & low, old & young showed their grief & sorrow & how they really mourned their beloved King."[102] The funeral was on the 18th, the German emperor had announced himself and Alexandra regretted her husband's absence even more intensely. "The Service itself was very holy & edifying but indescribably <u>sad</u> – all so simple & beautiful – just as he wld have liked. But oh, all these people around one & <u>we</u> all <u>convulsed</u> with grief! felt it doubly! hard! Of <u>course</u> I had to stand next to William!!! & Uncle Willy on my other side! ... I placed a large cross of flowers, from Papa, myself, all our Children & grandchildren in English colours on darling Apapa's bier, & another with my two sisters." Afterwards, they tried to come to terms with losing their parents and their old home, going again to pray at Roskilde, but "We are having very busy days too trying to arrange some of our beloved Parents' things & seeing about the things they left us, but it is all such sad work. And we are terribly disturbed by everybody coming in & out every moment of the day. We three sisters and three brothers have been working together & looking over everything. It is so horribly sad stirring up & touching their precious things." Uncle Hans had been reassured; he could still live in the same rooms and take his meals with his nephew, the new king. Frederick VIII and Queen Louise had both been kind and "it was nice meeting so many of the dear family & relations – Xenia I had not seen for 6 years, & dear little Minny[103] cheered us all up, nobody amuses me more than she does, & she is so sensible & sharp besides."[104]

Lord Esher commented; "the Queen of course feels the break-up of her Danish home, which she cared for much more than anything else."[105] The parting at Copenhagen had been a terrible wrench, and "all the poor Servants too came *en masse* to wish me good-bye as I left the dear old House & we all mingled our tears. I often wonder <u>how</u> one can live through it all! but God gives us strength at the time." Her loyalty to the past was actually helping her look to the future; the sisters had already discussed acquiring a Copenhagen property for themselves. Giving up Denmark was still unthinkable; if King Edward ever ventured to hope she would not need to go there quite so often now, he was going to be disappointed. However, he was much better and without the iron leg-support, although still walking with a stick. He was leaving for Biarritz on 2 March, which would do him good although Alexandra regretted his going so soon after her return. She and Victoria would stay quietly at Sandringham and join him in early April on the yacht at Marseilles for a cruise, perhaps meeting the Waleses at Athens or Corfu on their way back from India. They all needed a tonic and the trip would cover the time when she usually visited her father.

Until then, she needed to "<u>bury</u> myself for a little while, quite away from the world & its noise & bustle – one feels so out of place when all the world around one is jolly & happy." After many visitors, she and Victoria left on 7 March for three weeks of quiet country life. They spent evenings upstairs and after dinner Alexandra worked on her holiday album.[106] She enjoyed George's letter about a tiger hunt; "How I wish I could have been up that tree with you & seen it all." The children were well; "Dear David grown & such [a] sturdy, manly looking little fellow, & little Mary also grown a good deal, & sweet Bertie, my particular friend, looking strong & well, the three babies too – the youngest enormous, on <u>fat Gustaf's</u> lines – I can hardly carry him, & wonder how Charlotte[107] can do it all day long, she ought to have a prize for it. You say I am no exception in spoiling my grandchildren, & I say you are <u>no</u> exception in being impertinent to yr Mother! which I consider much worse." As for her own parents; "I am truly miserable when I sit still & think it all over. Darling Apapa & Amama both were

<u>so</u> much to us, & now that they both have been taken from us life can never be the same again."[108] Influenza had prevented Queen Maud from attending the funeral, although King Haakon had done so. Victoria Eugénie of Battenberg was engaged to the King of Spain; "they certainly seem very much in love with each other but what do you [think] of her being able to change her Religion so quickly & without a pang! Here, people are furious & we are getting endless letters about it!! The Archbishop[109] was very much against it & very indignant!! but Papa said he had nothing to do with it as she was not born an English P[rince]ss."[110] While Alexandra wrote again, "the dear Children are singing at the Piano where you all did the same in old days – do you remember? It is terrible to think how quickly time flies, & soon yr children will be grown up too & you will be the old ones then – they are so good & nice, only David dear must <u>not</u> get <u>grand</u>, he is a tiny bit inclined that way & gets a little important when <u>reporting</u> about his younger brothers; that must not be encouraged." They had had a good magic lantern lecture one evening, with Sydney Holland's twin brother Arthur[111] talking about India and the Waleses' tour.[112] She was still immersed in Nursing Board matters; in exchange for agreeing to supply better housing for the nurses, Haldane wanted the Matron of St Bartholomew's Hospital[113] elected to the board, which Holland strongly opposed, but after a "very civil but decided letter" from Haldane, Alexandra felt they should put a good face on it. Surely the lady would do her best and if by any chance they found she was talking about the meetings outside, it would not be tolerated. As she told Holland on another occasion, "I think we all learn to be Diplomats from experience."[114]

She planned to give "little Bobsy" a small birthday table for his 6th birthday before she and Victoria went to London; it would be a day early "but otherwise he wld have no fun at all. He is so sweet & always such an amusing little fellow, full of funny ideas, with a twinkle in his eye when he comes out with them." The head keeper, Charles Jackson, had recently married Mrs Elizabeth Butler;[115] both were of mature years but had now returned from their honeymoon, "looking supremely happy, he a little shy but she as proud as a peacock! Quite the <u>Duchess</u> as they call her here!"[116] Alexandra and Victoria returned to London where, on 3 April, they met the King and went on board *Victoria and Albert*. "Little Minny", staying at Cannes, joined them for a few days. Strong winds kept the yacht in harbour at Marseilles for several days, so they motored to Roynefavour to see the old Roman aqueduct and have coffee in Restaurant Arquère's garden, but sad news intervened; Frederick VIII's daughter Louise had died. They motored to Notre Dame de la Garde on the 5th and, with the King, again on the 7th. Landing at Messina two days later, they went to Taormina, for lunch at Hotel San Dominica, and to see the site of the ancient Greek amphitheatre. Arriving at Corfu on the 11th, they welcomed the Waleses, back from India on board *Renown*. King George also arrived and the English party drove round the town, and visited each other's yachts. The next day, Maundy

Thursday, they lunched at Mon Repos and drove to Villa Achilleon, dining on *Renown* later. For the next two days Alexandra watched torpedo drill on board Hedworth Lambton's[117] ship, *Leviathan*, and *Implacable*. Leonard Tyrwhitt[118] gave Holy Communion on board *Renown* on Easter Sunday and afterwards took a service on *Victoria and Albert*. They had tea at Mon Repos later. On the 16th the yacht, followed by *Renown*, left for the Piraeus; there was a great reception at Athens, and the King, Queen and Princess Victoria drove to the palace, where they stayed.

Alexandra visited the School of Art Needlework on 18 April and they drove next day to the new stadium and later to Phalerum. Their hosts took them to the museum, Acropolis and Temple of Theseus and the next day, Tatoï. On the 22nd King George opened the Olympic Games at the stadium, before 60,000 people, and the royal party attended over the next two days. On the 24th Alexandra also visited the Greek technical school. The next day they landed at Katakolo, travelled to Olympia and visited the museum. Passing Messina and Stromboli, the yacht arrived at Naples on the 27th after a rough night passage. They motored to see villages wrecked by lava from Mount Vesuvius, and had tea at Capo di Monte with the Aostas, as also on the 29th. On the 28th they visited Pompeii and lunched with Lord Rosebery at Posilippo the next day. On the 30th they went up Mount Vesuvius by electric railway for most of the way past the observatory, and saw the director,[119] who had remained there alone all through the eruption. King Edward later left for Paris[120] and London, while Alexandra and Victoria stayed on the yacht.

At Naples on 1 May, they visited the museum and took a long motor drive. The next day it was Rome, for sightseeing and shopping with Lady Egerton. Via Naples on the 4th, they left for Leghorn, motoring to Pisa to see the Leaning Tower, cathedral and baptistery on the 6th. There was more shopping and sightseeing at Florence on the 7th and at Venice on the 8th, staying overnight at the Grand Hotel after gondola trips; the next day they went with Lady Layard[121] to six "antiquity shops". On the 10th they saw Leghorn again, passed Menorca and Majorca, landed at Malaga and visited the cathedral and the town on the 12th; the next day they went by train to Granada, to see the Alhambra and Palace Gardens. They left Malaga on the 14th for Gibraltar and more sightseeing, then on the 15th went in a destroyer, *Angler*, to Algeciras, riding on donkeys to see a waterfall. On the 16th they toured the ships, *Edward VII* and *Victorious* and, after lunch, drove in "Spider" carriages on the sea shore, for tea at Pablo Larios's[122] house. They left on the 17th for Lisbon, spent the day at Cintra and invited King Carlos, Queen Amélie, their sons[123] and the Dowager Queen Maria Pia to tea on board. Back in England on 22 May, Alexandra called on Beatrice and her daughter on the 23rd and the next day the King and Queen saw them off for Spain at Victoria Station. The 25th was Helena's 60th birthday and they lunched with the Christians at Schomberg House. On the 26th they opened the "Hearts of

Oak" Benefit Society's new offices in Euston Road, while the Waleses left for the Spanish wedding. The King and Queen received Fridtjof Nansen,[124] the Norwegian minister, on the 28th and also Professor and Mrs Edvard Grieg,[125] who played and sang. A Danish deputation announced Frederick VIII's accession; the next day there was a dinner for the Norwegian envoys, when a choir, the Wiener Männergesang Verein, sang in the ballroom. Alexandra received Lady Emily Kingscote, who resigned as woman of the bedchamber,[126] on 30 May. On 1 June Victoria Eugénie of Battenberg married Alfonso XIII of Spain, but as they returned from the ceremony, a bomb killed 25 people and wounded over 100 others. The bridal pair were shaken but unhurt and King Edward considered it a miraculous escape "but I own I think very gloomily of the future, & he will have to be very careful, if he values his life & that of his Wife."[127]

Alexandra had received Landgrave Aleck and also a Polish boy pianist, Miecio Horszowski,[128] who played for her, on 1 June, when the second court was held, but deep mourning for her father kept her from most of the season's events. At Windsor there were official functions, inspections and presentations, and a reception of Japanese naval officers on the 7th. Alexandra drove with General and Mrs Haig to London to see Victoria (who had shingles), but returned later to Windsor until the 11th. The next day, Alexandra went to see Messrs Waring's furniture exhibition;[129] Julie d'Hautpoul and Soveral later came to tea in the garden. On the 13th the King and Queen opened a sanatorium for consumption and diseases of the chest, at Midhurst; Alexandra visited the Fine Art Gallery on the 14th and the next day the Waleses and Soveral came to tea. George and May were going to Norway on the 16th for the coronation, with Victoria and their nine-year-old daughter Mary, while Edward and Alexandra went to Sandringham, where Louise and her daughters arrived on the 18th for a week. The King left for Ascot but Alexandra took her daughter and granddaughters for tea on the beach at Heacham, and to the convalescent home and Appleton. On 22 June, King Haakon and Queen Maud were crowned at Trondhjem. Victoria thought it wonderful that her sister was a queen; "She does it all so well & it is nice to see how they all adore her already."[130]

Alexandra returned to London on the 28th for the third court, visited the Arts and Crafts exhibition at Alexandra House on 1 July, went driving and saw friends. On the 5th she attended the rose show at the botanical gardens but later met the returned Norwegian party at Charing Cross. On the 6th the Spartas and their children arrived and there was also a children's afternoon garden party.[131] The royal couple left for Newcastle on the 10th, opened the new High Level Bridge and drove to stay at Alnwick Castle;[132] miners clog-danced as entertainment. The next day they opened Armstrong College, inspected the electrical engineering laboratory in Newcastle and later opened the Royal Victoria Infirmary, viewing the buildings and unveiling a statue of Queen

Victoria. After lunch at the Assembly Rooms with the Mayor, they returned to Alnwick, where the Duke drove them round the park to see the ruins of Hulm and Alnwick Abbeys. They were home next day for the fourth court on 13 July, and on the 14[133] Monsieur de Saint-Saëns[133] and Herr Hollman[134] played for the Queen. She visited the Austrian Exhibition at Earl's Court with Victoria and the Spartas on the 17th, lunching with Count Albert Mensdorff, the ambassador. The next day she received the Rani of Kapurthala. Driving and visiting as usual, Alexandra also gave three sittings to Mr Wade.[135] On the 24th there was a society wedding.[136] The next day the Rhymney Male Choir sang in the ballroom at Buckingham Palace and there was also an inspection of the soon disbanding 3rd Battalion Scots Guards in the gardens. Later, the Queen received the Lord Mayor,[137] John Burns,[138] Mr Cohen and Mr J Danvers Power,[139] with a final report of the "Unemployed Fund"; by 9 July, £153,635/4s/0d had been collected and distributed between various institutions, which then gave money to those in need. The Church Army and Salvation Army each received £1,000 and the rest went to central bodies and distress committees empowered under the Unemployed Workmen Act.

The couple visited the Royal Academy's Summer Exhibition's private view and the Queen received the Maharani of Cooch Behar on the 29th. On the 30th Alexandra and Victoria went to Sandringham, Constantine[140] arrived the next day and they motored to Holkham and to Melton Constable. Alexandra and Victoria joined the King on the yacht at Cowes on 4 August and saw the Spanish sovereigns, who were visiting the island. After a week of sailing and social events, the King and Queen returned to London on the 13th; the King left for Marienbad the next day. Alexandra paid calls, entertained friends and went shopping with Louise Gosford on the 15th. She and Victoria, on *Victoria and Albert* left for Norway on the 19th and, after a rough passage, reached Christiania on the 21st and were welcomed by the Norwegian Royal Family, with lunch at the King's country house, Bygdö Kongsgaard. In the next few days they explored the area, steamed up the fjörds and round the islands, took a beautiful drive along the coast and travelled up the mountain to Holmenkollen, with lunch at Voksenkollen at the top. Alexandra received the officers of English armed cruisers then in Norwegian waters on the 25th; they lunched on board *Euryalus* on the 27th, where King Haakon hoisted his flag as an English Admiral. There was also a three-hour drive, a tour of the palace, a cinematograph show, more drives and a visit to the art museum to see the Regalia and the ancient Viking ship. Alexandra and Victoria left for Denmark on 5 September and at Copenhagen lunched on *Polar Star*, which had brought Minny and her son, Michael. On the 7th, "Amama's" birthday, everyone went to Roskilde, except Minny, who had lumbago. Alexandra usually had meals with her sister on *Polar Star* but called briefly at Bernstorff and Charlottenlund. On 10 September she drove to the Villa Hvidöre, the sisters' new Danish home, and took her suite to see it on the 12th. The next day she went shopping but was "quite in despair; since darling 'Minny Minny's' arrival here on the 6th she has been laid up with a most horrible attack of lumbago, which made her suffer <u>tortures</u> and kept me by her <u>bedside</u> most of the time I have been here, so that I have hardly been on shore at all or seen much of the rest of the family, who are all in the country. It really is too hard on her, poor dear Minny, with all her many <u>heavy</u> sorrows & trials, to come here, only to be laid up & kept a prisoner here all the very short time we have here together, and to make things worse, dear Aunt Thyra has caught a bad cold & is in bed at Bernstorff the last three days, so she also is cut off from us two here." She had just called on relatives in the country, "and <u>twice</u> I have been to <u>my</u> & <u>Minny's</u> <u>charming</u> place near the sea, Hvidöre, which I & all who see it are perfectly delighted with. It really is going to be <u>lovely</u> both <u>in</u> & <u>outside</u>, & the view over the sea is splendid. I am quite excited about it all, and now poor Minny cannot even <u>see</u> it with me, but at present I have arranged it all & chosen everything by myself, but I hope she will like it all when she sees it; the grounds & garden too are so well laid out." It was a pretty white house with a garden, not large but pretty and well-kept; all the family and her English friends liked it.[141] This new project was giving her something positive to enjoy in the future.

Louise had had an acutely painful abscess. "I fear she has really been <u>seriously</u> ill and suffered <u>tortures</u> ... I am glad you saw her and that <u>excellent</u> MacDuff, & <u>best</u> <u>husband</u> <u>in the world</u>!! How he must have suffered too & what constant anxiety for him!! how <u>too sad</u>." Another patient was, ironically, Sir Francis Laking, "our dear & valued friend & <u>invaluable</u> <u>Doctor</u>", who had had severe gastric pains. Alexandra had to finish her letter quickly, as "Aunt Minny is calling & furious at my writing so much."[142] Minny was well enough to visit Bernstorff and later, Hvidöre, towards the end of Alexandra's visit; the Queen herself went there twice more and also visited an old friend, Miss Rosen, and received Petersen the sculptor.[143] She and Victoria returned to London on the 21st, leaving on the 25th for Balmoral. On the 27th the King and Queen opened and inspected new buildings at Marischal College, Aberdeen, and had lunch with the Lord Provost.[144] After ten days of shooting parties at Balmoral the King left for London on 8 October but Alexandra remained, visiting and going for excursions. On the 17th she and Victoria went to Sandringham, for her usual occupations and also fishing. After briefly visiting London, when they drove in Victoria's new motor car and Alexandra received the Spanish, Japanese and Italian ambassadors, the King, Queen and Princess returned to Sandringham and on the 5th opened King Edward VII Grammar School's new buildings at King's Lynn. The King knighted Mr WJ Lancaster,[145] who had built and endowed it and Alexandra unveiled the King's statue in the courtyard.

Shooting was postponed several times because of poor weather, but on the King's birthday, Frederick Harrison's[146] Haymarket Theatre Company performed *The Man from Blankney's*. On the 12th the King, Queen and Princess went to Windsor for the Norwegian state visit, with shooting, driving, two banquets in St George's Hall and the first Chapter of the Order of the Garter for 51 years, in the Throne Room on the 13th, when King Haakon was invested. The Norwegians had lunch at the Guildhall on the 14th and Lewis Waller's[147] Company performed *Robin Hood* in the Waterloo Gallery on the 16th. The court returned to London on the 19th and later Alexandra and Victoria went to the Symphony Society's concert at the Queen's Hall. On the 20th Alexandra received Colin Campbell, of the Church Army, and a Roumanian lady, Madame Balabou. She had more visitors the next day, shopped with her daughters, and later, Lady Antrim, and on the 22nd attended an opera (*La Bohême*), for the first time since her father's death. She and Victoria returned to Sandringham the next day, while the Norwegians (staying in England till 14 December) went to Appleton. Alexandra went out riding on the 29th and there were visits, meals at Appleton and the schoolchildren's tea party on her birthday; in the evening Herr Joachim and others played Lieberslieder and a Brahms quintet in the ballroom. Shooting parties continued, despite the weather. Back in London on the 12th, Alexandra went twice to the Queen's Hall to hear the pianists, Miss Struckmann, and Tovey,[148] and also visited Louise several times. On the 20th she and Victoria joined the King at Sandringham for Christmas; there were guests and "thought reading" by Mr and Mrs Zanzig,[149] as well as sledging through the heavy snow that had fallen.

On 1 January 1907 it was Chatsworth as usual. As it snowed heavily on the 2nd, the King did not shoot, although Alexandra motored to Haddon Hall. She joined the shooters after lunch next day and on the 4th there were theatricals in aid of local good causes. Lunching at Rangemore,[150] they celebrated Twelfth Night at Chatsworth with singing and dancing round the tree. On the 7th the King left for London and the Queen for Sandringham, where they met again on the 14th to remember Eddy's death fifteen years earlier. The court moved to Windsor for the mausoleum service on the 22nd and a large turnover of guests continued till the 28th, when there was a shooting lunch at Cumberland Lodge. The court returned to London; there were theatre visits and on 1 February Alexandra received Nansen.[151]

On the 2nd Victoria left for Norway and her parents for Paris, where they saw President and Madame Fallières[152] several times, although it was a cultural foray rather than a state visit. It included several plays; a tour of Versailles by the Director, M de Nolhac;[153] visiting the studios of Aimé Morot,[154] d'Epinay[155] and Détaille and also seeing Camille Groult's[156] collection and Samson's "Reproductions de Vieux Sèvres".[157] Alexandra went round the shops, "thought everything very cheap, and bought up half the town." Lord Esher thought she excelled at the 'receptions' and made the most favourable impression possible. "The Parisians had never seen anything like her. Of course the Faubourg St Germain was in ecstacies and mocked poor Mme Fallières, dressed in plum-coloured velvet, who trotted and waddled alternately behind her."[158] Returning home on the 9th, the passage in *Invicta* was "fair", according to Charlotte Knollys, but the Queen considered it "nasty!"[159] Parliament opened in state on the 12th; meanwhile there were plays (including *The Stronger Sex* and some French plays), Wagner operas and Gilbert and Sullivan operettas. The King sat to[160] Cope on the 13th, watched by Alexandra. On the 17th there was a dinner party in the Music Room; later there were two courts and the Queen received a number of people, including, on the 22nd, Vilhelm Herold.[161] The couple opened the South African Products exhibition on 23 February, and the next day saw paintings of the Arctic by the Russian painter, Borisoff,[162] at the Grafton Galleries. Alexandra sat to Mrs Massey[163] for her miniature on the 26th and drove with the King to open the new buildings of the "Old Bailey"[164] the next day.

On 4 March King Edward left for Biarritz, where Mrs Keppel was also staying, while Alexandra remained in London and saw Ernest Rowe's[165] pictures of "old world gardens" at the Dowdeswell Galleries in Bond Street; later hearing the Blackpool Glee Singers at the Queen's Hall. On the 6th she visited the Jubilee Nurses' Institute and the next day, to her delight, Minny arrived for ten strenuous days, including six theatre evenings. By day they saw Alexandra House, the London Hospital, St Paul's Cathedral, Windsor, the National Gallery, the National Portrait Gallery, the Wallace Collection, Hatfield House, the Tate Gallery, the Tower of London, and a jumping competition at the Agricultural Hall. They also called on friends and acquaintances. King Edward wrote; "A Minny's visit seems a great success & how happy Mama must be with her. They are indefatigably sight-seeing – by day & night. A Minny will have found Windsor much changed since she was here last." Meanwhile the weather at Biarritz was poor and his motor car had caught fire; luckily he had two with him. His cough was better and he was out walking and motoring a great deal, as well as dutifully keeping early hours and being careful with his diet. Women's suffrage demonstrations in England were becoming more strident and he suspected that, eventually, they would succeed. Meanwhile, "Thank Heaven those dreadful women have not yet been enfranchised. It would have been far more dignified if the PM had not spoken on the Bill – or backed it up – but he appears to wish to stand well with everyone!"[166]

Minny loved Windsor: the magnificent castle, her sister's beautiful, cosy rooms and the spring flowers, which were all out. She was thoroughly enjoying her visit and felt "a different person, and twenty years younger!"[167] On the 18th; "Mama & Aunt Minny having exhausted the sights of London have betaken themselves to the calm of Sandringham wh I am sure is good for them both."[168] Victoria returned from Norway on the 20th and sightseeing resumed on 1 April; the South Kensington and Natural History Museums, the Institute of Painters in Watercolours, Westminster Abbey, Borisoff's exhibition, and four theatre evenings. On 4 April there was a cinematograph performance in the Green Drawing Room; the Queen saw her dentist[169] and received Treves and Colonel Gildea. The next day, the three ladies left; Minny for Biarritz, Alexandra (as Duchess of Lancaster) and Victoria for Toulon, where they arrived at 7.30am and met the King on board *Victoria and Albert*, for a Mediterranean cruise, which, mainly for health reasons, had become a regular occurrence. Victoria unfortunately had caught cold on the journey and had completely lost her voice by the 7th. The yacht arrived at Cartagena on the 8th, where Alfonso XIII and his mother, Dowager Queen Maria Cristina, welcomed them. They visited each other's yachts and all left on the 10th. Victoria had heard on the 9th that "Maddie" (Mrs Johnson) had died. This was a great shock "as she was quite excellent & a great loss to Toria in every way!"[170]

At Minorca on the 11th, they had a picnic on the sea shore, and arrived at Malta on the 13th for four days, including a garden party (where it poured with rain the whole time), reviewing 4,500 Blue Jackets and Marines, and lunching on Louis of Battenberg's flagship, *Venerable,* on the 15th. They dined on board *HMS Queen*, where a young officer, CA Parker[171] was curious to see them. Because of the ship's name, they had a nightly custom of drinking the health of "The King and Queen" rather than just "The King". When Alexandra arrived, the first thing she said was "This is <u>my</u> ship." Parker and everyone else were much impressed with them both. "I of course have never seen either before. He is not so stout as I had imagined & was wonderfully well as far as appearances go – cheery, hearty & robust-looking. She I had always imagined from hearsay and from her photos etc to be a rather reserved & cold sort of person, but she was anything but that – she hardly stopped talking the whole evening & had any amount to say to everyone that came along. One of our fellows keeps a couple of marmosets – she heard of this & made him produce them, & so up they came. She simply screamed with delight at seeing them & when they jumped about & hid in some palms & things on the deck the hubbub was terrific." Alexandra looked wonderfully young, no older than her daughter. Parker also mentioned; "we have a tiny wee midshipman on board, who, though possessing the face of an angel, has many of the attributes of the proverbial trooper." When the Queen spotted him, "he was hailed forth & made much of". The other midshipmen "were praying that she would kiss him, but she spared him that." She then had to meet all the ladies and have "a long quack with each – the way she succeeded in this was wonderful." The King meanwhile was enjoying playing bridge below deck.[172]

On 16 April the King reviewed over 6,000 soldiers on the Marsa before visiting the Naval Hospital. They dined at Government House and saw *La Bohême,* and the next day lunched with the King of Italy on his yacht at Gaëta. They drove through Naples on the 19th, visited the museum and entertained Hélène d'Aosta, Olga and George William of Cumberland[173] to lunch on board. The King, Queen and others motored to Sorrento on the 20th, while Victoria had lunch at Capo di Monte. On the 21st, they motored to the Campo di Marte for a *Concours Hippique.*[174] The next day the royal couple shopped and visited the Churches of San Francesco di Paolo and Santa Chiara and also Galleria Vittoria. They went to the palace and saw *L'Amico Fritz* at San Carlo Theatre. At Palermo from 24–26 April they visited churches, palaces, gardens and a football match, a museum, the catacombs of the Cappucine monks, botanical gardens, Sidney Churchill's[175] private house and collection of antique jewellery. The yacht returned to Naples later on the 26th; the next day they visited Capo di Monte again and also saw the Hereditary Prince and Princess of Hohenlohe-Langenburg and Sir Thomas Lipton, who were staying nearby. Alexandra stayed on board the next day as it was raining but her Cumberland niece and nephew came to tea. They shopped and drove on the 29th.

On 30 April the King left for England via Paris. The Queen shopped again and the next day went to Capri with Hélène and saw an extinct volcano called "La Solferata". After tea at Capo di Monte, the yacht left Naples, passed the erupting Stromboli and steamed along all the next day to Corfu, for two days of visiting the King's palace, Mon Repos, One Gun Battery, and receiving local officials. Arriving at the Piraeus at midday on the 7th, they met the Greek Royal Family and continued to Athens. On the 12th, Alexandra gave prizes for some of the Olympic Games in the stadium. They heard on the 10th that the Spanish queen had had a son,[176] after a lot of unwelcome press speculation; "And so at last, after more than a month's waiting, Ena has got a son & heir born today. Well, I am delighted & the Spaniards will be pleased, after all the anxiety & waiting for so long! Poor girl, I pity her with all this publicity about it all, & she still so young – I think it disgusting & positively indecent!" Alexandra's relatives' health was mixed; King George was very well but Queen Olga had hurt her knee and was in a wheel chair. Prince George was so worried about Crete he had lost weight "& his face has got to be like Uncle Willy's – so odd as he was not like him before." The Spartas and their children were all well and so was Prince Nicholas, although his wife, recovering from heart failure, was white and frail. Prince and Princess Andrew and daughters were all flourishing. "Dear fat Christo is still the same & studies hard." It was very hot "now but everything very backward, hardly any trees out yet, & the lovely orange trees all cut down on account of the frost." Alexandra spared a thought for David, nearly thirteen, starting at the Royal Naval College at Osborne. "I remember so well when you & dear Eddy left us to join the Britannia. I was in despair, & you both miserable. It is indeed a terrible wrench ... Poor darling little David & quite by himself too. You & dear Eddy were at least together the first few years ... One good thing is he is not so far away yet, so that you <u>could</u> go & see him occasionally."[177]

They left Athens on the 16th and called at Corfu. A thunderous and squally gale forced the yacht to put into Messina on the 19th but they left next day, despite a great swell and a strong north wind, anchored overnight in Pozzuole Bay and arrived at Naples later on the 21st; the Aostas called on the 22nd. Because of the weather, Alexandra decided to return home overland, much to Victoria's disappointment; "I was in despair as I always love the ship best."[178] They left the yacht and travelled 24 hours to Rome, for the Villa Doria gallery and gardens, driving in the Pincio, visiting St Peter's and meeting the Dowager Duchess of Saxe-Coburg-Gotha[179] and her daughter, Beatrice.[180] On the 23rd it was driving, sightseeing and shopping in Florence. Leaving by special train on the 25th, they arrived in Paris on the 26th for three nights at the Hotel Bristol, paying calls, shopping, and eating at cafés. The King met them at Victoria Station on 29 May.

On 1 June *The Illustrated London News* reported that, at the HAIA's exhibition at the Albert Hall, the Sandringham technical school showed a set of Chippendale-style cane-seated satinwood chairs, made to the Queen's order for Hvidöre. The backs were decorated with inlaid darker wood and hand-painting. Alexandra's chairs had her cypher, two crossed "A"s, surrounded by wreaths of roses and groups of lilies of the valley and violets, surmounted by the imperial crown. Similar chairs, decorated with a little purple Russian flower, were made for the Dowager Empress's rooms.[181] Meanwhile the season began and the royal couple started attending operas by Wagner, Verdi, Puccini and others, as well as a levee, courts, the Military Tournament at Olympia, concerts and art galleries showing work by Walter Crane,[182] Philip de Laszlo[183] and Corlandi. Alexandra visited the South Kensington Museum on the 6th. Two days later the Danish sovereigns[184] arrived on a state visit, until the 13th, with a banquet in the Picture Gallery and a concert by Melba, Caruso and Gilibert. They saw Windsor, and then attended a banquet at the Mansion House on the 10th, when King Frederick received the Freedom of the City. On the 11th it was a horse show at Olympia, and a gala opera performance, but, as it began, Major-General Sir Arthur Ellis collapsed and died from heart failure. The royal party were not told until the opera was over.[185] Ellis, a friend and talented artist, had been in the King's household for many years. Despite this tragedy, the programme had to go on; an enormous review of 21,250 troops at Aldershot on the 12th, and a state ball. On the 13th Alexandra opened the Mansion House Bazaar for the Crippled Children's Fund.

On 14 June, the King and Queen saw *The Merry Widow* at Daly's. The next day the King unveiled the Duke of Cambridge's statue outside the new War Office in Whitehall. Later, Alexandra received International Red Cross Society delegates. The couple inspected the Corps of Commissionaires in Buckingham Palace gardens on the 16th before leaving on the 17th for Ascot Races, which

King Edward attended every day. There were many guests, and on the 22nd a garden party for 8,500 in Windsor Castle's grounds; two days later the court returned to London for more seasonal events. The Queen, Princess Victoria and Prince and Princess Andrew of Greece visited the Ladies' Kennel Association's Show in Regent's Park on the 26th. The next day, Alexandra and Victoria were present when the King laid the foundation stone of the British Museum's extension. Later, all three dined at Crewe House with the Crewes,[186] whose daughter, Lady Cynthia Crewe-Milnes,[187] studying the piano at the Royal College of Music, had invited two fellow students, May (seventeen)[188] and Beatrice (fifteen)[189] Harrison,[190] to play the violin and cello in some trios with her as after-dinner entertainment. The King's official birthday was celebrated at Horse Guards on the 28th; Alexandra went to the Hippodrome in the afternoon. Later they inspected the Honourable Artillery Company, where the King distributed Long Service Medals. The next day he inspected the Yeomen of the Guard.

On 1 July the King and Queen opened the Union Jack Club for Soldiers and Sailors, in Waterloo Road. On following days, Alexandra visited the Fine Art Society's Gallery, the Danish Exhibition at the Guildhall, the Rose Show at Regent's Park and polo at Ranelagh. Victoria had her birthday children's party on the 6th and the next day it was the Royal Academy's Summer Exhibition's private view. On the 8th the three embarked on the yacht at Holyhead, to lay the foundation stone of the University College of North Wales's new buildings at Bangor the next day. Lunching at the Bishop's Palace, they motored via Bethesda, Capel Carig, Llanberis, Caernarvon and the Menai Bridge to Baron Hill,[191] Beaumaris, for tea, walking in the grounds and planting trees. At Kingstown on the 10th, they saw the International Exhibition at Herbert Park, followed by a garden party at Viceregal Lodge and Leopardstown Races on the 11th. On the 12th the yacht left for Cardiff, and, on the 13th, steamed into the new Alexandra Dock; the ribbon was cut, the dock inaugurated and the Queen took a photograph of it. They toured the docks by rail and drove in procession to Cathays Park, received an address from the Lord Mayor outside City Hall and later opened King Edward VII Avenue. After lunch at Cardiff Castle,[192] they visited the ruined Caerphilly Castle before returning to London.

There were more calls, guests and theatres, as well as the second state ball. On the 18th Alexandra sat for a crayon drawing to Mademoiselle d'Epinay.[193] She and the King motored to Sandown on the 19th, for the "Eclipse Stakes". On the 20th they and Victoria went to Bowood[194] for two days; after motoring to Major Holford's house at Westonbirt, they were caught in a tremendous thunderstorm. On the 24th the couple visited the Royal Victoria Patriotic Asylum at Wandsworth; later, Alexandra opened a new wing of St Luke's Hostel for Clergy. On the 26th she received three officers commanding the regiment of Gurkhas, of which she was colonel, and later went with the King to open University College

Schools' new buildings at Frognal. There were more visits and operas; Alexandra saw Wade's[195] studio on the 30th and the next day received Flameng,[196] the French painter. On 1 August Mademoiselle Mercier[197] came to paint and Mademoiselle V Branica to sing; Alexandra also visited the Hospital for Incurable Children at Cheyne Walk. She sat to de Laszlo on the 2nd and on the 3rd she, her husband and daughter, on *Victoria and Albert*, inspected the Home Fleet at Portsmouth, passing down a treble line of ships to Cowes, with fireworks and illuminations later. The next day they visited the Royal Naval College at Osborne, the Convalescent Home and Barton Manor, where the Herveys[198] were staying, and had tea later with Princesses Beatrice and Helena at Osborne Cottage. They had also, on the 4th, gone on board the Swedish ship, *Oscar II* and the British Antarctic Exploration Expedition ship, *Nimrod*, which, under Ernest Shackleton, was leaving the next day for the South Pole. On the 5th, on board *HMS Dreadnought*, they steamed down the lines of the Home Fleet and watched target practice and exercises by the submarine flotilla. There was sailing in *Britannia* over the next few days, despite bad weather, and the Town Regatta, followed by fireworks, took place on the 9th. The court returned to London on the 12th, after the Fifes had lunched with the King and Queen; "[Louise] looks fairly well, & the others brown and healthy – though those girls were like mutes."[199]

The season had been exhausting; on 13 August King Edward left for Marienbad and his wife and daughter for Scotland. Alexandra immediately got a cold, but still motored to Mar Lodge on the 16th, and paid all her usual Balmoral visits. She was feeling sad and needing rest, but faced commitments in the near future. The Scottish visit was short and, writing to George, she regretted they now saw so little of each other; "It makes me quite sad to think of, as life is so short and the days go so fast and we are all getting on in age – and I am an old woman now – *au fond!!* Well we got here all right but I was not very well here & my neck and cough very troublesome. I cannot say that I feel much better now, but I have led a very quiet 10 days here, so ought to feel all right ... We have seen dear Louise most days & on the whole I think her looking better – she was quite happy & cheery with us & fished & played golf ... I am quite sorry to have had to say Goodbye again, & to have to tear myself away again from dear Scotland & this dear place but unfortunately my time is so limited & I have Harry to see first for a few days in Norway when I leave Toria with her while I must go to my new house in Denmark, which Aunt Minny & I will take possession of the first days in Sept."[200] She and Victoria boarded the yacht at Dundee on 23 August and, after a horrid passage, with a heavy swell, reached Christiania on the 25th, where the King and Queen met them. They apparently lived on the yacht during the visit, having meals either there, or at Bygdö, or on *Polar Star*, which brought Minny on the 30th. They visited places nearby, a "Kinomatograf" show and the theatre, for *Peer Gynt*, with music by Grieg, who died that morning, 4

September. Victoria remained with Maud when Alexandra and Minny left for Copenhagen and, on the 7th, Roskilde.

The sisters moved to Hvidöre on 9 September, while their suites remained at Amalienborg; when Alexandra came into town, she stayed on the yacht. On the 16th they heard Herold in *Bajadser (Pagliacci)* and saw the ballet, *Napoli*. They gave their first dinner party at Hvidöre on the 17th. There were visits and drives and then on the 23rd, Victoria arrived from Norway and came to stay at Hvidöre; other relatives also came to see it. They went to the opera, *Regimentals Datter*, with Herold singing, on 1 October. Writing at last to George, Alexandra gave him all the news; "I must say you are an excellent correspondent, which alas I am not." She was sorry Papa had caught a chill, with bronchitis, after returning from Marienbad; "he really is so very imprudent always! after all those hot baths & drinking waters he ought to be extra careful. I am sure he sat in a great draught or in the wet or something like it." But "now I must quickly tell you how <u>perfectly delighted</u> Aunt Minny & I are with this simply enchanting place! It <u>really</u> is quite <u>lovely</u> both <u>in</u> & <u>outside</u>, & so bright & cheery. Quite <u>plainly</u> furnished but lovely. Our bedrooms all <u>chintzy</u> & some silk in the drawingroom downstairs. <u>Inside</u> it has all the <u>comforts</u> & beauties of an English House & outside like an Italian Villa, with two charming verandahs & a small balcony in front of my bedroom, covered with flowers. How I wish you cld see it all. Our Maids have rooms exactly like their cabins on board the yacht, so nice & comfortable. And what pleases me most is that Victoria, who came from Norway last week, is as enchanted with it as we are, & loves her little room. She is so well here too, in this excellent bracing sea air … We keep our <u>English hours</u> too – dine at 8.30 and are quite independent. The rest of the family drops in occasionally & we give them excellent dinners & luncheons, which they enjoy immensely. We have each three servants & a Page between us, most of Apapa's dear old people who are all so pleased to be back. Our garden is also delightful, full of nice old fruit trees & masses of pears & apples, then we go through <u>our Tunnel</u> to our second garden full of flowers, which runs right down to the sea; here we sit basking ourselves in the sun. The weather has been <u>quite</u> perfect summer up till now. We do enjoy it all so, and the quiet & peace here has done us all good." They had all visited Roskilde, remembering "Amama & Apapa", but she felt that having "this <u>new</u> little place to ourselves here … makes all the difference."[201] She told Soveral it was "even better than your beautiful Cintra!!"[202] To her, Hvidöre was idyllic and the carved inscription over the fireplace in the billiard room, dated 1907, set the seal: 'Øst Vest, Hjemme Bedst'[203] echoing Sir William Armstrong's fireplace at Cragside in 1884.

Alexandra was much looking forward to seeing her nephew, George of Greece, before his marriage; "He writes that he is delighted now with his future wife & I am dying to hear what he says himself. I believe the marriage takes place at the end of October in Paris."[204] After the Tuborg Brewery, life boats, theatres and a Grieg concert, the Queen, her daughters and Olaf left on 24 October for London, via Flushing, and were met at Charing Cross on the 26th by the King, who thought his grandson "a dear, unspoilt little fellow."[205] On the 31st, Alexandra and Victoria went to Sandringham and Maud and her son to Appleton. The King and the first party of guests arrived on 2 November and the Spanish sovereigns on the 4th. King Edward celebrated his birthday with a dinner for 462 estate workmen; later there was a performance of *The Clandestine Marriage, French as He is Spoke* and *A Quiet Rubber*. On the 11th the court moved to Windsor to receive the German emperor and empress; a banquet in St George's Hall, a Welsh choir, other performances and, of course, shooting. Queen Maud, her son and the Fifes arrived and the next day, the Queen of Portugal, Duchess of Aosta, King and Queen of Spain, Grand Duke and Grand Duchess Vladimir of Russia, Infanta Isabella,[206] Princess Beatrice and Prince and Princess Johann of Saxony[207] came to lunch. It was an impressive muster of royalty. They all left on the 18th; King Edward stayed briefly at Ingestre, while Alexandra and Victoria went to Sandringham. He returned on the 25th to Castle Rising but moved to Sandringham on the 30th for the next shooting party. Guests came and went until 9 December, and on the 11th, the Queen, Victoria and the Norwegians left for London, visiting Maple's and Waring's, perhaps for Christmas presents. After more entertaining, they returned to Sandringham, where the King and guests joined them on the 23rd for Christmas.

Augusta had told May about "poor Marie",[208] who wanted a divorce; her husband, Count Jametel, had all the time been having an affair with "E" – Infanta Eulalie of Spain. Knowing Alexandra was on good terms with Eulalie, Augusta thought she should be more careful; "Alix is so innocent, she can't believe in such wickedness, therefore makes such sad mistakes."[209] Alexandra, however, was always loyal to people she liked and believed in fairness, even if she did not approve of their behaviour. She did not befriend "dubious" people out of naïvety; they often understood human nature and were far more amusing and endearing than the strictly moral. Without going out of her way to encounter Eulalie, she did see her again in 1913 and in 1922, when the Infanta called at Marlborough House.

❦

January 1908 was frosty and good for skating. Alexandra still had plenty to do but was trying to rest after Christmas and it was much better, and easier to have conversations, with fewer people about.[210] There was a better chance of her making sense of what was said. In larger groups, her responses were often anticipated and given by others, which annoyed her as, naturally, she wanted to speak for herself.[211]

King Edward returned on the 13[212]th from Elveden, with more guests for a week, and the Queen, with Victoria, drove, walked, paid calls and gave the schoolchildren at West Newton their Christmas presents. At Windsor, the mausoleum service was held on the 22nd but shooting was cancelled because of thick fog; Alexandra visited the dean,[213] and she and May called on Canon Dalton and the sub dean,[214] shopped in Windsor and motored to Taplow, Ascot and Great Fosters. The royal couple opened Parliament on the 29th and saw *Siegfried* at Covent Garden, in English, the next day. They were pleased the Wales family had been at Windsor, wrote Alexandra, especially as May was always "so dear & nice to me, & whenever I am not quite 'au fait' on account of my beastly ears, you always by a word or even a turn towards me make me understand, for which I am most grateful as nobody can know what I often have to go through."[215]

To Alexandra's distress, Nurse Fletcher, Victoria's nurse after her operation in 1905, got appendicitis herself. On the 31st, Alexandra's sister-in-law, Louise, brought a boy, Lionel Ovenden,[216] to play the piano and violin to her. The next day there was shocking news from Lisbon; the King and Queen, driving with their sons, had been fired at by an assassin, killing the King and Crown Prince. King Carlos was King Edward's distant cousin and Queen Amélie had been on friendly terms with the Wales family for years; like them, she had now lost her elder son. For the next few days Alexandra only felt able to drive with Victoria or walk in the palace garden. She sat to Flameng[217] on 5 February and again on the 11th and 24 March but the artist could not disguise her strained expression. Soveral, who had been at Lisbon, was distraught and called at Buckingham Palace several times. However, 6 February was Baba Knollys's twentieth birthday and Alexandra offered her the appointment of maid of honour, which she gladly accepted. On the 8th the royal couple attended a requiem mass for King Carlos and his son at St James's Church, Spanish Place; the next day there was a memorial service in St Paul's Cathedral, and court mourning for two weeks. King Edward stayed a week at the Fifes' house in Lewes Crescent, Brighton; Alexandra motored with May to Brighton for lunch with him on the 13th. On 14 February she drove with her grandson George. During this time she also visited the New Gallery, a women artists' exhibition in Suffolk Street and the Fine Art Society's Gallery. "Persimmon", the King's famous racehorse[218] had broken his pelvis and died on the 18th at Sandringham, where, on the 22nd a terrible blizzard blew down much of the lime avenue, doing enormous damage, which the King inspected on the 28th.

Alexandra meanwhile continued visiting art exhibitions and galleries, and driving. On 4 March Minny arrived for just over six weeks, spent mostly in London. According to Lord Esher, they were worrying about foreign affairs and were convinced that Germany "is effecting the pacific penetration of Denmark by getting millionaires to purchase estates across the border, gradually encroaching up on Denmark."[219] However, there were at least twelve plays and a number of dinner parties, two visits to the zoo and frequent drives and calls, once at Waring's on the 21st. Art visits included the Dowdeswell and Fine Art Society galleries, J Pierrepoint Morgan's[220] art collection, Martino's[221] studio and Abbey's[222] pictures at the South Kensington Museum. In the evening, Alexandra sometimes read aloud to her sister, "which I enjoy very much", wrote Minny.[223] They visited Agnes Keyser's Hospital, the military hospital at Millbank, the Medical College, and Alexandra Hospital for Children with Hip Disease in Queen's Square. Then it was the horse show at the Agricultural Hall, the United Service Institution, the Royal School of Art Needlework, the Royal Hospital at Chelsea, the Union Jack Club, a swimming display at the Bath Club, Kew Gardens, the British Museum, the Franco–British Exhibition buildings (not yet open) at Shepherd's Bush, and a society wedding. They heard Fauré[224] play his songs, which Miss Susan Metcalfe[225] sang, and the Société de Concerts d'Instruments Anciens played in the Music Room at Buckingham Palace. Alexandra also gave a children's party with conjurer for Bobsy's birthday on the 31st. Meanwhile Victoria stayed in Brighton for a week at the Sassoons' house.[226]

On 24 March the Duke of Devonshire died, and would be much missed, the King wrote; "as … a great personality with all classes, & most popular because he was such a straightforward & honest man & incapable of any mean act."[227] The Waleses had visited Cologne, Darmstadt and, later, Paris; from Darmstadt George told his mother he had got on fairly well speaking German at the military event at Cologne; they were now with the grand ducal pair and their little boy (sixteen months), who "is a little duck & walks about most independent".[228] In Paris they had visited the salon and studios, including Flameng's; "we saw your picture, he has greatly improved it since he brought it here & I think it is certainly a success & like."[229] The King was pleased that he and his son agreed about theatres in Paris; "All you say about French Theatres are entirely my views; the atmosphere is horrid, boxes uncomfortable, entr'actes endless, nowhere to smoke or conveniently relieve nature & the Plays either dull or very improper or coarse! This mania of undressing & scenes in bed – has been going on a long time."[230]

Alexandra, Victoria and Minny went to Sandringham on 11 April, visiting the King's horses at Egerton Lodge, Newmarket, en route.[231] Alexandra took Minny to see the boat-shaped "bungalow" on Snettisham Beach, which she had recently installed as a resting place when walking by the sea. On the 13th Lord Redesdale[232] and Major Holford advised her about restoring Sandringham's gale-damaged grounds. The two sisters returned to London on the 14th, to see the Waleses, back from Paris, and the King, back from Biarritz for official duties; Alexandra feared he would catch cold in the chilly English weather. She was feeling disgruntled; they were leaving for a Northern State Visit and she had hoped they could start on the 18th with Minny, who would then be going home, and spend Easter Saturday and Sunday in Paris before travelling north from there. The King preferred leaving from London on the 20th, so that he could visit Sandringham on the 18th, to inspect the gale-provoked alterations to the road leading to the house. So on 20 April, he, his wife and daughter left London for Copenhagen, arriving the next day for a four-day visit with a state banquet, gala opera, *Cavalleria Rusticana* and ballet, *Napoli,* an evening party at the King's Palace and a concluding dinner at the Christian VII Palace. On the 23rd Alexandra took her husband to see Hvidöre and, gratifyingly, he was "delighted with it. Really it is remarkably pretty & Waring[233] has done wonders in furnishing it, but I think the success is entirely owing to Mama's good taste, & I can well understand how 'the two Sisters' (who are so devoted to each other) must enjoy living there."[234] Charles Hardinge[235] told Lord Knollys that the visit had been an unqualified success. The King was well and in good spirits while the Queen was "naturally as happy as the day is long." She had taken them all to see her villa, "You would have laughed to see her running up and down the house showing us the attics, pantries, bath rooms &c. It is very prettily furnished and a regular dolls' house. I should not like it as there is no privacy at all but I fancy the Danish Royal Family rather like publicity."[236]

At Stockholm on the 26th, they went to a horse show, followed later by a state banquet. The next day, with King Gustav, they saw Ritterhalen Church, the Northern Museum, and had tea with the artist, Prince Eugène.[237] There was a gala opera performance of Verdi's *Otello* before they left for Norway, where King Haakon and Queen Maud met them at Christiania on the 28th. An official reception was followed by lunch at the palace, a carriage drive round the town and into the country, and a state dinner. On 29 April they saw the Oseberg and Viking ships, the Paintings and Sculptures Museum, lunched at the British Legation[238] and later drove to Bygdö, walking through a wood to Villa Victoria, by the sea. Later, the opera, *Mary Stuart in Scotland* was performed. The next day, they went to Holmenkollen and Voxenkollen, with a concert and a large reception at the palace later. They spent 1 May driving round the local area, with a dinner and ball at the palace afterwards. They left for Copenhagen by train on the 2nd, stopped for 15 minutes to greet the Royal Family, then continued their journey home, crossing the Channel in fog and arriving on the 4th.

The next day Alexandra and Victoria both had bad colds but started recovering within the week. The King and Queen saw a French play, *Robe Rouge* on the 11th and for the next three evenings (while he was at Chester for the races) Alexandra saw *La Traviata, Rigoletto* and *Götterdämmerung.* She also went round the Franco–British Exhibition at Shepherd's Bush on the 13th, the day before it opened. Edward Hughes had died, and Alexandra visited an exhibition of his work at the French Gallery on the 15th. Victoria spent the weekend at Barton Manor with the Waleses. The third court, on the 15th, lasted two hours, the longest so far in the reign. There were more operas and plays and on the 18th the royal couple motored to Aldershot to see field operations from "Caesar's Camp" and elsewhere. After Newmarket, they dined with the Dudleys at Carlton Gardens and saw some "classic dances" performed by Maud Allan,[239] the latest sensation. On the 22nd they watched the Royal Naval and Military Tournament at Olympia and the next day visited the Duke of York's Military School at Chelsea. President Fallières arrived on a state visit on the 25th; they received him at Buckingham Palace and there was a state banquet later. The next day it was the Franco–British Exhibition and a state ball. On the 27th the President went to the Guildhall, and to a gala opera performance at Covent Garden. He left on the 29th and Alexandra, curious about the arrangement of his rooms at York House, went to see them. Concerts, dinners and operas followed; the King presented colours to the 2nd Battalion, Grenadier Guards, and the Queen visited St Luke's Home for the Dying, at Bayswater. On 3 June, with Victoria, they attended the Derby at Epsom but the King's horse, "Perrier" failed to win. Louise, her daughters and Soveral came to lunch on the 4th and Alexandra heard the pianist, Adolphe Borchard.[240]

On 5 June, the royal couple and Victoria set off on *Victoria and Albert* for Reval in the Baltic, to meet the Russian sovereigns and their children. It was rough and stormy, with cold and showery weather, but the yacht arrived on the 9th, when Nicholas II came on board. The English party visited *Standard* and had lunch on *Polar Star*. The next day there was lunch on *Standard*, inspecting the King's new yacht, *Alexandra*, then tea with Minny on *Polar Star* and later a banquet for the Russians on *Victoria and Albert*. It was a pleasant family occasion, also marking the Russo–British friendly agreement, signed in 1907, but it was very brief; *Victoria and Albert* left Reval on 11 June, in a calm sea with an icy north wind, reaching London on the 14th. The court moved to Windsor for Ascot week on the 15th; as usual, Alexandra attended in state on two days, and otherwise motored and took a river trip in an electric launch, beyond Cliveden. On the 20th they gave a garden party for 6,000.

On 22 June the King laid the commemoration stone of the new King Edward VII Hospital and Dispensary, opposite Combermere Barracks in Windsor, later going with Alexandra to the International Horse Show at Olympia. The next day it was Hon John Ward's[241] wedding to the American Ambassador's daughter at the Chapel Royal. There were operas and plays in the evenings. Alexandra visited the Agnew and Dowdeswell Galleries and they both attended Madame Nellie Melba's[242] twentieth anniversary matinée concert at Covent Garden, raising money for the London Hospital. They also saw an exhibition of caricatures at the Fine Art Society's gallery and attended the Londesboroughs'[243] entertainment in aid of rebuilding Selby Abbey. Trooping the Colour was on the 26th. After a weekend at Wilton House,[244] the couple saw the Children's Happy Evenings Association's display at the Queen's Hall on the 29th. On the 30th the King was at Newmarket and Alexandra dined at Lady Gosford's party in the Garden Club at the Franco–British Exhibition. She saw the art students' exhibition at Alexandra House on 1 July and watched polo at Ranelagh on the 2nd. On the 3rd it was the Rose Show in Regent's Park and lunch at the Garden Club. On the 4th she and the King opened the Royal National Pension Fund for Nurses' new building on the Thames Embankment. After the Royal Academy private view on the 5th and a children's garden party on the 6th, the King, Queen and Princess left for Leeds the next day, opening the new university buildings and staying overnight at Harewood House.[245] They then went to *Victoria and Albert* at Avonmouth for an evening performance on deck by the British Madrigal Society. At Bristol the next day, they lunched at the art gallery with the Lord Mayor,[246] the King opened the new Royal Edward Dock and after dinner, the Bristol Harmonic Male Voice Choir sang. The next day they toured Badminton's house and stables and returned to London for the second and last state ball.

On 11 July the Queen took Sophie, Duchess of Sparta and her sister, Landgravine Frederick Charles of Hesse-Cassel (who both came to stay at Buckingham Palace) to the New Gallery in Regent Street. At 3 o'clock on the 13th the King and Queen drove in state to Shepherds Bush to open the Olympic Stadium at the Franco–British Exhibition and watch some of the Games. The Duchess of Wellington's[247] ball took place that evening. Alexandra sat three more times to Flamang; Soveral brought an Italian artist, Vittorio Corcos,[248] to see her on the 15th and she visited the Franco–British Exhibition again. On the 20th the royal couple received the prelates attending the Pan Anglican Congress at Lambeth Palace. Alexandra saw a number of people, dined on the 24th at the Pavilion at the Franco–British Exhibition, and then watched the finish of the marathon race, which had started at Windsor. The Italian runner, Dorando Pietri,[249] came first but had fallen several times and was helped over the finishing line, which disqualified him. The winner was the American runner, Hayes,[250] who came in second, but when Alexandra gave prizes the next day, they included a special gilt cup for Dorando. On the 27th the royal couple received a deputation from the International Peace Congress before leaving for Goodwood with Victoria. Pleasingly, the King's mare, "Princesse de Galles", won the Ham Stakes on the first day, but it was his only win that week. Alexandra attended the races but also motored to Arundel, for tea at the castle, and to Selsey, by the sea, and later to Bognor and Littlehampton, as Victoria did independently, perhaps in her own motor. She also went to Bisham and Chichester, seeing the cathedral, and St Mary's Hospital, with its almshouses for old ladies, which, on 1 August, she and her parents visited before crossing over to Cowes later. On the 2nd, Helena, Beatrice and her son Alexander (Drino), and David,[251] came to lunch; later the King, Queen and Victoria visited the Osborne Naval College and Convalescent Home, Barton Manor, the Swiss Cottage and Osborne Cottage, for tea with Beatrice. On the 3rd they went round the Island in *Alexandra* and that evening George returned from Canada in *HMS Indomitable*. They sailed on *Britannia*, cruised round the Island on *Indomitable* and visited *Agamemnon and Minotaur*. Crossing to Portland Harbour on the 7th, they steamed round the Channel Fleet; all the admirals and captains came to lunch and that evening there was the Town Regatta firework display. After leaving Cowes on the 8th, they visited the Haslar Royal Naval Hospital on the way back to London.

Alexandra motored in Richmond Park on 9 August; the next day, after the King had gone to Marienbad, she and Victoria left for Sandringham and on the 11th for Balmoral, arriving the next day. There were drives to Mar Lodge, Abergeldie Woods, Birkhall and the surrounding area, lunches and teas round the estate and, on the 21st, the Queen rode. They motored to Mar Lodge for her granddaughters' confirmation on the 22nd. Alexandra and Victoria left on the 24th for Norway, living on board the yacht but meeting Haakon and Maud frequently, driving and exploring the fjörds. Minny, with Xenia, her husband and three of their children, arrived in *Polar Star* on the 31st; later there was a performance of *Anne Pedersdotter* at the theatre. Next evening, Victoria went to a dance at Bygdö. It rained all day on 2 September, but Alexandra "assisted at a performance of the Kinomatograf."[252] Did she play a piano accompaniment? They had "a delightful fortnight in Norway & darling Harry, Charles & sweet Olaf were all looking well & happy. He really is such an excellent host & arranges everything so well, we were all very <u>dissipated</u> there, giving dances on board our various yachts & the girls danced five nights remaining ... At last they were really tired out & Maud collapsed the last day of our stay which was sad, as she had to stay in bed."[253] Victoria would remain with her a little longer. At Marienbad, the King had met Izvolsky[254] and Clémenceau[255] socially, but the German papers were suspicious. They were really too foolish, he complained, "always attributing intrigues on my part agst their Country, when I pay visits abroad or see men of note. Whatever faults I possess, intriguing is certainly not one of them. I only want peace & quiet amongst all Nations & to be left alone! but that is I fear asking too much fr the Press of any Country."[256]

On the 7th, the two yachts left for Copenhagen and for the next four weeks Alexandra, switching between *Victoria and Albert* and Hvidöre, visited all her relatives. "Beloved little Aunt Thyra, Ernest, their eldest son, such a dear & good looking boy, as well as their two daughters; <u>Marie Louise</u> with her two sweet fat babies, were here, but alas, I only spent their <u>last</u> week here with them, as he wished to hurry off for his vile shooting on the 16th. Little Alix Mecklenburg came for two nights to fetch them. She was looking so pretty & in such good spirits – luckily her <u>tiresome</u> husband did not come, he is such a prig & whenever he is present he makes her dull & silent – such a stuck up German fool. Even Uncle Ernest thinks so – while they all love Max of Baden. We remained on the yacht a few days longer at Copenhagen, as Thyra naturally wanted to see as much as possible of us all & we three sisters ran about shopping etc which was great fun & she liked dining on board so much. We also all went to the play together one night & heard Herold sing beautifully in 'Bajadser' & saw one of our favourite old Ballets called 'Fjerret fra Danmark'. Thyra's were all staying at Bernstorff with Waldemarias', where also Georgie[257] & his very nice & pretty wife Marie were stopping. She is quite simple & natural & pleasing with very pretty brown eyes & beautiful teeth ... looks a little like an Italian.[258] They seem very happy together but Georgie does not look well at all – still dreadfully thin & pulled down & has got so quiet, & still is very bitter poor boy! What a misfortune for him he ever was sent to Candia! and he will never get over the way the Consuls treated him the time of his departure from there!" Alexandra was sorry to hear of Augusta's grandson, Karl Borwin's sudden death, at under twenty.[259] Frederick VIII was worried about a financial scandal involving the Danish Justice Minister. Aunt Swan was "very flourishing but never, hardly, leaves her stuffy rooms; sits there surrounded by papers doing illumination painting." The others were pretty well and "We have given one big family dinner in our lovely abode before Aunt Thyra left."[260] Alexandra and Minny took up residence at Hvidöre on the 15th, although the Queen still sometimes stayed on the yacht; she was preparing a book of her snapshots, to be sold for charity.[261] On the 19th she called on Miss Rosen and Miss Knudsen. There were more plays, family dinners and concerts and on 5 October a three-hour long review of 25,000 Danish troops at Skulderigsgaar. On the 12th Victoria arrived from Norway, but other relatives, such as Uncle Willy, were already leaving. There were operas, more dinners, excursions, copious entertaining at Hvidöre and a visit to the Home Arts Exhibition. Finally, on the 30th, Maud and Olaf arrived and, with her mother, sister and cousin Michael, left for England.

Queen Alexandra's Christmas Gift Book, published by the *Daily Telegraph*, was on sale; on 4 November Ralph Hall Caine[262] gave the Queen £10,000. His father hoped the King would boost sales by endorsing the book publicly, but while Edward was glad so many orders had been received, he declined to interfere as "he thinks any work which may emanate from The Queen should stand entirely on its own merits and should not be in any way 'exploited'". He thus gracefully deferred to an achievement which was Alexandra's alone.[263] She left for Sandringham on the 5th, taking her relatives and Patricia of Connaught with her. The King, who had been at Newmarket since the 1st, joined them and on the 6th they went to see the bungalow at Snettisham. Whatever might have been hoped, Michael and Patricia did not get together and they both left on the 9th, when the King's birthday guests arrived. There was shooting, and he also planted some trees. On the 13th there was a performance of *The Flag Lieutenant* in the ballroom. More guests arrived until the court moved to Windsor for the Swedish state visit from the 16th to the 21st. The Hanley Glee and Madrigal Society gave a concert in St George's Hall; next evening there was a state banquet. On the 18th the Swedish sovereigns[264] went to London, while the King, Queen and Princess opened buildings at Eton College, commemorating old Etonians who had died in the Boer War. King Gustav and Queen Victoria returned and *The Corsican Brothers* was performed later in the Waterloo Gallery. There were three shooting luncheons and another banquet; on the 20th, *The Duke's Mother* was staged in the Waterloo Gallery. On the 21st, Messrs Levey and Asscher brought the Cullinan diamond[265] to show the King. On the 23rd he, Alexandra and Victoria returned to Norfolk; he shot at Castle Rising until the 28th, despite having a cold. Guests arrived but for nearly a week he was too ill to go out. There was a large dinner party on Alexandra's birthday and on 4 December *The Builder of Bridges* was performed. They came to London on the 7th; the King convalesced at Brighton with the Sassoons till the 14th, while Alexandra shopped on most days and also went four times to the theatre. The Norwegians went home on the 15th and the King had another week at Brighton, with Mrs Keppel nearby. He joined Alexandra and Victoria at Sandringham on the 23rd for a traditional Christmas, and on the 31st they all drank a toast to 1909 in the library.

All the guests left on 4 January 1909 and the King went to Elveden. On the 7th Alexandra and Victoria attended Xandra Hervey's[266] wedding to Sir Walter Chaytor in Sandringham Church and the reception, but they both caught influenza, which Alexandra did not want to pass on; "I am <u>too</u> sorry to have missed seeing you all this <u>one peaceful</u> week of my hurried life! Alas it was hard just to be ill thus & to <u>feel</u> so utterly wretched, as I am doing just now."[267] George replied sympathetically; they were all looking forward to being with her at Windsor soon, the only time of year they all lived under the same roof; "We will do all we can to help you & cheer you up & the children will amuse you, 4 of them, especially the two youngest, are more funny than ever & Johnny is most cheeky & impertinent. I am sure the change of air will do you good & Toria could later follow you there."[268]

However, Alexandra was too ill to leave Sandringham. The Waleses had glimpsed her at her window on the 19th [269] and from Windsor, George wrote; "Papa, '*unberufen*', is wonderfully well & in excellent spirits" but "I can't tell you how dreadfully we all miss you & Toria. It all seems so strange without you & I miss you so much at dinner & in the evening. I do hope you may be able to come here later." The children's colds were better and they were running up and down the castle corridors. David and Bertie seemed happy and comfortable at Osborne. Johnny "pulled Papa's hair at lunch today, I don't think [Papa] quite liked it, but we couldn't stop him."[270] On the 26th, he was pleased Alexandra had been out for a walk; "I do trust that horrible depression which always comes after that beastly influenza is less now & that you try to cheer up. Glad darling Toria has also been able to get up for a short time … I can't tell you how much we all miss you here darling Motherdear, it is not at all the same without you, everything seems different, & something is wanting without you which is difficult to describe. We are all so sorry that you are not here."[271] He wrote, bracingly, on the 28th, "[I] am so pleased that you are now really feeling better & more like yourself again."[272] She was not yet ready to be braced; "Thank you, my beloved Georgie boy for all yr precious letters to me during this vile time of this horrible Influenza. We are both <u>better</u> but still I am not happy. Darling Toria is also getting on but alas, as she is a week behind me, she cannot come up to town yet, & I am in <u>despair</u> to <u>leave</u> her just now when we both want each other."[273] They had missed Crichel as well as Windsor and in early February there was a state visit she was dreading.

Alexandra returned to London on 1 February, alone. She went driving and, with the King, attended a charity concert at the Albert Hall on the 4th, for the Messina earthquake victims. They saw *Penelope* at the Comedy and Alexandra also saw English productions of *Rhinegold* and *Valkyrie*. Perhaps this was as good a preparation as any for the Berlin state visit. They arrived on the 9th and drove to the palace.[274] Alexandra drove and walked in the afternoon, and visited Charlottenburg with Prince Henry, his wife Irène and sister, Victoria, Princess Adolf of Schaumburg-Lippe, before a large state banquet in the Weisse Saal. The next day Alexandra called on the Crown Prince and Crown Princess. She and the King lunched at the British Embassy, where he was taken ill with a choking fit. His doctor, Sir James Reid,[275] hastened over, but Edward recovered immediately when Alexandra unfastened his tight collar.[276] After driving and walking with the Empress in Bellevue's garden, the couple visited Empress Frederick's Institute for surgical inventions, and home for medical postgraduates. Fräulein Schumann Heink[277] sang at tea time; the royal couple dined alone but later attended a state ball in the Weisse Saal. On the 11th they visited the Marstall, with 240 horses and carriages kept on the first floor, and Kaiser Friedrich Museum. Later, they saw a gala opera performance of *Sardanapul*.[278] To compliment them, it was based on work by Sir Austen Layard[279] and his assistant, Hormuzd Rassam[280] on ancient Nineveh, especially the sculptured slabs from the Palaces of Sennacherib and Ashurpanipal in the British Museum. The King, tired and unwell, quietly allowed his eyes to close but was startled awake by the noise and a stage apparently in flames. The next day, Alexandra received Franz de Vecsey and drove with the Empress to Monbijou, the Hohenzollern Museum (where the Emperor joined them) and later the Virchow Hospital,[281] directed by Dr Ohlemüller. She was intensely irritated by William's insistence on explaining everything to her in the museum, which shortened their time at the hospital for seeing "all the latest Medical & Surgical discoveries."[282] But, when they returned home on the 13th, Victoria fancied "my Mother <u>has</u> enjoyed her visit, in spite of her unwillingness at starting."[283]

Opening Parliament and receiving ambassadors followed. On the 18th the couple attended a matinee, for the Royal Ear Hospital, at the Queen's Theatre.

The next day King Edward motored to Brighton, staying with the Sassoons.[284] Queen Alexandra received visitors and went out to tea, hearing Miss Mary Law[285] play the violin at Lady Antrim's daughter's house on the 20th. Later she saw *The Dashing Little Duke* at Hicks' Theatre, and called at sculptors' studios over the next week. The King returned and they received the Swedish Minister,[286] with Dr Sven Hedin,[287] explorer of Tibet. Alexandra heard the Spanish singer, Maria Galvany[288] on the 24th and in the evening the couple saw *Samson* at the Garrick. She visited the exhibition of *Fair Women* at the New Gallery on the 25th and the next day heard the singer, Madame Darlays,[289] (recommended by Cousin Lily)[290], accompanied by Signor Vannaccini. Despite feeling quite ill, Alexandra attended the first court that evening but next day was in bed with congestion of the lung. Her serious attack of influenza, followed so soon by the stress of the Berlin visit and the busy resumption of activities, made her more vulnerable to illness.[291] Victoria returned from Sandringham and the King, not particularly well himself, left for Biarritz. Mrs Keppel was there again, this time with her husband and two young daughters.[292]

Thankfully, Minny arrived on her annual visit; the King was sorry Laking (who had influenza) was ill but "I cannot help feeling that Mama will sooner get better now that he cannot come to see her. Aunt Minny will also do wonders & make Mama rouse herself. They will I hope go soon to Sandringham as it will act as a 'pick me up' to ensure Mama's recovery."[293] He felt the problem was no longer the infection but the consequent depression. May told her aunt; "Aunt Minny arrived Monday looking so well & this has cheered poor 'Mother dear' up, who is not well yet & has not been out for over a fortnight. Poor dear, she is so deaf it makes me quite sad & she looks so pathetic sometimes, trying to hear what we are saying & laughing about. The King is I fear not having good weather at Biarritz. Of course Victoria has again had influenza these last days, she is too unlucky in always being ill, but almost everybody at the Palace has influenza & London seems to be full of it."[294]

Charlotte was too ill with influenza to keep the engagement diary, which Alexandra and Victoria wrote over the next five weeks. On 9 March, Alexandra noted; "Minny & I spent the day together, I not very well, poor Victoria again unwell, poor dear Charlotte so unwell." The next day, "poor Charlotte has bronchitis & pneumonia" and over succeeding days the only entry was "My beloved Charlotte still so ill – am very anxious." Finally, on the 16th she wrote "Thank God dear Charlotte better."[295] The King agreed; "I am glad that the invalids are better, but I am sure Mama will not really get better, till she has a change of air, & if it is not too cold there, I am sure that Sandringham would be the best place, & where she has all her home comforts … That poor dear Toria should have influenza for the 3rd time is too cruel. Do tell her how much I feel for her."[296] Lady Hallé and Miss Neruda[297] came to play the piano the next day. Minny told her son how anxious Alexandra had been about "Good old

13 "Their Majesties' Gracious Smile", taken in 1907/8; postcard printed and published
by *J Beagles & Company Limited; private collection*

Charlotte, who is a difficult patient and does not want to obey anybody but Aunt Alix who because of this had to go and see her constantly", and "tear herself in two among the sick."[298] By 22 March the King was relieved "Mama is now well again, & Toria & Charlotte rapidly recovering but I fear that the latter will be weak for a long time." He had been intrigued by "Wright's[299] two 'flights' of his Aeroplane at Pau last week. It is a very graceful & at the same time delicate machine, & looks like a huge Dragonfly when up in the air. I enclose a photograph but I look upon it as an expensive toy, & do not see how it can be of any use for Military or scientific purposes."[300]

On the 25th they "went to Garrard's in pouring rain to see the Cullinan Diamond". Lady Hallé and her sister came four more times; finally, with royal cooperation, they played "8 hands" on two pianos. Now they were all feeling better, with outings, visitors and on the 31st, Bobsy's birthday party at Marlborough House. On 1 April Alexandra wrote in the diary; "We went to Badminton to the Duke & Dss of Beaufort.[301] Saw a meet of hunt – delightful." She also noted, sadly, Maurice Holzmann's death that afternoon; he had been her secretary for many years. She went to the theatre, drove with Minny, had guests to lunch and tea, motored to Windsor and visited the London Hospital. On the 6th she saw General Booth[302] and the next day attended a concert at the Queen's Hall, where Richter conducted Elgar's symphony.[303] A cruise was planned and the King was "living in hopes that A Minny may accompany us ... but have heard nothing for certain yet. I don't expect Mama to leave England before the 16th or the 17th as I don't think she is in a great hurry about it – I wonder if she is going to Sandringham this week. They showed wonderful energy in going to Badminton only for the day."[304]

In the end, there was no time to go to Sandringham. The King was pleased the Waleses had persuaded the sisters to spend Easter Sunday at Frogmore. "It is a pity that they spent Easter in Town, but Charlotte's illness & A Minny's devotions had a great deal to do with it."[305] On 14 April the Queen heard Bach's *St John Passion* "in our Chapel"; the next day she, Minny, Victoria and Charlotte were busy preparing to leave for Paris, where they joined the King on the 16th. The English party travelled through the Simplon Pass, while the Dowager Empress proceeded on her own train; they met at Genoa on the 17th and boarded *Victoria and Albert*. Alexandra was relieved to find "dear Papa very well & in excellent spirits; Biarritz did him much good."[306] He was glad to see "A Minny ... Mama & Toria looking so well but was dreadfully shocked at poor Charlotte's appearance, who has become quite an old woman & she seems very feeble. She bore the railway journey well & likes being on board ship, but we virtually let her do nothing & she takes her meals in her cabin." Like them, she was on holiday to recover her health, but was keeping the engagement diary again.

The yacht arrived at Girgenti on the 19th and all the next day they toured the ancient Greek temples of Castor and Pollux and Juno with Professor Salinas. After lunch in the Temple of Concord, they drove to see the cathedral, the Greek sarcophagus and "The Devil's Letter", "in most primitive carriages & awful horses. The heat & dust was tremendous". At Malta the next day, the Connaughts,[307] and various officials came on board. After lunch at the palace they motored round the island before tea at San Anton. "Both there & at the Palace U Arthur has greatly improved everything. Our weather is splendid & very hot, especially in the Cabins at night. We dined at the Palace the same evening, there was an Investiture afterwards & then a regular 'Court' in the newly decorated Ball Room (as at Buck: Palace) ... A 'stand up' Supper in the Armoury brought the entertainment to a conclusion & we were not sorry to return to the ship & get a good night's rest."[308] On the 22nd there were naval and military parades on the Marsa and the King opened the Connaught Hospital (Antica Corte) for consumptive patients. They visited the cathedral at Notabile and had tea with the Governor[309] and his wife at Verdala. On the 23rd they visited St John's Church, where the King admired the tapestries, which were only brought out once a year; later, acts from *Rigoletto, La Bohême* and *Adrienne Lecouvreur*, were "very fairly given". After the naval hospital, lunch at Verdala and a dinner and dance at the palace on the 24th, they left next day for Catania. On the 26th they circled Mount Etna by special train, rose 2,500 feet and later had tea with the Marquis di San Giuliano[310] and his family. Steaming slowly past Messina on the 27th, they "could perfectly see the terrible destruction to the town, with our glasses."[311]

At Palermo they "made a splendid long excursion all round that lovely spot, & saw all the plentiful Cathedrals and Churches & Castles" including the King's Palace, with a mosaic chapel. George William of Cumberland joined them and dined on board. Writing from Baia on the 29th, Alexandra remembered that David would soon start his first term at Dartmouth and that the brothers would be parted after their happy time at Osborne; "poor little Bertie will miss him very much there I am sure." At Baia they lunched with Victor Emanuel III, Queen Elena and the Aostas on board *Re Umberto*. They motored over the mountains for tea at the Monastery of Camaldoli, where the monks were only allowed to speak once a week. The yacht left on the 30th for Naples, where they motored and had tea at Bertolini's Palace Hotel. Near Vesuvius the next day the view was spoiled by the haze but they lunched at the Observatory Eremo Hotel. "Dear Aunt Minny Minny is enjoying herself <u>madly</u> & we are so happy together; everything is new to her & everything interests her & she had never been in Italy before." Victoria accompanied her parents everywhere but although Charlotte was much better, "she must be careful & keeps quiet on board & only has luncheon & tea with us."[312]

On 2 May the yacht steamed round Capri and on to Castellamare, meeting Hélène d'Aosta and her sister, Isabelle, Duchesse de Guise[313] at their hotel. The next day they all had lunch in Terme Stabiane, one of the excavated rooms at Pompeii. On the 4th King Edward left for England, while Alexandra and the others visited the museum at Naples, lunched at Hotel Bertolini and shopped, going the next day to Sorrento. After shopping and eating at hotels on the 6th and the 7th, they left, reaching the Piraeus on the 9th, going by train to Athens and walking in the palace gardens. The next day, Mademoiselle Mercatis and Colonel Palis[314] were married in the palace chapel. Later, Alexandra, Minny and Willy drove to Phalerum, visited the Russian hospital and had tea with Constantine. The next day and on the 13th they motored to Tatoii and later had tea with Prince George. On the 12th they visited Queen Olga's Hospital and School of Needlework. 14 May was tremendously hot and they visited the museum; on the 15th there was a large family dinner on *Victoria and Albert* in intense heat, 94° in the shade and 97° in the cabins. They left early in the morning of the 16th, with a calm sea but high temperature; Willy accompanied them to Corfu, where the next day they lunched at Mon Repos and motored to the Achilleion; he left on the 18th and the yacht started for Venice. Landing on 20 May, they stayed ashore all day, shopping, sightseeing and visiting, the Moisè shop[315] and Lady Layard's Hospital, and dined later on deck with the yacht's officers. This was followed by a grand fête with illuminations in gondolas, Venice's salutation to Alexandra. On the 21st were the Murano Glass factory, more social events, and gondola rides after dinner that evening and the next. There was more sightseeing, shopping, an art exhibition and a reception by the Prefetto, and on the 23rd they, the Russian suite and all the officers, dined on deck; the Dowager Empress and her attendants left afterwards for Russia. The Queen's party left on the 24th and, via Paris, crossed the Channel in *Alexandra*.

The royal couple went to the opera, *Samson et Delilah* that evening, and on the 26th watched the King's horse, "Minoru" win the Derby at Epsom. Thereafter Alexandra received visitors, attended the Oxford Choral Society's concert at the Queen's Hall and watched the Military Tournament at Olympia. On the 29th the couple and Victoria had a peaceful five-day break at Crichel,[316] motoring to Milton Abbey, Broadlands and Romsey Abbey for lunches, and watching Crichel's Motor Gymkhana on 2 June. Back in London on the 3rd, they had a family lunch and tea with the Waleses and later saw *The Arcadians*, a popular musical comedy, with the Fifes and their daughters. Within a few days Alexandra saw *La Somnambula, Aïda* and *Tosca* and also received the Japanese Prince and Princess Nashimoto,[317] who came to lunch on the 7th. The King and Queen attended the horse show at Olympia on the 8th and with Victoria, in the pouring rain, a charity garden fête in the grounds of Chelsea Hospital, held for poor crippled children by the Queen Alexandra League of Children.[318] A court was held on the 11th, and Adeline Genée[319] danced during a matinee at His Majesty's Theatre.

After Hatfield House and Knebworth, the royal couple and Victoria motored to Windsor for Ascot week, with tea at Adelaide Cottage before the party arrived. On the 16th Alexandra, Victoria and some of the guests lunched at the Fishing Temple at Virginia Water, fished and on the 18th went in a steam launch on the river. The King had a good Ascot; "Princesse de Galles" won the Coronation Stakes and "Minoru" the St James's Palace Stakes. He presented colours and guidons to Territorials in the Home Park on the 19th and on the 21st they motored to Wellington College for prize-giving on its Golden Jubilee. Alexandra saw *Les Huguenots*, and later, *Louise, Our Miss Gibbs* and *La Bohême*. The fourth court was on the 24th; there was a bazaar at Olympia for Great Ormond Street Hospital and the new chapel at Queen Alexandra's Military Hospital at Millbank was dedicated. Trooping the Colour, planned for the 25th, was rained off but the King did present new colours to the Corps of Gentlemen at Arms in the Picture Gallery, and later the couple received a deputation from the Russian Duma in the Throne Room.

On 26 June, the King, with his wife, daughter and other royalties, opened the Aston Webb building of the Victoria and Albert Museum at South Kensington. Alexandra saw the play, *Penelope* later. They received the Turkish and Panamanian Ministers on the 28th, and saw *La Bohême* that evening. While the King was at Newmarket, Alexandra saw *The Merry Widow* and *Samson et Delilah* on two evenings. She also visited Lady Egerton's sale of Cretan and Greek embroideries and received 180 members of the Jubilee Nurses Committee. Reynaldo Hahn's[320] Orchestra played and Hahn sang for her on 1 July. The state ball was the next day. Alexandra saw *Le Voleur* at the Adelphi and *La Somnambula*, sung by children, at Terry's Theatre. She attended the Rose Show in Regent's Park, a swimming competition at the Bath Club and also motored to Ranelagh for an Anglo–American polo match. On the 5th the couple and Victoria left to stay at Knowsley[321] during a three-day visit to Lancashire, starting with a large territorial review in the park. They opened the Manchester Royal Infirmary and visited some wards on the 6th; after lunch at Worsley,[322] the King reviewed and presented colours to the East Lancashire Territorials. There were evening cinematograph shows and dancing at Knowsley. On the 7th the royal party motored to Liverpool, were received by the Lord Mayor at the station and took a train to Birmingham, lunching at the Council Chamber with the Mayor, opening the university's great hall and visiting the electrical and civil engineering departments before returning to London.

On the 8th they laid the foundation stone of the Imperial College of Science and Technology's new buildings at South Kensington; later the King inspected the Honourable Artillery Company in Buckingham Palace garden. That evening they saw Ethel Smyth's[323] opera, *The Wreckers* at His Majesty's. The next day they reviewed the boys of Greenwich Hospital School in the garden and later saw *His Borrowed Plumes*, by Mrs George Cornwallis-West,[324] at the Globe. In the evening they attended the American Ambassador and Mrs Whitelaw

Reid's[325] dinner and dance at Dorchester House. During the next week, Alexandra received the French author, Pierre Loti and saw *Fires of Fate* at the Lyric. A children's party for 620 was given on the 12th in the ballroom and garden of Buckingham Palace; there was *Otello* in the evening and the next day Alexandra and Victoria, with Greek relatives, dined with the Farquhars at the White City[326] and saw a firework display at the former Olympic Stadium. On 14 July Alexandra received the composer, Madame Ferrari; an Australian, Mrs Wrohan; and heard Dagmar Wiehe[327] sing. She saw the opera *Tess* in the evening. There were more lunches, dinners and social calls. Prince and Princess Kuni of Japan[328] came to lunch on 19 July; the King and Queen received a deputation from the imperial Turkish parliament and saw the London Fire Brigade's display in Hyde Park. The next day they laid the foundation stone of King's College Hospital at Denmark Hill. Alexandra saw *La Bohème* and *Our Miss Gibbs* again, and on the 23rd the royal couple opened the Royal National Orthopaedic Hospital's new in-patient department in Great Portland Street. They gave a large lunch party to the delegates of the South African Union and Defence Conference and their wives, on the 24th and two days later received the first contingent of petty officers and men from Australia and New Zealand, who were to serve in the Royal Navy. After Goodwood,[329] the King, Queen and Princess boarded *Victoria and Albert* at Portsmouth on the 30th.

The next day they reviewed the 1st and 2nd Divisions of the Home Fleet at Spithead. On 1 August there was a Sunday service on the yacht; later they called on Empress Eugénie on *Thistle*, motored to Barton Manor, where the Wales family were staying and then to the Convalescent Home and Osborne Cottage. They returned in *Victoria and Albert* on the 2nd to Spithead, where the Russian imperial yacht *Standard*, with the Emperor and Empress, their five children and suite, arrived at noon; Edward and Alexandra brought them back to *Victoria and Albert* for lunch. The yacht steamed up and down the line of warships, from Spithead to Cowes; later, there was a dinner on board for 44 royalties, suites, politicians and officers. On the 3rd, the imperial couple sailed with the royal couple on *Britannia* in the Solent, watching the Regatta; that evening there was a state dinner on board *Standard*. The next day they all visited the Royal Naval College at Osborne, had tea with the Waleses at Barton and visited the Swiss Cottage and Osborne Cottage. Alexandra, Victoria and their suite dined later on *Standard*, while the King entertained Nicholas II on *Victoria and Albert* to a Yacht Squadron dinner. On the 5 August the English party lunched on *Standard* and, taking leave of their uncle and aunt at 3pm, the Russians left for home shortly afterwards. After more sailing in *Britannia* and George's yacht, *Corisande*, the King and Queen gave a large family lunch on the 8th and later called on Empress Eugénie again, leaving on the 9th for London and a theatre that evening.

After an exceptionally busy time, the King left for Marienbad and, on the 12th,

Alexandra and Victoria started for two weeks in Scotland. Alexandra told George; "We are a very nice quiet little party here this time & Doris Haig with her two sweet babies came here on Tuesday. I have been twice to see dear Louise, she really seems quite well this time, & never complained once of her health; she was in very good spirits too. Yesterday after lunch we all went fishing in that upper Lake of theirs & caught 68 fish, lovely trout to look at but don't taste as well as they look. I caught 24, twice <u>two at a go</u> – most exciting." On the 21st they went to ask after Bertie, quarantined at Altnaguithasach with whooping cough, but were not allowed to see him. Alexandra was paying visits round the estate and on the 23rd had a cinematograph show in the ballroom, to which 100 people were invited; the next day the Gillies' Ball was held. Sadly, she told George; "I do miss you ... so dreadfully at times. Really on board the yacht at Cowes now seems the only time we ever sleep under the same roof, which makes me quite low & unhappy when I think of how much formerly we were ... together & to each other. Of course I know it can't be helped but that does not make it better. If I had not my darling Toria with me, I shd indeed be quite miserable & lonely as Papa is always so much away now from home. I heard twice from him, he is very well out there & thank God the Cure agrees with him so well."[330] Victoria wrote despondently to May; "Thank God for your dear friendship, love & kindness always, such as a kindly word now & then, helps one <u>on so much</u>!"[331]

Cretan affairs were critical and Alexandra worried about her brother, who wanted the Great Powers to intervene. The Cretans believed they would ultimately become part of Greece and, after waiting eleven years, had hoisted the Greek flag. "How cld they believe the Great P & <u>we</u> in particular wld have so utterly changed & left them to their fate at the critical moment; in fact having now <u>undone</u> all the good we were supposed to do for their cause during the 11 years. <u>Today</u> our ships were supposed to haul down the flag ... The Turks behave infamously to Greece who has behaved so well."[332] Edward VII wrote; "Indeed the Cretan state of affairs is most serious, but we with the other 3 Great Powers are doing our utmost to prevent a conflict betwixt Turkey & Greece. The former is suffering fr 'swelled head' & is very difficult to restrain fr setting the East in a blaze. Poor U Willy is much to be pitied & has I fear a new & radical Govt to deal with." Also, "Mama & Toria leave tomorrow for Dundee but whether the yacht takes them to Christiania or Copenhagen I have <u>not</u> been told!!"[333]

It was Christiania, and they arrived on the 28th, meeting "the Norwegian trio" for meals, but staying on the yacht. They saw *Madama Butterfly* on the 30th and the next day went to inspect King Haakon's new house at Voxenkollen, later walking down to Holmenkollen for tea. On 1 September Minny and her daughter Olga arrived in *Polar Star*. They saw *Erasmus Montanus* at the theatre that evening; the next day there were excursions and a dinner and dance on *Victoria and Albert*; on the 3rd there was a lunch party on board and later, an evening dance on *Polar Star*. They visited each other's yachts and toured the local area, motoring up into the mountains for beautiful views over the fjörds. Minny and Olga left for Copenhagen on the 9th and, after more trips, including calling on Nansen on the 13th, Alexandra and Victoria reached Copenhagen on the 15th. King Edward had expected her to go there on the 8th but then "she studiously avoids telling me her plans, wh seems a quaint fashion of the Danish Royal Family!"[334] First of all Alexandra called on Uncle Hans, who had gallstones,[335] and visited him constantly during the next five and a half weeks. On the 16th she and Minny moved to Hvidöre. Alexandra attended the theatre and there were visits, relatives, shopping and trips; on 7 October Alexandra visited Finsen's Institute. She told May how delightful it was at Hvidöre; "The dear little place is looking its very best – the garden with its profusion of lovely flowers & colours right down to the sea is perfection and the house <u>so bright</u> & comfortable. How I wish I cld show it to you." But the familiar emotional turmoil made her think wistfully of Balmoral; "I am so glad you all liked the Gillies' ball which I am sure was nice. I only regret not having been there myself, & all the time while you all were there – too provoking really, only this is the only time of year I can meet all my people here."[336]

On the 8th she lamented that, unlike her son, "I am always, or at least appear so from here, to be such a bad correspondent, but I positively hardly ever have a moment to myself, & have to write to Papa & so many other things to attend to that you must forgive your poor old loving Motherdear!" Happily, Charlotte was now well and resting at Copenhagen, with the Russian suite. Uncle Hans was better, but had unfortunately fallen over, hurting his nose and hand; "we go to see him almost daily in our <u>Motor</u> which saves us a lot of time." They dined every Sunday at Charlottenlund and entertained at Hvidöre; "Our lovely place here is looking beautiful this year, both in & outside, with lovely flowers & fruit trees laden with excellent fruit we pick ourselves." They had called with birthday greetings for their nephew Harald at his "charming little house in Jagersborg, very bright & prettily arranged, & his wife is very nice, & has a very pleasant kind face, rather pretty, but like a <u>fat</u> dairy maid." His brother was transformed; "our <u>fat</u> Gustaf you wld hardly recognise – he is <u>almost</u> <u>thin</u> now & so <u>brown</u> & a most <u>active</u> soldier, to the wonder of the world – he has just come back from manoeuvres, where he was the keenest of them all, & he is very much liked in his regiment by high & low, & really seems a different being." The Greek situation was very grave; her brother was being badly treated, especially by the army and she feared he might abdicate; "I will say no more about it now, but you know well whose fault I consider it all to be; we have utterly left him & his country in the lurch, & this is the result & which he foresaw wld be the end of it all. If <u>we</u> had <u>last year</u> <u>agreed</u> with Clémenceau & the other Great Powers who wished to settle the Greek question in favour for Greece, all this wld have been avoided, and England has lost its chance with Turkey anyhow, as that is quite in German hands." Willy's sons were not supporting him adequately; "<u>I</u> think it very wrong that George & <u>Tino</u> particularly left Greece now; of course poor Tino has been treated infamously by the Army, yet I shld have stayed with my Father at this most critical moment! instead of now being in Paris!! Of course he was perfectly <u>miserable</u> & dreadfully humbled, poor boy, yet it looks as if he now simply wanted to <u>console</u> himself abroad. You know what I mean."[337]

On 9 October Alexandra attended a lecture by Ernest Shackleton and on the 13th an Icelandic concert, both in the Concert Sal. Victoria arrived from Norway, and, after more trips and visits, Alexandra, Victoria, Maud and Olaf, who had joined them, left on the 25th for England, where King Edward met them the next day at Victoria Station. They saw several plays, including *Dear little Denmark* at the Prince of Wales's Theatre on the 29th, and went to Sandringham on 1 November; Queen Maud and her son going to Appleton. The King arrived on the 5th for the first shooting party the next day; on the 9th they had partridge driving at Shernbourne and Ling House and the shooters, including Montague Guest,[338] an old friend, were walking along after lunch. Without warning, Guest had a seizure and fell dead; shooting the next day was cancelled out of respect. On 9 November 1914 Alexandra recalled "that last birthday in 1909 when poor dear Monty Guest died while out shooting with you all, & both you & Papa suddenly came back about three o'clock! when I was so surprised to see you come in while I was changing my clothes & Papa <u>burst</u> out telling me at once that 'poor M Guest has just fallen down <u>dead</u> after luncheon'! I remember so well it gave me such an awful shock, & I thought to <u>myself</u> at the time, Oh, what a bad omen on dear Papa's birthday – and alas it proved but too true, it was his last birthday on earth with us."[339]

On the 15th the court moved to Windsor for King Manuel of Portugal's state visit and a concert that evening in St George's Hall by the North Staffordshire District Choral Society. There was shooting, a chapter of the Order of the Garter in the Throne Room, where Manuel was invested, and a banquet in St George's Hall on the 16th. The next day he received the Freedom of the City at the Mansion House. Queen Alexandra, as Honorary Colonel, presented new colours to a deputation of the 2nd Battalion, Princess of Wales's Own Yorkshire Regiment in the Red Drawing Room. *Trilby* was staged in the Waterloo Gallery later. There was more shooting, and in the evenings a banquet and *The Lyons Mail*, performed by HB Irving's Company.[340] The official visit ended but Manuel (twenty) stayed on, was shown over Eton College and Chapel and watched a football match on the 20th; after all, he himself was little more than a schoolboy. The couple received Prince Tsai Hsun[341] and gave him lunch, and the Russian Balalaika Court Orchestra played in the evening. On the 22nd the court and Manuel moved to London; Alexandra and Victoria took him to see *The Whip* at Drury Lane and he had lunch next day at Soveral's residence. Alexandra and Victoria returned to Sandringham; the Balalaika Orchestra played in the ballroom on Alexandra's birthday and Charles Hawtrey's[342] Company presented

The Little Damozel on 3 December. Alexandra visited her bungalow at Snettisham the next day but heard sad news; her sister-in-law, Marie, Princess Waldemar, had died after a short illness at Copenhagen. In London, she shopped with Julie d'Hautpoul, received visitors and paid calls before returning to Sandringham on the 18th for Christmas.

Notes

1   RA GV/PRIV/AA24/3, King Edward VII to Prince of Wales, 1905: 9 January
2   John Fisher (1841–1920), 1st Baron Fisher, Admiral of the Fleet, innovator, strategist and developer of the Navy, m Kitty, née Broughton (d 1918)
3   RA VIC/ADDU/417/1, Soveral Papers, Queen Alexandra to Marquis de Soveral, 1905: 13 January
4   Prince and Princess Alexander of Teck lived there
5   RA GV/PRIV/AA24/4, King Edward VII to Prince of Wales, 1905: 31 January
6   Annie Fletcher (1865–1933) Lancashire-born nurse to King Edward VII, Queen Alexandra, Princess Victoria and their household; she was introduced to them because of her association with Sister Agnes' hospital
7   Ethel McCaul (1867–1931), a Royal Red Cross nurse, established a private nursing home (the McCaul Hospital for Officers during the First World War) in Welbeck Street, W1
8   RA GV/ADD/COPY/140/44 Rosebery Papers, Princess Victoria to Lord Rosebery, 1905: 28 February
9   RA GV/PRIV/AA33/3, Queen Alexandra to Prince of Wales, 1905: 7 February
10   At Buckingham Palace
11   RA VIC/ADDX13/42, Queen Alexandra to Lady Curzon, 1905: 9 March
12   Manuel Garcia (1805–1906), famous Spanish singing teacher, who is credited with inventing the laryngoscope
13   Albums, Mediterranean Cruise, 1905, RCIN 2923718, RCIN 2923795; Dimond, pp 107–8
14   Princess Maria Pia of Savoy (1847–1911), m King Luis I of Portugal (1838–1889)
15   RA GV/PRIV/AA33/4, Queen Alexandra to Prince of Wales, 1905: 8 April
16   Sir Maurice de Bunsen, 1st Baronet (1852–1932), diplomat who in 1905 was British Envoy Extraordinary and Minister Plenipotentiary at Lisbon
17   RA VIC/ADDC07/2/Q/28/3/1905, Maurice de Bunsen to Lord Knollys, 1905: 28 March
18   This is likely to mean that she rode cattle, as Queen Amélie did.
19   Ferdinand d'Orléans (1884–1924), Duke de Montpensier
20   Louise d'Orléans (1882–1958), m Prince Carlos of Bourbon-Parma
21   RA GV/PRIV/AA33/4, Queen Alexandra to Prince of Wales, 1905: 8 April
22   Sir George White (1835–1912), Field Marshal, Governor of Gibraltar (1900–1905), m Amelia, née Baly
23   Prince Louis of Battenberg and his nephew, Prince Alexander; both were serving in the Royal Navy
24   Dimond, p 108
25   Princess Marie of Greece had married Grand Duke George Michaelovitch of Russia in 1900.
26   RA GV/PRIV/AA24/7, King Edward VII to Prince of Wales, 1905: 7 April
27   RA GV/PRIV/AA33/4, Queen Alexandra to Prince of Wales, 1905: 8 April
28   RA GV/PRIV/AA24/8, King Edward VII to Prince of Wales, 1905: 15 April
29   RA GV/PRIV/AA24/9, King Edward VII to Prince of Wales, 1905: 23 April
30   Alexandra called them "Arabs on their prancing steeds", RCIN 2923718/58c

31 RA GV/PRIV/AA24/10, King Edward VII to Prince of Wales, 1905: 27 April

32 RA GV/PRIV/AA24/11, King Edward VII to Prince of Wales, 1905: 28 April

33 Princess Olga Lobanov-Rostovsky m Sir Edwin Egerton (1841–1916), British Envoy Extraordinary and Minister Plenipotentiary to Greece from 1892–1903. She took an interest in the Royal Hellenic School of Needlework and Lace, set up in 1897, and was chairwoman of its committee.

34 Dimond, p 108

35 Written at the end of the cruise album

36 RA VIC/ADDA21/228/6, Sir Dighton Probyn to Viscount Hayashi, 1905: 12 April

37 RA VIC/ADDA21/228/115, Sir Dighton Probyn to Mr Phillips, 1914: 30 May; King Edward shared her fondness for dogs

38 Sometimes called Japanese spaniels

39 Empress Haruko (1849–1914, b Masako Ichijo), m Emperor Meiji; known as Empress Shōken after death

40 RA VIC/ADDA21/228/8, Viscount Hayashi to Sir Dighton Probyn, 1905: 18 May

41 Viscount Hayashi Tadasu (1850–1913), Japanese diplomat who had worked for the successful conclusion of the Anglo–Japanese Alliance of 1902. He was resident minister in London and became ambassador in December 1905.

42 RA VIC/ADDA21/228/3, Viscount Hayashi to Charlotte Knollys, 1905: 2 April

43 RA VIC/ADDA21/228/12, Queen Alexandra to Sir Dighton Probyn, 1905: 20 May

44 Tschumi, pp112–3

45 King Alfonso XIII of Spain (1886–1941), m Princess Victoria Eugénie of Battenberg

46 Prince Gustav Adolf of Sweden (1882–1973), Crown Prince, and King from 1950–1973, m (1) Princess Margaret of Connaught (1882–1920), (2) Lady Louise Mountbatten (1889–1965)

47 RA GV/PRIV/AA24/13, King Edward VII to Prince of Wales, 1905: 11 July

48 Dorothy (Doris), née Vivian (1879–1939) m Major General Douglas Haig (1861–1928), later Field Marshal and 1st Earl, renowned army commander; Mary Hart Dyke m Captain Matthew Bell. Both brides were maids of honour to Queen Alexandra.

49 Seat of Earl of Derby, then Frederick Stanley (1841–1908), the 16th Earl, m Lady Constance, née Villiers (1840–1922)

50 Prince John Charles Francis (1905–1919)

51 RA GV/PRIV/AA33/5, Queen Alexandra to Prince of Wales, 1905: 18 July

52 RA GV/PRIV/AA33/7, Queen Alexandra to Prince of Wales, 1905: 24 September

53 Princess Margaret of Connaught, recently married to Prince Gustaf Adolf of Sweden

54 RA GV/PRIV/AA33/7, Queen Alexandra to Prince of Wales, 1905: 24 September

55 Which had moved out of London in 1902

56 RA GV/PRIV/AA33/8, Queen Alexandra to Prince of Wales, 1905: 19 October

57 Giacomo Puccini (1858–1924), famous Italian opera composer

58 Christian IX

59 RA GV/PRIV/AA33/9, Queen Alexandra to Prince of Wales, 1905: 26 October

60 Prince Alexander George of Teck, who had been plump as a child

61 Henry Peter Hansell (1863–1935), tutor to George V's sons

62 Mademoiselle José Dussau (d 1924), French Governess to Princess Mary

63 RA QM/PRIV/CC42/65, Queen Alexandra to Princess of Wales, 1905: 2 November

64 Lt Colonel John Henry Patterson (1867–1947), army officer, hunter, author and Christian Zionist, built railway bridge over the Tsavo River in British East Africa (Kenya) in 1898-9.

65 RA GV/PRIV/AA33/10, Queen Alexandra to Prince of Wales, 1905: 2 November

66 RA GV/PRIV/AA24/25, King Edward VII to Prince of Wales, 1905: 3 November

67 Leopold Greville (1882–1928), later 6th Earl of Warwick

68 Ie. not like any of his mother, Lady Warwick's lovers

69 Miss Jane Thornewell, a local lady and regular visitor

70 Mrs George Keppel, suffering from Alexandra's version of "tummy ache"

71 RA GV/PRIV/AA33/11, Queen Alexandra to Prince of Wales, 1905:10 November

72 RA GV/PRIV/AA33/12, Queen Alexandra to Prince of Wales, 1905:17 November

73 RA GV/PRIV/AA33/13, Queen Alexandra to Prince of Wales, 1905: 23 November

74 RA GV/PRIV/AA24/29, King Edward VII to Prince of Wales, 1905: 1 December; Peter Carl Fabergé (1846–1920), Russian jeweller, famous for jewelled bibelots and Easter eggs

75 RA GV/PRIV/AA33/14, Queen Alexandra to Prince of Wales, 1905: 1–7 December

76 With the Duke and Duchess of Portland

77 RA QM/PRIV/CC42/66, Queen Alexandra to Princess of Wales, 1905: 14 December

78 RA GV/PRIV/AA33/15, Queen Alexandra to Prince of Wales, 1905: 15 December

79 Richard Burdon Haldane (1856–1928), 1st Viscount Haldane of Cloan, politician, lawyer and philosopher

80 RA VIC/ADDA21/233/77,78, pencil note by Sydney Holland; Queen Alexandra to Sydney Holland, 1905: 18 December

81 RA GV/PRIV/AA33/16, Queen Alexandra to Prince of Wales, 1905: 22 December

82 Grand Duchess Elizabeth; her husband, Grand Duke Serge, had been assassinated earlier in the year

83 RA GV/PRIV/AA33/17, Queen Alexandra to Prince of Wales, 1905: 29 December

84 RA QM/PRIV/CC47/67, Queen Alexandra to Princess of Wales, 1905: 29 December

85 RA GV/PRIV/AA24/33, King Edward VII to Prince of Wales, 1905: 29 December

86 William Thomas Temple (c1832–1906), overseer at Sandringham, m Sarah Phillips (c1833–1891); parents of Netty (Mrs Cole) and Bessie (Mrs Sinclair), Alexandra's dressers

87 RA QM/PRIV/CC42/69, Queen Alexandra to Princess of Wales, 1906: 12 January

88 Munshi Hafiz Abdul Karim (1863–1909), Indian attendant, secretary and teacher of Hindustani to Queen Victoria from 1887–1901; although he had been unpopular with the household, Alexandra apparently sympathised with him.

89 Alexandra's name for her grandson, born a Prince of Denmark

90 RA GV/PRIV/AA33/19, Queen Alexandra to Prince of Wales, 1906: 11 January

91 RA QM/PRIV/CC42/70, Queen Alexandra to Princess of Wales, 1906: 19 January

92 Whose affair with the King was over; she had taken up Socialism

93 Sidney Greville was Lady Warwick's brother-in-law

94 RA GV/PRIV/AA33/20, Queen Alexandra to Prince of Wales, 1906: 19 January

95 RA GV/PRIV/AA33/21, Queen Alexandra to Prince of Wales, 1906: 26 January

96 RA QM/PRIV/CC42/68, Queen Alexandra to Princess of Wales, 1906: 26 January

97 Princess May of Teck (1906–1994), later m Colonel Sir Henry Abel Smith (1900–1993), Governor of Queensland

98 RA GV/PRIV/AA33/22, Queen Alexandra to Prince of Wales, 1906:

99 She had inflammation of the brain and spine (RA GV/PRIV/AA33/19, Queen Alexandra to Prince of Wales, 1906:1 January)

100 His brother, Christian IX, had let him live in rooms in the Palace.

101 Louise, née Petersen (1816–1914), Danish actress, m the actor, Joachim Ludvig Phister

102 RA GV/PRIV/AA33/24, Queen Alexandra to Prince of Wales, 1906: 16 February

103 Grand Duchess George of Russia (born Princess Marie of Greece)

104 RA GV/PRIV/AA33/25, Queen Alexandra to Prince of Wales, 1906: 23 February

105 Esher, Vol II, pp 140–141

106 RA VIC/ADDU/417/3, Several Papers, Queen Alexandra to Marquis de Soveral, 1906: 12 March

107 Charlotte Bill (1875–1964), nurse to children of King George V and Queen Mary, 1896–1919

[108] RA GV/PRIV/AA33/27, Queen Alexandra to Prince of Wales, 1906: 9 March

[109] Archbishop of Canterbury, Randall Davidson

[110] RA GV/PRIV/AA33/28, Queen Alexandra to Prince of Wales, 1906: 15 March; Princess Victoria Eugénie had been born and brought up in Britain but technically she was a Princess of Battenberg and thus part of the Grand Ducal House of Hesse

[111] Arthur Holland-Hibbert (1855–1935), 3rd Viscount Knutsford

[112] RA GV/PRIV/AA33/29, Queen Alexandra to Prince of Wales, 1906: 29 March

[113] Isla Stewart (1856–1910), Matron of St Bartholomew's Hospital from 1887

[114] RA VIC/ADDA21/82,83,100, note by Sydney Holland; Queen Alexandra to Sydney Holland, 1906: 13 March; Queen Alexandra to Sydney Holland, undated, c. 1907

[115] Former Housekeeper at Sandringham

[116] RA QM/PRIV/CC42/73, Queen Alexandra to Princess of Wales, 1906: 29 March

[117] Hon Hedworth Lambton (1856–1929), Admiral of the Fleet, later took the surname Meux, m Mildred, née Sturt (1869–1942), widow of Viscount Chelsea

[118] Revd Leonard Tyrwhitt (1863–1921), Chaplain to King Edward VII and later Canon of Windsor (1910–1921)

[119] Professor Raffaele Vittorio Matteucci (1846–1909), Director of the Royal Observatory on Mount Vesuvius, had remained at his post, monitoring the progress of the eruption in April 1906

[120] Where Mrs Keppel was among the guests at a dinner at the British Embassy on 2 May

[121] Mary Enid Evelyn, née Guest (1843–1912), Sir Austen Layard, diplomat and Assyrian archaeologist

[122] Pablo Larios, later Marqués de Marzales (1862–1938) was Master of the Royal Calpe Hunt from 1891–1932 and 1934–1938. King Edward VII and King Alfonso XIII became joint Patrons of the Hunt in 1906.

[123] Luis Felipe (1887–1908), Prince Royal of Portugal, and Manuel (1889–1932), later King Manuel II between 1908 and 1910

[124] Fridtjof Nansen (1861–1930), Norwegian explorer, scientist, diplomat and humanitarian

[125] Edvard Grieg (1843–1907), Norwegian composer and pianist, m his cousin Nina, née Hagerup (1845–1935), Danish/Norwegian lyric soprano

[126] Through ill health

[127] RA GV/PRIV/AA24/48, King Edward VII to Prince of Wales, 1906: 8 June

[128] Mieczyslaw Horszowski (1892–1993), Polish/American pianist

[129] This was probably in connection with the Villa in Denmark which she and her sister had now acquired; the furnishings there were by Waring.

[130] RA GV/ADD/COPY/140/50, Rosebery Papers, Princess Victoria to Lord Rosebery, 1906: 7 July

[131] For Victoria's birthday

[132] With Henry Percy (1846–1918), 6th Duke of Northumberland and his wife, née Lady Edith Campbell (c 1850–1913)

[133] Camille Saint-Saëns (1835–1921), French composer, organist, conductor and pianist

[134] Joseph Hollman (1852–1927), Dutch cellist

[135] George Edward Wade, (1853–1933), sculptor

[136] Captain Hon Robert Ward (1871–1942) married Lady Mary Acheson (b 1881), daughter of Lord and Lady Gosford; Lady Gosford was one of Queen Alexandra's ladies-in-waiting from 1901–1925

[137] In 1905-6 the Lord Mayor was Sir Walter Morgan (1831–1916), businessman and 1st Baronet

[138] John Burns (1858–1943), trade unionist and politician, president of the Local Government Board,1905–1914

139 John Danvers Power (1858–1927), barrister and philanthropist

140 Duke of Sparta

141 RA VIC/ADDU/417/4, Soveral Papers, Queen Alexandra to Marquis de Soveral, 1906: 24 September

142 RA GV/PRIV/AA33/31, Queen Alexandra to Prince of Wales, 1906: 14 September

143 Perhaps Christian Petersen (1885–1961), Danish/American sculptor

144 Sir Alexander Lyon (1850–1927), Lord Provost of Aberdeen from 1905–1908

145 Sir William Lancaster (1841–1929), businessman, philanthropist and politician, and educated at the school

146 Frederick Harrison was the lessee of the theatre.

147 William Waller Lewis (1860–1915), stage name Lewis Waller, actor and theatre manager, m Florence West (1862–1912), actress

148 Donald Tovey (1875–1940), knighted in 1935; composer, conductor, pianist, musicologist, musical analyst and writer on music

149 The Danish-American telepathists, Julius Zanzig (1857–1929) and his wife Agnes

150 With Michael Bass (1837–1909), 1st Baron Burton, brewer, politician and philanthropist, m Harriett, née Thornewill (d 1931)

151 Fridtjof Nansen (1861–1930), Norwegian explorer, scientist, diplomat and humanitarian

152 Armand Fallières (1841–1931), French statesman and President of France, 1906–13. His wife was Jeanne (née Bresson), (1839–1939)

153 Pierre Girauld de Nolhac (1859–1936), French historian and poet, Curator at Versailles, 1892–1919

154 Aimé Morot (1850–1913), French painter and sculptor

155 Charles d'Epinay (1836–1914), French sculptor and caricaturist (as "Nemo"); he made a polychrome statue of Joan of Arc, later put in Rheims Cathedral

156 Camille Groult (1832–1909), French industrialist and art collector

157 Edmé Samson (1810–1891) founded porcelain firm, Samson, Edmé et Cie, which made high-quality copies of earlier styles of porcelain

158 Esher, Vol II, p 222

159 RA VIC/MAIN/QAD/1907: 9 February

160 Arthur Stockdale Cope (1857–1940), portrait painter, knighted in 1927; he was the son of Charles West Cope, the history and genre painter

161 Vilhelm Christoffer Herold (1865–1937), Danish operatic tenor, voice and drama coach and theatre director

162 Alexander Alexeievitch Borisov (1866–1934), Russian painter noted for his Arctic landscapes

163 Gertrude Massey (née Seth) (1868–1957), artist specialising in portrait miniatures

164 The Central Criminal Court

165 Ernest Arthur Rowe (1862–1922), watercolourist specialising in garden scenes; Queen Alexandra apparently noticed him painting (under an old umbrella) in Hampton Court Palace gardens. He later gave her the painting and she bought more from the gallery. https://thegardenstrust.blog/2018/12/8

166 RA GV/PRIV/AA25/7, King Edward VII to Prince of Wales, 1907: 12 March

167 Edward J Bing (editor) *The Letters of Tsar Nicholas and Empress Marie*, p 22

168 RA GV/PRIV/AA25/8, King Edward VII to Prince of Wales, 1907: 19 March

169 Sir Henry Bell Longhurst (b 1835), surgeon-dentist to the King

170 RA GV/PRIV/AA25/11, King Edward VII to Prince of Wales, 1907: 10 April

171 Captain Charles Avison Parker (1879–1965)

172 RA VIC/ADDU/260, CA Parker to his mother, 1907: 21 April, © private collection

[173] The youngest daughter and eldest son of the Duke and Duchess of Cumberland

[174] Horse racing and jumping

[175] Sidney Churchill (1862–1921), diplomat, art connoisseur and author

[176] Alfonso, Prince of the Asturias (1907–1939)

[177] RA GV/PRIV/AA33/32, Queen Alexandra to Prince of Wales, 1907: 9 May

[178] RA QM/PRIV/CC45/302, Princess Victoria to Princess of Wales, 1907: 24 May

[179] Alexandra's sister-in-law, Marie

[180] Princess Beatrice of Saxe-Coburg-Gotha and Edinburgh (1884–1966), m Alfonso d'Orléans y Borbón (1886–1975), Infant of Spain, Duke of Galliera

[181] *Illustrated London News*, 1907: 1 June, p 850

[182] Walter Crane (1845–1915), artist and book illustrator, especially of children's books

[183] Philip de László (1869–1937) (b Fülöp Laub), Anglo–Hungarian painter, especially of royalty and nobility

[184] King Frederick VIII and Queen Louise

[185] RA VIC/MAIN/EVIID/1907: 11 June

[186] Robert Crewe-Milnes (1858–1945), 1st Marquess of Crewe and his second wife, née Lady Margaret Primrose

[187] Lady Cynthia Crewe-Milnes (1884–1968), woman of the bedchamber to Queen Mary, and social worker, m Hon George Colville

[188] May Harrison (1890–1959), violinist

[189] Beatrice Harrison (1892–1965), noted cellist; recorded playing in company with nightingale song

[190] This was the Harrisons' introduction to the Royal Family

[191] Home of Sir Richard Williams-Bulkeley (1862–1942), the 12th Baronet, Lord Lieutenant of Anglesey, and his wife, Lady Magdalen, née Yorke (b 1865)

[192] With John Crichton-Stuart (1881–1947), 4th Marquess of Bute and wife Augusta, née Bellingham (1880–1947)

[193] Marie d'Epinay (1870–1960), painter of flowers, genre scenes and portraits

[194] Seat of the Marquess of Lansdowne

[195] George Edward Wade (1853–1933), sculptor, especially of royalty and politicians

[196] François Flameng (1856–1923), successful French painter

[197] Louise Mercier (1862–1925), French artist

[198] Perhaps the Rector of Sandringham and his wife

[199] RA GV/PRIV/AA25/17, King Edward VII to Prince of Wales, 1907: 13 August

[200] RA GV/PRIV/AA33/33, Queen Alexandra to Prince of Wales, 1907: 21 August

[201] RA GV/PRIV/AA33/34, Queen Alexandra to Prince of Wales, 1907: 30 September

[202] RA VIC/ADDU/417/5, Several Papers, Queen Alexandra to Marquis de Soveral, 1907: 9 October, original in French

[203] Danish for 'East, West, Home's Best'

[204] RA GV/PRIV/AA33/34, Queen Alexandra to Prince of Wales, 1907: 30 September

[205] RA GV/PRIV/AA25/26, King Edward VII to Prince of Wales, 1907: 29 October

[206] Infanta Isabella, (1851–1931) d of Queen Isabella II of Spain, m Prince Gaetan, Count of Girgenti (1846–71)

[207] Johann Georg of Saxony (1869–1938) and second wife, Maria Immaculata of Bourbon-Two Sicilies (1874–1942)

[208] They were divorced in 1908; Marie later had a happier marriage with Prince Julius Ernst of Lippe

[209] RA QM/PRIV/CC33/30, Dowager Grand Duchess of Mecklenburg-Strelitz to Princess of Wales, 1907: 4 December

210 RA VIC/ADDU/417/6, Soveral Papers, Queen Alexandra to Marquis de Soveral, 1908: 7 January

211 Pope-Hennessy/Vickers, p 218

212 The home of Edward Guinness (1847–1927), 1st Earl of Iveagh, m cousin Adelaide, née Guinness (1844–1916)

213 Philip Eliot (1835–1917), Dean from 1891–1917

214 Canon Edgar Sheppard (1845–1921), Sub Dean of the Chapels Royal from 1884, m Mary, née White

215 RA QM/PRIV/CC42/75, Queen Alexandra to Princess of Wales, 1908: 31 January

216 Lionel Ovenden (1894–1976), pianist and composer

217 François Flameng (1856–1923), French painter

218 He won £34,000 in stakes

219 Esher, Vol II, p 294

220 John Pierpont Morgan (1837–1913), influential and successful American financier and banker

221 Edoardo de Martino (1938–1912), Italian-British painter of naval scenes and battles; Marine Painter in Ordinary to King Edward VII

222 Edwin Austin Abbey (1852–1911), American muralist, illustrator and painter, who settled in England; work included a painting of King Edward VII's coronation

223 Bing, p 233

224 Gabriel Fauré (1845–1924), French composer, organist, pianist and teacher

225 Susan Metcalfe (1878–1959), American mezzo-soprano

226 Arthur Sassoon (1849–1912), banker and socialite, m Louise, née Perugia (1854–1943) lived at 8, King's Gardens, Brighton

227 RA GV/PRIV/AA25/32, King Edward VII to Prince of Wales, 1908: 25 March

228 This was Prince George Donatus of Hesse (1906–1937) later m Princess Cecilie of Greece (1911–1937)

229 RA GV/PRIV/AA37/7, Prince of Wales to Queen Alexandra, 1908: 28 March; as his second wife, the Grand Duke had married Princess Eleonore of Solms-Hohensolms-Lich; they eventually had two sons

230 RA GV/PRIV/AA25/35, King Edward VII to Prince of Wales, 1908: 8 April; the King also thought Rodin's statues were indecent (RA GV/PRIV/AA25/33, King Edward VII to Prince of Wales, 1908: 31 March)

231 RA VIC/MAIN/QAD/1908: 11April

232 Algernon Freeman-Mitford (1837–1916), 1st Baron Redesdale, m Lady Clementine, née Ogilvy (1854–1932)

233 Waring & Gillow, well-known London furniture emporium, founded in 1897 from two established businesses

234 RA GV/PRIV/AA25/37, King Edward VII to Prince of Wales, 1908: 23 April

235 Charles Hardinge (1855–1944), 1st Baron Hardinge of Penshurst, diplomat, statesman, Viceroy and Governor-General of India, 1910–1916

236 RA VIC/ADDC07/2, Charles Hardinge to Lord Knollys, 1908: 25 April

237 The King's brother, Prince Eugene of Sweden (1865–1947), Duke of Närke; painter, art collector and patron

238 With Sir Arthur Herbert (1855–1921), diplomat and 1st British Envoy to Norway, m Harriet, née Gammell

239 Maud Allan (Beulah Maude Durrant), (1873–1956), Canadian pianist, actress, dancer and choreographer, sometimes controversial

240 Adolphe Borchard (1882–1967), French pianist and composer

241 Hon John Ward (1870–1938), Major Sir, courtier, m Jean Templeton, née Reid (1884–1962), d of Whitelaw Reid, the American Ambassador

242 Nellie Melba (born Helen Mitchell), (1861–1931), Australian operatic soprano, and teacher; created a Dame in 1918 for war charity work

243 William Denison (1864–1917), 2nd Earl of Londesborough, m Lady Grace, née Fane (1860–1933)

244 Home of Sidney Herbert (1853–1913), the 14th Earl of Pembroke, m Lady Beatrix, née Lambton (1859–1944)

245 Home of Henry Lascelles (1846–1929), 5th Earl of Harewood, m Lady Florence, née Bridgeman (1859–1943)

246 Edward Robinson (1853–c1913), Lord Mayor of Bristol in 1908

247 Kathleen, née Williams, m Arthur Wellesley (1849–1934), 4th Duke of Wellington

248 Vittorio Corcos (1859–1933), Italian painter of portraits and genre pictures

249 Dorando Pietri (1885–1942), Italian long-distance runner

250 John Joseph Hayes (1886–1965), American athlete

251 David was training at the Royal Naval College, Osborne; "Drino" was already serving in the Royal Navy

252 RA VIC/MAIN/QAD/2/9/1908

253 RA GV/PRIV/AA33/37, Queen Alexandra to Prince of Wales, 1908: 19 September

254 Alexander Petrovitch Izvolsky (1856–1919), Russian diplomat, Foreign Minister, 1906–1910; he and King Edward VII favoured the signing if the Anglo–Russian Convention of 1907

255 Georges Clemenceau (1841–1929), French statesman, Prime Minister, 1906–1909 and 1917–1920

256 RA GV/PRIV/AA25/43, King Edward VII to Prince of Wales, 1908: 2 September

257 Prince George of Greece

258 Princess Marie Bonaparte (1882–1962), of partly Italian ancestry; she was an author and psychoanalyst

259 He had been killed in a duel with Count Jametel, his sister's unfaithful husband

260 RA GV/PRIV/AA33/37, Queen Alexandra to Prince of Wales, 1908: 19 September

261 Dimond, pp 118–134

262 Gordon Ralph Hall Caine (1884–1962), son of the writer, Hall Caine; he was a publisher and politician

263 RA PPTO/PP/EVII/MAIN/D/28119/1908: 7, 8 November

264 King Gustav V (1858–1950), m Princess Victoria of Baden (1862–1930)

265 Joseph Asscher & Company, of Amsterdam, had cut the Cullinan, the largest gem-quality rough diamond ever found. It had been discovered at the Cullinan Mine in South Africa in 1905.

266 Alexandra Hervey (1883–1970), the former rector's daughter, m 1) Sir Walter Chaytor; 2) George Gore

267 RA GV/PRIV/AA33/38, Queen Alexandra to Prince of Wales, 1909: 14 January

268 RA GV/PRIV/AA37/9, Prince of Wales to Queen Alexandra, 1909: 18 January

269 RA GV/PRIV/AA37/10, Prince of Wales to Queen Alexandra, 1909: 20 January

270 RA GV/PRIV/AA37/11, Prince of Wales to Queen Alexandra, 1909: 22 January

271 RA GV/PRIV/AA37/12, Prince of Wales to Queen Alexandra, 1909: 26 January

272 RA GV/PRIV/AA37/13, Prince of Wales to Queen Alexandra, 1909: 28 January

273 RA GV/PRIV/AA33/39, Queen Alexandra to Prince of Wales, 1909: 30 January

274 Album, *State Visit to Berlin, 1909*; RCIN 2924277, see Dimond, p 134–137

275 Sir James Reid (1849–1923), 1st Baronet, physician to Queen Victoria, Edward VII and George V, m Hon Susan, née Baring (1870–1961)

276 Michaela Reid, *Ask Sir James*, p 237

277 Ernestine Schumann-Heink (1861–1936), Austrian-born German/American operatic contralto

278 Sardanapale, unfinished opera by Franz Liszt, based loosely on Lord Byron's 1821 verse play, *Sardanapalus*.

279 Sir Austen Henry Layard (1817–1894), traveller, archaeologist, cuneiformist, art historian, draughtsman, collector, politician and diplomat

280 Hormuzd Rassam (1826–1910), Assyrian (from Syriac Christian community), noted Assyriologist and archaeologist. He assisted Layard, and became a naturalised British subject, settling in England.

281 Rudolf Virchow Hospital, built between 1898 and 1906, with 57 individual buildings, 2,000 beds, and living accommodation in the grounds for 700 physicians, nurses and other staff. Rudolf Virchow (1821–1902) was an eminent German physician, known especially for his work in modern pathology and social medicine.

282 Dimond, p 142–3

283 RA/GV/ADD/COPY/140/66, Rosebery Papers, Princess Victoria to Lord Rosebery, 1909: 18 February

284 Where the dinner guests included Alice Keppel

285 Mary Law (1889–1919), violinist

286 Count Herman Wrangel (1857–1934), Swedish ambassador from 1906–1920

287 Sven Hedin (1865–1952), Swedish geographer, topographer, explorer, photographer, travel writer and illustrator

288 Maria Galvany (c1878–1927), Spanish coloratura soprano

289 Jeanne Darlays (1874–1958), French opera singer whose repertoire included Wagner operatic roles

290 Princess Frederica of Hanover, Baroness Pawel-Rammingen

291 RA VIC/MAIN/QAD/1909: 1 March

292 Her daughters were Violet (1894–1972), m Denys Trefusis, and Sonia (1900–1986), m Roland Cubitt (1899–1962), 3rd Baron Ashcombe

293 RA GV/PRIV/AA25/49, King Edward VII to Prince of Wales, 1909: 9 March

294 RA QM/PRIV/CC25/22, Princess of Wales to Dowager Grand Duchess of Mecklenburg-Strelitz, 1909: 14 March

295 RA VIC/MAIN/QAD/1909: 9–16 March

296 RA GV/PRIV/AA25/50, King Edward VII to Prince of Wales, 1909: 16 March

297 This may be Olga Neruda (1858–1945), pianist; they had another sister, Maria (1840–1920), violinist

298 Bing, p 238

299 The brothers, Orville (1871–1948) and Wilbur (1867–1912) Wright were American aviation pioneers

300 RA GV/PRIV/AA25/51, King Edward VII to Prince of Wales, 1909: 22 March

301 Henry Somerset (1847–1924), 9th Duke of Beaufort, m Louise, née Harford (1864–1945)

302 Of the Salvation Army

303 Check RA VIC/MAIN/QAD/1909: 25 March – early April

304 RA GV/PRIV/AA25/53, King Edward VII to Prince of Wales, 1909: 6 April

305 RA GV/PRIV/AA25/54, King Edward VII to Prince of Wales, 1909: the Empress could attend a Russian Orthodox service in London

306 RA GV/PRIV/AA33/40, Queen Alexandra to Prince of Wales, 1909: 29 April – 1 May

307 The Duke was Commander-in-Chief of British troops in the Mediterranean

308 RA GV/PRIV/AA25/55, King Edward VII to Prince of Wales, 1909: 24 April

309 General Sir Henry Grant (1848–1919), governor of Malta, 1907–1909

310 Antonio Paterno Castello (1852–1914), Marquis di San Giuliano, Italian diplomat and foreign minister
311 RA GV/PRIV/AA25/56, King Edward VII to Prince of Wales, 1909: 29 April; the Messina earthquake had occurred on 28 December 1908
312 RA GV/PRIV/AA33/40, Queen Alexandra to Prince of Wales, 1909: 29 April – 1 May
313 Princess Isabelle d'Orléans (1878–1961) m Prince Jean (1874–1940), Duc de Guise
314 Lady and gentleman in waiting to Prince and Princess Nicholas of Greece
315 Might have been to do with the renaissance Church of St Moisè, or was in the same street
316 Lord Alington's house
317 Prince Nashimoto (1874–1951) m Princess Nabeshima Itsuko (1882–1976)
318 This seems to have been connected with an initiative by Sir William Purdie Treloar (1843–1923), Lord Mayor of London in 1906–7, who established a "Cripples' Fund" as his mayoral appeal and raised £10,000 in donations for his Alton Hospital and Treloar School and College, providing education, independence training and opportunities for young people with physical disabilities. Queen Alexandra started the League, it seems, to encourage other, able-bodied children to take part in the fundraising.
319 Danish/British ballet dancer, born Anina Jensen (1878–1970)
320 Reynaldo Hahn (1874–1947), Venezuelan/French composer, conductor, music critic etc.
321 Seat of Earl of Derby, then Edward Stanley (1865–1948), the 17th Earl, m Lady Alice, née Montagu (1862–1957), lady of the bedchamber to Queen Alexandra from 1901–10
322 Seat of Earl of Ellesmere
323 Ethel Smyth (1858–1944), Dame, composer and member of the women's suffrage movement
324 Formerly Lady Randolph Churchill
325 Whitelaw Reid (1837–1912), American politician and newspaper editor, m Elisabeth, née Mills (1857–1931)
326 The site of the Franco–British Exhibition, with white buildings
327 Dagmar Wiehe (d1975), actress
328 Prince Kuni Kunyoshi (1873–1929) m Princess Shimazu Chikako (1879–1956)
329 Where the King's horse, "Minoru" won the Sussex Stakes on the 28th
330 RA GV/PRIV/AA33/41, Queen Alexandra to Prince of Wales, 1909: 19 August
331 RA QM/PRIV/CC45/318, Princess Victoria to Princess of Wales, 1909: 2 August
332 RA GV/PRIV/AA33/41, Queen Alexandra to Prince of Wales, 1909: 19 August
333 RA GV/PRIV/AA25/61, King Edward VII to Prince of Wales, 1909: 25 August
334 RA GV/PRIV/AA25/63, King Edward VII to Prince of Wales, 1909: 8 September
335 RA GV/PRIV/AA33/43, Queen Alexandra to Prince of Wales, 1909: undated
336 RA GV/PRIV/CC42/77, Queen Alexandra to Princess of Wales, 1909: 7 October
337 RA GV/PRIV/AA33/42, Queen Alexandra to Prince of Wales, 1909: 8 October
338 Montague Guest (1839–1909), politician
339 RA GV/PRIV/AA34/43, Queen Alexandra to King George V, 1914: 9 November
340 Harry Brodribb Irving (1870–1919), actor and manager, son of Sir Henry Irving
341 Tsai Hsun, or Zaixun (1885–1949), of the Qing dynasty and Chinese naval minister
342 Charles Hawtrey (1858–1923), actor and theatre manager

Chapter 13

1910–1913

"My overwhelming sorrow and unspeakable anguish"

❦

The year 1910 began uneventfully, but soon Alexandra's page, Frederick Eggleden,[1] with 32 years' service, died, and the palace at Athens was partially burned down. After visiting Elveden, and then Brighton, the King brought guests back on the 15th. He went to London on the 18th and Alexandra joined him at Windsor for the mausoleum service and the court. There were guests and theatres and the King received a number of people before returning to Brighton on 7 February for a week with the Sassoons.[2]

May had confided in Alexandra, who quickly responded; "We so thoroughly understand each other, and you need never fear to speak out to me on any subject & you may be sure of my sympathy & help. It always gives me the greatest pleasure when you confide in me, the same as you wld have done to yr own blessed Mother, who you know I always was so devoted to."[3] Meanwhile she went to the theatre, visited Cruft's Dog Show[4] at the Agricultural Hall on the 10th and walked in the palace garden with her husband when he returned on the 14th. She visited the United Services Museum alone on the 16th and the Natural History Museum with the King on the 19th. Two days later they opened Parliament in state. Alexandra heard Elgar's symphony[5] during the philharmonic concert at the Queen's Hall on the 24th. The couple received the Greek minister[6] on the 26th and attended the Royal Academy's private view of an exhibition of Old Masters and British artists the next day. They both had visitors, the King a great many, including his doctors. The first levee was held on 1 March, and Alexandra attended concerts, the theatre and three equine shows at the Agricultural Hall. She gave badges to 400 Territorial Army nurses in the Throne Room on the 12th and visited the grounds of the Japanese–British Exhibition on the 14th. Four days later she and Victoria left for Sandringham.

Several sources[7] have asserted that, before the King left for Paris on 6 March, he and Alexandra had a furious row, supposedly about Mrs Keppel. Given that raised voices could merely mean that the King was trying to make the Queen hear, their subsequent relationship appears to have been amiable and affectionate, as usual. If there was a row, it blew over very quickly. The King, suffering from a chill, arrived on the 9th at the Hotel du Palais, Biarritz, with Mrs

Keppel at hand. He wrote to Alexandra every few days but by the 14th had severe bronchitis and stayed indoors for a week. As she told May, Alexandra was "in despair entre nous & thought really of going out there! My only fright was that I might have alarmed Papa by suddenly appearing. These terrible attacks of bronchitis are so bad for him & always frighten me." Luckily the nurse and doctor had been excellent.[8] On Easter Sunday, 27 March, Alexandra, regretting they were not all at Sandringham, told George how worried she had been; "Thank God dear Papa is really all right again now – such a relief!! I confess I was really <u>dreadfully</u> anxious knowing but too well what these horrid bronchial attacks mean with him! and what makes it doubly anxious when he is so far away too. It really was bad luck after having been so well all the winter & escaped all colds to go abroad for <u>that</u>!! & <u>immediately</u> catching this horrid one in Paris on his way to Biarritz & then <u>there</u> to find cold damp weather to welcome him. He writes quite cheery letters now & says he feels almost himself again. By the papers I see he has been walking [&] driving about & been playing <u>Crocket</u>!!![9] which <u>sounds complete</u>!! Laking & I were ready to have started any moment had it been necessary. I do so hate when he goes so far away by himself now always."[10]

It was warm and sunny at Sandringham, "& everything trying to burst out with Spring – we have plenty of primroses, violets etc. etc. & even some bushes of <u>red</u> rhododendrons quite in bloom. We go as often as possible to my little house by the sea, where it is lovely." On 1 April she motored to Norwich for lunch with the Herveys, showing them her bungalow at Snettisham on the 4th. In London on the 11th she attended debates in the House of Commons,[11] in the Speaker's box. On the 14th she and Victoria crossed in *Alexandra* to Calais for a cruise, which King Edward regretted had not been arranged earlier; "Mama thought I might be able to accompany her, but it was quite out of the question, as it might be necessary at any moment for me to return home (& I can do so under 24 hours at any time) should the Govt resign, dissolve or commit any act wh might entail my presence at home."[12] On the 19th he continued; "Now that the PM & the Govt have given way more than ever to the Redmondites,[13] the 'People's Budget' (as it is called), has passed! & P Minister[14] telegraphed to me, that as result of Debate showed there was no prospect of any ministerial crisis until after the Recess, there was no reason why I should alter my arrangements! Rather cool…" Current politics depressed him and when an old friend, Sir John Clark of Tillypronie,[15] died, he lamented that while he, despite radical ideas, had been a thorough gentleman, "that does not exist in that class of politicians of the present day, & as for their statements – the word truth does not exist in their vocabulary!" Still at the Hotel du Palais, socialising, driving, walking along "La Plage", picnicking and playing croquet, he left on the 26th and came home next day.

The Queen boarded *Victoria and Albert* at Genoa but was delayed by the weather until 19 April. Nevertheless, they reached Corfu safely on the 20th and the Greek Royal Family, having waited several days,[16] came on board for dinner. Alexandra visited the Achilleon, Mon Repos and the Monastery of Palaiokastritza in an old fort; one evening Eustratiou (fifteen) played music on the yacht and on the 23rd the ship's company entertained them. On the 24th they watched the Procession of St Spiridion; on the 25th the yacht crossed to the Albanian coast and they went up a river and round Buthrinto Lake in launches. Alexandra visited *Aboukir* and two destroyers, *Desperate* and *Angler*, on the 28th. She motored with her brother several times, perhaps discussing affairs in Greece, as George had suggested.[17] There were family lunches, entertainments, and receiving the former Greek minister in London's relatives. But on 2 May she left for England, having heard from George, who wrote again on the 4th, catching her at Calais the next day; "As I said in my telegram, dear Papa arrived home looking very well & in capital spirits. He went down to Sandringham last Saturday & only returned on Monday. I regret to have to tell you that he caught a chill there on the Sunday standing about, although he did not feel very well on the Saturday. And now he has got another bad bronchial attack I am sorry to say & he feels very miserable. I saw him yesterday & today for a short time but did not remain long as they don't want him to talk. Both Laking & Reid & the nurse are looking after him & are doing all they can for him. His cough troubles him very much & he has slept very badly the last two nights. I cannot disguise the fact that I am anxious about him, as one always must be when he gets one of these attacks & this one following so soon after the one he had at Biarritz. I know Laking is writing to you so I will not say more, but thank God you are coming home tomorrow to look after him."[18]

Despite everything, the King kept receiving visitors up to 6.45pm on 4 May, before dining alone at 8pm. Queen Alexandra was travelling as fast as she could but, after a rough crossing on the 5th she finally reached Buckingham Palace at 5.20pm and found him with bronchitis and a heart attack. Her distress was complete; it was bad enough that she had not been able to care for him at Biarritz, and that Alice Keppel had been in attendance, but Alice had even been at the palace earlier on the very day Alexandra returned. Now Alice revealed a letter from the King,[19] written in 1901, in which he hoped that, if he should ever be taken seriously ill, she would be allowed to come and say goodbye. Fulfilling his wishes, the Queen allowed Alice to be admitted, to find that the King could barely recognise her. It seems that Alexandra said to her, in effect; "I am sure you always had a good influence on him", but murmured to her attendants, "Get this woman away" when Alice, oblivious to everything else, was unable to control a hysterical outburst of grief. As Victoria tried to calm her and lead her out of the room, she cried "I never did any harm, there was nothing wrong between us".[20]

King Edward was in a critical state all day on 6 May and finally died that night at 11.45. His illness had so rapidly become terminal that it caused Alexandra maximum pain. She had so nearly been too late; their last shared hours had been disrupted by Mrs Keppel and there had barely been time to care for him, to be alone together, or even to say goodbye; no wonder she found the final parting so difficult. He looked peaceful and in good health, which she attributed to the oxygen administered to assist his breathing, but his life-like appearance was deceptive and heartrending. According to Wilfred Scawen Blunt,[21] the Queen, in deep despair, confided her feelings about the King and Mrs Keppel to Sir Francis Laking at this time; "Twelve years ago, when I was so angry about Lady Warwick, and the King expostulated with me and said I should get him into the divorce court, I told him once for all that he might have all the women he wished, and I would not say a word; and I have done everything since that he desired me to do about them. He was the whole of my life and, now he is dead, nothing matters."[22] At a service in Buckingham Palace's private chapel on the 8th the anthem, "Brother, Thou art gone before us", from Sullivan's *The Martyr of Antioch*, was sung.[23]

There was much to do. Relatives started arriving; the Norwegians on 9 May; Minny and her son Michael on the 11th; Freddy and Willy on the 12th and the 13th. The Connaughts arrived from Africa on the 13th. On the 10th Alexandra sent for Lord Esher, to say goodbye to the King. Wearing a simple black dress, she moved gently about as he lay on his bed, with his head to one side, smiling peacefully as though comfortably asleep. Alexandra talked for half an hour, her natural gaiety only slightly diminished, "but with a tenderness which betrayed all the love in her soul, and oh! so natural feeling that she had got him there altogether to herself. In a way she seemed, and is, I am convinced, happy. It is the womanly happiness of complete possession of the man who was the love of her youth and, as I fervently believe, of all her life." She spoke about their final resting place together; of the deathbed photographs for which she had given permission, and of the time when he would be taken away from her. "Once she said, 'What is to become of me?'" She gripped Esher's arm, a typical gesture, and he kissed both her hands; as he left, she sat down in tears on the little chair next to the King's bed. All his possessions were just as he had left them; his hats still hanging on their pegs.

Knollys had asked Esher to write a message for the Queen to issue publicly but, as they were reading it together, Alexandra sent down a note with her own draft. They were so impressed that they decided to publish it the next day. "These are the things that women, and especially Queens, do better than any man."[24] This is what she wrote:

"From the depths of my poor broken heart, I wish to express to the whole Nation and our kind people we love so well, my deep-felt thanks for all their touching sympathy in my overwhelming sorrow & unspeakable anguish. Not alone have I lost everything in him, my beloved husband, but the Nation too has suffered an irreparable loss in losing their best friend, Father & Sovereign, thus suddenly called away. May God give us all His divine help to bear this heaviest of crosses which He has seen fit to lay upon us – 'His Will be done'. Give me a thought in your prayers which will comfort & sustain me in all I still have to go through. Let me take this opportunity of expressing my heartfelt thanks for all the touching letters & tokens of sympathy I have received from all classes, high & low, rich & poor, which are so numerous that I fear it will be impossible for me ever to thank everybody individually. I confide my dear Son into your care, who I know will follow in his dear Father's footsteps, begging you to show him the same loyalty & devotion you showed his dear Father. I know that both my dear son and daughter in law will do their utmost to merit & keep it."[25]

The King's funeral was held two weeks after he died; after all, Christian IX and Alexander III had been buried some twenty days after death. Meanwhile, Queen Alexandra received many official condolences, from both Houses of Parliament on the 11th, and from foreign royalty on the 18th and the 19th. On the 21st she received military and civil deputations from Norway, Sweden, Russia, Denmark, Portugal, Spain, France, Germany, Austria–Hungary, Marienbad and Biarritz. On the 24th Theodore Roosevelt[26] and Canadian and Australian representatives were received; the next day she met Mrs Roosevelt. King Edward lay in state, face uncovered, in the Throne Room, with guards in attendance, from the 14th May. On the 15th, when Alexandra wore her widow's cap for the first time, there were services in the private chapel and the Throne Room; the anthem sung at the former had been sung at Prince Eddy's funeral in 1892.[27] On the 16th she allowed the King's household, friends[28] and servants to bid him farewell in the Throne Room, where there was another service at 10pm. One of those invited was Lord Rosebery, to whom she wrote "Do come & see him who looks so beautiful & noble even after death & so peaceful & at rest after all his toils & troubles for his Country, which cost him his life."[29] On the 17th the sealed coffin was taken on a gun carriage to lie in state in Westminster Hall, where Alexandra went on the 19th. On 20 May the cortège left Buckingham Palace at 9.10am, and took the King from Westminster Hall to Paddington Station. Accompanying him, with all the royalty and officials, were his horse and his dog, Caesar,[30] a gesture surely prompted by Alexandra. After the sombre 140-minute journey to Windsor, the funeral was held in St George's Chapel at 1.30pm. Nine sovereigns, George V, Frederick VIII of Denmark, George of the Hellenes, Haakon VII of Norway, Albert of the Belgians, William II of Germany, Ferdinand of Bulgaria, Manuel II of Portugal and Alfonso XIII of Spain, were present; all related to King Edward by blood or through marriage. Almost 2,500 floral tributes had arrived; Alexandra's was a cross, 4' 6" x 3', with orchids, lilies of the valley, carnations, lilies and ferns, inscribed "For my Beloved Husband from his broken-hearted lonely wife Alix. Rest in Peace."[31]

On the following day, Alexandra wrote to her son, King George V; "I really do not know how I cld have borne that fearful ordeal without you by my side. You were indeed my <u>only</u> consolation here on Earth & yr kind & affte support helped me through it. God was indeed merciful to me in the midst of such grief, such deep felt sorrow & pain, to allow me to keep <u>one</u> of my darling sons, who now indeed has shown me more than ever his blessed, loving & affectionate heart. <u>Thank</u> you again & again, for all you ever have been & are to yr poor old Mother dear ... I do hope you are none the worse for that long, <u>long</u> tiring & saddest of days – last night I was half dead. May God bless & keep you forever, darling Georgie & may you ever walk in beloved Papa's footsteps."[32] Minny had come to comfort her, just as Alexandra had done for her in 1894, and stayed till 16 August. King George called on his mother every day and she received more visitors and deputations. It was warm enough to walk in the garden and have tea there. There had been rumours which she felt she must refute publicly. One was that the King had died because of an influenza vaccination, taken before leaving for Biarritz; "Queen Alexandra wishes it to be known that before the late King left England he had never felt better in health and spirits than after this treatment, for it had kept him in excellent health, to his Majesty's entire satisfaction, for no less that fifteen months. Queen Alexandra wishes it stated that his Majesty's attack in Biarritz was in no way related to his previous course of treatment." The other rumour was that she was going back to Denmark, and this too was denied; "Queen Alexandra has received many kind letters expressing a hope that there is no truth in the report that her Majesty intended to leave England and take up her residence in Denmark. Queen Alexandra has lived in England for forty-seven years, during which time she has received countless tokens of love and affection, especially in her recent sorrow, shared, as she so truly knows it is, by the nation. Her Majesty will ever look upon England as her home."[33]

Nevertheless Alexandra had always helped compatriots, in England as well as Denmark. She gave generously to the Scandinavian Benevolent Society, made recommendations for employment and was a patron to Danish artists and musicians, including her old music master, Frits Hartvigsen;[34] Johan Hartmann, the distinguished composer and organist at the Frue Kirke in Copenhagen, was also a friend.[35] When the Anglo–Danish Society was founded in 1924, she gave it her support. She helped a Captain Petersen, epileptic and partially paralysed, who lived at the sailors' home "from where he writes to me quite happy – but he is to be pitied, his life is a burden to him without a home or friends ... & wishes so much to be taken on board a ship by some kind Captain & end his days at sea – poor man." He had called on her, grateful for all she had done.[36] Alexandra subscribed for many years to the Danish churches for sailors in London and Hull; she visited the Sailors' Church at Poplar several times; Pastor Storm, presiding there, also officiated at the "German Chapel" by Marlborough House, where Danish services had been held regularly since 1881. Three services had been held on Sundays; an English one in early morning for the Waleses' household, a Lutheran service in German at 12.00 and a Danish one at 4.30. When her husband decided it should be known as the Marlborough House Chapel and the German services discontinued, Alexandra asked that the Danish congregation should still be able to worship there.[37]

Apart from going to Westminster Hall and Windsor, Alexandra had not left the grounds of Buckingham Palace since 5 May but on 9 June went out for the first time, to a sculptor's studio. She still received many short condolatory visits but could not yet face longer ones, telling George; "The days are coming & going very quickly and make me <u>sadder</u> every day as I feel the <u>space</u> gets wider & wider since we had beloved Papa still with us. It all is <u>too</u> sad for words & I miss him more & more as days go on." Minny's company was very welcome as Victoria, heartbroken about her father, had gone to Bognor, where the young daughters of Prince and Princess Nicholas of Greece[38] were also staying "& the quiet & peace at Bognor has already done her good." At Buckingham Palace, Alexandra had "a great deal to do every day putting things straight & trying to arrange everything which keeps my mind occupied altho' I cannot sleep much yet & am always tired. Every afternoon I spend in the lovely garden."[39] The main concern was moving back to Marlborough House but Probyn was also worried about her financial affairs. As the King's widow, she had an annuity of £70,000 but after tax it would shrink to about £64,000, which would certainly be inadequate. Removal costs alone would be considerable; in 1902 her son had paid over £34,000. Probyn asked Lloyd George[40] to increase the Queen's allowance, in vain.

On 23 June, David (sixteen) was created Prince of Wales; the next day his grandmother motored to Windsor Castle for his confirmation in the private chapel. On the 25th she received the explorer Captain Robert Falcon Scott and gave him a flag to plant at the South Pole. She was beginning to re-engage in everyday events, receiving more visitors and also attending the King's review of the 3rd Battalion Grenadier Guards in Buckingham Palace garden on the 29th. For their wedding anniversary on 6 July she sent "two little cases off beloved Papa's table for you & sweet May – a small lighter box for you & tiny evening cigarette case for May – also two photos of him we loved best – the one with frame is for you."[41] She visited the Royal Vault and the gardens at Windsor on the 15th and two days later called at Marlborough House to consider her move. Victoria left for Harrogate on the 19th, with Marie[42] and Christopher of Greece but her deputy, Aunt Minny, was confined by lumbago until the 26th. Alexandra went over Marlborough House again on the 28th and received more visitors, including Aksel Broström,[43] a Danish priest living in London. She was extremely busy; Minny felt she would be better at Sandringham, spending more time out of doors; at present, "she spent a couple of hours in the garden from time to time while the rest of the day she ... stood about packing and arranging all her things. She looks very tired now and coughs incessantly, which keeps her awake at night."[44] On 7 August Alexandra attended service in the private chapel for the last time before leaving; on the 8th the King and Queen came to say goodbye before going to Scotland. She left at 2.30pm on the 9th, when all the servants had assembled in Buckingham Palace's Grand Entrance Hall. As she told George, it had been "a terrible ordeal to go through, leaving the dear last joined old home where we were together & where he was taken from me! & the leave taking of all the many & dear old Servants – all was pain & agony! but had to be gone through, as you said in yr blessed letter."[45]

The sisters reached Sandringham at 6pm. Over the next week they sometimes took lunch or tea at the Bungalow. Canon Hervey had recently died in Norwich; there was a memorial service for him and on 11 August he was buried in Sandringham Churchyard. On the 12th Alexandra motored to Sir John Fisher's place, some 40 miles, and the next day to Holkham. Victoria returned from Harrogate on the 15th with her cousins; Marie later remembered Alexandra showing her "Uncle Bertie's private rooms, which she always kept untouched. Everything remained as it was during his lifetime". Alexandra's own rooms overflowed with her possessions; most of the chairs had albums or other things on them, and it was difficult to move. "Her desk always amused me, as there was little space left on it for writing. She adored all her objects, and woe to anyone who tried to change the place of anything." She would never get rid of anything that had been given to her and, when challenged, would reply "So and so gave it to me and I cannot throw it away." This conglomeration included Fabergé objects, jades and paintings. Marie also saw Alexandra's favourite places in the grounds, and, after lunch on Sundays, watched her at the stables, giving the horses carrots and sugar, and at the kennels, where the kennel man tied an apron round her waist and gave her a basket of neat little squares of white bread. She would go from one kennel to another, flinging handfuls of bread to her dogs, which surrounded her, barking and yelping and nearly pushing her over. Later she would feed the cows at the farm and would finish at the racing stud.[46]

Augusta, Dowager Grand Duchess of Mecklenburg-Strelitz wrote to her nephew, Adolphus, Duke of Teck, about Queen Mary's relationship with her mother-in-law; "It interests me to hear that she is rather shy of Q Alix, they never were on a very intimate footing, both cling to their own family not making friends with others – at least this is my impression, so at this very trying time, their want of reciprocal confidence has made matters even more unpleasant than they might have been." Augusta blamed Minny; "the sister being near and advising also was a pity. I trust all may come right now she has gone, I agree in all your remarks, most fully."[47] The two Queens had their differences, of which Alexandra was aware (and may have tried to mitigate by more than one promise to May that "you know how fond I am of you") but, only in February, she had assured May of her pleasure that they thoroughly understood one another, and pledged her sympathy and help. She may have been too optimistic, or perhaps May had backed off in the face of the more forceful Dowager Empress.

Some later sources assert that Alexandra was sometimes "beastly" to May[48] and that she and her daughters never forgot that May was only partly royal. Contemporary documents, however, show that Alexandra always sought, and believed she had, a fundamentally good relationship with her daughter-in-law, whom she loved and to whom she would never have been deliberately unkind. Even Victoria seemed to want to be friends with May. May herself appreciated Alexandra's kindness (especially after Eddy's death), which she returned, and ultimately remembered her with affection.[49] However, Alexandra would have liked May to confide in her more often and was sometimes hurt by mis-understandings, while May could be impatient of what she saw as Alexandra's dilatoriness and sentimentality. She was irritated at her mother-in-law's remaining at Sandringham House after 1910, and letting it go to pieces,[50] while she, King George and their family were cramped in York Cottage. But King Edward had left the house to his wife; she loved it as it was, in memory of their life there together, and could not in any case have afforded renovations with her much-reduced income after 1910. It would have been churlish to turn her out and the new sovereigns should have rented a larger property[51] in the meantime.

Both Queens were, in their own way, diffident; Alexandra, for all her liveliness and spontaneity, was dignified and reserved, only revealing her innermost thoughts to close friends and relatives. Any negative feelings were strictly private. May's shyness perhaps began as a reaction against her embarrassing (although loved) parents, her mother overwhelmingly large and exuberant, and her father prone to anger and increasing eccentricity. Her morganatic inheritance also mattered a great deal to her,[52] and she would have been sensitive to slights, even if unintended. If she sensed criticism from her in-laws, it could easily be that their chaffing and joking tipped over accidentally into something darker. Louise was reported as saying, when annoyed with her sister-in-law, "Poor May, poor May, with her Württemberg hands".[53] This sounds rather pointed and not particularly amiable, given Louise's own "morganatic" marriage, but what if it reflected something May herself had said? She thought that she had a "vulgar"[54] laugh and may have expressed an opinion, good or bad, about her hands too; Louise, privately, may have been teasing rather than intentionally beastly, but who can tell?

There were visitors, drives, social calls and tea in the woods. Alexandra was filling the time but was completely worn out. She had not managed to write to George for some time but in the letter of 25/27 August described how "I have been <u>longing</u> & <u>trying</u> to write ever since I came here, but somehow I <u>could not</u> – I really felt as 'one collapsed', & had no energy or courage left in me. After all those <u>terrible</u> months & ever since beloved Papa was taken from us I have gone through such a terrible miserable strain so that I never fully realized all I have lost in him till I came back here to our beloved & formerly so happy & bright old home! – in which every nook & corner both inside & outside remind me of him

& seem to reopen the dreadful wound afresh." It was like a severe illness; "I feel so weak, so miserably tired with that same detestable cough always disturbing me, & my legs so weak & shaky too." His kind letters greatly touched her; "Thank God my darling Georgie that He has given me such a dear & blessed boy as you really are & always have been to me. I do not believe that there is a better or more loving or honestly devoted son in the world, than mine. Really ever since yr birth I do not think or remember the least misunderstanding ever between us. We have always understood & sympathised together, and now in our mutual terrible sorrow & irreparable loss we feel alike & share all misery. And you have indeed been such an inexpressible comfort to me. Thank you over & over again."[55] His father had told George something similar in 1894; both parents felt very close to him and his reply to his mother in 1910 shows how mutual this was; "only time can soften the hard feeling in your heart when all the world seems cold & miserable. But being out as much as possible & being able to rest & be quiet must be good for you & will help to soothe your aching heart. You are quite right when you say that we have never had any misunderstandings, you know, darling Motherdear how devoted I am to you & have always told you everything since I was a little child, we have never had any secrets. My great object now is to try & help & comfort you in any way I can & make your life easier & your sorrow lighter to bear ... & shall take care that nobody or anything ever comes between us."[56]

Marie and her children had left but Christopher[57] remained, "the dear boy trying to cheer us up – I am so glad [Toria] has him as cheery companion just now." Victoria was much better and "looks rounder in the face than I have seen her for years – Harrogate has put her all right. Laking I know will be pleased to hear this, and tell him thanks to him we sent her there." Sandringham looked its best, with hundreds of lovely flowers, "the gardens really are too beautiful, quite a sight & I only wish poor beloved Papa cld have seen them once in their real glory." There had been changes and Probyn had instigated a little brook, with flowers and several little wooden bridges.[58] "It is simply charming & I sit under that big oak tree & read very often when fine after luncheon; you will all be delighted with it & I hope you will have the little island opposite the cottage laid out in the same way. My little house by the sea we go to very often and dear Aunt Minny loved it."[59] On the 26th she watched the servants' cricket match and the next day drove out for the first time in her new white motor car. She was thinking of them all at Balmoral and whether May had made any changes "as I confess dear Grd Mama's taste in wallpapers was rather sad & very doubtful! That washed out pink moiré paper in the sitting room is sickly & the one in the bedroom appalling but I never liked to touch anything of hers so left it all exactly as she had it. Only downstairs the two drawing rooms were too awful for words & had to be redone & I thought looked very pretty & comfortable now." She planned to visit Louise later but "to tell the truth I for my own selfish part wld now prefer to stay here in <u>peace</u> & <u>quiet</u>, particularly as it is so lovely here just now ... It was <u>terrible</u> leaving the Old Home & then coming here to find it <u>empty</u>, but thank God Aunt Minny was with me, or I shld have been quite by myself as Toria had not then come back from Harrogate. The faithful Christo is still with us & cheers us up & he is such a nice companion to poor Victoria with whom he rides every morning."[60]

They left for Scotland on 5 September and, breakfasting the next day at Balmoral, motored to Mar Lodge later. Alexandra was looking forward to quiet days with Louise and indeed they did enjoy picnics and *al fresco* lunches, but it was entirely spoiled by a family row. According to Christopher (22), writing his memoirs later,[61] Victoria tried to bring him and the Fifes' elder daughter, Alix (19), together.[62] Her parents were horrified; their strictly-brought-up daughters were not allowed to talk to young men. Queen Alexandra, caught in the middle, was dreadfully upset "by their <u>inconceivable</u> <u>behaviour</u> towards that poor dear excellent Christo who behaved in the <u>most</u> gentlemanlike & <u>honest</u> way, to both Parents, & poor little Alix whom he really likes for <u>herself</u> only and <u>she him</u>! But she poor child is not allowed even to have a voice in the matter. They may one day <u>regret</u> their <u>cruelty</u> towards both and the next one they themselves may choose or pick out will only marry her for <u>money's</u> sake as the children are treated like <u>babies</u> & are <u>never</u> allowed to speak to anybody, so love would be out of the question." Love, to her, was the most important reason for marriage. "I shall never forget that scene as long as I live, and the extraordinary way they abused both Victoria & me. What wld dear Papa have said to all this! he who always told me he wished some Prince to marry them particularly as Louise herself <u>asked</u> for the <u>title</u> for the girls! – he also mentioned little Arthur[63] – but of course the girls were promptly forbidden to speak to him, & Louise said he had bad manners!! But I will not worry myself further about it & we must leave the future to Providence but whatever excuses they may still make their conduct remains unpardonably <u>rude</u> & <u>insulting</u>."[64]

Something else, which may have been brewing at the time of Augusta's earlier comments, had occurred. There had been some awkwardness and misunderstanding about the ownership of crown jewels and now Alexandra was angry and hurt at being accused of keeping six Garter Stars and other crown jewels, which should have been handed over to the King. The accusation had apparently started with Henry Bell,[65] of Messrs Garrard, the crown jewellers. In fact the items in dispute were Alexandra's own property and not crown jewels; one was Queen Victoria's diamond Garter Star and the other was a silver one; Queen Victoria had left them to King Edward, who gave them to Alexandra after having them re-set for her in the same way as some turquoises mounted by Garrard's. Alexandra had in fact offered the Garter Star to May earlier.[66] So, "Her Majesty is naturally very much annoyed therefore that anything should have been said by Mr Bell, or anybody else, to give rise to such false reports being circulated."[67] She asked for some work which Bell had been doing for her to be sent back forthwith, but first Garrard's and then Bell himself vehemently denied the accusation.[68] All was revealed when Alexandra mentioned the Garter Stars to May on 14 September but the only answer she got was "Oh! Yes – that was a mistake – but it's all right now – we have found them." Anything more unsatisfactory, Sir Arthur Davidson never knew; "to make an accusation – spread it broadcast & then to let it <u>remain</u> instead of contradicting it when it's found out to be groundless."[69] Probyn at once sent Bell Alexandra's apologies.[70] Every excuse should be made to him for her unjust suspicions, as "It all arose by Queen Mary's saying I had kept <u>6</u> stars <u>orders</u> – which she now owns having found among the King's property." Bell accepted the apology and Alexandra made sure the work he had been doing for her was returned for him to finish.[71] King Edward's will let her keep any of his property she wished, while crown jewels were for reigning sovereigns and consorts. Alexandra's own diamond Garter Star and Badge would go to her son after her death.[72]

Queen Alexandra's financial position was now grave, as Probyn confided to the Postmaster General, Herbert Samuel;[73] "My post is not an easy one. Ever since Her Majesty's marriage, now more than 47 years ago, she has had everything she wanted. She has always been allowed to give full vent to her generous propensities, and she has never been denied anything. Now however on Her Majesty's most terribly reduced income, I find it falls to my painful duty to endeavour to curtail expenses in every possible way. I beg of you to assist me in this unpleasant and difficult task, as it is in your power to do." During the King's lifetime, Alexandra had sent her official letters and telegrams free of charge; might this continue? Mr Samuel replied the next day, having already arranged for her to retain these privileges.[74]

Alexandra and Victoria left Mar on the 19th for Dundee, where *Victoria and Albert* was waiting, and started at 3.30pm but were delayed by a storm, finally reaching Copenhagen at 3.30pm on the 21st. The whole family came on board for tea, but "even here all my former pleasure has gone & everything seems <u>too sad</u> everywhere I go. We are still on board & even going to our dear pretty little bright house here I seem to shun. We are going there on Monday next however, & then the ship will go home. It was <u>so nice</u> being on board once again altho' I miss dear Papa dreadfully here too. It seems all to get sadder & worse as days go by."[75] As usual, she met relatives, made the pilgrimage to Roskilde Cathedral and visited the zoo, always a favourite outing. On 3 October, with Minny, Victoria and Christopher, she went to stay at Hvidöre; Charlotte Knollys and Davidson stayed at Amalienborg because Hvidöre was too small. Victoria and Christopher, with Davidson, had tea with Charlotte at Amalienborg several times before Davidson left for England on the 12th. There were more tea parties and visits but also bad news of the Portuguese revolution and expulsion of Dowager Queen Maria Pia, Queen Amélie and King Manuel, who stayed first at Gibraltar but were bound for England. "I was too thankful & pleased to hear that you sent them the dear yacht to bring them over to England in, & now thank God they are at least safely land[ed] in our hospitable country" Alexandra told her son. "I am glad too you are going to pay them a visit at Wood Norton to show them personally your sympathy in their dreadful misfortune! no words can say how deeply I feel for them all." She understood how upset Soveral would be "& how ashamed he must feel on the disgraceful behaviour of his countrymen and he loved his own country!" The other anxiety, in England, was Frank of Teck's health; minor nasal surgery had led to pleurisy, requiring a "tapping operation". "I do pray to God that his life may be spared." But Frank died on 22 October; Alexandra sent her heartfelt sympathy to May.

Her Danish visit was nearly over and she was thinking of home and her imminent move. She supposed it would be George's and May's "last stay at dear old Marlboro' House, the same as our very last at dear Buckingham Palace when I pack up my last remaining things in my two rooms. I feel it very much but all this cannot be helped & must be gone through. The only thing I hope is that you also will clear out now, or I shall never get the house cleaned & get my poor things straight or be able to get into the house before the summer."[76] With Victoria, Maud and Olaf, she left on 4 November and reached Buckingham Palace early next evening. The next day she wrote from "my now sad & empty home" to Lady Brownlow, missing the King intensely; everything seeming so desolate and changed; "I am here in this dear place packing up! which is dreadful – such a wrench besides & weary work which must be got through. I had a nice time with my dear Sister in our dear little House in my old Home, but even there everything seemed changed & clouded over, but I fear this will be so wherever I may be for the rest of my life."[77] Visitors called, then on the 8th, "King George and Queen Mary vacated Marlborough House."[78] A service in the Albert Memorial Chapel on King Edward's birthday included a special prayer; "Grant him, O Lord, light and rest, peace, joy and ever ampler employment in the spacious fields of Eternity; perfect cleansing from all earthly stain, endless growth of divine beauty as the face of God and the presence of Christ transform him more and more unto Thyself."[79]

On 10 November Alexandra inspected Marlborough House. It had changed substantially since Sir Christopher Wren[80] built it in 1709; for example, in 1860 the original ceiling in the south-west drawing room on the ground floor had been replaced by a coffered one. When George and May moved into the house in 1902, this was changed to a neo-Georgian one, which Alexandra now decided to replace with a new plaster ceiling with a central shallow dome, like one in the Amalienborg Palace in Copenhagen. The work was later carried out by Jackson's.[81] On the 11th the Queen and her daughters visited the Portuguese Royal Family at Wood Norton. They planned to leave Buckingham Palace the following week, but Victoria was unwell with dental problems. Peace was restored with Louise who, with her daughters, came to tea several times. Alexandra sent Sydney Holland a letter and photograph, for the lady superintendent of the children's hospital at Mandalay; "There, you see, yr letter was not put aside as you thought amongst my numerous papers on my table!"[82] On the 20th, "for positively the last time"[83] she attended service in the private chapel, Victoria's indisposition having delayed them for a week. They went to Sandringham the next day. May had been "thinking so much of you today, when you left your dear old home, for I know I felt very miserable a fortnight ago when I left Marlborough House. You cannot think how dreadfully we miss beloved Papa and you here, it seems so strange to be here alone & one feels rather bewildered."[84] Staying at Windsor for the first time since his father's death, George felt "so strange to be living in his rooms, one expects to see him come in every minute." Johnnie was "quite happy here & plays about in the corridor as usual with Alice's Children."[85] Alexandra told May she was longing to know how they were getting on at Windsor "without us!" and I do hope you missed us both a little, as I also feel like one dead already and my life seems ended with his!" She was eager to know how they would arrange the rooms, but, more widely, lamented; "Politics are in an awful mess and it is heartrending to see them trying their best to upset our old & solid constitution. I fear poor Georgie must be terribly worried." At Sandringham, "we are very busy unpacking & getting everything straight here, and everything has now been taken away from Buckingham Palace."[86]

King Haakon, the Fife family, King Manuel, his mother and their attendants had all arrived by early December. George and May were at York Cottage and on the 4th four queens and three kings were at dinner. The Norwegian Royal Family went home on the 13th. King George, now at Buckingham Palace, reported; "We are living in the rooms Aunt Minny had & they are most comfortable, it seems so strange being there without you, & it all seems wrong. Papa's rooms are getting on fairly well & I have hung some pictures in them already."[87] The elections were nearly over but the respective strength of the parties would be the same, which would make his position extremely difficult. The weather was dreadful; gales made many of the fires in Buckingham Palace smoke and they had to be put out. There were floods at Windsor and all over the country and the Fifes had had a rough passage to Gibraltar.

Alexandra had been very busy at Sandringham, "trying to do all those terrible Xmas presents & which I find terribly irksome to do this year! when my heart is not in it." She sympathised about the election results and the action George had taken, "& I know for certain Papa wld have been obliged to act exactly in the same way, it was unavoidable, & the only course open to you ... Do not worry ... and pray to God as we all do that He will continue to lead you on the right path all through this serious & difficult crisis."[88] The household arrived and the York Cottage party dined at the big house on Christmas Day; the clergy came in the evening. Alexandra and others went for walks and on the 31ˢᵗ the servants had their tree in the ballroom.

As 1911 began, scandal simmered. A journalist, Edward Mylius,[89] libellously resurrected an "odious lie"[90] that the King, as a young man in Malta, had married a Miss Seymour, making his marriage to Queen Mary bigamous. The King was determined to have it publicly disproved and urged Mylius' arrest and trial, which led to George's complete vindication. "Thank God" said Alexandra, "that vile trial is over, and those <u>infamous</u> lies & foul accusations at an end for <u>ever</u> & cleared up before the whole world – to <u>us</u> all it was a ridiculous story, yr having been <u>married</u> before! <u>too silly</u> for words, but as the public seems to have believed it this trial was the only way to let them hear & know the truth and to have your good name vindicated for ever." They were doing far too much; "I am sure you will both break down – you ought not – the Coronation year! [to] have engaged yourself to visit both Ireland & Scotland, besides all the functions you must do in London, & then on the top of all go to India to <u>begin</u> it all over again."[91] At the Opening of Parliament her thoughts had followed them "step by step to Westminster ... Were you both very alarmed & *shy & émotionné* as we were the <u>first time</u> particularly! I wished all the same I cld have had a peep at you! What did you wear?" she asked May, "did the cloak of Grandmama's do? Did you wear the big or small Crown – please tell me, it interests me to hear also what jewels you wore etc. I always <u>heard</u> & felt my heart beating loud all the time we were seated there on that very auspicious place & thanked our stars when it was well over." She sympathised with their having to arrange their rooms, but being nearby would be easier than trying to organise Marlborough House from Norfolk, which she dreaded. Poor little Johnnie had been worse lately and "I do hope the Doctors will be able to cure him quite, as it wld be too sad were he to go on like this."[92]

Her son assured her that he was not really tired and there were certain things he must do. Opening Parliament was "the most terrible ordeal I have ever gone through & I was horribly nervous, besides feeling so sad thinking of the many times we had seen you & beloved Papa do it that I nearly broke down."[93] Alexandra agreed. "Both dear Papa and I always rather dreaded it every time particularly ... with so many acquaintances & friends so near one all the time! makes one feel still more shy & awkward."[94] Louise and Lorne, now Duke and Duchess of Argyll, had written after staying at Windsor under the new regime; "You do not know! – nor can you <u>ever</u> believe what <u>real</u> pleasure your very dear & kind letter gave me after yr first stay at Windsor without <u>us</u>! ... I know well how everybody <u>really</u> does miss my beloved Bertie, but still it does one's sore heart good to hear them say so, and you two dear ones, were the only ones, except my darling Georgie, who wrote it to me." Everything was going on as usual but her life alone was becoming harder to bear and her future looked bleak; "But I try hard to cheer up for others' sake, particularly for my poor Victoria, whose life is not to be spoilt through me." At present she had no plans whatsoever, although the papers had kindly sketched some out for her. She would stay quietly at Sandringham before coming "to arrange poor dear old Marlborough House – and I have a great deal to do here just now, so am fully occupied, which is a good thing for mind & body."[95] Several of the grandchildren were ill; Mary with suspected mumps and her elder brothers with measles at Dartmouth. Johnnie's problems were different; epileptic episodes for two years and imperfect mental development. The doctors thought he would outgrow this by the age of seven and there were always hopes for improvement. Alexandra took an especial interest in him and had talked to his nurse, but "poor little Johnnie is still the same, it really [is] too sad for that dear little fellow who looks the picture of health."[96]

A memorial to Queen Victoria, in front of Buckingham Palace, would be ready for unveiling in May and the King had arranged to do it on the 16th, writing that "I know dearest Papa had always intended to invite William[97] to be present at the ceremony & W when he was here the other day said that he would come for it. So I thought it much better to invite him, which I did two days ago, & his wife, than that he should propose himself. I don't suppose for a minute she will come, & if he does it will be quite a private visit & I shall not ask any other representatives at all. I thought it would interest you to know what I had done."[98] Alexandra was interested, but said nothing in her reply. She had heard George had lost two of his best carriages in a fire at the coach-makers and offered him another; "I shld be so pleased if you wld use our glass coach for the Levee next Tuesday, the one dear Papa always drove in to St James." She had seen the plans for King Edward's statue, proposed for the Mall, near Marlborough House, "which I certainly think much nicer than in Green Park which we cld never really see unless walking by. Schomberg McDonnell[99] has certainly worked hard at it all which dear Papa wld have appreciated." Her son was pleased she approved, and gladly accepted the offer of the coach.

Alexandra was busy sorting things out at Sandringham; "my time has been so taken up by putting everything away & straight … Now I am nearly all right, but it is an awful undertaking & I brought about 8 great boxes from Buckingham Palace which I have now cleared, & hope in consequence to begin with empty Drawers at Marlborough House."[100] She hoped they were settling into the rooms at Buckingham Palace and were not too tired; they should not do too much at first, especially in view of the many important duties to be undertaken this year. It would disappoint the public much more if they had to cancel engagements on health grounds; "I speak like an old woman from sad experience. So please both of you remember my words & act accordingly." She also mentioned an essay on

Marlborough House that Mr Hood[101] had written for her earlier, which May now had, and requested a copy; "I shld like so much to have it now I go back there again, & it has the greatest interest for me now."[102] Probyn (78) was in bed at Sandringham with gout; he had been over-doing things, attending relatives' funerals and inspecting Marlborough House, where he had knocked his knee. Alexandra felt so sorry for him that she sent for Laking, knowing they were friends. Unfortunately, Probyn was "mortally affronted"; "I believe he was perfectly furious (he has an awful temper you know!) & never even allowed poor Laking to look at the knee – too bad, as he wld have been able to help him & suggest some treatment together with Manby. Really too bad! but he is the most obstinate Mule of a man I ever came across. He worked himself up into such a rage that he says he is much worse since Laking has been – most ungrateful as I only asked poor Laking to come all that way to give him ease & help & this is all the thanks we got. Catch me doing anything else for him now & those who won't hear must feel. It really worries & distresses me much as he must suffer tortures poor man – he even refuses to have any kind of help, tho' we have our excellent Nurse in the house!"[103]

Other nurses, the Territorial ones, wanted the same uniform as the military nurses. As patron of the latter, Alexandra could not allow this, "as our Military nurses must keep their distinction above all the other nurses and that even our own Reserve Nurses are not allowed to wear it, and as I hitherto, in all other nurses' dress, have been asked to choose it, I now ask them to have the Territorials in khaki colour like the men's dress, with a dark blue cape with red stripes and lining, which will look very well on that yellowish skirt, & a dark blue bonnet to match. I hope this will be adopted and please everybody, even Miss Haldane[104] & Co. What bores these old women are about dress!!! It is a pity that the Director General rather took their part, & I think he too might have asked me", she complained to Holland.[105]

Probyn struggled on, got up on the 6th and went out on the 9th. Meanwhile Alexandra felt a wreck, with an awful cold and bad cough, and was "ready to cry about everything." She could not go to bed as there were visitors to entertain but tried to go out, hoping to feel better. Then, as though the mist had cleared, she made a rapid decision; it was time to get away from all this pain and grief. She asked George on the 15th "if we may have the Yacht for a short cruise in April? I suddenly think it wld perhaps do me good to have a complete change for a little & take me a little out of myself … & also I think it wld do dear Toria good. So if you don't want the Yacht at this moment might we have her for a bit. I shld like only just to go & see Uncle Willy & come back the first day of May." She would also like to come up to Marlborough House as soon as Probyn was well enough but, in case it was not yet finished, could she stay for a few days just across the road at St James's Palace "as I suppose that is always ready & that wld be nearer for us to run over?"[106] The King gladly agreed to both requests, but she had been feeling really ill, aching all over and was no better; moreover Victoria now had a violent cold. "Whenever I make any plans something is sure to happen to me or somebody else which generally ends by a postponement." However, Probyn had said "that we can quite well go up to Marlborough House, so perhaps this will be the best plan after all. He went up there yesterday and is coming back tonight."[107] On the 25th they went to stay there for the first time since leaving in 1902 but it seemed so sad and desolate; Alexandra missed her husband more and more "and the house is in a dreadful state, nothing arranged yet!!!"[108]

A week later they had what Charlotte Knollys called the worst passage on record to Calais. As Alexandra told George from Corfu; "You know all about our <u>horrid</u> crossing from Dover to Calais – never did I see anything so <u>awful</u> & my only fear was that we shld not have been able to get into Calais and as it was it was by a hair's breadth. I think I was the only one who was not ill – even the <u>Admiral</u> Colin Keppel[109] who said he wld look after me on deck in the Captain's Cabin had to rush out twice & came back like a drowned rat as the seas were running over us all the time. Our passages from Genoa to Naples and here were not enjoyable either." At Corfu it was calm again and her relatives welcomed her on 13 April. Not so welcome was "The Great William very much *en evidence* [who] also came on board the first day & she & the whole family came next day. We are going to pay them a visit this afternoon!!" He had come to see some "very interesting excavations to which we all went & spent hours there. W spends his days there & all his enormous suites!! He seems in <u>very</u> good spirits I suppose about the Bagdad railway & all his last <u>really</u> <u>important</u> achievements Diplomatically! which alas will be a most <u>terrible blow</u> to England in the near future I fear & has cost us our <u>prestige</u> for ever in the East. How cld we be so <u>blind</u> & <u>slow</u>." On the 19th she and her party spent the whole afternoon with the Germans at the "lovely Achilleon", built for the late Austrian empress, whose daughter had sold it to William; "I do wish one of the Greek boys had got it instead". It was very comfortable, "bright & nice in that lovely place" with a beautiful garden and grand views. "They showed us everything both in and outside the place & were most amiable." Alexandra was enjoying the holiday, with trips, visits, large family lunches and dinners, but still had her chronic cough. "I very often cough without ceasing for an hour & a half" and sometimes could "neither breathe or speak. I think it is bronchitis or whooping cough or croup or some such vile thing." Medicine was useless. Above all, "How I miss beloved Papa's letters here you cannot think; only one little short year ago he wrote continually."[110] They left Corfu on the 27th and, via Trieste, reached London on 4 May. There was a service at the Albert Memorial Chapel at Windsor on the 6th, the first anniversary of King Edward's death; afterwards they laid flowers on his coffin in the Royal Vault. A family lunch in the castle followed. Queen Mary wrote; "Mama kept up well & was very nice & kind. She still has a nasty cough which she cannot get rid of & she does not look well & is terribly depressed. It is very sad seeing her like this, so 'hopeless & helpless' & one feels so sorry for her. I think it worries her that Marl: House is not finished yet & that the exertion & trouble of arranging it all is more than she can manage, poor thing."[111]

Alexandra had naturally attended her husband's memorial service, but made it clear she would not to be present at another ceremony.[112] When the imperial couple, with their daughter, Victoria Louise, arrived on the 15th for the unveiling of Queen Victoria's statue, she was staying at Lord Howe's house, Woodlands, at Uxbridge, having had as much as she could bear of William for the time being. She remained until the 22nd, meeting old friends and visiting Windsor on the 21st, when she had tea at Norman Tower with Probyn. On the 27th she and Victoria went to Sandringham, where for a few days they entertained King Manuel and Queen Amélie. On 1 June Alexandra inspected the works at Sandringham Church, drove her pony carriage to Appleton and called on old friends at Wolferton. She returned to London the next day, partly to see Queen Mary's coronation dress on the 8th. There were visits and guests, then on the 14th Alexandra went to Olympia at 9am for the horse show, perhaps privately, before it was open to the public. That evening Victoria attended the opera for the first time since her father's death. The next day Alexandra visited Feodore Gleichen's studio, to see her statue of King Edward for his Windsor hospital, and on the same day received the wife of Sir Solomon Obeyesekere,[113] a member of the Ceylon Legislative Council.

By tradition, a King's widow did not attend his successor's coronation; in any case Alexandra was still feeling unwell and the emotional strain would have been too much. Minny arrived from Russia on 17 June and they went to Sandringham together two days later. On the eve of the coronation she sent her son a "Mother's blessing", praying God "to guard & protect you and take you in His Holy keeping till yr life's end. May He guide you in the difficult path which you have to tread, & make you a blessing to our beloved Country as yr beloved Father & Grandmother were before you. It seems but so short a while ago that our Coronation took place! And you will <u>feel</u> & <u>know</u> that <u>both</u> our spirits are hovering near you!"[114] King George and Queen Mary were crowned in Westminster Abbey on the 22nd, while Alexandra attended a service in Sandringham Church. She inspected the tents in which over 2,000 men, women and children would be given dinner and tea and later watched games in the park. May sent her a description of the coronation, which pleased her; "nothing in this world comes up to it – having felt & gone through it all myself only 9 short years ago – <u>how</u> beautiful & solemn it was & quite ineffaceable from one's mind for ever, & the heavenly music adding to it all. My thoughts as you know never left you or darling Georgie for one moment, but alas! I cld not have <u>faced</u> being present now!"[115] Back in London, she paid several unofficial visits: the Radium Institute on 10 July, the Surgical Museum on the 11th, dinner at the Dominion

Club, and a pageant on the 12th, the Millbank Military Hospital on the 13th and picture galleries on the 14th. She was feeling better. She saw the Duchess of Devonshire, King Manuel and his mother on the 14th but heard on the 15th that the Duchess had died of apoplexy after attending Sandown Races. After more calls Alexandra, Minny and Victoria returned on the 17th to Sandringham where, the next day, Minny had to retire to bed with lumbago.

The King had been so busy there was no time for letter-writing; he and his mother sent daily telegrams instead. Finally he wrote from Plas Machynlleth during his official visits to Ireland, Wales and Scotland. Queen Alexandra replied on the 21st, pleased everything had gone off so well. David had been invested as Prince of Wales at Caernarvon Castle on the 13th and she admitted; "I wld have given anything to have been present to see him do his part. How well I can understand yr feelings when you had to lead him between you two & present him to the Welsh people by Queen Eleanor's[116] Gate, it must have been quite overwhelming in every sense of the word. Who wrote the speech for him? It was excellent & very well worded."[117] She only regretted that her husband, Prince of Wales for almost 60 years, had not been mentioned. The hot weather at Sandringham had "quite knocked me out"; neuralgia and toothache prevented her eating and "poor dear Aunt Minny" had only just felt well enough to get up, "so that my time was entirely taken up looking after her. She is now sitting up in another room, on the cool side of the house, while I am writing this." Alexandra still hoped a cure might be found for "sweet fat Johnnie"; Minny had told her about a French doctor who "<u>entirely</u> <u>cures</u> people of that sad illness,[118] & she herself knows a person who suffered from it for upwards [of] 38 years." Alexandra would tell Laking this, in case he could find out more. She also supported the King in the current, serious crisis, suggesting that, on the wave of patriotism following the coronation, he should personally appeal to the people and say he could not sanction something he believed to be to their detriment. "I think honestly that the <u>effect</u> of yr speaking out like this wld have such a startling & unexpected effect on all right-minded people, that all might <u>still</u> be <u>saved</u> & at any rate put off for a while."[119] The King's reply has not survived; perhaps he proceeded quietly as already decided. [120]

There were more visitors and outings and on the 28th some Red Cross Society demonstrations at Thornham. On the 29th Charles Urban's[121] "Kinemacolor" was shown in the ballroom. Victoria, with Blanche Lascelles,[122] left for Harrogate on the 31st, while her mother and aunt motored and had tea at the Bungalow. Alexandra had written; "Here in this beloved place it is simply stifling & I never remember anything like it anywhere. Thank God poor Aunt Minny has got over her horrible lumbago ... we spend most evenings by the sea & dine outside by my little house, & come home later in our open Motors which is delightful. I am so looking forward to yr little visit here on the 9th when I hope it will be cooler.[123] We had actually some refreshing showers today which quite revived one. We all & I in particular miss darling Toria dreadfully, but I know Harrogate will do her good."[124] On the 11th Probyn went to London, but his intended return was thwarted by *angina pectoris* and so he left for Birkhall on the 29th. Alexandra and Minny stayed at Studley Royal[125] from 15–22 August; they motored to Harrogate to see Victoria, toured the grounds and ruins of Fountains Abbey, motored to York, had tea at the treasurer's house, visited the cathedral and shopped. The railway strike began on the 18th; Alexandra motored to Harrogate again, and saw Studley Church, Fountains Abbey (for tea) and Ripon Cathedral. They had to motor 56 miles to Doncaster on the 22nd but got a special train there to King's Cross.

Victoria came home and on 23 August went to the zoo with her mother, Cousin Marie and children. In the next few days, Alexandra and Minny visited the Doré Gallery, the City and Richmond. On the 28th Alexandra's party embarked on *Victoria and Albert* for Norway and Denmark, when "We had on the whole an excellent passage altho' we rolled a good deal the second day & night tho' not very disagreeable; it was rather fun at meals when our chairs ran about & our bottles & things upset all over the table & there was a tremendous thunderstorm, which frightened all the dogs." Minny had left at Sheerness, being "hurried off by her Admiral Wiasemski[126] & not even allowed a cup of tea as he said they must start at once on account of the tide at Esbjerg." Alexandra's party had arrived safely at Christiania, with an old friend; "You will be glad to hear that I actually persuaded Soveral to come with us here & that the change has already done him a lot of good, as he was very low & depressed in London, both Charles & Maud were delighted to see him & show him everything worth seeing here." As for another old friend, "dear General Probyn is better tho' slow – since his arrival at Birkhall. I do hope the tiresome attack of gout will be the means of curing all his present heart troubles."[127]

They took a long motor drive to Ringerike on 9 September and a boat trip to Lysaker for tea with Nansen on the 10th. On the 11th they lunched at Bygdö, walked to Victoria Cottage and later had a dinner for 27 and entertainment by the Yacht's company. On the 13th, while Victoria and Christopher stayed at Christiania, Alexandra and the others left for Copenhagen, where Minny had already arrived on *Polar Star*. They visited Rosenborg, Charlottenlund and of course the zoo in the next couple of days then, on the 15th, the Queen and her sister went to see their little house. After more sightseeing, Soveral left for England on the 20th, "I think the thorough change after all he has gone through lately did him a lot of good & he got quite cheery & jolly as he used to be during beloved Papa's life time." She had shown him all the most interesting things in Copenhagen and outskirts and was happy that Hvidöre had left him with "une impression impérissable."[128] She went there on the 20th but almost immediately collapsed with a bad cold. Victoria and Christopher arrived on the 25th and on the 29th the whole party went to Roskilde to place flowers on the graves of King

Christian IX, Queen Louise, Prince William of Glücksburg and for the first time Uncle Hans, who had died earlier in the year. "How we miss him no words can say & every minute we expect him to come in & hear his never failing cheery voice ... How soon he went after beloved Papa – the year after on May the 29th, & only last year he was so unhappy about poor Papa & cld hardly bear seeing me at first & never ceased lamenting him, or talking about him."[129]

She was anxious about Probyn, at Birkhall. The doctors had said he could not go back to Sandringham, which he took to mean ever and was so upset, that "they might have knocked me down with a feather & it was a terrible blow to me & kept me awake all night long." He got up to write a long account of everything he had gone through that night "with his Doom before him". Alexandra very sensibly thought the doctors should just have told him it was too cold for him in Scotland and to go somewhere warmer, such as Barton in the Isle of Wight, for a bit. "I do pray & hope now if they won't worry him afresh about the future that he may get stronger and gradually get [to be] himself again." Meanwhile foreign affairs, especially Crete and the Italian–Turkish war, were a constant anxiety; "How will it all end – most likely lead to a European War, or religious war in the East! What will you now do about going to India!!!?"[130] Davidson was now back in England, after long, interesting talks with Uncle Willy "about everything in the East, which he can tell you". In addition, the Maharajah of Cooch Behar[131] had died and the Russian prime minister[132] had been shot at a state performance in the theatre in Kiev "before poor Nicky & his two eldest daughters' eyes – the poor girls cannot get over it at all."[133]

Alexandra was pleased that a reredos, in her husband's memory, had been installed in Crathie Church. In Copenhagen they were going to unveil a memorial in St Alban's; the portrait by Emil Fuchs, a version of which she had already placed in Sandringham Church. She expected to come home soon, so as to see as much as possible of George and May before they left for India but "as you know it is always so difficult to get away from here & I hate to see poor little Aunt Minny being left quite alone, & none of her children with her." Italy and Turkey were still at war "& who can tell where & how this may end or lead to. I confess I am very anxious about everything just now."[134] The Danish holiday continued a little longer, with Prince Harald's birthday celebrations on 8 October and the removal of Princess Waldemar's coffin to Roskilde. Marie visited Hvidöre, which they had furnished "with much care and very good taste ... they both loved this place and were very proud of it". Alexandra had sent for her gardener to arrange the grounds, so there was a profusion of flowers in the English style. The two sisters spent hours on the beach, collecting pieces of amber.[135] Prince George Schervashidze,[136] the Dowager Empress's chief steward, put on a cinematograph show for the sisters and Victoria on the 12th. Two days later they visited St Alban's to see King Edward's memorial. Alexandra and Victoria finally left on the 19th, reaching London, after a rough crossing, on the 20th.

The next day Queen Alexandra returned to Sandringham, and spent time with her two daughters, Crown Prince Olaf and later the King and Queen. On 27 and 28 October she was in bed with a bad cold but on the 29th the Bishop of Norwich[137] dedicated Sandringham Church's chancel and east window to King Edward's memory. Back in London, they commemorated his birthday on 9 November with lunch and dinner at Buckingham Palace and tea at 15, Portman Square. The next day the King and Queen came to dinner, before setting sail in the *Medina* for India on the 11th, when Alexandra, Victoria and Maud saw them off at Portsmouth. At sea between Portsmouth and Gibraltar on the 14th, the King told his mother the parting had been horrible, "& I felt it most acutely, leaving you especially now, when you have only darling Toria to look after you & all my other dear ones. Of course it was nice your coming to see the last of us, but it made it worse when the moment for saying goodbye came."[138] Yes, Alexandra replied, "but we understood & felt alike. I was indeed quite miserable … and yet I do not regret having gone all that way to Portsmouth with you, it was on the contrary my only comfort & I was so pleased for that last drive with you when we were able to talk a little together too."[139] Despite rough weather, George was pleased that all on *Medina* were getting on well together. It had also been wet and boisterous at home, replied Alexandra, but "the sisters have been to the play several times & very busy shopping & I have had a lot to do & seen a good many people & had to write endless tiresome letters every night when the sisters were out. Louise & Family have come here every day." They were soon going for their regular holiday, taken for health reasons. "Louise, Macduff & girls stayed with us for two days & were in good spirits & the poor girls quite delighted to be here; they leave for Egypt on the 7th but hurried back to pack!"[140] she told her son on the 24th. But the main subject of this letter was something else entirely.

The Rector of Sandringham, F Percival Farrar, incumbent since 1907, also had charge of the school.[141] In 1910 he was appointed Domestic Chaplain to the Royal Family and in 1911 his wife presented a parish hall to West Newton. All was, however, not well. "And now you have heard what awful things have happened here with our Clergyman of all people, such a disgrace & horror, it all gave me an awful shock. On Sunday last he was still preaching to us about our sins & performed the service as usual, not having the slightest idea or suspicion of what was hanging over him & that he was found out, & the police *en masse* here to arrest him!! Next day Monday he was gone & fled! & his poor, good, innocent & brave wife, Mrs Farrar fled with him!" With the King and Probyn both away, Queen Alexandra had to deal with this alone, although she immediately telegraphed to George at Port Said. Instinctively, she sympathised with Mrs Farrar. "It really is too sad & hard on her poor woman. How wicked of him to have married at all under such circumstances. The whole place is up in arms against him." She was anxious not to cause unnecessary speculation; "I tell everybody who asks or comes here [that] he was called away as he did something dishonourable, which shuts up all further questions." She had no idea what was to happen to the family; "How I feel for his poor old mother & that wretched wife who was so happy here & thought her home & house a little Paradise. What will they do now & where did they go to. They crossed to Calais & that ends their life's story. I do hope she may have a little money or else they must starve as he had only his pay." The sub dean was shortly coming to discuss things with her and make plans for Farrar's successor. She had some ideas of her own but meanwhile was "in perfect terror that poor dear Probyn should hear anything about it as that wld <u>kill</u> him, I feel sure, as he liked [Farrar] so much & had such confidence in him & had so much to do with him all this summer & autumn about the Church." Probyn was still away but beginning to ask for news, "so it is very difficult to hide things from him."

There was more. "It seems the Police had been warned & any number of detectives came down to get proofs, & directly he heard on Sunday evening they fled the next day! I had only seen them a few days before when they seemed so happy ... And <u>now</u> they are <u>homeless</u> exiles & everything has been removed from their pretty little home." He was a "poor miserable man & I fear that he has done an endless lot of harm to so many wretched boys."[142] Alexandra felt it would not have become such a public scandal if there had simply been a statement in the papers that Mr Farrar had resigned. As it was, the press announced that Queen Alexandra and the King had cancelled his appointment, which set everybody "writing & asking horrid questions". Probyn would have organised it better, with more consideration for Mrs Farrar and her mother-in-law; "it ought as I said, have been kept <u>quiet</u> like with poor Mr Mitchell." she wrote. Meanwhile "about his <u>successor</u>, I am making every kind of enquiry about several through the Bishop of Norwich." Although some people wanted a local clergyman appointed, she thought it wiser to take time to make the right choice. One suggestion was a "Mr Grant[143] who preaches very well & is a kind man & his wife was my Maid of Honour, [Margaret] Dawnay who is <u>very</u> <u>nice</u>."[144]

This was an extremely difficult situation. Queen Alexandra condemned wrong-doing absolutely, while feeling compassion for the wrong-doer as well as the victims; typical of her time, she thought scandal should be hushed rather than trumpeted. The event reveals the Royal Family's relationship to the clergy at Sandringham; the family were church-goers, and, especially Alexandra, held strong religious beliefs. They respected the clergy, seeing them as community leaders on a special footing, who might, for example, be asked to make up the numbers at a house party and were often invited in their own right as guests on Christmas Day and other festivals. Their families became friends; Canon Hervey's daughter Alexandra was the Queen's god-daughter. Mr Farrar's actions thus betrayed not only his calling, his young victims, his wife and mother, but also the Royal Family's trust.

General Clarke[145] died at the Ranger's Lodge on 29 November. At Sandringham, Alexandra celebrated her birthday with an afternoon cinematograph performance. She enjoyed reading George's letters from India; they had arrived at Delhi on 7 December and the Coronation Durbar on the 12th had been "the most wonderful & beautiful sight I have ever seen & one I shall remember all my life … It was tiring of course & lasted a long time, we left the Camp at 11.30 & only got back at 3.0. The whole thing was most beautifully arranged & thought out & it went without a hitch."[146] The Hardinges had been so helpful and had managed everything so well. At the Durbar the King had proclaimed that Delhi would once again become India's capital, instead of Calcutta. This was quite popular in India but some criticism was expected in England and Alexandra commented; "To my mind as far as I can judge I think it a very good & sensible idea to re-make Delhi India's future Capital as it used to be formerly, but what about Bengal & the rest of the Proclamation!!!? I do trust & hope it will all be for the best, tho' at present criticism runs high! … I hear Lord Curzon of K[147] was speechless with fury in the House, & nearly broke down from emotion or frenzy, at his plans for the future of India or Bengal having been dropped like a hot potato … But *entre nous*, I must say I cannot help laughing at the slyness & trickery of the present Ministry, to make use of this 'occasion' & of 'their King' to proclaim these vital changes for India, which they never wld have dared or had the courage to propose by themselves!! that beats all."[148]

She went on 13 December to see Whiteley's new store in Bayswater[149] but there was alarming news; the Fifes, on *HMS Delhi*, had been wrecked off the coast of Morocco. Knowing there was bad weather there, she had worried at not hearing from them for five days. "Thank God I only heard of it when they were safe … What an awful time the poor things must have had & particularly in their rescue boat, which at last actually filled & sank & they were all thrown out of it into the boisterous sea & roaring waves, & poor little Alix quite disappeared until pulled out by a Mr Gilbert McCaull Bell[150] who also had been in their boat & was thrown out too, & swam on shore with her. This last account is in the *Pall Mall Gazette* of this evening Dec. the 15th which I am told is quite correct. It really is too awful for words & to think how nearly they were all lost."[151] The King agreed, "What an awful thing to have happened & to poor Louise of all people."[152] They were now at Tangiers, waiting to see whether their luggage could be rescued from *Delhi*. They had all nearly drowned; Alix had been knocked unconscious by a blow from an oar, and, surprisingly, "One & all praised dear little Louise for her great pluck & bravery! which gladdens my heart", wrote her mother. "Thank God I heard they were all right & none the worse & it may be in her case kill or cure! which latter I do hope will be the case!"[153] Later, the King "received two letters from dear Louise giving me a description of all the terrible experiences they went through on bd the 'Delhi', she certainly seems to have behaved most bravely & I am proud that she is my sister. She hadn't much time to write very fully of course, such a pity that one of the girls didn't write, but I suppose that wasn't allowed, I should like to have heard what they thought of it & it would have been such a good opportunity, as they couldn't say they had nothing to write about this time."[154]

Alexandra had attended Louvima Knollys' wedding to Allan Mackenzie[155] in the Guards' Chapel on the 19th, as well as "preparing & choosing those everlasting Xmas presents – I quite envy you being well out of it this time!" Back at Sandringham, she was "nearly off my head arranging the tables & the rest of it – Ah what a business!"[156] Christmas guests arrived and afterwards she told George; "We missed [you] both dreadfully but I did all I could to amuse [the] dear Children who I think were pleased with their presents and enjoyed themselves. They came every afternoon & had great romps. The three eldest, Mlle Dussau & Mr Hansell dined with us on Xmas day. They are all very well & little Johnnie quite happy & was very good & civil to all ... Tomorrow we expect the Farquhars & Treves & on Saturday Amelie & Manuel, & after that I will shut up shop & recover from all the hard work of this month."[157]

❦

By January 1912 Alexandra "really could lie down & die I feel so tired, & we have the house still full of people." Admiral Cradock[158] had given "full & thrilling accounts of poor dear Louise's fearful shipwreck & how they all were saved by a miracle."[159] Lady Macclesfield, who had seen Alexandra safely through her first confinement and whom she had loved like a second mother, had died. The King, convinced it was right to make Delhi the capital of India, was interested in the home reaction, as "In fact most people in India welcome the changes."[160] Their time there was crammed with official events and the King also rode early every morning, "the only exercise I get. I must say, up till now everything has been a most wonderful success & we have had [an] extraordinary reception everywhere." They would leave on the 10th. Alexandra was still amazed at how much they had achieved; "I wonder whether you found time to write yr diary?" she asked May, "that I fear I cld not have done."[161]

"Thank God all ended well & was a success from beginning to end", she told George. Wishing him a good passage home and a good rest, she cautioned him about the Bay of Biscay which "is more dangerous than ever all through this winter & every ship going through has nearly been lost – and we can never forget poor Louise's fearful experience which we now realize might happen to the biggest & best of ships." She could understand; "you felt quite sad at having to leave that beautiful India (which was my one wish in life to see but which now I never shall!!!!)" and was sure "my Bena"[162] had done her best to make them comfortable in the camps at Delhi and Calcutta. Probyn was recovering and the children were well, except David, who, after measles, had had severe indigestion and lost weight. "Dear little Johnnie is certainly better & had none of his tiresome attacks this winter." She agreed that a thanksgiving service should be held at St Paul's Cathedral after the King and Queen returned, "& I will certainly come too. I am waiting to hear all particulars about it from the Archbishop and we will all go in semi-State; this will be my first appearance like that & alone since beloved Papa's funeral!"[163] She told May she wanted to help Lady Hallé's younger sister, both friends of hers. Alexandra had often played the piano with Miss Neruda,[164] who "entirely has taught Victoria & made her appreciate good music, & thanks to her she really plays well now. She, Olga Neruda, is a very good pianist herself, but since the death of her sister is very badly off – so if she could get some lessons to keep her going it wld be everything for her, poor lonely girl. We will have her twice a week while in London & perhaps you cld let Mary also play twice a week with her, which wld help her greatly, and I am sure you wld not regret it as she wld get Mary on wonderfully & is such a charming girl, cheery & pleasant manners! – and the advantage for Mary wld be that she speaks beautiful German – Austrian – she is fr Bohemia."[165]

Before afternoon tea, as she told Soveral, Alexandra often used to sit in her little library at Sandringham, reading or writing undisturbed.[166] Writing to George; "You will be glad to hear that at last we have found our Rector in Mr Grant who was so highly recommended by the Archbishop & all who know him speak highly of him! So I sent for him! & here he is, in person! just arrived. He seems very nice & pleasing, with a very earnest kind expression, much younger looking than I expected & rather good looking too. Poor man he seemed very shy when he first came in, but soon recovered & I feel sure by all he said that we shall like him, & what is more our poor people & all on the Estate will look up to him – he has nice quiet manners too. So I do hope & trust all will be well & that I found the right man for the place ... Margaret his wife wrote me such a delighted letter & they both mean to do their best for our dear Parish here." Johnnie had spent a happy afternoon with her, "& so much improved in every way; really quite well now & pays attention when one speaks to him & bows when he leaves & kisses one, which he never did before; really his mind is developing gradually now & since all those vile medicines were stopped he seems to have lost all those horrid attacks which bothered him so & must have stupefied the poor Child."[167] Everything looked hopeful; above all, the King and Queen were coming home, but on the 27th they heard Macduff had been taken ill in Egypt. Two days later he died of pneumonia at Assouan.

George wrote sadly; "Poor darling Louise & those two poor children, I can't think of anything else ... When one knows what she & Macduff were to one another one can partly realise what her grief & sorrow must be like. May God comfort her in her terrible trial. Think of the last few days & the terrible strain & anxiety she must have suffered & her nerves, poor dear child, my heart bleeds for her & I wish I could help her in some way. Lord Kitchener,[168] who has been so kind, has just telegraphed that she is quite calm & bearing up wonderfully. We know that she is brave & plucky & that will carry her through." Louise planned to take the coffin to Cairo and he would arrange for a cruiser to bring it back to England. "It is dreadful to think that we shall never see dear Macduff again, I was always very fond of him & know you were too & I am sure he was the best, most devoted & unselfish husband in the world, which fact makes it all the harder for dear Louise to bear." This, alas, would "cast a gloom on our happy home coming which we are all so looking forward to."[169] On 5 February, Alexandra and Victoria met *Medina* at Portsmouth; the next day, the thanksgiving service was held at St Paul's. Engagements were reduced because of Macduff's death, although Alexandra saw *The Miracle* at Olympia on the 15th and attended the late Princess Victor of Hohenlohe-Langenburg's memorial service at the Chapel Royal, St James's, on the 16th. On the 15th Alexandra had begun a course of treatment for deafness with Dr Zünd-Burguet,[170] having sixteen more sessions until the 23rd, and also received Lady Lamington, "poor dear little woman, so young & I fear <u>worse</u> than me – she only hears now through a splendid <u>tortoiseshell</u> horn! which however does not show much, but we sympathised & compared notes."[171] By the 20th Alexandra had influenza but was determined to meet her daughter and granddaughters at Portsmouth on the 24th. "Thank you darling Georgie I have not felt over well today [the 23rd] but am sure to be all right tomorrow & must go with you both to receive poor darling Louise & girls at Portsmouth, don't worry about me, I am alright really."[172] She insisted on meeting them but became so unwell that she could not attend Macduff's funeral at St George's Chapel on the 28th. Neither could Victoria. "Alas – I feel a wreck after a bad night & terrible coughing & as I <u>promised</u> you all if no better I wld not go, I now reluctantly must give it up. I feel it <u>terribly</u>! as I had so hoped & prayed to be near our poor darling Louise at this last sad ceremony but it was <u>not to</u> be & I must submit to God's will. If only Toria & I had the service book we cld follow every word & the beautiful hymns."[173] She would "like so much to pay this last loving tribute to our poor excellent Macduff – as for poor dear Louise she is a perfect '<u>Transformation</u>'!! in everything & in every way, this is her <u>real nature</u> & <u>self</u>. She wanted but to be spurred into it, 'A great sorrow recasts a Soul' & her great courage & <u>Faith</u> have changed her into this <u>strong Soul</u> & Being."[174] Charlotte Knollys had "never seen an instance of such <u>practical</u> faith & <u>perfect trust</u> in God."[175]

Alexandra's influenza lasted another fortnight. Current events were troubling: a Suffragette raid on 1 March, and the great miners' strike. By the 2nd King George had seen Louise, "she was as calm as possible & told us all about her affairs & what she was going to do &c. She sees people every day, a thing she never would do before, she is wonderful." On the other hand, "What do you think of the Suffragettes, nice ladies aren't they, breaking everybody's windows, I hope they will be severely punished."[176] Alexandra resumed her treatment with Zünd-Burguet on the 4th, having 36 sessions until the 23rd. On her 49th wedding anniversary, the King and Queen sent her a basket of flowers "to show you how much you are in our thoughts".[177] She was well enough on the 16th to drive to Buckingham Palace and to see Louise and her daughters; go to the new museum in Kensington Palace on the 18th[178]; attend a memorial service[179] in the Chapel Royal on the 20th; and on the 23rd call on Evie James,[180] newly widowed. On the 25th she watched an Australian, Mills,[181] demonstrating the use of a long stockwhip, and also visited Dowdeswell's Galleries. She and Victoria called on Alma Tadema on 26 March and on the 30th attended Landon Ronald's[182] concert in the Queen's Hall. After visitors, social calls and dental appointments, they returned to Sandringham on 3 April for Easter. Sydney Holland had asked Alexandra to open Tredegar House for London Hospital probationers and she gladly agreed, "if only I can be sure of myself when the time comes, as since my great sorrow two years ago, I have not been able to do anything of the kind, and have never been to any great public function by myself without the King, so I am sure you will understand my feelings! As the opening is in June you must ask me again when nearer the time!"[183]

The miners' strike ended on 9 April and she continued her usual occupations. Her grandson Bertie was confirmed by the Bishop of Ripon[184] on the 18th in Sandringham Church. On the 26th Minny, with her daughter, Olga and son-in-law Peter of Oldenburg,[185] arrived. Alexandra entertained them, visiting the convalescent home at Hunstanton, the Almshouses and ruins at Castle Rising, and Lynn Hospital, before they all left on 4 May. A memorial service for King Edward at Windsor on the 6th, a visit to Hampton Court on the 8th and then lunch at "The Mermaid Tavern" at the Shakespeare Memorial exhibition at Earl's Court, followed. On 10th the Queen visited Doré's Gallery. She had been attending events privately, being still in mourning for King Edward and now Macduff too, but on the 11th she saw the Delhi Durbar in "Kinemacolor" at the Scala Theatre; her first "public" appearance since her husband's death. On the 13th she started going to the opera (*Aïda*) again. The next day she and her relatives motored to Brighton for an exhibition of Danish pictures. Life was returning to normal at last.

It was too good to be true. On 15 May came the totally unexpected news that Frederick VIII had collapsed and died in the street while visiting Hamburg. Losing her eldest brother in this way was terrible but naturally Alexandra, with Minny, Charlotte Knollys and Davidson, crossed at Dover in *Alexandra* on the 21st and travelled day and night in Minny's Russian train to Fredericia and then Hvidöre. The late king's funeral was held at Christiansborg Church on the 24th and he was later interred near his parents at Roskilde. Everyone was grieving and Alexandra was doing her best to comfort them, visiting her widowed sister-in-law and seeing her relatives, who called for lunch, dinner and at all hours of the day. She attended church, shopped, gave Charlotte and Davidson tea at Hvidøre, and sent George "Just one line while all the others have gone & Aunt 'Minny Minny' is resting, but I want to wish you joy & God's richest blessings on yr beloved birthday the 3rd. I only regret not being able to spend [it] with you this year, but under these very sad circumstances I am better out of the way just then. It also being poor dear Freddy's birthday it was better for me to remain for another week with the poor bereaved family here, particularly as poor Aunt Minny would have been quite by herself till the 8th when she goes to Moscow."[186] The funeral had been heartrending and, to compound this, George William of Cumberland (31), travelling to Copenhagen for his uncle's funeral, had been killed in a motor accident on 20 May. "Poor darling Thyra in her awful sorrow we have hitherto only heard by telegr from her – they are all quite miserable about their darling blessed Plumpy's untimely & awful death." Prince Waldemar left Denmark straight after his brother's funeral for his nephew's at Gmunden. The new king, Christian X, had begun his task admirably and at a review of troops, which his aunts watched from Rosenborg Castle, he made an excellent speech but it reduced Alexandra to tears. On 5 June King George had sent *Victoria and Albert* to bring her home; she started on the 8th and reached Marlborough House on 10th.

In 1912 it was 50 years since Alexandra had first arrived in England as the Prince of Wales's fiancée, to stay "on approval" with Queen Victoria. The public loved and respected her and she had declared, after King Edward's death, that she would always regard England as her home. A group of women ("The Ladies of Great Britain") decided to inaugurate a floral fête, Alexandra Rose Day, in her honour, selling little pink fabric roses in aid of charity. It was organised by the Executive Committee at 1, Hyde Park Place and the Queen was asked to nominate the beneficiaries. The main event would be in Central London, with at least fifteen, mostly titled, ladies on duty at depots all over the West End; the flowers would be sold by young girls in white. This was put to Queen Alexandra, who, although in mourning, agreed to drive round the West End and then the City, receiving bouquets of flowers en route. It was a pretty and pleasing idea; she loved pink roses and wild flowers, such as "dog roses", which the little blossoms resembled; perhaps she chose the emblem herself. There was another factor; Alexandra would have known about "White Flower Day", started in Sweden in 1908 and spreading to Norway, Denmark, Germany and other European countries, although not to England. The white flower, usually a daisy, real or artificial, symbolised the fight against tuberculosis. Empress Alexandra of Russia adopted it in the Crimea in 1911, where it was held annually till 1914; the whole community took part and the Empress and her four daughters worked hard all day, driving and walking round selling white flowers in aid of the local sanatoria for tuberculosis patients.[187] The first Rose Day drive was on 26 June; the Queen and Victoria drove round the West End in a barouche and then into the City by motor. Alexandra entirely approved of supporting good causes, although, as a widow, she shrank from being the centre of public attention. Newsreels show what happened on these occasions. There was little time for decorous presentations; as the carriage bowled along, excited young women hurried forward to proffer their flowers, which the Queen gamely grasped. By the end of the drive she was exhausted; no wonder she grew to dread the event, while always taking care to appear gracious and happy.

She visited the horse show at Olympia, and Crystal Palace's Handel Festival for *The Messiah*. On the 28[188] she received the German and Italian ambassadors, and the Danish Mission announcing King Frederick's death. On 2 July Paderewski[188] played the piano for her and she had ten more sessions with Zünd-Burguet between the 1st and 5th. Victoria's birthday party for children was held at Marlborough House on the 6th. The next three weeks included the Rose Show at Regent's Park, the Home at Streatham, a dress rehearsal of the tournament and a grand performance the next day at Earl's Court. Alexandra received 200 members of Queen Victoria's Jubilee Nurses' Ladies' Committee on the 15th and gave them tea in the garden. That evening she saw *La Fanciulla del West* at the opera. The next day there was a garden party at Marlborough House for 1,000 members of the Red Cross Society. On the 17th there was a wedding,[189] and the Russian ballet at Covent Garden. Alexandra visited several galleries, the East End Horticultural Show and on the 19th finally opened Tredegar House for the London Hospital probationers. She had tea with Queen Amélie at Richmond, saw the dentist and received a number of people including Nielsen,[190] who sang for her after lunch on the 24th. On the 26th she visited the Cripples' Home at Alton. At last, on the 27th, with Victoria, "Little Minny", her husband[191] and daughters, Xenia and her daughter and other guests, Alexandra left for Sandringham at the end of her busiest season since 1909.

Relaxing a little, she told her son. "First as you know we had the house full of nieces, Christo, George of Russia & the various children of little Minny & Xenia, then last Sunday [4 August] my darling Toria left me too for Buxton & now I am utterly alone & by myself. I confess I feel rather low & wretched & miss her terribly! I do not think I ever was quite alone here without any of my blessed Children, but so it is & I must bear this & cheer up & try & be thankful for all the good & the many mercies still left for me in this sad world, & in my now lonely lot without beloved Papa by my side. And in this my beloved house I have always got plenty to do & many occupations so I am never dull or idle for a moment. I am out a great deal too & have visited every spot & seen all our blessed people. The mares & foals are very well & I was delighted to see Lord & Lady Falmouth[192] here the other day."[193] She was writing herself into cheerfulness and at least it was warm. Princess Beatrice was giving up Osborne Cottage; "I cannot understand B how she can make up her mind to sell that home her Mother gave her & made for her, but I fear she is very extravagant!! – or manages things badly!" Alexandra bemoaned the success of German yachts at Cowes, when, near Kiel, they had recently captured an English yacht containing doctors, and baselessly accused them of spying. Four days later she left in the evening and, travelling all night, arrived at Aberdeen for Ballater and then motored to Mar Lodge for the next ten days, seeing her grandsons at Balmoral, visiting poor people at Corby Hall and on 20 and 22 August fishing in the trout pond at Old Mar. She had found "dear Louise & the dear girls quite bright & pleased to have me here although alas the place to me seems dreadfully sad & changed without poor dear Macduff, who was the soul & spirit here. It all makes me feel dreadfully low & oppressed, but I try to hide it & cheer them up. Unfortunately the weather is horrid, dark, damp & muggy – I quite miss my dear bright & bracing Sandringham." She left on the 23rd but needed two days in London before going to Norway and Denmark on the 26th. "It is all so difficult to fit in ... this year in particular as I am so very anxious to see poor Thyra after all she has gone through & her stay [in Denmark] will be short as she has to go to Schwerin where little Alix expects her confinement."194

Getting to Norway was not going to be easy. The yacht left Port Victoria on 26 August but, delayed and diverted by severe weather, in which two other vessels were wrecked, they arrived at Christiania at last on the 31st and were welcomed by Haakon and Maud. After eight days of social visits, motoring, shopping and entertainments by the ship's company, they left for Denmark on 9 September, joining the new King and Queen, Minny and all the family the next day. On the 14th Alexandra and her party lunched on board the Russian yacht; some of the English sailors had saved two Russians from drowning and were given watches in gratitude by Minny. Thyra and others had lunch on board *Victoria and Albert* on the 16th and tea on the 27th. Alexandra visited a flower show at Arnager on the 17th and the Copenhagen Porcelain Manufactory two days later, when she also saw a zeppelin airship cruising over Copenhagen. A British squadron was stationed nearby; on the 20th the Queen went on board *Lion*, the largest battleship in the world, and gave lunch on the yacht to the admirals and captains of the squadron. She went motoring again and visited the old palace of Jaegersprees. On the 28th the whole family went to Roskilde and on 1 October Alexandra went to stay at Hvidöre.

Relaxing in her little house, she wrote to George; "What must you think of yr lazy old Mother dear – I know & feel it is too bad, but somehow or other I could not write all this time & I hope you will forgive me." Victoria had gone back to Norway to stay with Maud "who wanted her so much". Alexandra had enjoyed visiting the squadron and had liked Admiral Bayly,195 "he seemed very keen & straightforward & honest, I shld think a first rate Officer." The Russian fleet had arrived a few days later; "I am glad to say our men behaved very well on shore, while I am sorry to say the Russians had a good many escapades of various kinds & 6 deserters!" There was trouble in the Balkans and Willy was "very sad & low about everything in general & only hoped the Great Powers could still impose on Turkey <u>not to</u> monopolise all the Frontiers, otherwise none of the small countries cld restrain their Armies. He even said, as I do, oh, if only beloved Papa was still alive to use his great influence & powerful voice at this most serious moment. My great fear is that once the war breaks out down there, <u>everybody</u> in Europe, great & small, will gradually be dragged into it and what then?!! Oh I do hope & pray for Peace." George had explained that the Great Powers were doing all they could to keep Turkey and the smaller states quiet, "but it is not easy".[196] One complication was the effect on Muslims in India and other parts of the Empire if they perceived that their fellow Muslims in Turkey were being coerced in any way.

Alexandra had managed to see her youngest sister, "Thank God we saw dear Aunt Thyra here for nearly three weeks, she & I must say Uncle Ernest too, were wonderful in their great & overwhelming sorrow." Happily, their second daughter, Alexandra, had had a son[197] on 29 September, coincidentally his mother's and grandmother's birthday and his great-grandmother, Queen Louise's death day. Alexandra had found her sister-in-law, "Poor dear 'Swan'" very good and brave, though feeling her loss keenly. "We miss beloved Uncle Freddy here more that I can say & to us brothers & sisters the dear old Home from former bright & happy days is sadly changed. Dear Christian does very well & has a great deal to do just now, he is also like you my darling Georgie – an admirable & blessed son to his poor widowed Mother, full of kind thoughts and *égards* for her."[198] George tried to reassure her about the Balkans; "the mobilizing of the Armies of the Balkan States, Greece & Turkey, naturally causes us great anxiety, but if the Powers continue to work together as they are now, I trust that if war should alas break out, that they will be able to localize it & prevent it spreading. Everything that is possible to prevent a conflagration is I assure you being done by the Powers, they are fully alive to the seriousness of the situation."[199] He now faced a stormy session in Parliament, where Asquith's Liberal government was trying to force Home Rule for Ireland through the Commons. How they were going to do this "with Ulster staring them in the face" the King could not conceive and thought it would be most unwise; it looked as though the government would not last long. On the other hand, relations with Russia were now very good. He and May had had lunch with Louise the day before and she was considering going abroad for the winter but not to Egypt, which would be too painful.

Alexandra was still worrying about Greece, writing hastily to tell George that her brother was upset about England's apparent attitude; having read in the Viennese papers that England and the Powers were going to re-occupy Crete, he was worried about the effect on Greece. War had indeed broken out between Greece and Turkey and George assured his mother that the four occupying Powers had decided not to interfere in any way with Crete during the war, except to protect the Muslims if they were attacked by the Christians, which seemed unlikely. There was news that Tsesarevitch Alexis[200] had been very ill but "Nicky has just telegraphed that he is better now. Another anxiety added to his many."[201] Alexandra, with Minny and the Danish sovereigns, went to unveil a statue of Christian IX at Odense on the 10th. On the 28th she, her daughters and grandson returned to England.

There was tribulation at home. An entry for King Edward VII had appeared in the latest edition of the *Dictionary of National Biography*, written by the editor, Sir Sidney Lee.[202] It had outraged the late king's household, who found it inaccurate and unjust. During summer and early autumn, Davidson, consulting with colleagues, took it upon himself to try to put things right. He was inspired by duty, affectionate respect for the King's memory and loyalty to the Queen but also by his feelings for Princess Victoria, who had been devoted to her father; their shared grief probably brought them closer together. In mid-June Davidson had had the King's biography detached from the main, weighty volume and given to Alexandra to read, pointing out the various problems it contained. "Your Majesty will see the extreme difficulty there is, of selecting suitable grounds on which to successfully attack the Author." It was not that he had made an accusation which could be denied and disproved, "but the whole Article is one of general depreciation, written to try and show that The King's influence in Politics was not what it was generally supposed to be, and, as Sir S Lee says his information is derived mainly from 'conversations with most of the leading men of the day, especially those who came into contact with the late King', it becomes a most difficult & delicate matter to disprove opinions formed on such authoritative sources. Your Majesty will see therefore that a mere letter or Newspaper Article contradicting Sir S Lee's impression would be quite inadequate & would do no good." Perhaps a critique of the article, by an authoritative writer, could be published, Lee being merely a "hack" writer who just put information received from others into literary form. But who could this be?[203]

Queen Alexandra was indeed upset by the article and, when Lord Esher told Lee, he was contrite; "The knowledge that anything I had written was, however remotely, a cause of pain to her, has naturally distressed me greatly. I am most desirous that Queen Alexandra should know how alien it was from my whole intention & sentiment, whatever my conception of an historical writer's obligation on details, to say other than a just & loyal tribute to the late King's honoured memory. My aim was to show ... how his personality greatly strengthened the hold of Royalty in public affection & how probably no King won effectively the goodwill at once of foreign peoples & of his own subjects."[204] Certain politicians, with their professional reputations at stake, had apparently played down the King's role, for example, in foreign affairs, when talking to Lee. They were opposed to the idea of a critique and Esher agreed with them.

Davidson was incensed, not just with Lee but even more with those who had given him material which could create a false impression about the King and who almost certainly included Esher himself, despite his denial.

Letters and arguments flew about all summer and Davidson became increasingly heated and distressed. Lee had protested the article was correct according to the information he had received and he could not change it without destroying his authorial credit, although he was prepared to listen to opposing views. After further discussions, in which Esher was dismissed as a reliable reviser, Davidson wrote; "Lord Knollys has apparently been in consultation with others and yesterday he and Sir Dighton asked me to undertake the revision if Sir S Lee can be brought to regard it in anything like a reasonable light."[205] Although Davidson did not feel "intellectually equipped", he accepted, as he had been the one who had so deeply resented the article. It would not be easy and could fail completely but at least he would have made the effort to restore the King's prestige. For Alexandra, his long, complicated letters on this sensitive subject must have been exhausting. She was glad he had been asked to revise the production but would really have preferred an entirely new article. Probyn assured her Davidson was managing a difficult job in the best possible way, but poor Davidson had now worked himself up into a frenzy and, thinking she had misunderstood the situation, wrote again to her at length. Alexandra meekly replied on 24 October; "So sorry I expressed myself wrong & made you re-write your letter which I had perfectly understood in every way but simply intended to say I feared that a cheap edition by the same author could only make things worse altho' revised by you who so kindly & bravely are undertaking to point out to the author all the many misconceptions & untruths he has told the world."[206] It seems Probyn also wrote and she replied from Denmark in affectionate exasperation; "Very many thanks long letter understand everything perfectly have done so all the time, don't tire yourself writing so much hope to find you very well DV on the 29th."[207]

However, there was a further complication. Another author, Edward Legge, had written *King Edward in His True Colours* and had also suggested to Alexandra Rose Day's organising committee that they should sell an article by him on the Queen in aid of their funds.[208] His book on the King was intended to be complimentary, but Probyn and Davidson thought it vulgar rubbish and, although they had helped Legge by answering some simple questions, were anxious to distance themselves from it as far as possible. Davidson did not want to worry Alexandra with the correspondence, as, rightly or wrongly, he felt it would upset and confuse her. He was preparing to issue a disclaimer if the press suggested that the household had assisted Legge. Davidson was currently in Denmark in the Queen's suite, and Soveral was one of the party; "He is, as usual, priceless. We should be terribly dull without him." Davidson found the inactivity and the rich food served on the Russian yacht highly indigestible.[209] Back in

England by 4 October, he complained to Probyn about the cost of Alexandra's entertaining; the food was not extravagant but the sisters often changed their minds at the last moment about the number of guests, which meant food for a certain number had to be ordered every day, whether or not it was ultimately needed. He thought Alexandra did not appreciate how difficult this was for the kitchen staff. She had been well when he left but Victoria had had a bad cough and throat and did not want to see the local doctors.[210]

By 16 November Davidson had reverted to Lee's article. Lord Morley,[211] an author himself, sympathised with Lee's writerly feelings; it might be possible to delete some of the more offensive passages from the *DNB* but Lee was difficult to deal with and might object. Davidson begged Probyn not to make too much of his share, feeling that Alexandra would not understand or appreciate it. "The Queen, as you know, hates anything being <u>forced</u> on her. She likes to think she finds out everything for herself."[212] It would be impossible to explain things to her, as she "has absolutely <u>no</u> idea of logic – that if you <u>say</u> a thing is wrong, you must <u>prove</u> it so, & also the Queen has no sense of appreciation. I mean it's a constitutional deficiency, & she will only think, whatever she may say – a great deal of unnecessary fuss – 'much better have told Lee he was mistaken & get him to alter his article.' All the paraphernalia of the <u>means</u> of getting him to do so will be so much <u>Sanskrit</u> to her. I could see that at once, the only time I ever spoke on the subject to her, & HM will only retain the general idea that I have made a great deal of fuss & bother about what might have been done quite simply & easily, so please dear Sir Dighton, don't praise me etc & the other reason is, that I have done this, <u>solely</u> from the love & devotion I bear the King's memory & I don't want to be praised etc by anyone. I value what <u>you</u> say & what Pcess Victoria says – more than I can say, & I don't want anything from anyone else."[213] He was sore and disgruntled and it is hard not to sympathise with his sincere exertions and obvious affection for Victoria, which he could not hide and of which Probyn must have known. However, Alexandra had clearly not been fully briefed or given credit for understanding what was going on. People tended to be intimidated or embarrassed by her deafness; it was easiest to avoid telling her things. Thus she might well have thought Davidson was making an unnecessary fuss.[214] Could she herself have managed Lee better? Meanwhile Davidson sought help from Asquith, Arthur Balfour[215], Haldane, Sir Edward Grey, Lansdowne and Morley, as well as Sir Fairfax Cartwright[216] and Lord Hardinge of Penshurst. The two latter provided valuable evidence about the King; the others gave a mixed but mostly positive response. On 3 December Davidson had a successful two-hour meeting with Lee.[217]

At home in London, Alexandra paid visits, saw relatives, went to the Fine Arts Gallery and the Hippodrome and on 7 November saw a matinée performance of *A Winter's Tale* at the Savoy. The next day she and Victoria went to Sandringham and Maud and Olaf to Appleton. Alexandra was still worrying about the

Balkans; both Greeks and Turks were suffering misery and she was praying for peace and no interference "from outsiders, which I fear wld mean a European War. Really the Austrians are behaving too badly & selfishly, they ought to be satisfied indeed having already previously pocketed two large Provinces without Europe interfering."[218] At Sandringham, she saw relatives, went to tea parties at Appleton and on the 30th many of her old friends and staff began to arrive for her birthday the next day. It was a house party in the old style but, as Charlotte Knollys had written, "There is no light or life in this season's festivities without him, who was the ruling power & centre of it all!"[219] Alexandra and Victoria went shopping in London from 16 December but returned two days later to get ready for Christmas. Relatives and friends arrived; there was a tree and tables in the ballroom on the 24th. The servants had a fancy-dress ball on the 30th and a tree in the ballroom on the 31st.

All the guests left as 1913 began. David went to Oxford on 10 January, while Bertie joined his ship on the 16th. Alexandra gave presents and prizes to the schoolchildren and went to see the decorations in the parish room at West Newton, where the servants' ball was being held this year. On the 21st Probyn celebrated his 80th birthday and his colleagues, neighbours and personal friends all gave him presents. Unfortunately the Queen could not attend as she was in bed with a cold; Laking was called but she stayed in her room until the 31st. On 6 February she went to London, straight to the Guards' Chapel, where Baba Mackenzie's son,[220] born on 4 January, was christened; Alexandra and the King were sponsors. During February Alexandra was busy paying calls and receiving visitors, and went to Alma Tadema's exhibition at Burlington House on the 12th. Operas included Strauss's[221] *Rosencavalier* on the 8th and the 12th; his *Salome* on the 18th and the 25th and Wagner's *Meistersinger* on the 22nd, beginning at 6.30 and ending at 11.45; Alexandra ate her dinner in the box. She went to the Russian ballet four times. On the 14th she attended, privately, the requiem at St Paul's Cathedral for Captain Scott and his four companions, lost on returning from the South Pole.[222] After lunch on the 16th, Joseph Hollman played the cello, accompanied by Mr C Keith. The Queen called at Alexandra House[223] on the 27th, visited the Fine Arts Gallery on 1 March, and the Hackney Show at the Agricultural Hall on the 6th, with a cinematograph show at Buckingham Palace later.

On 7 March it was 50 years since Alexandra's arrival at Gravesend in 1863 and the Lord Mayor[224] and eight members of Guildhall gave her a celebratory address. A Danish service in Marlborough House Chapel at 4.30 on the 9th preceded a Danish reception at Marlborough House. On 10 March it was her 50th wedding anniversary and she motored to Windsor to visit the Royal Vault, where her husband lay. During the following week she motored to Coombe and

Hampton Court, attended the hunter and polo pony shows at Islington and was present at Princess Mary's confirmation in Buckingham Palace's chapel on the 16th. The next day Lord Knollys, having served King Edward and King George for 50 years, retired.

There had been three golden anniversaries in ten days. In Greece another was due on 30 March,[225] when Alexandra's brother would celebrate his golden jubilee. But on the 18th came the appalling news that he had been assassinated by a Greek at Thessaloniki.[226] It was one of the cruellest blows Alexandra ever received. As Charlotte Knollys told a friend, "HM was so devoted to this – her favourite Brother – that you may imagine, she is almost broken-hearted at the terrible fate that has befallen him."[227] Alexandra herself wrote, one year later; "I was so touched by yr dear kind words on this saddest & one of my most miserable days of my life! I have really never got over that awful & quite unexpected shock, which nearly killed me then when I suddenly was told my darling blessed brother Willy was killed shot down by a murderer! & all within the year when beloved brother Freddy also died so suddenly in the streets at Hamburg. Oh it has been & always will be a terrible deep deep sorrow for the remaining days of my poor life."[228] She later admitted to her nephew, Prince Nicholas; "I have never felt the same person since".[229] George visited her on 19 March 1913 and on Easter Day she took Holy Communion at St Paul's Cathedral. She had a small operation for a nasal abscess on the 25th then, on 2 April, the day of King George's funeral in Greece, a memorial service was held in the Chapel Royal, St James's Palace. Alexandra had received many condolatory visits and, as distractions, drove to Hendon to see the aeroplanes, to the zoo, and to walk in the gardens at Gunnersbury. On the 22nd she received a condolatory address from Parliament. Her one remaining brother, Waldemar, came for a few days; this was comforting, and gradually she began to attend events again: the Royal Academy, a cinematograph show, Melba's concert at the Albert Hall and Bach's *Requiem* at Westminster Abbey. The last was on 6 May, when she also went to the annual memorial service for King Edward at Windsor. She visited Julie d'Hautpoul, and also Louise, widowed for over a year, at Brighton. The 14th was the first anniversary of King Frederick's death; wherever she turned there was mourning and lamentation. There were more visits to art galleries and exhibitions and on the 20th she attended a new event, a great flower show at Chelsea.

On the 22nd Alexandra and Victoria, with Johnnie, went to Sandringham for a peaceful week; the Queen fished in the mill stream and enjoyed tea parties at the Dairy and Bungalow, but returned to London on the 29th because Minny had arrived from Russia. The King and Queen were due home from Berlin, after attending the marriage of William II's only daughter, Victoria Louise,[230] to Ernest Augustus, the Cumberlands' only surviving son. For some, this must have been as unwelcome as it was unexpected. The Duke of Cumberland[231] had no more reason to love the German emperor than the Danish Royal Family had; Prussia had defeated Hanover in 1866 and deprived him of the title of King, which he should have inherited on his father's death in 1878. The idea of his son marrying the Emperor's daughter must have been anathema to him but, faced with the young couple's determination, the matter was resolved. Alexandra, with her love of romance, made the best of it, "the wedding itself must have been a very pretty and interesting sight. And dear Poll & [Victoria Louise] are a very happy couple now, to the general satisfaction to both Parents & Parents-in-law! Dear Aunt Thyra writes how happy she was to see you both there & that you were of the greatest help … & made things much more comfortable to them in every way." She added that Johnnie had "been so happy here & I was delighted to have him" and described how beautiful Sandringham was looking; "I myself have never seen it like this before as generally we come too soon or too late. At this moment everything, trees & flowers, are in bloom & blossom."[232]

Although grief for Willy never left her, Alexandra wisely trusted to the soothing effects of time and diversions. She was taking part in her normal activities with some of her former energy, privately rather than officially and often with Minny. This included a visit, on 30 May, to the HAIA's exhibition at the Albert Hall but she was not yet attending theatres or balls. Victoria, with fewer mourning restrictions, attended the dinner and dance at Derby House on "Derby Day", 4 June, and the Versailles Fête Ball at the Albert Hall on the 5th. Alexandra went to the Military Tournament on 2 June and to Trooping the Colour the next day. On the 5th, with Minny and Victoria, she visited a new development called Hampstead Garden Suburb, and had tea the next day at Stafford House, sold by the Duke of Sutherland to become a museum.[233] Naturally she fostered Greek contacts at this time, receiving a Greek delegate on the 9th and visiting Mr Ralli's[234] house in Belgrave Square privately to see Greek needlework sent by Princess Nicholas for sale in aid of the war fund. On 22 July she received official Greek deputations announcing her brother's death.

Alexandra Day was approaching again and it was the last thing the Queen wanted to do. She begged May to help her; "I have one, one very great wish near my heart, & it wld please me immensely if you wld fulfil it. It is to ask you to spare me half an hour or so on the 25th, & drive with me on that tiresome Alexandra day, which I dread, & it wld be the greatest help to me if you wld accompany me! I know it is not amusing, but you wld give me & the people too, the greatest pleasure. I tried hard to get out of it this time but as Mr Poincaré[235] arrives the day before I cannot get away before that, & am told it wld be the greatest snub to all the poor people who put in their penny, so go I must, but it wld make all the difference if you wld kindly come with me. We wld take Toria & little Mary which wld make it all the better. Please think kindly about it & do come."[236] There were more sales; Irish industries at Londonderry House on 10 June and one for the London Hospital, on the 11th at the Albert Hall. Alexandra also attended a garden party at Devonshire House for the Jubilee Institute for Nurses, of which 1,100 were present. As ever, she enjoyed professional singing and heard Caruso, Melba, Granier[237] (twice) and Chaliapin,[238] but she always encouraged young musicians too; May and Beatrice Harrison played on 12 June and a young girl violinist, Ibolyka Gyarfas,[239] on 8 July. Miss Carrie Pringle[240] sang before her on the 17th.

On 16 June Victoria, with Violet Vivian, went for a week to Violet's uncle's[241] house, Glyn, in Wales. It was now very hot and Alexandra either motored or sat in the garden. On the 20th she presented Drum Banners to her regiment, the 19th (Queen Alexandra's Own) Royal Hussars, at Hounslow. She had already attended horse shows at Richmond on the 14th and Olympia on the 21st. King Manuel was engaged to Princess Augusta Victoria of Hohenzollern[242] and they, with Queen Amélie, came to lunch on the 24th. The French president, Poincaré, on an official visit to England, called that afternoon. The 25th was Alexandra Day; the Queen, with May, Victoria and Mary, drove 14 miles through central London and the City. A total of £18,391 was collected, and later much increased by collections outside London. It was more than in 1912 and about £15,000 was in pence, implying contribution by poor people. Alexandra did not attend the state ball on the 26th (although Victoria did). She visited two more horse shows at Olympia and on 28 June witnessed a torchlight tattoo at Chelsea Hospital. She also saw members of the Russian Imperial Family, visiting Grand Duke Michael[243] and his wife at Highgate on 2 July. Grand Duchess Elizabeth[244] called twice, once with her brother, the Grand Duke of Hesse. Minny was still in England and her children, Xenia and Michael, visited.

On the afternoon of 3 July Queen Alexandra toured the docks and the Cutler Street Warehouse. She went down the river in *Conservator* and was received at Cutler Street by Lord Devonport,[245] Lord Ritchie[246] and Sydney Holland. Ascending by lift, she was shown ostrich feathers, carpets, silk and "piece goods", later seeing the "Curio Show" on the ground floor. She then motored to London Dock, where first she saw the ivory department and then quicksilver, iodine, India rubber, tortoiseshell, mother-of-pearl shells and boxes of nutmegs and cloves. Next stop was Albert Dock but meanwhile tea was provided on *Conservator*, which then steamed along to the west end of Victoria Dock. Later, Alexandra landed at the meat department and saw the storage chambers. The visit had been carefully planned; "A card showing description and value of the different classes of goods should be placed on each exhibit" and "Foreman who is responsible for the working of the goods and who knows something interesting about them should be in attendance at each Department visited."[247] Alexandra had noticed a beautiful 200-year-old China blue glass bowl, which Holland obtained and gave her as a memento of the visit. She was absolutely delighted and asked Charlotte Knollys to send him a photograph which she had taken from *Conservator*.[248]

Davidson continued working towards a satisfactory outcome to Lee's biography of King Edward, but had made himself ill and suffered a nervous breakdown. He took a rest cure at Harrogate but was kept up to date by his colleagues. Lord Knollys, who had refused to have anything to do with Lee, finally saw him, with Ponsonby, and gathered that Lee had gained a wrong impression about the King from many if not most of the people he had seen, "& that he is beginning to realise this now himself." Knollys had also seen Queen Alexandra, who was very kind and sympathetic about Davidson and some of the things he had written to her.[249] There were more family meetings, a children's garden party on Victoria's birthday and the presentation of medals on the 8th to members of the Red Cross who had served during the Balkan War. The Queen visited Alexandra Court at Wimbledon on the 9th; on the 12th she received Lady Scott, widow of the Antarctic explorer, with her little son, Peter,[250] and on the 14th Rodman Wanamaker.[251] The next day she had tea with Louise and heard that Alix, now Duchess of Fife in her own right, was engaged to Arthur of Connaught. As Minny told her son, "Aunt Alix is very pleased indeed at her granddaughter's betrothal. It happened quite unexpectedly and was a <u>great</u> surprise. We all were very much astonished when Louise lost no time in giving her consent! They are, it seems, blissfully happy; Louise has even allowed them both to motor alone from London to Bagshot to spend the day with the Connaughts."[252]

More foreign visitors and relatives arrived and on the 21st Alexandra motored to Farnborough to see Empress Eugénie. She received the Archbishop of Canterbury on the 28th and returned the call on the 29th. The next day, after a very busy season she, Minny and Victoria went to Sandringham for the usual visits, drives and tea parties, and Minny's "name day" on 4 August. Grand Duchess George, with members of the Stoeckl family,[253] arrived on the 5th for a short break. On the 7th Charlotte Knollys fell backwards down some stairs, affecting her hearing and hurting her wrist[254] but she was able to accompany Alexandra to Balmoral on the 16th. The King was at Cowes; "We have sailed in 'Britannia' every day but yesterday and she really sails as well as ever. On Monday & today we raced & won both times I am glad to say."[255] Bertie and Mary were there; Bertie was now "a Midshipman & is very proud of himself." They were all looking forward to seeing Alexandra and the others in Scotland, but it was only a brief visit, with time for little more than tea at Mar Lodge and Birkhall and fishing at the Glassalt Shiel. Then Alexandra's party was off again, leaving on the 22nd, travelling all night to London, embarking on *Victoria and Albert* and reaching Aarhus on the 25th. The Danish King and Queen were at their house, Marselisborg, and between the 25th and 30th there were meetings on the yacht, sightseeing by day and dancing and singing by the sailors after dinner.

Alexandra left for Copenhagen on 30 August and Minny went to live on the Russian yacht. George told his mother they had been so delighted to see them at

Balmoral, "but it was such a pity you could not stay longer. I miss you dreadfully & it was so nice being all together again. I do hope you feel better now & less weak, as I did not think you were at all well when you were here. I beg of you to rest more & not always be running about, it would be splendid for you if you would stop in bed for a few days, till you felt stronger."[256] But Alexandra would never stay in bed unless forced by illness and, while Victoria left for Norway on 4 September, she went to the zoo, met her family, went sightseeing and watched her parents' memorial near Bernstorff being unveiled. At last, utterly exhausted, she wrote on the 9th, apologising for the delay, "but really I have felt very seedy & tired beyond all words & stupid & incapable of doing anything ... I am rather better now in some ways but still even here in my former dear old home feel dreadfully depressed at times. No doubt it all comes from all the many sad shocks I have received following each other so quickly during these last sad three years. I was so pleased, in spite of all, to be once more at dear old Balmoral I always loved so much formerly! with you & beloved May who both were so nice & kind to yr old Mother dear ... We were all dreadfully sad at the shortness of our stay with you, but alas it could not be helped."[257] She had enjoyed being in Jutland, and seeing Marselisborg; a wedding present to the King and Queen from the local people. As usual, there were constant family visits. "Greek Georgie" and his family were staying with Waldemar at Bernstorff; he was depressed about recent events in Greece and, after earlier problems as Governor of Crete, felt he could never again serve in his country. The new king, Constantine, was visiting abroad, beginning with Germany, which offended the French, who had previously worked in Greece's favour. Alexandra begged her son to see Constantine "before the Triple Alliance get hold of him – we must now as I told [Sir Edward] Grey[258] be Greece's friend for ever – they will now form our <u>chief</u> support for the future (with Turkey) in the Mediterranean against the Triple Alliance." Losing control there would lead to the same results as losing Heligoland in the North Sea. King Edward had been aware of this and had often discussed it with his brother-in-law, who had always pointed out that one day Greece might be of great use to England, but times were changing and it was all too clear Germany would try to draw Greece into its orbit. Alexandra was right to be concerned.

By 6 September Davidson was back in London, where a new horror awaited him. Edward Legge had published another book, *More about King Edward*. Davidson was in despair; it was far worse than the first, just a jumble of stories. Meanwhile Victoria left Norway and, skirting round Denmark, arrived in England on the 13th. Her mother wrote; "I miss my beloved Victoria more than I can say but for her sake I am willing to make this great sacrifice so that she might have a little peace & rest before the winter which we all seem in want of."[259] She motored to Hvidöre several times and on the 13th had tea at Captain Kaufman's, where she saw an aeroplane go up. The next day there was a "Harvest Home" service at St Alban's and later a visit to the stadium to see a "tug-of-war" between English and Russian sailors. On the 15th Alexandra moved to Hvidöre. The Cumberlands and their daughter, Olga, went home on the 17th; Alexandra was sorry they had gone so soon but Ernest always had to get back to Gmunden for stag-hunting. Infanta Eulalie had suddenly appeared with an American friend, "qu'elle m'a fait voir á Londres l'autre jour!"[260] The two ladies, with the American's husband, were going to Norway.[261]

While "seated in the garden close up to the sea in the most heavenly weather" the Queen told her son, "I am writing on my lap, César[262] lying by my side & surrounded by beautiful different shaded butterflies & bees! How I wish you cld see this really lovely spot once – we could quite well put you up as we have two or three small spare rooms." Minny had been "waylaid in the upper garden just as we were coming down here so I bolted just to send you these lines at 11 o'clock. We breakfast at 10, so you see I am earlier here." The latest was that the commodore of the yacht had an embarrassing ailment; "he has, I am sorry to say been very suffering ever since we came here with inflammation of the bladder, which however we are <u>not</u> supposed to know – he is supposed to suffer from great pain in his side, & he is very anxious no one shld know. Thank God he is <u>better</u> now, & was moved to a first rate Klinick under a first rate Specialist where he is very comfortable & well looked after, & where he has rest & <u>quiet</u> & they all speak English." She had seen in the papers that King Constantine had taken his wife and family to Eastbourne while he went to Paris to try to mend fences. Harry was off to Eton, George to his preparatory school at Broadstairs and Bertie to *Collingwood*, a large battleship which was to cruise the Mediterranean for a few months. "How you will miss them", she told her son. Also, "Thank God all is going on well at Mar Lodge & little Alix & young Arthur have really had a good time together."[263] The Duchess of Connaught was unwell and it was uncertain whether she would go back to Canada with her husband.[264]

Alexandra herself was feeling "better since I came here & my native air seems to do me good. The whole family here is well & most kind and drop in whenever they can." Her son reassured her about Greece; "we should do all we can to encourage & help them, as they could be of great service to England in looking after the eastern end of the Mediterranean. I have been talking to Sir Arthur Nicolson (who is here) & he says that is our policy. We have sent an Admiral & Naval Officers to Athens to help to reorganise & improve & increase their Navy & England has always been the friend of Greece. Tino must know this … Of course W is making up to him but I am sure Tino sees through it all. Greece may order some ships to be built in Germany; that does not matter, the fact is that all our shipbuilding yards in England are so busy that they can't build any more for anyone else at present."[265] This did not stop Alexandra from worrying. On the 23 and 24 September the yacht was coaled and painted and meanwhile the Queen enjoyed family gatherings, singing by the Danish tenor, Vilhelm Herold on the 23rd and a pantomime performed by sailors from *Bellona* at the Hotel d'Angleterre on the 25th. Two days later she called on the convalescent commodore in hospital, saw Danish torpedoes dive on the 28th and then motored with Minny to Roskilde to visit their parents' graves. On 2 October she watched military manoeuvres.

On 1 October Queen Mary had asked her whether she would like to wear "dear Grandmama's little diamond crown" at Alix's and Arthur's wedding, "because if you wish to do so I shall be only too glad to send it over to Marlborough House any time you say."[266] Alexandra responded gratefully on the 7th; "It is very kind yr offering me to wear the little Crown of beloved Grandmama, and I shld be very glad to have it for the occasion if I can manage it!" She added, "Poor Davidson is getting on so slowly which is most distressing."[267] He was still anguishing about Lee and Legge. On 9 October the Norwegian Royal Family boarded the royal yacht and the next day Alexandra left Hvidöre, giving the Commodore's wife and daughter a passage home. King George had told her about the new Duchess of Fife's[268] wedding plans; "Louise ... leaves for London towards the end of this week as she & Alix have to get all their things before the wedding ... We are giving an evening party at St James's Palace on the Monday the 13th & all the people who have given presents will be asked, I don't know whether you would wish to come to that. There will be no luncheon after the wedding as there were too many difficulties with regard to who should be asked. So as soon as the wedding is over, we all go home to change & have luncheon & later in the afternoon Louise wants us to come to Portman Square from where the young couple will start for the honeymoon, this will be the best arrangement."[269] Alexandra arrived home on the 12th and the next day saw her granddaughter's wedding presents at St James's Palace; the marriage took place in the Chapel Royal on the 15th.

Davidson was no better and now had phlebitis in his leg, so Alexandra had allowed him to remain at Marlborough House. He was grateful, despite his reservations about her. Probyn exploded; "My dear David – I have said it 100, no, 1,000 times – in the world there is nobody with a kinder heart than our beloved Queen has! Blessed Lady – think of her goodness to me – before, through and since my illness! Of course she wishes you to stop at M House."[270] Two days later he confided that she appeared to like Legge's book, as well as another, by the elderly Lord Suffield, commenting "I really don't know which [book] is the more vulgar or more stupid."[271] He advised Davidson to "give up bothering yourself about it ... I cannot help thinking that we are making a great deal too much fuss about this poor creature, Legge."[272]

Alexandra went to the London Hippodrome, Drury Lane and an exhibition at Olympia before returning to Sandringham with Victoria on 21 October and receiving many relatives over the next three weeks. On 15 November they went to London; the next day Archduke Franz Ferdinand and his wife, Countess

Hohenberg, called at Marlborough House. There were several shopping expeditions and theatre visits before Alexandra returned to Sandringham on the 22nd. Guests began arriving and her 69th birthday was celebrated with a kinematograph showing of *The British Soldier* in the evening. Unusually, Charlotte Knollys kept copious details of birthday presents in the engagement diary, perhaps because of Alexandra's golden jubilee in England.[273] More guests arrived; there were motoring expeditions and walks. On 8 December Alexandra, with Victoria, began a three-day visit to Knowsley,[274] visiting Southport and the lady chapel in the new Liverpool Cathedral, touring the town and docks and motoring on the 11th to Hoghton Tower, reputedly where King James I[275] knighted the "Sir Loin of beef". On the 9th two people from Chester demonstrated a new dance, the tango. Back in London, Alexandra visited shops, galleries and theatres before returning on the 22nd with Victoria for Christmas at Sandringham.

Notes

[1] Frederick Eggleden (c1853–1910), appointed footman, 1878; sergeant footman, 1891; wine butler,1892

[2] Mrs Keppel was nearby on both visits to Brighton

[3] RA QM/PRIV/CC42/78, Queen Alexandra to Princess of Wales, 1910: 6 February

[4] Started by Charles Cruft (1852–1938) in 1891; he originally worked for Spratt's, the dog food provider

[5] Perhaps the 1st; the 2nd was composed from 1909–1911 and dedicated to the memory of King Edward VII

[6] Ioannis Gennadios (1844–1932), diplomat and historian

[7] Raymond Lamont-Brown, *Edward VII's Last Loves*, p 127; James Lees-Milne's *The Enigmatic Edwardian: The Life of Reginald, 2nd Viscount Esher*, p 206; Wilfred Scawen Blunt Papers, MS10–1975, 1910, April 27 (footnote), quoting memories of "Skittles" (Catherine Walters, 1839–1920; famous courtesan), who asserted, rightly or wrongly, that the quarrel was the greatest the King and Queen ever had, although, "as a rule they are very good friends and the King always talks of her as the best little woman in the world."

[8] RA QM/PRIV/CC42/79, Queen Alexandra to Princess of Wales, 1910: 26 March

[9] Croquet

[10] RA GV/PRIV/AA34/44, Queen Alexandra to Prince of Wales, 1910: 26 March

[11] Perhaps to monitor the state of politics and estimate the possibility of the King's return

[12] RA GV/PRIV/AA25/74, King Edward VII to Prince of Wales, 1910: 12 April; Biarritz, on the Atlantic coast of France, gave easier and quicker access to England than the Mediterranean area

[13] Supporters of John Redmond (1856–1918), leader of the moderate Irish Parliamentary Party and of the Irish National Volunteers

[14] Herbert Henry Asquith (1852–1928), 1st Earl of Oxford and Asquith, politician

[15] Sir John Clark of Tillypronie (1821–1910), 2nd baronet, diplomat son of Sir James Clark, the royal physician

[16] RA GV/PRIV/AA25/75, King Edward VII to Prince of Wales, 1910: 19 April

[17] RA GV/PRIV/AA37/15, Prince of Wales to Queen Alexandra, 1910: 21 April

[18] RA GV/PRIV/AA37/16, Prince of Wales to Queen Alexandra, 1910: 4 May

[19] RA VIC/ADDA5/471, King Edward VII to Mrs Keppel, 1901: May, from Marlborough House: "My dear Mrs George, Should I be taken very seriously ill I hope you will come and cheer me up but should there be no chance of my recovery you will I hope still come and see me – so that I may say farewell and thank you for all your kindness and friendship since it has been my good fortune to know you. I feel convinced that all those who have any affection for me will carry out the wishes which I have expressed in these lines."

[20] Ridley, pp 457–8

[21] Fitzwilliam, Wilfrid Scawen Blunt papers, MS 11–1975 Diaries, 14 December 1910: Wilfred Scawen Blunt (1840–1922), poet and writer

[22] Although this, if genuine, is historically interesting, it was a serious breach of confidence; Laking should never have revealed such a private conversation to anyone else.

[23] Sir Arthur Sullivan, who had died in 1900, had been on friendly terms with the late King

[24] *Journals and Letters of Reginald, Viscount Esher*, Vol.III, pp 1–2

[25] RA VIC/ADDA21/238, Queen Alexandra to the Nation, 1910: May; in fact, in a typescript of the otherwise unaltered message, "unspeakable anguish" had become "irreplaceable loss". Not only did this emasculate Alexandra's grief, but it marred her eloquence by repeating a phrase which she would use in the next line.

[26] Theodore Roosevelt (1858–1919), the 26th American President, m Edith Kermit Carow

[27] This was Sullivan's "Brother, Thou art gone before us", from *The Martyr of Antioch*

[28] Mrs Keppel was not invited but was admitted to Westminster Hall to pay her respects to the King.

[29] RA GV/ADD/COPY/140/139, Rosebery Papers, Queen Alexandra to Lord Rosebery, 1910: undated (Sunday); had the parliamentary crisis been resolved sooner, the King would have been able to go on the Mediterranean cruise, which might well have safe-guarded his health and postponed his death

[30] Caesar, a wire-haired fox terrier (1898–1914)

[31] RA MRH//MRH/SOV/MIXED/244/54

[32] RA GV/PRIV/AA33/45, Queen Alexandra to King George V, 1910: 21 May

[33] *The Times, Court Circular*, 24 May 1910

[34] Frits Hartvigsen (1841–1919), Danish pianist and teacher; Alexandra had occasionally played in quartet with him, Lady Carmarthen and Sir Charles Hallé at Marlborough House.

[35] Johan Hartman (1805–1900), Danish composer; Tooley, pp17, 18, 20

[36] RA VIC/ADDA21/233/122, Queen Alexandra to Sydney Holland, 1912: 9 April

[37] Tooley, p 125

[38] Princesses Olga, Elizabeth, and Marina, who married Prince George, Duke of Kent, in 1934

[39] RA GV/PRIV/AA33/49, Queen Alexandra to King George V, 1910: 16 June

[40] David Lloyd George (1863–1945), 1st Earl Lloyd George of Dwyfor; Chancellor of the Exchequer in 1910

[41] RA GV/PRIV/AA33/49, Queen Alexandra to King George V, 1910: 6 July

[42] Grand Duchess George

[43] Aksel Broström, later rector of the Danish church in London

[44] Bing, p 255

[45] RA GV/PRIV/AA33/50, Queen Alexandra to King George V, 1910: 25–27 August

[46] Grand Duchess George, pp 142–3

[47] RA QM/PRIV/CC50/941, Dowager Grand Duchess of Mecklenburg-Strelitz to Duke of Teck, 1910: 20 August

[48] Pope-Hennessy/Vickers, pp 132, 303

[49] RA QM/PRIV/CC45/646, Queen Alexandra to Queen Mary, 1923: 26 May; "For my darling and beloved May on her the 56th birthday. God bless you and keep you for ever? From your

very deeply loving old Mother Alix." Queen Mary noted: "Paper written by my beloved mother in law (Queen Alexandra) for my birthday when she sent me a Russian parasol handle – an agate top with small stones – 1923."

50 Pope-Hennessy/Vickers, p 87
51 Such as Houghton Hall
52 Pope-Hennessy/Vickers, p 132
53 Pope-Hennessy/Vickers, p 137
54 Pope-Hennessy/Vickers, p 132
55 RA GV/PRIV/AA33/50, Queen Alexandra to King George V, 1910: 25–27 August
56 RA GV/PRIV/AA37/17, King George V to Queen Alexandra, 1910: 29 August
57 Prince Christopher of Greece
58 Within a few years he had a little hut, "The Queen's Nest", with its interior walls covered in blue and white tiles, made for Alexandra's use as a seat near the lake
59 RA GV/PRIV/AA33/50, Queen Alexandra to King George V, 1910: 25–27 August
60 RA QM/PRIV/CC42/81, Queen Alexandra to Queen Mary, 1910: 30 August
61 Prince Christopher of Greece, *Memoirs*, pp 94–7
62 Many years later, Princess Alix remembered Victoria as being "full of tricks. We all suffered from her, trying to make mischief between my parents and then between my parents and us children. Not bad mischief, ye know, but just old maid's tricks." James Pope Hennessy and Hugo Vickers, *The Quest for Queen Mary*, p 138.
63 Prince Arthur of Connaught, who did, in the end, marry Princess Alexandra in 1913. Princess Maud had to wait a further ten years before a bridegroom was found for her.
64 RA GV/PRIV/AA33/51, Queen Alexandra to King George V, 1910: 30 September
65 Henry J Bell was one of the directors of Garrard's
66 RA GV/PRIV/AA33/50, Queen Alexandra to King George V, 1910: 25–27 August
67 RA VIC/ADDA21/228/70, Sir Dighton Probyn to Messrs Garrard, 1910: 7 September
68 RA VIC/ADDA21/228/72,73, Garrards to Sir Dighton Probyn, 1910: 8 September; Henry J Bell to Sir Dighton Probyn, 1910: 12 September
69 RA VIC/ADDA21/228/75, Sir Arthur Davidson to Sir Dighton Probyn, 1910: 15 September
70 RA VIC/ADDA21/228/76, Sir Dighton Probyn to Henry J Bell, 1910: 18 September
71 RA VIC/ADDA21/228/77,78, undated note from Queen Alexandra; Henry J Bell to Sir Dighton Probyn, 1910: 21 September
72 RA VIC/ADDA21/228/59,60, notes about King Edward VII's will relating to jewels etc
73 Herbert Samuel (1870–1963), Postmaster-General; 1st Viscount Samuel; leader of Liberal Party, 1931–35
74 RA VIC/ADDA21/174,175, Sir Dighton Probyn to Herbert Samuel, 1910: 14 September
75 RA GV/PRIV/AA33/51, Queen Alexandra to King George V, 1910: 30 September
76 RA GV/PRIV/AA33/52, Queen Alexandra to King George V, 1910: 21 October
77 Queen Alexandra to Lady Brownlow, 1910: 6 November, private collection
78 RA VIC/MAIN/QAD/1910: 8 November
79 Typed prayer placed between the pages of the engagement diary
80 Sir Christopher Wren (1632–1723), acclaimed architect
81 NA PRO Work 19/698
82 RA VIC/ADDA21/233/117, Queen Alexandra to Sydney Holland, 1910: 16 November
83 Charlotte Knollys's underlining in the engagement diary
84 RA GV/O2548/18, Queen Mary to Queen Alexandra, 1910: 21 November
85 RA GV/PRIV/AA37/18, King George V to Queen Alexandra, 1910: 18 November; Alice was Princess Alexander of Teck, living at Henry III Tower; her children were May and Rupert.
86 RA GV/PRIV/CC42/87, Queen Alexandra to Queen Mary, 1910: 25 November
87 RA GV/PRIV/AA37/19, King George V to Queen Alexandra, 1910: 11 December

[88] RA GV/PRIV/AA33/53, Queen Alexandra to King George V, 1910: 19 December

[89] Edward Frederick Mylius (1878-?1947)

[90] RA GV/PRIV/AA37/22, King George V to Queen Alexandra, 1911: 6 February

[91] RA GV/PRIV/AA33/54, Queen Alexandra to King George V, 1911: 4 February

[92] RA QM/PRIV/CC42/88, Queen Alexandra to Queen Mary, 1911: 6 February

[93] RA GV/PRIV/AA37/22, King George V to Queen Alexandra, 1911: 6 February

[94] RA GV/PRIV/AA34/1, Queen Alexandra to King George V, 1911: 15 February

[95] RA VIC/ ADDA/17/1086, Queen Alexandra to Princess Louise, Duchess of Argyll, 1911: 31 January

[96] RA GV/PRIV/AA34/1, Queen Alexandra to King George V, 1911: 15 February

[97] As Queen Victoria's eldest grandchild, who had been present at her death

[98] RA GV/PRIV/AA37/23, King George V to Queen Alexandra, 1911: 12 February

[99] Major Hon Sir Schomberg McDonnell (1861-1915), army officer, politician, civil servant; private secretary to Lord Salisbury as prime minister; secretary to the office of works, with duties relating to royal palaces

[100] RA GV/PRIV/AA34/1, Queen Alexandra to King George V, 1911: 15 February

[101] Perhaps Sir Alexander Nelson Hood, 5th Duke of Brontë (1854-1937), courtier, including being private secretary to Princess May as Princess of Wales, and later her treasurer when she became Queen Mary

[102] RA QM/PRIV/CC42/89, Queen Alexandra to Queen Mary, 1911: 27 February; the essay was later found between the pages of her "Kodak" photograph album

[103] RA GV/PRIV/AA34/2, Queen Alexandra to King George V, 1911: 1 March; she should really have consulted Probyn before sending for Laking, but was so anxious to help that she acted on impulse

[104] Elizabeth Sanderson Haldane (1862-1937), author, philosopher, historian, suffragist, nursing administrator, social welfare worker and the sister of Lord Haldane of Cloan.

[105] RA VIC/ADDA21/233/120, Queen Alexandra to Sydney Holland, 1911: 2 March

[106] RA GV/PRIV/AA34/3, Queen Alexandra to King George V, 1911: 15 March

[107] RA GV/PRIV/AA34/4, Queen Alexandra to King George V, 1911: 21 March

[108] RA VIC/ADDA17/1112, Queen Alexandra to Princess Louise, Duchess of Argyll, 1911: undated (Sunday)

[109] Admiral Sir Colin Keppel (1862-1947), courtier

[110] RA GV/PRIV/AA34/5, Queen Alexandra to King George V, 1911: 18 April

[111] RA QM/PRIV/CC25/100, Queen Mary to Dowager Grand Duchess of Mecklenburg-Strelitz, 1911: 7 May

[112] RA GV/PRIV/AA37/30, King George V to Queen Alexandra, 1911: 14 April

[113] Sir Solomon Obeyesekere (1848-1927) married Ezline Maria De Alwis

[114] RA GV/PRIV/AA34/6, Queen Alexandra to King George V, 1911: 21 July

[115] RA QM/PRIV/CC42/91, Queen Alexandra to Queen Mary, 1911: 3 July

[116] Eleanor of Castile (1241-90), w of King Edward I; after her death, near Lincoln, her husband had 12 memorial stone crosses erected at the places where her funeral cortège had stopped between Lincoln and London; the last was at Charing Cross

[117] RA GV/PRIV/AA34/7, Queen Alexandra to King George V, 1911: 21 July

[118] Epilepsy

[119] RA GV/PRIV/AA34/7, Queen Alexandra to King George V, 1911: 21 July

[120] This was perhaps the curtailing of the powers of the House of Lords, resulting in the Parliament Act, which received the Royal Assent on 18 August 1911. The Prime Minister had threatened to create enough Liberal peers to overcome the Conservative majority in the House of Lords, which the King was reluctant to do, but felt he could not oppose the Prime Minister.

121 Charles Urban (1867–1942), Anglo–American film producer and distributer
122 Blanche, née Lascelles (1880–1969), m George Lloyd, 1ˢᵗ Baron Lloyd, in 1911, was a Maid of Honour to Queen Alexandra from 1905–1911
123 When the King arrived on 9 August, it was 97° in the shade
124 RA GV/PRIV/AA34/8, Queen Alexandra to King George V, 1911: 3 August
125 With the Marquis and Marchioness of Ripon
126 Admiral Prince Nicholas Wiasemsky, commander of *Polar Star*
127 RA GV/PRIV/AA34/10, Queen Alexandra to King George V, 1911: 6 September
128 RA VIC/ADDU/417/9, Soveral Papers, Queen Alexandra to Marquis de Soveral, 1911: 1 October
129 RA GV/PRIV/AA34/11, Queen Alexandra to King George V, 1911: 28 September
130 RA GV/PRIV/AA34/11, Queen Alexandra to King George V, 1911: 28 September
131 Nripendra Natayan Bhup Bahadur, Maharaja of Cooch Behar (1862–1911); he had died at Bexhill-on-Sea, where he was convalescing.
132 Peter Arkadyevitch Stolypin, (1862–1911), who was also Minister of the Interior
133 RA GV/PRIV/AA34/9, Queen Alexandra to King George V, 1911: 6 October
134 RA QM/PRIV/CC42/93, Queen Alexandra to Queen Mary, 1911: 10 October
135 Grand Duchess George, p144
136 Prince George Schervashidze (1847–1918)
137 Bertram Pollock (1863–1943), Bishop of Norwich from 1911–43
138 RA GV/PRIV/AA37/32, King George V to Queen Alexandra, 1911: 14 November
139 RA GV/PRIV/AA34/12, Queen Alexandra to King George V, 1911: 15 November
140 RA GV/PRIV/AA34/13, Queen Alexandra to King George V, 1911: 24 November
141 He was also Librarian and Chairman of Sandringham Estate Cottage Horticultural Society
142 RA GV/PRIV/AA34/14, Queen Alexandra to King George V, 1911: 7 December
143 Arthur Rowland Harry Grant (d 1961), later Canon, m Margaret, née Dawnay (1880–1948), maid of honour to Queen Alexandra from 1905–08
144 RA GV/PRIV/AA34/16, Queen Alexandra to King George V, 1911: 20 December
145 Lt Colonel Sir Stanley Clarke, Equerry since 1878 and later Alexandra's private secretary
146 RA GV/PRIV/AA37/36, King George V to Queen Alexandra, 1911: 13, 14 December
147 George Curzon, 1ˢᵗ Marquess Curzon of Kedleston (1859–1925), statesman; Viceroy of India, 1899–1905; Foreign Secretary, 1919–24
148 RA GV/PRIV/AA34/15, Queen Alexandra to King George V, 1911: 15 December
149 William Whiteley (1831–1907), entrepreneur, began the business, which became a large shopping emporium in Bayswater, London, in the 1870s. A new building, in Queensway, was opened on 21 November 1911. Whiteley had claimed to be "The Universal Provider" and sold a wide variety of goods.
150 A Scottish engineer
151 RA GV/PRIV/AA34/15, Queen Alexandra to King George V, 1911: 15 December
152 RA GV/PRIV/AA37/36, King George V to Queen Alexandra, 1911: 13,14 December
153 RA GV/PRIV/AA34/16, Queen Alexandra to King George V, 1911: 20 December
154 RA GV/PRIV/AA37/40, King George V to Queen Alexandra, 1912: 15 January
155 Captain Allen Keith Mackenzie (1887–1916)
156 RA GV/PRIV/AA34/16, Queen Alexandra to King George V, 1911: 20 December
157 RA GV/PRIV/AA34/17, Queen Alexandra to King George V, 1911: 28 December
158 Sir Christopher Cradock (1862–1914), Rear-Admiral, served on royal yacht
159 RA GV/PRIV/AA34/18, Queen Alexandra to King George V, 1912: 4 January
160 RA GV/PRIV/AA37/39, King George V to Queen Alexandra, 1912 : 3 January
161 RA QM/PRIV/CC42/97, Queen Alexandra to Queen Mary, 1912: 4 January
162 Lady Hardinge, formerly Hon. Winifred Sturt (1868–1914), known as "Bena", had been a

young friend of the Wales Princesses. She was later woman of the bedchamber (1893–1901) and extra lady of the bedchamber (1910–14) to Queen Alexandra.

163   RA GV/PRIV/AA34/19, Queen Alexandra to King George V, 1912: 11 January

164   Olga Neruda (1858–1945), pianist

165   RA QM/PRIV/CC42/98, Queen Alexandra to Queen Mary, 1912: 16 January

166   RA VIC/ADDU/417/10, Soveral Papers, Queen Alexandra to Marquis de Soveral,1912: 17 January; many of her books (some with fine bindings), of which she had 3,000–4,000 in total, on many subjects, were kept here

167   RA GV/PRIV/AA34/20, Queen Alexandra to King George V, 1912: 20 January

168   Field Marshal Lord Kitchener was at this time British agent and consul-general in Egypt

169   RA GV/PRIV/AA.37/42, King George V to Queen Alexandra, 1912: 30 January

170   Dr Adolphe Zünd-Burguet; his method of vibro-massaging the ear with an electrophonoid was recommended for treating vertigo, neuralgia, tinnitus and hearing loss, including otosclerosis, from which Queen Alexandra suffered. The treatment's success rate was variable.

171   RA QM/PRIV/CC42/100, Queen Alexandra to Queen Mary, 1912: undated (Friday night)

172   RA GV/PRIV/AA34/21, Queen Alexandra to King George V, 1912: 23 February

173   RA GV/PRIV/AA34/23, Queen Alexandra to King George V, 1912: 28 February

174   RA GV/PRIV/AA34/24, Queen Alexandra to King George V, 1912: undated

175   Bodleian Library. Acland MSS, d.177/132/ 2054/26, Charlotte Knollys to Sara Acland, 1912: 25 March

176   RA GV/PRIV/AA37/45, King George V to Queen Alexandra, 1912: 3 March; the Suffragettes held a meeting in Parliament Square three days later

177   RA GV/PRIV/AA37/46, King George V to Queen Alexandra, 1912: 10 March

178   The state apartments had been opened as the London Museum (1911–14 and later 1950–76), which then moved to London Wall as the Museum of London

179   For Louisa, Duchess of Buccleuch

180   Evelyn James (1867–1929), wife of William (Willie) James.

181   Roderick William Mills, known as "Saltbush Bill" (1869–1940), larger-than-life character, stockman, market gardener and entertainer; the Duke of Cornwall and York had met him in Australia in 1901 and enjoyed his display with a long stockwhip. One of the whips was 65' long. Mills later raised money for the 1914–18 war effort with his entertainment. https://midwestwhips.com/HendersonSundayHerald1950.html; https://localhistory.kingston.vic.gov.au/articles/89, article by Silvia Roberts

182   Landon Ronald (Russell) (1873–1938), later knighted, was a conductor, composer, pianist, teacher and administrator

183   RA VIC/ADDA21/233/122, Queen Alexandra to Sydney Holland, 1912: 9 April

184   Thomas Wortley Drury (1847–1926), Bishop of Ripon from 1912–20

185   Duke Peter of Oldenburg (1868–1924)

186   RA GV/PRIV/AA34/25, Queen Alexandra to King George V, 1912: 1 June

187   Anna Vyroubova, *Memories of the Russian Court*, publ. 1923, Chapter 4; http://home.mts-nn-ru/~tbd/whiteflower/history_en.htm

188   Ignacy Jan Paderewski (1860–1941), Polish pianist, composer and spokesman for Polish independence; in 1919 he was Poland's prime minister

189   Sir George Holford married Mrs Menzies in the Chapel Royal

190   Perhaps Carl Nielsen (1865–1931), renowned Danish composer, conductor, violinist and song-writer

191   Grand Duke George Michaelovitch of Russia (1863–1919)

192   Major-General Evelyn Boscawen, 7th Viscount Falmouth (1847–1918) m Hon Kathleen, née Douglas-Pennant (1861–1953), horticulturalist

193 RA GV/PRIV/AA34/26, Queen Alexandra to King George V, 1912: 8 August

194 RA GV/PRIV/AA34/27, Queen Alexandra to King George V, 1912: 17 August; Princess Alexandra of Cumberland had married Hereditary Grand Duke Friedrich Franz of Mecklenburg-Schwerin in 1904.

195 Sir Lewis Bayly (1857–1938), Admiral

196 RA GV/PRIV/AA37/52, King George V to Queen Alexandra, 1912: 30 September

197 Duke Christian Ludwig of Mecklenburg-Schwerin (1912–96)

198 RA GV/PRIV/AA34/28, Queen Alexandra to King George V, 1912: 1 October

199 RA GV/PRIV/AA37/53, King George V to Queen Alexandra, 1912: 7 October

200 Who had haemophilia

201 RA GV/PRIV/AA37/54, Queen Alexandra to King George V, 1912: 9 October

202 Sir Sidney Lee (1859–1926), biographer, writer and critic

203 RA AEC/GG/9/16, Sir Arthur Davidson to Queen Alexandra, 1912: 16 June

204 RA AEC/GG/9/40, Sir Sidney Lee to Lord Esher, 1912: 24 August

205 RA AEC/GG/9/98, Sir Arthur Davidson to Queen Alexandra,1912: 17 October

206 RA AEC/GG/9/133, Queen Alexandra to Sir Arthur Davidson, 1912: 24 October

207 RA AEC/GG/9/16,40–1,58–9,77–8,82,98,111–15,122,140,142,147

208 RA AEC/GG/9/12, Edward Legge to Charlotte Knollys, 1912: 10 June

209 RA AEC/GG/9/78, Sir Arthur Davidson to Sir Dighton Probyn, 1912: 21 September

210 RA AEC/GG/9/82, Sir Arthur Davidson to Sir Dighton Probyn, 1912;4 October

211 John Morley (1838–1923), 1st Viscount Morley of Blackburn, statesman, writer and newspaper editor

212 For example, she had at first been slightly piqued about being rescued from the fire in her room in 1903 and pointed out that she had not been at all frightened

213 RA AEC/GG/9/175a, Sir Arthur Davidson to Sir Dighton Probyn, 1912: 16 November

214 The weight of the files rather supports this

215 Arthur James Balfour (1848–1930), 1st Earl of Balfour, politician and Prime Minister

216 Sir Fairfax Cartwright (1857–1928), author and diplomat; then British Ambassador at Vienna

217 RA AEC/GG/9/183, Sir Arthur Davidson, 1912: 3 December

218 RA VIC/ADDA/17/1118, Queen Alexandra to Princess Louise, Duchess of Argyll, 1912: 13 November

219 Acland MSS, d.177/132/ 2054/28, Charlotte Knollys to Sarah Acland, 1912: 29 November

220 Alexander George Anthony Allan Mackenzie of Glenmuick (1913–1993), 4th Baronet

221 Richard Strauss (1864–1949), German composer, conductor, pianist and violinist

222 It was discovered on 17 January 1912 by Scott's team, almost five weeks after Roald Amundsen's expedition

223 Accommodation for women students of the Royal Colleges of Music, Art and Science

224 Sir Thomas Vansittart Bowater (1862–1938), MP; Lord Mayor of London, 1913–14

225 The day in 1863 when he was elected King; he did not arrive in Greece until October that year

226 He was shot while walking informally in the town

227 Acland MSS, d 177/132/2054/29, Charlotte Knollys to Sarah Acland, 1913: 10 April

228 RA GV/PRIV/AA34/37, Queen Alexandra to King George V, 1914: 18 March

229 RA VIC/ADDA21/229, Queen Alexandra to Prince Nicholas of Greece, 1915: 19 January

230 Princess Victoria Louise of Prussia (1892–1980), m Ernest Augustus of Cumberland, now styled Duke of Brunswick-Lüneburg

231 Title inherited from his grandfather, Ernest, Duke of Cumberland, King of Hanover from 1837 when his niece Queen Victoria succeeded to the British throne; she could not succeed as Queen of Hanover because the Salic Law was in force there

[232] RA GV/PRIV/AA34/30, Queen Alexandra to King George V, 1913: 28 May

[233] It was the home of the London Museum from 1924 to just after the end of the Second World War

[234] Pandeli Ralli, (1845–1928), Liberal MP, of Greek ancestry

[235] Raymond Poincaré (1860–1934), French statesman, President from 1913–1920

[236] RA QM/PRIV/CC42/102, Queen Alexandra to Queen Mary, 1913: 12 June

[237] Jeanne Granier (1852–1939), French soprano

[238] Feodor Ivanovitch Chaliapin (1873–1938), Russian operatic bass singer

[239] Ibolyka Gyarfas (1901–86), Hungarian violin virtuoso performer

[240] Carrie Pringle (1859–1930), Austrian-born British soprano, who had sung some Wagner roles

[241] Violet's uncle was Hon Walter Vivian (1856–1943)

[242] Princess Augusta Victoria of Hohenzollern-Sigmaringen (1890–1966), m King Manuel II of Portugal

[243] Grand Duke Michael Michaelovitch of Russia (1861–1929) not to be confused with Alexandra's nephew, Grand Duke Michael Alexandrovitch; he m Sophie Nicholaievna von Merenberg (1868–1927), created Countess de Torby

[244] Widow of Grand Duke Serge, assassinated in 1905

[245] Hudson Ewbanke Kearley (1856–1934), 1st Viscount Devonport, grocer and politician

[246] Charles Ritchie (1866–1948), 2nd Baron Ritchie of Dundee

[247] Notes referring to the visit, kept in the Engagement Diary.

[248] RA VIC/ADDA21/233/127, Queen Alexandra to Sydney Holland, 1913: undated (Saturday)

[249] RA AEC/GG/9/279, Lord Knollys to Sir Arthur Davidson, 1913: 30 July

[250] Peter Markham Scott (1909–89), Sir, ornithologist, conservationist, painter, naval officer, broadcaster and sportsman. His mother was Kathleen, née Bruce (1878–1947), sculptor, m (1) Captain Robert Falcon Scott; after his death she was granted the rank of a widow of a KCB and was called Lady Scott; she m (2) Edward Hilton Young, created Baron Kennet in 1935

[251] Lewis Rodman Wanamaker (1863–1928), American department store magnate and patron of the arts. He donated a silver altar and reredos in memory of King Edward, and other silver items, to Sandringham Church

[252] Bing, p 287

[253] Agnes, née Barron (1874–1968), m Alexander, Baron de Stoeckl (1862–1926), a Russian diplomat; they had one daughter, Zoia. The couple were in the household of Grand Duke George Michaelovitch.

[254] RA GV/PRIV/AA37/56, King George V to Queen Alexandra, 1913: 28 August

[255] RA GV/PRIV/AA37/55, King George V to Queen Alexandra, 1913: 7 August

[256] RA GV/PRIV/AA37/56, King George V to Queen Alexandra, 1913: 28 August

[257] RA GV/PRIV/AA34/31, Queen Alexandra to King George V, 1913: 9–10 September

[258] Sir Edward Grey (1862–1933), 1st Viscount Grey of Falloden, statesman, including being foreign secretary

[259] RA GV/PRIV/AA34/32, Queen Alexandra to King George V, 1913: 20 September

[260] Whom she made me see in London the other day

[261] RA VIC/ADDU/417/11, Soveral Papers, Queen Alexandra to Marquis de Soveral, 1913: 19 September

[262] King Edward's dog, Caesar

[263] RA GV/PRIV/AA34/32, Queen Alexandra to King George V, 1913: 20 September

[264] RA GV/PRIV/AA37/56, King George V to Queen Alexandra, 1913: 28 August; the Duke was Governor-General of Canada from 1911–16

[265] RA GV/PRIV/AA37/59, King George V to Queen Alexandra, 1913: 20 September

266 RA GV/O2548/25, Queen Mary to Queen Alexandra, 1913: 1 October
267 RA QM/PRIV/CC42/103, Queen Alexandra to Queen Mary, 1913: 7 October
268 Princess Alexandra succeeded her father as Duchess of Fife in her own right.
269 RA GV/PRIV/AA37/60, King George V to Queen Alexandra, 1913: 29 September
270 RA AEC/GG/9/303, Sir Dighton Probyn to Sir Arthur Davidson, 1913: 3 November
271 RA AEC/GG/9/311, Sir Dighton Probyn to Sir Arthur Davidson, 1913: 5 November
272 RA AEC/GG/9/322, Sir Dighton Probyn to Sir Arthur Davidson, 1913: 10 November
273 She was also photographed officially in 1913.
274 Seat of the Earl of Derby
275 King James I of England and VI of Scotland (1566–1625)

Chapter 14

1914–1918

"A horrible butchery on innocent people"

⚜

The year 1914 was Queen Alexandra's 70th and would have been Eddy's 50th.[1] Probyn was trying to control a current situation, as he told Lord Ripon;[2] "Heaps of letters come now to the 'Private Secretary' or perhaps to the 'Comptroller', or to Her Majesty direct, which she may give to the Private Secretary to deal with, letters which finally often have to be referred to Queen Alexandra to ask whether she will help the cases with money. When this is done, in 9 cases out of 10, the 'Blessed Lady', instead of giving £1 or £2, in all probability says 'Yes' and sends £5, or £10, or more, from her own quarterly allowance[3] to be forwarded to the 'begging applicant'."[4] He and Sir Henry Streatfeild[5] suggested that, if Ripon gave Streatfeild some money, say £50, as required, he could pay sums out of it on his own responsibility without needing to refer to the Queen, perhaps saving Ripon trouble and Alexandra money.[6]

Davidson told Probyn that Lee planned to revise his article or write a new memoir of King Edward; this needed further discussion. Meanwhile he was speechless. Edward Legge's first book[7] had appeared in 1912 after the household had warned him that, if it were published, they would strongly disclaim having helped him. Miss Knollys had seen the correspondence, yet, without telling them, had congratulated Legge on having "done his utmost to place our beloved King's <u>character & career</u> in its <u>true</u> & proper light." Legge of course mentioned in his second book[8] that "I have been honoured by the most gracious recognition of the accuracy of my portrait of the King." This implied Alexandra's approval and she had indeed asked Charlotte to thank Legge for the copy of his first book. But Davidson felt "more sore & indignant about it than about anything I can remember."[9] "What on earth does it matter if she did write it", replied Probyn, "I mean, what is there in it, of sufficient importance to let you worry yourself to death about it, my dear old friend? If she wrote it, she wrote it <u>heedlessly,</u> not <u>thinking</u>; most certainly not with any evil intentions."[10]

King Edward in his True Colours was wholly sympathetic. Legge steadily provided evidence against Lee's belittling allegations, while stating, justifiably, that as the King had only recently died, it was too soon for a complete evaluation. He produced a credible portrait, emphasising the King's strengths, while admitting his faults. What Davidson had objected to in Legge's work, which included an article in the *Fortnightly Review*, was that, among other things, he over-emphasised the King's sadness at a friend's death and mentioned the Mordaunt and Tranby Croft cases, which "in the interests of kindness & generosity had better be forgotten." However, this all showed Edward VII as fallible but likeable; far better than as an historically-discounted nonentity. Mordaunt and Tranby Croft were in the public domain; could not be ignored and had both vindicated the then Prince of Wales; Legge also praised Alexandra for supporting her husband during the Tranby Croft affair. Her liking the book suggests that she preferred sympathetic and honest authors. She enjoyed biographies and memoirs and owned a large collection; her husband had given her a life of Madame de Pompadour[11] for Christmas in 1896.[12]

Victoria was unwell again and Charlotte had influenza. Davidson had painful blood clots in his legs, but just needed rest; his heart trouble was dormant "as long as I keep quiet & don't get tired or agitated." He decided that Nurse Fletcher, whom Alexandra had left with him, ought to be looking after the patients at Sandringham, and wired that he would get another nurse for himself. Soon after, Alexandra telephoned to say Nurse Fletcher was to stay at Marlborough House, thus turning the tables on Davidson's cry that she did not appreciate him. He gratefully acknowledged her "<u>extraordinary</u> kindness in allowing me to remain here, & providing me with every possible comfort. It is <u>indeed</u> good of her."[13] The King and his mother had decided that Lee himself should re-write his work on King Edward, probably because revising it had seriously affected Davidson's health, but Lee would not do it without fresh facts.[14] It had been a "tiresome time ... with everybody ill etc ... So we came up here on Monday to try and cheer up poor dear Davidson", wrote Alexandra from Marlborough House; "I do not know what I shall do if anything were to happen to him too! We can indeed ill afford to lose another friend". Probyn had bronchitis and she herself succumbed "<u>at last!</u>" to a bad cold and cough. "Such a bore, so I feel in a vile temper & everything worries me doubly".[15] She managed to attend the first performance in England of Wagner's *Parsifal* (six and a half hours) on 2 February but then stayed indoors until late March. Victoria wrote three letters to Rosebery, all mentioning Davidson's ill health; on 12 March he was "still in bed <u>14</u> weeks without moving! So patient – much touched at your kind enquiry."[16]

Alexandra had plenty to worry her but, primarily, was still mourning; since her father's death in 1906, significant bereavements had relentlessly occurred and no-one, except the 87-year-old Christian IX, had reached a ripe old age. King Carlos and Crown Prince Luis Filipe of Portugal were killed in 1908 at 44 and 20; her sister-in-law, Marie, Princess Waldemar, died in 1909 at 44; and her beloved husband, Edward VII in 1910, at 68. In January 1912 her son-in-law, the Duke of Fife, died at 62 and she had hardly taken this in before her eldest brother, Frederick VIII died unexpectedly at almost 69, and her nephew, George William of Cumberland, at only 31. Within a year, her second brother, King George of the Hellenes, was assassinated at 67 in March 1913, which, even a year later, made her feel ill and wretched. Greek politics frightened her; at home the Suffragettes' campaign was causing concern. Most alarming was the turbulent question of Home Rule for Ireland. She begged her son to "<u>speak</u> out and put your foot down! while there yet is time – to save your Country from such a <u>calamity</u> which now is threatening it. <u>How</u> I feel for you – you know, and how I wish I could help you!"[17] Lord Suffield died on 9 April. Poor Caesar, whose jaw was broken during a tooth extraction on the 17th, had to be chloroformed the next day because he was in such agony. Sir Francis Laking died on 21 May and on the 24th so did "dear little Togo", one of Alexandra's Japanese dogs. She mourned her pet animals almost as much as her human friends, Caesar because of his special connection with her husband. Jacques Fehr, the trusted courier, became mixed up in the trafficking of honours. The King dismissed him on the spot but Alexandra took his part, convinced he had been stupid rather than depraved. She persuaded George to let Fehr resign instead of being sacked, with a pension, "but <u>nothing</u> will induce me to give him up. I <u>first</u> got him & will stick to him always." Quoting Probyn, she agreed Fehr had indeed been "a d. fool", but he was quite honest. She would double his salary, compensating him for the loss of his previous earnings, and employ him to look after her affairs in Denmark at Hvidöre.[18] Fehr remained and justified her loyalty.

The Duke of Argyll was seriously ill and Alexandra assured Louise that "indeed to me you have <u>always</u> been the dearest sister & I too think of all former happy times when we were young together & saw so much of each other. Life has so many ups & downs but I have never changed." When the Duke died on 2 May at Kent House in the Isle of Wight, she wrote in condolence; "there is no earthly comfort for a broken heart. My thoughts have never left you for a single moment in all those terrible 6 days & nights … when you watched by his side … I do hope you will let me come to you either on the Thursday you come up or Friday after the last heartrending ceremony at Westminster. A telephone message will bring me to you at once." Later, she sent her own widow's bonnet for Louise to copy if she liked it.[19] Alexandra was still meeting friends and relatives, visiting galleries, flower shows, dog shows and the theatre. She saw Adeline Genée dance at the Coliseum on 27 April and received the boy conductor, Willy Ferrero,[20] on 16 May. The Danish sovereigns,[21] on a state visit from 9–15 May, had tea with Aunt Alix at Marlborough House as well as visiting the Tower of London and the Wallace Collection with her. On the 14th she gave a Danish evening party for them, with Danish musicians and entertainers and the British comedian Harry Tate,[22] who performed his sketch, *Motoring*. She inspected a Grand Muster of 10,000 Boy Scouts at Horse Guards on 13 June, visited the HAIA's exhibition at the Albert Hall on the 20th, chaired a meeting of the Red Cross Society at

Brooklands and drove with Victoria through London on "Alexandra Day". This time a newspaper reported; "By Queen Alexandra's wish none of the sellers will be under the age of 16, and those who undertake the work will go in couples." She had realised there might be problems.[23]

On 21 May, the Suffragettes, led by Mrs Emmeline Pankhurst,[24] reached Buckingham Palace, seeking redress for their grievances from the King. Queen Alexandra thought they behaved foolishly, and deplored their sometimes violent actions (she might well have felt more sympathy for the non-violent Suffragists), but she supported and promoted women's education, whether domestic, academic, artistic, musical or medical, and approved, for example, of women working in aid of good causes, as she did herself. One of her books was *Notable Women Authors of the Day; biographical sketches,*[25] by Helen C Black and another was the intriguingly titled *Woman, the Predominant Partner,*[26] by Sir Edward Sullivan. Alexandra had little sympathy for certain politicians; did she ever think women could do better? The suffragettes' leaflet residing in her engagement diary for 1914 could simply have been an interesting souvenir; retaining it could also indicate private sympathy for the general idea of women's rights which, as a member of the Royal Family, she could not show publicly.[27] She would have been shocked at the mistreatment of women by the guardians of law and order, which was one reason for the appeal to the King.

On 18 May Minny had arrived from Russia and they spent a lot of time visiting, motoring and opera-attending. Queen Olga joined them on 21 June. This companionable interlude was rattled by the shocking news, on the 28th, of the assassination of Archduke Francis Ferdinand and his wife at Sarajevo; Alexandra had met them in London only the previous autumn. On 11 July there was yet another premature death: "Bena", Lady Hardinge at 46. Meanwhile Sir Sidney Lee had fully acknowledged his mistakes in the *DNB* article. There had been no compulsion; he simply could not ignore the facts. He was now anxious to write an accurate historical record of King Edward's reign and had begun it[28] but in view of unfolding events, decided to postpone the book until a better time. On the 16th Queen Alexandra visited Sir Ernest Shackleton's[29] ship, *Endurance,* starting for the South Pole. Queen Olga had left on the 15th but Minny was still in England; she and Alexandra were terribly anxious about current affairs and now time was running out. On 1 August Germany declared war on Russia and Minny had to leave precipitately in order to get home before it was too late. Victoria, Princess Louis of Battenberg who, with her daughter Louise,[30] had been visiting her sisters in Russia, was struggling to get back to England. Germany declared war on France on the 3rd. Alexandra's niece, Margrethe, and her governess, Miss Ramsen, who had been staying in Paris, managed to get a passage to England and arrived unexpectedly. At midnight on 4 August, England declared war on Germany; on the 12th she declared war on Austria too and the ambassador, recalled to Vienna, came to take leave. Count Albert Mensdorff was a distant relative and old friend, and the leave-taking must truly have been poignant.

In August 1914 few believed the war would last longer than several months, but its general impact would be catastrophic. Specifically, it would change Alexandra's life irrevocably, although this only became clear as it dragged out its bloody course. Her Danish visit in 1913 had been the last to her beloved homeland.[31] She would never visit Norway, Greece or Russia again, or receive most of her overseas relatives in England for the duration, as travelling in wartime was too risky. She corresponded with them[32] when she could, and they kept her up to date with news, but her pleasure in travelling was lost forever.[33] Anglo–Greek relations were imperfect and King Constantine came under unjust public suspicion because his wife was the German emperor's sister. Russia's troubles were temporarily masked by patriotic fervour but who could tell what the future held? Nevertheless Russia was an ally, while Austria, where the Cumberlands lived, was not. Alexandra's affection for them was thus at odds with her British loyalties; ironically, as the Duke of Cumberland had an English title and was descended from George III. Of course she still loved Thyra but, politically, could not make this too obvious.[34] Effectively, Alexandra had lost her sisters; she would never see Thyra again and was only reunited with Minny in 1919. She had already lost her parents and two of her brothers. The happy gatherings at Rumpenheim, Fredensborg, Bernstorff and Hvidøre were over in the natural order, but also through the machinations of fate. Denmark was neutral in the war, however, and her brother Waldemar, an admiral in the Danish Navy, sometimes managed to visit her. Thus in August 1914 Alexandra was a widow approaching 70, deaf, separated from relatives and interests abroad and desperately worried. This was increased by lesser sorrows, such as the death on 5 August of Mrs Rosalie Dodds.[35] The Queen felt affection for her, as for all her faithful old servants, and attended the memorial service at Marlborough House Chapel. Now she had to give all her support to the fight for victory, which, with her abiding hatred of Prussian-led Germany, would not be difficult.

On 5 August Alexandra called on her son at Buckingham Palace and during the next few days witnessed troops departing "on foreign service". She gave Probyn £2,000 in bank notes, for SSFA, the Red Cross and other relief funds, from her personal quarterly allowance; Ripon was thankful he would not have to find the money from the depleted sum he was responsible for, but now war had been declared, no one knew what would happen in the future.[36] The announcement that an Expeditionary Force had been sent to France was not published until 18 August. Anxious to keep up to date with war news and following a longstanding habit, Alexandra read newspapers from cover to cover and cut out items of interest to place in large albums; she took 15 daily papers, 26 weekly papers and 7 monthly periodicals.[37] She could not always hear what people said and probably suspected that confidential or upsetting information was kept from her; indeed the King had ordered that she should not be given any news which was to be treated as secret but that anything for publication should be shown to her shortly beforehand.[38] But she was able to find out a great deal from the press; more than was good for her peace of mind, and was thus quite well-informed, although at the mercy of exaggeration, jingoism and inaccuracy, all reinforcing the hatred of Prussia which she had felt since 1864. The war did not surprise her; she had always distrusted the German Empire's ambition.

On 7 October she wrote to Margaret, Duchess of Teck,[39] whose husband had just left for the front. "God guard & protect him throughout the whole of this long & terrible campaign & bring him back safely to his dear & devoted little Meg!" She enclosed a "chain letter"; "This little prayer which was sent to me to copy 9 days in succession, & send to 9 different people, when on the 10th day you will experience a <u>great joy</u>. We must not break the chain which goes all over the world, but write it 9 days running – this is the little prayer: Oh! Lord Jesus I pray Thee bless us and keep us from all evil, and bring us to dwell with Thee! Amen."[40] She wrote agitatedly to George; "This horrible, brutal & awful war is getting more fierce and appalling as days go on, and one trembles to hear what next. Now those awful Germans are actually carrying their submarines by rail across country to torpedo our ships. If only we can stop them from carrying out this devilish effort, there really remains nothing mean or bad for them to do. Even their making use of their confiscated Dreadnought under [a] Turkish name, without the declaration of war by Turkey, & bombarding Odessa & a number of unfortified Russian towns on the Black Sea – is quite beyond words."[41] Casualties increased, some close to home. Baba's husband, Allan Mackenzie, was wounded at the Battle of the Aisne in September and one of the King's equerries, Lord Charles Mercer Nairne,[42] was killed. In late October news came that Prince Maurice of Battenberg,[43] Princess Beatrice's 23-year-old youngest son, had died of wounds in France: "poor dear little ... Maurice ... <u>was</u> a real hero & so brave & it is too sad he was killed so young & promising too."[44]

Another casualty, although not a fatality, was Maurice's uncle, Louis of Battenberg, a family friend ever since Albert Edward had taken him under his wing when he came to England, aged fourteen, in 1868. Louis made a fine career in the Royal Navy, rising to the rank of First Sea Lord; he also married one of Queen Victoria's granddaughters, Princess Victoria of Hesse.[45] His German name and ancestry now seemed disadvantageous, and he was obliged to resign his office. Alexandra warmly supported him, justifiably feeling that he had been very badly treated: "Poor dear Louis B, it is too hard on him, but he is of a noble character & has sacrificed himself to the Country he has served so well."[46] Soon afterwards she got a bad cold and stayed indoors for most of November. Lord Roberts (82) had died of pneumonia while on a visit of inspection to British and Indian soldiers in France. At his funeral at St Paul's Cathedral on the 19th Queen Alexandra was officially represented by Probyn, but in fact, with Victoria,

Charlotte Knollys and John Ward, attended privately, refusing to let illness stop her paying her personal respects.

Alexandra had been in London since 26 January, intending then to return to Sandringham soon, but illness and events had forestalled her and she was still there by the end of 1914. Except for eight days in October, she had spent most of the year in London, including Christmas, when the King, Queen and their family were at York Cottage. This was unusual but she was committed to the war effort and most of her obligations to it were in London. After May 1910 her public engagements had decreased; from August 1914 they began to multiply again. From January to early August she had twelve official engagements, but between 10 August and 30 December there were some 30 war-related occasions, which she attended in an official capacity. They included visiting hospitals, clinics and convalescent homes to see repatriated wounded servicemen; events connected with the Red Cross; visits to work depots and premises where work funds were administered and where the emergency women's corps carried out their duties; and seeing the troops off to France. She contributed to schemes such as collecting money for "stockings" or long socks for the troops; 300,000 were required and she was delighted to help, sending £25 to Queen Mary to add to the fund.[47] Alexandra's love of the theatre would have been starved had it not been for the many charity events which she attended, "got up" by amateurs instead of professionals, some of whom were on active service. Theatres were shut in the evening because of black-out restrictions but there was nothing to prevent their use in the afternoon. Charity matinées became popular and were often organised by society ladies and other enthusiasts in aid of causes like "the sick and wounded", "the Arts fund for the relief of members of the artistic profession in distress owing to the war" or "the soldiers of the Royal Engineers". On 10 September the Queen went to see "the Ballet Girls" working for the Red Cross at the Alhambra.

One member of Alexandra's extended family in England was Marie, Grand Duchess George, who, with her daughters Nina[48] and Xenia[49] had been prevented from leaving by the German declaration of war on Russia on 1 August. They became part of the Queen's intimate circle. Alexandra was pleased to get a letter from her grandson, David, on her birthday; he was in France but she worried that "he will always drive himself about without a chauffeur even in that strange country with dangers <u>all around</u> him and <u>awful</u> roads – when any accident might happen."[50] She liked bronze statuary and among her Christmas presents in 1914 was a little old bronze figure with outstretched arms, from Viscount Knutsford, as Sydney Holland had become after his father's death in January. Through collaborating over the Nursing Board and the London Hospital he and Alexandra had become firm friends; in a note with the little statue, he wrote, "It is bubbling over with affection & sympathy & wishes to give both to someone. So do I. It finds great difficulty in putting this into words. So do

I." Rather sentimental, perhaps, but she responded gracefully, "Cannot thank you sufficiently for beautiful bronze figure and for your more than kind letter."[51] During the winter, she gave £1,000 to J Danvers Power[52] to distribute amongst the poor as he thought best. Nearly £652 was dedicated to the very poorest people, while the rest went to others, including small merchants ruined by the war, actors, artists, clergy families, writers, musicians and individual special cases in difficulties.[53] On 24 December Alexandra gave a dinner for twelve, with a Christmas table and tree, at Marlborough House. On Christmas Day she attended morning service in Marlborough House Chapel and an afternoon one in St Paul's Cathedral, followed on Boxing Day by evening service and carols in Westminster Abbey; she was worshipping and celebrating with the public at a time of national crisis. It was wonderful to see David, on leave from the front, on the 27th; three days later she visited wounded soldiers in St Bartholomew's Hospital. She sent George "a few lines to thank you for all yr love in the old, & to wish you & our Country a blessed New Year – and above all let us pray for <u>Peace</u> after a glorious <u>Victory</u>" adding, slightly mischievously "I am glad you all missed me a little at Xmas, when the dear house was shut up & no Xmas tree this time. I was sorry for the dear Children's sake!"[54]

Zeppelin raids began in earnest in 1915. Queen Alexandra had been told officially, at 11.20pm on 10 October 1914, to cover up the skylights at Marlborough House. On 19 January there was a raid over Norfolk and between 18 February and October further enemy bombardments caused casualties, destruction and general alarm. By favouring London and East Anglia they put the Royal Family, especially Alexandra, under particular strain. On 20 January she told her nephew, Prince Nicholas; "those *canailles*[55] sent a Zeppelin to <u>Norfolk</u>, passed actually over my beloved home <u>Sandringham</u> & dropped a lot of bombs over Lynn, where they killed people & ruined houses, & at various other places on the coast. It is too infamous & I am sure they will destroy my dear little house by the sea! Oh if I only had a cannon on that shore that cld destroy them all!" Since aerial attacks began, they had lived in constant terror and misery; it was not a war "but a horrible butchery on innocent people". Airship and submarine warfare was what frightened her most. There were now thousands of refugees in England and thousands of German prisoners had been captured; the British troops were fighting splendidly and were "not quite that <u>despicable</u> little Army that *canaille* the <u>arrogant</u> <u>despicable</u> German K ... r looked upon us."[56] It felt as though a whole generation was being wiped out and every house was in mourning. War work, however, flourished; "We are all hard at work for our poor brave soldiers both with sending warm clothes out to the Front, which I do every week, and also for the sailors & <u>nurses</u>. We have an enormous lot of Hospitals both in Belgium and France besides all over England. I have a Hospital Ship too & there are ambulance motors & trains all very well organised, and I have visited a great number of our hospitals here in London." There were so many sad cases, but the wounded were brave, cheerful and uncomplaining. Princess Victoria supported a scheme for having clothes for soldiers, sailors and refugees cut out and sent to unemployed girls to make up. In 1915 she became president of a committee founding "Rest Clubs" for nursing sisters in France; the first started at Wimereux by Lady Ponsonby[57] and Mrs Cyril Ward.[58] Grand Duchess George had her own large hospital at Harrogate, where Princess Margrethe was nursing; she could not yet go home because of the danger of mines at sea.[59]

Early in 1915 Alexandra became concerned over horror stories about women in Belgium, including nuns and nurses, giving birth after being raped by German soldiers. She had heard of other cases at Salisbury.[60] Alexandra wanted to start a scheme to help them, and asked Knutsford for his advice. Circumspectly, he doubted whether women could become pregnant as a result of rape;[61] if they did, they might have "willingly surrendered themselves". He was sorry about the cases but enquiries had been made; there were none at the Belgian refugee centres and a number of alleged rapes had been disproved, including those involving nurses. The Foundling Hospital in London[62] would take any resulting babies and bring them up as English girls and boys. Genuine cases in Belgium, including nuns, would be properly cared for by the religious authorities. Knutsford assured Alexandra it would be impossible to enquire into the background of every woman claiming to have been raped and if she started a scheme to help such women it could be abused by women who had not been raped and would risk becoming a laughing stock. She must not be associated with a failed enterprise and it would be best to make use of available resources. The matter was problematic; possibly there was unwillingness to investigate more thoroughly. Alexandra apologised for having caused Knutsford so much trouble, but would not be fobbed off; she sincerely wished to help and "I shld ... be very pleased to talk it all over with you some day whenever suits you best."[63]

By 18 February Alexandra had visited nine hospitals, four charity performances and exhibitions[64] and a kinematograph of war pictures at the Scala. She had also inspected five motor ambulance cars which the Salvation Army was sending to the front, and received a Japanese Red Cross unit. Such events continued.[65] Grand Duchess George, with her daughters, stayed at Marlborough House and, with Alexandra, attended a service at "the little Chapel in Bayswater"[66] on 18 March, the second anniversary of her father's assassination. On 15 April, suffering from a bad cold and cough, Alexandra told her son she had just seen a Dane, Andersen[67] ("the great man who invented & owns all those beautiful oil ships with no funnels"). He was in England for the third time ("I think on a secret mission") and had important contacts, having just come from meeting Nicholas II and the Dowager Empress and then the

German emperor, "who asked him to come again on his way back but I strongly advised him <u>not</u> to do so as W[illiam] will only <u>pump</u> him & try to get him into <u>his power</u>". Andersen was on good terms with Sir Edward Grey,[68] and also Lord Grey.[69] He had a letter to George V from Christian X, proposing a peace conference at Copenhagen. Alexandra thought it was "<u>too</u> soon for <u>us</u> to think of <u>Peace yet</u> – <u>we</u> must crush them first of all." She assured her son he could speak quite openly to Andersen, who was most discreet. The King did indeed meet him in September and had a long and interesting talk with him.

Anti-German feeling in England was growing. Alexandra ("although as a rule I never interfere") drew her son's attention on 12 May to "those hateful German banners in our sacred Church St George's at Windsor", warning that he was "bound to the Nation who demands to have these hateful ... banners removed ... I would not say so if I did not think it yr <u>duty</u> to do so. I know Papa wd have done so at once."[70] It had already happened, George told her. Not just the Prussian ones, however; all the other German ones had gone too; the sheep had been thrown out with the goats. She protested: "that was not necessary, as all of them are simply <u>soldiers</u> or <u>vassals</u> under that brutal German emperor's orders. Poor dear Ernie[71] for instance who was dead against the war and loves England and poor Uncle Ernest[72] whose name is English; also poor stupid Charlie[73] for his Mother's sake might have been left. I think it was a mistake particularly as it was to punish the Head of the German Nation."[74] Nothing was simple and this was only one of the effects the war had on the Royal Family; the King was being forced to take revenge on his relatives in the name of patriotism.

Probyn was now permanently worried about Alexandra's financial position, but hesitated to shock her with too much reality. They discussed it and this time she had agreed; "certainly have less flowers in the house, but I thought coming fr Sandringham wld have been cheaper. I must keep some in the hall & two drawing rooms & I really have not many upstairs in my own rooms, but they <u>change</u> them <u>much too often</u> which always makes me furious." She asked May for "*a résumé* of yr plants & flowers while at Marlborough House – and I have at once compared it with what I have been spending here now for 5 years; I have showed it to General Probyn and we are doing our utmost to cut it down a bit. It is very difficult as I do like to have a lot of lovely flowers about the house & in my own rooms."[75] In 1895, in the season, there had been 300–400 vases of cut flowers daily in the royal apartments; two men were employed exclusively to do the work.[76] It had been suggested that Alexandra's quarterly allowance should be cut to £2,000; "At <u>present</u> I cannot spare the 500 extra per quarter, but Lord de Grey can tell you I have not touched any of his money since last summer, so I am sure with <u>less eating</u> ... things ought to be getting better financially". Probyn was sure there was no over-eating either upstairs or downstairs, "although Her Majesty says she thinks there is."[77] She did not miss a thing on her regular visits to the kitchens.

Alexandra was chief patroness of the Universal Cookery and Food Association (founded in 1885) promoting the science of cookery and domestic economy. In March 1915 she accepted a copy of their *War-time Cookery Guide*.[78] She was not unwilling to practise frugality; she had learned about household economy as a girl from her mother in Denmark. She liked her clothes to last; favourites were sometimes kept for years, such as the sealskin cloak she brought from Denmark in 1863 and still wore on the Norwegian cruise in 1893.[79] Between 1888 and 1890 she had had six of her good brocade dresses unpicked, cleaned and re-used as furniture covers at Sandringham.[80] However, before May 1910 she had never had so much to pay for. From 1863 to 1910 her husband paid large expenses, including the maintenance of Sandringham, staff wages, electricity, gas and coal bills and general household costs, and Alexandra's annual "pocket money" of £10,000 out of her allowance was usually enough for personal needs; clothes, presents, hobbies like photography,[81] or impromptu donations to charity. The rest of her annual allowance of £40,000 paid for travelling and other matters appropriate to her status. King Edward had paid income tax voluntarily but not super-tax and was, when he died, personally solvent. In 1910 Alexandra was granted an annuity of £70,000 by Parliament and had some small private savings as well. She paid income tax on this but, by an oversight, had not been exempted from paying super-tax and within two years of the King's death was made liable for it, with no abatement, while still having to meet the general running costs of two establishments as well as her personal expenditure. This seemed very unfair, especially as it hampered her ability fully to carry out what she regarded as her particular responsibility: charitable donations. Probyn had complained in 1901 when the government fixed £70,000 as her allowance if the King died, fearing it would not be enough. William IV's widow, Queen Adelaide had been granted £100,000 in 1837. Probyn prayed that the King would live long and be able to save a reasonable "purse" for his wife.

When King Edward died at 68, Probyn requested the prime minister, Herbert Henry Asquith, to grant Queen Alexandra £100,000 a year. Asquith asked several times whether the King had not died in debt; Probyn assured him not. "What, no debts?" said Asquith, in amazement. "None" retorted Probyn; in fact the King had saved enough to leave sums to his widow and younger daughters. If he had not done so, Probyn doubted whether Alexandra would be able to live even on £100,000 a year. Finally Probyn was told that any increase for her would have to be deducted from King George's younger children's allowances. Thus the request for more money was knocked on the head.[82] However, there was another possible small source. In 1885 Alexandra had started her own branch of the National Aid Fund, to assist relief for the Sudan campaign. The branch had closed in March 1886, but the fund still existed[83] and by 1915 still held a few thousand pounds. As she had collected this herself, for war purposes, she could appropriately use it currently and money could be made available to her from

14 Group taken in the dining room, Sandringham, October 1916; left to right, *clockwise round the table*, Sir Dighton Probyn (white beard); Princess Mary (hat only); Princess Victoria; King George V; Queen Alexandra; Sir Arthur Davidson; Hon Charlotte Knollys.

RCIN 2919530

time to time. She was very glad to receive the first £1,000 on 27 May. Probyn told Lord Farquhar; "It was cruel of the Govt only granting Her Majesty such a scanty allowance in the first instance, and now still further reducing it by heavy taxation. If she was trying to hoard money, or spending it lavishly on herself, I should not feel for her, but it all goes on others. We must, I think be prepared to let her have more from this Fund if she wants it, which the Blessed Lady is sure to do ... provided the expenditure is confined to legitimate war charities, which it may certainly be considered as doing ... Nobody knows what the Queen has paid away from her own private income on War Charities since this war began."[84] Alexandra was grateful for this and careful with the money. By December she said she could manage a bit longer without another instalment, and asked how the balance of the account now stood.[85]

By 10 June, Probyn was very worried; in the past year Alexandra had spent £8,000 over her income and now, because of extra taxation, would lose a further £8,000. "God knows I am doing all I can to reduce expenditure – to cut down the expenses where I feel justified in doing so, and can obtain the Queen's permission ... however ... I would far sooner see the Queen spend more than she ought to, than give anybody a just cause to complain of meanness on Her Majesty's part." He had been preaching economy to her for months if not years past, to little avail. He was trying to get her to let him dispose of the aged horses and dogs at Sandringham, "but she won't". As for his colleagues, some had military responsibilities and Davidson was not really well enough to fulfil his duties as equerry. "As regards myself", the 82-year-old mused, "I feel I am a useless bit of lumber, but as, thank goodness, I don't cost the Queen anything, I ease my conscience and hang on. My successor, I am afraid, will have to be paid." However, Alexandra had apparently managed to pay all but one bill out of her personal allowance during the past year.[86]

On 10 August she wrote again to Prince Nicholas about Greece. Although it was not involved in the main war in Europe, there was anxiety because of nearby unrest and because King Constantine had been seriously ill. Bulgaria supported the Central Powers but it was hoped that Roumania and other countries would join the Allies "at the end of our terrific struggle", when Turkey and Germany had been vanquished. There was dismay at the fall of Warsaw and the threat that William's youngest son, Joachim,[87] would be made King of Poland.[88] There were changes in the ministry;[89] Lord Fisher, whom the Queen loyally supported, was about to resign as First Sea Lord, in protest at "that stupid young foolhardy Winston C[hurchill]'s"[90] ill-fated Dardanelles Campaign, to which men from Sandringham, including the agent, Frank Beck, had been sent. There were more casualties among friends and acquaintances. Through it all, Alexandra kept visiting the wounded, attending charity events, inspecting depots, workshops and ambulances and visiting the "huts" and "Buffets" set up at railway stations, often by charitable ladies, for returning troops. A matinee on 2 July at the

Haymarket in aid of Invalid Kitchens of London,[91] under Alexandra's patronage, benefited the "Home Front" by raising money to provide suitable, reasonably-priced food for invalids, convalescents and maternity cases among two million of London's poorest people. Her support for all kinds of enterprises was eagerly sought and generously given, even if sometimes reluctantly: "I will certainly come this afternoon as soon as I can after Mrs Asquith's[92] play which she has bothered my life out to attend and see her daughter act."[93] She appreciated being invited to Buckingham Palace on 3 August, when colours were presented to the newly formed Welsh Guards, and told May; "Dear George's speech was excellent & went straight to my heart and I only wish the whole regiment had been ordered to come closer up & heard his touching words too. I was so sorry that the thunderstorm at the end wetted them all to the skin, & must have ruined their new uniforms, and am looking forward to meeting you tomorrow at St Paul's for the great & solemn service."[94]

Through the Invalid Kitchens of London, Queen Alexandra was in touch with Lady Muriel Paget.[95] In August 1915 the London Committee to establish an Anglo–Russian Hospital in Petrograd[96] was set up, with Lady Muriel as its honorary organising secretary. Alexandra was invited to be patron; she and Minny headed the Red Cross Societies in Britain and Russia and the new project interested them both. The hospital, suggested by the Foreign Office, was funded by public subscription and donations from the British Red Cross and other societies, although not as an official British Red Cross Society hospital. Its base was Grand Duke Dmitri Pavlovitch's palace[97] in Petrograd. As a present from Britain to Russia, it was run by British medical staff, for Russian officers, with donated money and equipment, such as motor ambulances. Queen Alexandra gave £100, dressing gowns and clothing.[98] She received Lady Muriel Paget on 30 August.

Meanwhile on 18 August a British submarine, E13, ran aground in shallow water near Saltholm Island and was torpedoed by the Germans. Fourteen bodies were brought back to Hull on the 28th on a Danish steamer, *Vidar*, and Alexandra sent fourteen wreaths to be placed on the coffins before the public procession through Hull to the railway station. The Danish Society in London sent a 5' high floral tribute, with 500 red and white carnations, and on the 31st Alexandra received the Danish officer who had brought the bodies home. Her son wrote; "I see you are pretty busy & go somewhere every day, hope you are not too tired."[99] But the submarine tragedy and Denmark's help seem to have been a catalyst. Alexandra was already miserable without Victoria, at Harrogate with Marie. On 2 September, taking the luggage that had been packed for some time and leaving her standard flying, Alexandra, with Charlotte Knollys, fled London by motor and travelled the 115 miles to Sandringham in five hours, lunching on the way without stopping. Unluckily there were two thunderstorms, with deluges of rain; travelling on bumpy roads gave her a headache and when they arrived, unexpected and in the cold, "everything seemed so sad and empty here at this beloved place that I really wished I had never come!"[100] Reinforcement and black-out precautions were on the roof over a little passage upstairs "on account of those beastly Zeppelins" and walking there unwarily the next day in the dim light, Alexandra lost her balance on some steps and sprained her ankle. Forced to rest in her room, she wrote a letter on her lap to Nicholas; "Nobody knows I am here … I have lately had so many worries & so much to do that I felt quite broken up … but I tried to keep up as long as possible, going to all the Hospitals & seeing our <u>thousands</u> or even millions of poor wounded. Now I have hurt my foot here badly so probably shall have to lay up!!"[101] She had some "very good stuff" to put on it until Dr Manby arrived; it ached all night long but her "stuff" reduced the swelling "to Manby's surprise" and she could "hobble to Church with the help of a stick & Ellinger's[102] support on the other side, such a nuisance." "Don't have a fit when you see where I write from!" she informed George; "I came here quite in <u>secret</u> & hope that <u>no one knows</u>! Otherwise I shall have <u>no peace</u> & dear kind excellent Probyn immediately wld fly after me from Scotland! And as much as I love him I [would] rather be quite alone & with no one near me! … in London I never had a moment's peace & I feel so horribly low spirited, which I hate anybody seeing, & both my <u>head</u> and <u>legs</u> hurt so I felt like a poor old cab horse when it cannot go any further."[103]

Alexandra hoped May and George were "not doing <u>too</u> much at once, as I can tell from experience that there are certain limits to one's strength! I am sure I broke down at last from a kind of nervous prostration, my head was so bad & when I first came here I really was miserable & thought this was the beginning of the end. <u>Now</u> thank God after this complete rest & by myself! I really feel much better & hope to return all right & to begin afresh" perhaps at some time after 2 October. Sandringham looked lovely; many spring and early summer flowers were out and she had picked a lot of rhododendrons the day before. Frank Beck was still missing; "Poor little Mrs Beck is so wonderfully brave & calm in her terrible grief & anxiety and she still hopes he may be alive as Prisoner! though I fear the worst has happened & none of those [who have] come back give the least hope. I saw two of the wounded here from the Dardanelles who never saw him again altho' they had been fighting close to him! Oh it is indeed too sad & he will ever be an irreparable loss to us all here!"[104]

Alexandra usually tried to find a silver lining in adversity; her spirits revived as the weather improved and once again she started paying visits round the estate. She was still there on 4 October, having enjoyed the warm weather and beautiful gardens during September, but it was now chilly enough to need a fire in the hall. She shrugged off a cold and acknowledged feeling much better after a good long rest "and I think a new lease of life, as I really thought it was the beginning of my end." No wonder; she was probably under greater strain than ever before and physically less able to bear it. Although trying to be brave and optimistic, she always worried about people and things she valued. Now there were so many more, constant, anxieties. Sandringham was always comforting, with its fresh air and quietness, beautiful flowers and trees, beloved house and memories, and familiar, friendly faces, but tragedy was there too, and not just Beck's probable fate at Gallipoli. On 1 October the gardener, Thomas Cook, was driving with his wife when the pony bolted; the cart upset and Mrs Cook[105] tried to jump out but slipped and fell, landing on her chin and breaking her neck. "Really it is <u>too sad</u> & they were so happy & [she] looked so young & pretty when I saw them together on the Sunday in their pretty & bright home. And she told me <u>how</u> happy she was that he had not to go to the war! & now <u>he</u> is left & <u>she</u> taken."[106]

Knutsford had asked Alexandra if she would allow the new nursing home at London Hospital to be called after her and she had agreed, while reminding him that another nurses' home which she had already opened also bore her name. However, the latest horrifying news from the front was that Edith Cavell,[107] born in Norfolk and trained partly at London Hospital, had been executed on 12 October by the Germans occupying Belgium. She had helped save the lives of the wounded from both sides and also helped over 200 Allied soldiers escape. She was arrested, with 33 others, and found guilty of assisting the enemy. Her forgiveness of her executioners; "I realise that patriotism is not enough: I must have no hatred or bitterness towards anyone" made her the greatest heroine of the war. This and her link with London Hospital prompted naming the new nursing home after her. Knutsford mentioned this to Alexandra, who was all in favour; "It is a splendid idea of yours, suggesting that our new Nursing Home ... shld instead bear the name of <u>Nurse Cavell</u> in everlasting memory of that brave & heroic woman who died the death of a martyr."[108] He therefore announced the new name as though it had been Alexandra's idea. She was "frantic when I saw <u>what</u> a <u>humbug</u> you have made me appear!!" She felt very uncomfortable at getting the credit; "I <u>abhor</u> <u>humbugs</u>! & now thanks to yr kindness you have made <u>me</u> one of the <u>biggest</u>!!" She was telling everyone it was his good idea.[109] He responded good-humouredly that the person who deserved thanks was not the one who started the idea but the one who acted upon it. Besides, surely someone who suggested to a Queen that she should give up her own name in favour of another deserved to be "hung, drawn & quartered & his remains scattered to the 4 winds?" She had always been so kind to him and allowed him to say just what he thought; in any case, it would have been "odious ... if I had given out, or let it be known, that I had made the suggestion."[110]

There had been a victory around Loos but a high loss of life; among those killed was "my poor charming Myles Ponsonby!"[111] It looked as though Greece would be dragged into the war, but Russian news was brighter. Alexandra returned to London on 19 October and resumed her life there. She and May went to a ballet[112] and were both rather shocked; "I quite agree with you",

Alexandra wrote, "about part of the performance the other day. Really it is too disgusting to see both <u>women</u> & <u>men</u> likewise with barely a shred to cover them! I think it a disgrace to our stage, & ballets can be very pretty in proper clothes!"[113] On the 29th she attended the memorial service at St Paul's Cathedral for Edith Cavell. But on the 28th, the King, who had gone to inspect troops in France, had fallen from his horse; "no bones broken but he was squashed", Alexandra wrote.[114] He was brought back in great pain to Buckingham Palace on 1 November; his mother visited him every day until the 5th, when "Although I did not see you today, my thoughts & prayers were with you! How can I ever thank God enough for having spared yr precious life to us all ... The thought alone makes me shudder, & to think what an escape you had. I do hope you are really feeling better & that the pain is less ... Thank God too that you were able to be moved home so soon, which was such a relief & comfort to you both, & <u>me too</u>!"[115] She had intended just seeing May on the 5th, as he had been rather tired, but had first been to Roehampton, "where they walked us outside in pelting rain & mud to see the various new additions & workrooms, which made me <u>so wet</u> & cold that I was obliged to pass yr door & come home to change everything, & then it was too late for yr tea. I do hope dear Georgie feels all the better for a quiet & peaceful day."[116]

Taxation had risen steadily for everyone since war began. From being taxed just under £7,000 in 1911/12, Alexandra was, in 1915/16, having to pay £26,687 11s 10d, which rose in 1916/17 to £28,777 11s 10d. On 26 November 1915 the King asked Asquith whether she could be exempted from the new taxes. There was sympathy for her plight but he was told it could not be done without an Act of Parliament, which could risk great unpopularity for her and might bring up the whole question of the civil list for critical debate. Probyn was prepared to chance this in the face of the heavy debts which could otherwise ensue. It was decided not to bring the matter before Parliament, although Probyn could not help feeling excuses were being made and it was a mistake that Alexandra had ever been required to pay so much tax when King George did not.[117] Her annuity had now virtually shrunk from £70,000 to £46,000.[118] As Probyn pointed out, she could not reduce her expenses like a private individual; she had to pay charities and subscriptions at a fitting level; her servants could not be reduced or dismissed without pensions; she had to pay rates and taxes, and £2,000 annually for garden maintenance at Marlborough House. She was responsible for keeping two establishments, horses, carriages and servants, at an appropriately high standard and for the proper upkeep and maintenance of the Sandringham grounds, which she held in trust for her descendants. When talking to Probyn about money, "Her Majesty said, and I know she has spoken in the same way to others, that if she could not afford to keep up Marlborough House and Sandringham, that she would have to leave London and live entirely at Sandringham." He now suggested she pay income and super-tax on her annuity as in 1913/14 and the current income tax on her private income, which ought to be enough to convince Asquith that she was prepared to put up with a reduced income like everyone else. In fact, some "big tradesmen" with whom he had talked recently about tax could hardly believe she paid any at all. Most of them knew, because it was published, that Alexandra had an allowance of £70,000, but they all thought it was paid in full with no deductions. People might well sympathise with her; no one seemed to mind the King not paying tax. Asquith probably thought she lived rent, rate and tax free at Marlborough House, as he did in Downing Street.[119] Probyn was reducing expenses as much as possible and some of the household had offered to work for nothing, but Alexandra would not allow this.

Marie had accompanied her aunt on a number of hospital visits and noticed that she spoke to every single man, shaking hands, asking where they had been wounded and about their families; she comforted those in pain and "the joy of seeing her was visible on every face."[120] She also saw Alexandra's response to the multitude of begging letters which she received and often read out. "She never hesitated sending these people sums of money. Once I suggested it would be a good thing to get information through the police concerning [them], as she could not possibly know if they really needed money. She got quite cross with me and answered 'How would you like to ask for help and not get it?'"[121] After all, she had personal experience of that with her own allowance. Alexandra attended three charity matinees in mid-November, for the Nurse Cavell Memorial Fund, "Russia Day" and the Australian War Contingent Association. She was once again seeing as many people and working as hard as ever, visiting hospitals and attending events such as Lady Farquhar's[122] tea party on the 24th at the Grosvenor Hall, arranged by an organisation, (of which Alexandra was patron), providing afternoon tea and entertainment for wounded servicemen. On 13 December she inspected the motor ambulances presented by the Ladies' Park Club to the Red Cross Hospital at Netley. Two days later she attended a "Grand Slav Concert" at the Queen's Hall, for the Serbian Relief Fund. On the 17th she received the Japanese Red Cross unit, who had been working at Netley Hospital for a year. They were going home and she gave them medals. She thanked Canon Dalton for remembering her birthday; "71 seems a great age; in fact I am a very old woman now!! and ought to keep no more birthdays." The war had made it a very sad one too, although she had been so thankful that her son had not died from the accident in France.[123] It was nearly Christmas and on the 20th she went shopping; two days later the King and Queen left for Sandringham (the King returning on the 30th). Alexandra had decided to spend Christmas in London again and attended a Christmas Eve entertainment at King George's Hospital in Westminster Bridge Road. On Christmas Day she received Holy Communion at Millbank Military Hospital and afterwards toured the wards giving presents. She visited the Kensington and Fulham General Hospital on Boxing Day. On the 30th she received Ian Malcolm,[124] attached to the British Red Cross unit going to Russia.

Alexandra had heard about a new venture, perhaps from Lord Esher. In September 1914, informally investigating military matters, he had visited a military hospital in Paris, based in Claridge's Hotel, which was efficiently run and staffed by women. In charge were former suffragettes, Dr Flora Murray[125] (administrator) and Dr Louisa Garrett Anderson,[126] (surgeon). Initially sceptical, Esher was converted and, when the women opened a London hospital at Endell Street, Covent Garden, in the renovated St Giles' and St George's Workhouse, it too became renowned and widely approved,[127] although not without many difficulties from the authorities. Among the original staff were 14 professionally-trained doctors (all loyal to the suffrage movement), 29 trained nurses and a large number of orderlies, a minority being men. This aroused Alexandra's attention and support, not just as a hospital and a war project, but as a novelty; she must have been impressed by a female-run military hospital and a suffragette-run enterprise of which she could fully approve. The hospital, renowned for medical skill, also became famous for entertainments for the wounded soldiers in its care, and on 28 December 1915, Alexandra, with Victoria, Louise and Maudie (seated in St Anne's Ward) witnessed the start of a fancy-dress parade, dancing and the singing of carols, which spread throughout the hospital.

By 9 January 1916 Probyn had been able to reduce the comptroller's account considerably, as there had been almost no travelling and hardly any entertaining for two years. Secretly, the King and Princess Victoria contributed £10,000 and £1,000 to their mother's "purse". Street lighting was now restricted; there would be over 50 zeppelin raids over England this year. Of more personal concern to Alexandra was the health of Miss Luckes,[128] about whom she called to enquire on the 19th. Within a week she herself had a bad cough, bronchitis and shingles, which prevented her sleeping; "So altogether I am not in a happy state, & shut up in the house ever since which is most depressing, particularly in the semi darkness we are having here for nearly a week now, always a thick fog! today it was as dark as night – too horrid."[129] She felt well enough by 10 February to attend a children's matinee[130] at the Ritz, for the Children's Convalescent Home at Holt in Norfolk. May had told Alexandra on 13 January how much she would be thinking of her the next day, "the anniversary of that saddest of days when beloved Eddy left us. It seems impossible to believe that 24 years have passed since those dreadful days when we went through so much together, I can never forget your special kindness to me then, which helped me so much."[131]

Greece was now in a thankless position; Alexandra hoped the Allies could stop the Central Powers invading but, even so, there were foreign troops on Greek soil. Montenegro and Serbia were suffering and there were lies about Emperor William sending for his sister, Queen Sophie. Newspapers hinted at a secret understanding between Bulgaria and Turkey about Salonika, a Greek town "which that brute F[erdinand][132] always wanted!!" Alexandra told Prince Nicholas about the terrible cases she had seen in the hospitals: amputees "& so many <u>blind</u> ones which are too pathetic for words. Thank God there is a splendid house arranged for them in Regent's Park,[133] where these poor blind men are taught various trades & typewriting etc. which will be of the greatest service to them hereafter. Then we have another institution where they make artificial limbs,[134] and already a quantity have very good <u>flexible</u> new arms or legs."[135] On 11 February she received Indian officers who had been in hospitals in England. She was shocked to hear, on 2 March, that Knutsford had been knocked down by a motor car; he was recovering in Putney Hospital.[136] There were charity concerts, functions, receptions and hospital visits – and enemy raids; a great zeppelin raid over East Anglia and the Midlands on 31 January had claimed 160 casualties. On 6 March another raid killed and injured 46, introducing a volley of five more raids and the German fleet's bombardment of the east coast during April. On the 22nd, two days before a raid over East Anglia, Alexandra went to Sandringham until 5 May.

Alexandra's finances were scarcely improved and her household was depleted because some men were on active service. Probyn now wrote to her "in a terrible fix". At least six stablemen were being called up and suitable replacements had been impossible to find. "What are we to do? Blessed Lady, there is no help for it. I must beg of your Majesty to sanction a reduction of some of the Horses and Ponies in the Stable at Sandringham <u>at once</u>. Please look at the accompanying list of 6 of the Horses and Ponies there, and tell me you will be prepared <u>not to see them again</u>." They were old, useless, unsafe to ride, expensive and it was wrong to keep them. Several other decrepit horses could remain as pensioners, but younger horses would be neglected if enough men to look after them all properly could not be found. "Blessed Lady, you know how I love Horses, and how I idolize Your Majesty. You will I hope therefore understand what pain it gives me to write this letter. But there is no help for it; I must not, because I dislike it, hesitate to perform what I know to be my duty."[137] Three days later Alexandra replied, heartbroken that the war should cause her old friends to be slaughtered; "It is all such <u>pain</u> to me that I will say no more. But one thing I will add – that as we have now made <u>so many</u> reductions in my household & in <u>every way already</u>, & the Finances are much relieved by it, we must <u>not be</u> in a hurry to do more at present, and my Kennels & dogs[138] <u>I</u> will not have touched." She signed the letter "Yr poor <u>not</u> blessed Lady." Probyn thanked her at once; of course there would be no "'slaughtering' … It is not only a kind, necessary, good & charitable action, but the best for the animals and all concerned." The finances indeed looked more hopeful than 1915, which had been terrible.[139]

At 2am on 20 May all clocks were advanced by an hour for national "daylight saving", not unlike "Sandringham Time". British morale took a devastating blow on 6 June; Alexandra was just going out to open a sale when news came that Lord Kitchener and his staff had been lost when their ship, *HMS Hampshire*, was destroyed by enemy action in the North Sea, not far from the Orkney Islands. She wrote in great distress "at these <u>dreadful</u> and <u>awful news</u> of our beloved <u>Kitchener's</u> untimely loss – at <u>sea</u> too! on his way to Russia! which I felt & told you only last Sunday, was unnecessary at <u>this</u> very important moment too ... He had the whole Empire's full confidence and did so splendidly. My poor Georgie, I am sorry for you indeed, just on the top of your having lost so many of our precious ships too!" She begged him to telephone her about "how you are & feel as I get so upset about all you have to go through & are doing at this moment".[140] Soon afterwards she invited May and young George to lunch, when May saw that "Lady Paget[141] has given Mama such a sweet little Pekinese dog, quite small & so sprightly! running about all over her room. Quite a relief & contrast to the old broken down dogs Mama has had for so many years which really became a nuisance at last to everybody."[142] Alexandra wrote again to George, who had been unwell. She had been unable to visit him "but I have had such a lot to do every day that it was impossible, & besides I was half dead myself".[143] She mused that David was 22, the age her husband had been when Eddy was born; perhaps reflecting that he had been a very young father or hinting she would like to see David married, with a son of his own. Victoria, unwell and unnerved, was going to stay with Violet Vivian[144] in Wales for a while. Alexandra dreaded being without her, "but ... I must make the sacrifice".[145] By July, despite severe losses, the Allies were making progress in France, but in Greece there was a terrible fire on the Tatoii estate; the old forest and the King's house had been destroyed. Willy's and Olga's house was saved, but "Poor unfortunate <u>dear</u> Tino, how many misfortunes have persecuted him for all these many month[s] together. I am <u>too</u> sorry for him & poor Sophie and all of them."[146] The Christians' golden wedding was approaching and Alexandra immediately responded to George's request for a donation, "of course I will at once send you my share for the gold vase ... <u>£10</u> enclosed!"[147]

Alexandra continued her support for Russia and on 7 March had presented four motor ambulances from the Wounded Allies Relief Committee to the Russian Red Cross Society. On 18 April she had received Lady Muriel Paget on her departure for Russia, and on 21 July attended a matinee at the Empire for the Anglo–Russian Hospital. She remembered other interests too; in 1904 she had become patron of Bedford College for Women[148] and had given £100 towards the building of its new premises. On 8 October 1914 she had visited the Emergency Women's Corps at the college's rooms in York Place, where the students made hospital supplies. They also organised parties for wounded soldiers and arranged help in canteens and in a Women's War Club. The college was a centre for special classes in First Aid and Hospital Cookery, under the Red Cross Society. Alexandra was a good friend to Bedford College and visited it several times; on 26 June 1916, at its new premises in Regent's Park, she took them entirely by surprise, found her way to the hall, where an examination was under way, and was nearly asked to leave; fortunately Professor Spurgeon[149] recognised her and showed her round the building.[150] This year Queen Alexandra visited Endell Street twice, on 29 July and 16 August, to see the 570 wounded soldiers and to show her deep compassion in practical kindness. As often on such occasions, she gave them presents, such as monogrammed handkerchiefs and walking sticks, which might well have been made in her technical schools at Sandringham. She later sent cigarettes, pillows and more walking sticks, and on 29 July gave her parasol to one man lying in his bed in the hospital's courtyard, to keep the sun from his eyes.[151]

During the night of 19 August a zeppelin raid on Sandringham dropped over 30 bombs. The war had, seemingly, become personal. Defiantly, Alexandra returned there three days later, to more raids on the 24th and the 25th. Davidson arrived on the 26th and the next day the Queen and household went to church as usual and were snap-shotted on the terrace in their best Sunday clothes. One shows Victoria and Davidson sitting close together on a bench, his arm round hers; his hand, originally light-coloured and obvious, inked over. Taken where others were nearby, the snap seems to imply a tacit sanction of the romance, almost an unofficial engagement, but nothing changed and Alexandra may have been influenced by her husband's views. He would have done his best to dissuade Victoria from her affection for Davidson. Alexandra's own anguish at the thought of losing her was real but she had always been able to come to terms, gradually, with loss, and could have done so if her daughter had married. Victoria being drawn to a member of staff was not ideal; Davidson was also in poor health. The ailing, middle-aged Princess would have had to care for a chronic invalid before shortly being widowed[152] but Alexandra could see they were in love and mourned for the circumstances which kept them apart. As in other matters, her feelings were conflicted and apparently insoluble. In fact, rules would soon relax and, but for Davidson's frail condition, there might have been a happy ending. But, agonisingly respectable though the couple were, Alexandra dreaded gossip;[153] if they finally got together after so long and so often living under the same roof, with her sanction, it would provide ample spice for the ill-natured.[154]

During Saturday evening, 2 September, there was a five-zeppelin raid near Sandringham, lasting until 5am the next day. Alexandra reported; "We have been living through some gruesome moments here – just a fortnight today we had those beastly Zepps over us ... We were all sitting upstairs in Victoria's room when we suddenly were startled by that awful noise! & lo & behold there was that awful monster over our heads – everybody rushed up & wanted us to go downstairs. I must confess I was not a bit afraid, but it was a most uncanny feeling. Poor Victoria was quite white in the face & horror struck – but we all wanted to see it. The House was pitch dark & at last I & Charlotte stumbled down in the darkness & found Col Davidson & Hawkins scrambling about outside. So I also went out, but saw nothing and for the time [being] the Zepps had flown off somewhere, but came back about 4 o'clock in the night dropping bombs all over the place!! There was an awful cannonading going on & search lights all round, but luckily they missed us here but further on they did a great havoc & destroyed six poor little cottages on Dothill[155] [sic] … I am sure they take that part for Sandringham as they have been there so frequently lately. I went to see those poor people the next day, it was an <u>awful</u> sight, everything destroyed both <u>inside</u> and outside & several people had been badly hurt & taken to Lynn Hospital – there were crowds of motors & cars & people of all description to see the havoc, & everybody tumbled about in the great holes made by the bombs. I am so glad you sent £50 to those poor stricken people – we had a collection in Church & all together I think about £80 was collected."[156]

She visited Lynn Hospital on 18 September to see a Mrs Dunger,[157] dying of wounds received during the last raid at Dersingham, and on the 22nd viewed a wrecked aeroplane in a field near Anmer. Nineteen zeppelins raided on the 23rd and the 25th, and news came that Allan Mackenzie had died from wounds received at the Battle of the Somme. Among other activities, Alexandra visited the soldiers' convalescent home at Hunstanton and later gave tea to 54 (with 15 Australians) on the 28th. "We trotted them about everywhere & finished up with a grand tea and <u>crackers</u> in the ball room, which they the poor Anzacs in particular were delighted with."[158] She returned to Marlborough House on 16 October and her Greek nephews, George and Nicholas, and niece Marie, called several times; Greek and Russian news grew steadily worse and Marie's only consolation was visiting her aunt, who "was always so full of sympathy in my troubles and anxieties and invariably saw things in the right light and never misunderstood."[159]

On 26 October Alexandra visited the Russian Hospital in South Audley Street; a corollary to the Anglo–Russian Hospital. It had been opened on the 17th for British officers and was entirely financed by Monsieur Mouravieff-Apostol, once Chamberlain at the Russian court, whose wife was the hospital's commandant.[160] Baba Mackenzie and her son Tony came to tea on the 28th. There were more functions, visits and entertainments and on 13 November Alexandra went to see Countess Nada Torby's[161] trousseau and wedding presents at Kenwood. Coming back, she was caught in "a tremendous fog".[162] On the 17th, with Victoria, Louise and Maudie,[163] she attended a matinee at the London Opera House, raising £1,600 for the Plum Pudding Fund for the soldiers at the front at Christmas. Sad news arrived; Aunt Augusta had died on 5 December, and Alexandra's cousin, Adelaide, Dowager Grand Duchess of

Luxemburg, had also died, to her sorrow. Her thoughts were with Adelaide's daughter Hilda, Grand Duchess of Baden, and her sister, Princess Hilda of Anhalt-Dessau; "she herself almost an invalid & so very <u>lonely</u> at Dessau!" Alexandra was also "sorry about the poor old Emperor of Austria dying in the midst of this awful war, altho' for him what a relief after so tragic a life as his has been all through those <u>68</u> years of his reign."[164] By the 7th she had a bad cold, having planned to receive three nurses the next day. Colonel Streatfeild told Charlotte Knollys "Her Majesty says they are to come anyhow & if she does not feel up to coming downstairs I am to give the nurses the cards etc from her."[165] She did receive two, but her cold lasted until the end of the year and she could only go out to Marlborough House Chapel on the 25th and the 31st.

On 9 December Davidson suggested to Probyn that Alexandra should be told about George's and Victoria's financial help. He felt that, while everyone was doing their utmost to help her, she was not helping herself but squandering her allowance. Perhaps he thought Victoria was sacrificing more than she could afford. Alexandra had spoken to him several times that year about money but always in the same way, "I don't care – I shall do as I like & if I get into debt <u>they</u> can pay." Davidson said "Who will pay, Madam – certainly not the Nation for they won't pay a <u>penny</u>. It will all fall on King George & Princess Victoria & it isn't either right or fair on them." Alexandra would wave her hand, decline to hear, and end the conversation. Davidson now thought it essential that she be told of her son's generosity, despite the King's objection to her knowing.[166] Alexandra probably felt that, as she had been brought to England to fulfil a particular role, it was the government's business to make sure her resulting expenses were covered. The war had deprived her of so much already, and now, despite retrenching, she was being forced to give up her old horses, reduce her charitable donations and live with anxiety and debt. Although fond of Davidson, she disliked being lectured by a member of staff who lacked Sir Dighton's bardic eloquence; she may also have been irritated by his mentioning Victoria. By now everyone was weary, depressed and tetchy. On the 23rd she sent the Knutsfords some engravings for Christmas, and £100 for his children's hospital in the East End ("altho' I am penniless myself!) and trust it may be of some use towards keeping that valuable Hospital going."[167] Sadly she told George on the 28th; "I am better but not right yet & feel utterly collapsed & useless altho' I work hard with all the numerous things I have to do just now & the endless tiresome letters I am persecuted by. I am glad for all yr sakes you are going to beloved Sandringham, where I am longing to be, but do not feel up to it yet. I shall be sorry too not to spend New Year with you & darling May & all yr blessed Children, but nothing matters now in these terribly sad & depressing days. God be with us all & give us a Victorious Peace in the coming year is all I pray for."[168]

The year 1917 started ominously. Alexandra had a bad sore throat, and sensational news had arrived from Russia. Grigori Rasputin[169] had been killed, "but only regretted by poor dear Alicky who might have ruined the whole future of Russia through his influence! Since yr letter to me about it there is nothing new & Benckendorff knew nothing more about it either. Aunt Minny telegr [that] neither Dmitri[170] or Felix[171] have anything to do with it, but the former was still arrested by A's order! I am sure she thinks herself like their Empress Katherine." Greece was still in trouble; Alexandra, always loyal to Constantine, blamed German meddling and questioned British actions in Salonika. The Germans would "make use of the 75,000 men they stole from Kavolo & in this way, drag [Tino] in on their side! Oh it is a cruel way, and only all he wanted was to be left outside the war, but I will say no more, it makes me ill." Bitterly, she hoped they were "all happy together at beloved S, where I hope I am missed a little; now you can imagine or picture to yrselves how it will be when I am no longer among the living."[172] At least, through careful management, there was some money in hand for 1917 and some light relief; on 18 January, Louise and Maudie accompanied Alexandra to Endell Street Military Hospital for a seasonal entertainment.

On 11 January Count Benckendorff,[173] Russian ambassador in London, died suddenly of influenza. Shocked, the King reflected that he would "be a great loss to me, as he was the only one I could talk to, quite openly, about Russia, I fear things there are most unsatisfactory & even dangerous on account of the bad influence of Alicky over Nicky, I do trust things will come right, but I own that I am very anxious."[174] Later, Benckendorff's loss might well hamper him in understanding the true state of Russia and its impact on the Imperial Family. On the 12th another friend, Countess Castenskijold,[175] died. Lady Ripon was seriously ill and until she died on 27 October, Alexandra faithfully called and enquired after her at least 66 times. When on 17 February William Church[176] died, at 68, she attended his funeral, as also the Duchess of Connaught's, who died at 56 on 14 March of complications from measles and pneumonia. There had been a terrible explosion at a munitions factory on 19 January and zeppelin raids were increasing. On 3 and 10 March George went to Marlborough House with bad news about Russia; Alexandra was extremely upset. On the 16th they learned of the Emperor's abdication. Six days later, Minny wrote; "broken hearted, having had to part from her beloved Nicky, who was made to leave ... but she thanks God for having let her spend these two heaviest saddest of days with him & only prays God to protect & bless her darling child." Alexandra felt crushed and overwhelmed.[177]

The Emperor had abdicated for himself and his 12-year-old son Alexis, from whom he could not bear to be parted, naming his brother, Michael, as his successor. The British ambassador at Petrograd, Sir George Buchanan,[178] thought Alexis' succession would have been the best solution, but hoped the monarchy might return after the war; he doubted Russia was ready for a republic. Once the provisional government was in control, it could work towards permanent constitutional government.[179] George V sent a supportive message to Nicholas II on the 19th; "Events of last week have deeply distressed me. My thoughts are constantly with you and I shall always remain your true and devoted friend as you know I have been in the past."[180] On the same day, General Hanbury Williams,[181] doyen of the Allied representatives at Petrograd, had a long talk with the Dowager Empress. Nicholas would go nowhere without his wife and the provisional government had been asked to let him join her and their family at Tsarskoe Selo. But what then? Hanbury Williams had asked the British government about asylum in England but Minny, alarmed at the long sea voyage, seemed to prefer Denmark. Her son-in-law, Grand Duke Alexander, urged the allied representatives at Petrograd to ask their governments to acknowledge the provisional government, which had pledged to continue the war as an ally. Hanbury Williams and Alexander agreed that Grand Duke Nicholas[182] should be reinstated as Commander-in-Chief of the Russian army but feared the revolutionaries might object.[183] Hanbury Williams and Buchanan reported from Russia throughout March and April; the provisional government respected them and the British alliance and sought to protect the Imperial Family as close relatives of the King. But Britain feared Russia's inability to play a full part in the war; the army was torn between duties at the front and keeping order in Petrograd, where the government was imperceptibly weakening as anarchists gained influence over soldiers and workers. The British Labour Party therefore sent a message to the Socialist and workers' unions in Petrograd, reminding them that, to safeguard the future of labour in Europe, the enemy still needed defeating.[184]

Having seen Alexander Kerensky,[185] Buchanan reported that factories were reopening and the newly formed Council of Workers' and Soldiers' Deputies was losing ground. There were disturbances on the northern and western fronts but all was quiet on the south-western one. Whether or not the Emperor went to England rather depended on the British government promising to deter any attempt at a counter-revolution. There was now considerable feeling in Russia against the Romanovs, and left-wing fear that, with Gouchkoff[186] as Minister of War, reinstating Grand Duke Nicholas as Commander-in-Chief could lead to the re-establishment of the dynasty.[187] The army was, so far, intact and the extreme left party was losing ground; there was complete order in Moscow and hope that the government would soon have things under control,[188] but Hanbury Williams reported that the general situation, especially regarding the soldiers, was still serious.[189]

British public opinion about Russia was crystallising. Sir Harry Verney[190] was worried about "the welfare of our Monarchy" and winning the war if the Imperial Family came to England, surrounded by "a vast system of intrigue and espionage" and possibly followed by most of the grand dukes and their entourages. Buchanan's unique persona at Petrograd could be lost, as Russia would distrust every communication sent to him from England, and it could compromise the King's position if people realised that British influence in Russia had thus been sacrificed. George might find an appeal to receive his cousin and friendly ally difficult; if Buchanan could find out secretly what the imperial plans were, he could, if necessary, "pour cold water on the idea" of them coming here just now. There might be good reasons for welcoming the Romanovs, but Verney was convinced that "for our own King's welfare and in order to maintain and increase our present influence in Russia, we ought to be very careful how we move in this matter." Perhaps they could go to a palace at Venice or Corfu.[191]

On 21 March David Lloyd George[192] sent Prince Lvoff[193] a supportive message, anticipating stable constitutional rule and Russia's strengthened resolve to fight and win the war.[194] The next day, Minny left for Kiev[195] and Buchanan reported that Miliukoff[196] was urging Nicholas's earliest possible departure to asylum in England. Denmark was too near Germany, where there was serious danger he would become a focus of intrigue. Further danger to him might come from discontented Russian generals encouraging the army to support a counter-revolution to reinstate him. Lord Hardinge and Mr Bonar Law[197] agreed that, as the British government was doing its utmost to support the Russian one it could not refuse their request for asylum. Possible land and sea routes were discussed, but the King was apprehensive about the sea voyage and there was also the question of living costs and accommodation. Lloyd George's suggestion of "one of the King's houses" was vetoed; the only possible one was Balmoral, which would be unsuitable at that time of year. Perhaps the British government could make Nicholas an allowance[198] but Lord Hardinge thought it perfectly reasonable to hint that the Russian government might do this. Finally they decided to draft an official telegram to Buchanan stating that, as the Russian government had proposed it, the King and government would be prepared to receive the Imperial Family in England.[199]

General Alexieff[200] told Hanbury Williams, unofficially, that, to appease the anarchists, the Romanovs[201] were now under arrest at Tsarskoe Selo. Fearing for their safety, Alexeieff begged him to press the British government to insist on their being given safe conduct to Port Romanov and England immediately. Nicholas did not yet realise that danger was increasing, as the anarchists had become "top dogs". Alexeieff hoped the Allied governments would urge the Russian government to keep the popular Grand Duke Nicholas as Commander-in-Chief; otherwise he feared for Russia's future part in the war.[202] Buchanan, on the same day, said it would be impossible; there was considerable opposition and hope that the Grand Duke would resign voluntarily.[203] Hanbury

Williams had actually been told he had been received very enthusiastically at all the stations through which his train had passed.[204] In fact, no-one really knew what the Russian people thought and, in the general confusion, decisions were delayed and opportunities lost.

On 23 March *The Times* published Lloyd George's message to Prince Lvoff, showing that the war was a struggle for democracy as well as liberty. There was trouble about the King's telegram of the 19th to his cousin, despite it being a private, sympathetic message and not a formal pledge to help. Unfortunately Nicholas had left army headquarters before it was delivered; Buchanan had shown it to Miliukoff and then to the British Foreign Office where, unknown to the King, it was discussed at the War Cabinet. Learning this, George was extremely perturbed; as the message had never reached Nicholas it had better be cancelled.[205] He now considered the matter very carefully. He loved his cousin and would be glad to help him but a sea journey in wartime would be dangerous and it might be inadvisable "on general grounds of expediency" for the family to take up residence in Britain.[206] This included indefinite financial and housing obligations; the compromising of Anglo–Russian relations if a potential rival government had its centre in England; and the consequent danger from any anarchists who wanted to destroy it. British opposition was also growing and, even if Nicholas was allowed to leave Russia, his coming here would cause much criticism. Nevertheless, the British government was determined to honour the Russian government's request.[207] Miliukoff wanted Nicholas to leave Russia immediately and hoped he would be offered asylum in Britain; he had been told this would happen, but his own government had not yet decided. The King accepted that the invitation had been sent, and was irrevocable and final unless the Russian government decided otherwise.[208] Grand Dukes Michael and George[209] could come to England; the former had a country house here and wanted to send a lump sum towards rent and other expenses, but this was problematic.[210]

A letter for Alexandra from Minny was sent by Buchanan on 3 April but he refused to forward any return letters, as two telegrams from the Queen had been held up. One was harmless "but the other I fear was rather compromising in its language. It is useless for Her Majesty to telegraph at present." The King had to break this to his mother[211] while being bombarded with protests against the Imperial Family coming to England; he was keenly alive to the problems and deeply worried. Stamfordham[212] told Balfour on the 6th how awkward their close relationship to the Romanovs was for the Royal Family; people were either assuming the plan was the King's idea, or deprecating the unfair position in which he would be placed if it were carried out. George hoped the Russian government could be encouraged to make other arrangements for his cousins' future residence. Stamfordham had gathered that their living in England "would be strongly resented by the public, and would undoubtedly compromise the position of the King and Queen from whom it is already generally supposed the invitation had emanated." Buchanan should be asked to tell Miliukoff that opposition was so strong that Britain should be allowed to withdraw its consent to the proposal.[213] Buchanan was told on 13 April that a considerable anti-monarchical movement was developing in the UK, including personal attacks on the King because he had supported Nicholas II ("a tyrant") and King Constantine; both accused of being pro-German. This completely unjustified outcry had erupted in the frenzy of anti-German war fever; had the Russian revolution happened at any other time, Nicholas might well have ended his days peacefully in England. Now Buchanan was told that, if he came to England, this movement might dangerously increase; perhaps he should go to France when he was allowed to leave Russia. Buchanan agreed; Will Thorne,[214] then in Russia with a British Labour delegation, had told him Nicholas should not be allowed to stay in England under any circumstances during the war. The provisional government wanted to get Nicholas out of Russia secretly as soon as possible; he wanted to go to Livadia but Prince Lvoff thought the journey too risky. As long as he was in Russia there could always be a counter-revolution, which would seriously endanger his life.[215] Buchanan was depressed; "though the majority of the nation would prefer a constitutional monarchy, there is not a single acceptable candidate among all the members of the Imperial Family."[216]

Unfortunately the Imperial Family did not seem to realise its present position. Minny was in despair at not hearing from Alexandra, but Buchanan, who had been forwarding mail in both directions, asked to be excused in future, as it could always be captured and both sides compromised. Prince Felix Yusupov would tell Minny that Alexandra had instructed Buchanan to keep all her letters until he could deliver them personally. Buchanan conceded that it would be harmless if perhaps Alexandra sent him a telegram saying how relieved she was that her sister was safe and in good health, with news of herself. Yusupov was very pessimistic and thought Nicholas should be sent away from Russia at once.[217] On 27 April Lord Bertie[218] in Paris doubted whether France would welcome Nicholas there and if he came to England, the Germans would have told the Russian Socialists that the British government was keeping him for use against them, whenever it might suit British policy.[219] Meanwhile, Vladimir Lenin[220] returned secretly to Russia from exile and took over the Bolshevik party, an extreme Socialist group.

There was great uncertainty now about Russia's worth as an ally but things were changing. No one had been sure whether America would enter the war and, if so, on which side, as her many citizens of German, Irish and Russian Jewish ancestry were thought unlikely to support the Allied cause. But German U-boats threatened American shipping and America declared war on Germany on 6 April, augmenting the Allied forces and encouraging hopes of success. All Alexandra's thoughts were now of Russia and her sister's fate. Minny, formerly respected and loved, had lived in Russia for 50 years devoted to its welfare. Now she was just another Romanov scapegoat and had been arrested. "She ... is sent away as if <u>she</u> had committed a crime! Oh! It <u>pains</u> & worries me more than any words cld possibly describe", Alexandra told George on Easter Monday. "And not being able to hear from her either by letter or telegraph makes it naturally ten times worse. They say she has been sent to the Crimea, the place she has not revisited since her beloved husband Uncle Sasha died there, so you can imagine what extra pain this must be to her!"[221] Alexandra spent Easter in London, but on 30 April heard that Captain Donald Davidson,[222] one of her pages at the coronation in 1902, had been killed flying in action in France. Meanwhile she maintained her interest in the Anglo–Russian Hospital, receiving Lady Muriel Paget on 27 April and on 4 May attending her Russian Exhibition and sale in aid of the hospital, at the Grafton Galleries from 30 April till 31 May. Alexandra also contributed items to the exhibition.[223]

As Socialism grew, hatred of anything German also flourished in England. Murmurings against the Royal Family's German ancestry and associations led to the adoption of the surname Windsor by the King and the abolition of his relatives' German titles. Nevertheless most people still supported the Royal Family and the public attitude was naïve; anyone of Anglo–Saxon origin had Germanic roots too. The Hanoverian dynasty had been British by legislation, loyalty and domicile for over 150 years; despite some German forebears and connections they were also descended from Kings of England and Scotland.[224] George III had gloried in the name of Briton.[225] Victoria had been proud to be Queen of such a nation.[226] But the government had recognised the provisional government in Russia and, despite imperial Russia's loyalty as England's ally, some public opinion turned against Nicholas and his "German" wife, as it already had against King Constantine and his "German" wife.[227] Constantine's sister, Marie, married to Nicholas II's second cousin, was being targeted and it was thought some of this could reflect against Queen Alexandra, who was assisting her. Marie had been helping with the war effort and, rather reluctantly, the King told his mother about these fears. Alexandra, furiously indignant, responded; "I know what that letter of yrs cost you to write! But I know that <u>we both</u> feel alike about this sad subject of our poor dear beloved little Minny who is *au fond* here <u>now</u> as an Immigrant or outcast & <u>homeless</u>!! as she cannot return to Russia or to her old home in Greece. She was kept here originally through the war, & unable to return while this is going on, with her children, and now made impossible by this awful Revolution. So people ought to understand that she is really kept here against her will. I quite agree with you it wld have been wiser for her to have stayed on at Harrogate where she did such splendid work for <u>our</u> wounded in her various hospitals, but alas she has <u>no money left</u> & cannot keep them up any longer ... it seems to me a very <u>cruel</u> idea to suspect her of intriguing here on behalf of her poor unfortunate brother, who I feel sure

& fear is done for anyhow.[228] I wish you could make people understand this. It worries me all to death & particularly if these vile people think or say to imagine that through my being seen with her in public, (my own niece! the daughter of my beloved brother) I shld be doing you! my own beloved son, harm! or even injuring the Monarchy! that is really beyond all words. And yet as you say the people & the world in general are really going mad & have been stirred up through our welcoming the Revolution in Russia. I will do my best not to be seen in public with the poor Child, but will not give her up – and see her in private here! ... In fact as things are now we never mention poor Greece any more although I know how she must suffer & feel it all most acutely."[229]

Marie and her daughters had moved to London and she dined with Alexandra nearly every evening; they were close, and could talk openly for hours. Marie admired Alexandra's generosity and how she "felt everyone's sufferings, worries or anxieties acutely, just as if they were her own. No matter what people did, she always found some excuse for them. She never cherished a grudge against anyone." At the same time, she had a "wonderful childlike nature, and was up for any fun or mischief. I often teased her, and she never resented it." The Queen "never had any servants to serve, but the food was put on the table in silver tureens with hot water underneath to keep them warm." After dinner they would sit in her boudoir, on a sofa standing back to back with her desk, facing the fireplace, which was screened, to keep the heat from their faces; "two tables [stood] in front of us with cards, and we both played patience, of which my aunt was very fond." There was not much space, as the tables were piled high with newspapers and illustrated reviews, all of which Alexandra would read with a magnifying glass, as she said she saw better that way than with spectacles. She read everything and cut out items which interested her, to be pasted into special albums. On another little table were bottles of orangeade and lemonade.[230]

Alexandra had been "very busy lately & never had a minute to myself ... I have just seen all the American Nurses here, & also those of ours who got the Red Cross today at B Palace; there were such a lot altogether that I am so hot & my feet ache from standing so long ... We went to rather a dull & very long performance yesterday under Feo Alington's[231] patronage; I feel still quite collapsed from it."[232] Attacks were increasing dramatically. Zeppelin raids had been augmented by aeroplane raids and they had bombarded Dover on 25 May, with some 250 casualties. On 13 June 15 enemy aeroplanes raided London, killing and injuring over 580. Queen Alexandra and Princess Victoria visited churches and war shrines in South Hackney and Poplar and the scenes of the raid. As Charlotte Knollys told Miss Acland, on the 17th; "Her Majesty takes this dreadful war terribly to heart and is almost tiring herself out in her efforts to help and comfort all the many sufferers – both in body and mind."[233] On the 18th she visited the air raid victims at the London and Poplar Hospitals. On 7 July there was another big raid over London; over 20 aeroplanes caused 240 casualties and again, Alexandra visited the victims on the 10th and the 18th. Between 22 July and 22 December there were twenty more raids, including at least ten over London; on 1 October shrapnel and bits of bombs landed in Marlborough House gardens and on the roof.[234] But five zeppelins returning from a raid on October the 20th were brought down by the French. Zeppelins came when it was dark, but every time there was moonlight there would be terrible aeroplane raids. Sometimes Marie would be caught when dining at Marlborough House and would have to wait until they were over. Alexandra seemed quite unafraid "and I remember once, when the bombardment was at its worst, her going to the window and opening the curtains to look out. She entirely ignored strict orders of keeping everything dark, and I had to rush all over the room to put the lights out. She even laughed at me for doing this." Alexandra collected all the bits of shrapnel and bombs from her garden and kept them in a box.[235]

As president of the British Red Cross, Alexandra would meet the nurses who had been awarded the Red Cross badge, which they usually received from the King at Buckingham Palace, and would greet them individually at Marlborough House, giving them cards and books. She met at least 740 Red Cross and other nurses on 26 occasions in 1917 and continued visiting hospitals and attending charity matinees; one on 11 July at the Vaudeville, for the Wives and Children of the French Cooks from London serving at the Front – something perhaps only amateur endeavour would support or even recognise.[236] It was typical of Alexandra to help minor charities[237] just as much as better-known ones.

On 24 July, Buchanan reported that the Russian government would be sending the Imperial Family to Siberia for greater safety. They left for Tobolsk on the night of the 25th, to live in the governor's house and have more personal liberty than at Tsarskoe Selo. Nicholas would have preferred the Crimea but seemed pleased with the proposed change of residence. It would have been dangerous for him to go out driving at Tsarskoe Selo but it was hoped he could do so at Tobolsk, as, despite everything, he "was not a criminal and deserved to be treated with as much consideration as possible." Kerensky[238] was anxious to do what he could to meet Nicholas' wishes, such as choosing who went with him, and he would have a very comfortable house with a large garden. The real reason for moving him was the Socialists' fear of counter-revolution; this seemed unlikely, as there was no intention of restoring the dynasty, although there was a decided reaction in favour of order and strong government, which was quite a different thing.[239]

Queen Alexandra may well have longed to see something unconnected with the war; she was still interested in all kinds of things, including London Docks, where she went on 24 July, having enjoyed her 1913 visit so much.[240] On 4 September she returned to Sandringham, to relax in fine weather on the terrace. As she told George on the 8th, "Thank goodness before I got away I cleared everything & made it all tidy after that long spell I had in London since last October!" Russian affairs daily seemed worse and she had heard nothing of Minny lately, although there was news that her daughter Olga, who had married her second husband, Colonel Nicholas Kulikovsky[241] in 1916, had recently had a son. Of more local interest was the elderly Dean of Windsor's retirement.[242] Alexandra suggested replacing him with Canon Dalton "who so fully deserves it in every way & brought you & Eddy up & has been so faithful to you all these many years now, & he is a very clever & excellent man in every way & loved by his congregation & by all who know him, & it wld be a worthy ending to his busy unselfish life."[243] Sadly, her son told her, Dalton was nearly 78 and had ruled himself out on that account already.[244] Lord Knutsford had started a collection of half crowns[245] in aid of the London Hospital, flatteringly choosing Queen Alexandra's birthday as the collecting day. She was also delighted at "what endless good the Finsen's Light for the cure of Lupus has done at our great Hospital, & which I was proud to be the giver, & which you tell me has already in 14 years cured 420,000!"[246]

The Russian government had agreed that Grand Duke George could join his family in England; he proposed to go incognito, as Mikailoff. However no grand dukes were welcome in England at present; his coming might attract attention and endanger other Romanovs, in particular the Dowager Empress, whose safety and protection were paramount. Buchanan believed the Russian government would make her an exception if she wished to go to England, and as Queen Alexandra's sister, with strong anti-German feelings, she was on the right side of British public opinion. By 11 September it was agreed that, if she wished to come, she could bring Grand Duchess Xenia with her.[247] Secretly, the Russian government had already decided that certain Romanovs would be allowed to leave; the Dowager Empress first, then Grand Duke Michael, followed probably by Grand Duke George, but all this changed when the Bolsheviks, dominated by Lenin, seized power in October and catapulted Russia into armed uprising and revolution.

Marie still remained cheerful and uncomplaining[248] and by 22 October was at Sandringham, where Alexandra took her and her lady-in-waiting, Agnes de Stoeckl, to see the horses, getting them to suggest names for the new foals. A few airships had passed over Sandringham and wrought havoc in London, much to Alexandra's distress but "Thank God they forgot us here this time, though we are now prepared with guns & soldiers."[249] She was already feeling "so out of everything here" and asked her son to let her know "if there is anything going on or if you hear any details of the horrible ghastly war".[250] She was still there on 2 November, when she recommended an elderly French Roman Catholic mother superior[251] for a Red Cross badge. Prince Christian had died at Windsor on 28 October, "but [I] did not feel equal to attending [the funeral] ... poor Helena herself was not able to go." Lady Ripon had died the previous day at Studley: "All too sad for words & she is a real loss to me! Their charming home at Coombe was always open to me & I shall miss her terribly next Summer. She has been such a dear & faithful friend of mine for so many, many years now. I feel deeply for him too ... they were equally devoted to each other, & his poor life now will be terribly lonely ... without her by his side."

Alexandra was disappointed at not seeing, or even hearing from, David lately, "but now I hear nothing from any of the family, I might just as well be dead & buried, but no matter, I love you all just the same, but sometimes it makes me sad."[252] Her hard-pressed son hastily reassured her; "Yes, I fear I have been very remiss in not having written to you for a fortnight. But I telephone to Toria every morning & very often in the evening & give her all the news & ask her to pass it on to you. My work seems to increase every day ... [and] you must not think because I have not written that you are out of my thoughts, as the reverse is the case."[253] Alexandra was touched; "All what I wrote was not meant as a reproach, simply it was a <u>cry</u> of my heart! as I was longing so for you all, & my mind & spirits are low & sometimes now everything around me seems dark & dreary – but never mind, I know it is wrong to give way & I have <u>so</u> much to be grateful for & have my beloved Victoria near me ... My poor dear Lady de Grey's[254] death upset me greatly I must say."[255] She tried to "buck up" and make the best of things, and there were pleasant times too. She had always loved Prince John, whose condition had not improved and who now lived apart, with his own staff, at Wood Farm on the Sandringham estate, although he still saw his family. On 8 August Alexandra wrote to May "about yr darling Johnnie who is looking the picture of health & had tea with me at my Cottage by the sea, when he was full of fun & talked incessantly, telling me about his bathing & his <u>own</u> house, which he is very proud of. Next day I called on him & found him playing football with his tutor, the faithful excellent Charlotte & the other two women of <u>his Household</u>!! He was so hot, but came rushing to me & showed me his garden & all over the House which certainly is very nice & comfortable & he seemed quite happy – but all the same I think he is longing for a companion!"[256] She made sure to visit him at home or invite him to tea at the Dairy nine times until 13 November, when "Your dear little Johnnie had tea with us yesterday & was in very good spirits & health."[257]

She herself, as she had told May, was feeling "terribly <u>low</u> & <u>lonely</u> – altho' I try to be brave – it is not always easy to face so many various troubles at once, which seem to surround me, wherever I look. And this awful cruel and endless war seems to crush one's spirits more & more!" There was constant anxiety about the relatives in Russia, grief for Lady Ripon and sorrow for "Poor Aunt Helena ... as she will miss her dear old Christian terribly after [over 50] years of happy marriage."[258] 13 November was foggy; for the rest of her stay Alexandra remained indoors or nearby. On the 27th she sent Lord Knutsford her and Victoria's contributions to the Half Crown Collection.[259] On her 73rd birthday she watched a football match between the Seaforth Highlanders and the Royal Artillery, quartered in the grounds on guard duty. The next day the Grants' baby son was christened in Sandringham Church; the King and Victoria were sponsors. On 3 December Alexandra returned to London after three months and resumed her engagements, receiving more nurses, visiting relatives and attending functions; on the 20th she unveiled a memorial in St John's Churchyard to the 600 patients who had died in King George Hospital[260] since the war started. There had been another air raid on the 18th, beginning at 6.15pm and lasting nearly four hours. On Christmas Day Alexandra took Holy Communion in Marlborough House Chapel and afterwards visited King Edward's Hospital for Officers in Grosvenor Gardens. On the 28th she went to an entertainment for 800 former child patients, at the London Hospital.

Buchanan had reported on 12 December that the Dowager Empress was better and able to go out. Everything was quiet in Petrograd. He could not get any news about Nicholas and his family but feared their living conditions were very trying. The guard had been changed, for stricter security and they were to be moved elsewhere; Kerensky took responsibility for their safety.[261] As to their having been refused asylum in England, the King, as a good constitutional monarch, had been bound to let his people's wishes and welfare override his considerable anxiety for his cousins, especially when it still seemed that they could be safeguarded in some other way. He could not have known that they would soon be in danger and it would be too late to rescue them.

In 1918 there were more visitors, Red Cross nurses and charity events. Alexandra recommended Sister Agnes Keyser, "such a great friend & admirer of dear Papa's" for a Red Cross medal. "She really deserves it having worked incessantly at her hospital[262] ever since the war began. She works from 8 in the morning till 8 at night & had I think about 900 or a thousand officers, very bad cases too and I think she feels having been left out ... I shld so much like to give [the medal to] her <u>myself</u> in yr name."[263] She told May; "I was only too glad to have had yr darling little Georgie here, even for one night, & only regretted it was not for a few days instead. He was so dear & sweet, he & I dined together alone & he talked away all the time. I was so sorry he had a bad cold, & the journey up made him much worse as his carriage was so cold, so I gave him a hot foot bath with mustard & some Febrifuge & he said he felt better the next day." She had been feeling unwell, which must be "old age creeping over me, so I ought not to complain."[264] On 20 January the Queen met an inspiring figure, Sergeant Major Flora Sandes,[265] an Englishwoman who served in the Royal Serbian Army from 1914–1922. She had been seriously wounded in action in 1916, spent the rest of the war running a hospital and was then commissioned as Captain.

Air raids continued and in a particularly bad one on 28 January there were 231 casualties; on the 29th 20 more and in February four raids, one on the 16th destroying a house at Chelsea Hospital and killing six members of one family. The next day 35 were killed during a raid on St Pancras' Station and Hotel. Official food rationing began on the 25th and all[266] were issued with ration cards; Alexandra's household was already on strict rations. Charlotte Knollys agreed that the food question was most serious but wondered "how people can find it worth their while to stand for hours in the street for the sake of getting a little <u>Margarine</u>. Meat and Bread are of course quite a different thing."[267] On the 25th Alexandra inspected a motor dental surgery, bought from the Silver Thimble Fund, an imaginative scheme of which, typically, she was patron. Miss Elizabeth Hope-Clarke[268] had started it in July 1915, collecting old silver thimbles, broken or worn silver or gold trinkets, jewellery, cigarette cases and coins, to be melted down and sent to the Bank of England. Anything too good, or unmeltable, was valued and sold in aid of the fund. By February 1918, £33,000 had been raised; £16,500 was divided between the Navy Employment Agency for Disabled Sailors, the "Star and Garter" Fund, St Dunstan's Hostel for the Blind and Disabled Soldiers and Sailors. The rest bought twelve motor ambulances, one disinfector, five motor hospital launches for Mesopotamia, and the motor dental surgery; the remaining £222 provided small grants. It had been a truly splendid effort.[269]

Gas prices had risen; Marlborough House's March bill was £10 more than in 1917, even with reduced consumption.[270] Savings continued, automatically when Alexandra was away from London, but she was usually there to carry out most of her public duties. On 4 March she launched two war carrier pigeons from Marlborough House.[271] Within a few days air raids started again; on the 7th there was one over London, killing 100 and injuring 79. The next day Alexandra drove to see the destruction. There were air raids on Paris and, on the 12th, on Hartlepool, with twenty casualties. On 19 March Alexandra decided to visit Endell Street again, finding her way, unexpected, to the operating theatre. The anaesthetist,[272] who was pregnant, was sitting at her work but tried to get up as the Queen entered; Alexandra insisted she remain seated. On the 24th Summer Time began, now five weeks longer as urged by the Food Production Department and the coal controller. As life at home became more regulated, so news from the front improved, due partly to American support. The air offensive was decreasing and there would only be a couple more air raids over England, the last, on 19 May, a big one lasting from 11.00pm to 2.45am, causing 223 casualties, but losing seven German Gotha planes. In May 1918 healthy men under 51 became eligible for military service; by the 13th, 26 members of Alexandra's staff were serving with the forces.[273]

The Russian Imperial Family had been transferred to the Ipatieff house in Ekaterinburg. Minny, in the Crimea, was well and able to take long walks every day. There had been an unconfirmed press report about her finances but, as Charlotte Knollys told Sarah Acland, "for that matter the Queen has lost more than half of her income owing to the war!"[274] Alexandra visited Handley Page's large aerodrome at Cricklewood on 25 March, an exhibition of war pictures by Lieutenant Brookes at the Grafton Galleries the next day and Messrs du Cros' Munitions Factory at Acton on the 28th. She saw the film, *Christus* at the Philharmonic Hall in Great Portland Street on the 30th and motored on 1 April to the Vickers' Ammunition Factory at Clayford in Kent to see 27 acres of buildings and 37 miles of shops, where 9,000 people were employed. She visited the Park Royal Munitions Factory for motor engines and aeroplanes on the 4th. More public engagements, charity performances, exhibitions and Red Cross nurses followed and she insisted on a memorial service for King Edward on 6 May at Windsor, which George and May thought unnecessary.[275]

Despite everything, Alexandra was feeling "out of it", lonely and desperately sad in these troubled times to have had none of her usual private conversations with her son, especially as there were things she wanted to talk about. She knew "how terribly hard you are worked & how little time you have to yrself! but yet as yr Mother I feel I want you too sometimes & you are now my only boy! and you know well my great love for all of my darling Children … so that I cannot help feeling…'my utter loneliness' now! & quite out of everything!! & not wanted by anybody. I know I am getting old and stupid but there is life in me yet and I cling to my beloved Children & my Georgie boy … "[276] She had a cold, was not feeling particularly well, and it was a cry of despair, although the King was overwhelmed with work and anxiety and she should have realised he had not meant to neglect her. But ever since 1863 Alexandra had wanted above everything to help her husband and later, her son. Love of her family and the desire for this to be returned was the most important thing in her life. What was the good of anything now? Bertie and Eddy were dead, Louise had her own family, Victoria was about to go away for three and a half weeks to stay with Julie d'Hautpoul, Maud was inaccessible and George was too busy to see her. She was consumed with anxiety about Minny in Russia and may well have been worrying about Victoria for other reasons. She missed the Danish family holidays and the cheerful house parties of which her husband had been the life and soul; in the same letter she asked George whether their old friends, Rosebery and Soveral, were still with him.

Louise, Maudie and Marie spent more time with her during Victoria's absence and by 1 June she was writing more cheerfully and sending her miniature as a birthday present for George. His response was all she could have wished; "I shall put your picture on my table & have it always with me. Rest assured darling Motherdear that you have the same place in my heart that you have had ever since I was a little child."[277] During their recent visit to Yorkshire they had had "a splendid reception from many hundreds of thousands of people, many of them are supposed to be Socialists, anyhow they were most friendly to us." The growth of socialism had seemed a threat; now the King was reassured of people's loyalty, whichever party they belonged to. Also, at Aldershot he had seen troops training, and a good many Americans working as mechanics with the Royal Air Force.[278]

Even though she had "escaped from London", Alexandra was still bothered by "interference" with the Nursing Board; the War Office had sent her a paper adding "an <u>endless</u> number of names & Hospitals … to <u>our</u> working party." She was going to tell them they should do nothing in a hurry and wait until she had consulted Lord Knutsford, which, on 1 June, she did. The existing board had worked splendidly and satisfactorily since it was started after the South African War following her appeal to him and Lady Roberts and she really could not sanction any alterations, as "this new plan with so large an addition of members (of tiresome interfering ladies) will I feel sure upset all our old work." Expanded committees were not necessarily better ones and she signed herself "Yours very sincerely but <u>tiresome</u> <u>bully</u> Alexandra."[279] By 15 June she was enjoying the fine weather and gardens at Sandringham. "I have never seen this beloved place looking better smothered in flowers, & the rhododendrons both in the garden & everywhere in all the woods & commons too quite too beautiful & of every colour." She had finally heard, via the Danish legation, from Minny in the Crimea but was anything but comforted; "Her life there already, was too awful & they nearly starved & haven't got a <u>penny</u> left, & were never allowed to leave the place for a moment even & her beautiful <u>Motor</u> confiscated." Worse, she had lost her greatest ally. "<u>Since</u> then I have been told that her beloved faithful Prince Chervachidze has died suddenly from heart failure! <u>Too</u> awfully sad! if true!! her only faithful friend, companion, support & guide taken from her <u>now</u> in the midst of all her trials & horrors wld really be <u>too</u> much for her to bear!! & I quite tremble to think of her future, she says she has already grown into a perfect skeleton & has no flesh left [on her] bones!! And God knows <u>where</u> she is at this moment." Alexandra herself had lost a stone in weight since 1917.[280]

She and Victoria drove to London for Alexandra Rose Day on the 19th, in pouring rain; happily, £25,000 was collected, over £3,000 more than in 1917. Perhaps inspired by George's comment about the American mechanics at Aldershot, Alexandra had mentioned earlier that she would so much like to see a baseball match.[281] Sure enough and appropriately on 4 July, with her daughters and Maudie, she watched a match between the American Army and Navy at Chelsea Football Ground; a good chance to see Britain's new allies in friendly rivalry. Feelings about the war were more hopeful; aerial combat was being won and battle lines on the ground were, on the whole, being held by the Allies, although the situation was still serious. Amid cautious optimism George and May's silver wedding anniversary on 6 July was marked by a state service at St Paul's Cathedral and a reception at the Mansion House, where a cheque for £50,000, for charity, was presented. There was a family luncheon at Buckingham

Palace, the Belgian king and queen[282] arrived by aeroplane from France, and on the 10th a concert, *Belgium's Tribute to England*, was held at the Albert Hall. Alexandra also received over 100 Red Cross nurses by the 16th.

Life seemed brighter and continued normally for Alexandra: a charity performance, a Girl Guides' rally, receiving Lady Muriel Paget[283] on the 18th and visiting a naval war photograph exhibition at Prince's Galleries on the 21st. But terrible, although unconfirmed, news was received; it was feared that Nicholas II had been shot by the Bolsheviks at Ekaterinburg. The Duke of Connaught surmised that, once it was certain that the poor Emperor was dead, "I suppose His Majesty would order the usual mourning for a Sovereign and near relative, who was also an Ally, and a very true one too."[284] By the 25th there was sufficient confirmation, and a memorial service was held in the Russian Chapel in Welbeck Street, which the King and Queen, Queen Alexandra and other members of the Royal Family attended. Stamfordham was aghast at the callous indifference of the public and press to this "sickening horror". The government had not been represented at the service. Lord Esher's letter in *The Morning Post* of the 27th, however, was excellent: "The Emperor no doubt was a weak man, but there are plenty of them in places high and low in the world. Whatever he was, he was a true friend to this country, and as long as he was on the Throne his Army fought, which is more than can be said for it under a Republic!"[285]

It was thought that Empress Alexandra and her children might have survived and a government telegram was sent to General Poole[286] at Archangel on 9 August; "King of Spain having offered the Empress, her children and the Dowager Empress his hospitality is believed to have asked the Germans to help them to leave Russia. If you have a chance of helping and saving them, Mr Balfour desires that you should do so." The King drafted a telegram to King Alfonso on the 14th; "I shall be most grateful if you will exert all your influence in whatever direction you think best to rescue the Imperial Family of Russia from their present pitiable position." However, dread that they, the Dowager Empress and all the others might also be dead, was consuming their relatives in England. No letters between the King and his mother survive for July and they only resume towards the end of August. Perhaps they kept in touch by telephone, or in person. They could only wait, hope and pray. A shakily-written letter to May reveals Alexandra's state of mind; "Excuse my late answer but I have been very busy the last few days & am not feeling over well & perfectly miserable about my beloved Sister Minny & her blessed son, Nicky, the perfect Martyr & cruelly sacrificed by his own Country."[287] Two days earlier, she had written to the sub dean about "this awful cruel tragedy". It was indeed "the most wicked & cruellest of deeds. May God in His mercy give [my sister] & her poor children strength to bear it. Please thank yr dear wife for all her kind sympathy in this truly overwhelming sorrow!"[288]

Intensive activity helped her: functions, hospitals, ever more Red Cross nurses, and seeing relatives. Miss Luckes was very ill and she visited her on 30 July. A young black woman had written to Alexandra, asking if she could help with the war effort. She was directed to Endell Street and taken on as a nursing orderly and on 1 August Alexandra made a special visit there to see her.[289] This seems to have been Alexandra's last visit to the hospital, which had begun to treat cases in the first wave of "Spanish flu" as well as war wounds. On 4 August a service at St Margaret's, Westminster marked the fourth anniversary of the war's outbreak. On the 9th Alexandra motored to St Jude's Church at Hampstead Garden Suburb, returning three days later to plant a rose bush at the shrine there. She went motoring again; Crystal Palace, Clapham Common, Streatham, Hampstead and Richmond. Finally, she, Victoria and Charlotte returned to Sandringham for an extended visit. Johnnie came to tea at least ten times and Harry, training at Sandhurst but "rather run down", stayed with Alexandra for a week, as his doctor had recommended the bracing Norfolk climate. George wrote; "The news from France is most satisfactory in every way & I am glad to say we continue to make good progress & are still driving back the enemy, we have captured a great many prisoners, a considerable number of guns & inflicted heavy losses on him ... During the last 5 weeks he has sustained the greatest defeat that he has had during the last four years & I think it will be very difficult to hide the fact from the German people."[290]

Alexandra replied the next day but the optimistic news had failed to cheer her. She was feeling unwell, with acute pain in her side and back; perhaps lumbago, which she had never had before. It had been very hot, which had made her feel worse but she was really suffering because of her state of mind. There had been disturbing news from Minny; still alive in June but having heard nothing from her sons, and "had again an awful time to go through with those brutes the Red Guards, who wanted to kill them all; they were protected by some faithful sailors, but none of the family went to bed or undressed for fourteen nights, excepting she herself, who said she did not care what became of her!! ... I dread to think what may be in store for them yet. I can think of nothing else, which nearly drives me mad."[291] It was like 1906, when Alexandra had felt unwell at Claremont, almost exactly when her father died. In 1918 she found herself unexpectedly in great pain from lumbago, like her sister. Her close affinity with those she loved sometimes showed itself physically.

Reports from Murmansk on 31 August suggested that the Russian empress and children had been murdered at the same time as the Emperor[292] and the King tried to break the bad news gently to his mother. "I am so sorry to hear that you have not been feeling well ... Of course you are worried & anxious which makes you feel worse. I fear those foul brutes in Russia have killed poor Alicky & those lovely girls & the little boy, but the news is not confirmed, but the source from which it came is fairly reliable. I wrote to poor Victoria[293] to tell her what I had heard & she has written to me a miserable letter & she fears the worst ... But in the South things seem to be more quiet & I am sure that darling Aunt Minny & her children are quite safe & are being treated well."[294] George continued with good news of the war which he was now convinced the Allies would ultimately win. Alexandra did not want to accept the bad news; "I wonder ... whether those awful rumours are true about poor dear unfortunate Alicky & all their lovely daughters & precious son!! It would indeed be too scandalous & horrible. What mad brutes they have all become out there."[295] Alas, despite rumours of their survival, by 20 September there was little room for doubt.[296] Marie was now desperately anxious about her husband, imprisoned at Petrograd.

Despite everything, life at Sandringham had brighter aspects. Georgie was staying with his grandmother and enjoying bicycling with his Aunt Victoria, "which does them both good".[297] Also, Victoria had friends staying in a cottage on the estate: the Harrisons, a mother[298] and her four musical daughters. Alexandra had already met May, the violinist, and Beatrice, the cellist; the others were Margaret,[299] another violinist, and Monica,[300] who sang. From 4–30 September they came to play the piano with Victoria about eleven times. Earlier, as Alexandra wrote, "Dear Johnnie comes here very often & enjoys the music so much when Victoria plays, accompanied by several young girls, violinists & violoncellos, who come from London and are staying at Dersingham."[301]

Lord Rosebery had written sympathetically about Russia, to which Alexandra replied gratefully; "I feel you understand exactly what I am going through now on account of & for my beloved darling Sister, my tried Sister as you so rightly call her. We shared every thought & feeling for each other during all our life, and to think of her now in this agony & misery about her beloved eldest son's cruel & dastardly murder should she know it by this time!! is almost more than I can bear!! ... Indeed her precious life is now a most terrible tragedy! and that beloved, most excellent eldest son, who you also appreciated in the right way, that he shld have been sacrificed in this brutal way seems too hard." She could scarcely realise that the Empress, their daughters and "his precious & beautiful son" had also been murdered. "Oh! it is indeed too fearful to think of, and I cannot help asking myself why should she, my beloved sister, really the best woman in the world, Why shld she be made to suffer so much. May God give her strength to bear this heaviest of crosses laid upon her!" Rosebery too had sorrows; he had lost his son Neil[302] in the war. Other deaths broke links with the happy past at Sandringham, when she and her husband were surrounded by their many friends. "It is sad to think how quickly all happiness & bright days pass, and how soon we have to face the Shadow of the Valley of Death.[303] May God lead us on towards the path He has chosen for each of us."[304] By the 28th Alexandra was reassured; good news of Minny had been sent to Davidson for her information. But Charles Jackson, the head keeper, died at Sandringham after 47 years of service, then on 11 October news was received that Phyllis Hamilton had been drowned when the *Leinster*, crossing to Ireland, was torpedoed.[305] The war was still claiming innocent victims, although there was hope of victory. But there was no hope for Grand Duke George and the other grand dukes in the Peter and Paul Fortress at Petrograd.

Hostilities were now moving towards conclusion, as the King told his mother; there had been correspondence between Germany and the American President, Woodrow Wilson.[306] Lloyd George and his colleagues were going to Paris the next day for an Allied conference, with an American representative, to "draw up our terms for an armistice. I know that these terms will be so drastic & humiliating that I do not believe Germany will accept them, unless their internal state is much worse than we have any idea [of]. If they don't accept our terms, the war will have to continue & we shall go on hammering at them until we have driven them back to the Rhine but it will take some time, I fear."[307] Alexandra thanked God the news was good, but "I do hope & trust <u>no</u> peace or <u>armistice</u> till we have smashed & crushed them forever … [but] I am sorry for poor <u>Austria</u> she is done for & split up forever I fear; if it had only been that <u>hateful Germany</u>." She was fearful of the chaos in Austria, "the poor young Emperor & Empress[308] I hope will escape before too late!"[309] and spared a kindly thought for the German empress, who "I see by the papers … is again very ill & suffering from her heart, & where is <u>he</u>, the beast, I wonder & <u>how</u> does he <u>feel</u> now? after all his <u>pride</u> & glory!" She warned that "Lots of people here have the flu & in London it seems terribly bad – Do all of you please be careful as it is so very catching."[310] Events were moving almost as quickly as in August 1914. King Ferdinand of Bulgaria had abdicated on 4 October; Turkey made an armistice and withdrew from the German alliance on the 31st. The Austrian armistice was signed on 4 November.[311] On the 9th William II abdicated and an armistice between Germany and the Allies was signed at 5am on the 11th.

On Sunday 10 November a prayer, written by Davidson, was read during the service at Sandringham Church:

"Almighty God, before whom all Nations and Rulers must bow, whose Power is infinite and Mercy everlasting, we Thy servants do give Thee humble thanks in that it had pleased Thee to listen to our prayers. We called upon Thee in our trouble & Thou, O Lord, hast heard our supplication. We thank Thee, O Lord, for the talent of our Commanders, and the steadfast courage of our Soldiers and Sailors. Thou hast given ascendency to our Arms and to those of our Allies, and through the fierce tumult of War hast given us the light of Victory and shown us the vision of Peace. May we remember the trials through which we passed lest we forget that it is Thou, O God, who hast enabled us to meet them with faith, and to overcome them with endurance. Grant, O Lord, that the peace when it comes may be lasting, that it be not impaired by discord or disturbed by civil strife, but that it may be one in which all can join with mutual help for the common good. Comfort, O Lord, in Thine infinite compassion, those who in the war have lost those they most love, and grant, O most merciful Saviour, that we who remain may strive to follow in the noble footsteps of those who have fallen, and like them may prove ourselves worthy to share the glory of the Life Eternal, which they have died to gain."[312]

When peace was declared Alexandra was still at Sandringham. George had written; "I fear at this moment Monarchies are pretty cheap anyhow in the Central Powers & their Allies ... But please God this dear old country will remain calm & collected, I have great faith in the British race who are full of common sense & I believe a monarchy suits them best. Anyhow I shall never give them any cause to complain of [my] being an Autocrat & shall do my best to keep in close touch with the people & help them all I can & do what I consider my duty."[313] He had recognised the public mood and offered an exemplary pattern for a constitutional monarch. Alexandra responded, "My thoughts are always near you, & I know you work hard & conscientiously for yr Country & people, & God will help & keep you in yr place & for yr people's sake! This country thank God, is not like anywhere abroad, where everything now is topsy turvy & Revolutions seem everywhere."[314] On the 17th she returned to London and resumed her motoring trips, exhibitions, charity performances and visits to centres which had worked hard for the war effort: on 27 November, Miss Knowles'[315] depot for sending parcels to prisoners of war, and, on the 30th, the Field Force Fund sale. To boost the RSPCA's fund for sick and wounded horses, Captain Fairholme[316] was organising shops in Central London:[317] two selling fruit and vegetables (supplied by Messrs Sutton & Sons of Reading and Messrs Barr & Sons of Covent Garden) and the others selling donated antiques. Fairholme asked whether Queen Alexandra might visit any of them during the week of the sale; no promise was given, but there was really no doubt and she visited five on 5 December. The Daltons had sent her a birthday present; "It does one good to feel how one's old & most valued friends never forget you, & happy times gone by. Thank you over and over again for so kindly remembering me!"[318] On the 13th Alexandra received fourteen Red Cross nurses and the Doctor and five nurses from Highgate Hospital. The next day she saw *The Pirates of Penzance*, given by the patients of the Orthopaedic Hospital (under King Manuel's patronage) at Shepherd's Bush Empire. She also visited the Duchess of Marlborough's[319] dolls' show in aid of the Children's Jewel Fund. On the 17th there was a wonderful reunion; Queen Maud and Crown Prince Olaf, whom she had not seen since 1913, arrived from Norway. On the 19th Sir Douglas Haig, his generals and staff had a public welcome and, after lunch at Buckingham Palace, visited Alexandra at Marlborough House. She received more Red Cross nurses, and on the 23rd met the Arab Prince Feisal,[320] with Colonel Lawrence[321] and Mr Synge.

On 23 November, Vice Admiral Arthur Calthorpe,[322] on board *HMS Superb* at Constantinople, told the King that his officer, Commander Turle,[323] and a White Russian naval officer, Lt-Commander Korostovzeff, had seen the

Dowager Empress in the Crimea. She did not believe her son and his family had been murdered and refused to leave Russia, but gave Turle a letter for Queen Alexandra. Davidson and Stamfordham asked the Admiralty to give Alexandra any details about her sister that they received, and she sent a message on the 18th via the Admiralty, asking Minny to leave Russia for England at once and bring everyone she wished, but all she got was "Though I long to see you awfully see no real necessity to leave now for the moment."[324] Christmas was again spent in London, Alexandra distributing gifts in the drawing room on the 24th and receiving Holy Communion in the chapel the next day. On Boxing Day, President Woodrow Wilson and his wife arrived in London and stayed with the King at Buckingham Palace. Alexandra received them at Marlborough House but later attended a pantomime at Drury Lane with Victoria and Maud; the next day they and Olaf saw a children's entertainment at London Hospital. On the 28th Alexandra received a Russian visitor and two days later Colonel Boyle[325] from Russia. She was trying to find out what was happening.

Notes

[1] RA GV/PRIV/AA34/34, Queen Alexandra to King George V, 1914: 14 January; May had been with her at the little service that was held

[2] Queen Alexandra's treasurer

[3] £2,500

[4] George, 2nd Marquess of Cambridge (1895–1981), Queen Mary's nephew, later remembered a story about batches of £5 notes being sent to Queen Alexandra by the bank every month, to send out in answer to appeals. Pope-Hennessy/Vickers, *The Quest for Queen Mary*, p 265.

[5] Colonel Sir Henry Streatfeild (1857–1938), Queen Alexandra's equerry and private secretary

[6] RA VIC/ADDA21/228/262, Sir Dighton Probyn to Lord Ripon, 1914: 17 January

[7] *King Edward in his True Colours*; the household had helped by answering some simple questions

[8] *More about King Edward*

[9] RA AEC/GG/9/356, Sir Arthur Davidson to Sir Dighton Probyn, 1914: 7 January

[10] RA AEC/GG/9/328, Sir Dighton Probyn to Sir Arthur Davidson, 1913: 15 November

[11] Jeanne Antoinette Poisson (1721–1764), Marquise de Pompadour, chief mistress and favourite of Louis XV of France. This seems a slightly insensitive gift – but perhaps Alexandra was amused by the Marquise's surname and intrigued by her having been a patron of the arts. The book was by Edmond (1822–1896) and Jules (1830–1870) de Goncourt.

[12] Private information

[13] RA AEC/GG/9/356, Sir Arthur Davidson to Sir Dighton Probyn, 1914: 7 January

[14] RA AEC/GG/9/385, Sir Frederick Ponsonby, 1914: 19 February

[15] RA GV/PRIV/AA34/35, Queen Alexandra to King George V, 1914: 29 January

[16] RA GV/ADD/COPY/140/95,96,97, Rosebery Papers, Princess Victoria to Lord Rosebery, 1914: 1 February, undated, 12 March

[17] RA GV/PRIV/AA/34/38, Queen Alexandra to King George V, 1914: 21 March

18 RA VIC/ADDA21/56,59, Queen Alexandra to Sir Dighton Probyn, 1914: 26, 28 March

19 RA VIC/ADDA/17/1164,1173–4, Queen Alexandra to Princess Louise, Duchess of Argyll, 1914: 30 April; 5 May; undated (Saturday)

20 Willy Ferrero (1906–54), conductor, as a child and as an adult

21 King Christian X and Queen Alexandrine

22 Ronald Macdonald Hutchison (1872–1940), known as Harry Tate, was a music hall and film comedian. He had worked for Henry Tate & Sons, sugar refiners, and took his stage name from them.

23 Unidentified press cutting, 24/6/1914

24 Emmeline, née Goulden (1858–1928), m Richard Pankhurst, was a political activist and suffragette

25 RCIN 1033746

26 RCIN 1232313

27 During the coming war, she supported a military hospital which was run by suffragettes, of which more anon.

28 RA AEC/GG/9/507, Sir Arthur Davidson to Sir Dighton Probyn, 1914: 14 June

29 Sir Ernest Shackleton (1874–1922), Antarctic explorer

30 Princess Louise of Battenberg (1889–1965), became Lady Louise Mountbatten in 1917, m Gustav VI Adolf, King of Sweden, as his second wife

31 This must have affected her deeply, although no references to it by her have yet been found. Perhaps she could not bear to put it into words.

32 Sometimes by way of relatives in neutral countries, such as Crown Princess Margaret of Sweden

33 To remind her of past or wished-for travels she did possess books about Greece, Denmark, Russia, India and elsewhere and subscribed to *The Story of the Nations*, which ran comprehensively to over 50 volumes. She also had a copy of Sir Henry H Johnston's *A History of the Colonisation of Africa by Alien Races*, RCIN 1033829.

34 Letters to Thyra during most of the war have not survived, although they resumed afterwards for the rest of Alexandra's life. Information from Niedersächsisches Landesarchiv, Hannover, Dep103 II Nr 164/02

35 Mrs Rosalie Dodds, housekeeper at Marlborough House from 1880; she was housekeeper at Buckingham Palace from 1901–1910 but returned with Queen Alexandra to Marlborough House later

36 RA VIC/ADDA21/228/121–2, Sir Dighton Probyn to Lord Ripon, 1914: August; Lord Ripon to Sir Dighton Probyn, 1914: 9 August

37 RA VIC/ADDA21/228/220, List of newspapers and periodicals supplied to Queen Alexandra by Messrs May & Williams, 1917: April

38 RA GV/Q2554/2, Lord Stamfordham to Lord Kitchener, 1914: 24 August

39 Lady Margaret, née Grosvenor (1873–1929), m Adolphus, 2nd Duke of Teck; in 1917 they became the Marquess and Marchioness of Cambridge

40 RA QM/PRIV/CC50/1085, Queen Alexandra to the Duchess of Teck, 1914: 7 October

41 RA GV/PRIV/AA34/41 Queen Alexandra to King George V, 1914: 31 October

42 Lord Charles Petty-Fitzmaurice (1874–1914), took the surname Mercer-Nairne; soldier and courtier

43 Prince Maurice of Battenberg (1891–1914), Lieutenant

44 RA GV/PRIV/AA34/41, Queen Alexandra to King George V, 1914: 31 October

45 Their wedding had been popularly marked in England by the creation of a new cake, the Battenberg.

46 RA GV/PRIV/AA34/41, Queen Alexandra to King George V, 1914: 31 October

47 RA QM/PRIV/CC42/105, Queen Alexandra to Queen Mary, 1914: 21 September

48   Princess Nina Georgievna of Russia (1901–74), artist, m Prince Paul Chavchavadze
49   Princess Xenia Georgievna of Russia (1903–65), m (1) William Bateman Leeds, (2) Herman Jud
50   RA QM/PRIV/CC42/106, Queen Alexandra to Queen Mary, 1914: 2 December
51   RA VIC/ADDA21/234/19,20, Viscount Knutsford to Queen Alexandra, 1914: Christmas; Queen Alexandra to Lord Knutsford, 1914: undated [December]
52   Formerly on her Unemployed Fund committee
53   RA VICADDA21/228/149–154
54   RA GV/PRIV/AA34/45, Queen Alexandra to King George V, 1914: 31 December
55   Blackguards, ruffians
56   He had called it a "contemptibly little Army" but the version which had gained wide credence was "contemptible little Army".
57   Victoria, née Kennard (1874–1955) m Sir Frederick Ponsonby (later Lord Sysonby)
58   RA/GV/ADD/COPY/40,98,100; Baroness Irene van Brienen (1883–1974) m Hon Cyril Augustus Ward
59   RA VIC/ADDA21/229, Queen Alexandra to Prince Nicholas of Greece, 1915: 19 January
60   It is not clear whether this refers to a hospital in Salisbury, or the military camp on Salisbury Plain
61   A comforting fiction, which the Queen could privately have countered with her knowledge of Duchess Marie of Mecklenburg-Strelitz's experience
62   Founded in 1739 by Thomas Coram (1668–1751) a philanthropic sea captain; new premises for it were built in Bloomsbury between 1742–52, where they still were in 1915; the institution later moved to Redhill and then Berkhamsted before being reconstituted as the Thomas Coram Foundation for Children ("Coram")
63   RA VIC/ADDA21/233/135,137, Lord Knutsford to Queen Alexandra, 1915: 23 February; Queen Alexandra to Lord Knutsford, 1915: undated [Tuesday]
64   One on 13 February to raise money to fund an ambulance for Russia
65   On 5 March Alexandra saw a parade of 10 Ambulance Motor Cars; a present from the British Red Cross to the Russian
66   Perhaps the Greek Orthodox Church in Moscow Road
67   Hans Niels Andersen (1852–1937), Danish shipping magnate, businessman, diplomat and founder of the East Asiatic company
68   Foreign Secretary
69   Albert Grey (1851–1917), 4th Earl Grey
70   RA GV/AA34/47, Queen Alexandra to King George V, 1915: 12 May; they were the Garter Banners of William II and others who had been made Knights of the Order in happier times.
71   Ernest Louis, Grand Duke of Hesse and by Rhine
72   The Duke of Cumberland
73   Charles Edward, Duke of Saxe-Coburg-Gotha and of Albany, whose mother, Helen, Duchess of Albany was living in England
74   RA GV/PRIV/AA34/48, Queen Alexandra to King George V, 1915: 23 May
75   RA QM/PRIV/CC42/108, Queen Alexandra to Queen Mary, 1915: undated
76   Beavan, p 77
77   RA VIC/ADDA21/228/140–2, Queen Alexandra to Sir Dighton Probyn, 1915: 8 June; Lord Ripon to Sir Dighton Probyn, 1915: 11 July; Sir Dighton Probyn to Lord Ripon, 1915: 10 June
78   RA MRH/MRH/SOV/MIXED/227/08
79   Dimond, p 70
80   RA QM/PRIV/CC58/162, note
81   By this time she had virtually given up photography and so was economising on that too

[82] RA VIC/ADDA21/228/172, memorandum by Sir Dighton Probyn, 1915: 11 November

[83] And was used during the Boer War

[84] RA VIC/ADDA21/228/195, Sir Dighton Probyn to Lord Farquhar, 1915: 27 May

[85] RA VIC/ADDA21/228/210, Queen Alexandra to Sir Dighton Probyn, 1915: 31 December

[86] RA VIC/ADDA21/228/141-2, Lord Ripon to Sir Dighton Probyn, 1915: 11 July; Sir Dighton Probyn to Lord Ripon, 1915: 10 June

[87] Prince Joachim of Prussia (1890–1920)

[88] RA VIC/ADDA21/230, Queen Alexandra to Prince Nicholas of Greece, 1915: 10 August

[89] RA GV/PRIV/AA34/48, Queen Alexandra to King George V 1915: 23 May

[90] Winston Spencer Churchill (1874–1965), army officer, writer, painter and statesman; prime minister,1940–5 and 1951–5; in 1915 he was first lord of the Admiralty but resigned

[91] Lady Muriel Paget was honorary secretary of the organisation

[92] Emma, née Tennant (1864–1945), second w of Herbert Henry Asquith, was a socialite, author and wit. Her daughter was Elizabeth, née Asquith (1897–1945), m Prince Antoine Bibesco

[93] RA GV/PRIV/AA34/49, Queen Alexandra to King George V, 1915: 13 July

[94] RA QM/PRIV/CC42/156, Queen Alexandra to Queen Mary, 1915: [undated, 3 August?]; the service was to commemorate the first anniversary of the beginning of the war

[95] Lady Muriel, née Finch-Hatton (1876–1938), m Richard Paget of Cranmore, 2nd Baronet; she was a philanthropist and humanitarian relief worker

[96] St Petersburg's wartime name, seen as patriotically more Slavic

[97] Grand Duke Dmitri Pavlovitch of Russia (1891–1942); the building was also known as the Beloselsky Belozhersky Palace

[98] RA VIC/ADDA21/228/143-9; information board at *The Last Tsar – Blood and Revolution*, shown at the Science Museum, London, in 2019; Internet; Foreign and Commonwealth Office blog by Keith Allan, 4 February 2016

[99] RA GV/PRIV/AA37/62, King George V to Queen Alexandra, 1915: 2 September

[100] RA GV/PRIV/AA34/51, Queen Alexandra to King George V, 1915: 6 September

[101] RA VIC/ADDA21/231, Queen Alexandra to Prince Nicholas of Greece, 1915: 3 September

[102] Walter Ellinger, the Queen's Sergeant Footman; he was appointed as footman in 1900

[103] RA GV/PRIV/AA34/51, Queen Alexandra to King George V, 1915: 6 September

[104] RA QM/PRIV/CC42/110, Queen Alexandra to Queen Mary, 1915: 29 September

[105] Her name was Isabella Mary ("Mabel")

[106] RA GV/PRIV/AA34/52, Queen Alexandra to King George V, 1915: 4 October

[107] Edith Cavell (1865–1915), heroic nurse

[108] RA VIC/ADDA21/233/130, Queen Alexandra to Lord Knutsford, 1915: 26 October

[109] RA VIC/ADDA21/233/131, Queen Alexandra to Lord Knutsford, 1915: 2 November

[110] RA VIC/ADDA21/233/132, Lord Knutsford to Queen Alexandra, 1915: un dated

[111] RA GV/PRIV/AA34/52, Queen Alexandra to King George V, 1915: 4 October; she had sanctioned Myles Ponsonby's appointment as equerry but the war had intervened before this could be gazetted. Major Cyril Myles Ponsonby (1881–1915) was the second son of the 8th Earl of Bessborough

[112] This may have been part of the entertainment at Lady Paget's matinée at the Empire Theatre, in aid of Red Cross funds, on 21 October, as no other theatre visits are recorded in the engagement diary at this time

[113] RA QM/PRIV/CC42/112, Queen Alexandra to Queen Mary, 1915: 23 October

[114] RA VIC/ADDA21/233/131, Queen Alexandra to Lord Knutsford, 1915: 2 November; in fact the King had fractured his pelvis after his horse shied and he was thrown

[115] RA GV/PRIV/AA34/53, Queen Alexandra to King George V, 1915: 5 November

[116] RA :QM/PRIV/CC42/117, Queen Alexandra to Queen Mary, 1915: 5 November

117 RA VIC/ADDA21/228/170, Sir Frederick Ponsonby to Sir Dighton Probyn, 1915: 26 November

118 In the following tax year it would be £43, 313 and the one after that £41, 223

119 RA VIC/ADDA21/228/172, memorandum by Sir Dighton Probyn, 1915: 11 November

120 Grand Duchess George, p 163

121 Grand Duchess George, p 165

122 Emilie, née Packe (d 1922) m (1) Sir Edward Scott, 5ᵗʰ Baronet, (2) Horace Farquhar, 1ˢᵗ Earl Farquhar

123 RA GV/PRIV/AA6/543, Queen Alexandra to Canon Dalton, 1915: 16 December

124 Sir Ian Malcolm (1868–1944), the 17ᵗʰ Laird of Poltalloch, British Red Cross officer in France, Switzerland, Russia and America during the war. He married Lillie Langtry's daughter, Jeanne.

125 Dr Flora Murray (1869–1923), doctor, medical pioneer and suffragette

126 Dr Louisa Garrett Anderson (1873–1943), medical pioneer, physician, surgeon and suffragette; d of Mrs Elizabeth Garrett Anderson (1836–1917), the first woman to qualify in Britain as a physician and surgeon

127 As the Military Hospital, Endell Street; for the full story see *Endell Street*, by Wendy Moore

128 Eva Luckes (1854–1919), Matron of the London Hospital from 1880–1919

129 RA QM/CC42/118, Queen Alexandra to Queen Mary, 1916: 30 January

130 In which Alice Keppel's daughters, Violet and Sonia, were among those who took part

131 RA GV/O/2548/ref, Queen Mary to Queen Alexandra, 1916: 13 January

132 Prince Ferdinand of Saxe-Coburg-Gotha (1861–1948), created ruling Prince, and then King, of Bulgaria

133 St Dunstan's

134 Roehampton

135 RA VIC/ADDA21/232, Queen Alexandra to Prince Nicholas of Greece, 1916: 20 January

136 RA VIC/ADDA21/234/24,26, Queen Alexandra to Lord Knutsford, 1916: 2 March; 16 April

137 RA VIC/ADDA21/228/162, Sir Dighton Probyn to Queen Alexandra, 1916: 19 March

138 Sadly enough, Little Marvel died on 19 May.

139 RA VIC/ADDA21/228/164,165, Queen Alexandra to Sir Dighton Probyn, 1916: 22 March; Sir Dighton Probyn to Queen Alexandra, 1916: 22 March

140 RA GV/PRIV/AA34/54, Queen Alexandra to King George V, 1916: 6 June; the Battle of Jutland was a British victory but only because it facilitated the blockade of the German fleet for the rest of the war; many lives were lost. Prince Albert's ship had taken part.

141 Louise, née Paget (1881–1958), humanitarian, created Dame; m her cousin, Sir Ralph Paget

142 RA QM/PRIV/CC8/200, Queen Mary to King George V, 1916: 15 June

143 RA GV/PRIV/AA34/55, Queen Alexandra to King George V, 1916: 23 June

144 Hon Violet Vivian (1879–1962) twin sister of Lady Haig, maid of honour to Queen Alexandra from 1901–1925; she created a notable garden at Cestyll, on the Isle of Anglesey

145 RA GV/PRIV/AA34/55, Queen Alexandra to King George V, 1916: 23 June

146 RA GV/PRIV/AA35/2, Queen Alexandra to King George V, 1916: 18 July

147 RA GV/PRIV/AA35/3, Queen Alexandra to King George V, 1916: 24 July

148 Queen Mary became joint Patroness with her in 1913

149 Caroline Spurgeon (1869–1942), head of the department of English at Bedford College from 1915; she was a literary critic and the first female professor at London University, starting at Bedford College in 1901. She specialised in the works of Geoffrey Chaucer (1343–1400, famous poet and author).

150 *The Sphere*; Woman's Sphere, 6 January 1906; Margaret J Tuke, *A History of Bedford College for Women, 1849–1937*, p 209; Linna Bentley, *Educating Women; a History of Bedford College, University of London, 1849–1985*, p 34

[151] Moore, p 186

[152] This might have carried weight with Davidson, although Princess Victoria would have accepted it

[153] Such as that which had been rife about her own relatives in 1862

[154] Recalling her own grandmother's dilemma in supposedly "encouraging her daughter's passion for a groom in her stables"

[155] Dod Hill, near West Newton

[156] RA GV/PRIV/AA35/4, Queen Alexandra to King George V, 1916: 17 September

[157] Violet Ellen, née Green (1881–1916), m George Dunger; she died on 21 September 1916; http://dersinghamhistory.info/darkening_skies.html

[158] RA VIC/ADDU/417/13, Soveral Papers, Queen Alexandra to Marquis de Soveral, 1916: 5 October

[159] Grand Duchess George, p 164

[160] RA VIC/MAIN/QAD/1916: 26 October; Internet; ezitis.myzen.co.uk, *Lost Hospitals of London*

[161] Countess Nadejda Michaelovna Torby (1896–1963), d of Grand Duke Michael and Countess Torby; she was to marry Prince George of Battenberg (1892–1938), later 2nd Marquess of Milford Haven, two days later

[162] RA VIC/MAIN/QAD/1916: 13 November

[163] Alexandra's granddaughter, known as Maudie to distinguish her from her aunt, Queen Maud

[164] RA QM/PRIV/CC42/121, Queen Alexandra to Queen Mary, 1916: 25 November, referring to the Emperor's son's suicide and his wife's murder.; Francis Joseph (1830–1916) had died on 21 November

[165] Letter placed between pages in Queen Alexandra's engagement diary

[166] RA VIC/ADDA21/228/184, Sir Arthur Davidson to Sir Dighton Probyn, 1916: 9 December

[167] RA VIC/ADDA21/234/28, Queen Alexandra to Lord Knutsford, 1916: 23 December

[168] RA GV/PRIV/AA35/5, Queen Alexandra to King George V, 1916: 28 December

[169] Grigori Yefimovitch Rasputin (1869–1916) Russian peasant, mystic and self-proclaimed holy man, on whom the Empress had depended to help her haemophiliac son and on whom she increasingly relied for spiritual and, unfortunately, political advice

[170] Grand Duke Dmitri Pavlovitch, son of Grand Duke Paul and his first wife, Princess Alexandra of Greece

[171] Prince Felix Yusupov (1887–1967), m the Emperor's niece, Princess Irina Alexandrovna of Russia

[172] RA GV/PRIV/AA35/6, Queen Alexandra to King George V, 1917: 8 January

[173] Count Alexander von Benckendorff (1849–1917), Russian ambassador from 1903–1917; he had previously been ambassador in Denmark

[174] RA GV/PRIV/AA37/69, King George V to Queen Alexandra, 1917: 13 January

[175] D of Count Frijs of Frijsenborg, m Count Henrik Grevenkop-Castenskjiold (1862–1921), Danish ambassador

[176] Carpenter and then tapissier at Marlborough House for 38 years

[177] RA GV/PRIV/AA35/7, Queen Alexandra to King George V, 1917: 22 March

[178] Sir George Buchanan (1854–1924), diplomat, British ambassador to Russia, 1910–1917

[179] RA PS/PSO/GV/C/M/1067/17, Sir George Buchanan, 1917: 18 March

[180] RA PS/PSO/GV/C/M/1067/20, King George V to Emperor Nicholas II of Russia, 1917: 19 March

[181] Major-General Sir John Hanbury-Williams (1859–1946), at this time head of the British Military Mission with the Russian Stavka (high command of the armed forces), with direct access to the Emperor.

182 Grand Duke Nicholas Nicholaievitch of Russia (1856–1929), commander-in-chief of the Russian army before the Emperor assumed this role in 1915

183 RA PS/PSO/GV/C/M/1067/21, General Hanbury Williams to CIGS, 1917: 19 March

184 RA PS/PSO/GV/C/M/1067/15, General Hanbury Williams to Sir W Robertson, 1917: 16 March

185 Alexander Fyodorovitch Kerensky (1881–1970) Justice Minister and only Socialist member of the provisional government

186 Alexander Ivanovitch Gouchkoff (1862–1936), first war minister of the provisional government

187 RA PS/PSO/GV/C/M/1067/22, Sir George Buchanan to King George V and war cabinet, 1917: 19–20 March

188 RA PS/PSO/GV/C/M/1067/23, Sir George Buchanan, 1917: 19 March

189 RA PS/PSO/GV/C/M/1067/25, General Hanbury Williams to CIGS, 1917: 20 March

190 Sir Harry Verney (1881–1974), 4th baronet, politician

191 RA PS/PSO/GV/C/M/1067/26, Sir Harry Verney to Lord Stamfordham, 1917: 21 March

192 Prime Minister

193 Prince George Yevgenyevitch Lvov (1861–1925), 1st post-Imperial Russian premier

194 RA PS/PSO/GV/C/M/1067/27, David Lloyd George to Prince Lvoff, 1917: 21 March

195 RA PS/PSO/GV/C/M/1067/28, General Hanbury Williams, 1917: 22 March

196 Pavel Nicholaievitch Miliukoff (1859–1943), historian, politician and foreign minister in the provisional government, working to prevent Russia's exit from the war

197 Andrew Bonar Law (1858–1923), politician, prime minister from 1922–3

198 Judging by their attitude to Queen Alexandra's finances, this seems highly unlikely.

199 RA PS/PSO/GV/C/M/1067/29, memorandum by Lord Stamfordham, 1917: 21 March

200 General Michael Vasilyevitch Alexeieff (1857–1918), chief of staff of the Stavka and its commander-in-chief under the provisional government

201 The children suffering from measles

202 RA PS/PSO/GV/C/M/1067/30, General Hanbury Williams to CIGS, 1917:1917: 22 March

203 RA PS/PSO/GV/C/M/1067/32, Sir George Buchanan, 1917: 22 March

204 RA PS/PSO/GV/C/M/1067/35, General Hanbury Williams, 1917: 23 March

205 RA PS/PSO/GV/C/M/1067/38, Lord Stamfordham to Sir George Buchanan, 1917: 29 March

206 RA PS/PSO/GV/C/M/1067/39, Lord Stamfordham to Arthur Balfour, 1917: 30 March

207 RA PS/PSO/GV/C/M/1067/41, 42, Lord Carnock to Lord Stamfordham, 1917: 1 April; Lord Stamfordham's notes, 1917: 2 April

208 RA PS/PSO/GV/C/M/1067/44, 45, Arthur Balfour to Lord Stamfordham, 1917: 2 April; note [1917: 3 April]

209 Michael Alexandrovitch, the Emperor's brother, and George Michaelovitch, Marie of Greece's husband

210 RA GV/M/1067/46, Sir George Buchanan, 1917: 4 April

211 RA PS/PSO/GV/C/M/1067/47, 48, Eric Drummond to Stamfordham, 1917: 5 April; Sir George Buchanan, 1917: 4 April

212 Arthur Bigge (1849–1931), 1st Baron Stamfordham, private secretary to Queen Victoria and to George V

213 RA PS/PSO/GV/C/M/1067/51, 52, Lord Stamfordham to Arthur Balfour, 1917: both 6 April

214 William James Thorne (1857–1946), trade unionist, activist and one of the first Labour MPs

215 RA PS/PSO/GV/C/M/1067/62, 63, Government telegram to Sir George Buchanan, 1917: 13 April; Sir George Buchanan's reply, 1917: 15 April

216 RA PS/PSO/GV/C/M/1067/64, Sir George Buchanan, 1917: 16 April

217 RA PS/PSO/GV/C/M/1067/66, Sir George Buchanan, 1917: 25 April

218 Francis Bertie (1844–1919), 1st Viscount Bertie of Thame, diplomat, ambassador to France, 1905–1918

219 RA PS/PSO/GV/C/M/1067/68, Lord Bertie to Lord Stamfordham, 1917: 27 April

220 Vladimir Ilyich Ulyanov (Lenin) (1870–1924), Russian revolutionary, politician and political theorist; head of government from 1917–1924

221 RA GV/PRIV/AA35/8, Queen Alexandra to King George V, 1917: 9 April

222 Captain Donald Davidson (c 1892–1917), Royal Flying Corps

223 Leeds Russian Archive, MS 1405; "Garrard has all my things for the exhibition & they must arrange all together – & we can keep them at night." Queen Alexandra to unknown addressee, 1917: undated

224 As were Queen Alexandra, Queen Mary, William II, Nicholas II and his wife, Constantine and his wife and many others

225 In his speech at his first Opening of Parliament, 1760: 18 November, delivered in the House of Lords.

226 RA VIC/MAIN/QVJ/1838: 28 June

227 In fact, both, as granddaughters of Queen Victoria, had spent part of their youth in England. They loved this country and neither would have raised a finger against it.

228 Indeed; the King abdicated in favour of his second son, Prince Alexander, on June the 12th.

229 RA GV/PRIV/AA35/9, Queen Alexandra to King George V, 1917: 29 May

230 Grand Duchess George, p 165

231 Feodorovna, née Yorke (1864–1934), m 2nd Baron Alington

232 RA QM/PRIV/CC/42/124, Queen Alexandra to Queen Mary, 1917: 22 May

233 Acland MSS, d 154/2054/1, Charlotte Knollys to Sarah Acland, 1917: 27 June

234 RA VIC/MAIN/QAD/1917: many references, as dated in the text

235 Grand Duchess George, pp 167–8

236 As dependents of French soldiers, they could probably not claim from charities like SSFA, and being British residents (and possibly British-born) it would be difficult for them to appeal to French charities in France.

237 Including the National Egg Collection

238 Now Russian premier

239 RA PS/PSO/GV/C/M/1067/70, Sir George Buchanan, 1917: 25 July

240 Document enclosed in RA VIC/MAIN/QAD/1917: 24 July

241 Colonel Nicholas Alexandrovitch Kulikovsky (1881–1958)

242 Philip Eliot (1835–1917), Dean of Windsor from 1891–1917

243 RA GV/PRIV/AA35/11, Queen Alexandra to King George V, 1917: 8 September

244 RA GV/PRIV/AA37/70, King George V to Queen Alexandra, 1917: 10 September

245 Worth about 12 ½ pence after decimalisation in 1971

246 RA VIC.ADDA21/234/32, Queen Alexandra to Lord Knutsford, 1917: 15 September

247 RA PS/PSO/GV/C/M/1067/71–75, Sir George Buchanan, 1917: 3, 4 September; Foreign Office to Sir George Buchanan, 1917: 5 September; Sir George Buchanan to Arthur Balfour, 1917: 8 September; Foreign Office to Sir George Buchanan, 1917: 12 December

248 RA GV/PRIV/AA35/12, Queen Alexandra to King George V, 1917: 22 October

249 RA VIC/ADDA21/234/33, Queen Alexandra to Lord Knutsford, 1917: 24 October

250 RA GV/PRIV/AA35/12, Queen Alexandra to King George V, 1917: 22 October

251 Who had been working with British wounded soldiers and to whom Alexandra had already sent her usual card and thanks

252 RA GV/PRIV/AA35/13, Queen Alexandra to King George V, 1917: 2 November

253 RA GV/PRIV/AA/37/71, King George V to Queen Alexandra, 1917: 4 November

254 Lady Ripon's other title

255 RA GV/PRIV/AA35/14, Queen Alexandra to King George V, 1917: 6 November
256 RA QM/PRIV/CC42/127, Queen Alexandra to Queen Mary, 1917: 8 August
257 RA GV/PRIV/AA35/15, Queen Alexandra to King George V, 1917: 14 November
258 RA QM/PRIV/CC42/128, Queen Alexandra to Queen Mary, 1917: 3 November
259 RA VIC/ADDA21/234/35, Queen Alexandra to Viscount Knutsford, 1917: 27 November
260 Then operating as a military hospital, this was at Newbury Park
261 RA PS/PSO/GV/C/M/1067/76, Sir George Buchanan to Lord Stamfordham, 1917: 12 December
262 King Edward VII's Hospital for Officers (Sister Agnes's Hospital); at its future premises in Beaumont Street, St Marylebone, it was the hospital of choice for members of the royal family later in the 20th and the 21st centuries
263 RA GV/PRIV/AA35/16, Queen Alexandra to King George V, 1918: 3 January
264 RA QM/PRIV//CC42/129, Queen Alexandra to Queen Mary, 1918: 21 January
265 Flora Sandes (1876–1956)
266 It is not clear whether members of the royal family were personally issued with ration cards, but it seems that they had the use of them
267 Acland MSS, d.177/132 /2054/35, Charlotte Knollys to Sarah Acland, 1918:28 January
268 Elizabeth Hope-Clarke (1870–1950), charity campaigner
269 RA VIC/MAIN/QAD/1918: information inserted between pages at the end of February
270 RA VIC/ADDA21/228/221, Average annual consumption of electric light, gas and coal for 1916–17 at Marlborough House
271 She had always been fond of pigeons and doves, once buying some which had been destined for the table and then releasing them during a Mediterranean cruise. At one time Princess Victoria had a pet dove, "Dovey".
272 Evelyn Windsor, a Canadian; Moore, p 248
273 RA VIC/ADDA21/228/228
274 Acland MSS, d.177/132 /2054/36, Charlotte Knollys to Sarah Acland, 1918: 21 March
275 RA/GVI/PRIV/RF/11/280, Queen Mary to Prince Albert, 1918:3 May
276 RA GV/PRIV/AA/35/17, Queen Alexandra to King George V, 1918: 21 April
277 RA GV/PRIV/AA37/74, King George V to Queen Alexandra, 1918: 2 June
278 RA GV/PRIV/AA37/75, King George V to Queen Alexandra, 1918: 11 June; an early use of this term; soldiers using aeroplanes had previously formed the Royal Flying Corps, while sailors similarly employed were the Royal Naval Air Service. They combined and the Royal Air Force came officially into being in 1918.
279 RA VIC/ADDA21/234/37, Queen Alexandra to Lord Knutsford, 1918: 1 June
280 RA GV/PRIV/AA35/19, Queen Alexandra to King George V. 1918: 15 June
281 RA GV/PRIV/AA35/19, Queen Alexandra to King George V, 1918: 15 June
282 King Albert I (1875–1934) and Queen Elisabeth, née Duchess in Bavaria (1876–1965)
283 The Anglo–Russian Hospital had closed in 1918 after the revolution and Russia's withdrawal from the war
284 RA PS/PSO/GV/C/M/1344a/1, Duke of Connaught, 1918: 23 July
285 RA PS/PSO/GV/C/M/1344a/8, Lord Stamfordham to Rt Hon George Russell, 1918: 28 July
286 Major-General Sir Frederick Poole (1869–1936), commanded North Russian expeditionary force in 1918-9
287 RA QM/PRIV/CC42/131, Queen Alexandra to Queen Mary, 1918: 30 July
288 RA GV/PRIV/DD2/22, Queen Alexandra to Canon Edgar Sheppard, 1918: 28 July
289 Moore, p 251; the identity of the young woman has not yet been established, but it is interesting that on 21 August 1916 Alexandra had received Mrs Victoria Randle, daughter of "black Sally", Sarah Forbes Bonetta, who had once been sponsored by Queen Victoria. Mrs Randle had a daughter, Beatrice, who in 1918 would have been in her 20s. Even if the young

woman was not Beatrice, perhaps there was a connection.

290 RA GV/PRIV/AA37/76, King George V to Queen Alexandra, 1918: 26 August

291 RA GV/PRIV/AA35/20, Queen Alexandra to King George V, 1918: 27 August

292 RA PS/PSO/GV/C/M/1344a/20, DMI to General Poole, 1918: 9 August; 22, Draft telegram from King George V to King Alfonso XIII of Spain, 1918: 14 August; 30, Lord Milner to Lord Stamfordham, 1918: 31 August; 31, Lord Stamfordham to Lord Milner, 1918: 1 September

293 Marchioness of Milford Haven, formerly Princess Victoria of Hesse, eldest sister of the Russian Empress

294 RA GV/PRIV/AA37/77, King George V to Queen Alexandra, 1918: 5 September

295 RA GV/PRIV/AA35/21, Queen Alexandra to King George V, 1918: 12 September

296 RA GV/PRIV/AA35/22, Queen Alexandra to King George V, 1918: 20 September

297 RA GV/PRIV/AA35/21, Queen Alexandra to King George V, 1918: 12 September

298 Annie, née Martin, (c 1862–1934), m Colonel John Harrison (d 1936)

299 Margaret Harrison (1899–1995), violinist

300 Monica Harrison (1897–1983), mezzo-soprano

301 RA QM/PRIV/CC42/132, Queen Alexandra to Queen Mary, 1918: 12 September

302 Captain Hon Neil Primrose (1882–1917), politician and soldier

303 She meant "the Valley of the Shadow of Death" but her version is compelling. She may have remembered Tennyson's *The Charge of the Light Brigade*; "into the Valley of Death rode the six hundred".

304 RA GV/ADD/COPY/140/142, Queen Alexandra to Lord Rosebery, 1918: 26 September

305 RA VIC/ADDU/417, Queen Alexandra to Marquis de Soveral, 1918: 15 October. Lady Alexandra Phyllis Hamilton (1876–1918), her goddaughter, was the Duchess of Abercorn's third child to be lost in the war.

306 Thomas Woodrow Wilson (1856–1924), the 28th American president, m (2) Edith Bolling, née Galt (1872–1961)

307 RA GV/PRIV/AA37/79, King George V to Queen Alexandra, 1918: 27 October

308 Emperor Karl (1887–1922), m Princess Zita of Bourbon-Parma (1892–1989), Empress Zita

309 RA QM/PRIV/CC42/133, Queen Alexandra to Queen Mary, 1918: 5 November

310 RA GV/PRIV/AA35/23, Queen Alexandra to King George V, 1918: 29 October; this was the "Spanish flu"

311 Emperor Karl and Empress Zita of Austria; he abdicated on 13 November 1918

312 Found between the pages of Queen Alexandra's engagement diary for November 1918

313 RA GV/PRIV/AA38/1, King George V to Queen Alexandra, 1918: 3 November

314 RA GV/PRIV/AA35/24, Queen Alexandra to King George V, 1918: 6 November

315 Christine Knowles (1890–1965); in the Second World War she founded and directed the British Prisoners of War Games and Books Fund and the Forget-me-not League

316 Captain Edward George Fairholme (1873–1956), Royal Army Veterinary Corps, secretary of the RSPCA

317 To be supervised by Queen Amélie, the Duchess of Portland (Winifred, née Dallas-Yorke (1863–1954), m 6th Duke of Portland), Mary, née Dawson (1852–1935), m 5th Earl of Ilchester) and Lady Cowans (possibly Eva Mary, née Coulson, m General Sir John Cowans)

318 RA GV/PRIV/AA6/549, Queen Alexandra to Canon and Mrs Dalton, 1918: 11 December

319 Consuelo, née Vanderbilt (1877–1964) 1st wife of 9th Duke of Marlborough

320 Faisal I bin Hussein bin Ali al-Hashemi (1883–1933) later King of Greater Syria and of Iraq

321 Thomas Edward Lawrence (1888–1935), archaeologist, army officer, diplomat and writer; took part in the Arab revolt and the Sinai and Palestine campaign against the Ottoman Empire during the First World War. He used two aliases in later life but is remembered as Lawrence of Arabia.

322 Admiral Sir Somerset Arthur Gough-Calthorpe (1865–1937), commander-in-chief of the Mediterranean fleet in the closing years of the war

323 Commander Charles Edward Turle (1883–1966), mine clearance officer for the Aegean and Black Seas

324 RA PS/PSO/GV/C/M/1344a/35, RH Campbell to Lord Wigram, 1918: 28 September; 47, Vice-Admiral Arthur Calthorpe to King George V, 1918: 23 November, 50, Sir Arthur Davidson to Lord Stamfordham, 1918: 27 November; 51, Lord Stamfordham to Sir Arthur Davidson, 1918: 27 November; 69, Dowager Empress Marie Feodorovna to Queen Alexandra, 1918: 25 December; 76, RE Wemyss to Sir Ronald Graham, 1919: 14 January

325 Honorary Colonel Joseph ("Klondike Joe") Boyle (1867–1923), Canadian adventurer, then businessman and entrepreneur in the UK, undertaking a mission to Russia in 1917 to help reorganise its railway system; he also took part in clandestine operations against German and Bolshevik forces in Bessarabia and SW Russia

Chapter 15

1919–1925

"How I wish he was still with me"

Queen Alexandra, her daughters and grandson returned to Sandringham on 8 January 1919 and on the 12th the Archbishop of Canterbury confirmed Prince George in Sandringham Church. It was foggy and wet at first, but later there were motoring trips. Sadly Johnnie, aged thirteen, died on the 18th after one of his attacks, and was buried on the 21st near his baby uncle, Alexander John. Alexandra, with Victoria and Maud, returned to London the next day and the customary visits, hospitality and receiving Red Cross nurses,[1] resumed, although some things had changed irrevocably. Marie heard that her husband and other Grand Dukes[2] had been shot by the rebels at Petrograd. On 5 February there was a memorial service at St Paul's Cathedral for 14,359 war casualties from the Brigade of Guards. Alexandra, suffering from a bad cold, heard on the 16th that Miss Luckes had died. On the 25th the Queen stood at Marlborough House's gate to welcome the Grenadier Guards home and the next day went to St James's Palace to see Princess Patricia's wedding presents before she married Commander Hon. Alexander Ramsay[3] in Westminster Abbey on the 27th. They had been in love for many years but the Duchess of Connaught, with traditional views, had disapproved of Patricia marrying a commoner who had also been on the Duke's staff in Canada. However, she had died in 1917 and the war had changed everything. This first post-war royal wedding heralded future alliances with British upper-class families instead of foreign royalty; the cruel lesson of divided loyalties in wartime had been learned. Troops came home, while hospital visits and charity shows, still raising money for deserving causes like the East London Children's Hospital claimed Alexandra's attention. Queen Marie of Roumania and two of her daughters called on 13 March.[4] On 1 April, Prince Waldemar and his daughter came to stay; Queen Amélie and Marie[5] remained welcome guests. Minny was still refusing to leave Russia but George had sent *HMS Marlborough* to fetch her.

On 9 April Alexandra received Baroness Isa Buxhoeveden,[6] who had just returned from Siberia. On the same day, George sent her a note; Minny and family were "actually on a British ship coming over here! but the simple thought of her feeling[s] on being obliged to leave her beloved country, which she loved so truly, breaks my heart! as I know <u>what</u> <u>that</u> will <u>cost her</u> & how miserable she must feel! ... Of course she must come here to me – but how am I to hear anything of her or about it all! To whom & where to cld I teleg[raph]? Please tell the Admiral that they must come straight here first. Are you quite <u>sure</u> they are all on board & off already – please let me hear [anything] as I feel so terribly anxious about it all."[7] Alexandra could hardly take in the wonderful news, but her many occupations helped her keep calm. On the 11th she visited Nurse Cavell's Home at London Hospital, where a Danish deputation presented a cheque for £7,000 to fund a bed. Alexandra thanked them in English and Danish, and gave them two framed pictures of herself for their club. She told Knutsford how glad she was that "my poor little speech of thanks to you & all there present" was audible.[8] By the 12th, HMS *Marlborough* had arrived safely at Constantinople and Minny telegraphed that all was well, although it had been heartbreaking to leave Russia.[9] Alexandra continued duties and events as usual, standing outside Buckingham Palace's gate on 25 April as 5,000 Anzacs marched past. On the 24th she had heard of the Comtesse de Paris's death in Spain but many other friends and relatives were now visiting her. Finally, Minny and her suite arrived on 9 May at Portsmouth, where Alexandra and Victoria met them.

Crying over spilt milk and mopping it up takes much longer than spilling it. So it was with the First World War; cleaning up the war zones at home and abroad was a monstrous task that some might say was never completed. There was overwhelming gratitude that fighting was over, although traces of the war were everywhere. Returning combatants were simply glad to be alive, although some had severe after-effects. In May Alexandra attended four memorial services; on the 14th at St Paul's Cathedral for 18,957 railwaymen; on the 15th at Westminster Abbey for Edith Cavell; on the 17th at the Abbey for 350 members of the police force; and again on the 24th for the colonial troops. On 13 June there was another at St Paul's for 57,000 sailors. There were more obsequies but the war's legacy persisted. The epidemic, "Spanish Flu", perhaps brought back by the troops, was killing thousands, many of them young.[10] Returning ex-servicemen, resuming their pre-war employment, found that women, who had done their work in 1914–1918, could potentially be on the job market too. The "land fit for heroes" had been severely battered; most families had lost someone, or knew someone who had been killed; air raids had caused shock, damage and death. Extreme political views, albeit among a minority, had been encouraged by the Bolsheviks' success in Russia.

There were compensations; for Alexandra the reopening of the Covent Garden Opera season, with *Carmen*, which she saw on 12 May, or a visit to the Amateur Artists' exhibition at Carlton House Terrace on the 19th. Best of all, she could take motor drives with Minny, trying to recuperate at Marlborough House after two years of insecurity and fear. There were visits from family and friends; Red Cross nurses to meet; theatres, concerts, exhibitions and Chelsea Flower

Show to attend. There was also a new, interesting diversion; the success of air power during the war was encouraging peacetime aviation and now Hawker and Grieve[11] were attempting to fly across the Atlantic. The plane came down in the sea but they were rescued by a Danish ship and arrived in London on 27 May, to be received by Alexandra three days later. When Alcock and Brown[12] made another attempt on 14 June, crossing the Atlantic non-stop from Newfoundland to Ireland in 16 hours, she received them too, on the 20th. She was intrigued by aviation and motored to Hendon on the 21st to see Captain Gathergood[13] win the Aerial Derby Aeroplane Race, flying the 190-mile course in 87 minutes. Generally she was carrying out more traditional duties. On 22 May a deputation from the Grocers' Association presented £10,000 to build a convalescent home at Brighton for St Dunstan's patients. Writing to Knutsford, Alexandra mentioned "yr interview with Mr Brown about his new invention of sound … and I do hope you are feeling happier about it. Oh if they only cld help poor suffering creatures, as no one can understand what has to be gone through & suffered in silence!!"[14] If this was an invention to help deaf people, she spoke from bitter personal experience. On 29 May she and Minny went to a Russian bazaar. After meeting Hawker and Grieve, they motored alone to Sandringham but returned in time for Trooping the Colour on 3 June in Hyde Park. On the 5th the Queen presented the "Silver Thimble Fund's" cheque for £10,000 to the Dreadnought Hospital for Seamen, of which the Marquess of Milford Haven[15] was president, at Greenwich. She attended a march past of 20,000 special constables and reserve police force at Buckingham Palace on 14 June and on the 15th a service for the Dannebrog's[16] 700th Anniversary at St Clement Danes Church must have pleased her particularly. On the 28th the peace treaty was signed at Versailles, officially ending the war and Alexandra watched from the garden terrace as peace was proclaimed in Friary Court. On 6 July[17] a solemn state thanksgiving service for peace was held at St Paul's Cathedral.

Accounts of the Russian Imperial Family's last days were arriving. On 4 July Stamfordham wrote that the King had read Colonel Robertson's despatch with horror.[18] He had heeded popular opinion and stopped them coming to England, but never could have imagined his poor cousins would suffer such a fate. Circumstances arising from the war had demanded cruel sacrifices, but functions relating to it continued. On 9 July Queen Alexandra's Hostel for Discharged Soldiers and Sailors was opened at Gifford House, Roehampton and on the 15th Alexandra saw an exhibition of war memorials at the Victoria and Albert Museum. On the 17th she attended a service dedicating the new bells at St Clement Danes. There was a peace celebration outside Buckingham Palace; a march past the King in his pavilion at Queen Victoria's Memorial, fireworks and a bonfire, on the 19th. Alexandra received General Maitland and Captain Scott[19] who, in an R34 Airship, had cruised from England to New York and back. She saw the Russian ballet at the Alhambra on 28 July and a cinema show and thought-reading performance at Marlborough House on the 30th, recalling her pre-war entertainments. Elsewhere there were constant celebrations of peace. On the 29th at the Mansion House, the King received an address on the conclusion of peace. On 4 August, five years since war was declared, a great water pageant was held on the Thames from Westminster to Chelsea; Queen Alexandra and Princess Victoria were with the King in his state barge. England seemed punch-drunk on peace and, not surprisingly, there would soon be a reaction.

On 13 August Alexandra, Minny and Waldemar motored to Farnborough to see Empress Eugénie and the next day all members of the Russian Imperial Family then in London were invited to a film show in Marlborough House's dining room. This marked Minny's departure for Denmark on the 16th, although some of her family stayed behind. When the court left for Balmoral on the 18th, Alexandra motored, entertained and paid calls before going on the 29th to Sandringham, where the hot weather made it more comfortable to spend most afternoons near the sea, although even there it felt airless. She told May; "The little Cross on our beloved little Johnnie's grave is very pretty, & our two darling Johnnies lie peacefully side by side."[20] On the 11th she called, as usual, on the Wolfe sisters who, after 20 years in England, were leaving for America, with pensions for their services at the technical school.[21] The girls' school may then have closed[22] but the carving school continued until 1957, producing bespoke small items of furniture for Sandringham House, shops, exhibitions and the new royal apartments for Kempton Park Race Course in 1933.

Queen Alexandra was still feeling "so low & depressed, & bodily weary! And during the last week we have had the most <u>fearfully</u> hot days I ever remember here or anywhere; walking was impossible, & even sitting out was killing; the only cool place was the hall with every window open, in the whole House." Luckily the harvest had been good and everyone seemed well and happy. But Lord Charles Beresford had died suddenly on the 6th; "that bright and cheery Charlie ... has gone forever!" Alexandra was glad they had seen a lot of Louise while in Scotland, and delighted with letters from her grandchildren, while rather surprised – or perhaps quietly amused – at something Princess Mary had been allowed to do. "And so you let Mary go off by <u>herself</u>!! to see & take leave of her Regiment. I wonder <u>you</u> approve of that! as <u>Papa</u> was always so very particular about letting the Sisters [do] anything of that sort, <u>quite</u> by <u>themselves</u>. He never <u>wld allow</u> anything of that sort! The boys of course are different, but to let girls get in the habit of this sort wld end by making them so very independent etc, etc! Excuse this dreadful scrawl but the heat is killing me!"[23] King Edward held old-fashioned views; Alexandra's emphatic assertion may indicate agreement – or amusement. She herself had always had an independent spirit, when she got the chance, while being mindful of propriety and the need to look after young girls. George failed to comment; she responded, "So you did not deign to take any notice of my remarks about little Mary! Never mind, I meant it kindly anyhow."[24] Times were changing; Mary was 22 and within ten years women that age had the vote. Some women over 30 already had it.

Alexandra was extremely concerned about the state of the country "such terrible unrest in every corner & strikes going on right & left. I see Mr Balfour has at last returned from Paris! if only he had been able to bring <u>real</u> <u>Peace</u> with him. Everything with the Allies & the brutal Huns is still far from settled."[25] George suggested having a friend to stay and trying not to be depressed as it was bad for her; he could not give her the longed-for reassurance about peace.

The railway strike which had begun on 27 September was causing difficulty at Sandringham; they were "entirely cut off from the rest of the world & get neither papers or letters – too bad really, but the whole world seems to have gone bad & mad, and we must all try & have patience a little longer, when people will come to their senses once more & gradually will settle down & see how useless this is. Some people think they are being stirred up to make a revolution <u>all</u> over the Country, but I do not think so myself. Anyhow it is all very unpleasant & disagreeable & makes me furious to think what all <u>Foreigners</u> will say about <u>England</u> at this moment too!! when the whole world is still so upset & unsettled. I only hope things may soon get better." Davidson had come back last night and was "in such a state at my being alone here just now, but there is nothing whatever to fear, everybody is quiet here; simply we are cut off from the rest of the world."[26] Davidson shared Edward VII's view that women needed protection. A woman was considered to be "alone" if she had no husband, adult male relative or other responsible man with her; it made no difference if she was with her daughter, other women or servants. Davidson, especially in view of his feelings for Victoria, would have seen himself as the responsible man. Even Alexandra, (and indeed Queen Victoria) could describe herself as "alone" because her husband was dead, irrespective of the houseful of people living alongside her.

She continued as usual; tea outdoors, local visits and, on the 24th and the 29th, Women's Institute meetings in the parish room at West Newton. On 6 October the railway strike ended and on the 25th the King gave a dinner in the stable yard to 450 demobilised soldiers on the estate. There was a new anxiety; Germany wanted to keep Flensborg, in Schleswig, as a base for its new fleet. Horrified, Alexandra begged George to put a stop to it "Do look at the map & see <u>what</u> a <u>gain</u> Flensborg means to that vile nation – think it well over ... Let us <u>here</u> in <u>England</u> remember <u>what</u> we lost by giving up Helgoland."[27] If the King commented on this he must have done so verbally, as there are no reassuring letters. Nevertheless, her fear of a future German threat was not unjustified.

The weather was dreadful, poor Victoria had had bad toothache and Alexandra was suffering from "terrible noises in my poor old head which nearly drives me mad & nothing seems to stop that <u>terrible</u> ordeal!"[28] May found her greatly changed; "She looks so frail, the deafness is awful!"[29] She remained at Sandringham and on 11 November the first anniversary of the Armistice was marked, as proclaimed by the King throughout the Empire, by a silence of two minutes for praise and prayer. The next day Alexandra telegraphed to the editor of the *Daily Mail*; "We all pray that God will hear our silent prayers in remembrance of all our brave departed who laid down their precious lives on the battlefield."[30] The two minutes' silence and the telegram were intended to calm an unsettled population, reminding them of what had been lost and prompting quiet reflection. Queen Maud celebrated her 50th birthday at Appleton on 26 November and three days later, with her mother and sister, went to London. Here Alexandra received more visitors, called on friends and relatives and, by 18 December, had met over 200 Red Cross nurses. She left for Sandringham on the 20th for her first Christmas there since 1913, in the old style, with Christmas tables in the ballroom on the 24th, Church, Holy Communion, dinner for 24 on Christmas Day and on the 30th a tree with over 700 presents for the servants and people on the estate.

They came to London on 13 January 1920 and the next day Maud and Olaf went home. Alexandra saw David and, after receptions and visits, returned to Sandringham on the 28th. Another old friend and household member had died and she sent a wreath for the memorial service on 3 February in the Chapel Royal, St James's; "In loving memory of my beloved Lady Katherine Coke,[31] whose loss we all so deeply deplore, from her old friend Alexandra. Now comes rest." Queen Mary, despite having known "Lady Katty", her mother's friend, all her life, just put "Mary R" on her own wreath.[32] Nothing shows more clearly the temperamental difference between the two Queens.

On 16 February Alexandra returned to her usual London life; dozens of Red Cross nurses, weddings, christenings, church services, exhibitions, bazaars and relatives. David, about to leave for New Zealand and Australia, lunched with her on 15 March. On St Patrick's Day[33] at Chelsea Barracks, Alexandra presented the shamrock to all ranks of the Irish Guards, an annual ceremony which she is credited with starting and which became a tradition. Also, at a short ceremony in St Martin's Place, she unveiled a statue of Edith Cavell.[34] On 16 April it was the Royal Drawing Society's exhibition of the King Edward VII Memorial Collection of Natural Drawing, at the Guildhall Art Gallery. She attended Lady Dorothy Cavendish's wedding to Harold Macmillan[35] at St Margaret's Church, Westminster on the 21st. Lord Fisher had been ill; she hoped he would soon feel "your old, strong, splendid old self again! Please let me hear how you are getting on, as I never forget our precious old Admiral Fisher."[36]

Mary's 23rd birthday was on 25 April; Alexandra wanted to see her and the others at Windsor and drove there for lunch, but was overcome by "some fearful attacks of coughing" on the way. At home that evening she felt "very bad – I must have burst something in my good eye." Hardly able to see, she managed to tell George; "everything is crooked. Newspapers I cannot see a word of, so you can imagine my despair"[37] Victoria was very worried; "it is so sad to see her so very low & depressed & not being able to read is a terrible deprivation to her."[38] "My good eye" implies that the other one was not so good,[39] and now "poor old blind & deaf old loving Motherdear", was unable to enjoy many of her occupations, although she did have a lot of visitors, particularly the King and Queen, and by 12 May managed to receive about twenty Red Cross nurses. To stem public concern, *The Times* reported that "Queen Alexandra has been suffering from a severe bronchial attack, which is now subsiding. During a violent attack of coughing, a small blood vessel burst in one of the Queen's eyes, which has, of necessity, caused a troublesome impairment of vision. It is hoped that with care and rest this inconvenience will pass away, but in the meantime her Majesty's engagements must be to some extent dependent upon the progress made."[40] She began going out, went to church and met more Red Cross nurses, but Alexandra Rose Day on 23 June was beyond her and she asked Louise and Victoria to go instead, which they did; "It was a nightmare, that drive without Her, but as she wished it I hardened my heart & thoughts and did it" wrote Victoria.[41]

Davidson had been very busy. On 8 June he told the King he had seen Colonel Rodzianko,[42] attached to General Knox's[43] military mission and recently back from Russia. He and General Dietrichs[44] were investigating the Imperial Family's murder and the story was appalling. Among other things, the Bolsheviks had apparently tried to force the Emperor to sign the Brest–Litovsk Treaty with Germany by threatening to kill the Tsesarevitch. Calling their bluff, Nicholas bravely refused to have anything to do with it; eventually they gave up.[45] Another matter was Sir Sidney Lee's biography of King Edward. Despite the past, Davidson thought it was time to treat him as a friend and Ponsonby agreed to start the ball rolling. Lee was to have access to documents from the archives at Windsor and his proofs were to be submitted to Ponsonby and Lord Morley. Lord Hardinge of Penshurst had promised to help and Davidson had a friendly interview with Lee on 29 July. On the same day Davidson told Messrs Coutts that the treasury lords under their statutory powers had decided to exempt 5/7ths of Queen Alexandra's annual pension of £70,000 from taxation, taking effect from 1 April 1919.[46] A refund of the previous year's excess payment was now due, but it was needed at once, as £16,500 was required to reimburse the King and Princess Victoria, pay the staff (including extra bonuses and wages) and settle the Daimler Motor Company's repairs bill.

The King and Queen had gone to Holyrood in early July and George told his mother what he was doing. He had laid the foundation stone of Edinburgh

University's new buildings; it was pouring with rain and cold enough for a fire in his room. At an afternoon reception they had shaken hands with over 1,100 people, and also held an Investiture. David, still abroad, had narrowly escaped injury on the railway.[47] George wrote again[48] from London; by now Alexandra had returned to Sandringham, still not up to writing. Later, from Balmoral, he sent the latest news, which looked grim everywhere. The Mayor of Cork[49] had been arrested and things in Ireland were very bad. The Poles had driven the Bolsheviks out of Poland but still had to make peace with Russia. At home, the miners' leader, Mr Smillie,[50] was threatening a strike. Some articles had appeared in The Times about the Romanovs' fate; "it is very sad reading but I fear it is all true."[51] He sent Alexandra "a bit of white heather for luck which I picked on the hill". It looked as though everyone was going to need it.

This time she responded the next day, cheered by the letter and the "lovely white heather". She would have written sooner to him and May, who had also sent her a kind letter, but "Today for the first time I feel more like myself so hurry off at once to write these few words to tell you how much I appreciate every kind word from either of you." She supported his views about the Mayor of Cork ("go on insisting upon his release before it is too late") and hoped the Poles would now stop fighting "& stick to their own country & we & the Allies support them in this." She also sent up a prayer for "real peace in the world soon! and here in our own beloved country too, where Mr Smillie tries to upset everything." She remembered fondly her visits to Balmoral and was glad Probyn was well and happy in semi-retirement at Birkhall. But she had been horrified by The Times articles "about Russia & our poor beloved excellent Nicky & poor dear Alicky & their charming family ... and today the whole account of their cruel & awful murder is told! ... and to think of what they must have gone through and suffered makes me quite miserable ... I loved them all! I do hope to God that my beloved Minny will not read these horrors! She luckily does not keep The Times!"[52] Minny had steadfastly denied that her son and his family had been killed and insisted they were in hiding somewhere safe. She declined to be disabused of this forlorn hope. Alexandra thus had the pain of knowing the truth but being unable to discuss it with her sister.

Her eye was recovering; George wrote that her letter had been "so beautifully written, the lines quite straight & I could read every word, which shows how much better your eyes are; I am so glad also that you feel better, more like yourself again."[53] Her finances were also improving, although on the 30th Probyn calculated that the whole deficit was £20,000 and really the only answer was to get another remission from the treasury. If the tax-free amount were increased to £64,000, and the tax due reduced to approximately £11,000, there would be some hope of a solution.[54] On 9 October Alexandra came up to London and, two days later, was among those who greeted David at Victoria Station on his return from Australia, New Zealand and British territories in the

Pacific and West Indies. After receiving some Red Cross nurses on the 12th she returned to Sandringham on the 16th and the next day, with George, May and other relatives, attended the dedication of King Edward's completed memorial in Sandringham Church and the unveiling and dedication of a memorial cross erected by King George in memory of the 77 men from the estate who had died in the war.

The Dowager Duchess of Coburg and the young King of the Hellenes[55] both died on 25 October. Alexander had been made King by the Greek government, which would not accept his father, Constantine, or elder brother, George, Duke of Sparta;[56] he died of septicaemia after being bitten by a monkey. As for the Dowager Duchess, King George had always been fond of Aunt Marie, who had been kind to him in his youth but "she had a lot of sorrow lately & had been unwell for a long time."[57] Alexandra was surprised that court mourning had not been ordered for her but George had "thought the matter over very carefully & came to the conclusion that it would have been difficult to have called her the Duchess of Coburg just at this moment. Of course she was my aunt & once had been Duchess of Edinburgh, but by law she was a German subject. Of course we the family will wear mourning for her. And now the Court is in mourning for poor Alexander of Greece so it really comes to the same thing. I hope you are not annoyed with me, but it was a difficult question to settle. You know how fond I was of her, so it was not because I did not want to show all respect for her memory."[58] The war still overshadowed their private grief.

The elections after Alexander's death complicated Greek affairs but it seemed unlikely that Constantine would be allowed to return, as he was still wrongly considered a traitor to his country and the Allies. George was "very sorry for him but he has played his cards badly I fear."[59] On 8 November Queen Alexandra returned to London and on the morning of the 11th attended the King's unveiling of the Cenotaph in Whitehall, and was later present at the burial of "An Unknown Warrior" in Westminster Abbey. After a weekend at Sandringham she returned on the 30th to greet the Danish sovereigns at Victoria Station on a state visit. On her 76th birthday she received eighteen relatives and friends and even more callers over the next three weeks. Returning on 20 December, she spent Christmas at Sandringham with her family, including "the Norwegian three".[60]

❦

On 5 January 1921 some tableaux were performed at the Club at Dersingham; Alexandra also attended George's shooting luncheon on the 7th at the back of the kitchen garden, and meets of the hounds at Congham and Grimston. On the 22nd she presented a prize to Dorothy Woollstoncroft, chosen by the pupils of the Lynn High School for Girls,[61] attended a Women's Institute party at West Newton on the 27th and soon afterwards gave presents to schoolchildren at West

Newton and Wolferton. She had caught a cold, which became a cough, and had to stay indoors until 22 February. George and May had returned to London on the 7th and George assured her; "Our weather here has been cloudy & dark & there has been East wind. It is certainly much better for you to remain quietly in the country; London is no place to be in, in February, where you would only be worried by people wishing to see you."[62] Alexandra replied the next day, sad at being "cut off from you all" and feeling "worse every day. I begin to think it is softening of the brain, as I feel such an utter fool & up to nothing ... Thank God Victoria is much better the last few days & has been out today ... I do hope you are not doing too much which is also bad for you my dear."[63] She was surprised at their having lunch with Aunt Helena ("You never did that before!") who had the Ramsays'[64] baby son staying with her while his parents were away. Ireland's and Greece's difficulties, Lord Farquhar's serious operation, and the sad death of Lord Ranksborough[65] were all upsetting her.

Victoria was still not really well and Alexandra had a bad headache. She had also heard from Minny, who had been under severe strain for so long and whose heart trouble had finally caught up with her; "alas [she] is still very <u>weak</u> & not able to do anything ... I fear it will be a long time before she will get over this terrible attack (of heart)."[66] Thankfully, her two daughters were with her; Alexandra was miserable at being so far away but confessed to Soveral that she no longer had the courage or the desire to travel so far or to go on journeys.[67] She begged her son to do all he could for Greece and Constantine "who has been so infamously treated by the world ... Don't let <u>England</u> <u>forget</u> that we put my excellent <u>brother</u> on the Greek throne and the only cause of dear <u>honest</u> <u>Tino's</u> <u>present</u> awkward position is simply & solely his having married poor dear Sophie – the <u>sister</u> of that ass William. Point it out plainly to all our Ministers & tell them, from me if you like, that I know for <u>certain</u> that Papa wld have <u>insisted</u> upon our <u>duty</u> being carried out concerning Greece & its future. So please promise me to do everything possible in this very important question."[68] George replied tactfully, "The Conference to try & settle the Near East is still sitting & I am sure that everything that is fair & just will be done both by Greece & Turkey, but it is a very difficult question to settle & will take some little time." The reparations conference was starting the next day and "it will be by no means easy to settle how much Germany has got to pay."[69] On 6 March he told her; "The Germans were very foolish at the conference the first day & everyone was furious with them, but I think you will see that they will be more reasonable when they meet tomorrow. The Greeks are very obstinate & have refused the Allies' proposal, while the Turks have accepted it. It is no good putting yourself in the wrong. The only alternative is that they must go on fighting the Turks until one side wins or becomes exhausted, but it will take a long time & in meantime their country will be ruined."[70] He sent home news on the 13th; Sandringham Church needed a new roof, which would be expensive and would take until August to finish.[71] Meanwhile Bertie, in Belgium, had written to his grandmother from Laeken. She replied on the 15th; Laeken had been "that very place where I was <u>engaged</u> to marry yr Grandpapa! We were walking together in the pretty garden, following my Mother & the late Queen of the Belgians, when he suddenly proposed to me! My <u>surprise</u> was great & I accepted him with <u>greatest</u> delight! I hope you enjoyed yr stay there & that the Court or the life there was not very stiff & formal."[72]

On 16 March a treasury minute stated that, after consideration, it had been decided to increase the tax-free part of Alexandra's income from £50,000 to £64,000.[73] Her total net annual income would thus amount to approximately £75,000. Satisfactory as this was, it raises questions. If it was impossible to allow her more money without passing an Act of Parliament during the war, why was it apparently so easy in 1921? Could there not have been a treasury minute in 1915 or earlier? Apparently through fear of anti-Royal agitation, the government had been taking as much money as possible from Alexandra towards the war effort, while she was draining what was left of her own personal resources for the same cause. Meanwhile, Messrs Coutts continued to make regular payments on her behalf to some 60 charities and a few individuals for the rest of her life.

One problem was solved but another emerged; the 19th Hussars Regiment, of which Alexandra was honorary colonel, was to be disbanded. She was deeply upset. It was a famous Regiment which had fought in the Boer War as well as the Great War; most importantly, "it was given to me by yr Father & I say straight out I will <u>never consent</u> to it & I <u>beg you</u> to <u>support</u> me in this … Please use all yr influence at once … as I am <u>very old now</u>, so they can wait till after my death, and I shall always look upon this while I am alive as a personal insult & particularly as it was beloved Papa who gave it to me! I am sure you can understand my feelings about it & <u>will insist</u> upon my keeping it as long as I live."[74] Sadly, George told her he could do nothing; the three junior cavalry regiments, including the 19th, were to be disbanded through economic necessity, "but if you would allow it, I should be delighted to make you Colonel of another Cavalry regiment, which I hope you will agree to."[75] No, she replied, "I can <u>never</u> accept a new after having been robbed of this dear old one, given me by Papa & of which I was so proud, & they distinguished themselves so splendidly during this last terrible war." Apropos the coal strike, just begun; "I fear we will soon see the whole beloved country in a state of Revolution as it has already begun in dear old Ireland."[76] George agreed; "This strike of the miners is criminal, just when things were getting a little better, probably all racing will be stopped & less trains will run & coal, food & petrol may have to be rationed again, it is really shameful & will do an awful lot of harm & one can never tell where or when it will stop."[77] Two days later; "On Friday the Railwaymen & Transport workers informed us that they were also going to strike on Tuesday next, so I at once decided to return to London & we all came up yesterday morning. There is no doubt that we are passing through as grave a crisis as this country has ever had. All the troops have been called out, Kensington Gardens are full [of] them, they have come from Aldershot & the Government have made all their preparations for distributing food &ct, & the public are entirely with the Govt., so perhaps these delightful people who want a revolution will come to their senses before it is too late and give in."[78] The railway and transport workers decided not to strike after all, but the miners were determined, despite public opposition, to go ahead.

Alexandra agreed; "We are indeed going through dreadful & anxious times now, but still hope & trust the strikers will open their eyes & come to their senses before too late & before causing such a dreaded Calamity to the whole Country, which means a revolution. It is all so <u>unlike</u> English people, and one can hardly believe that miners wish to follow those terrible Bolsheviks' example. I wish you could hold a meeting and speak out yr mind to them & what they owe to their Country. I think that wld have a splendid effect and quiet them all … What a terrible time you yrself must have [had] and are going through still about it all. The whole world is topsy turvey at this moment wherever we look & Peace on Earth seems still very far off." But something else had happened; Augusta Victoria, William II's wife, had died. Alexandra wrote; "The poor Empress' death was very sad indeed poor woman, what she must have gone through & suffered besides! She will be a terrible loss to him particularly now in his loneliness & exile! did you telegraph to him? or not – if you do, I will do the same, otherwise not. His only daughter & her husband, my sister Thyra's son, are still with him."[79] All her rancour had been replaced by pity for the sick Empress and the sad, widowed Emperor. The King agreed; "It was a happy release for the poor Empress, as she must have suffered a great deal these last years, he will be terribly lonely now she has gone." He was more cheerful about Britain's state, having attended a football match "at which there were 73,000 people; at the end they sang the National Anthem & cheered tremendously, there were no bolshevists there, at least I never saw any. The country is all right, just a few extremists are doing all the harm."[80] The strike continued, however, despite causing hardship to the country and the miners themselves. Coal was being imported but the miners had no money and thousands of others were unemployed because most of Britain's industries had stopped.

May wrote sympathetically; Alexandra had told her how tired she was and how she could not do as much as she would like. "I fear, as you rightly say, that your age is beginning to tell on you, but you have always been so wonderful all your life & so energetic & looked so <u>young</u>, that one scarcely believes you really are <u>76</u>."[81] Alexandra was planning to return to London but could not yet predict when, "as unfortunately I do not feel well yet & <u>always</u> so dreadfully <u>tired</u> & <u>idiotic</u>!!"[82] The weather at Sandringham was lovely, the leaves green and the flowers blooming; it was easier to stay there and she enjoyed motoring, paying calls, having tea at the Bungalow and receiving visitors. After all, her son kept her in touch with news from London; the Japanese crown prince's[83] state visit had gone off well, although he spoke no English; the strike was still on; there were problems in Poland; and David was in the Scilly Isles, after a successful West Country tour. When Alexandra did return to London, on 24 May, she found plenty to do; attending the Royal Tournament at Olympia on the 26th and taking the salute at the Empire Day Parade on the Guards' Parade Ground in Hyde Park two days later. Trooping the Colour took place at Horse Guards on 4 June. There were also visits and guests, concerts, private views, Richmond Horse Show and the International Polo Match at Hurlingham, where the home team was beaten by the Americans by 11 goals to 4. Alexandra went to see the Unknown Warrior's grave at Westminster Abbey on the 16th. Then on 22 June, inevitably, there was Alexandra Rose Day. She drove for an hour and a quarter, acclaimed by an enormous crowd, who were delighted to see her again after her absence in 1920. £38,667 was collected, £3,000 more than in 1920, which, considering the industrial unrest and unemployment, was splendid. Alexandra was now going out every day; her energy had returned. If not driving, visiting friends or galleries, she was attending a polo match at Ranelagh with David (on the 29th), watching George present new colours to the Grenadiers, Coldstream and Scots Guards at Horse Guards and, on the same day (2 July) motoring to Hendon to see the air pageant. With her family, she received the Belgian king and queen at Victoria Station on 4 July. At 12 o'clock on the 6th she opened the nurses' bazaar at the London Hospital but, as it was also Victoria's 53rd birthday, she gave her a garden party, with over 200 adult and child guests. The next day, she, her daughters and Maudie went to the Queen's Hall to see the Russian dancer, Anna Pavlova.[84]

On "France's Day" (14 July) Alexandra laid a wreath at the Cenotaph and later went to Ivy Titchfield's[85] sale of articles in aid of disabled soldiers; charity events connected with the war continued. Now she was playing her full part as a senior member of the Royal Family; on the 16th she received a deputation of 40 Danes, on the 20th she met the Canadian prime minister[86] and his wife, as well as Sir Ernest Shackleton.[87] On the 21st she received the French, German, American and Brazilian ambassadors, with their wives, as well as the Belgian and Italian Ambassadors. She had been touched by a letter from Miss Acland, including, as Charlotte Knollys wrote, "all the kind things you say about her beloved husband." Charlotte herself had "always thought that hitherto all his great and good qualities have never been adequately recognised and dwelt upon." Now Lee's articles about King Edward were repairing the omission "and rejoicing the hearts of his innumerable friends."[88] London was hot and stuffy and people were leaving; Probyn for Scotland on 26 July, Louise and Maudie for Scotland on 5 August, Victoria for Harrogate on the 10th and May for Balmoral on the 19th. Alexandra still had a few lunch guests before going to Sandringham but on the 13th had bad toothache. Her dentist, Sir Francis Farmer,[89] called eight times before the problem was resolved. Ready to leave at last on the 23rd, with the motor waiting at the door, her departure was prevented by a sudden violent thunderstorm. She went by train the next day.

News was received on 28 August of the death of M Castenskîjold, the Danish minister, on his 59th birthday and two days later the sub dean of the Chapels Royal, Canon Edgar Sheppard, died of a stroke in the cloisters at Windsor Castle. Alexandra was "so <u>dreadfully</u> & deeply affected by the sudden loss of <u>two</u> of our dear old friends", whom she would greatly miss.[90] She hoped Mrs Sheppard[91] would be allowed to keep the rooms in St James's Palace which King Edward had allocated to the Canon; George reassured her.[92] Alexandra was feeling unwell, with an irritating cough and dental trouble and was longing for Victoria to come home, but she planned to visit Violet Vivian in Wales after leaving Harrogate, so her return date was uncertain. But there was one bright spot: "the <u>only</u> one of the family who ever writes to me is darling <u>Georgie</u>! & such interesting charming letters during his sail & cruise in his ship which I appreciate greatly." She finished her letter light-heartedly: "And now … I must tear myself away again & go to the seaside for tea & fresh air."[93] Probyn wrote to Davidson on the 13th from Birkhall, glad Princess Victoria was having a happy time at Glyn; "I wish you could be there too. But I quite understand your declining the invite."[94] Meanwhile, Lee had been studying archives and negotiating with publishers, despite heart trouble.[95]

The Marquess of Milford Haven died in London on 11 September and King Edward's old friend, Sir Ernest Cassel,[96] on the 22nd.[97] Miss Adams[98] died at Marlborough House, after a long illness, on the 27th. There was serious trouble in Ireland and once again, King Constantine's fate was distressing Alexandra, who continued to insist it was England's duty to support him. Alas, there was nothing he could do, George patiently explained to her, several times. She had not seen Queen Olga since 1914 but now she was at Brussels, having been ill and undergone a serious operation in Paris. Alexandra had always been fond of her and wanted to see her. Mary and David had written to their grandmother, "so I suppose you told them that I regretted never to hear from them. Well I was <u>delighted</u> & thank you very much for having told them. One appreciates letters from one's dear ones doubly, when quite alone"[99] Alexandra told her son. Things were improving. On 25 September Alexandra attended the consecration[100] of an altar cross given by her, and other gifts given by the King and Queen, at Sandringham Church, which now had a new roof. On 4 October, to her mother's great relief, Victoria returned after six weeks. Four days later there was a parade of Boy Scouts in the park, and a service on the 16th prior to David's departure for India on the 26th. On the 18th, to Alexandra's delight, Queen Olga, with Grand Duchess George and Mademoiselle Baltazzi, finally arrived for ten days, but on a strictly private visit, which for political reasons was not reported in the press and neither was Olga photographed.[101] Maud had arrived on the 10th and regularly visited her mother. May had decided it would be a good idea to start planning early for Christmas and suggested this to Alexandra, who replied on 24 October; "I wanted to thank you for yr dear letter asking me about our joint Xmas presents for our people here. Yes certainly I quite agree with you to have them chosen now in time to be all settled before Xmas. I do wish our darling David a happy prosperous journey to India and may God keep him in His blessed keeping during his long visit there."[102]

Alexandra returned to London with her daughters on 24 November; they celebrated Maud's 52nd birthday on the 26th with a large family lunch, tea and dancing by Madame Kauner in the dining room, but Alexandra had caught another cold. George was sure "you will soon be well again if you remain in one temperature for a day or two. You must be well by Thursday as we all want to come & see you on your birthday. Please don't smoke so much, it only makes you cough."[103] They did come, but her cold kept her indoors until 17 December, although she ventured out on the 14th to see the procession going to the Opening of Parliament. Haakon VII and Olaf arrived in England on the 20th and, with Maud and Victoria, accompanied Alexandra back to Sandringham for Christmas.

New Year, 1922, was celebrated with a film show, *Fresh Air, The Kid* and *The Runaway Train*, for 400 people on 2 January, and a ball for 400 servants and tenants the next day, although the housemaid Priscilla Hall's[104] death on the 6th was a grim augury of the coming year. However, Princess Mary was now engaged to Viscount Lascelles[105] and on the 16th the King introduced him to his future grandmother-in-law. Alexandra made her usual benefactions to the schoolchildren; Christmas presents locally on the 18th and the 20th and chocolate for the Dersingham children on the 27th. Probyn, still not fully retired, was 89 on the 21st. Alexandra had sent a Christmas present and letter to the Daltons; "It seems such ages since we met, but my thoughts are very often with you and <u>here</u> I always miss you very <u>much</u> and the happy old days gone by alas for ever. I very often go into yr & the dear boys' rooms here, when all those happy days seem to revive in my memory."[106]

As usual, the Queen attended meets of the foxhounds on 9 January and the 30th, when news came of Shackleton's death on board the *Quest* in the South Sea; Alexandra had met him several times and was interested in his exploits and discoveries. On 1 February Charlotte Knollys's sister, Mirabel Grey[107] died at Cannes. Alexandra called on neighbours and tenants, motored and attended church. The dress code for Mary's wedding was issued; Alexandra was "glad we are going to wear high gowns for the wedding, as a low frock in this extra cold winter weather wld have been very disagreeable. I am coming up on the 15th about 4 o'clock – should you be disengaged about tea time may we look in then and I am so anxious to see some of darling Mary's numerous wedding presents … Poor Colonel Davidson is still quite shut up & mostly in bed with a very bad cough still, which frightens me; he looks so ill & suffering, he is obliged to remain here till he is able to walk & stronger. I have sent for a nurse from London, when we leave."[108] Returning to London with Victoria on the 15th, Alexandra gave the King, Queen and bridal couple lunch on the 19th and later went to see the presents at St James's Palace. Lady Feodora Gleichen[109] died on the 22nd.

Princess Mary and Lord Lascelles were married in Westminster Abbey on 28 February, amid great public enthusiasm; although some years older than her, he was British. It must have been a bitter-sweet occasion for Princess Victoria, with her own would-be British groom lying ill at Sandringham. She endured this while her mother visited the Ideal Home Exhibition at Olympia on 1 March, the pony show at the Agricultural Hall on the 3rd and had another look at Mary's presents on the 5th. Then Victoria could bear her absence from Davidson, now dangerously ill, no longer. She impulsively made a request which rather startled her mother but they motored to Sandringham on 6 March. As Alexandra told George on the 10th; "We are still here as poor dear Davidson is still so ill & I think it has quite revived him seeing us all, as he was so terribly lonely which I am sure made him feel much weaker. I am glad his 2nd sister is going to stay on with him to cheer him up."[110] They had left hurriedly, without saying goodbye to Probyn, who, as George told his mother, "was very much hurt that you did not tell him that you were going. After all there was no mystery about it, poor Davidson was very ill & you wanted to see him & it was quite natural that you should go. But Probyn said 'I have served the 'Blessed Lady' for 50 years & she doesn't even trust me now.'"[111] Alexandra was sorry but "I was so upset & taken [a]back by Toria's sudden wish to go down here by herself, that I told her I wld drive back … with her; as I thought I was coming back that evening I did not want to frighten General Probyn, who himself was not well at all, but Charlotte who quite understood & was very nice about it, I thought wld have explained it all to him, but never mind, I both wrote & telegr it all to him & now he quite understands my reasons why I did not tell him!"

Clearly she was determined Victoria's relationship with Davidson must remain private, although Charlotte and Probyn doubtless knew. Alexandra was now in a quandary, "At present I do not yet know how long I can stay but as you will understand it all worries me dreadfully & makes me feel quite ill myself, but I really cannot leave Victoria here by herself as I am sure you will agree too – it all seems so sad!"[112] While feeling deeply for Victoria, she was still aware of what was "done" and what was "not done". The King thought she was worrying unnecessarily and stated some plain facts; "I quite understand that it must be very sad for you all at Sandringham on account of poor Davidson being so critically ill; no doubt you & Toria having gone down to see him will have cheered him up ... I quite see that you don't know how long you will stay. But when you leave I really do not see why Toria should not remain a little longer as she will be there with his sister & they will do him good & cheer him up. After all, it is her own home & she has not been well lately & the rest & quiet there will do her good. And therefore it is quite natural that she should remain there a little. And really no one knows that poor Davidson is there. I am sure it would set her mind at rest if you told her she could remain as long as his sister does."[113] He was doing his best for Victoria but what seemed simple to a man was causing their mother, who could see all kinds of pitfalls, endless anxiety. In the end Victoria developed a terrible cold and cough and Alexandra did not "feel well at all but I suppose it is age & so many worries just now".[114] Davidson had not recovered but the mother and daughter finally returned to London on 28 March.

On 1 April Alexandra watched Cambridge win the boat race by 5 lengths. There were lunch parties, meetings with relatives, and two more old friends died; Lady Farquhar on the 6th and Lord Gosford,[115] who had been ill for a long time, on the 11th. The next day Alexandra and Victoria went back to Sandringham where Davidson was slowly improving. On 20 April Mr Goddard,[116] a ventriloquist, gave a performance in the ballroom. Alexandra visited the kennels on the 22nd; Mr RW Binks[117] was portraying one of her pet dogs, "Tutsy". On 23 April, Lord Leopold Mountbatten[118] (33), Princess Beatrice's haemophiliac second son, died at Kensington Palace of peritonitis following internal bleeding, but "with that dreadful illness, he was always having these attacks when he suffered terribly & one must be thankful that he has been spared further suffering",[119] George told Alexandra. She felt great sympathy for Beatrice, who had been on holiday at Palermo; "It must have been heart breaking for poor Beatrice & her two remaining children. I am so glad her daughter Ena & girls will stay with her for a month ... It really is very sad for poor dear Beatrice to have been absent when he died, & his loss will be dreadful in her lonely home." Alexandra had had tea with Mary in her new home on 9 April "where I saw them both so happy together, & it was really beautifully arranged by him, with all his beautiful pictures & furniture. I only wonder <u>where</u> they will be able to put all their masses of beautiful wedding presents." The yacht *Alexandra* was to be sold, "the little yacht <u>Papa</u> called <u>after me</u>" and she referred to this again later. It belonged to the Navy, cuts had to be made and nothing could be done but it and her regiment were linked with her husband's affection for her; losing them was like losing him all over again, "but nothing matters now any more as I shall soon be out of this world myself I feel." Victoria was ill in bed with a cough, cold and joint pains. The news was no better; "The world is still standing on its head everywhere ... everything seems to be getting more complicated & unsettled every day! – <u>how</u> will it end."[120]

On 4 May Davidson told Ponsonby, who had also been ill, to "go slow" on convalescence. He had found that any attempt to pull himself together and go ahead "has resulted in an instantaneous collapse – like a pricked balloon." He was afraid the "psychological moment" for Lee's book was being lost; however, Lee had published articles on the King in two recent editions of *The Times* and Davidson warmly congratulated him on them, while regretting the full biography was not yet ready. He himself was now more or less a complete invalid but hoped Lee had recovered.[121] The King, who was going to Belgium, sent his mother some comforting thoughts; "I trust that our trade will soon begin to improve, which will help to reduce the number of unemployed. I hope you were pleased to see that two of my horses won races at Chester this week, it looks as though my bad luck of last year was changing." He added; "Tomorrow will be the 12th anniversary of the day that beloved Papa was taken from us; I shall think of you more than ever; I shall always continue to miss his good advice, thank God he has been spared this ghastly war & all that it has left behind it."[122]

Alexandra was delighted at the success of the Belgian visit, "& yr speeches particularly the last one about all our brave soldiers & their graves was really so touching & did so much good. And all the French papers are full of them. I have cut everything out and will keep them carefully." But "I feel worse every day & quite idiotic with everlasting pain & noises in my wretched old head, which really drives me quite mad. I am quite dreading to come up to London now in this idiotic state but will try to do so at the end of the month. Everybody asks me to open this & that, but how can I promise in my present state! Poor Probyn is quite annoyed that I won't go up at once, but he does not know how I feel! and besides dear Toria is not at all well yet which also worries me dreadfully! And then our poor dear Col Davidson is again very weak & bad with a horrid cough; he had been out several times in his bath chair but is now again in bed all day long. So you will understand how everything worries me."[123] The next day she went to a muster of the Sandringham and Hillington Scouts in Laycock's field. On the 25th she and Victoria returned to Marlborough House to continue the round of functions and visits. On Alexandra Rose Day, 21 June, £46,230 was collected, £6,000 more than in 1921, which was wonderful. Better still was David's return, after eight months in India and the East, on the same day. On 3 July Victoria, Marchioness of Milford Haven, brought her younger son, Lord Louis Mountbatten,[124] and his fiancée, Edwina Ashley, to tea. They were married at St Margaret's, Westminster, on the 18th. Miss Ashley was granddaughter and heiress of Sir Ernest Cassel, King Edward's old friend. Alexandra was present; unfortunately a small blood vessel in her eye burst during the day but this time it did not stop her going out or, for example, attending the grand review of 10,000 territorial troops in Hyde Park on the 22nd. She gave Mary and Lascelles lunch two days later and then had tea with them at Chesterfield House, afterwards calling on her sisters-in-law, Helen Albany, Louise and Beatrice. On 2 August she met Queen Alexandrine of Denmark[125] at Paddington Station.

Victoria had had severe toothache and three extractions "which has not yet helped or removed the pain. It makes me all very anxious to see her in this sad painful state – as soon as we can I suppose we shall go back to dear Sandringham."[126] Alexandra wrote sympathetically from there after George had admitted to missing his daughter. "How well I understand how you must miss yr beloved girl & only daughter, Mary, up in Scotland, where she always accompanied you everywhere; it is dreadful for us parents when they marry." She was enjoying Sandringham; "Yesterday was splendid here, and very hot. I went all over the dear place, & fed all my ... horses & dogs, & finished in the glorious kitchen garden, which I have never seen so beautiful before crammed with flowers; we had tea at the farm in my little house & visited the horses there afterwards, a lot of little foals."[127] Although Davidson looked slightly better he was, as she told May, "still in the same & hopeless state as he was before we left him in the Spring! too sad for words; he is driven out twice a day but goes to bed on his return in the afternoon; he looks terribly thin & weak & it gives me such pain to see him like that, his Sister has left him for a week while we are looking after him, & Victoria drives with him in the afternoon."[128] Probyn was at Marlborough House but expected soon; "his poor neck & head is bent very much which always gives me a great pain to see & must be a terrible trial for him." Davidson was still taking an interest in King Edward's biography, which Lee had now begun writing.[129]

When Alexandra wrote to George again, things were no better. She was feeling ill and, as all her old doctors had died, there was "nobody really to consult" who would understand her medical history. As for poor Davidson, "I fear his lungs are affected, it is too sad to see him ill & helpless like this now for so many months; his dear Sister is still here with him & I make her stop on as long as ever she can; his head is quite clear & we have long talks together, but he is so thin & cannot walk now as his veins are so swelled. It is all most distressing & does not cheer up our stay here now."[130] However, the Harrisons were again staying on the estate; they came to tea on the 14th and played the piano and their presence comforted Victoria. In letting Davidson stay so long in these circumstances, Alexandra was acting with Christian charity and showing her appreciation of him as a member of her household, and personally. Perhaps it was also for Victoria's sake. But there was little hope now and George tried to prepare her for the worst (of which she was already aware) in his next letter. "I am much distressed at the bad account you give of dear Davidson, I fear he can never recover & of course it makes you all very sad & it is always depressing having someone that you are fond of, lying ill in your house; I feel for you & Toria very much."

Affairs abroad were worrying the King. "Turkey has driven the Greek army out of Asia Minor & it is most difficult to know what the Turks will do next. The Powers are doing all they can to get peace. But the situation is very serious."[131]

He commiserated with his mother about the plight of her Greek relatives; the restored King Constantine had abdicated voluntarily, realising the people were against him. "I am very sorry for him as he has been very badly treated & has been entirely misunderstood." Constantine's eldest son, George, Duke of Sparta, had become King, while Constantine, Sophie and their other relatives had left Greece the previous day in a British man-of-war. This time George V was not going to risk a repetition of his Russian cousins' fate. "But where they are going to I do not know. I am greatly worried by the whole situation in the Near East & no one can say what might happen. We certainly do not wish to fight the Turks, but Kemal[132] & his army who are elated at their victory over the Greeks, may do anything. It is an anxious time, as we certainly don't wish to have another war!" There was more bad news; Soveral was "sinking, one could not wish him to live as I fear he was suffering … Everything is sad & depressing."[133]

Helen, Duchess of Albany, a widow since 1884, died at 61 on 1 September at Hinterriss in the Tyrol, where she was buried. She left a cross to Alexandra, which "touched me deeply as I was very fond of her & we were always such good friends."[134] Alexandra and Victoria came to London for the wedding on 3 September of Marie's elder daughter, Princess Nina, to Prince Chavchavadze. There was a large family lunch next day and Queen Olga, Princess Nicholas and two daughters and Marie, as well as Xenia, visited Alexandra for lunch or tea. On the 9th the Queen motored back to Sandringham, Victoria travelling faster by train. In the next couple of weeks Alexandra motored several times with Miss Davidson and on the 21st Dr Perkins came from London to see Davidson. On the 26th they heard that Bobby Spencer,[135] another old friend, had died. The Harrisons had tea with the Queen at the Bungalow on the 28th. On 5 October the expected news came of the Marquis de Soveral's death, at a nursing home in Paris. As Alexandra told her son; "The death of our beloved & faithful old friend Soveral has given me the greatest pain, I cannot get over it at all, he was such a faithful & honest friend of ours for so many years now. I shall always miss him greatly, & he spent his last Xmas with us here & then he already began losing his voice & did not feel well at all – how he must have suffered, poor man & lately the accounts of him through dear Amélie were most painful & too sad for words, particularly as his mind was always clear up to the last."[136] She was in despair about Greece; Queen Olga was now in Denmark with Minny, "who I hope will keep her there as long as possible! Poor little Minny[137] was here last week for two days to say goodbye before joining her mother to go to Greece together – and now she does not know what to do & has given up her London house & her two daughters[138] are married & left her … How will it all end & the Turks are getting very troublesome! If only we cld force them into Peace now … Only God alone knows when Peace will come back to the world."[139] Happily, a Danish friend, Carl Rothe, was spending that day with them on his way home from the South, where he had been staying for his health.

The next day, Alexandra carried out the usual "Sunday round" and was photographed at the kennels with the dogs. On 10 October Sir Stanley Hewett[140] came to see Davidson, whose eldest sister arrived for two days. Alexandra was distraught, both about Greece and because "Our beloved dear Col Davidson gets worse every day now & is so weak that he can hardly speak & looks so thin & suffering with swelled legs which they say is a very bad sign. It is too sad to see him thus & what a loss he will be to me & all his friends is beyond words – his two poor sisters were here together the last few days altho' the eldest will leave already tomorrow; the second will stay on, she has been here for months now."[141] Colonel Sir Arthur Davidson died at 9am on 16 October. On the same day Queen Maud arrived from Norway and Violet Vivian came "into waiting" on the 18th. Perhaps they were due anyway but it does look like a concerted effort to comfort Victoria. Alexandra told May; "our beloved Col Davidson … died quite calmly this morning. I only saw him last night about 7 o'clock when he just looked at me once but was gradually sinking. It is all too sad for words, & I feel quite ill & collapsed. What a loss he will be to us all & everybody who loved him."[142] Did she include Victoria in the first category or the second? In any case, May sent a kind reply.

Lee was distressed about Davidson's death; his help and encouragement had been invaluable and "I greatly admired his loyal affection for King Edward's memory." He was working hard at the book.[143] Davidson's body was taken to his own place, the Red House at Warnham in Sussex, on the 19th. The King wrote to his mother; "Thinking so much of you today when dear Davidson starts for his last resting place".[144] On the 20th memorial services for him were held at Sandringham and in London. Maud spent a lot of time with her mother and sister over the next few weeks and Marie arrived on a visit on the 26th. Lord Marcus Beresford,[145] old friend and manager of King Edward's thoroughbred stud, came to lunch next day and there were more visits and the usual occupations. They heard that Baba Mackenzie had married her second husband, Richard Checkley, in Edinburgh on 8 November. Lady Haig, Violet Vivian's twin sister, arrived with her two children on the 9th and left the next day, letting them stay for a while. The 11th was Armistice Day and was marked by two minutes' silence at 11am; there was a collection in the house for Haig's "Remembrance Day" Fund, augmented the next day by a collection in church. On the 21st Queen Alexandra and her daughter came to Marlborough House, although Victoria went back to Sandringham from the 25th to the 27th. Two days later, she wrote to Lord Rosebery about their three late friends; "the last the worst!! & the utter blank! is not to be described. He was just everything to us here, & I simply do not know how Life is to go on without that wonderful help, as adviser – everything that was human, kind and understanding … I am heartbroken but have to struggle on somehow!!"[146]

On the 27th, the day after her 75th birthday, Minny arrived at Marlborough

House for the first time since 1919. Alexandra celebrated her own 78th birthday with a family lunch for 34. More lunches and teas followed; the two sisters visited a Russian picture exhibition on the 11th; Queen Olga arrived from Paris on the 13th and Queen Amélie called. But there were more deaths; Sarah Lindley, Sandringham's housekeeper, on the 11th; Lord Marcus Beresford, so recently a visitor, on the 16th; and Sir Adolphus FitzGeorge, Uncle George's second son, on the 17th. On the 19th Alexandra received the Danish pastor, Mr Brodström and also wrote to her son sympathising that Georgie, recovering from appendicitis, would have to spend Christmas in King Edward VII's Hospital, where she visited him the next day, his twentieth birthday. On the 21st she, with Victoria, Minny, Olga and their suites, left to join the Norwegians at Sandringham.

Victoria began 1923 with bronchitis. Maud was still at Appleton, although her husband and son had gone home. Olga had left but Minny remained, taking drives with Alexandra. On 11 January they were grieved to hear that King Constantine had died suddenly from a stroke. However, there was some very good news on the 15th; Prince Albert[147] was engaged to Lady Elizabeth Bowes Lyon[148] and he hurried round to tell his grandmother personally. As George told Alexandra on the 16th; "Bertie ... has been in love with her for some time. It is a particularly nice family & she is a nice little girl & was one of Mary's bridesmaids but I hardly know her. I trust she will make him a good wife & be a help to him in his various duties, he seems very happy. We have invited the parents, Lord & Lady Strathmore[149] & the girl to come here next Saturday."[150] In response, Alexandra gave a tea party on the 20th. Queen Olga, with her son, George, returned and ten days later, May and the young couple came to tea again. On the 31st Alexandra and Olga called on Mrs Eleanor Tylden, a local lady[151] who was celebrating her 100th birthday. Xenia arrived on 1 February and on the 3rd there was another tea party for George, May and the young couple. Victoria returned to London on 5 February but Alexandra stayed at Sandringham because Minny had been ill. On the 7th Mary had her first child, the Hon. George Lascelles.[152] Alexandra, with Minny, left for London on the 12th and three days later went to see her granddaughter at Chesterfield House. She told the King on the 16th that "I was so delighted to see yr blessed little Mary with my newborn Great Grandson, who is a sweet little Child & she was looking very well & happy & her dear husband too."[153] As she told May, she herself had just been through a difficult time "with my beloved Minny being ill & laid up ever since you left. Thank God I kept the nurse here when Victoria went to London & she has been looking after her ever since." Alexandra continued; "Did you see my beloved Toria again today. Thank God she is so much better now that she is able to leave tomorrow, unfortunately before my return. I do hope the South will do her good & quite restore her general good health. I am so glad Sir F Treves will be at Mentone to look after her, as I hate not being with her & miss her dreadfully."[154] Queen Olga was awaiting her daughter, who had recently re-married. George had invited his mother and aunt to lunch at Buckingham Palace on the Sunday "as we thought it would be a little change for you. We would be delighted if you could come."[155] They planned to visit the Royal Academy. While happily accepting the lunch invitation, Alexandra feared "we can't go to the Academy as our legs are weak – anyhow we shall see what we are up to."[156] In the end she did go, and saw an exhibition of decorative art.

On the previous day her niece, once again Princess Marie of Greece, had introduced her new, Greek, husband, Admiral Pericles Joannides.[157] Alexandra visited Julie d'Hautpoul; there were more outings and family visits and on 22 February she accompanied Minny to the doctor for some x-rays. Other friends, including Carl Rothe and Lady Mary (Tooka) de Mauny came to see her. Alexandra had resumed an active life, which she was finding quite demanding. She accompanied George and May to the horse show at the Agricultural Hall on the 28th and went to the pony show there on 3 March, "from 3o'clock till 5.30 so I was nearly dead of such an endless time."[158] On the 6th it was the dedication of Canon Edgar Sheppard's memorial tablet in the Chapel Royal, St James's Palace, and on the 7th it was 60 years since her arrival in England in 1863. George wrote, "We want of course to come & see you on Saturday the 10th the 60th anniversary of your wedding day; would you like May & I & George to come to luncheon with you on that day? Perhaps you would send me a message. I thought of you yesterday when I am sure you got heaps of letters & telegrams from all over the country. I hope Aunt Minny is feeling better & that she walks in the garden every day which is what the Drs want her to do."[159] Alexandra replied the next evening; "I am nearly mad with all I have had to do today, so you must excuse this late answer. Yes darling boy, you & beloved May and dear little Georgie are all welcome to lunch here tomorrow on beloved Papa & my wedding day, 60 years ago!! how I wish he was still with me."[160] The party also included Louise, Maudie and Xenia.

Minny was now feeling much better and the sisters regularly took motor drives. On the 22nd they visited the Ideal Home Exhibition at Olympia. Alexandra received many family visitors, not just those living in England but others, like Waldemar who had recently been to America and who came to stay on 31 March, triggering several Danish events; on 1 April they had a Danish service in Marlborough House Chapel and Alexandra received the Danish minister, Count Ahlefeldt,[161] on the 5th and the 18th. Alexandra, Minny and Waldemar had tea at the Danish legation on the 10th; he went home on the 12th but the Danish theme continued. On 13 April, when Marie and Admiral Joannides came to lunch, Kammerherr Rothe was there too. The Duke of York's marriage to Lady Elizabeth Bowes Lyon was now imminent; Alexandra went to an afternoon party at Buckingham Palace, where the presents were on display, and the wedding took place in Westminster Abbey on the 26th, followed by the breakfast at the palace. Among those on the balcony being cheered by the crowd were Queen Alexandra and her sister; the past looking into the future.

Alexandra was taking on fewer public duties but continued to visit things that interested her, such as the Royal Academy Exhibition on 3 May, a revue at the Empire on the 5th and the matinee at the Hippodrome on the 12th. She spent much of her time paying calls or receiving visitors, mostly relatives; she motored with Minny and Victoria, called on Arthur[162] on his 73rd birthday on 1 May and often had tea with George and May. Christopher of Greece and David came to lunch on the 7th and so, the following day, did Alexandra's sisters-in-law, Louise and Beatrice. She received Mr Larsen and Mr Bang, members of London's Danish community, on the 11th and entertained, or went out, every day until the 19th, when she was unwell. Two days later she was visiting the Cart Horse Parade in Regent's Park, giving lunch to Count Ahlefeldt on the 23rd and calling on Helena on the 25th, to wish her joy on her 77th birthday. She also sent a Russian parasol handle, with an agate top, set with small stones, "For my darling and beloved May on her 56th birthday. God bless you & keep you for ever! From yr very deeply loving old Mother Alix."[163] On the 28th she received Lady Curzon of Kedleston[164] who presented a cheque for £3,300 for Queen Victoria's Jubilee Nurses. Later she attended the christening of Xenia's grandson. On 2 June, she, Minny and Victoria watched Trooping the Colour at Horse Guards Parade.

Princess Helena was taken ill at the end of May. Alexandra had been fond of her since coming to England in 1862, when she had made friends with her fiancé's younger sisters. They had met and attended social events together after the Waleses' marriage, but there had been a little difficulty over Helena's marriage, arranged by Queen Victoria, with Christian of Schleswig-Holstein, much older than Helena and, worse, an Augustenburg.[165] The Waleses bowed to the inevitable and embraced "the Christians" as part of their circle, sometimes offering them hospitality. There was also nursing patronage; both Alexandra and Helena were sincerely interested in hospitals and medical matters. Helena regarded this as her particular sphere but, after the King's accession in 1901, his wife felt it should be hers, as Queen, and she carried her point. Again, there was some friction but this was resolved and, after all, the two couples had been close and amiable neighbours for many years.[166] Their children were of a similar age; in 1892 the Christians had seemed to hope their elder daughter might marry George and Christian Victor had been on friendly terms with the Waleses. After King Edward's death, Alexandra continued to show affection and loyalty to Helena, as his sister, but by 6 June Helena was seriously ill. Alexandra called on her that day but she died on the morning of 9th. Alexandra and Minny paid a "farewell visit" and Alexandra placed a wreath on the coffin in Marlborough

House Chapel, where a memorial service was held on the 14th. The funeral was at St George's Chapel the next day. Queen Victoria's surviving children, Louise, Arthur and Beatrice, would outlive Alexandra by many years.

Meanwhile, Princess Maud of Fife was engaged to Lord Carnegie[167] and Alexandra Rose Day had taken place on 13 June. This was the twelfth year of the event and just over £44,113 had been collected; although this was "a splendid amount for our hospitals etc",[168] it was not quite as good as had been expected. This was the last time Queen Alexandra undertook the drive. Despite being so deaf, she still enjoyed music and could hear it to a certain extent. On the 23rd Mischa Elman[169] played and on 4 July Madame Melba and Prince Obolensky[170] sang for her. She received more Danes; Count Ahlefeldt on 26 June and Fru Tövslepp and daughters on 5 July. On 20 June, the Danish composer, Carl Nielsen,[171] had visited Marlborough House. He thought the sisters completely different; Queen Alexandra rather frail and indecisive but "exceedingly sweet and engaging", while the Dowager Empress, perhaps less loveable, was "undoubtedly wise and steadfast". They showed him the house and the Queen asked him to write his name in an album[172] given her in 1905 by her husband. Nielsen added a few bars of music from his opera, Masquerade to the two old ladies' delight. "It was actually all perfectly fantastic: a world of unreality that I have never before seen."[173] On 27 June Alexandra went to the horse show at Olympia and the next day the rose show in Regent's Park. On the 30th she attended the air pageant at Hendon. Victoria Milford Haven called on 2 July with her daughter, Lady Louise Mountbatten, just engaged to the widowed Crown Prince of Sweden. It was becoming very hot and on the 7th reached 87° in the shade in London and 90° in the country; to keep cool, Alexandra and Minny motored every day, while the thermometer fluctuated between 80° and 90°. Overnight on 10 July was one of the biggest thunderstorms in recent years, starting at 11pm and raging for 6 hours. By the 13th it was 91° in the shade but had started to cool down by the 15th. On the 18th Alexandra attended the police horse show at Thames Ditton. By the 25th Minny was ill, while Alexandra continued to see her family; on the 27th she was photographed in a "four generations" group, with George, Mary and baby George Lascelles. Waldemar arrived on the 29th and the next day Alexandra inspected 150 Danish Boy Scouts in Marlborough House garden. He left for Paris on 2 August and the next day Victoria joined the King on board the yacht for Cowes Week.

Minny was anxious to go home; she was beginning to feel better and had made plans to start on 25 August. Alexandra wanted to go to Sandringham but not before Minny had left. Entertaining her, and her family, had tired the Queen out. There were more visits from relatives and motoring trips until Waldemar returned and he, with Minny and her staff, left for Denmark on the 27th. Alexandra wrote; "I shall miss her dreadfully but it will do us both good."[174] The devoted sisters had found that they could no longer get along together so well.

Minny had been through terrible experiences in Russia, so far removed from Alexandra's life in England that some threads of connection had been lost. Moreover, although both were elderly and frail, Minny lacked the patience to come to terms with her sister's deafness and the fact that she was slowing down. She herself still had the energy to travel abroad. She also found the loss of her status difficult and altogether it was easier to face being mistress of Hvidöre than a guest at Marlborough House or Sandringham. The souring of such an important relationship must have seemed almost like bereavement; they did not meet again, although they still corresponded.[175]

George had written from Balmoral on 20 August, anticipating his mother's return to Sandringham; "I am sure peace & quiet there will do you a great deal of good & I hope you will have some nice warm weather."[176] May was staying with their daughter at Goldsborough while he had gone to Mar Lodge to see Louise, whom he had never seen in better spirits. Maudie and her fiancé were there too, looking very happy. Alexandra was delighted to hear from him, as she was feeling low and tired and wishing she could have got away sooner, although "Thank God dear General Probyn & dear Charlotte are quite well in spite of their long stay here!" Victoria had enjoyed being on the yacht and it had done her good. Alexandra was still thinking of her eldest grandson's prospects, "Does yr blessed David think of being married soon? like his dear brother who is <u>so happy</u> now? It will be difficult for him to marry an English girl like his brother has done – but God grant him to find a perfect wife for his future & in <u>his position</u>."[177] The King thanked her; she certainly needed a long rest "and it will be everything for dear Charlotte & Probyn getting to Sandringham again, they are really wonderful old people." He agreed "David ought to marry, he is more than 29, but who is he to marry? & it is not easy to find anyone who is suitable & he is very obstinate & I don't think has any wish at all to marry & one can't force him; that is impossible. Anyhow Bertie & Elizabeth are very happy & she is quite charming & everyone likes her."[178]

On 1 September Alexandra left for Sandringham and Victoria went to visit Blanche Leigh.[179] Only two days before there had been deaths: Princess Christopher of Greece,[180] and Molly Sneyd[181] and Lord Farquhar, both old friends. The King wrote again on the 9th; "I do hope you have had fairly fine weather & have been able to get out & that the peace & quiet has already done you much good, after the long time you spent in London with all your many worries, & anxiety about Aunt Minny, with all the relations coming in & out all day. I am sure Sandringham must be looking lovely with all the pretty flowers."[182] She could now relax, going nearly every day to the bungalow on Dersingham beach for tea; 29 times by 6 October.[183] Alexandra visited all her old friends on the estate, including on 4 September Mrs Beck, widow of the agent who had never returned from Gallipoli. She had been "out of her mind" for a long time but was now at home. The Queen also visited the garden, her dogs and horses. In church, "I sit quite alone in our pew, & Charlotte opposite & Probyn in his usual place by himself. We three took yesterday the Holy Communion! And [I] prayed so to give me strength to live on & do my duty towards you, all my beloved Children & my beloved Country where I have now lived … 60 years and I am nearly 80! I am still so worried about myself as I feel I am getting more & more an <u>idiot</u> & forget everything." But she had a new interest; "Here, my garden is full of dear lovely pheasants which I feed every day on the steps where we drive from & they all run after me every time I come out & [there is] one white one & one brown one who had one bad foot & is lame. I shall be dreadfully sorry when they are shot; there are lots who come running towards me when they see me and I feed them with bread which they enjoy very much." She had been pleased with some nice letters from Georgie and also hoped "the <u>young pair</u> are very happy together; she is such a dear bright little one."[184] George replied on the 21st, rather "amused to hear that you feed the pheasants every day, they spoil the flowers & some of them are bound to be shot later, I fear."[185]

By the 27th Alexandra had had "a nice peaceful time so far here with dear Probyn & Charlotte but tomorrow afternoon comes my beloved Olga with dear Toria." Olga was mourning her daughter-in-law, in whose London house she and other relatives had been staying and which they now had to leave. Alexandra felt she could not cope with more troubles. "I love dear Olga but now I feel so <u>idiotic</u> & get worse every day so that I think I have got softening of the brain & can never remember any name etc."[186] Extra company, however beloved, was now a strain. Alexandra was used to her own ways and to a small circle of familiar faces. She went out every day but was eating very little. By contrast, "I have never seen anyone with such an enormous appetite as Queen Olga",[187] wrote Charlotte in wonderment. Lord Ripon[188] had died while out grouse-shooting on 22 October and Alexandra lamented, "if it had only been <u>me</u> instead as I am utterly useless now in the world."[189] Probyn (90) now became treasurer as well as comptroller. Queen Maud arrived at Wolferton on 8 October "looking very well … I took her first to see Aunt Olga & we all had tea together, then I & Toria took her home to her <u>lovely</u> little house which was perfect – everything so tidy."[190] On 19 October her great-grandson George Lascelles came to stay until the 30th. There were tea parties every day now and more relatives arrived before Alexandra, Victoria, Probyn and Charlotte returned on 1 November to Marlborough House, where they were joined by Queen Maud for two royal weddings; the Crown Prince of Sweden and Lady Louise Mountbatten, at the Chapel Royal on the 3rd and Princess Maud, (whose presents Alexandra went to see at St James's Palace on the 8th) who married Lord Carnegie in the Guards' Chapel on the 12th. On the 14th Alexandra heard that the Duke of Cumberland had died at Gmunden, and on the same day received the Misses Wolfe, over from America; some of her last visitors at Marlborough House.[191]

Minny had been impoverished by the Russian revolution and from 24 January 1924, George, May, Alexandra and Victoria would, jointly, pay her a quarterly allowance. Alexandra's share was to be £850 annually, from her private allowance of £10,000.[192] On 16 November she and Victoria returned to Sandringham, the last time Alexandra would make this journey. London life was now too tiring; it was much more comfortable to remain at Sandringham. George commented; "I suppose you still feed the white pheasant after luncheon, as we did not shoot him."[193] On Maud's birthday, the 26th, at Appleton, "Motherdear & all her party of 6 came to lunch, & we were 5, so we were quite a lot for my small dining room! They all enjoyed my food & praised up my French cook! ... We go every day over to tea at S. I prefer it than to lunch! Poor dear M[otherdear] is not over well & complains more than ever about the noises in her head ... Just fancy, we actually dance after tea at S on the thick carpet, it amuses M & we all take turns & play the pianola."[194] Alexandra motored, gave tea parties and celebrated her 79th birthday. When the others went to London on 10 December, she went motoring with Charlotte and visited the "motor show" at Lynn on the 17th. Victoria and the others returned on the 19th and relatives started to arrive; on Christmas Day there was a dinner for 24, including Alexandra, nearly all her family and household. The servants' Christmas tree was ready on the 29th; as usual the Queen presented all the gifts herself and there was a party in the ballroom on the 31st for the tenants and estate workers.

Charlotte Knollys kept engagement diaries for the Queen from 1873–1923, although some years are missing. Court circulars for 1924 report her church attendance and very little else. She was becoming frailer and Lord Dawson[195] was consulted. Queen Mary sent his report to Queen Maud, who had been very upset "& feared really that last evening that it might be the last time I saw her, as she looked so dreadfully delicate & tired out, & she kept on holding my arm & repeating 'I shall never see you again, & I am sure I shall die soon as I feel so odd.'" Poor Victoria was in a terrible state, being left "alone with all 'The Old Ones' (as we call them!)" and Maud feared she might collapse from the emotional strain, as there was no one with whom to talk or go out. "I do wish Ld Dawson could have given some strengthening tonic to dear M[other dear] & Toria, I am sure they need it."[196]

George still kept his mother in touch with current affairs and told her on 22 January that he had asked the Labour Party leader, Ramsay Macdonald,[197] to form a government after Stanley Baldwin's[198] had been defeated. "So by tomorrow the Labour party will be in power & today is the 23rd anniversary of dear Grandmama's death. I wonder what she would have thought of it. Mr Macdonald made a very good impression (I met him before) & I am sure he will carry on without resorting to any extreme measures certainly in this House of Commons." There was more news; "They say Lenin is dead, what a good thing!!!"[199] On 17 February he mentioned that "I have been making the acquaintance of all the Ministers in turns & I must say that they all seem to be very intelligent & they take things very seriously. They have different ideas to ours, as they are all Socialists but they ought to be given a chance & ought to be treated fairly. I regret to say the dockers' strike began yesterday, which if it lasts for any length of time will do great harm to the Country & destroy all the trade we have got left."[200] Marie visited Alexandra again and found that, every day, regardless of the weather, "she insisted upon going straight after lunch to throw bread crumbs to the numerous pheasants strutting about on the lawn in front of the house. I usually ran after her with a cape, being terrified she might catch cold, but the moment I put it on her shoulders she flung it off; we sometimes had regular fights! Every Sunday afternoon she went to feed her various animals, and treated them like human beings. She always had a small Peke with her, which she addressed as 'Tootsie dog'. During meals she threw all the food she did not eat to this beast, which I regret to say we all hated."[201]

Alexandra still corresponded with Knutsford and maintained her interest in London Hospital, but on 10 January wrote "Please accept this little Almanack & think of me as I used to be, <u>now</u> I am breaking up."[202] Knutsford did indeed think of her; in an undated letter on one of her wedding anniversaries, 1923 or 1924, he hoped she would remember "a long past day & all the happiness it brought you then. I always feel that happy days help one to bear others which have brought sorrow. Happy recollections help to lessen sorrow. It is well that it should be so or sorrow would just be unbearable." In 1863, when he was eight, he had seen the Waleses driving past St George's Hospital in London; "I felt that I could swagger over the other boys at school because 'I saw them married' which they had not." He would have been very surprised if he had been told that one day the lady in the carriage would be very kind to him, "But so it has happened, and grateful for the many kindnesses I venture to send this my dutiful greeting." He also sent pictures of the wedding procession, which he was going to have put on a screen, for her to see.[203]

The progress of Lee's biography of King Edward, to be published in two volumes, was hampered by his poor health and over-work; he was 64 and had other academic commitments too. Queen Alexandra now wrote far fewer letters; only three to her son have survived for 1924 but she was glad to receive news from him. She felt she was "<u>falling slowly</u> down and get worse every day & forget everything." She was miserable about this but still managed to go out every day to see her dogs and horses. Victoria was away, consulting doctors in London; her mother missed her greatly and seems to have feared she might die before Victoria returned. She was concerned that David had hurt himself falling during a point-to-point race near Aldershot; "tell him to stop all this – it [is] so dangerous."[204] George told her he had seen Victoria, who had had a cold. He and May had visited the exhibition site at Wembley, progressing but with still a lot to do before the opening on April the 23rd. "It is an enormous place & will be very interesting."[205] Later he told her they had been showing Queen Olga round the state rooms at Windsor, which had fascinated her.[206]

On 15 April Waldemar arrived at Sandringham for a couple of days. Victoria and Louise arrived on the 17th. There was public concern about Alexandra and on 8 May Charlotte Knollys reassured Miss Acland that "in spite of all the Newspaper reports the Queen is not ill. She goes to church regularly on Sundays and takes long Motor drives every day. Her Majesty however greatly prefers Sandringham to London, as when in London she is overwhelmed with requests to attend Charitable Functions – Hospitals, Opera etc, and as she is now very deaf, she cannot derive much pleasure from the association of her friends, and greatly prefers the peace & quiet of the Country."[207] Alexandra's greatest pleasure now was receiving letters from her son. She kept worrying about her health and was convinced she would soon die; her memory was faulty and the distressing noises in her ears stopped her thinking clearly. It was a miserable time, which little could alleviate. Queen Olga came to stay on 14 May and after a few days Victoria left for London, having told May; "Dear A Olga is peaceful here, but I don't think it has yet! done my poor M[otherdear] much good! – as she thinks she must entertain her? which is so unnecessary ... All here is more sad & terrible than ever – poor Dear – she hears nothing & A Olga can't see – so you can imagine what I have to go through."[208] In June Alexandra remembered; "next week is Ascot where I loved being". She hoped to see George for lunch at Sandringham on 3 July "I think Aunt Olga will still be here – she sits close to me as I write & she is reading all the time".[209] She was worried at not hearing from Victoria, who was supposed to be at Marlborough House.

More old friends had died but the saddest loss was Sir Dighton Probyn, at 91, on 20 June. Alexandra attended his memorial service at Sandringham Church on the 24th. George had written; "I feel for you deeply in the fresh sorrow & I am sure you must be very unhappy at losing such an old & faithful friend, who had been with you for over fifty years. I am so sorry for poor Charlotte who was so devoted to him, what will she do without him. I fear you will both miss him terribly. But he is happy now & at peace." Another old friend, Harry Legge,[210] had also died on 20 June. But George was able to tell his mother that Victoria was quite happy, doing a rest cure "in a charming little house among the fir trees" near Windsor.[211] This was Shepherd's Corner at Ascot;[212] when Victoria returned to Sandringham on 29 November, she had been there for nearly six months.

Louise came to stay at Sandringham from 18–23 July and on the 30th Queen Alexandra and Queen Olga attended the Sandringham Estate Cottage Horticultural Society's annual show. Cecil Beaton,[213] (twenty) on holiday in

Norfolk, was visiting Sandringham with his mother and aunt. They were delighted to find the flower show taking place, especially when Queen Alexandra arrived and they were near enough for Mrs Beaton to curtsey to her. Beaton, who had never seen her before, had always been fascinated by the idea of the Queen and had imagined her now to be "an old painted hag", hung about with ropes of pearls and wearing a black sequinned gown. But as everyone hurried to the tent to see her, he "nearly wept when I saw the old Queen. She wasn't at all as I had imagined. She was not a bit painted or enamelled & grotesque. She was merely a perfectly charming old lady, with ... a very beautiful face & ... a marvellous wig, a mass of curls, tight to the head ... & so frail. She has been left a mess, a perfectly charming mess, with a deep, jerky voice, a charming thin neck, & very delicate & lovely." Her hand was "like an egg stuck on a hatpin." She smiled and went to talk to "a weeping baby & she looked in at all the flowers. And crowds waited patiently & silently for her to comment & drive away. She is a ... lovely old hag with marvellous frail black clothes & a feathered sequin hat perched on the front of her high coiffure." He and his relatives thought about her all day as they walked round the garden, enjoying the flowers, wondering what she would have to eat and imagining her moving about the house. When they got close enough, they peered through the windows and "saw her tottering about the rooms & she looked at a photo of the Duke & Duchess of York."[214]

Victoria was "getting on very well with her rest cure, but she will have to remain in the home for some time yet."[215] George wrote again on 10 August from *Victoria and Albert* at Cowes; "I have been thinking so much of you all this week on bd this dear old Yacht, where we have spent so many happy days together in old times."[216] Julie d'Hautpoul had been there too and would be able to tell Alexandra all about it when she came to stay. George was distressed that Lord Knollys, at 87, was seriously ill; Charlotte had gone to be with him. By the time he wrote again, on the 21st, Knollys had died. His funeral had been at St Peter's Church, Eaton Square, on the 18th. "I shall miss him greatly. I have known him all my life, one of my oldest & best friends. Too sad for dear Charlotte who must feel his loss terribly & was so devoted to him."[217] But there was good news too; Mary had had another son.[218] Replying to George's letter of the 25th from Balmoral, Alexandra, despite an irritating cough, was interested in everything he had told her about Scotland. She was glad "Bertie & Elizabeth" were so happy together and that he and May liked them so much.[219] On 3 October George commented that Olaf was going to Oxford, just as his grandfather, Frederick VIII, had done.[220] Queen Olga stayed briefly in London but later returned to Sandringham until the 13th. Mary and Lascelles visited Alexandra and by now Maud had arrived for her regular stay. On 11 November, Sir Henry Streatfeild placed a wreath at the Cenotaph on Alexandra's behalf. Victoria returned on the 29th and a party of relatives, friends and household gathered to wish the Queen a happy 80th birthday on 1 December. The Gaumont Company showed

Monsieur Beaucaire in the ballroom that evening. Many guests remained to share the Christmas festivities, with Alexandra, as usual, handing out presents from the tree to the staff herself.

〰

At the beginning of 1925 Victoria was enjoying a visit to Lugano.[221] Queen Alexandra needed a companion however and, in addition to Charlotte, she was often accompanied by Marie or Louise. She no longer took part in official functions but went driving and attended church regularly, at least until 17 May. Sometimes the sermon at the Sunday service was preached by a visiting cleric; on 18 January he was "Tubby" Clayton, Vicar of All Hallows, Barking-by -the-Tower and Honorary Padre of TocH,[222] which he had founded in 1915 at Poperinghe in Belgium. On 1 February the King sent his mother an urgent note, "I hear from the Drs that you have a bad cough. It is really <u>bitterly cold</u> today with a strong wind, although there is sun & I beg of you <u>not</u> to go to Church this morning, just to <u>please me</u>. You really must take care of your health & it makes us all miserable when you go out in this weather when you know that your cough is so troublesome. I will come up & see you later. If you go out it will only make you ill & it is very unkind to all of us. <u>So please do not go to church</u> today to please me."[223] He might have saved paper and ink. When Alexandra made up her mind, nothing would stop her; the *Court Circular* for 1 February records that she did indeed attend church that morning. Back at Buckingham Palace on the 8th George wrote again; "We were all sorry to leave dear Sandringham last week & we miss you very much & enjoyed seeing you at tea & doing puzzles afterwards. I do hope your cough is better now & that you take more care of yourself."[224] Marie was now staying with her aunt, as George commented in his next letter: "I suppose you have just been to church & that you missed me there, but I am sure Minny helped you to find the place in the prayer book ... like I always do."[225] Marie had noticed that Alexandra "was beginning to lose her wonderful energy and had moments of great lassitude."[226] She was worrying about Victoria, who had been away for so long, and she no longer felt up to writing letters. Marie used to sit with her while she had breakfast in her dressing room, never very much; sometimes an egg and usually fruit (especially grapes), with a cup of coffee. At about 10am Marie went out for a walk or a drive and at 1.30 there was lunch. She, Alexandra and sometimes Charlotte went for a motor drive at about three o'clock every day. On Sundays they went to church; later, everyone had tea together in the hall, after which Alexandra put together jigsaw puzzles, her one amusement, helped by the others, while Admiral Joannides played the pianola and King George called him "organ-grinder". Dinner was upstairs in a private room at 9.00 and usually included the household. Alexandra always appeared in a black velvet tea gown, wearing pearls, jewels, a floral corsage and a delicious scent called "Daphne". She was still beautiful; her complexion was quite out of the ordinary, which made some people believe she was "enamelled" and painted up, neither of which was true; Alexandra's skin was as soft and fresh as a child's,[227] due to her regime of soap and water and cold cream. Sometimes she used a little powder but never lipstick. She wore a toupée for many years but her own hair never turned white, apart from a few silvery threads. Her worst problem was lifelong deafness; "she was terribly sensitive about this and absolutely refused, even *en famille*, to use any kind of instrument. She only spoke about this defect in her later years, never even mentioning it before. It was a terrible torture to her, as she was so full of life and interest, and always felt she was missing something. When anyone shouted at her, it gave her physical pain which she could hardly bear."[228] Charlotte had to write down her responses to the Queen on pieces of paper and sometimes by late evening the waste paper basket was full of them.[229]

The King meanwhile had had a sharp attack of bronchitis, telling his mother that it was the third day he had been allowed up for a few hours and he still felt a bit weak, but was looking forward to a Mediterranean cruise that had been planned. "I hope that Toria will join us on board the Yacht & go for the cruise with us, it will do her so much good & we will bring her home with us."[230] Later; "The doctors say it is much too cold for dear Toria to come home now, so we have arranged to take her with us, so that she will really come home sooner than was intended."[231] To this his mother replied in her only surviving letter to him for 1925; it was perhaps her last letter to him: "How do you feel today, I hope much better. Have you been out today? Here it was horrid <u>snowing</u> all the morning; we drove out today all the same, Minny, me & Charlotte. I think of you darling boy so much – I miss you so <u>much</u>. I feel <u>completely</u> collapsed – I shall soon go. You & my darling May are in my thoughts all day long, & all yr Children, I wonder if I ever see you again. I hope you <u>haven't</u> taken <u>Toria</u> with you. I so hope to <u>see</u> her <u>soon</u> – I <u>long</u> for her <u>so much</u>, and she is a dear to me. I <u>miss her so</u> for <u>so long</u>. Now [I haven't] got any of my children with me which is <u>so dreadful</u>, I can't live long … excuse this bad letter. I can't write any more today & I hope you are better."[232] George was very moved by this letter and the effort she had made to write it. He replied that they were planning to leave for Genoa the following Thursday to join *Victoria and Albert* for the cruise and were hoping to find fine, warm weather. He supposed she would "go & feed your animals this afternoon & hope it is not cold."[233] By 22 March they were at sea, off Leghorn and Victoria had joined them at Genoa, "she looks thin, we will take great care of her & bring her home very soon."[234] By 5 April they had reached Messina and visited Queen Amélie at Capodimonte; "she was not looking very well & has got thinner. May did a lot of sightseeing which she loves & I took her to Pompeii one day which interested her very much."[235] On the 9th Louise arrived at Sandringham to take over as her mother's companion, staying over

Easter until the 27th. Then at last, on 29 April, Victoria came home. George visited Alexandra the next day.

Esher had written to Stamfordham on 26 April, about the first volume of Sir Sidney Lee's book, which had just come out. This time "the dear old Queen will, I trust, be left in peace." He felt people tended to dismiss her; "the attitude of so many people towards her infuriates me. I don't mean the <u>young</u> people ... But others, who are still middle aged, should recollect how they would, and did, lick the dust under her very small feet."[236] The first volume was a success but before Lee could complete the second he became terminally ill and died on 3 March 1926. When it was finally published, a year later, Lord Hardinge of Penshurst thought it "a monumental work, admirably done & contains a quantity of indiscreet material which will ensure its success." He had seldom read a more interesting biography, but it had been a great pity Lee himself had not known King Edward, as he could then have included examples showing the charm of his personality.[237]

Lee, who was Jewish, had been looked at askance by the establishment, who found him difficult to deal with. In fact, each party was wary of the other. Most members of the household only gradually began to trust him but one had always been a good friend, advising him about pictures and listening sympathetically to his concerns. This was Lionel Cust, who wrote about him to Ponsonby on 3 November 1927. Lee had been rather a recluse; a bachelor who was a much-respected scholar but who knew little of society, or women, although he had three sisters. One particular difficulty with the book, which he had not had time to resolve, was how to estimate Queen Alexandra's part in the King's reign, especially in domestic life. "He was very anxious to do justice to the Queen as a factor in the reign. When he began the second volume he was given to understand, I do not know by whom, that Queen Alexandra would wish to read his text before it was actually printed. He was certainly relieved at the last, when it became evident, that the state of the Queen's health would not permit of her reading, or even being told what he had said, for he was very nervous about the Queen's possible criticism." People might therefore find the biography extremely meagre regarding her contribution to the reign but "I say with some confidence that any such fault of omission was due to Sidney Lee's health and death, & not to any lack of appreciation."[238] Ironically, if Lee could only have met the King, who had many Jewish friends, and the kindly Queen, who would have forgiven him for the *DNB* article when she saw his efforts to do justice to the King, his path would have been immeasurably smoother and he would have seen for himself that the couple's real power was not political but personal.[239]

This was in the future and, from Oslo on 6 May 1925, Maud told May that Louise, although writing happily from Sandringham and getting on well with her mother, had been quite ill. Victoria also was still nervous, restless and upset at Alexandra's state of health; the Queen wanted to tell people things and could not, as her power of speech was going.[240] On 3 June King George celebrated his 60th birthday and was delighted to receive from his mother "that lovely cigarette case & writing those kind words for my old 60th birthday. I thank you a thousand times for them. You are always in my thoughts."[241] She had hoped to listen to a wireless programme celebrating his birthday, but could no longer hear well enough. However, Miss Acland was able to get a transcript for her from the British Broadcasting Company. Alexandra was delighted and declared that "she shall always value and treasure it as long as she lives."[242] There was little left for her to do; she was losing weight and growing weaker. Marie returned to Sandringham on 1 September and was distressed by a great change; Alexandra had become very thin "and somehow had lost her interest in everything and continually fell asleep." They had to write everything down, as her deafness was much worse, but she would not give in and continued her usual life, including her regular motor drives. After these she would usually lie down on a sofa in a darkened room and sleep until tea time. Sadly, they watched her getting weaker every day, just as Alexandra herself had watched her mother in 1898. Xenia came for a visit, which gave her great pleasure. Maud arrived at Appleton on 12 October and visited her mother and on 11 November Colonel Streatfeild placed a wreath at the Cenotaph on Alexandra's behalf.

On 19 November Marie and Victoria went to Alexandra's room before their morning walk. She seemed all right, asked where they were going, and to come back soon. "Just when we were going downstairs, the nurse came running to say that the Queen had had a heart attack … We of course rushed up to the bedroom. The Queen was quite conscious and even smiled to see us back so soon. My cousin and I stood at either side of her bed and she gave a hand to each and kept looking at us pathetically." George, May and Maud were summoned and came immediately but were only allowed to stay a few minutes. The doctor said Alexandra must be kept as quiet and calm as possible, but she was so happy to see George again and even tried to talk to him. When the physician Sir Thomas Horder[243] examined her, he acknowledged that the end was not far away. "Victoria and I were in and out of her room all the time, and she always stretched out her dear hands to us, which we held for hours." That night Marie did not go to bed but slept on a sofa in her dressing room, ready to be called if needed. At 5am she went to look at her aunt, who was sleeping peacefully. She returned later and found Victoria there but Alexandra's strength was waning and she suffered more heart attacks during the morning. The rest of the family came and went; Louise arrived from London during the afternoon and went straight to her mother, who still seemed to recognise her. Queen Alexandra died quietly at 5.25pm on 20 November. Louise, Victoria, Nurse Fletcher and Marie stood by her to the last. It was "Such a calm and peaceful death. A short time after, all her wonderful beauty returned, and she lay on her deathbed with a happy smile, the picture of peace and so beautiful."

The Duke of Connaught told his sister, Louise that "poor Charlotte Knollys threw herself on Alix's bed & kept on talking to her some time after she had passed away & had at last to be led away."[244] Next morning there was a short service by Queen Alexandra's bed, in the presence of all her family, and her household and servants filed past all day, to see her for the last time. Later she was put into her coffin and taken to Sandringham Church at 9am on the 22nd, accompanied by Victoria, Marie and her husband, and the suite. The coffin, covered with Alexandra's Royal Standard, faced the altar and crowds visited the church, which was "one mass of floral offerings". On the 26th the Queen's close relatives attended a private service for her there. Afterwards her coffin was taken to Wolferton Station, conveyed to King's Cross and then placed privately in the Chapel Royal, St James's Palace, to be watched overnight by Gentlemen at Arms and Yeomen of the Guard. Foreign guests arrived and on the 27th the funeral cortège moved slowly through the cold London streets, which were lined with troops and thousands of spectators, many in tears. Snow was falling and everything was quiet. At 11.30 the coffin, borne by eight Life Guards, entered Westminster Abbey to the strains of Chopin's *Funeral March*. At that moment, a ray of sunshine appeared and touched the coffin. It was placed on a high catafalque, surrounded by tall candles in gilded candelabra. "The whole scene was impressive in its grand simplicity. One could feel that every single person in the church was sincerely praying for the repose of the soul of a beloved Queen, who had spent all her life doing kind deeds to everyone."[245] A member of the household later commented; "there is no question that Queen Alexandra was really beloved in this country, and earned the title which someone has bestowed upon her of 'The Queen of Hearts'."[246] The coffin remained in the Abbey, guarded as before, and the next day was taken to Windsor, where a private funeral service was held in the Albert Memorial Chapel, near Prince Eddy's tomb.

Many messages of condolence were received. Lord Revelstoke, son of Alexandra's friend, Mrs Baring, recalled the Queen's charm and the many kindnesses she had shown him since he was a little boy.[247] Prince Nicholas of Greece told his cousin, "Whatever I say, I feel I shall never be able to tell you how deeply I am affected by an event which put an end to a whole chapter of my life, as your beloved mother was not only the sweetest and kindest of close relatives, but has always and invariably been the best and staunchest of friends to me and mine throughout the most bitter trials of my life. May God bless her and rest her beautiful soul in His Kingdom of love and everlasting peace."[248]

Sir Thomas Horder and Dr FJ Willans[249] prepared a report for *The Lancet* of 5 December, although it was ultimately not published. It stated that Alexandra had been in general good health and carrying on as usual before her heart attack on 19 November. Her speech difficulty was not due to mental failure but to a localised cerebral thrombosis.[250] This issue of *The Lancet* carried a message which Alexandra had recently sent to the annual meeting of Queen Victoria's Jubilee Institute, with good wishes for its prosperity and thanks to all the workers for "the good cause which is so near to my heart."[251] Encouraging the work of district nurses was thus one of the last things she did.

On 23 December, the King wrote to the Archbishop of York, Cosmo Gordon Lang,[252] thanking him for his kind letter and sympathy and paying Queen Alexandra a special tribute:

"No man had a more perfect mother than I had, & I was devoted to her & she still looked upon me as her child. The blank she has left can never be filled, but thank God her end was beautiful & most peaceful. She is happy now & will have no more worries & no more sorrows. I admired her greatly; besides being a beautiful woman she spent her life in helping the poor & suffering & trying to make them happy. The universal sympathy shown us from all over the world is a consolation in our sorrow. She now lies beside my Father in the Memorial Chapel at Windsor, where they will remain until St George's is restored & then placed in their tombs which have been prepared for them."[253]

Later, they were laid to rest in the sarcophagus to the right of the altar in St George's Chapel. King Edward VII and Queen Alexandra were thus reunited in death only a few yards away from where, in 1863, they had been united in life.[254]

Notes

[1]   Miss Bertha Marion Martin, serving in Queen Alexandra's Royal Naval Nursing Service from 1913–1940, and matron-in-chief from 1938–1940, received her ARRC from the King at Buckingham Palace on an occasion in 1919, after which she and other nurses were asked to go to Marlborough House to see Queen Alexandra. Miss Martin was the only naval sister and went in first. "She took my cape in both her hands and said; 'this pretty uniform – you know I chose it – I do hope you like it and I hope it will not be altered.'" She had approved this uniform as well as the one for the military nurses; "They sent figures dressed in the suggested uniform to the Palace for the Queen's approval; she was interested in every detail and had many suggestions." Alexandra was "a very sweet little frail old lady and so different to what I had expected. It is a happy memory." QARNNS Archives, U/-/7/L 247/letter from Miss Martin, 25 July 1948.

[2]   Grand Duke Nicholas Michaelovitch (1859–1919), scholar and eminent historian, and Grand Duke Dmitri Constantinovitch (1860–1919), army officer, were shot on January the 28th; Grand Duke Paul Alexandrovitch and Grand Duke George Michaelovitch on January 30th

[3]   Admiral Sir Alexander Ramsay (1881–1972), naval officer

[4]   They were in England from 12–29 March

[5]   Grand Duchess George

[6]   Baroness Sophie ("Isa") Buxhoeveden (1883–1956), author and former lady-in-waiting to the murdered Russian empress

[7]   RA GV/PRIV/AA35/25, Queen Alexandra to King George V, 1919: 9 April

[8]   RA VIC/ADDA21/234/39, 41, Queen Alexandra to Lord Knutsford, 1919: 3 February, 12 April

[9]   RA GV/M/1344a/86, 92, Admiralty, 1919: 29 March, 8 April; 96, 106, Dowager Empress

Marie to Queen Alexandra, 1919: 12, 15 April

10   Endell Street Military Hospital remained open to deal with three waves of the disease; patients and staff fell ill and some died. The hospital wound down gradually and finally closed in January 1920, but its professional and disciplined ethos had played a part in gaining the first step in achieving women's suffrage in 1918.

11   Harry Hawker (1889–1921) Australian aviation pioneer, and his navigator, Lt Commander Kenneth Mackenzie-Grieve (b1880)

12   Captain John Alcock (1892–1919), Arthur Brown (1886–1948), aviators who made the first non-stop transatlantic flight

13   Captain Gerald William Gathergood (1895–1966) First World War pilot and aviator

14   RA VIC/ADDA21/234/42, Queen Alexandra to Lord Knutsford, 1919: 27 May

15   Prince Louis of Battenberg

16   The Danish flag

17   The King's and Queen's 26th wedding anniversary (and Princess Victoria's 51st birthday)

18   RA PS/PSO.GV/C/M/1344a/136, Lord Stamfordham to Sir Ronald Graham, 1919: 4 July

19   Edward Maitland (1880–1921) and the pilot, George Scott (1888–1930)

20   RA QM/PRIV/CC42/135, Queen Alexandra to Queen Mary, 1919: 8 September

21   RA VIC/ADDA21/117

22   No further references to it have been found; after the war working-class women did not just want to do needlework and domestic service. Perhaps the school was also a victim of Alexandra's need to economise.

23   RA GV/PRIV/AA35/26, Queen Alexandra to King George V, 1919: 12 September

24   RA GV/PRIV/AA35/27, Queen Alexandra to King George V, 1919: 30 September

25   RA GV/PRIV/AA35/26, Queen Alexandra to King George V, 1919: 12 September

26   RA GV/PRIV/AA35/27, Queen Alexandra to King George V, 1919: 30 September; Davidson may also have thought that, as Queen Mother, she was entitled to special protection.

27   RA GV/PRIV/AA35/28, Queen Alexandra to King George V, 1919: 9 October

28   RA VIC/ADDA/17/1304, Queen Alexandra to Princess Louise, Duchess of Argyll, 1919:10 November

29   RA QM/PRIV/CC50/1443, Queen Mary to Marquis of Cambridge, 1919: 16 October

30   Daily Mail, 12 November 1919

31   Lady Katherine, née Egerton (1835–1920), m Hon Henry Coke; woman of the bedchamber to Queen Mary

32   According to her woman of the bedchamber, Hon Margaret Wyndham (1879–1965), Queen Mary would have liked "above all else" to be Queen Regnant; Pope-Hennessy/Vickers, p 115. Alexandra apparently did not use the style "Alexandra R"; she had wanted to be "The Queen" but of course with "The King" too.

33   17 March

34   She met the Cavell Memorial Committee and a delegation from the Ecole Edith Cavell in Brussels, and presented the Union Flag to be placed on the statue, receiving a Belgian flag presented by the Queen of the Belgians. Buglers of the 2nd Coldstream Guards sounded the "Last Post" and "Reveille".

35   Lady Dorothy, née Cavendish (1900–1966), m Harold Macmillan (1894–1986), later 1st Earl of Stockton, statesman, prime minister, 1957–63

36   RA VIC/ADDU38/24, Queen Alexandra to Lord Fisher, 1919: 18 April © Reserved

37   RA GV/PRIV/AA35/29, Queen Alexandra to King George V, 1920: 30 April

38   RA GV/ADD/COPY/140/122, Rosebery Papers, Princess Victoria to Lord Rosebery, 1920: 2 June

39   Some photographs of her suggest astigmatism in her left eye

40   *The Times*, 25 May 1920

41 Princess Victoria to Beatrice Harrison, [no date but probably 1920: 24 June] © The Harrison Sisters' Trust
42 Lt-General Alexander Pavlovitch Rodzianko (1879–1970), sought British financial support for anti-Bolshevik combat
43 General Sir Alfred Knox (1870–1964), head of British Mission under Admiral Kolchak
44 General Michael Constantinovitch Dietrichs (1874–1937), key figure in the "White" monarchist movement in Siberia
45 RA PS/PSO/GV/C/M/1067/89, Sir Arthur Davidson to King George V, 1920: 8 June
46 RA VIC/ADDA21/228/248, Sir Arthur Davidson to Messrs Coutts, 1920: 29 July
47 RA GV/PRIV/AA38/5, King George V to Queen Alexandra, 1920: 8 July
48 RA GV/PRIV/AA38/6, King George V to Queen Alexandra, 1920: 15 August
49 Terence MacSwiney (1879–1920), elected in 1920 as Sinn Fein Lord Mayor of Cork, but later died on hunger strike in Brixton Prison
50 Robert Smillie (1857–1940), miners' leader, trade unionist and Labour party politician
51 RA GV/PRIV/AA38/7, King George V to Queen Alexandra, 1920: 27 August
52 RA GV/PRIV/AA35/30, Queen Alexandra to King George V, 1920: 28 August
53 RA GV/PRIV/AA38/8, King George V to Queen Alexandra, 1920: 6 September
54 RA VIC/ADDA21/228/253, Sir Dighton Probyn to Lord Ripon, 1920: 30 September; 254, Sir Arthur Davidson to Mr Dunphie, 1921: 11 March
55 King Alexander of the Hellenes (1893–1920), second son of King Constantine
56 George, Duke of Sparta (1890–1947), later King George II of the Hellenes, 1922–4 and 1935–47
57 RA GV/PRIV/AA38/10, King George V to Queen Alexandra, 1920: 22 October
58 RA GV/PRIV/AA38/11, King George V to Queen Alexandra, 1920: 27 October
59 RA GV/PRIV/AA38/12, King George V to Queen Alexandra, 1920: 18 November
60 Something which must have given the Queen pleasure in 1920 was that North Schleswig was reunited with Denmark, not as a separate duchy but properly within the realm. Although South Schleswig was incorporated into Germany, many of its inhabitants began yearning for closer ties with Denmark and gradually a cultural programme was drawn up, providing subsidies for such things as Danish schools and Danish church services.
61 The Queen signed and presented similar books in successive years; in 1922 on 13 February to Ellen Fulton and in 1923 on 3 February to Joan le Grice
62 RA GV/PRIV/AA38/13, King George V to Queen Alexandra, 1921: 13 February
63 RA GV/PRIV/AA35/31, Queen Alexandra to King George V, 1921: 14 February
64 Princess Patricia, now Lady Patricia Ramsay, and her husband; their son was Captain Alexander Ramsay of Mar (1919–2000), m Flora Fraser, 1st Lady Saltoun
65 John Brocklehurst, Baron Ranksborough,(1852–1921), "Brock", had been her Equerry from 1901–10 and Extra Equerry from 1910–21
66 RA GV/PRIV/AA35/32, Queen Alexandra to King George V, 1921: 27 February
67 RA VIC/ADDU/417/15, Soveral Papers, Queen Alexandra to Marquis de Soveral, 1921: 4 March
68 RA GV/PRIV/AA35/32, Queen Alexandra to King George V, 1921: 27 February
69 RA GV/PRIV/AA38/15, King George V to Queen Alexandra, 1921: 28 February
70 RA GV/PRIV/AA38/16, King George V to Queen Alexandra, 1921: 6 March
71 RA GV/PRIV/AA38/17, King George V to Queen Alexandra, 1921: 13 March
72 RA VIC/ADDA21/159, Queen Alexandra to Prince Albert, 1921: 15 March
73 RA VIC/ADDA21/228/256a, Treasury Minute, 1921: 16 March
74 RA GV/PRIV/AA35/33, Queen Alexandra to King George V, 1921: 22 March
75 RA GV/PRIV/AA38/18, King George V to Queen Alexandra, 1921: 24 March
76 RA GV/PRIV/AA35/34, Queen Alexandra to King George V, 1921: 1 April

77 RA GV/PRIV/AA38/19, King George V to Queen Alexandra, 1921: 2 April
78 RA GV/PRIV/AA38/20, King George V to Queen Alexandra, 1921: 10 April
79 RA GV/PRIV/AA35/35, Queen Alexandra to King George V, 1921: 20 April
80 RA GV/PRIV/AA38/22, King George V to Queen Alexandra, 1921: 24 April
81 RA PS/PSO/GV/C/O/2548/40, Queen Mary to Queen Alexandra, 1921: 24 April
82 RA GV/PRIV/AA35/35, Queen Alexandra to King George V, 1921: 20 April
83 Hirohito (1901–1989), later Emperor from 1926–1947, and head of state in Japan from 1947–1989
84 Anna Pavlova (1881–1931)
85 Ivy, Marchioness of Titchfield (1887–1982), her husband later became 7th Duke of Portland; she had been a Maid of Honour to Queen Alexandra
86 Arthur Meighen (1874–1960), prime minister in 1920–1 and in 1926, Canadian lawyer and politician
87 Starting in August on a new expedition to the South Pole
88 Acland MSS, d.177/132/ 2054/43, Charlotte Knollys to Sarah Acland, 1921: 26 July; Sidney Lee's articles about the King were published in *The Times* in 1922. Miss Knollys may be anticipating these or may be referring to others, as yet unidentified, or may have misdated the letter
89 Sir Francis Farmer (1866–1922) dental surgeon; worked at Queen Alexandra Military Hospital at Millbank
90 RA GV/PRIV/AA35/36, Queen Alexandra to King George V, 1921: 1 September
91 Née Mary White
92 RA GV/PRIV/AA38/30, King George V to Queen Alexandra, 1921: 4 September
93 RA GV/PRIV/AA35/36, Queen Alexandra to King George V, 1921: 1 September; Prince George, later Duke of Kent, seems to have had a special rapport with his grandmother; in future years his two elder children would be christened Edward and Alexandra. Queen Alexandra would have been delighted that he had married Princess Marina of Greece, her nephew Nicholas's youngest daughter.
94 RA AEC/GG/9/835, Sir Dighton Probyn to Sir Arthur Davidson, 1921: 13 September
95 RA AEC/GG/9/677, 1921: 8 September
96 Sir Ernest Cassel (1852–1921), merchant banker and capitalist
97 Curiously, the Marquess's younger son would marry Sir Ernest's granddaughter the following year
98 The Queen's dresser
99 RA GV/PRIV/AA35/37, Queen Alexandra to King George V, 1921: 11 September
100 By the Bishop of Thetford
101 RA GV/M1723/3,5, Lord Stamfordham to Sir Arthur Davidson, 1921: 13 September; note from Buckingham Palace to War Office, 1921: 17 October
102 RA QM/PRIV/CC42/145, Queen Alexandra to Queen Mary, 1921: 24 October
103 RA GV/PRIV/AA38/36, King George V to Queen Alexandra, 1921: 27 November
104 This may be a housemaid called Priscilla Hall (1855–1922) who died in Nottinghamshire
105 Henry Lascelles (1882–1947), later 6th Earl of Harewood
106 RA GV/PRIV/AA6/555, Queen Alexandra to Canon Dalton, 1922: 24 January
107 Mirabel, née Knollys (1844–1922), m Charles Grey (1841–1903)
108 RA GV/CC42/147 Queen Alexandra to Queen Mary, 1922: 13 February
109 Lady Feodore Gleichen (1861–1922) sculptress and granddaughter of Queen Victoria's half-sister; her father, Prince Victor of Hohenlohe-Langenburg, had married, morganatically, Miss Laura Seymour, daughter of Admiral Sir George Francis Seymour, and their children had been given the surname Gleichen. The daughters, Feodore, Victoria (Valda) and Helena, were bridesmaids at Princess Louise's wedding in 1889, perhaps a nod

to the fact that she also was marrying outside the close royal family circle.

[110] RA GV/PRIV/AA35/40, Queen Alexandra to King George V, 1922: 10 March

[111] RA GV/PRIV/AA38/37, King George V to Queen Alexandra, 1922: 7 March

[112] RA GV/PRIV/AA35/40, Queen Alexandra to King George V, 1922: 10 March

[113] RA GV/PRIV/AA38/38, King George V to Queen Alexandra, 1922: 12 March

[114] RA GV/PRIV/AA35/41, Queen Alexandra to King George V, 1922: 21 March

[115] Archibald Acheson (1841–1922), 3rd Earl of Gosford, vice-chamberlain in Queen Alexandra's household from 1901

[116] John Goddard, from Leicester, performed ventriloquism with marionettes at this time

[117] Reuben Ward Binks (1880–1950), artist who painted dogs, Lakeland landscapes and wildlife

[118] Lord Leopold Mountbatten (1889–1922), formerly known as Prince Leopold of Battenberg

[119] RA GV/PRIV/AA38/41, King George V to Queen Alexandra, 1922: 23 April

[120] RA GV/PRIV/AA35/42, Queen Alexandra to King George V, 1922: 3 May

[121] RA AEC/GG/9/864, Sir Arthur Davidson to Sir Frederick Ponsonby, 1922: 4 May

[122] RA GV/PRIV/AA38/43, King George V to Queen Alexandra, 1922: 5 May

[123] RA GV/PRIV/AA35/43, Queen Alexandra to King George V, 1922: 19 May

[124] Lord Louis Mountbatten (1900–79), later 1st Earl Mount batten of Burma, 1st Sea Lord, last Viceroy of India, m Edwina, née Ashley (1900–60), socialite and relief worker

[125] Who had been visiting her son, Prince Knud, at Dartmouth

[126] RA GV/PRIV/AA35/44, Queen Alexandra to King George V, 1922: 2 August

[127] RA GV/PRIV/AA35/45, Queen Alexandra to King George V, 1922: 21 August

[128] RA QM/PRIV/CC42/150, Queen Alexandra to Queen Mary, 1922: 29 August

[129] RA AEC/GG/9/879, Sir Arthur Davidson to Sir Frederick Ponsonby, 1922: 19 August

[130] RA GV/PRIV/AA35/46, Queen Alexandra to King George V, 1922: 13 September

[131] RA GV/PRIV/AA38/47, King George V to Queen Alexandra, 1922: 17 September

[132] Mustafa Kemal Atatürk (1881-1938), first President of Turkey from 1923–1938

[133] RA GV/PRIV/AA38/48, King George V to Queen Alexandra, 1922: 1 October

[134] RA QM/PRIV/CC42/151, Queen Alexandra to Queen Mary, 1922: 16 October

[135] Charles Robert Spencer, 6th Earl Spencer (1857–1922)

[136] RA GV/PRIV/AA35/47, Queen Alexandra to King George V, 1922: 7 October

[137] Grand Duchess George

[138] Her younger daughter, Princess Xenia, had married William Leeds, son of Princess Christopher of Greece from an earlier marriage, in October 1921

[139] RA GV/PRIV/AA35/47, Queen Alexandra to King George V, 1922: 7 October

[140] Sir Stanley Hewett (1880–1954), surgeon and apothecary to the royal family.

[141] RA GV/PRIV/AA35/48, Queen Alexandra to King George V, 1922: 12 October

[142] RA QM/PRIV/CC42/151, Queen Alexandra to Queen Mary, 1922: 16 October; she refers here to Queen Mary's kind reply

[143] RA AEC/GG/9/896, Sir Sidney Lee to Sir Frederick Ponsonby, 1922: 18 October

[144] RA GV/PRIV/AA38/49, King George V to Queen Alexandra, 1922: 19 October

[145] Lord Marcus Beresford (1848–1922), equerry and racing manager

[146] RA GV/ADD/COPY/140/124, Rosebery Papers, Princess Victoria to Lord Rosebery, 1922: 29 November, referring to Davidson

[147] Now Duke of York

[148] Lady Elizabeth, née Bowes Lyon (1900–2002), m the future King George VI and became Queen Elizabeth; after his death she was known as Queen Elizabeth The Queen Mother

[149] Claude Bowes Lyon (1855–1944), the 14th Earl of Strathmore and 1st of Kinghorne, m Cecilia, née Cavendish-Bentinck (1862–1938)

[150] RA GV/PRIV/AA38/52, King George V to Queen Alexandra, 1923: 16 January

151 Eleanor, née Bellamy, Mrs Tylden (1823–1928), lady of the manor of Ingoldisthorpe

152 Hon George Lascelles (1923–2011), later 7th Earl of Harewood, music director and author

153 RA GV/PRIV/AA35/50, Queen Alexandra to King George V, 1923: 16 February

154 RA QM/PRIV/CC42/153, Queen Alexandra to Queen Mary, 1923: 11 February

155 RA GV/PRIV/AA38/53, King George V to Queen Alexandra, 1923: 16 February

156 RA GV/PRIV/AA35/50, Queen Alexandra to King George V, 1923: 16 February

157 Admiral Pericles Joannides (1881–1965)

158 RA GV/PRIV/AA35/52, Queen Alexandra to King George V, 1923: 3 March

159 RA GV/PRIV/AA38/55, King George V to Queen Alexandra, 1923: 8 March

160 RA/GV/PRIV/AA35/51, Queen Alexandra to King George V, 1923: 9 March (filed out of sequence)

161 Count Preben Ferdinand Ahlefeldt-Laurvig

162 Duke of Connaught

163 RA QM/PRIV/CC45/646, Queen Alexandra to Queen Mary, 1923: 26 May

164 Grace, née Hinds (1885–1958), second w of Marquess Curzon of Kedleston

165 RA AEC/GG/9/1031, Sir Frederick Ponsonby to Sir Sidney Lee, 1924: 18 November; apparently Prince Christian would insist that he was Danish and not German

166 The Waleses at Marlborough House and the Christians at Schomburg House, Piccadilly

167 Charles Carnegie (1893–1992), Lord Carnegie, later the 11th Earl of Southesk

168 RA VIC/MAIN/QAD/1923: 21 June

169 Mischa (Moishe) Elman (Russian name Mikhail Saulovitch Elman) (1891–1967), Ukrainian Jewish violinist who later settled in America

170 Prince Alexis Obolensky (1883–1942), Russian aristocrat who had become a singer

171 Carl Nielsen (1865–1931) prominent Danish composer, conductor and violinist

172 RA VIC/ADDW/28

173 Letter from Nielsen to his wife, 21 June 1923, Royal Library, Copenhagen, MSS collection, CN-AMCN, quoted in Kejserinde Dagmar, Ulstrup, p110, Maria Feodorovna through Diaries and personal Letters

174 RA GV/PRIV/AA35/53, Queen Alexandra to King George V, 1923: 22 August

175 Alexandra's last letter to Minny was on 23 March 1925; private information

176 RA GV/PRIV/AA38/56, King George V to Queen Alexandra, 1923: 20 August

177 RA GV/PRIV/AA35/53, Queen Alexandra to King George V, 1923: 22 August

178 RA GV/PRIV/AA38/57, King George V to Queen Alexandra, 1923: 24 August

179 Helen Blanche, née Forbes (1870–1934) m John Blundell Leigh; she was a friend of Princess Victoria and sister of Evelyn, Mrs "Willie" James

180 Prince Christopher's American wife; as Mrs Nancy Leeds, she had married him as her third husband.

181 Mary, née Ellis (1865–1923), m Ralph Sneyd (1863–1949); she was a daughter of Sir Arthur Ellis

182 RA GV/PRIV/AA38/58, King George V to Queen Alexandra, 1923: 9 September

183 RA VIC/ADDA21/13,142: the bungalow had been looked after since 1908 by Mrs Parsons, who lived nearby, for £20 per year, which in 1923 was raised to £30 in recognition of her invaluable and faithful service

184 RA GV/PRIV/AA35/54, Queen Alexandra to King George V, 1923: 17 September

185 RA GV/PRIV/AA38/59, King George V to Queen Alexandra, 1923: 21 October

186 RA GV/PRIV/AA35/55, Queen Alexandra to King George V, 1923: 27 September

187 RA VIC/MAIN/QAD/1923: 17 October

188 The Queen's Treasurer and Gwladys's widower

189 RA GV/PRIV/AA35/55, Queen Alexandra to King George V, 1923: 27 September

190 RA GV/PRIV/AA35/56, Queen Alexandra to King George V, 1923: 8 October

[191] RA VIC/MAIN/QAD/1923: 14 November

[192] RA VIC/ADDA21/145, note, 1923: 22 November

[193] RA GV/PRIV/AA38/63, King George V to Queen Alexandra, 1923: 25 November

[194] RA QM/PRIV/CC45/651, Queen Maud to Queen Mary, 1923: 27 November

[195] Bertrand Dawson (1864–1945), later 1st Viscount Dawson of Penn, physician to the royal family

[196] RA QM/PRIV/CC45/653, Queen Maud to Queen Mary, 1924: 11 January

[197] Ramsay MacDonald (1866–1937), Prime Minister in 1924 and from 1929–35

[198] Stanley Baldwin (1867–1947), later 1st Earl Baldwin of Bewdley, Prime Minister three times

[199] RA GV/PRIV/AA38/64, King George V to Queen Alexandra, 1924: 22 January

[200] RA GV/PRIV/AA38/65, King George V to Queen Alexandra, 1924: 17 February

[201] Grand Duchess George, p 259

[202] RA VIC/ADDA21/234/50, Queen Alexandra to Lord Knutsford, 1924: 10 January

[203] RA VIC/ADDA21/234/53, Lord Knutsford to Queen Alexandra, undated, 1923 or 1924

[204] RA GV/PRIV/AA35/58, Queen Alexandra to King George V, 1924: 17 March

[205] RA GV/PRIV/AA38/67, King George V to Queen Alexandra, 1924: 25 March

[206] RA GV/PRIV/AA38/68, King George V to Queen Alexandra, 1924: 10 April

[207] Acland MSS.d.177/2054/50, Charlotte Knollys to Sarah Acland, 1924: 8 May

[208] RA QM/PRIV/CC45/657, Princess Victoria to Queen Mary, 1924: 16 May

[209] RA GV/PRIV/AA35/59, Queen Alexandra to King George V, 1924: 10 June

[210] Colonel Sir Henry Legge (1852–1924), army officer and courtier

[211] RA GV/PRIV/AA38/69, King George V to Queen Alexandra, 1924: 21 June

[212] Princess Victoria to Beatrice Harrison, 1924: 19 November ©The Harrison Sisters' Trust

[213] Cecil Beaton (1904–80), Sir, noted photographer, diarist, painter, interior, stage and costume designer

[214] Beaton's unpublished diary for Wednesday 30/7/1924, © The Literary Executors of the late Sir Cecil Beaton

[215] RA GV/PRIV/AA38/73, King George V to Queen Alexandra, 1924: 29 July

[216] RA GV/PRIV/AA38/74, King George V to Queen Alexandra, 1924: 10 August

[217] RA GV/PRIV/AA38/75, King George V to Queen Alexandra, 1924: 21 August

[218] Hon Gerald Lascelles (1924–98)

[219] RA GV/PRIV/AA35/60, Queen Alexandra to King George V, 1924: 27 September

[220] RA GV/PRIV/AA38/78, King George V to Queen Alexandra, 1924: 3 October

[221] RA GVI/PRIV/RF/11/342, Queen Mary to Duke of York, 1925: 3 January

[222] The Revd Philip Thomas Byard Clayton (1885–1972) founded Talbot House, (known as TocH in the parlance of radio signallers) as a rest home for soldiers at the Front. Many branches were opened after the war in Britain and elsewhere, as clubs.

[223] RA GV/PRIV/AA38/79, King George V to Queen Alexandra, 1925: 1 February

[224] RA GV/PRIV/AA38/80, King George V to Queen Alexandra, 1925: 8 February

[225] RA GV/PRIV/AA38/81, King George V to Queen Alexandra, 1925: 15 February

[226] Grand Duchess George, p 259

[227] As her grandmother, Landgravine Charlotte of Hesse-Cassel's had been

[228] Grand Duchess George, pp 165–6, 258–9

[229] RA GV/ADD/COPY/118, *Memoirs of Robert Charles Marrington* (cabinet maker and tapissier at Sandringham)

[230] RA GV/PRIV/AA38/82, King George V to Queen Alexandra, 1925: 3 March

[231] RA GV/PRIV/AA38/83 King George V to Queen Alexandra, 1925: 8 March; Victoria would join them at Genoa from Lugano

[232] RA GV/PRIV/AA35/61, Queen Alexandra to King George V, 1925: 9 March

[233] RA GV/PRIV/AA38/84, King George V to Queen Alexandra, 1925: 15 March

234 RA GV/PRIV/AA38/85, King George V to Queen Alexandra, 1925: 22 March

235 RA GV/PRIV/AA38/86, King George V to Queen Alexandra, 1925: 5 April

236 RA AEC/GG/9/1064, Lord Esher to Lord Stamfordham, 1925: 26 April

237 RA AEC/GG/9/1132, Sir Frederick Ponsonby to Mr Macmillan, 1927: 11 April

238 RA AEC/GG/9/1170, Sir Lionel Cust to Sir Frederick Ponsonby, 1927: 3 November

239 Cust, p 207

240 RA QM/PRIV/CC45/687, Queen Maud to Queen Mary, 1925: 6 May

241 RA GV/PRIV/AA38/87, King George V to Queen Alexandra, 1925: 4 June

242 Acland MSS d.177/132 /2054/56, Charlotte Knollys to Sarah Acland, 1925: 6 October

243 Sir Thomas Horder (1871–1955), 1st Baron Horder, physician-in-ordinary to the royal family

244 RA VIC/ADDA17/1411, Duke of Connaught to Princess Louise, Duchess of Argyll, 1925: 5 December

245 Descriptions of the Queen's last illness, death and funeral are from Grand Duchess George, pp 260–1

246 RA PS/PSO/GV/C/N/2556/39, [Lord Stamfordham] to Field Marshal Sir William Birdwood, 1925: 1 December

247 RA GV/PRIV/AA56/9, Lord Revelstoke to King George V, 1925: 20 November

248 RA GV/PRIV/AA56/103, Prince Nicholas of Greece to King George V, 1925: 23 Novenber

249 Frederick Jeune Willans (1884–1949), Sir, surgeon-apothecary to the royal family at Sandringham; he was Sir Alan Manby's son-in-law

250 RA BP31/Box 31/20A

251 The Lancet, 5 December 1925

252 Cosmo Gordon Lang (1864–1945), Archbishop of York (1908–28) and of Canterbury (1928–42)

253 Lambeth Palace Library, Lang 318 f.2, King George V to Cosmo Gordon Lang, 1925: 23 December

254 RA VIC/ADDA17/1411, Duke of Connaught to Princess Louise, Duchess of Argyll, 1925: 5 December; the burial place had been arranged in advance by Alexandra

Genealogical Tables

Descendants of King Christian IX and Queen Louise of Denmark

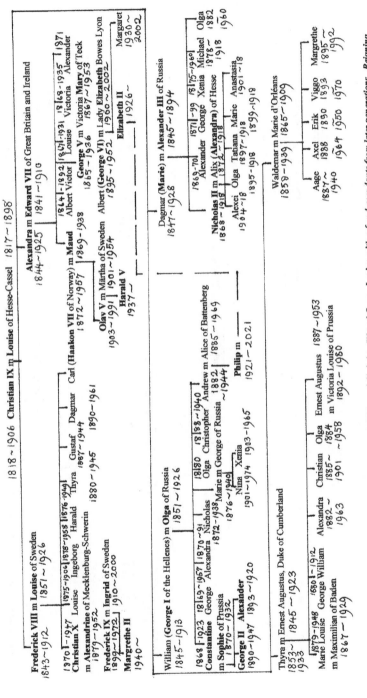

1818~1906 **Christian IX** m **Louise** of Hesse-Cassel 1817~1898

Frederick VIII m **Louise** of Sweden
1843~1912 | 1851~1926

1870†~1947 1878†~1953 1876~1949
Christian X Louise Ingeborg Harald Thyra Gustaf Dagmar Carl (**Haakon VII** of Norway) m **Maud**
m Alexandrine of Mecklenburg-Schwerin 1880~1945 1887~1944 1890~1961 1872~1957 | 1869–1938
1879~1952

Frederick IX m **Ingrid** of Sweden
1899~1972 | 1910~2000
Margrethe II
1940~

Olav V m Märtha of Sweden
1903~1991 | 1901~1954
Harald V
1937~

Alexandra m **Edward VII** of Great Britain and Ireland
1844~1925 | 1841~1910

1864~1892 1867~1931 1868~1935 1871
Albert Victor Louise Victoria Alexander
George V m Victoria Mary of Teck
1865~1936 | 1867~1953

Albert (**George VI**) m Lady **Elizabeth** Bowes Lyon
1895~1952 | 1900~2002
Elizabeth II
1926~

Margaret
1930~
2002

Dagmar (Marie) m **Alexander III** of Russia
1847~1928 | 1845~1894

1868~70 1871~99 1875~960
Alexander George Xenia Michael Olga
1878~ 1882
1918 1960

Nicholas II m Alix (**Alexandra**) of Hesse
1868~1918 | 1872~1918
Alexei Olga Tatiana Marie Anastasia
1904~18 1895~1918 1897~1918 1899~1918 1901~18

Waldemar m Marie d'Orléans
1858~1939 | 1865~1909
Aage Axel Erik Viggo Margrethe
1887~ 1888 1890 1893 1895~
1940 1964 1950 1970 1992

William (George I of the Hellenes) m **Olga** of Russia
1845~1913 | 1851~1926

1868†~1923 1869~1957 1870~91
Constantine George Alexandra Nicholas
1872~1938 Marie m George of Russia
1876~1940
Nina Xenia
1901~1974 1903~1965

1880 1888~1940
Olga Christopher Andrew m Alice of Battenberg
1882~ | 1885~1969
1944
Philip m
1921~2021

George II Alexander
1890~1947 1893~1920

Thyra m Ernest Augustus, Duke of Cumberland
1853~ | 1845~1923
1933

1879~1948 1880†~1912
Marie Louise George William
m Maximilian of Baden
1867~1929

Alexandra Christian Olga Ernest Augustus 1887~1953
1882~ 1885~ 1884~ m Victoria Louise of Prussia
1963 1901 1958 1892~1980

Sophie of Prussia
1870~1932

This table, which is incomplete, shows the children and grandchildren of Christian IX and Queen Louise, with a few descendants from later generations. Reigning monarchs and consorts are in bold type.

Connections between the British and Danish Royal Families and the Houses of Glücksburg and Hesse-Cassel

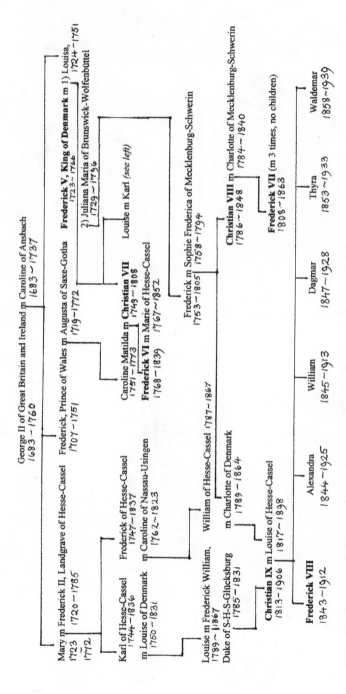

This table is incomplete and has been simplified to show the main lines of descent. Reigning Danish monarchs are in bold type.

Some descendants of King George III of Great Britain and Ireland

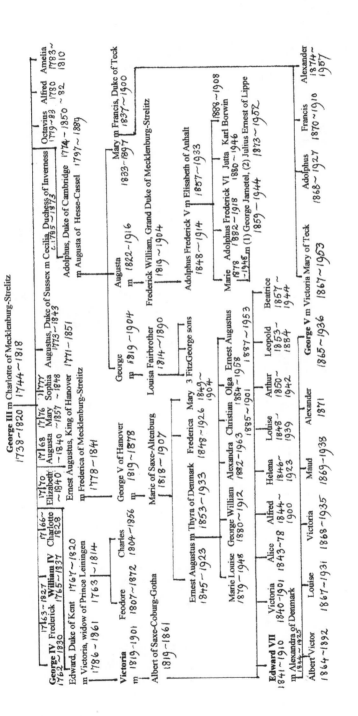

This table is incomplete. Reigning British monarchs are in bold type.

The family of Queen Victoria of Great Britain and Ireland

Edward, Duke of Kent m Victoria of Saxe-Coburg-Saalfeld, m (1) Emich Charles, 2nd Prince of Leiningen
1767~1820 / 1786~1861 / 1763~1814

Feodore m Ernest I, Prince of Hohenlohe-Langenburg 1807~1872 / 1794~1860

Charles, 3rd Prince of Leiningen m Countess Maria von Klebelsberg 1804~1856 / 1806~1880
Ernest, 4th Prince of Leiningen 1830~1904
Edward 1833~1914

Victoria m Albert of Saxe-Coburg-Gotha 1819~1901 / 1819~1861

Victoria m Frederick III, German Emperor 1840~1901 / 1831~1888
- William II 1859~1941
- Charlotte 1860~1919
- Henry 1862~1929
- Sigismund 1864~66
- Victoria 1866~1929
- Waldemar 1868~79
- Sophie 1870~1932
- Margaret 1872~1954

Edward VII m Alexandra of Denmark 1841~1910 / 1844~1925
- Albert Victor 1864~92
- George V m Victoria Mary of Teck 1865~1936 / 1867~1953
- Louise 1867~1931
- Victoria 1868~1935
- Maud 1869~1938
- Alexander 1871

Alice m Louis IV, Grand Duke of Hesse-Darmstadt 1843~1878
- Victoria 1863~1950
- Elizabeth 1864~1918
- Irene 1866~1953
- Ernest Louis 1868~1937
- Alix 1872~1918
- Marie 1874~1878

George V m Victoria Mary of Teck
- Edward VIII 1894~1972
- George VI m Lady Elizabeth Bowes Lyon 1895~1952 / 1900~2002
- Mary, Princess Royal 1897~1965
- Henry, Duke of Gloucester 1900~1974
- George, Duke of Kent 1902~1942
- John 1905~1919

Alfred, Duke of Edinburgh and Saxe-Coburg-Gotha m Grand Duchess Marie of Russia 1844~1900 / 1853~1920
- Alfred 1874~99
- Marie 1875~1938
- Victoria Melita 1876~1936
- Alexandra 1878~1942
- Beatrice 1884~1966

Helena m Christian of Schleswig-Holstein-Sonderburg-Augustenburg 1846~1923 / 1831~1917
- Christian Victor 1867~1900
- Albert 1869~1931
- (Helena) Victoria 1870~1948
- (Marie) Louise 1872~1956
- Harold 1876

Louise m John, 9th Duke of Argyll 1848~1939 / 1845~1914

Arthur, Duke of Connaught m Louise Margaret of Prussia 1850~1942 / 1860~1917
- Margaret 1882~1920
- Arthur 1883~1938
- Patricia 1886~1974

Leopold, Duke of Albany m Helen of Waldeck-Pyrmont 1853~1884 / 1861~1922
- Alice 1883~1981
- Charles Edward 1884~1954

Beatrice m Prince Henry of Battenberg 1857~1944 / 1858~1896
- Alexander 1886~1960
- Victoria Eugénie 1887~1969
- Leopold 1889~1922
- Maurice 1891~1914

George VI m Lady Elizabeth Bowes Lyon
- Elizabeth II m Philip, Duke of Edinburgh 1926~ / 1921~2021

Elizabeth II
- Charles, Prince of Wales m (1) Diana Spencer, (2) Camilla Parker-Bowles 1948~ / 1961~1997 / 1947~
- Anne, Princess Royal 1950~
- Andrew, Duke of York 1960~
- Edward, Earl of Wessex 1964~

Charles
- William, Duke of Cambridge m Catherine Middleton 1982~ / 1982~
- Henry, Duke of Sussex 1984~

William, Duke of Cambridge
- George 2013~
- Charlotte 2015~
- Louis 2018~

This table is incomplete; it shows Queen Victoria's parents, half-siblings, children and grandchildren but only a few in later generations.

Unpublished Sources

The Royal Archives, Windsor Castle (RA)

Queen Alexandra's Photograph Albums (Royal Collection)

National Archives, PRO, Work 19/698; Marlborough House

Hampshire Record Office; the papers of Dr George Vivian Poore

Norfolk Record Office; description by Louisa Buxton

The Bodleian Library; Acland Papers

Fitzwilliam Museum; Wilfrid Scawen Blunt's diaries

The Harrison Sisters' Trust; Princess Victoria's letters

The Royal Borough of Kensington and Chelsea, Leighton House; Lord
Leighton's papers

The Rosebery Papers; Princess Victoria's letters

Archivo General de Palacio, Madrid; Queen Alexandra's letter to Infanta Eulalia

Lambeth Palace Library, Lang Papers; King George V's letter to Cosmo Gordon
Lang

Leeds Russian Archive; Queen Alexandra's support of the Anglo–Russian
Hospital

Niedersächsisches Landesarchiv, Hannover; advice

Literary Executors of the late Sir Cecil Beaton; unpublished diary entry

Bibliography

Palle Lauring, *A History of Denmark*, Copenhagen 1999

Sarah A Tooley, *The Life of Queen Alexandra*, London 1902

David Williamson, *Queen Alexandra*, London and Edinburgh 1919

Georgina Battiscombe, *Queen Alexandra*, London 1969

David Duff, *Alexandra, Princess and Queen*, London 1980

Frances Dimond, *Developing the Picture, Queen Alexandra and the Art of Photography*, The Royal Collection, 2004

Kate Strasdin, *Inside the Royal Wardrobe, a Dress History of Queen Alexandra*, London 2017

Sidney Lee, *Dictionary of National Biography*; article about King Edward VII

Edward Legge, *King Edward VII in his True Colours*, London 1912

Edward Legge, *More about King Edward*, London 1913

Sidney Lee, *King Edward VII, a biography*, London 1925

Lionel Cust, *King Edward VII and His Court*, London 1930

Philip Magnus, *King Edward the Seventh*, London 1964

Raymond Lamont-Brown, *Edward VII's Last Loves*, Gloucestershire 1998

Jane Ridley, *Bertie*, London 2012

Victor Mallet (ed), *Life with Queen Victoria*, London 1968

Michaela Reid, *Ask Sir James*, London 1987

Theodore Martin, *The Life of The Prince Consort*, London 1875-80

Prince Michael of Greece, *Eddy and Hélène, an Impossible Match*, Sweden 2013

Clement Kinloch Cooke, *A Memoir of Princess Mary Adelaide, Duchess of Teck*, London 1900

James Pope-Hennessy, *Queen Mary*, London 1959

James Pope-Hennessy, edited by Hugo Vickers, *The Quest for Queen Mary*, London 2018

Reginald Brett, Viscount Esher, *Journals and Letters*, London 1938

James Lees-Milne, *The Enigmatic Edwardian: the life of Reginald, 2nd Viscount Esher*, 1986

Exhibition catalogue, *Kejserinde Dagmar, Maria Feodorovna, Empress of Russia*: essay by Preben Ulstrup, Maria Feodorovna through Diaries and Personal Letters, Copenhagen 1997

Andrei Maylunas and Serge Mironenko, *A Lifelong Passion*, London 1996

Grand Duchess George of Russia, *A Romanov Diary*, New York, 1988

Charlotte Zeepvat, *From Cradle to Crown*, Gloucestershire 2006

Arthur H Beavan, *Marlborough House and Its Occupants*, London 1896

Gabriel Tschumi, *Royal Chef*, London 1954
Michael Howell and Peter Ford, *The History of the Elephant Man*, London 1980
Hugh Dixon and Andrew Saint, *Cragside*, The National Trust 2007
Richard G G Price, *A History of Punch*, London 1957
Margaret J Tuke, *A History of Bedford College for Women*, 1849–1937, OUP 1939
Linna Bentley, *Educating Women: a History of Bedford College*, 1849–1985, 1991

Journals, Periodicals and Newspapers

The Court Circular
British Medical Journal, 3 August 1877
The Medical Examiner, 9 August 1877
The Spectator, 14 September 1861
The Danemark, 26 February 1863
The Graphic, 30 May, 27 June 1903
The Illustrated London News, 1 June 1907
The Daily Mail, 12 November 1919
The Times, Court Circular, 24 May 1910
The Times, 26 April 1930
The William Shipley Group for RSA History, Bulletin 64, March 2020
Unidentified press cuttings, cut out and stuck in scrap books

Reference Books and Search Engines

Burke's *Royal Families of The World, Volume 1, Europe & Latin America,* 1977
Wikipedia and other online search tools

15 Queen Alexandra at Sandringham, with "Tootsie dog" in the distance, c 1916–20.
RCIN 2106386

Index Notes

This Index is in three parts

1) Queen Alexandra and King Edward VII
2) Index of Persons
3) General Index

As the book is overwhelmingly chronological, events and encounters can be found throughout in the order in which they happened. It is hoped that they can thus be tracked without too much difficulty, with the aid of the indexes and the dates which appear at the beginning of each chapter.

The first part of the index deals with Queen Alexandra's and King Edward's personal characteristics, such as their views, appearance, and health, as well as some of their relationships. An overview of their interests and occupations can be found by referring to the General Index, under headings such as Denmark, visits to; Dogs; Horses; Galleries; Museums; Theatres; Music and Exhibitions. Headings such as Hospitals; Charities; Army; and Navy, indicate some of their formal duties, and Alexandra's experience of the war effort can be found under War, First World. The General Index also contains headings for royal residences and other places visited by or associated with the royal couple.

A large number of the people whom the King and Queen met, heard about, or to whom they were related, can be found in the Index of Persons. Some, especially their parents, children, siblings and close associates, appear a great many times in the book. Their entries have been divided according to dates, so as to make it easier to find specific information, as it would have been too repetitive and cumbersome to split each of them in the same way as for the King and Queen in the first part of the index. By contrast, anyone wishing to get a broad impression of the kind of company the royal couple kept can do so by glancing down the columns of names of the artists, musicians, actors, authors, statesmen and others. There may, regrettably, be some idiosyncrasies in the spelling of some names, such as Russian ones. This has largely arisen from a conflict between how they were known during Queen Alexandra's lifetime and afterwards, and how they now appear, a hundred years later, in current works of reference. In general, but not always, the author has preferred Queen Alexandra's version, but she is aware, and apologises, that inconsistencies may grate with some readers.

Pages on which illustrations appear are shown in bold type.

Index of Queen Alexandra
and King Edward VII

Index of Persons

General Index